INTRODUCTION TO
GEOMETRY

INTRODUCTION TO GEOMETRY

JAMES M. STAKKESTAD
LIN WYANT
Cabrillo College

Saunders College Publishing
Harcourt Brace Jovanovich College Publishers
Fort Worth Philadelphia San Diego
New York Orlando Austin San Antonio
Toronto Montreal London Sydney Tokyo

About the cover
The three midpoints of the sides of a triangle determine a unique circle. This circle also passes through the feet of the altitudes and the midpoints of the line segments joining the vertices to the intersection of the altitudes. Part of the folklore of geometry, this figure is called the nine-point circle and is more fully discussed in Appendix D.

Academic Press, Inc.
Orlando, Florida 32887

United Kingdom edition published by
Academic Press, Inc. (London) Ltd.
24/28 Oval Road, London NW1 7DX

ISBN: 0-12-766140-9
Library of Congress Catalog Card Number: 85-70900
Printed in the United States of America

CONTENTS

Preface ix

1 Preliminaries 1
1.1 The Nature of Geometry 2
1.2 The Language of Sets 6
Exercises for 1.1 and 1.2 8
1.3 The Set of Real Numbers 10
Exercises for 1.3 13
1.4 Some Relations Between Real Numbers 14
Exercises for 1.4 18
1.5 Basic Properties of Real Numbers 20
Exercises for 1.5 23
Summary • Facts to Know • Problems to Master 24

2 Points and Lines 25
2.1 Introduction 26
2.2 Lines and Subsets of Lines 27
Exercises for 2.1 and 2.2 31
2.3 Measuring Line Segments 32
Exercises for 2.3 35
2.4 Congruent Line Segments 37
Exercises for 2.4 39
2.5 Geometric Proofs 40
Exercises for 2.5 44
Summary • Facts to Know • Problems to Master 50

3 Angles 51
3.1 Introduction 52
3.2 Measuring Angles 56
Exercises for 3.1 and 3.2 62
3.3 Congruent Angles 65
Exercises for 3.3 71
3.4 Problems Involving Angles 74
Exercises for 3.4 77
Summary • Facts to Know • Problems to Master 85

4 Triangles 86
4.1 Introduction 88
4.2 Congruent Triangles 90
Exercises for 4.1 and 4.2 96
4.3 Problem Solving with Triangles 103
Exercises for 4.3 106
4.4 More About Proofs 112
Exercises for 4.4 116
4.5 Special Line Segments and Triangles 124
Exercises for 4.5 127
4.6 Inequalities in Triangles: Indirect Proof 135
Exercises for 4.6 140

4.7 More Problem Solving with Triangles 145
Exercises for 4.7 149
Summary • Facts to Know • Problems to Master 158

5 Parallel Lines 159

5.1 Introduction 161
5.2 Proving Lines Parallel 162
Exercises for 5.1 and 5.2 165
5.3 The Parallel Postulate and Some Consequences 172
Exercises for 5.3 175
5.4 More Consequences of the Parallel Postulate 185
Exercises for 5.4 188
Summary • Facts to Know 196
Problems to Master 197

6 Quadrilaterals and Other Polygons 198

6.1 Introduction 200
6.2 Parallelograms 203
Exercises for 6.1 and 6.2 206
6.3 Special Parallelograms 213
Exercises for 6.3 216
6.4 Proving Special Quadrilaterals 222
Exercises for 6.4 226
6.5 Other Four-Line Figures 232
Exercises for 6.5 235
6.6 Polygons Having more than Four Sides 239
Exercises for 6.6 245
Summary • Facts to Know 250
Problems to Master 251

7 Circles 252

7.1 Introduction 254
7.2 Central Angles, Arcs, and Chords 259
Exercises for 7.1 and 7.2 262
7.3 Inscribed Angles 270
Exercises for 7.3 275
7.4 Chords, Tangents, and Secants 282
Exercises for 7.4 288
Summary • Facts to Know • Problems to Master 297

8 Area and Perimeter 298

8.1 Introduction 300
8.2 Parallelograms, Triangles, and Trapezoids 304
Exercises for 8.1 and 8.2 309
8.3 Polygons and Circles 314
Exercises for 8.3 320
Summary 326
Facts to Know • Problems to Master 327

9 Similarity 328

9.1 Introduction 330
9.2 Similar Triangles 334
Exercises for 9.1 and 9.2 337
9.3 Right Triangles 342
Exercises for 9.3 346
9.4 More About Similar Triangles 352
Exercises for 9.4 356
9.5 Circles, Similarity, and Sectors 361
Exercises for 9.5 367
9.6 Applications 373
Exercises for 9.6 375
Summary • Facts to Know • Problems to Master 380

10 Solid Geometry 381

10.1 Introduction 383
10.2 Lines and Planes in Space 384
Exercises for 10.1 and 10.2 387
10.3 Polyhedrons 392
Exercises for 10.3 397
10.4 Volumes of Prisms and Pyramids 403
Exercises for 10.4 407
10.5 Cylinders, Cones, and Spheres 413
Exercises for 10.5 418
Summary • Facts to Know • Problems to Master 422

Appendix A The System of Real Numbers A-1

Appendix B Definitions, Postulates, and Theorems in This Text A-4

Appendix C Loci A-16

Appendix D Concurrent Lines and Triangles A-23

Appendix E Geometric Date Line A-33

Answers to Selected Exercises A-35

Index I-1

PREFACE

Geometry at the introductory college level may be taught in a variety of ways. The approach may be synthetic, analytic, transformational, or a mix of all three. This text, by contrast, is an up-to-date version of the traditional, Euclidean synthetic approach. It presents the fundamentals of geometry in a straightforward and sequential manner, beginning with simple figures and proceeding, step-by-step, to complicated ones. Our experience suggests that this is the best approach for teaching the facts of geometry, cultivating the student's geometric intuition, and fostering the practice of deductive reasoning. Such a foundation firmly prepares the student to study analytic geometry, trigonometry, and calculus.

The text is suited for a one-term course at the introductory college level with elementary algebra (one year at the high school level) as a prerequisite. The material can be covered in three or four semester hours per week or five quarter hours per week. We have chosen only those topics fundamental to the development of geometry and have designed each section to fit the usual class period. Additional topics in the exercises and the appendixes and a separate chapter on solid geometry allow flexibility in assignments. The format also enables the instructor to choose between or to integrate the teaching of intuition versus rigor.

The text begins with some fundamental concepts about sets and numbers that are used in the geometric development. Included is a list of the axioms about relations and numbers that have direct application in geometry. (Appendix A contains a complete list of the axioms for the real numbers.) Although the selected list appears lengthy, each axiom is simple to motivate and most are familiar to students from their work in algebra. Thus, Chapter 1 need not be pored over but rather may be used as a basis that becomes more meaningful as the student proceeds in the text.

Our discussion of geometry proceeds naturally from points and lines to increasingly complicated linear figures, circles, and solid geometry. These concepts are first developed through the congruence relation; the same figures are subsequently discussed with respect to the similarity relation. This gradual development, we believe, provides the best format for students to learn geometry and to cultivate an intuitive grasp of geometric relationships. Furthermore, our inclusion of three-dimensional topics only in the final chapter simplifies the learning process by avoiding frequent shifts between two- and three-dimensional figures.

We uniformly treat length, angular measure, area, and volume by covering the set of points that make up a geometric figure with standard units that are themselves geometric figures of the same type. This approach is not only mathematically sound but also underlines the different types of units used to measure line segments, angles, areas, and volumes. We include many applications involving mensuration formulas.

One of the most important features of this text is the large number of exercises. Except for the chapter introductions, every section has an exercise set, each containing exercises with various degrees of difficulty. Among the types of exercises are true-false, identification, discussion, fill-in-the-blank, "find what is wrong with the figure," number problems, constructions, and four different kinds of proof problems. These exercises provide an abundant supply of assignments to fit the student's needs. Answers to most odd-numbered problems and representative proof problems from each exercise set are given at the back of the book.

Our approach to geometric proofs starts with clear, detailed examples with no steps omitted. Only later are clearly spelled out shortcuts introduced. Reasons are shown as abbreviations that indicate the content of the definition, axiom, postulate, or theorem rather than referencing them by number. This device speeds the memorization of geometric facts and makes the reading of proofs more meaningful. In the exercises, the student is guided into proof-writing by supplying missing reasons in proofs and by rearranging provided statements into a correct order for a proof. We also include many original proof exercises of varying difficulty. Hence, proofs may be treated minimally or extensively.

Constructions appear throughout the text. They are used to motivate some of the postulates, thus meshing the constructions with the logical development of geometry. This technique helps the student understand the content of the postulate and develop geometric intuition. Proofs of constructions and problems to be solved using constructions are given in the exercises.

The history of geometry and its place in the development of mathematics is presented through historical notes at the beginning of each chapter, comments in the text itself, and the inclusion of exercises and constructions of special historical interest. Thus, we show geometry as a human endeavor, its past rich with dynamic individuals.

This text is a fourth revision resulting from several years of use at Cabrillo College. We thank the several hundred students who worked through our earlier manuscripts and made useful suggestions. We also thank Dave Viglienzoni, Adele Miller, and Bob Stidham, whose adoption of our material for their own classes enhanced this textbook. Special gratitude goes to our production editor Jennifer Keith, our production supervisor Iris Medina, and the rest of the staff at Academic Press for their patience and energetic production of this book.

We appreciate the following reviewers for their helpful suggestions:

Steve Blasberg
West Valley College, California

Beth Hooper
Golden West College, California

Michael Sanchez
Sacramento City College, California

Ed Harris
College of San Mateo, California

Jack Rotman
Lansing Community College, Michigan

Maurice Ngo
Chabot College, California

Tina Levy
Diablo Valley College, California

Paige Yuhn
Santa Barbara City College, California

Daniel Reeves
Sam Houston State University, Texas

John Huber
Sam Houston State University, Texas

Reta Parrish
Lamar University, Texas

Gerald Skidmore
Alvin Community College, Texas

Rudy Maglio
Oakton Community College, Illinois

We especially thank Bob Stidham for preparing the answer key and Suzanne Stidham for her unflagging help in preparing the manuscript.

1

PRELIMINARIES

MAJOR TOPICS

- $\subseteq$ Geometric figures as models of physical objects
- $\subseteq$ Content of a mathematical system
  1. Undefined terms
  2. Definitions
  3. Axioms and postulates
  4. Theorems
- $\subseteq$ Real numbers and the number line
- $\subseteq$ Distance on the number line

HISTORICAL NOTE

GEOMETRY AND NUMBERS

The history of mathematics shows that numbers and geometric figures have long been linked together. Although plane geometry in its present form began in Greece during the years 650–300 B.C., the peoples of the earlier Babylonian and Egyptian civilizations (1800–650 B.C.) had used numbers and geometric figures to solve practical problems. Both groups knew, for example, that a right angle could be obtained by forming a triangle whose sides were three, four, and five units long. The ability to lay out a square corner in this way had many applications.

There were two certainties in ancient Egypt. One was the annual flooding of the Nile River, and the other was taxes on land. Since the flood waters destroyed many landmarks, surveying to determine tax assessments was a regular necessity. Early Egyptian surveyors were known as rope-stretchers because, using a rope with knots tied at equal intervals, they stretched it into the form of a 3-4-5 triangle to obtain an accurate square corner.

The early Egyptians and Babylonians did not content themselves with the 3-4-5 triangle. They knew that if the sides a, b, and c satisfied the equation $a^2 + b^2 = c^2$, the angle opposite side c (the hypotenuse) would be a right angle, but they were troubled by the simple case $1^2 + 1^2 = c^2$, or $2 = c^2$. Although the Babylonians knew about fractions as well as integers, the best they could do for c was $\frac{14}{10}$ or 1.4 ($[\frac{14}{10}]^2 = \frac{196}{100} = 1.96$), and this was doubtless good enough for practical purposes.

Today we refer to the number c where $c^2 = 2$ as *the square root of two* ($\sqrt{2}$), and much better decimal approximations than 1.4 are available. We know, too, that there is no fraction that is exactly equal to this troublesome number; we call it an *irrational* number, meaning that it is not expressible as a ratio (fraction).

But for the Greeks of 650–300 B.C., not having "exact" numbers (i.e., integers or fractions) for the irrationals was as genuine and important a problem as was land surveying for the earlier Egyptians. To overcome this difficulty they decided to work with all numbers geometrically. They began with a certain length to represent the number 1. Other rational numbers were then represented in terms of this length. The irrational number $\sqrt{2}$ was represented by the length of the hypotenuse of a right triangle whose other two sides were each one unit long.

Arithmetic operations were done geometrically. The answer to $1 + \sqrt{2}$, for example, was represented by the line segment formed by adjoining a segment representing 1 to a segment representing $\sqrt{2}$. The answer to a multiplication of two numbers was represented by the area of a rectangle, and the product of three numbers was a volume. A product of four numbers, however, was inconceivable because there was no geometric figure to represent it.

Although clumsy in some ways, the geometric arithmetic of the early Greeks was, in fact, remarkably sophisticated. For example, they were able to develop a workable theory of ratio and proportion involving both rational and irrational numbers. Indeed, the geometry of classical Greece was a masterpiece of mathematics, and it had a profound influence on the development of European mathematics for many hundreds of years. Its effect, in a very small way, may be noted today in our practice of referring to the multiplication of 5×5, for example, as "squaring" and to the multiplication of $5 \times 5 \times 5$ as "cubing."

1.1 THE NATURE OF GEOMETRY

The word geometry comes from the Greek language and means "earth measure," but the study of geometry involves more than just the size of our planet. Indeed, our world is filled with objects that have size, shape, and position and that are separated by varying distances, and geometry is a systematic study of these observable properties. Hence, "earth measure" should suggest such figures as triangles, rectangles, and circles and the use of numbers to measure their sizes.

This book is primarily about *plane* geometry, that is, about figures that can be drawn on a flat surface. The first systematic study of the properties of plane figures was begun in Greece by Thales (640–546 B.C.), who had learned about geometry from the Egyptians. Thales' most famous student was Pythagoras, whose name still identifies an important property of right triangles. Perhaps the most creative mathematician of ancient Greece was Archimedes (287–212 B.C.), whose many achievements include a good estimate of the numerical relation, denoted π, between the circumference (length) of any circle and its diameter. Probably the most famous of the Greek geometers was Euclid (330–275 B.C.), the first to systematically organize in book form the then-known facts of plane geometry. For this reason, the geometry we will study is often termed *Euclidean geometry*. Euclid's method, now called a deductive system, has had a profound effect on the nature of scientific study, and his books, called *Elements,* are probably the most famous textbooks of all time.

There are countless examples of ways in which geometric facts may be used. It is said that Thales was able to find the height of an Egyptian pyramid by measuring the length of its shadow. As shown in Figure 1.1, this involves the idea of representing the physical situation by a geometric figure or model. No doubt Thales knew enough about triangles to relate his measurements to a geometric model and determine the unknown height.

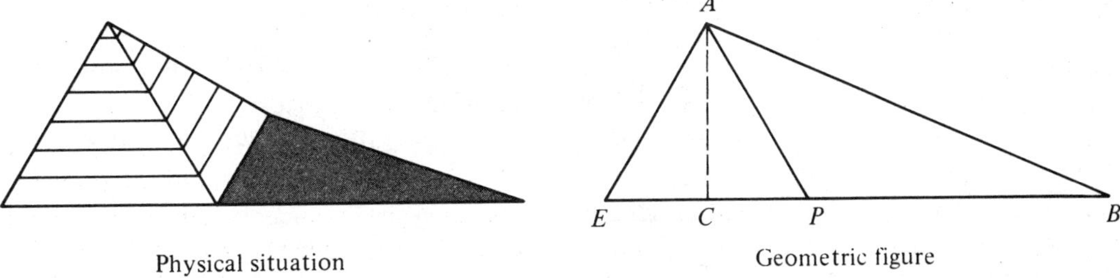

Figure 1.1

This example points up the fact that to apply geometry we must learn about basic geometric figures containing points, lines, angles, triangles, and so on. It is these figures that are used to model physical reality and thus bridge the gap between the things we observe and the mathematical concepts we use to answer questions. We can learn about geometric figures by making useful *comparisons*. For example, the triangles Thales measured at the pyramid were much larger than any he could draw. As shown by Figure 1.1, however, triangles having the same *shape* can be drawn, a comparison that provides a way to solve Thales' problem.

Comparisons in mathematics are called *relations*. In geometry some comparisons, like the "same shape" relation suggested above, do not involve numbers. Others are numerical—for example, "is less than" or "has the same length as."

The relations and facts of geometry will be developed in this text in the form of a mathematical system, a modern version of Euclid's approach. To begin, we will need definitions of the terms we use, and here we face a logical difficulty, as illustrated by the following "definitions" of the words *statue* and *pedestal*:

> A statue is something that stands on a pedestal.
>
> A pedestal is something that holds up a statue.

Obviously, if the two words were unknown to you, you would not learn much from these definitions. To be useful, then, a definition must be in simpler (already-understood) terms. This means that we must begin with a set of simplest terms whose meanings are intuitively understood but that we do not attempt to define formally. These are called *undefined terms*.

It is also logically necessary to start with some basic properties that can be accepted without proof. In geometry, these are called *postulates*. They are like the basic properties called axioms in algebra, but they will deal with basic properties of simple geometric figures.

Using the undefined terms, the definitions, the postulates, and occasionally some axioms from algebra, we will deduce more complicated geometric properties, stated as *theorems*. There are, of course, an enormous number of geometric properties, but those we state as theorems have been found to have wide application. They may be thought of as basic strategies for problem solving.

A theorem is a statement to be proved, and it has two parts: a *hypothesis*, which states the given facts, and a *conclusion*, which states the property to be proved based on the hypothesis and on previously established properties. Here is a nongeometric example of the theorem form:

> If an animal is a normal cat, then it has four legs.

The hypothesis (the "if" part) is "an animal is a normal cat," and the conclusion (the "then" part) is "it has four legs."

In summary, a mathematical system may be outlined as follows:

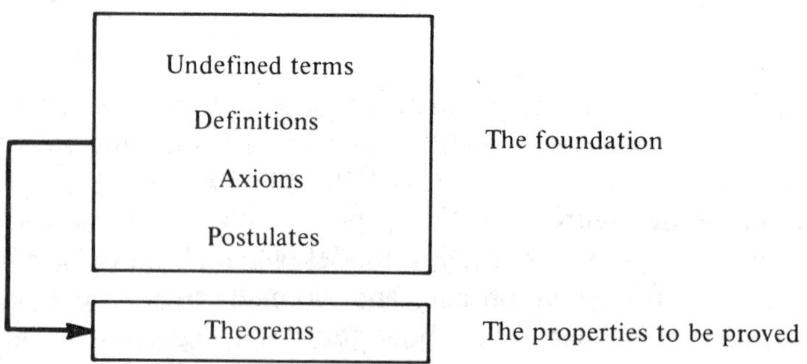

In addition to the format just outlined, whose parts contain the basic concepts and facts of geometry, we will present a few geometric constructions, for which we use only a compass, for copying lengths and drawing circles, and an unmarked straightedge, for drawing lines. These are presented without proof, as motivations for certain important concepts and relationships. Their correctness can be proved, and a few such proofs are given as exercises.

Another feature of our development is that we will begin with the simplest geometric figures and proceed through increasingly complex ones, as outlined in Figure 1.2. Some of the terms in the diagram may be unfamiliar now, but the outline is given here so that you will know where we begin and where we are going at any point in the text.

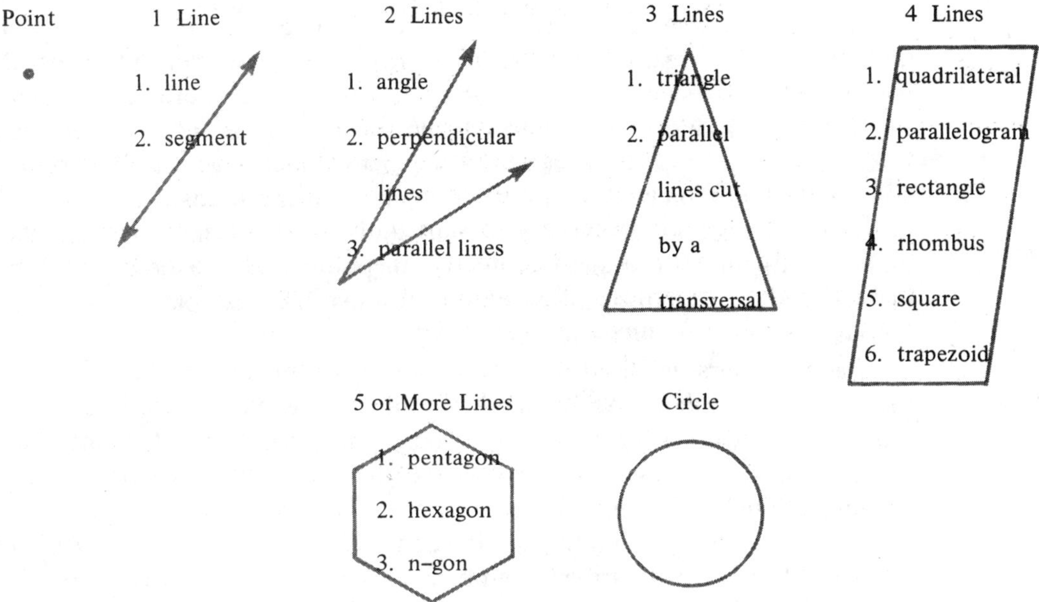

Figure 1.2

Finally, it is important to outline the broad objectives you, as a student, should have in studying geometry. These are

1. A knowledge of the *facts*.
   These facts are the definitions, postulates, and theorems.
2. The development of *geometric intuition*.
   Knowledge of the facts should improve your ability to "see" geometric relationships.
3. An ability to *analyze problems*.
   Here our main tool will be the geometric figure. It holds the known facts in view, suggests geometric relationships, and is an important aid to your intuition.
4. An ability to write *proofs*.
   You will learn that a proper proof of a theorem is a chain of statements that link the hypothesis to the conclusion, and that the correctness of each statement in the proof must be clearly established. Proof writing in geometry affords excellent practice in logical, deductive thinking. It is a bit like writing a list of instructions directing someone, say, from your college to your home. If a person followed your instructions step by step, would he or she in fact find your home? Clearly your instructions would have to be complete and in the proper order. How many times have you asked directions, been told, "You can't miss it," and then missed it! Why?

Our study of geometry will begin in Chapter 2. The rest of this chapter presents some preliminary topics that will be needed in the development.

1.2 THE LANGUAGE OF SETS

The concept of a set of objects, and certain related concepts and notations, will be useful in organizing some of our ideas about geometric figures. A *set* is any well-defined collection of objects, where "well-defined" means that there must be a rule for deciding whether or not a given object is in the set. For example, we may talk about the set of freshmen attending a certain college or the set of books owned by a student. In these cases a listing of the objects in the set would be a sufficient rule for specifying the contents. Of course, geometry is concerned with sets of points and lines and with the sets of numbers used to measure geometric figures. This chapter, however, will be confined to nongeometric examples.

Capital letters are used to name sets in algebra, and this practice is followed in this chapter. As we shall see later, however, in geometry capital letters are used to name *points,* so other symbols are used to name the important *sets of points* (lines, for example) that we study. In both subjects, it is conventional to list the contents of a set in braces: $\{\ \}$. Thus, we may name the set of even numbers between 7 and 17 set D and write $D = \{8, 10, 12, 14, 16\}$. Further examples of this notation are $A = \{0, 1, 2\}$, $B = \{-5, -3, \frac{1}{2}, 6.1\}$, and $C = \{\sqrt{2}\}$.

Sometimes we need the concept of the set that contains no objects at all. This set is called the *empty set* or the *null set* and is denoted by $\emptyset$. For example, the set containing all the negative numbers that are greater than 100 is assuredly empty!

It is essential to distinguish between the objects in a set and the concept of the set itself. The objects in a set are called its *elements*. The symbol $\in$ means "is an element of" while the symbol $\notin$ means "is not an element of." Thus, for the sets defined above,

$10 \in D$, is read "10 is an element of D."

$0 \in A$, is read "0 is an element of A."

$6 \notin B$, is read "6 is not an element of B."

$2 \notin C$, is read "2 is not an element of C."

If $E = \{3, 4, 5\}$ and $G = \{1, 2, 3, 4, 5, 6\}$, it is *not* correct to write $E \in G$, because E itself is not an element of G, although the *elements* of E are also elements of G. The distinction between the set and the elements that are in the set is clarified by the concept of a *subset*.

Definition 1.1 A set A is a *subset* of a set B, written $A \subseteq B$, if and only if every element of A is also an element of B.

Now, for sets E and G as defined above, it is correct to write $E \subseteq G$, since every element of E is also an element of G.

EXAMPLE 1

Given	Are the following true or false? Justify answers.
$A = \{0, 1, 2, 3\}$	**(a)** $B \subseteq A$
$B = \{0, 1, 2\}$	**(b)** $C \subseteq B$
$C = \{1, 2, 3\}$	**(c)** $B \in A$
$D = \{1, 2, 3, 4\}$	**(d)** $3 \in D$
	(e) $A \subseteq A$

Answers

(a) True, because every element of B is also in A.
(b) False, because $3 \in C$ but $3 \notin B$.
(c) False, because set B is not an element of A.
(d) True, because 3 is in D.
(e) True, because every element of A is certainly in A.

In Definition 1.1 the words "if and only if" imply two statements: (1) If $A \subseteq B$, then every element of A is also an element of B; and (2) if every element of A is also an element of B, then $A \subseteq B$. All definitions in mathematics can be written this way, and for this reason they are said to be reversible. Hereafter "if and only if" will be abbreviated *iff*.

As another example of the subset concept, if $S = \{-5, -3, -1\}$, then the statement $S \subseteq \emptyset$ is clearly false according to the definition, for there is certainly at least one element of S that is not in the empty set. But is the statement $\emptyset \subseteq S$ true or false? We cannot find at least one element of $\emptyset$ that is not in S; thus, $\emptyset \subseteq S$ does not seem to be false by definition. For this reason it is standard practice to define $\emptyset \subseteq S$ to be true where S is *any set whatever*.

So far we have defined sets by listing their elements, that is, by the *list method,* but this listing notation is inconvenient if a set is large. No one is eager to write the whole numbers from zero through one hundred, but this set may be partially listed as $\{0, 1, 2, 3, \ldots, 99, 100\}$, in which the three dots indicate that the established pattern continues. Similarly, the entire set of whole numbers may be denoted by $\{0, 1, 2, 3, \ldots\}$. Note here that the pattern continues indefinitely. Can you supply the missing numbers in the following sets?

$$\{1, 3, 5, \ldots, 37, 39\}$$

$$\{5, 10, 15, 20, \ldots\}$$

$$\{\tfrac{1}{2}, \tfrac{1}{4}, \tfrac{1}{8}, \tfrac{1}{16}, \ldots, \tfrac{1}{512}\}$$

Another useful way to designate the contents of a set is called the *set-builder* notation, in which a variable such as x is used to name any element in the set and a rule is given telling exactly what elements the variable can represent. The notation $\{x|x$ is any whole number less than $12\}$ is read, "the set of all x such that x is any whole number less than 12," and denotes the set $\{0, 1, 2, 3, 4, 5, 6, 7, 8, 9, 10, 11\}$.

EXAMPLE 2 Define the following sets by using the list method.

(a) $\{x|x$ is a negative integer greater than $-8\}$

(b) $\{y|y \text{ is a multiple of } 3\}$
(c) $\{2n|n \text{ is any whole number less than } 51\}$

Answers
(a) $\{-7, -6, -5, -4, -3, -2, -1\}$
(b) $\{0, 3, 6, 9, 12, \ldots\}$
(c) $\{0, 2, 4, 6, 8, \ldots, 98, 100\}$

Two set operations will be used in the work that follows. Recall that in arithmetic the addition operation "acts on" two numbers and produces a third number as the answer. Similarly, the set operations defined below act on two sets to produce a third set.

Definition 1.2 Let A, B, and C name three sets and the symbol $\cup$ name the set operation called *union*. Then $A \cup B = C$ iff C contains all those elements and only those elements that are either in A or in B or in both.

For example, if $A = \{-3, -2, -1, 0, 1\}$ and $B = \{0, 1, 2, 3,\}$, then $A \cup B = \{-3, -2, -1, 0, 1, 2, 3\}$.

Definition 1.3 Let A, B, and C name three sets and the symbol $\cap$ name the set operation called *intersection*. Then $A \cap B = C$ iff C contains all those elements and only those elements that are in both A and B.

For the sets A and B given in the example of union, $A \cap B = \{0, 1\}$. The next example further illustrates these operations.

EXAMPLE 3

Given
$A = \{\frac{1}{2}, \frac{1}{3}, \frac{1}{4}, \frac{1}{5}\}$
$B = \{\frac{1}{2}, \frac{1}{4}, \frac{1}{6}\}$
$C = \{\frac{1}{7}, \frac{1}{8}, \frac{1}{9}, \frac{1}{10}\}$

Find
(a) $A \cup B$
(b) $A \cup C$
(c) $A \cap B$
(d) $A \cap C$
(e) $A \cup \emptyset$
(f) $B \cap \emptyset$

Answers
(a) $A \cup B = \{\frac{1}{2}, \frac{1}{3}, \frac{1}{4}, \frac{1}{5}, \frac{1}{6}\}$
(b) $A \cup C = \{\frac{1}{2}, \frac{1}{3}, \frac{1}{4}, \frac{1}{5}, \frac{1}{7}, \frac{1}{8}, \frac{1}{9}, \frac{1}{10}\}$
(c) $A \cap B = \{\frac{1}{2}, \frac{1}{4}\}$
(d) $A \cap C = \emptyset$
(e) $A \cup \emptyset = A$
(f) $B \cap \emptyset = \emptyset$

EXERCISES FOR 1.1 AND 1.2

In exercises 1–20 answer true or false.

1. Plane geometry is primarily the study of figures that can be drawn on a flat surface.
2. Euclid was the author of the first geometry textbook.
3. Before defining geometric terms it is necessary to state a set of undefined terms.
4. A theorem is a statement to be proved.
5. Comparisons of one geometric figure with another are called dimensions.
6. A set of simplest terms whose meanings are intuitively clear is called a set of definitions.

7. Basic properties in geometry that are accepted without proof are called definitions.
8. The given facts in a theorem are called the hypothesis.
9. Theorems may be thought of as basic strategies for problem solving.
10. A set is any collection of objects.
11. A set containing no objects is called the zero set.
12. The objects in a set are called subsets.
13. If $A = \{3, 5, 7\}$ and $B = \{5, 3, 7\}$, then $A \subseteq B$.
14. The empty set is a subset of every set.
15. If $E = \{0, 2, 4\}$ and $J = \{6, 8, 10\}$, then $E \cup J = \emptyset$.
16. If $E = \{1, 3\}$ and $J = \{1, 3, 5, 7\}$, then $E \cap J = E$.
17. If $3 \in E$, $5 \in J$, $E \subseteq K$, and $J \subseteq K$, then $3, 5 \in K$.
18. If $2 \notin E$, $7 \in J$, $E \subseteq K$, and $J \subseteq K$, then $2 \notin K$.
19. If $A \cap B = \emptyset$, then A and B have only one element in common.
20. If $A \cup B = B$, then $A = B$.

In exercises 21–25 write a brief paragraph about the given topic.

21. Name four early Greek geometers and give a reason each is remembered.
22. Compare the use of undefined terms and defined terms in geometry.
23. Compare the use of postulates and theorems in geometry.
24. Describe the deductive reasoning process.
25. Name four broad objectives that the student should have for the course.

In exercises 26–35 answer true or false, given that $A = \{1, 2, 5, 7\}$, $B = \{3, 4, 5, 6, 7, 8\}$, and $C = \{1, 2, 3, 4, 5, 6, 7\}$.

26. $2 \in A$
27. $8 \notin C$
28. $5, 8 \in A$
29. $A \subseteq B$
30. $A \subseteq C$
31. $5 \subseteq A$
32. $B \not\subseteq C$
33. $8 \in B$
34. $A \in C$
35. $\emptyset \subseteq B$

In exercises 36–45 do the indicated operations, given that $U = \{x|x$ is a letter in the English alphabet$\}$, $E = \{x|x$ is a vowel$\}$, $J = \{x|x$ is the letter i or one of the next six letters in the alphabet$\}$, and $K = \{x|x$ is one of the first five letters in the alphabet$\}$.

36. $E \cap J$
37. $J \cap K$
38. $E \cup K$
39. $U \cap E$
40. $E \cup J$
41. $U \cup E$
42. $U \cap J$
43. $E \cap (J \cup K)$
44. $(J \cap K) \cup U$
45. $(U \cap E) \cup (U \cap J)$

In exercises 46–50, under what conditions on sets A and B would each statement be true?

46. $A \cap B = A$
47. $A \cup B = B$
48. $A \cup B = \emptyset$
49. $A \cup \emptyset = \emptyset$
50. $(A \cup B) \cap (A \cap B) = A$

In each of exercises 51–55 copy Figure 1.3 and shade in the indicated set. A is the set of points of the square and its interior, B is the set of points of the circle and its interior, and C is the set of points of the triangle and its interior.

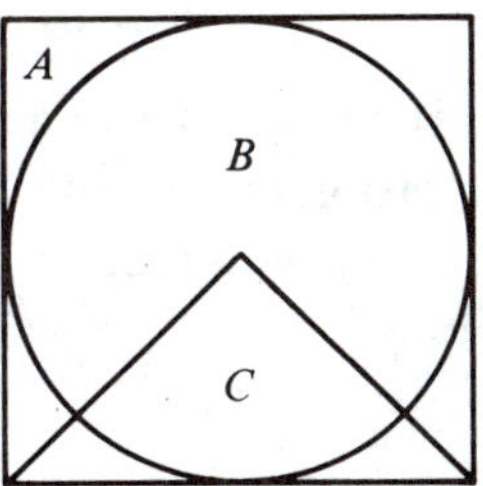

Figure 1.3

51. $B \cap C$
52. $B \cup C$
53. $A \cap B \cap C$
54. $A \cap (B \cup C)$
55. $(B \cup C) \cup (A \cap C)$

In exercises 56–65 use Figure 1.4, in which A represents the triangle and its interior, B represents the rectangle and its interior, and C represents the circle and its interior. Draw a figure for each exercise and shade in the region represented by the indicated set.

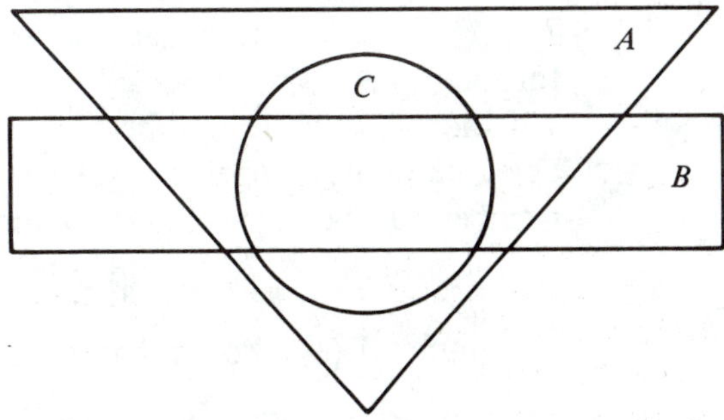

Figure 1.4

56. $A \cup B$ **57.** $A \cap C$ **58.** $B \cap C$ **59.** $B \cup C$
60. $A \cap (B \cap C)$ **61.** $B \cup (A \cap C)$ **62.** $(A \cup B) \cup C$ **63.** $(B \cap C) \cup C$
64. $(A \cup C) \cap (A \cup B)$ **65.** $(A \cap B) \cup (A \cap C)$

1.3
THE SET OF REAL NUMBERS

Numbers are needed in geometry to measure the sizes of various geometric figures. You are probably already familiar with the ways in which line segments and angles are measured. Nonetheless, Chapters 2 and 3 contain a detailed discussion of these concepts. This section reviews the types of numbers that will be used.

Perhaps the simplest set of numbers is the set W of *whole numbers,* which may be written as

$$W = \{0, 1, 2, 3, 4, 5, 6, 7, \ldots\}$$

This familiar set of numbers has the weakness that it cannot supply answers to subtraction problems of the "smaller-take-away-larger" variety, for example, $2 - 10$. This defect is remedied by defining the set J of *integers,* which we write as

$$J = \{\ldots, -3, -2, -1, 0, 1, 2, 3, 4, \ldots\}$$

Now we have $2 - 10 = -8$, as you should recall from algebra. Note also that $W \subseteq J$.

A further extension is needed, of course, because many division problems with integers do not have answers in J. An example is $13 \div 5 = 2\frac{3}{5}$, a number that is not an integer. To handle this difficulty, we need the set F of rational numbers, a set that, although awkward to list even partially, may be defined as follows.

Definition 1.4 A number is called a *rational number* iff it can be written as a fraction $\frac{a}{b}$, where $a, b \in J$, but $b \neq 0$.

Thus, $\frac{1}{3}$, $4 = \frac{4}{1}$, $-\frac{2}{7}$, $2\frac{3}{5} = \frac{13}{5}$, and $-10 = -\frac{10}{1}$ all name rational numbers. Such numbers and their uses as answers to division problems should be familiar to you. It should be emphasized that the integers have not been lost; that is, $J \subseteq F$. This is true because every integer can be represented as a fraction; for example, $9 = \frac{9}{1}$, $-6 = -\frac{6}{1}$, and $0 = \frac{0}{1}$. In fact, note the way Definition 1.4 includes whole numbers, integers, and fractions, all in one set of numbers, certainly a useful result. It should also be recalled that each rational number can be represented by many fractions. Thus, any element of the set

$$\{\tfrac{1}{2}, \tfrac{2}{4}, \tfrac{3}{6}, \ldots, \tfrac{-1}{-2}, \tfrac{-2}{-4}, \tfrac{-3}{-6}, \ldots\}$$

is a numeral (symbol) for the rational number one-half.

EXAMPLE 1 Answer true or false.
(a) $-7 \in F$ **(b)** $J \subseteq W$ **(c)** $11\frac{1}{6} \in F$ **(d)** $W \subseteq F$ **(e)** $\frac{-25}{10} \in F$

Answers

(a) True, because $-7 = \frac{-7}{1}$, a fraction.
(b) False, because $-1 \in J$, but $-1 \notin W$.
(c) True, because $11\frac{1}{6} = \frac{67}{6}$, a fraction.
(d) True, because if $x \in W$, then $x = \frac{x}{1}$, a fraction.
(e) True, because $\frac{-25}{10}$ is a fraction.

Note that in Example 1(e) $\frac{-25}{10} = -\frac{5}{2} = -2\frac{1}{2}$. Again, there are many numerals that represent a given rational number.

One further extension of our number concepts is used in geometry. It may be introduced by recalling the *square root* concept. The equation $x^2 = 9$ has two roots, 3 and -3, and these two numbers are called the square roots of 9. The positive square root of 9 is denoted $\sqrt{9}$ so that $\sqrt{9} = 3$, whereas the negative square root of 9 is denoted $-\sqrt{9}$ and thus $-\sqrt{9} = -3$.

Definition 1.5 Let c be a positive rational number. Then

1. $\sqrt{c} = x$ iff $x^2 = c$ and x is positive;
2. $-\sqrt{c} = x$ iff $x^2 = c$ and x is negative;
3. $\sqrt{0} = 0$.

At the end of this section we will show that the number c of Definition 1.5 need not be restricted to set F.

EXAMPLE 2 Find the indicated square roots, and justify the answers.
(a) $\sqrt{64}$ **(b)** $\sqrt{\frac{4}{49}}$ **(c)** $-\sqrt{121}$ **(d)** $-\sqrt{\frac{50}{72}}$ **(e)** $\sqrt{3\frac{6}{25}}$

Answers

(a) $\sqrt{64} = 8$ because $8^2 = 64$ and 8 is positive.
(b) $\sqrt{\frac{4}{49}} = \frac{2}{7}$ because $(\frac{2}{7})^2 = \frac{4}{49}$ and $\frac{2}{7}$ is positive.
(c) $-\sqrt{121} = -11$ because $(-11)^2 = 121$ and -11 is negative.
(d) $-\sqrt{\frac{50}{72}} = -\sqrt{\frac{25}{36}} = -\frac{5}{6}$ because $(-\frac{5}{6})^2 = \frac{25}{36} = \frac{50}{72}$ and $-\frac{5}{6}$ is negative.
(e) $\sqrt{3\frac{6}{25}} = \sqrt{\frac{81}{25}} = \frac{9}{5}$ because $(\frac{9}{5})^2 = \frac{81}{25} = 3\frac{6}{25}$ and $\frac{9}{5}$ is positive.

The numbers in Example 2 were carefully chosen. There are many rational numbers c for which $\sqrt{c}$ is not rational. Examples are $\sqrt{2}$, $\sqrt{\frac{1}{3}}$, and $-\sqrt{5}$. To understand these numbers properly and to extend our number concepts to include these nonrational numbers, we need to review the decimal numerals for rational numbers.

EXAMPLE 3 Express the rational numbers as decimals.
(a) $\frac{1}{8}$, **(b)** $\frac{15}{4}$, **(c)** $\frac{2}{3}$, **(d)** $\frac{2}{11}$

Answers

(a)
$$\begin{array}{r} 0.125 \\ 8\overline{)1.000} \\ \underline{8} \\ 20 \\ \underline{16} \\ 40 \\ \underline{40} \end{array}$$
$\frac{1}{8} = 0.125$

(b)
$$\begin{array}{r} 3.75 \\ 4\overline{)15.00} \\ \underline{12} \\ 30 \\ \underline{28} \\ 20 \\ \underline{20} \end{array}$$
$\frac{15}{4} = 3.75$

(c)
```
   0.66
3)2.00
  1 8
    20    2/3 = 0.66 ···
    18
     2
```

(d)
```
    0.1818
11)2.0000
   1 1
     90    2/11 = 0.1818 ···
     88
      20
      11
       90
```

The quotients in Example 3(a) and (b) are *terminating* decimals because a zero remainder was reached in each case. In (c) and (d), however, the quotients are *nonterminating* decimals, because a zero remainder can never be obtained. They are also *repeating* decimals, since a block of digits will be repeated as the division is continued. Such decimals are indicated either by writing the repeating block twice, followed by three dots, or by placing a bar over the repeating block. Thus $\frac{2}{3} = 0.66\cdots = 0.\overline{6}$ and $\frac{2}{11} = 0.1818\cdots = 0.\overline{18}$. Although we omit the proof, it is a fact that *every rational number has either a terminating decimal numeral or a nonterminating repeating decimal numeral,* and conversely, *such decimals always represent rational numbers.*

One reason for reviewing the types of decimal numerals that represent rational numbers is to alert you to the possibly startling fact that *there are decimal numerals that do not name rational numbers*. It is easy to write such decimals. Clearly they may neither terminate nor repeat, although they may contain a pattern that enables us to continue writing them indefinitely. Two such decimals are shown in the next example.

EXAMPLE 4 Explain why the numbers represented cannot be rational.
(a) $0.5252252225\cdots$ **(b)** $-0.135791113\cdots$

Answers
(a) There is no repeating block here, because the pattern calls for an additional 2 between each successive pair of 5s.
(b) In this negative nonrepeating, nonterminating decimal, the pattern is to continue writing the odd whole-number numerals. Clearly there cannot be a repeating block of digits.

It was stated earlier that a number may be rational and yet have nonrational square roots. Such square roots have nonterminating, nonrepeating decimal numerals. For example, $\sqrt{7} = 2.64575131106\cdots$. It can be shown that this decimal never terminates and never repeats.

Many numbers that occur in mathematics and its applications have nonterminating, nonrepeating decimal numerals. One such number is π (mentioned in Section 1.1), which is very important in geometry. In the next definition we formally identify these nonrational numbers.

Definition 1.6 The numbers represented by the nonterminating, nonrepeating decimals are called *irrational* numbers. The set of irrational numbers is named set I.

It is essential to understand that there is no number that is both rational and irrational. This may be stated briefly as $F \cap I = \emptyset$. We would like, however, to group these two distinct types of numbers into one set that contains *all* of the decimals.

Definition 1.7 The numbers represented by the terminating, the nonterminating repeating, and the nonterminating, nonrepeating decimals are called *real numbers*. The set of real numbers is named set R. Symbolically, $R = \{x|x \text{ has a decimal numeral}\}$.

The set R can be defined more briefly: $R = F \cup I$. Note also that $W \subseteq J \subseteq F \subseteq R$ and $I \subseteq R$. The diagram in Figure 1.5 will aid in relating the various types of numbers.

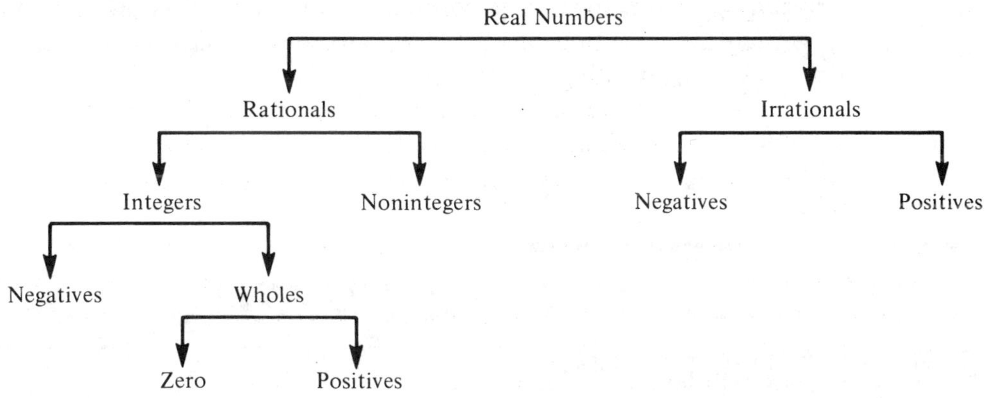

Figure 1.5

Finally, note that Definition 1.5 can be extended to include the cases where c is a positive irrational number. Thus $\sqrt{\pi} = x$ iff $x^2 = \pi$ and x is positive. For practical purposes a terminating decimal (i.e., rational) approximation may be found for such square roots by using a hand-held calculator.

EXERCISES FOR 1.3

In exercises 1–20 answer true or false.

1. Numbers are used in geometry to measure the sizes of geometric figures.
2. The set of integers is a subset of the set of whole numbers.
3. Any number that can be represented by a decimal numeral is called a real number.
4. $0.878878887\cdots$ is a rational number.
5. A number is a rational number if it can be written as a fraction $\frac{a}{b}$ where a and b are integers.
6. All fractions can be written either as terminating decimals or as nonterminating repeating decimals.
7. $-0.1212\cdots$ is a real number.
8. A number cannot be both rational and irrational.
9. $0.123123\cdots$ is an irrational number.
10. $W \subseteq J \subseteq F \subseteq R$
11. $F \cap I = R$
12. If $x \in I$, then x cannot be written as a fraction.
13. The square root of every positive number is an irrational number.
14. The integer zero is a rational number.
15. The numeral $\sqrt{25}$ represents both $+5$ and -5.
16. If $x \in I$, then $x \notin R$.
17. A number cannot be both real and irrational.
18. If $x \in R$, then $x \in F$ or $x \in I$.
19. Many different numerals can represent a given rational number.
20. $0.66\cdots + 0.33\cdots$ must equal one because $\frac{2}{3} + \frac{1}{3} = 1$.

In exercises 21–25 change the given number to a decimal. Name the type of decimal in your answer.

21. $\frac{7}{8}$ **22.** $-\frac{5}{6}$ **23.** $\frac{5}{7}$ **24.** $-\frac{23}{11}$
25. $-\frac{11}{13}$

In exercises 26–35 replace the comma with $\in$, $\notin$, $\subseteq$, or $\not\subseteq$ so that the resulting statement is true.

26. J, R **27.** $\{-\sqrt{3}\}, R$
28. $\sqrt{121}, R$ **29.** $\frac{2}{3}, I$ **30.** $-5, J$
31. $-2, W$ **32.** $\emptyset, R$ **33.** F, I
34. $\{\pi, 2, 3\}, I$ **35.** $\{.77\cdots\}, F$

In exercises 36–45 replace the comma with $\cup$ or $\cap$ so that the resulting statement is true.

36. $F, I = \emptyset$ **37.** $F, I = R$
38. $W, J = J$ **39.** $J, F = J$
40. $F, R = R$ **41.** $F, R = F$
42. $\emptyset, R = \emptyset$ **43.** $\{.33\cdots\}, F = F$
44. $J, R = R$ **45.** $F, (W \cap J) = W$

In exercises 46–49 write short answers to the questions.

46. If $r \in I$, why can r not be written as $\frac{a}{b}$, where $a, b \in J$ and $b \neq 0$?
47. Why is $-\frac{2}{3}$ a square root of $\frac{4}{9}$?
48. In this section, we changed fractions to decimals to develop what type of decimal numeral representing what type of number?
49. Why cannot a given real number be both rational and irrational?
50. Find five unequal fractions between $\frac{2}{3}$ and $\frac{7}{10}$.

1.4

SOME RELATIONS BETWEEN REAL NUMBERS

Comparisons between geometric figures or between numbers are called *relations*, and the *equals relation* is the most fundamental one in mathematics. In general, $x = y$ means that x and y represent the same mathematical object. Certainly if $x, y \in R$—that is, if x and y are variables naming real numbers—and if $x = y$, then x and y must name the same real number. Clearly $5 = 5$, $-\frac{3}{4} = -\frac{3}{4}$, and $11 = 11$. On the other hand, if $x, y \in R$ and $x \neq y$, then there are two possibilities: either x is less than y ($x < y$) or x is greater than y ($x > y$). You should be familiar with these *order relations* from algebra. For example, $7 < 15$, $-\frac{9}{4} < 2$, $-6 < -1$, $4 > 0$, and $0 > -2$.

These relations between real numbers may be visualized on the *number line* for set R. This is an imaginary line consisting of an infinite number of points, which are placed in a one-to-one correspondence with the real numbers according to the order relation "is less than"; that is, the numbers are *ordered* along the line. Although the number line is an abstract concept, it can be diagrammed by drawing a line and selecting a point that we mark 0 (zero) and another that we mark 1, thus establishing a unit interval and a positive direction. Then, after marking the unit intervals as far as desired in both directions and matching integers to the points so obtained, we have

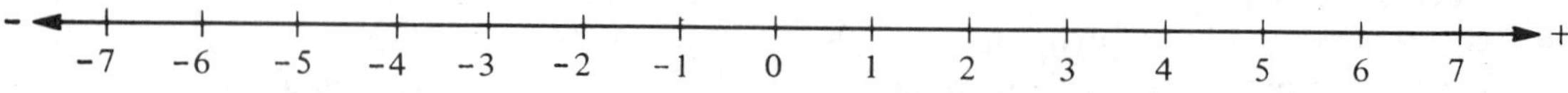

Note that an understanding of the less-than relation is needed to do this.

Next the concept of fractional parts enables us to match each rational number to a unique point on the line. For example,

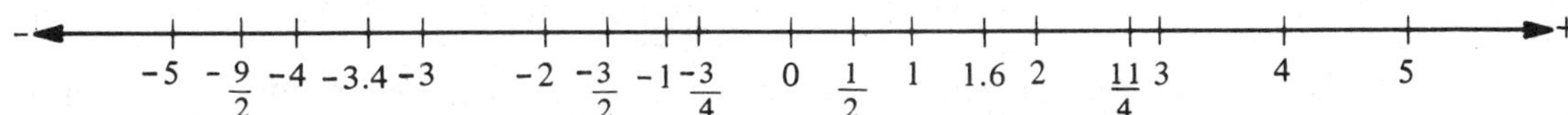

Physical considerations limit the number of fractions that can be marked on the line, but by thinking of a point as having no thickness, we can visualize a unique point for each rational number.

Finally each irrational number may be matched to a unique point on the number line, if we think of the irrational numbers as decimals. Accurately marking such points is more difficult than approximating the locations of such numbers as 2 or $\frac{1}{3}$. There is a procedure that may be used, however. We have stated that $\sqrt{7} = 2.64575131106\cdots$, an irrational number. It follows that $2.6 < \sqrt{7}$ and $\sqrt{7} < 2.7$. These order relations enable us to mark approximately the proper point for $\sqrt{7}$ as shown.

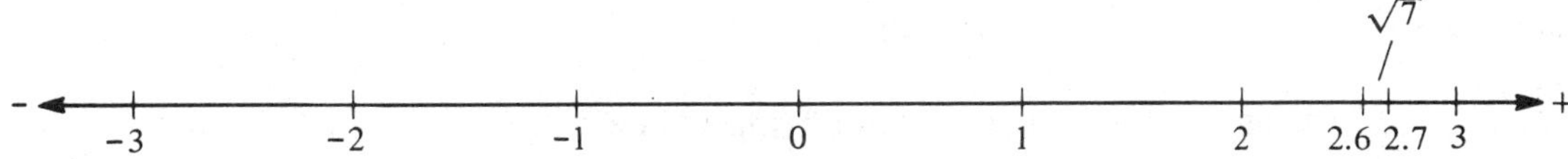

Thus each real number may be matched to exactly one point on a number line, and if $x, y \in R$ and $x < y$, then on a horizontal number line the point for x is to the left of that for y, whereas if $x > y$, the point for x is to the right of that for y. The number that is matched to each point is called the *coordinate* of the point.

Coordinates are useful in defining the distance between two points on the number line. Doing so, however, requires the concept of the absolute value of a real number.

Definition 1.8 Let $x \in R$ and let $|x|$ denote the *absolute value* of x. Then

1. $|x| = x$ if $x > 0$;
2. $|x| = 0$ if $x = 0$;
3. $|x| = (-1)x$ if $x < 0$.

A consequence of this definition is that $|x|$ is always nonnegative, as shown in the next example.

EXAMPLE 1

Find

(a) $|10|$ **(b)** $|0|$ **(c)** $|-\frac{1}{2}|$ **(d)** $|\sqrt{2}|$

Answers

(a) $|10| = 10$ **(b)** $|0| = 0$ **(c)** $|-\frac{1}{2}| = (-1)(-\frac{1}{2}) = \frac{1}{2}$ **(d)** $|\sqrt{2}| = \sqrt{2}$

Now consider the following diagram, in which capital letters (as is the practice in geometry) are used to name certain points.

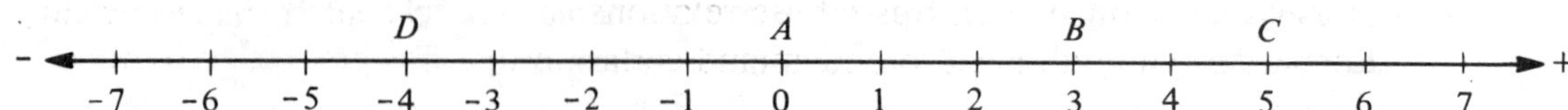

Using the notation AB to denote the *distance* between point A and point B, we see that AB should be 3 units, BC 2 units, and DA 4 units. Note that, using coordinates, we can write

$$AB = 3 - 0 = 3$$
$$BC = 5 - 3 = 2$$
$$DA = 0 - (-4) = 4$$

Since distance is nonnegative, however, we cannot reverse the order of these subtractions; that is, $0 - 3 = -3 \neq AB$, $3 - 5 = -2 \neq BC$, and $-4 - 0 = -4 \neq DA$. It is nonetheless possible to use subtraction of coordinates to correctly define distance by using the absolute value of a real number.

Definition 1.9 Let P and Q name two points on a number line, with x the coordinate of P and y the coordinate of Q. Then the *distance* between P and Q is $PQ = |x - y| = |y - x|$.

Using this definition and referring to the above diagram, we have

$$AB = |3 - 0| = |3| = 3 \quad \text{or} \quad AB = |0 - 3| = |-3| = 3$$
$$BC = |5 - 3| = |2| = 2 \quad \text{or} \quad BC = |3 - 5| = |-2| = 2$$
$$DA = |0 - (-4)| = |4| = 4 \quad \text{or} \quad DA = |-4 - 0| = |-4| = 4$$

When computing distances by using coordinates, care must be taken to subtract correctly, particularly when negative numbers are involved. The order of subtraction is immaterial, however, because of the final, absolute-value step. These points are illustrated in the next example.

EXAMPLE 2

Given

Points P, T, Q, V, W, and S as shown.

Find

(a) QS **(b)** PQ **(c)** TV **(d)** VW

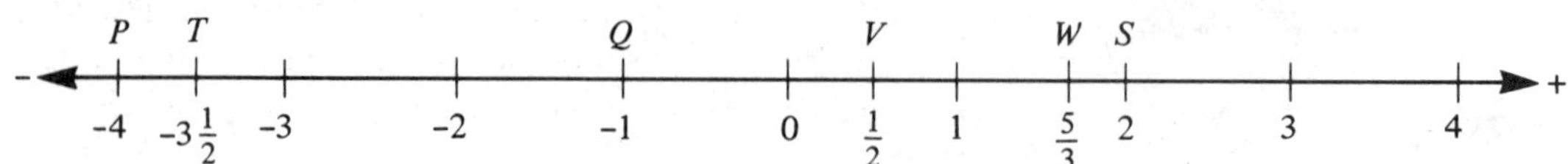

Answers

(a) $QS = |2 - (-1)| = |2 + 1| = |3| = 3$

(b) $PQ = |-4 - (-1)| = |-4 + 1| = |-3| = 3$

(c) $TV = |\frac{1}{2} - (-3\frac{1}{2})| = |\frac{1}{2} + \frac{7}{2}| = |4| = 4$

(d) $VW = |\frac{1}{2} - \frac{5}{3}| = |\frac{3}{6} + \frac{-10}{6}| = |-\frac{7}{6}| = \frac{7}{6}$ or $1\frac{1}{6}$

We have discussed the equals, less-than, and greater-than relations between real numbers, and we have seen how they may be visualized on a number line. Later we will use these relations to compare sizes of geometric figures, and you will need to understand certain properties possessed by these relations among the elements of set R. For example, suppose that three distances AB, BC, and CD on a number line are such that $AB = BC$ and $BC = CD$. May we then conclude that $AB = CD$? The answer, of course, is yes. This is an illustration of a simple but important property of the equals relation in set R.

There are three fundamental properties of the equals relation in set R, which we state as axioms. (Remember that an axiom is a fundamental property that is accepted without proof.)

Axiom 1 *Reflexive Property of Equals*
If $x \in R$, then $x = x$.

This merely indicates that any real number is equal to itself. For example $-8 = -8$.

Axiom 2 *Symmetric Property of Equals*
If $x, y \in R$ and $x = y$, then $y = x$.

This may seem trivial, but remember that there are many ways to represent a given real number. Thus, by this property, since $2 + 3 = 5$, we may write $5 = 2 + 3$. Also, since $\frac{2}{3} = 0.666\cdots$, $0.666\cdots = \frac{2}{3}$.

Axiom 3 *Transitive Property of Equals*
If $x, y, z \in R$ such that $x = y$ and $y = z$, then $x = z$.

An example of this has already been mentioned, where x, y, and z were distances on a number line. A further example: Since $\frac{18}{30} = \frac{9}{15}$ and $\frac{9}{15} = \frac{3}{5}$, we conclude that $\frac{18}{30} = \frac{3}{5}$.

The above three properties are briefly called the RST properties. Although all three are valid for the equals relation in set R, they are not all true for all relations in set R. For example, consider the less-than relation.

Is the less-than relation reflexive in set R?
Consider the statement $2 < 2$. Clearly this is false and we conclude that the less-than relation does *not* have the reflexive property.
Is the less-than relation symmetric in set R?
For example, we know $2 < 9$. May we then conclude that $9 < 2$? No! Thus, the less-than relation does *not* have the symmetric property.
Is the less-than relation transitive in set R?
Because $2 < 9$ and $9 < 11$, it follows that $2 < 11$, and, in general, if $x < y$ and $y < z$, then $x < z$, although we will not prove it so. Therefore, the less-than relation *does* have the transitive property.

Hence, we say that the less-than relation is transitive, but *not* reflexive or symmetric in set R. The important point is that we now know certain things that can and cannot be done with the less-than relation in set R.

It should now be evident that checking the validity of the RST properties for a relation requires clear definitions of

1. a *set* of elements
2. the *relation* to be checked among the elements of the set

In the examples above, the *set* was R and the *relations* were the equals and less-than relations. Of course, the relation must be one that makes sense for the set in question. The next example further illustrates these points.

EXAMPLE 3 For each of the RST properties and the greater-than relation in set R, (a) state the property, (b) give a numerical example, and (c) state whether or not the property is valid.

Answers

Reflexive:
(a) Let $x \in R$. Then $x > x$.
(b) Let $x = 12$. Then $12 > 12$.
(c) Clearly *not* valid.

Symmetric:
(a) If $x, y \in R$ and $x > y$, then $y > x$.
(b) If $x = 17$, $y = 0$, and $17 > 0$, then $0 > 17$.
(c) Clearly *not* valid.

Transitive:
(a) If x, y, and $z \in R$, $x > y$, and $y > z$, then $x > z$.
(b) If $x = 23$, $y = 19$, and $z = \frac{1}{8}$, and if $23 > 19$ and $19 > \frac{1}{8}$, then $23 > \frac{1}{8}$.
(c) Valid.

In geometry there are many relations between geometric figures, some of which will be familiar to you. One such relation, the parallel relation, concerns lines. In writing proofs, you will need to know which of the RST properties may be used for some of these geometric relations. Therefore, this section concludes with a nonmathematical example as a further aid in identifying and understanding the RST properties. The general symbol ® stands for the relation in question.

EXAMPLE 4 Let A name the set of all women and ® stand for the relation "is the sister of." For each of the RST properties, (a) state the property, (b) give a specific example, and (c) state whether or not the property is valid.

Answers

Reflexive:
(a) If $x \in A$, then x ® x.
(b) Karen ® Karen.
(c) Not valid.

Symmetric:
(a) If $x, y \in A$ and x ® y, then y ® x.
(b) If Wendy ® Jenny, then Jenny ® Wendy.
(c) Valid.

Transitive:
(a) If $x, y, z \in A$, and if x ® y and y ® z, then x ® z.
(b) If Joyce ® Janet and Janet ® Joan, then Joyce ® Joan is valid, but if Joyce ® Janet and Janet ® Joyce, then Joyce ® Joyce is not.
(c) Not valid.

EXERCISES FOR 1.4

In exercises 1–20 answer true or false.

1. Comparisons between geometric figures or between numbers are called operations.
2. Each point on the number line is matched with a rational number.

3. The number line is an imaginary line consisting of an infinite number of points.
4. If $a = b$, then a and b represent the same mathematical object.
5. Seven is less than nine because it lies to the right of nine on the number line.
6. Real numbers are ordered on the number line using the less-than relation.
7. The real number matched to a point on the number line is called the coordinate of that point.
8. The absolute value of a real number is always a positive number.
9. If the coordinate of a point is -6, then the coordinate of a second point 3 units to its left is -3.
10. The distance from -8 to -1 on the number line is 9 units.
11. A relation defined on a set is a comparison that can be applied to any two objects in the set.
12. The less-than relation in R is symmetric but not reflexive or transitive.
13. If $|n| = 6$, then $n = 6$.
14. In order to check the validity of the RST properties, a set of elements and a relation must first be clearly defined.
15. The equals relation in R is reflexive, symmetric, and transitive.
16. If the coordinate of E is -11, and the coordinate of J is -19, then the distance from J to E is -8.
17. The greater-than relation in R is not symmetric, because a number is not greater than itself.
18. The reflexive property is valid for the less-than-or-equal-to relation in the set of real numbers.
19. If $n \leq 3$, then $|n - 3|$ is always less than or equal to zero.
20. If the coordinates of two points are given by $|-1 - \sqrt{3}|$ and $|-1 + \sqrt{3}|$, then the distance between them is given by $|-2|$.

Complete the statements in exercises 21–35 by using Figure 1.6.

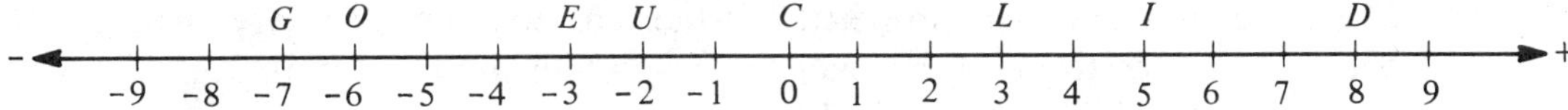

Figure 1.6

21. The coordinate for point E is ________.
22. The coordinate for point U is ________.
23. The point with coordinate 0 is labeled ________.
24. The point with coordinate 8 is labeled ________.
25. The coordinate of a point 10 units to the right of point G is ________.
26. The coordinate of a point 7 units to the left of point I is ________.
27. The distance from point O to point L is ________ units.
28. The distance from point I to point G is ________ units.
29. A point (or points) 7 units from C is (or are) labeled ________.
30. A point (or points) 5 units from L is (or are) labeled ________.
31. The distance from point E to point D is ________.
32. The distance from point L to point E is ________.
33. The distance from point G to point E is ________.
34. The distance from point U to point G is ________.
35. The distance from point D to point G is ________.

In exercises 36–40 write a short but complete answer.

36. Describe the number line concept.
37. Explain how the less-than relation is used to order the number line.
38. What numbers could be substituted for r to make $|r| = \pi$ a true statement?
39. Show that the less-than-or-equal-to relation in R is reflexive and transitive but not symmetric.
40. Explain the role of absolute value in finding the distance between two points.

In exercises 41–50, give an example, using the given set and relation, that shows that the assertion is true.

41. The less-than relation is not symmetric in F.
42. The less-than relation is not reflexive in F.
43. The less-than relation is not symmetric in I.
44. "Is 5 units to the right of" is not transitive on the number line for R.
45. "Is 3 units to the left of" is not symmetric on the number line for R.
46. The greater-than-or-equal-to relation is not symmetric in R.
47. "Is a point distinct from" is not transitive for the points on the number line for R.
48. "Is a multiple of" is not symmetric in W.
49. "Is the absolute value of" is not symmetric in R.
50. "Is the square root of" is not reflexive in R.

In exercises 51–55 tell whether the given relation ® defined on the given set S has the reflexive, symmetric, and transitive properties. Show why or why not.

51. S is the set of real numbers, and ® is the relation less than or equal to ($\leq$).
52. S is the set of points on the number line, and ® is the relation "lies to the right of."
53. S is the set of whole numbers, and ® is the relation "is a factor of."
54. S is the set of all sets, and ® is the subset relation ($\subseteq$).
55. S is the set of points on the number line, and ® is the relation "is at a distance of 5 units from."

1.5 BASIC PROPERTIES OF REAL NUMBERS

There are certain simple properties of the real numbers that serve as a foundation on which to build the many more-complicated manipulations that are required in applying these numbers. These properties are stated as axioms, that is, as fundamental statements that are accepted without proof. The axioms reflect the ways in which real numbers are used in counting, measuring, and calculating, and you should be familiar with most of these axioms from your work in algebra. In this section we state only those axioms that will be needed explicitly in our development of geometry. A complete list of the axioms for the system of real numbers is given in Appendix A.

Axiom 4 *Commutative Property for Addition*
If $x, y \in R$, then $x + y = y + x$.

In words, the order of two numbers being added may be reversed without changing the sum. For example, $20 + 9 = 9 + 20$.

Axiom 5 *Associative Property for Addition*
If $x, y, z \in R$, then $(x + y) + z = x + (y + z)$.

This axiom is necessary because addition involves only two numbers at a time. An expression such as $2 + 6 + 5$ is ambiguous: Which operation is to be done first, and how does the choice affect the answer? According to Axiom 5, the order in which the additions are done does not matter, for the answer is unchanged. Thus, we define $2 + 6 + 5$ to mean $(2 + 6) + 5$ or $2 + (6 + 5)$ and obtain 13 either way.

Axiom 6 *Commutative Property for Multiplication*
If $x, y \in R$, then $x \cdot y = y \cdot x$.

The order of two numbers being multiplied may be reversed without changing the product. For example, $7 \cdot 5 = 5 \cdot 7$.

Axiom 7 *Associative Property for Multiplication*
If $x, y, z \in R$, then $(x \cdot y) \cdot z = x \cdot (y \cdot z)$.

The similarity of this axiom to Axiom 5 should be clear. An expression like $8 \cdot 2 \cdot 3$ is defined to mean $(8 \cdot 2) \cdot 3$ or $8 \cdot (2 \cdot 3)$. Either way, the answer is 48.

Axiom 8 *Distributive Property*
If $x, y, z \in R$, then $x \cdot (y + z) = (x \cdot y) + (x \cdot z)$.

For example, if $x = -5$, $y = 8$, and $z = 2$, then

$$-5 \cdot (8 + 2) \stackrel{?}{=} (-5 \cdot 8) + (-5 \cdot 2)$$
$$-5 \cdot 10 \stackrel{?}{=} (-40) + (-10)$$
$$-50 = -50$$

This verification suggests that the definitions of addition and multiplication are consistent with the axiom. It can be shown that they indeed are.

Axioms 4–8 justify many of the familiar manipulations of arithmetic and algebra. For example:

$2x + 3y + 4x + 5y = 2x + (3y + 4x) + 5y$	Associative for addition
$= 2x + (4x + 3y) + 5y$	Commutative for addition
$= (2x + 4x) + (3y + 5y)$	Associative for addition
$= (2 + 4) \cdot x + (3 + 5) \cdot y$	Distributive
$= 6x + 8y$	Addition facts

These steps suggest calling the associative, commutative, and distributive axioms *rearrangement properties*. We will do this, and we will also omit writing out the detailed steps just shown.

As indicated in Section 1.4, the less-than relation in the set of real numbers has the transitive property. This fact may be stated formally as follows:

Axiom 9 *Transitive Property of Order*
If $x, y, z \in R$, $x < y$, and $y < z$, then $x < z$.

Note that this property is also valid for the greater-than relation, as shown in Example 3 in Section 1.4.

In Section 1.4 we discussed the way in which each real number can be matched to a unique point on a number line, but in doing so, we implied an important question: Does this matching process use up all the points on the line, or are there points left over that do not correspond to real numbers? This question bothered mathematicians for many years and was finally resolved rigorously in 1872 by the German mathematician Richard Dedekind. The answer is that there are no points left over; we say that the real numbers *complete* the number line. This fact may be stated as follows:

Axiom 10 *Completeness*

There exists a one-to-one correspondence between the elements of R and the points on a line.

This formal language means simply that to each real number there corresponds a unique point on the number line and that, conversely, to each point on the number line there corresponds a unique real number. Note that this would not be true without the irrationals; that is, there are points on the number line that do *not* correspond to fractions.

Using the axioms for the system of real numbers (Appendix A) and the RST properties of the equals relation (Section 1.4), many useful theorems can be proved although we will not do this here. We will, however, state as axioms seven additional properties that are particularly useful in geometry.

Axiom 11 *Addition of Equals*

If $a = b$ and $c = d$, then $a + c = b + d$

This means that, given two correct equals relations, if the left members are added and the right members are added, the resulting sums will be equal. For example, it is true that

$$2 + 7 = 6 + 3 \quad \text{and} \quad 5 = 5$$

Adding left members and right members, we obtain

$$(2 + 7) + 5 = (6 + 3) + 5 \quad \text{or} \quad 14 = 14$$

Axiom 12 *Subtraction of Equals*

If $a = b$ and $c = d$, then $a - c = b - d$.

Thus, since $2 + 7 = 6 + 3$ and $5 = 5$, we may write $(2 + 7) - 5 = (6 + 3) - 5$, or $4 = 4$.

Axiom 13 *Multiplication of Equals*

If $a = b$ and $c = d$, then $a \cdot c = b \cdot d$.

Again, using $2 + 7 = 6 + 3$ and $5 = 5$, we have $(2 + 7) \cdot 5 = (6 + 3) \cdot 5$ or $45 = 45$.

Axiom 14 *Division of Equals*

If $a = b$, $c = d$, $c \neq 0$, and $d \neq 0$, then $a \div c = b \div d$.

For example, since $-30 = -30$ and $10 = 10$, we may write $-30 \div 10 = -30 \div 10$, or $-3 = -3$.

Axiom 15 *Whole Greater than Part*

If $x, y, z \in R$, $z > 0$, and $x = y + z$, then $x > y$.

For example, since $10 = 7 + 3$ and $3 > 0$, we have $10 > 7$.

Axiom 16 *Addition of Inequalities*

If $a < b$ and $c < d$, then $a + c < b + d$, or if $a > b$ and $c > d$, then $a + c > b + d$.

Thus, since $5 < 11$ and $3 < 13$, we may write $5 + 3 < 11 + 13$ or $8 < 24$. Also, since $4 > -1$ and $-7 > -10$, we have $4 + (-7) > (-1) + (-10)$, or $-3 > -11$.

Often, when using mathematical symbols, we must replace one expression with another that is equal to it. Thus, in algebra we may wish to replace the polynomial expression $(3x - 2) - (x - 7)$ with the equal (and simpler) expression $2x + 5$. This substitution process is the content of our final axiom.

Axiom 17 *Substitution*
If a and b name two mathematical expressions such that $a = b$, then a may replace b or b may replace a in any mathematical statement.

While a list of 17 axioms may seem lengthy, remember that these fundamental properties form the basis needed for those parts of our work that involve the real numbers and the equals relation.

EXERCISES FOR 1.5

In exercises 1–20 answer true or false.

1. The equation $7 \cdot \frac{1}{2} = \frac{1}{2} \cdot 7$ is true because of the commutative axiom for multiplication.
2. Axioms are statements about the real numbers that are proved to be true.
3. The distributive axiom involves both the addition and the multiplication operations.
4. The equation $(\frac{5}{3} \cdot \frac{2}{11}) \cdot \frac{3}{2} = \frac{3}{2} \cdot (\frac{5}{3} \cdot \frac{2}{11})$ is true because of the associative axiom for multiplication.
5. There are points on the number line that do not correspond to rational numbers.
6. The equation $\pi + \sqrt{2} = \sqrt{2} + \pi$ is true because of the commutative axiom for addition.
7. The collective term *rearrangement properties* refers to the commutative, associative, and distributive axioms.
8. Every point on the number line has a coordinate that is a real number.
9. Since there are an infinite number of points on the number line and an infinite number of fractions, the fractions name all the points on the line.
10. Since every point on the number line has a decimal coordinate, the distance between any two points can be found.
11. If equal real numbers are added to equal real numbers, the sums are equal real numbers.
12. If two mathematical expressions are equal, one may be substituted for the other in any mathematical statement.
13. Since $11 < 14$ and $5 < 20$, it follows that $11 + 5 < 14 + 20$.
14. Since $12 = 18 + (-6)$, it follows that $12 > 18$.
15. If $a = b + c$, then $a > b$ because "the whole is greater than the part."
16. Since $10 > 7$ and $7 > 6$, then $10 > 6$ because of the symmetric property of the greater-than relation.
17. If $a < b$ and $c > d$, then $a + c < b + d$.
18. If $u = v + w$ and $w > 0$, then $u > v$ because "the whole is greater than the part."
19. If $a < b + c$ and $b + c < d$, then $a < d$ because of the transitive axiom for order.
20. The completeness axiom for R states that to each point on the number line there corresponds a real number and that to each real number there corresponds a point on the line.

In exercises 21–28 verify the indicated axiom for the given numbers.

21. distributive; $x = 5$, $y = \frac{3}{10}$, $z = -\frac{1}{20}$
22. associative for multiplication; $x = \frac{18}{5}$, $y = -5$, $z = \frac{1}{45}$
23. commutative for addition; $x = \frac{5}{17}$, $y = \frac{11}{51}$
24. addition of inequalities ($<$); $a = 27$, $b = 61$, $c = 39$, $d = 48$
25. addition of inequalities ($>$); $a = 8$, $b = 5$, $c = -9$, $d = -15$
26. addition of equals; $a = \frac{1}{6}$, $b = \frac{1}{6}$, $c = \frac{2}{9}$, $d = \frac{2}{9}$
27. multiplication of equals; $a = 14.2$, $b = 14.2$, $c = 7.9$, $d = 7.9$
28. division of equals; $a = 49.56$, $b = 49.56$, $c = 12$, $d = 12$

In exercises 29–46 name the axiom from this section that justifies the statement.

29. $\frac{1}{2} \cdot 9 = 9 \cdot \frac{1}{2}$

30. $2.13113\cdots + 5.1212\cdots = 5.1212\cdots + 2.13113\cdots$
31. Since $5 < 8$ and $4 < 10$, then $5 + 4 < 8 + 10$.
32. Since $26 = 21 + 5$, then $26 > 21$.
33. $\frac{2}{15}(-6 + \frac{1}{12}) = \frac{2}{15} \cdot (-6) + \frac{2}{15} \cdot \frac{1}{12}$
34. $(-\frac{3}{8} + \frac{1}{4}) + \frac{12}{5} = -\frac{3}{8} + (\frac{1}{4} + \frac{12}{5})$
35. If $x = y + z$ and $a = y$, then $x = a + z$.
36. $(6.43) \cdot \sqrt{7} = \sqrt{7} \cdot (6.43)$
37. If $a > \frac{1}{2}$ and $b > \frac{1}{3}$, then $a + b > \frac{1}{2} + \frac{1}{3}$.
38. Since $-5 < 0$ and $0 < 0.99\cdots$, then $-5 < 0.99\cdots$.
39. $(\frac{3}{4} + \frac{1}{2}) + 2 = \frac{3}{4} + (\frac{1}{2} + 2)$
40. $(.57676\cdots) \cdot [2 + 3] = (.57676\cdots) \cdot 2 + (.57676\cdots) \cdot 3$
41. $(7 + 3) + (\frac{1}{2} + 3) = (7 + 3) + (3 + \frac{1}{2})$
42. If $x < \sqrt{5}$ and $y < \pi$, then $x + y < \sqrt{5} + \pi$.
43. There is a point on the number line corresponding to the number $5.171819\cdots$.
44. If $a + c > 90$ and $a + c = b$, then $b > 90$.
45. $(\frac{1}{2} + \frac{1}{3}) + \frac{1}{5} = \frac{1}{5} + (\frac{1}{2} + \frac{1}{3})$
46. If $x < 501$ and $501 < y$, then $x < y$.

Exercises 47–50 show applications of the axioms called *rearrangement properties*. Name the axiom that justifies each step.

47. $11x + 17y + 13x$
    $= 11x + (17y + 13x)$ ________
    $= 11x + (13x + 17y)$ ________
    $= (11x + 13x) + 17y$ ________
    $= (11 + 13)x + 17y$ ________
    $= 24x + 17y$ Addition facts
48. $(5a) \cdot (19b)$
    $= 5 \cdot (a \cdot 19) \cdot b$ ________
    $= 5 \cdot (19 \cdot a) \cdot b$ ________
    $= (5 \cdot 19) \cdot (a \cdot b)$ ________
    $= 95ab$ Multiplication facts
49. $9a + [2(3b) + 10a]$
    $= 9a + [(2 \cdot 3)b + 10a]$ ________
    $= 9a + [6b + 10a]$ Multiplication facts
    $= 9a + [10a + 6b]$ ________
    $= [9a + 10a] + 6b$ ________
    $= [9 + 10] \cdot a + 6b$ ________
    $= 19a + 6b$ Addition facts
50. $11(x + 4y) + 13x + 2y$
    $= 11x + 11(4y) + 13x + 2y$ ________
    $= 11x + (11 \cdot 4)y + 13x + 2y$ ________
    $= 11x + 44y + 13x + 2y$ Multiplication facts
    $= 11x + (44y + 13x) + 2y$ ________
    $= 11x + (13x + 44y) + 2y$ ________
    $= (11x + 13x) + (44y + 2y)$ ________
    $= (11 + 13)x + (44 + 2)y$ ________
    $= 24x + 46y$ Addition facts

CHAPTER 1 SUMMARY

The way geometry is organized, the approach used in this book, and the broad objectives of a study of geometry are presented in this chapter, setting the stage for the chapters that follow. Some of the fundamental concepts about sets and real numbers that aid in the study of geometry are given so that they may be reviewed along with their accompanying notation. The chapter may also be used as a reference for the underlying ideas about real numbers.

FACTS TO KNOW

1. Definitions
   a. Subset
   b. Union
   c. Intersection
   d. Rational numbers
   e. Square root
   f. Irrational numbers
   g. Real numbers
   h. Absolute value
   i. Distance on the number line
2. Axioms for the equals relation in set R
   a. Reflexive
   b. Symmetric
   c. Transitive
3. Fundamental properties of the real numbers: Axioms 4–17 (See text for list.)

PROBLEMS TO MASTER

1. Find unions and intersections of sets.
2. Find distances on the number line.
3. Test the validity of the RST properties for a relation defined on a set.
4. Name axioms that justify given statements.

2

POINTS AND LINES

MAJOR TOPICS

- Concept of space as the set of all points
- Role of undefined terms and definitions in a logical development
- Segment as an important subset of a line in that it can be measured
- Difficulties in measuring a segment and the role of axioms and postulates in overcoming these difficulties
- RST properties of congruence for line segments
- Concept of a proof as a justifiable sequence of steps leading from the hypothesis to the conclusion

HISTORICAL NOTE

THALES AND GEOMETRIC PROOF

The ancient Egyptians were masters of practical geometry, as evidenced by their abilities to survey and to build. Their knowledge, however, consisted of a large number of distinct rules, which they obtained by generalizing from specific examples, that is, by inductive reasoning. They do not seem to have possessed an overall theory. Indeed, Proclus (412–485 A.D.), the author of an early history of geometry, credits the practical needs of the Egyptians as the motivation for the later development of a geometric theory by the Greeks, who traveled to Egypt to acquire their geometric knowledge.

One of these early travelers was Thales of Miletus (640–546 B.C.), a successful merchant and public servant, who was among the first to learn Egyptian geometry and to present it to the scholars of Greece. He retired at an early age and devoted himself to the pursuit of mathematics, science, and philosophy.

From Proclus we learn that Thales presented Egyptian geometry as a set of isolated propositions not arranged in any logical order. He did, however, present them as conclusions obtained by arguing step by step from basic premises, that is, by deductive reasoning. This achievement gave Thales a distinctive place in history, for it is deductive reasoning that permits the development of a unified and cohesive mathematical theory.

It is interesting to note that at that time in Greece people were ready to move from the practical world of everyday affairs to the abstract world of ideas. Philosophical discussions about the why and the how of things were the fashion of the day. The time was right for a person of Thales' talents.

Thales' introduction of proof by deductive reasoning was a remarkable phenomenon in the world, but it was not his only achievement. He gave new impetus to astronomy as an abstract science, dedicated to discovering geometric laws governing the observed motions of the moon, the sun, and the planets, rather than simply cataloging how they appeared to behave. He successfully predicted a solar eclipse in 585 B.C.

To Greeks of later generations, Thales was known as one of the Seven Sages of Greece, and many anecdotes about him were told. One relates that during an evening when he was observing the stars, his concentration was so intense that he fell into an open ditch. An old woman accompanying him exclaimed, "How can you know what is doing in the heavens, when you don't see what is at your feet?"

We live at a time so distant from the beginnings of rational thought that it is easy to miss the major importance of Thales' introduction of proof by deductive reasoning. It was truly a giant step forward in the development of human thought.

2.1 INTRODUCTION

The simplest of all geometric figures is a point. Most of us have a fairly clear concept of a point. Physical examples include a pinhole, the tip of a pencil, the intersection of two roads as shown on a map, and a dot on a piece of paper. These all suggest a geometric point. Conceptually, a point has no size: we do not think of a point as being large or small or short or long. We do think of a point as having a position, however. These comments are meant to help achieve an understanding of the term *point* without giving it a formal definition. Indeed, it is so fundamental that we take it as our first undefined term (recall Section 1.1).

It is convenient to think of geometric models of physical objects as subsets of the space around us. Thus, we have the following definitions.

Definition 2.1 *Space* is the set of all points.

Definition 2.2 A *geometric figure* is any nonempty subset of space.

According to Definition 2.2, anything consisting of one or more points is a geometric figure. Of course, many special sorts of figures will be defined as we proceed. First, however, we must consider a type that is left undefined.

Recall from Section 1.1 that this text is primarily about plane geometry. A *plane* is suggested by any flat surface, such as a tabletop, with the added idea that it extends without end in all directions. Since "flat" is difficult to define in simpler words and since most people can easily imagine such a geometric figure, we take *plane* as our second undefined term. *Chapters 2–9 are about geometric figures in a plane unless specifically stated otherwise.*

There are countless geometric figures that are subsets of a plane. Some consist of a *finite number* of points; that is, a whole number may be assigned as the number of points by the usual counting process. A few examples appear in Figure 2.1. Note that capital letters are used to name the points and that the subscript notation A_1, A_2, . . . may be convenient when several related points are involved. Figure 2.1(c) is called a lattice (a useful figure in electronics). Figure 2.1(b) suggests a line, but it is not one; it is merely five distinct points. A line, as discussed in the next section, is an infinite (uncountable) set of points.

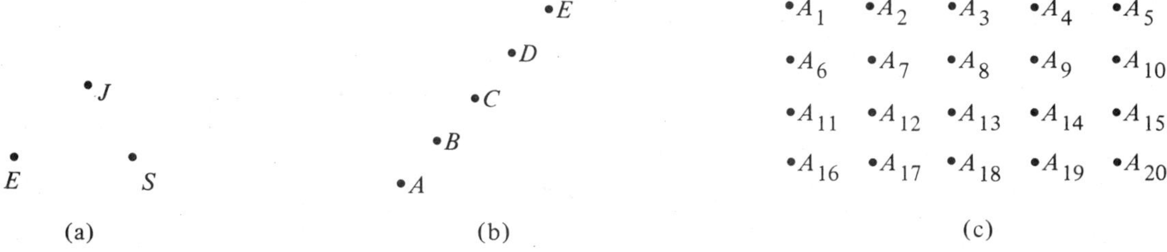

Figure 2.1 Finite sets of points.

2.2 LINES AND SUBSETS OF LINES

The most fundamental infinite set of points used in geometric figures is the *straight line*. Numerous examples appear in physical objects around us. The edge of a table, a carpenter's stretched string, and a rail of a railroad track may all suggest the abstract concept of a line. We think of it as determining the shortest distance between two points, as having no bends, and as extending indefinitely in both directions. A mathematical example we have already met is the number line. With these ideas in mind, since straight is difficult to define, we take *straight line* or, more briefly, *line* as an undefined term in the systematic development of geometry.

Recall from Section 1.1 that, in addition to undefined terms, we need to accept without proof certain properties of simple geometric figures. These assumptions are called postulates, and they are cornerstones on which are based more complicated properties, given in the form of theorems to be proved. We state two postulates about points and lines:

Postulate 1 Any two points determine exactly one line.

Postulate 2 Any line contains at least two points.

The first postulate is often stated, "Two points determine a unique line." Thus, given any two points, there is one and only one line containing them. Postulate 2 may seem unnecessary. We want to clearly state, however, that the undefined term *line* means a *nonempty* set of points, which certainly cannot contain less than two points!

Two standard notations are used to name lines in geometric figures. In one, a lowercase letter such as l is written next to the line, as shown in Figure 2.2(a). The other requires naming two points on the line, say E and J as shown in Figure 2.2(b). Then the line is denoted by $\overleftrightarrow{EJ}$. Note that a line is drawn with an arrowhead on each end to show the infinite extension, and that this notation appears in two-point names for lines, such as $\overleftrightarrow{EJ}$. Note also that the symbols $\overleftrightarrow{EJ}$ and l are names for *sets* of points. Recall from Section 1.2 that capital letters are not the only symbols used to name sets.

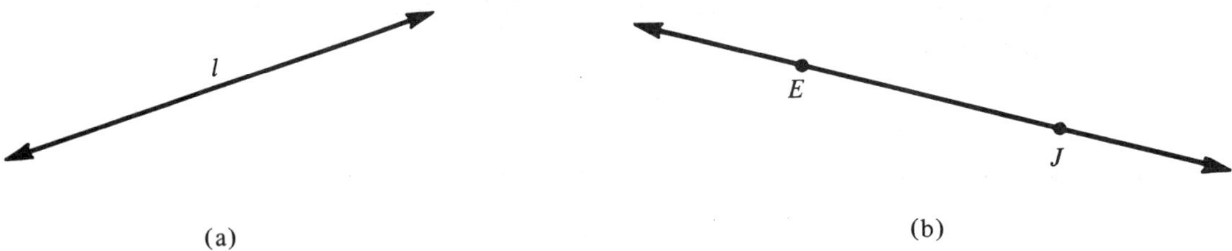

Figure 2.2

Postulate 2 asserts that any line contains at least two points. There are, of course, many more, and we may want to refer to points that are between two given points on a line. In Figure 2.3 points M, K, J, and C are all in some sense between E and S.

Figure 2.3

The term *between*, however, will be used to refer only to points *on the line* that are, in the usual sense, between two given points. Thus, in Figure 2.3, J is the only named point that is between E and S. The fact that J is between E and S is denoted E-J-S. With these understandings, we adopt *between* as an undefined term.

Three or more points that lie on the same line are said to be collinear, a term whose formal definition is as follows:

Definition 2.3 A set of three or more points is *collinear* iff it is a subset of a line.

We may now define three other important types of subsets of a line.

Definition 2.4 A set of points is a *line segment* iff it consists of two points and all the points between them.

Figure 2.4 shows a line segment that is denoted $\overline{AC}$. Note that arrowheads are omitted here because line segments do *not* extend without end. Of course, given points A and C, we know there is a line $\overleftrightarrow{AC}$ by Postulate 1. It follows that line segment $\overline{AC}$ is a subset of line $\overleftrightarrow{AC}$ ($\overline{AC} \subseteq \overleftrightarrow{AC}$), because every point of $\overline{AC}$ is also a point of $\overleftrightarrow{AC}$.

Figure 2.4

Next consider a line $\overleftrightarrow{ES}$ and one of its points, J (Figure 2.5). The point J separates $\overleftrightarrow{ES}$ into three distinct subsets: the set of points to the left of J, the set of points to the right of J, and the set consisting solely of J itself. The sets to the left and right are called *half lines* and are denoted $\overset{\circ\!\!\rightarrow}{JE}$ and $\overset{\circ\!\!\rightarrow}{JS}$, with J the *endpoint* of each. Note, however, that J is not part of either half line. In such notations as $\overset{\circ\!\!\rightarrow}{JE}$, the symbol for the endpoint must appear first. Thus, in the figure below, the half line $\overset{\circ\!\!\rightarrow}{EJ}$ consists of all the points to the right of endpoint E, and $\overset{\circ\!\!\rightarrow}{EJ} \neq \overset{\circ\!\!\rightarrow}{JE}$. We take *half line* and *endpoint* as undefined terms and use them to define an important subset of a line called a ray.

Figure 2.5

Definition 2.5 A set of points is a *ray* iff it is the union of a half line and its endpoint.

The notation $\overrightarrow{AB}$ is used to name the ray consisting of the endpoint A and all the points of half line $\overset{\circ\!\!\rightarrow}{AB}$. To summarize, in Figure 2.6,

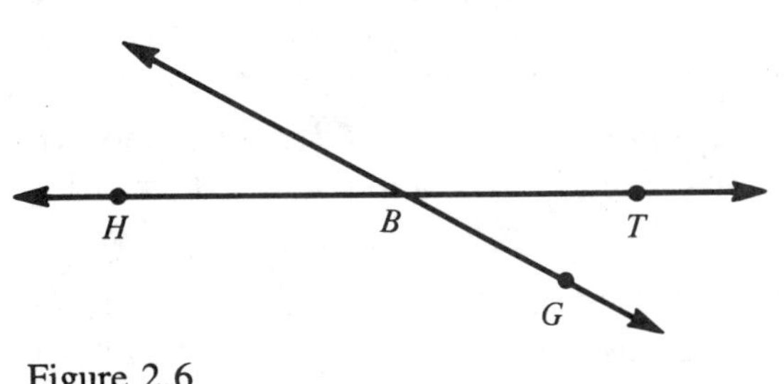

Figure 2.6

1. $\overleftrightarrow{HT}$ and $\overleftrightarrow{BG}$ are lines;
2. $\overleftrightarrow{HB}$ and $\overleftrightarrow{HT}$ name the same line;
3. $\overline{HB}$, $\overline{BT}$, $\overline{HT}$, and $\overline{BG}$ are line segments;
4. $\overline{HB}$ and $\overline{BH}$ name the same segment;
5. $\overrightarrow{HB}$, $\overrightarrow{BG}$, and $\overrightarrow{BT}$ are rays;
6. $\overrightarrow{HB}$ and $\overrightarrow{HT}$ name the same ray;
7. $\overrightarrow{BT}$ and $\overrightarrow{TB}$ are different rays;
8. $\overset{\circ\!\!\rightarrow}{BT}$ and $\overset{\circ\!\!\rightarrow}{BG}$ are half lines;
9. H-B-T, but G is not between H and T.

Many geometric figures may be viewed as unions or intersections involving lines or subsets of lines. This section concludes with three examples designed to illustrate this idea. In reading these examples, remember that notations such as $\overline{AB}$, $\overleftrightarrow{AB}$, $\overrightarrow{AB}$, and $\overset{\circ}{\overrightarrow{AB}}$ are *names* for sets of points, whereas braces { } are used to enclose the *contents* of a set. Thus, $\{A, B, C\}$ denotes an unnamed set consisting of three points named A, B, and C. Also, a ray $\overrightarrow{AB}$ may be defined briefly as $\overrightarrow{AB} = \overset{\circ}{\overrightarrow{AB}} \cup \{A\}$, where $\overset{\circ}{\overrightarrow{AB}}$ names a half line (a set of points) and $\{A\}$ denotes the set consisting of the endpoint A.

EXAMPLE 1 For the figure shown, find

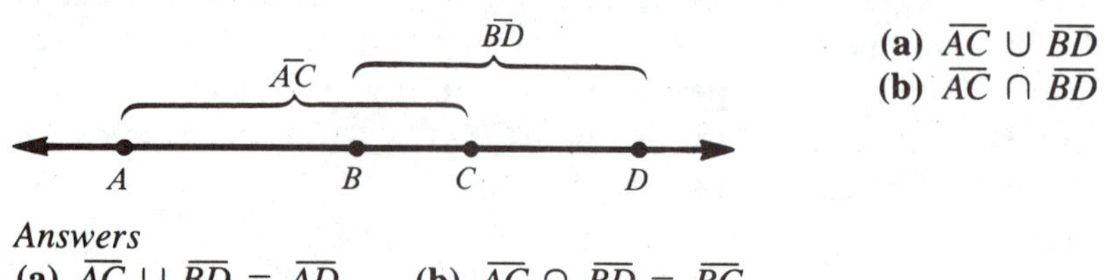

(a) $\overline{AC} \cup \overline{BD}$
(b) $\overline{AC} \cap \overline{BD}$

Answers
(a) $\overline{AC} \cup \overline{BD} = \overline{AD}$ **(b)** $\overline{AC} \cap \overline{BD} = \overline{BC}$

Note the marking technique used in the figure for Example 1. This technique aids in visualizing the union (all points in $\overline{AC}$ or $\overline{BD}$ or both) and the intersection (all points in both $\overline{AC}$ and $\overline{BD}$). You should mark the figure in the next example in a similar way.

EXAMPLE 2 For the figure shown, find

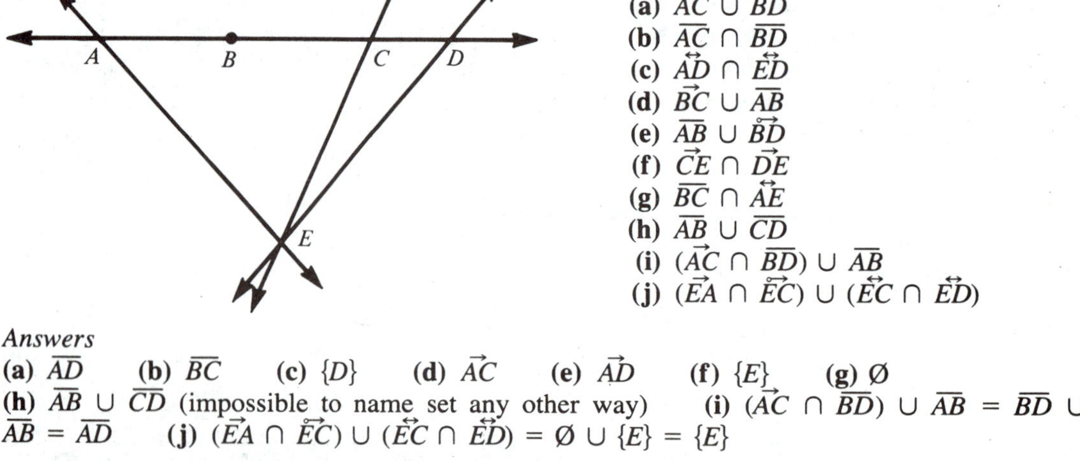

(a) $\overline{AC} \cup \overline{BD}$
(b) $\overline{AC} \cap \overline{BD}$
(c) $\overleftrightarrow{AD} \cap \overleftrightarrow{ED}$
(d) $\overrightarrow{BC} \cup \overline{AB}$
(e) $\overline{AB} \cup \overset{\circ}{\overrightarrow{BD}}$
(f) $\overrightarrow{CE} \cap \overrightarrow{DE}$
(g) $\overline{BC} \cap \overleftrightarrow{AE}$
(h) $\overline{AB} \cup \overline{CD}$
(i) $(\overrightarrow{AC} \cap \overline{BD}) \cup \overline{AB}$
(j) $(\overrightarrow{EA} \cap \overset{\circ}{\overrightarrow{EC}}) \cup (\overleftrightarrow{EC} \cap \overleftrightarrow{ED})$

Answers
(a) $\overline{AD}$ **(b)** $\overline{BC}$ **(c)** $\{D\}$ **(d)** $\overrightarrow{AC}$ **(e)** $\overrightarrow{AD}$ **(f)** $\{E\}$ **(g)** $\varnothing$
(h) $\overline{AB} \cup \overline{CD}$ (impossible to name set any other way) **(i)** $(\overrightarrow{AC} \cap \overline{BD}) \cup \overline{AB} = \overline{BD} \cup \overline{AB} = \overline{AD}$ **(j)** $(\overrightarrow{EA} \cap \overset{\circ}{\overrightarrow{EC}}) \cup (\overleftrightarrow{EC} \cap \overleftrightarrow{ED}) = \varnothing \cup \{E\} = \{E\}$

Using geometry to solve problems often requires drawing a figure that satisfies certain given facts. The technique is illustrated in the final example of this section.

EXAMPLE 3 Draw a figure satisfying all the given facts: $\overrightarrow{AB}$, $\overline{CD}$, $\overset{\circ}{\overrightarrow{CE}}$, and $\overline{BE}$ are such that $\overrightarrow{AB} \cap \overline{CD} = \overline{CD}$, $\overrightarrow{AB} \cap \overset{\circ}{\overrightarrow{CE}} = \varnothing$, $\overrightarrow{AB} \cap \overline{BE} = \{B\}$, and $\overset{\circ}{\overrightarrow{CE}} \cap \overline{BE} = \{E\}$.

Answer

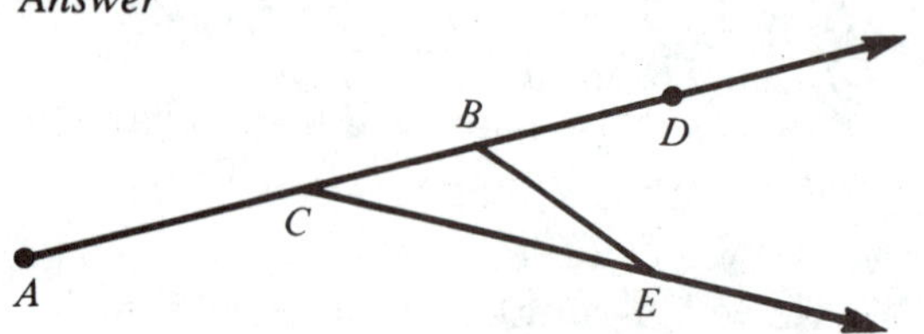

EXERCISES FOR 2.1 AND 2.2

In exercises 1–20 answer true or false.

1. The term *point* in geometry is undefined.
2. A plane is defined to be a flat surface.
3. Postulates are statements to be proved in geometry.
4. If A lies on the same line as B, and B lies on the same line as C, then A, B, and C are collinear.
5. A geometric point is a dot on a paper.
6. Space is the set of all points.
7. A-B-C means B is between A and C and on the same line as A and C.
8. Two points determine exactly one line.
9. $\overline{AB} \cup \overline{BC} = \overline{AC}$ for every location of A, B, and C.
10. Undefined terms are used to give definitions of more complex terms.
11. If E-J-S and K-J-S, then E-K-S.
12. If $\overleftrightarrow{AB} \cap \overleftrightarrow{CD} = \emptyset$, then the lines intersect in only one point.
13. If $\overline{AB} \cup \overline{BC} = \overline{AC}$, then A-B-C.
14. If A-B-C, then $\overline{AB} \cup \overline{BC} = \overline{AC}$.
15. A ray is the union of a half line and its endpoint.
16. $\{K, E, S\} \subseteq \{K, S\}$
17. $\{E, J\} \cap \{E, S\} = \{E, J, S\}$
18. If E-J-S, then $\overrightarrow{JS} \subseteq \overline{ES}$.
19. $\overset{\circ\!\!\longrightarrow}{AJ} \cup \{A\} = \overleftrightarrow{AJ}$
20. If A-B-C and B-C-D, then $(\overline{AB} \cup \overline{BC}) \cup \overline{CD} = \overline{AD}$.

In exercises 21–25 list all the named points on Figure 2.7 that are contained in the indicated set.

Figure 2.7

21. $\overline{KS}$ 22. $\overleftrightarrow{KJ}$ 23. $\overset{\circ\!\!\longrightarrow}{HS}$
24. $\overrightarrow{EJ}$ 25. $\overline{CJ} \cap \overline{EH}$

In exercises 26–30 use Figure 2.8 to name the geometric figures requested.

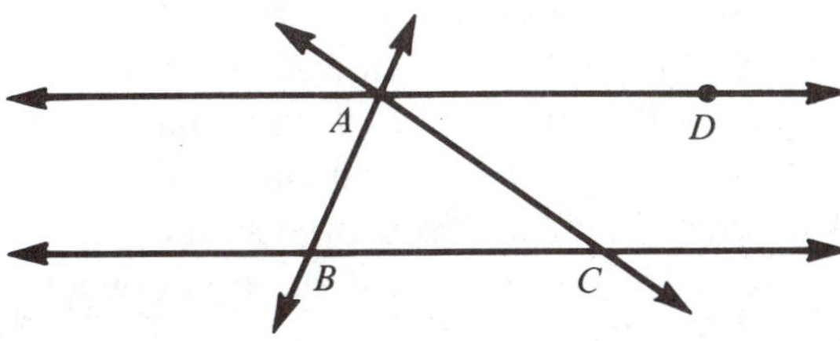

Figure 2.8

26. four lines 27. four line segments
28. eight rays 29. nine subsets of $\overleftrightarrow{AD}$
30. two segments whose intersection is empty

In exercises 31–40 use Figure 2.9 to find the indicated sets.

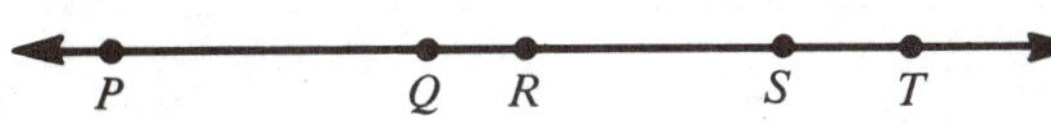

Figure 2.9

31. $\overline{PR} \cup \overline{QR}$ 32. $\overline{RS} \cap \overrightarrow{ST}$
33. $\overrightarrow{QP} \cap \overrightarrow{RS}$ 34. $\overline{QS} \cap \overline{RT}$
35. $\overline{PR} \cup \overrightarrow{PR}$ 36. $\overleftrightarrow{QT} \cup \overline{QT}$
37. $\overleftrightarrow{QT} \cap \overline{QT}$ 38. $(\overrightarrow{PQ} \cup \overline{QR}) \cap \overrightarrow{ST}$
39. $\overline{PR} \cup \overrightarrow{ST}$
40. $(\overline{PQ} \cup \overline{QR}) \cap (\overline{RS} \cup \overline{ST})$

In exercises 41–45 use Figure 2.10 to fill in the blank.

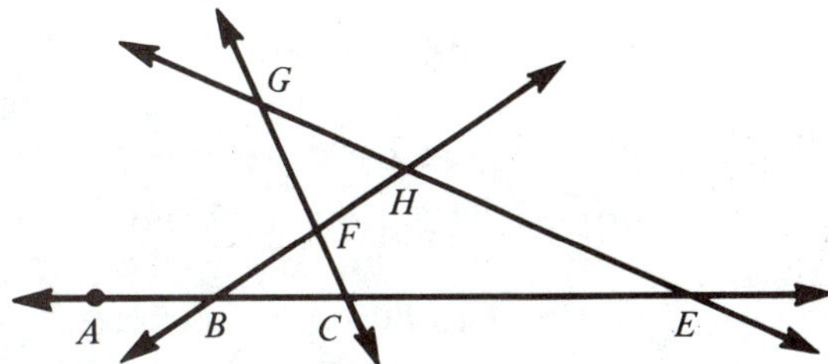

Figure 2.10

41. $\overrightarrow{AB} \cap \overrightarrow{EC} =$ ______________.
42. $(\overline{GF} \cup \overline{FC}) \cap \overline{BH} =$ ______________.
43. $(\overrightarrow{EH} \cap \overrightarrow{CF}) \cup (\overline{AC} \cap \overset{\circ\!\!\longrightarrow}{CE}) =$ ____________.
44. $(\overline{AC} \cap \overline{BE}) \cup (\overline{GC} \cap \overrightarrow{FG}) =$ ____________.
45. $(\overleftrightarrow{BH} \cap \overleftrightarrow{CG}) \cup (\overrightarrow{FG} \cap \overrightarrow{HG}) \cup (\overset{\circ\!\!\longrightarrow}{GH} \cap \overline{BH}) =$ ______________.

In each of exercises 46–60, draw a figure satisfying all the given facts.

46. $\overline{AB} \cup \overline{CD} = \overline{AB}$.
47. $\overline{AB} \cap \overline{CD} = \overline{AD}$.

48. $\overrightarrow{AB} \cap \overrightarrow{CD} = \overline{AC}$.
49. $\overrightarrow{AB} \cup \overrightarrow{AC}$ such that $\overrightarrow{AB} \cap \overrightarrow{AC} = \{A\}$.
50. $\overline{EJ} \cup \overline{JS} \cup \overline{SE}$ such that $\overline{SE} \cap \overline{JS} = \{S\}$.
51. $\overline{AB}$, $\overline{BC}$, and $\overline{AC}$ such that $\overline{AB} \cap \overline{BC} = \{B\}$ and $\overline{AC} \cap \overline{BC} = \{C\}$.
52. $\overleftrightarrow{ES}$, $\overleftrightarrow{JM}$, $\overset{\circ\!\!\longrightarrow}{RS}$, and $\overset{\circ\!\!\longrightarrow}{RM}$ such that $\overleftrightarrow{ES} \cap \overleftrightarrow{JM} = \emptyset$, $\overset{\circ\!\!\longrightarrow}{RS} \cap \overset{\circ\!\!\longrightarrow}{RM} = \emptyset$, and $\overset{\circ\!\!\longrightarrow}{RS} \cap \overleftrightarrow{ES} = \{S\}$.
53. $\overrightarrow{AB}$, $\overrightarrow{AC}$, and $\overrightarrow{CD}$ such that $\overrightarrow{AB} \cap \overrightarrow{AC} = \{A\}$, and $\overrightarrow{CD} \cap \overrightarrow{AB}$ such that A-B-D.
54. $\overrightarrow{JE}$, $\overrightarrow{JS}$, and $\overline{KR}$ such that $\overrightarrow{JE} \cap \overrightarrow{JS} = \{J\}$, $\overline{KR} \cap \overrightarrow{JE} = \{E\}$, and $\overline{KR} \cap \overrightarrow{JS} = \{S\}$.
55. $\overline{EJ}$, $\overline{JS}$, $\overline{ES}$, and $\overrightarrow{KC}$ such that $\overline{EJ} \cap \overrightarrow{KC} = \emptyset$, $\overline{JS} \cap \overrightarrow{KC} = \emptyset$, and $\overline{ES} \cap \overrightarrow{KC} \neq \emptyset$.
56. $\overline{AD}$, $\overline{DE}$, $\overline{AB}$, and $\overline{CD}$ such that $\overline{AD} \cup \overline{DE} = \overline{AE}$, $\overline{AB} \cap \overline{CD} = \overline{CD}$, and $\overline{AD} \cap \overline{BE} = \emptyset$.
57. $\overleftrightarrow{AC}$, $\overrightarrow{DB}$, and $\overrightarrow{EC}$ such that $\overrightarrow{DB} \cap \overleftrightarrow{AC} = \{B\}$, $\overrightarrow{EC} \cap \overleftrightarrow{AC} = \{C\}$, and $\overrightarrow{DB} \cap \overrightarrow{EC} = \emptyset$.
58. $\overrightarrow{AB}$, $\overrightarrow{JC}$, $\overrightarrow{KD}$, and $\overrightarrow{AE}$ such that $\overrightarrow{AB} \cap \overrightarrow{JC} = \{A\}$, $\overrightarrow{JC} \cap \overrightarrow{KD} = \{A\}$, $\overrightarrow{AD} \cap \overrightarrow{AE} = \{A\}$, and $\overrightarrow{JC} \cap \overrightarrow{AE} = \{A\}$.
59. $\overleftrightarrow{AB}$, $\overleftrightarrow{CD}$, $\overleftrightarrow{EF}$, and $\overleftrightarrow{JS}$ such that $\overleftrightarrow{AB} \cap \overleftrightarrow{JS} = \{S\}$, $\overleftrightarrow{AB} \cap \overleftrightarrow{CD} = \emptyset$, $\overleftrightarrow{AB} \cap \overleftrightarrow{EF} = \emptyset$, and $\overleftrightarrow{EF} \cap \overleftrightarrow{JS} = \{J\}$.
60. $\overleftrightarrow{AB}$, $\overleftrightarrow{AC}$, $\overleftrightarrow{CD}$, and $\overleftrightarrow{BD}$ such that $\overleftrightarrow{AB} \cap \overleftrightarrow{CD} = \emptyset$, $\overleftrightarrow{AB} \cap \overleftrightarrow{AC} = \{A\}$, $\overleftrightarrow{BD} \cap \overleftrightarrow{CD} = \{D\}$, and $\overleftrightarrow{AC} \cap \overleftrightarrow{BD} = \emptyset$.

2.3

MEASURING LINE SEGMENTS

Almost all of us have used a tape measure or ruler to measure the width of a table, the height of a person, the length of a roof rafter, and so on. We often compare such measurements by noting that one table is wider than another or that one person is the same height as another. Such measurements and comparisons can be modeled with the use of geometric figures—recall Thales and the pyramid (Section 1.1)—and this requires the assignment of lengths to segments.

Certainly a ruler may be used to measure a line segment in the same way it is used to measure the edge of a table. Some careful thought is in order here, however. First, note that a unit length is needed. Of course, many are available. To measure a table edge, the unit might be 1 inch or 1 foot or 1 centimeter. Longer lengths, such as distances run at track meets, are measured in larger units—meters or yards—and, of course, the distance between two cities is normally given in miles or kilometers.

Having chosen a unit length, we measure a line segment by "covering" it with unit lengths as shown in Figure 2.11, where for clarity the ruler is

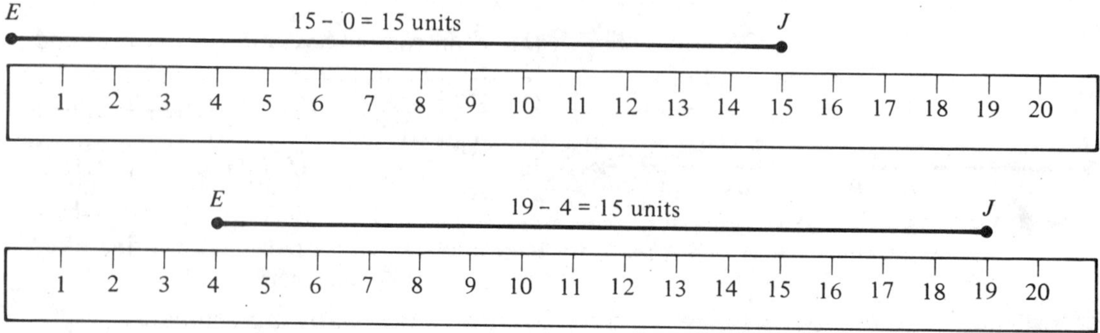

Figure 2.11

separated slightly from the line segment. The figure shows that, whether or not the covering process begins at the zero point of the ruler, a length of 15 units is assigned to $\overline{EJ}$.

A problem, however, immediately arises. How can we be sure that the marks on the ruler are accurately matched to the endpoints E and J? Clearly, any mark has some "thickness." The answer is that we cannot *exactly* match the ruler to the segment and hence any measurement obtained must be, in some sense, an approximation.

There is a second difficulty. Even if we could match a ruler mark very accurately to point E, the other endpoint J might fall between two unit interval marks. This problem is handled, of course, by subdividing each unit interval on the ruler into fractional parts. We then obtain the measurement by using the mark that seems to be nearest to J, but again the measurement must be termed an approximation.

If, then, a measurement of a line segment is only an approximation, what quantity does it, in fact, approximate? Putting it another way, given a line segment, can we assign a *unique* positive number as its real length? Such an assignment seems logically desirable, for then any measurement would become simply an approximation of this unique length. We can accomplish the trick mathematically by using the concepts of the number line and of distance, as developed in Section 1.4. The unique length assigned is called the *measure* of the line segment.

Recall that the real numbers may be placed in a one-to-one correspondence with the points of any line. Thus, a number line may be established on a given line, or on the extension of a line segment, in such a way that each point on the line has a unique real-number coordinate. Then the *distance* between any two given points is defined as the absolute value of the difference between their coordinates. Note that the distance has nothing to do with the *number of points* between the two given ones. All of this is stated formally in the next postulate.

Postulate 3 *The Ruler Postulate*. The points of any line may be placed in one-to-one correspondence with the real numbers, and a unique positive number may be assigned as the distance between two given points.

With this postulate we can now define the length of any line segment.

Definition 2.6 The *length*, or *measure*, of a line segment is the distance between its endpoints.

It is important to stress that *distance* in the above definition is a mathematical term that has been precisely defined. Further, once a number line is established containing any given line segment, that line segment's length is unique. Finally, we will use the same notation for length as we used for distance in Section 1.4. Thus, if a line segment is named $\overline{AB}$, its length is denoted AB. Note carefully that the symbol $\overline{AB}$ represents a *set of points*, whereas the symbol AB stands for a *number*.

EXAMPLE 1 In the given figure, find the lengths of the following segments:
(a) $\overline{AB}$ **(b)** $\overline{BD}$ **(c)** $\overline{CB}$ **(d)** $\overline{CD}$ **(e)** $\overline{PQ}$ **(f)** $\overline{EJ}$

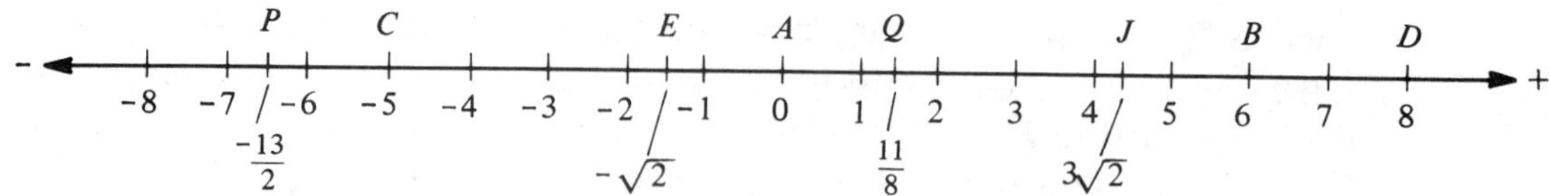

Answers

(a) $AB = |6 - 0| = |6| = 6$ **(b)** $BD = |8 - 6| = |2| = 2$

(c) $CB = |-5 - 6| = |-11| = 11$ **(d)** $CD = |8 - (-5)| = |13| = 13$

(e) $PQ = |\frac{11}{8} - (-\frac{13}{2})| = |\frac{11}{8} + \frac{13}{2}| = |\frac{11 + 52}{8}| = |\frac{63}{8}| = \frac{63}{8} = 7\frac{7}{8}$

(f) $EJ = | -\sqrt{2} - 3\sqrt{2}| = |-4\sqrt{2}| = 4\sqrt{2}$

In the example above, notice that *C-B-D* and that $CB + BD = CD$. These facts illustrate a general property about lengths of line segments, which is stated in the next postulate.

Postulate 4 If $\overline{ES}$ is a line segment and J is a point such that *E-J-S*, then $EJ + JS = ES$.

A less precise form of Postulate 4 is "The length of a segment equals the sum of the lengths of its parts," a statement that suggests that in some cases there might be more than two "parts." In some cases there are more than two parts, and it is easy to see how Postulate 4 can be extended to include such cases. For example, consider Figure 2.12. Remember that such symbols as AC and CD represent *numbers*. Since *A-C-D*, we have $AC + CD = AD$ by Postulate 4, and then $AD = AC + CD$ by the symmetric property of equals. Also, since *A-D-B*, it follows that $AD + DB = AB$. Then, using substitution (Axiom 17, Section 1.5), we may write $(AC + CD) + DB = AB$ or, by the associative axiom for addition, simply $AC + CD + DB = AB$. In later work we will apply Postulate 4 to segments having two parts or any larger whole number of parts.

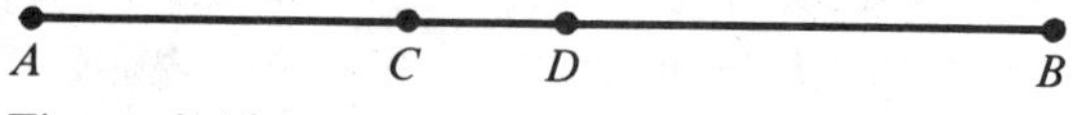

Figure 2.12

We can obtain another useful variation of Postulate 4 by using elementary algebra and by recognizing that subtraction of real numbers is done by adding additive inverses (or "negatives"). Thus, if $EJ + JS = ES$, we may write

$$\begin{aligned} [EJ + JS] + (-JS) &= ES + (-JS) \\ EJ + [JS + (-JS)] &= ES + (-JS) \\ EJ + 0 &= ES + (-JS) \\ EJ &= ES - JS \end{aligned}$$

This result can be stated, "One part of a segment equals the whole minus the other part." Later we shall use Postulate 4 to justify statements of this type.

Next we have two important definitions and our first geometric construction.

Definition 2.7 Point J is called the *midpoint* of $\overline{ES}$ iff *E-J-S* and $EJ = JS$.

In less precise words, the midpoint of a line segment is the point that is exactly halfway from one end to the other. Note that we have referred to *the* midpoint. Although we omit a proof, a line segment does have one and only one midpoint.

Definition 2.8 A line, half line, ray, or line segment is a *bisector* of a given line segment iff it contains the midpoint and no other points of that given segment.

It is possible to construct a bisector and the midpoint of a line segment. Recall (from Section 1.1) that to construct a figure geometrically only an unmarked straightedge, a pencil, and a compass for drawing circles may be used. The point and pencil of the compass may be matched to any two given points. Also, with the compass point at a circle's center, the circle or any part of it, called an *arc* of the circle, may be drawn. The distance from the center to any point of the circle is called the *radius*. With the straightedge any line may be drawn if we have two points on it. The straightedge is unmarked because points are not located by measuring, which is an approximate process. Instead, points are located as intersections of lines or arcs. You may object that this intersection method is as approximate as measuring, but bear in mind that we can prove the correctness of these constructions by using definitions, postulates, and theorems. We could not do so if measuring were used. As noted earlier, however, we will not give formal proofs of the constructions, although a few appear as exercises. Rather, we focus on the steps in those constructions that will assist you in understanding certain geometric properties when those properties appear as definitions, postulates, or theorems.

Construction 1 To construct a bisector and the midpoint of a line segment.

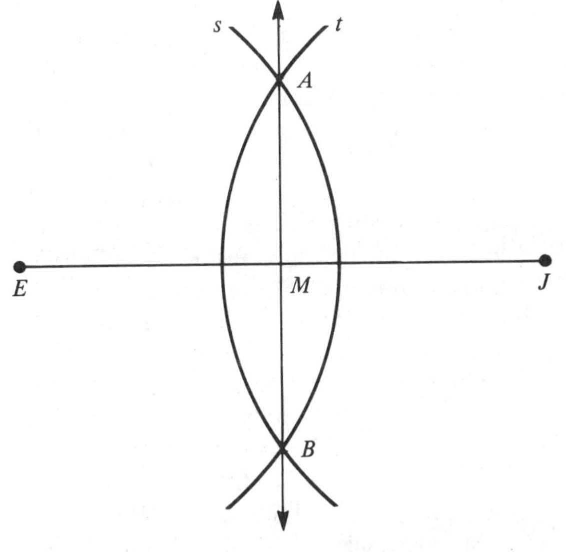

Given
$\overline{EJ}$

To Construct
bisector $\overleftrightarrow{AB}$ and midpoint M of $\overline{EJ}$

Steps

1. With E as center and a radius longer than $\frac{1}{2}EJ$, draw arc s.
2. With J as center and the same radius used in step 1, draw arc t so that it intersects arc s in points A and B.
3. Match a straightedge to points A and B, and draw bisector $\overleftrightarrow{AB}$ intersecting $\overline{EJ}$ in midpoint M.

EXERCISES FOR 2.3

In exercises 1–20 answer true or false.

1. A line segment is measured by covering it with unit lengths.
2. If the measurement of a segment is 6 feet, then 3 yards can also be its measurement.

3. Every line has exactly one length.
4. The measurement of a ray is greater than the measurement of a half line.
5. $\overline{EJ}$ represents a segment, and EJ represents its length.
6. If E-J-S and if $EJ = 3$ units and $ES = 7$ units, then $JS = 4$ units.
7. If $AB = 2$ units and $BD = 11$ units, then $AD = 13$ units.
8. The length of a segment is determined by the number of points in the segment.
9. If $EJ = 8$ units and $JS = 8$ units, then J is the midpoint of ES.
10. The measure of a segment is always a positive number.
11. The measure of a segment is the distance between its endpoints.
12. Every half line has exactly one midpoint.
13. The distance between any two given points is the absolute value of the difference between the coordinates of the points.
14. The Ruler Postulate states that the points of any line may be placed in a one-to-one correspondence with the rational numbers.
15. If $EJ = 4$ units, $JS = 4$ units, and $ES = 8$ units, then E-J-S.
16. A bisector of a line segment contains at least one of the endpoints of the segment.
17. A half line cannot be the bisector of a segment.
18. If A, B, and C are three points in a plane, then they always determine three distinct lines.
19. Using a ruler to measure a segment results in only an approximation of the length of that segment.
20. If $AD = 12$ units, $AB = 7$ units, and $BC = 2$ units and if A, B, C, and D are collinear, then there are four possibilities for the length of CD.

Complete the statements in exercises 21–35, using Figure 2.13.

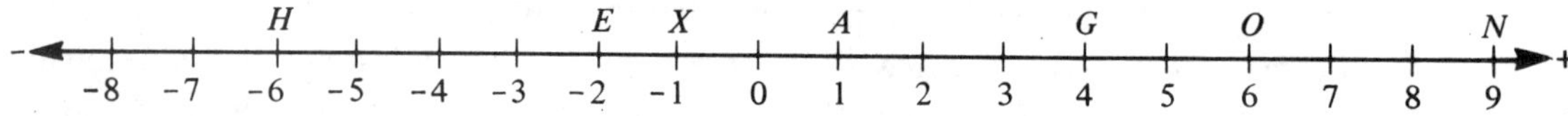

Figure 2.13

21. The coordinate of E is __________.
22. The coordinate of G is __________.
23. The coordinate of the point 8 units to the left of N is __________.
24. The coordinate of the point 8 units to the right of E is __________.
25. The length of $\overline{XN}$ is __________.
26. The length of $\overline{EO}$ is __________.
27. Distance $HA =$ __________.
28. The midpoint of $\overline{HG}$ is point __________ which has the coordinate __________.
29. The midpoint of $\overline{XN}$ is point __________ which has the coordinate __________.
30. Point A is the midpoint of segment __________.
31. The endpoints of $\overline{HN}$ have coordinates __________ and __________.
32. The length of $\overrightarrow{EX} \cap \overrightarrow{GA}$ is __________.
33. The length of $(\overline{XA} \cup \overline{AO}) \cap \overline{HG}$ is __________.
34. Two segments of length 5 units are __________ and __________.
35. Two segments of length 10 units are __________ and __________.

Complete the statements in exercises 36–39.

36. If the coordinate of E is -3 and the coordinate of S is 7, the coordinate of the midpoint of $\overline{ES}$ is __________.
37. If the coordinate of E is 2 and the coordinate of J is 11, the coordinate of the midpoint of $\overline{EJ}$ is __________.
38. If the coordinate of E is -5 and the coordinate of the midpoint of ES is 2, then the coordinate of S is __________.
39. If the coordinate of E is $-3\frac{1}{2}$ and the coordinate of the midpoint of ES is $2\frac{1}{4}$, then the coordinate of S is __________.
40. Given $\overline{KS}$, use only a compass and straightedge to construct (a) a bisector $\overleftrightarrow{CD}$ of $\overline{KS}$ intersecting $\overline{KS}$ in point M, and (b) the midpoint E of $\overline{MS}$.
41. The coordinate of A is 8. What are the possible coordinates of B if $AB = 17$?
42. The coordinates of 5 points are as follows: S, 7; T, 0; A, -5; O, 3; and P, -1. State the sequence of points in order from left to right.

43. If $EJ + JS > ES$ and J is not between E and S, what is true about E, J, and S?

44. If the coordinate of E is -2, the coordinate of J is 5, $EJ = JS$, and $EK = 20$, find (a) the coordinate of S, (b) the coordinate of K, (c) the length of $\overline{ES}$, and (d) SK.

45. Six points, L, U, E, Q, S, and O, are collinear. Find their order on a line if all of the following conditions are true: (1) five points are to the left of L; (2) U is between E and Q; (3) Q is the midpoint of $\overline{SL}$; (4) O is between S and Q; and (5) E is to the right of Q.

2.4 CONGRUENT LINE SEGMENTS

With our ideas about lengths of line segments properly organized, let us compare the following line segments.

$\overline{EJ}$ appears to be longer than either $\overline{CM}$ or $\overline{KS}$, and $\overline{CM}$ and $\overline{KS}$ seem to have the same length. More briefly, we may write $EJ > CM$, $EJ > KS$, and $CM = KS$, in which, of course, we are relating numbers (lengths) by using the greater-than and equals relations for real numbers. Note that it would be *incorrect* to write $\overline{EJ} > \overline{CM}$, since sets of points cannot be related by $>$. Also, we did not write $\overline{CM} = \overline{KS}$, for this would mean that $\overline{CM}$ and $\overline{KS}$ name the *same* line segment, that is, *identical* sets of points.

The fact that two different line segments have the same length is a comparison of fundamental importance in geometry. Such line segments are said to be congruent.

Definition 2.9 Two line segments are *congruent* (denoted $\cong$) iff their lengths (measures) are equal.

Recall that "iff" implies two statements. Thus, for two line segments $\overline{AB}$ and $\overline{CD}$, if $AB = CD$, it follows from Definition 2.9 that $\overline{AB} \cong \overline{CD}$; conversely, if $\overline{AB} \cong \overline{CD}$, we conclude from the same definition that $AB = CD$.

In Section 1.4 we saw that a relation in mathematics provides a way to compare the objects in a given set. Now we have, in Definition 2.9, the congruence relation in the set of all line segments. In later work certain properties of this relation will be used, and the important ones are the very RST properties that were found to be valid for the equals relation in set R (Section 1.4). Therefore, we now examine these three properties for the congruence relation as defined above. Note carefully how we establish the validity of the properties for congruence by using the corresponding properties for equals, a typical technique in mathematics.

Is the reflexive property valid?

That is, is a line segment $\overline{EJ}$ "congruent to itself?" Symbolically, is $\overline{EJ} \cong \overline{EJ}$? We know that $EJ = EJ$, since a line segment has a unique length and since the equals relation is reflexive in set R. Therefore, $\overline{EJ} \cong \overline{EJ}$.

Is the symmetric property valid?

Symbolically, if $\overline{EJ} \cong \overline{KS}$, does it follow that $\overline{KS} \cong \overline{EJ}$? The answer is yes, because if $\overline{EJ} \cong \overline{KS}$, then $EJ = KS$ by definition of congruent segments (Definition 2.9). According to the symmetric property of equals in set R, $KS = EJ$, which means $\overline{KS} \cong \overline{EJ}$, again by Definition 2.9.

Is the transitive property valid?

That is, if $\overline{EJ} \cong \overline{KS}$ and $\overline{KS} \cong \overline{CM}$, is $\overline{EJ} \cong \overline{CM}$? This is proved formally in the next section. The proof is based on the transitive property of equals in set R.

Thus, the RST properties are valid for congruence of line segments. This validity is based on the RST properties of equality of real numbers and the definition of congruence. Intuitively, we see that this means that we may rearrange congruence relations concerning line segments just as we rearrange equals relations concerning numbers in arithmetic and algebra.

We summarize the foregoing discussion by stating our first three geometric theorems. Recall that a theorem, unlike an axiom or postulate, requires proof. We omit formal proofs of Theorems 1 and 2, however. The preceding informal discussion is sufficient justification of their correctness. Theorem 3 is proved in Example 1 of the next section.

Theorem 1 *Reflexive Property for Congruence of Line Segments.* If $\overline{EJ}$ is any line segment, then $\overline{EJ} \cong \overline{EJ}$.

Theorem 2 *Symmetric Property for Congruence of Line Segments.* If $\overline{EJ}$ and $\overline{KS}$ are line segments and $\overline{EJ} \cong \overline{KS}$, then $\overline{KS} \cong \overline{EJ}$.

Theorem 3 *Transitive Property for Congruence of Line Segments.* If $\overline{EJ}$, $\overline{KS}$, and $\overline{CM}$ are line segments such that $\overline{EJ} \cong \overline{KS}$ and $\overline{KS} \cong \overline{CM}$, then $\overline{EJ} \cong \overline{CM}$.

For help in understanding the important RST properties, consider another example of a geometric relation in a set, with an informal discussion of the validity of the RST properties.

EXAMPLE 1 Let S be the set of all line segments in a plane, and let ® be the relation "intersect in at least one point." Are the RST properties valid?

Answers

(a) Reflexive: Does $\overline{AB}$ ® $\overline{AB}$? Yes, because they are the same line segment and hence have at least one point in common.

(b) Symmetric: If $\overline{AB}$ ® $\overline{CD}$, does $\overline{CD}$ ® $\overline{AB}$? Yes, because the point of intersection guaranteed by the hypothesis may be used as the point needed to make $\overline{CD}$ ® $\overline{AB}$ true.

(c) Transitive: If $\overline{AB}$ ® $\overline{CD}$ and $\overline{CD}$ ® $\overline{EF}$, does $\overline{AB}$ ® $\overline{EF}$? No, for the property to be valid, the conclusion must *always* follow from the hypothesis, and in Figure 2.14, for example, the hypothesis is true, but the conclusion is false.

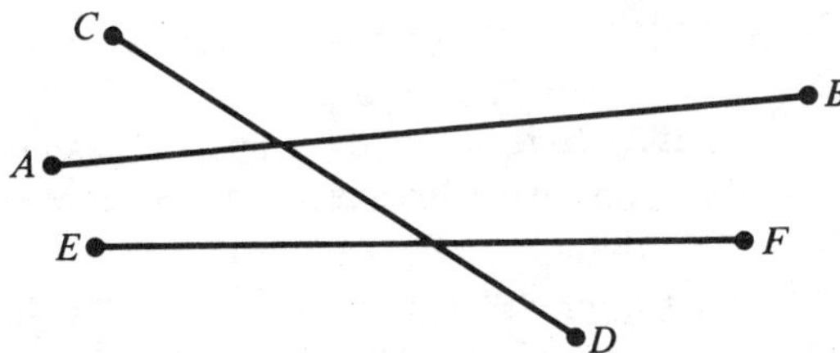

Figure 2.14

Figure 2.14, as used in Example 1(c), is called a *counterexample*. It shows that the proposed conclusion does not always follow from the stated hypothesis. Thus, if a theorem is proposed and one example can be produced for which the conclusion is false, the theorem is shown to be *invalid by counterexample*.

We now show how to construct on a given ray a line segment congruent to another given one.

Construction 2 To copy a given line segment onto a given ray.

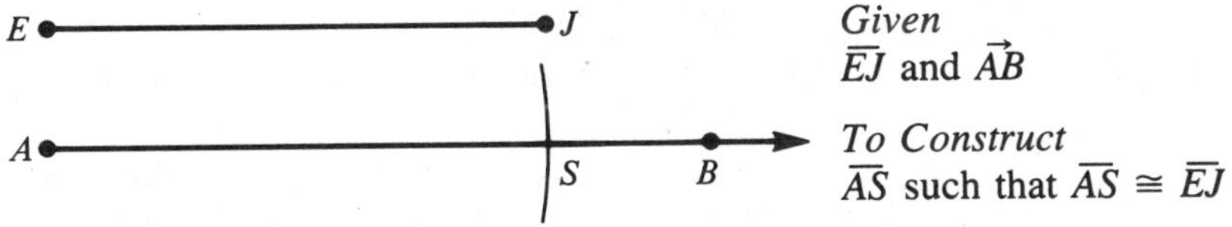

Given
$\overline{EJ}$ and $\overrightarrow{AB}$

To Construct
$\overline{AS}$ such that $\overline{AS} \cong \overline{EJ}$

Steps

1. Match the point and pencil of a compass to points E and J.
2. With A as center, draw an arc intersecting $\overrightarrow{AB}$.
3. Label the intersection point S.

The next postulate is the formal basis for the foregoing construction.

Postulate 5 Given any $\overline{EJ}$ and any $\overrightarrow{AB}$, there exists a unique point S on $\overrightarrow{AB}$ such that $\overline{AS} \cong \overline{EJ}$.

EXERCISES FOR 2.4

In exercises 1–20 answer true or false.

1. EJ represents the length of $\overline{EJ}$.
2. If $EJ = JS$, then $\overline{EJ} \cong \overline{JS}$.
3. If $\overline{AB} \cong \overline{CD}$, then $AB = CD$.
4. If $EJ > JS$, then $\overline{EJ} \cong \overline{JS}$.
5. If $\overline{TJ} \cong \overline{KR}$, then TJ could be less than KR.
6. Proofs involving congruent segments are often based on properties of the equals relation in R.
7. Congruence of segments is reflexive and transitive but not symmetric.
8. To construct a figure geometrically only a straightedge and a pencil may be used.
9. If J is the midpoint of $\overline{ES}$ and if Q is the midpoint of $\overline{PR}$, then $\overline{EJ} \cong \overline{PQ}$.
10. If the coordinates of A, B, C, and D are -7, -2, 6, and 12, respectively, then $\overline{AB} \cong \overline{CD}$.
11. If $MN = PR$ and M, N, P, and R are points on the number line, in that order, with coordinates of M, N and P being -11, 3, and 5, respectively, then the coordinate of R must be 19.
12. The reflexive property for congruence of segments states that a segment is congruent to itself.

13. Given any $\overline{AB}$ and any $\overrightarrow{LM}$, there exists a unique point P on $\overrightarrow{LM}$ such that $\overline{LP} \cong \overline{AB}$.
14. The measure of a segment is sometimes a negative number.
15. The congruence relation in the set of line segments is like the equals relation in R in that both satisfy all the RST properties.
16. If $\overline{BC} \cong \overline{FG}$, it is not true that $\overline{FG} \cong \overline{BC}$.
17. Theorems are like postulates in that they are accepted as true without proof.
18. A set of objects must be given and a proper relation defined before the validity of the RST properties can be considered.
19. The relation "has more area than" is a meaningful relation for comparing two line segments.
20. The relation "has the same length as" is a meaningful relation for comparing two rays.

In exercises 21–30 provide an example of the given relation in the given set to show that the stated assertion is false; that is, produce a counterexample.

21. "Has at least one point in common with" is transitive in the set of segments in a plane.
22. "Is a point distinct from" is reflexive in the set of points on the number line.
23. "Has a greater length than" is symmetric in the set of segments on a plane.
24. "Has at least two points in common with" is transitive in the set of rays in a plane.
25. "Is a subset of" is symmetric in the set of segments on the number line.
26. "Extends in the opposite direction to" is transitive in the set of rays on the number line.
27. "Lies on the same segment as" is transitive in the set of points in two segments forming a cross.
28. "Is distinct from" is reflexive in the set of half lines in a plane.
29. "Extends in the opposite direction to" is reflexive in the set of half lines on a given line.
30. "Is not a subset of" is symmetric in the set of segments in a given line.

In exercises 31–36 tell whether the relation ® defined for the given set S has the RST properties. Show why or why not.

31. S is the set of points on a line segment; ® is "is a point distinct from."
32. S is the set of points in two segments that form a V-shaped figure; ® is "lies on the same segment as."
33. S is the set of the points of a plane that are not on a line that divides the plane into two half planes; ® is "lies on the opposite side of the line from."
34. S is the set of line segments in a plane; ® is "is collinear with."
35. S is the set of all half lines in a plane; ® is "has at least two points in common with."
36. S is the set of all lines in space; ® is "lies in the same plane as."

In exercises 37–40 do the constructions using only a compass and straightedge.

37. Given $\overline{AB}$ and $\overrightarrow{EJ}$, construct (a) $\overline{ES}$ on $\overrightarrow{EJ}$ such that $\overline{ES} \cong \overline{AB}$ and (b) a bisector $\overleftrightarrow{CD}$ of $\overline{ES}$.
38. Given $\overline{RS}$, $\overline{ST}$, and $\overrightarrow{WY}$, construct $\overline{WG}$ on $\overrightarrow{WY}$ such that $WG = RS + ST$.
39. Given ray $\overrightarrow{ES}$ and line ℓ containing points A, B, and C such that A-B-C, construct (a) $\overline{EJ}$ on $\overrightarrow{ES}$ such that $EJ = AB + AC$, and (b) the midpoint M of $\overline{EJ}$.
40. Given $\overline{EJ}$, $\overline{JS}$, $\overline{ST}$, and $\overrightarrow{AB}$, construct $\overline{AK}$ on $\overrightarrow{AB}$ such that $AK = EJ + JS + ST$.

2.5

GEOMETRIC PROOFS

Using undefined terms, definitions, axioms, and postulates as a basis, we can prove other geometric properties. These will be simple properties at first but will become more complicated later. The most important results to be proved will be stated as theorems, but many other interesting properties will appear in the examples and exercises.

Recall from Section 1.1 that a proof may be thought of as a chain that leads from the hypothesis (the given facts) to the conclusion (the property to be proved). Each link in the chain is a statement, the correctness of which must be shown by giving a reason. Valid reasons are definitions, postulates, axioms, and previously proved theorems.

For simplicity in writing the reasons in proofs, we will use abbreviations that indicate the *content* of each reason. This procedure is a significant aid to learning and is therefore far better than writing simply "Postulate 3" or "Definition 2.6." In the following lists we repeat those established definitions, axioms, postulates, and theorems that will be needed in proofs, followed by the abbreviations to be used. Axioms 4–8 of Section 1.5—the associative, commutative, and distributive axioms—are not repeated here, because we will freely use algebraic and arithmetic manipulations based on these axioms and give "rearrangement properties" (abbreviated rearr props) as the reason. Also, it was noted informally that a line segment has one and only one midpoint (seg has 1 and only 1 midpt), and this fact will be used as needed in proofs.

Definitions

2.7. Point J is called the midpoint of $\overline{ES}$ iff E-J-S and $EJ = JS$ (midpt iff 2 lengths =).

1.8. A line, half line, ray, or line segment is a bisector of a given line segment iff it contains the midpoint and no other points of that given segment (bis seg iff contains midpt).

2.9. Two line segments are congruent iff their lengths (measures) are equal (≅ iff meas =).

Axioms

1. *Reflexive Property of Equals.* If $x \in R$, then $x = x$ (refl =).
2. *Symmetric Property of Equals.* If $x, y \in R$ and $x = y$, then $y = x$ (symm =).
3. *Transitive Property of Equals.* If $x, y, z \in R$ such that $x = y$ and $y = z$, then $x = z$ (trans =).
9. *Transitive Property of Order.* If $x, y, z \in R$, $x < y$, and $y < z$, then $x < z$ (trans <).
   We will also use the fact that the greater-than relation is transitive (trans >).
11. *Addition of Equals.* If $a = b$ and $c = d$, then $a + c = b + d$ (= + =, sums =).
12. *Subtraction of Equals.* If $a = b$ and $c = d$, then $a - c = b - d$ (= − =, diff =).
13. *Multiplication of Equals.* If $a = b$ and $c = d$, then $a \cdot c = b \cdot d$ (= · =, prod =).
14. *Division of Equals.* If $a = b$, $c = d$, $c \neq 0$, and $d \neq 0$, then $a \div c = b \div d$ (= ÷ =, quot =).
15. *Whole Greater than Part.* If $x, y, z \in R$, $z > 0$ and $x = y + z$, then $x > y$ (whole > part).
16. *Addition of Inequalities.* If $a < b$ and $c < d$, then $a + c < b + d$, or if

$a > b$ and $c > d$, then $a + c > b + d$ ($<$ + $<$, sums $<$ or $>$ + $>$, sums $>$).

17. *Substitution.* If a and b name two mathematical expressions such that $a = b$, then a may replace b or b may replace a in any mathematical statement (subst).

Postulates

1. Any two points determine exactly one line (2 pts determ line).
4. If $\overline{ES}$ is a line segment and J is a point such that E-J-S, then $EJ + JS = ES$ (whole = sum parts).
5. Given any $\overline{EJ}$ and any $\overrightarrow{AB}$, there exists a unique point S on $\overrightarrow{AB}$ such that $\overline{AS} \cong \overline{EJ}$ (can copy seg).

Theorems

1. If $\overline{EJ}$ is any line segment, then $\overline{EJ} \cong \overline{EJ}$ (refl $\cong$).
2. If $\overline{EJ}$ and $\overline{KS}$ are line segments and $\overline{EJ} \cong \overline{KS}$, then $\overline{KS} \cong \overline{EJ}$ (symm $\cong$).
3. If $\overline{EJ}$, $\overline{KS}$, and $\overline{CM}$ are line segments such that $\overline{EJ} \cong \overline{KS}$ and $\overline{KS} \cong \overline{CM}$, then $\overline{EJ} \cong \overline{CM}$ (trans $\cong$).

There are seven steps that should be followed when developing a geometric proof. They are listed in the order in which they should be applied.

1. Read the problem and identify the type of figure involved.
2. If a figure is not given, draw one and label it.
3. Write the hypothesis (the given facts) and the conclusion (the statement to be proved).
4. Mark the given facts on the figure.
5. Analyze the problem. It may be helpful to mark on the figure the results that can be derived from the given facts.
6. Make an informal plan or outline.
7. Write a logical sequence of statements and reasons leading from the hypothesis to the conclusion.

You will see as we proceed that geometric figures fall into types. For now we will study simple cases involving line segments. Step 2 gives a picture of the problem, and step 3 eliminates frequent referral to the book. Standard ways to mark the figure will be explained, marks that place the given facts in front of you. Step 5 requires practice, and the examples and exercises in the text, together with classwork, are the best help here. Step 6 may sometimes be done mentally, but often some written notes are helpful. Step 7, the writing of the proof, does not begin until the first six steps are completed.

In Example 1, which follows, we prove that congruence of line segments has the transitive property. The given facts are marked on the figure with short slashes called hash marks. If each of two line segments shows a single hash mark, then the segments are given as congruent. Another congruent pair may be identified with double hash marks, and so on.

EXAMPLE 1 Prove that if $\overline{EJ} \cong \overline{KS}$ and $\overline{KS} \cong \overline{CM}$, then $\overline{EJ} \cong \overline{CM}$.

Steps

1. Identify that the problem is about line segments.
2. Draw and label a figure.
3. Write the hypothesis (the "given") and the conclusion (the "to prove.")
4. Mark the figure using hash marks.

(Steps 2–4: See below)

5. Analysis: congruent line segments have equal lengths and the equals relation is transitive.
6. Plan: show that the given facts imply $EJ = KS$ and $KS = CM$. We then have $EJ = CM$ and the conclusion follows.
7. Write the proof as shown.

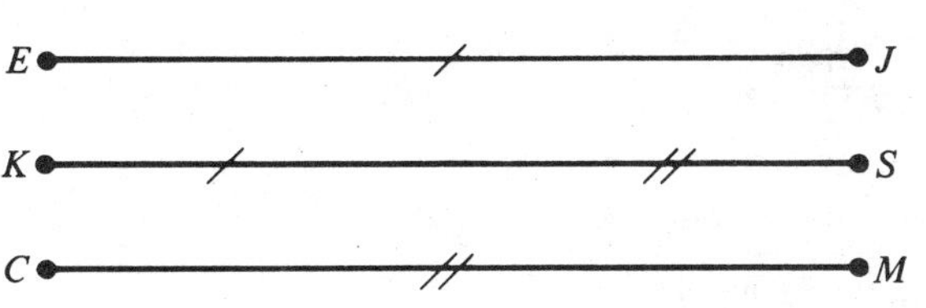

Given
$\overline{EJ} \cong \overline{KS}$
$\overline{KS} \cong \overline{CM}$

To Prove
$\overline{EJ} \cong \overline{CM}$

Statement	*Reason*
1. $\overline{EJ} \cong \overline{KS}$	1. given
2. $EJ = KS$	2. $\cong$ iff meas =
3. $\overline{KS} \cong \overline{CM}$	3. given
4. $KS = CM$	4. $\cong$ iff meas =
5. $EJ = CM$	5. trans =
6. $\therefore \overline{EJ} \cong \overline{CM}$	6. $\cong$ iff meas =

The symbol $\therefore$ in statement 6 means *therefore* and shows that the required conclusion has been reached.

Note that statements and reasons are paired by numbering them. Also note that the proof begins with a given fact followed by a useful consequence of it (the congruence in step 1 implies the equal lengths of step 2). Finally, study carefully the order in which the statements are written. Remember that a correct proof links the given facts to the conclusion step by step and that each step must be justified by a valid reason. Example 2 draws further attention to the importance of a proper order for the statements in a proof.

EXAMPLE 2

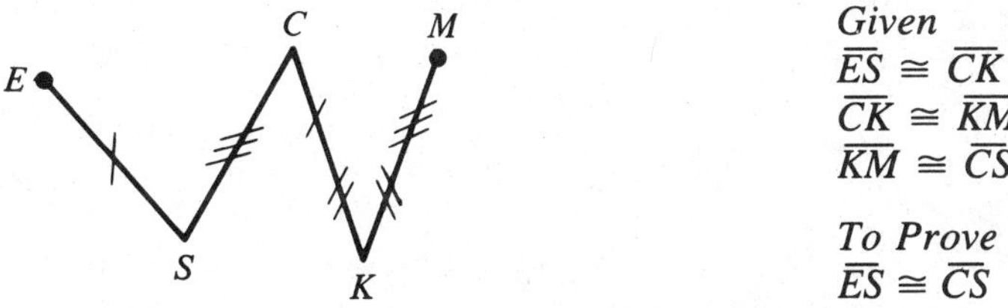

Given
$\overline{ES} \cong \overline{CK}$
$\overline{CK} \cong \overline{KM}$
$\overline{KM} \cong \overline{CS}$

To Prove
$\overline{ES} \cong \overline{CS}$

Rearrange the following statements into a proper order leading from the hypothesis to the conclusion:

(a) $ES = CK$ **(b)** $KM = CS$ **(c)** $ES = CS$ **(d)** $\overline{CK} \cong \overline{KM}$
(e) $\overline{ES} \cong \overline{CK}$ **(f)** $CK = KM$ **(g)** $\overline{ES} \cong \overline{CS}$ **(h)** $\overline{KM} \cong \overline{CS}$

Answer
e, a, d, f, h, b, c, g

The answer given in Example 2 is not the only correct one. Another is d, f, e, a, h, b, c, g, and others are possible, but in all cases g must be the last statement. Also, (e) $\overline{ES} \cong \overline{CK}$ must come *before* (a) $ES = CK$, because (e) is given and (a) is a useful consequence of it.

Another example concludes our introduction to geometric proofs.

EXAMPLE 3 Prove: If L-M-N and P-Q-R such that $\overline{LM} \cong \overline{PQ}$ and $\overline{MN} \cong \overline{QR}$, then $\overline{LN} \cong \overline{PR}$.

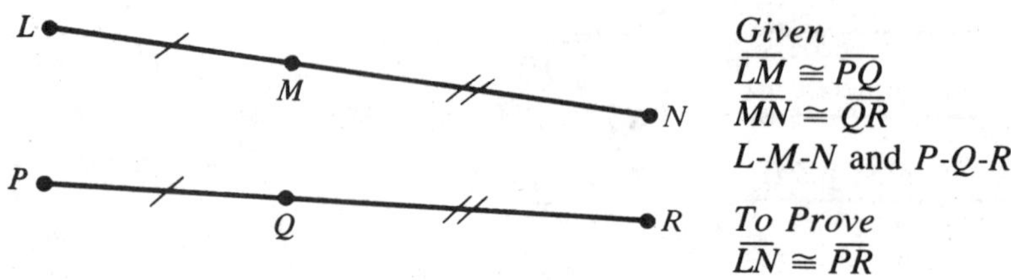

Given
$\overline{LM} \cong \overline{PQ}$
$\overline{MN} \cong \overline{QR}$
L-M-N and P-Q-R

To Prove
$\overline{LN} \cong \overline{PR}$

Statement	*Reason*
1. $\overline{LM} \cong \overline{PQ}$	1. given
2. $LM = PQ$	2. $\cong$ iff meas $=$
3. $\overline{MN} \cong \overline{QR}$	3. given
4. $MN = QR$	4. $\cong$ iff meas $=$
5. $LM + MN = PQ + QR$	5. $= + =$, sums $=$
6. L-M-N	6. given
7. $LN = LM + MN$	7. whole $=$ sum parts
8. P-Q-R	8. given
9. $PQ + QR = PR$	9. whole $=$ sum parts
10. $LN = PR$	10. trans $=$
11. $\therefore \overline{LN} \cong \overline{PR}$	11. $\cong$ iff meas $=$

Reason 10 applies because from statements 7 and 5 we have $LN = PQ + QR$, and this, together with statement 9, gives $LN = PR$.

EXERCISES FOR 2.5

In exercises 1–20 answer true or false.

1. A geometric proof may be thought of as a chain, leading from the given facts to the conclusion, in which each link is a statement justified by a valid reason.

2. The reasons used to justify statements in a proof are definitions, axioms, postulates, or previously proved theorems.

3. Postulates are statements that must be proved.

4. Theorems are statements that are assumed to be true without proof.

5. A line has only one midpoint.

6. A bisector of a line segment contains the midpoint and no other point of the segment.

7. Of all the subsets of a line, only line segments have midpoints.

8. A half line can bisect a segment.

9. If $\overline{AB} \cong \overline{CD}$, then $AB = CD$.

10. Congruence of segments is reflexive and symmetric but not transitive.

11. "If $\overline{AB} \cong \overline{CD}$, then $\overline{CD} \cong \overline{AB}$" is valid because $\cong$ is transitive.

12. If $AB = AC + CB$, then A-C-B.

13. The length of a segment does not depend on the number of points in the segment.
14. If $EJ = 5$ units and $JS = 7$ units, then $ES = 12$ units.
15. Axioms are basic statements that are assumed to be true about real numbers.
16. Marking a figure with the given facts helps to keep the known information readily available.
17. The final statement in a proof should be the conclusion that was to be proved.
18. There is exactly one correct sequence of statements for a geometric proof.
19. Each reason used in a proof must justify the statement that it accompanies.
20. A valid proof shows that the conclusion is a necessary consequence of the hypothesis.

In exercises 21–25 state which segments are congruent as shown by the marks.

21.

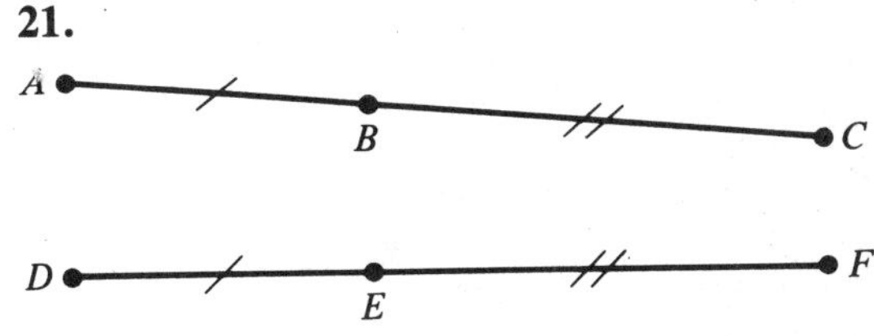

22.

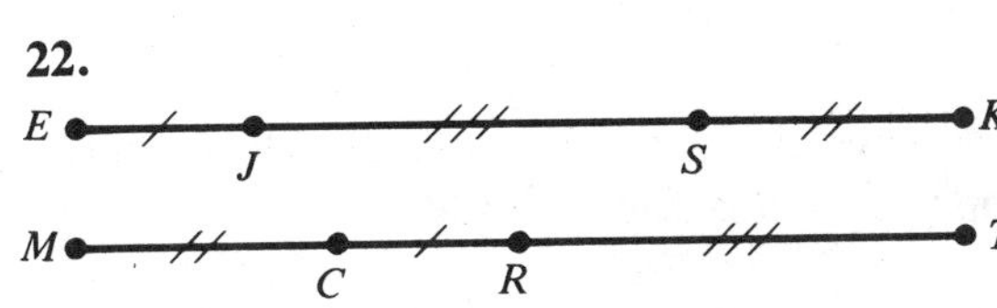

23.

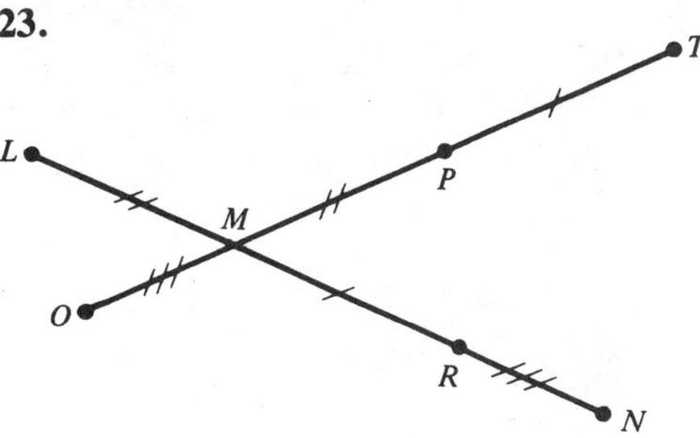

24.

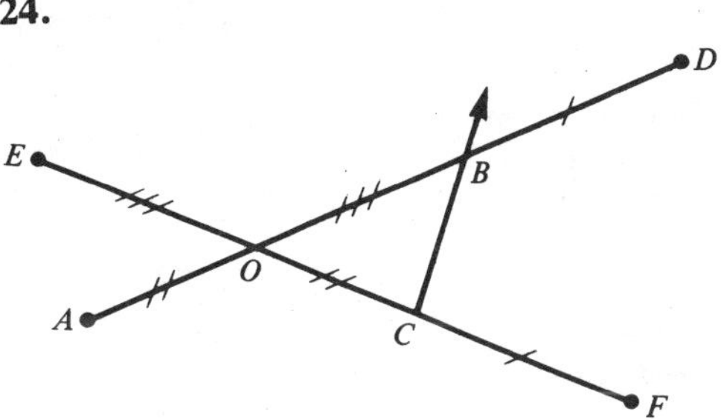

25.

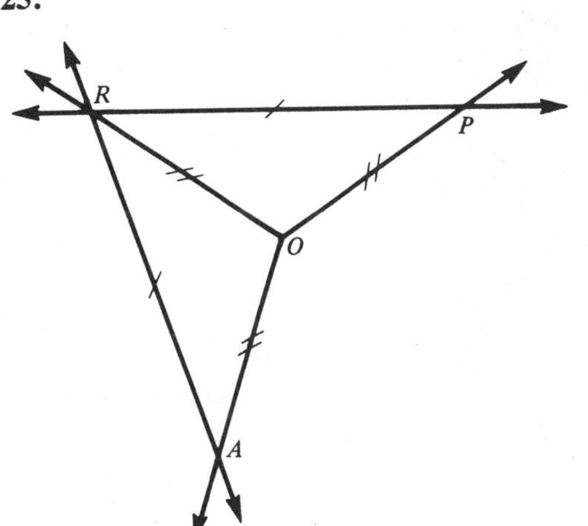

In exercises 26–29 copy the figure, mark it, and supply the missing reasons in the proof.

26. Given
$\overline{AB} \cong \overline{CD}$

To Prove
$\overline{CD} \cong \overline{AB}$

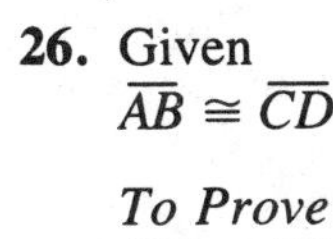

Statement	*Reason*
1. $\overline{AB} \cong \overline{CD}$	1. ?
2. $AB = CD$	2. ?
3. $CD = AB$	3. ?
4. $\therefore \overline{CD} \cong \overline{AB}$	4. ?

27. *Given*
S-T-U-V
$\overline{ST} \cong \overline{UV}$

To Prove
$\overline{SU} \cong \overline{TV}$

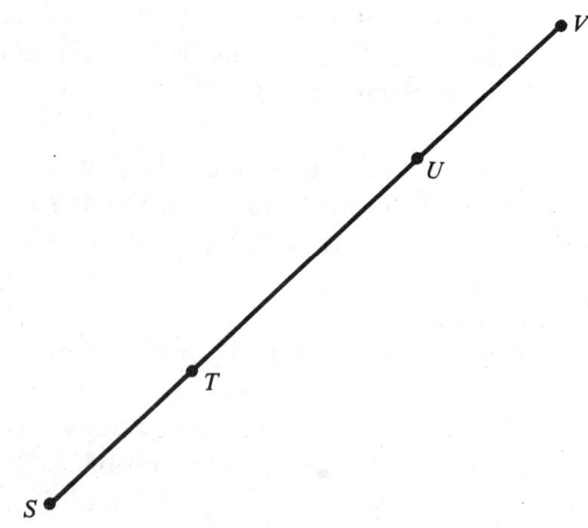

Statement	*Reason*
1. *S-T-U-V*	1. ?
2. $\overline{ST} \cong \overline{UV}$	2. ?
3. $ST = UV$	3. ?
4. $\overline{TU} \cong \overline{TU}$	4. ?
5. $TU = TU$	5. ?
6. $ST + TU = UV + TU$	6. ?
7. $SU = ST + TU$	7. ?
8. $UV + TU = TV$	8. ?
9. $SU = TV$	9. ?
10. $\therefore \overline{SU} \cong \overline{TV}$	10. ?

28. *Given*
$\overline{ES}$ inters $\overline{MK}$ at J
$\overline{EJ} \cong \overline{MJ}$
$\overline{JS} \cong \overline{JK}$

To Prove
$\overline{ES} \cong \overline{MK}$

Statement	*Reason*
1. $\overline{ES}$ inters $\overline{MK}$ at J	1. ?
2. $\overline{EJ} \cong \overline{MJ}$	2. ?
3. $EJ = MJ$	3. ?
4. $\overline{JS} \cong \overline{JK}$	4. ?
5. $JS = JK$	5. ?
6. $EJ + JS = MJ + JK$	6. ?
7. $ES = EJ + JS$	7. ?
8. $MJ + JK = MK$	8. ?
9. $ES = MK$	9. ?
10. $\therefore \overline{ES} \cong \overline{MK}$	10. ?

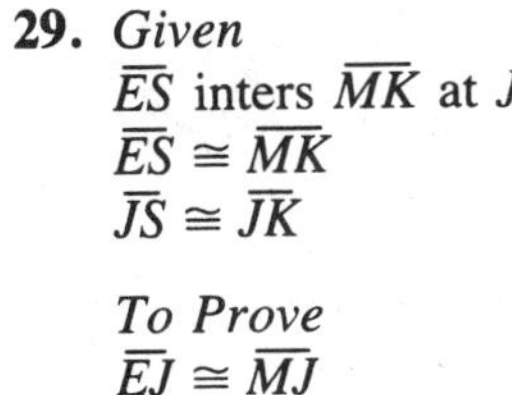

29. *Given*
$\overline{ES}$ inters $\overline{MK}$ at J
$\overline{ES} \cong \overline{MK}$
$\overline{JS} \cong \overline{JK}$

To Prove
$\overline{EJ} \cong \overline{MJ}$

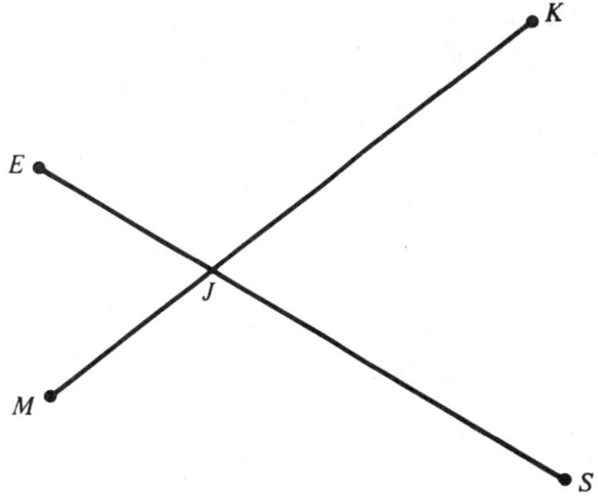

Statement	Reason
1. $\overline{ES}$ inters $\overline{MK}$ at J	1. ?
2. $\overline{ES} \cong \overline{MK}$	2. ?
3. $ES = MK$	3. ?
4. $\overline{JS} \cong \overline{JK}$	4. ?
5. $JS = JK$	5. ?
6. $ES - JS = MK - JK$	6. ?
7. $EJ = ES - JS$	7. ?
8. $MK - JK = MJ$	8. ?
9. $EJ = MJ$	9. ?
10. $\therefore \overline{EJ} \cong \overline{MJ}$	10. ?

In exercises 30 and 31 copy the figure, mark it, and rearrange the given statements into a correct order for a proof.

30. *Given*
A-B-C-D-E
$\overline{AB} \cong \overline{DE}$
$\overline{BC} \cong \overline{CD}$

To Prove
$\overline{AC} \cong \overline{CE}$

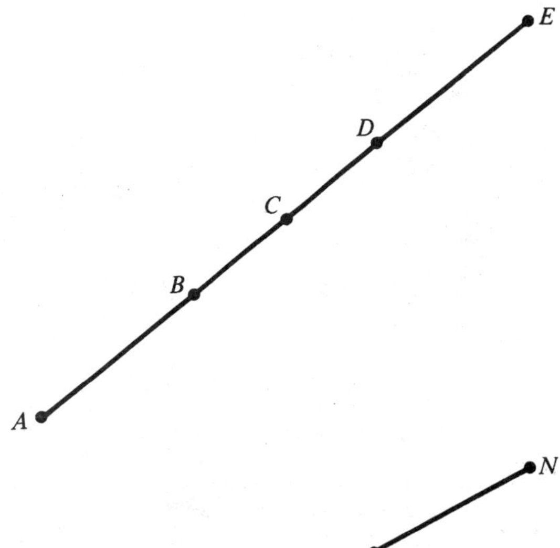

(a) $AB + BC = DE + CD$
(b) $AB = DE$
(c) $AC = CE$
(d) $AC = AB + BC$
(e) $\overline{AB} \cong \overline{DE}$
(f) A-B-C-D-E
(g) $\overline{BC} \cong \overline{CD}$
(h) $DE + CD = CE$
(i) $\overline{AC} \cong \overline{CE}$
(j) $BC = CD$

31. *Given*
L-K-M-N
$\overline{LM} \cong \overline{KN}$

To Prove
$\overline{LK} \cong \overline{MN}$

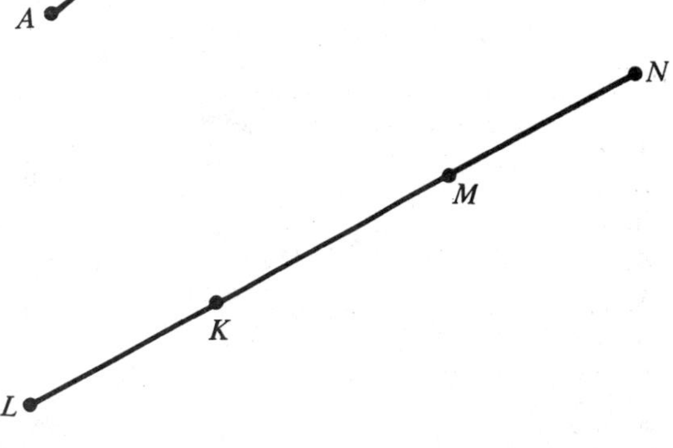

(a) $KM = KM$
(b) $LM = KN$
(c) $LK = LM - KM$
(d) $LM - KM = KN - KM$
(e) $\overline{LK} \cong \overline{MN}$
(f) $KN - KM = MN$
(g) L-K-M-N
(h) $\overline{LM} \cong \overline{KN}$
(i) $\overline{KM} \cong \overline{KM}$
(j) $LK = MN$

In exercises 32–40 copy the figure, copy the hypothesis and the conclusion, mark the figure, and write a proof.

32. *Given*
A-B-C-D
$\overline{AB} \cong \overline{CD}$

To Prove
$\overline{AC} \cong \overline{BD}$

33. *Given*
E-J-S
K-C-M
$\overline{ES} \cong \overline{KM}$
$\overline{JS} \cong \overline{KC}$

To Prove
$\overline{EJ} \cong \overline{CM}$

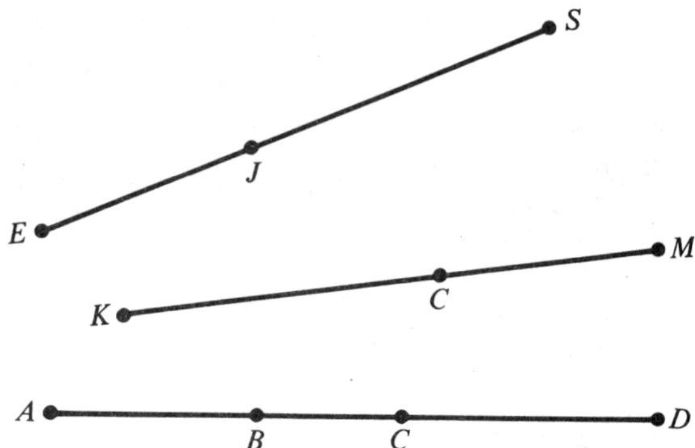

34. *Given*
A-B-C-D
E-J-S-K
$\overline{AB} \cong \overline{EJ}$
$\overline{BC} \cong \overline{JS}$
$\overline{CD} \cong \overline{SK}$

To Prove
$\overline{AD} \cong \overline{EK}$

35. *Given*
$\overline{ES}$ inters $\overline{LW}$ at *J*
J midpt $\overline{ES}$
J midpt $\overline{LW}$
$\overline{ES} \cong \overline{LW}$

To Prove
$\overline{JS} \cong \overline{JW}$

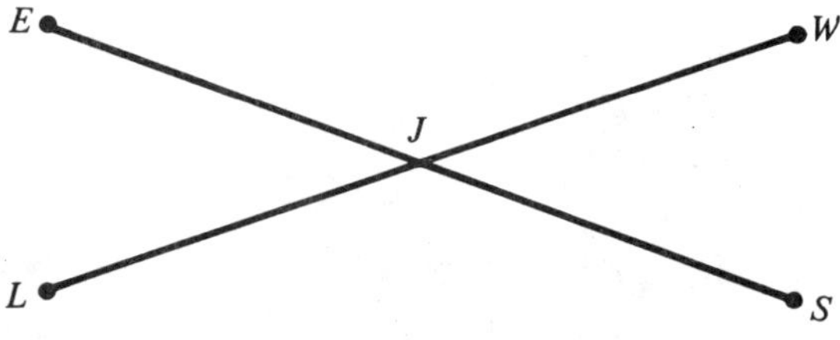

36. *Given*
$\overline{ES} \cong \overline{JS}$
K midpt $\overline{ES}$
C midpt $\overline{JS}$

To Prove
$\overline{SK} \cong \overline{SC}$

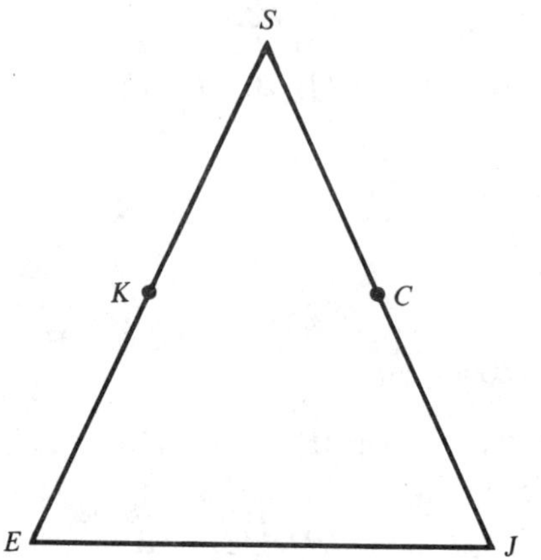

37. *Given*
A-B-C
D-B-F
$\overline{AC} \cong \overline{FD}$
$\overline{BC} \cong \overline{BD}$

To Prove
$\overline{AB} \cong \overline{FB}$

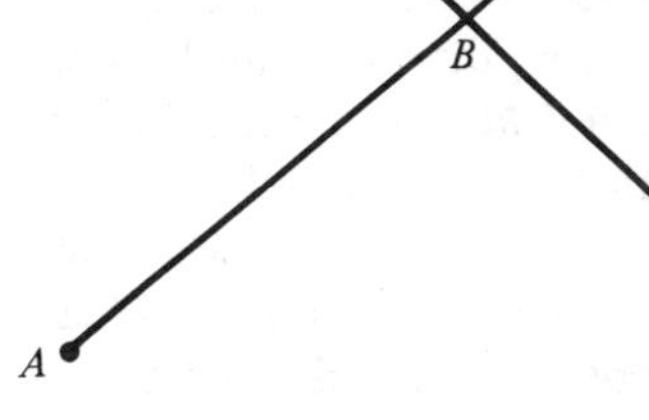

38. *Given*
H-E-X-A-G-O-N
A midpt $\overline{HN}$
A midpt $\overline{EO}$

To Prove
$\overline{HO} \cong \overline{EN}$

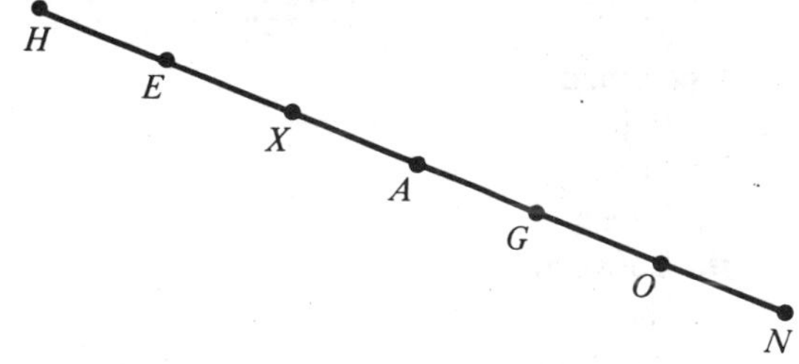

39. *Given*
A-D-G
B-E-H
C-F-I
$\overline{DG} \cong \overline{EH}$
$\overline{BE} \cong \overline{CF}$
$\overline{EH} \cong \overline{FI}$
$\overline{AD} \cong \overline{BE}$

To Prove
$\overline{AG} \cong \overline{CI}$

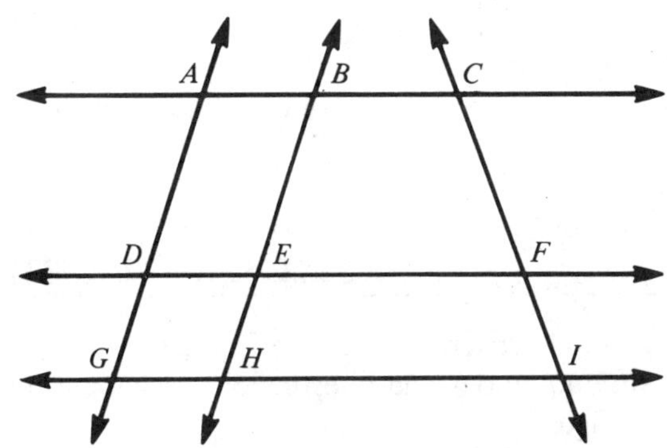

40. *Given*
R-S-T-U
E-J-K-C
$\overline{RS} \cong \overline{JK}$
$\overline{TU} \cong \overline{KC}$
S midpt $\overline{RT}$
J midpt $\overline{EK}$

To Prove
$\overline{RU} \cong \overline{EC}$

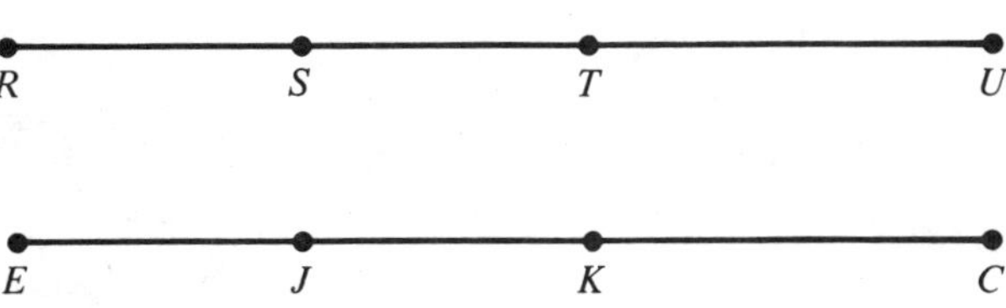

CHAPTER 2 SUMMARY

This chapter begins the development of Euclidean plane geometry with a discussion of certain undefined terms, the most fundamental of which are *point* and *line*. Important subsets of a line are identified, namely half lines, rays, and line segments. A discussion of the manner in which line segments may be measured leads us to use the number line for the set of real numbers to assign an exact length or measure to any line segment. We define the congruence relation for line segments and observe that it behaves as the equals relation does for numbers, in that the RST properties are valid for both. The chapter concludes with an introduction to the techniques involved in writing proofs.

FACTS TO KNOW

1. Undefined terms
- **a.** Point
- **b.** Plane
- **c.** Line
- **d.** Between
- **e.** Half line
- **f.** Endpoint

2. Definitions
- **a.** Space
- **b.** Geometric figure
- **c.** Collinear points
- **d.** Line segment
- **e.** Ray
- **f.** Length or measure of a line segment
- **g.** Midpoint of a line segment
- **h.** Bisector of a line segment
- **i.** Congruent line segments

3. Postulates
- **a.** 2 pts determ line
- **b.** Any line contains at least two points.
- **c.** Ruler Postulate
- **d.** whole = sum parts
- **e.** can copy seg

4. Theorems
- **a.** refl ≅
- **b.** symm ≅
- **c.** trans ≅

PROBLEMS TO MASTER

1. Find the length of a line segment.
2. Find unions and intersections of geometric figures.
3. Test validity of RST properties of a relation in a set.
4. Mark figures.
5. Write proofs.
6. Construct a bisector and the midpoint of a line segment.
7. Construct on a ray a line segment congruent to a given line segment.

3

ANGLES

MAJOR TOPICS

- ∡ Distinction between an angle and its measure
- ∡ The unit angle of one degree and the protractor
- ∡ Postulates about the measure of an angle
- ∡ Identification of special pairs of angles
- ∡ Congruence of angles
- ∡ RST properties of congruence of angles
- ∡ Perpendicular lines and right angles

HISTORICAL NOTE

PYTHAGORAS AND IRRATIONAL NUMBERS

One of Thales' students was Pythagoras (584–495 B.C.) who is perhaps better known to us than his teacher because of the right-triangle theorem that bears his name. Thales never forgot his geometrical learning in Egypt and advised Pythagoras to visit the priests, who were the scholars, of that country. This he did, and the experience became the basis for much of his later work.

Pythagoras was born on the island of Samos, belonging, like Thales, to the Ionian colony of Greeks living on the western shores and islands of Asia Minor. After his travels, Pythagoras settled at Crotona, a town in southern Italy, where he gathered students of his own and lectured on philosophy and mathematics. So powerful were his teachings that his more zealous students formed a secret society, the Order of the Pythagoreans. Members were required to share everything and to take an oath not to reveal the teachings of the society. In time they gained a great influence in the Grecian world, especially in religious matters. Their symbol was the five-pointed star formed by the five diagonals of a regular pentagon. This star was also used at that time to symbolize health, and indeed the Order was much interested in medicine.

The Pythagoreans are credited with achieving for mathematics a special and independent status. They were the first to treat mathematical concepts as clearly identified abstractions and to establish theorems deductively and systematically using the pattern set by Thales and his followers.

Pythagoras discovered and investigated many phenomena concerning numbers, including the harmonic progressions formed by the notes of the musical scale. His greatest achievement, however, was the discovery of irrational numbers. Pythagoras arrived at these by considering a seemingly simple question related to the well-established practice of measuring lengths with a marked measuring stick (a ruler). He wondered whether it is always possible to find a common measuring unit for any two given lengths p and q. In other words, if q is shorter than p, is it always possible to express p as a whole number multiple of q plus fractional parts of q? To attempt this we would successively mark off the length q onto p until nothing remains or until a piece shorter than q remains. If nothing remains, we can express p as a whole number multiplied times q. If a shorter piece remains, we subdivide q into equal parts and mark these off onto the remaining part of p. The process would then be repeated as many times as necessary until no part of p remains. Pythagoras thought this should always be possible, a view probably grounded in his belief that numbers were the ultimate reality, the stuff of which everything was made! To his dismay, however, he found that if q is the side of a square and p is the diagonal, then the fractional process never terminates. In other words, the diagonal of a square cannot be expressed as a multiple of the side using whole numbers and fractions. (The correct multiplier is $\sqrt{2}$, a nonterminating nonrepeating decimal.) Thus, Pythagoras proved the existence of irrational numbers, a piece of advanced mathematics remarkable for its time.

Perhaps it is fitting that Pythagoras, with his religious view of numbers, has achieved a kind of immortality, for his name has been given to the best-known theorem in mathematics. It is a less well-known fact that he invented the very word "mathematics."

3.1 INTRODUCTION

In following our progression from simple to more complex geometric figures, we next consider figures that can be formed by two lines or two subsets of lines. The two possible types using two lines are shown in Figure 3.1. You will probably recognize that four angles are formed by the two intersecting

Figure 3.1

lines l and m and that a and b are two parallel (nonintersecting) lines. These figures are in a sense more complicated than those formed using two subsets of lines. Some of the possibilities using line segments and rays are shown in Figure 3.2. A comparison of these figures with familiar physical objects suggests that the most valuable of the figures are those containing angles or parallel lines. For example, an arm bent at the elbow forms an angle; the two rails of a straight railroad track illustrate parallel lines. There are countless other examples of such figures around us. This chapter develops the fundamental geometric concepts concerning angles. Parallel lines are discussed in Chapter 5.

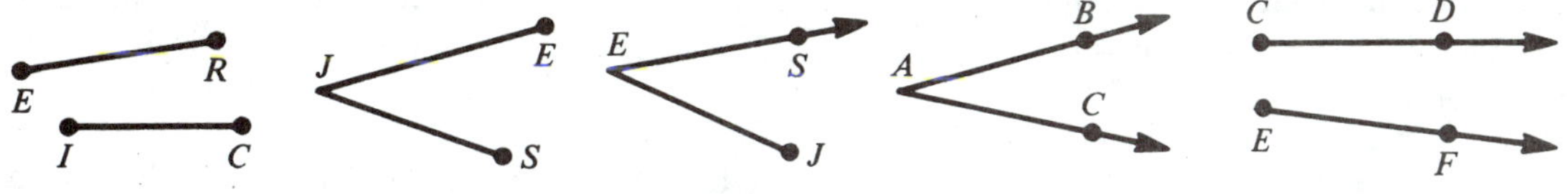

Figure 3.2

We begin with a definition.

Definition 3.1 A set of points is an *angle* iff it is the union of two rays having the same endpoint.

Note that an angle is the *set of points in two rays*. It is not the "opening" between the rays, a concept that is related to the numerical measure of an angle (Section 3.2). A similar distinction was made for line segments. A line segment is a set of points to which is assigned a numerical measure called its length.

The rays in Definition 3.1 are called the *sides* of the angle, and the common endpoint is called the *vertex*. In Figure 3.3 $\overrightarrow{JE}$ and $\overrightarrow{JS}$ are the sides, and point J is the vertex. There are three standard ways to name angles. All use the symbol $\measuredangle$ to stand for "angle." Figure 3.3 shows $\measuredangle EJS$ or $\measuredangle J$ or $\measuredangle 1$.

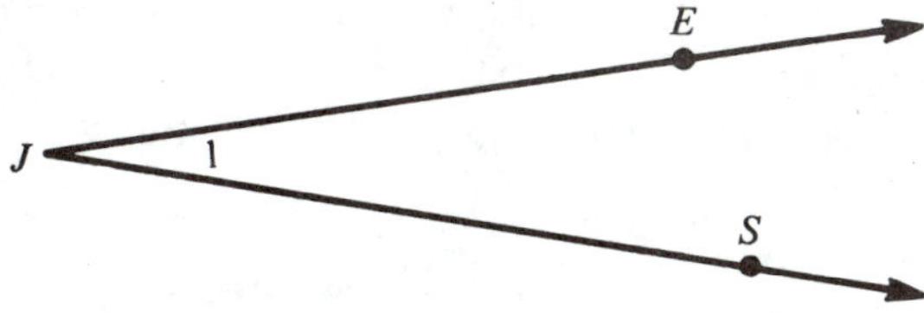

Figure 3.3

The three-letter notation, $\measuredangle EJS$, may also be written $\measuredangle SJE$. In this notation the vertex letter *must* appear in the middle. In the second notation, $\measuredangle J$, only the vertex letter appears. This may be used only if there is no confusion as to which angle is named (see Example 1). The third notation, $\measuredangle 1$, is often convenient in a figure containing several angles.

EXAMPLE 1

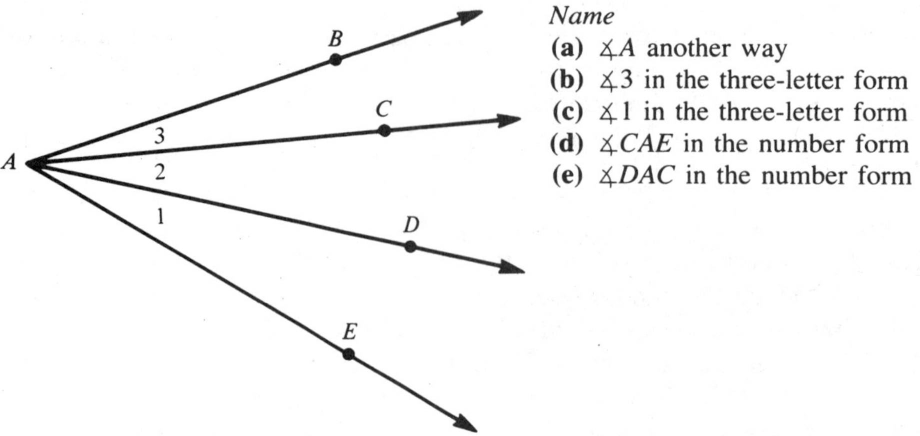

Name

(a) ∡A another way
(b) ∡3 in the three-letter form
(c) ∡1 in the three-letter form
(d) ∡CAE in the number form
(e) ∡DAC in the number form

Answers

(a) Since there are several angles having vertex A, it is not clear which angle is meant. The question cannot be answered.
(b) ∡BAC or ∡CAB
(c) ∡DAE or ∡EAD
(d) Since ∡CAE is formed by a ray of ∡1 and a ray of ∡2, the number form should not be used.
(e) ∡2

We next discuss some terminology about angles. Formal definitions are omitted to avoid the excessive detail required to develop them.

It is important to notice that the definition of an angle makes no restriction on the relative positions of the two rays except that they have the same endpoint. Thus, the rays could be subsets of the same line, as are $\overrightarrow{JE}$ and $\overrightarrow{JS}$ in Figure 3.4. Such rays are called *opposite rays* and are said to form a *straight angle*. Evidently, a straight angle is simply a line with one of its points as the vertex.

Figure 3.4

We will occasionally refer to the *interior* and the *exterior* of an angle that is not a straight angle. In Figure 3.5 points K and M are in the interior of ∡EJS, whereas points P and Q are in the exterior. Although this illustration may sufficiently explain these terms, some further discussion will be useful.

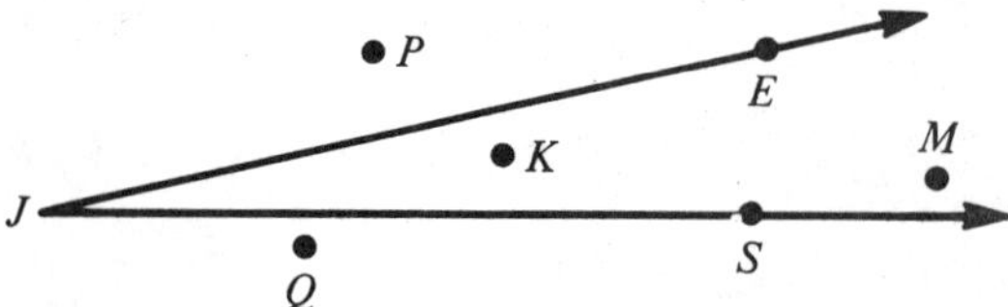

Figure 3.5

There is exactly one plane that contains any given angle. The angle may be viewed as separating the plane into three distinct sets of points, namely (1) the angle itself, (2) the interior of the angle, and (3) the exterior of the angle.

These sets are shown in Figure 3.6. The interior has a property not shared by the exterior. If *any* two points of the interior are joined by a line segment, all points of the line segment lie in the interior. For example, all points of $\overline{KM}$ lie in the interior in Figure 3.6. Such a set of points is said to be *convex*. The same is *not* true of the exterior. Thus, not all points of $\overline{PQ}$ in Figure 3.6 lie in the exterior. Thus, the interior of an angle is a convex set, but the exterior is not.

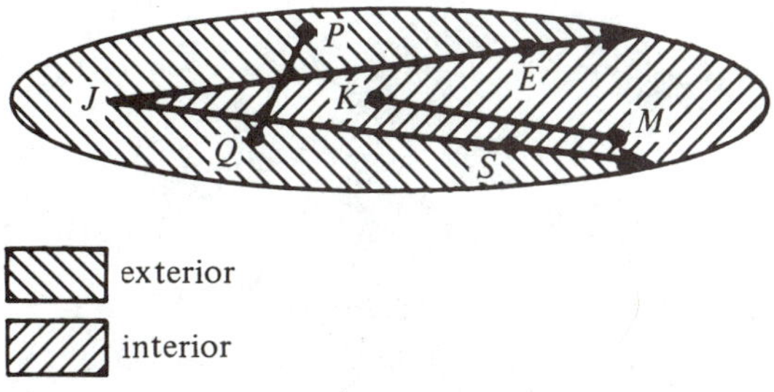

Figure 3.6

Although our approach has been informal, we will use the foregoing terms in the work that follows. In particular, we need the following definition.

Definition 3.2 Let $\overrightarrow{OA}$, $\overrightarrow{OB}$, and $\overrightarrow{OC}$ name three rays with the same endpoint O. Then $\overrightarrow{OB}$ is *between* $\overrightarrow{OA}$ and $\overrightarrow{OC}$ iff B is in the interior of $\measuredangle AOC$.

This definition is illustrated in Figure 3.7. Note that $\overrightarrow{OD}$ is *not* between $\overrightarrow{OA}$ and $\overrightarrow{OC}$ because D is in the exterior of $\measuredangle AOC$. Now Definition 3.2 may be used to define a useful term that identifies angles that are next to each other.

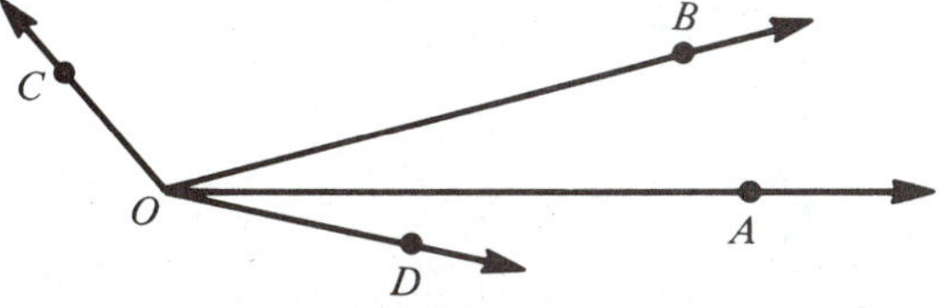

Figure 3.7

Definition 3.3 Two angles are called *adjacent angles* iff they have the same vertex and a common side between their other two sides (adj $\measuredangle$s iff same vtx and com side betw).

In Figure 3.8 $\measuredangle EJM$ and $\measuredangle MJS$ are adjacent angles because they have the same vertex J and common side $\overrightarrow{JM}$ between $\overrightarrow{JE}$ and $\overrightarrow{JS}$. Angle EJS and $\measuredangle MJS$, however, are not adjacent because their common side $\overrightarrow{JS}$ is not between their other two sides $\overrightarrow{JE}$ and $\overrightarrow{JM}$.

Definition 3.4 identifies another pair of angles that occurs in geometric figures where two lines intersect.

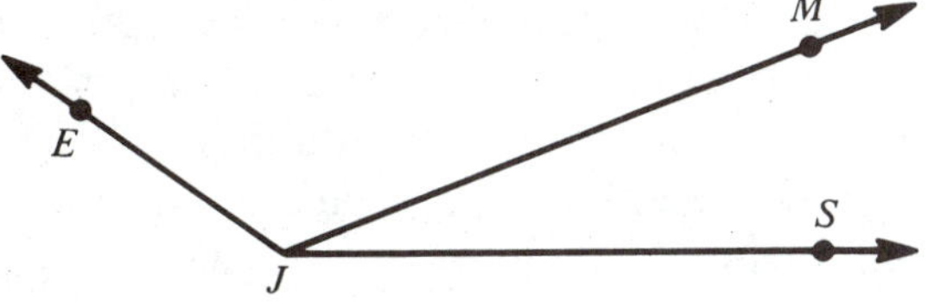

Figure 3.8

Definition 3.4 Two angles are called *vertical angles* iff the sides of one are rays opposite to the sides of the other (vert $\measuredangle$s formed by opp rays).

In Figure 3.9 $\measuredangle 1$ and $\measuredangle 3$ are one pair of vertical angles, and $\measuredangle 2$ and $\measuredangle 4$ are the other pair.

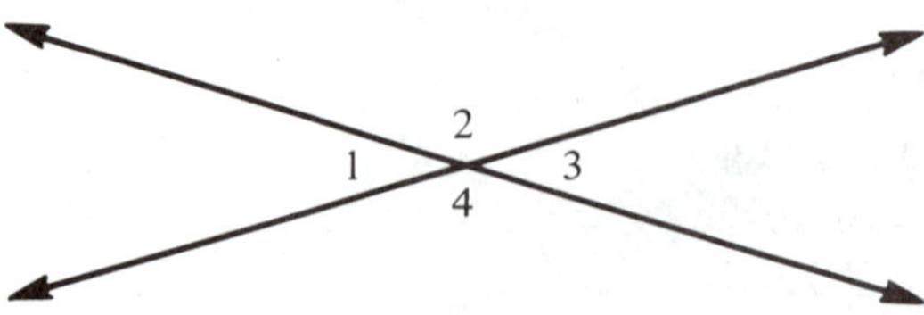

Figure 3.9

A frequently met geometric figure is shown in Figure 3.10, which shows $\overleftrightarrow{AC}$ with A-B-C and $\overrightarrow{BD}$ forming $\measuredangle 1$ and $\measuredangle 2$. Such angles are said to be a *linear pair*.

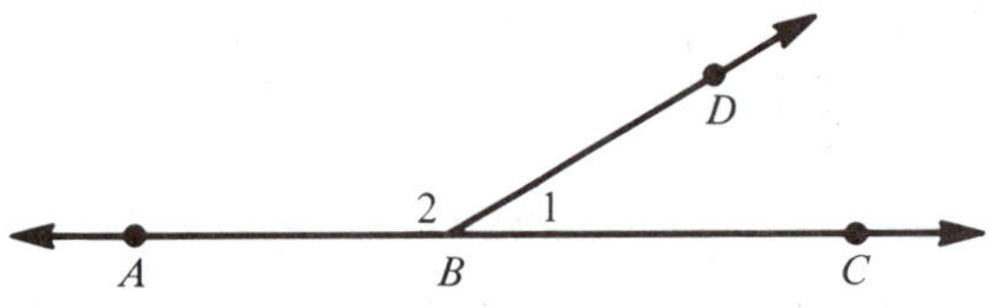

Figure 3.10

Definition 3.5 Two angles are a *linear pair* iff they have a common side and the other two sides are opposite rays (lin pr iff com side and opp rays).

It is common practice to refer to a linear pair as adjacent angles even though their common side is not in the interior of an angle.

3.2 MEASURING ANGLES

Many of the underlying ideas in our discussion of measuring line segments apply to measuring angles. Recall that a line segment is measured by covering it with *unit line segments*. The number of units needed, together with the name of the unit (e.g., inches, centimeters), is the measurement of the line segment. In the same way, an angle is measured by covering it with *unit angles*. The number needed, together with the name of the unit angle, will give the angle's measurement.

But how do we establish a unit angle? The sides are rays and thus are infinitely long. Similarly, the interior of an angle is of infinite extent. It appears, therefore, that the size of a unit angle cannot be established by any measurement involving its sides or interior. An examination of the angles in Figure 3.11 suggests that the size of an angle should be related in some way to the "amount of opening" between its sides. The curved arrows convey a sense of rotation from the horizontal side to the other side. It is this "amount

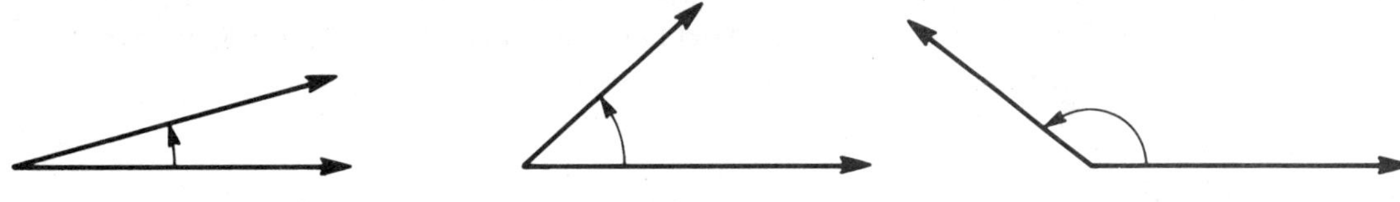

Figure 3.11

of rotation" that we wish to measure; therefore, this must be the concept leading to our unit angle.

The foregoing discussion is the basis for an instrument called a *protractor*. One is pictured in Figure 3.12. It is a half circle having 180 equally marked spaces. The circle's center is point A. Using the points marked 0 and 1, a unit angle is established with its vertex at A. Unit $\measuredangle BAC$ is drawn in the figure. It is called an angle of *one degree* (abbreviated 1°). Thus 1° is $\frac{1}{180}$ of a half rotation and $\frac{1}{360}$ of a full rotation. This use of the number 360 is inherited from the ancient Babylonians who, more than 4000 years ago, divided a full circle into 360 equal parts as their basis for measuring angles. (They chose 360 because they estimated one year as 360 days.)

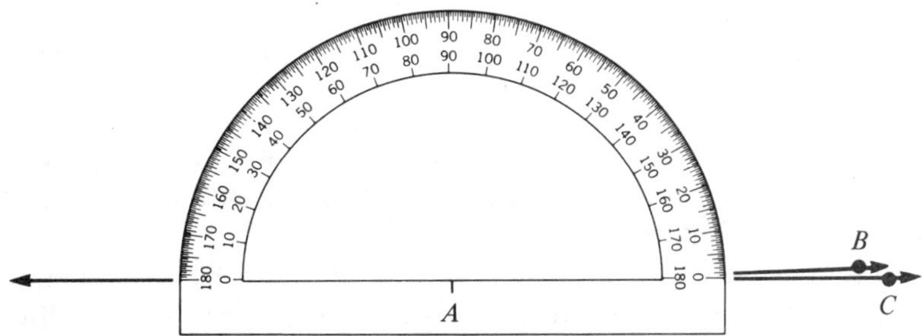

Figure 3.12

Now, to measure any angle—that is, to cover it with unit angles of 1°—place the protractor's center at the angle's vertex and the zero mark on one of the angle's sides. The degree measurement of the angle may now be read at the mark matching the other side of the angle. The process is pictured in Figure 3.13 in which $\measuredangle EJS$ is measured as 60°.

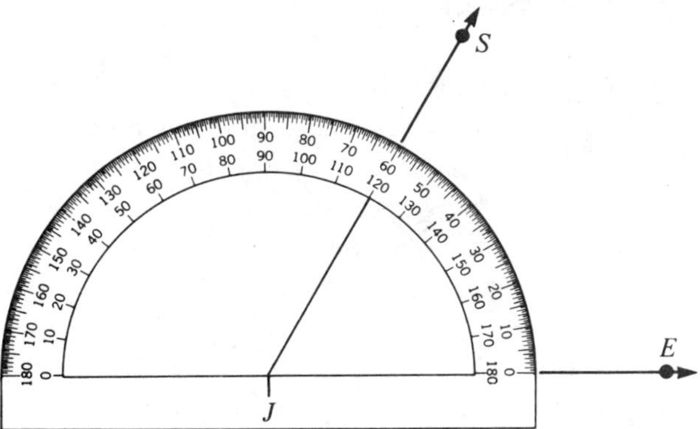

Figure 3.13

For more precise measurements, each degree is subdivided into 60 equal parts called *minutes*. Each minute is subdivided into 60 equal parts called *seconds*. (These terms, of course, have nothing to do with time!) Most protractors do not show these small subdivisions because, for example, to mark minutes on the half circle would require $60 \cdot 180 = 10{,}800$ marks. The above equivalent measurements are sometimes briefly shown as:

$$1^\circ = 60' \qquad \text{and} \qquad 1' = 60''$$

Here the symbol $'$ stands for minutes and $''$ stands for seconds. Angle measurements in degrees, minutes, and seconds may be added or subtracted as shown in Example 1.

EXAMPLE 1

Given

$82^\circ 8' 21''$ and $47^\circ 51' 39''$

Find

(a) the sum of the two angle measurements,

(b) the difference of the two angle measurements.

Answers

(a)
$$\begin{array}{r} 82^\circ\ 8'21'' \\ +\underline{47^\circ 51'39''} \\ 129^\circ 59'60'' \end{array} = 129^\circ 60' = 130^\circ$$

(b)
$$\begin{array}{r} 82^\circ 8'21'' = 81^\circ 67'81'' \\ -\underline{47^\circ 51'39''} \\ 34^\circ 16'42'' \end{array}$$
(borrowing $1^\circ = 60'$ and $1' = 60''$)

Measuring with a protractor, just as with a ruler, gives an approximation whose precision is limited by the nature of the instrument and by our ability to accurately match points, rays, and marks. We will now introduce a mathematical process whereby an exact number of degrees is assigned as the measure of a given angle. The procedure is similar to that used for line segments in Section 2.3.

Experience with a protractor suggests that the set of rays in one half of a rotation about a point may be put in a one-to-one correspondence with the set of real numbers from zero to 180, inclusive. This is indeed true, and a few examples are shown in Figure 3.14. The number matched to each ray is called the coordinate of the ray. The *angular distance* between two rays is the absolute value of the difference between their coordinates. Thus, the angular distance between $\overrightarrow{AB}$ and $\overrightarrow{AD}$ is $|89^\circ - 17^\circ| = |72^\circ| = 72^\circ$.

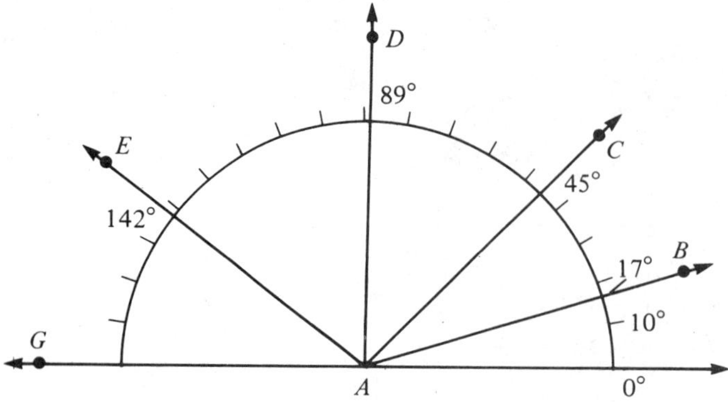

Figure 3.14

Our discussion leads to Postulate 6.

Postulate 6 *Protractor Postulate*. The rays in a half rotation around a point may be placed in one-to-one correspondence with the real numbers from zero to 180, inclusive, and a unique positive number may be assigned as the angular distance between two given rays.

Since the one-to-one correspondence in Postulate 6 may be established for the vertex of any angle, we may now define angular measure.

Definition 3.6 The *degree measure* of an angle is the angular distance between its sides.

Thus, a unique degree measure is assigned to each angle and it is this number that is approximated using a protractor. It should be noted that other systems of angular measure have been devised. One, called radian measure, is used extensively in trigonometry and calculus. Degree measure, however, is the only system used in this text.

Recall that we use the symbol $\measuredangle$ in naming an angle. To distinguish between an angle (which is a set of points) and its measure (which is a number) we will use the symbol $\angle$ when denoting measure. Thus, if $\measuredangle EJS$ has measure 20°, we write $\angle EJS = 20°$.

Next are postulates and definitions that involve the concept of angular measure.

Postulate 7 If K is any point in the interior of $\measuredangle EJS$, then $\angle EJK + \angle KJS = \angle EJS$ (whole = sum parts).

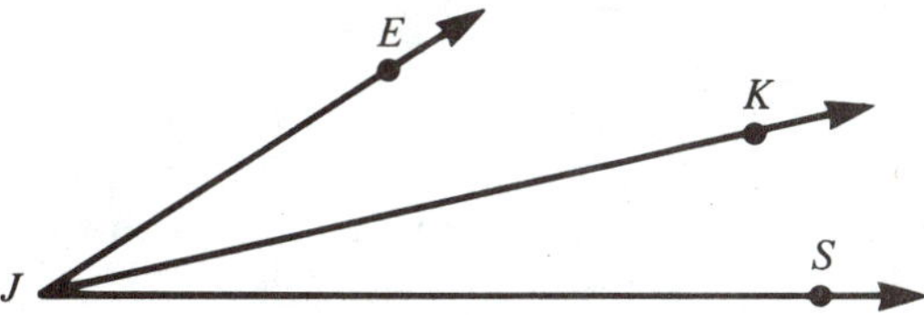

Figure 3.15

Figure 3.15 illustrates this postulate. We use the same abbreviation for Postulate 7 as that for Postulate 4 (concerning line segments) because of their similar content. Also, as with Postulate 4, Postulate 7 may be used to justify subtraction statements such as $\angle EJS - \angle EJK = \angle KJS$ (Figure 3.15) and statements about angles involving more than two "parts." We will also use Postulate 7 in connection with straight angles even though they have no interiors. Thus, in Figure 3.16 we have $\angle EJK + \angle KJS = \angle EJS$ because the "whole = sum parts."

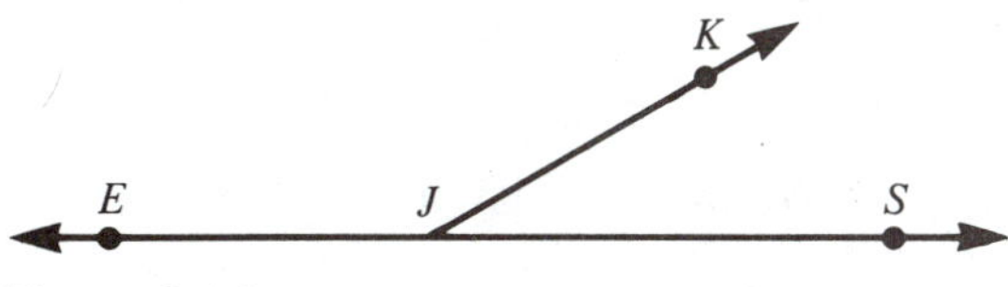

Figure 3.16

Recall that in Section 2.3 the concept of length was used to define the midpoint of a line segment (Definition 2.7) and a bisector of a line segment

(Definition 2.8). In a similar way, angular measure may be used to define the midray of an angle and the bisector of an angle.

Definition 3.7 $\overrightarrow{JK}$ is called the *midray* of ∡*EJS* iff *K* is in the interior of ∡*EJS* and ∠*EJK* = ∠*KJS* (midray iff 2 ∠s =).

Roughly speaking, an angle's midray is exactly "halfway from one side to the other." Although we will not prove it, any angle other than a straight angle has one and only one midray.

Definition 3.8 Either the midray of an angle or the line determined by the midray is a *bisector* of the angle (midray or its line is ∡ bis).

It follows that an angle has one and only one line as its bisector (∡ has 1 and only 1 bis), and we will use this fact as needed in subsequent proofs. Construction 3 describes how this unique angle bisector can be constructed for any given angle.

Construction 3 To construct the bisector of an angle.

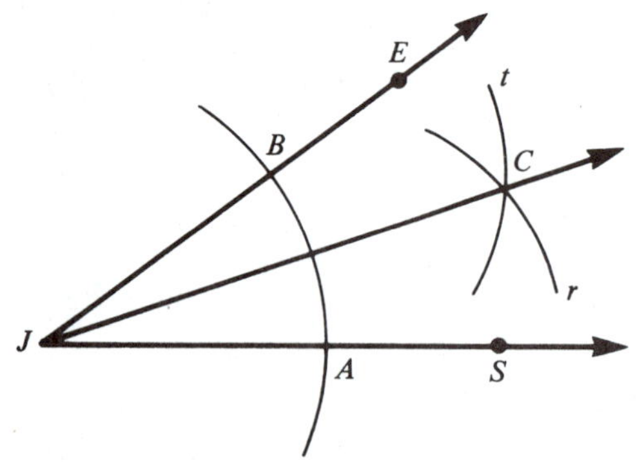

Given
∡*EJS*

To Construct
$\overrightarrow{JC}$, the bisector of ∡*EJS*

Steps

1. With *J* as center, mark an arc intersecting $\overrightarrow{JS}$ and $\overrightarrow{JE}$. This determines points *A* and *B*.
2. With *A* as center and a convenient radius (see step 3), mark arc *r* in the interior of ∡*EJS*.
3. Using the same radius as in step 2 and with *B* as center, mark arc *t* intersecting arc *r*. This determines point *C*. (Note that the radius used in steps 2 and 3 must be sufficiently long for arcs *r* and *t* to intersect.)
4. Match a straightedge to *J* and *C* and draw $\overrightarrow{JC}$.

Three special types of angles are described in the following definitions.

Definition 3.9 An angle is an *acute angle* iff its measure is greater than 0° but less than 90°.

Definition 3.10 An angle is a *right angle* iff its measure is 90° (rt ∠ = 90°).

Definition 3.11 An angle is an *obtuse angle* iff its measure is greater than 90° but less than 180°.

Our informal definition of a straight angle (Section 3.1) makes the following postulate reasonable.

Postulate 8 The measure of a straight angle is 180° (st $\angle$ = 180°).

These types of angles are illustrated in Example 2.

EXAMPLE 2

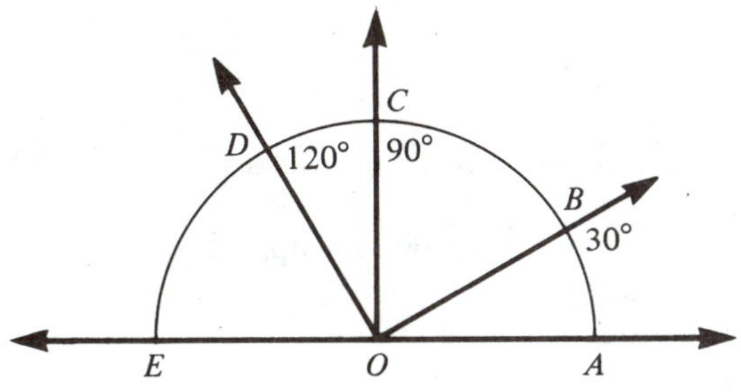

Given
the figure as marked

Name
(a) Three acute angles
(b) Two right angles
(c) One obtuse angle
(d) One straight angle

Answers
(a) $\measuredangle AOB$, $\measuredangle BOC$, $\measuredangle COD$, or $\measuredangle DOE$
(b) $\measuredangle AOC$, $\measuredangle BOD$, or $\measuredangle COE$
(c) $\measuredangle AOD$ or $\measuredangle BOE$
(d) $\measuredangle AOE$

In Section 3.1 we defined three special pairs of angles called adjacent angles, vertical angles, and a linear pair. Two other useful pairs are defined next.

Definition 3.12 Two angles are *supplementary* iff the sum of their measures is 180° (supp iff sum = 180°).

Definition 3.13 Two angles are *complementary* iff the sum of their measures is 90° (comp iff sum = 90°).

These two definitions do not require the angles to be adjacent. Thus, in Figure 3.17 $\measuredangle E$ is supplementary to $\measuredangle J$ because $\angle E + \angle J = 180°$, and $\measuredangle K$ is complementary to $\measuredangle S$ because $\angle K + \angle S = 90°$.

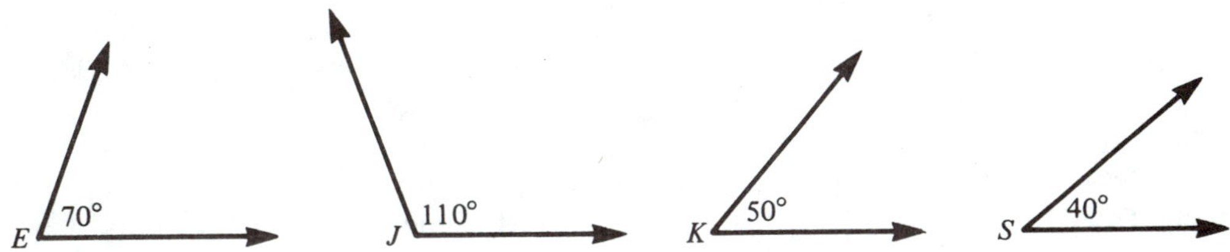

Figure 3.17

When two angles are supplementary, either is called the *supplement* of the other. Thus, in Figure 3.17 $\measuredangle E$ is the supplement of $\measuredangle J$ and $\measuredangle J$ is the supplement of $\measuredangle E$. Similarly, $\measuredangle K$ is the *complement* of $\measuredangle S$ and $\measuredangle S$ is the complement of $\measuredangle K$.

We next prove the evident fact that the angles in a linear pair are supplementary.

Theorem 4 If two angles are a linear pair, then the two angles are supplementary (lin pr supp).

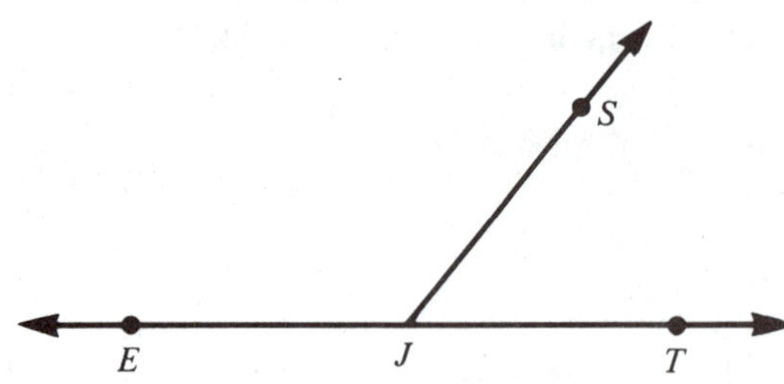

Given
∡*EJS* and ∡*SJT* lin pr

To Prove
∡*EJS* supp ∡*SJT*

Statement	*Reason*
1. ∡*EJS* and ∡*SJT* lin pr	1. given
2. ∡*EJT* st ∡	2. lin pr iff com side and opp rays
3. $\angle EJT = 180°$	3. st $\angle = 180°$
4. $\angle EJS + \angle SJT = \angle EJT$	4. whole = sum parts
5. $\angle EJS + \angle SJT = 180°$	5. trans =
6. ∴ ∡*EJS* supp ∡*SJT*	6. supp iff sum = 180°

Example 3 illustrates many of the foregoing definitions.

EXAMPLE 3

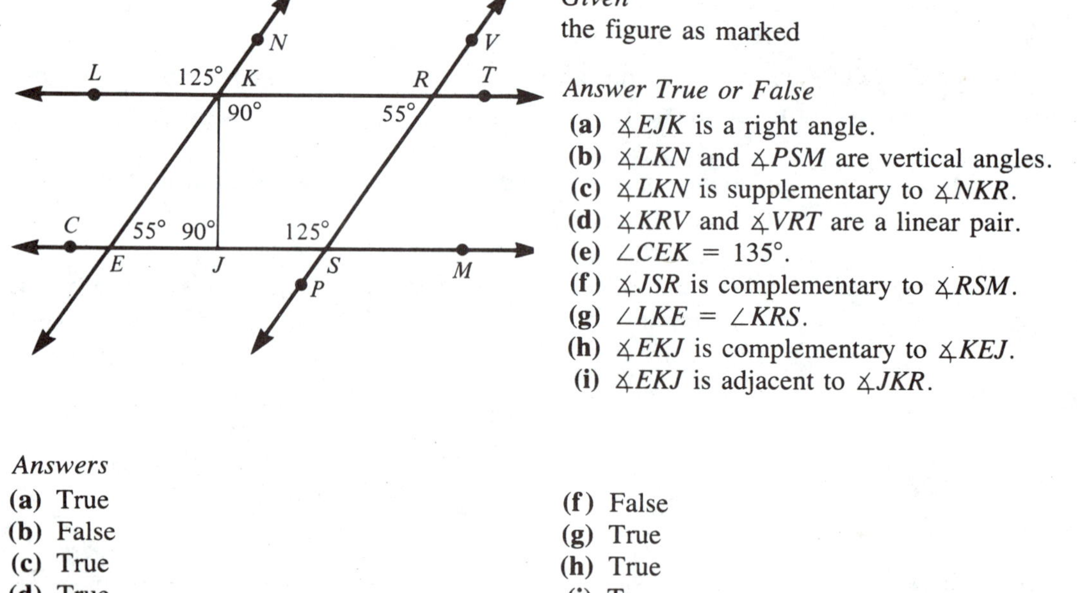

Given
the figure as marked

Answer True or False

(a) ∡*EJK* is a right angle.
(b) ∡*LKN* and ∡*PSM* are vertical angles.
(c) ∡*LKN* is supplementary to ∡*NKR*.
(d) ∡*KRV* and ∡*VRT* are a linear pair.
(e) $\angle CEK = 135°$.
(f) ∡*JSR* is complementary to ∡*RSM*.
(g) $\angle LKE = \angle KRS$.
(h) ∡*EKJ* is complementary to ∡*KEJ*.
(i) ∡*EKJ* is adjacent to ∡*JKR*.

Answers
(a) True
(b) False
(c) True
(d) True
(e) False
(f) False
(g) True
(h) True
(i) True

EXERCISES FOR 3.1 AND 3.2

In exercises 1–20 answer true or false.

1. If two rays have the same endpoint, then they form a figure called an angle.

2. The measure of an angle is the length of its longest side.

3. An angle is a convex set of points.

4. Two opposite rays with a common endpoint form a right angle.

5. A half plane is a convex set of points.

6. If $\angle EJK + \angle KJS = \angle EJS$, then K is in the exterior of $\measuredangle EJS$.

7. If $\measuredangle ABC$ names an angle, then A names the vertex of the angle.

8. Vertical angles are the nonadjacent angles formed when two lines intersect.

9. If an obtuse angle is bisected, each of the two angles formed is an acute angle.

10. All rays passing through the vertex of an angle are midrays.

11. All pairs of angles with a common side are adjacent angles.

12. The symbol $\angle EJS$ means the set of points in the angle.

13. The supplement of 112°12′12″ is 67°48′48″.

14. The compass is an instrument used to measure angles.

15. The measurement of an angle is accomplished by covering the angle with standard units that are also angles.

16. A linear pair consists of any two angles whose measures total 180°.

17. If the coordinate of $\overrightarrow{OA}$ is 16°, of $\overrightarrow{OB}$ is 37°, and of $\overrightarrow{OC}$ is 58°, then B is in the interior of $\measuredangle AOC$.

18. An angle measuring 72°15′38″ is complementary to an angle measuring 17°44′22″.

19. If $\measuredangle E$ is supplementary to $\measuredangle J$, then one of the two angles must be an obtuse angle.

20. It is impossible for two acute angles to form a linear pair.

In exercises 21–25 use Figure 3.18 to answer the questions.

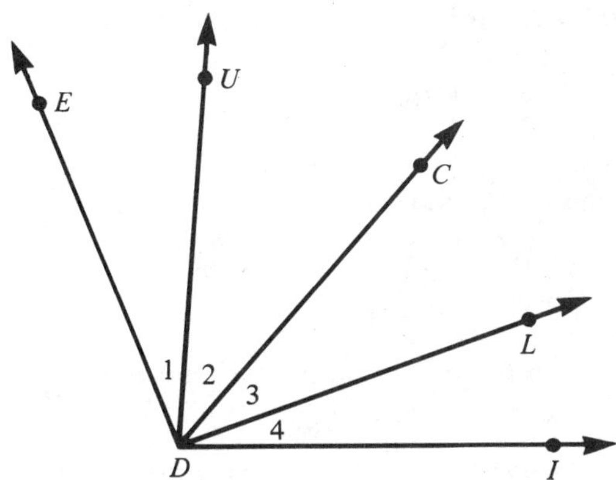

Figure 3.18

21. **(a)** Name $\measuredangle 2$ using three letters.
(b) Name $\measuredangle 3$ using three letters.

22. **(a)** Name $\measuredangle IDL$ using a number.
(b) Name $\measuredangle EDU$ using a number.

23. **(a)** Name the side that $\measuredangle EDC$ and $\measuredangle CDI$ have in common.
(b) Name the side that $\measuredangle UDC$ and $\measuredangle UDI$ have in common.

24. **(a)** Is C in the interior or exterior of $\measuredangle EDU$?
(b) Is L in the interior or exterior of $\measuredangle UDI$?

25. **(a)** U is in the exterior of which three angles?
(b) L is in the interior of which three angles?

In exercises 26–30 refer to Figure 3.19 to answer true or false.

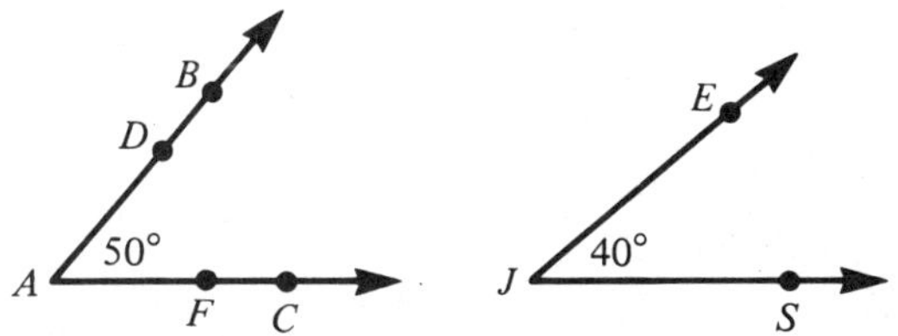

Figure 3.19

26. $\measuredangle BAC$ is the same angle as $\measuredangle BAF$.

27. $\measuredangle SJE$ is complementary to $\measuredangle CAD$.

28. $\measuredangle EJS$ is an obtuse angle.

29. $\angle DAC + \angle EJS = 90°$.

30. $\overrightarrow{AB} \cup \overrightarrow{AC} = \measuredangle DAF$.

In exercises 31–35 use Figure 3.20 and numbered angles only to answer the questions.

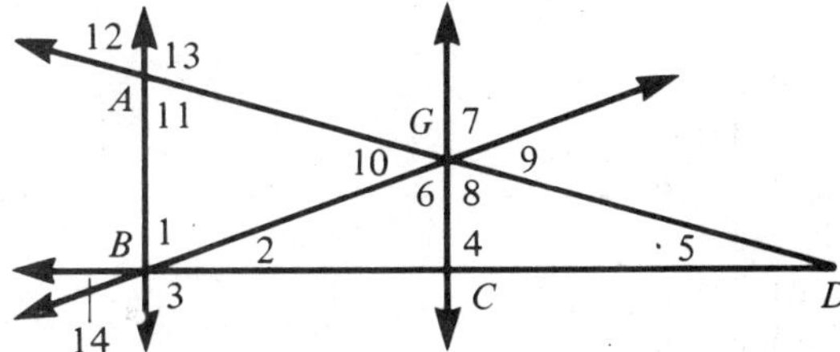

Figure 3.20

Given
$\measuredangle 3$ and $\measuredangle 4$ rt $\measuredangle$s
$\angle 8 = \angle 11$
$\measuredangle 5$ comp $\measuredangle 8$

31. Name four pairs of vertical angles.

32. Name three pairs of supplementary angles.
33. Name four pairs of complementary angles.
34. Name two linear pairs.
35. Name eight pairs of adjacent angles.

In exercises 36–40 use Figure 3.21 and numbered angles only to answer the questions.

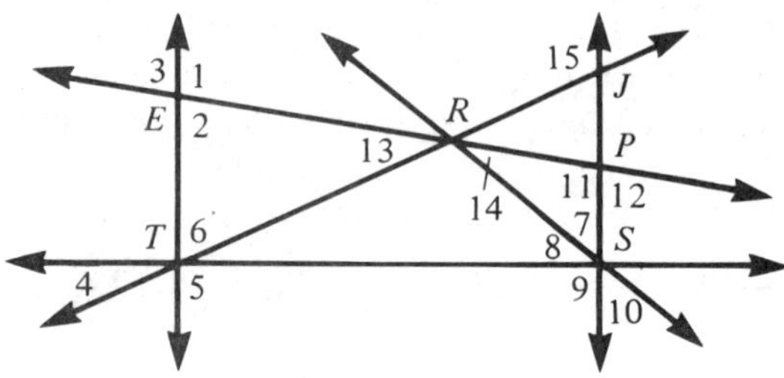

Figure 3.21

Given
$\angle 9 = 90°$
∡15 supp ∡6

36. Name three obtuse angles.
37. Name ten acute angles.
38. Name four pairs of supplementary angles.
39. Name three linear pairs.
40. Name eight pairs of nonadjacent angles that share a common vertex.

Complete the statements in exercises 41–50 using Figure 3.22.

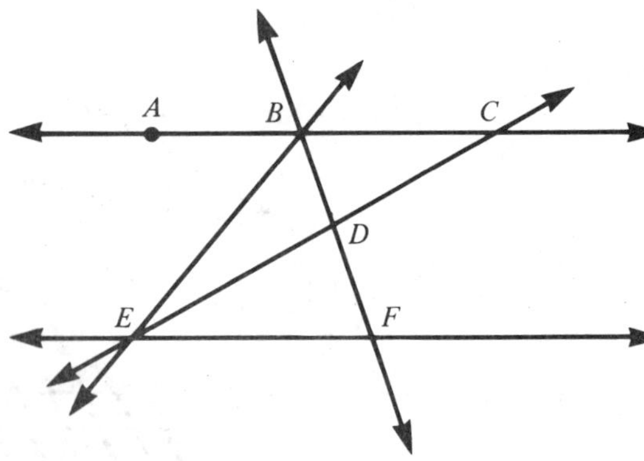

Figure 3.22

41. $\overrightarrow{EB} \cup \overrightarrow{ED}$ = ____________.
42. $\overrightarrow{EB} \cap \overrightarrow{ED}$ = ____________.
43. $\overrightarrow{CA} \cup \overrightarrow{CE}$ = ____________.
44. $\overrightarrow{AC} \cup \overrightarrow{EC}$ = ____________.
45. $\overrightarrow{DB} \cup \overrightarrow{DF}$ = ____________.

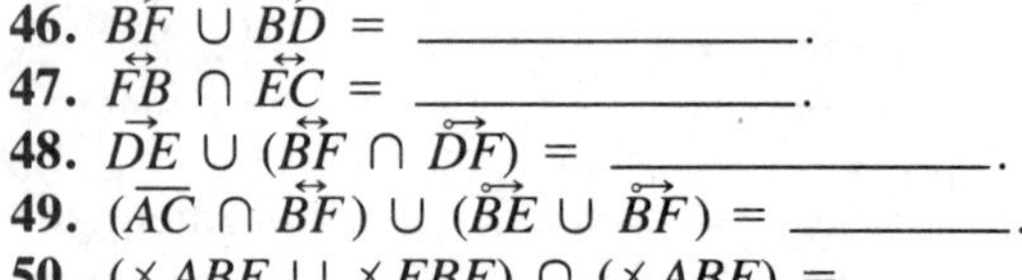

46. $\overrightarrow{BF} \cup \overrightarrow{BD}$ = ____________.
47. $\overleftrightarrow{FB} \cap \overleftrightarrow{EC}$ = ____________.
48. $\overrightarrow{DE} \cup (\overrightarrow{BF} \cap \overrightarrow{DF})$ = ____________.
49. $(\overline{AC} \cap \overleftrightarrow{BF}) \cup (\overrightarrow{BE} \cup \overrightarrow{BF})$ = ________.
50. $(∡ABE \cup ∡EBF) \cap (∡ABF)$ = ______.

In exercises 51–60 use Figure 3.23 and numbered angles only to answer the questions.

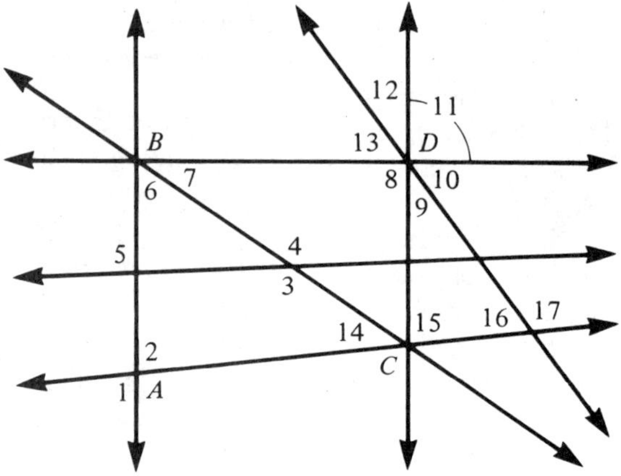

Figure 3.23

Given
angles as drawn
∡*CDB* rt ∡

51. Name eleven acute angles.
52. Name two right angles.
53. Name four obtuse angles.
54. Name eight pairs of adjacent angles.
55. Name five pairs of vertical angles.
56. Name two pairs of supplementary angles.
57. Name four pairs of complementary angles.
58. Why aren't ∡9 and ∡13 vertical angles?
59. Why aren't ∡14 and ∡15 adjacent angles?
60. Name one linear pair.

In exercises 61–65 find the complement of each of the given angles.

61. 57°27′ **62.** $a°$ **63.** 69°14′23″
64. 3°13″ **65.** 11′29″

In exercises 66–70 find the supplement of each of the given angles.

66. 119°38′ **67.** $b°$ **68.** 62°19′29″
69. 111°11′11″ **70.** 169°23″

71. Add the following: 32°11′29″; 57°49′; 23°17′16″; and 100°58″.

72. Subtract 37°53′12″ from 103°3′8″.

73. Find the complement and supplement of 43°3′29″. What is the difference between the supplement and the complement? Is the difference always the same for all acute angles?

74. **(a)** If one angle of a linear pair is an acute angle, is the other angle acute, right, or obtuse?

(b) If one angle of a linear pair is a right angle, is the other acute, right, or obtuse?

75. If the measure of an angle is twice that of its complement, what is the angle's measure?

76. If the measure of an angle is five times that of its supplement, what is the angle's measure?

77. If $\measuredangle A$ is supplementary to $\measuredangle B$, $\angle 1 = \frac{1}{2}\angle A$, and $\angle 2 = \frac{1}{2}\angle B$, then what is the relationship between $\measuredangle 1$ and $\measuredangle 2$?

78. What is the measure of an angle whose supplement is 30° more than twice that of the angle?

79. The measure of the supplement of an angle is nine times that of the angle. Find the angle.

80. Two angles have a sum of 67°15′ and a difference of 37°48′. Find the angles.

81. **(a)** Using a straightedge draw an acute angle and an obtuse angle.

(b) Using only a compass and straightedge construct the angle bisectors of the angles you drew in exercise 81(a).

3.3 CONGRUENT ANGLES

The concept of angular measure enables us to compare angles just as the concept of length allows us to compare line segments. Figure 3.24 shows $\angle A > \angle B$, $\angle A > \angle C$, and $\angle B = \angle C$. Note that these relations involve degree measures, that is, *numbers*. When two different angles have the same degree measures, they are said to be *congruent*.

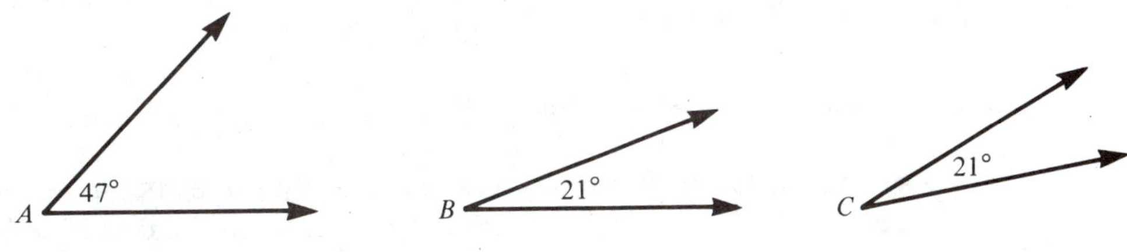

Figure 3.24

Definition 3.14 Two angles are *congruent* (denoted ≅) iff their measures are equal (≅ iff meas =).

This definition is the same as Definition 2.9 for congruent line segments so the same abbreviation is used for each.

In Figure 3.24 we can state that $\measuredangle B \cong \measuredangle C$ because $\angle B = \angle C$. On the other hand, if it is known that two angles are congruent, it follows from Definition 3.14 that their measures are equal.

As a line segment may be copied onto a ray (Construction 2, Section 2.4), so may an angle be copied, as in Construction 4.

Construction 4 To copy an angle using a given ray as one side.

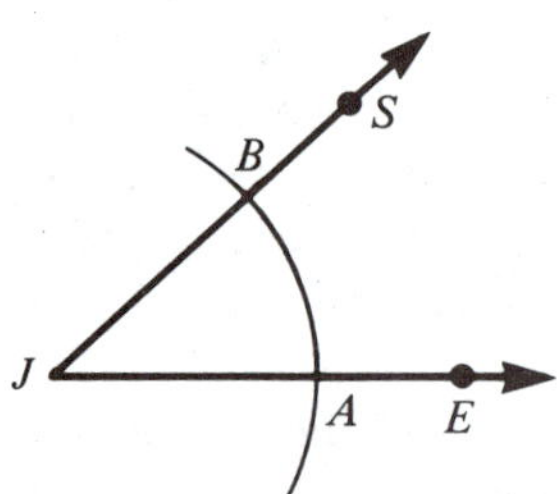

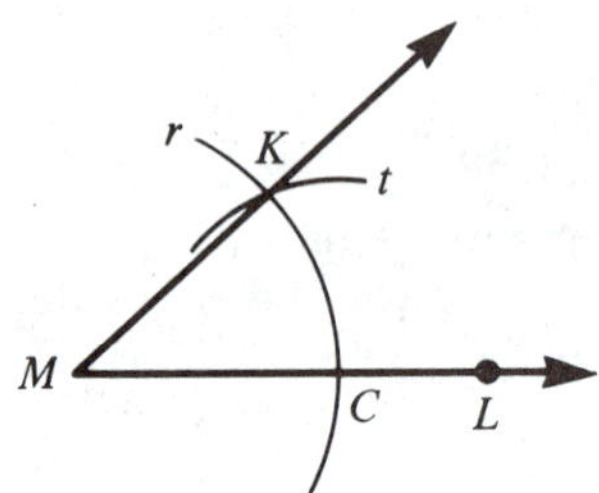

Given
∡*EJS* and $\overrightarrow{ML}$

To Construct
∡*LMK* such that ∡*LMK* ≅ ∡*EJS*

Steps
1. With *J* as center, mark an arc intersecting $\overrightarrow{JE}$ and $\overrightarrow{JS}$. This determines points *A* and *B*.
2. Using *M* as center and the same radius, draw a sufficiently long arc *r* intersecting $\overrightarrow{ML}$. This determines point *C*.
3. Match the point and pencil of the compass to points *A* and *B*; using this radius and with *C* as center, draw arc *t* intersecting arc *r*. This determines point *K*.
4. Match a straightedge to *M* and *K* and draw $\overrightarrow{MK}$.

The language "sufficiently long" in step 2 means to make the arc long enough to establish the necessary intersection. Our work suggests Postulate 9.

Postulate 9 Given any ∡*EJS* and $\overrightarrow{ML}$, there exists a $\overrightarrow{MK}$ such that ∡*LMK* ≅ ∡*EJS* (can copy ∡).

Later it will be possible to prove that using Construction 4 we do obtain the congruence described in Postulate 9. Note, too, that the $\overrightarrow{MK}$ in Construction 4 is not unique. The construction can be done such that $\overrightarrow{MK}$ is below, rather than above, $\overrightarrow{ML}$.

Recall that the equals relation for numbers and the congruence relation for line segments both have the RST properties. It should be no surprise that these properties are also valid for congruence of angles.

Theorem 5 If ∡*E* is any angle, then ∡*E* ≅ ∡*E* (refl ≅).

This theorem may be informally proved by noting that if ∡*E* is any angle, then $\angle E = \angle E$, from which we have ∡*E* ≅ ∡*E* by Definition 3.14.

Theorem 6 If ∡*E* and ∡*J* are angles such that ∡*E* ≅ ∡*J*, then ∡*J* ≅ ∡*E* (symm ≅).

The proof of this theorem is left as an exercise.

Theorem 7 If ∡*E*, ∡*J*, and ∡*S* are angles such that ∡*E* ≅ ∡*J* and ∡*J* ≅ ∡*S*, then ∡*E* ≅ ∡*S* (trans ≅).

The proof of this theorem is almost identical to that of the transitive property for congruence of line segments (see Example 1, Section 2.5).

The RST properties for equals and congruence relations enable us to usefully rearrange statements involving them. The same, however, is not necessarily true for various other relations that occur in geometry. Example 1 illustrates this point.

EXAMPLE 1 Let S name the set of all angles in a plane. Let ® mean "is complementary to." Are the RST properties valid for ® in set S?

Answers

(a) *Reflexive*. No, because $\measuredangle E$ ® $\measuredangle E$ is false. For example, if $\angle E = 10°$, then $\measuredangle E$ is not complementary to $\measuredangle E$ as the sum of 10° and 10° is not 90°.

(b) *Symmetric*. Yes, because if $\measuredangle E$ ® $\measuredangle J$, we have $\angle E + \angle J = 90°$, which implies $\angle J + \angle E = 90°$, so $\measuredangle J$ ® $\measuredangle E$.

(c) *Transitive*. No, for suppose $\angle E = 30°$, $\angle J = 60°$, and $\angle S = 30°$. Then $\measuredangle E$ ® $\measuredangle J$ and $\measuredangle J$ ® $\measuredangle S$, but $\measuredangle E$ ®̸ $\measuredangle S$.

Because the transitive property in Example 1 is not valid, we know that two angles that are complementary to the same angle are not, in general, themselves complementary. The example does suggest, however, that the angles are congruent, and this fact is established in Theorem 8.

Theorem 8 If two angles are complementary to the same (or congruent) angle(s), then the two angles are congruent ($\measuredangle$s comp same $\measuredangle$ [or $\cong$ $\measuredangle$s] are $\cong$).

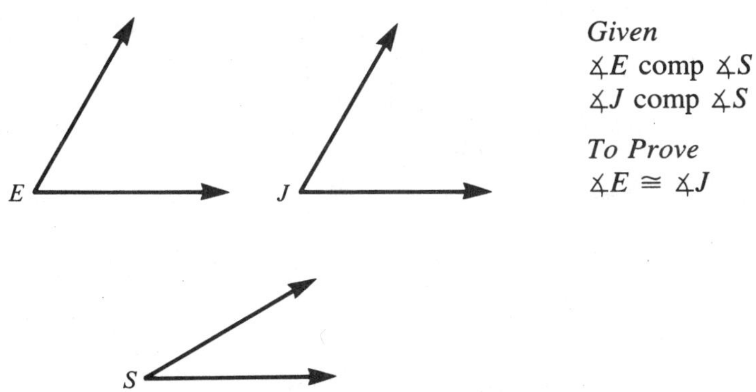

Given
$\measuredangle E$ comp $\measuredangle S$
$\measuredangle J$ comp $\measuredangle S$

To Prove
$\measuredangle E \cong \measuredangle J$

Statement	*Reason*
1. $\measuredangle E$ comp $\measuredangle S$	1. given
2. $\angle E + \angle S = 90°$	2. comp iff sum = 90°
3. $\measuredangle J$ comp $\measuredangle S$	3. given
4. $\angle J + \angle S = 90°$	4. comp iff sum = 90°
5. $90° = \angle J + \angle S$	5. symm =
6. $\angle E + \angle S = \angle J + \angle S$	6. trans =
7. $\angle S = \angle S$	7. refl =
8. $\angle E = \angle J$	8. = − =, diff =
9. $\therefore \measuredangle E \cong \measuredangle J$	9. $\cong$ iff meas =

Note that the above proof relies on the RST properties of equals. While some of these statements may seem obvious, their inclusion emphasizes the step-by-step nature of proofs. Later we will shortcut some of this detail.

As shown in brackets, Theorem 8 is also correct if the two angles are complementary to *congruent* angles. This is true because the congruent angles have equal measure. The above proof may be slightly altered to include this case.

Theorem 9 If two angles are supplementary to the same (or congruent) angle(s), then the two angles are congruent (∡s supp same ∡ [or ≅ ∡s] are ≅).

The proof of Theorem 9 is almost the same as that for Theorem 8 and is left as an exercise.

The next two theorems provide additional facts about congruent angles. In proving the first of these, we omit the statements establishing that *A*-*B*-*C* and *D*-*B*-*E* (true because the sides of vertical angles are opposite rays). Thus, we have $\overleftrightarrow{AC}$ and $\overleftrightarrow{DE}$.

From now on, except where desirable for clarity, we will agree to shorten proofs by assuming from the figure the following relationships:

1. Betweenness of points
2. Collinearity of points
3. Betweenness of rays
4. Intersections of lines and subsets of lines

Theorem 10 If two angles are vertical, then they are congruent (vert ∡s ≅).

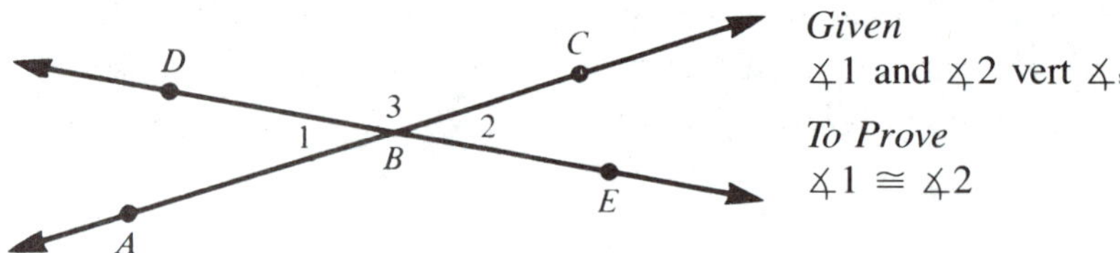

Given
∡1 and ∡2 vert ∡s

To Prove
∡1 ≅ ∡2

Statement	*Reason*
1. ∡1 and ∡2 vert ∡s	1. given
2. ∡1 and ∡3 lin pr ∡2 and ∡3 lin pr	2. lin pr iff com side and opp rays
3. ∡1 supp ∡3 ∡2 supp ∡3	3. lin pr supp
4. ∴ ∡1 ≅ ∡2	4. ∡s supp same ∡ are ≅

In the above proof, notice the use of Theorem 9 as reason 4. Keep in mind that established theorems may be used to prove new theorems. This use of previously proved theorems often shortens the new proof significantly.

Theorem 11 All right angles are congruent (rt ∡s ≅).

This theorem is obviously true because all right angles measure 90°. Also, all straight angles are congruent (st ∡s ≅). We omit a formal proof.

The rest of this section describes an important type of geometric figure formed when lines or subsets of lines intersect in a special way.

Definition 3.15 Two lines or subsets of lines are *perpendicular* (denoted ⊥) iff they intersect and form a right angle (⊥ iff a rt ∡).

Figure 3.25 shows (a) $\overrightarrow{EJ} \perp \overrightarrow{ES}$, (b) $\overleftrightarrow{CD} \perp \overrightarrow{AB}$, and (c) line $l \perp$ line m. The language "*a* right angle" is used in Definition 3.15 to cover all the possible figures even though some of them evidently contain more than one right angle.

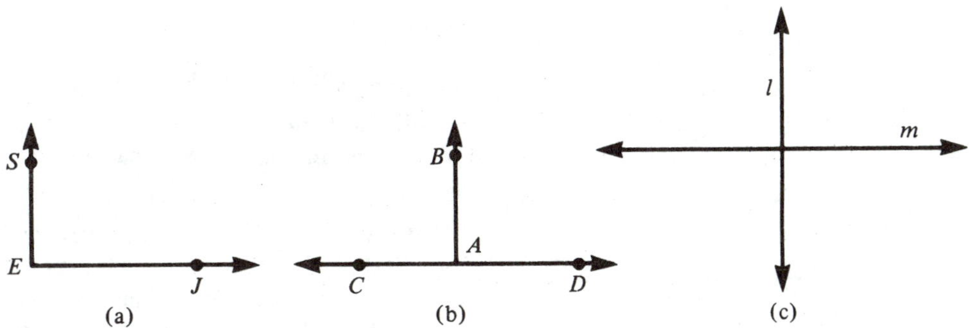

Figure 3.25

Perpendicular lines and right angles appear in many physical situations. It is well-known that a fence built on level ground looks best if the posts are perpendicular to a line on the ground, that the edges of a pane of glass to fit a window should form a right angle, and that the shortest route for a swimmer heading for a straight beach is along a line perpendicular to the beach. Many of these varied applications are related to two fundamental geometric properties that we now state as postulates. Each is motivated by a geometric construction.

Construction 5 To construct a line perpendicular to a given line through one of its points.

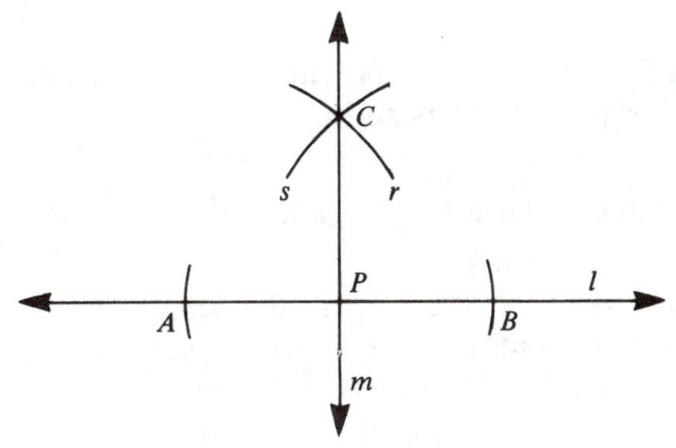

Given
line l and point P on l

To Construct
line m through P such that $m \perp l$

Steps

1. With P as center, draw two arcs having the same radius, each intersecting l. This determines the two points labeled A and B.
2. With A as center and a radius longer than AP, draw an arc r above l.
3. Repeat step 2 using the same radius but with B as center. This second arc s must intersect arc r determining point C.
4. Match a straightedge to C and P and draw line m.

With material developed later we can prove $m \perp l$ as constructed above. Our work suggests the following postulate.

Postulate 10 There is one and only one line perpendicular to a given line through one of its points (1 ⊥ thru pt on line).

Note that this postulate not only asserts that line m of Construction 5 exists, but also that it is unique (one and only one).

Construction 6 To construct a line perpendicular to a given line through a point not on the given line.

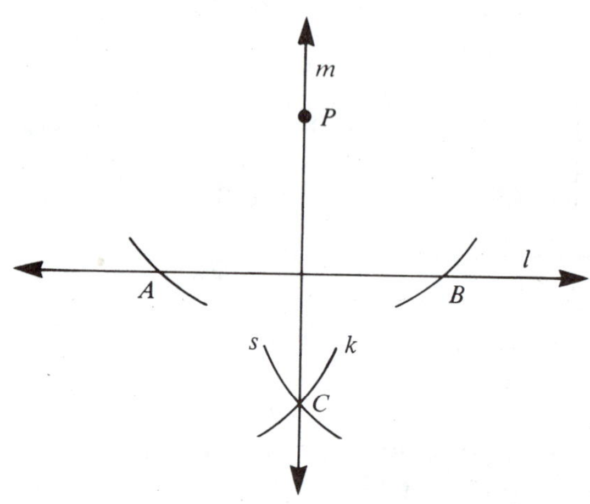

Given
line l and point P not on l

To Construct
line m through P such that $m \perp l$

Steps

1. With P as center and a sufficiently long radius, draw two arcs, each intersecting l. This determines points A and B.
2. With A as center and a sufficiently long radius, draw arc k as shown. This arc may be on either side of l but not too close to P.
3. Repeat step 2 using the same radius but with B as center. This second arc, s, must intersect arc k to determine point C.
4. Match a straightedge to C and P and draw line m.

The words "sufficiently long" in Construction 6 again mean that the radius must be long enough to establish the required intersections. Just as for Construction 5, later we can prove $m \perp l$ in Construction 6. Postulate 11 should now seem reasonable.

Postulate 11 There is one and only one line perpendicular to a given line through a point not on the given line (1 ⊥ from pt to line).

This postulate enables us to define the distance from a point to a line.

Definition 3.16 The *distance from a point to a line* is the length of the perpendicular line segment joining the point and the line (dis pt to line is length of ⊥ seg).

This distance is, of course, unique according to Postulate 11.

This section concludes with a particularly useful theorem. In the figure for Theorem 12, perpendicular lines are marked with a "square corner" (⏋). This mark is also used to show right angles.

Theorem 12 If two lines are perpendicular, then they form four congruent right angles (⊥s form ≅ rt ∡s).

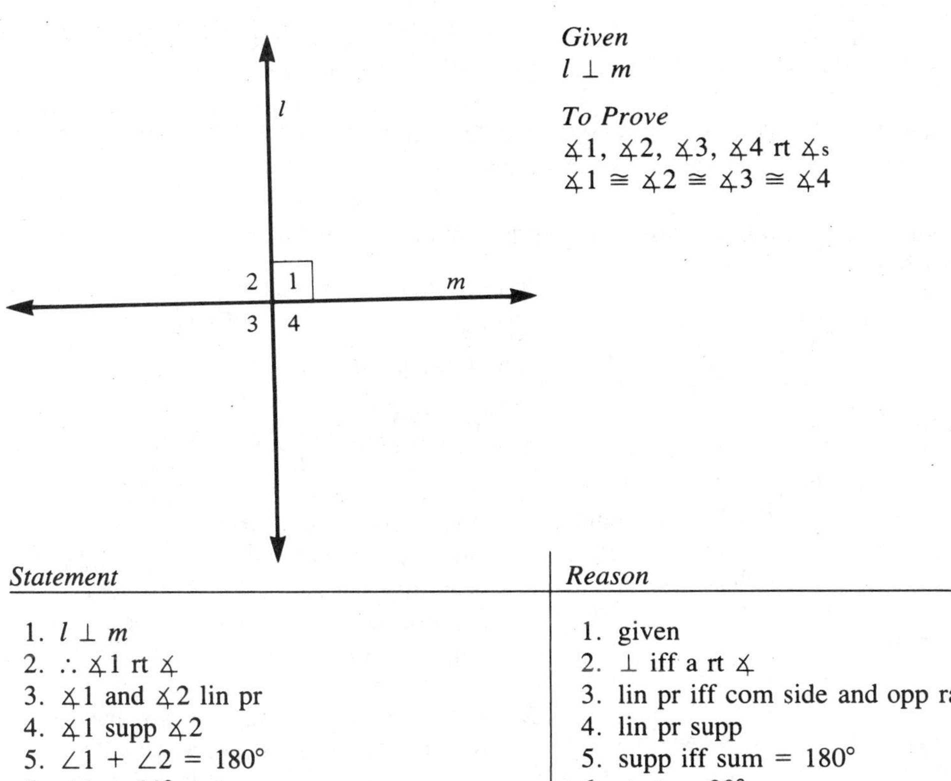

Given
$l \perp m$

To Prove
$\measuredangle 1, \measuredangle 2, \measuredangle 3, \measuredangle 4$ rt $\measuredangle$s
$\measuredangle 1 \cong \measuredangle 2 \cong \measuredangle 3 \cong \measuredangle 4$

Statement	*Reason*
1. $l \perp m$	1. given
2. $\therefore \measuredangle 1$ rt $\measuredangle$	2. $\perp$ iff a rt $\measuredangle$
3. $\measuredangle 1$ and $\measuredangle 2$ lin pr	3. lin pr iff com side and opp rays
4. $\measuredangle 1$ supp $\measuredangle 2$	4. lin pr supp
5. $\angle 1 + \angle 2 = 180°$	5. supp iff sum = 180°
6. $\angle 1 = 90°$	6. rt $\angle$ = 90°
7. $\angle 2 = 90°$	7. = − =, diff =
8. $\therefore \measuredangle 2$ rt $\measuredangle$	8. rt $\angle$ = 90°
9. $\measuredangle 1$ and $\measuredangle 3$ vert $\measuredangle$s $\measuredangle 2$ and $\measuredangle 4$ vert $\measuredangle$s	9. vert $\measuredangle$s formed by opp rays
10. $\measuredangle 3 \cong \measuredangle 1$, $\measuredangle 4 \cong \measuredangle 2$	10. vert $\measuredangle$s $\cong$
11. $\angle 3 = \angle 1$, $\angle 4 = \angle 2$	11. $\cong$ iff meas =
12. $\angle 3 = 90°$, $\angle 4 = 90°$	12. trans =
13. $\therefore \measuredangle 3$ and $\measuredangle 4$ rt $\measuredangle$s	13. rt $\angle$ = 90°
14. $\therefore \measuredangle 1 \cong \measuredangle 2 \cong \measuredangle 3 \cong \measuredangle 4$	14. rt $\measuredangle$s $\cong$

Statement 2 above may worry the beginning student. "Why $\measuredangle 1$?" and "If I can assume $\measuredangle 1$ is a right angle, can't I just as well assume that $\measuredangle$s 2, 3, and 4 are right angles?" are typical questions. But remember that we must reason from the given fact. By definition, $l \perp m$ means there is *a* right angle. We may assume it to be any one but *only* one of the angles in the figure. The proof then may be written as above starting with any one of the four angles.

EXERCISES FOR 3.3

In exercises 1–20 answer true or false.

1. Congruence for angles has the reflexive, symmetric, and transitive properties.

2. If $\measuredangle E \cong \measuredangle J$ and one side of $\measuredangle E$ is made longer, then $\measuredangle E$ is still congruent to $\measuredangle J$.

3. If $\measuredangle E$ is complementary to $\measuredangle J$ and $\measuredangle J$ is complementary to $\measuredangle S$, then $\measuredangle E$ is complementary to $\measuredangle S$.

4. Two angles supplementary to the same angle are supplementary.

5. Theorems are statements that are proved to be true.

6. Vertical angles are also adjacent angles.

7. Some right angles have a greater measure than others.

8. If two angles are complementary and congruent, each angle is a right angle.

9. From a point not on a line, one and only one perpendicular line can be drawn to the given line.

10. If two angles are congruent and form a linear pair, the lines forming the angles are perpendicular.

11. $\overrightarrow{JK}$ separates $\measuredangle EJS$ such that $\angle EJK + \angle KJS = \angle EJS$ for all positions of point K.

12. If $\measuredangle 1$ is supplementary to $\measuredangle 2$ and $\measuredangle 2$ is a vertical angle with $\measuredangle 3$, then $\measuredangle 1$ is supplementary to $\measuredangle 3$.

13. If $\overleftrightarrow{AB} \perp \overleftrightarrow{CD}$ and $\overleftrightarrow{CD} \perp \overleftrightarrow{EJ}$, then $\overleftrightarrow{AB} \perp \overleftrightarrow{EJ}$.

14. If $\overrightarrow{JK}$ separates $\measuredangle EJS$ such that $\measuredangle EJK \cong \measuredangle KJS$, then $\overrightarrow{JK}$ is a midray.

15. There is a unique distance from a point to a line not containing the point because there is one and only one perpendicular to a line through a point not on the line.

16. Given $\overleftrightarrow{AB}$ and point C with A-C-B, there is exactly one line l such that $l \perp AB$ and l contains point C.

17. If $\angle ABC = 40°$ and $\angle DBC = 50°$, then $\measuredangle DBA$ is a right angle.

18. To prove that two lines are perpendicular, it is sufficient to show that they form one right angle.

19. If $\overleftrightarrow{AB}$ and $\overleftrightarrow{CD}$ intersect at O, then $\measuredangle AOB \cong \measuredangle BOD$.

20. If $\angle EJS = 60°$ and $\angle KJS = 120°$, then either $\measuredangle KJE$ is a straight angle or $\measuredangle KJE \cong \measuredangle EJS$.

In exercises 21–30 use Figure 3.26 to answer true or false.

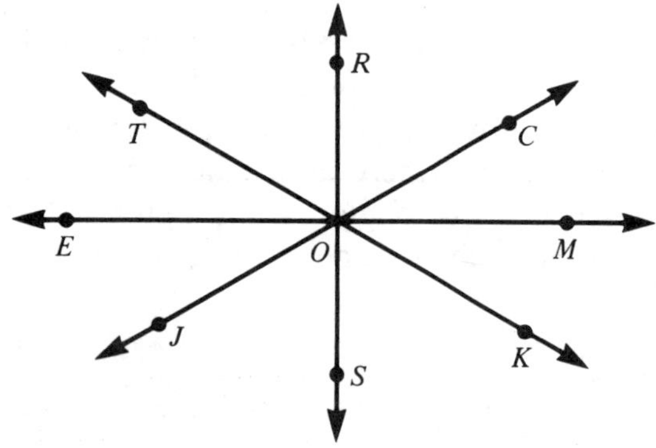

Figure 3.26

Given
$\overleftrightarrow{RS} \perp \overleftrightarrow{EM}$
$\angle TOE = \angle JOE = 30°$

21. $\measuredangle MOS$ is a right angle.

22. $\measuredangle JOE \cong \measuredangle MOC$.

23. $\angle EOR = \angle EOT + \angle TOR$.

24. $\measuredangle ROC$ and $\measuredangle KOS$ are vertical angles.

25. $\measuredangle JOS$ is supplementary to $\measuredangle EOJ$.

26. M is in the interior of $\measuredangle ROK$.

27. C, M, and S are all in one of the half planes formed by $\overleftrightarrow{TK}$.

28. $\measuredangle TOR$ and $\measuredangle SOJ$ are adjacent angles.

29. $\measuredangle TOR \cong \measuredangle MOK$.

30. $\angle EOC = 135°$.

In exercises 31–38 which of the RST properties does the given relation ® have in the given set S?

31. S is the set of all angles in a plane.
® is the relation "is supplementary to."

32. S is the set of all lines in a plane.
® is the relation "is perpendicular to."

33. S is the set of all right angles and obtuse angles in a plane.
® is the relation "is supplementary to."

34. S is the set of all acute angles and right angles in a plane.
® is the relation "is complementary to."

35. S is the set of all angles in a plane.
® is the relation "is adjacent to."

36. S is the set of all rays with the same endpoint O.
® is the relation "is *not* perpendicular to."

37. S is the set of all rays with the same endpoint O.
® is the relation "forms an obtuse angle with."

38. S is the set of all acute angles in a plane whose vertices lie on a horizontal line in that plane.
® is the relation "has its vertex to the left of the vertex of."

In exercises 39–40 use Figure 3.27 to answer the questions.

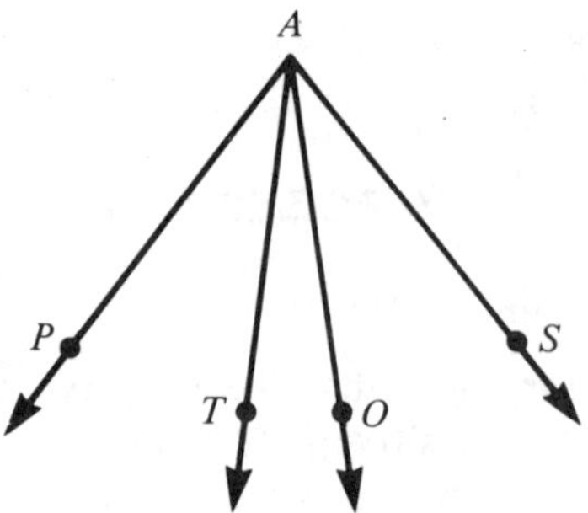

Figure 3.27

39. **(a)** If $\angle PAT = 32°44'$ and $\angle PAO = 59°4'$, what is $\angle TAO$?
(b) If $\angle PAS = 87°5'$, $\angle TAO = 27°49'$ and $\measuredangle PAT \cong \measuredangle OAS$, what is $\angle PAT$?

40. (a) If $\measuredangle PAT \cong \measuredangle OAS$, then $\measuredangle PAO$ is congruent to what angle?
(b) If $\measuredangle PAO \cong \measuredangle TAS$, then $\measuredangle PAT$ is congruent to what angle?

In exercises 41–44 copy the figure, mark it, and supply the missing reasons in each proof.

41. *Given*
$\measuredangle E \cong \measuredangle J$

To Prove
$\measuredangle J \cong \measuredangle E$

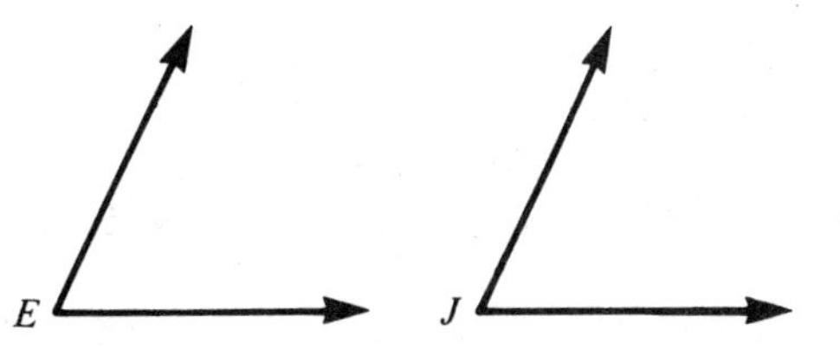

Statement	*Reason*
1. $\measuredangle E \cong \measuredangle J$	1. ?
2. $\angle E = \angle J$	2. ?
3. $\angle J = \angle E$	3. ?
4. $\therefore \measuredangle J \cong \measuredangle E$	4. ?

42. *Given*
$\measuredangle E \cong \measuredangle J$
$\measuredangle J \cong \measuredangle S$

To Prove
$\measuredangle E \cong \measuredangle S$

Statement	*Reason*
1. $\measuredangle E \cong \measuredangle J$	1. ?
2. $\angle E = \angle J$	2. ?
3. $\measuredangle J \cong \measuredangle S$	3. ?
4. $\angle J = \angle S$	4. ?
5. $\angle E = \angle S$	5. ?
6. $\therefore \measuredangle E \cong \measuredangle S$	6. ?

43. *Given*
$\measuredangle E$ supp $\measuredangle J$
$\measuredangle S$ supp $\measuredangle J$

To Prove
$\measuredangle E \cong \measuredangle S$

Statement	*Reason*
1. $\measuredangle E$ supp $\measuredangle J$	1. ?
2. $\angle E + \angle J = 180°$	2. ?
3. $\measuredangle S$ supp $\measuredangle J$	3. ?
4. $\angle S + \angle J = 180°$	4. ?
5. $180° = \angle S + \angle J$	5. ?
6. $\angle E + \angle J = \angle S + \angle J$	6. ?
7. $\angle J = \angle J$	7. ?
8. $\angle E = \angle S$	8. ?
9. $\therefore \measuredangle E \cong \measuredangle S$	9. ?

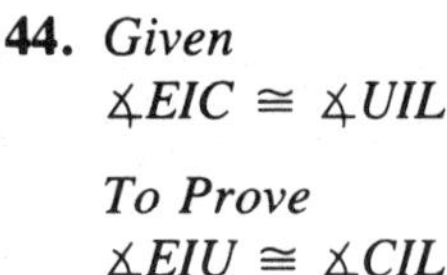

44. *Given*
$\measuredangle EIC \cong \measuredangle UIL$

To Prove
$\measuredangle EIU \cong \measuredangle CIL$

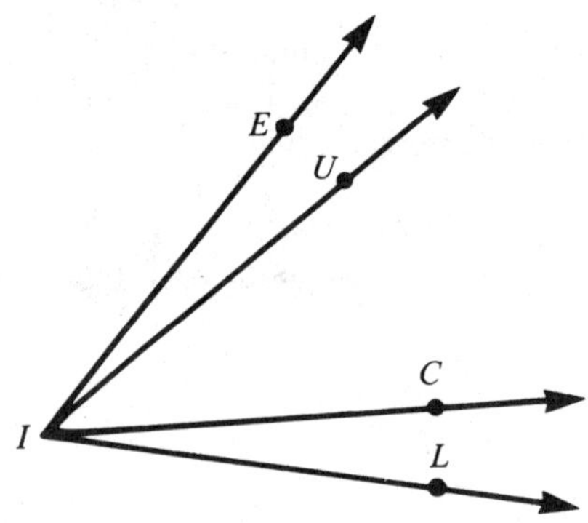

Statement	*Reason*
1. $\measuredangle EIC \cong \measuredangle UIL$	1. ?
2. $\angle EIC = \angle UIL$	2. ?
3. $\measuredangle UIC \cong \measuredangle UIC$	3. ?
4. $\angle UIC = \angle UIC$	4. ?
5. $\angle EIC - \angle UIC = \angle UIL - \angle UIC$	5. ?
6. $\angle EIU = \angle EIC - \angle UIC$	6. ?
7. $\angle CIL = \angle UIL - \angle UIC$	7. ?
8. $\angle UIL - \angle UIC = \angle CIL$	8. ?
9. $\angle EIU = \angle CIL$	9. ?
10. $\therefore \measuredangle EIU \cong \measuredangle CIL$	10. ?

In exercises 45–48 use Figure 3.28 to answer the questions.

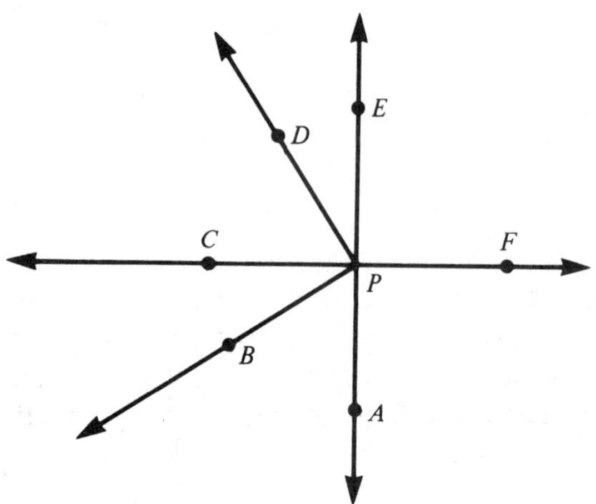

Figure 3.28

Given
$\overleftrightarrow{AE} \perp \overleftrightarrow{CF}$; $\overrightarrow{PB} \perp \overrightarrow{PD}$

45. Name five pairs of perpendicular rays.

46. Name ten pairs of supplementary angles.

47. Name two pairs of complementary angles.

48. Name ten pairs of congruent angles.

49. Using only a compass and straightedge, (a) draw an obtuse angle and label it $\measuredangle JES$, (b) construct midray $\overrightarrow{EK}$, the bisector of $\measuredangle JES$, and (c) from K, construct $\overleftrightarrow{KM} \perp \overrightarrow{ES}$.

50. Using only a compass and straightedge, (a) draw a line $\overleftrightarrow{EJ}$, (b) construct $\overrightarrow{ES} \perp \overleftrightarrow{EJ}$, (c) construct midray $\overrightarrow{EK}$, the bisector of $\measuredangle SEJ$, and (d) copy $\measuredangle KEJ$ on $\overrightarrow{ES}$ with E as the vertex.

3.4 PROBLEMS INVOLVING ANGLES

This section contains no new definitions, postulates, or theorems. Its purpose is to use the material in the preceding sections to develop some problem-solving skills.

We have already seen that marking a figure to show known facts is effective in problem solving. Congruent angles may be marked with arcs and hash marks or small circles as in Figure 3.29. The marks show that $\measuredangle 2 \cong \measuredangle 4$, $\measuredangle 1 \cong \measuredangle 3$, and $\measuredangle LPM \cong \measuredangle MPN$. The technique is further illustrated in Example 1.

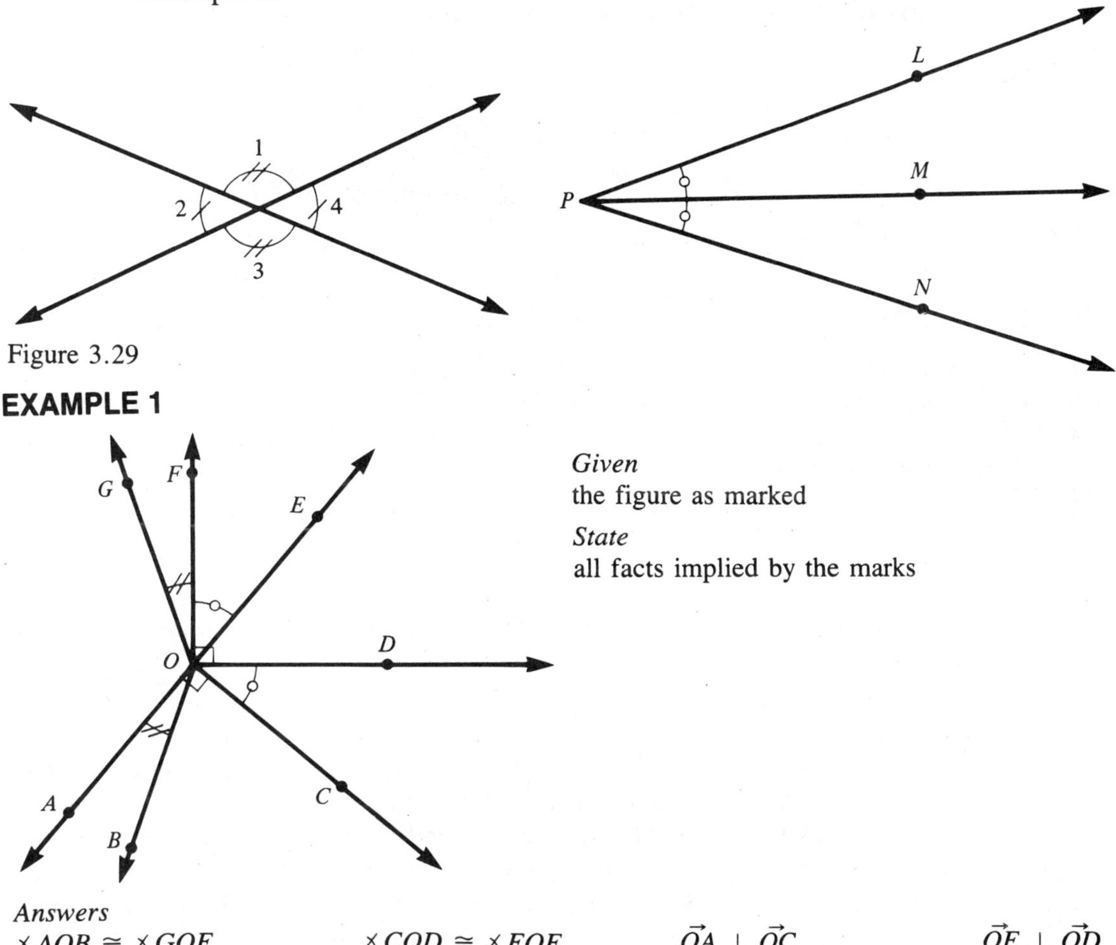

Figure 3.29

EXAMPLE 1

Given
the figure as marked

State
all facts implied by the marks

Answers

$\measuredangle AOB \cong \measuredangle GOF$ $\quad$ $\measuredangle COD \cong \measuredangle FOE$ $\quad$ $\vec{OA} \perp \vec{OC}$ $\quad$ $\vec{OF} \perp \vec{OD}$

In the next example certain facts are given to find the measures of ten angles. Here the first step is to mark the figure according to the given facts. Then, using suitable definitions, postulates, axioms, or theorems, relationships must be deduced that will lead to the correct answers. You are encouraged to copy the figure, mark it, and try to find the answers for yourself. No proof is required.

EXAMPLE 2

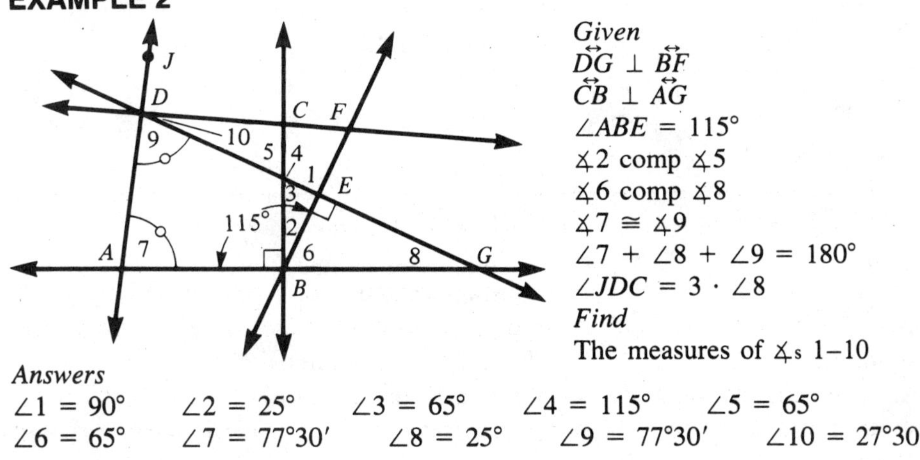

Given
$\overleftrightarrow{DG} \perp \overleftrightarrow{BF}$
$\overleftrightarrow{CB} \perp \overleftrightarrow{AG}$
$\angle ABE = 115°$
$\measuredangle 2$ comp $\measuredangle 5$
$\measuredangle 6$ comp $\measuredangle 8$
$\measuredangle 7 \cong \measuredangle 9$
$\angle 7 + \angle 8 + \angle 9 = 180°$
$\angle JDC = 3 \cdot \angle 8$

Find
The measures of $\measuredangle$s 1–10

Answers

$\angle 1 = 90°$ $\quad$ $\angle 2 = 25°$ $\quad$ $\angle 3 = 65°$ $\quad$ $\angle 4 = 115°$ $\quad$ $\angle 5 = 65°$
$\angle 6 = 65°$ $\quad$ $\angle 7 = 77°30'$ $\quad$ $\angle 8 = 25°$ $\quad$ $\angle 9 = 77°30'$ $\quad$ $\angle 10 = 27°30'$

The following Examples 3 and 4 further illustrate the techniques involved in writing proofs. Example 3 stresses the importance of a proper order for the statements in a proof. Remember, there must be a chain of steps that clearly links the hypothesis to the conclusion.

EXAMPLE 3

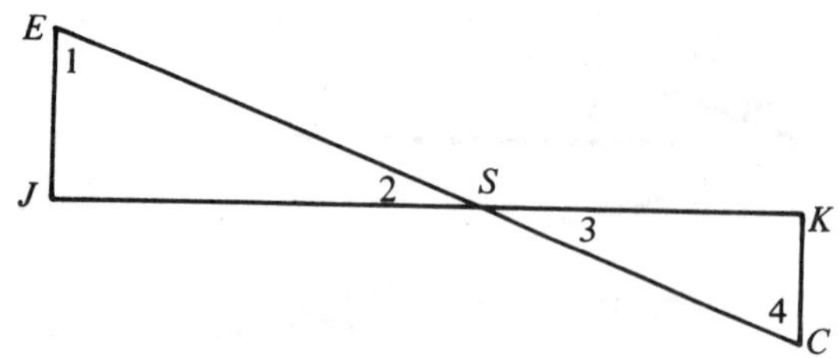

Given
∡1 comp ∡2
∡4 comp ∡3

To Prove
∡1 ≅ ∡4

Rearrange the following statements into a correct order for a proof.

	One Possible Answer
(a) ∡2 ≅ ∡3	e
(b) ∡4 comp ∡3	b
(c) ∡2 and ∡3 vert ∡s	c
(d) ∡1 ≅ ∡4	a
(e) ∡1 comp ∡2	d

What previously proved theorem is the reason justifying statement (d) in Example 3?

A complete proof is required in Example 4. You may want to review the seven steps to use in developing a proof (Section 2.5) before studying the example. It may also be helpful when creating a list of statements to "reason backwards" from the conclusion to the hypothesis. This idea applied in Example 4 leads us to consider what is needed to prove the two rays perpendicular. Since the definition of perpendicularity requires a right angle to be formed, we must try to show that $\angle KJM = 90°$. From the figure we see that $\angle KJM = \angle 2 + \angle 3$; hence, we should try to prove that $\angle 2 + \angle 3 = 90°$. This seems possible knowing that ∡*EJS* is a straight angle (measure 180°) and the given bisection facts.

EXAMPLE 4

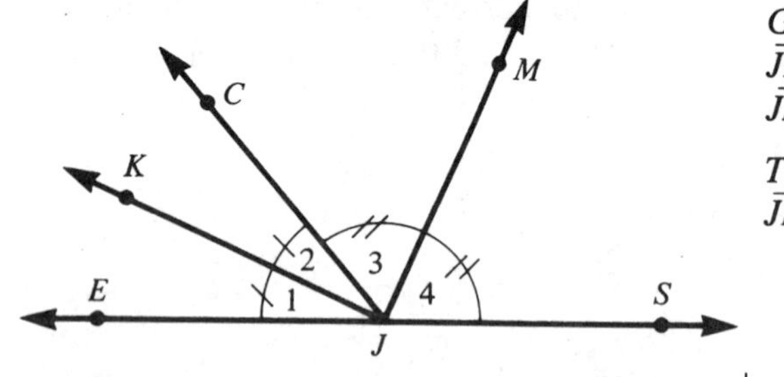

Given
$\overrightarrow{JK}$ bis ∡*EJC*
$\overrightarrow{JM}$ bis ∡*CJS*

To Prove
$\overrightarrow{JK} \perp \overrightarrow{JM}$

Statement	*Reason*
1. $\overrightarrow{JK}$ bis ∡*EJC*	1. given
2. $\overrightarrow{JK}$ midray ∡*EJC*	2. midray or its line is ∡bis
3. $\angle 1 = \angle 2$	3. midray iff 2 ∡s =
4. $\overrightarrow{JM}$ bis ∡*CJS*	4. given
5. $\overrightarrow{JM}$ midray ∡*CJS*	5. midray or its line is ∡bis
6. $\angle 3 = \angle 4$	6. midray iff 2 ∡s =

7. $\angle 1 + \angle 2 + \angle 3 + \angle 4 = \angle EJS$	7. whole = sum parts
8. $\angle EJS = 180°$	8. st $\angle$ = 180°
9. $\angle 1 + \angle 2 + \angle 3 + \angle 4 = 180°$	9. trans =
10. $\angle 2 + \angle 2 + \angle 3 + \angle 3 = 180°$	10. subst
11. $2 \cdot \angle 2 + 2 \cdot \angle 3 = 180°$	11. rearr props
12. $2 \cdot (\angle 2 + \angle 3) = 180°$	12. rearr props
13. $\angle 2 + \angle 3 = 90°$	13. = ÷ =, quot =
14. $\angle KJM = \angle 2 + \angle 3$	14. whole = sum parts
15. $\angle KJM = 90°$	15. trans =
16. $\measuredangle KJM$ rt $\measuredangle$	16. rt $\angle$ = 90°
17. $\therefore \overrightarrow{JK} \perp \overrightarrow{JM}$	17. $\perp$ iff a rt $\measuredangle$

EXERCISES FOR 3.4

In exercises 1–6 state the facts shown by the marks.

1.

2.

3.

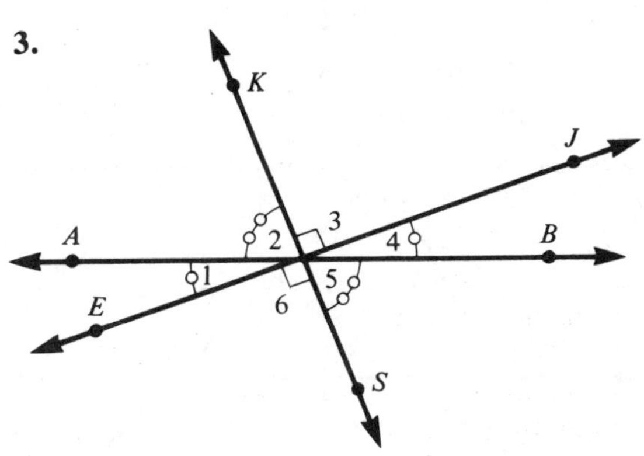

4.

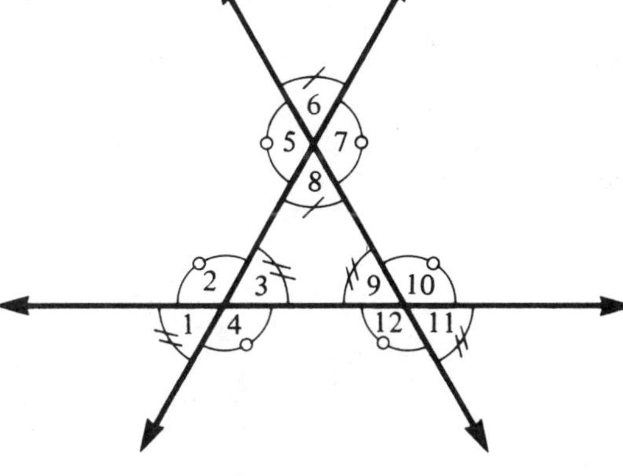

5.

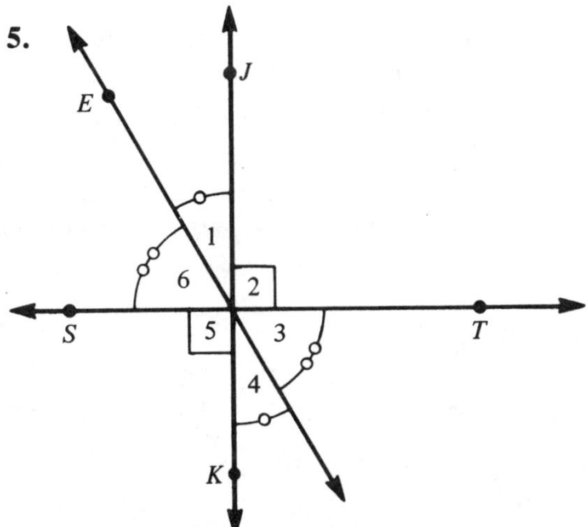

6.

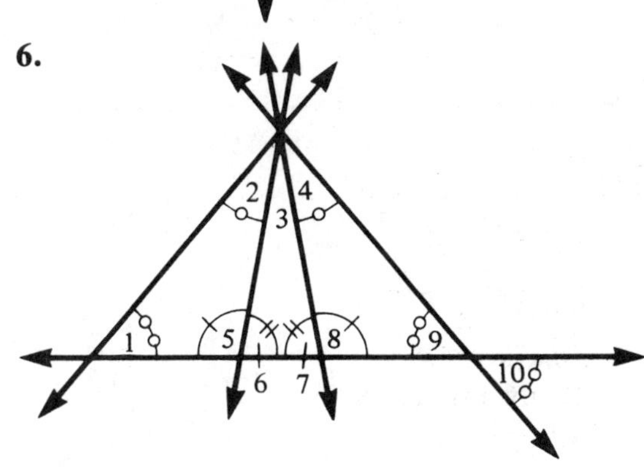

In exercises 7–18 copy the figure, mark it, and find the requested measures.

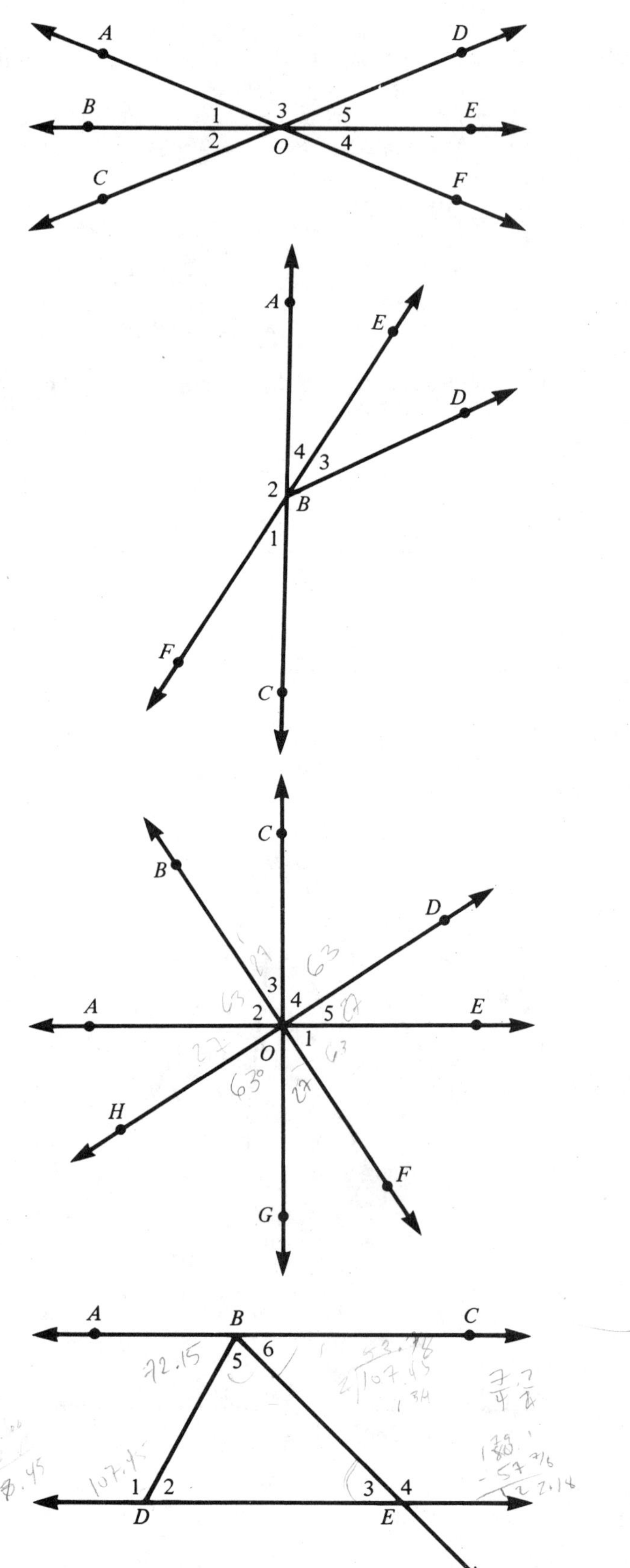

7. *Given*
$\overleftrightarrow{BE}$ bis $\measuredangle AOC$
$\angle COF = 137°$

Find
$\measuredangle$s 1–5

8. *Given*
$\overrightarrow{BE}$ midray $\measuredangle DBA$
$\angle CBD = 117°28'$

Find
$\measuredangle$s 1–4

9. *Given*
$\angle HOG = 63°$
$\overleftrightarrow{BF} \perp \overleftrightarrow{HD}$
$\overleftrightarrow{CG} \perp \overleftrightarrow{AE}$

Find
$\measuredangle$s 1–5

10. *Given*
$\overrightarrow{BE}$ midray $\measuredangle DBC$
$\angle ABD = 72°15'$
$\measuredangle 3 \cong \measuredangle 6$
$\measuredangle 1$ supp $\measuredangle ABD$

Find
$\measuredangle$s 1–6

11. *Given*
$\angle 8 = 115°$
$\measuredangle 6 \cong \measuredangle 2$

Find
∡s 1–8

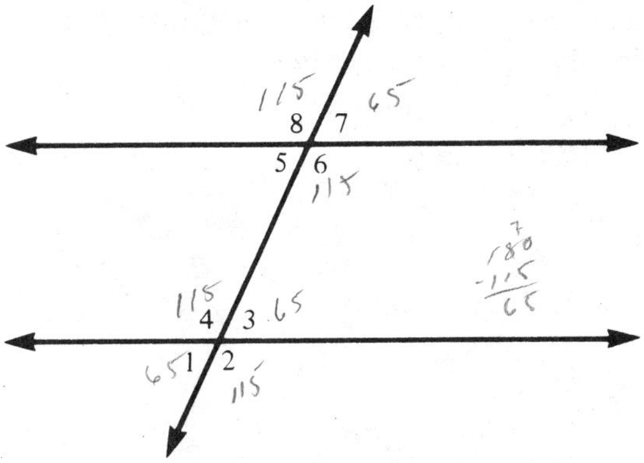

12. *Given*
$\angle BDC = 44°$
$\overleftrightarrow{DH}$ bis $\measuredangle CDG$
$\overleftrightarrow{DA}$ bis $\measuredangle BDE$
$\overleftrightarrow{AB} \perp \overleftrightarrow{AD}$ and $\overleftrightarrow{BC}$
$\measuredangle OBD$ supp $\measuredangle ADB$

Find
∡s 1–10

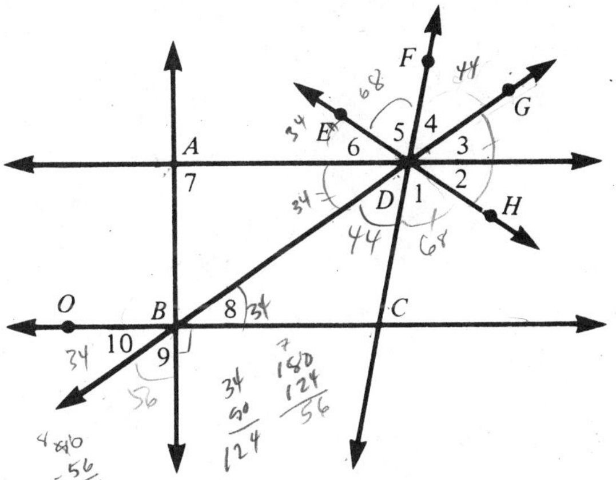

13. *Given*
$\overleftrightarrow{JK} \perp \overleftrightarrow{SM}$
$\angle EJK = 118°$

Find
∡s 1–5

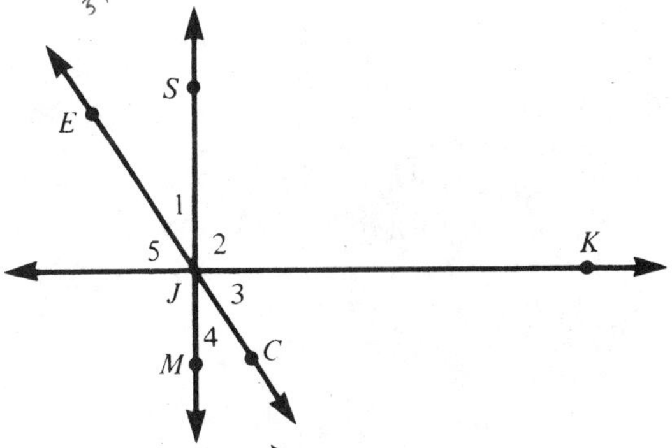

14. *Given*
$\measuredangle 2$ comp $\measuredangle 7$
$\angle 8 = 129°11'37''$

Find
∡s 1–7

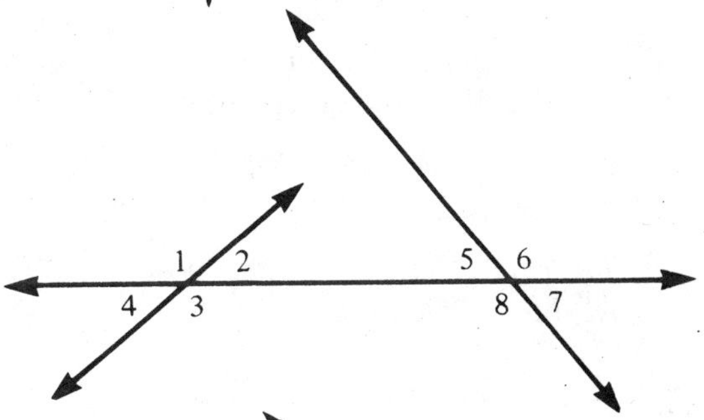

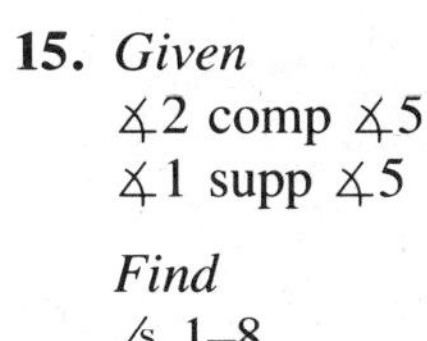

15. *Given*
$\measuredangle 2$ comp $\measuredangle 5$
$\measuredangle 1$ supp $\measuredangle 5$

Find
∡s 1–8

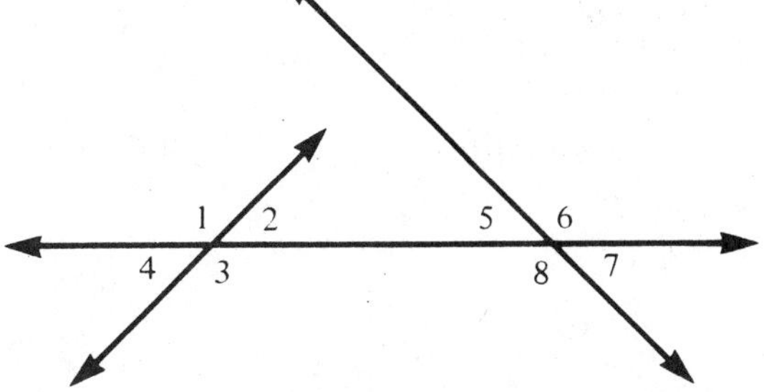

16. *Given*
$\overleftrightarrow{DB} \perp \overleftrightarrow{AC}$
$\angle FDA = 117°$
$\overleftrightarrow{BE}$ bis $\measuredangle DBC$
$\angle HAM = 36°$
$\angle ADG = \angle BAD + \angle 6$
$\angle CBD + \angle BCD + \angle CDB = 180°$
$\measuredangle 9$ comp $\measuredangle BAD$

Find
$\measuredangle$s 1–10

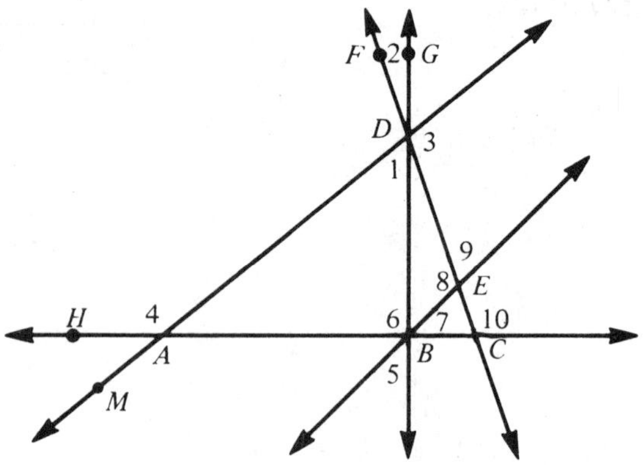

17. *Given*
$\overleftrightarrow{DE} \perp \overleftrightarrow{BF}$
$\overleftrightarrow{BC} \perp \overleftrightarrow{AG}$
$\angle ABE = 121°$
$\measuredangle 7 \cong \measuredangle 9$
$\angle 7 + \angle 8 + \angle 9 = 180°$
$\measuredangle 2$ comp $\measuredangle 5$, $\measuredangle 6$ comp $\measuredangle 8$
$\measuredangle 10 \cong \measuredangle 2$

Find
$\measuredangle$s 1–10

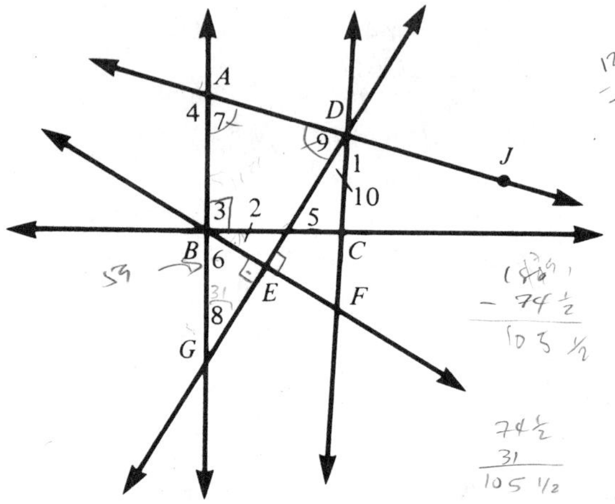

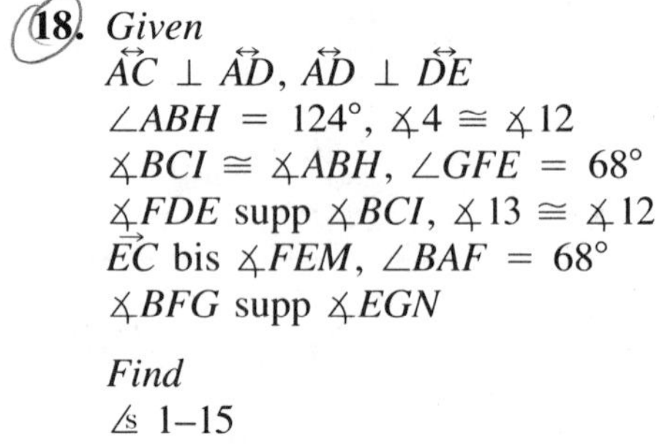

18. *Given*
$\overleftrightarrow{AC} \perp \overleftrightarrow{AD}$, $\overleftrightarrow{AD} \perp \overleftrightarrow{DE}$
$\angle ABH = 124°$, $\measuredangle 4 \cong \measuredangle 12$
$\measuredangle BCI \cong \measuredangle ABH$, $\angle GFE = 68°$
$\measuredangle FDE$ supp $\measuredangle BCI$, $\measuredangle 13 \cong \measuredangle 12$
$\overrightarrow{EC}$ bis $\measuredangle FEM$, $\angle BAF = 68°$
$\measuredangle BFG$ supp $\measuredangle EGN$

Find
$\measuredangle$s 1–15

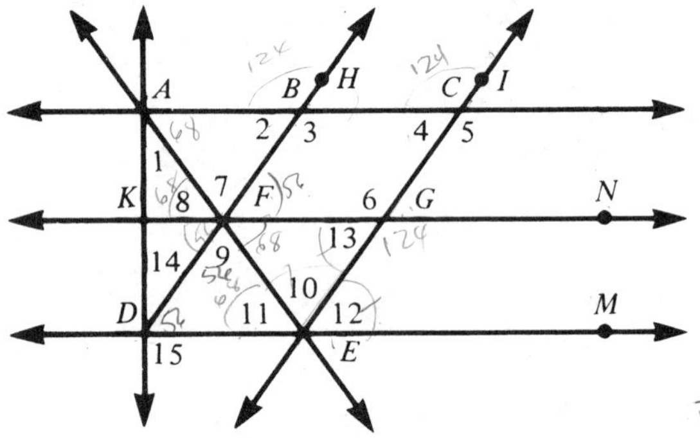

In exercises 19 and 20 copy the figure, mark it, and supply the missing reasons in each proof.

19. *Given*
$\overleftrightarrow{AB}$ bis $\measuredangle EOC$

To Prove
$\overleftrightarrow{AB}$ bis $\measuredangle DOF$

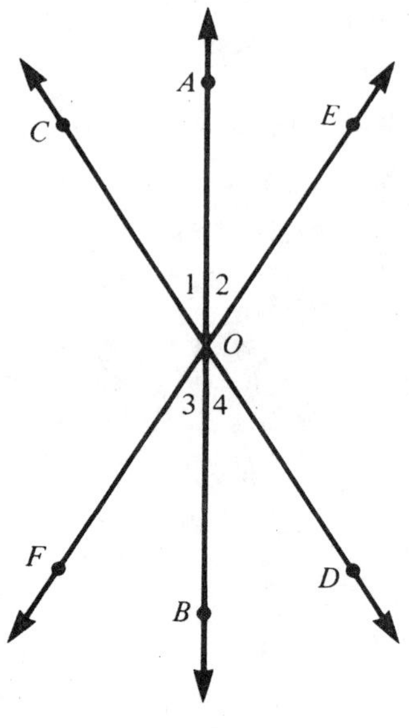

Statement	*Reason*
1. ∡1 and ∡4 vert ∡s	1. ?
2. ∡1 ≅ ∡4	2. ?
3. ∡2 and ∡3 vert ∡s	3. ?
4. ∡3 ≅ ∡2	4. ?
5. $\overleftrightarrow{AB}$ bis ∡*EOC*	5. ?
6. $\overrightarrow{OA}$ midray ∡*EOC*	6. ?
7. ∠2 = ∠1	7. ?
8. ∡2 ≅ ∡1	8. ?
9. ∡3 ≅ ∡4	9. ?
10. ∠3 = ∠4	10. ?
11. ∴ $\overleftrightarrow{AB}$ bis ∡*DOF*	11. ?

20. 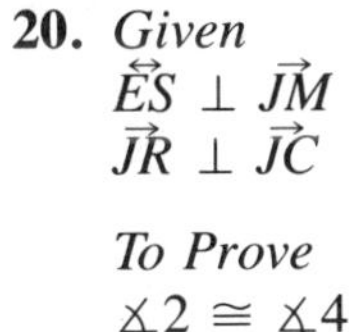
Given
$\overleftrightarrow{ES} \perp \overrightarrow{JM}$
$\overrightarrow{JR} \perp \overrightarrow{JC}$

To Prove
∡2 ≅ ∡4

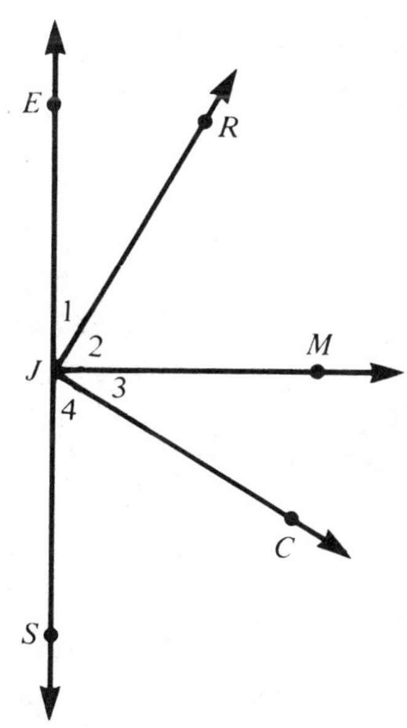

Statement	*Reason*
1. $\overleftrightarrow{ES} \perp \overrightarrow{JM}$	1. ?
2. ∡*MJS* rt ∡	2. ?
3. ∠*MJS* = 90°	3. ?
4. ∠3 + ∠4 = ∠*MJS*	4. ?
5. ∠3 + ∠4 = 90°	5. ?
6. ∡4 comp ∡3	6. ?
7. $\overrightarrow{JR} \perp \overrightarrow{JC}$	7. ?
8. ∡*RJC* rt ∡	8. ?
9. ∠*RJC* = 90°	9. ?
10. ∠2 + ∠3 = ∠*RJC*	10. ?
11. ∠2 + ∠3 = 90°	11. ?
12. ∡2 comp ∡3	12. ?
13. ∴ ∡2 ≅ ∡4	13. ?

In exercises 21 and 22 copy the figure, mark it, and rearrange the statements into a correct order for a proof.

21. *Given*
∡3 ≅ ∡2

To Prove
$\overleftrightarrow{ON}$ bis ∡*SOA*

(a) ∡1 ≅ ∡2
(b) ∡1 and ∡3 vert ∡s
(c) ∠1 = ∠2
(d) ∡3 ≅ ∡2
(e) $\overleftrightarrow{ON}$ bis ∡*SOA*
(f) ∡1 ≅ ∡3
(g) $\overleftrightarrow{ON}$ midray ∡*SOA*

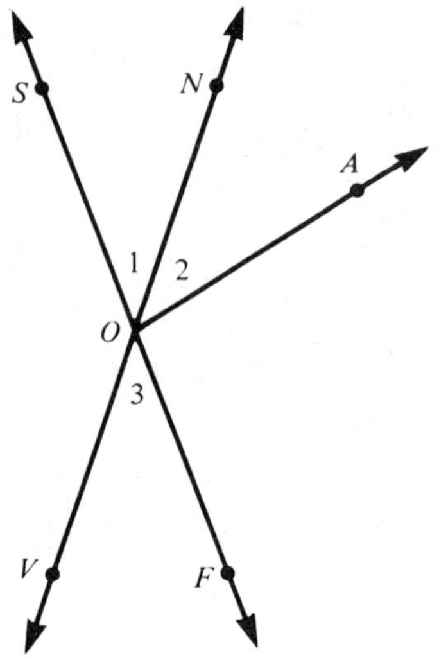

22. *Given*
∡3 ≅ ∡1

To Prove
∡2 ≅ ∡4

(a) ∡1 and ∡4 vert ∡s
(b) ∡2 ≅ ∡3
(c) ∡2 ≅ ∡4
(d) ∡3 ≅ ∡1
(e) ∡2 and ∡3 vert ∡s
(f) ∡1 ≅ ∡4

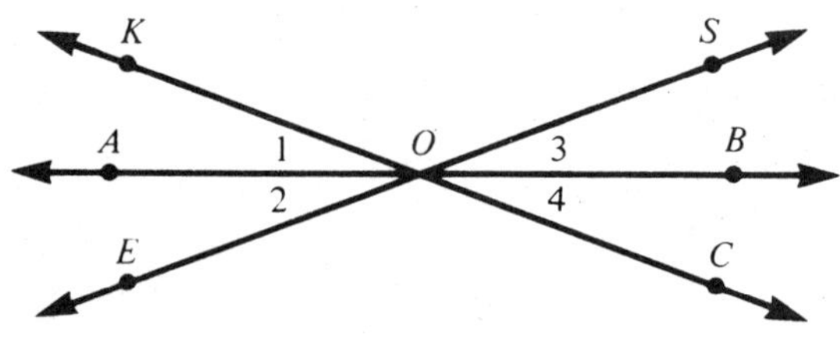

In exercises 23–34 copy the figure, the hypothesis, and the conclusion. Mark the figure and write a proof.

23. *Given*
∡*HOE* ≅ ∡*AON*

To Prove
∡*HOT* ≅ ∡*AOM*

24. *Given*
∡1 ≅ ∡4

To Prove
∡2 ≅ ∡3

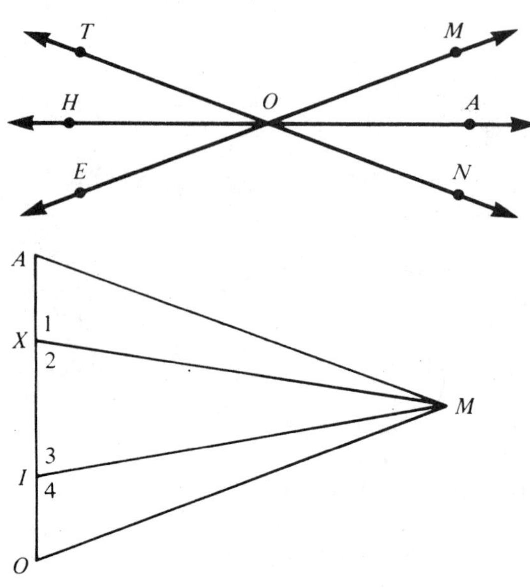

25. *Given*
$\measuredangle EJS \cong \measuredangle EKT$

To Prove
$\measuredangle EJS$ supp $\measuredangle TKM$

26. *Given*
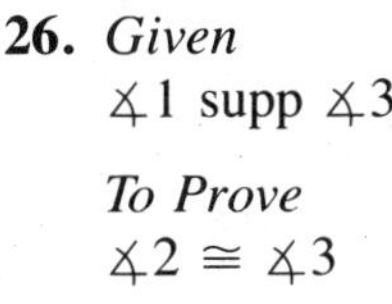
$\measuredangle 1$ supp $\measuredangle 3$

To Prove
$\measuredangle 2 \cong \measuredangle 3$

27. *Given*
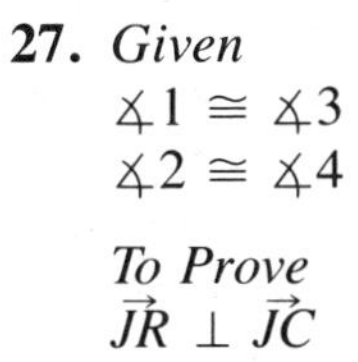
$\measuredangle 1 \cong \measuredangle 3$
$\measuredangle 2 \cong \measuredangle 4$

To Prove
$\overrightarrow{JR} \perp \overrightarrow{JC}$

28. *Given*
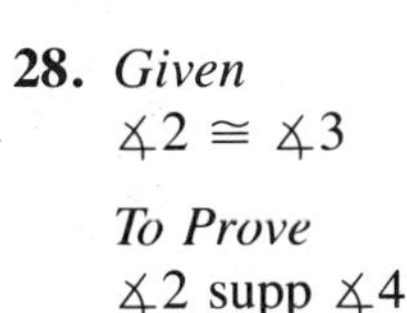
$\measuredangle 2 \cong \measuredangle 3$

To Prove
$\measuredangle 2$ supp $\measuredangle 4$

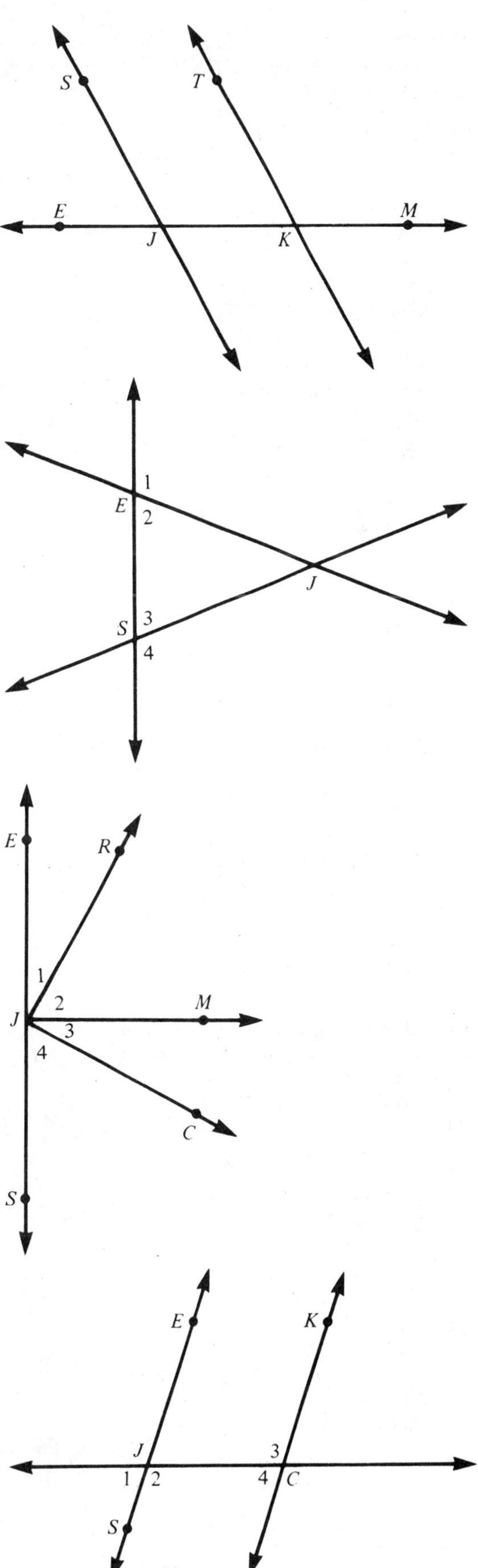

29. *Given*
∡1 ≅ ∡3

To Prove
∡*TOA* ≅ ∡*ROP*

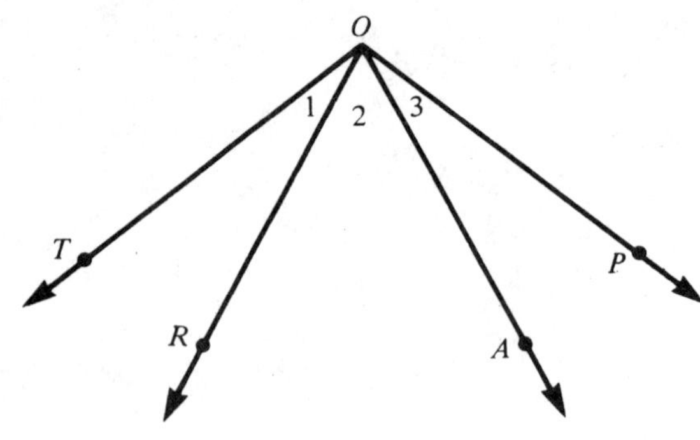

30. *Given*
$\overleftrightarrow{SJ} \perp \overleftrightarrow{KJ}$

To Prove
∡1 comp ∡3

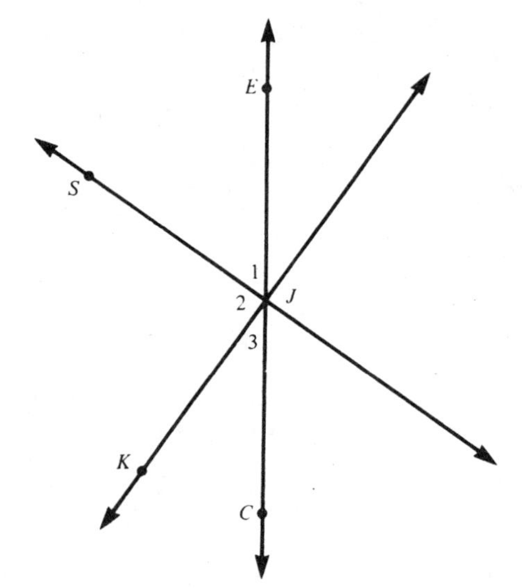

31. *Given*
$\overrightarrow{EN}$ bis ∡*IET*
$\overrightarrow{EN}$ bis ∡*OES*

To Prove
∡2 ≅ ∡5

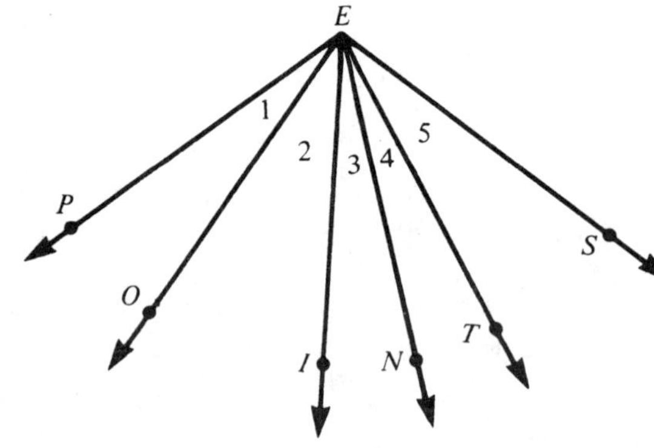

32. *Given*
$\overrightarrow{OA} \perp \overrightarrow{OC}$
∡1 ≅ ∡4
∡2 ≅ ∡3

To Prove
∡3 comp ∡4

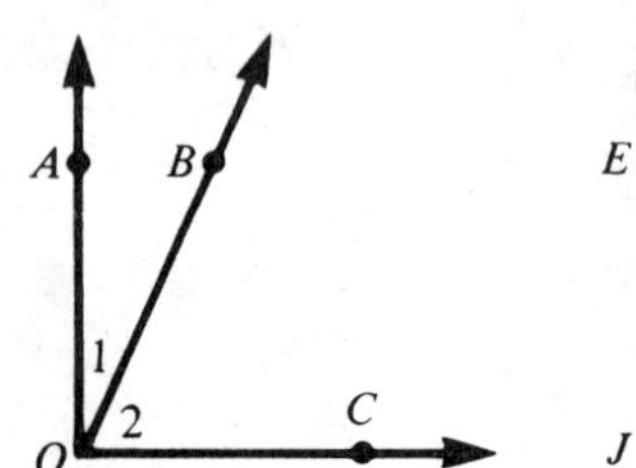

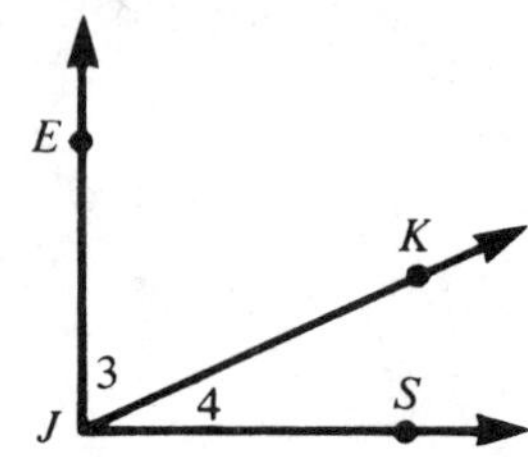

33. *Given*
∡5 ≅ ∡3
∡4 ≅ ∡2

To Prove
∡6 ≅ ∡1

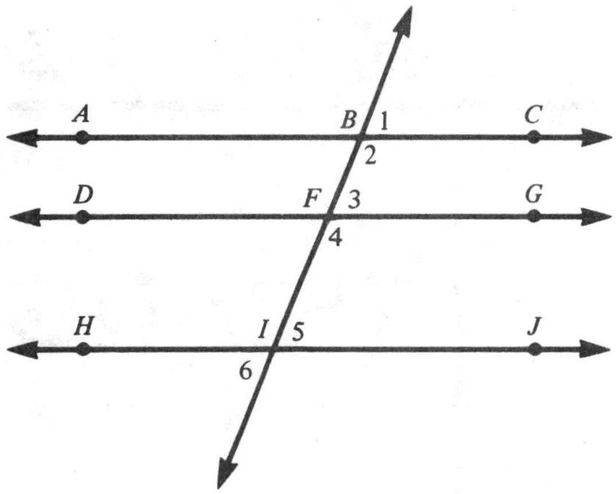

34. *Given*
∡1 comp ∡5
∡2 supp ∡3

To Prove
$\overrightarrow{IU} \perp \overrightarrow{IC}$

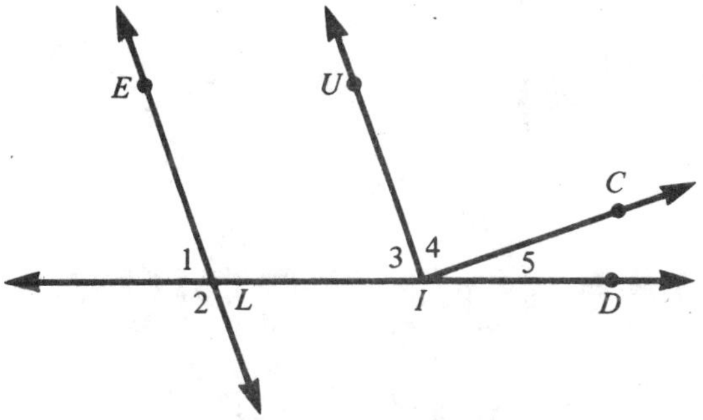

CHAPTER 3 SUMMARY

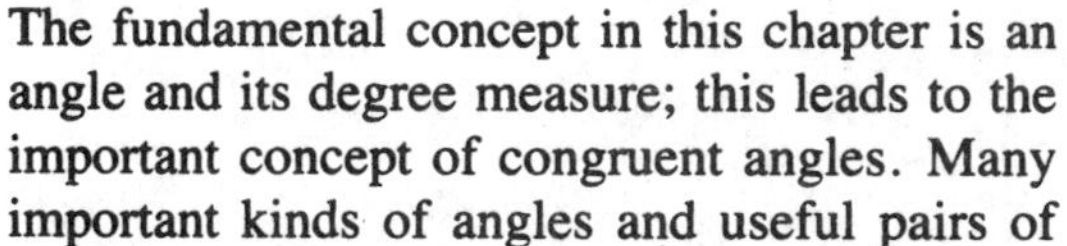

The fundamental concept in this chapter is an angle and its degree measure; this leads to the important concept of congruent angles. Many important kinds of angles and useful pairs of angles are identified. Further use of the RST properties of relations involving angles and associated relations helps us to better understand their roles in the development of geometry.

FACTS TO KNOW

1. Definitions
   a. Angle
   b. Betweenness for rays
   c. Adjacent angles
   d. Vertical angles
   e. Linear pair
   f. Degree measure
   g. Midray
   h. Angle bisector
   i. Acute angle
   j. Right angle
   k. Obtuse angle
   l. Supplementary angles
   m. Complementary angles
   n. Congruent angles
   o. Perpendicularity

2. Postulates
   a. Protractor postulate
   b. whole = sum parts
   c. st ∠ = 180°
   d. can copy ∡
   e. 1 ⊥ thru pt on line
   f. 1 ⊥ from pt to line

3. Theorems
   a. lin pr supp
   b. refl ≅
   c. symm ≅
   d. trans ≅
   e. ∡s comp same ∡ (or ≅ ∡s) are ≅
   f. ∡s supp same ∡ (or ≅ ∡s) are ≅
   g. vert ∡s ≅
   h. rt ∡s ≅
   i. ⊥s form ≅ rt ∡s

PROBLEMS TO MASTER

1. Identify types of angles and pairs of angles.
2. Test validity of RST properties of a relation in a set.
3. Mark figures containing angles.
4. Find measures of angles from given information.
5. Write proofs involving angles.
6. Construct
   a. Angle bisector
   b. Copy an angle
   c. Perpendicular to a line through a point on the line
   d. Perpendicular to a line through a point not on the line

4

TRIANGLES

MAJOR TOPICS

- △ Types of triangles
- △ Congruent triangles
- △ Ways to prove triangles congruent (sss, sas, asa)
- △ RST properties for congruence of triangles
- △ Use of congruent triangles to prove segments or angles congruent (cpctc)
- △ Shortcuts in proofs using congruence rather than equals relations
- △ Auxiliary lines in proofs
- △ Order relations and triangles
- △ Indirect proof

HISTORICAL NOTE

EUCLID

In the fourth century B.C., Alexander the Great, King of Macedonia, conquered the Grecian world. He dreamed of forming a great empire with a major city, Alexandria, at the mouth of the Nile river in Africa. Although he died at the early age of 33, two years after founding Alexandria, the city prospered and became a great center of learning. Ptolemy, Alexander's successor in Africa, established in Alexandria a great library, reputed to have contained 700,000 books. The library was largely destroyed in a series of wars with the Arabs culminating in the fall of Alexandria in 642 A.D.

When Ptolemy built the library he also established a university, among whose early teachers was Euclid. Little is known about Euclid's life, but undoubtedly he studied in Athens where he learned the mathematics of Thales and Pythagoras. During his twenty to thirty years in Alexandria, Euclid unified, in one masterful book called *Elements,* the geometrical work that had been accomplished over many years by many individuals throughout the world. This most famous and influential of all geometry books is not only the first logically organized presentation of the subject, but with its exhaustive account of contemporaneous mathematical knowledge it is also the mathematical history of an age. *Elements'* format became a standard for geometry texts still followed today. This master work earned for Euclid the accolade "Father of Geometry."

Some understanding of Euclid's work must be based on the fact that for him and his contemporary Greek geometers, points, lines, angles, planes, triangles, circles, and the like were abstractions of physical objects rather than replications of the objects themselves. For example, a stretched rope suggests a straight line, but attributes of the rope such as color, thickness, and the material of which it is made, are not part of the concept of the line. Thus it was necessary for Euclid to attempt to define precisely what his terms meant. Many of his definitions are crude by today's standards (e.g., a point is "that which has no parts"), but his recognition of their necessity in establishing a mathematical system was a key insight.

Euclid also saw the need for axioms and postulates (i.e., elementary properties) to be accepted without proof, from which he could deduce as theorems the accumulated geometry of his time. In his selection of these he displayed great insight and judgment: from a few well-chosen axioms and postulates he succeeded in proving all the important results of the Greek masters, some five hundred theorems!

Euclid's *Elements* is organized in thirteen books (each equivalent to a chapter today) discussing points, lines, triangles, and other plane figures; congruence, circles, and similar figures; proportion; and the theory of numbers. Although its compilation of the mathematical knowledge of its day is truly impressive, its organization and proof of that knowledge in the form of a deductive system (what we call the axiomatic method) was Euclid's more significant intellectual advance.

History paints Euclid as a genial, patient, and fair-minded man. His patience may have been strained, however, by a student who once asked him, "What shall I get by learning these things?" Euclid called his slave and instructed, "Give him threepence, since he must make gain out of what he learns."

Euclid's intellectual leap forward had such a profound effect that for centuries his work was regarded as indisputable truth. More than two thousand years after his death, Euclid's *Elements* still ranks as one of the most significant steps forward in the development of mathematics.

4.1 INTRODUCTION

Figures containing three lines or three subsets of lines are among the most useful in plane geometry. Some of the possibilities are shown in Figure 4.1. Of these, the familiar triangle shown in (a), and in (b) with its sides extended, is by far the most important. It is used in designing roof trusses, bridge girders, geodesic domes, and in bracings of many types. The triangle is also important in surveying and navigation. Figure 4.1(c) shows two parallel lines "cut" by a third line called a transversal. This figure is central to the systematic development of geometry and will be discussed in Chapter 5. In Figure 4.1(d) we see three lines intersecting in one point (*concurrent* lines) and in (e) three parallel lines. These seldom occur and are less important than the others.

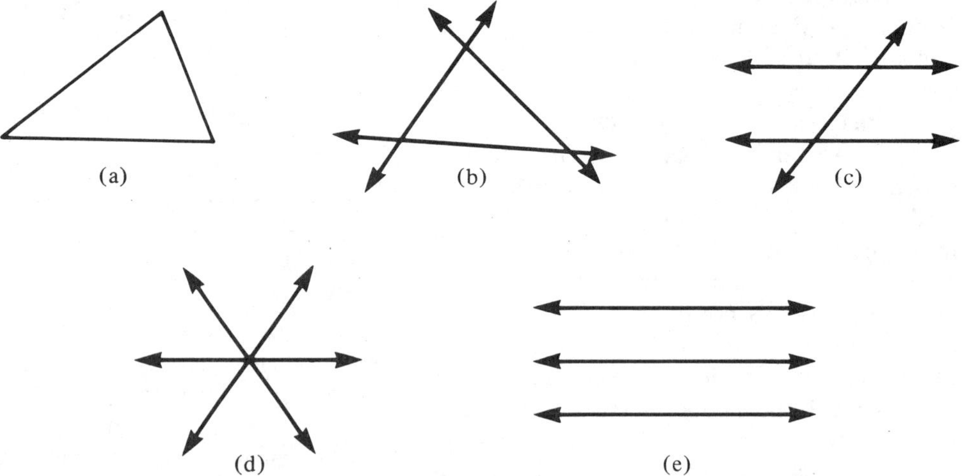

Figure 4.1

This chapter is devoted to the triangle, and we begin with its definition.

Definition 4.1 A figure is a *triangle* iff it is the union of three line segments determined by three noncollinear points.

Each of the three line segments is a *side* of the triangle and each of the three noncollinear points is a *vertex* (plural, vertices). Triangles are named using the symbol "$\triangle$" and either the three letters labeling the vertices or a single Roman numeral. The triangle in Figure 4.2 is named either $\triangle EJS$ or $\triangle$I.

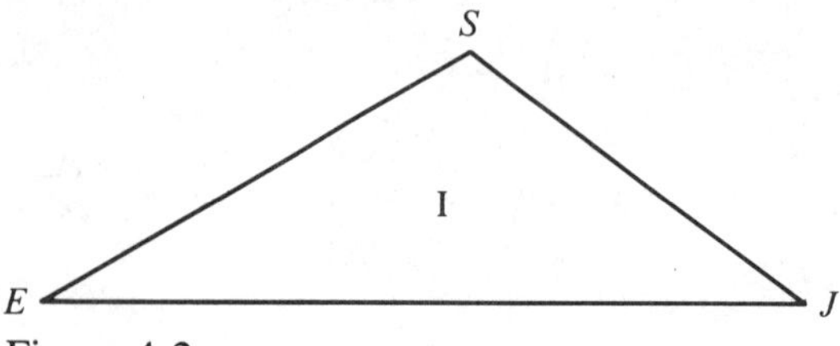

Figure 4.2

It is interesting to note that the word "triangle" means "three angles" and yet Definition 4.1 contains no reference to angles. This is because the sides of angles are rays, not line segments. Since line segments, however, may be extended to form rays, we do refer to the angles of a triangle. The triangle in Figure 4.2 has ∡*E*, ∡*J*, and ∡*S*. Thus, a triangle contains the more elementary figures already studied: three line segments and three angles.

The *interior* of a triangle is the intersection of the interiors of its three angles. Intuitively it is the set of points inside the triangle. The *exterior* is the set of all points that are neither on the triangle nor in its interior, that is, the points that are outside the triangle.

The positions of the sides and angles of a triangle are related using the words "opposite" and "included." In Figure 4.2 side $\overline{EJ}$ is *opposite* ∡*S* and *included* between ∡*E* and ∡*J*. Similar statements may be made for each of the other two sides. We also say that ∡*S* is *opposite* side $\overline{EJ}$ and *included* between sides $\overline{SE}$ and $\overline{SJ}$, with similar statements for ∡*E* and ∡*J*.

Special types of triangles are identified by the relative lengths of their sides.

Definition 4.2 A triangle is *scalene* iff no two of its sides are congruent.

Definition 4.3 A triangle is *isosceles* iff at least two of its sides are congruent (isos △ iff 2 ≅ sides).

Definition 4.4 A triangle is *equilateral* iff all three of its sides are congruent (equilat △ iff 3 ≅ sides).

Note that, by definition *an equilateral triangle is also isosceles*. In Figure 4.3 the marks show that △*EJS* is equilateral and isosceles, △*CDE* is scalene (no marks), and △*KER* is isosceles. In an isosceles triangle that is not equilateral, the congruent sides are called the *legs* and the third side is the *base*. The angle opposite the base and included between the legs is the *vertex angle*, and the other two angles are the *base angles*. In △*KER*, $\overline{RK}$ and $\overline{RE}$ are the legs, $\overline{KE}$ is the base, ∡*R* is the vertex angle, and ∡*K* and ∡*E* are the base angles.

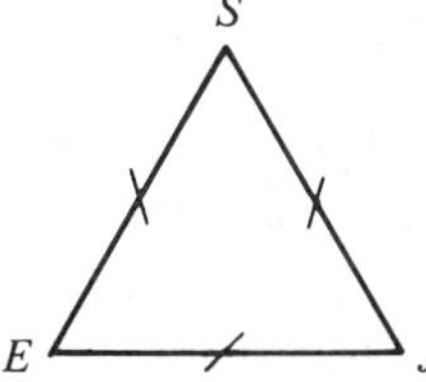

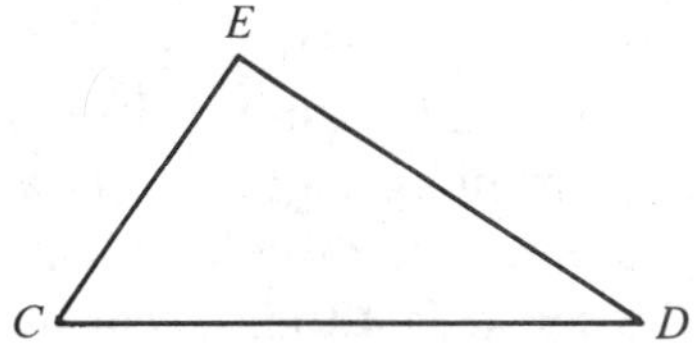

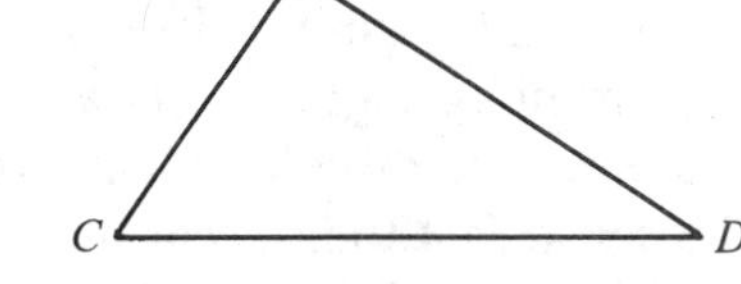
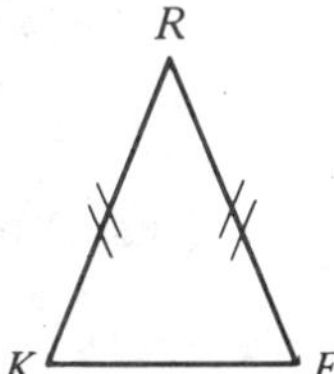

Figure 4.3

Triangles are also classified according to the sizes of their angles.

Definition 4.5 A triangle is *acute* iff all three of its angles are acute.

Definition 4.6 A triangle is *right* iff one of its angles is a right angle (rt △ iff a rt ∡).

Definition 4.7 A triangle is *obtuse* iff one of its angles is an obtuse angle.

Definition 4.8 A triangle is *equiangular* iff all three of its angles are congruent (equiang △ iff 3 ≅ ∡s).

In Figure 4.4 △I is acute, △II is obtuse, △ABC is right since $\angle C = 90°$, and △EJS is equiangular. In a right triangle, the two sides that include the right angle are the *legs,* and the side opposite the right angle is the *hypotenuse*.

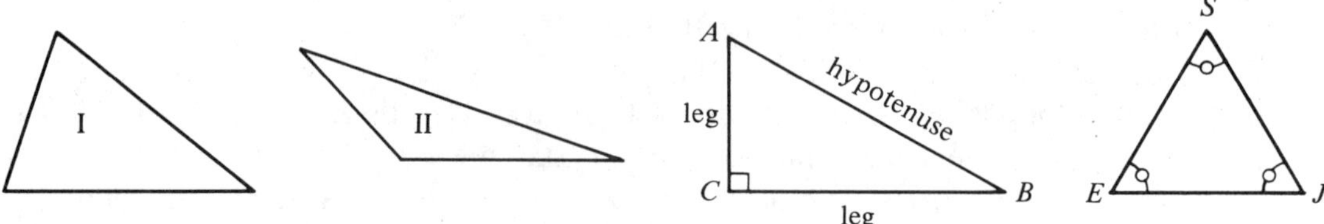

Figure 4.4

4.2 CONGRUENT TRIANGLES

Two line segments or two angles are congruent iff their measures are equal. There is more, however, to the concept of congruence than simply a dependence on equal measure. If two line segments are congruent, then a tracing of one can be made to coincide with the other, that is, can be made to match it point for point. This is not only because the segments have the same length, but also because they have the same shape. An arc of a circle that is 1 inch long is *not* congruent to a 1-inch line segment. Angles are more straightforward since they are all formed by two rays. If two angles have the same degree measure, they must have the same shape and are certainly congruent. A tracing of one would coincide with the other.

Congruence of two geometric figures, then, requires that they have the *same size and shape*. This concept is the basis for the technology of mass production and the interchangeability of parts and is, therefore, of great practical importance. The congruence of two geometric figures is central to the systematic development of plane geometry. We begin with some comparisons of triangles.

Triangles I and II in Figure 4.5 seem to have the same shape but not the same size. They are not congruent. Triangles II and III do not have the same shape so they are not congruent. (It is worth noting that they do have the same size in the sense that their areas are equal. Area is discussed in Chapter 8.) Triangles I and IV are the only pair in the figure that are congruent. They have the same size and shape, and a tracing of one could coincide with the

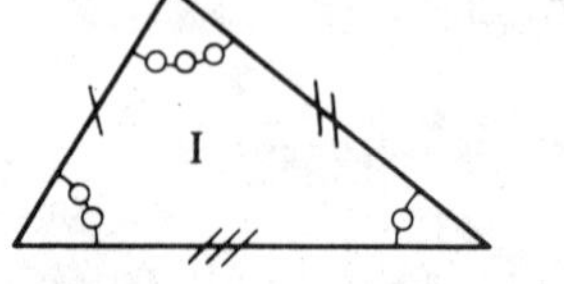

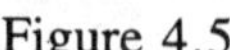
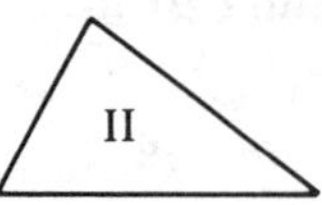

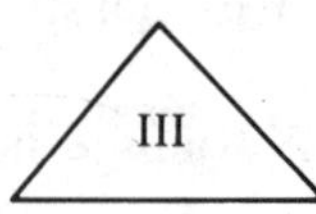

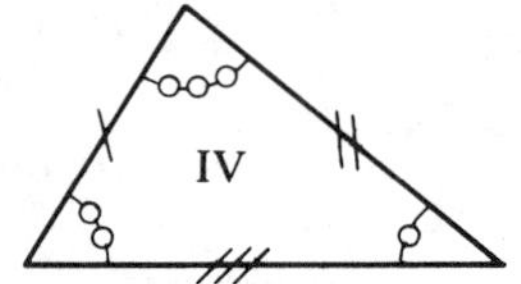

Figure 4.5

other. To make these ideas precise we need to establish a one-to-one correspondence between the vertices of two triangles.

Figure 4.6 shows two congruent triangles. To make them coincide we would match vertex A with vertex D, vertex B with vertex E, and vertex C with vertex F ($ABC \leftrightarrow DEF$). In this way, the following matching between the triangles's sides and between its angles may be established:

$$\overline{AB} \leftrightarrow \overline{DE}, \quad \overline{BC} \leftrightarrow \overline{EF}, \quad \overline{AC} \leftrightarrow \overline{DF},$$
$$\measuredangle A \leftrightarrow \measuredangle D, \quad \measuredangle B \leftrightarrow \measuredangle E, \quad \measuredangle C \leftrightarrow \measuredangle F$$

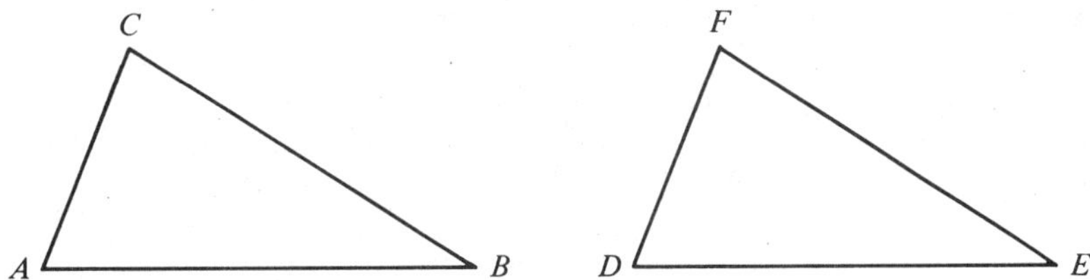

Figure 4.6 $A \leftrightarrow D$, $B \leftrightarrow E$, and $C \leftrightarrow F$, or briefly $ABC \leftrightarrow DEF$.

Thus, the two triangles have six pairs of corresponding parts. Our work suggests that the triangles should be called congruent iff the six pairs of corresponding parts are congruent.

Definition 4.9 Two triangles are *congruent* iff there is a one-to-one correspondence between their vertices such that three pairs of corresponding sides are congruent and the three pairs of corresponding angles are congruent (cpctc).

The abbreviation "cpctc" stands for "corresponding parts of congruent triangles are congruent."

To further illustrate this key definition, Figure 4.7 shows two congruent triangles in "mirror-image" position. With the vertices matched $E \leftrightarrow C$, $J \leftrightarrow K$, and $S \leftrightarrow M$ ($EJS \leftrightarrow CKM$), we have $\measuredangle E \cong \measuredangle C$, $\measuredangle J \cong \measuredangle K$, $\measuredangle S \cong \measuredangle M$, $\overline{EJ} \cong \overline{CK}$, $\overline{JS} \cong \overline{KM}$, $\overline{SE} \cong \overline{MC}$, and so $\triangle EJS \cong \triangle CKM$. Note that in naming the triangles we preserve the correspondence $EJS \leftrightarrow CKM$. *Thus, when we write* $\triangle ABC \cong \triangle DEF$ *we will mean* $ABC \leftrightarrow DEF$, *and, if* $ABC \leftrightarrow DEF$ *we will,* in three-letter notation, *write* $\triangle ABC \cong DEF$.

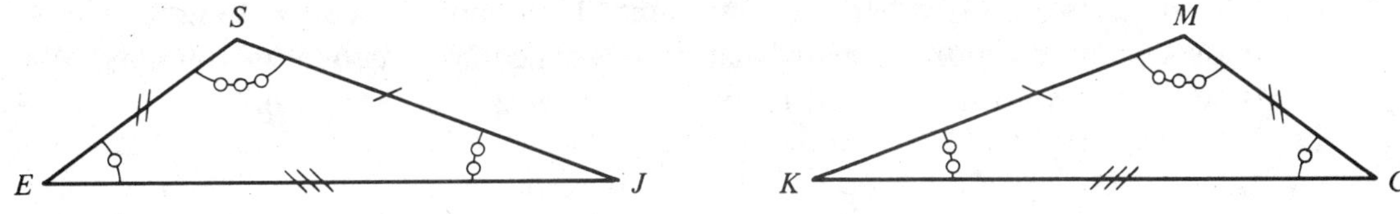

Figure 4.7

Triangle congruences may be rearranged in the same way as congruences concerning line segments or angles and as equals relations about numbers. This is because the congruence relation between triangles has the RST properties as stated in Theorems 13–15. Two of the proofs are left as exercises.

Theorem 13 If $\triangle EJS$ is any triangle, then $\triangle EJS \cong \triangle EJS$ (refl $\cong$).

Theorem 14 If $\triangle EJS$ and $\triangle CKM$ are triangles such that $\triangle EJS \cong \triangle CKM$, then $\triangle CKM \cong \triangle EJS$ (symm $\cong$).

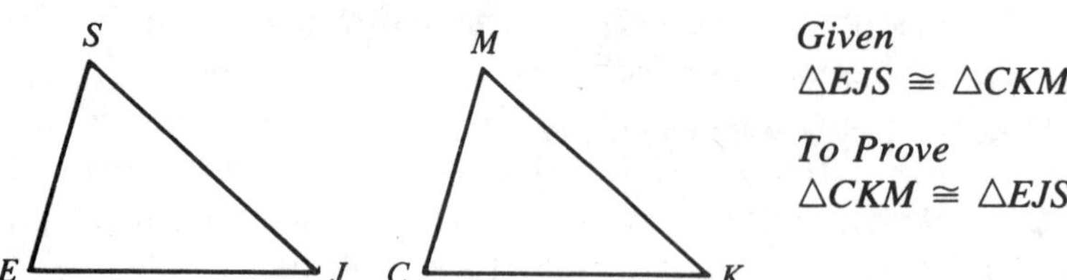

Given
$\triangle EJS \cong \triangle CKM$

To Prove
$\triangle CKM \cong \triangle EJS$

Statement	*Reason*
1. $\triangle EJS \cong \triangle CKM$	1. given
2. $\overline{EJ} \cong \overline{CK}$ $\overline{JS} \cong \overline{KM}$ $\overline{SE} \cong \overline{MC}$	2. cpctc
3. $\overline{CK} \cong \overline{EJ}$ $\overline{KM} \cong \overline{JS}$ $\overline{MC} \cong \overline{SE}$	3. symm $\cong$ (line segments)
4. $\measuredangle E \cong \measuredangle C$ $\measuredangle J \cong \measuredangle K$ $\measuredangle S \cong \measuredangle M$	4. cpctc
5. $\measuredangle C \cong \measuredangle E$ $\measuredangle K \cong \measuredangle J$ $\measuredangle M \cong \measuredangle S$	5. symm $\cong$ (angles)
6. $\therefore \triangle CKM \cong \triangle EJS$	6. cpctc

Theorem 15 If $\triangle EJS$, $\triangle CAM$, and $\triangle LRW$ are such that $\triangle EJS \cong \triangle CAM$ and $\triangle CAM \cong \triangle LRW$, then $\triangle EJS \cong \triangle LRW$ (trans $\cong$).

To prove that two triangles are by definition congruent, we must match their vertices and show that the resulting six pairs of corresponding parts are congruent. But is this much work really necessary? If you were designing a geodesic dome, how much matching would be necessary to insure that the triangles used were congruent? Perhaps fewer than six pairs of congruent parts are enough to insure that the triangles have the same size and shape. Some experimentation with triangles shows that, in fact, *three* pairs of congruent parts are sufficient *if they occur in certain arrangements*. Figure 4.8 is a warning to be careful! Although $\measuredangle A \cong \measuredangle D$, $\measuredangle B \cong \measuredangle E$, and $\measuredangle C \cong \measuredangle F$, the triangles are certainly not congruent. There are, however, three arrangements of three congruent pairs that do guarantee congruence of triangles. We state these as postulates and motivate each with a construction.

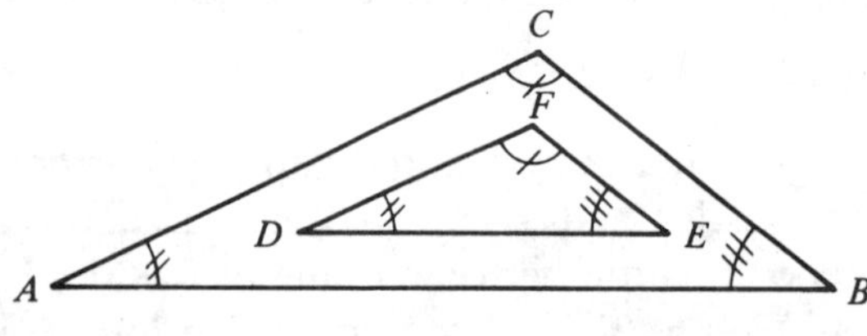

Figure 4.8

Construction 7 To construct a triangle having its sides congruent to the corresponding parts of a given triangle.

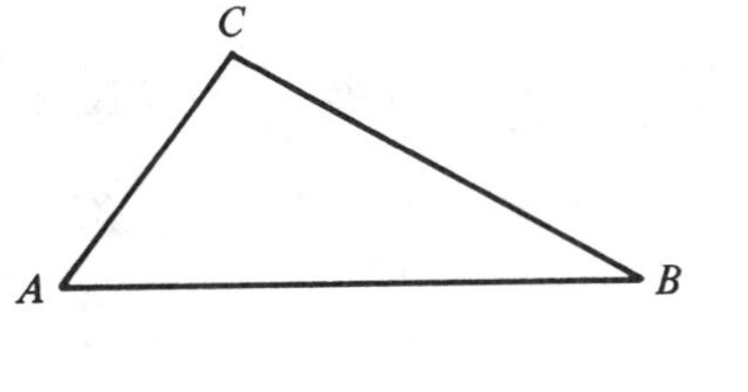

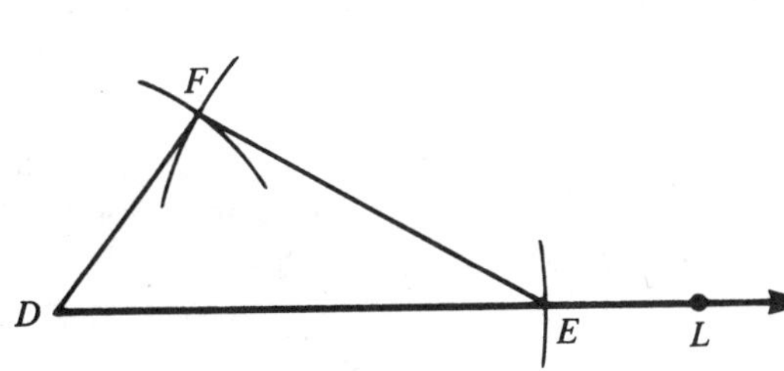

Given
$\triangle ABC$

To Construct
$\triangle DEF$ with $\overline{DE} \cong \overline{AB}$, $\overline{EF} \cong \overline{BC}$, and $\overline{FD} \cong \overline{CA}$

Steps
1. Draw $\overrightarrow{DL}$ and on it construct $\overline{DE} \cong \overline{AB}$ (Construction 2).
2. With D as center and $\overline{AC}$ as radius, draw an arc on one side of $\overrightarrow{DL}$.
3. With E as center and $\overline{BC}$ as radius, draw an arc intersecting the arc of step 2. This determines vertex F.
4. Draw $\overline{EF}$ and $\overline{DF}$.

You should draw any $\triangle ABC$ and do Construction 7 to satisfy yourself that $\triangle DEF \cong \triangle ABC$.

Postulate 12 If there is a correspondence between two triangles such that the three sides of one are congruent to the corresponding parts of the other, then the triangles are congruent (sss $\cong$ sss).

Construction 8 To construct a triangle having two sides and the included angle congruent to the corresponding parts of a given triangle.

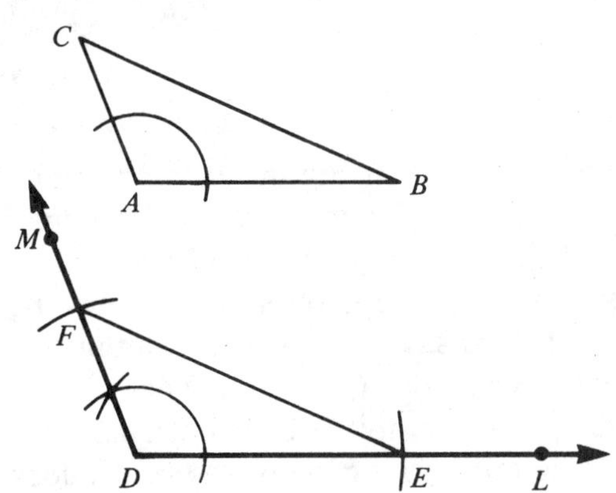

Given
$\triangle ABC$

To Construct
$\triangle DEF$ with $\overline{DE} \cong \overline{AB}$, $\angle D \cong \angle A$, and $\overline{DF} \cong \overline{AC}$

Steps
1. Draw $\overrightarrow{DL}$ and construct $\angle D \cong \angle A$ (Construction 4). This determines $\overrightarrow{DM}$.
2. On $\overrightarrow{DL}$ construct $\overline{DE} \cong \overline{AB}$ and on $\overrightarrow{DM}$ construct $\overline{DF} \cong \overline{AC}$ (Construction 2).
3. Draw $\overline{EF}$.

Again, you should do this construction and check that $\triangle DEF \cong \triangle ABC$.

Postulate 13 If there is a correspondence between two triangles such that two sides and the included angle of one are congruent to the corresponding parts of the other, then the triangles are congruent (sas $\cong$ sas).

Construction 9 To construct a triangle having two angles and the included side congruent to the corresponding parts of a given triangle.

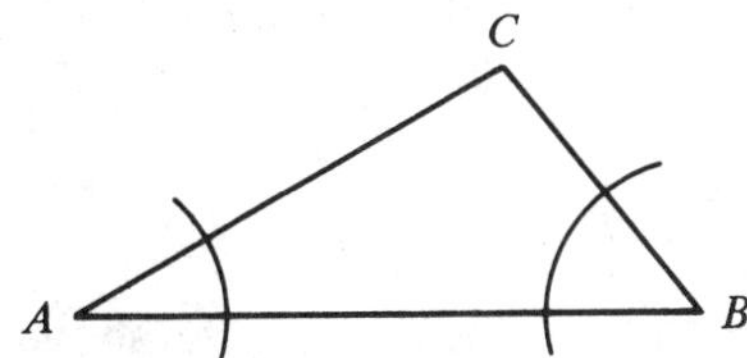

Given
$\triangle ABC$

To Construct
$\triangle DEF$ with $\angle D \cong \angle A$, $\overline{DE} \cong \overline{AB}$, and $\angle E \cong \angle B$

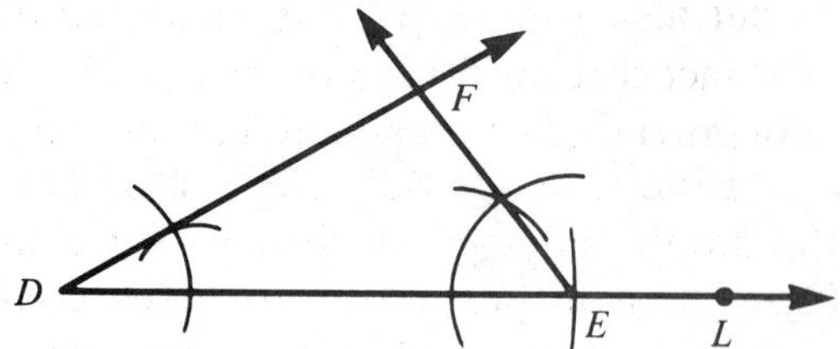

Steps

1. Draw $\overrightarrow{DL}$ and construct $\overline{DE} \cong \overline{AB}$ (Construction 2).
2. Construct $\angle D \cong \angle A$ and $\angle E \cong \angle B$ (Construction 4). This determines vertex F.

Postulate 14 If there is a correspondence between two triangles such that two angles and the included side of one are congruent to the corresponding parts of the other, then the triangles are congruent (asa ≅ asa).

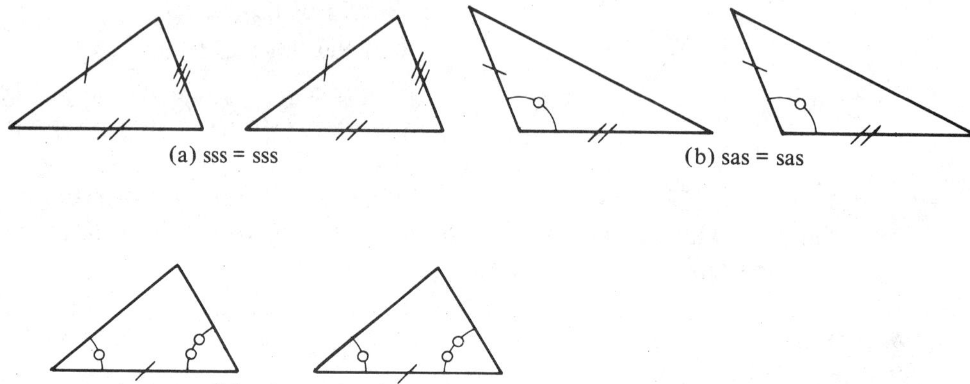

(a) sss = sss (b) sas = sas

(c) asa = asa

Figure 4.9

The three congruence postulates are illustrated in Figure 4.9. The pairs of congruent corresponding parts are marked in the usual way. You may wonder whether any other arrangements of three pairs of congruent parts might guarantee congruence of the triangles. The remaining possibilities may be abbreviated aaa ≅ aaa, ssa ≅ ssa, and aas ≅ aas. Figure 4.8 shows that the first of these does not assure congruence of triangles (although it does mean that they have the same shape). That the second possibility does not guarantee congruence is indicated in Figure 4.10. The third arrangement aas ≅ aas does mean that the triangles are congruent, and it will be proved as Theorem 41 in Chapter 5.

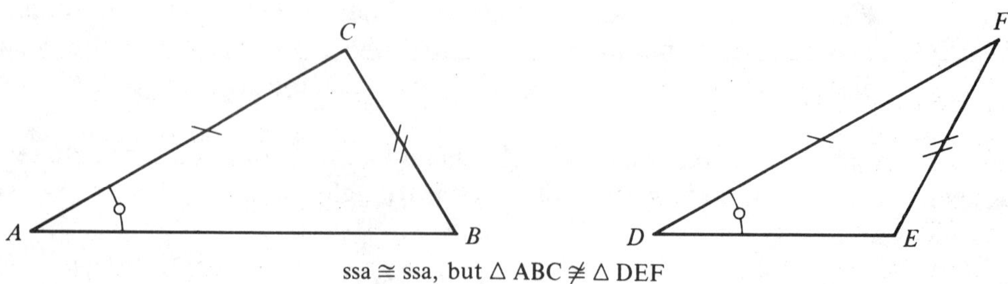

ssa ≅ ssa, but $\triangle ABC \not\cong \triangle DEF$

Figure 4.10

This section concludes with three examples illustrating the use of the above postulates to prove two triangles congruent. Note how the figures have been marked not only with the given facts but also with *direct consequences* of the given facts. Thus, in Example 1 the fact that $\triangle EJS$ is isosceles leads us to mark its two legs, $\overline{ES}$ and $\overline{JS}$, as congruent. This technique can be very helpful as a preliminary to designing the steps in a proof. Note, too, how given facts are stated separately in the proofs followed by their useful consequences. Finally, each example shows that to prove two triangles congruent, it is necessary to prove three pairs of corresponding parts congruent that fit the conditions of one of the above postulates (sss, sas, or asa).

EXAMPLE 1

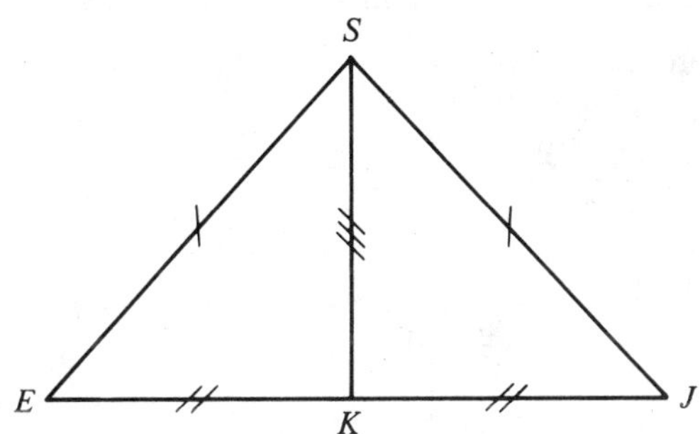

Given
$\triangle EJS$ isos ($\overline{EJ}$ base)
K midpt $\overline{EJ}$

To Prove
$\triangle EKS \cong \triangle JKS$

Statement	*Reason*
1. $\triangle EJS$ isos ($\overline{EJ}$ base)	1. given
2. $\overline{ES} \cong \overline{JS}$	2. isos $\triangle$ iff 2 $\cong$ sides
3. K midpt $\overline{EJ}$	3. given
4. $EK = JK$	4. midpt iff 2 lengths =
5. $\overline{EK} \cong \overline{JK}$	5. $\cong$ iff meas =
6. $\overline{SK} \cong \overline{SK}$	6. refl $\cong$
7. $\therefore \triangle EKS \cong \triangle JKS$	7. sss $\cong$ sss

EXAMPLE 2

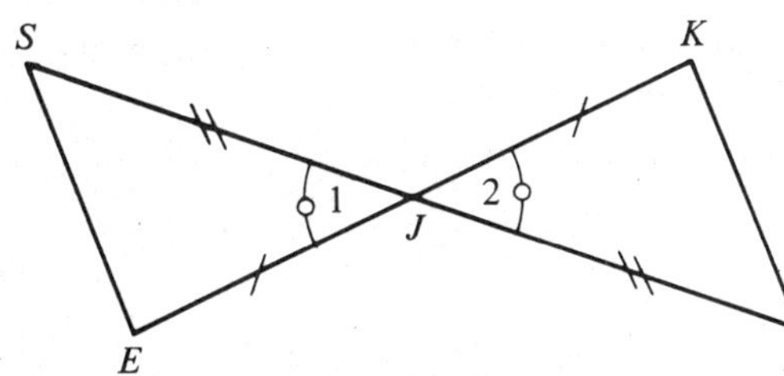

Given
$\overline{SF}$ bis $\overline{EK}$
$\overline{EK}$ bis $\overline{SF}$

To Prove
$\triangle EJS \cong \triangle KJF$

Statement	*Reason*
1. $\overline{SF}$ bis $\overline{EK}$	1. given
2. J midpt $\overline{EK}$	2. bis seg iff contains midpt
3. $EJ = KJ$	3. midpt iff 2 lengths =
4. $\overline{EJ} \cong \overline{KJ}$	4. $\cong$ iff meas =
5. $\overline{EK}$ bis $\overline{SF}$	5. given
6. J midpt $\overline{SF}$	6. bis seg iff contains midpt
7. $SJ = FJ$	7. midpt iff 2 lengths =
8. $\overline{SJ} \cong \overline{FJ}$	8. $\cong$ iff meas =
9. $\measuredangle 1$ and $\measuredangle 2$ vert $\measuredangle$s	9. vert $\measuredangle$s formed by opp rays
10. $\measuredangle 1 \cong \measuredangle 2$	10. vert $\measuredangle$s $\cong$
11. $\therefore \triangle EJS \cong \triangle KJF$	11. sas $\cong$ sas

EXAMPLE 3

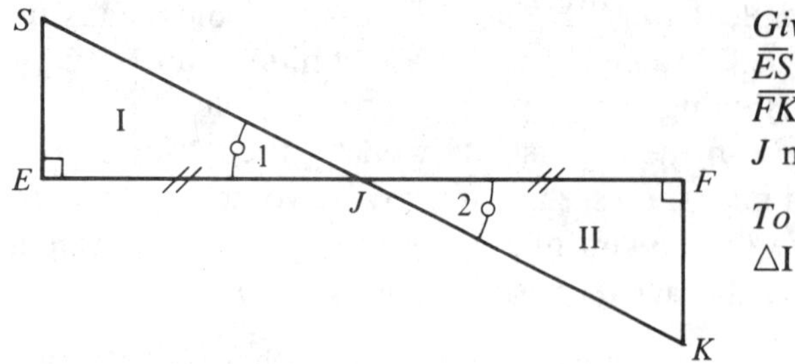

Given
$\overline{ES} \perp \overline{EF}$
$\overline{FK} \perp \overline{EF}$
J midpt $\overline{EF}$

To Prove
$\triangle I \cong \triangle II$

Statement	*Reason*
1. $\overline{ES} \perp \overline{EF}$	1. given
2. $\measuredangle E$ rt $\measuredangle$	2. $\perp$ iff a rt $\measuredangle$
3. $\overline{FK} \perp \overline{EF}$	3. given
4. $\measuredangle F$ rt $\measuredangle$	4. $\perp$ iff a rt $\measuredangle$
5. $\measuredangle E \cong \measuredangle F$	5. rt $\measuredangle$s $\cong$
6. J midpt $\overline{EF}$	6. given
7. $EJ = FJ$	7. midpt iff 2 lengths =
8. $\overline{EJ} \cong \overline{FJ}$	8. $\cong$ iff meas =
9. $\measuredangle 1$ and $\measuredangle 2$ vert $\measuredangle$s	9. vert $\measuredangle$s formed by opp rays
10. $\measuredangle 1 \cong \measuredangle 2$	10. vert $\measuredangle$s $\cong$
11. $\therefore \triangle I \cong \triangle II$	11. asa $\cong$ asa

In the above examples the correspondences between the vertices were not stated. They are easy to see, however, once the figures have been marked. Care must be taken to match the parts correctly. For example, in Figure 4.11 the marks show that $E \leftrightarrow F$, $S \leftrightarrow K$, and $J \leftrightarrow J$. This is *not* the same correspondence as the one in Example 2.

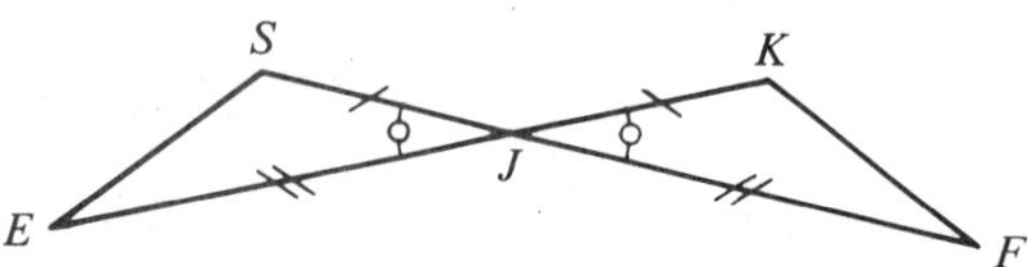

Figure 4.11

EXERCISES FOR 4.1 AND 4.2

In exercises 1–20 answer true or false.

1. A scalene triangle has at least one right angle.
2. The hypotenuse is the side opposite one of the acute angles in a right triangle.
3. Congruent triangles have the same size and shape.
4. If A, B, and C are three collinear points, the union of $\overline{AB}$, $\overline{BC}$, and $\overline{AC}$ is $\triangle ABC$.
5. A triangle is the set of points enclosed by three segments.
6. In $\triangle EJS$ $\overline{EJ}$ is opposite $\measuredangle S$.
7. An isosceles triangle can have an obtuse angle as one of its angles.
8. In $\triangle ABC$ $\measuredangle A$ is included between sides $\overline{AB}$ and $\overline{BC}$.
9. If $\triangle EJS \cong \triangle LRW$, then $\overline{JS} \cong \overline{RW}$.
10. A right isosceles triangle has two right angles.
11. Congruence for triangles is symmetric and transitive but not reflexive.
12. The hypotenuse of a right isosceles triangle is the base of the triangle.
13. The interior of a triangle is a convex set of points.
14. If three angles of one triangle are congruent to three angles of a second triangle, then the two triangles are congruent.
15. The measures of the three sides of an isosceles triangle could be 8, 8, and 17 units. (Hint: Try to draw the triangle.)

16. A triangle could have an acute angle, a right angle, and an obtuse angle as its three angles. (Hint: Try to draw the triangle.)
17. If E-K-S on a side of $\triangle EJS$, then $\overline{JK}$ is in the interior of $\triangle EJS$.
18. The vertex angle of an isosceles triangle is the angle included between the congruent sides.
19. If in $\triangle ABC$ and $\triangle EJS$, $\measuredangle A \cong \measuredangle E$, $\overline{AC} \cong \overline{ES}$, and $\overline{CB} \cong \overline{SJ}$, then $\triangle ABC \cong \triangle EJS$.
20. If $\triangle ABC$ is isosceles with $\measuredangle A$ the vertex angle and D and E the midpoints of $\overline{AB}$ and $\overline{AC}$, respectively, then $\overline{BD} \cong \overline{CE}$.

In exercises 21 and 22, use Figure 4.12 to answer the questions.

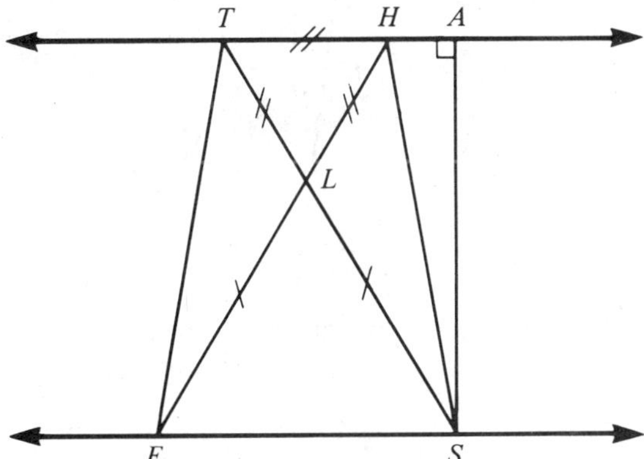

Figure 4.12

21. **(a)** Name four acute triangles.
    (b) Name four obtuse triangles.
    (c) Name one right triangle.
22. **(a)** Name two isosceles triangles.
    (b) Name one equilateral triangle.
    (c) Name six scalene triangles.

In exercises 23–25 use Figure 4.13 to answer the questions.

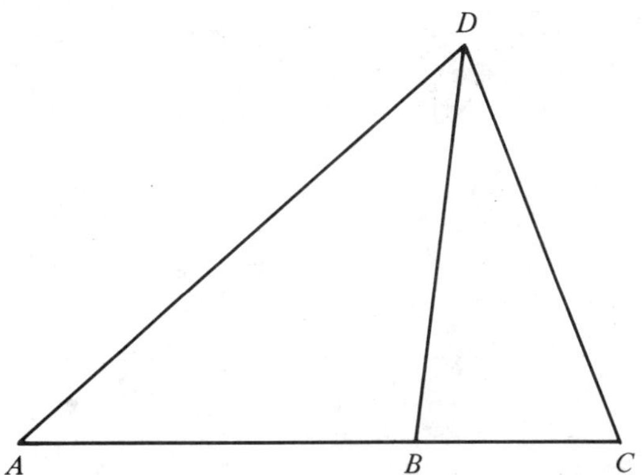

Figure 4.13

23. **(a)** In $\triangle ABD$ what angle is opposite $\overline{BD}$?
    (b) In $\triangle ABD$ what angle is included between $\overline{AD}$ and $\overline{BD}$?
24. **(a)** In $\triangle ACD$ what side is opposite $\measuredangle ACD$?
    (b) In $\triangle ACD$, what side is included between $\measuredangle ADC$ and $\measuredangle ACD$?
25. **(a)** In $\triangle BCD$, $\overline{DC}$ is opposite which angle?
    (b) In $\triangle ACD$, $\overline{DC}$ is opposite which angle?

In exercises 26–37, (a) write the congruences given by the indicated measures or marks, (b) state whether from the given congruences only you may conclude that triangles I and II are congruent, and (c) if so, write sss ≅ sss, sas ≅ sas, or asa ≅ asa as appropriate.

26.

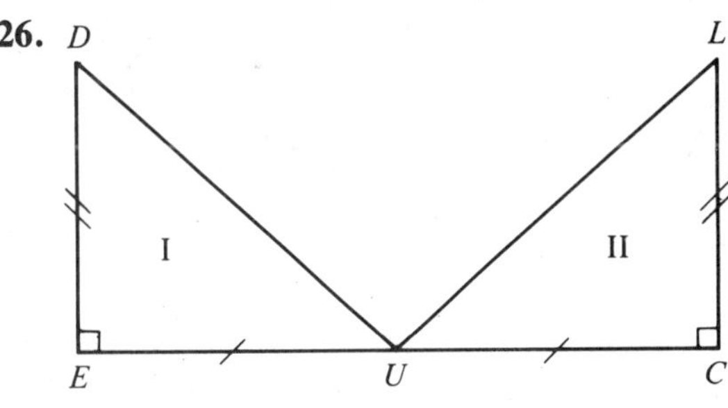

27.

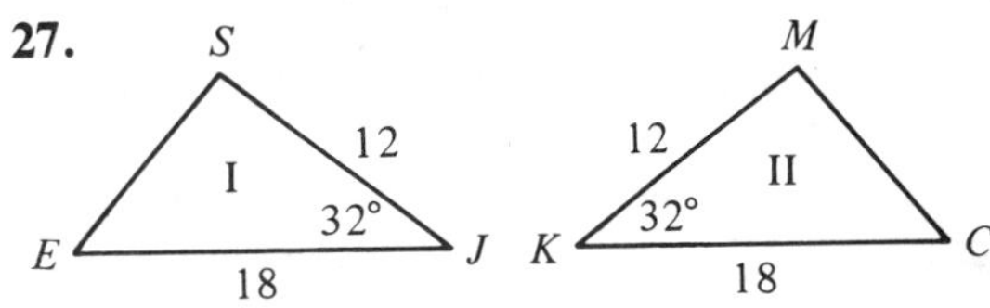

28.

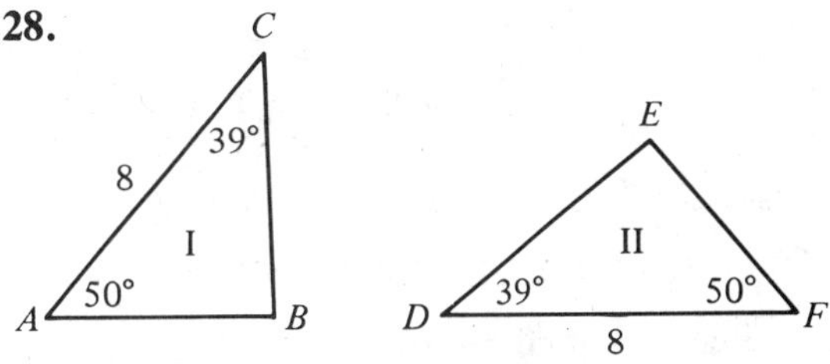

29.

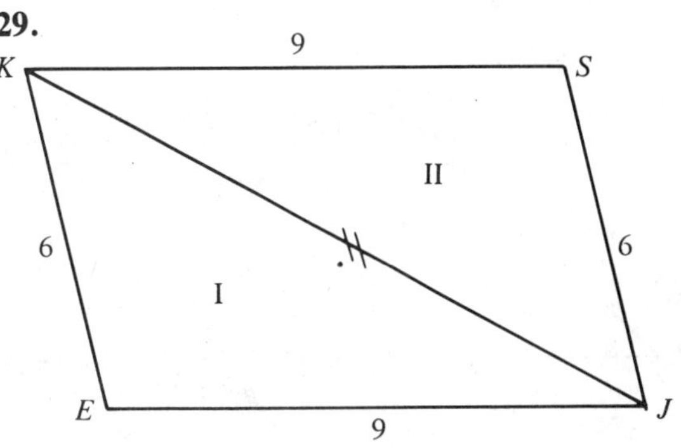

30.

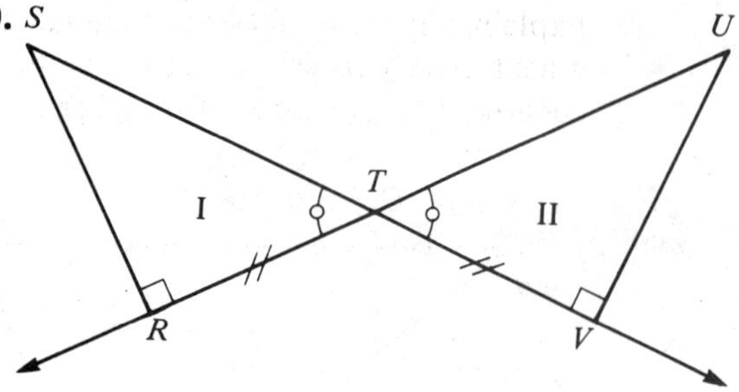

31.

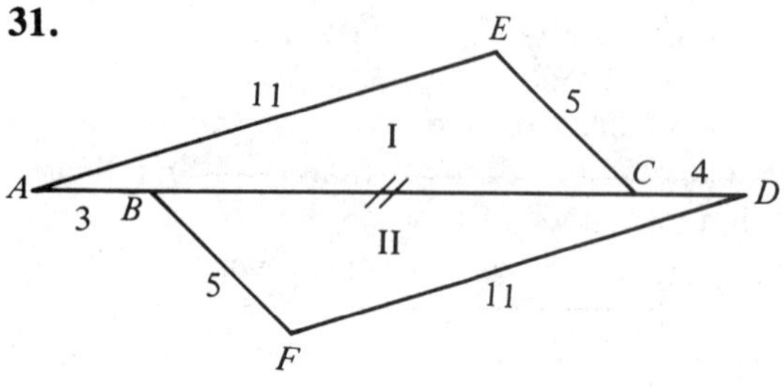

32.

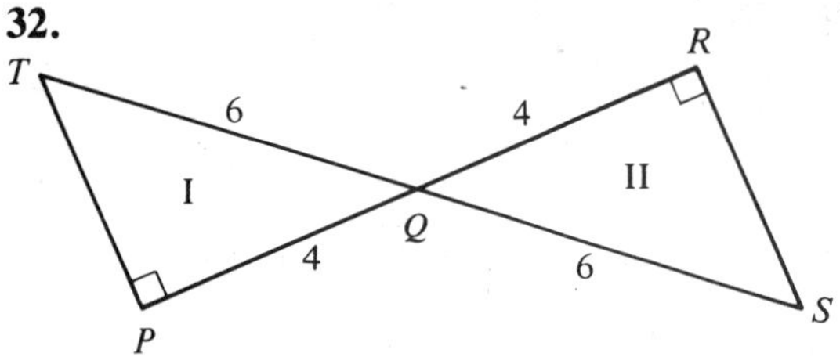

33.

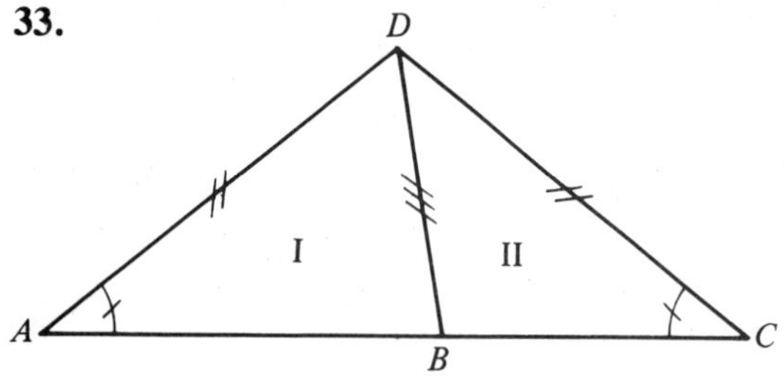

34.

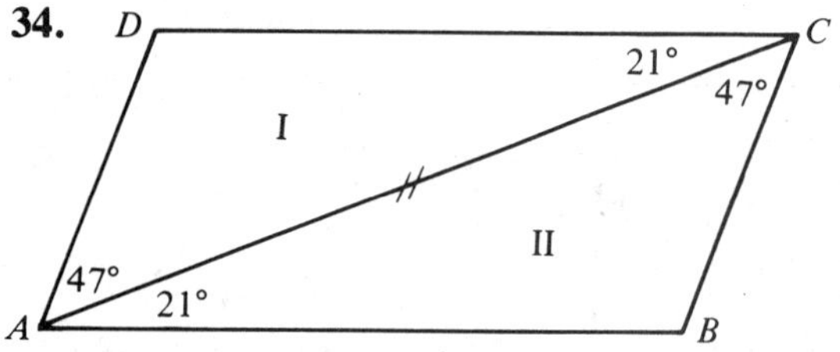

35.

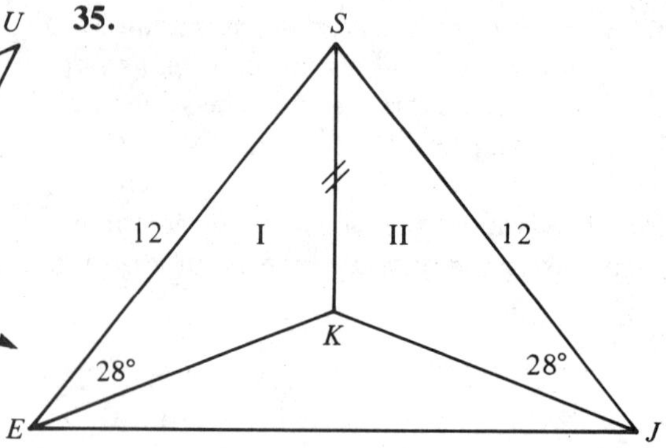

36.

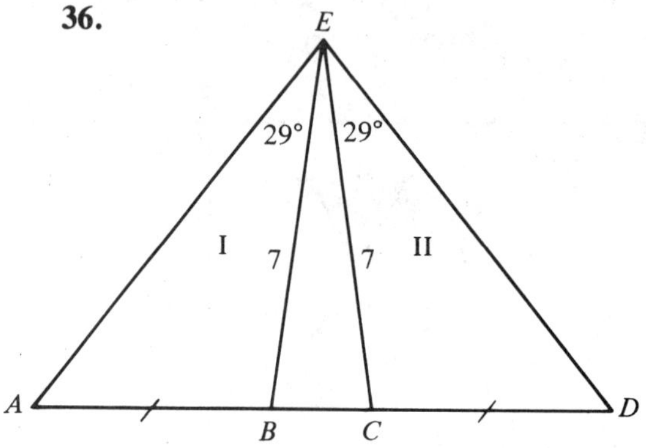

37.

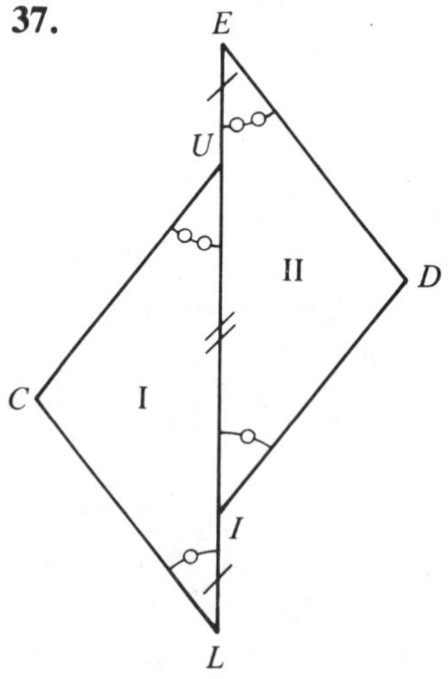

In exercises 38 and 39 use Figure 4.14 to answer the questions.

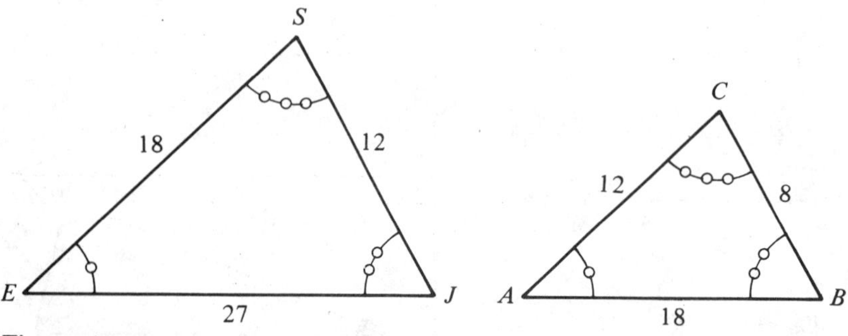

Figure 4.14

38. **(a)** Name three pairs of congruent angles.
(b) Name two pairs of congruent sides.
(c) Name one pair of sides that are not congruent.

39. Explain why the two triangles are not congruent even though five parts of one are congruent to five parts of the other.

In exercises 40–43 copy the figure, mark it, and supply the missing reasons in each proof.

40. *Given*

$\overline{EK} \cong \overline{SJ}$
$\overline{EJ} \cong \overline{SK}$

To Prove
$\triangle I \cong \triangle II$

Statement	*Reason*
1. $\overline{EK} \cong \overline{SJ}$	1. ?
2. $\overline{EJ} \cong \overline{SK}$	2. ?
3. $\overline{KJ} \cong \overline{KJ}$	3. ?
4. $\therefore \triangle I \cong \triangle II$	4. ?

41. *Given*
$\overline{MP} \cong \overline{OP}$
$\overrightarrow{PN}$ midray ∡MPO

To Prove

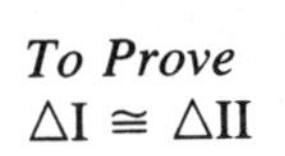

$\triangle I \cong \triangle II$

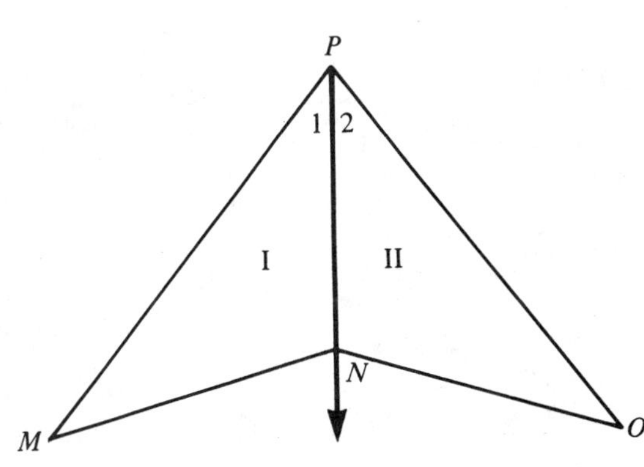

Statement	*Reason*
1. $\overline{MP} \cong \overline{OP}$	1. ?
2. $\overrightarrow{PN}$ midray ∡MPO	2. ?
3. $\angle 1 = \angle 2$	3. ?
4. ∡1 ≅ ∡2	4. ?
5. $\overline{PN} \cong \overline{PN}$	5. ?
6. $\therefore \triangle I \cong \triangle II$	6. ?

42. *Given*

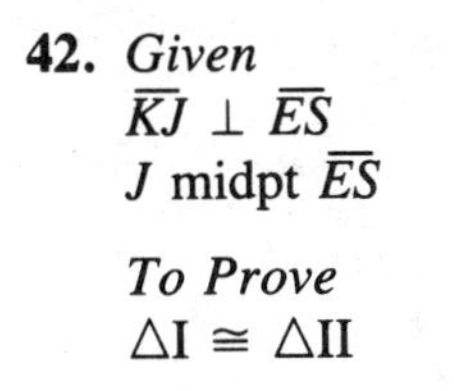

$\overline{KJ} \perp \overline{ES}$
J midpt $\overline{ES}$

To Prove
$\triangle I \cong \triangle II$

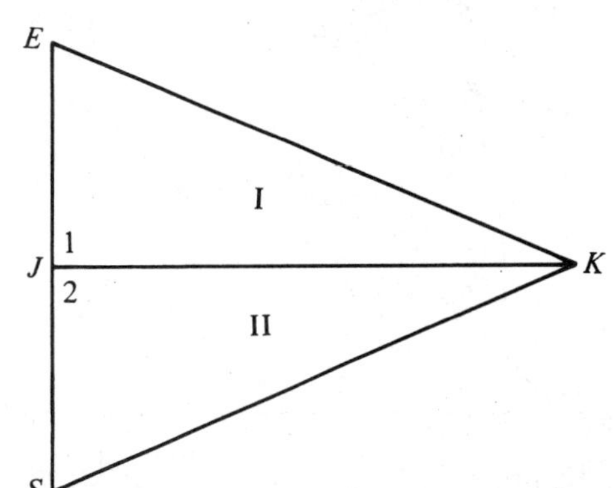

Statement	*Reason*
1. $\overline{KJ} \perp \overline{ES}$	1. ?
2. $\measuredangle 1 \cong \measuredangle 2$	2. ?
3. $\overline{JK} \cong \overline{JK}$	3. ?
4. J midpt $\overline{ES}$	4. ?
5. $EJ = SJ$	5. ?
6. $\overline{EJ} \cong \overline{SJ}$	6. ?
7. $\therefore \triangle\text{I} \cong \triangle\text{II}$	7. ?

43. *Given*

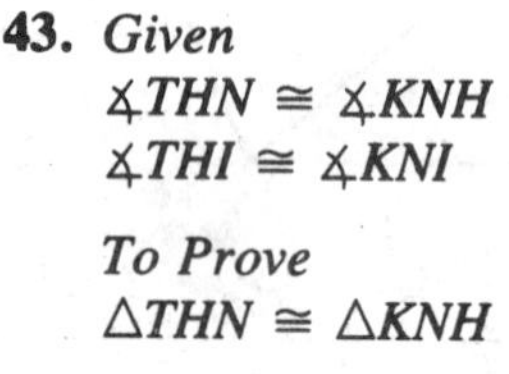

$\measuredangle THN \cong \measuredangle KNH$
$\measuredangle THI \cong \measuredangle KNI$

To Prove
$\triangle THN \cong \triangle KNH$

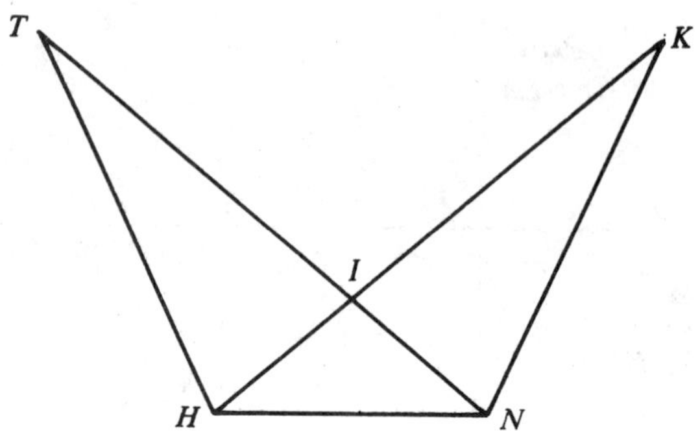

Statement	*Reason*
1. $\measuredangle THN \cong \measuredangle KNH$	1. ?
2. $\angle THN = \angle KNH$	2. ?
3. $\measuredangle THI \cong \measuredangle KNI$	3. ?
4. $\angle THI = \angle KNI$	4. ?
5. $\angle THN - \angle THI = \angle KNH - \angle KNI$	5. ?
6. $\angle IHN = \angle THN - \angle THI$	6. ?
7. $\angle INH = \angle KNH - \angle KNI$	7. ?
8. $\angle KNH - \angle KNI = \angle INH$	8. ?
9. $\angle IHN = \angle INH$	9. ?
10. $\measuredangle IHN \cong \measuredangle INH$	10. ?
11. $\measuredangle INH \cong \measuredangle IHN$	11. ?
12. $\overline{HN} \cong \overline{HN}$	12. ?
13. $\therefore \triangle THN \cong \triangle KNH$	13. ?

In exercises 44 and 45 copy the figure, mark it, and rearrange the given steps into a correct order for a proof.

44. *Given*
$\overrightarrow{KJ}$ midray $\measuredangle EKS$
$\measuredangle 1 \cong \measuredangle 2$

To Prove
$\triangle\text{I} \cong \triangle\text{II}$

(a) $\measuredangle 3 \cong \measuredangle 4$
(b) $\triangle\text{I} \cong \triangle\text{II}$
(c) $\overrightarrow{KJ}$ midray $\measuredangle EKS$
(d) $\measuredangle 1 \cong \measuredangle 2$
(e) $\overline{JK} \cong \overline{JK}$
(f) $\angle 3 = \angle 4$

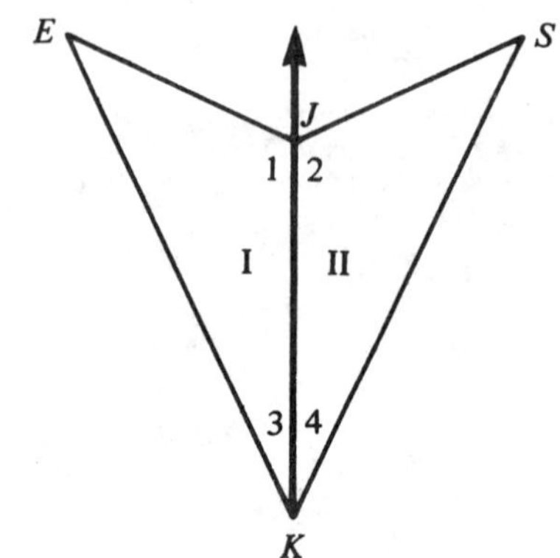

45. *Given*
$\triangle MPR$ isos ($\overline{MP}$ base)
$\overline{MN} \cong \overline{PO}$
$\triangle NOR$ isos ($\overline{NO}$ base)

To Prove
$\triangle \text{I} \cong \triangle \text{II}$

(a) $\overline{MR} \cong \overline{PR}$
(b) $\triangle \text{I} \cong \triangle \text{II}$
(c) $\triangle MPR$ isos ($\overline{MP}$ base)
(d) $\overline{NR} \cong \overline{OR}$
(e) $\overline{MN} \cong \overline{PO}$
(f) $\triangle NOR$ isos ($\overline{NO}$ base)

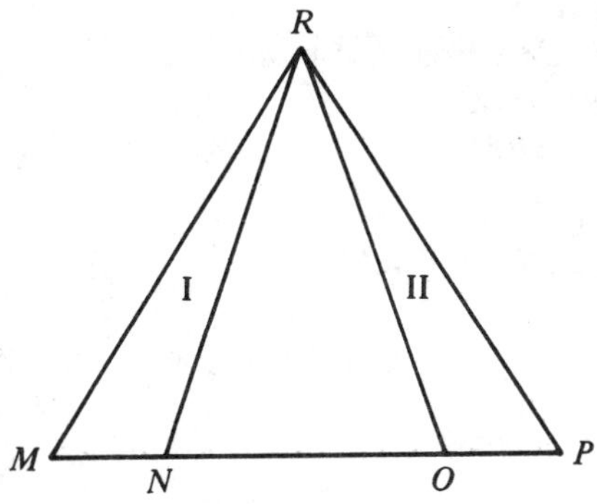

In exercises 46–55 copy the figure, the hypothesis, and the conclusion. Mark the figure and write a proof.

46. *Given*
$\triangle ESK$ isos ($\overline{ES}$ base)
J midpt $\overline{ES}$

To Prove
$\triangle EJK \cong \triangle SJK$

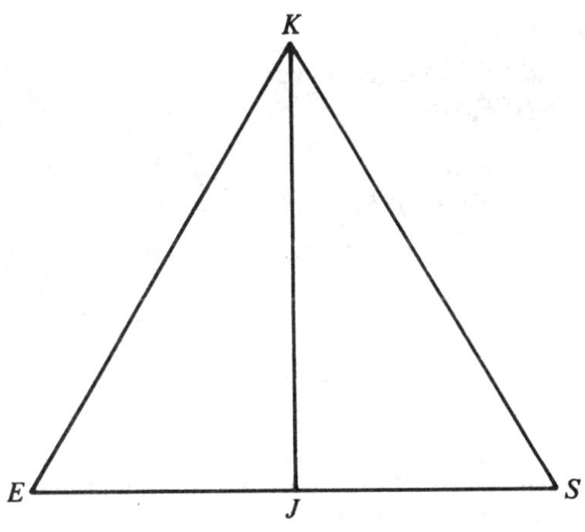

47. *Given*
$\triangle ABC$ isos ($\overline{AB}$ base)
$\overrightarrow{CD}$ midray $\measuredangle ACB$

To Prove
$\triangle \text{I} \cong \triangle \text{II}$

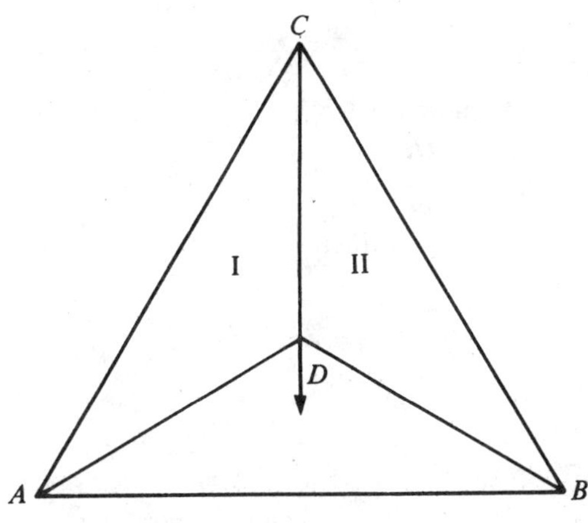

48. *Given*

$\triangle LMO$ isos ($\overline{LM}$ base)
$\measuredangle LON \cong \measuredangle MON$

To Prove
$\triangle LON \cong \triangle MON$

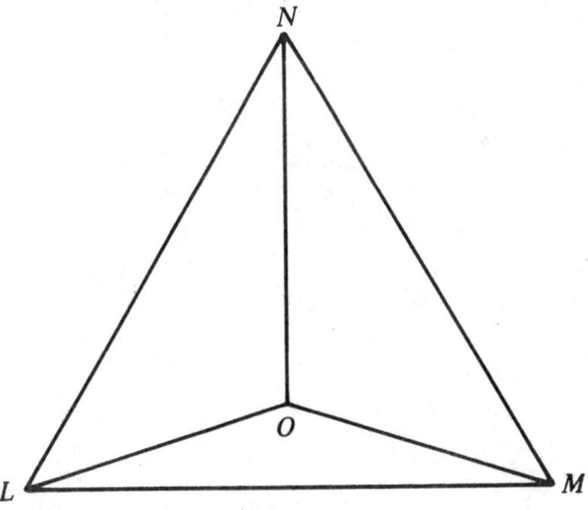

49. *Given*
$\triangle RMA$ isos ($\overline{RM}$ base)
$\angle R \cong \angle M$
$\overline{RP} \cong \overline{MN}$

To Prove
$\triangle RAN \cong \triangle MAP$

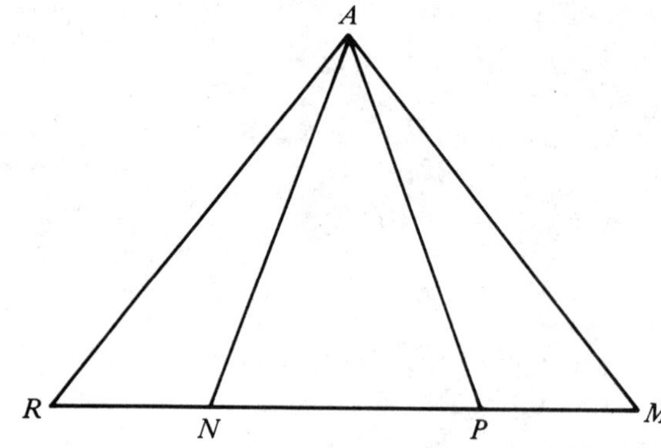

50. *Given*
$\triangle SKJ$ isos ($\overline{SJ}$ base)
$\triangle SEJ$ isos ($\overline{SJ}$ base)

To Prove
$\triangle EKS \cong \triangle EKJ$

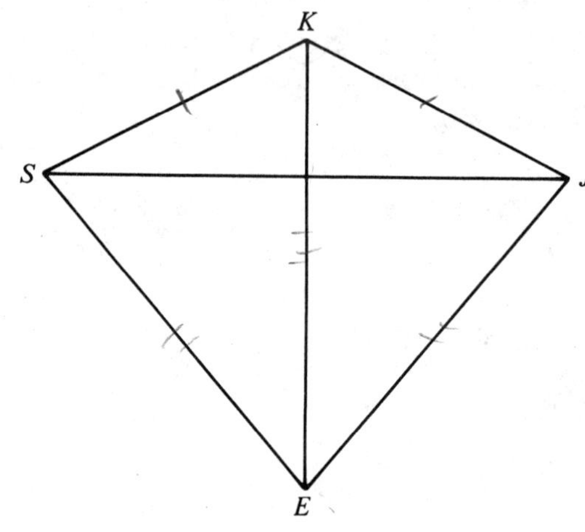

51. *Given*
$\overrightarrow{KA}$ midray $\angle MKR$
$\overrightarrow{KA} \perp \overline{MR}$

To Prove
$\triangle MAK \cong \triangle RAK$

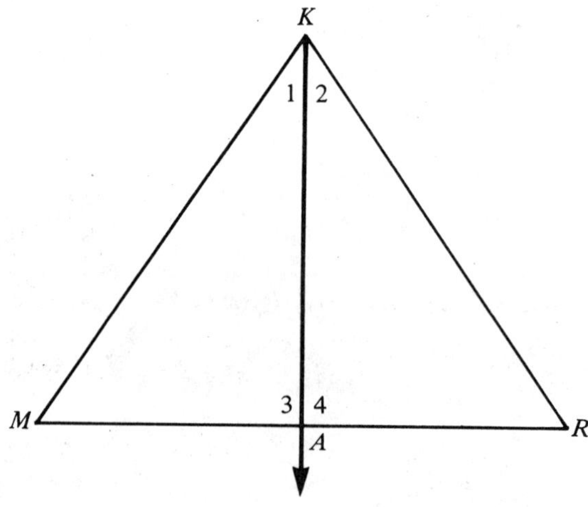

52. *Given*
$\overrightarrow{HL}$ bis $\angle PHE$
$\overrightarrow{LH}$ bis $\angle PLE$

To Prove
$\triangle HPL \cong \triangle HEL$

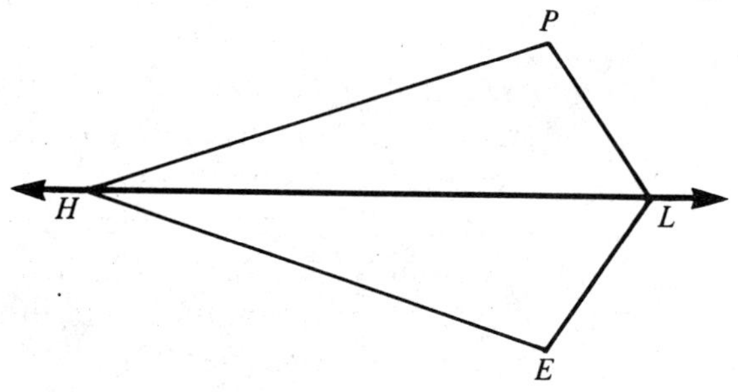

53. *Given*
$\overline{IU} \perp \overline{EC}$
$\overline{EL} \perp \overline{IC}$
$\overline{CL} \cong \overline{CU}$

To Prove
$\triangle ECL \cong \triangle ICU$

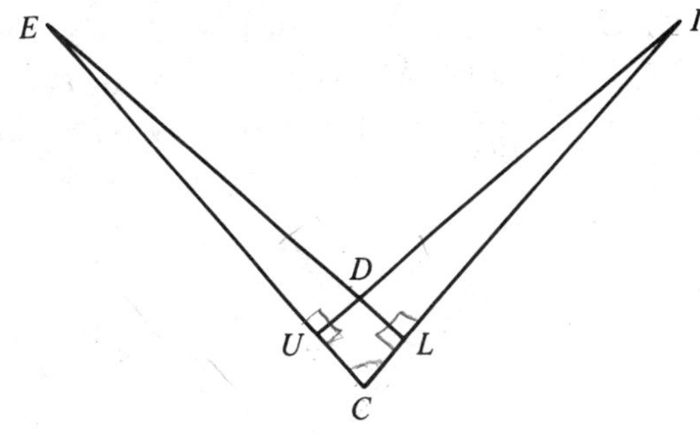

54. *Given*
$\measuredangle 1 \cong \measuredangle 4$
J midpt $\overline{ES}$
$\overline{EK} \cong \overline{SC}$

To Prove
$\triangle EJK \cong \triangle SJC$

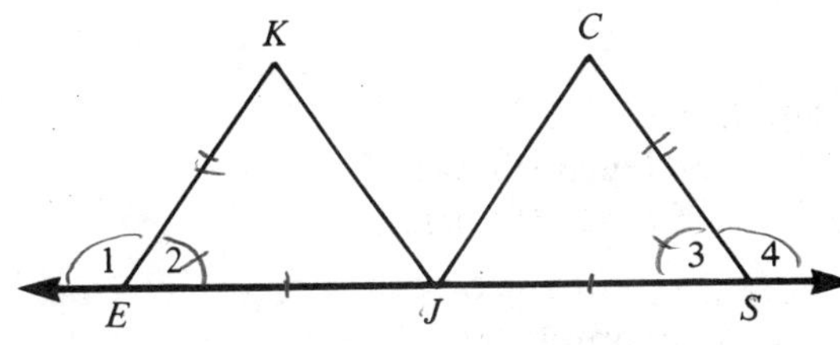

55. *Given*
$\measuredangle 1 \cong \measuredangle 4$
$\overline{AB} \cong \overline{DC}$
$\overline{FC} \cong \overline{EB}$

To Prove
$\triangle CFA \cong \triangle BED$

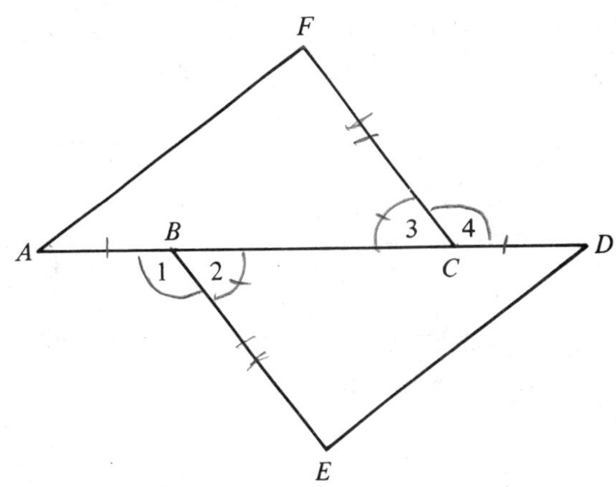

4.3
PROBLEM SOLVING WITH TRIANGLES

The theory of congruent triangles is very useful in mathematics and its applications. One possible use is in measuring inaccessible lengths. Recall the problem about the pyramid (Section 1.1) in which Thales wished to measure the height AC (Figure 4.15). One solution may be obtained by measuring $\measuredangle ABC$ and side $\overline{BC}$ (half of the pyramid's edge). Then, since $\angle C = 90°$, a triangle congruent to $\triangle ABC$ may be marked out on the ground (asa $\cong$ asa), and the side corresponding to $\overline{AC}$ may then be measured. Admittedly, a large piece of flat ground would be needed, and, in fact, it is unlikely that Thales used this method since there are more sophisticated ways to find the answer. Nonetheless, the underlying idea of finding the length indirectly is important. It is likely that you will meet this idea again in science and mathematics. The problem of measuring height AC goes beyond plane geometry since a pyramid is a three-dimensional figure. Still, the methods of plane geometry apply because the triangles of the three-dimensional figure are plane figures. (Chapter 10 is an introduction to three-dimensional, or solid, geometry.)

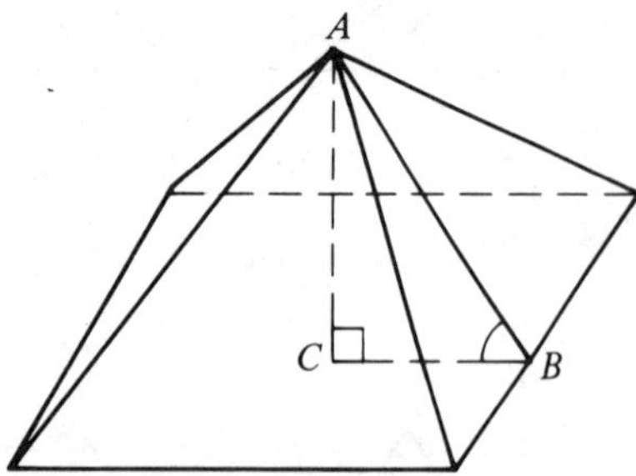

Figure 4.15

In geometry congruent triangles are helpful in proving facts about more complicated figures. This is done by dividing the figure to be analyzed into two or more congruent triangles as shown by the Roman numerals in Figure 4.16. Then, facts about the given figure may be derived using known facts about congruent triangles. This idea will be applied in Chapter 6.

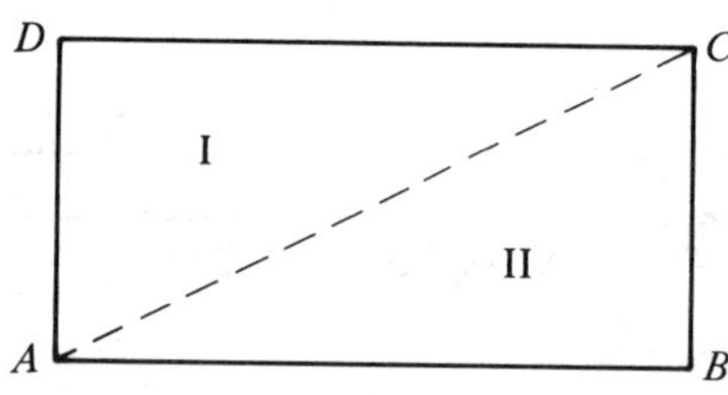

Figure 4.16

The purpose of this section is to provide practice in applying the theory of congruent triangles. We begin with a problem in which congruent triangles assist in finding the sizes of some angles.

EXAMPLE 1

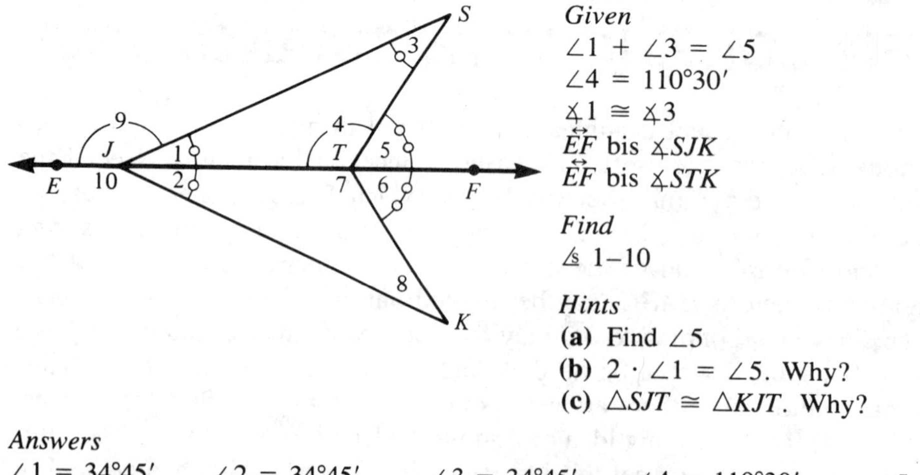

Given
$\angle 1 + \angle 3 = \angle 5$
$\angle 4 = 110°30'$
$\measuredangle 1 \cong \measuredangle 3$
$\overleftrightarrow{EF}$ bis $\measuredangle SJK$
$\overleftrightarrow{EF}$ bis $\measuredangle STK$

Find
$\measuredangle$s 1–10

Hints
(a) Find $\angle 5$
(b) $2 \cdot \angle 1 = \angle 5$. Why?
(c) $\triangle SJT \cong \triangle KJT$. Why?

Answers

$\angle 1 = 34°45'$	$\angle 2 = 34°45'$	$\angle 3 = 34°45'$	$\angle 4 = 110°30'$	$\angle 5 = 69°30'$
$\angle 6 = 69°30'$	$\angle 7 = 110°30'$	$\angle 8 = 34°45'$	$\angle 9 = 145°15'$	$\angle 10 = 145°15'$

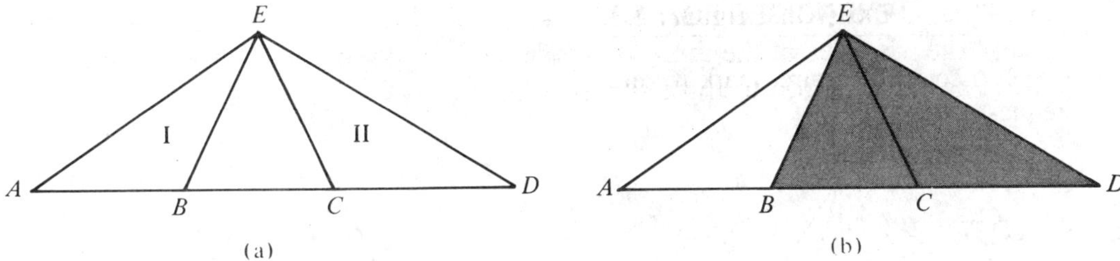

Figure 4.17 (a) Identify $\triangle ABE$ and $\triangle DCE$ and number them. (b) Identify $\triangle DBE$ and $\triangle ACE$ and shade one of them.

Geometric figures often contain several triangles. Figure 4.17 shows two ways to identify pairs of triangles that have the same shape, making them candidates for congruence. Another approach is to draw the two triangles separately as in Figure 4.18. This is particularly useful when the triangles "overlap." You may wish to use it when studying the next example.

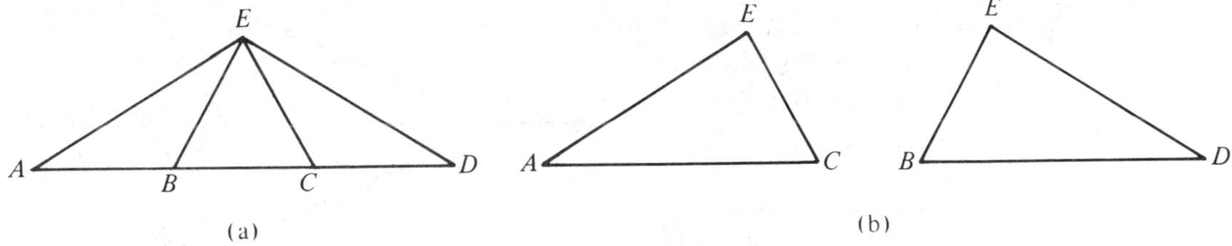

Figure 4.18 (a) Given figure. (b) Identify $\triangle ACE$ and $\triangle DBE$ and draw them separately.

EXAMPLE 2 State the facts implied by the marks in the given figure.

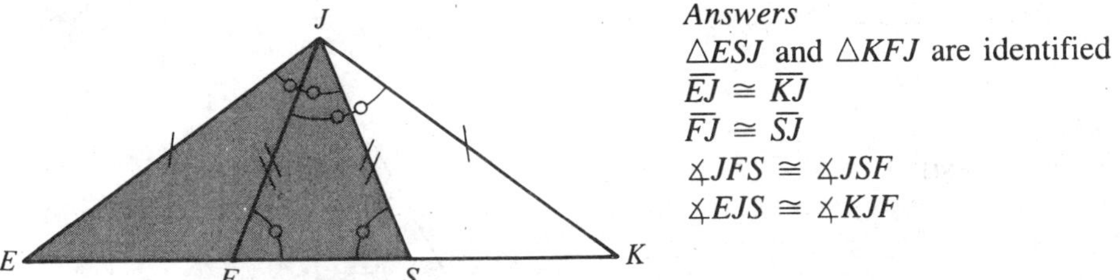

Answers

$\triangle ESJ$ and $\triangle KFJ$ are identified

$\overline{EJ} \cong \overline{KJ}$

$\overline{FJ} \cong \overline{SJ}$

$\measuredangle JFS \cong \measuredangle JSF$

$\measuredangle EJS \cong \measuredangle KJF$

Our concluding example illustrates a way to prove that two line segments are congruent by showing that they are corresponding parts of two congruent triangles. The shading indicates one choice of the two triangles to be used.

EXAMPLE 3

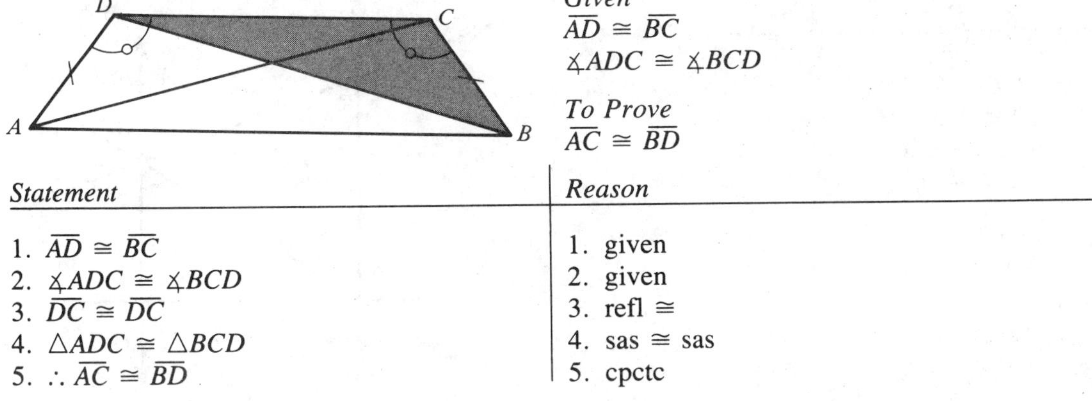

Given

$\overline{AD} \cong \overline{BC}$

$\measuredangle ADC \cong \measuredangle BCD$

To Prove

$\overline{AC} \cong \overline{BD}$

Statement	*Reason*
1. $\overline{AD} \cong \overline{BC}$	1. given
2. $\measuredangle ADC \cong \measuredangle BCD$	2. given
3. $\overline{DC} \cong \overline{DC}$	3. refl $\cong$
4. $\triangle ADC \cong \triangle BCD$	4. sas $\cong$ sas
5. $\therefore \overline{AC} \cong \overline{BD}$	5. cpctc

EXERCISES FOR 4.3

In exercises 1–6 copy the figure, mark it, and find the requested measures.

1. *Given*

$\measuredangle 1 \cong \measuredangle 2$
$\overrightarrow{CE}$ bis $\measuredangle DCF$
$\angle ABD = 117°$
$\angle 1 + \angle 2 + \angle 5 = 180°$

Find

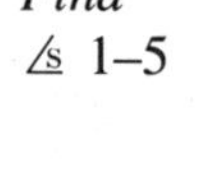

$\measuredangle$s 1–5

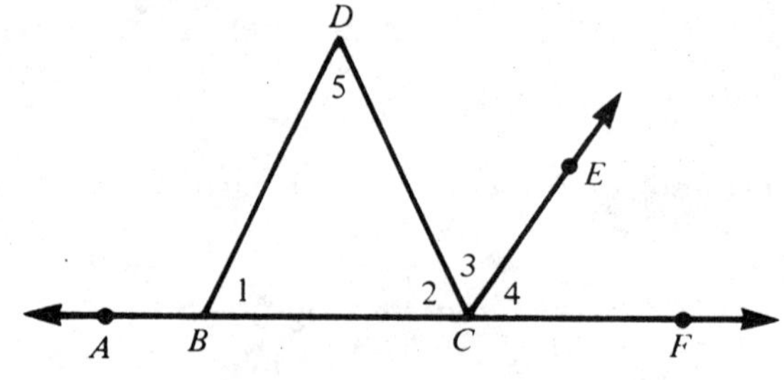

2. *Given*

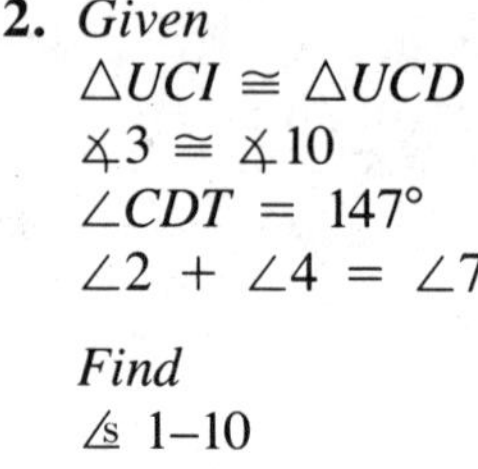

$\triangle UCI \cong \triangle UCD$
$\measuredangle 3 \cong \measuredangle 10$
$\angle CDT = 147°$
$\angle 2 + \angle 4 = \angle 7$

Find

$\measuredangle$s 1–10

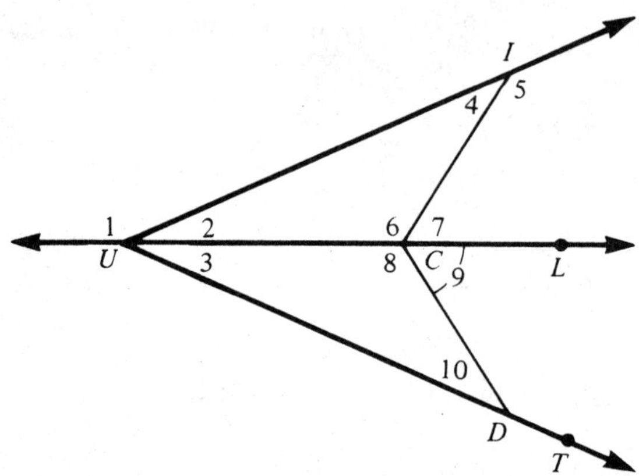

3. *Given*

$\overline{SR} \perp \overline{EJ}$
$\overline{SK}$ bis $\measuredangle ESR$
$\measuredangle 3$ comp $\measuredangle 8$
$\angle 1 + \angle 5 + \angle 6 = 180°$
$\angle SKR = 74°$
$\angle 2 + \angle 7 = \angle 6$
$\triangle EKS \cong \triangle JTS$

Find

$\measuredangle$s 1–10

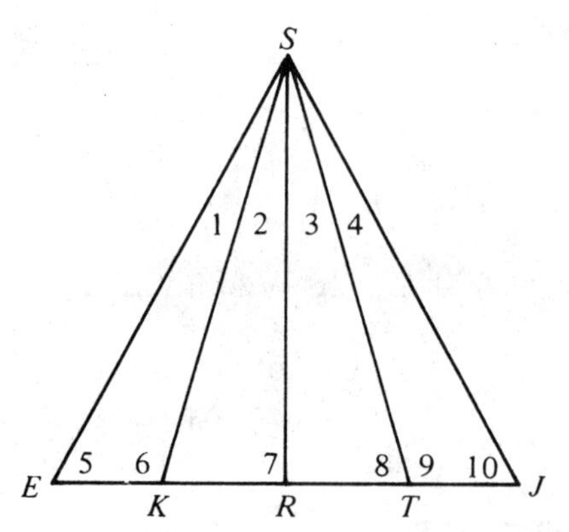

4. *Given*

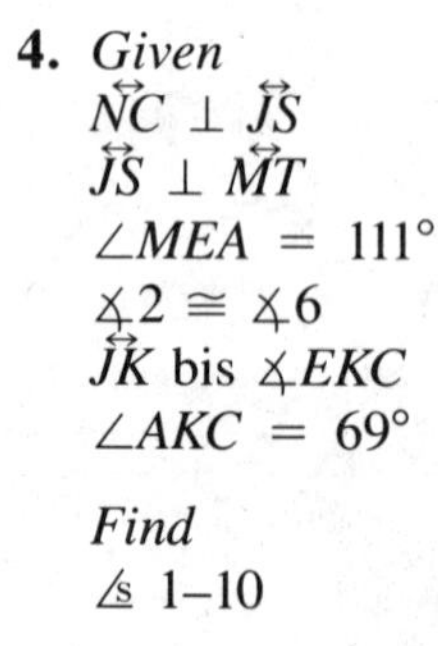

$\overleftrightarrow{NC} \perp \overleftrightarrow{JS}$
$\overleftrightarrow{JS} \perp \overleftrightarrow{MT}$
$\angle MEA = 111°$
$\measuredangle 2 \cong \measuredangle 6$
$\overleftrightarrow{JK}$ bis $\measuredangle EKC$
$\angle AKC = 69°$

Find

$\measuredangle$s 1–10

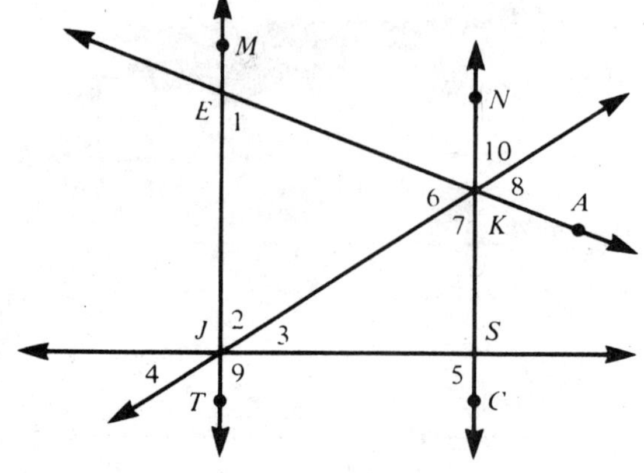

5. *Given*

$\overline{EC}$ bis $\measuredangle FCD$
$\measuredangle 2 \cong \measuredangle 3$
$\angle BFC = 41°$
$\measuredangle 1$ supp $\measuredangle 10$
$\angle 2 + \angle 3 + \angle 9 = 180°$
$\angle 6 = \angle 8 + \angle 4$

Find

$\measuredangle$s 1–10

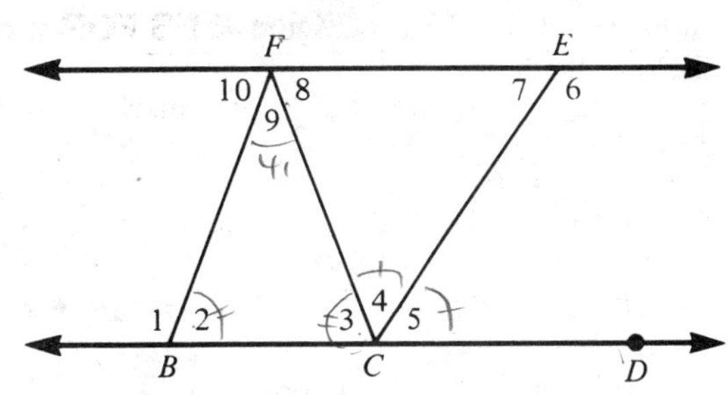

6. *Given*

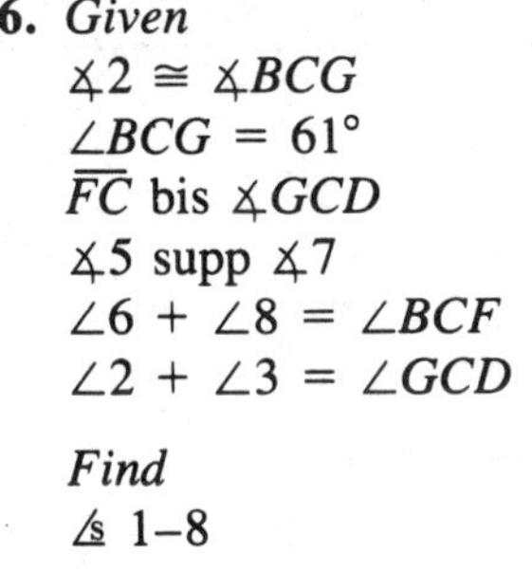

$\measuredangle 2 \cong \measuredangle BCG$
$\angle BCG = 61°$
$\overline{FC}$ bis $\measuredangle GCD$
$\measuredangle 5$ supp $\measuredangle 7$
$\angle 6 + \angle 8 = \angle BCF$
$\angle 2 + \angle 3 = \angle GCD$

Find

$\measuredangle$s 1–8

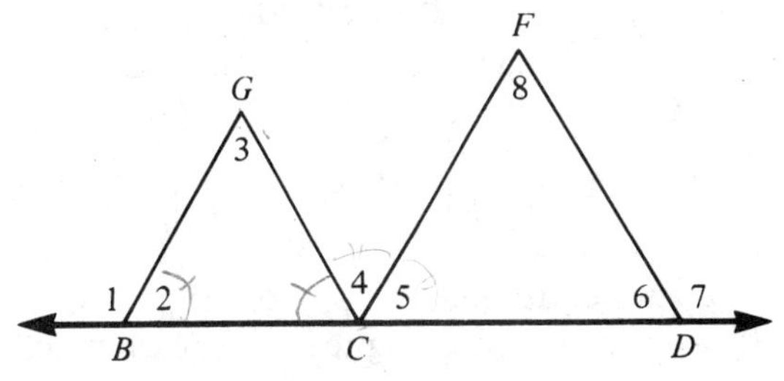

In exercises 7–10, (a) name the triangles being considered, (b) write the congruences given by the marks, (c) state whether or not the triangles are congruent, and (d) if they are congruent, write sss ≅ sss, sas ≅ sas, or asa ≅ asa as appropriate.

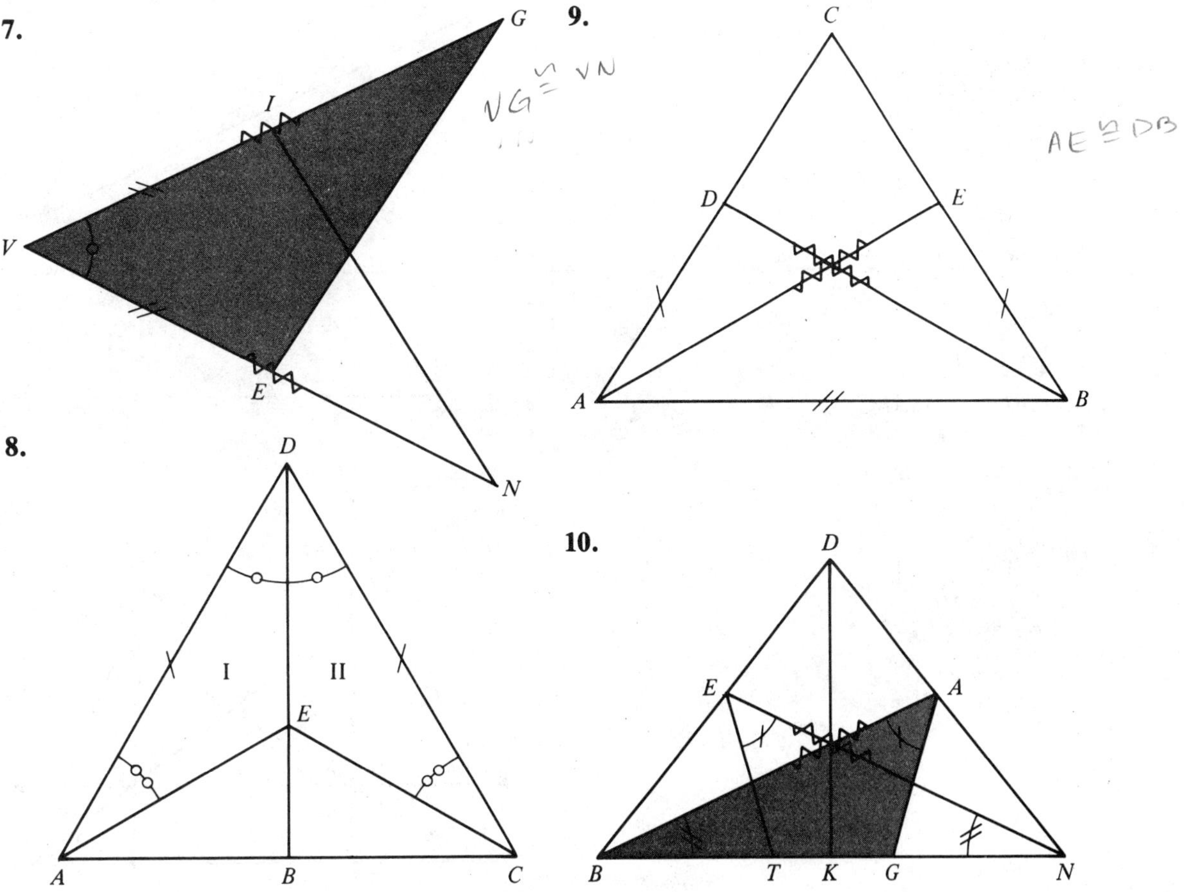

In exercises 11–15 use Figure 4.19 to answer the questions.

11. If $\overline{FC} \perp \overline{AE}$ and $\overline{AC} \cong \overline{EC}$, is $\triangle ACF \cong \triangle ECF$? Why?

12. If $\overline{FC} \perp \overline{AE}$ and $\overline{FC}$ bisects $\measuredangle AFE$, is $\triangle ACF \cong \triangle ECF$? Why?

13. If $\measuredangle 7 \cong \measuredangle 10$ and $\overline{BC} \cong \overline{DC}$, is $\triangle BCF \cong \triangle DCF$? Why?

14. If $\overline{AB} \cong \overline{ED}$, $\measuredangle 10 \cong \measuredangle 7$ and $\overline{BF} \cong \overline{DF}$, is $\triangle ADF \cong \triangle EBF$? Why?

15. If $\measuredangle 1 \cong \measuredangle 4$, $\overline{FC} \perp \overline{AE}$, $\overline{FB}$ bisects $\measuredangle AFC$ and $\overline{FD}$ bisects $\measuredangle EFC$, is $\triangle BCF \cong \triangle DCF$? Why?

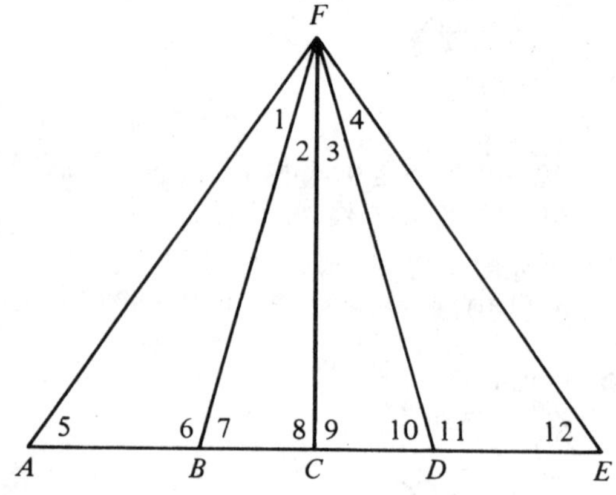

Figure 4.19

In exercises 16 and 17 copy the figure, mark it, and supply the missing reasons in each proof.

16. *Given*
$\overline{AD} \cong \overline{AB}$
$\measuredangle 1 \cong \measuredangle 2$

To Prove
$\overline{DC} \cong \overline{BC}$

Statement	*Reason*
1. $\overline{AD} \cong \overline{AB}$	1. ?
2. $\measuredangle 1 \cong \measuredangle 2$	2. ?
3. $\overline{AC} \cong \overline{AC}$	3. ?
4. $\triangle ADC \cong \triangle ABC$	4. ?
5. $\therefore \overline{DC} \cong \overline{BC}$	5. ?

17. *Given*
$\overline{KE} \cong \overline{SJ}$
$\overline{KJ} \cong \overline{SE}$

To Prove
$\measuredangle K \cong \measuredangle S$

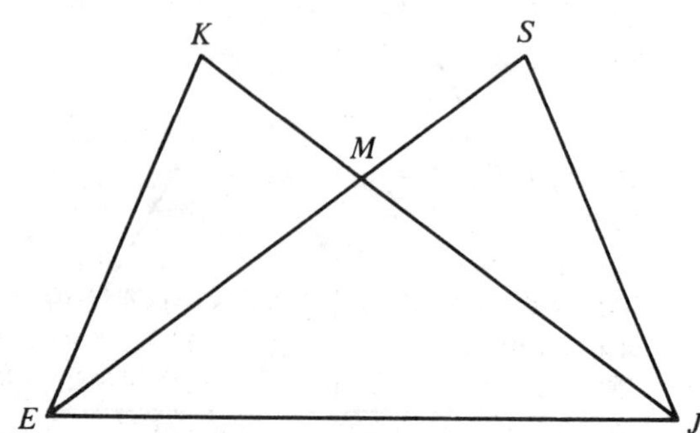

Statement	*Reason*
1. $\overline{KE} \cong \overline{SJ}$	1. ?
2. $\overline{KJ} \cong \overline{SE}$	2. ?
3. $\overline{EJ} \cong \overline{EJ}$	3. ?
4. $\triangle EJK \cong \triangle JES$	4. ?
5. $\therefore \measuredangle K \cong \measuredangle S$	5. ?

In exercises 18–20 copy the figure, mark it, and rearrange the statements into a correct order for a proof.

18. *Given*
$\overline{AC} \cong \overline{DB}$
$\measuredangle 1 \cong \measuredangle 4$
$\measuredangle A \cong \measuredangle D$

To Prove
$\measuredangle AEC \cong \measuredangle DEB$

(a) $\measuredangle 1 \cong \measuredangle 4$
(b) $\measuredangle 1$ and $\measuredangle 2$ lin pr
(c) $\overline{AC} \cong \overline{DB}$
(d) $\measuredangle 3 \cong \measuredangle 2$
(e) $\measuredangle 3$ supp $\measuredangle 4$
(f) $\measuredangle AEC \cong \measuredangle DEB$
(g) $\measuredangle A \cong \measuredangle D$
(h) $\measuredangle 3$ and $\measuredangle 4$ lin pr
(i) $\measuredangle 2$ supp $\measuredangle 1$
(j) $\triangle ACE \cong \triangle DBE$

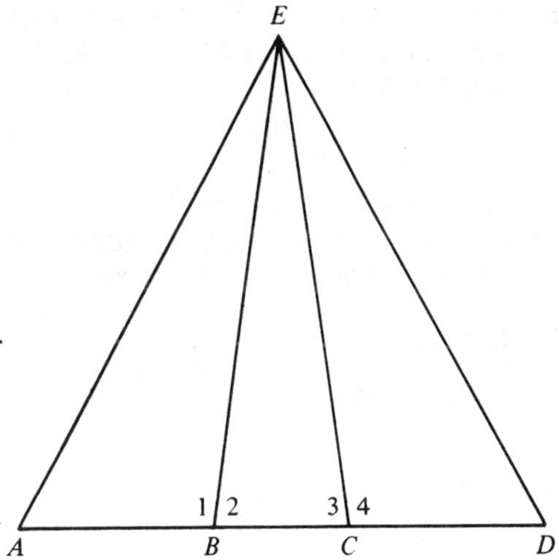

19. *Given*
$\overline{ES} \cong \overline{EJ}$
$\overline{SC} \cong \overline{JK}$

To Prove
$\overline{KS} \cong \overline{CJ}$

(a) $\overline{SC} \cong \overline{JK}$
(b) $EC = ES + SC$
(c) $\measuredangle E \cong \measuredangle E$
(d) $\overline{ES} \cong \overline{EJ}$
(e) $SC = JK$
(f) $\overline{EC} \cong \overline{EK}$
(g) $EJ + JK = EK$
(h) $\overline{KS} \cong \overline{CJ}$
(i) $ES = EJ$
(j) $ES + SC = EJ + JK$
(k) $EC = EK$
(l) $\triangle KSE \cong \triangle CJE$
(m) $\overline{EK} \cong \overline{EC}$

20. *Given*
$\measuredangle 1 \cong \measuredangle 4$
$\measuredangle 2 \cong \measuredangle 3$

To Prove
$\measuredangle D \cong \measuredangle C$

(a) $\angle 1 + \angle 2 = \angle 3 + \angle 4$
(b) $\measuredangle 1 \cong \measuredangle 4$
(c) $\measuredangle D \cong \measuredangle C$
(d) $\angle DAB = \angle 1 + \angle 2$
(e) $\measuredangle 2 \cong \measuredangle 3$
(f) $\angle DAB = \angle CBA$
(g) $\triangle BAD \cong \triangle ABC$
(h) $\angle 1 = \angle 4$
(i) $\angle 3 + \angle 4 = \angle CBA$
(j) $\measuredangle DAB \cong \measuredangle CBA$
(k) $\angle 2 = \angle 3$
(l) $\overline{AB} \cong \overline{AB}$
(m) $\measuredangle 3 \cong \measuredangle 2$

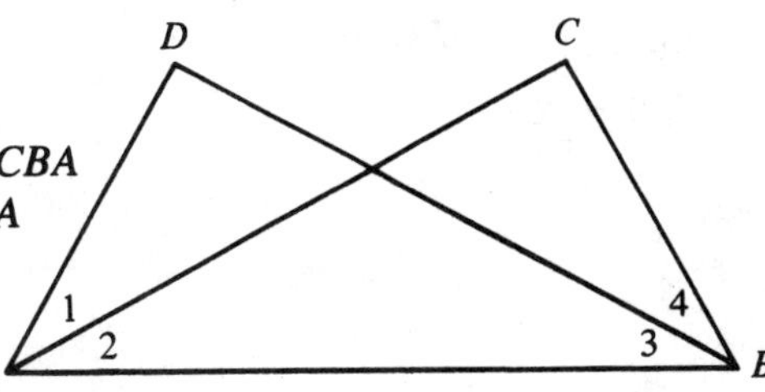

In exercises 21–30 copy the figure, the hypothesis, and the conclusion. Mark the figure and write a proof.

21. *Given*
$\overline{JC} \perp \overline{CR}$
$\overline{ER} \perp \overline{CR}$
I midpt $\overline{CR}$

To Prove
$\overline{ER} \cong \overline{JC}$

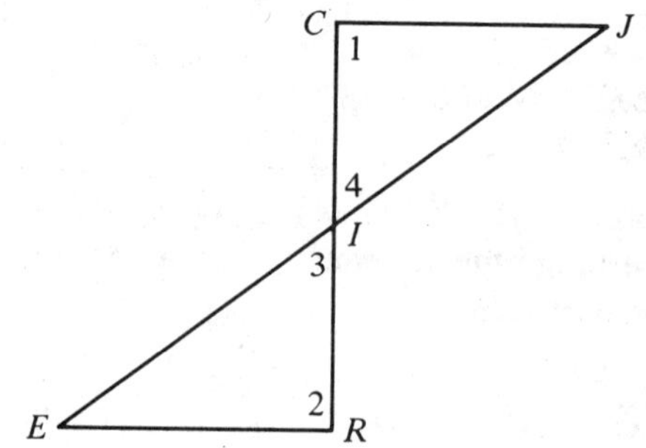

22. *Given*
$\overline{AD} \cong \overline{BD}$
$\measuredangle 1 \cong \measuredangle 6$

To Prove
$\overline{ED} \cong \overline{CD}$

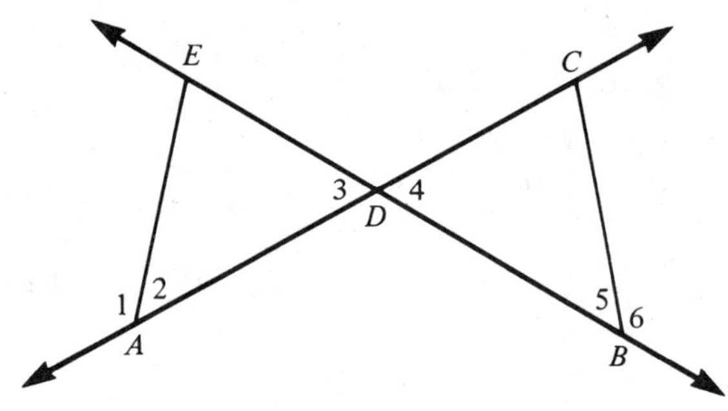

23. *Given*
$\overline{IE}$ bis $\measuredangle KIT$
$\overline{IE}$ bis $\measuredangle KET$

To Prove
$\measuredangle K \cong \measuredangle T$

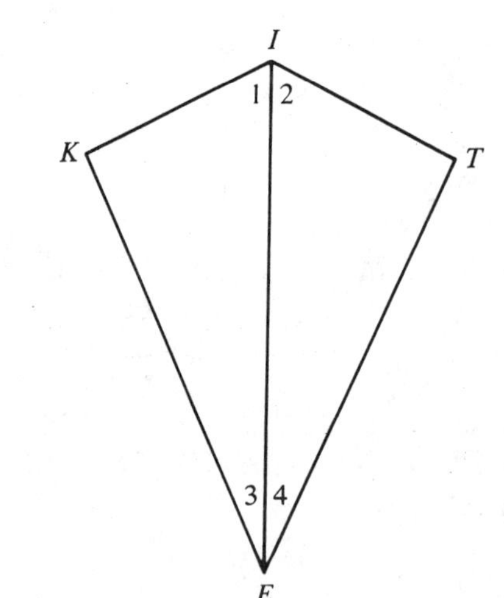

24. *Given*
$\overline{AB} \perp \overline{BC}$
$\overline{DC} \perp \overline{BC}$
$\measuredangle ACB \cong \measuredangle DBC$

To Prove
$\overline{AB} \cong \overline{DC}$

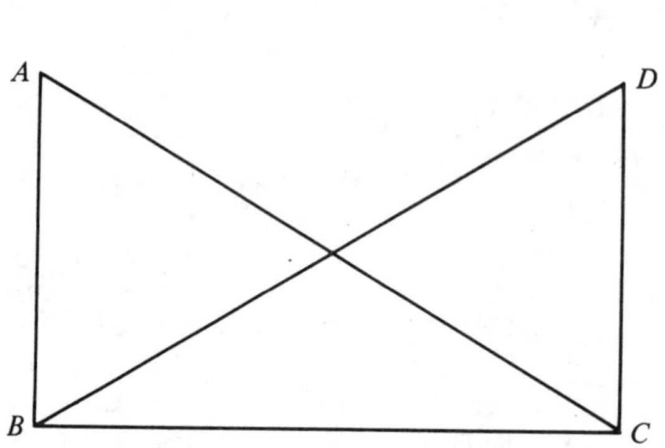

In exercises 25–27 refer to Figure 4.20.

25. *Given*
$\triangle EJS$ isos ($\overline{EJ}$ base)
$\measuredangle 8 \cong \measuredangle 5$

To Prove
$\overline{SK} \cong \overline{ST}$

26. *Given*
$\overline{ET}$ bis $\measuredangle SEJ$
$\overline{JK}$ bis $\measuredangle SJE$
$\measuredangle 5 \cong \measuredangle 8$

To Prove
$\overline{ET} \cong \overline{JK}$

27. *Given*
$\measuredangle 2 \cong \measuredangle 4$
$\overline{SK} \cong \overline{ST}$

To Prove
$\measuredangle 8 \cong \measuredangle 5$

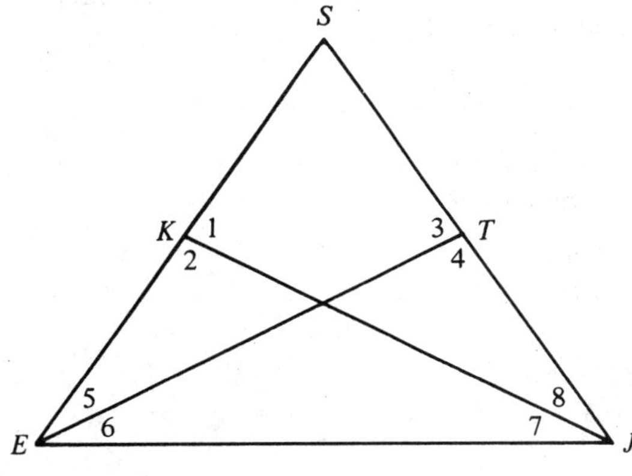

Figure 4.20

28. *Given*
$\overline{EU} \cong \overline{LC}$
$\measuredangle 1 \cong \measuredangle 4$
$\overline{CD} \cong \overline{UI}$

To Prove
$\measuredangle D \cong \measuredangle I$

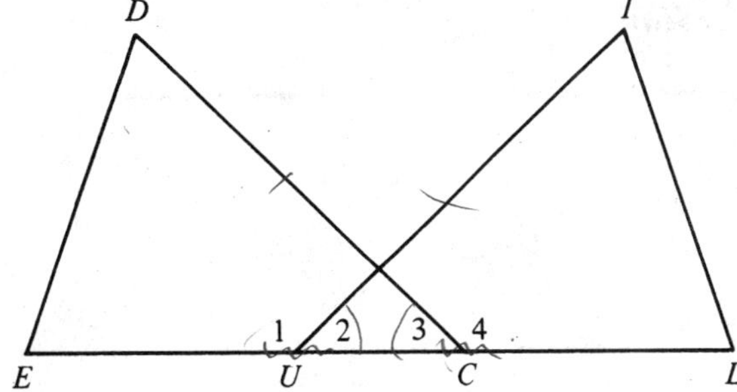

29. *Given*
S midpt $\overline{ET}$
L midpt $\overline{EA}$
$\overline{SH} \cong \overline{LA}$
H midpt $\overline{TA}$
$\overline{HA} \cong \overline{SL}$

To Prove
$\measuredangle 1 \cong \measuredangle 2$

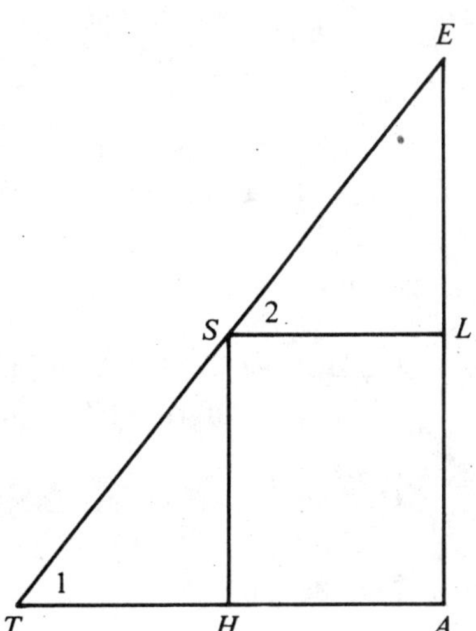

30. *Given*
$\triangle AOT$ isos ($\overline{OT}$ base)
$\overline{AO}$ bis $\measuredangle SAT$
$\overline{AT}$ bis $\measuredangle PAO$
$\overline{SA} \cong \overline{PA}$

To Prove
$\overline{SO} \cong \overline{PT}$

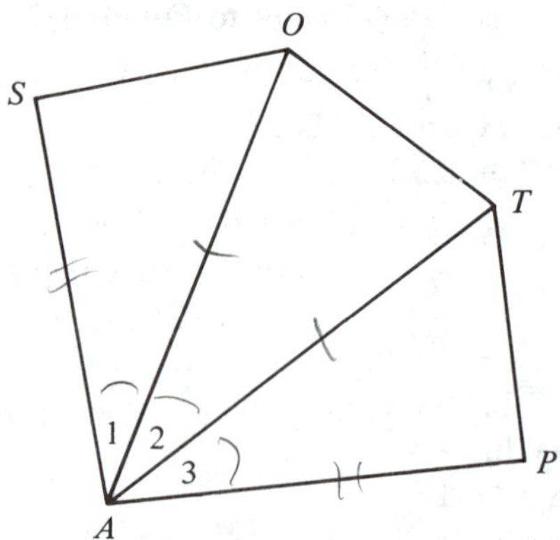

4.4
MORE ABOUT PROOFS

Certain fundamental ideas occur frequently in geometric proofs. Once these ideas are understood, we may abbreviate them to shorten proofs. We illustrate such abbreviations with the concept of bisection.

EXAMPLE 1

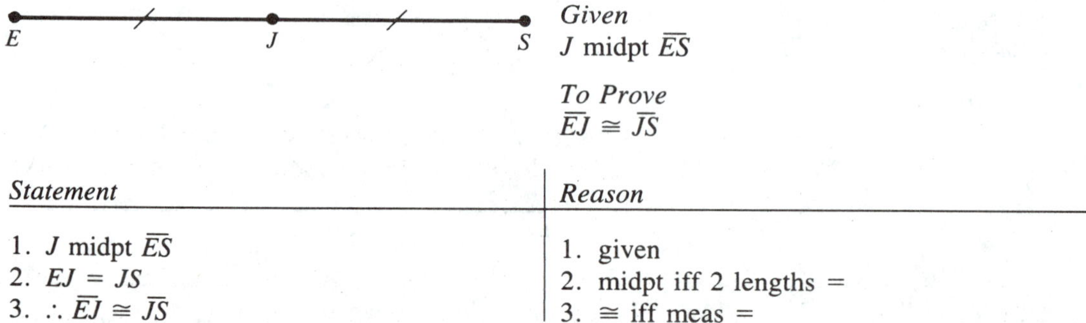

Given
J midpt $\overline{ES}$

To Prove
$\overline{EJ} \cong \overline{JS}$

Statement	*Reason*
1. J midpt $\overline{ES}$	1. given
2. $EJ = JS$	2. midpt iff 2 lengths =
3. $\therefore \overline{EJ} \cong \overline{JS}$	3. ≅ iff meas =

A similar example may be written involving an angle and its midray. In both cases it seems clear that bisection means "to divide into two congruent parts." We therefore adopt the following alternate definitions for *midpoint* and *bisector*.

Definition 4.10 A point is the *midpoint* of a line segment iff it divides it into two congruent line segments (midpt ÷ seg into 2 ≅ segs).

Definition 4.11 A line, half line, ray, or line segment is a *bisector* of a line segment iff it divides it into two congruent line segments (bis ÷ seg into 2 ≅ segs).

Definition 4.12 A ray or the line it determines is a *bisector* of an angle iff it divides it into two congruent angles (bis ÷ $\measuredangle$ into 2 ≅ $\measuredangle$s).

The use of these definitions not only unifies our ideas about bisection but also eliminates a step (e.g., statement 2, Example 1) in proofs.

Another approach that abbreviates proofs involves showing that two line segments or two angles are congruent using the addition, subtraction, multiplication, or division properties of equals (Axioms 11–14). This method is used in Example 2, after which we show how the proof may be shortened.

EXAMPLE 2

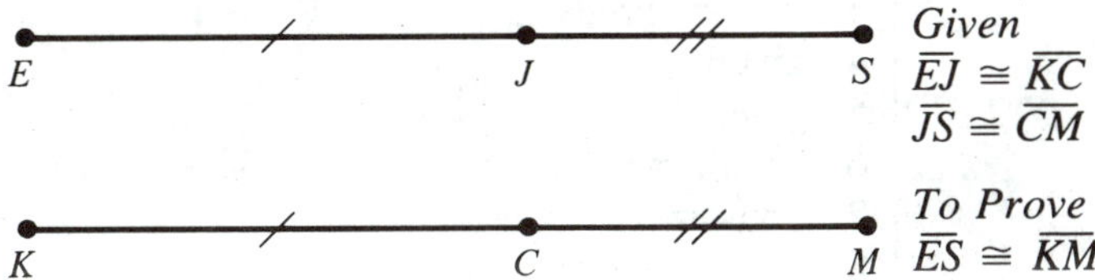

Given
$\overline{EJ} \cong \overline{KC}$
$\overline{JS} \cong \overline{CM}$

To Prove
$\overline{ES} \cong \overline{KM}$

Statement	*Reason*
1. $\overline{EJ} \cong \overline{KC}$	1. given
2. $EJ = KC$	2. ≅ iff meas =
3. $\overline{JS} \cong \overline{CM}$	3. given
4. $JS = CM$	4. ≅ iff meas =
5. $EJ + JS = KC + CM$	5. = + =, sums =
6. $ES = EJ + JS$ $KC + CM = KM$	6. whole = sum parts
7. $ES = KM$	7. trans =
8. $\therefore \overline{ES} \cong \overline{KM}$	8. ≅ iff meas =

Going from congruence to measure and back, as in Example 2, also occurs in proving angles congruent by addition. In both cases, proofs may be shortened by using Theorems 16 and 17.

Theorem 16 *Addition Property of Congruence.* If congruent line segments (or angles) are "added" to congruent line segments (or angles), the "sums" are congruent (≅ + ≅, sums ≅).

Example 2 proves the theorem for line segments; the proof for angles is similar.

The subtraction property of equals can be applied more briefly by the use of Theorem 17. The proof is left as an exercise.

Theorem 17 *Subtraction Property of Congruence.* If congruent line segments (or angles) are "subtracted" from congruent line segments (or angles), the "differences" are congruent (≅ − ≅, diff ≅).

The multiplication and division properties of equals have counterparts for congruence. The proof in Example 3 illustrates this idea.

EXAMPLE 3

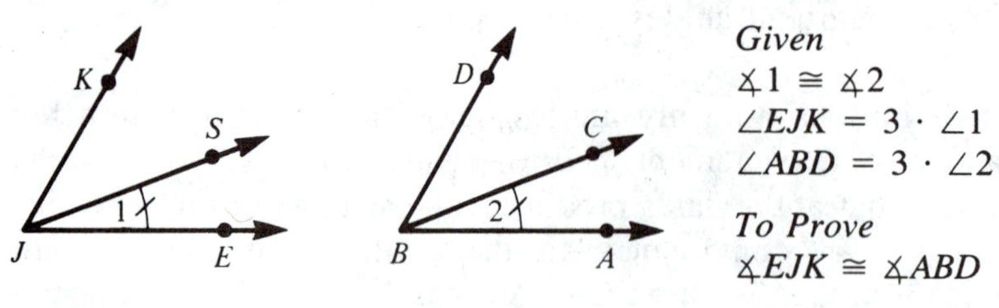

Given
$\measuredangle 1 \cong \measuredangle 2$
$\angle EJK = 3 \cdot \angle 1$
$\angle ABD = 3 \cdot \angle 2$

To Prove
$\measuredangle EJK \cong \measuredangle ABD$

Statement	*Reason*
1. $\measuredangle 1 \cong \measuredangle 2$	1. given
2. $\angle 1 = \angle 2$	2. $\cong$ iff meas =
3. $3 \cdot \angle 1 = 3 \cdot \angle 2$	3. = · =, prod =
4. $\angle EJK = 3 \cdot \angle 1$	4. given
5. $\angle ABD = 3 \cdot \angle 2$	5. given
6. $3 \cdot \angle 2 = \angle ABD$	6. symm =
7. $\angle EJK = \angle ABD$	7. trans =
8. $\therefore \measuredangle EJK \cong \measuredangle ABD$	8. $\cong$ iff meas =

A proof similar to that in Example 3 may be written for line segment congruence. Such examples suggest Theorems 18 and 19.

Theorem 18 *Multiplication Property of Congruence.* If congruent line segments (or angles) are "multiplied" by a positive number, the "products" are congruent (≅ · pos, prod ≅).

Theorem 19 *Division Property of Congruence.* If congruent line segments (or angles) are "divided" by a positive number, the "quotients" are congruent (≅ ÷ pos, quot ≅).

An important special case of Theorem 19 occurs when the divisor is 2, or equivalently when two congruent line segments (or angles) are known to be bisected. We will abbreviate this case "$\frac{1}{2}$s of ≅ are ≅."

A final shortcut refers to Postulates 4 and 7 concerning line segments and angles (whole = sum parts). These may be combined as follows:

Postulates 4 and 7 (Alternate) The whole of a line segment or angle is congruent to the "sum" of its parts (whole ≅ sum parts).

We illustrate the shortcuts for writing proofs by redoing Example 2:

EXAMPLE 4

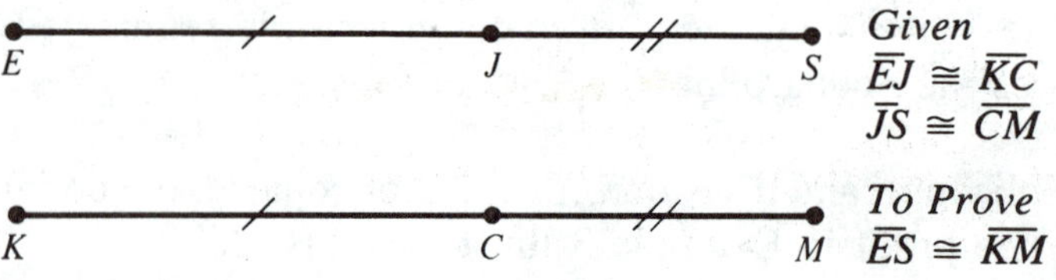

Given
$\overline{EJ} \cong \overline{KC}$
$\overline{JS} \cong \overline{CM}$

To Prove
$\overline{ES} \cong \overline{KM}$

Statement	*Reason*
1. $\overline{EJ} \cong \overline{KC}$	1. given
2. $\overline{JS} \cong \overline{CM}$	2. given
3. $\overline{EJ} + \overline{JS} \cong \overline{KC} + \overline{CM}$	3. $\cong + \cong$, sums $\cong$
4. $\overline{ES} \cong \overline{EJ} + \overline{JS}$ $\overline{KC} + \overline{CM} \cong \overline{KM}$	4. whole $\cong$ sum parts
5. $\therefore \overline{ES} \cong \overline{KM}$	5. trans $\cong$

Our development so far has established a number of ways to prove two line segments or two angles congruent. It is useful to list these here, particularly since it is first necessary to prove line segments and angles congruent before proving two triangles congruent.

Ways to prove two line segments congruent:

1. Equal lengths
2. Transitive property of congruence
3. Midpoint of a line segment
4. Bisector of a line segment
5. Addition or subtraction of congruences
6. Multiplication or division of congruence by a positive number
7. Corresponding parts of congruent triangles (cpctc)

Ways to prove two angles congruent:

1. Equal measures
2. Transitive property of congruence
3. Angle bisector
4. Addition or subtraction of congruences
5. Multiplication or division of congruence by a positive number
6. Vertical angles
7. Right angles
8. Complements of the same or congruent angles
9. Supplements of the same or congruent angles
10. Corresponding parts of congruent triangles (cpctc)

Example 5 further demonstrates how the theorems of this section streamline a typical geometric proof.

EXAMPLE 5

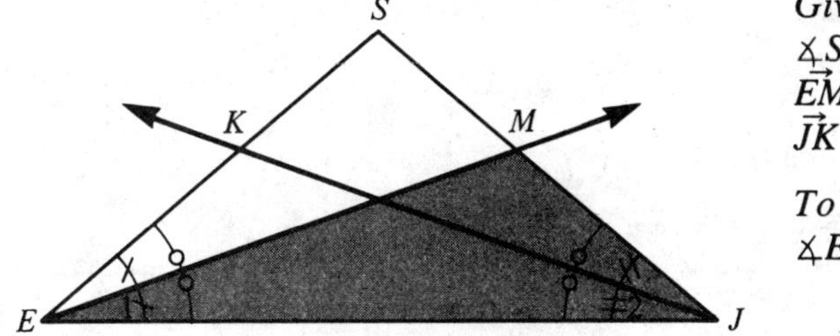

Given
$\measuredangle SEJ \cong \measuredangle SJE$
$\overrightarrow{EM}$ bis $\measuredangle SEJ$
$\overrightarrow{JK}$ bis $\measuredangle SJE$

To Prove
$\measuredangle EKJ \cong \measuredangle JME$

Statement	*Reason*
1. $\measuredangle SEJ \cong \measuredangle SJE$	1. given
2. $\overrightarrow{EM}$ bis $\measuredangle SEJ$	2. given
3. $\measuredangle SEM \cong \measuredangle 1$	3. bis $\div$ $\measuredangle$ into 2 $\cong$ $\measuredangle$s
4. $\overrightarrow{JK}$ bis $\measuredangle SJE$	4. given
5. $\measuredangle SJK \cong \measuredangle 2$	5. bis $\div$ $\measuredangle$ into 2 $\cong$ $\measuredangle$s
6. $\measuredangle 2 \cong \measuredangle 1$	6. $\frac{1}{2}$s of $\cong$ are $\cong$
7. $\overline{EJ} \cong \overline{EJ}$	7. refl $\cong$
8. $\triangle KEJ \cong \triangle MJE$	8. asa $\cong$ asa
9. $\therefore \measuredangle EKJ \cong \measuredangle JME$	9. cpctc

EXERCISES FOR 4.4

In exercises 1–10 use the figures and "new" definitions, postulates, and theorems to answer the questions.

In exercises 1–5 refer to Figure 4.21.

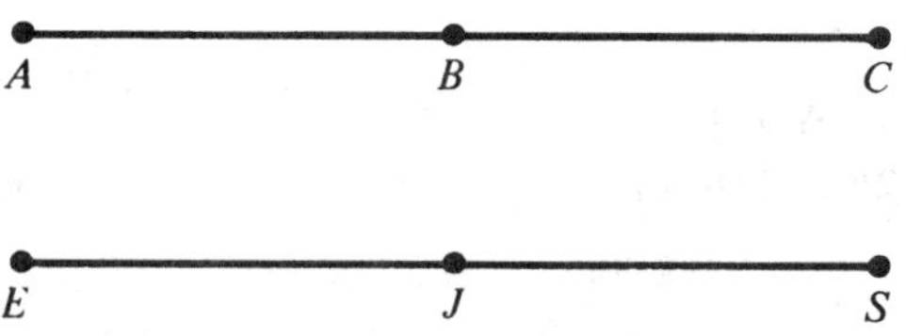

Figure 4.21

1. If $\overline{AB} \cong \overline{EJ}$ and $\overline{BC} \cong \overline{JS}$, why is $\overline{AB} + \overline{BC} \cong \overline{EJ} + \overline{JS}$?
2. If $\overline{AC} \cong \overline{ES}$ and $\overline{BC} \cong \overline{JS}$, why is $\overline{AC} - \overline{BC} \cong \overline{ES} - \overline{JS}$?
3. Why is $\overline{ES} \cong \overline{EJ} + \overline{JS}$?
4. If B is the midpoint of $\overline{AC}$, why is $\overline{AB} \cong \overline{BC}$?
5. If $\overline{AC} \cong \overline{ES}$ and B is the midpoint of $\overline{AC}$ and J is the midpoint of $\overline{ES}$, why is $\overline{BC} \cong \overline{EJ}$?

In exercises 6–10 refer to Figure 4.22.

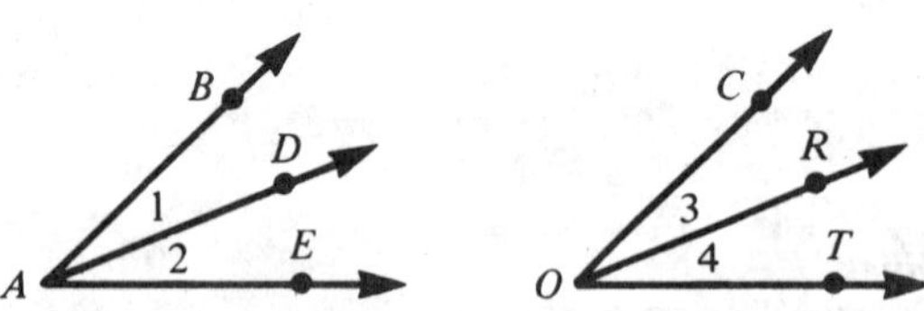

Figure 4.22

6. Why is $\measuredangle BAE \cong \measuredangle BAD + \measuredangle DAE$?
7. If $\overrightarrow{AD}$ bisects $\measuredangle BAE$, why is $\measuredangle BAD \cong \measuredangle DAE$?
8. If $\measuredangle 1 \cong \measuredangle 3$ and $\measuredangle 2 \cong \measuredangle 4$, why is $\measuredangle 1 + \measuredangle 2 \cong \measuredangle 3 + \measuredangle 4$?
9. If $\overrightarrow{AD}$ bisects $\measuredangle BAE$ and $\overrightarrow{OR}$ bisects $\measuredangle COT$ and $\measuredangle 1 \cong \measuredangle 3$, why is $\measuredangle BAE \cong \measuredangle COT$?
10. If $\measuredangle BAE \cong \measuredangle COT$, $\overrightarrow{AD}$ is the midray of $\measuredangle BAE$, and $\overrightarrow{OR}$ is the midray of $\measuredangle COT$, why is $\measuredangle 2 \cong \measuredangle 3$?

In exercises 11–14 copy the figure, mark it, and supply the missing reasons in each proof. Note that exercises 11 and 13 are done *without* the new shortcuts and that exercises 12 and 14 (the same problems) use the new shortcuts.

In exercises 11 and 12 refer to Figure 4.23.

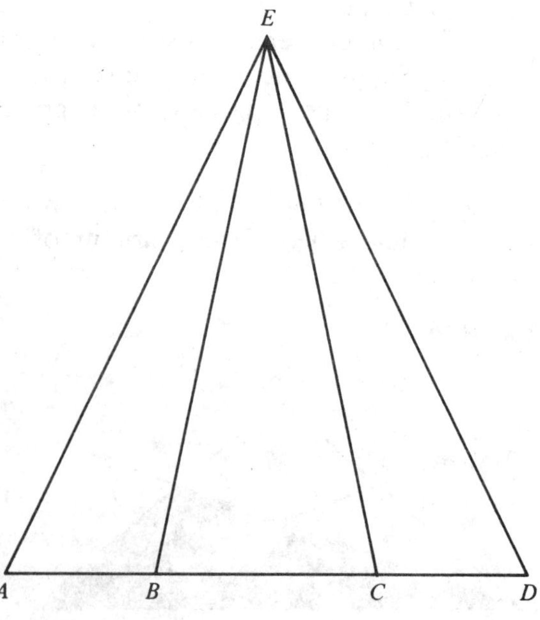

Figure 4.23

11. *Given*
$\overline{AB} \cong \overline{DC}$
$\triangle ADE$ isos ($\overline{AD}$ base)
$\triangle BCE$ isos ($\overline{BC}$ base)

To Prove
$\measuredangle AEC \cong \measuredangle DEB$

Statement	*Reason*
1. $\overline{AB} \cong \overline{DC}$	1. ?
2. $AB = DC$	2. ?
3. $\overline{BC} \cong \overline{BC}$	3. ?
4. $BC = BC$	4. ?
5. $AB + BC = DC + BC$	5. ?
6. $AC = AB + BC$	6. ?
7. $DC + BC = DB$	7. ?
8. $AC = DB$	8. ?
9. $\overline{AC} \cong \overline{DB}$	9. ?
10. $\triangle ADE$ isos ($\overline{AD}$ base)	10. ?
11. $\overline{AE} \cong \overline{DE}$	11. ?
12. $\triangle BCE$ isos ($\overline{BC}$ base)	12. ?
13. $\overline{EC} \cong \overline{EB}$	13. ?
14. $\triangle AEC \cong \triangle DEB$	14. ?
15. $\therefore \measuredangle AEC \cong \measuredangle DEB$	15. ?

12. *Given*
$\overline{AB} \cong \overline{DC}$
$\triangle ADE$ isos ($\overline{AD}$ base)
$\triangle BCE$ isos ($\overline{BC}$ base)

To Prove
$\measuredangle AEC \cong \measuredangle DEB$

Statement	*Reason*
1. $\overline{AB} \cong \overline{DC}$	1. ?
2. $\overline{BC} \cong \overline{BC}$	2. ?
3. $\overline{AB} + \overline{BC} \cong \overline{DC} + \overline{BC}$	3. ?
4. $\overline{AC} \cong \overline{AB} + \overline{BC}$	4. ?
5. $\overline{DC} + \overline{BC} \cong \overline{DB}$	5. ?
6. $\overline{AC} \cong \overline{DB}$	6. ?
7. $\triangle ADE$ isos ($\overline{AD}$ base)	7. ?
8. $\overline{AE} \cong \overline{DE}$	8. ?
9. $\triangle BCE$ isos ($\overline{BC}$ base)	9. ?
10. $\overline{EC} \cong \overline{EB}$	10. ?
11. $\triangle AEC \cong \triangle DEB$	11. ?
12. $\therefore \measuredangle AEC \cong \measuredangle DEB$	12. ?

In exercises 13 and 14 refer to Figure 4.24.

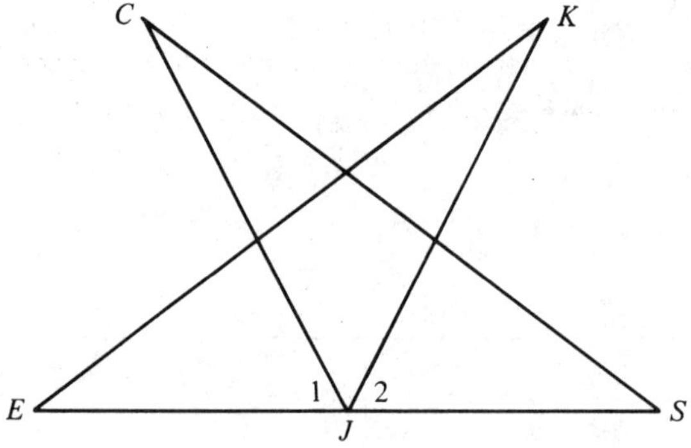

Figure 4.24

13. *Given*
J midpt $\overline{ES}$
$\overline{JK} \cong \overline{JC}$
$\measuredangle 1 \cong \measuredangle 2$

To Prove
$\measuredangle K \cong \measuredangle C$

Statement	*Reason*
1. J midpt $\overline{ES}$	1. ?
2. $EJ = SJ$	2. ?
3. $\overline{EJ} \cong \overline{SJ}$	3. ?
4. $\overline{JK} \cong \overline{JC}$	4. ?
5. $\measuredangle 1 \cong \measuredangle 2$	5. ?
6. $\angle 1 = \angle 2$	6. ?
7. $\measuredangle CJK \cong \measuredangle CJK$	7. ?
8. $\angle CJK = \angle CJK$	8. ?
9. $\angle 1 + \angle CJK = \angle 2 + \angle CJK$	9. ?
10. $\angle EJK = \angle 1 + \angle CJK$	10. ?
11. $\angle 2 + \angle CJK = \angle SJC$	11. ?
12. $\angle EJK = \angle SJC$	12. ?
13. $\measuredangle EJK \cong \measuredangle SJC$	13. ?
14. $\triangle EJK \cong \triangle SJC$	14. ?
15. $\therefore \measuredangle K \cong \measuredangle C$	15. ?

14. *Given*
J midpt $\overline{ES}$
$\overline{JK} \cong \overline{JC}$
$\measuredangle 1 \cong \measuredangle 2$

To Prove
$\measuredangle K \cong \measuredangle C$

Statement	*Reason*
1. J midpt $\overline{ES}$	1. ?
2. $\overline{EJ} \cong \overline{SJ}$	2. ?
3. $\overline{JK} \cong \overline{JC}$	3. ?
4. $\measuredangle 1 \cong \measuredangle 2$	4. ?
5. $\measuredangle CJK \cong \measuredangle CJK$	5. ?
6. $\measuredangle 1 + \measuredangle CJK \cong \measuredangle 2 + \measuredangle CJK$	6. ?
7. $\measuredangle EJK \cong \measuredangle 1 + \measuredangle CJK$	7. ?
8. $\measuredangle 2 + \measuredangle CJK \cong \measuredangle SJC$	8. ?
9. $\measuredangle EJK \cong \measuredangle SJC$	9. ?
10. $\triangle EJK \cong \triangle SJC$	10. ?
11. $\therefore \measuredangle K \cong \measuredangle C$	11. ?

In exercises 15 and 16 copy the figure, mark it, and rearrange the statements into a correct order for a proof.

15. *Given*
$\overline{ID} \cong \overline{IL}$
$\overline{DE} \cong \overline{LC}$
U midpt $\overline{EC}$

To Prove
$\measuredangle EUI \cong \measuredangle CUI$

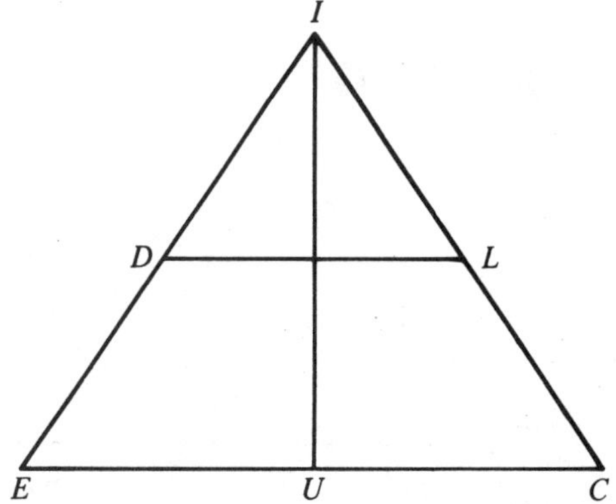

(a) $\overline{ID} + \overline{DE} \cong \overline{IL} + \overline{LC}$
(b) $\measuredangle EUI \cong \measuredangle CUI$
(c) $\overline{IL} + \overline{LC} \cong \overline{IC}$
(d) $\overline{EU} \cong \overline{CU}$
(e) $\overline{IU} \cong \overline{IU}$
(f) $\overline{DE} \cong \overline{LC}$
(g) $\triangle EUI \cong \triangle CUI$
(h) $\overline{IE} \cong \overline{ID} + \overline{DE}$
(i) $\overline{IE} \cong \overline{IC}$
(j) $\overline{ID} \cong \overline{IL}$
(k) U midpt $\overline{EC}$

16. *Given*
$\measuredangle 3 \cong \measuredangle 1$
$\measuredangle 4 \cong \measuredangle 2$
$\triangle EAL$ isos ($\overline{EA}$ base)

To Prove
$\overline{TA} \cong \overline{HE}$

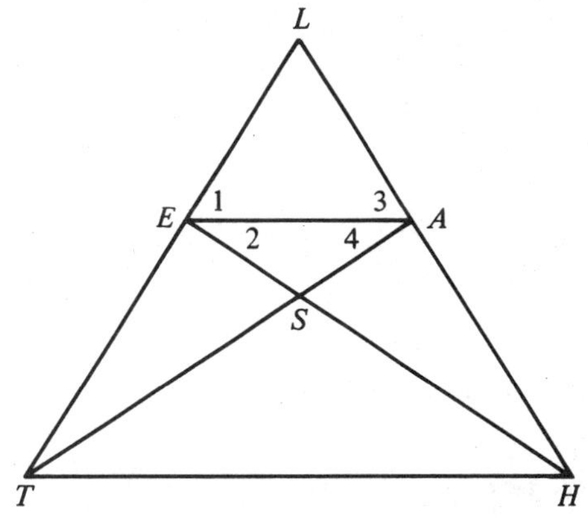

(a) $\overline{LA} \cong \overline{LE}$
(b) $\measuredangle 4 \cong \measuredangle 2$
(c) $\measuredangle 1 + \measuredangle 2 \cong \measuredangle HEL$
(d) $\triangle TAL \cong \triangle HEL$
(e) $\measuredangle TAL \cong \measuredangle HEL$
(f) $\measuredangle 3 \cong \measuredangle 1$
(g) $\measuredangle TAL \cong \measuredangle 3 + \measuredangle 4$
(h) $\measuredangle 3 + \measuredangle 4 \cong \measuredangle 1 + \measuredangle 2$
(i) $\overline{TA} \cong \overline{HE}$
(j) $\triangle EAL$ isos ($\overline{EA}$ base)
(k) $\measuredangle L \cong \measuredangle L$

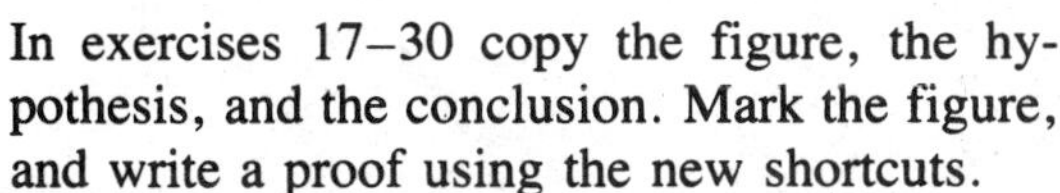
In exercises 17–30 copy the figure, the hypothesis, and the conclusion. Mark the figure, and write a proof using the new shortcuts.

17. *Given*
$\triangle UCE$ isos ($\overline{UC}$ base)
$\overline{EL}$ bis $\measuredangle UEC$

To Prove
$\triangle UCL$ isos

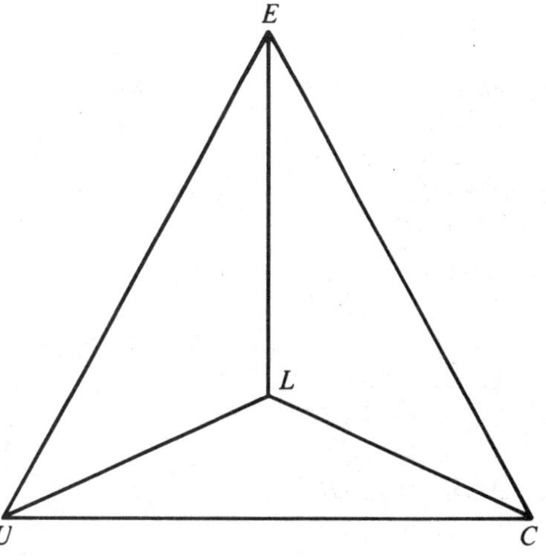

18. 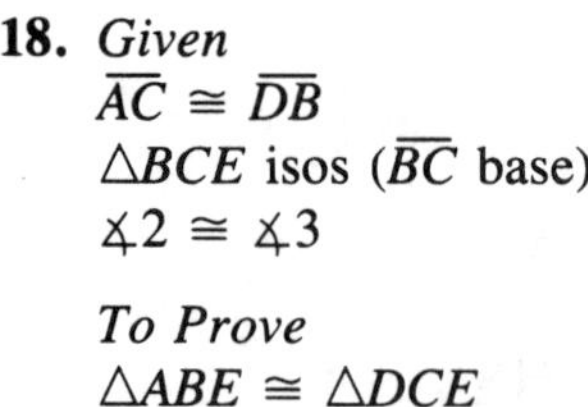
Given
$\overline{AC} \cong \overline{DB}$
$\triangle BCE$ isos ($\overline{BC}$ base)
$\measuredangle 2 \cong \measuredangle 3$

To Prove
$\triangle ABE \cong \triangle DCE$

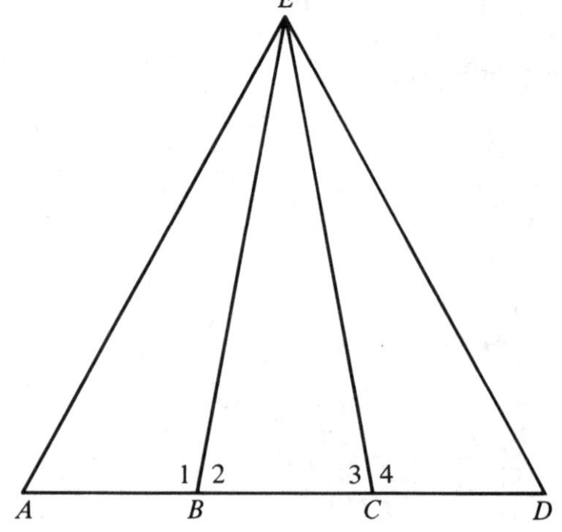

19. 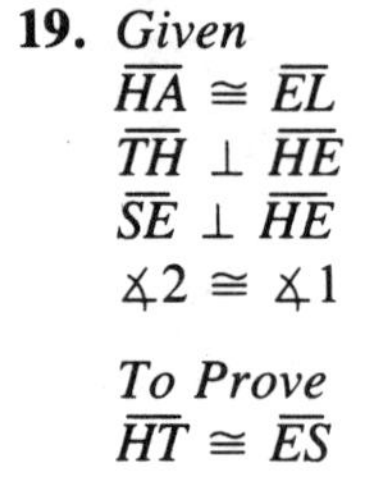
Given
$\overline{HA} \cong \overline{EL}$
$\overline{TH} \perp \overline{HE}$
$\overline{SE} \perp \overline{HE}$
$\measuredangle 2 \cong \measuredangle 1$

To Prove
$\overline{HT} \cong \overline{ES}$

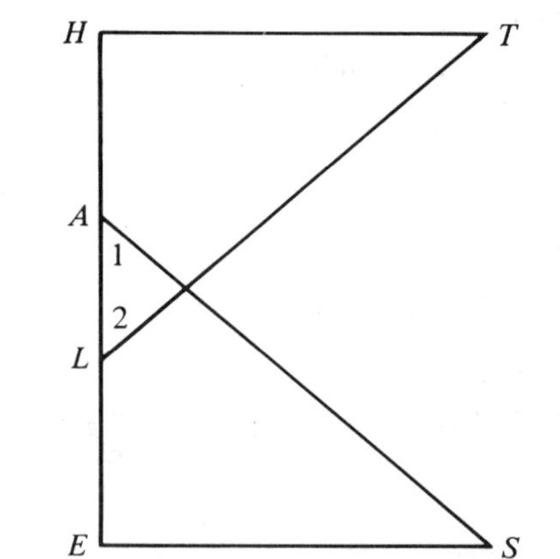

20. 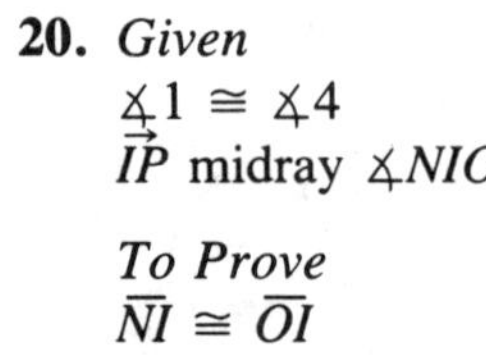
Given
$\measuredangle 1 \cong \measuredangle 4$
$\overrightarrow{IP}$ midray $\measuredangle NIO$

To Prove
$\overline{NI} \cong \overline{OI}$

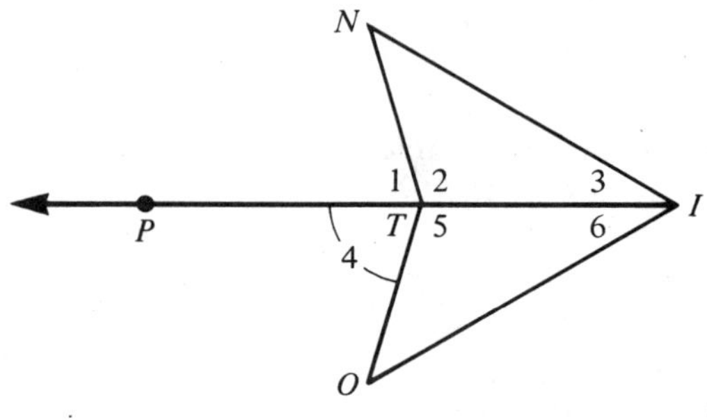

21. *Given*
$\overline{EJ} \cong \overline{CK}$
$\overline{JS} \cong \overline{KS}$

To Prove
$\measuredangle SJC \cong \measuredangle SKE$

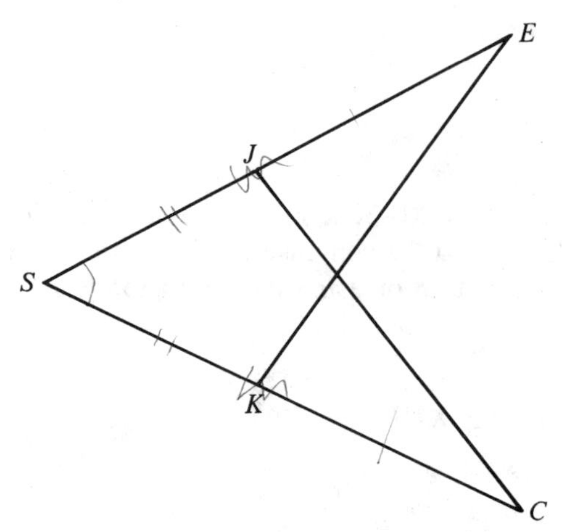

22. *Given*
$\overline{MC} \cong \overline{RS}$
$\overline{MS} \cong \overline{RC}$

To Prove
$\measuredangle 1 \cong \measuredangle 3$

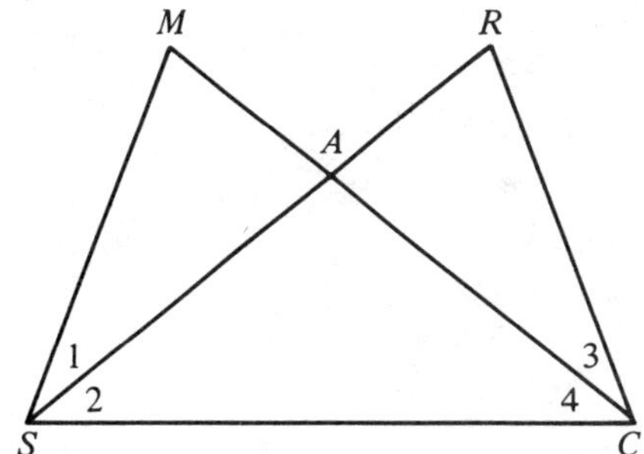

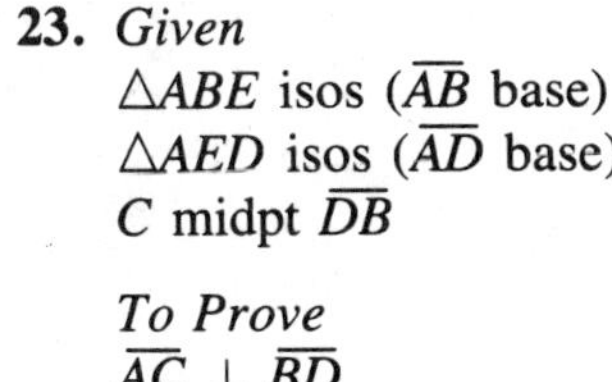

23. *Given*
$\triangle ABE$ isos ($\overline{AB}$ base)
$\triangle AED$ isos ($\overline{AD}$ base)
C midpt $\overline{DB}$

To Prove
$\overline{AC} \perp \overline{BD}$

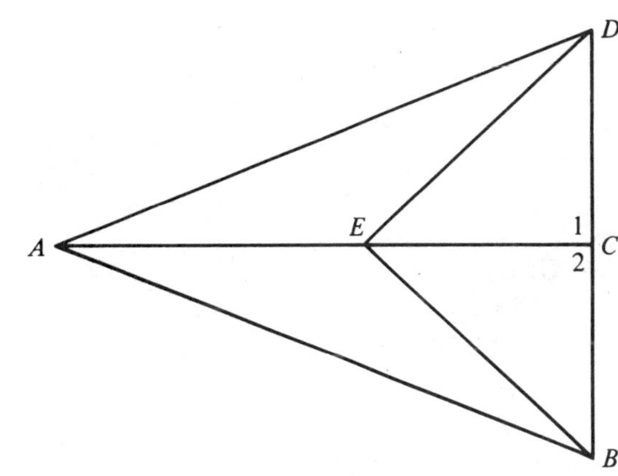

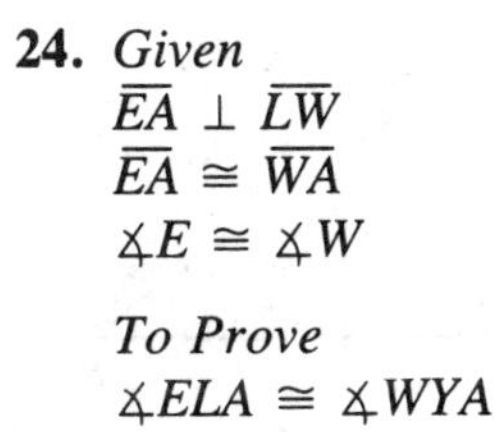

24. *Given*
$\overline{EA} \perp \overline{LW}$
$\overline{EA} \cong \overline{WA}$
$\measuredangle E \cong \measuredangle W$

To Prove
$\measuredangle ELA \cong \measuredangle WYA$

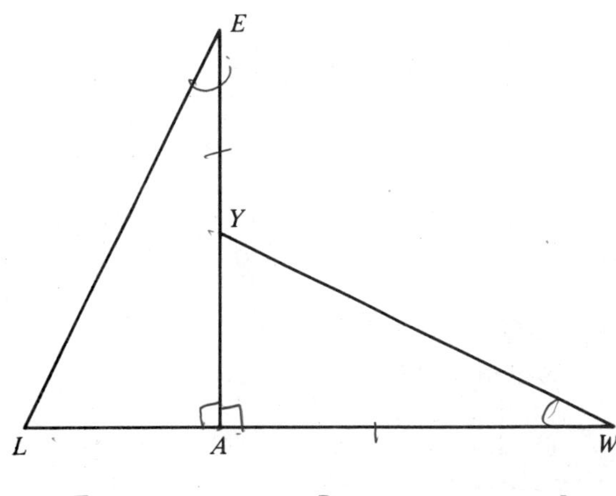

25. *Given*
$\overline{TC}$ bis $\overline{EI}$
$\overline{DU}$ bis $\measuredangle TLI$
$\triangle TIL$ isos ($\overline{TI}$ base)
$\measuredangle T \cong \measuredangle E$

To Prove
$\overline{TD} \cong \overline{EU}$

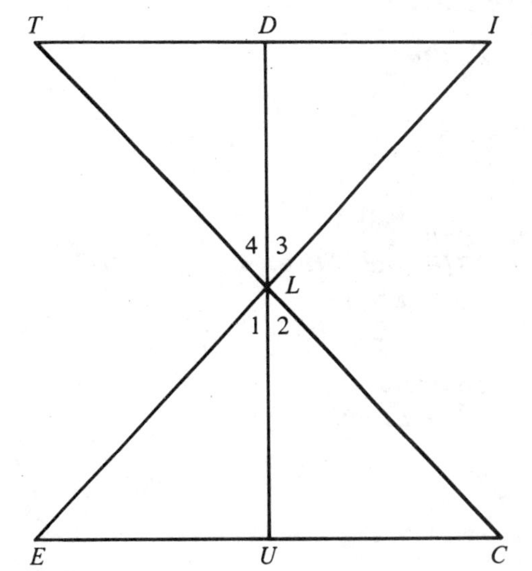

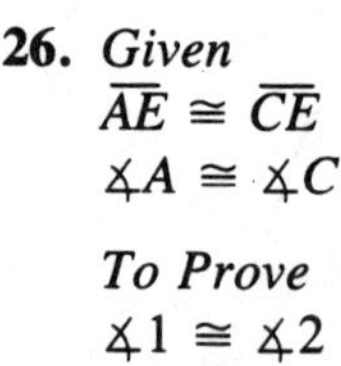

26. *Given*
$\overline{AE} \cong \overline{CE}$
$\angle A \cong \angle C$

To Prove
$\angle 1 \cong \angle 2$

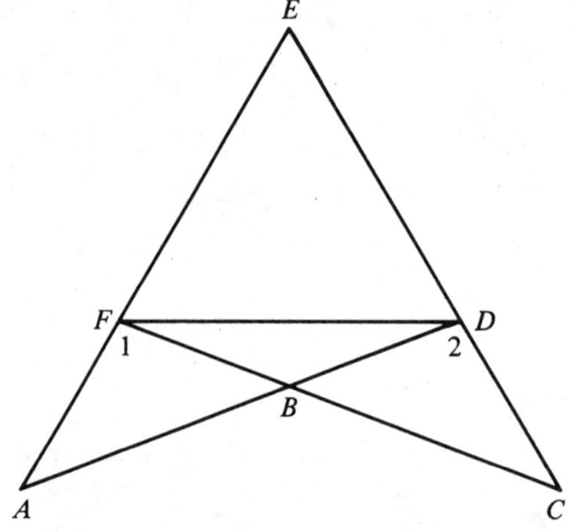

27. *Given*
$\overline{AS} \cong \overline{PT}$
$\triangle APO$ isos ($\overline{AP}$ base)

To Prove
$\overline{AT} \cong \overline{PS}$

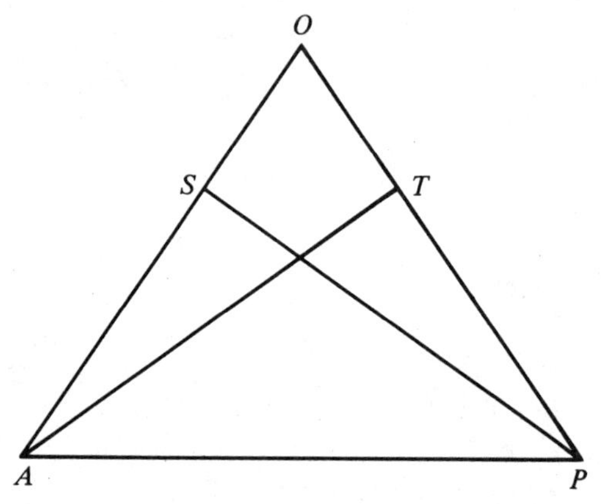

28. *Given*
O midpt $\overline{MR}$
$\overline{OE}$ bis $\angle MON$
$\overline{ON}$ bis $\angle ROE$
$\angle M \cong \angle R$

To Prove
$\overline{OE} \cong \overline{ON}$

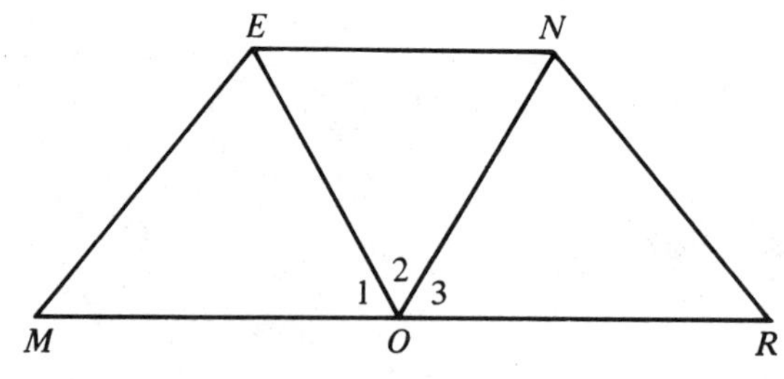

29. *Given*
$\triangle THE$ isos ($\overline{TH}$ base)
$\angle 3 \cong \angle 5$
$\angle 1 \cong \angle 2$

To Prove
$\overline{TA} \cong \overline{HL}$

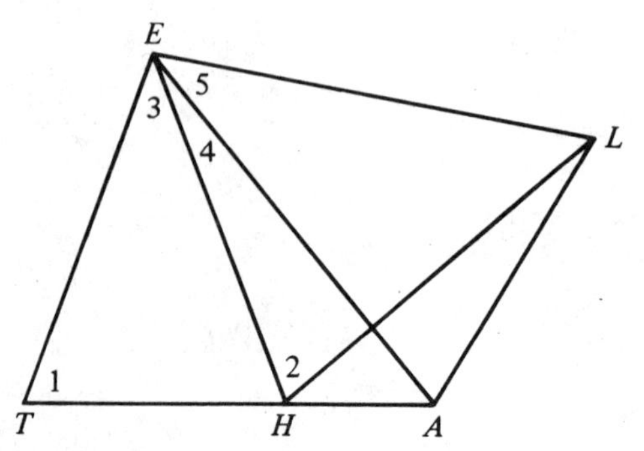

30. *Given*
$\overline{SR} \cong \overline{WA}$
$\angle A \cong \angle 4$
$\angle JSR \cong \angle JWA$

To Prove
$\angle 1 \cong \angle 3$

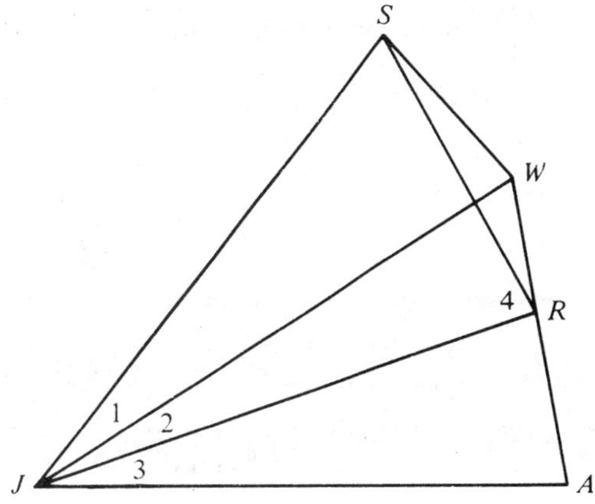

31. Describe how the distance across a lake might be measured using the following diagram and congruent triangles.

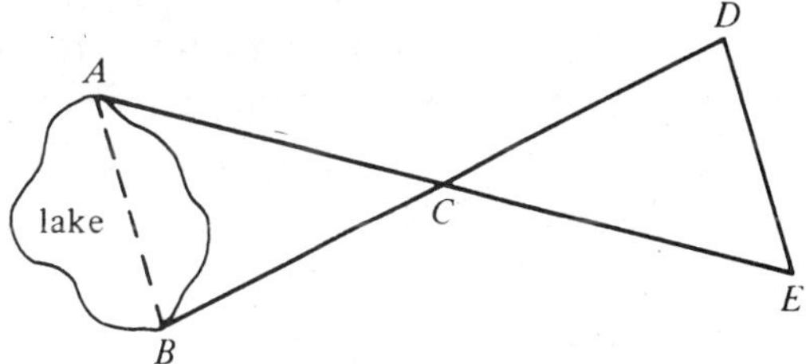

32. Describe how the height of a building might be found by measuring parts of the triangle shown and constructing a second triangle congruent to it.

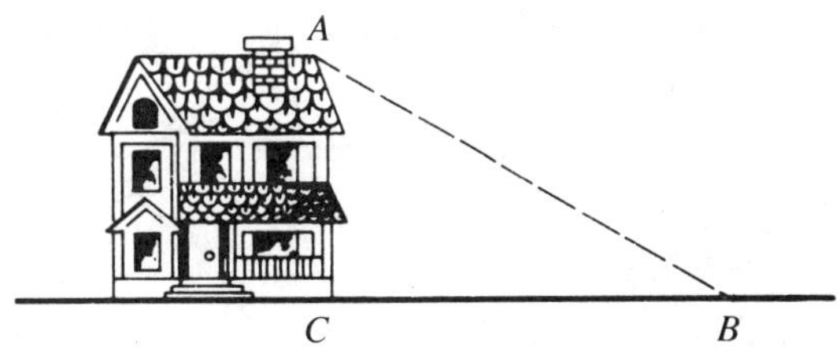

33. Describe how the distance CE across a river might be found by measuring the triangle on land ($\triangle ACB$) and by using congruent triangles.

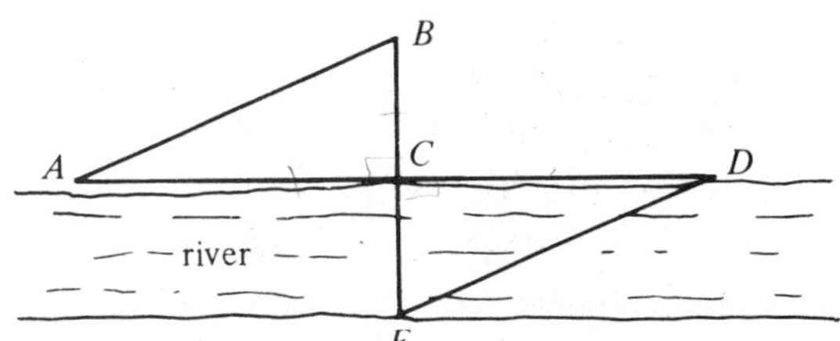

34. Two volleyball players are on opposite sides of the net standing at points A and B. Use congruent triangles to show that the players' feet are equidistant from the top of the net.

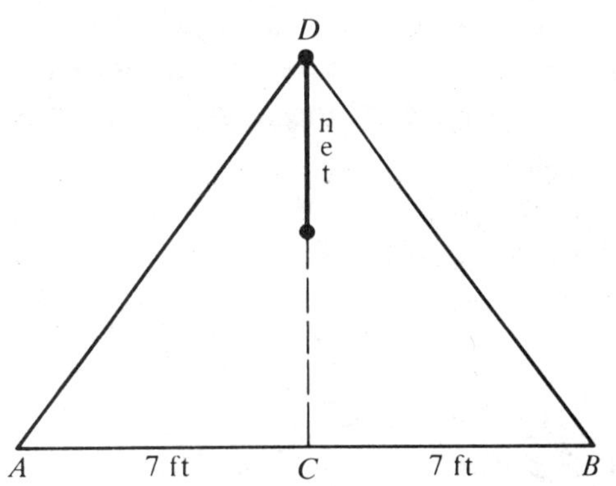

35. Two telephone poles of equal length form right angles with a line on the ground between them. Using congruent triangles, show that guy wires from the base of each pole to the top of the other have the same length.

4.5 SPECIAL LINE SEGMENTS AND TRIANGLES

The bisectors of the angles of a triangle are called the *angle bisectors* of the triangle. Figure 4.25(a) shows them as rays whereas (b) shows them as line segments with endpoints on the triangle's sides. Note that the three angle bisectors are shown intersecting at one point. In Appendix D, Theorem D1 we prove that this single point of intersection exists for every triangle.

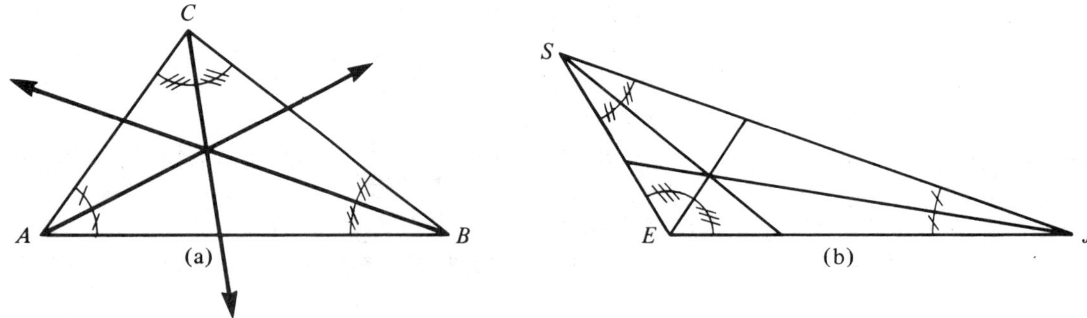

Figure 4.25

As stated in Definitions 4.13 and 4.14, every triangle has two other important sets of line segments.

Definition 4.13 A line segment is a *median* of a triangle iff its endpoints are a vertex and the midpoint of the opposite side (med from vtx to midpt opp side).

The three medians of an acute and an obtuse triangle are shown in Figure 4.26. They always intersect at one point as shown (Appendix D, Theorem D.4). By looking at vertex J in Figure 4.26 we see that a median is *not*, in general, the angle bisector. Only in special cases do they coincide.

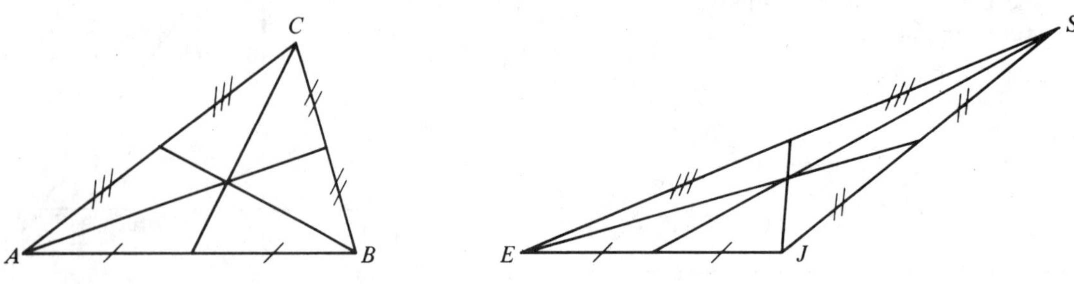

Figure 4.26

Definition 4.14 An *altitude* of a triangle is a line segment from one vertex perpendicular to the line containing the opposite side (alt from vtx $\perp$ opp side).

Figure 4.27 shows the three altitudes for acute $\triangle ABC$ and obtuse $\triangle EJS$. As shown, an altitude does not always lie in the interior of a triangle. The three altitudes of $\triangle ABC$ intersect at one point. The altitudes for $\triangle EJS$ would also intersect at one point if they were extended. See Appendix D, Theorem D.3, for a proof.

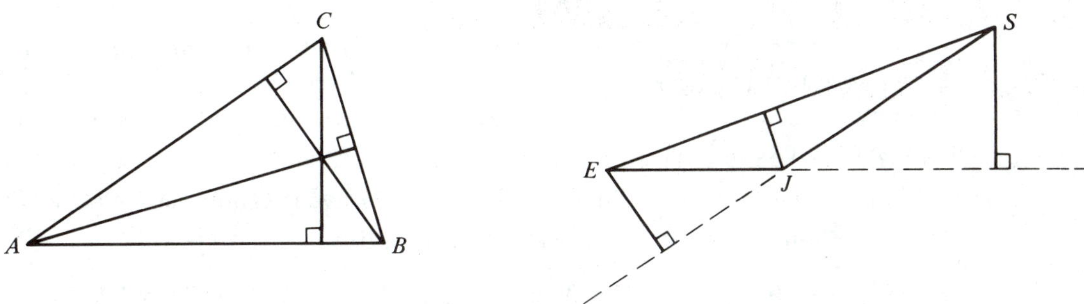

Figure 4.27

Some proofs in geometry require the addition of lines, line segments, or rays to the given figure. These are called *auxiliary lines* and are drawn in dashed form. Their relation to the given figure must be clearly stated and justified in the proof. *Great care must be taken not to impose too many conditions* (restrictions) *on one auxiliary line*. For example, in $\triangle EJS$ (Fig. 4.28) $\overline{EM}$ is an auxiliary line from vertex E to the midpoint M of the opposite side. In a proof we would state that $\overline{EM}$ is a median of $\triangle EJS$, but we *could not* also assert that it is an angle bisector or an altitude even if it appeared to be one or both of these in the figure.

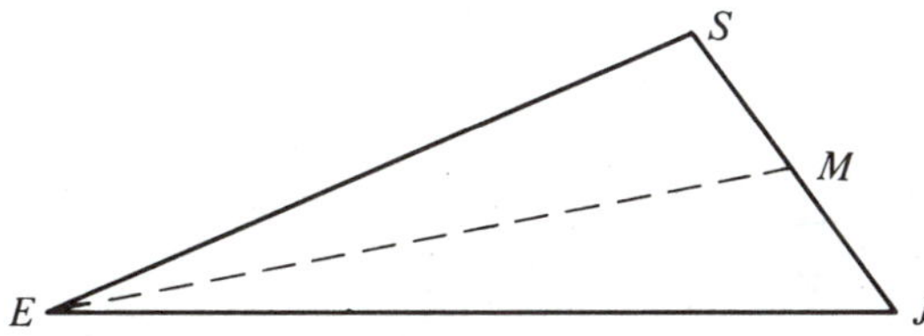

Figure 4.28

Auxiliary lines are often used to create two triangles that may be proved congruent. We now use this idea to prove a famous theorem concerning isosceles triangles.

Theorem 20 If two sides of a triangle are congruent, then the angles opposite the congruent sides are congruent (if 2 sides $\triangle \cong$, opp $\measuredangle$s $\cong$).

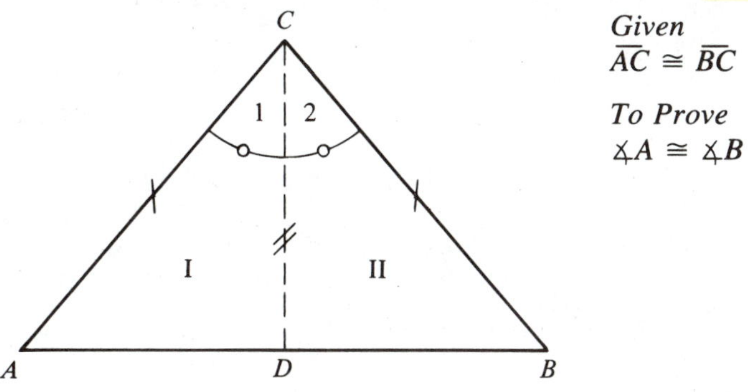

Given
$\overline{AC} \cong \overline{BC}$

To Prove
$\measuredangle A \cong \measuredangle B$

Statement	*Reason*
1. Draw ∡ bis $\overline{CD}$.	1. ∡ has 1 and only 1 bis
2. ∡1 ≅ ∡2	2. bis ÷ ∡ into 2 ≅ ∡s
3. $\overline{AC} \cong \overline{BC}$	3. given
4. $\overline{CD} \cong \overline{CD}$	4. refl ≅
5. △I ≅ △II	5. sas ≅ sas
6. ∴ ∡A ≅ ∡B	6. cpctc

For every theorem in geometry there is a related "if-then" statement called the *converse* that is formed by interchanging the hypothesis and conclusion. The converse statement, however, may or may not be a valid theorem. A nongeometric example is

Theorem: If I live in Los Angeles, then I live in California.

Converse: If I live in California, then I live in Los Angeles.

Clearly, the theorem is valid and its converse is not (because there are cases for which it is false). On the other hand, some theorems and their converses may both be valid. This is the case in Theorem 20 with its converse stating: If two angles of a triangle are congruent, then the sides opposite the congruent angles are congruent. This may be proved using auxiliary lines, but the proof is lengthy. A shorter proof is based on the fact that although every triangle is congruent to itself (refl ≅), *some triangles are congruent to themselves in more than one way*. In Figure 4.29(a) the correspondence $ABC \leftrightarrow ABC$ is the only one such that $\triangle ABC \cong \triangle ABC$, whereas in 4.29(b) with ∡A ≅ ∡B either $ABC \leftrightarrow ABC$ or $ABC \leftrightarrow BAC$ makes the triangle congruent to itself. This point of view is the basis for the proof of Theorem 21.

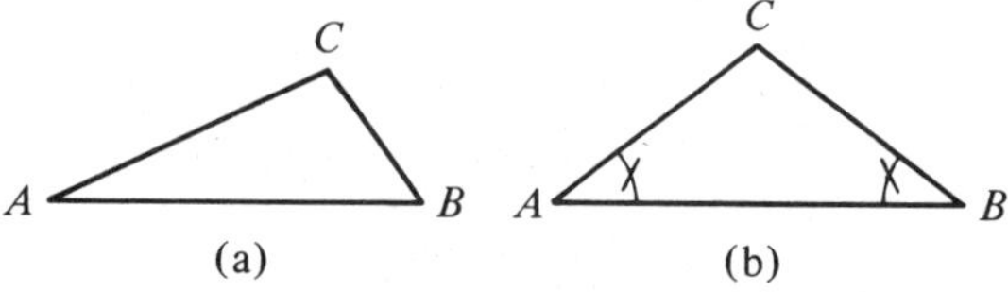

Figure 4.29 (a) Only $ABC \leftrightarrow ABC$ makes $\triangle ABC \cong \triangle ABC$. (b) $ABC \leftrightarrow ABC$ makes $\triangle ABC \cong \triangle ABC$, and $ABC \leftrightarrow BAC$ makes $\triangle ABC \cong \triangle BAC$.

Theorem 21 *(Converse of Theorem 20.)* If two angles of a triangle are congruent, then the sides opposite the congruent angles are congruent (if 2 ∡s △ ≅, opp sides ≅).

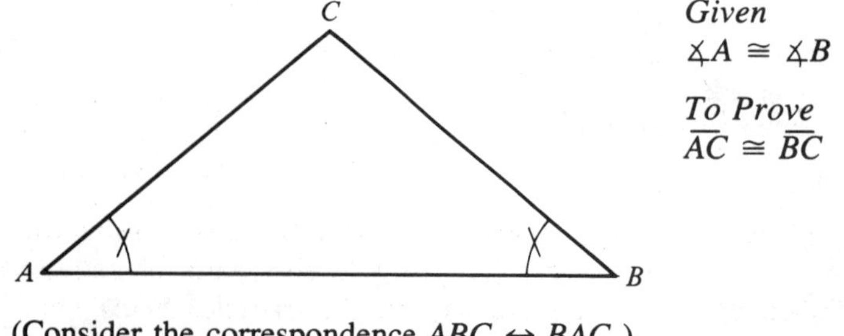

Given
∡A ≅ ∡B

To Prove
$\overline{AC} \cong \overline{BC}$

(Consider the correspondence $ABC \leftrightarrow BAC$.)

Statement	*Reason*
1. $\angle A \cong \angle B$	1. given
2. $\angle B \cong \angle A$	2. symm $\cong$
3. $\overline{AB} \cong \overline{BA}$	3. refl $\cong$
4. $\triangle ABC \cong \triangle BAC$	4. asa $\cong$ asa
5. $\therefore \overline{AC} \cong \overline{BC}$	5. cpctc

Once a theorem is proved, there are often others that are easy to prove by referring to it. These new, related theorems are called *corollaries*. Theorem 22 is an important corollary of Theorem 20.

Theorem 22 An equilateral triangle is also equiangular (if equilat $\triangle$, then equiang $\triangle$).

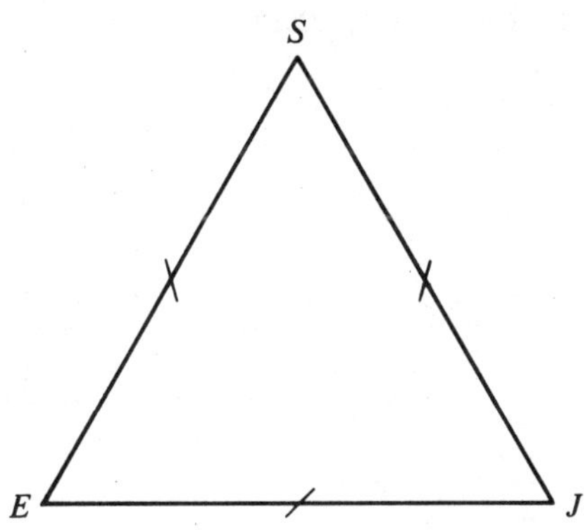

Given
$\triangle EJS$ equilat

To Prove
$\triangle EJS$ equiang

Statement	*Reason*
1. $\triangle EJS$ equilat	1. given
2. $\overline{ES} \cong \overline{EJ}$	2. equilat $\triangle$ iff 3 $\cong$ sides
3. $\angle S \cong \angle J$	3. if 2 sides $\triangle$ $\cong$, opp $\angle$s $\cong$
4. $\overline{JE} \cong \overline{JS}$	4. equilat $\triangle$ iff 3 $\cong$ sides
5. $\angle E \cong \angle S$	5. if 2 sides $\triangle$ $\cong$, opp $\angle$s $\cong$
6. $\angle E \cong \angle J$	6. trans $\cong$
7. $\therefore \triangle EJS$ equiang	7. equiang $\triangle$ iff 3 $\cong$ $\angle$s

The converse of Theorem 22 is a corollary of Theorem 21. The statement and proof are left as exercises. There are other corollaries that could be stated here. For example, the bisector of the vertex angle of an isosceles triangle is also the median and the altitude from that vertex. This is proved using the properties of the congruent triangles in the proof of Theorem 20. Similarly, the three angle bisectors in an equilateral triangle coincide with its medians and altitudes. The proofs of these corollaries and some similar properties are left as exercises.

EXERCISES FOR 4.5

In exercises 1–20 answer true or false.

1. Triangles can be proved congruent using ssa $\cong$ ssa.

2. In triangle *EJS*, side $\overline{JS}$ is included between $\angle S$ and $\angle J$.

3. It is possible to have five parts of one triangle congruent to five parts of another triangle without the triangles being congruent.

4. If an angle is supplementary to another angle, then one of the angles is an obtuse angle.
5. Corresponding parts of congruent angles are congruent.
6. If $\triangle CAT \cong \triangle DOG$, then $\overline{AT} \cong \overline{OG}$.
7. An altitude of a triangle is sometimes a ray.
8. If $\overline{TD}$ is a median in $\triangle CAT$, then C-D-A.
9. If $\overline{JK}$ is an altitude of $\triangle EJS$, then E-K-S.
10. The three altitudes of a right triangle meet in the interior of the triangle.
11. The three medians of an obtuse triangle meet in the interior of the triangle.
12. The angle bisectors of the angles of a triangle are always rays.
13. A triangle is a convex set of points.
14. In an obtuse triangle the altitudes are perpendicular to the sides of the triangle.
15. Auxiliary lines may be drawn in figures to aid in developing a proof.
16. In an equilateral triangle its three medians are congruent to each other.
17. A point in the interiors of two angles of a triangle must be in the interior of the triangle.
18. The median to the base of an isosceles triangle bisects the vertex angle.
19. If $\overrightarrow{AD}$ bisects $\measuredangle A$ of $\triangle ABC$, then $\overrightarrow{AD}$ intersects $\overline{AB}$.
20. If a median of a triangle is perpendicular to a side of a triangle, then the triangle is isosceles.

In exercises 21–26 copy the figure, mark it, and find the requested measures.

21. *Given*
    $\overline{BD} \perp \overline{FD}$
    $\overline{BD} \perp \overline{AB}$
    $\measuredangle 2 \cong \measuredangle 10$
    $\overleftrightarrow{CB}$ bis $\measuredangle ACD$
    $\angle ABE = 122°$
    $\angle FCG = 116°$

    Find
    $\measuredangle$s 1–10

22. *Given*
    $\measuredangle 3 \cong \measuredangle 5$
    $\measuredangle 1$ supp $\measuredangle 5$
    $\overline{FI}$ bis $\measuredangle KFR$
    $\triangle DFR$ isos ($\overline{DF}$ base)
    $\angle 4 = 55°$
    $\measuredangle 8$ supp $\measuredangle 10$

    Find
    $\measuredangle$s 1–10

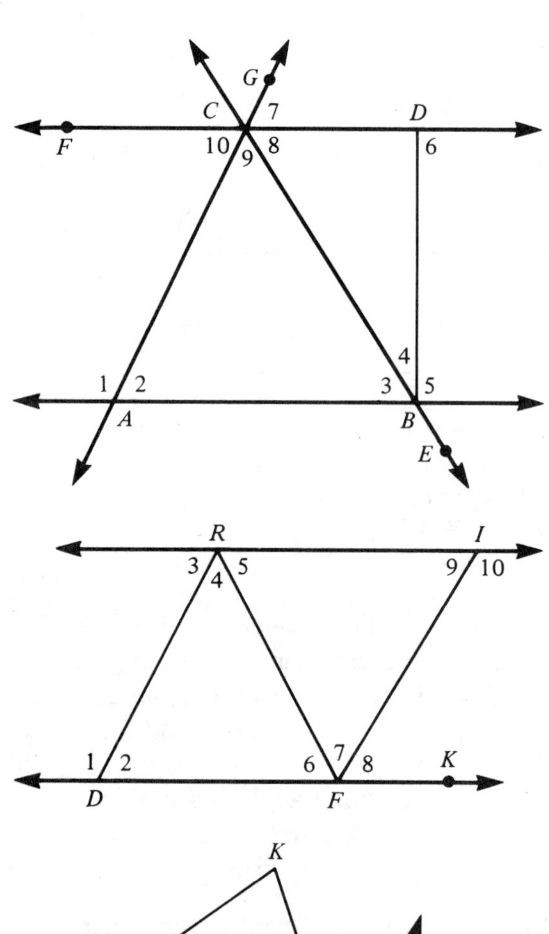

23. *Given*
    $\overline{KR} \cong \overline{IR}$
    $\angle K = 72°$
    $\triangle MCI$ isos ($\overline{CI}$ base)
    $\measuredangle 2 \cong \measuredangle 9$
    $\angle 8 = 2 \cdot \angle 2$

    Find
    $\measuredangle$s 1–9

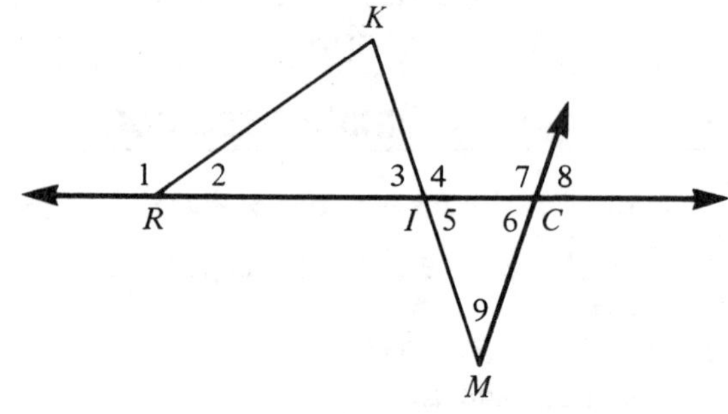

24. *Given*
$\angle CME = 118°$
$\overline{ME} \cong \overline{DE}$
$\overline{DA} \cong \overline{IA}$
$\angle IAN = 119°30'$
$\angle 1 + \angle 2 + \angle 3 = 180°$
$\angle NAI = \angle 5 + \angle 6$

Find
$\angle$s 1–7

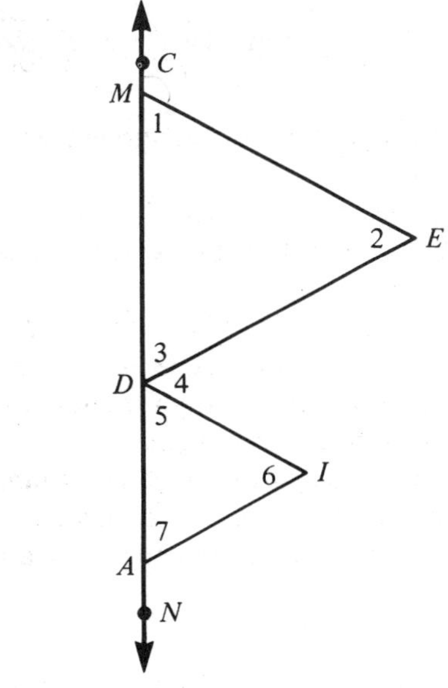

25. *Given*
$\angle AKD = 150°$
$\angle BCJ = 120°$
$\overline{KB} \cong \overline{DB} \cong \overline{DC} \cong \overline{BC}$

Find
$\angle$s 1–8

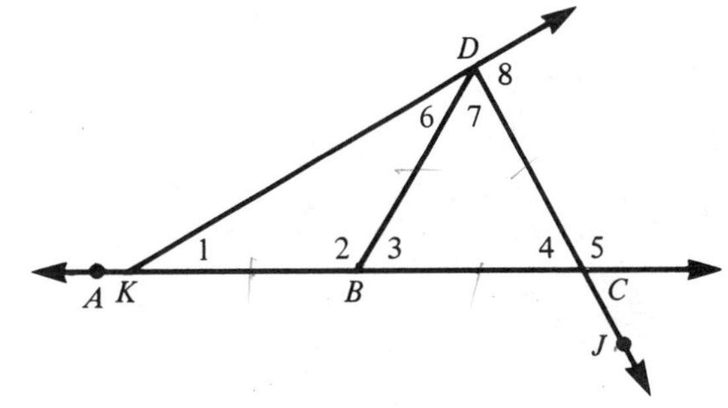

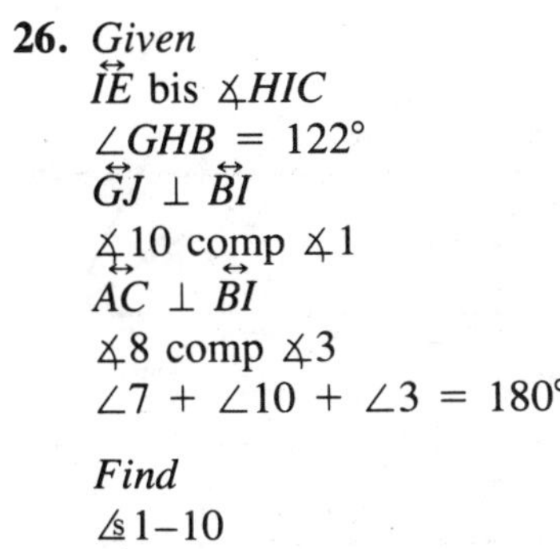

26. *Given*
$\overleftrightarrow{IE}$ bis $\measuredangle HIC$
$\angle GHB = 122°$
$\overleftrightarrow{GJ} \perp \overleftrightarrow{BI}$
$\measuredangle 10$ comp $\measuredangle 1$
$\overleftrightarrow{AC} \perp \overleftrightarrow{BI}$
$\measuredangle 8$ comp $\measuredangle 3$
$\angle 7 + \angle 10 + \angle 3 = 180°$

Find
$\angle$s 1–10

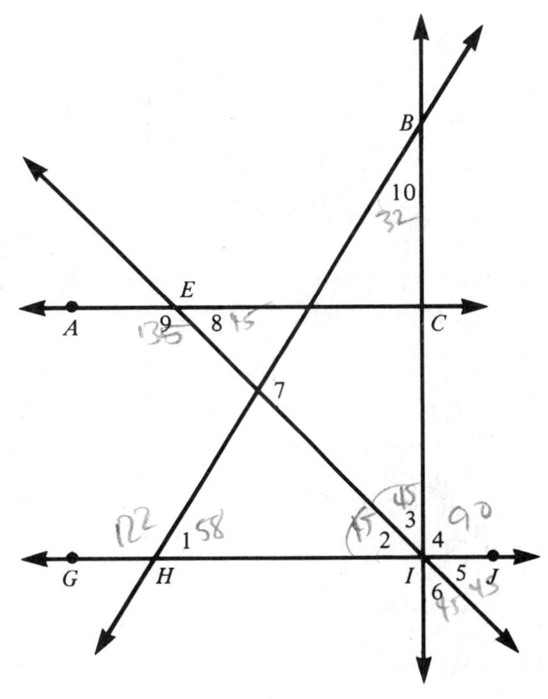

In exercises 27 and 28 copy the figure, mark it, and supply the missing reasons in each proof.

27. *Given*
$\overline{DB}$ alt
$\overline{DB}$ bis $\measuredangle ADC$

To Prove
$\triangle ACD$ isos

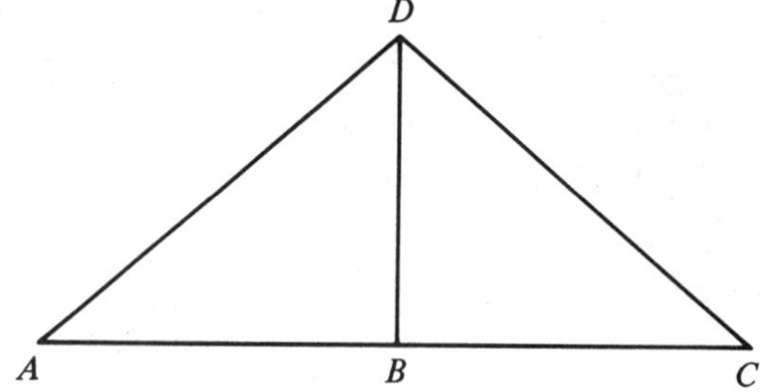

Statement	*Reason*
1. $\overline{DB}$ alt	1. ?
2. $\overline{DB} \perp \overline{AC}$	2. ?
3. $\measuredangle DBA \cong \measuredangle DBC$	3. ?
4. $\overline{DB} \cong \overline{DB}$	4. ?
5. $\overline{DB}$ bis $\measuredangle ADC$	5. ?
6. $\measuredangle ADB \cong \measuredangle CDB$	6. ?
7. $\triangle ABD \cong \triangle CBD$	7. ?
8. $\overline{AD} \cong \overline{CD}$	8. ?
9. $\therefore \triangle ACD$ isos	9. ?

28. *Given*
$\triangle SPR$ isos ($\overline{SP}$ base)
$\overline{PT}$, $\overline{SO}$ medians

To Prove
$\overline{SO} \cong \overline{PT}$

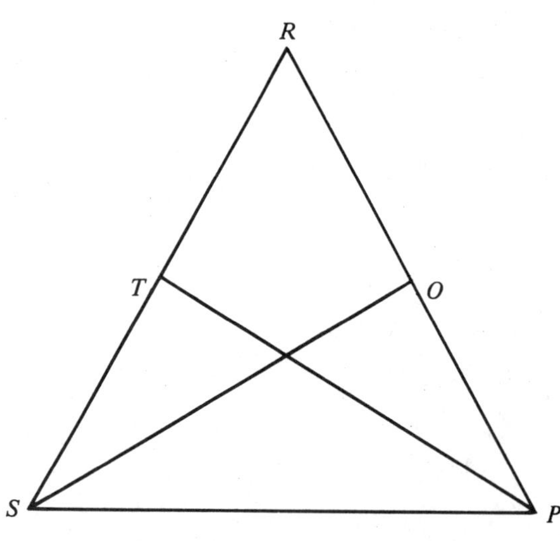

Statement	*Reason*
1. $\triangle SPR$ isos ($\overline{SP}$ base)	1. ?
2. $\overline{RS} \cong \overline{RP}$	2. ?
3. $\overline{PT}$ median	3. ?
4. T midpt $\overline{SR}$	4. ?
5. $\overline{ST} \cong \overline{RT}$	5. ?
6. $\overline{SO}$ median	6. ?
7. O midpt $\overline{PR}$	7. ?
8. $\overline{PO} \cong \overline{RO}$	8. ?
9. $\overline{RO} \cong \overline{RT}$	9. ?
10. $\measuredangle R \cong \measuredangle R$	10. ?
11. $\triangle SOR \cong \triangle PTR$	11. ?
12. $\therefore \overline{SO} \cong \overline{PT}$	12. ?

In exercises 29–37 copy the figure, the hypothesis, and the conclusion. Mark the figure and write a proof.

29. *Given*
$\overline{KO}$ alt
$\overline{KO}$ med

To Prove
$\overline{KO}$ bis $\measuredangle MKR$

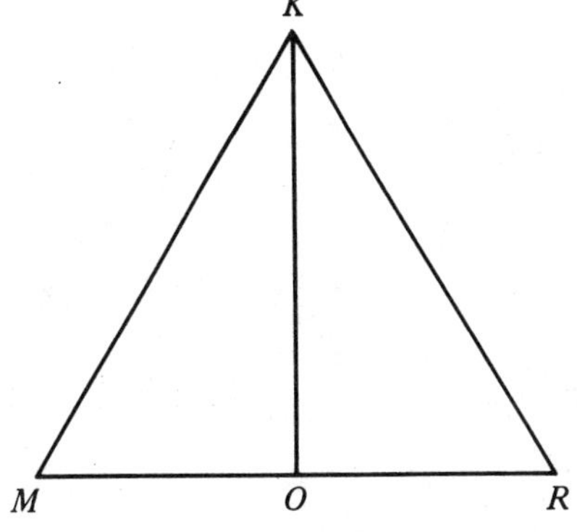

30. *Given*
$\overline{SA}$ bis $\measuredangle JSW$
$\triangle JWS$ isos ($\overline{JW}$ base)

To Prove
$\overline{SA}$ med

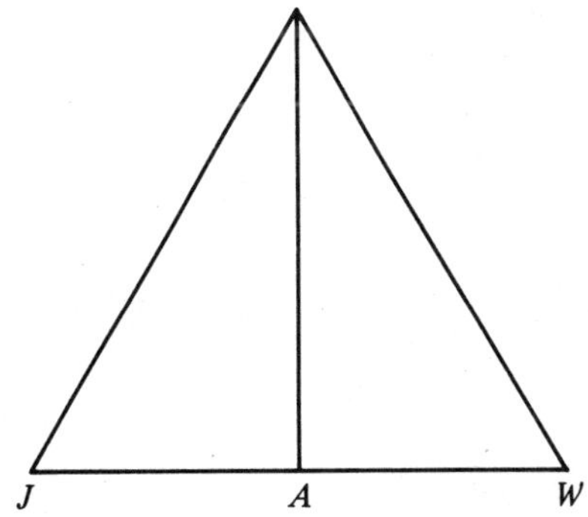

31. *Given*
$\triangle ACD$ isos ($\overline{AC}$ base)
$\overline{DB}$ bis $\measuredangle ADC$

To Prove
$\overline{DB}$ alt

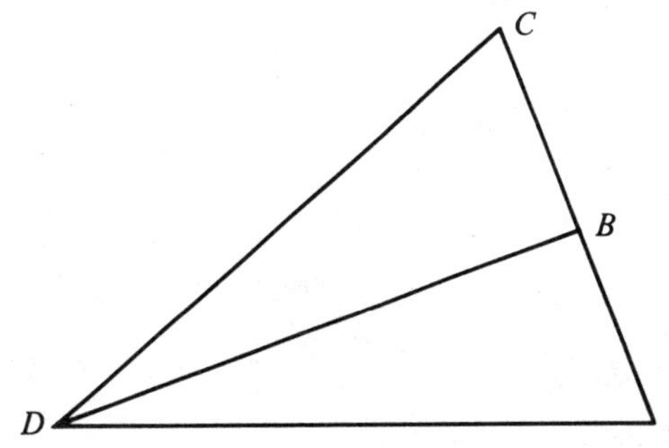

32. *Given*
$\triangle WID$ isos ($\overline{WI}$ base)
$\measuredangle 3 \cong \measuredangle 4$

To Prove
$\overline{YE} \cong \overline{NE}$

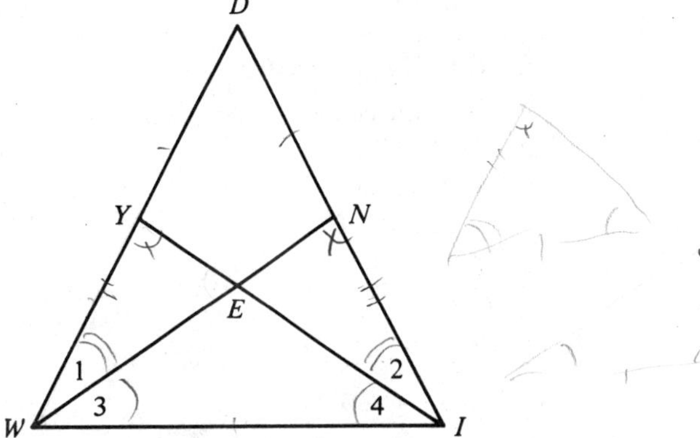

33. *Given*
$\triangle SAI$ isos ($\overline{SA}$ base)
$\overline{IL}$ bis $\measuredangle SIA$

To Prove
$\measuredangle LSA \cong \measuredangle LAS$

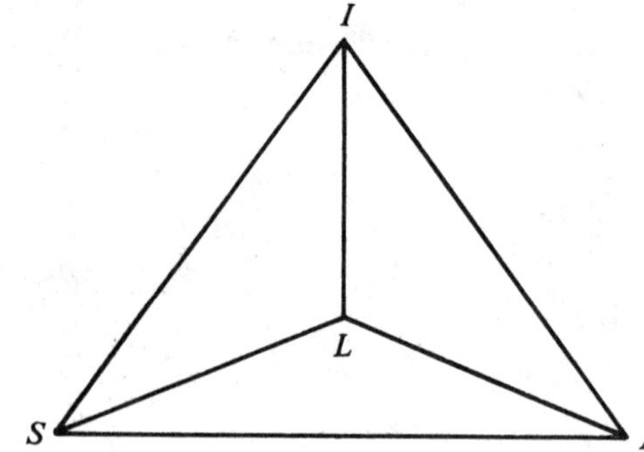

34. *Given*
$\triangle CEL$ isos ($\overline{CL}$ base)
$\measuredangle 2 \cong \measuredangle 4$

To Prove
$\overline{LI} \cong \overline{CU}$

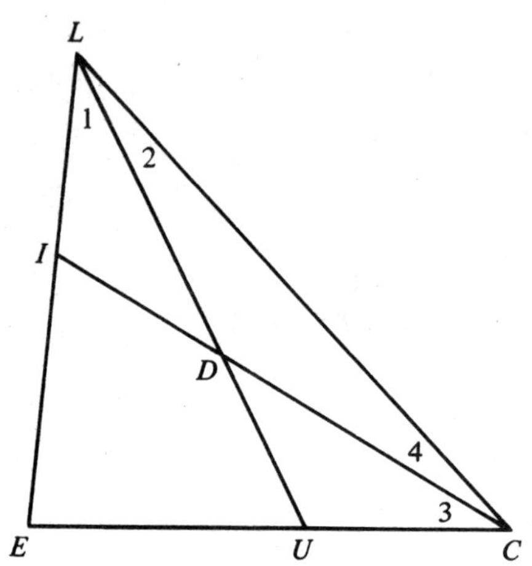

35. *Given*
$\measuredangle 1$ supp $\measuredangle 3$

To Prove
$\triangle ABC$ isos

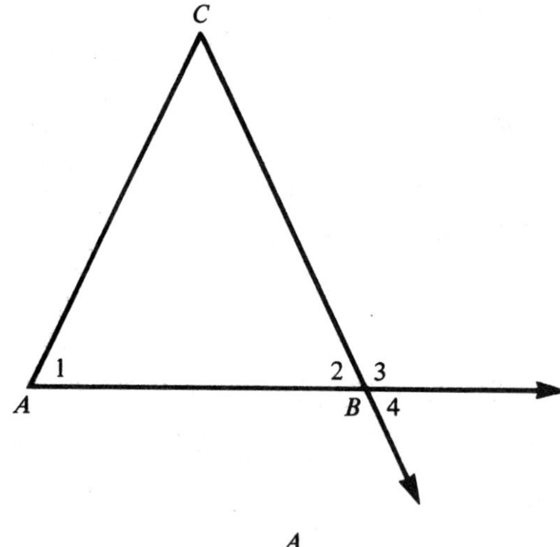

36. *Given*
$\measuredangle C \cong \measuredangle G$
$\measuredangle CAU \cong \measuredangle GAO$

To Prove
$\triangle OUA$ isos

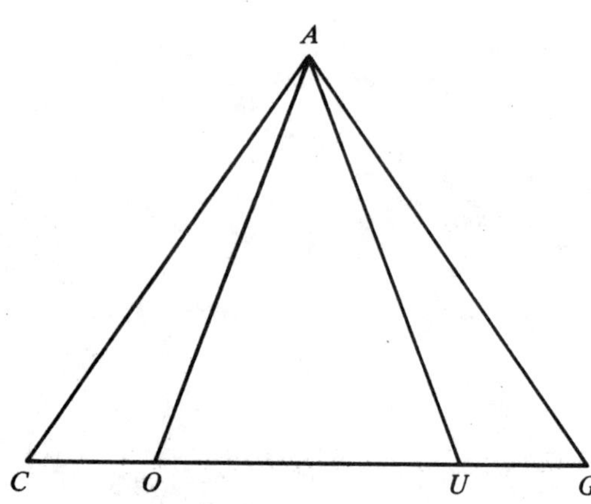

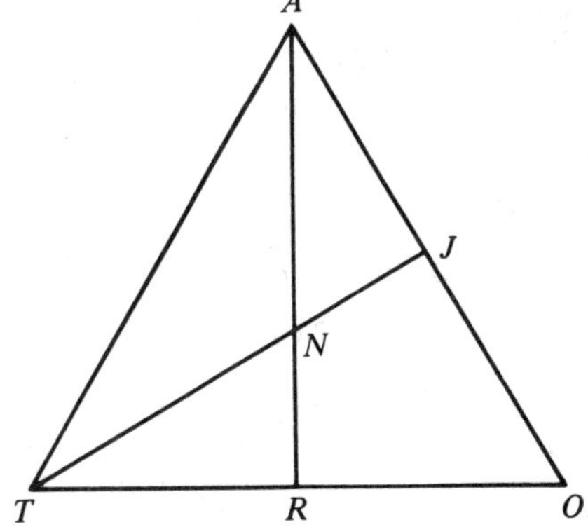

37. *Given*
$\triangle TOA$ equilat
$\overline{TJ}$ med
$\overline{AR}$ med

To Prove
$\overline{TJ} \cong \overline{AR}$

In exercises 38–42 draw a figure and write the hypothesis and conclusion. Mark the figure and write a proof.

38. If two line segments are medians of an equilateral triangle, then they are congruent.

39. If the bisector of an angle of a triangle is perpendicular to the opposite side, then the triangle is isosceles.

40. If a line segment is the median from the vertex angle of an isosceles triangle, then it bisects the vertex angle.

41. If the median of a triangle is perpendicular to one of its sides, then the triangle is isosceles.

42. In a triangle if an angle bisector is an altitude, then it is also a median.

In exercises 43–47 copy the figure, the hypothesis, and the conclusion. Mark the figure and write a proof. (Hint: In each problem it is necessary to draw one or more auxiliary lines.)

43. *Given*

$\overline{HO} \cong \overline{RN}$
$\overline{HN} \cong \overline{RO}$

To Prove
$\measuredangle H \cong \measuredangle R$

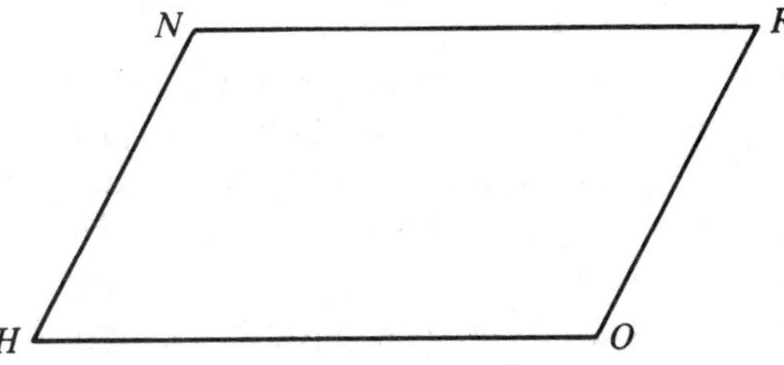

In exercises 44 and 45 refer to Figure 4.30.

44. *Given*

$\overline{KE} \cong \overline{CJ}$
$\overline{KJ} \cong \overline{CE}$

To Prove
$\measuredangle K \cong \measuredangle C$

45. *Given*
$\overline{KE} \cong \overline{CJ}$
$\overline{EC} \cong \overline{JK}$

To Prove
$\measuredangle E \cong \measuredangle J$

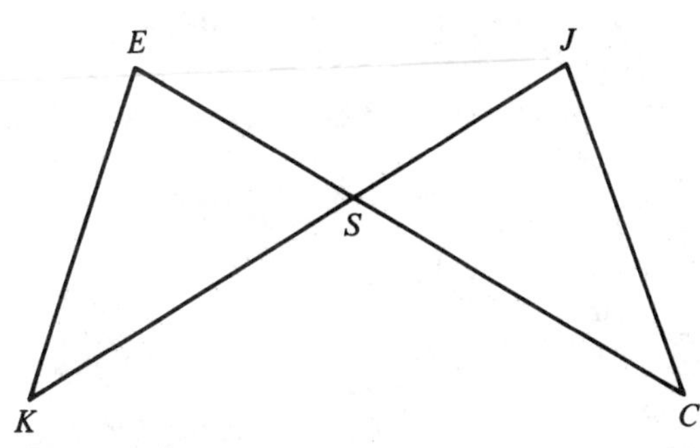

Figure 4.30

46. *Given*
$\overline{ER} \cong \overline{IR}$
$\measuredangle CER \cong \measuredangle CIR$

To Prove
$\overline{EC} \cong \overline{IC}$

47. *Given*
$\overline{PU} \cong \overline{OS}$
$\overline{UO} \cong \overline{SP}$

To Prove
$\overline{PT} \cong \overline{OT}$

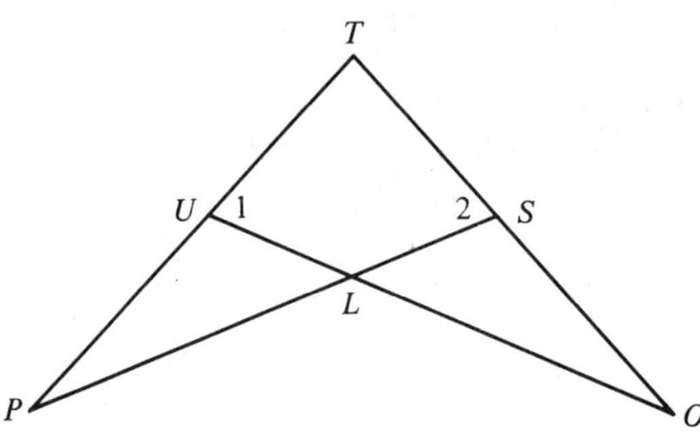

In exercises 48–50 use only a compass and straightedge.

48. (a) Construct a right triangle by constructing a perpendicular through a point on a line.
(b) Construct the three angle bisectors of this right triangle.

49. Draw an acute $\triangle TAD$. Construct the three medians of $\triangle TAD$.

50. Draw an obtuse $\triangle EJS$. Construct the three altitudes of $\triangle EJS$.

In exercises 51–53 three constructions are to be proved using the properties of congruent triangles. These proofs are based on Postulate 5 (can copy seg), the construction for copying a segment (Construction 2), and Theorem 65 (Section 7.1) stating that all radii of the same circle are congruent.

51. Do the construction, mark the figure, and supply the missing reasons in the proof.

Construction 4 To copy an angle using a given ray as one side.

Given
$\measuredangle A$
$\measuredangle E$ as constructed
$\overline{ES} \cong \overline{AB}$
$\overline{EK} \cong \overline{AC}$

To Prove
$\measuredangle E \cong \measuredangle A$

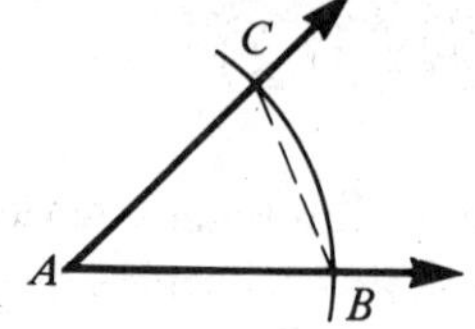

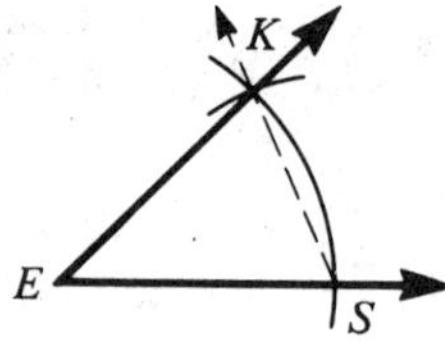

Statement	*Reason*
1. $\measuredangle A$	1. ?
2. $\measuredangle E$ as constructed	2. ?
3. $\overline{ES} \cong \overline{AB}$	3. ?
4. $\overline{EK} \cong \overline{AC}$	4. ?
5. Draw $\overrightarrow{SK}$ and $\overline{BC}$.	5. 2 pts determ line
6. $\overline{SK} \cong \overline{BC}$	6. can copy seg
7. $\triangle ESK \cong \triangle ABC$	7. ?
8. $\therefore \measuredangle E \cong \measuredangle A$	8. ?

In exercises 52 and 53 do the construction, mark the figure, and write a proof.

52. Construction 3 To construct the bisector of an angle.

Given
$\measuredangle RST$
$\overrightarrow{SU}$ as constructed
$\overline{ST} \cong \overline{SR}$

To Prove
$\overrightarrow{SU}$ bis $\measuredangle RST$

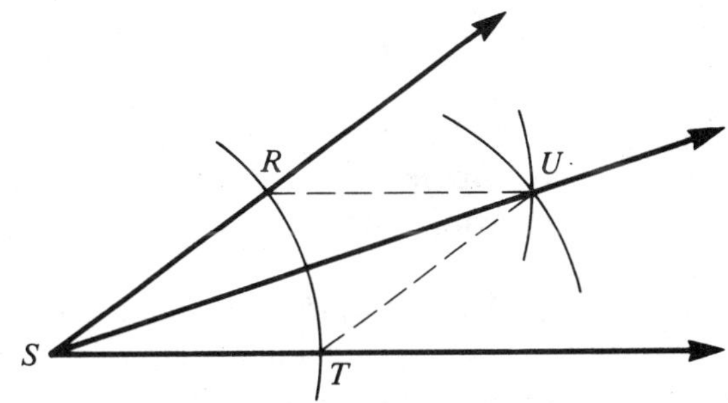

53. Construction 5 To construct a line perpendicular to a given line through one of its points.

Given
$\overline{DA} \cong \overline{DB}$
$\overleftrightarrow{CD}$ as constructed

To Prove
$\overleftrightarrow{CD} \perp \overleftrightarrow{AB}$

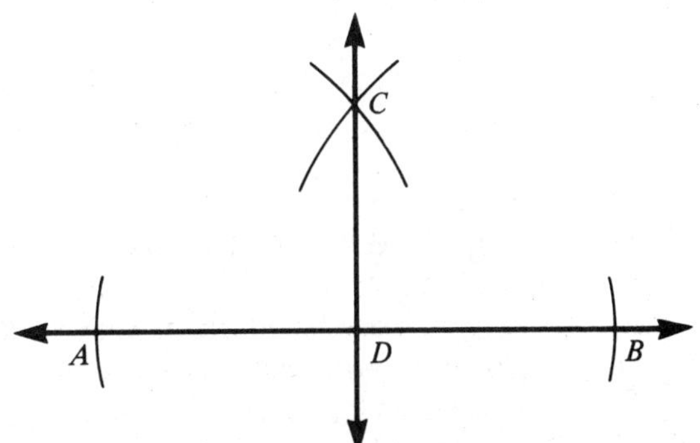

4.6

INEQUALITIES IN TRIANGLES: INDIRECT PROOF

There are several important order relations involving the measures of the sides and angles of a triangle. Four of these relations are presented as theorems in this section. Our study of these relations begins with two geometric definitions.

Definition 4.15 An angle is an *exterior angle* of a triangle iff it forms a linear pair with one of the angles of the triangle (ext ∡ of △ iff lin pr with 1 ∡).

In Figure 4.31 ∡*AES* and ∡*BEJ* are exterior angles, but ∡*AEB* is not. There are four more exterior angles, two at vertex *S* and two at vertex *J*. Thus, every triangle has six exterior angles.

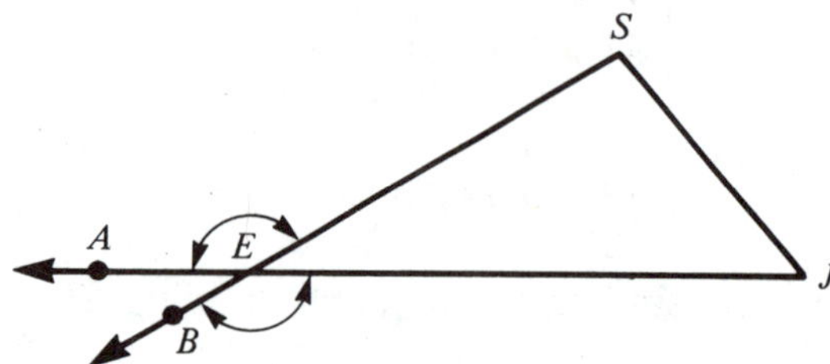

Figure 4.31

There are two remote interior angles associated with each exterior angle. In Figure 4.31 ∡*S* and ∡*J* of the triangle are the remote interior angles for exterior ∡*AES* and exterior ∡*BEJ*.

Definition 4.16 A *remote interior angle* associated with an exterior angle of a triangle is either one of the interior angles not forming a linear pair with the exterior angle.

Section 1.5 included three axioms about the order relation for real numbers. Since these axioms will be needed in proofs involving inequalities in triangles, we restate them for easy reference:

Axiom 9 *Transitive Property of Order*
If $x, y, z \in R$, $x < y$, and $y < z$, then $x < z$ (trans <).

Axiom 15 *Whole Greater than Part*
If $x, y, z \in R$, $z > 0$, and $x = y + z$, then $x > y$ (whole > part).

Axiom 16 *Addition of Inequalities*
If $a < b$ and $c < d$, then $a + c < b + d$, or if $a > b$ and $c > d$, then $a + c > b + d$ (< + <, sums < or > + >, sums >).

Theorem 23 The measure of an exterior angle of a triangle is greater than the measure of either remote interior angle (ext ∠ > rem int ∠).

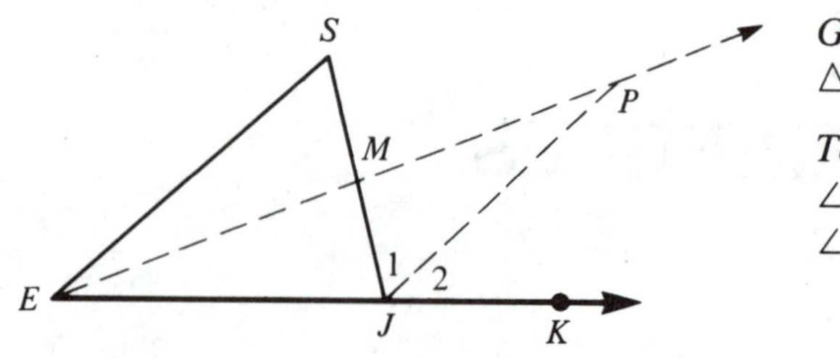

Given
△*EJS* with ext ∡*SJK*

To Prove
∠*SJK* > ∠*S*
∠*SJK* > ∠*E*

Statement	*Reason*
1. △*EJS* with ext ∡*SJK*	1. given
2. let *M* be midpt $\overline{SJ}$	2. seg has 1 and only 1 midpt

3. Draw $\overrightarrow{EM}$.	3. 2 pts determ line
4. Construct $\overline{MP} \cong \overline{ME}$, such that E-M-P.	4. can copy seg
5. Draw $\overline{JP}$.	5. 2 pts determ line
6. $\overline{MJ} \cong \overline{MS}$	6. midpt $\div$ seg into 2 $\cong$ segs
7. $\measuredangle PMJ$ and $\measuredangle EMS$ vert $\measuredangle$s	7. vert $\measuredangle$s formed by opp rays
8. $\measuredangle PMJ \cong \measuredangle EMS$	8. vert $\measuredangle$s $\cong$
9. $\triangle PMJ \cong \triangle EMS$	9. sas $\cong$ sas
10. $\measuredangle 1 \cong \measuredangle S$	10. cpctc
11. $\angle 1 = \angle S$	11. $\cong$ iff meas $=$
12. $\angle SJK = \angle 1 + \angle 2$	12. whole $=$ sum parts
13. $\angle SJK = \angle S + \angle 2$	13. subst
14. $\therefore \angle SJK > \angle S$	14. whole $>$ part

The proof that $\angle SJK > \angle E$ is similar but requires drawing $\overrightarrow{SN}$ where N is the midpoint of $\overline{EJ}$.

Figure 4.32 shows a triangle with side $\overline{AC}$ longer than side $\overline{BC}$. It appears that the angles opposite these sides are of unequal size and that $\angle B > \angle A$. The next theorem establishes that this relationship is always true.

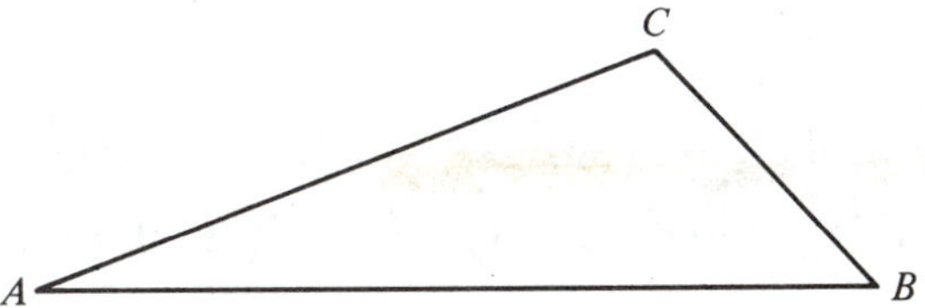

Figure 4.32 Since $AC > BC$, $\angle B > \angle A$.

Theorem 24 If the lengths of two sides of a triangle are unequal, then the measures of the angles opposite them are unequal and the larger angle is opposite the longer side (2 sides $\triangle \neq$, opp $\measuredangle$s $\neq$ same order).

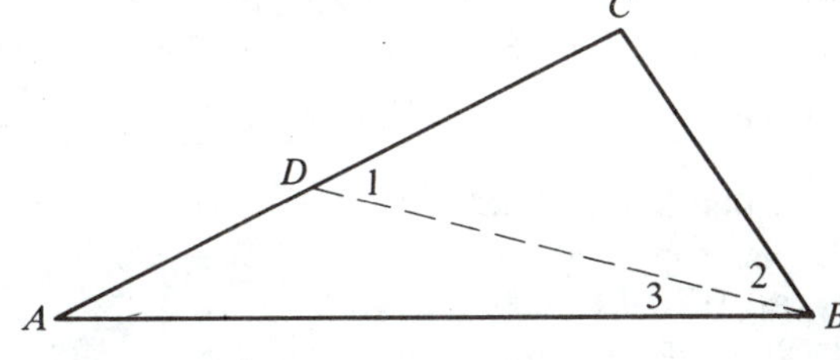

Given
$\triangle ABC$ with $CA > CB$

To Prove
$\angle ABC > \angle A$

Statement	*Reason*
1. $\triangle ABC$ with $CA > CB$	1. given
2. Construct $\overline{CD} \cong \overline{CB}$ such that C-D-A.	2. can copy seg
3. Draw $\overline{DB}$.	3. 2 pts determ line
4. $\measuredangle 1 \cong \measuredangle 2$	4. if 2 sides $\triangle \cong$, opp $\measuredangle$s $\cong$
5. $\angle 1 = \angle 2$	5. $\cong$ iff meas $=$
6. $\angle ABC = \angle 2 + \angle 3$	6. whole $=$ sum parts
7. $\angle ABC = \angle 1 + \angle 3$	7. subst
8. $\angle ABC > \angle 1$	8. whole $>$ part
9. $\measuredangle 1$ ext $\measuredangle$ of $\triangle ADB$	9. ext $\measuredangle$ of $\triangle$ iff lin pr with 1 $\measuredangle$
10. $\angle 1 > \angle A$	10. ext $\angle >$ rem int $\angle$
11. $\therefore \angle ABC > \angle A$	11. trans $>$

The converse of Theorem 24 is also true:

Theorem 25 If the measures of two angles of a triangle are unequal, then the lengths of the sides opposite them are unequal and the longer side is opposite the larger angle (2 ∡s △ ≠, opp sides ≠ same order).

This theorem will be proved at the end of this section by a new method.

Theorem 26 is often called the *Triangle Inequality Theorem*. Its content is suggested in Figure 4.33. Triangle I cannot be constructed because 10 + 5 = 15. Triangle III is also impossible because 9 + 5 < 15. If you are skeptical, use a ruler and try to draw them. Triangle II, however, can be constructed because if the lengths of any two of its sides are added, the sum is greater than the length of the third side.

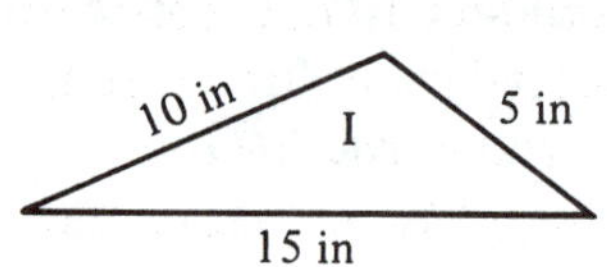

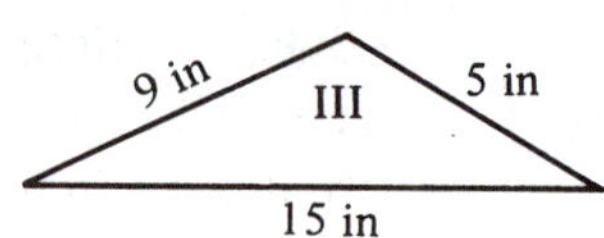

Figure 4.33

Theorem 26 *The Triangle Inequality Theorem.* The sum of the lengths of any two sides of a triangle is greater than the length of its third side (sum 2 sides △ > 3d side).

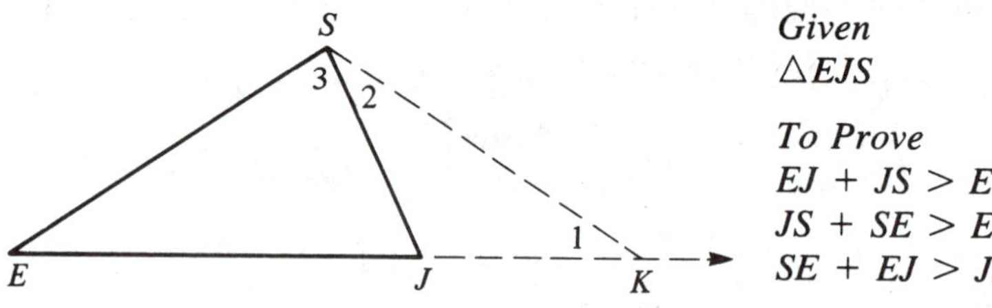

Given
$\triangle EJS$

To Prove
$EJ + JS > ES$
$JS + SE > EJ$
$SE + EJ > JS$

Statement	*Reason*
1. Draw $\overrightarrow{EJ}$.	1. 2 pts determ line
2. Construct $\overline{JK} \cong \overline{JS}$ such E-J-K.	2. can copy seg
3. $JK = JS$	3. ≅ iff meas =
4. Draw $\overline{KS}$.	4. 2 pts determ line
5. ∡1 ≅ ∡2	5. if 2 sides △ ≅, opp ∡s ≅
6. $\angle 1 = \angle 2$	6. ≅ iff meas =
7. $\angle ESK = \angle 2 + \angle 3$	7. whole = sum parts
8. $\angle ESK > \angle 2$	8. whole > part
9. $\angle ESK > \angle 1$	9. subst
10. in $\triangle ESK$, $EK > ES$	10. 2 ∡s △ ≠, opp sides ≠ same order
11. $EJ + JK = EK$	11. whole = sum parts
12. $EJ + JK > ES$	12. subst
13. $\therefore EJ + JS > ES$	13. subst

Proofs of the other two order relations are similar.

The method of proof that we have used so far is called the direct method because it involves a sequence of statements leading *directly* from the hypothesis to the conclusion. There are, however, valid theorems that are difficult to prove in this way. It should be emphasized that the inability to find a direct proof does *not* prove the theorem to be wrong—it only shows that the attempts have been fruitless! When this happens, the *indirect method* of proof should be tried. We will not present a detailed analysis of the method. Instead, a brief description will be given, followed by two simple examples.

An indirect proof is similar to the process-of-elimination method often used by students when taking a true-false or multiple-choice examination. Suppose there are exactly two possible answers to a question and only one is correct. We may *assume* one of the possibilities to be true and then explore whether this leads to the contradiction of some known fact. If this is the case, our assumption must be wrong and we conclude that the other possible answer is the correct one. The process is similar when there are exactly three possible answers and only one is correct. We try to show that by assuming each of two of the possibilities to be true we find a contradiction. If this can be accomplished, we may conclude that the remaining possibility is the correct one. The process may of course be extended to questions involving four or more possibilities. Note that this indirect approach is most easily applied when you can make a good guess of the correct possibility. Unfortunately, like the direct method, this method does not always work. Again, this does not mean that what we are attempting to prove is incorrect, but only that so far we have been unable to prove it!

EXAMPLE 1 Prove using the indirect method that the following statement is false: If $\angle 1 = 18°$ and $\angle 2 = 73°$, then $\measuredangle 1$ and $\measuredangle 2$ are complementary.

Answer
Assume that $\measuredangle 1$ and $\measuredangle 2$ are complementary.

Statement	*Reason*
1. $\angle 1 + \angle 2 = 90°$	1. comp iff sum $= 90°$
2. $\angle 1 = 18°$, $\angle 2 = 73°$	2. given
3. $\angle 1 + \angle 2 = 91°$	3. $= + =$, sums $=$
4. $\therefore \measuredangle 1$ and $\measuredangle 2$ not comp	4. statement 3 contradicts statement 1

EXAMPLE 2 Prove using the indirect method that (b) is the correct answer to the following: Exactly one of the given numbers is the root of the equation $9x - 1 = 17$. Is it (a) 7, (b) 2, or (c) 1?

Answer

(1) Assume that (a) is the correct answer.
$9x - 1 = 17$
$9 \cdot 7 - 1 = 17$
$63 - 1 = 17$
$62 = 17$, a contradiction

(2) Assume that (c) is the correct answer.
$9x - 1 = 17$
$9 \cdot 1 - 1 = 17$
$9 - 1 = 17$
$8 = 17$, a contradiction

Therefore, (b) is the correct answer.

We now prove Theorem 25 using the indirect method. There are exactly three possibilities: (a) $BC < AC$, (b) $BC = AC$, and (c) $BC > AC$.

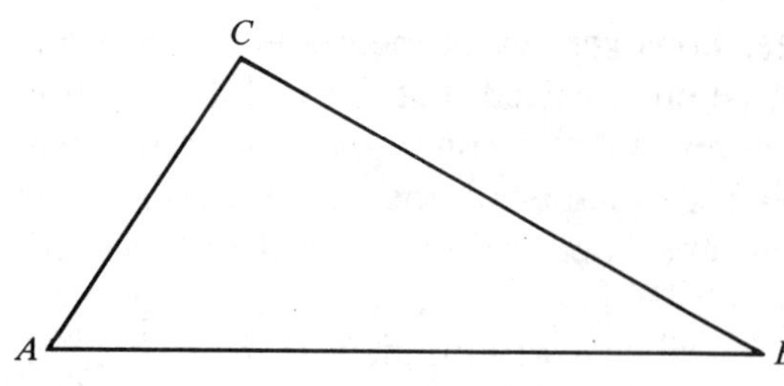

Given
$\triangle ABC$ with $\angle A > \angle B$

To Prove
$BC > AC$

Statement	*Reason*
(a) assume $BC < AC$	
1. $\angle A < \angle B$	1. 2 sides $\triangle \neq$, opp $\measuredangle$s $\neq$ same order
2. $\angle A > \angle B$	2. given
3. $\therefore BC \not< AC$	3. statement 2 contradicts statement 1
(b) assume $BC = AC$	
1. $\overline{BC} \cong \overline{AC}$	1. $\cong$ iff meas $=$
2. $\measuredangle A \cong \measuredangle B$	2. if 2 sides $\triangle \cong$, opp $\measuredangle$s $\cong$
3. $\angle A = \angle B$	3. $\cong$ iff meas $=$
4. $\angle A > \angle B$	4. given
5. $\therefore BC \neq AC$	5. statement 4 contradicts statement 3
(c) $\therefore BC > AC$ because (a) and (b) lead to contradictions	

The method of indirect proof is used relatively infrequently in elementary mathematics. There are, however, a few geometric theorems such as the one above for which the indirect proof works well. Another name for the indirect method is "proof by contradiction."

EXERCISES FOR 4.6

In exercises 1–20 write the abbreviation for the theorem that justifies each statement.

In exercises 1–10 refer to Figure 4.34.

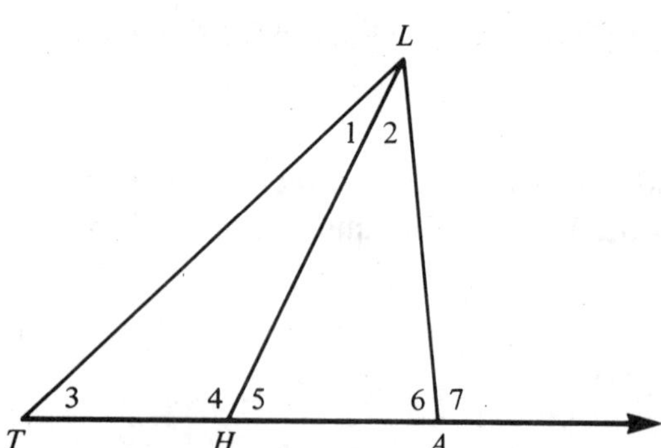

Figure 4.34

1. $\angle 7 > \angle 5$
2. $\angle 4 > \angle 6$
3. If $LH < TL$, then $\angle 3 < \angle 4$
4. If $\angle 6 > \angle 3$, then $TL > LA$
5. $LA + TA > TL$
6. If $LA < HL$, then $\angle 5 < \angle 6$
7. If $\angle TLA < \angle TAL$, then $TA < TL$
8. $LH + HA > LA$
9. $\angle 3 < \angle 5$
10. If $TA < TL$, then $\angle TLA < \angle TAL$

In exercises 11–15 refer to Figure 4.35.

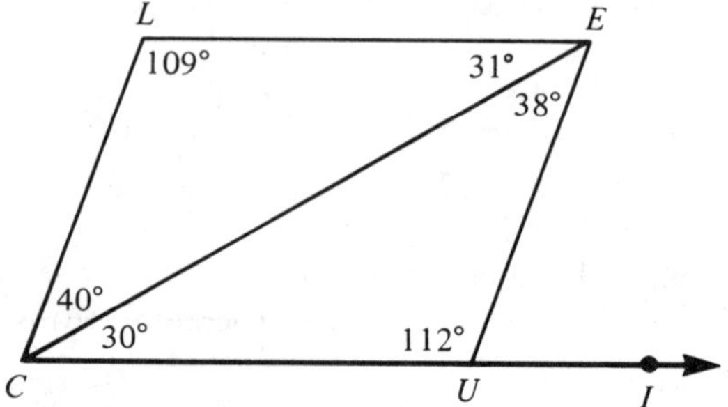

Figure 4.35

11. $LE > LC$
12. $EU + UC > EC$
13. $LE < LC + EC$
14. $EU < UC$
15. $\angle EUI > \angle ECU$

In exercises 16–20 refer to Figure 4.36.

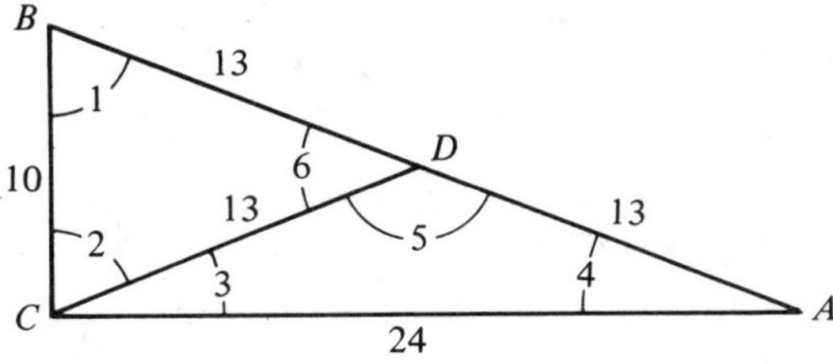

Figure 4.36

16. $\angle 1 > \angle 6$
17. $\angle 5 > \angle 2$
18. $\angle 4 < \angle 5$
19. $\angle 1 > \angle 4$
20. $\angle 3 < \angle 5$

In exercises 21–30 use Figure 4.37 to answer the questions.

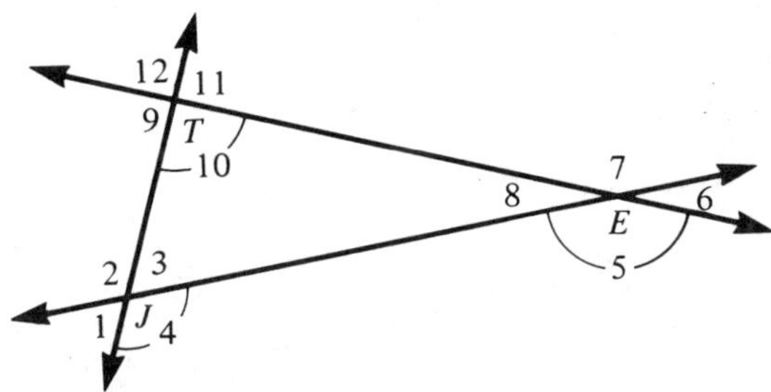

Figure 4.37

21. (a) Name the six exterior angles of $\triangle JET$.
(b) Why is $\measuredangle 6$ not an exterior angle of $\triangle JET$?

22. If $\measuredangle 10$ is a right angle, name the types of angles that the six exterior angles of $\triangle JET$ would be.

23. Name six angles that have a smaller measure than $\measuredangle 2$.

24. **(a)** If $\angle 3 > \angle 8$, side ______ is greater than side ______.
(b) If $\angle 10 > \angle 3$, side ______ is greater than side ______.

25. **(a)** If side $\overline{JE}$ is longer than side $\overline{JT}$, $\angle$______ $> \angle$______.
(b) If side $\overline{JE}$ is longer than side $\overline{TE}$, $\angle$______ $> \angle$______.

26. **(a)** If $JT = 7$ units, $TE = 17$ units, could $JE = 22$ units? Why or why not?
(b) If $JE = 19$ units, $JT = 6$ units, could $ET = 25$ units? Why or why not?

27. **(a)** If $TE = 12$ units, $JT = 7$ units, could $JE = 23$ units? Why or why not?
(b) If $TE = 12$ units, $JT = 7$ units, is $\angle 3 > \angle 8$? Why or why not?

28. If $\angle 3 = 58°$, $\angle 10 = 98°$, and $\angle 8 = 24°$, state in order of shortest to longest the three sides of $\triangle JET$.

29. If $JT = 6$ units, $TE = 11$ units, and $JE = 15$ units, state in order of smallest to largest the three angles of $\triangle JET$.

30. If $\measuredangle 10$ is an obtuse angle, name the types of angles that the six exterior angles of $\triangle JET$ would be.

In exercises 31–33 copy the figure, mark it, and supply the missing reasons in each proof.

31. *Given*
$\overline{GS} \cong \overline{GN}$

To Prove
$SO > SN$

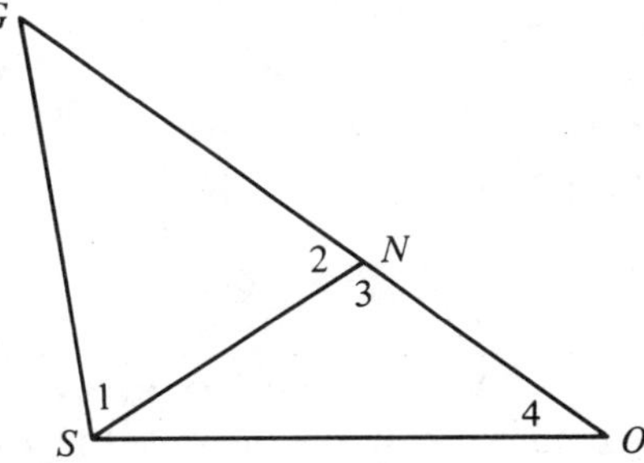

Statement	*Reason*
1. $\overline{GS} \cong \overline{GN}$	1. ?
2. $\measuredangle 1 \cong \measuredangle 2$	2. ?
3. $\angle 1 = \angle 2$	3. ?

4. $\angle 3 > \angle 1$	4. ?
5. $\angle 2 > \angle 4$	5. ?
6. $\angle 1 > \angle 4$	6. ?
7. $\angle 3 > \angle 4$	7. ?
8. $\therefore SO > SN$	8. ?

32. *Given*
$\angle E > \angle SKE$

To Prove
$SK > SJ$

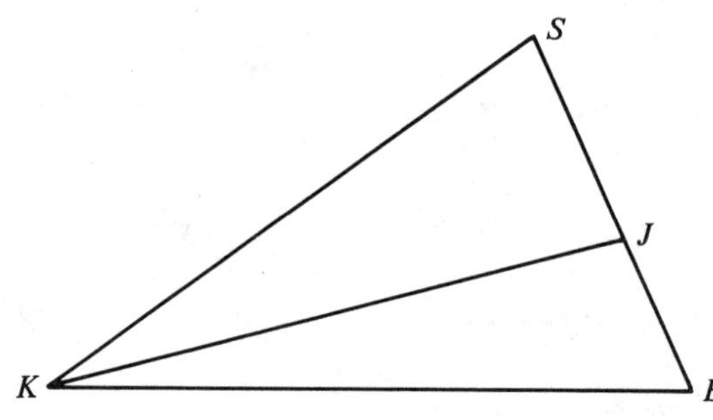

Statement	*Reason*
1. $\angle E > \angle SKE$	1. ?
2. $SK > SE$	2. ?
3. $SE = SJ + JE$	3. ?
4. $SE > SJ$	4. ?
5. $\therefore SK > SJ$	5. ?

33. *Given*
$\triangle ABC$ isos ($\overline{AB}$ base)

To Prove
$\angle A > \angle 2$

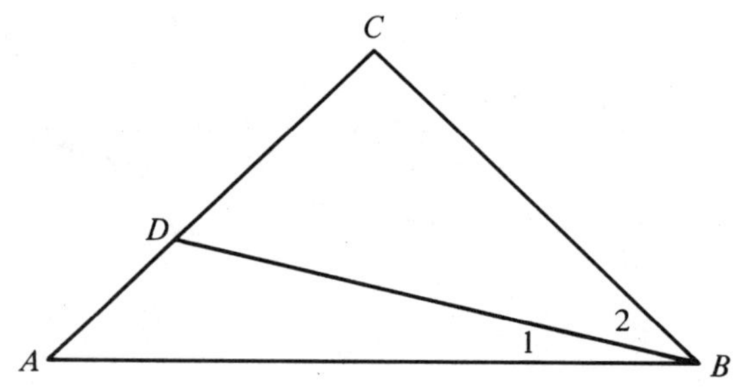

Statement	*Reason*
1. $\triangle ABC$ isos ($\overline{AB}$ base)	1. ?
2. $\overline{AC} \cong \overline{BC}$	2. ?
3. $\measuredangle A \cong \measuredangle CBA$	3. ?
4. $\angle A = \angle CBA$	4. ?
5. $\angle CBA = \angle 1 + \angle 2$	5. ?
6. $\angle CBA > \angle 2$	6. ?
7. $\therefore \angle A > \angle 2$	7. ?

In exercises 34–40 some of the proofs may require as reasons two axioms stated in Appendix A. These are

Addition for Order. If $x, y, z \in R$ and $x < y$, then $x + z < y + z$.

Multiplication for Order. If $x, y, z \in R$, $x < y$, and $z > 0$, then $xz < yz$.

34. Copy the figure, mark it, and supply the missing reasons in each proof.

Given
$JW > WA$
$\overline{JS}$ bis $\measuredangle WJA$
$\overline{AS}$ bis $\measuredangle WAJ$

To Prove
$JS > AS$

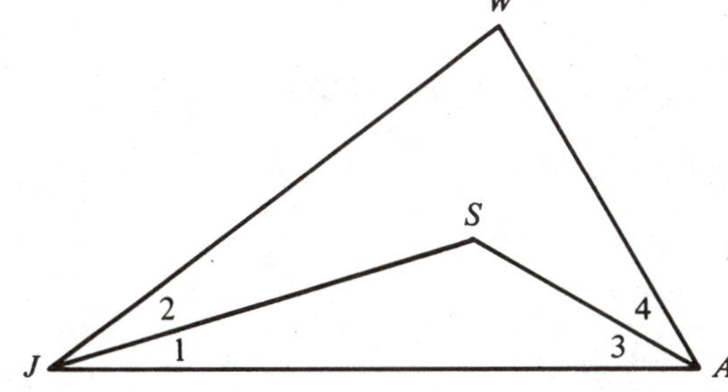

Statement	*Reason*
1. $JW > WA$	1. ?
2. $\angle WAJ > \angle WJA$	2. ?
3. $\angle WAJ = \angle 3 + \angle 4$ $\angle WJA = \angle 1 + \angle 2$	3. ?
4. $\angle 3 + \angle 4 > \angle 1 + \angle 2$	4. ?
5. $\overline{JS}$ bis $\measuredangle WJA$ $\overline{AS}$ bis $\measuredangle WAJ$	5. ?
6. $\measuredangle 1 \cong \measuredangle 2$, $\measuredangle 3 \cong \measuredangle 4$	6. ?
7. $\angle 1 = \angle 2$, $\angle 3 = \angle 4$	7. ?
8. $\angle 3 + \angle 3 > \angle 1 + \angle 1$	8. ?
9. $2 \cdot \angle 3 > 2 \cdot \angle 1$	9. ?
10. $\angle 3 > \angle 1$	10. Multiplication for Order
11. $\therefore JS > AS$	11. ?

In exercises 35–40 copy the figure, the hypothesis, and the conclusion. Mark the figure and write a proof.

35. *Given*
$\overline{TE} \cong \overline{RE}$
$YR > YT$
$\overline{ER}$ bis $\measuredangle YRT$

To Prove
$\angle 1 > \angle 2$

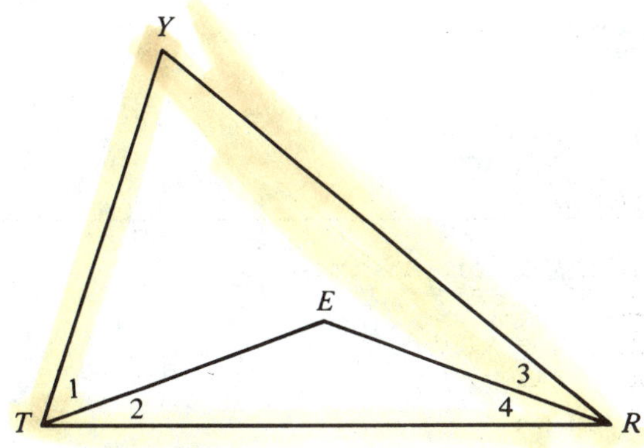

36. *Given*
$AW > WS$
$AJ > JS$

To Prove
$\angle WSJ > \angle WAJ$

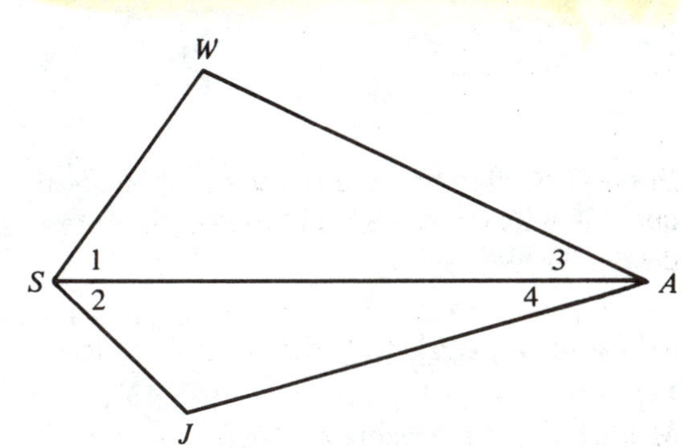

37. *Given*
quadrilateral *MORK*
(A quadrilateral is a four-sided figure.)

To Prove
$MK + KR + RO > MO$

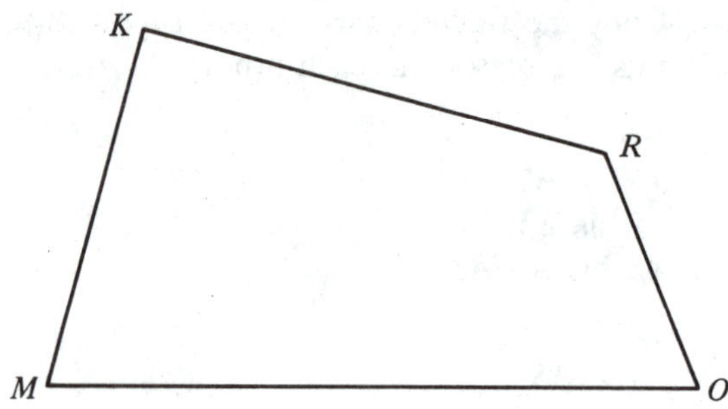

38. *Given*
$\overline{CD} \cong \overline{BD}$

To Prove
$\angle ACB > \angle 3$

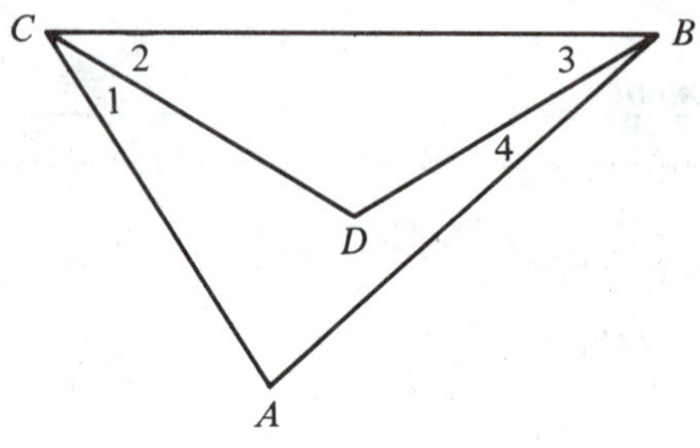

39. *Given*
$\overline{CU} \cong \overline{EU}$

To Prove
$EL > EC$

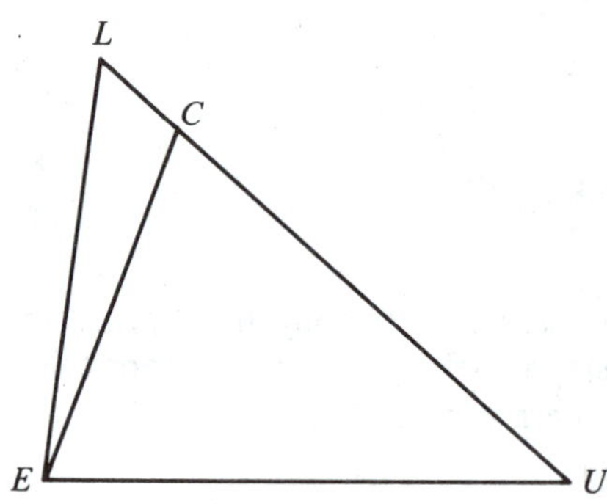

40. *Given*
$\overline{EK} \cong \overline{SK}$

To Prove
$EK > KJ$

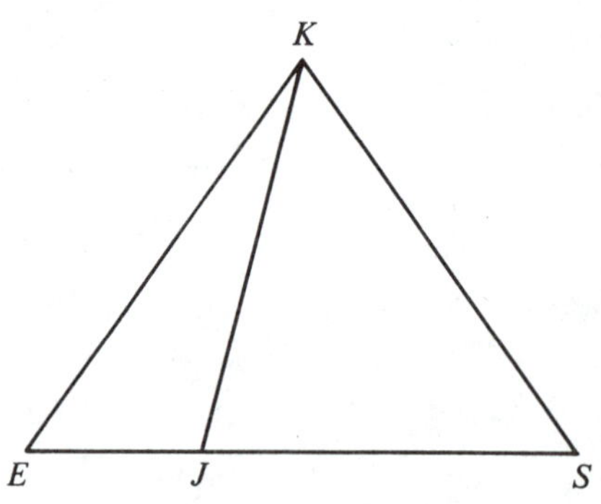

In exercises 41–44 use the indirect method to prove that the statements are false. See the examples in this section for a format.

41. If $\angle 1 = 43°$ and $\angle 2 = 37°$, then ∡1 is complementary to ∡2.

42. If $\angle 1 = 35°17'$ and $\angle 2 = 55°43'$, then ∡1 is complementary to ∡2.

43. If $\angle 1 = 111°11'11''$ and $\angle 2 = 68°49'49''$, then ∡1 is supplementary to ∡2.

44. If $\angle 1 = a°$ and $\angle 2 = 181° - a°$, then ∡1 is supplementary to ∡2.

In exercises 45–48 exactly one of the given numbers is a root of the equation. In each exercise use the indirect method to prove that (c) gives the root. See the examples in this section for a format.

45. $3x + 2 = 4x + 3$;
(a) 2 **(b)** 0 **(c)** -1

46. $3(x - 2) = 14 - 7x$;
(a) 1 **(b)** -3 **(c)** 2

47. $2x^2 + x - 6 = 0$;
(a) 1 **(b)** 0 **(c)** $\frac{3}{2}$

48. $(2x - 3)^2 - (x - 2)^2 = (x - 3)^2$;
(a) 0 **(b)** 4 **(c)** 2

4.7

MORE PROBLEM SOLVING WITH TRIANGLES

The facts developed so far allow us to derive many useful geometric relationships in complex figures from only a few given facts. Example 1 illustrates some of these derivations.

EXAMPLE 1

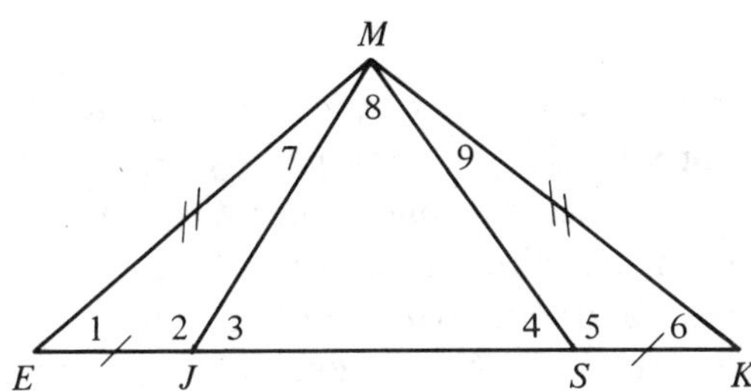

(a) State the facts indicated by the marks.
(b) Given the marked facts, state others that may be derived from these facts.

Answers

(a) $\overline{EM} \cong \overline{KM}$ $\overline{EJ} \cong \overline{KS}$

(b) $\triangle EMK$ isos $\angle 1 \cong \angle 6$ $\triangle EMJ \cong \triangle KMS$ $\angle 7 \cong \angle 9$ $\angle 2 \cong \angle 5$ $\overline{JM} \cong \overline{SM}$
$\triangle JMS$ isos $\angle 3 \cong \angle 4$ $\overline{ES} \cong \overline{KJ}$ $\triangle ESM \cong \triangle KJM$ $\angle EMS \cong \angle KMJ$

In studying Example 1 first try to see intuitively how the given facts in (a) insure that the derived ones are true; then find the reasons that justify each of the derived facts.

Example 2 shows that the sizes of angles in a complicated figure may be found from given facts. Mark the figure as fully as possible and then try to find the answers for yourself.

EXAMPLE 2

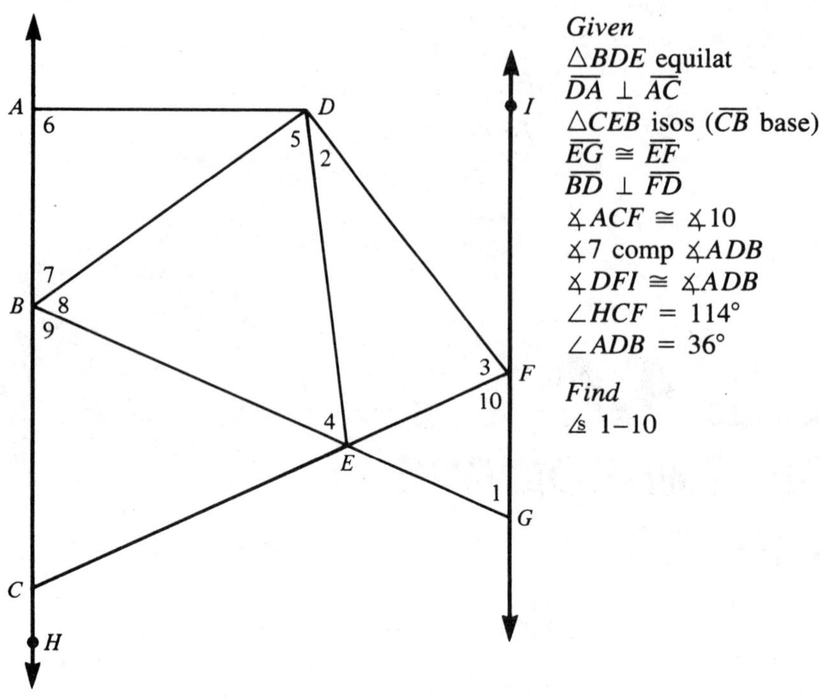

Given
$\triangle BDE$ equilat
$\overline{DA} \perp \overline{AC}$
$\triangle CEB$ isos ($\overline{CB}$ base)
$\overline{EG} \cong \overline{EF}$
$\overline{BD} \perp \overline{FD}$
$\measuredangle ACF \cong \measuredangle 10$
$\measuredangle 7$ comp $\measuredangle ADB$
$\measuredangle DFI \cong \measuredangle ADB$
$\angle HCF = 114°$
$\angle ADB = 36°$

Find
$\measuredangle$s 1–10

Answers

$\angle 1 = 66°$	$\angle 2 = 30°$	$\angle 3 = 78°$	$\angle 4 = 60°$	$\angle 5 = 60°$	$\angle 6 = 90°$
$\angle 7 = 54°$	$\angle 8 = 60°$	$\angle 9 = 66°$	$\angle 10 = 66°$		

Example 3 contains a long proof that uses two pairs of congruent triangles to reach the conclusion. The plan of the proof may be developed by reasoning in reverse; that is, by beginning with the conclusion and attempting to find a sequence of steps that leads to the hypothesis. Note in the following format that each requirement becomes the next statement to be proved. Once the plan is outlined, a proof must then be written with its steps in the proper order.

To prove	*We require*
$\overline{KJ} \perp \overline{ES}$	a right angle, for example, $\measuredangle 1$
$\measuredangle 1$ rt $\measuredangle$	$\angle 1 = 90°$
$\angle 1 = 90°$	$\angle 1 + \angle 2 = 180°$ and $\angle 1 = \angle 2$
$\angle 1 = \angle 2$	$\triangle EKM \cong \triangle SKM$

Now consider the three congruence postulates. In Example 3 the given fact $\overline{EK} \cong \overline{SK}$ and the obvious fact that $\overline{KM} \cong \overline{KM}$ suggest either sas or sss. For sas we require that $\measuredangle 3 \cong \measuredangle 4$, and this may be established by proving $\triangle JEK \cong \triangle JSK$ using sss.

EXAMPLE 3

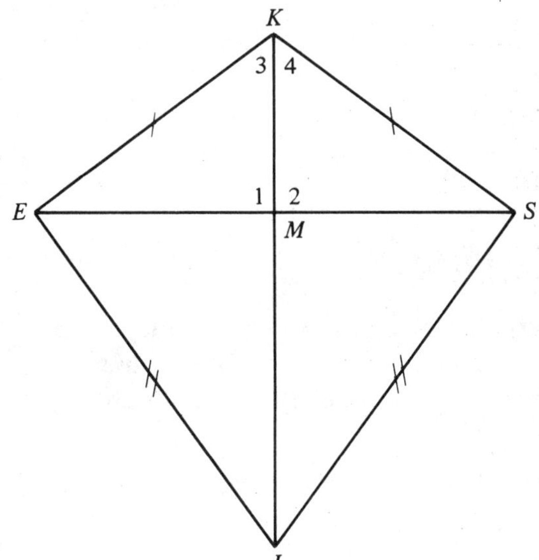

Given
$\overline{EK} \cong \overline{SK}$
$\overline{EJ} \cong \overline{SJ}$

To Prove
$\overline{KJ} \perp \overline{ES}$

Statement	*Reason*
1. $\overline{EK} \cong \overline{SK}$, $\overline{EJ} \cong \overline{SJ}$	1. given
2. $\overline{KJ} \cong \overline{KJ}$	2. refl ≅
3. $\triangle JEK \cong \triangle JSK$	3. sss ≅ sss
4. ∡3 ≅ ∡4	4. cpctc
5. $\overline{KM} \cong \overline{KM}$	5. refl ≅
6. $\triangle EKM \cong \triangle SKM$	6. sas ≅ sas
7. ∡1 ≅ ∡2	7. cpctc
8. $\angle 1 = \angle 2$	8. ≅ iff meas =
9. ∡1 and ∡2 lin pr	9. lin pr iff com side and opp rays
10. ∡1 supp ∡2	10. lin pr supp
11. $\angle 1 + \angle 2 = 180°$	11. supp iff sum = 180°
12. $\angle 1 + \angle 1 = 180°$	12. subst
13. $\angle 1 = 90°$	13. = ÷ =, quot =
14. ∡1 rt ∡	14. rt ∠ = 90°
15. ∴ $\overline{KJ} \perp \overline{ES}$	15. ⊥ iff a rt ∡

An important type of geometric problem is the location of all points that satisfy a certain requirement. Such exercises are called *locus* problems. (Locus problems are discussed in more detail in Appendix C.) For example, let us try to locate all points that are equidistant (equally distant) from the endpoints of a given line segment. One such point is of course the line segment's midpoint. Hence the remaining points must lie on a figure containing the midpoint. Figure 4.38 illustrates that the appropriate figure is the bisector of the line segment that is also perpendicular to it. We now define this special bisector and show how to construct it.

Definition 4.17 A line is the *perpendicular bisector* of a line segment iff it bisects the given segment and is perpendicular to it (⊥ bis iff bis seg and is ⊥).

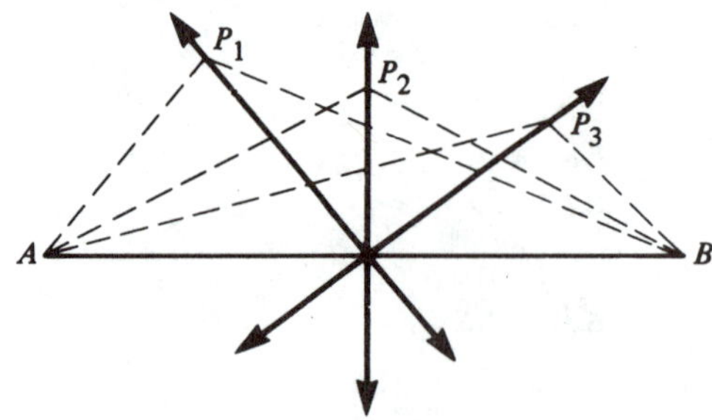

Figure 4.38 $P_1A \neq P_1B$, $P_2A = P_2B$, and $P_3A \neq P_3B$.

The perpendicular bisector appears in many practical types of constructions (e.g., king posts in gable roofs). If you are to prove that a line is the perpendicular bisector of a segment, note that you must find *both* a right angle and two congruent segments.

Construction 10 To construct the perpendicular bisector of a line segment.

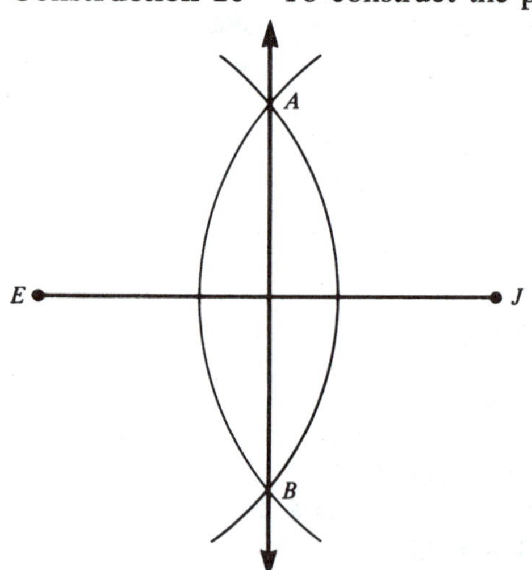

Given
$\overline{EJ}$

To Construct
$\overleftrightarrow{AB} \perp$ bis $\overline{EJ}$

Steps

1. With E as center and a radius longer than $\frac{1}{2}EJ$, draw an arc extending above and below $\overline{EJ}$.
2. With the same radius and J as center, draw an arc intersecting the first one. This determines points A and B.
3. Draw $\overleftrightarrow{AB}$, the perpendicular bisector of $\overline{EJ}$.

Note that the steps in Construction 10 are a slightly abbreviated version of those used earlier to construct a bisector and the midpoint of a line segment (Construction 1, Section 2.3). In fact, the two results are identical.

We now establish the fact proposed earlier that the perpendicular bisector of a line segment is the set of all points and only those points that are equidistant from the line segment's endpoints. This requires two theorems.

Theorem 27 If a point is on the perpendicular bisector of a line segment, then it is equidistant from the line segment's endpoints.

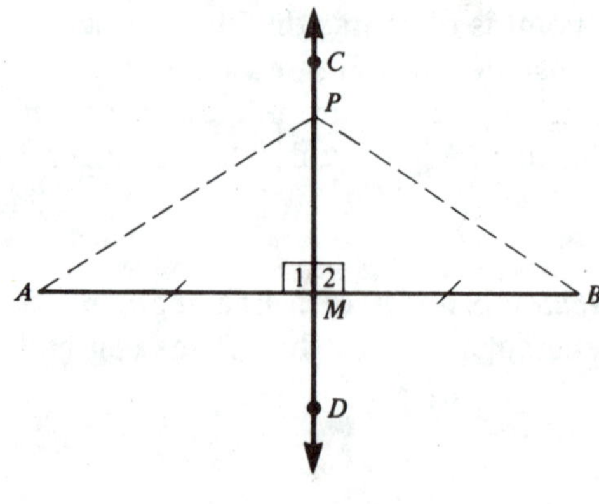

Given
$\overline{AB}$
$\overleftrightarrow{CD} \perp$ bis $\overline{AB}$
P any point on $\overleftrightarrow{CD}$
If P is the midpoint of $\overline{AB}$, $PA = PB$ by definition. Therefore, we suppose P is not the midpoint of $\overline{AB}$ and so is not on $\overline{AB}$.

To Prove
$PA = PB$

Statement	Reason
1. Draw $\overline{PA}$ and $\overline{PB}$.	1. 2 pts determ line
2. $\overleftrightarrow{CD} \perp$ bis $\overline{AB}$	2. given
3. $\overleftrightarrow{CD}$ bis $\overline{AB}$	3. $\perp$ bis iff bis seg and is $\perp$
4. $\overline{AM} \cong \overline{BM}$	4. bis $\div$ seg into 2 $\cong$ segs
5. $\overleftrightarrow{CD} \perp \overline{AB}$	5. $\perp$ bis iff bis seg and is $\perp$
6. $\measuredangle 1 \cong \measuredangle 2$	6. $\perp$s form $\cong$ rt $\measuredangle$s
7. $\overline{PM} \cong \overline{PM}$	7. refl $\cong$
8. $\triangle AMP \cong \triangle BMP$	8. sas $\cong$ sas
9. $\overline{PA} \cong \overline{PB}$	9. cpctc
10. $\therefore PA = PB$	10. $\cong$ iff meas =

Theorem 27 shows that every point on the perpendicular bisector is in the set of points we seek. Now we must show that if a point is known to be equidistant from the endpoints of a line segment, then it must be on the perpendicular bisector of the line segment.

Theorem 28 *(Converse of Theorem 27.)* If a point is equidistant from the endpoints of a line segment, then it is on the perpendicular bisector of the line segment.

The proof is left as an exercise; an approach to the proof may be found in Example 3. For convenience, both Theorem 27 and Theorem 28 will be abbreviated as follows: "pt on $\perp$ bis of seg iff equidis from endpts."

EXERCISES FOR 4.7

In exercises 1–20 answer true or false.

1. The measure of an exterior angle of a triangle is always greater than the measure of one of its interior angles.

2. If $n, r, a \in R$ and $n = r + a$, then $r > n$ if $a > 0$.

3. If $EJ > JS$ in $\triangle EJS$, then $\angle S > \angle E$.

4. If $\angle A < \angle B$ in $\triangle ABC$, then $AB > AC$.

5. An exterior angle of a triangle forms a linear pair with one of the angles of the triangle.

6. According to the Triangle Inequality Theorem (Theorem 26), no triangle can have sides of 5, 6, and 12 units.

7. A triangle with sides measuring $3\frac{1}{4}$, $5\frac{1}{2}$, and $8\frac{7}{8}$ units can be constructed.

8. The perpendicular bisector of a segment can be constructed at one of the endpoints of the segment.

9. A point equidistant from the endpoints of a segment lies on any bisector of the segment.

10. If in $\triangle ABC$ and $\triangle EJS$, $\overline{CB} \cong \overline{SJ}$, $\overline{CA} \cong \overline{SE}$, and $\measuredangle A \cong \measuredangle E$, then $\triangle ABC \cong \triangle EJS$.

11. Locus problems are those seeking all points that satisfy a certain requirement.

12. An exterior angle of a triangle is the supplement of one of the interior angles of the triangle.

13. If the lengths of two sides of a triangle are 9 and 14 units, then the length of the third side must be greater than 5.

14. If $\triangle DFG \cong \triangle GFD$, then $\triangle DFG$ must be equilateral.

15. If in $\triangle TAP$ $\angle T = 35°$, $\angle A = 65°$, and $\angle P = 80°$, then $PA < TP < TA$.

16. If in $\triangle DOG$ $\angle D = 90°$, $\angle O = 23°$, and $\angle G = 67°$, then $GO > GD > DO$.

17. If in $\triangle CAT$, $CA = 12$ units, $AT = 15$ units, and $TC = 23$ units, then $\angle T < \angle A < \angle C$.

18. If two isosceles triangles have a common side, then the two isosceles triangles must be congruent.

19. If two sides of a triangle measure 10 and 13 inches, then the third side must be greater than 3 inches and less than 23 inches.

20. If a point is on the perpendicular bisector of the base of an isosceles triangle, then the point is on the median from the vertex angle of the triangle.

In exercises 21 and 22 copy the figure: (a) write the congruences given by the marks, and (b) write the congruences and other facts that can be derived from the congruences in (a).

21.

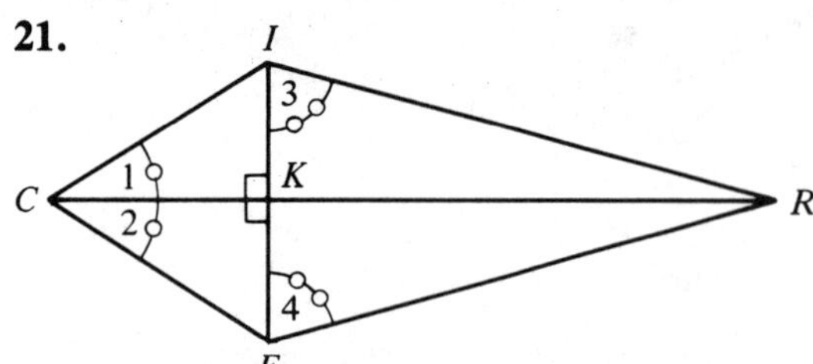

22.

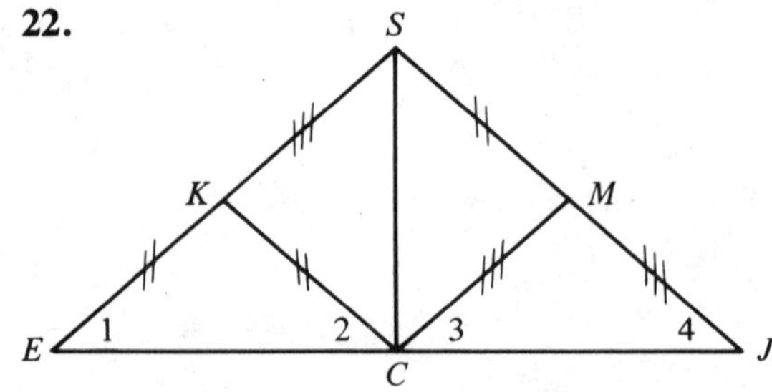

In exercises 23–30 copy the figure, mark it, and find the requested measures.

23. *Given*
$\overline{KA} \perp \overline{JC}$
$\angle BOC = 29°$
$\angle KFO = 82°$
∡6 supp ∡KFO
Sum of ∡s in a △ is 180°

Find
∡s 1–10

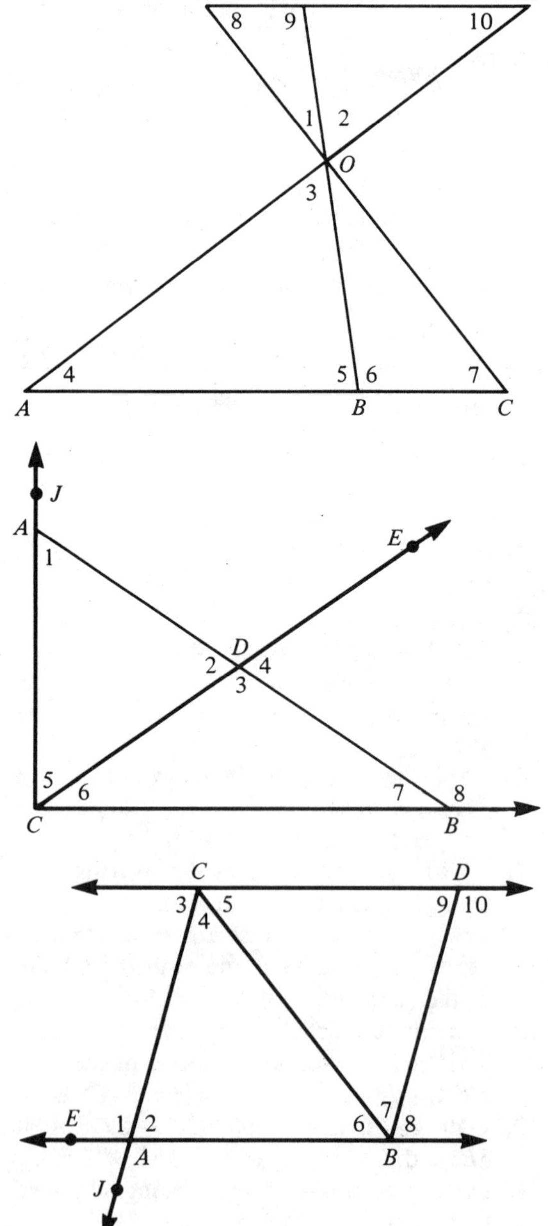

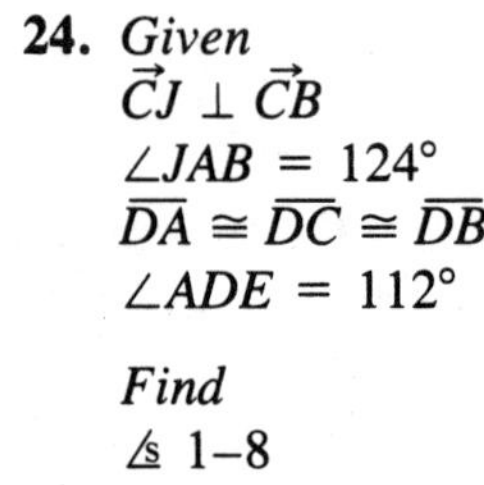

24. *Given*
$\overrightarrow{CJ} \perp \overrightarrow{CB}$
$\angle JAB = 124°$
$\overline{DA} \cong \overline{DC} \cong \overline{DB}$
$\angle ADE = 112°$

Find
∡s 1–8

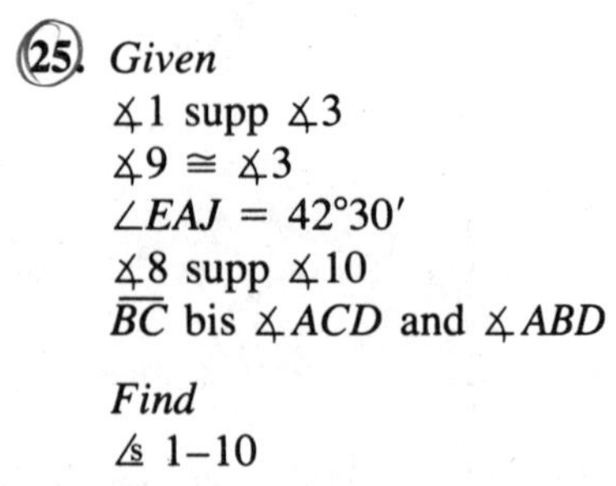

25. *Given*
∡1 supp ∡3
∡9 ≅ ∡3
$\angle EAJ = 42°30'$
∡8 supp ∡10
$\overline{BC}$ bis ∡ACD and ∡ABD

Find
∡s 1–10

26. *Given*
$\measuredangle 5$ supp $\measuredangle 9$
$\overrightarrow{JS}$ bis $\measuredangle EJK$
$\overrightarrow{AB}$ bis $\measuredangle JAC$
$\measuredangle 1 = 120°30'$

Find
$\measuredangle$s 2–10

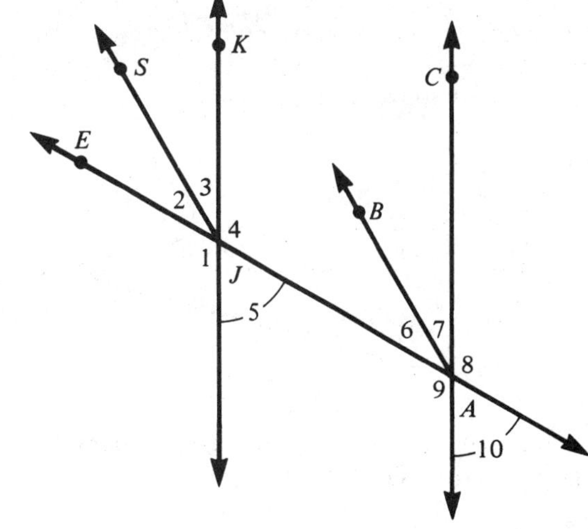

27. *Given*
$\triangle EJS$ isos ($\overline{EJ}$ base)
$\triangle I \cong \triangle II$
$\overrightarrow{JK}$ bis $\measuredangle EJS$
$\angle 1 + \angle 7 + \angle EJK = 180°$
$\angle 2 + \angle 5 + \angle 3 = 180°$
$\angle EJS = 72°15'$

Find
$\measuredangle$s 1–8

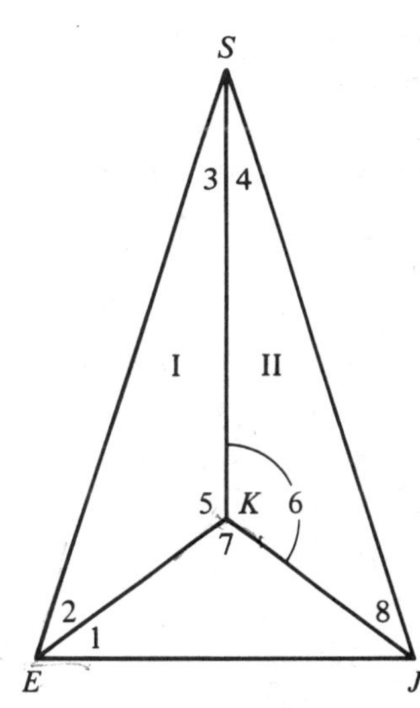

28. *Given*
$\triangle CBA$ isos ($\overline{CB}$ base)
$\triangle CEF$ isos ($\overline{CE}$ base)
$\angle B = 68°13'$
$\angle 6 + \angle 7 = \angle 9$
$\angle 3 + \angle B = \angle 1$
$\overrightarrow{CD}$ bis $\measuredangle BCF$

Find
$\measuredangle$s 1–9

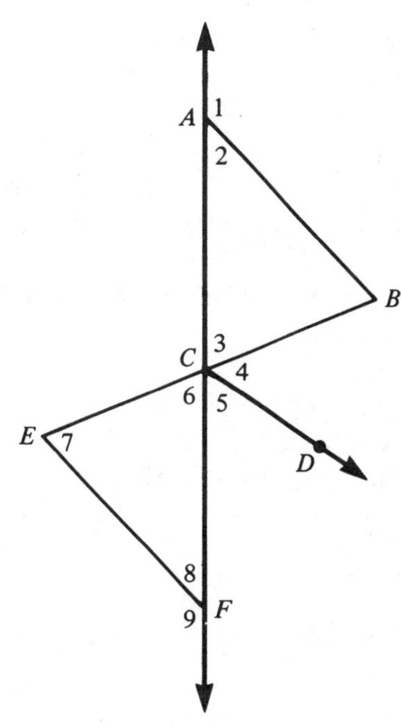

29. *Given*
$\overrightarrow{CE} \perp \overrightarrow{ES}$, $\measuredangle 3 \cong \measuredangle CJT$, $\angle LEM = 12°$, $\measuredangle 1 \cong \measuredangle 8$, $\overrightarrow{MJ}$ bis $\measuredangle CJS$, $\measuredangle 10 \cong \measuredangle 4$, $\measuredangle 8$ comp $\measuredangle 4$, $\angle 6 + \angle 7 + \angle 10 = 180°$

Find
$\measuredangle$s 1–10

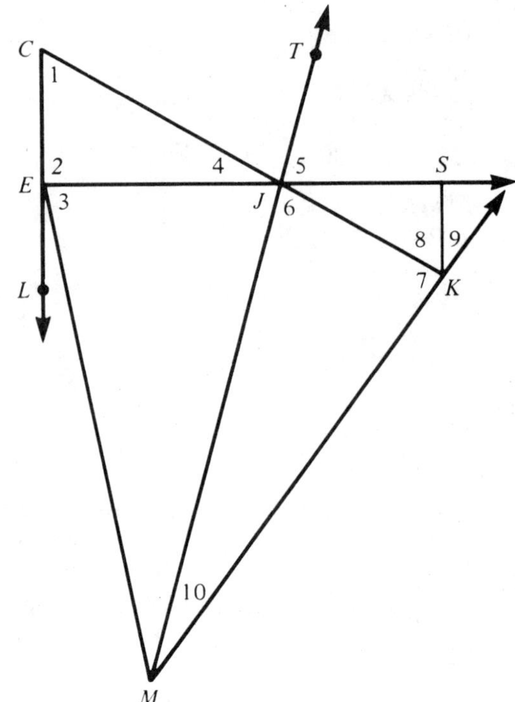

30. *Given*
$\measuredangle 1 \cong \measuredangle GFA$, $\overline{BC} \perp \overline{DC}$, $\overrightarrow{DC}$ bis $\measuredangle FDB$, $\angle EFD = 57°$, $\overline{ED} \cong \overline{EF}$, $\angle 1 + \angle 3 + \angle 7 = 180°$, $\measuredangle 7$ supp $\angle 12$, $\measuredangle 4$ comp $\measuredangle 8$, $\measuredangle FDC$ supp $\measuredangle 11$

Find
$\measuredangle$s 1–12

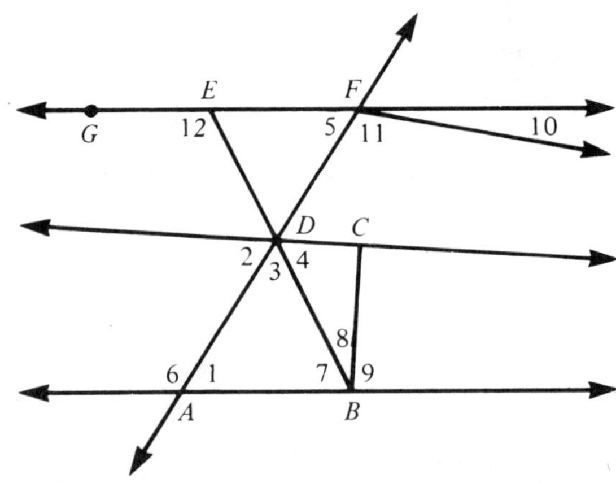

In exercises 31 and 32 copy the figure, mark it, and supply the missing reasons in each proof. (Note that both proofs require showing that two pairs of triangles are congruent.)

31. *Given*
U midpt $\overline{EC}$
$\measuredangle 3 \cong \measuredangle 4$
$\overline{UD} \cong \overline{UL}$

To Prove
$\measuredangle 1 \cong \measuredangle 2$

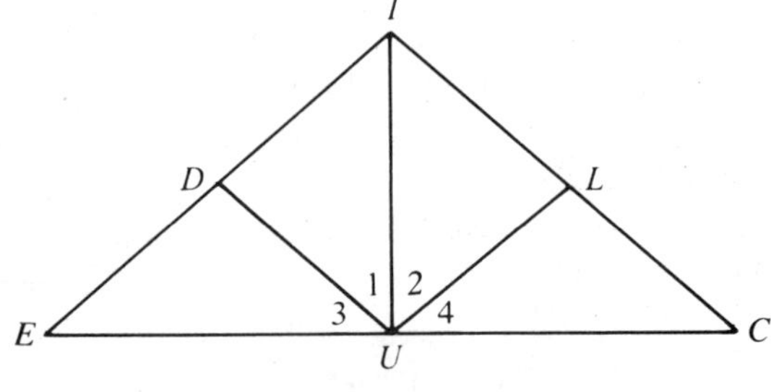

Statement	*Reason*
1. U midpt $\overline{EC}$	1. ?
2. $\overline{UE} \cong \overline{UC}$	2. ?
3. $\measuredangle 3 \cong \measuredangle 4$	3. ?
4. $\overline{UD} \cong \overline{UL}$	4. ?
5. $\triangle EUD \cong \triangle CUL$	5. ?
6. $\measuredangle E \cong \measuredangle C$	6. ?
7. $\overline{EI} \cong \overline{CI}$	7. ?
8. $\triangle EUI \cong \triangle CUI$	8. ?
9. $\measuredangle EUI \cong \measuredangle CUI$	9. ?
10. $\measuredangle EUI - \measuredangle 3 \cong \measuredangle CUI - \measuredangle 4$	10. ?
11. $\measuredangle 1 \cong \measuredangle EUI - \measuredangle 3$	11. ?
12. $\measuredangle CUI - \measuredangle 4 \cong \measuredangle 2$	12. ?
13. $\therefore \measuredangle 1 = \measuredangle 2$	13. ?

32. Proof of Construction 10. To construct the perpendicular bisector of a line segment. This proof is based on Postulate 5 (can copy seg) and the construction for copying a segment (Construction 2).

Given
$\overline{AB}$
$\overleftrightarrow{EC}$ as constructed

To Prove
$\overleftrightarrow{EC} \perp$ bis $\overline{AB}$

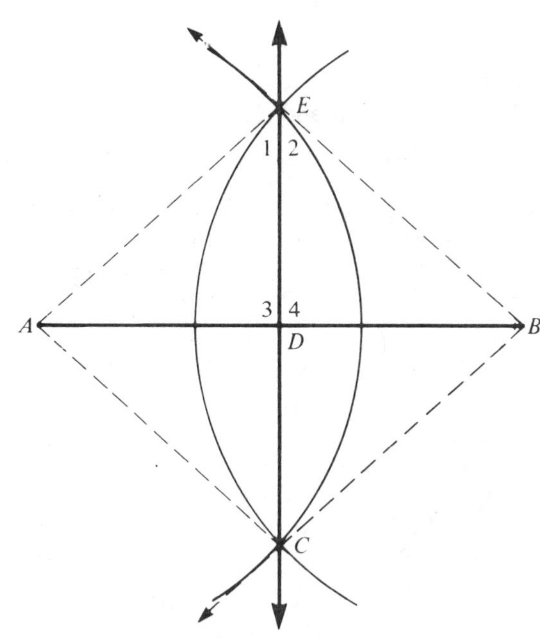

Statement	*Reason*
1. $\overline{AB}$	1. ?
2. $\overleftrightarrow{EC}$ as constructed	2. ?
3. Draw $\overline{AE}$, $\overrightarrow{BE}$, $\overline{AC}$, $\overrightarrow{BC}$.	3. ?
4. $\overline{AE} \cong \overline{BE}$	4. radii of ≅ Ⓢ are ≅
5. $\overline{AC} \cong \overline{BC}$	5. ?
6. $\overline{EC} \cong \overline{EC}$	6. ?
7. $\triangle ACE \cong \triangle BCE$	7. ?
8. $\measuredangle 1 \cong \measuredangle 2$	8. ?
9. $\overline{ED} \cong \overline{ED}$	9. ?
10. $\triangle ADE \cong \triangle BDE$	10. ?
11. $\overline{AD} \cong \overline{BD}$	11. ?
12. $\overleftrightarrow{EC}$ bis $\overline{AB}$	12. ?
13. $\measuredangle 3 \cong \measuredangle 4$	13. ?

14. $\angle 3 = \angle 4$	14. ?
15. $\measuredangle 3$ and $\measuredangle 4$ lin pr	15. ?
16. $\measuredangle 3$ supp $\measuredangle 4$	16. ?
17. $\angle 3 + \angle 4 = 180°$	17. ?
18. $\angle 3 + \angle 3 = 180°$	18. ?
19. $2 \cdot \angle 3 = 180°$	19. ?
20. $\angle 3 = 90°$	20. ?
21. $\angle 3$ rt $\measuredangle$	21. ?
22. $\overleftrightarrow{EC} \perp \overline{AB}$	22. ?
23. $\therefore \overleftrightarrow{EC} \perp$ bis $\overline{AB}$	23. ?

In exercises 33–47 copy the figure, the hypothesis, and the conclusion. Mark the figure and write a proof.

33. *Given*
E midpt $\overline{AD}$
$\overline{DB}$ and $\overline{EF}$ bis each other

To Prove
$\overline{EA} \cong \overline{FB}$

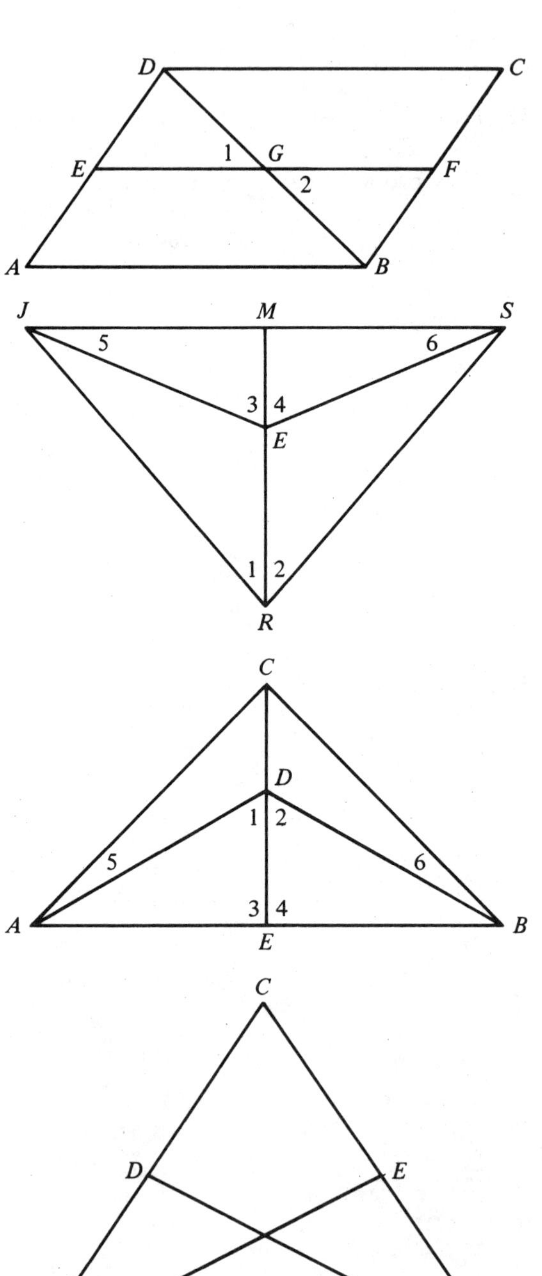

34. *Given*
$\overline{RM}$ bis $\measuredangle JRS$ and $\measuredangle JES$

To Prove
$\measuredangle 5 \cong \measuredangle 6$

35. *Given*
$\overline{CE} \perp$ bis $\overline{AB}$

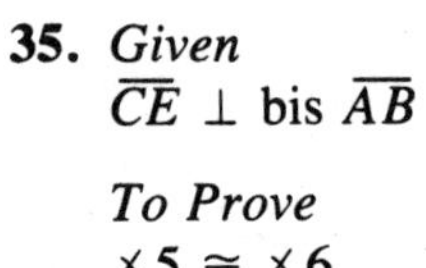

To Prove
$\measuredangle 5 \cong \measuredangle 6$

36. *Given*
$\triangle ABC$ isos ($\overline{AB}$ base)
$\overline{AE}$ med
$\overline{BD}$ med

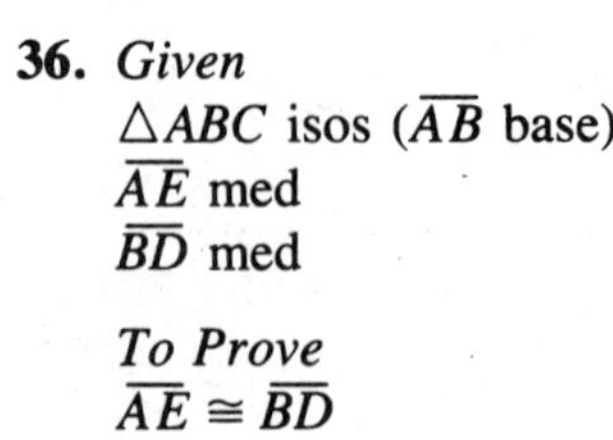

To Prove
$\overline{AE} \cong \overline{BD}$

37. *Given*
$\triangle TAE$ equilat
$\overline{TH} \cong \overline{AL} \cong \overline{ES}$

To Prove
$\measuredangle 1 \cong \measuredangle 2 \cong \measuredangle 3$

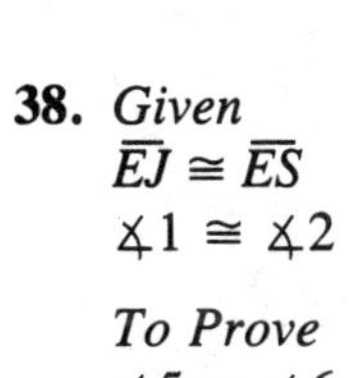

38. *Given*
$\overline{EJ} \cong \overline{ES}$
$\measuredangle 1 \cong \measuredangle 2$

To Prove
$\measuredangle 5 \cong \measuredangle 6$

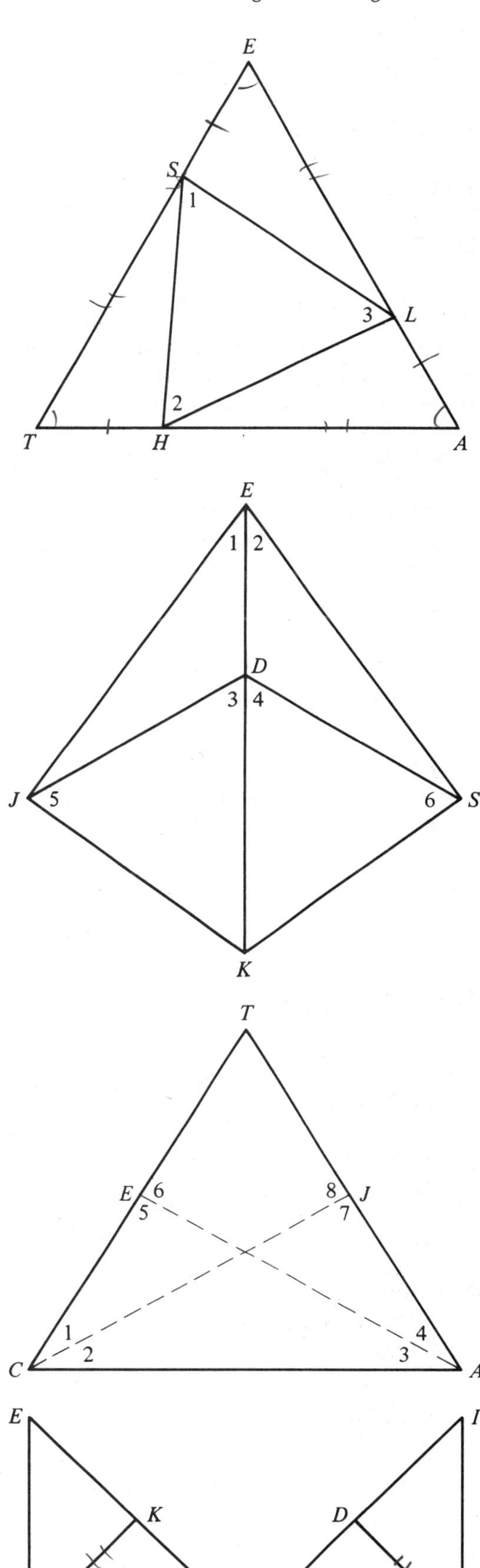

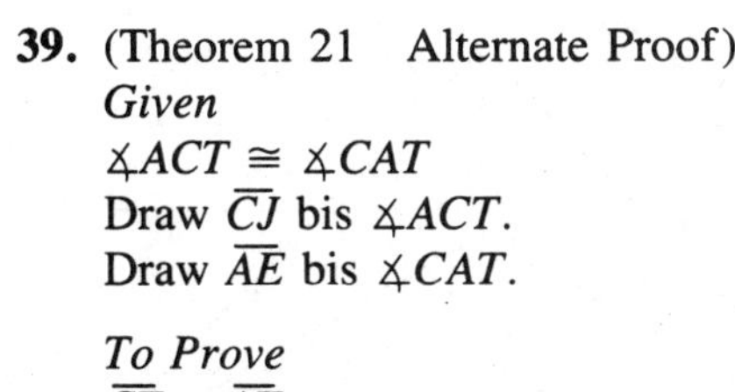

39. (Theorem 21 Alternate Proof)
Given
$\measuredangle ACT \cong \measuredangle CAT$
Draw $\overline{CJ}$ bis $\measuredangle ACT$.
Draw $\overline{AE}$ bis $\measuredangle CAT$.

To Prove
$\overline{CT} \cong \overline{AT}$

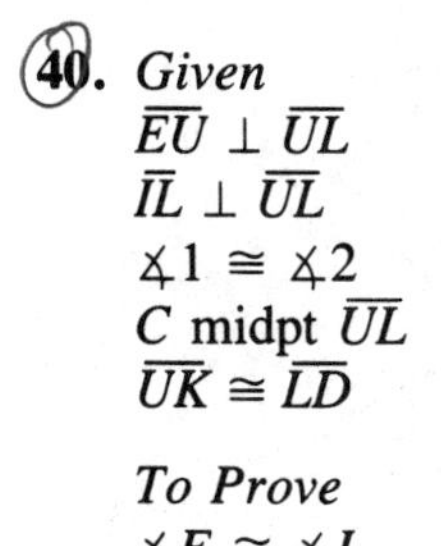

40. *Given*
$\overline{EU} \perp \overline{UL}$
$\overline{IL} \perp \overline{UL}$
$\measuredangle 1 \cong \measuredangle 2$
C midpt $\overline{UL}$
$\overline{UK} \cong \overline{LD}$

To Prove
$\measuredangle E \cong \measuredangle I$

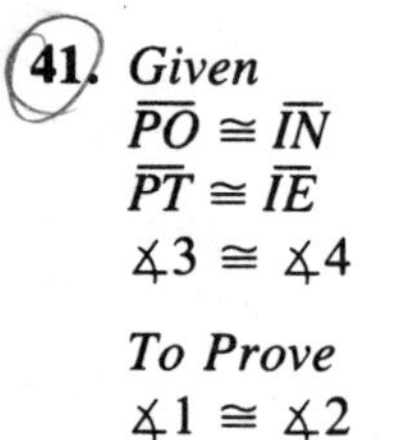

41. *Given*
$\overline{PO} \cong \overline{IN}$
$\overline{PT} \cong \overline{IE}$
$\measuredangle 3 \cong \measuredangle 4$

To Prove
$\measuredangle 1 \cong \measuredangle 2$

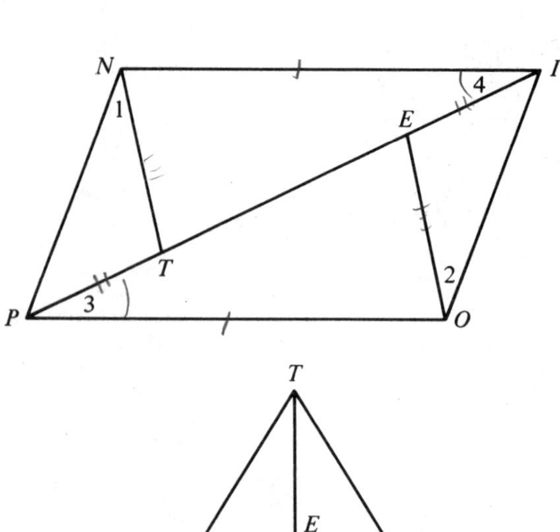

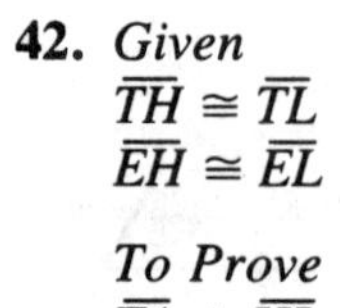

42. *Given*
$\overline{TH} \cong \overline{TL}$
$\overline{EH} \cong \overline{EL}$

To Prove
$\overline{TA} \perp \overline{HL}$

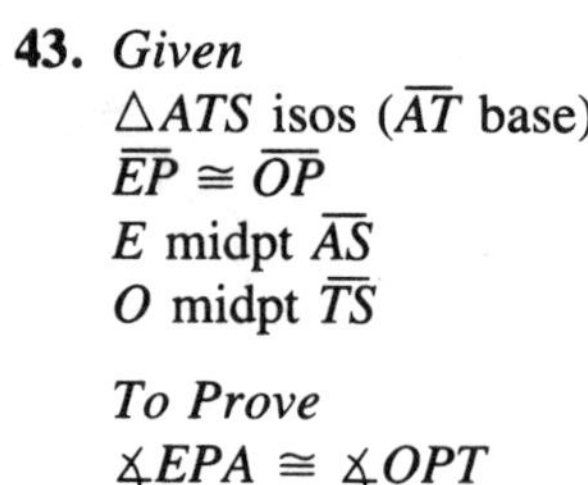

43. *Given*
$\triangle ATS$ isos ($\overline{AT}$ base)
$\overline{EP} \cong \overline{OP}$
E midpt $\overline{AS}$
O midpt $\overline{TS}$

To Prove
$\measuredangle EPA \cong \measuredangle OPT$

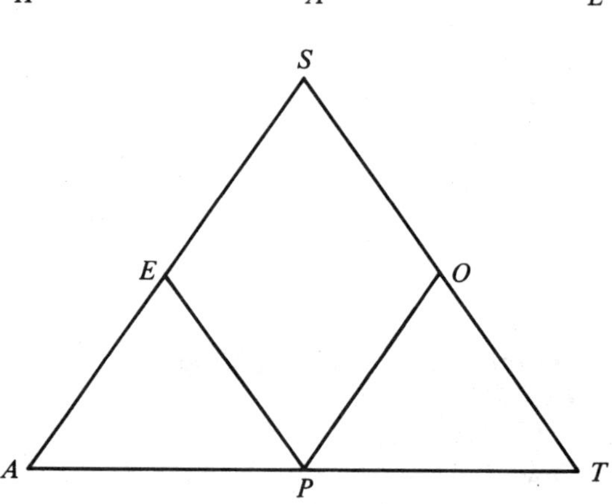

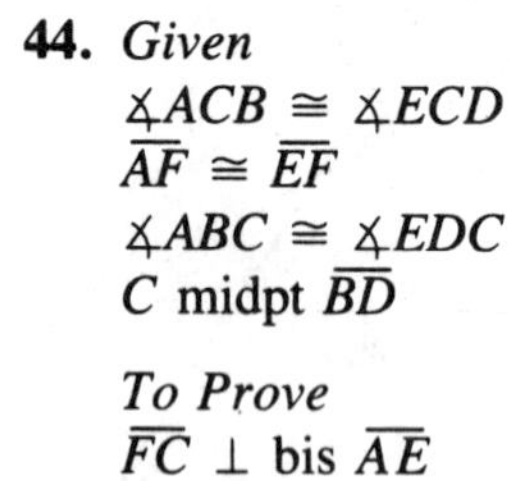

44. *Given*
$\measuredangle ACB \cong \measuredangle ECD$
$\overline{AF} \cong \overline{EF}$
$\measuredangle ABC \cong \measuredangle EDC$
C midpt $\overline{BD}$

To Prove
$\overline{FC} \perp$ bis $\overline{AE}$

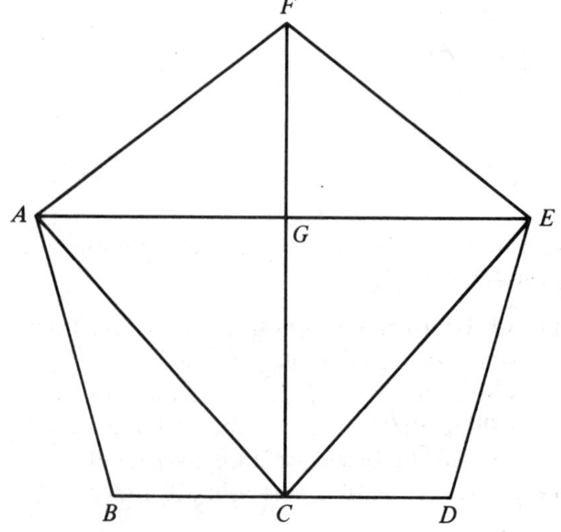

45. *Given*
$\overline{EC} \cong \overline{UC}$
$\overline{CI} \cong \overline{CL}$
$\measuredangle 1 \cong \measuredangle 2$

To Prove
$\measuredangle 4 \cong \measuredangle 3$

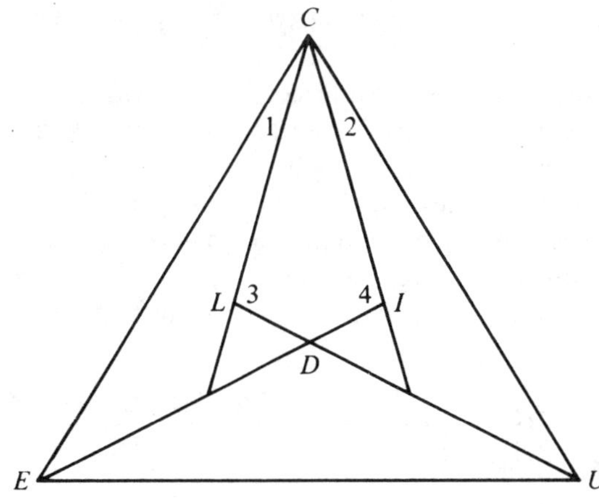

46. *Given*
$\overline{KE} \cong \overline{GE}$
$\triangle KGC$ isos ($\overline{KG}$ base)

To Prove
$\measuredangle DAJ \cong \measuredangle BAJ$

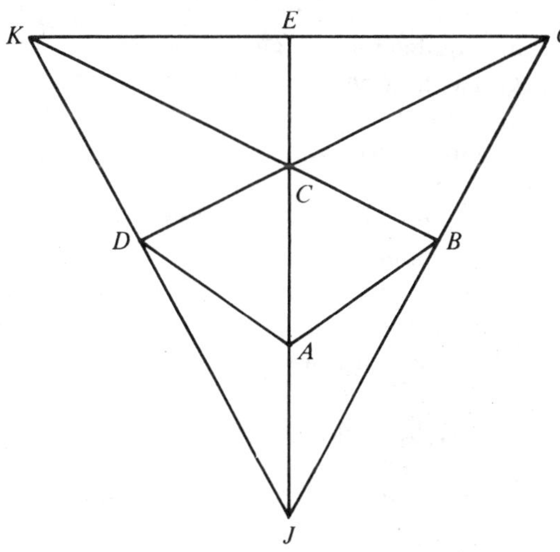

47. *Given*
$\measuredangle GOA \cong \measuredangle GCK$
$\overline{OG} \cong \overline{CG}$
$\overline{KN} \cong \overline{AT}$

To Prove
$\triangle EJS$ isos

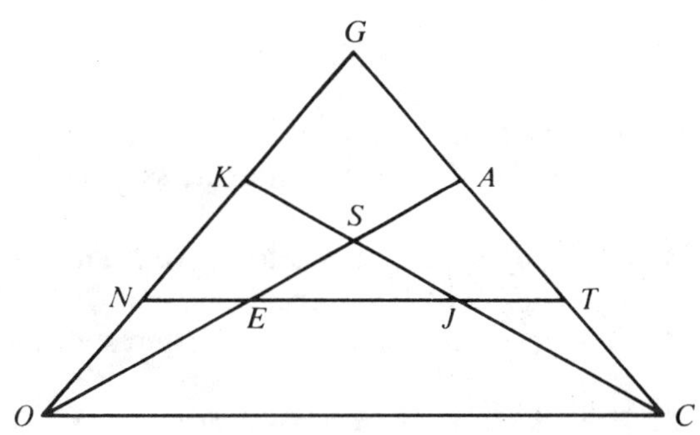

In exercises 48–50 use only a compass and straightedge.

48. **(a)** Construct a right triangle by constructing a perpendicular to $\overrightarrow{EJ}$ at E.
(b) Construct the perpendicular bisectors of the three sides of the triangle in (a); extend the bisectors until they meet.

49. Draw an obtuse triangle. Construct the perpendicular bisectors of the three sides; extend the bisectors until they meet.

50. Construct an isosceles $\triangle BIG$ with $\overline{BI}$ as the base. Construct the perpendicular bisector of the base $\overline{BI}$; extend the bisector until it intersects the triangle.

CHAPTER 4 SUMMARY

Among the possible three-line figures, the triangle is the most important because it forms the basis of much geometry and appears in many more complex figures. The concept of congruent triangles provides a powerful tool for problem solving. For example, the congruence of triangles permits indirect measurement through the "corresponding parts of congruent triangles are congruent" (cpctc) technique. In developing the numerous facts about triangles, we have extended our proof-writing techniques; in particular, the notion of inequalities in triangles allows us to introduce indirect proofs.

FACTS TO KNOW

1. Definitions
- **a.** Triangle
- **b.** Scalene triangle
- **c.** Isosceles triangle
- **d.** Equilateral triangle
- **e.** Acute triangle
- **f.** Right triangle
- **g.** Obtuse triangle
- **h.** Equiangular triangle
- **i.** Congruent triangles
- **j.** Midpoint of segment
- **k.** Bisector of segment
- **l.** Bisector of angle
- **m.** Median of triangle
- **n.** Altitude of triangle
- **o.** Exterior angle of triangle
- **p.** Remote interior angle
- **q.** Perpendicular bisector of segment

2. Postulates
- **a.** sss ≅ sss
- **b.** sas ≅ sas
- **c.** asa ≅ asa
- **d.** whole ≅ sum parts

3. Theorems
- **a.** refl ≅
- **b.** symm ≅
- **c.** trans ≅
- **d.** ≅ + ≅, sums ≅
- **e.** ≅ − ≅, diff ≅
- **f.** ≅ · pos, prod ≅
- **g.** ≅ ÷ pos, quot ≅
- **h.** if 2 sides △ ≅, opp ∡s ≅
- **i.** if 2 ∡s △ ≅, opp sides ≅
- **j.** if equilat △, then equiang △
- **k.** ext ∠ > rem int ∠
- **l.** 2 sides △ ≠, opp ∡s ≠ same order
- **m.** 2 ∡s △ ≠, opp sides ≠ same order
- **n.** sum 2 sides △ > 3d side
- **o.** pt on ⊥ bis of seg iff equidis from endpts

PROBLEMS TO MASTER

1. Identify types of triangles.
2. Prove triangles congruent using sss, sas, or asa.
3. Use congruent triangles to prove segments or angles congruent (cpctc).
4. Find measures of angles in figures using triangles.
5. Use shortcuts (≅ for =) in proofs.
6. Write proofs involving inequality relations.
7. Write indirect proofs.
8. Construct a triangle congruent to another, given
   - **a.** three sides,
   - **b.** two sides and the included angle
   - **c.** two angles and the included side.
9. Construct the perpendicular bisector of a segment.

5

PARALLEL LINES

MAJOR TOPICS

|| Parallel lines in a plane

|| Role of transversal with parallel lines

|| Identification of certain pairs of angles when two lines are cut by a transversal

|| Role and need for Parallel Postulate

|| Congruent pairs of angles when two parallel lines are cut by a transversal

|| Ways to prove lines parallel

|| New methods for proving triangles congruent (aas and hs)

|| The "180° in a triangle" theorem

HISTORICAL NOTE

THE PARALLEL POSTULATE

Euclid's geometric postulates, the foundation of his proofs, were so simple and plausible that no thinking person of his time (except Euclid himself) questioned their truth. Here "truth" means that the postulates stated self-evident properties of physical objects that suggested geometric figures in the minds of the Greek geometers. To Euclid, however, one of his postulates was not so self-evident. In fact, it disturbed him enough that he tried to prove as many theorems as possible without using it. This was the now-famous Parallel Postulate, which Euclid stated in this way:

> If a straight line meets two straight lines, so as to make the two interior angles on the same side of it taken together less than two right angles, these straight lines, being continually produced, shall at length meet on that side on which are the angles which are less than two right angles.

The modern equivalent of this complicated statement asserts:

> In a plane there is one and only one line parallel to a given line and containing a given point not on that line.

Euclid was troubled by his Parallel Postulate because it was difficult to verify by experiment. He conceived of a line as extending indefinitely in both directions, but who could in practice continually produce a line? All his other postulates concerned finite geometric figures and thus were capable of physical verification. It was the "infinite extent" aspect of the Parallel Postulate that stymied Euclid.

To state the problem differently, suppose that plane geometry were restricted to figures inside a circle and that parallel lines were defined as those that do not intersect. Then there would be infinitely many lines parallel to a given line and containing a given point not on that line!

Euclid hoped that he could overcome these concerns by proving the Parallel Postulate as a theorem. This would show it as a necessary consequence of his other, more self-evident, postulates. In this attempt, however, he failed, and it remained as a postulate in his text.

For many centuries after Euclid's death, attempts were made to either prove the Parallel Postulate or to rewrite it in a way that would eliminate the problem. Proclus, in the fifth century A.D., proposed redefining a line parallel to a given line as the locus (collection) of points at a given fixed distance from the line. This idea, however, only shifted the problem to that of proving that such a locus of points formed a straight line, and this Proclus could not do. In fact, his definition and the Parallel Postulate are equivalent, and accepting one amounts to accepting the other.

One of the most original efforts to prove the Parallel Postulate, and one that foreshadowed the future, was made by Girolamo Saccheri (1667–1733), a Jesuit priest and professor of mathematics at the University of Pavia in northern Italy. Saccheri attacked the problem indirectly. He assumed that there are at least two lines through a given point and parallel to a given line. He was sure that such an absurd assumption would lead to a contradiction, leaving Euclid's postulate as the only acceptable alternative. But, to his amazement, Saccheri found instead that he could prove many new and remarkable theorems, all free of contradiction. So strong was his (and the scientific community's) faith in Euclid's infallibility, however, that he concluded that the strange nature of these new theorems was sufficient proof that his assumption was wrong. Thus, despite the evident originality of his mind, Saccheri—nearly two thousand years after Euclid—could not make the next leap forward. Another century would pass before the implications of the Parallel Postulate were confronted.

5.1 INTRODUCTION

Many physical objects suggest the notion of parallel lines; such as, railroad tracks, the edges of a tall building, and lines painted on a straight highway. All these suggest lines that do not intersect however far they extend. Before using this idea to *define* parallel lines, we must recognize that there are lines that never intersect and yet do not fit the usual notion of parallelism. Figure 5.1 shows a rectangular box with three of its edges extended. Lines l_1, and l_2 are parallel, but l_1 and l_3 are not *even though they do not intersect*. This is because l_1 and l_3 are not in the same plane. Lines that do lie in the same plane are *coplanar*. As stated in Section 2.1, Chapters 2–9 describe plane geometry (figures that lie in a plane) unless specifically stated otherwise, but the distinction between the pairs l_1, l_2 (parallel lines) and l_1, l_3 (skew lines) in Figure 5.1 is so important that we account for it in Definition 5.1.

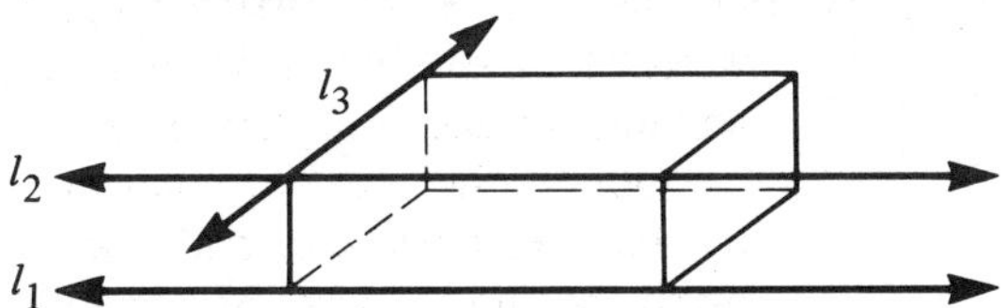

Figure 5.1

Definition 5.1 Two coplanar lines, l and m, are parallel (abbreviated $l \parallel m$) iff $l \cap m = \emptyset$.

The term "parallel" is also applied to line segments and rays when the lines they determine are parallel.

In developing the geometry of parallel lines we will focus on the three-line arrangement in Figure 5.2. Lines l and m may or may not be parallel, and line t is called a transversal. A *transversal* is a line that intersects two or more coplanar lines in *different* points. In any such figure, ∡s 3, 4, 5, and 6 are called *interior* angles, and ∡s 1, 2, 7, and 8 are called *exterior* angles. Certain pairs of nonadjacent angles are given special names.

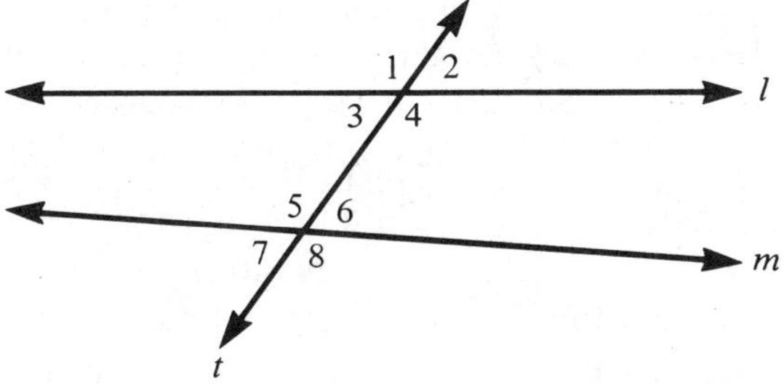

Figure 5.2

Definition 5.2 Two *nonadjacent* angles formed by two lines and a transversal are

1. *Alternate interior angles* iff they are interior angles whose interiors are on opposite sides of the transversal (alt int ∡s iff int ∡s opp sides t).
2. *Alternate exterior angles* iff they are exterior angles whose interiors are on opposite sides of the transversal (alt ext ∡s iff ext ∡s opp sides t).
3. *Corresponding angles* iff one is an interior angle, the other is an exterior angle, and their interiors are on the same side of the transversal (corr ∡s iff 1 int, 1 ext, same side t).

These types of angles are illustrated in Example 1 together with other types of angles that may be identified in the figure.

EXAMPLE 1

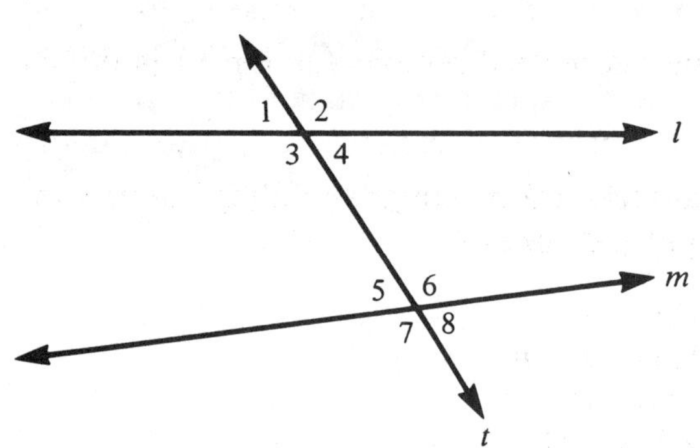

List all pairs of
(a) alternate interior angles
(b) alternate exterior angles
(c) corresponding angles
(d) interior angles on the same side of the transversal
(e) adjacent interior angles
(f) adjacent exterior angles

Answers
(a) ∡s 3 and 6, ∡s 4 and 5 **(b)** ∡s 1 and 8, ∡s 2 and 7
(c) ∡s 1 and 5, ∡s 2 and 6, ∡s 3 and 7, ∡s 4 and 8 **(d)** ∡s 3 and 5, ∡s 4 and 6
(e) ∡s 3 and 4, ∡s 5 and 6 **(f)** ∡s 1 and 2, ∡s 7 and 8

5.2

PROVING LINES PARALLEL

The definition of parallel lines cannot normally be used to prove that two lines are parallel. This is because lines are infinitely long, and there is usually no practical way to decide whether or not they ever intersect. There are other ways, however, to prove that two lines are parallel as shown in the theorems of this section. In stating these, we continue with our practice of discussing figures in a plane unless stated otherwise. We begin with a construction.

Construction 11 To construct a line parallel to a given line and containing a given point not on that line.

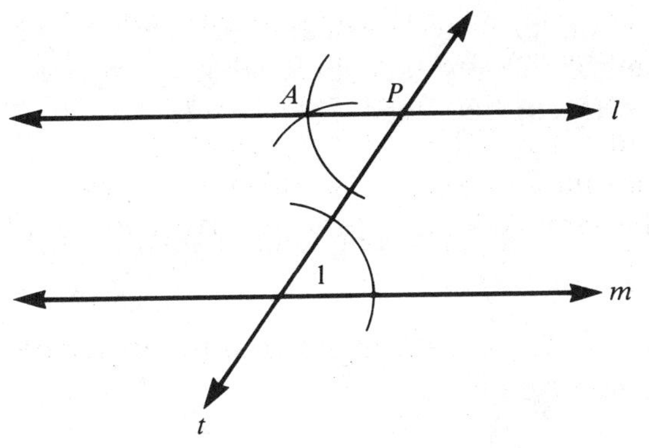

Given
line m
point P not on m

To Construct
line $l \parallel m$ and containing P

Steps
1. Draw any line t containing P and intersecting m.
2. Copy $\measuredangle 1$ at vertex P in alternate interior angle position (Construction 4). This determines $\overrightarrow{PA}$.
3. Extend $\overrightarrow{PA}$ to form line l.

The next theorem proves that the line l described in Construction 11 is in fact parallel to m.

Theorem 29 If two lines and a transversal form congruent alternate interior angles, then the two lines are parallel ($\cong\measuredangle$, lines $\parallel$).

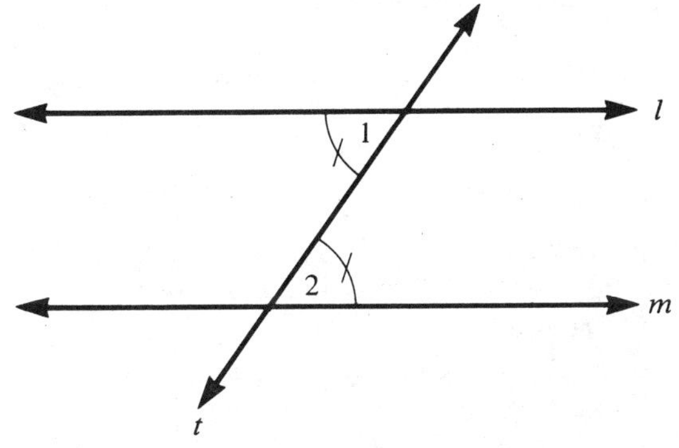

Given
lines l and m
transversal t
$\measuredangle 1$, $\measuredangle 2$ alt int $\measuredangle$s
$\measuredangle 1 \cong \measuredangle 2$

To Prove
$l \parallel m$

Our proof is indirect. Assume l is not parallel to m. Then l intersects m, for example, at A, forming a triangle as shown.

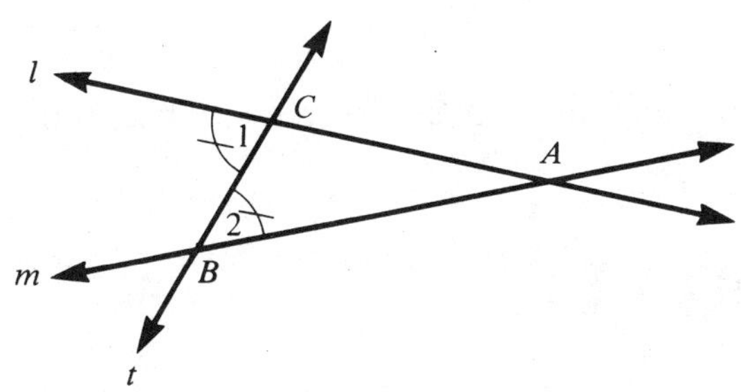

Statement	*Reason*
1. lines l, m, t $\measuredangle 1$, $\measuredangle 2$ alt int $\measuredangle$s	1. given
2. $\measuredangle 1$, ext $\measuredangle$ of $\triangle ABC$	2. ext $\measuredangle$ of $\triangle$ iff lin pr with 1 $\measuredangle$
3. $\angle 1 > \angle 2$	3. ext $\angle$ > rem int $\angle$
4. $\measuredangle 1 \cong \measuredangle 2$	4. given
5. $\angle 1 = \angle 2$	5. $\cong$ iff meas =
6. $\therefore l \parallel m$	6. statement 5 contradicts statement 3

There are four more theorems about proving lines parallel. These may be proved easily using the indirect method. To illustrate an alternative approach, however, the next proof uses the direct method and Theorem 29.

Theorem 30 If two lines and a transversal form congruent alternate exterior angles, then the two lines are parallel (≇, lines ∥).

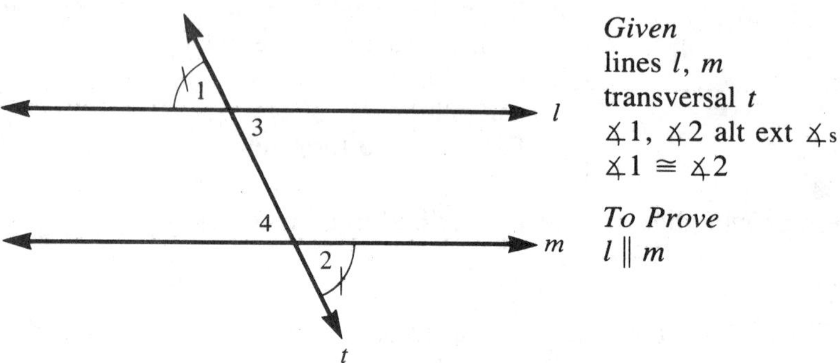

Given
lines l, m
transversal t
$\measuredangle 1$, $\measuredangle 2$ alt ext $\measuredangle$s
$\measuredangle 1 \cong \measuredangle 2$

To Prove
$l \parallel m$

Statement	*Reason*
1. lines l, m, t $\measuredangle 1$, $\measuredangle 2$ alt ext $\measuredangle$s	1. given
2. $\measuredangle 3$, $\measuredangle 1$ vert $\measuredangle$s	2. vert $\measuredangle$s formed by opp rays
3. $\measuredangle 3 \cong \measuredangle 1$	3. vert $\measuredangle$s $\cong$
4. $\measuredangle 1 \cong \measuredangle 2$	4. given
5. $\measuredangle 3 \cong \measuredangle 2$	5. trans $\cong$
6. $\measuredangle 2$, $\measuredangle 4$ vert $\measuredangle$s	6. vert $\measuredangle$s formed by opp rays
7. $\measuredangle 2 \cong \measuredangle 4$	7. vert $\measuredangle$s $\cong$
8. $\measuredangle 3 \cong \measuredangle 4$	8. trans $\cong$
9. $\measuredangle 3$, $\measuredangle 4$ alt int $\measuredangle$s	9. alt int $\measuredangle$s iff int $\measuredangle$s opp sides t
10. $\therefore l \parallel m$	10. ≇, lines ∥

The proofs of the next three theorems are left as exercises. The proofs are similar to that of Theorem 30.

Theorem 31 If two lines and a transversal form congruent corresponding angles, then the two lines are parallel (≇, lines ∥).

Theorem 32 If two lines and a transversal form supplementary interior angles on the same side of the transversal, then the two lines are parallel (≇, lines ∥).

Theorem 33 If two lines are perpendicular to a third line, then the two lines are parallel (2 lines ⊥ 3d line ∥).

In Example 1 two line segments are proved parallel by proving an appropriate pair of angles congruent.

EXAMPLE 1

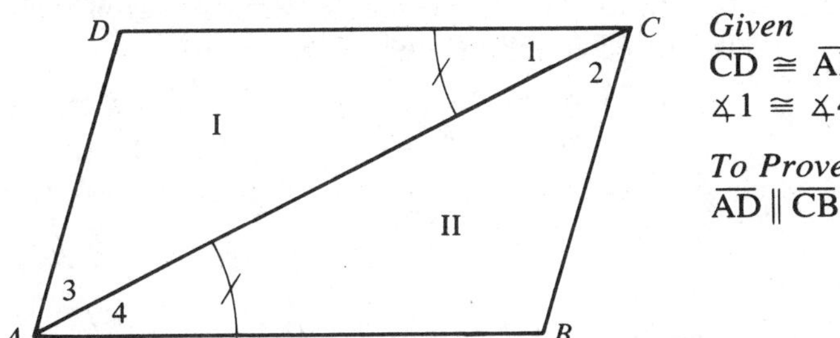

Given
$\overline{CD} \cong \overline{AB}$
$\measuredangle 1 \cong \measuredangle 4$

To Prove
$\overline{AD} \parallel \overline{CB}$

Statement	*Reason*
1. $\overline{CD} \cong \overline{AB}$, $\measuredangle 1 \cong \measuredangle 4$	1. given
2. $\overline{AC} \cong \overline{AC}$	2. refl $\cong$
3. $\triangle I \cong \triangle II$	3. sas $\cong$ sas
4. $\measuredangle 3 \cong \measuredangle 2$	4. cpctc
5. $\measuredangle 2$, $\measuredangle 3$ alt int $\measuredangle$s	5. alt int $\measuredangle$s iff int $\measuredangle$s opp sides t
6. $\therefore \overline{AD} \parallel \overline{CB}$	6. $\not\cong\measuredangle$, lines $\parallel$

Note the importance in the Example 1 proof of identifying $\measuredangle$s 2 and 3 as alternate interior angles formed by $\overline{AD}$, $\overline{CB}$, and transversal $\overline{AC}$. Note, too, that for these line segments, $\measuredangle$s 1 and 4 are *not* alternate interior angles. These facts are easily seen by extending $\overline{AD}$ and $\overline{CB}$ (the line segments to be proved parallel) and omitting $\overline{AB}$ and $\overline{CD}$ as in Figure 5.3. This Z-shaped configuration is the key to properly identifying alternate interior angles formed by two lines and a transversal.

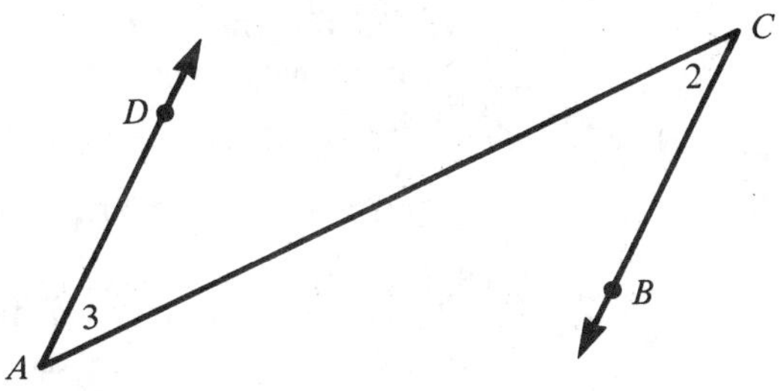

Figure 5.3

EXERCISES FOR 5.1 AND 5.2

In exercises 1–20 answer true or false.

1. Two lines in a plane either intersect or are parallel.
2. Transversals are only used with parallel lines.
3. Corresponding angles lie on the same side of the transversal.
4. If $\overleftrightarrow{AB}$, $\overleftrightarrow{CB}$, and $\overleftrightarrow{DB}$ intersect at B, then $\overleftrightarrow{AB}$ is a transversal for $\overleftrightarrow{CB}$ and $\overleftrightarrow{DB}$.
5. If S is the set of all lines in a plane and ® is the relation "is parallel to," then ® is not reflexive in S.
6. Two lines can be both parallel and perpendicular to each other.
7. Two lines perpendicular to a third line are parallel to each other.
8. Two lines parallel to a third line are perpendicular to each other.
9. In $\triangle EJS$, $\overline{JS}$ is a transversal for $\overline{EJ}$ and $\overline{ES}$.
10. If two interior angles on the same side of a transversal are complementary, the lines are parallel.
11. Alternate interior angles are nonadjacent angles.
12. If two alternate interior angles are supplementary, then the lines are parallel.
13. Two lines that intersect to form congruent adjacent angles are parallel.

14. The set of points between two parallel lines is a convex set.
15. The perpendicular bisectors of any two sides of a triangle are parallel to each other.
16. The intersection of a line and a ray can be empty even though the two are not parallel.
17. If $\overline{EJ} \cap \overline{KS} = \emptyset$, then $\overline{EJ} \parallel \overline{KS}$.
18. If m, n, and q are lines and $m \perp n$ and $n \parallel q$, then $m \perp q$.
19. If p and q are two lines that are not coplanar and $p \cap q = \emptyset$, then p and q are skew lines.
20. The median of a triangle is a transversal for the two sides of the triangle that intersect at one endpoint of the median.

In Exercises 21–25 refer to Figure 5.4 and answer with numbered angles only.

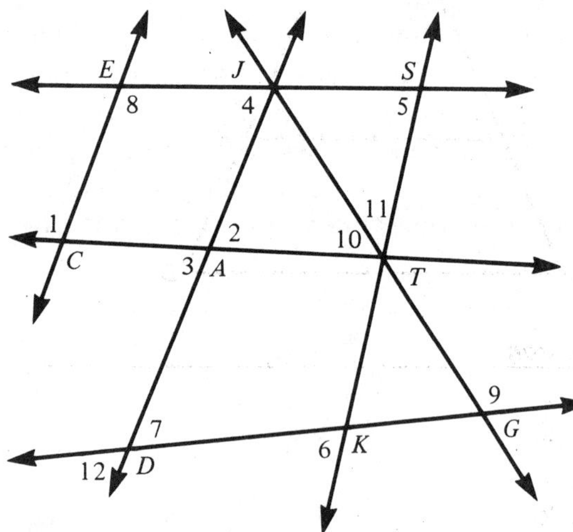

Figure 5.4

21. Name five pairs of alternate interior angles.
22. Name three pairs of alternate exterior angles.
23. Name nine pairs of corresponding angles.
24. Name four pairs of interior angles on the same side of the transversal.
25. If $\angle 4 = 62°$, $\angle 9 = 102°$, $\angle 12 = 62°$, $\angle 8 = 118°$, and $\angle 10 = 78°$, name four pairs of parallel lines.

In exercises 26–30 refer to Figure 5.5 to answer the questions.

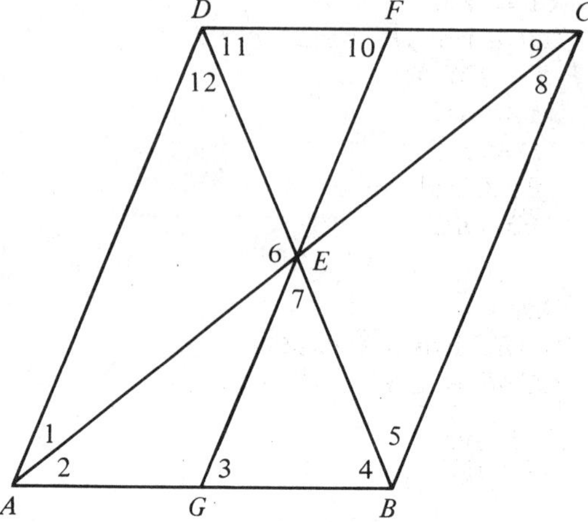

Figure 5.5

26. (a) Name five transversals for $\overline{AB}$ and $\overline{CD}$.
    (b) Name four transversals for $\overline{AD}$ and $\overline{BC}$.
27. (a) Is $\overline{BC}$ a transversal for $\overline{AB}$ and $\overline{BD}$? Why or why not?
    (b) Is $\overline{BC}$ a transversal for $\overline{AC}$ and $\overline{BD}$? Why or why not?
28. (a) If $\measuredangle 12 \cong \measuredangle 5$, is $\overline{AB} \parallel \overline{DC}$? Why or why not?
    (b) If $\measuredangle 9 \cong \measuredangle 2$, is $\overline{AB} \parallel \overline{DC}$? Why or why not?
29. (a) If $\overline{DC}$ is a transversal for $\overline{GF}$ and $\overline{AC}$, are $\measuredangle 10$ and $\measuredangle 9$ corresponding angles? Why or why not?
    (b) If $\overline{BC}$ is a transversal for $\overline{AC}$ and $\overline{BD}$, are $\measuredangle 5$ and $\measuredangle 9$ corresponding angles? Why or why not?
30. (a) Name eight pairs of alternate interior angles.
    (b) Name two pairs of corresponding angles.

In exercises 31 and 32 copy the figure, mark it, and supply the missing reasons in each proof.

31. *Given*
    $\triangle EJS$ isos ($\overline{EJ}$ base)
    $\triangle JCK$ isos ($\overline{JC}$ base)

    To Prove
    $\overline{ES} \parallel \overline{KC}$

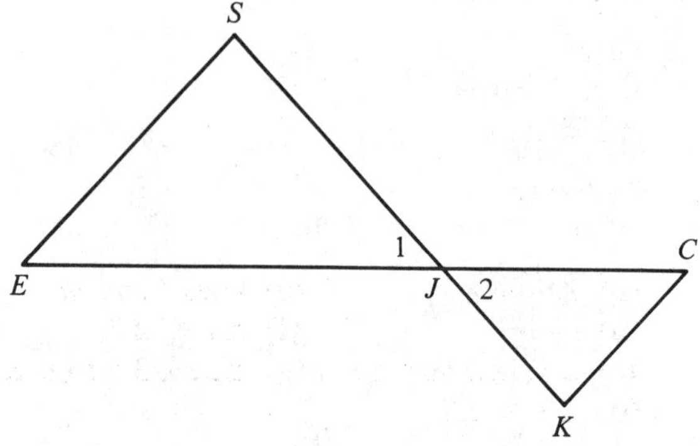

Statement	*Reason*
1. $\triangle EJS$ isos ($\overline{EJ}$ base)	1. ?
2. $\overline{ES} \cong \overline{JS}$	2. ?
3. $\measuredangle E \cong \measuredangle 1$	3. ?
4. $\measuredangle 1$, $\measuredangle 2$ vert $\measuredangle$s	4. ?
5. $\measuredangle 1 \cong \measuredangle 2$	5. ?
6. $\triangle JCK$ isos ($\overline{JC}$ base)	6. ?
7. $\overline{JK} \cong \overline{CK}$	7. ?
8. $\measuredangle 2 \cong \measuredangle C$	8. ?
9. $\measuredangle E \cong \measuredangle C$	9. ?
10. $\measuredangle E$, $\measuredangle C$ alt int $\measuredangle$s	10. ?
11. $\therefore \overline{ES} \parallel \overline{KC}$	11. ?

32. *Given*
$\triangle ABC$ isos ($\overline{AB}$ base)
$\measuredangle CDE \cong \measuredangle B$

To Prove
$\overline{AB} \parallel \overline{DE}$

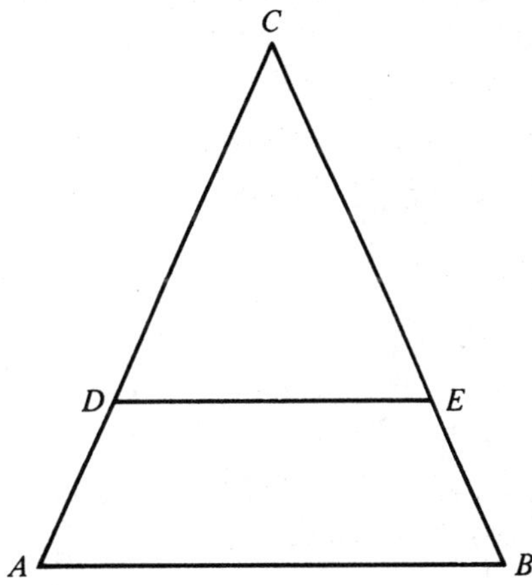

Statement	*Reason*
1. $\triangle ABC$ isos ($\overline{AB}$ base)	1. ?
2. $\overline{AC} \cong \overline{BC}$	2. ?
3. $\measuredangle A \cong \measuredangle B$	3. ?
4. $\measuredangle CDE \cong \measuredangle B$	4. ?
5. $\measuredangle B \cong \measuredangle CDE$	5. ?
6. $\measuredangle A \cong \measuredangle CDE$	6. ?
7. $\measuredangle A$, $\measuredangle CDE$ corr $\measuredangle$s	7. ?
8. $\therefore \overline{AB} \parallel \overline{DE}$	8. ?

In exercises 33–35 copy the figure, mark it, and rearrange the statements into a correct order for a proof.

33. (Theorem 31)

Given
lines l and m
$\measuredangle 3 \cong \measuredangle 1$

To Prove
$l \parallel m$

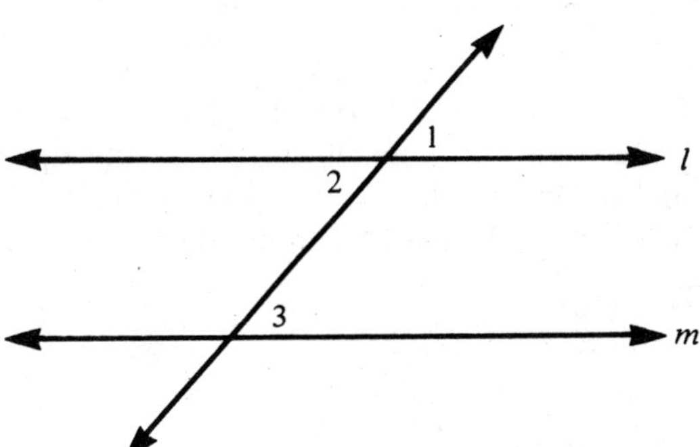

(a) $\measuredangle 3 \cong \measuredangle 1$
(b) $l \parallel m$
(c) $\measuredangle 1$, $\measuredangle 2$ vert $\measuredangle$s
(d) $\measuredangle 3 \cong \measuredangle 2$
(e) lines l and m
(f) $\measuredangle 1 \cong \measuredangle 2$
(g) $\measuredangle 2$, $\measuredangle 3$ alt int $\measuredangle$s

34. *Given*
E midpt $\overline{AD}$
E midpt $\overline{BC}$
$\measuredangle 2 \cong \measuredangle 5$

To Prove
$\overline{CD} \parallel \overline{FG}$

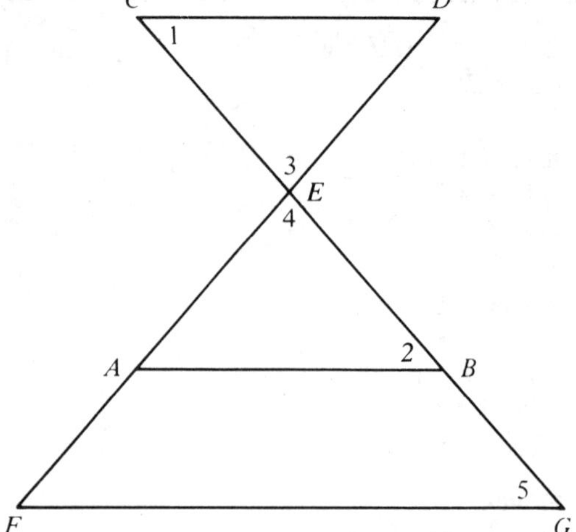

(a) $\overline{DE} \cong \overline{AE}$
(b) E midpt $\overline{BC}$
(c) $\triangle DCE \cong \triangle ABE$
(d) $\measuredangle 2 \cong \measuredangle 5$
(e) $\overline{CD} \parallel \overline{FG}$
(f) $\measuredangle 3$, $\measuredangle 4$ vert $\measuredangle$s
(g) $\measuredangle 1 \cong \measuredangle 5$
(h) $\overline{CE} \cong \overline{BE}$
(i) $\measuredangle 3 \cong \measuredangle 4$
(j) $\measuredangle 1 \cong \measuredangle 2$
(k) $\measuredangle E$ midpt $\overline{AD}$
(l) $\measuredangle 1$, $\measuredangle 5$ alt int $\measuredangle$s

35. *Given*
$\triangle JBE$ isos ($\overline{EB}$ base)
$\overrightarrow{JA}$ bis $\measuredangle BJS$
$\angle 1 + \angle 2 = \angle BJS$

To Prove
$\overline{EB} \parallel \overrightarrow{JA}$

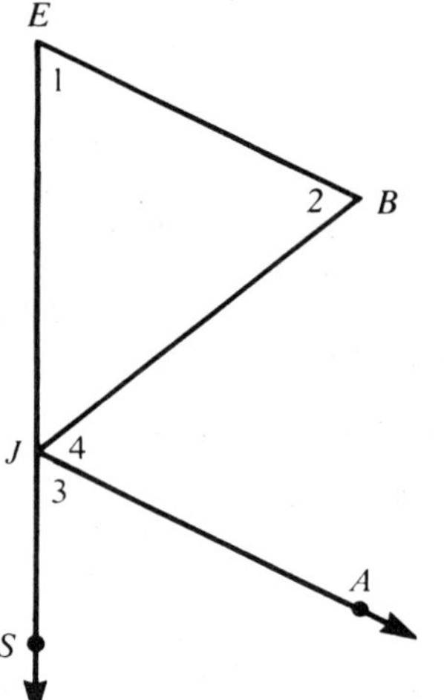

(a) $\overline{JE} \cong \overline{JB}$
(b) $\overline{EB} \parallel \overrightarrow{JA}$
(c) $\measuredangle 1 \cong \measuredangle 3$
(d) $\triangle JBE$ isos ($\overline{EB}$ base)
(e) $\angle 1 + \angle 2 = \angle 4 + \angle 3$
(f) $\measuredangle 1 \cong \measuredangle 2$
(g) $\overrightarrow{JA}$ bis $\measuredangle BJS$
(h) $\angle 1 = \angle 2$
(i) $\angle BJS = \angle 4 + \angle 3$
(j) $2 \cdot \angle 1 = 2 \cdot \angle 3$
(k) $\angle 1 + \angle 2 = \angle BJS$
(l) $\angle 4 = \angle 3$
(m) $\angle 1 = \angle 3$
(n) $\measuredangle 4 \cong \measuredangle 3$
(o) $\angle 1 + \angle 1 = \angle 3 + \angle 3$
(p) $\measuredangle 1$, $\measuredangle 3$ corr $\measuredangle$s

In exercises 36–50 copy the figure, the hypothesis, and the conclusion. Mark the figure and write a proof.

36. (Theorem 33)

Given
$l \perp n$
$m \perp n$

To Prove
$l \parallel m$

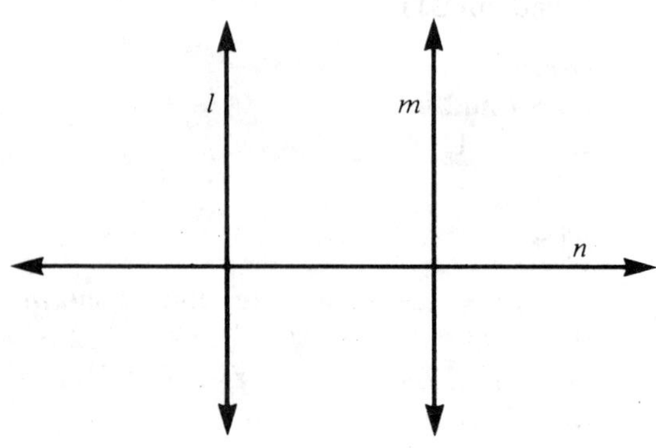

37. *Given*
$\triangle POI$ isos ($\overline{PO}$ base)
$\overline{IE}$ med $\triangle POI$
$\overline{IE} \perp \overline{NT}$

To Prove
$\overline{NT} \parallel \overline{PO}$

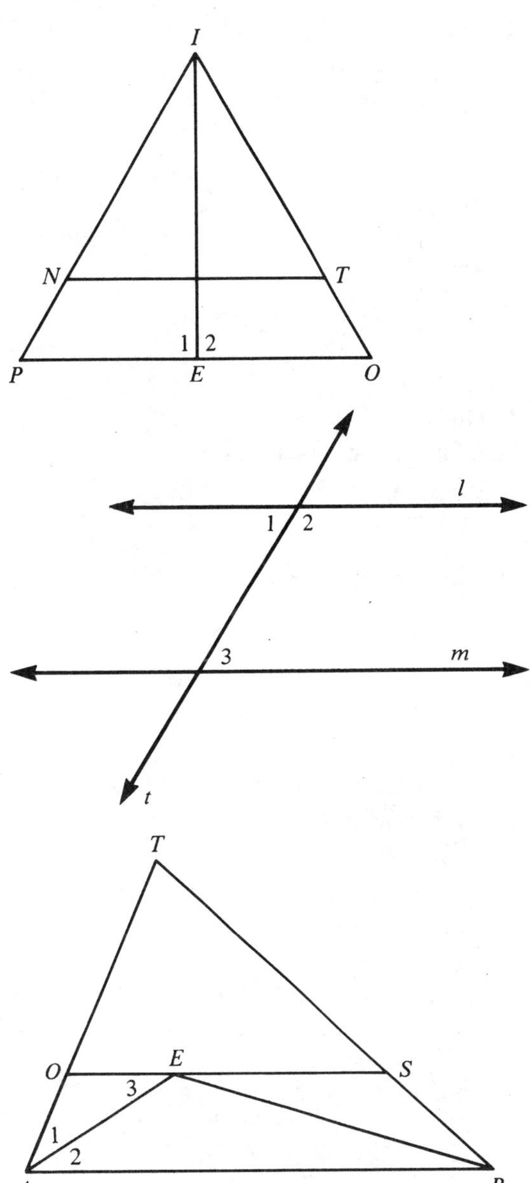

38. (Theorem 32)

Given
lines l, m
$\measuredangle 2$ supp $\measuredangle 3$

To Prove
$l \parallel m$

39. *Given*
$\overline{AE}$ bis $\measuredangle OAP$
$\triangle AEO$ isos ($\overline{AE}$ base)

To Prove
$\overline{OS} \parallel \overline{AP}$

40. *Given*
$\angle XAM = 90°$
$\overline{AO} \cong \overline{MO}$
$\overline{OI}$ med $\triangle AOM$

To Prove
$\overline{OI} \parallel \overline{XA}$

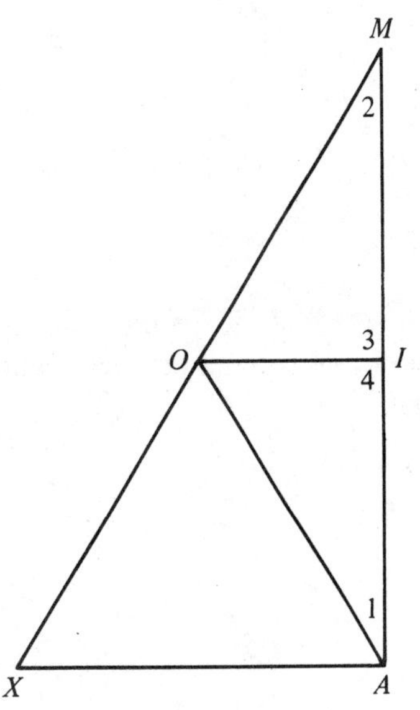

41. *Given*
$\overline{AE}$ bis $\measuredangle CAB$
$\overline{DG}$ bis $\overline{AE}$ at F
$\overline{DG} \perp \overline{AE}$ at F

To Prove
$\overline{DE} \parallel \overline{AB}$

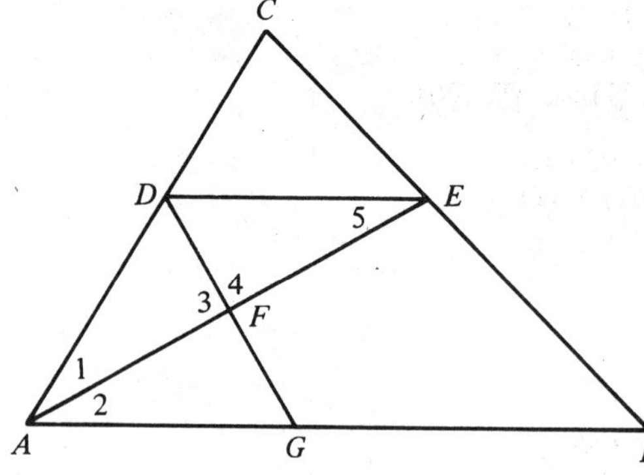

42. *Given*
$\overline{KJ}$ and $\overline{ES}$ bis each other

To Prove
$\overline{EK} \parallel \overline{JS}$

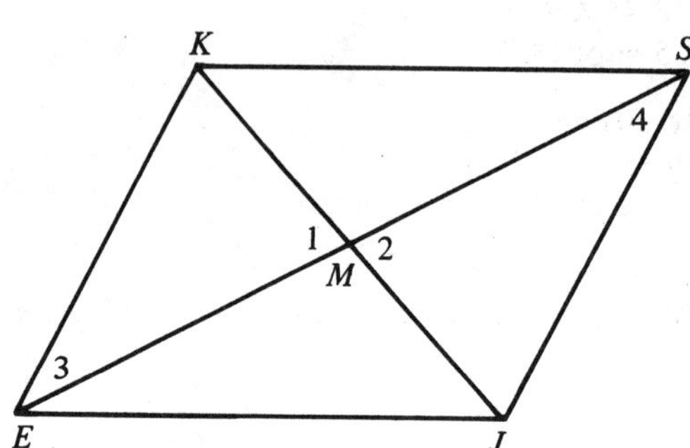

43. *Given*
$\overline{EO} \cong \overline{SO}$
$\overline{SE}$ bis $\overline{JM}$ at O

To Prove
$\overline{ME} \parallel \overline{SJ}$

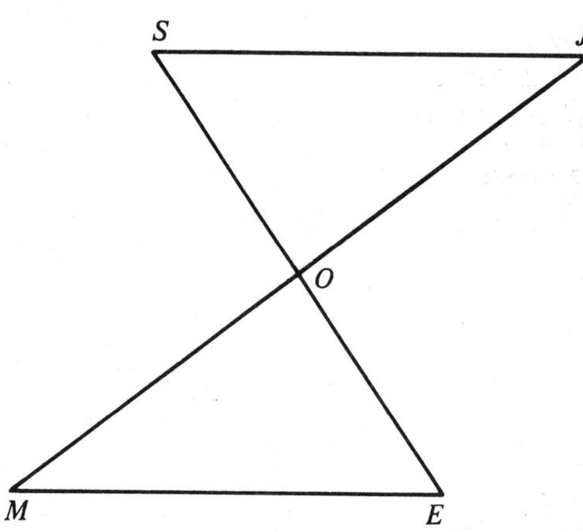

44. *Given*
$\overline{ED} \cong \overline{CI}$
$\overline{EC} \cong \overline{UL}$
$\overline{DU} \cong \overline{IL}$

To Prove
$\overline{ED} \parallel \overline{CI}$

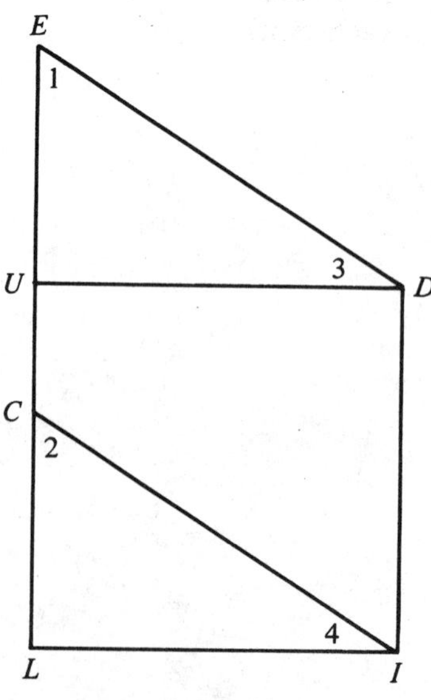

45. *Given*
$\angle 1 \cong \angle 2$
$\overline{AO}$ bis $\overline{ST}$ at P

To Prove
$\overline{AT} \parallel \overline{SO}$

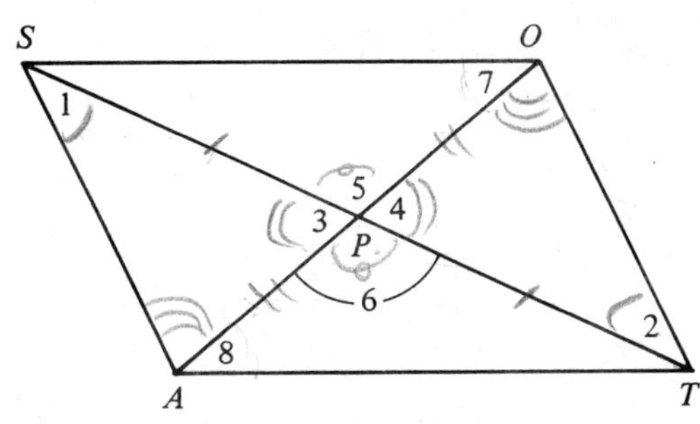

46. *Given*
$\angle 2 \cong \angle 9$
$\angle 5$ supp $\angle 7$

To Prove
$l \parallel m$

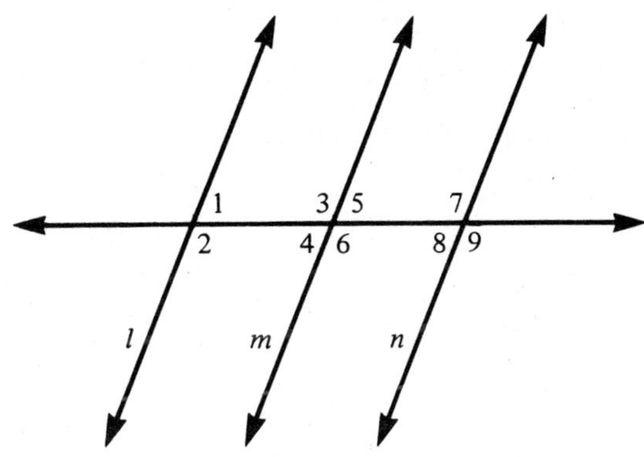

47. *Given*
$\overline{OP}$ ⊥ bis $\overline{AT}$
$\overline{AT}$ bis $\angle OAP$

To Prove
$\overline{OT} \parallel \overline{AP}$

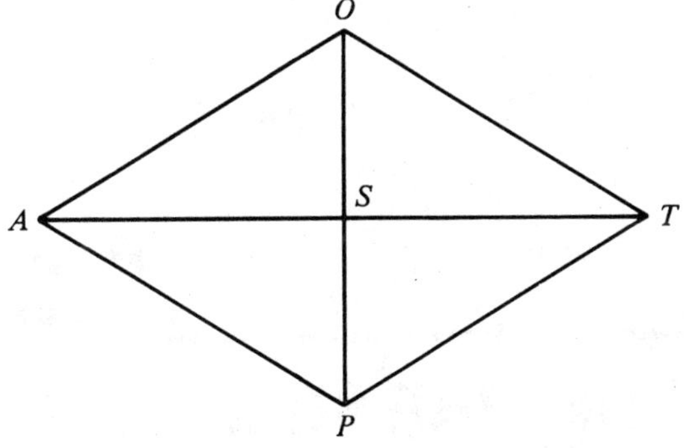

48. *Given*
$\overline{AE}$ and $\overline{BF}$ bis each other
$\overline{HF}$ and $\overline{EC}$ bis each other

To Prove
$\overline{AB} \parallel \overline{CH}$

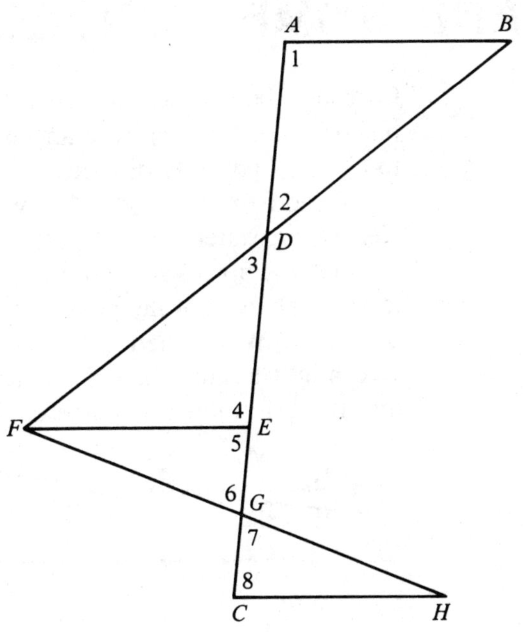

49. *Given*
$\triangle TSJ$ isos ($\overline{SJ}$ base)
$\measuredangle 3 \cong \measuredangle 1$

To Prove
$\overline{TE} \parallel \overline{SJ}$

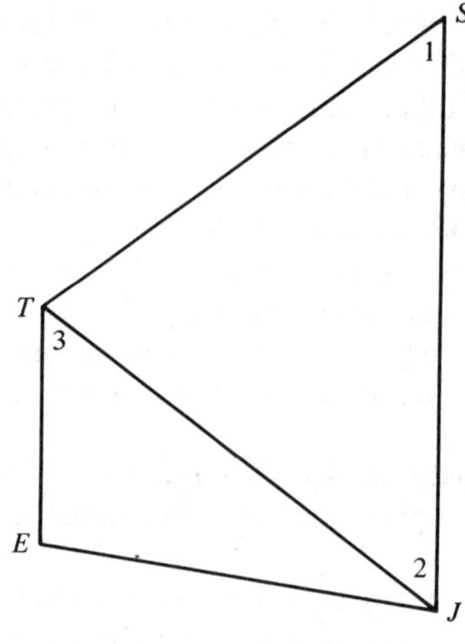

50. *Given*
$\overline{JM}$ bis $\measuredangle SJA$
$\overline{JM} \perp \overline{SA}$
$\overline{JS} \cong \overline{AM}$

To Prove
$\overline{JS} \parallel \overline{AM}$

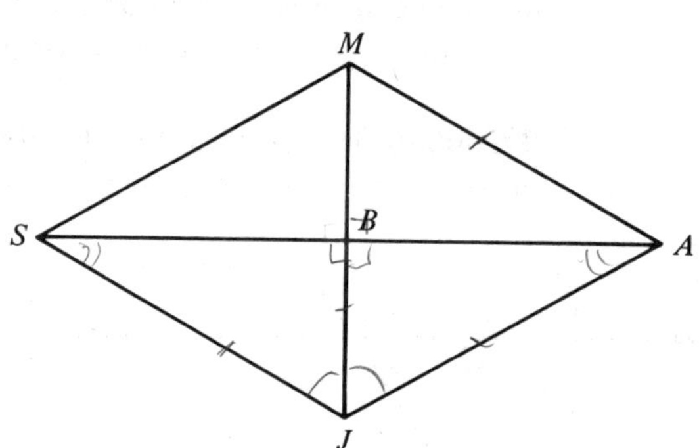

5.3 THE PARALLEL POSTULATE AND SOME CONSEQUENCES

Consider the simple geometric figure consisting of a line l and a point P not on l (Figure 5.6). How many lines are there that contain P and are parallel to l? The seemingly obvious answer is exactly 1. Euclid, the pioneer organizer of geometry, thought this was the case, but he was unable to prove it. Hence, he stated the property as a postulate. During the next 2000 years various attempts were made to prove Euclid's postulate but all failed. Finally it was realized that the postulate states a property that is fundamental to plane geometry. What, then, would result if a different property were postulated? One might assume that there are no lines containing P and parallel to l, or that there is more than one such line. These ideas were investigated inde-

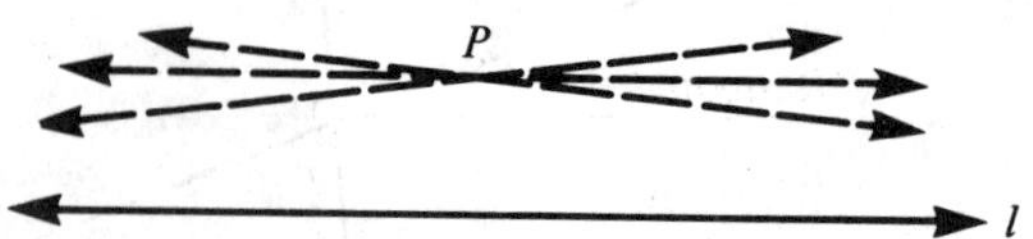

Figure 5.6

pendently by Karl Friedrich Gauss (1777–1855), Nicolai Ivanovich Lobachevski (1793–1856), and Janos Bolyai (1802–1860). Their work, and that of others after them, led to geometries about figures that are not in a plane. Spherical geometry is one example, important to us because the earth is approximately a sphere, not a plane. The theory of navigation rests on the properties of spherical geometry. The discovery of these non-Euclidean geometries is generally regarded as the birth of modern mathematics. We must return to Euclidean geometry, however, for it is both the subject of this book and the basis for many facets of our culture.

We now state the modern version of Euclid's famous postulate.

Postulate 15 *The Parallel Postulate*. There is one and only one line parallel to a given line and containing a given point not on that line (∥ post).

Many theorems in plane geometry are consequences of this postulate. Five are stated in this section and several more in the next section. We begin with four theorems about angles formed by two parallel lines and a transversal.

Theorem 34 If two parallel lines are cut by a transversal, then both pairs of alternate interior angles are congruent (⧣, alt int ∡s ≅).

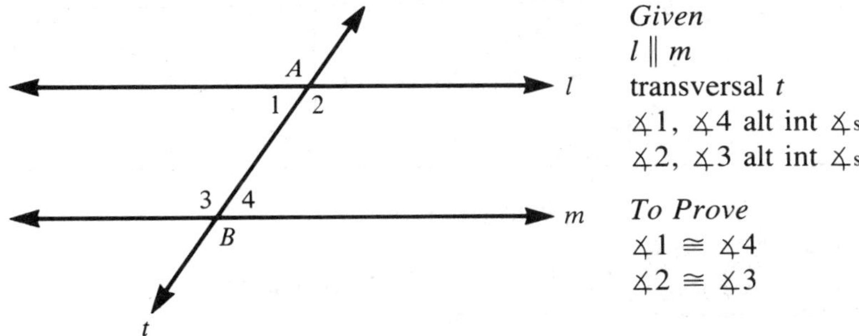

Given
$l \parallel m$
transversal t
∡1, ∡4 alt int ∡s
∡2, ∡3 alt int ∡s

To Prove
∡1 ≅ ∡4
∡2 ≅ ∡3

We prove ∡1 ≅ ∡4 by the indirect method. Assume ∡1 ≇ ∡4; then there is an ∡*BAC* ≅ ∡4 as shown in Figure 5.7.

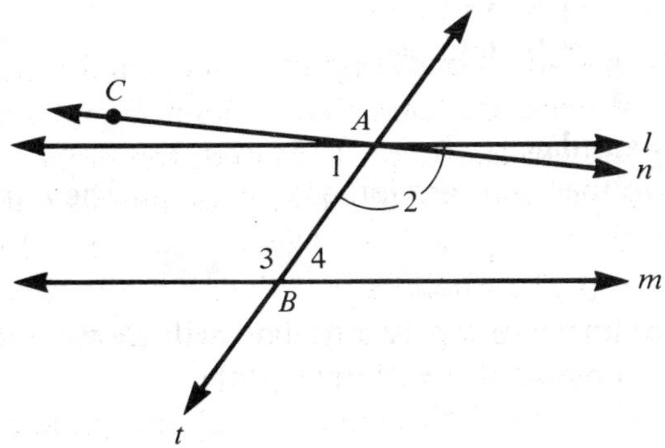

Figure 5.7

Statement	*Reason*
1. transversal t ∡1, ∡4 and ∡2, ∡3 alt int ∡s	1. given
2. Construct ∡*BAC* ≅ ∡4.	2. can copy ∡

3. Draw line n.	3. 2 pts determ line
4. $n \parallel m$	4. ∦, lines ‖
5. $l \parallel m$	5. given
6. ∴ ∡1 ≅ ∡4	6. statements 4 and 5 contradict the Parallel Postulate
7. ∡1, ∡2 lin pr ∡3, ∡4 lin pr	7. lin pr iff com side and opp rays
8. ∡2 supp ∡1 ∡3 supp ∡4	8. lin pr supp
9. ∴ ∡2 ≅ ∡3	9. ∡s supp ≅ ∡s are ≅

Note that after proving ∡1 ≅ ∡4, the proof that ∡2 ≅ ∡3 is direct.

Theorem 35 If two parallel lines are cut by a transversal, then both pairs of alternate exterior angles are congruent (≠, alt ext ∡s ≅).

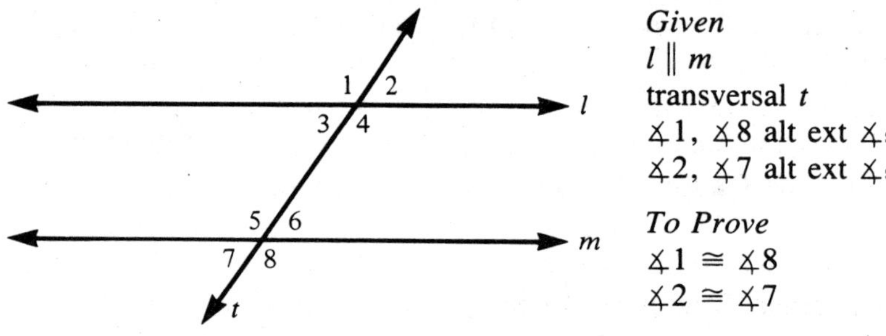

Given
$l \parallel m$
transversal t
∡1, ∡8 alt ext ∡s
∡2, ∡7 alt ext ∡s

To Prove
∡1 ≅ ∡8
∡2 ≅ ∡7

Statement	*Reason*
1. $l \parallel m$, transversal t ∡1, ∡8 and ∡2, ∡7 alt ext ∡s	1. given
2. ∡4, ∡5 alt int ∡s	2. alt int ∡s iff int ∡s opp sides t
3. ∡4 ≅ ∡5	3. ≠, alt int ∡s ≅
4. ∡1, ∡4 vert ∡s	4. vert ∡s formed by opp rays
5. ∡1 ≅ ∡4	5. vert ∡s ≅
6. ∡1 ≅ ∡5	6. trans ≅
7. ∡5, ∡8 vert ∡s	7. vert ∡s formed by opp rays
8. ∡5 ≅ ∡8	8. vert ∡s ≅
9. ∴ ∡1 ≅ ∡8	9. trans ≅

The proof that ∡2 ≅ ∡7 is similar.

The proofs of the next two theorems are left as exercises. They are similar to the proof of Theorem 35.

Theorem 36 If two parallel lines are cut by a transversal, then all four pairs of corresponding angles are congruent (≠, corr ∡s ≅).

Theorem 37 If two parallel lines are cut by a transversal, then both pairs of interior angles on the same side of the transversal are supplementary (≠, int ∡s same side t supp).

One or more of the above four theorems may be used to find the angle measures in Example 1.

EXAMPLE 1

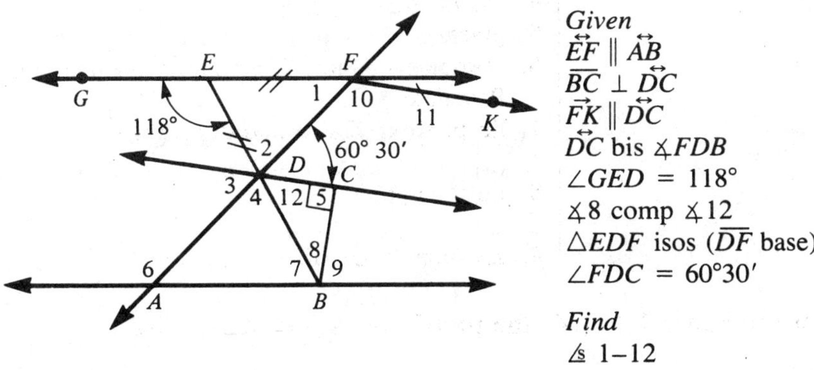

Given
$\overleftrightarrow{EF} \parallel \overleftrightarrow{AB}$
$\overline{BC} \perp \overleftrightarrow{DC}$
$\overrightarrow{FK} \parallel \overleftrightarrow{DC}$
$\overleftrightarrow{DC}$ bis ∡FDB
$\angle GED = 118°$
∡8 comp ∡12
$\triangle EDF$ isos ($\overline{DF}$ base)
$\angle FDC = 60°30'$

Find
∡s 1–12

Answers
$\angle 1 = 59°$ $\angle 2 = 59°$ $\angle 3 = 60°30'$ $\angle 4 = 59°$ $\angle 5 = 90°$ $\angle 6 = 121°$
$\angle 7 = 62°$ $\angle 8 = 29°30'$ $\angle 9 = 88°30'$ $\angle 10 = 119°30'$ $\angle 11 = 1°30'$
$\angle 12 = 60°30'$

A formal proof of the next theorem is omitted. We do, however, give an informal discussion of an indirect proof that shows how the theorem is a direct consequence of the Parallel Postulate and the definition of parallel lines.

Theorem 38 If two lines are each parallel to a third line, then the two lines are parallel to each other (2 lines ∥ 3d line ∥).

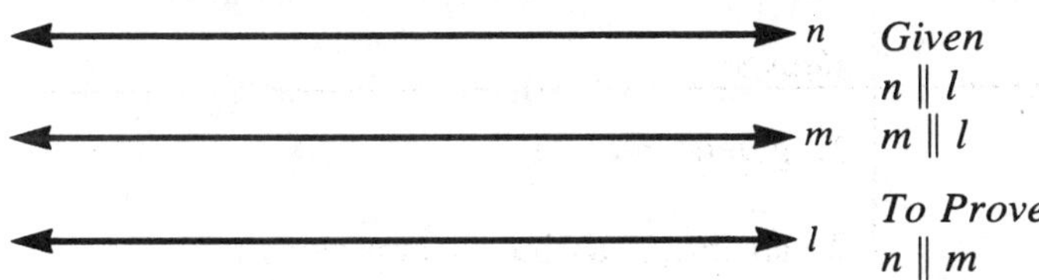

Given
$n \parallel l$
$m \parallel l$

To Prove
$n \parallel m$

Assume n is *not* parallel to m ($n \nparallel m$). Then n and m intersect in some point P, and there are two lines (n and m) both parallel to l and containing P. But according to the Parallel Postulate, there can be only one line parallel to l and containing P. This is a contradiction, so the assumption must be wrong and we conclude that $n \parallel m$.

EXERCISES FOR 5.3

In exercises 1–4 refer to Figure 5.8 and answer with numbered angles only.

Given
$l \parallel m \parallel n$

1. Name five pairs of congruent alternate interior angles.
2. Name nine pairs of congruent corresponding angles.
3. Name four pairs of congruent alternate exterior angles.
4. Name five pairs of nonadjacent supplementary angles.

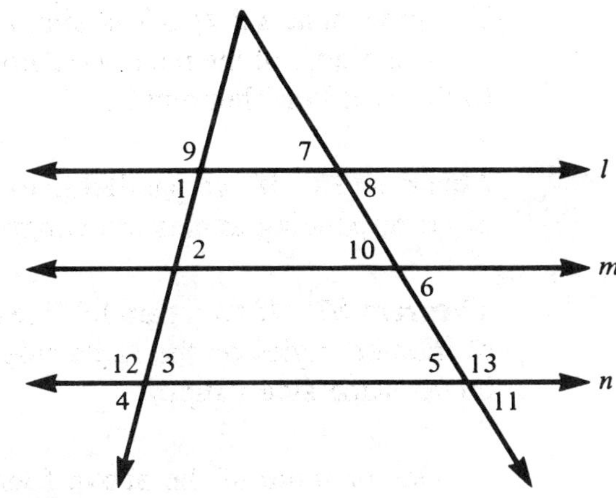

Figure 5.8

In exercises 5–8 refer to Figure 5.9 and answer with numbered angles only.

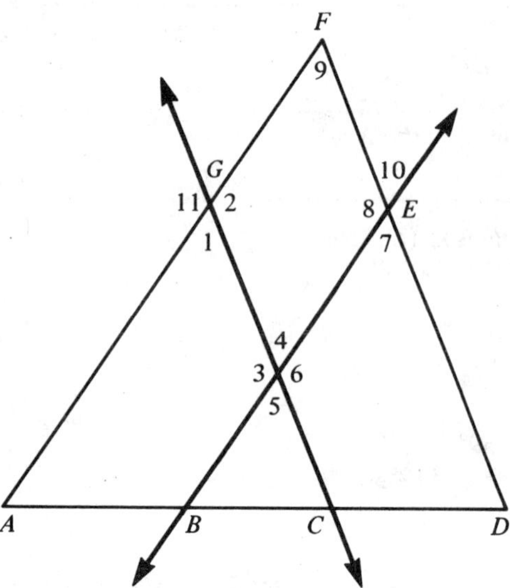

Figure 5.9

Given
$\overline{AF} \parallel \overleftrightarrow{BE}$
$\overline{FD} \parallel \overleftrightarrow{GC}$

5. Name five pairs of congruent alternate interior angles.
6. Name two pairs of congruent alternate exterior angles.
7. Name eight pairs of congruent corresponding angles.
8. Name fifteen pairs of nonadjacent supplementary angles.

In exercises 9 and 10 refer to Figure 5.10 and answer with the three-letter notation for angles.

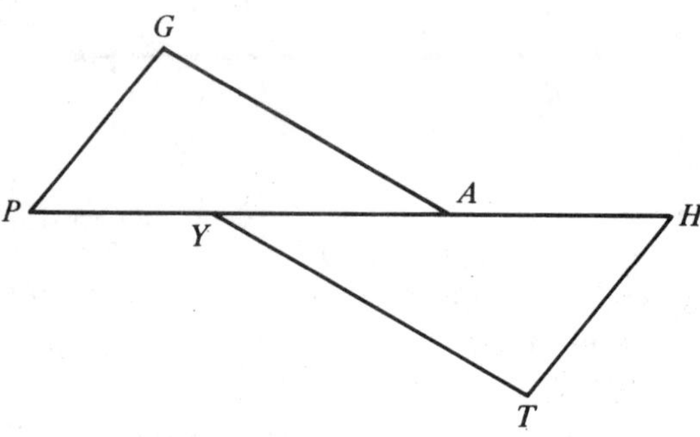

Figure 5.10

Given
$\overline{GA} \parallel \overline{YT}$
$\overline{PG} \parallel \overline{TH}$

9. Name two pairs of congruent alternate interior angles.
10. Name one pair of congruent alternate exterior angles.

In exercises 11–22 copy the figure, mark it, and find the requested measures.

11. *Given*
$\overleftrightarrow{OS} \parallel \overleftrightarrow{AP}$
$\triangle APT$ isos ($\overline{AT}$ base)
$\angle APT = 78°47'$
$\angle APT + \angle T + \angle 7 = 180°$

Find
$\measuredangle$s 1–10

12. *Given*
$\overleftrightarrow{AB} \parallel \overleftrightarrow{CD}$
$\overrightarrow{EF} \parallel \overrightarrow{GH}$
$\overrightarrow{EF}$ bis $\measuredangle IEB$
$\angle AEI = 116°$

Find
$\measuredangle$s 1–9

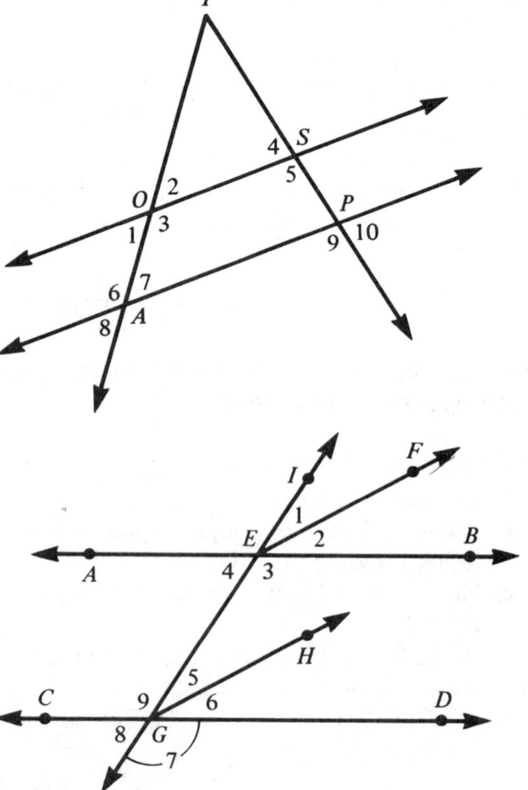

13. *Given*
$\triangle LAE$ isos ($\overline{AE}$ base)
$\overleftrightarrow{TJ} \parallel \overleftrightarrow{HS} \parallel \overleftrightarrow{AE}$
$\angle HTJ = 67°52'$

Find
$\angle$s 1–10

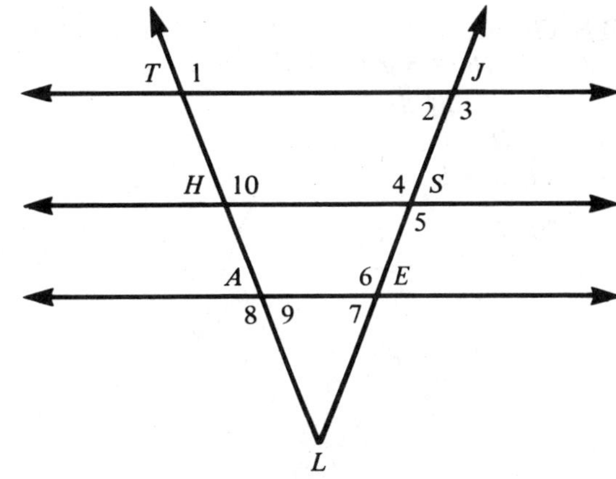

14. *Given*
$\overleftrightarrow{JK}$ bis $\measuredangle SJC$
$\overrightarrow{SE} \parallel \overleftrightarrow{KJ}$
$\angle S = 60°$

Find
$\angle$s 1–8

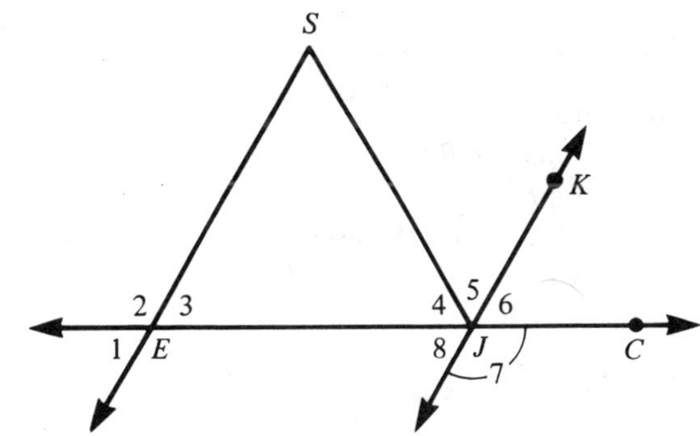

15. *Given*
$\overleftrightarrow{DE} \parallel \overleftrightarrow{AC}$
$\triangle BDC$ isos ($\overline{BD}$ base)
$\angle BDC = 57°23'$

Find
$\angle$s 1–9

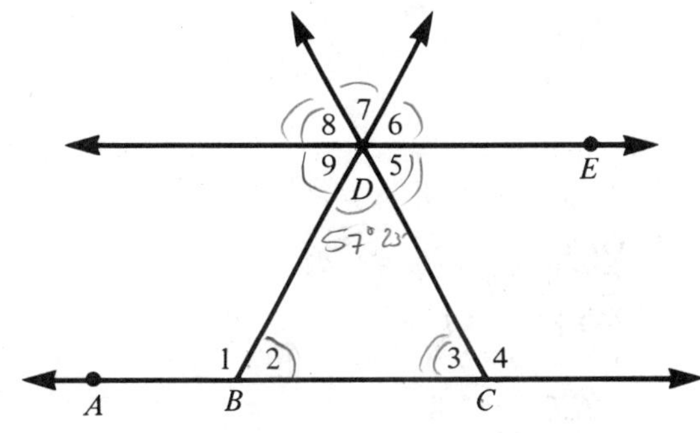

16. *Given*
$\overleftrightarrow{AB} \parallel \overleftrightarrow{DC}$
$\overleftrightarrow{DA} \parallel \overleftrightarrow{CB}$
$\angle HDC = 87°47'$
$\overleftrightarrow{EF}$ bis $\measuredangle DCJ$
$\overleftrightarrow{AC}$ bis $\measuredangle DCB$

Find
$\angle$s 1–10

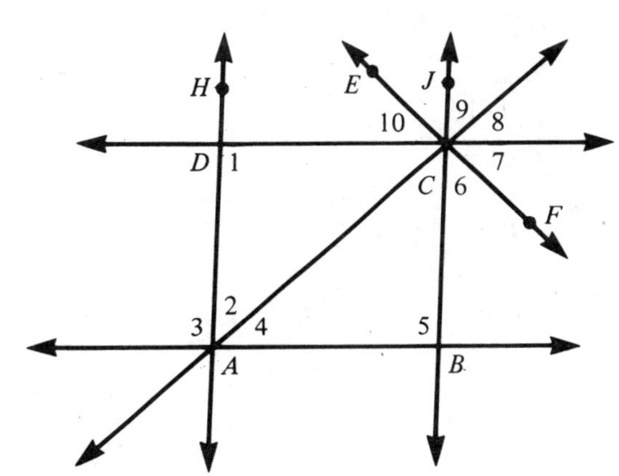

17. *Given*
$\angle LTH = 55°$
$\overleftrightarrow{TH} \parallel \overleftrightarrow{EL} \parallel \overleftrightarrow{SJ}$
$\triangle SJL$ isos ($\overline{SJ}$ base)
$\overleftrightarrow{TE} \perp \overleftrightarrow{EL}$

Find
∠s 1–12

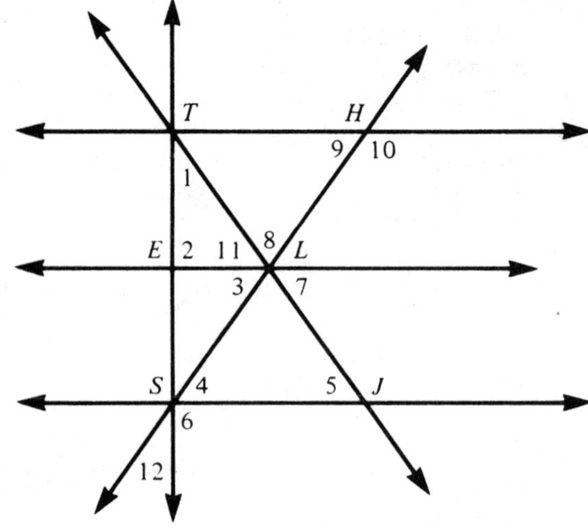

18. *Given*
$\overline{BE}$ bis $\angle CBA$
$\overrightarrow{CB} \parallel \overrightarrow{EF}$
$\triangle ADE$ isos ($\overline{DE}$ base)
$\angle ABG = 115°$
$\overline{BD} \cong \overline{BF}$

Find
∠s 1–10

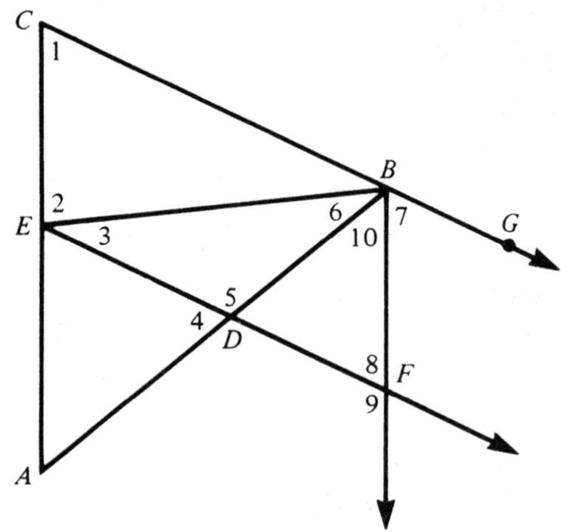

19. *Given*
$\overline{ED} \perp \overline{UI}$
$\overline{ED}$ bis $\angle ULI$
$\overline{UE} \parallel \overline{LI}$
$\angle ILD = 118°$
$\overline{IL} \cong \overline{DL}$
$\angle 5$ comp $\angle 1$
$\angle 8 + \angle IDL = \angle ELI$

Find
∠s 1–10

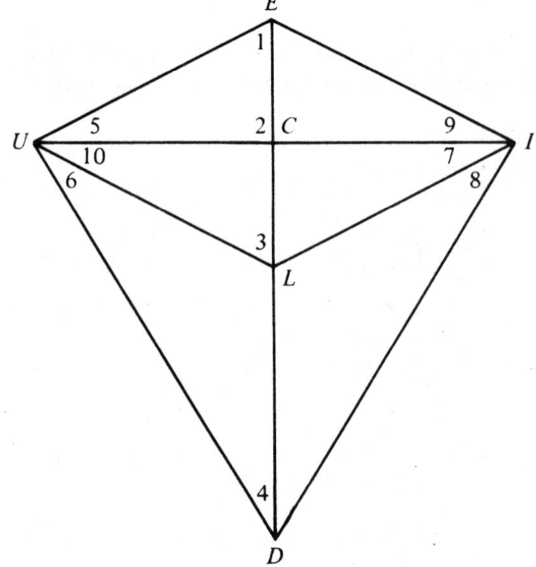

20. *Given*
$\overleftrightarrow{IB} \parallel \overleftrightarrow{CS}$
$\overleftrightarrow{IS} \parallel \overleftrightarrow{CT}$
$\angle ECT = 137°14'$

Find
∡s 1–9

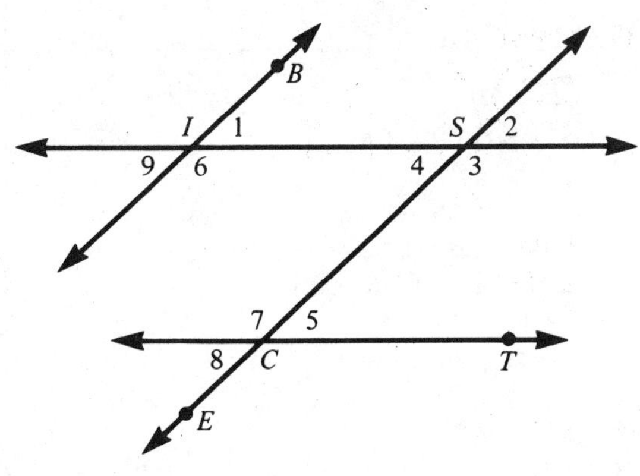

21. *Given*
$\overline{MO} \parallel \overline{KR}$
$\overline{MK} \parallel \overline{OR}$
$\angle KOR = 73°12'$
$\angle MOR = 118°3'$
$\angle 7 = 37°23'$
$\angle 4 + \angle 6 + \angle 7 = 180°$

Find
∡s 1–10

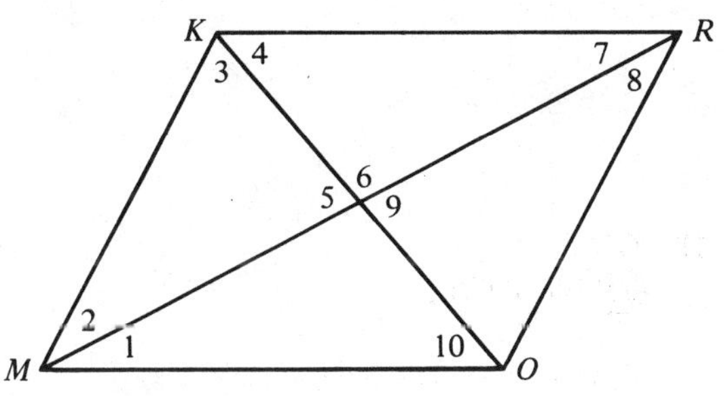

22. *Given*
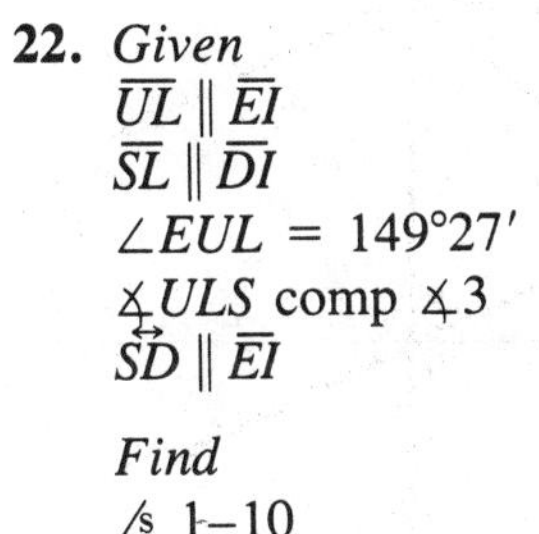
$\overline{UL} \parallel \overline{EI}$
$\overline{SL} \parallel \overline{DI}$
$\angle EUL = 149°27'$
∡ULS comp ∡3
$\overleftrightarrow{SD} \parallel \overline{EI}$

Find
∡s 1–10

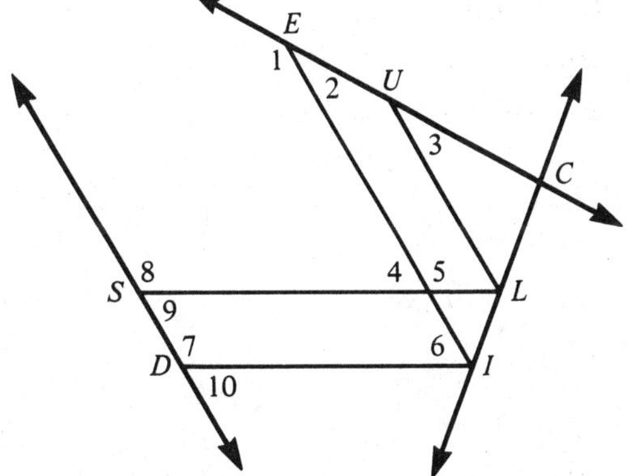

In exercises 23 and 24 copy the figure, mark it, and supply the missing reasons in each proof.

23. *Given*
$\overrightarrow{CE} \parallel \overline{AB}$
$\triangle ABC$ isos ($\overline{AB}$ base)

To Prove
$\overrightarrow{CE}$ bis ∡BCD

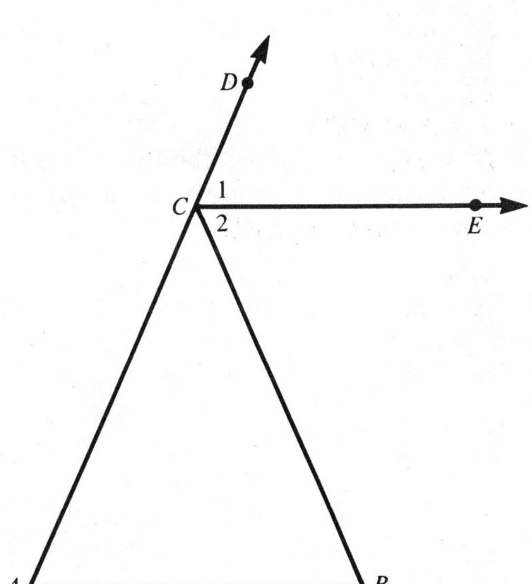

Statement	*Reason*
1. $\overrightarrow{CE} \parallel \overline{AB}$	1. ?
2. $\measuredangle 1$, $\measuredangle A$ corr $\measuredangle$s	2. ?
3. $\measuredangle 1 \cong \measuredangle A$	3. ?
4. $\measuredangle 2$, $\measuredangle B$ alt int $\measuredangle$s	4. ?
5. $\measuredangle 2 \cong \measuredangle B$	5. ?
6. $\triangle ABC$ isos ($\overline{AB}$ base)	6. ?
7. $\overline{CA} \cong \overline{CB}$	7. ?
8. $\measuredangle A \cong \measuredangle B$	8. ?
9. $\measuredangle B \cong \measuredangle 2$	9. ?
10. $\measuredangle 1 \cong \measuredangle 2$	10. ?
11. $\therefore \overrightarrow{CE}$ bis $\measuredangle BCD$	11. ?

24. 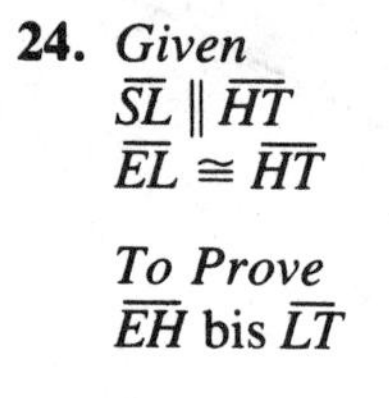
Given
$\overline{SL} \parallel \overline{HT}$
$\overline{EL} \cong \overline{HT}$

To Prove
$\overline{EH}$ bis $\overline{LT}$

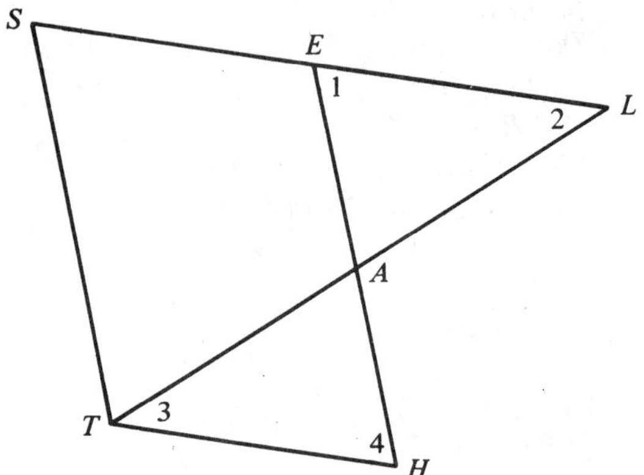

Statement	*Reason*
1. $\overline{SL} \parallel \overline{HT}$	1. ?
2. $\measuredangle 1$, $\measuredangle 4$ alt int $\measuredangle$s	2. ?
3. $\measuredangle 1 \cong \measuredangle 4$	3. ?
4. $\measuredangle 2$, $\measuredangle 3$ alt int $\measuredangle$s	4. ?
5. $\measuredangle 2 \cong \measuredangle 3$	5. ?
6. $\overline{EL} \cong \overline{HT}$	6. ?
7. $\triangle ELA \cong \triangle HTA$	7. ?
8. $\overline{LA} \cong \overline{TA}$	8. ?
9. $\therefore \overline{EH}$ bis $\overline{LT}$	9. ?

In exercises 25 and 26 copy the figure, mark it, and rearrange the statements into a correct order for a proof.

25. 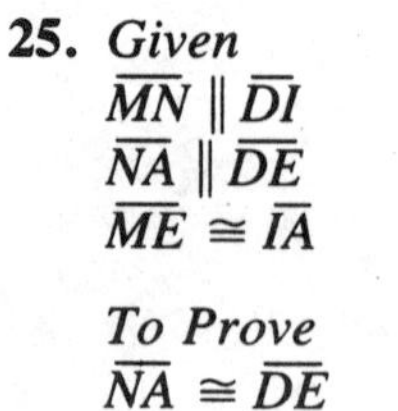
Given
$\overline{MN} \parallel \overline{DI}$
$\overline{NA} \parallel \overline{DE}$
$\overline{ME} \cong \overline{IA}$

To Prove
$\overline{NA} \cong \overline{DE}$

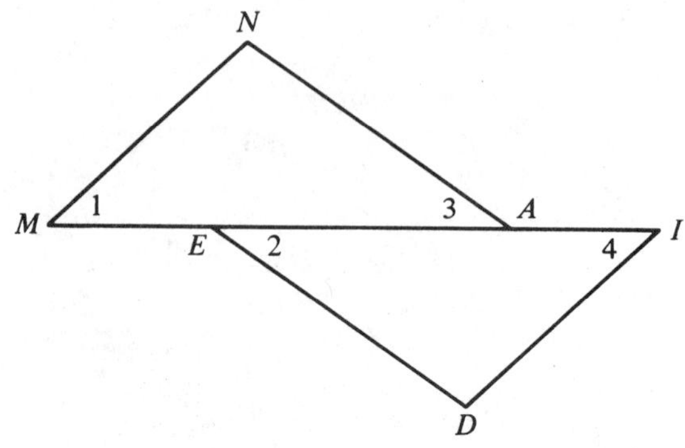

(a) $\overline{EA} \cong \overline{EA}$
(b) $\overline{MA} \cong \overline{ME} + \overline{EA}$
(c) ∡3, ∡2 alt int ∡s
(d) $\overline{NA} \cong \overline{DE}$
(e) ∡1, ∡4 alt int ∡s
(f) $\overline{ME} + \overline{EA} \cong \overline{IA} + \overline{EA}$
(g) ∡3 ≅ ∡2
(h) ∡1 ≅ ∡4
(i) $\overline{NA} \parallel \overline{DE}$
(j) $\triangle MAN \cong \triangle IED$
(k) $\overline{ME} \cong \overline{IA}$
(l) $\overline{IA} + \overline{AE} \cong \overline{IE}$
(m) $\overline{MN} \parallel \overline{DI}$
(n) $\overline{MA} \cong \overline{IE}$

26. *Given*
$\overleftrightarrow{AC} \parallel \overleftrightarrow{EG}$
∡1 ≅ ∡2

To Prove
$\overrightarrow{BH} \parallel \overrightarrow{FI}$

(a) ∡*DBC* ≅ ∡*BFG*
(b) ∡3 + ∡1 ≅ ∡4 + ∡2
(c) ∡1 ≅ ∡2
(d) ∡*BFG* ≅ ∡4 + ∡2
(e) $\overleftrightarrow{AC} \parallel \overleftrightarrow{EG}$
(f) ∡3 ≅ ∡4
(g) $\overrightarrow{BH} \parallel \overrightarrow{FI}$
(h) ∡*DBC*, ∡*BFG* corr ∡s
(i) ∡3 + ∡1 ≅ ∡*DBC*
(j) ∡3, ∡4 corr ∡s

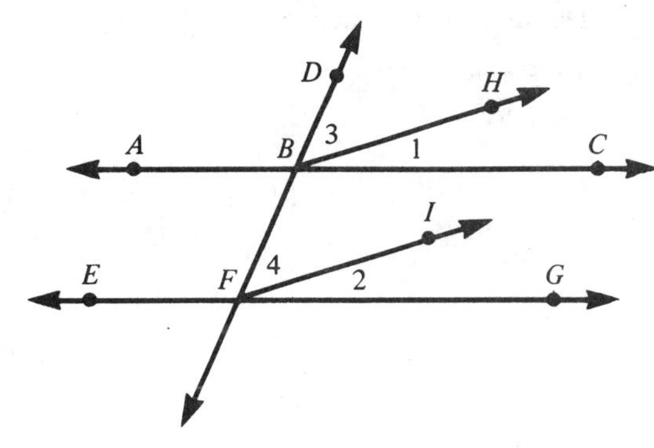

In exercises 27–43 copy the figure, the hypothesis, and the conclusion. Mark the figure and write a proof.

27. *Given*
$\overline{IU} \parallel \overline{LC}$
△*ECL* isos ($\overline{EC}$ base)

To Prove
$\overline{EI} \cong \overline{UI}$

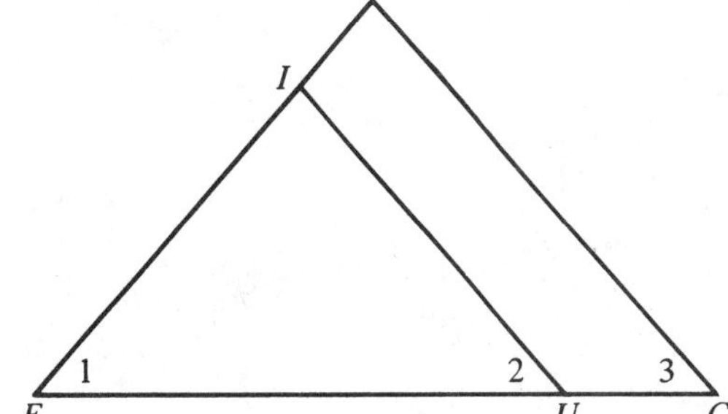

28. *Given*
$\overline{TS}$ bis ∡*LTH*
$\overline{EA} \parallel \overline{TH}$

To Prove
△*TSE* isos

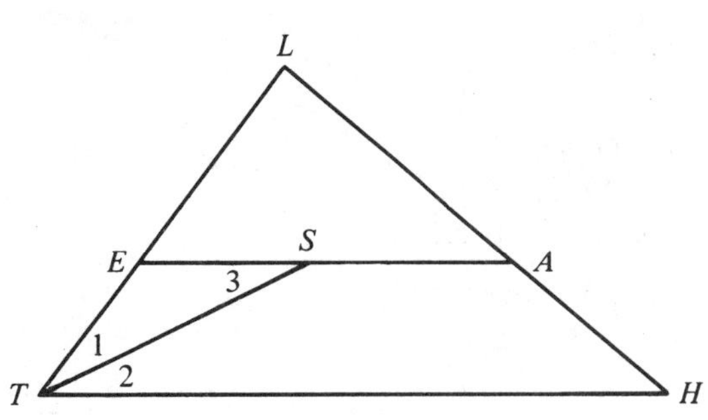

29. *Given*
$\overline{AB} \parallel \overline{CD}$
$\overline{AB} \cong \overline{CD}$

To Prove
$\overline{AD} \cong \overline{CB}$

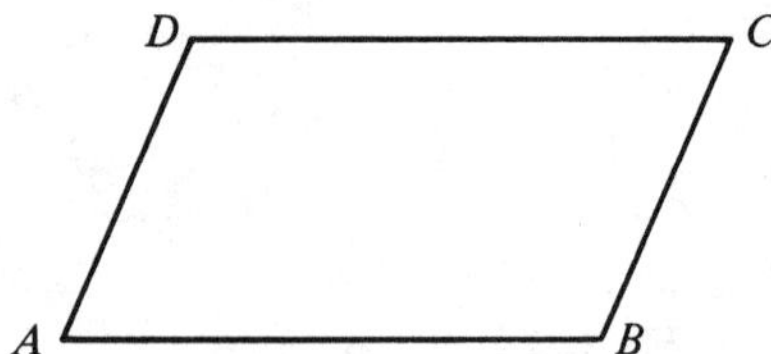

30. *Given*
$\overline{DC}$ and $\overline{EB}$ bis each other

To Prove
$\overline{AE} \parallel \overline{BC}$

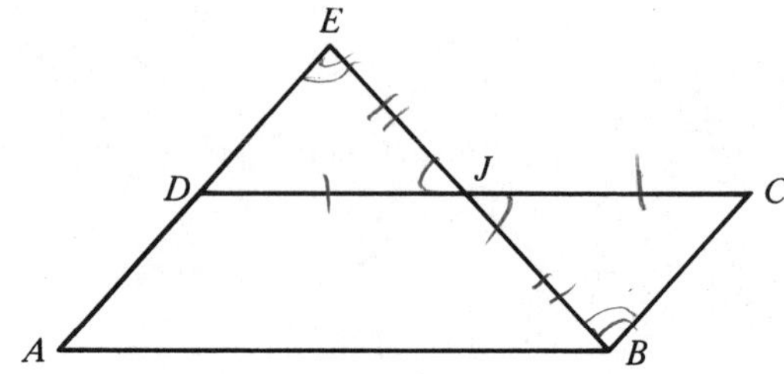

31. *Given*
$\overleftrightarrow{ES} \parallel \overleftrightarrow{CM}$
$\overrightarrow{JR}$ bis ∡EJK
$\overrightarrow{KT}$ bis ∡JKM

To Prove
$\overrightarrow{JR} \parallel \overrightarrow{KT}$

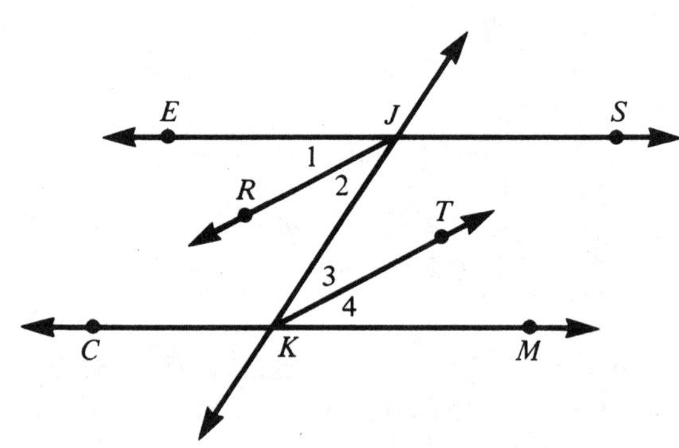

32. *Given*
$\overleftrightarrow{AP} \perp \overleftrightarrow{AT}$
$\overleftrightarrow{AP} \parallel \overleftrightarrow{TO}$

To Prove
$\overleftrightarrow{TO} \perp \overleftrightarrow{AT}$

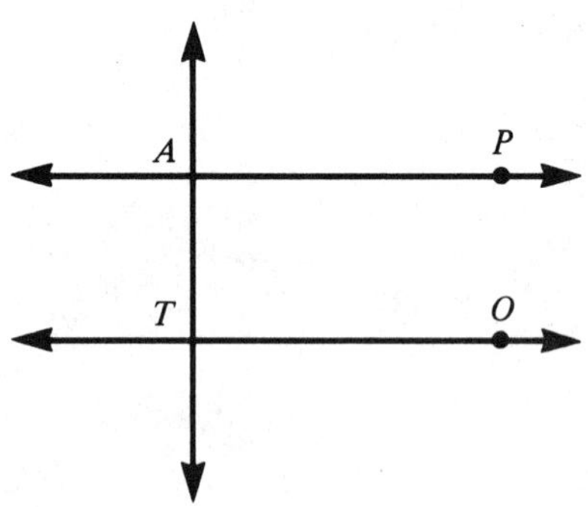

33. *Given*
$\overline{AX} \parallel \overline{MO}$
∡A supp ∡O

To Prove
∡$A \cong$ ∡X

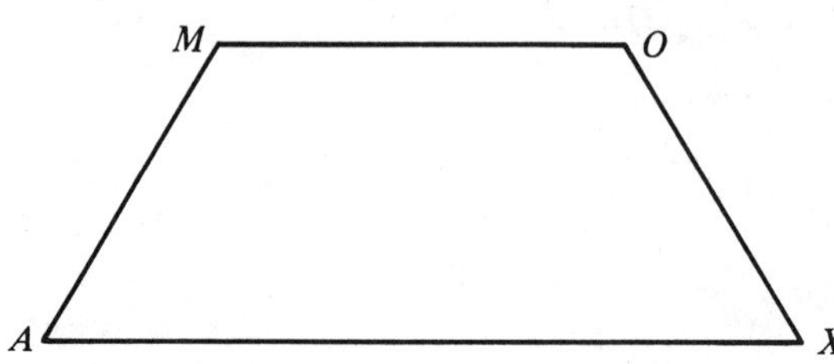

34. *Given*
$\overline{EG} \parallel \overline{AT}$
$\overline{ET} \parallel \overline{AG}$

To Prove
$\measuredangle E \cong \measuredangle A$

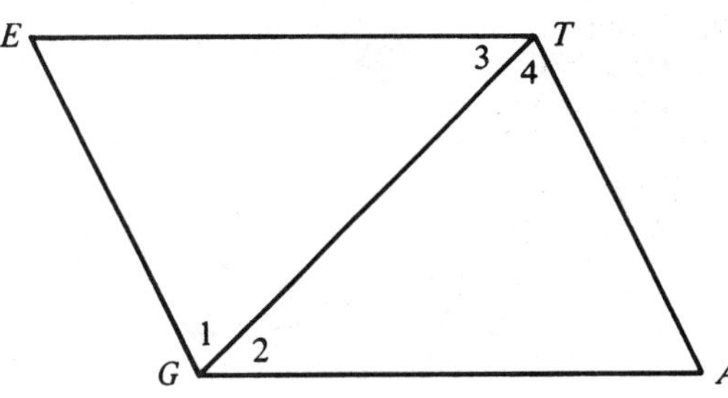

35. *Given*
$\overline{GE} \parallel \overline{LF}$
$\overline{GE} \cong \overline{LF}$

To Prove
$\overline{FE}$ bis $\overline{GL}$

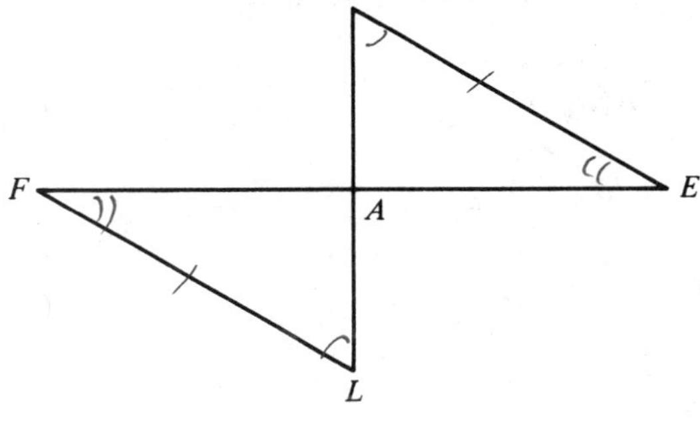

36. *Given*
$\triangle ABC$ isos ($\overline{AB}$ base)
$\overline{DE} \parallel \overline{AB}$

To Prove
$\triangle DCE$ isos

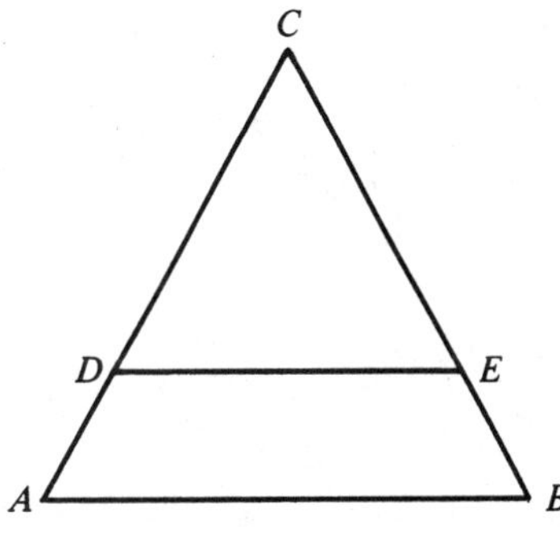

37. *Given*
$\overleftrightarrow{EJ} \parallel \overline{SK}$

To Prove
$\angle 1 + \angle 2 + \angle 3 = \angle 4 + \angle 2 + \angle 5$

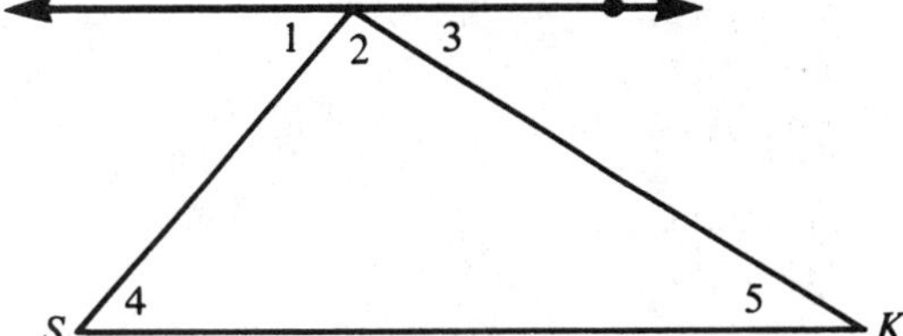

38. *Given*
$\overline{SJ} \parallel \overline{WA}$
$\overline{SW} \parallel \overline{JA}$

To Prove
$\overline{WJ}$ bis $\overline{SA}$

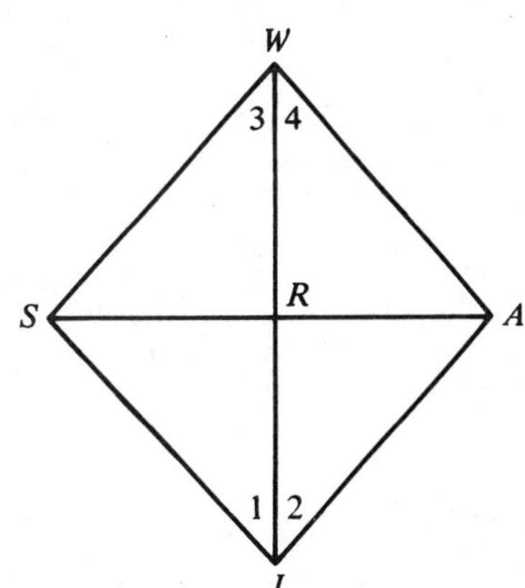

39. *Given*
$IC > RC$
$\overline{EJ} \parallel \overline{RC}$

To Prove
$\angle E > \angle I$

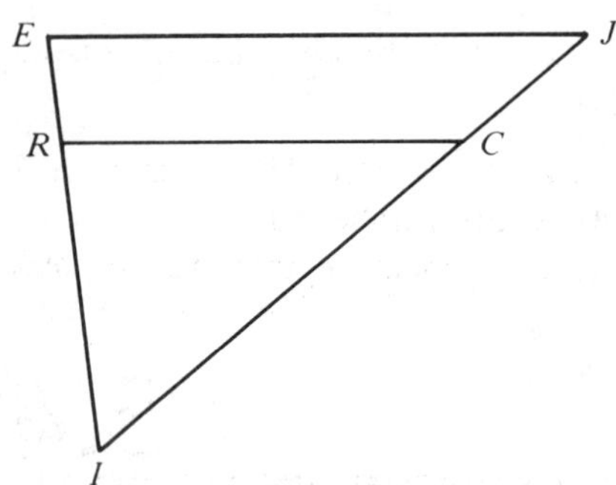

40. *Given*
$BR > BI$
$\overline{IR} \parallel \overline{CA}$

To Prove
$\angle A > \angle C$

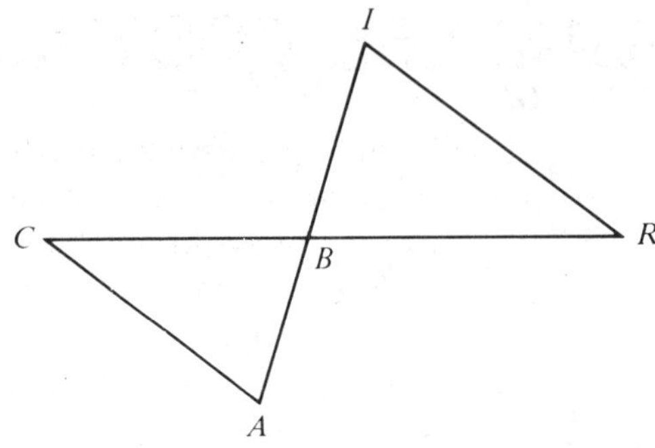

41. *Given*
$\overline{TS} \parallel \overline{PO}$
$\overline{PT} \cong \overline{TS}$

To Prove
$\overline{PS}$ bis $\measuredangle TPO$

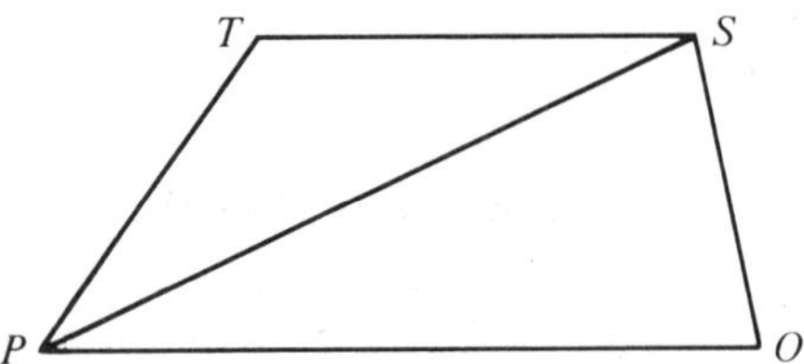

42. *Given*
$\overline{GT}$ bis $\measuredangle PGA$
$\overline{RY} \parallel \overline{GP}$
$\overline{RH} \parallel \overline{GA}$

To Prove
$\overline{GT}$ bis $\measuredangle YRH$

43. *Given*
$\overline{NG} \parallel \overline{TO}$
$\overline{CN} \perp \overline{NG}$
$\overline{ET} \perp \overline{OT}$
$\overline{GJ} \cong \overline{OA}$

To Prove
$\overline{NJ} \cong \overline{TA}$

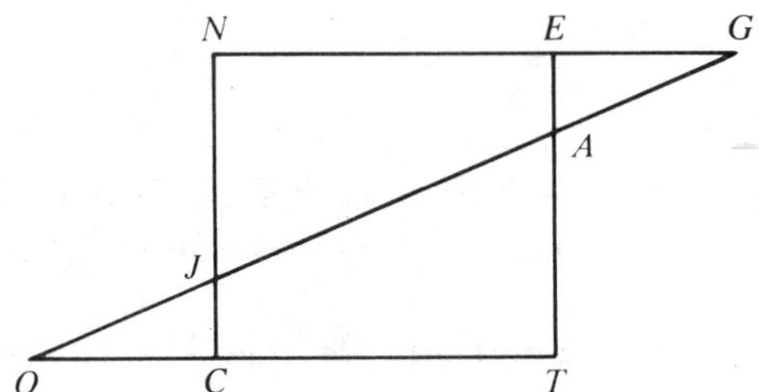

In exercises 44 and 45 use only a compass and straightedge.

44. Draw an acute triangle *ABC*. Through *A* construct a line parallel to $\overline{BC}$.

45. Draw a line segment $\overline{AC}$ and mark a point *B* such that *A-B-C*. At *B* construct $\overline{BD}$ perpendicular to $\overline{AC}$. Then, through *D* construct a line parallel to $\overline{AC}$.

5.4

MORE CONSEQUENCES OF THE PARALLEL POSTULATE

In our formal proofs we have been careful to state that certain pairs of angles are vertical angles, alternate interior angles, and so forth. These angles have been so designated to emphasize that only certain pairs are the correct ones to use. Once learned, however, this identification process in proofs becomes tedious and contributes nothing new to learning. Therefore, we will now shorten proofs by omitting statements identifying the following types of angles:

linear pair
vertical
alternate interior
alternate exterior
corresponding

These omissions, together with our earlier agreements, significantly streamline proofs as illustrated in Example 1. Note, however, that such proofs cannot be understood without a precise understanding of the terms involved.

EXAMPLE 1

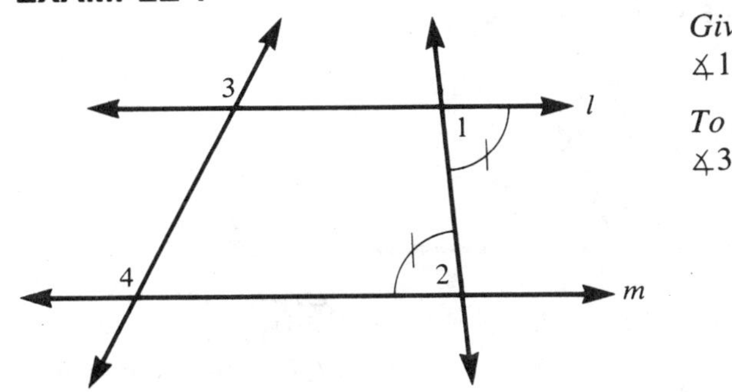

Given
∡1 ≅ ∡2

To Prove
∡3 ≅ ∡4

Statement	*Reason*
1. ∡1 ≅ ∡2	1. given
2. $l \parallel m$	2. ≇, lines ∥
3. ∴ ∡3 ≅ ∡4	3. ≠, corr ∡s ≅

The next theorem is one of the most famous and important ones in plane geometry. Observe how the proof depends on the Parallel Postulate.

Theorem 39 The sum of the measures of the angles of a triangle is 180° (180° in △).

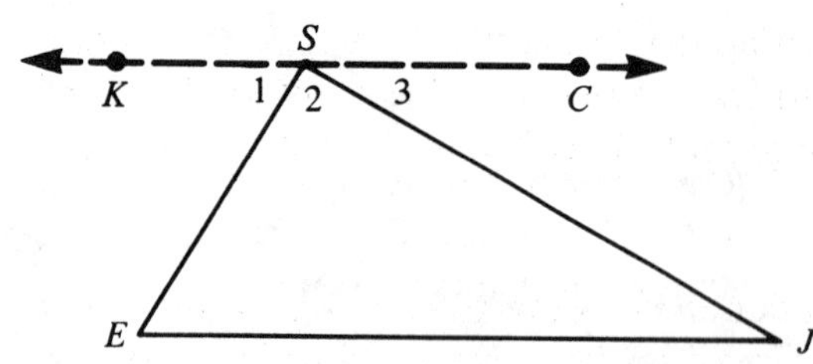

Given
$\triangle EJS$

To Prove
$\angle E + \angle 2 + \angle J = 180°$

Statement	*Reason*
1. $\triangle EJS$	1. given
2. Draw $\overleftrightarrow{KC} \parallel \overline{EJ}$ and containing S.	2. $\parallel$ post
3. $\measuredangle 1 \cong \measuredangle E$	3. $\nparallel$, alt int $\measuredangle$s $\cong$
4. $\angle 1 = \angle E$	4. $\cong$ iff meas $=$
5. $\measuredangle 3 \cong \measuredangle J$	5. $\nparallel$, alt int $\measuredangle$s $\cong$
6. $\angle 3 = \angle J$	6. $\cong$ iff meas $=$
7. $\angle 2 = \angle 2$	7. refl $=$
8. $\angle 1 + \angle 2 + \angle 3 = \angle E + \angle 2 + \angle J$	8. $= + =$, sums $=$
9. $\angle KSC = 180°$	9. st $\angle = 180°$
10. $\angle 1 + \angle 2 + \angle 3 = \angle KSC$	10. whole $=$ sum parts
11. $\angle 1 + \angle 2 + \angle 3 = 180°$	11. trans $=$
12. $\therefore \angle E + \angle 2 + \angle J = 180°$	12. subst

The following corollary of Theorem 39 has a simple proof that is omitted.

Theorem 40 If there is a correspondence between two triangles such that two angles of one are congruent to the corresponding parts of the other, then the third angles are congruent (if aa $\cong$ aa, 3d $\measuredangle$s $\cong$).

Theorem 39 makes it possible to calculate unknown sizes of angles in certain geometric figures. For example, if the measure of one angle of an isosceles triangle is known, then the measures of the other two angles are easy to find. This fact and some of the theorems about parallel lines may be used to find the angle measures in Example 2.

EXAMPLE 2

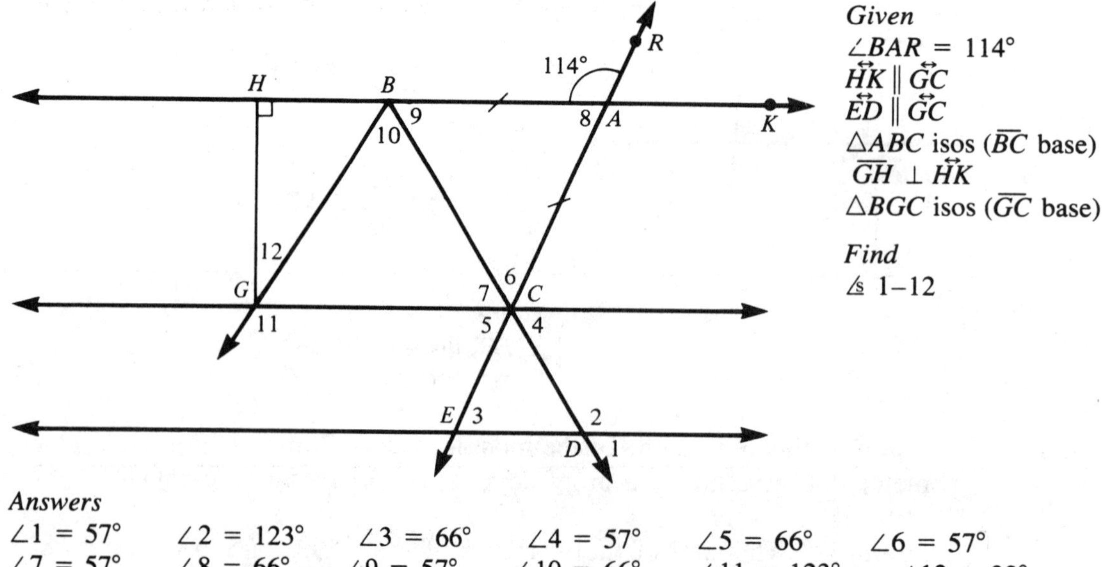

Given
$\angle BAR = 114°$
$\overleftrightarrow{HK} \parallel \overleftrightarrow{GC}$
$\overleftrightarrow{ED} \parallel \overleftrightarrow{GC}$
$\triangle ABC$ isos ($\overline{BC}$ base)
$\overline{GH} \perp \overleftrightarrow{HK}$
$\triangle BGC$ isos ($\overline{GC}$ base)

Find
$\measuredangle$s 1–12

Answers

$\angle 1 = 57°$	$\angle 2 = 123°$	$\angle 3 = 66°$	$\angle 4 = 57°$	$\angle 5 = 66°$	$\angle 6 = 57°$
$\angle 7 = 57°$	$\angle 8 = 66°$	$\angle 9 = 57°$	$\angle 10 = 66°$	$\angle 11 = 123°$	$\angle 12 = 33°$

In Section 4.2 we noted that if two angles and a nonincluded side of one triangle are congruent, respectively, to two angles and a nonincluded side of another, then the two triangles are congruent. This is the content of Theorem 41.

Theorem 41 If there is a correspondence between two triangles such that two angles and a side of one are congruent to the corresponding parts of the other, then the two triangles are congruent (aas ≅ aas).

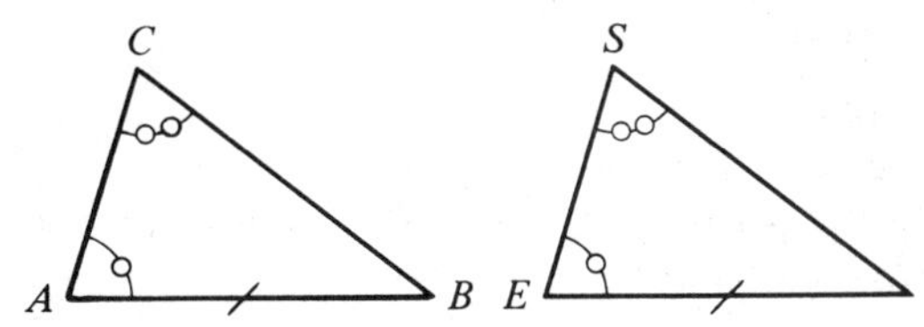

Given
$\triangle ABC$, $\triangle EJS$ with $ABC \leftrightarrow EJS$
$\measuredangle A \cong \measuredangle E$, $\measuredangle C \cong \measuredangle S$, $\overline{AB} \cong \overline{EJ}$

To Prove
$\triangle ABC \cong \triangle EJS$

Statement	*Reason*
1. $\triangle ABC$, $\triangle EJS$ with $ABC \leftrightarrow EJS$	1. given
2. $\measuredangle A \cong \measuredangle E$, $\measuredangle C \cong \measuredangle S$	2. given
3. $\measuredangle B \cong \measuredangle J$	3. if aa ≅ aa, 3d $\measuredangle$s ≅
4. $\overline{AB} \cong \overline{EJ}$	4. given
5. ∴ $\triangle ABC \cong \triangle EJS$	5. asa ≅ asa

It should be evident that the proof of Theorem 41 depends essentially on Theorem 39. Below are two more theorems that also follow from Theorem 39. The proofs are left as exercises.

Theorem 42 The acute angles in a right triangle are complementary (acute $\measuredangle$s rt $\triangle$ comp).

Theorem 43 The measure of an exterior angle of a triangle is equal to the sum of the measures of the two remote interior angles (ext $\angle$ = sum rem int $\angle$s).

Example 3 involves a proof that uses the new congruence theorem (aas ≅ aas). It also suggests another congruence theorem with which we conclude this section.

EXAMPLE 3

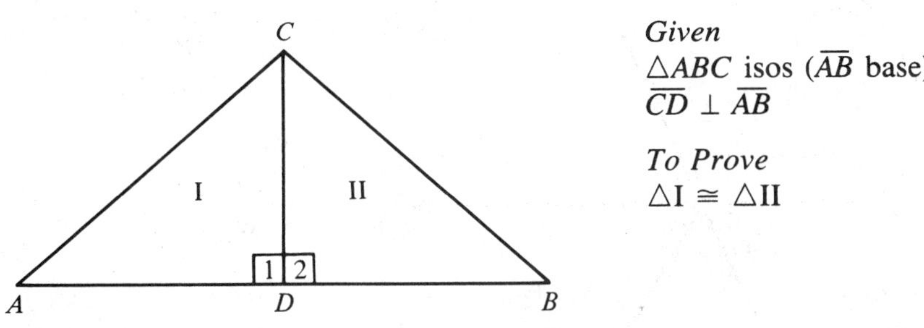

Given
$\triangle ABC$ isos ($\overline{AB}$ base)
$\overline{CD} \perp \overline{AB}$

To Prove
$\triangle$I ≅ $\triangle$II

Statement	*Reason*
1. $\triangle ABC$ isos ($\overline{AB}$ base)	1. given
2. $\overline{AC} \cong \overline{BC}$	2. isos $\triangle$ iff 2 ≅ sides
3. $\measuredangle A \cong \measuredangle B$	3. if 2 sides $\triangle$ ≅, opp $\measuredangle$s ≅

4. $\overline{CD} \perp \overline{AB}$	4. given
5. ∡1 ≅ ∡2	5. ⊥s form ≅ rt ∡s
6. ∴ △I ≅ △II	6. aas ≅ aas

If triangles I and II in Example 3 were "separated," we would have from the given facts two right triangles with congruent hypotenuses ($\overline{AC} \cong \overline{BC}$) and a pair of congruent legs ($\overline{CD} \cong \overline{CD}$). Considering this intuitive notion with the fact that △I can be proved congruent to △II, leads to the following important theorem concerning right triangles.

Theorem 44 If there is a correspondence between two right triangles such that the hypotenuse and a leg of one are congruent to the corresponding parts of the other, then the two triangles are congruent (hs ≅ hs).

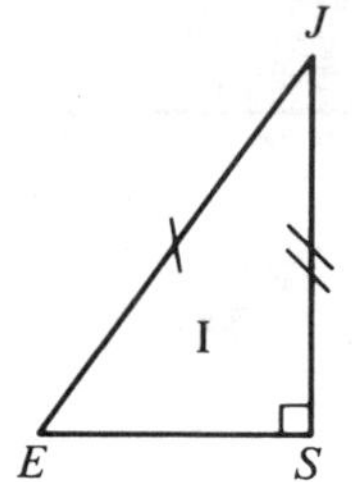

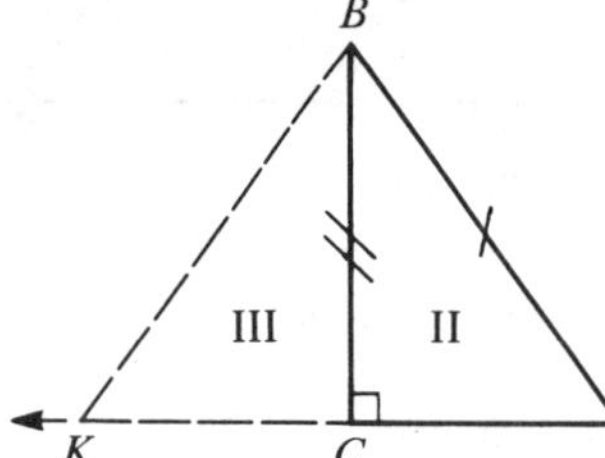

Given
rt △*EJS* (*S* rt ∡)
rt △*ABC* (*C* rt ∡)
$\overline{EJ} \cong \overline{AB}$
$\overline{JS} \cong \overline{BC}$

To Prove
△I ≅ △II

Statement	*Reason*
1. rt △*EJS* (*S* rt ∡) rt △*ABC* (*C* rt ∡)	1. given
2. Draw $\overrightarrow{AC}$.	2. 2 pts determ line
3. Construct $\overline{CK}$ so that $\overline{SE} \cong \overline{CK}$.	3. can copy seg
4. Draw $\overline{BK}$.	4. 2 pts determ line
5. $\overline{BC} \perp \overline{CA}$	5. ⊥ iff a rt ∡
6. ∡*BCK* rt ∡	6. ⊥s form ≅ rt ∡s
7. ∡*S* ≅ ∡*BCK*	7. rt ∡s ≅
8. $\overline{JS} \cong \overline{BC}$	8. given
9. △I ≅ △III	9. sas ≅ sas
10. $\overline{EJ} \cong \overline{KB}$	10. cpctc
11. $\overline{EJ} \cong \overline{AB}$	11. given
12. $\overline{KB} \cong \overline{AB}$	12. symm and trans ≅
13. ∡*K* ≅ ∡*A*	13. if 2 sides △ ≅, opp ∡s ≅
14. ∡*BCK* ≅ ∡ *BCA*	14. rt ∡s ≅
15. △III ≅ △II	15. aas ≅ aas
16. ∴ △I ≅ △II	16. trans ≅

EXERCISES FOR 5.4

In exercises 1–20 answer true or false.

1. The three angles of a triangle could measure 72°17′37″, 93°18′42″, and 13°23′41″.

2. If two angles of one triangle are congruent to two angles of a second triangle, the third angles are not necessarily congruent.

3. Only special triangles in a plane contain two right angles.

4. If one angle of a right triangle measures 32°10′, the other acute angle measures 58°50′.

5. If the vertex angle of an isosceles triangle measures 58°30′, a base angle measures 60°45′.

6. Two triangles can be proved congruent using ssa ≅ ssa.

7. The six exterior angles of an equilateral

triangle each measure 120°.

8. A triangle may have an acute angle, a right angle, and an obtuse angle for its three angles.
9. If two parallel lines are cut by a transversal and an exterior angle measures 111°51′, then two alternate interior angles each measure 68°9′.
10. If a transversal is perpendicular to one of two parallel lines, it is perpendicular to the other line also.
11. If two angles of a triangle are congruent and the third has a measure six times one of the others, the angles measure 22°30′, 22°30′, and 135°.
12. If two angles of a triangle each measure 45°, the triangle is an isosceles right triangle.
13. If an exterior angle at the vertex of an isosceles triangle measures 105°, an exterior angle at one of the base angles measures 126°30′.
14. If an exterior angle of a triangle measures 112°14′, two angles of the triangle could measure 43°28′ and 67°46′.
15. If the sum of the measures of two angles of a triangle equals that of the third angle, then the triangle is an equilateral triangle.
16. An equilateral triangle has three congruent angles each measuring 59°59′59″.
17. If in triangles *ABC* and *EJS*, angle *A* is congruent to angle *E*, angle *C* is congruent to angle *S*, and side $\overline{AC}$ is congruent to side $\overline{EJ}$, then triangle *ABC* is congruent to triangle *EJS* according to aas ≅ aas.
18. The hs ≅ hs method of proving two triangles congruent is a special case of ssa ≅ ssa.
19. If an exterior angle of a triangle is greater than 90°, then the triangle must be an acute triangle.
20. A perpendicular (not at the midpoint) to the base of an isosceles triangle intersecting one of the congruent sides and the other side extended, forms—with two segments from the congruent sides—an isosceles triangle.

In exercises 21–28 copy the figure, mark it, and find the requested measures.

21. *Given*
$\overline{SK}$ bis ∡*ESA*
$\overline{TK}$ bis ∡ *ETA*
$\angle KSA = 58°$, $\angle ATJ = 136°$

Find
∡s 1–10

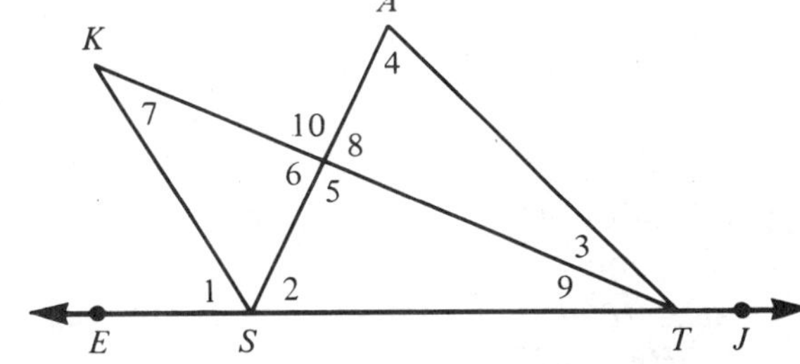

22. *Given*
$\overline{DC} \parallel \overline{EF}$
△*DCI* isos ($\overline{DC}$ base)
△*ABI* isos ($\overline{AB}$ base)
$\angle EGI = 137°15'$
$\overline{DC} \parallel \overline{AB}$
$\angle CBA = 87°30'$

Find
∡s 1–10

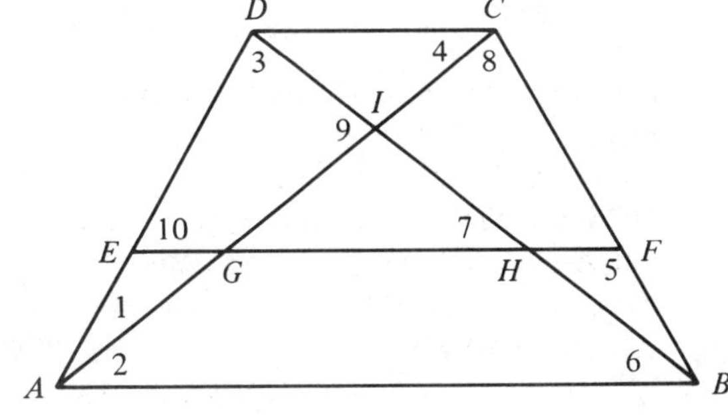

23. *Given*
$\overline{AB} \parallel \overline{ES}$
$\angle 2 = 53°33'$
$\overline{AD} \parallel \overline{BC}$
$\angle 1 = 41°$
$\angle 12 = 44°$
$\angle ABD = 38°$

Find
$\angle$s 3–11

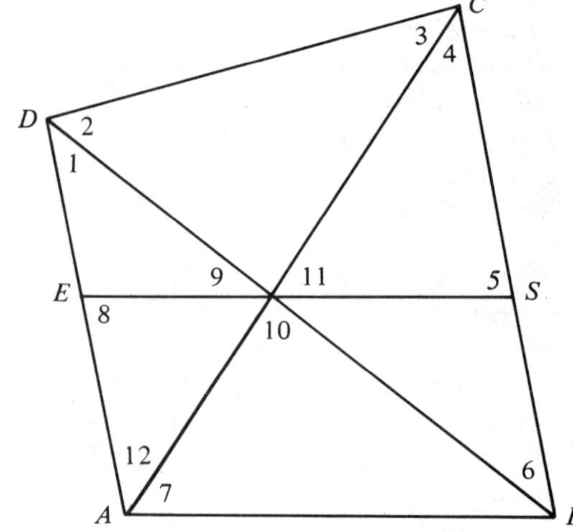

24. *Given*
$\triangle ABC$ isos ($\overline{BC}$ base)
$\angle BCD = 127°$
$\overleftrightarrow{BC} \parallel \overrightarrow{DE}$
$\overrightarrow{AE}$ bis $\measuredangle BAC$

Find
$\angle$s 1–10

25. *Given*
$\overleftrightarrow{GI} \perp \overleftrightarrow{IB}$
$\overleftrightarrow{AC} \perp \overleftrightarrow{IB}$
$\angle GHF = 122°$
$\overleftrightarrow{IE}$ bis $\measuredangle HIC$

Find
$\angle$s 1–12

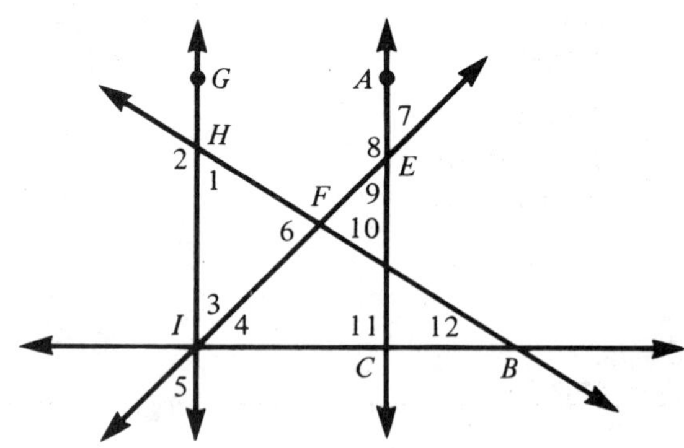

26. *Given*
$\overleftrightarrow{FG} \parallel \overleftrightarrow{BA}$
$\overline{BC} \perp \overline{CD}$
$\angle EFD = 59°$
$\overleftrightarrow{DC}$ bis $\measuredangle FDB$
$\overline{ED} \cong \overline{EF}$
$\overrightarrow{FK} \parallel \overleftrightarrow{CD}$

Find
$\angle$s 1–12

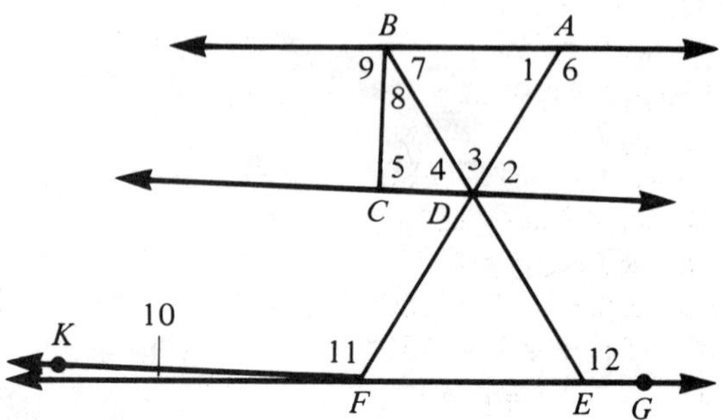

27. *Given*
$\angle 2 = 118°$
$\overline{EK}$ bis $\measuredangle SEJ$
$\overline{JK}$ bis $\measuredangle SJE$

Find
$\angle 1$

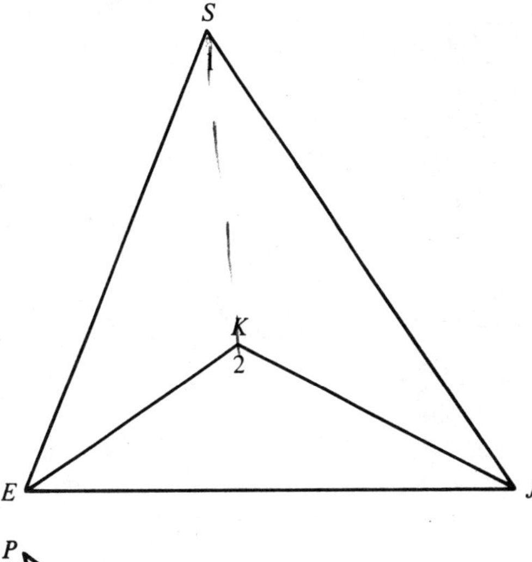

28. *Given*
$\overline{GP} \cong \overline{GR}$
$\overline{GE} \cong \overline{GO}$
$\angle 1 = 40°$

Find
$\angle 2$

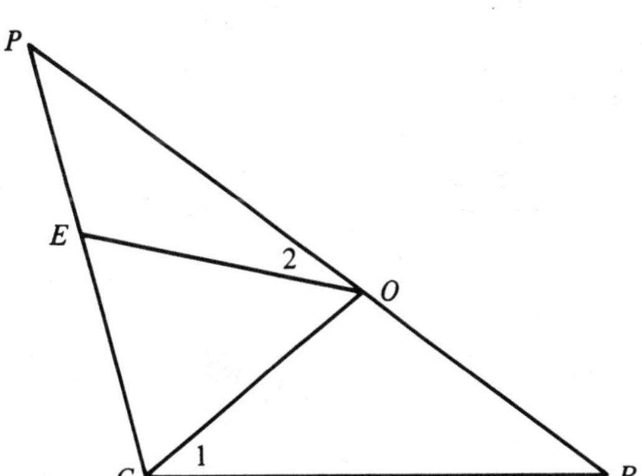

In exercises 29–31 copy the figure, mark it, and supply the missing reasons in each proof. Note the new shortcuts.

29. (Theorem 37)

Given
$l \parallel m$

To Prove
$\measuredangle 2$ supp $\measuredangle 4$
$\measuredangle 3$ supp $\measuredangle 1$

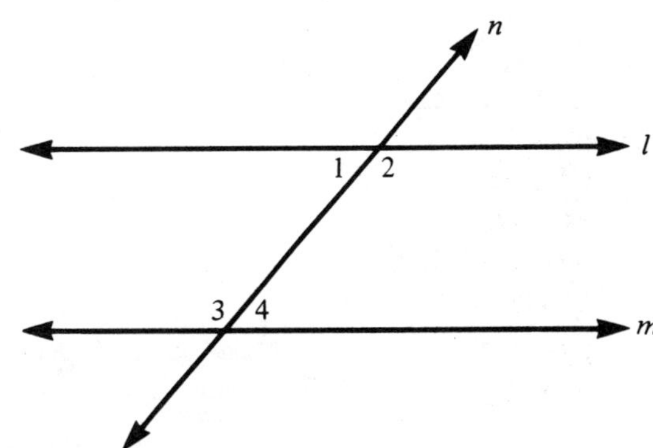

Statement	*Reason*
1. $l \parallel m$	1. ?
2. $\measuredangle 1 \cong \measuredangle 4$	2. ?
3. $\angle 1 = \angle 4$	3. ?
4. $\measuredangle 1$ supp $\measuredangle 2$	4. ?
5. $\angle 1 + \angle 2 = 180°$	5. ?
6. $\angle 4 + \angle 2 = 180°$	6. ?
7. $\therefore \measuredangle 2$ supp $\measuredangle 4$	7. ?
8. $\measuredangle 3$ supp $\measuredangle 4$	8. ?
9. $\angle 3 + \angle 4 = 180°$	9. ?
10. $\angle 3 + \angle 1 = 180°$	10. ?
11. $\therefore \measuredangle 3$ supp $\measuredangle 1$	11. ?

30. *Given*
$\overline{AD} \cong \overline{CB}$
$\overline{AD} \parallel \overline{CB}$
$\overline{DE} \perp \overline{AC}$
$\overline{BF} \perp \overline{AC}$

To Prove
$\overline{DE} \cong \overline{BF}$

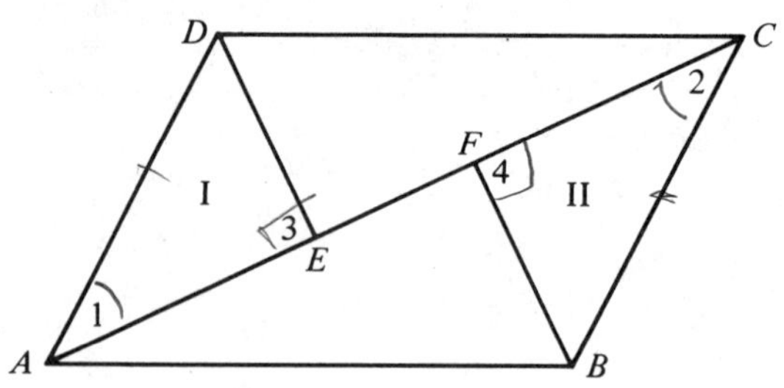

Statement	*Reason*
1. $\overline{AD} \cong \overline{CB}$	1. ?
2. $\overline{AD} \parallel \overline{CB}$	2. ?
3. $\angle 1 \cong \angle 2$	3. ?
4. $\overline{DE} \perp \overline{AC}$	4. ?
5. $\angle 3$ rt $\angle$	5. ?
6. $\overline{BF} \perp \overline{AC}$	6. ?
7. $\angle 4$ rt $\angle$	7. ?
8. $\angle 3 \cong \angle 4$	8. ?
9. $\triangle\text{I} \cong \triangle\text{II}$	9. ?
10. $\therefore \overline{DE} \cong \overline{BF}$	10. ?

31. (Theorem 36)

Given
$l \parallel m$

To Prove
$\angle 1 \cong \angle 5$
$\angle 2 \cong \angle 6$
$\angle 3 \cong \angle 7$
$\angle 4 \cong \angle 8$

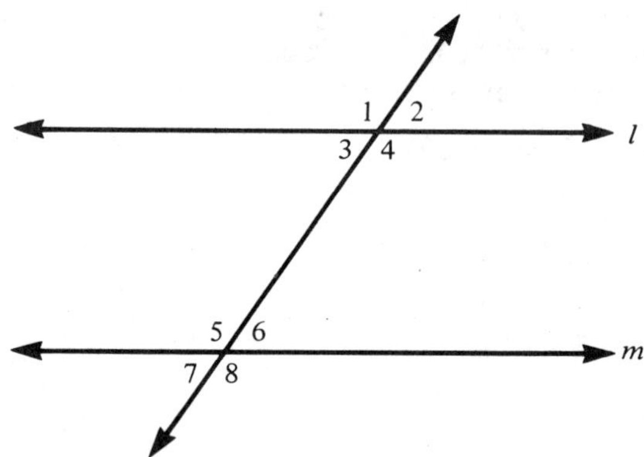

Statement	*Reason*
1. $l \parallel m$	1. ?
2. $\angle 1 \cong \angle 4$	2. ?
3. $\angle 4 \cong \angle 5$	3. ?
4. $\therefore \angle 1 \cong \angle 5$	4. ?
5. $\angle 2 \cong \angle 3$	5. ?
6. $\angle 3 \cong \angle 6$	6. ?
7. $\therefore \angle 2 \cong \angle 6$	7. ?
8. $\angle 6 \cong \angle 7$	8. ?
9. $\therefore \angle 3 \cong \angle 7$	9. ?
10. $\angle 5 \cong \angle 8$	10. ?
11. $\therefore \angle 4 \cong \angle 8$	11. ?

In exercises 32 and 33 copy the figure, mark it, and rearrange the statements into a correct order for a proof.

32. *Given*
$\overline{EM} \parallel \overline{CS}$
$\overline{CM}$ bis $\overline{ES}$ at J

To Prove
$\overline{MJ} \cong \overline{CJ}$

(a) $\overline{MJ} \cong \overline{CJ}$
(b) $\overline{EJ} \cong \overline{SJ}$
(c) $\overline{EM} \parallel \overline{CS}$
(d) $\measuredangle 2 \cong \measuredangle 3$
(e) $\overline{CM}$ bis $\overline{ES}$ at J
(f) $\measuredangle 1 \cong \measuredangle 4$
(g) $\triangle \text{I} \cong \triangle \text{II}$

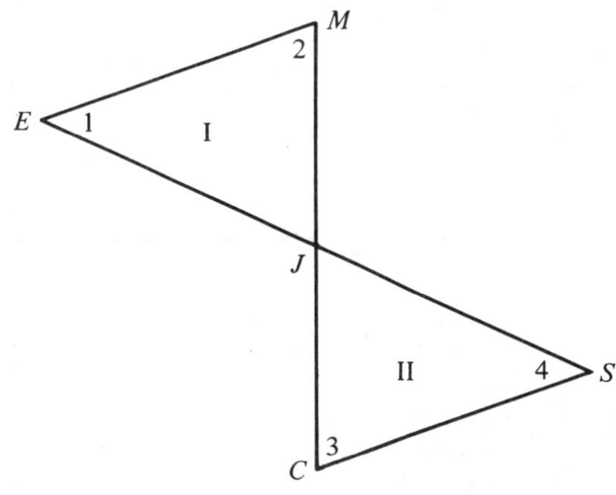

33. *Given*
$\overline{AD} \cong \overline{CB}$
$\overline{AD} \parallel \overline{CB}$
$\triangle ADE$ isos ($\overline{DE}$ base)
$\triangle BFC$ isos ($\overline{BF}$ base)

To Prove
$\overline{DE} \cong \overline{BF}$

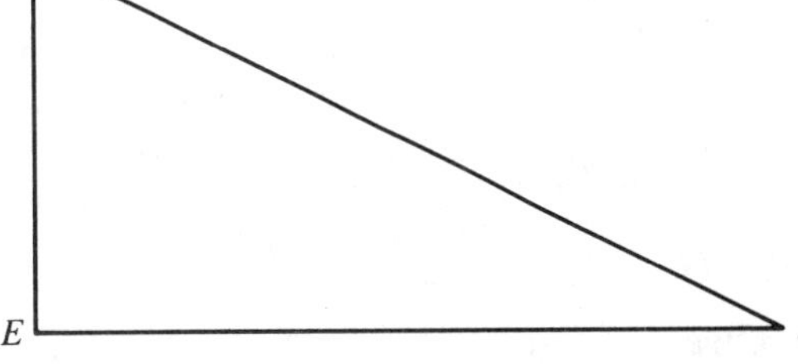

(a) $\measuredangle 1 \cong \measuredangle 2$
(b) $\overline{DE} \cong \overline{BF}$
(c) $\triangle BFC$ isos ($\overline{BF}$ base)
(d) $\overline{CB} \cong \overline{CF}$
(e) $\overline{AD} \parallel \overline{CB}$
(f) $\overline{AE} \cong \overline{AD}$
(g) $\triangle \text{I} \cong \triangle \text{II}$
(h) $\triangle ADE$ isos ($\overline{DE}$ base)
(i) $\overline{AD} \cong \overline{CB}$
(j) $\overline{AE} \cong \overline{CF}$

In exercises 34–45 copy the figure, the hypothesis, and the conclusion. Mark the figure and write a proof. Use the new shortcuts.

34. (Theorem 42)

Given
rt $\triangle$ EJS
$\measuredangle E$ rt $\measuredangle$

To Prove
$\measuredangle S$ comp $\measuredangle$ J

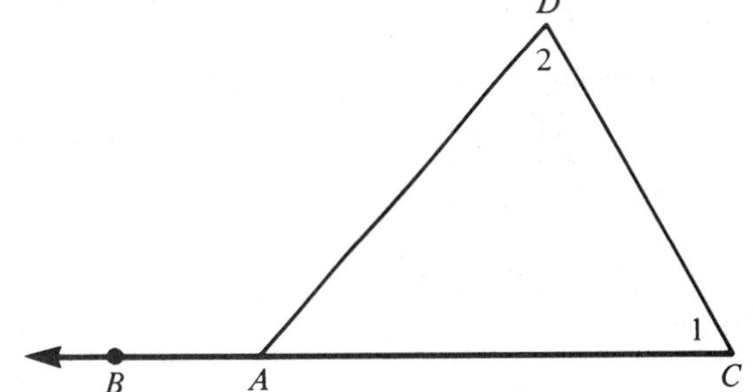

35. (Theorem 43)

Given
$\triangle CAD$
$\measuredangle BAD$ ext $\measuredangle$

To Prove
$\angle BAD = \angle 1 + \angle 2$

36. *Given*
$\overline{DL} \cong \overline{EU}$
$\overline{DL} \parallel \overline{EC}$
$\overline{DU} \parallel \overline{IC}$

To Prove
U midpt $\overline{EC}$

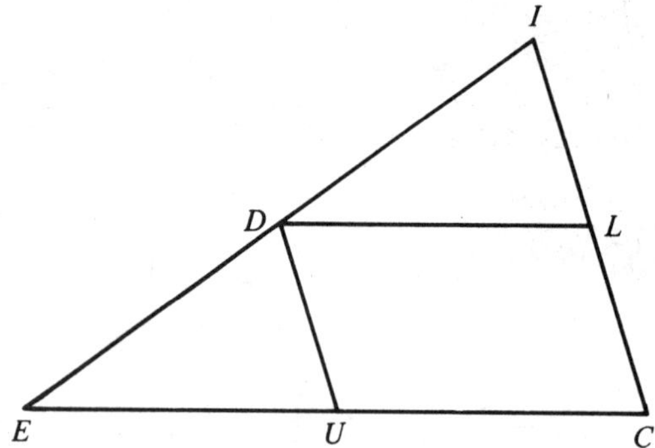

37. *Given*
$\overleftrightarrow{ES} \parallel \overleftrightarrow{CM}$
$\overrightarrow{JR}$ bis $\measuredangle SJK$
$\overrightarrow{KR}$ bis $\measuredangle JKM$

To Prove
$\measuredangle JRK$ rt $\measuredangle$

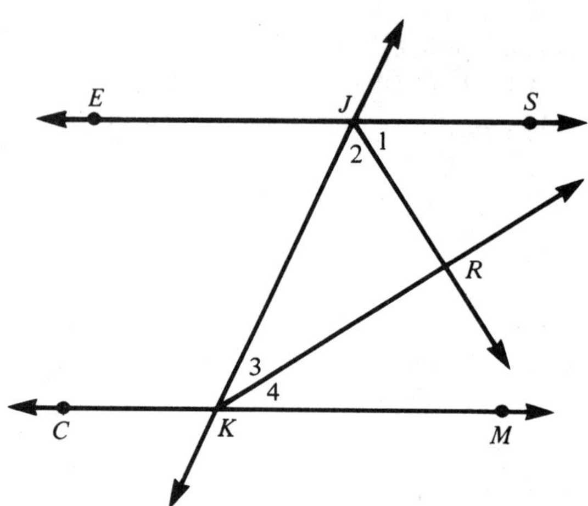

38. *Given*
$\overline{SH} \perp \overline{TL}$
$\overline{SA} \perp \overline{TE}$

To Prove
$\measuredangle 1 \cong \measuredangle 3$

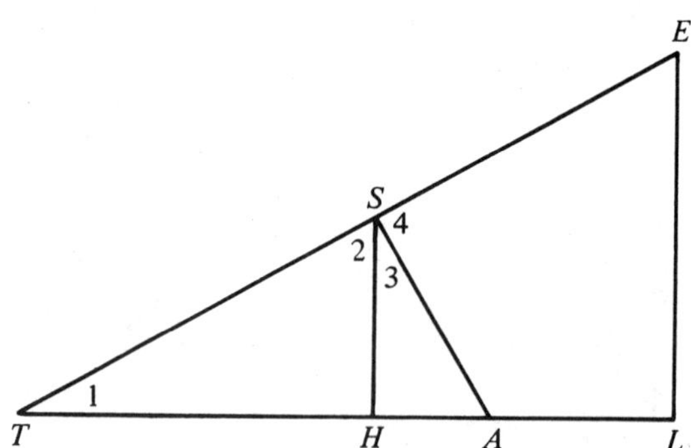

39. *Given*
$\overline{WN} \parallel \overline{AO}$
$\overline{TN} \parallel \overline{SO}$

To Prove
$\measuredangle N \cong \measuredangle O$

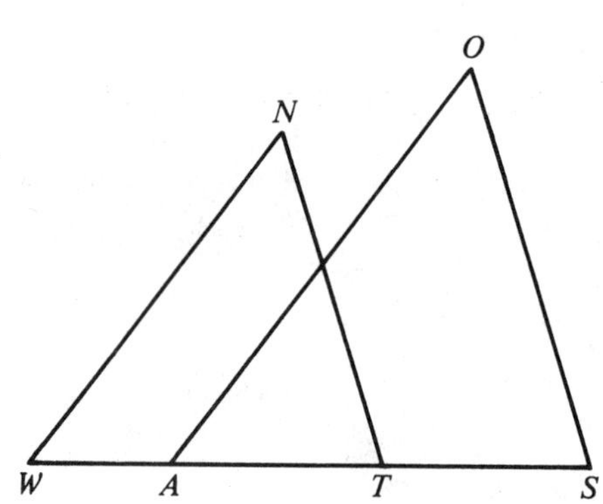

40. *Given*
$\overleftrightarrow{EC} \parallel \overline{LD}$
$\overline{UL}$ bis $\measuredangle EUI$
$\overline{UD}$ bis $\measuredangle CUI$

To Prove
$\overline{LI} \cong \overline{DI}$

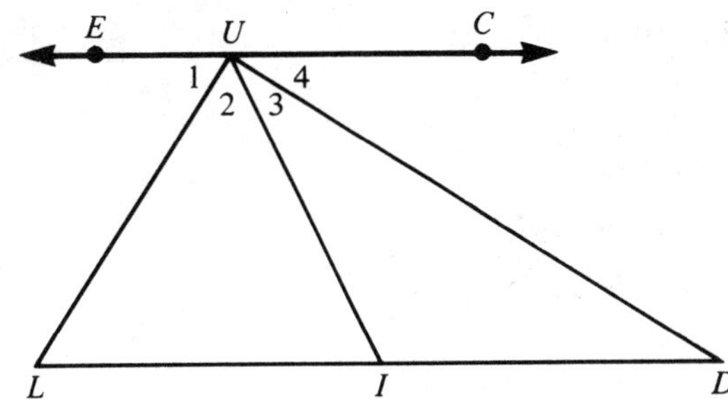

41. *Given*
$\overline{CA} \perp \overline{AB}$
$\overline{BE} \perp \overline{CE}$
$\overline{CD} \cong \overline{BD}$

To Prove
$\overline{CA} \cong \overline{BE}$

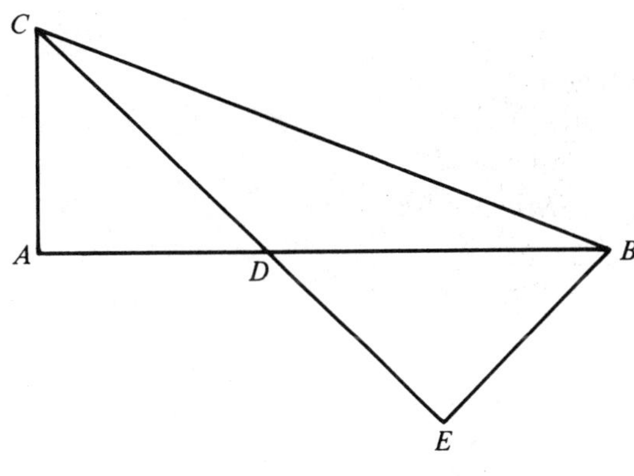

42. *Given*
$\overline{EL} \cong \overline{EU}$
$\overline{EU} \perp \overline{UC}$
$\overline{EL} \perp \overline{CL}$

To Prove
$\overline{UC} \cong \overline{LC}$

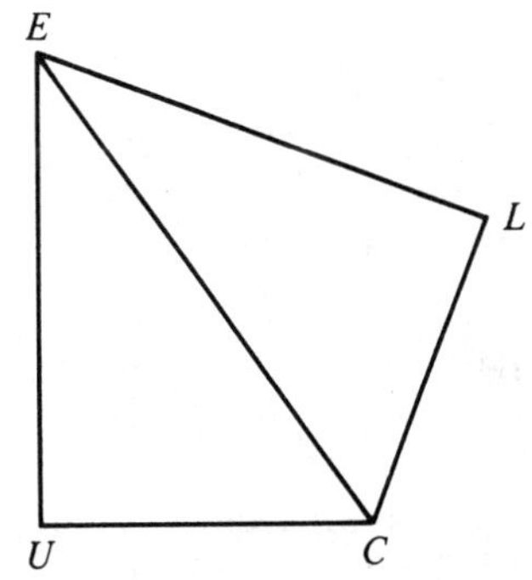

43. *Given*
$\triangle PNT$
P-O-I-N

To Prove
$\angle 1 + \angle 9 + \angle 4 = \angle 6 + \angle 7 + \angle 3$

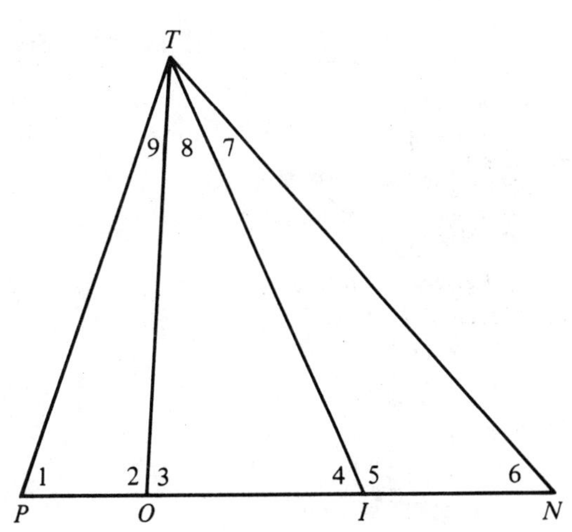

44. *Given*
$\overline{MJ} \perp \overline{ES}$
$\overline{CS} \cong \overline{CE}$

To Prove
$\measuredangle M \cong \measuredangle MAC$

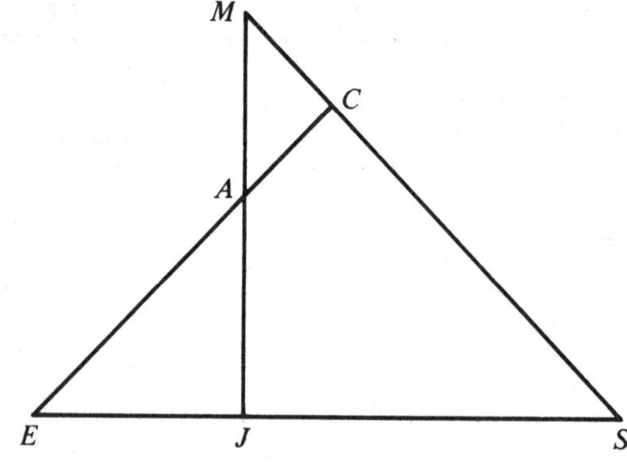

45. *Given*
$\overleftrightarrow{ES} \parallel \overleftrightarrow{AC}$

To Prove
$\angle JPB = \angle 1 + \angle 2$

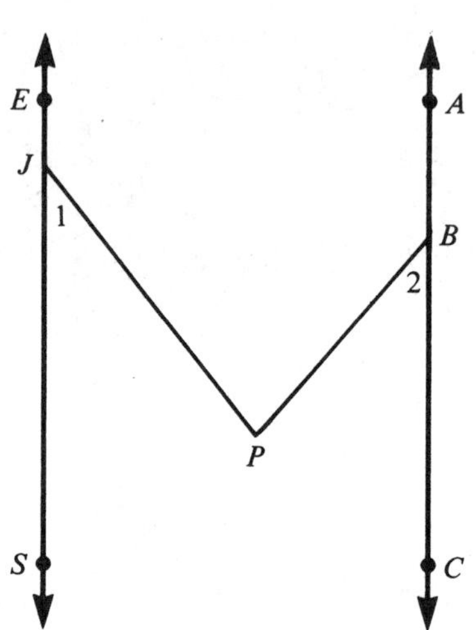

CHAPTER 5 SUMMARY

The practical uses of parallel lines and the efforts made (beginning with Euclid) to prove the Parallel Postulate lead to a detailed study of two parallel lines cut by a transversal. Two lines can be proved to be parallel if certain pairs of angles formed by them and a transversal can be shown to be congruent. The theory of parallel lines provides two more ways to prove triangles congruent; it also gives rise to the important 180°-in-a-triangle theorem.

FACTS TO KNOW

1. Definitions
   - **a.** Parallel lines
   - **b.** Alternate interior angles
   - **c.** Alternate exterior angles
   - **d.** Corresponding angles
2. The Parallel Postulate
3. Theorems
   - **a.** $\not\measuredangle$, lines $\parallel$
   - **b.** $\not\measuredangle$, lines $\parallel$
   - **c.** $\not\measuredangle$, lines $\parallel$
   - **d.** $\not\measuredangle$, lines $\parallel$
   - **e.** 2 lines $\perp$ 3d line $\parallel$
   - **f.** $\ne$, alt int ∡s ≅
   - **g.** $\ne$, alt ext ∡s ≅
   - **h.** $\ne$, corr ∡s ≅
   - **i.** $\ne$, int ∡s same side *t* supp
   - **j.** 2 lines $\parallel$ 3d line $\parallel$
   - **k.** 180° in △
   - **l.** if aa ≅ aa, 3d ∡s ≅
   - **m.** aas ≅ aas
   - **n.** acute ∡s rt △ comp
   - **o.** ext ∠ of △ = sum rem int ∡s
   - **p.** hs ≅ hs

PROBLEMS TO MASTER

1. Identify certain pairs of angles when two lines are cut by a transversal.
2. Find congruent angles given two parallel lines cut by a transversal.
3. Prove two lines are parallel using pairs of angles.
4. Prove triangles congruent using aas or hs.
5. Find degree measures of angles in figures using parallel lines and triangles.
6. Construct a line parallel to a given line through a point not on the given line.

6

QUADRILATERALS AND OTHER POLYGONS

MAJOR TOPICS

- ▱ Quadrilaterals, types of quadrilaterals, and their properties
- ▱ Polygons, types of polygons, and their properties
- ▱ Use of auxiliary lines and congruent triangles to prove properties of polygons
- ▱ Ways to show that a given quadrilateral is a special type
- ▱ Use of facts about congruent triangles and parallelograms to prove other theorems

HISTORICAL NOTE

THE PARALLEL POSTULATE CHALLENGED

Euclid's *Elements,* with its plausible postulates and its impeccable deductive logic, dominated mathematical thought for 2000 years. Indeed, it was considered to be nothing short of absolute truth. This view was reinforced by the controversy over the Parallel Postulate, for all efforts to replace it or to prove it as a theorem based on the other postulates had seemingly ended in failure. The fortress of Euclidean geometry appeared to be impregnable. True, Saccheri (1667–1733) had glimpsed a crack in the wall by assuming the Parallel Postulate to be false and trying to deduce contradictions, but he did not recognize the consequence of his work. Saccheri and other geometers of his time were not able to reject a 2000-year-old pattern of thought.

The early part of the nineteenth century, however, saw a change in the intellectual climate of the western world. Societies began to reexamine their fundamental beliefs. Doubtless such a climate accounted for the fact that three men, independently and without knowledge of each other's efforts, discovered during the 1800s the correct interpretation of Saccheri's work. The mathematical world was finally ready for a breakthrough.

One of these three discoverers was Karl Friedrich Gauss, born in Brunswick, Germany, in 1777. He was the son of a bricklayer, and it was his father's wish that his son would follow in this trade. At a very young age, however, Karl showed the talents of genius. When only three years old he found an error in his father's accounts. In his school years, he proved that a regular polygon of 17 sides could be inscribed in a circle using only a compass and straightedge. This impressive achievement convinced Gauss to pursue the study of mathematics rather than philology, his other major interest. His later accomplishments were so wide-ranging and numerous that he has been called the "Prince of Mathematicians" and ranked with Archimedes and Newton as one of the three greatest mathematicians of all time.

As a young man, Gauss followed Saccheri's methods, but he saw that the failure to deduce contradictions meant that *there can be valid geometries that are different from Euclid's!* Gauss did not publish his conclusions, however, because he did not wish to face the turmoil they would have created. Only after Gauss's death in 1855 did the world uncover his vision of non-Euclidean geometry.

One of Gauss's contemporaries, Nikolài Ivanovich Lobachevski, was born to a poor Russian family in 1793. At the young age of 23, Lobachevski became a full professor at the University of Kasan. He was fascinated by the fact that, for 2000 years, efforts by so many mathematicians had not settled the Parallel Postulate controversy. Like Saccheri and Gauss, he built a new geometry based on a different parallel postulate, understanding that the consistency of his theorems meant that his structure was as sound as Euclid's. Unlike Gauss, Lobachevski published his work, and its radical nature soon led to his dismissal from the university.

The third of the discoverers of new geometries was the Hungarian Janos Bolyai (1802–1860), the son of the mathematician Wolfgang Bolyai who had himself spent many years working on the Parallel Postulate problem. At age 23, Janos saw that the assumption of a parallel postulate different from Euclid's led to an equally valid geometry. His work was published as an appendix to one of his father's textbooks.

For approximately thirty years after their publication, the works of Lobachevski and Bolyai were largely ignored. But on the posthumous revelation that the great Gauss had reached similar conclusions, the validity of non-Euclidean geometries was finally admitted. The sweeping significance of this event cannot be overstated. It freed mathematicians to roam the fertile regions of new geometries but moreover it undermined the notion that mathematics is a system inherent in the world around us. The acceptance of non-Euclidean geometries suggested the view that mathematics, in essence, is a creation of the human intellect. This was the beginning of modern mathematics.

6.1 INTRODUCTION

The major part of this chapter examines geometric figures called *quadrilaterals*. These figures are a special type of *polygon,* a word of Greek origin that means *many angles;* hence, it implies *many sides*. The mathematical definition of polygon is in Section 6.6.

Some familiar quadrilaterals are the square and the rectangle; these and other four-sided figures emerge when we consider geometric figures that are the union of four lines. Figure 6.1 shows some of the possibilities. The figures in (a), (b), (d), and (e) contain nothing new at this stage of our geometric development. The quadrilateral in (c) is said to be *convex* because, if any two points in its interior are joined by a line segment all points will lie in the quadrilateral's interior. Segment $\overline{AB}$ illustrates this property. The quadrilateral in (f) is not convex as shown by $\overline{CD}$, many of whose points are not in the quadrilateral's interior. Such quadrilaterals are said to be *nonconvex* or *concave*.

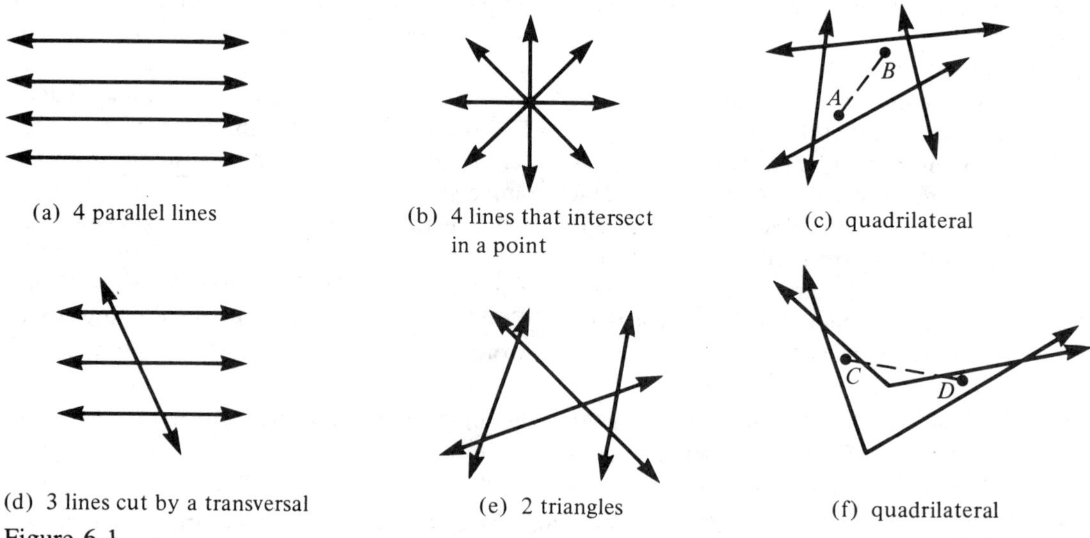

Figure 6.1

Nonconvex quadrilaterals are not frequently used; thus, we will concentrate on the convex quadrilateral. In fact, certain special cases of convex quadrilaterals having useful properties are the major emphasis of this chapter. These special quadrilaterals (squares, rectangles, rhombuses, parallelograms, and trapezoids) occur in various practical circumstances, such as, architectural design, construction materials, fabric design, and urban planning. We begin with a general definition.

Definition 6.1 The union of four line segments $\overline{EJ}$, $\overline{JS}$, $\overline{SK}$, and $\overline{EK}$ is a *quadrilateral* iff E, J, S, and K are coplanar points no three of which are collinear and each segment intersects exactly two others, one at each endpoint.

According to this definition, figures such as those in Figure 6.2 are *not* quadrilaterals. Although the definition does include nonconvex quadrilaterals, *we will use the term to mean convex quadrilaterals unless stated otherwise.*

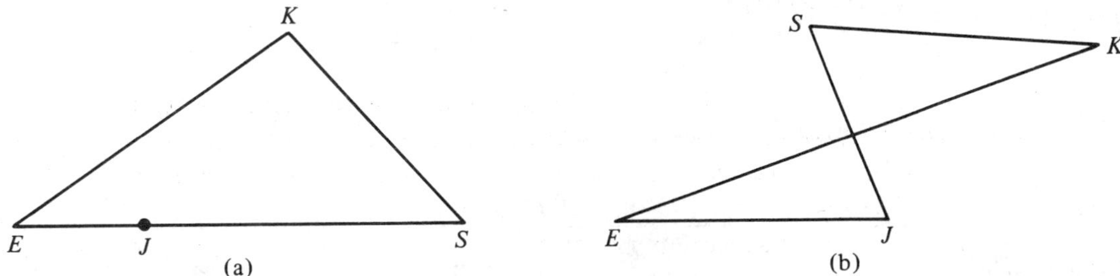

Figure 6.2 (a) Three points collinear. (b) $\overline{JS}$ and $\overline{EK}$ intersect more than two other segments.

The terms *sides* and *vertices* have their usual meanings. We also refer to *adjacent* and *opposite sides, consecutive vertices* and *angles,* and *opposite vertices* and *angles,* as shown in Figure 6.3.

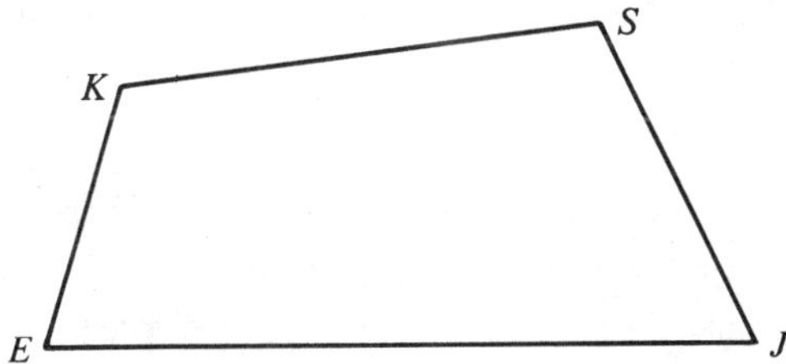

Figure 6.3 $\overline{EJ}$ is *adjacent* to $\overline{EK}$ and to $\overline{JS}$; $\overline{EJ}$ is *opposite* $\overline{KS}$; $\measuredangle E$ and $\measuredangle J$ are *consecutive;* $\measuredangle E$ is *opposite* $\measuredangle S$. (Similarly for other sides and angles.)

The four vertices of a quadrilateral in fact determine *six* lines. The sides are subsets of four of these lines; the other two contain important segments, which are defined as follows.

Definition 6.2 A line segment is a *diagonal* of a quadrilateral iff its endpoints are opposite vertices.

Note that each of the two diagonals divides the quadrilateral into two triangles, namely $\triangle KEJ$ and $\triangle KSJ$ or $\triangle EKS$ and $\triangle JSE$ (Figure 6.4). Also, each diagonal is a transversal for a pair of opposite sides. These facts are useful in proving a number of properties, one of which is described in Theorem 45.

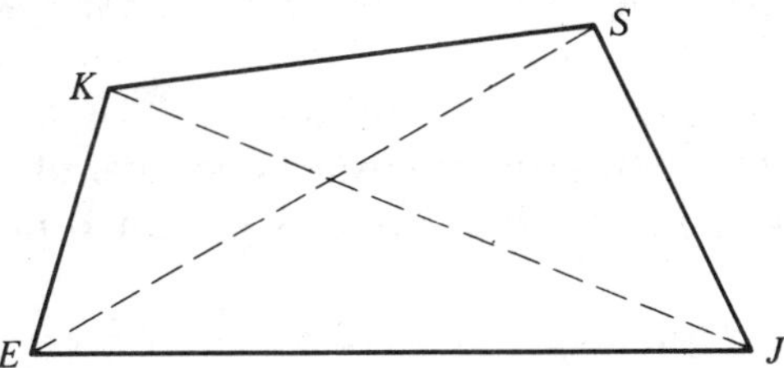

Figure 6.4 $\overline{ES}$ and $\overline{JK}$ are diagonals.

Theorem 45 The sum of the measures of the angles of a quadrilateral is 360° (360° in quad).

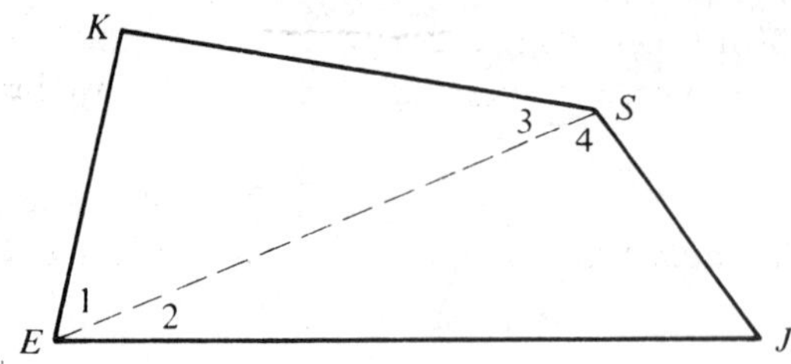

Given
quad *EJSK*

To Prove
$\angle E + \angle J + \angle S + \angle K = 360°$

Statement	*Reason*
1. quad *EJSK*	1. given
2. Draw $\overline{ES}$.	2. 2 pts determ line
3. $\angle 1 + \angle 3 + \angle K = 180°$ $\angle 2 + \angle 4 + \angle J = 180°$	3. 180° in △
4. $(\angle 1 + \angle 3 + \angle K) + (\angle 2 + \angle 4 + \angle J) = 360°$	4. = + =, sums =
5. $(\angle 1 + \angle 2) + \angle J + (\angle 3 + \angle 4) + \angle K = 360°$	5. rearr props
6. $\angle E = \angle 1 + \angle 2$ $\angle S = \angle 3 + \angle 4$	6. whole = sum parts
7. $\therefore \angle E + \angle J + \angle S + \angle K = 360°$	7. subst

We next define some special types of quadrilaterals, all of which have at least one pair of parallel sides. This special property of parallelism makes these figures important in geometry and its applications.

Definition 6.3 A quadrilateral is a *trapezoid* iff exactly one pair of its opposite sides are parallel (trap iff 1 pr sides ∥).

The parallel sides of a trapezoid are its *bases*. If the nonparallel pair of opposite sides are congruent, then the quadrilateral is an *isosceles trapezoid* (isos trap iff non ∥ sides ≅). See Figure 6.5.

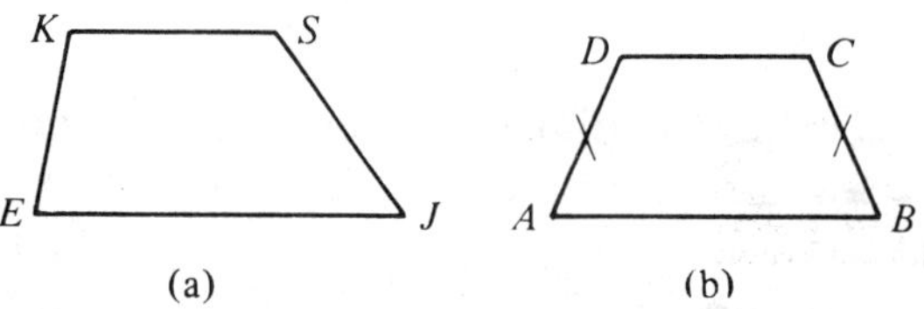

Figure 6.5 (a) Trapezoid *EJSK*; $\overline{EJ} \parallel \overline{KS}$; $\overline{EJ}$ and $\overline{KS}$ are the bases. (b) Isosceles trap *ABCD*; $\overline{AB} \parallel \overline{DC}$; $\overline{AD} \cong \overline{BC}$; $\overline{AB}$ and $\overline{DC}$ are the bases; ∡*A* and ∡*B* are the base angles.

The quadrilateral with both pairs of opposite sides parallel has many practical applications and occurs in several forms as indicated in Definitions 6.4–6.7.

Definition 6.4 A quadrilateral is a *parallelogram* iff both pairs of opposite sides are parallel (▱ iff opp sides ∥).

Definition 6.5 A parallelogram is a *rhombus* iff it has pair of adjacent sides that are congruent (rh iff ▱ with ≅ adjacent sides).

We will see later that all four sides of a rhombus are congruent. This fact is based on the above definition and a property of parallelograms soon to be proved.

Definition 6.6 A parallelogram is a *rectangle* iff it has a right angle (rect iff ⊡).

Using this definition and a property of parallelograms, we shall find that all four angles of a rectangle must necessarily be right angles.

Definition 6.7 A rectangle is a *square* iff it has a pair of adjacent sides that are congruent (sq iff ⊞).

A square has many properties in addition to those that define it. One of these properties is that all four of its sides are congruent. We have chosen, however, to minimize the number of properties in the foregoing definitions. This makes it easier to prove that a quadrilateral is a rhombus, rectangle, or square, and it emphasizes that all three figures are parallelograms, hence possessing all the properties of parallelograms. Our study of special quadrilaterals begins in the next section with the basic facts about parallelograms.

Figure 6.6(a) shows a parallelogram that is not a rhombus, rectangle, or square; it is followed by examples of these special types of parallelograms in (b), (c), and (d).

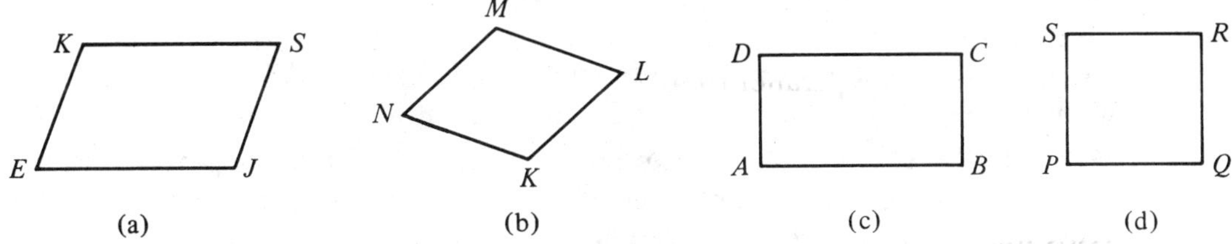

Figure 6.6 (a) ▱*EJSK;* (b) rh *KLMN;* (c) rect *ABCD;* (d) sq *PQRS.*

6.2 PARALLELOGRAMS

The defining property for a parallelogram is that it is a quadrilateral whose opposite sides are parallel. Many other properties follow from this; four of these are given in the theorems of this section. After studying these theorems and the methods used to prove them, you can discover other facts about parallelograms. In any case, rely on the geometric figure to display the basic facts and to assist you in seeing other correct properties. The most significant feature of the figure is that for either pair of opposite sides, the other two sides and the diagonals are transversals. Thus, the theory of parallel lines and transversals (Chapter 5) may be used to prove properties of parallelograms. This theory and that for congruent triangles provide the needed tools for the study of parallelograms.

Theorem 46 The opposite sides of a parallelogram are congruent (opp sides ▱ $\cong$).

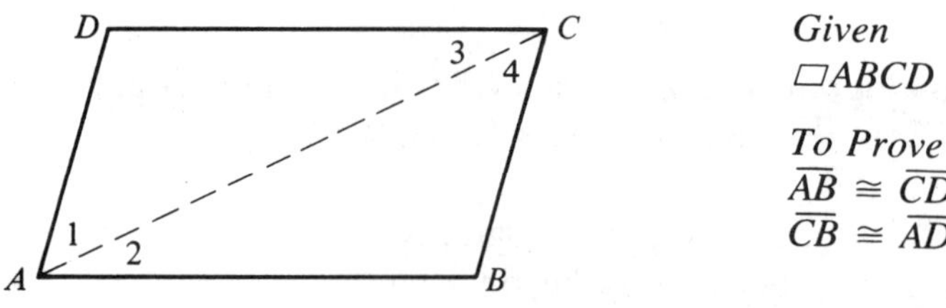

Given
▱$ABCD$

To Prove
$\overline{AB} \cong \overline{CD}$
$\overline{CB} \cong \overline{AD}$

Statement	*Reason*
1. ▱$ABCD$	1. given
2. $\overline{AB} \parallel \overline{CD}$	2. ▱ iff opp sides $\parallel$
3. Draw $\overline{AC}$.	3. 2 pts determ line
4. $\angle 2 \cong \angle 3$	4. $\nparallel$, alt int $\angle$s $\cong$
5. $\overline{AC} \cong \overline{AC}$	5. refl $\cong$
6. $\overline{AD} \parallel \overline{CB}$	6. ▱ iff opp sides $\parallel$
7. $\angle 4 \cong \angle 1$	7. $\nparallel$, alt int $\angle$s $\cong$
8. $\triangle CAB \cong \triangle ACD$	8. asa $\cong$ asa
9. $\therefore \overline{AB} \cong \overline{CD}$ $\overline{CB} \cong \overline{AD}$	9. cpctc

Theorem 47 The opposite angles of a parallelogram are congruent (opp $\angle$s ▱ $\cong$).

We omit the proof; however, by referring to the figure and proof for Theorem 46, it is easy to see that $\angle B \cong \angle D$ (cpctc). Similarly, using diagonal $\overline{BD}$, we can prove that $\angle A \cong \angle C$.

Theorem 48 Any two consecutive angles of a parallelogram are supplementary (consec $\angle$s ▱ supp).

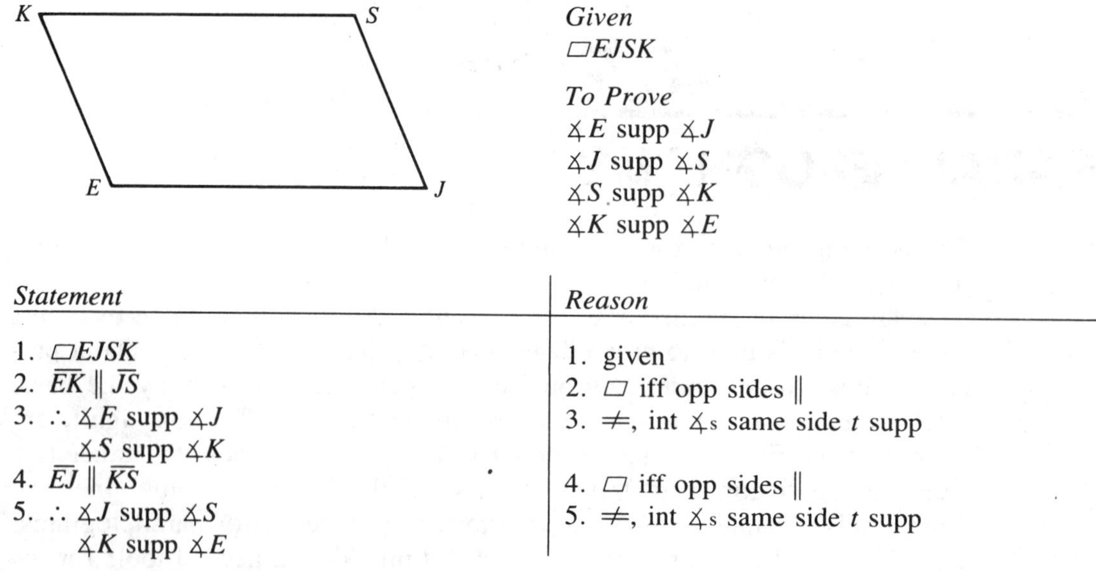

Given
▱$EJSK$

To Prove
$\angle E$ supp $\angle J$
$\angle J$ supp $\angle S$
$\angle S$ supp $\angle K$
$\angle K$ supp $\angle E$

Statement	*Reason*
1. ▱$EJSK$	1. given
2. $\overline{EK} \parallel \overline{JS}$	2. ▱ iff opp sides $\parallel$
3. $\therefore \angle E$ supp $\angle J$ $\angle S$ supp $\angle K$	3. $\nparallel$, int $\angle$s same side t supp
4. $\overline{EJ} \parallel \overline{KS}$	4. ▱ iff opp sides $\parallel$
5. $\therefore \angle J$ supp $\angle S$ $\angle K$ supp $\angle E$	5. $\nparallel$, int $\angle$s same side t supp

Theorem 49 The diagonals of a parallelogram bisect each other (diags ▱ bis ea other).

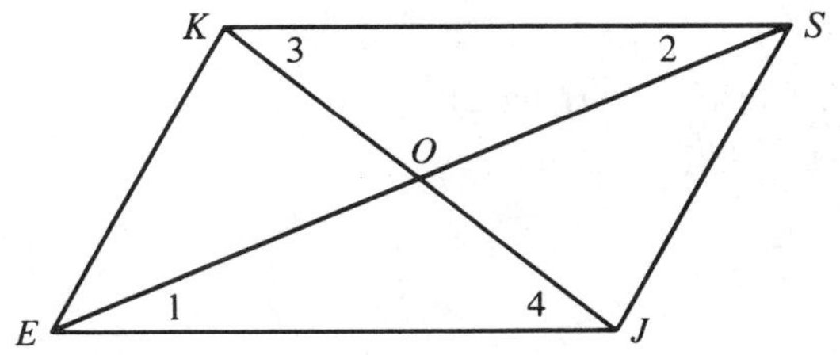

Given
▱$EJSK$, diags $\overline{ES}$ and $\overline{KJ}$

To Prove
$\overline{ES}$ bis $\overline{KJ}$
$\overline{KJ}$ bis $\overline{ES}$

Statement	*Reason*
1. ▱$EJSK$, diags $\overline{ES}$, $\overline{KJ}$	1. given
2. $\overline{EJ} \parallel \overline{SK}$	2. ▱ iff opp sides $\parallel$
3. ∡1 ≅ ∡2, ∡4 ≅ ∡3	3. ≠, alt int ∡s ≅
4. $\overline{EJ} \cong \overline{SK}$	4. opp sides ▱ ≅
5. △EJO ≅ △SKO	5. asa ≅ asa
6. $\overline{JO} \cong \overline{KO}$	6. cpctc
7. ∴ $\overline{ES}$ bis $\overline{KJ}$	7. bis ÷ seg into 2 ≅ segs
8. $\overline{EO} \cong \overline{SO}$	8. cpctc
9. ∴ $\overline{KJ}$ bis $\overline{ES}$	9. bis ÷ seg into 2 ≅ segs

These new facts about parallelograms together with earlier results about parallel lines and congruent triangles are applied in the examples below.

EXAMPLE 1

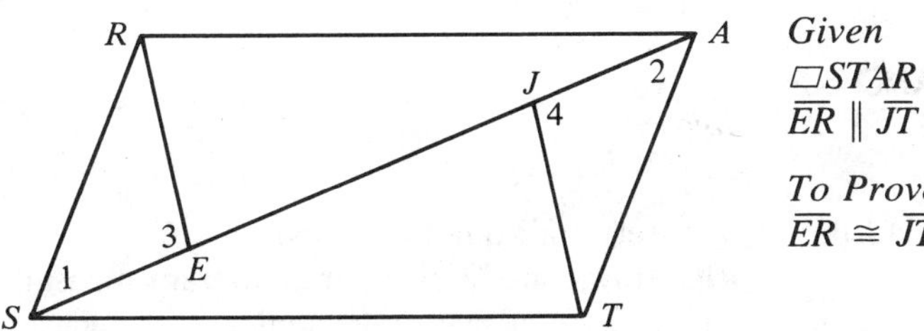

Given
▱$STAR$
$\overline{ER} \parallel \overline{JT}$

To Prove
$\overline{ER} \cong \overline{JT}$

Statement	*Reason*
1. ▱$STAR$	1. given
2. $\overline{SR} \cong \overline{AT}$	2. opp sides ▱ ≅
3. $\overline{SR} \parallel \overline{AT}$	3. ▱ iff opp sides $\parallel$
4. ∡1 ≅ ∡2	4. ≠, alt int ∡s ≅
5. $\overline{ER} \parallel \overline{JT}$	5. given
6. ∡3 ≅ ∡4	6. ≠, alt ext ∡s ≅
7. △SER ≅ △AJT	7. aas ≅ aas
8. ∴ $\overline{ER} \cong \overline{JT}$	8. cpctc

EXAMPLE 2

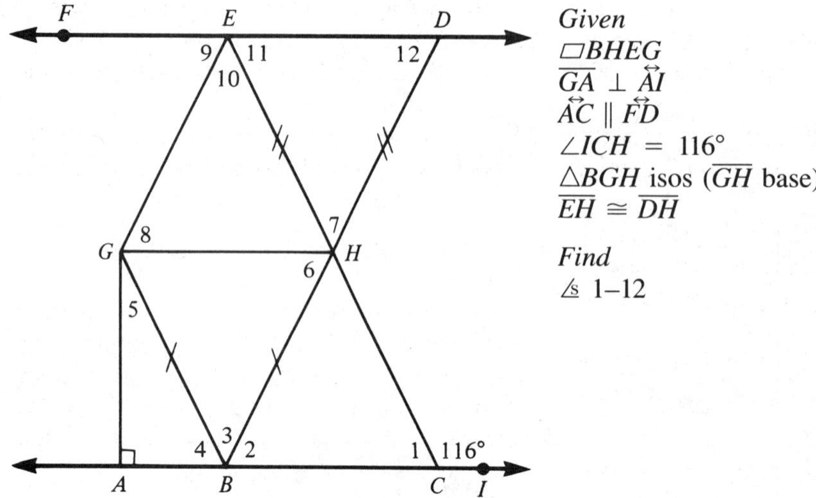

Given
▱$BHEG$
$\overline{GA} \perp \overleftrightarrow{AI}$
$\overleftrightarrow{AC} \parallel \overleftrightarrow{FD}$
$\angle ICH = 116°$
$\triangle BGH$ isos ($\overline{GH}$ base)
$\overline{EH} \cong \overline{DH}$

Find
$\angle$s 1–12

Answers

$\angle 1 = 64°$	$\angle 3 = 52°$	$\angle 5 = 26°$	$\angle 7 = 52°$	$\angle 9 = 64°$	$\angle 11 = 64°$
$\angle 2 = 64°$	$\angle 4 = 64°$	$\angle 6 = 64°$	$\angle 8 = 64°$	$\angle 10 = 52°$	$\angle 12 = 64°$

Finally, we have a theorem and a definition that are based on Theorem 46. The proof of the theorem is left as an exercise.

Theorem 50 If two lines are parallel, then every perpendicular segment joining one to the other has the same length (if lines $\parallel$, $\perp$ seg $=$).

This theorem allows us to define the distance between two parallel lines as follows:

Definition 6.8 The *distance between two parallel lines* is the length of any perpendicular line segment joining the lines.

EXERCISES FOR 6.1 AND 6.2

In exercises 1–20 answer true or false.

1. Four lines always determine a quadrilateral.
2. If two angles of a quadrilateral are right angles, the quadrilateral is a rectangle.
3. Every equiangular quadrilateral is also equilateral.
4. If three angles of a quadrilateral measure 87°45′22″, 63°23′, and 123°47″, the fourth angle measures 85° 50′51″.
5. A parallelogram is also a trapezoid.
6. The set of all rectangles is a subset of the set of all parallelograms.
7. The diagonals of a quadrilateral bisect each other.
8. A quadrilateral has four diagonals.
9. The set of all trapezoids is a subset of the set of all quadrilaterals.
10. If one angle of a parallelogram measures 75°, then two other angles each measure 105°.
11. In a trapezoid, two sides are always congruent.
12. In quadrilateral *MORK*, $\overline{MO}$ is opposite $\overline{RK}$.
13. If the four sides of a quadrilateral are congruent, then it must be a square.
14. In quadrilateral *NITE*, $\overline{IT}$ is called a diagonal.
15. If *J*, *A*, *W*, and *S* are four points in a plane, then *JAWS* names a quadrilateral.
16. The distance between two parallel lines is defined as the length of any segment whose

endpoints are points of the two lines, one from each line.

17. If one angle of a parallelogram is twice as large as a second, the angles measure 30° and 60°.

18. If three angles of a parallelogram are right angles, then the fourth angle must also be a right angle.

19. If two consecutive angles of a quadrilateral are right angles, then the bisectors of the other two angles are perpendicular to each other.

20. In quadrilateral *GOLD*, if $\measuredangle G$ is supplementary to $\measuredangle D$ and $\overline{GD} \cong \overline{OL}$, then *GOLD* is an isosceles trapezoid.

In exercises 21 and 22 use Figure 6.7 to answer the questions.

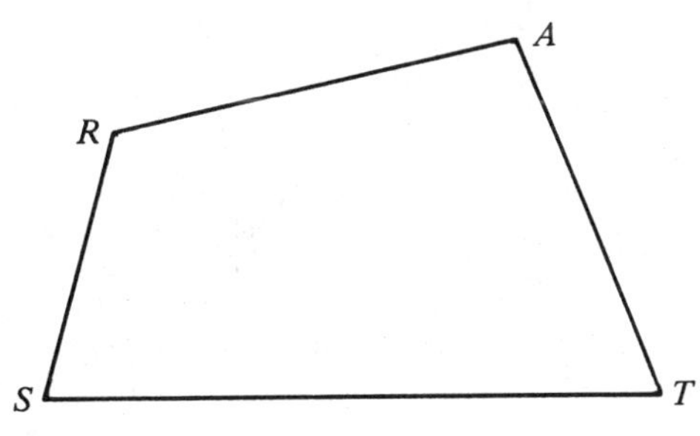

Figure 6.7

21. (a) Name two pairs of opposite sides.
(b) Name two pairs of opposite angles.

22. (a) Name four pairs of consecutive sides.
(b) Name four pairs of consecutive angles.

23. In how many ways can two congruent triangles be positioned so that they form a parallelogram? Draw the figures.

In exercises 24–30 use the given information about quadrilateral *WHAT* to choose the one name among the following that *best* describes the figure: quadrilateral, trapezoid, isosceles trapezoid, parallelogram, rectangle, rhombus, or square.

24. $\angle W = 90°$ and $\angle H = 90°$

25. $\angle W = 68°$, $\angle A = 68°$, and $\angle T = 112°$

26. $\angle T = 90°$, $\angle H = 90°$, and $\angle A = 90°$

27. $\overline{WT} \cong \overline{HA}$, $\angle H = 78°$, and $\angle A = 102°$

28. $\angle H = 73°$, $\angle A = 117°$, and $\angle W = 97°$

29. $\angle H = 92°$, $\angle A = 88°$, $\angle T = 92°$, and $\overline{WT} \cong \overline{TA}$

30. $\measuredangle W \cong \measuredangle A$, $\angle H = 90°$, $\angle T = 90°$, and $\overline{WH} \cong \overline{HA}$

In exercises 31–36 copy the figure, mark it, and find the requested measures.

31. *Given*
▱*EJSK*
$\overline{SK} \cong \overline{SC}$
▱*MTSC*
$\angle 13 = 66°17'$

Find
$\measuredangle$s 1–12

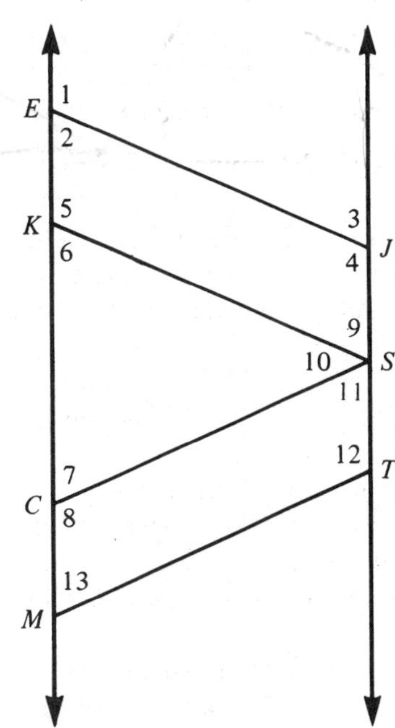

32. *Given*
□*ABCD*
□*HBED*
$\overline{BF} \perp \overline{AC}$
$\angle 13 = 61°$
$\angle 14 = 56°$

Find
∠s 1–12

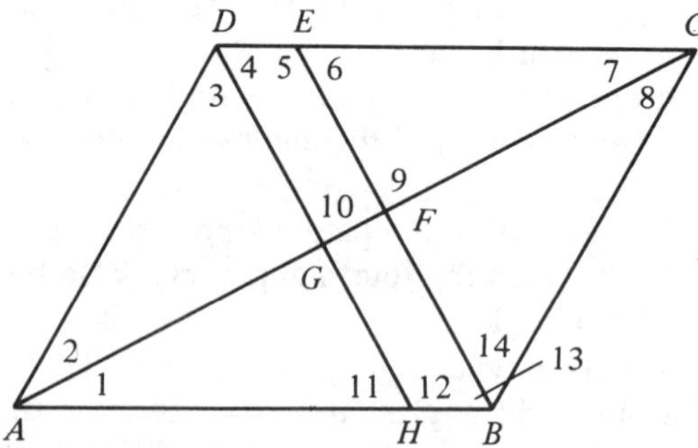

33. *Given*
□*EJSK*
△*EJK* isos ($\overline{KJ}$ base)
$\angle KEJ = 82°$

Find
∠s 1–12

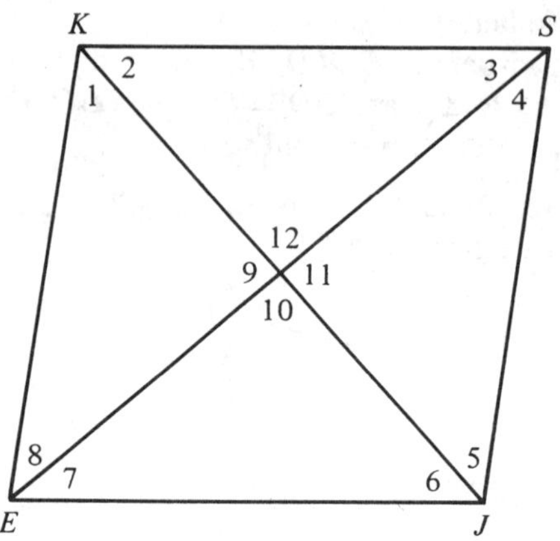

34. *Given*
△*JSB* isos ($\overline{JS}$ base)
$\overline{JD}$ bis ∡*BJS*
□*SKCB*
□*JSED*
$\angle ABJ = 57°$

Find
∠s 1–10

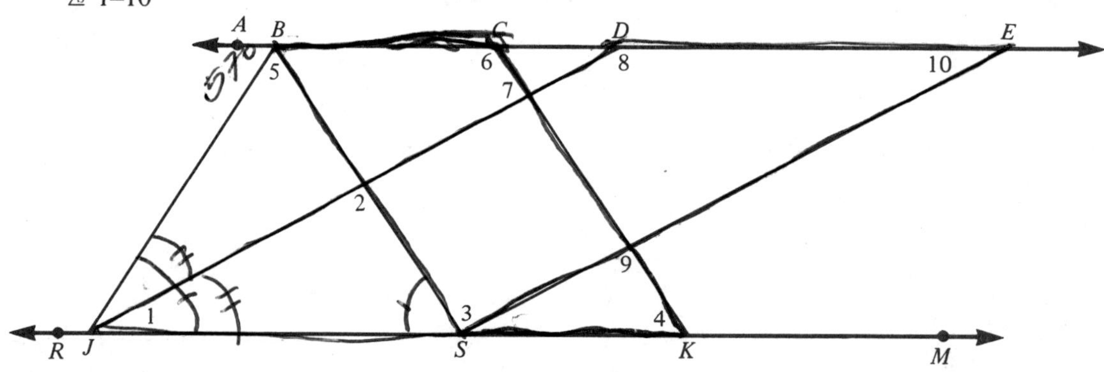

35. *Given*
□*SOQU*
$\overline{UL}$ bis ∡*U*
$\overline{QJ}$ bis ∡*Q*
$\overline{OJ}$ bis ∡*O*
$\overline{SL}$ bis ∡*S*
$\angle QUE = 37°30'$

Find
∠s 1–10

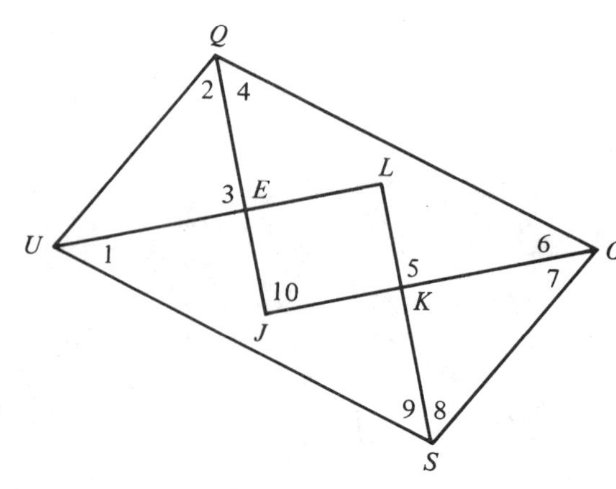

36. *Given*
$\square ATOS$
$\square PTES$
$\angle SAO = 52°12'$, $\angle APS = 46°13'$
$\angle AJT = 101°11'$

Find
$\measuredangle$s 1–10

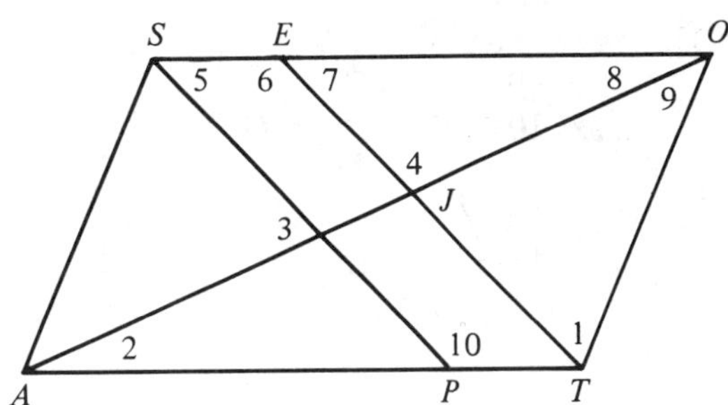

In exercises 37 and 38 copy the figure, mark it, and supply the missing reasons in each proof.

37. *Given*
$\square ABCD$
$\overline{DS} \cong \overline{BQ}$
$\overline{AP} \cong \overline{CR}$

To Prove
$\overline{SP} \cong \overline{QR}$

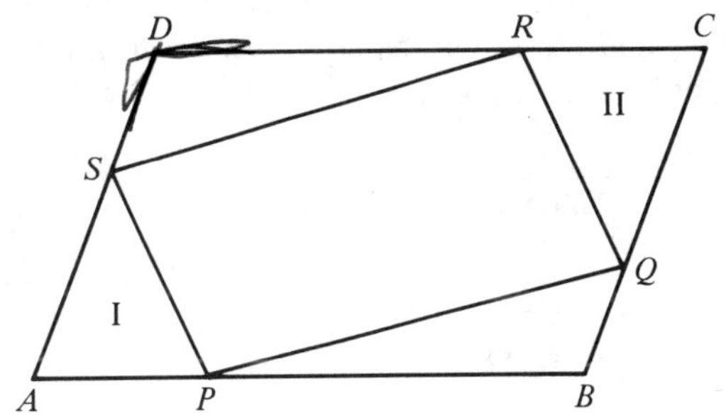

Statement	Reason
1. $\square ABCD$	1. ?
2. $\overline{AD} \cong \overline{CB}$	2. ?
3. $\overline{DS} \cong \overline{BQ}$	3. ?
4. $\overline{AD} - \overline{DS} \cong \overline{CB} - \overline{BQ}$	4. ?
5. $\overline{AS} \cong \overline{AD} - \overline{DS}$	5. ?
6. $\overline{CQ} \cong \overline{CB} - \overline{BQ}$	6. ?
7. $\overline{CB} - \overline{BQ} \cong \overline{CQ}$	7. ?
8. $\overline{AS} \cong \overline{CQ}$	8. ?
9. $\measuredangle A \cong \measuredangle C$	9. ?
10. $\overline{AP} \cong \overline{CR}$	10. ?
11. $\triangle I \cong \triangle II$	11. ?
12. $\therefore \overline{SP} \cong \overline{QR}$	12. ?

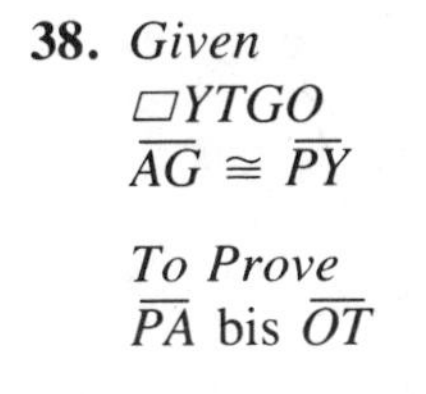

38. *Given*
$\square YTGO$
$\overline{AG} \cong \overline{PY}$

To Prove
$\overline{PA}$ bis $\overline{OT}$

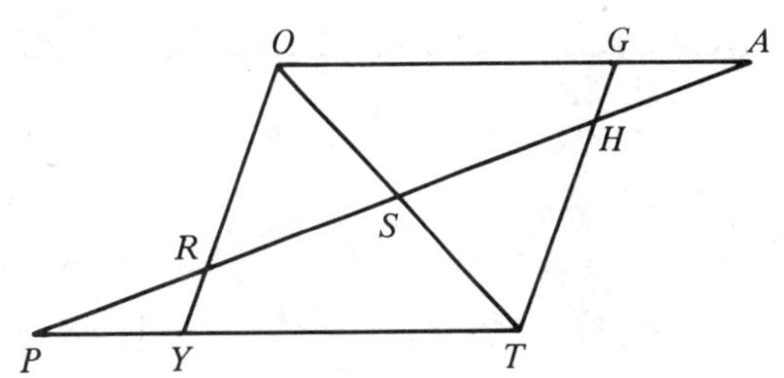

Statement	Reason
1. $\square YTGO$	1. ?
2. $\overline{YT} \parallel \overline{GO}$	2. ?
3. $\measuredangle AOS \cong \measuredangle PTS$	3. ?
4. $\measuredangle OAS \cong \measuredangle TPS$	4. ?
5. $\overline{OG} \cong \overline{TY}$	5. ?
6. $\overline{AG} \cong \overline{PY}$	6. ?
7. $\overline{OG} + \overline{AG} \cong \overline{TY} + \overline{PY}$	7. ?

8. $\overline{OA} \cong \overline{OG} + \overline{AG}$	8. ?
9. $\overline{TP} \cong \overline{TY} + \overline{PY}$	9. ?
10. $\overline{TY} + \overline{PY} \cong \overline{TP}$	10. ?
11. $\overline{OA} \cong \overline{TP}$	11. ?
12. $\triangle OAS \cong \triangle TPS$	12. ?
13. $\overline{OS} \cong \overline{TS}$	13. ?
14. $\therefore \overline{PA}$ bis $\overline{OT}$	14. ?

In exercises 39 and 40 copy the figure, mark it, and rearrange the statements into a correct order for a proof.

39. *Given*
□*WEST*
$\measuredangle 1 \cong \measuredangle 2$

To Prove
$\overline{WN} \cong \overline{SI}$

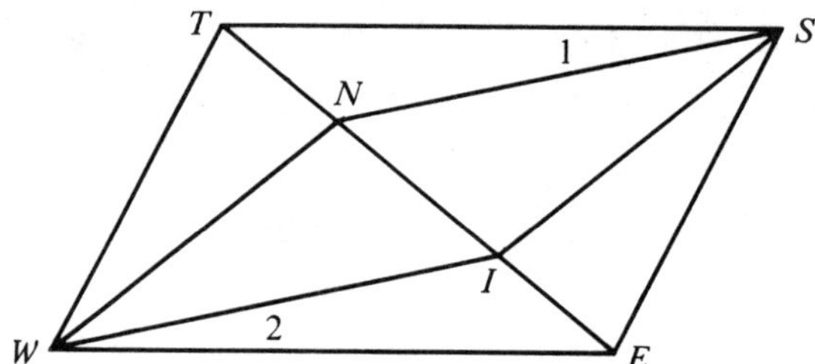

(a) $\measuredangle STN \cong \measuredangle WEI$
(b) □*WEST*
(c) $\measuredangle 1 \cong \measuredangle 2$
(d) $\overline{WN} \cong \overline{SI}$
(e) $\overline{ST} \cong \overline{WE}$
(f) $\measuredangle WTN \cong \measuredangle SEI$
(g) $\overline{ST} \parallel \overline{WE}$
(h) $\overline{WT} \cong \overline{SE}$
(i) $\triangle STN \cong \triangle WEI$
(j) $\overline{WT} \parallel \overline{SE}$
(k) $\overline{TN} \cong \overline{EI}$
(l) $\triangle WTN \cong \triangle SEI$

40. *Given*
□*EJSK*
□*MRSC*

To Prove
$\measuredangle E \cong \measuredangle M$

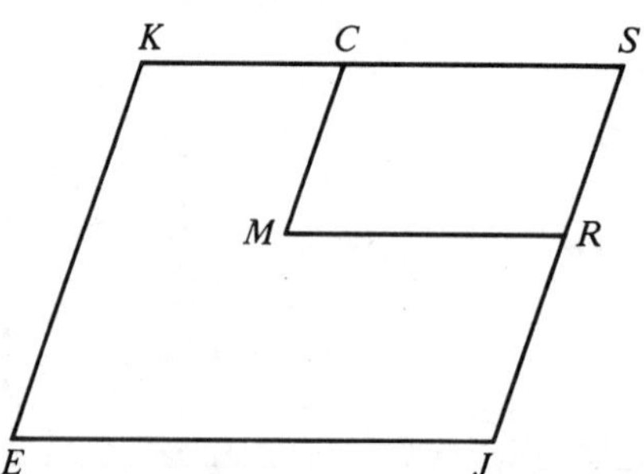

(a) $\overline{EJ} \parallel \overline{KS}$
(b) $\measuredangle M$ supp $\measuredangle MRS$
(c) □*MRSC*
(d) $\measuredangle E \cong \measuredangle M$
(e) □*EJSK*
(f) $\overline{EJ} \parallel \overline{MR}$
(g) $\overline{MR} \parallel \overline{CS}$
(h) $\measuredangle MRS \cong \measuredangle EJS$
(i) $\measuredangle E$ supp $\measuredangle EJS$

In exercises 41–50 copy the figure, the hypothesis, and the conclusion. Mark the figure and write a proof.

41. *Given*
$\square PQRS$
$\overline{ST} \cong \overline{QV}$

To Prove
$\overline{PT} \cong \overline{RV}$

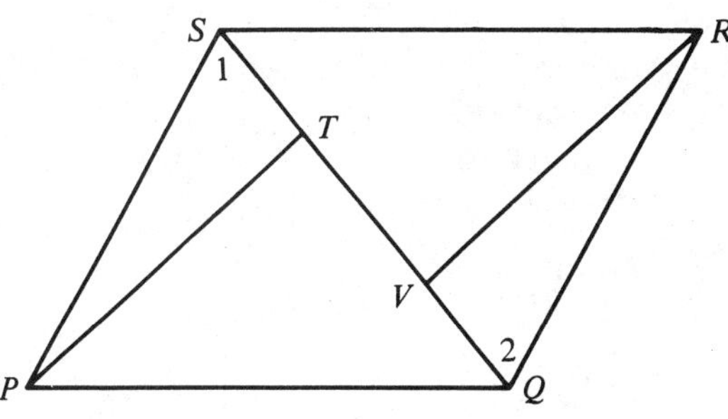

42. *Given*
$\square HERO$
$\overline{HK} \perp \overline{OE}$
$\overline{RJ} \perp \overline{OE}$

To Prove
$\overline{OJ} \cong \overline{EK}$

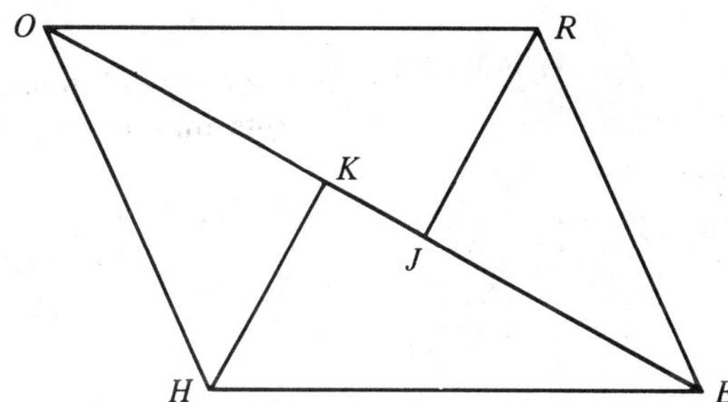

43. *Given*
$\square JACK$
O midpt $\overline{JA}$
S midpt $\overline{CK}$

To Prove
$\measuredangle 1 \cong \measuredangle 2$

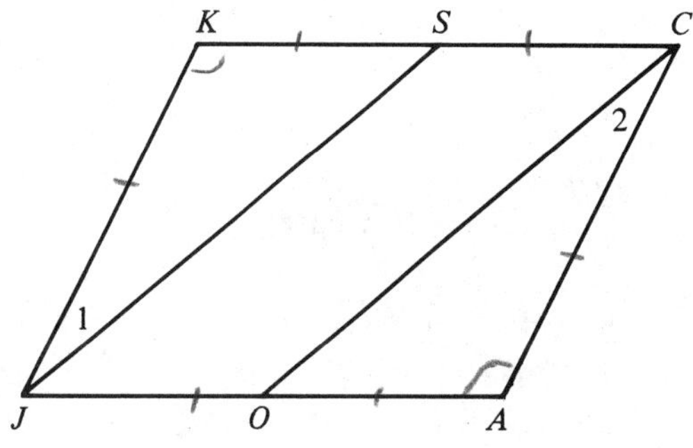

44. (Theorem 50)

Given
$\overleftrightarrow{AB} \parallel \overleftrightarrow{CD}$
$\overline{AC} \perp \overline{CD}$
$\overline{BD} \perp \overline{CD}$

To Prove
$\overline{AC} \cong \overline{DB}$

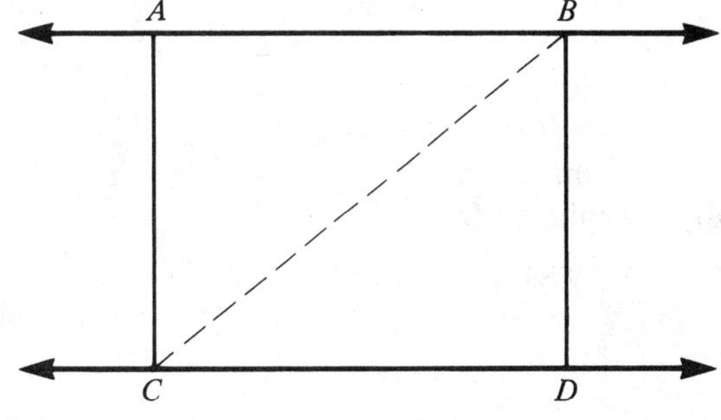

45. *Given*
$\square ABCD$
$\triangle ABD$ isos ($\overline{BD}$ base)

To Prove
$\overline{AC} \perp \overline{BD}$

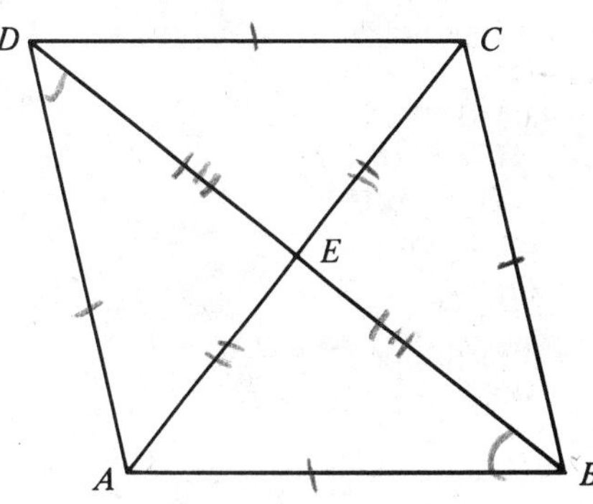

46. *Given*
▭$PQRS$
A midpt $\overline{PQ}$
K midpt $\overline{RS}$
$\overline{PT} \cong \overline{RL}$

To Prove
$\overline{TA} \parallel \overline{KL}$

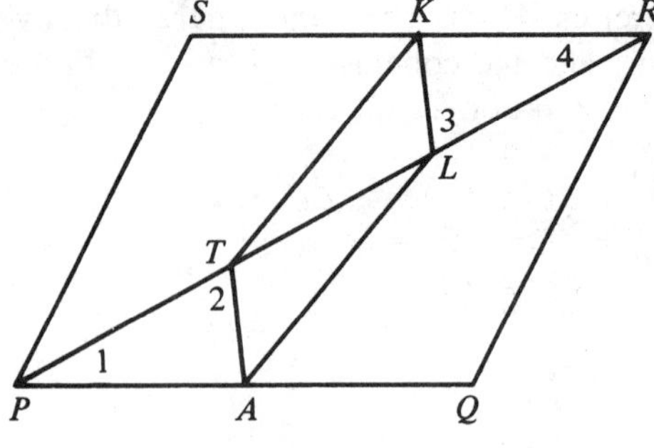

47. *Given*
$\triangle BAG$ isos ($\overline{BA}$ base)
▭$SING$

To Prove
$BG + AG = GS + SI + IN + NG$

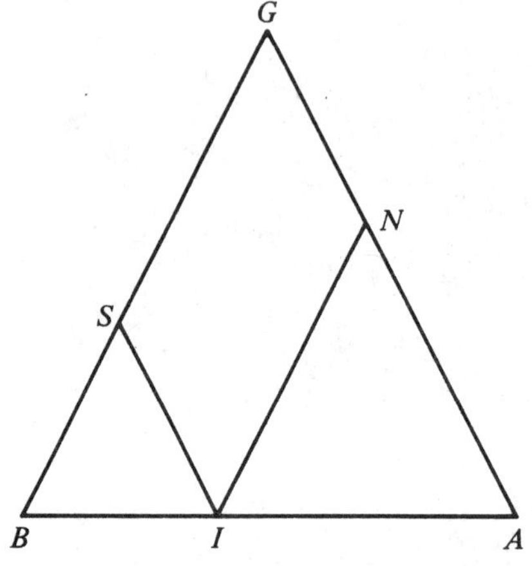

48. *Given*
trap $BANG$ ($\overline{BA}$ base)
$\overline{GB} \perp \overline{BA}$
$\measuredangle NGI \cong \measuredangle ABI$

To Prove
$\triangle BIG$ isos

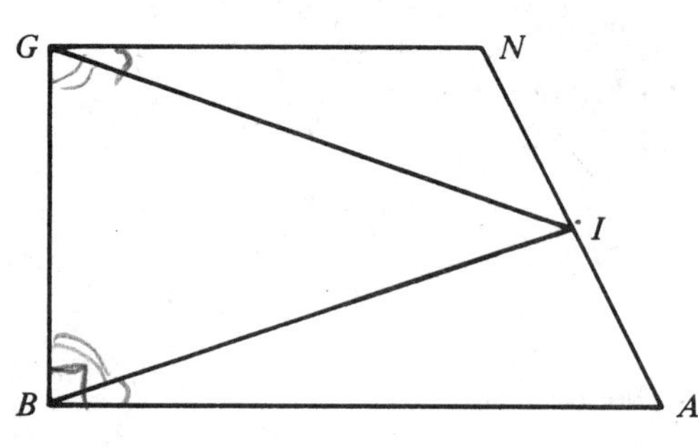

49. *Given*
▭$ECLD$
U midpt $\overline{EC}$
I midpt $\overline{LD}$

To Prove
$\overline{JU} \cong \overline{RI}$

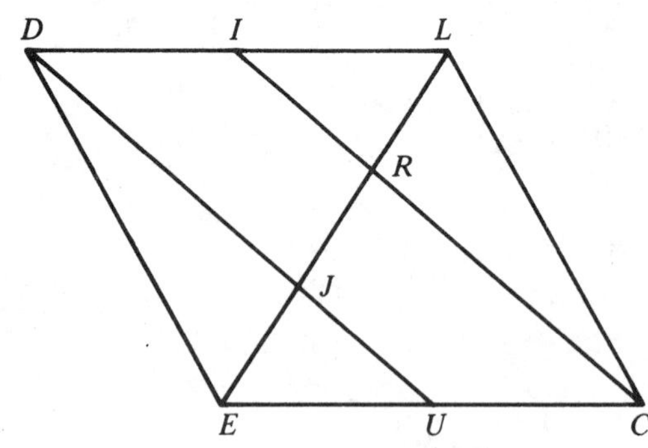

50. *Given*
▭$ABDF$
F midpt $\overline{AE}$
B midpt $\overline{AC}$

To Prove
D midpt $\overline{CE}$

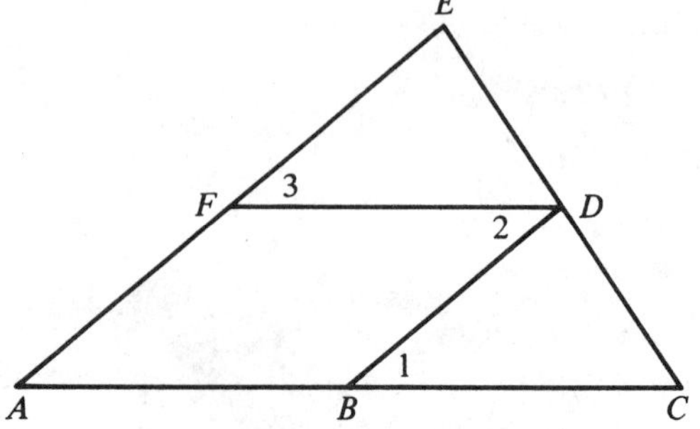

6.3

SPECIAL PARALLELOGRAMS

In Section 6.1, Definition 6.6, a rectangle was defined as a parallelogram having a right angle. The theorems concerning parallelograms (Section 6.2) now allow us to prove that all four angles of a rectangle are right angles (Theorem 51). Although this latter property could have been used to define rectangles, Definition 6.6 is preferable in that it allows us to prove that a parallelogram is also a rectangle by showing only that it has *one* right angle.

Theorem 51 The four angles of a rectangle are right angles (rect has 4 rt ∡s).

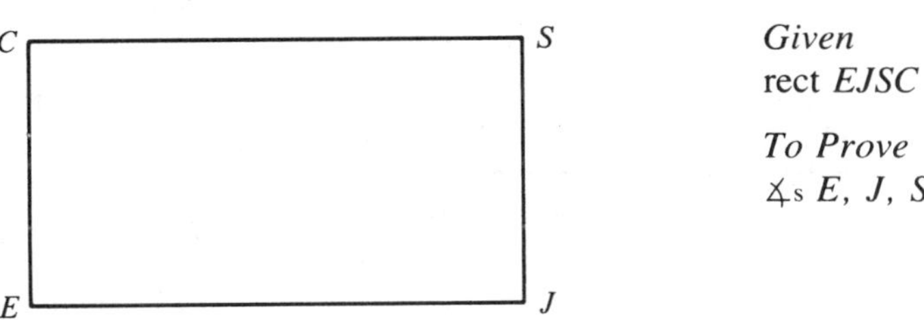

Given
rect $EJSC$

To Prove
∡s E, J, S, C rt ∡s

Statement	*Reason*
1. rect $EJSC$	1. given
2. $\measuredangle E$ rt ∡	2. rect iff ▭
3. $\measuredangle S \cong \measuredangle E$	3. opp ∡s ▱ (rect) ≅
4. $\angle S = \angle E$	4. ≅ iff meas =
5. $\angle E = 90°$	5. rt ∠ = 90°
6. $\angle S = 90°$	6. trans =
7. ∴ $\measuredangle S$ rt ∡	7. rt ∠ = 90°
8. $\measuredangle E$ supp $\measuredangle C$	8. consec ∡s ▱ supp
9. $\angle E + \angle C = 180°$	9. supp iff sum = 180°
10. $\angle C = 90°$	10. = − =, diffs =
11. ∴ $\measuredangle C$ rt ∡	11. rt ∠ = 90°
12. $\measuredangle J \cong \measuredangle C$	12. opp ∡s ▱ (rect) ≅
13. $\angle J = \angle C$	13. ≅ iff meas =
14. $\angle J = 90°$	14. trans =
15. ∴ $\measuredangle J$ rt ∡	15. rt ∠ = 90°

Since rectangles are parallelograms, any property of parallelograms is also true for rectangles. This fact was used to advantage in the proof of Theorem 51. The fact may also be used to prove another special property of rectangles, which is stated in the next theorem. The proof is left as an exercise.

Theorem 52 The diagonals of a rectangle are congruent (diags rect ≅).

Note carefully that the above theorem does *not* hold for parallelograms in general. The isosceles trapezoid (a quadrilateral that is not a parallelogram), however, does have congruent diagonals.

The rhombus, too, is a parallelogram. It is defined as one with two adjacent sides congruent (Section 6.1, Definition 6.5). We now use properties of parallelograms to show that all four sides of a rhombus must be congruent.

This circumstance is similar to that for rectangles. The "four-sides-congruent" property could have been used to define a rhombus. Definition 6.5, however, has the advantage that to prove a parallelogram is a rhombus it is only necessary to show that it has *one* pair of adjacent sides congruent. Keep in mind that since rhombuses are parallelograms, all the properties of parallelograms are also true for rhombuses.

Theorem 53 The four sides of a rhombus are congruent (rh has 4 ≅ sides).

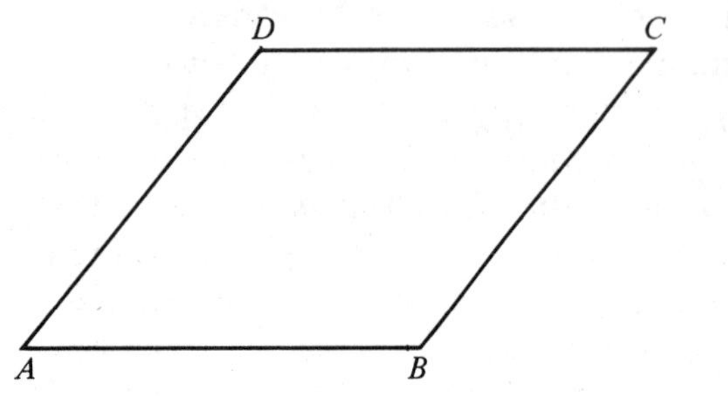

Given
rh *ABCD*

To Prove
$\overline{AB} \cong \overline{BC} \cong \overline{CD} \cong \overline{DA}$

Statement	*Reason*
1. rh *ABCD*	1. given
2. $\overline{DA} \cong \overline{AB}$	2. rh iff ▱ with adj sides ≅
3. $\overline{DA} \cong \overline{BC}$, $\overline{AB} \cong \overline{CD}$	3. opp sides ▱ ≅
4. ∴ $\overline{AB} \cong \overline{BC} \cong \overline{CD} \cong \overline{DA}$	4. symm and trans ≅

The proof above contains a shortcut. The conclusion as stated means $\overline{AB} \cong \overline{BC}$, $\overline{AB} \cong \overline{CD}$, $\overline{AB} \cong \overline{DA}$, $\overline{BC} \cong \overline{CD}$, $\overline{BC} \cong \overline{DA}$, and $\overline{CD} \cong \overline{DA}$. It is easy to see how all these congruence relations may be obtained by applying the symmetric and transitive properties to the congruences in statements 2 and 3 of the proof. We will use this type of shortcut when appropriate in any subsequent work.

The diagonals of a rhombus have special properties as do the diagonals of a rectangle.

Theorem 54 The diagonals of a rhombus bisect the angles of the rhombus (diags rh bis ∡s).

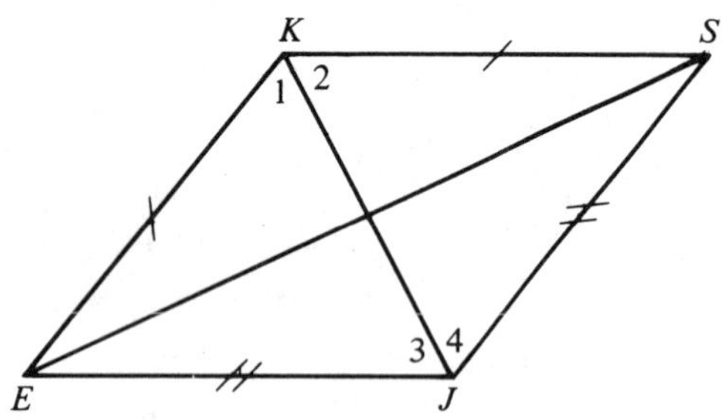

Given
rh *EJSK*
diags $\overline{KJ}$, $\overline{ES}$

To Prove
$\overline{KJ}$ bis ∡*SKE* and ∡*SJE*
$\overline{ES}$ bis ∡*KEJ* and ∡*KSJ*

Statement	*Reason*
1. rh *EJSK*, diags $\overline{KJ}$, $\overline{ES}$	1. given
2. $\overline{EK} \cong \overline{SK}$, $\overline{EJ} \cong \overline{SJ}$	2. rh has 4 ≅ sides
3. $\overline{KJ} \cong \overline{KJ}$	3. refl ≅
4. △*KEJ* ≅ △*KSJ*	4. sss ≅ sss
5. ∡1 ≅ ∡2, ∡3 ≅ ∡4	5. cpctc
6. ∴ $\overline{KJ}$ bis ∡*SKE* and ∡*SJE*	6. bis ÷ ∡ into 2 ≅ ∡s

The proof for $\overline{ES}$ is similar. Note the marking of the figure and statement 2 in the above proof. Although it is true that all four sides are congruent, we chose only the pairs needed to establish the correspondence $KEJ \leftrightarrow KSJ$ for the sss congruence between $\triangle KEJ$ and $\triangle KSJ$. This congruence would be impossible if *EJSK* were a parallelogram but *not* a rhombus.

Theorem 55 The diagonals of a rhombus are perpendicular to each other (diags rh $\perp$).

The proof of Theorem 55 is left as an exercise.

Finally, consider the square, a special parallelogram because it is defined as a rectangle with a pair of adjacent sides congruent. Thus, it is a parallelogram, rectangle, and rhombus, all in one figure! This means of course that all the theorems concerning these figures are valid for squares, and so there is no need to state special theorems for squares. Squares, however, do have some interesting properties, one of which is proved in Example 1. Note how this proof uses theorems about parallelograms, rhombuses, and rectangles.

EXAMPLE 1

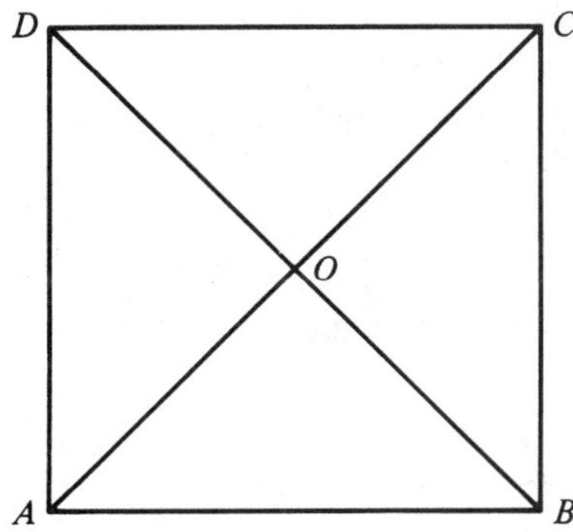

Given
sq *ABCD*

To Prove
$\triangle AOD$ isos rt $\triangle$

Statement	*Reason*
1. sq *ABCD*	1. given
2. $\overline{AC} \perp \overline{BD}$	2. diags rh (sq) $\perp$
3. $\measuredangle AOD$ rt $\measuredangle$	3. $\perp$s form $\cong$ rt $\measuredangle$s
4. $\therefore \triangle AOD$ rt $\triangle$	4. rt $\triangle$ iff a rt $\measuredangle$
5. $\overline{AC} \cong \overline{BD}$	5. diags rect (sq) $\cong$
6. $\overline{AO} \cong \overline{CO}$, $\overline{DO} \cong \overline{BO}$	6. diags $\square$ (sq) bis ea other
7. $\overline{AO} \cong \overline{DO}$	7. $\frac{1}{2}$s of $\cong$ are $\cong$
8. $\therefore \triangle AOD$ isos	8. isos $\triangle$ iff 2 $\cong$ sides

Two shortcuts are evident in this proof. First, the statement "$\overline{AC}$ bis $\overline{DB}$, $\overline{DB}$ bis $\overline{AC}$" is omitted. Instead, we went directly to statement 6, which follows from the fact that "to bisect" is "to divide into two congruent parts." Second, it is not explicitly stated that $\overline{AO}$ is congruent to half of $\overline{AC}$ and $\overline{DO}$ is congruent to half of $\overline{DB}$. Obviously, this follows from statement 6. Such shortcuts are desirable because, once understood, they permit a shorter proof that is nicely focused on the essential ideas involved.

EXERCISES FOR 6.3

In exercises 1–7 list those properties from the following List B that are true for each of the figures. (Most figures will have more than one property.)

1. Trapezoid
2. Rhombus
3. Square
4. Quadrilateral
5. Parallelogram
6. Isosceles trapezoid
7. Rectangle

List B

a. exactly four sides
b. sum of angles is 360°
c. at least one pair of parallel sides
d. two pairs of parallel sides
e. four congruent angles
f. four congruent sides
g. congruent diagonals
h. diagonals bisect each other
i. perpendicular diagonals
j. opposite angles are congruent
k. diagonals bisect the angles

In exercises 8–10 use Figure 6.8 to answer the questions.

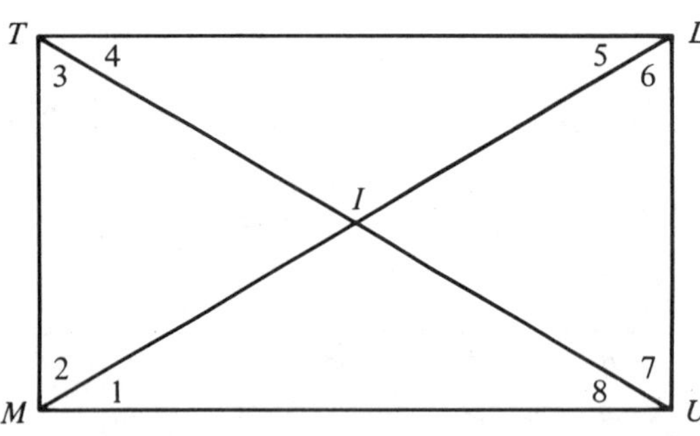

Figure 6.8

Given
rect *MULT*

8. Name five pairs of congruent segments.
9. Name four pairs of congruent alternate interior angles.
10. Name four congruent right angles.

In exercises 11–14 use Figure 6.9 to answer the questions.

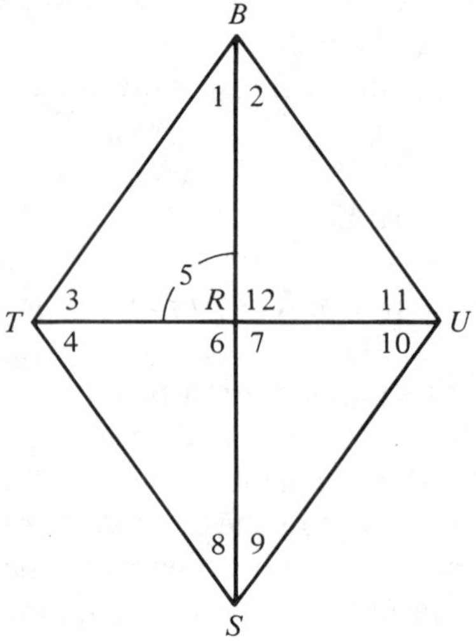

Figure 6.9

Given
rh *SUBT*

11. Name eight pairs of congruent segments.
12. Name four congruent right angles.
13. Name four pairs of congruent alternate interior angles.
14. Name ten pairs of congruent angles that are not alternate interior angles.

In exercises 15–18 use Figure 6.10 to answer the questions.

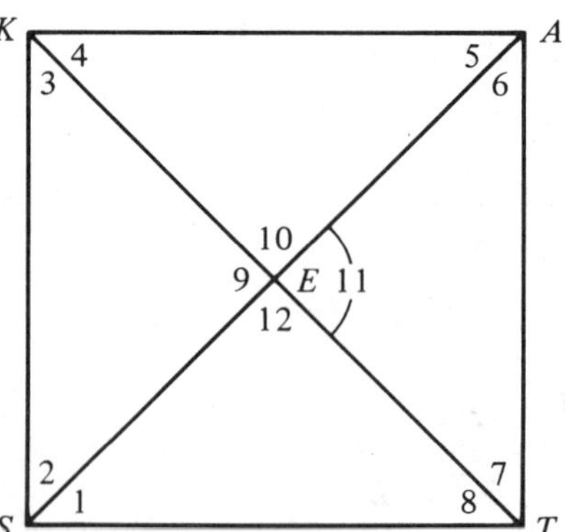

Figure 6.10

Given
sq *STAK*

15. Name seven pairs of congruent segments that are not sides of the square.
16. Name eight congruent right angles.
17. Name eight isosceles right triangles.
18. Name eight right triangles.

In exercises 19–25 copy the figure, mark it, and find the requested measures.

19. *Given*
$\square JSCK$
$\triangle EJR$ isos ($\overline{ER}$ base)
$\angle 16 = 72°$
$\angle 2 = 104°$

Find
∡s 1–16

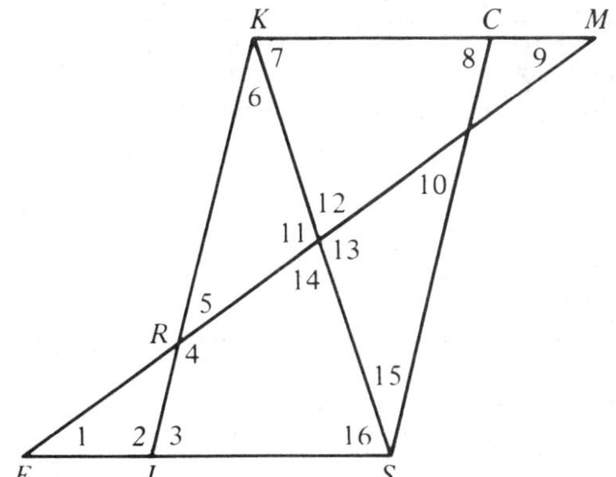

20. *Given*
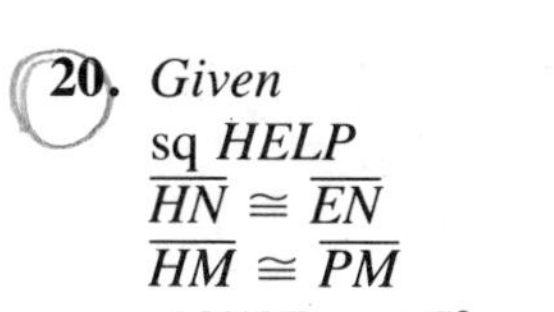
sq *HELP*
$\overline{HN} \cong \overline{EN}$
$\overline{HM} \cong \overline{PM}$
$\angle NHE = 15°$
$\measuredangle MPH \cong \measuredangle NHE$

Find
∡s 1–10

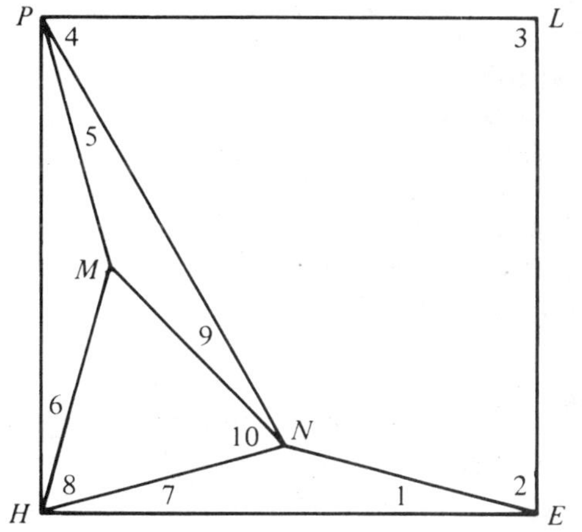

21. *Given*
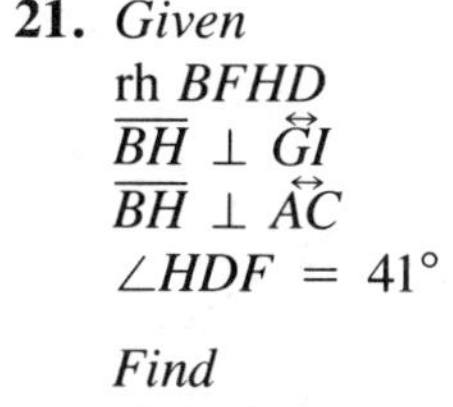
rh *BFHD*
$\overline{BH} \perp \overleftrightarrow{GI}$
$\overline{BH} \perp \overleftrightarrow{AC}$
$\angle HDF = 41°$

Find
∡s 1–10

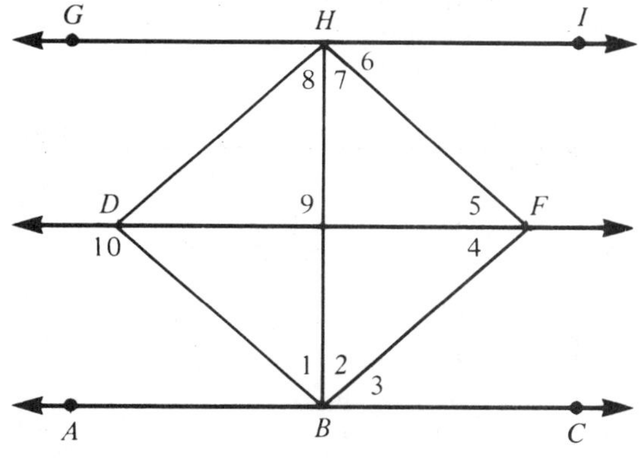

22. *Given*
isos trap *OCTN* ($\overline{OC}$, $\overline{NT}$ bases)
rect *GNTA*
$\triangle JAG$ isos ($\overline{GA}$ base)
$\angle OAG = 45°45'$
$\angle OCT = 60°12'$
$\measuredangle NOC \cong \measuredangle TCO$

Find
∡s 1–10

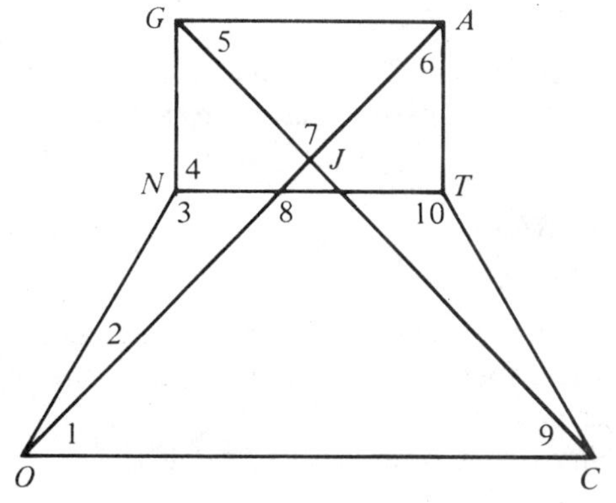

23. *Given*
isos trap *CRAM* ($\overline{CR}$, $\overline{MA}$ bases)
$\overline{TL} \parallel \overline{CR}$
$\overline{CJ} \cong \overline{RJ}$
$\angle TJC = 87°$
$\angle LAM = 81°$

Find
∠s 1–10

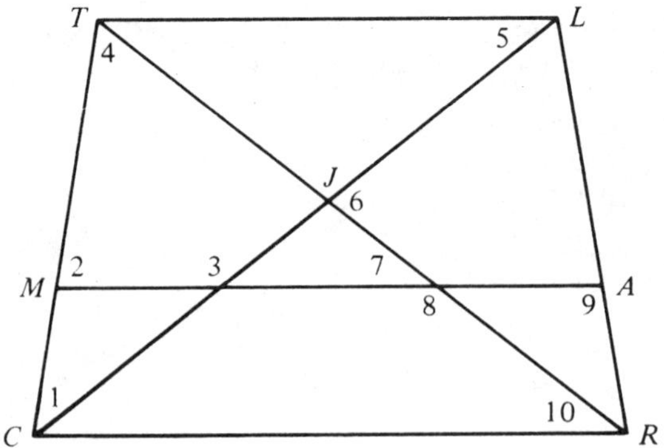

24. *Given*
▱ *SHAM*
rect *CORN*
$\overline{CO} \parallel \overline{SH}$
$\angle SHO = 79°$
$\angle OCS = 138°$
$\angle SMA = 111°$
$\angle CNM = 148°$
$\angle NRA = 155°$

Find
∠s 1–10

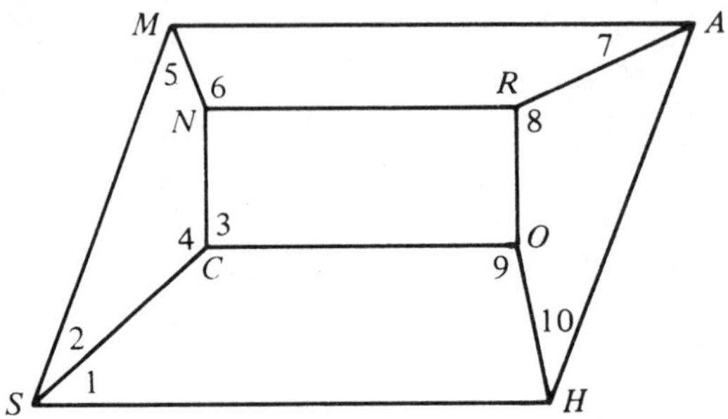

25. *Given*
rh *DEBC*
$\triangle DEA$ isos ($\overline{DA}$ base)
$\angle BEA = 112°$

Find
∠s 1–15

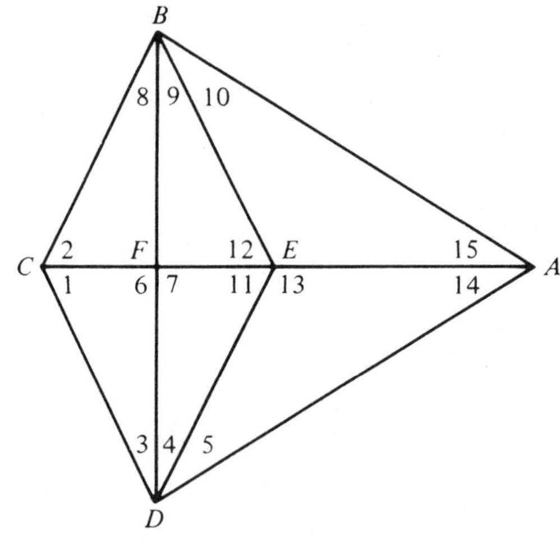

In exercises 26 and 27 copy the figure, mark it, and supply the missing reasons in each proof.

26. *Given*
rect *AXIO*
$\overrightarrow{IM}$ midray ∡*OIX*

To Prove
$\triangle MIO$ isos

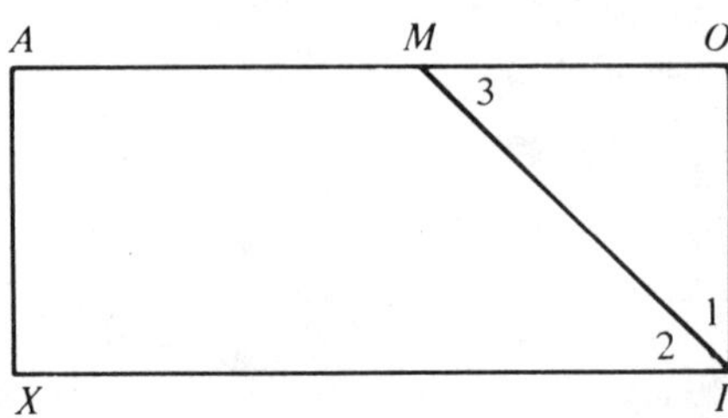

Statement	*Reason*
1. rect $AXIO$	1. ?
2. $\measuredangle O$, $\measuredangle OIX$ rt $\measuredangle$s	2. ?
3. $\angle O = \angle OIX = 90°$	3. ?
4. $\overline{IM}$ midray $\measuredangle OIX$	4. ?
5. $\angle 1 = \angle 2$	5. ?
6. $\angle 1 + \angle 2 = \angle OIX$	6. ?
7. $\angle 1 + \angle 2 = 90°$	7. ?
8. $\angle 1 + \angle 1 = 90°$	8. ?
9. $2 \cdot \angle 1 = 90°$	9. ?
10. $\angle 1 = 45°$	10. ?
11. $\angle 3 + \angle O + \angle 1 = 180°$	11. ?
12. $\angle 3 + \angle 1 = 90°$	12. ?
13. $\angle 3 = 45°$	13. ?
14. $\angle 1 = \angle 3$	14. ?
15. $\measuredangle 1 \cong \measuredangle 3$	15. ?
16. $\overline{MO} \cong \overline{IO}$	16. ?
17. $\therefore \triangle MIO$ isos	17. ?

27. *Given*
sq $SOQE$
U midpt $\overline{LO}$

To Prove
E midpt $\overline{LS}$

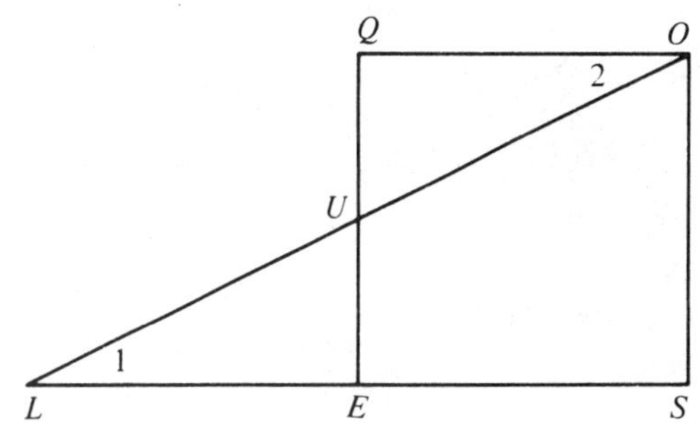

Statement	*Reason*
1. sq $SOQE$	1. ?
2. $\measuredangle QES$, $\measuredangle EQO$ rt $\measuredangle$s	2. ?
3. $\overline{QE} \perp \overline{LS}$	3. ?
4. $\measuredangle QEL$ rt $\measuredangle$	4. ?
5. $\measuredangle QEL \cong \measuredangle EQO$	5. ?
6. $\overline{ES} \parallel \overline{QO}$	6. ?
7. $\measuredangle 1 \cong \measuredangle 2$	7. ?
8. U midpt $\overline{LO}$	8. ?
9. $\overline{LU} \cong \overline{OU}$	9. ?
10. $\triangle LEU \cong \triangle OQU$	10. ?
11. $\overline{LE} \cong \overline{OQ}$	11. ?
12. $\overline{OQ} \cong \overline{ES}$	12. ?
13. $\overline{LE} \cong \overline{ES}$	13. ?
14. $\therefore E$ midpt $\overline{LS}$	14. ?

In exercises 28–40 copy the figure, the hypothesis, and the conclusion. Mark the figure and write a proof.

28. *Given*
rect *THAR*
$\overline{ET} \cong \overline{EH}$

To Prove
$\overline{RS} \cong \overline{AL}$

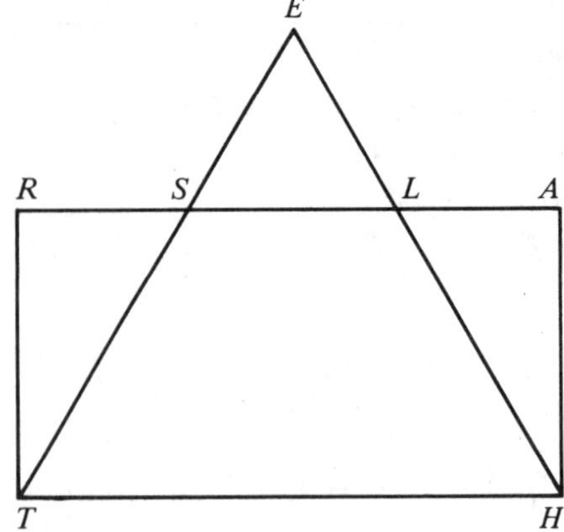

29. *Given*
sq *MATE*
B, R, O, P midpts

To Prove
$\overline{BP} \parallel \overline{RO}$

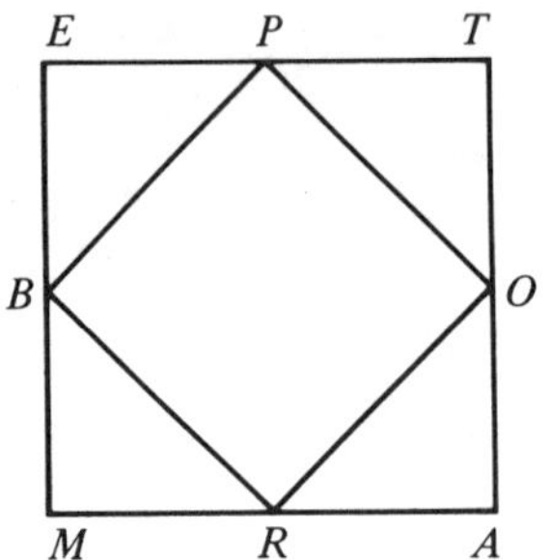

30. *Given*

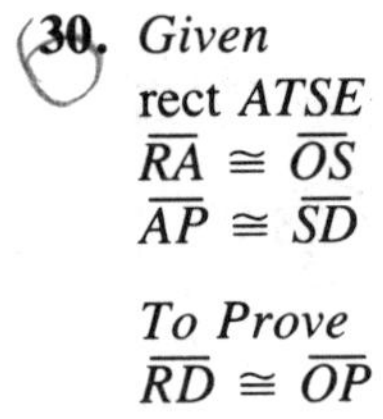

rect *ATSE*
$\overline{RA} \cong \overline{OS}$
$\overline{AP} \cong \overline{SD}$

To Prove
$\overline{RD} \cong \overline{OP}$

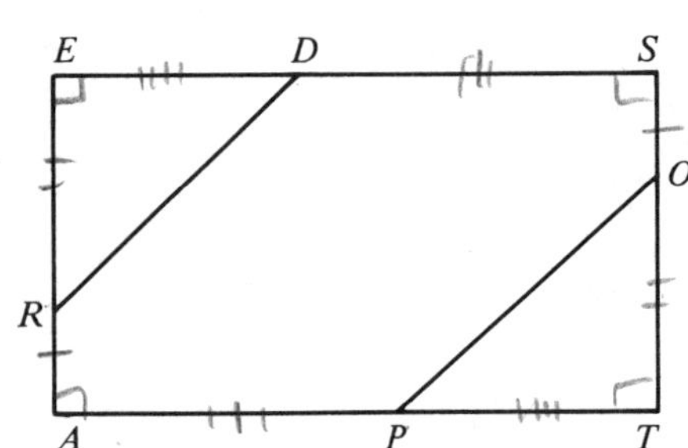

31. *Given*

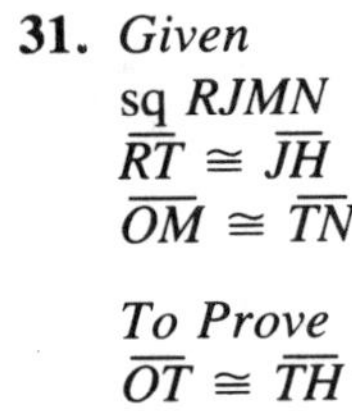

sq *RJMN*
$\overline{RT} \cong \overline{JH}$
$\overline{OM} \cong \overline{TN}$

To Prove
$\overline{OT} \cong \overline{TH}$

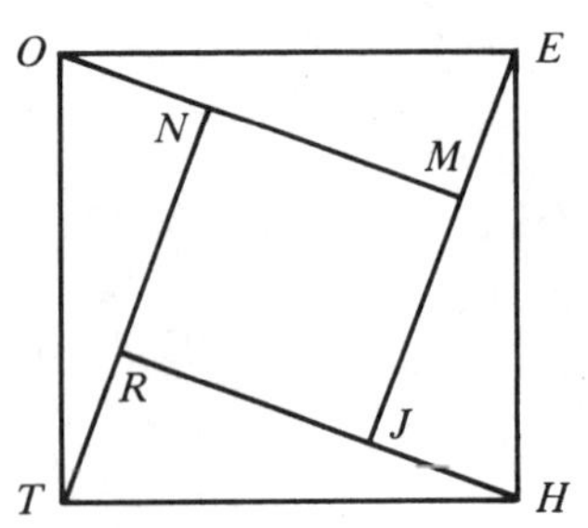

32. *Given*
rect *CAKE*
$\overline{CO}$ bis $\angle ACE$
$\overline{AO}$ bis $\angle CAK$

To Prove
$\overline{CO} \perp \overline{AO}$

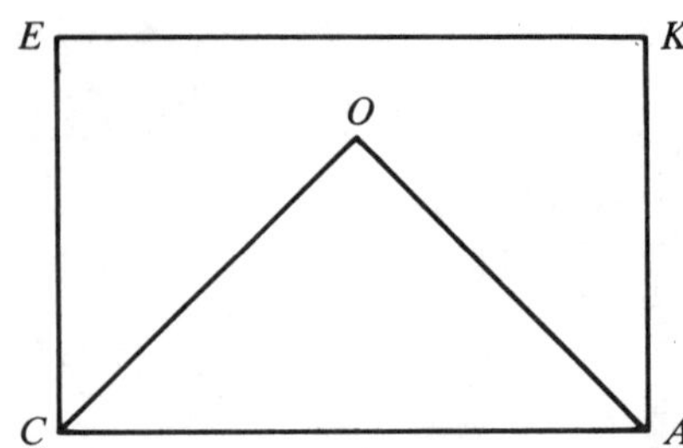

33. *Given*
$\square EULI$
$\overline{IC} \parallel \overline{UD}$

To Prove
$\overline{IC} \cong \overline{UD}$

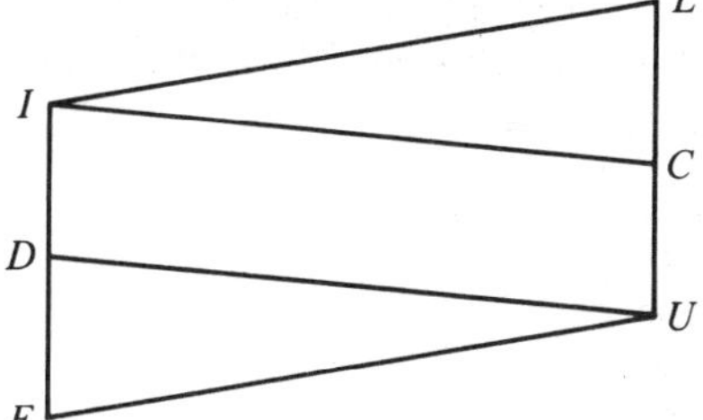

34. *Given*
rect *TAEJ*
K, *H*, *L*, *S* midpts

To Prove
$\overline{SL} \cong \overline{HK}$

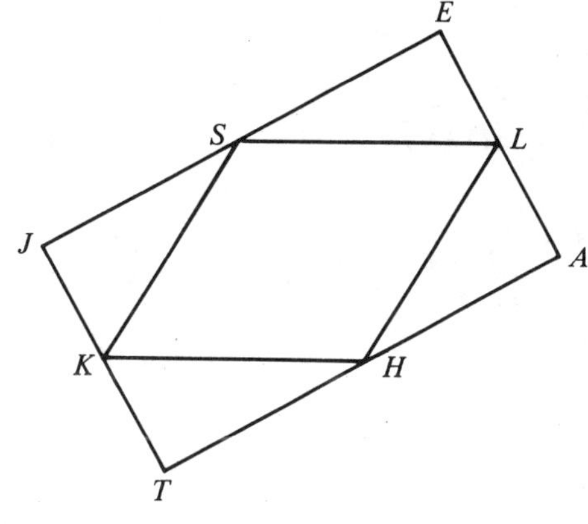

35. *Given*
rect *ABCD*
$\overline{AR}$ bis $\measuredangle DAB$
$\overline{CT}$ bis $\measuredangle DCB$

To Prove
$\overline{AR} \parallel \overline{CT}$

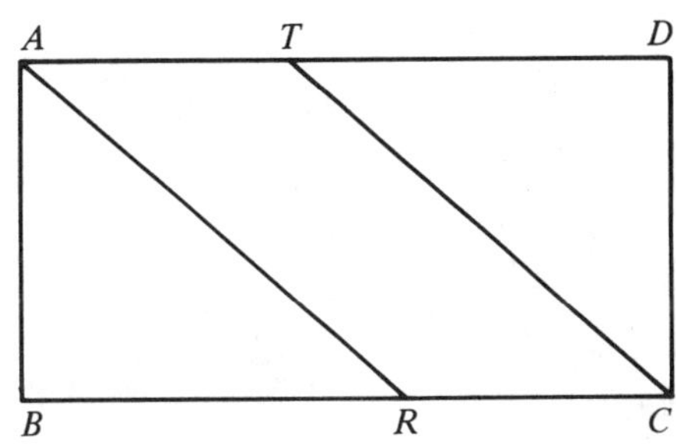

36. *Given*
sq *APTO*
$\triangle OAE$ isos ($\overline{OA}$ base)

To Prove
E midpt $\overline{TP}$

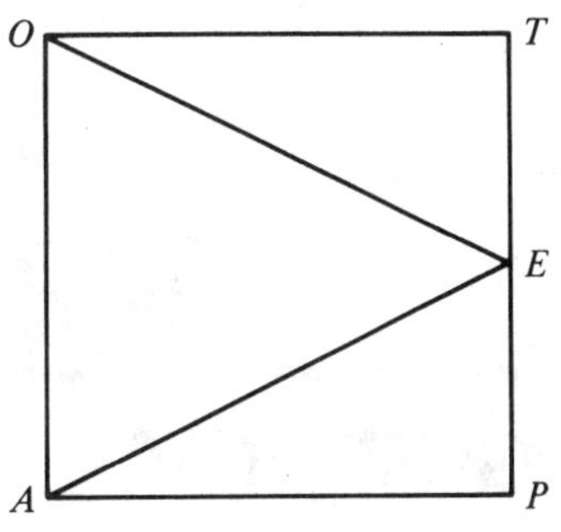

37. *Given*
sq *ABDE*
$\overline{CF} \perp \overline{AD}$

To Prove
$\triangle FCD$ isos

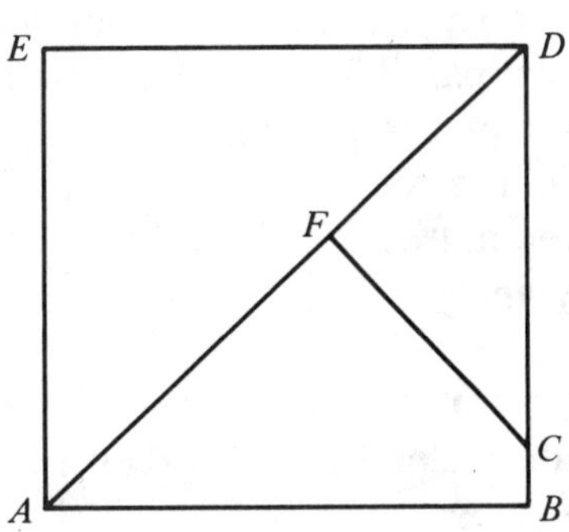

38. 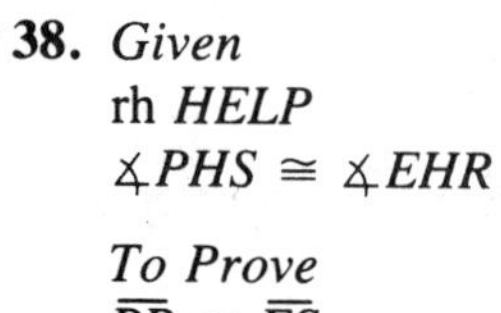
Given
rh *HELP*
$\measuredangle PHS \cong \measuredangle EHR$

To Prove
$\overline{PR} \cong \overline{ES}$

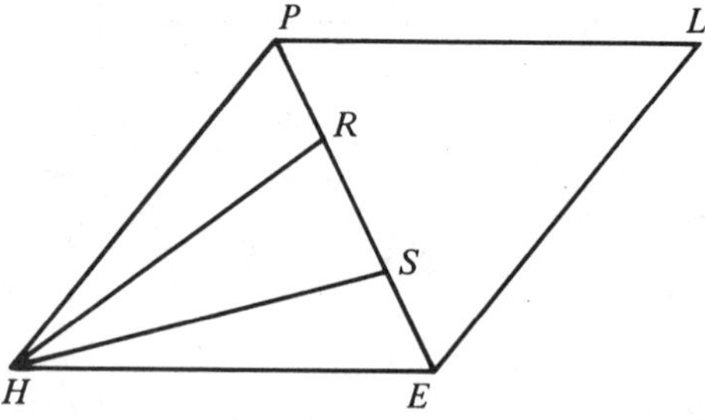

39. *Given*
sq *PYOG*
$\overline{AG} \cong \overline{HO} \cong \overline{TY}$

To Prove
$\overline{TH} \perp \overline{AH}$

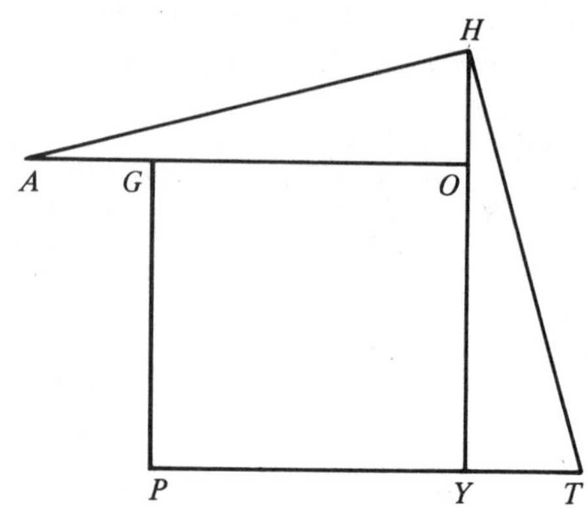

40. 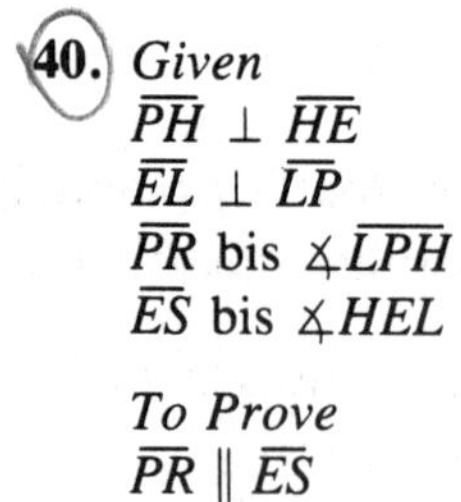
Given
$\overline{PH} \perp \overline{HE}$
$\overline{EL} \perp \overline{LP}$
$\overline{PR}$ bis $\measuredangle LPH$
$\overline{ES}$ bis $\measuredangle HEL$

To Prove
$\overline{PR} \parallel \overline{ES}$

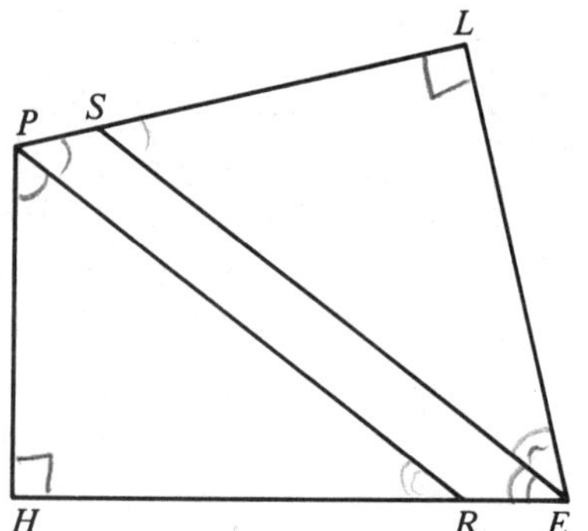

6.4

PROVING SPECIAL QUADRILATERALS

It is important to know when a quadrilateral is a parallelogram or one of the special parallelograms because then all the properties of the particular figure are known to be present. To prove that a quadrilateral is a parallelogram by definition requires showing that both pairs of opposite sides are parallel. If this is not easy or possible, one or the other of the following two theorems may apply.

Theorem 56 *(Converse of Theorem 46.)* If both pairs of opposite sides of a quadrilateral are congruent, then the quadrilateral is a parallelogram (quad opp sides ≅ is ▱).

Given
quad $ABCD$
$\overline{AB} \cong \overline{CD}$
$\overline{CB} \cong \overline{AD}$

To Prove
$ABCD$ ▱

Statement	*Reason*
1. quad $ABCD$, $\overline{AB} \cong \overline{CD}$, $\overline{CB} \cong \overline{AD}$	1. given
2. Draw $\overline{AC}$.	2. 2 pts determ line
3. $\overline{AC} \cong \overline{AC}$	3. refl $\cong$
4. $\triangle CAB \cong \triangle ACD$	4. sss $\cong$ sss
5. $\measuredangle 2 \cong \measuredangle 3$	5. cpctc
6. $\overline{AB} \parallel \overline{CD}$	6. $\not\measuredangle$, lines $\parallel$
7. $\measuredangle 4 \cong \measuredangle 1$	7. cpctc
8. $\overline{AD} \parallel \overline{CB}$	8. $\not\measuredangle$, lines $\parallel$
9. $\therefore ABCD$ ▱	9. ▱ iff opp sides $\parallel$

Theorem 57 If one pair of opposite sides of a quadrilateral is both parallel and congruent, then the quadrilateral is a parallelogram (quad 1 pr opp sides $\parallel$ and $\cong$ is ▱).

The proof is omitted. It is similar to that for Theorem 56 in that a diagonal may be drawn and two triangles proved congruent. Then using "cpctc" and Theorem 56, the conclusion follows.

The foregoing two theorems give the most useful ways to prove that a quadrilateral is a parallelogram. One of them is applied in Example 1.

EXAMPLE 1

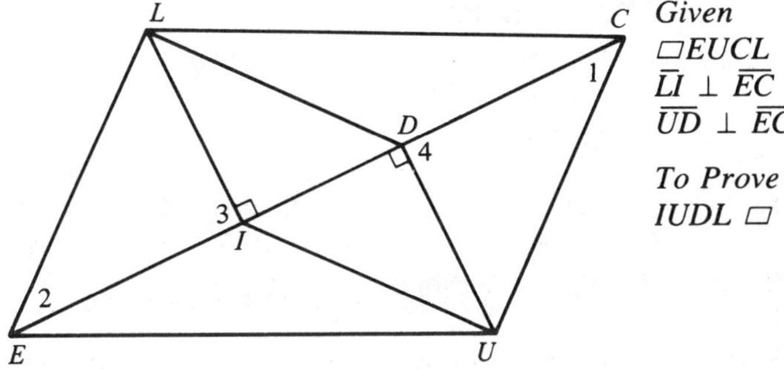

Given
▱$EUCL$
$\overline{LI} \perp \overline{EC}$
$\overline{UD} \perp \overline{EC}$

To Prove
$IUDL$ ▱

Statement	*Reason*
1. ▱$EUCL$	1. given
2. $\overline{EL} \cong \overline{CU}$	2. opp sides ▱ $\cong$
3. $\overline{EL} \parallel \overline{CU}$	3. ▱ iff opp sides $\parallel$
4. $\measuredangle 2 \cong \measuredangle 1$	4. $\nparallel$, alt int $\measuredangle$s $\cong$
5. $\overline{LI} \perp \overline{EC}$	5. given
6. $\measuredangle 3$ rt $\measuredangle$	6. $\perp$s form $\cong$ rt $\measuredangle$s
7. $\overline{UD} \perp \overline{EC}$	7. given
8. $\measuredangle 4$ rt $\measuredangle$	8. $\perp$s form $\cong$ rt $\measuredangle$s

9. ∡3 ≅ ∡4	9. rt ∡s ≅
10. $\triangle EIL \cong \triangle CDU$	10. aas ≅ aas
11. $\overline{LI} \cong \overline{UD}$	11. cpctc
12. $\overline{LI} \parallel \overline{UD}$	12. 2 lines ⊥ 3d line ∥
13. ∴ *IUDL* ▱	13. quad 1 pr opp sides ∥ and ≅ is ▱

A quadrilateral may be proved to be a rectangle by definition if we can show that it is a parallelogram having a right angle. Another way is to show that it is a parallelogram and then use Theorem 58.

Theorem 58 *(Converse of Theorem 52.)* If the diagonals of a parallelogram are congruent, then the parallelogram is a rectangle (▱ diags ≅ is rect).

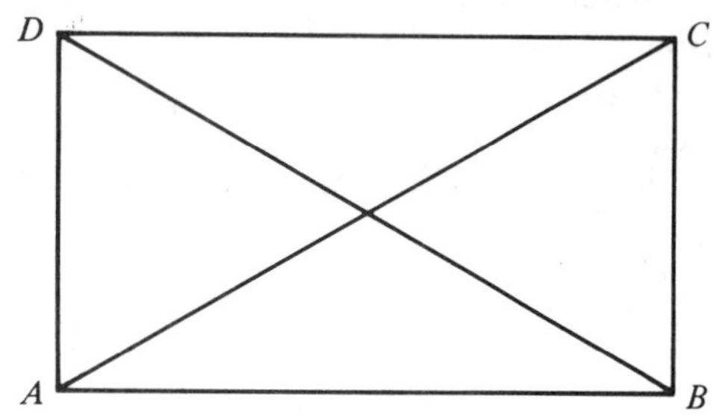

Given
▱*ABCD*
$\overline{AC} \cong \overline{BD}$

To Prove
ABCD rect

Statement	*Reason*
1. ▱*ABCD*	1. given
2. $\overline{BC} \cong \overline{AD}$	2. opp sides ▱ ≅
3. $\overline{AB} \cong \overline{AB}$	3. refl ≅
4. $\overline{AC} \cong \overline{BD}$	4. given
5. $\triangle ABC \cong \triangle BAD$	5. sss ≅ sss
6. ∡*CBA* ≅ ∡*DAB*	6. cpctc
7. $\overline{AD} \parallel \overline{BC}$	7. ▱ iff opp sides ∥
8. ∡*DAB* supp ∡*CBA*	8. ∦, int ∡s same side t supp
9. $\angle DAB + \angle CBA = 180°$	9. supp iff sum = 180°
10. $\angle CBA = \angle DAB$	10. ≅ iff meas =
11. $\angle DAB = 90°$	11. $\frac{1}{2}$s of = are =
12. ∡*DAB* rt ∡	12. rt ∠ = 90°
13. ∴ *ABCD* rect	13. rect iff ▭

To prove that a quadrilateral is a rhombus by definition, it must be shown to be a parallelogram having a pair of adjacent sides congruent. Another method is to show it is a parallelogram and then use Theorem 59.

Theorem 59 *(Converse of Theorem 55.)* If the diagonals of a parallelogram are perpendicular, then the parallelogram is a rhombus (▱ diags ⊥ is rh).

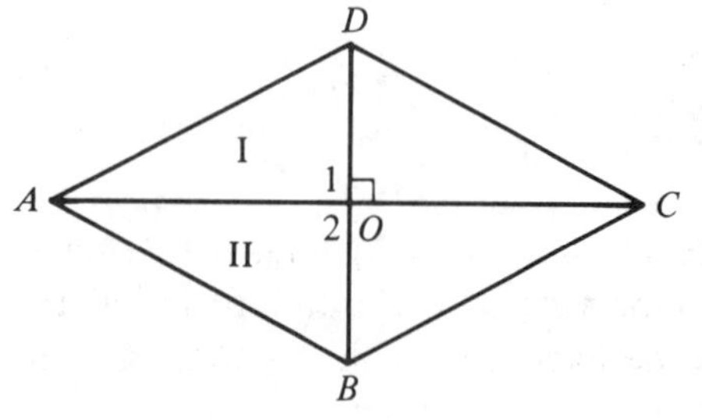

Given
▱*ABCD*
$\overline{AC} \perp \overline{BD}$

To Prove
ABCD rh

Statement	Reason
1. ▱$ABCD$	1. given
2. $\overline{DO} \cong \overline{BO}$	2. diags ▱ bis ea other
3. $\overline{AC} \perp \overline{BD}$	3. given
4. $\measuredangle 1 \cong \measuredangle 2$	4. ⊥s form ≅ rt ∡s
5. $\overline{AO} \cong \overline{AO}$	5. refl ≅
6. $\triangle I \cong \triangle II$	6. sas ≅ sas
7. $\overline{AD} \cong \overline{AB}$	7. cpctc
8. ∴ $ABCD$ rh	8. rh iff ▱ with adj sides ≅

Theorem 59 is used in Example 2. Note that most of the proof is devoted to proving that $EJSK$ is a parallelogram.

EXAMPLE 2

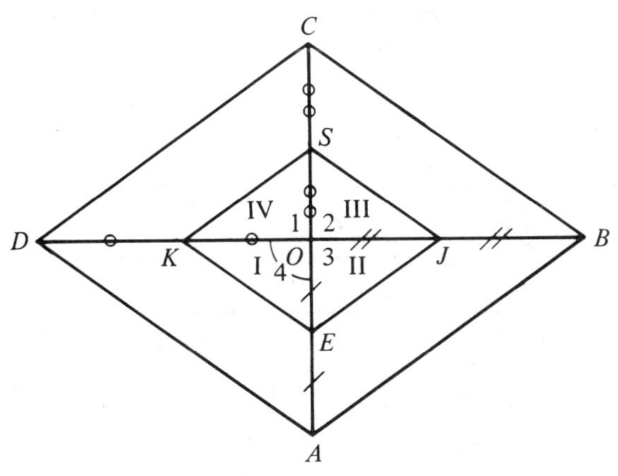

Given
rh $ABCD$
E, J, S, K midpts

To Prove
$EJSK$ rh

Statement	Reason
1. rh $ABCD$	1. given
2. $\overline{CO} \cong \overline{AO}$ and $\overline{DO} \cong \overline{BO}$	2. diags ▱ (rh) bis ea other
3. $\overline{CA} \perp \overline{DB}$	3. diags rh ⊥
4. E, J, S, K midpts	4. given
5. $\overline{CS} \cong \overline{SO}$ and $\overline{AE} \cong \overline{EO}$	5. midpt ÷ seg into 2 ≅ segs
6. $\overline{EO} \cong \overline{SO}$	6. $\frac{1}{2}$s of ≅ are ≅
7. $\overline{DK} \cong \overline{KO}$ and $\overline{BJ} \cong \overline{JO}$	7. midpt ÷ seg into 2 ≅ segs
8. $\overline{KO} \cong \overline{JO}$	8. $\frac{1}{2}$s of ≅ are ≅
9. $\measuredangle 1 \cong \measuredangle 2 \cong \measuredangle 3 \cong \measuredangle 4$	9. ⊥s form ≅ rt ∡s
10. $\triangle I \cong \triangle III$, $\triangle II \cong \triangle IV$	10. sas ≅ sas
11. $\overline{EK} \cong \overline{SJ}$, $\overline{JE} \cong \overline{KS}$	11. cpctc
12. ▱$EJSK$	12. quad opp sides ≅ is ▱
13. ∴ $EJSK$ rh	13. ▱ diags ⊥ is rh

To prove that a quadrilateral is a square requires proving that it is a parallelogram with a right angle (a rectangle) and that it has a pair of adjacent sides congruent (a rhombus). Problem 12 in the exercises of this section shows that this proof can be a lengthy task.

EXERCISES FOR 6.4

In exercises 1–10 use the marks on each quadrilateral (*not* its appearance) to choose the one name among the following that best describes the figure: quadrilateral, trapezoid, isosceles trapezoid, parallelogram, rectangle, rhombus, or square.

1.

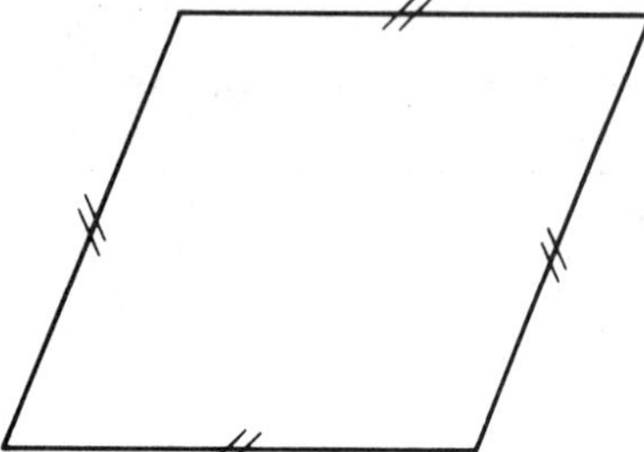

2.

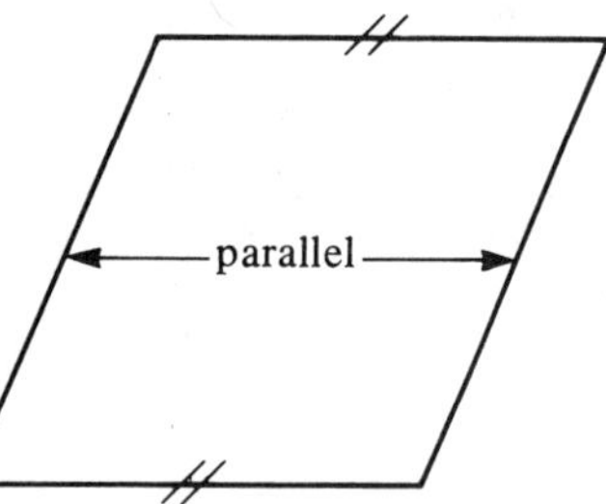

3.

4.

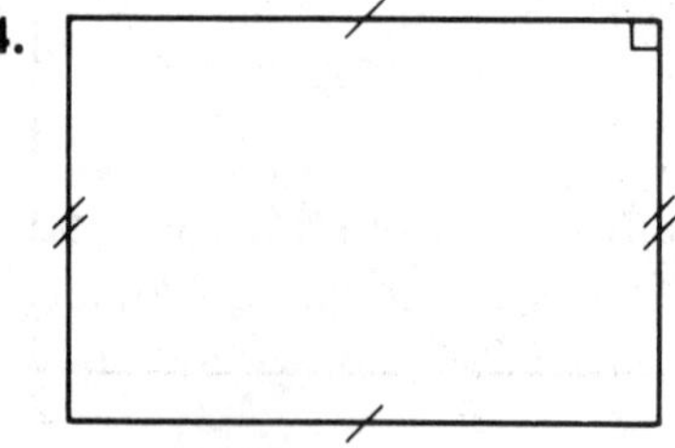

5.

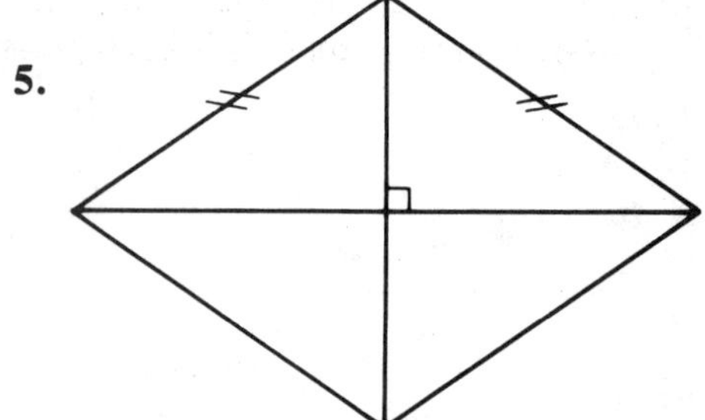

6.

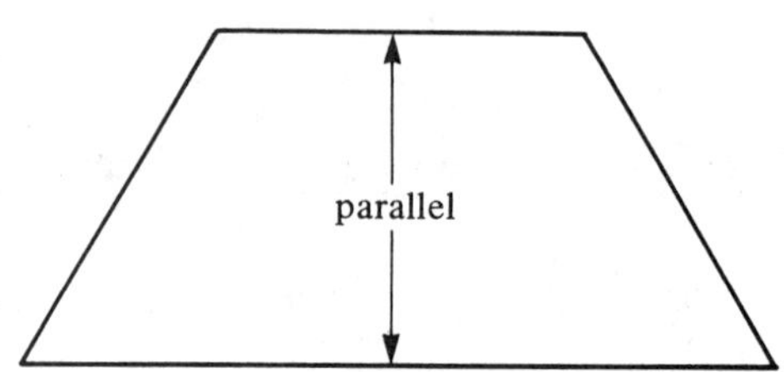

7.

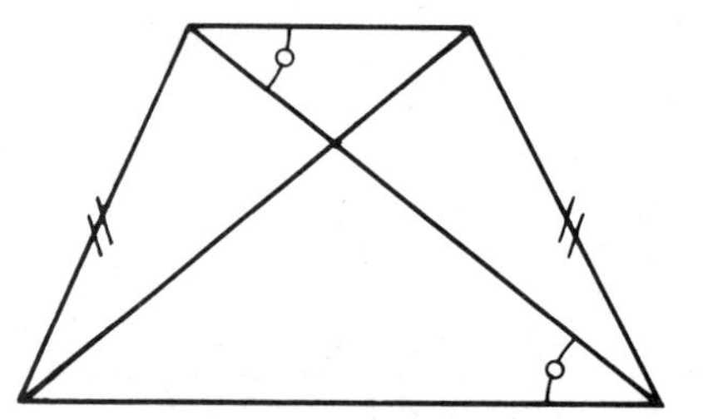

8.

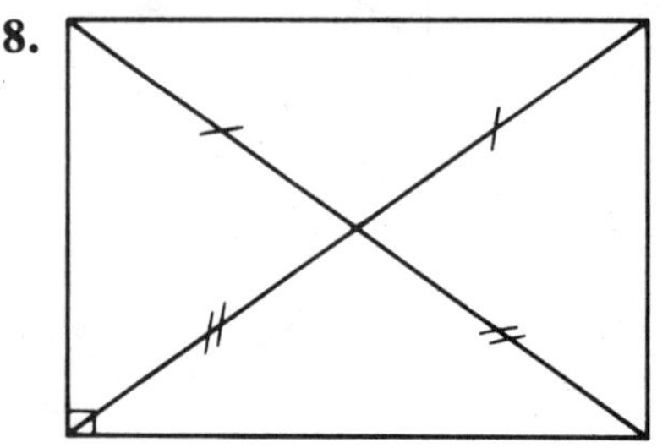

9.

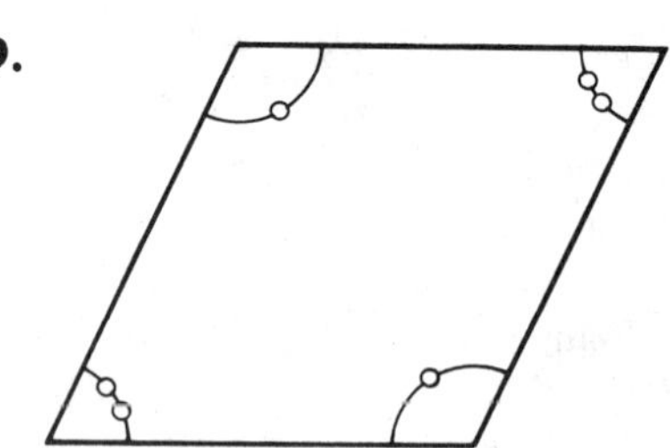

10.

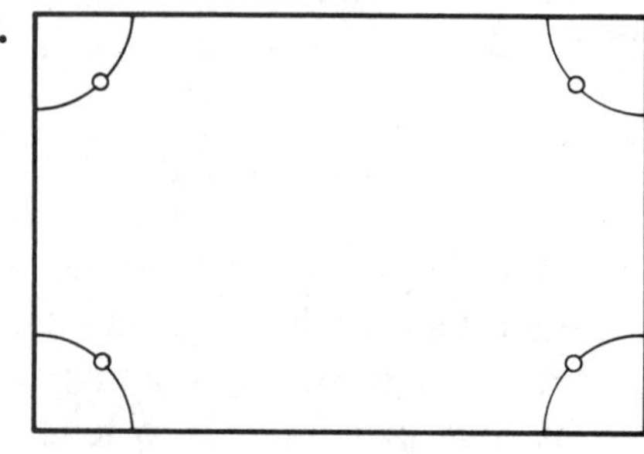

In exercises 11 and 12 copy the figure, mark it, and supply the missing reasons in each proof.

11. *Given*
$\square HERO$
$\overline{OG} \cong \overline{EA}$
$\overline{BE} \cong \overline{NO}$

To Prove
BANG $\square$

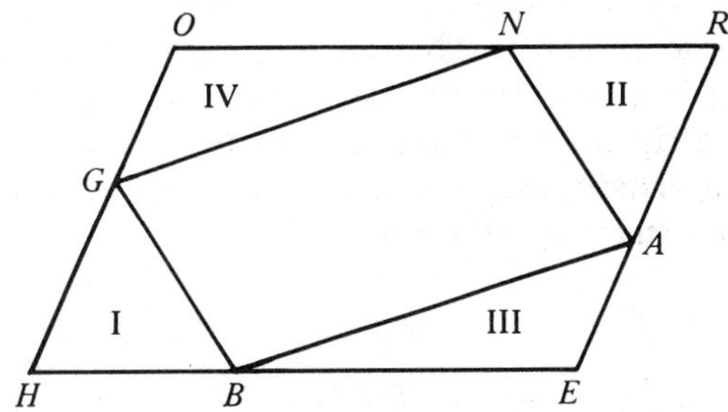

Statement	*Reason*
1. $\square HERO$	1. ?
2. $\overline{HO} \cong \overline{RE}$	2. ?
3. $\overline{OG} \cong \overline{EA}$	3. ?
4. $\overline{HO} - \overline{OG} \cong \overline{RE} - \overline{EA}$	4. ?
5. $\overline{HG} \cong \overline{HO} - \overline{OG}$	5. ?
6. $\overline{RE} - \overline{EA} \cong \overline{RA}$	6. ?
7. $\overline{HG} \cong \overline{RA}$	7. ?
8. $\measuredangle H \cong \measuredangle R$	8. ?
9. $\overline{HE} \cong \overline{RO}$	9. ?
10. $\overline{BE} \cong \overline{NO}$	10. ?
11. $\overline{HE} - \overline{BE} \cong \overline{RO} - \overline{NO}$	11. ?
12. $\overline{HB} \cong \overline{HE} - \overline{BE}$	12. ?
13. $\overline{RO} - \overline{NO} \cong \overline{RN}$	13. ?
14. $\overline{HB} \cong \overline{RN}$	14. ?
15. $\triangle \text{I} \cong \triangle \text{II}$	15. ?
16. $\overline{BG} \cong \overline{NA}$	16. ?
17. $\measuredangle E \cong \measuredangle O$	17. ?
18. $\triangle \text{III} \cong \triangle \text{IV}$	18. ?
19. $\overline{BA} \cong \overline{NG}$	19. ?
20. $\therefore$ *BANG* $\square$	20. ?

12. *Given*
sq *PQRS*
E, *J*, *M*, *K*, midpts

To Prove
EJMK sq

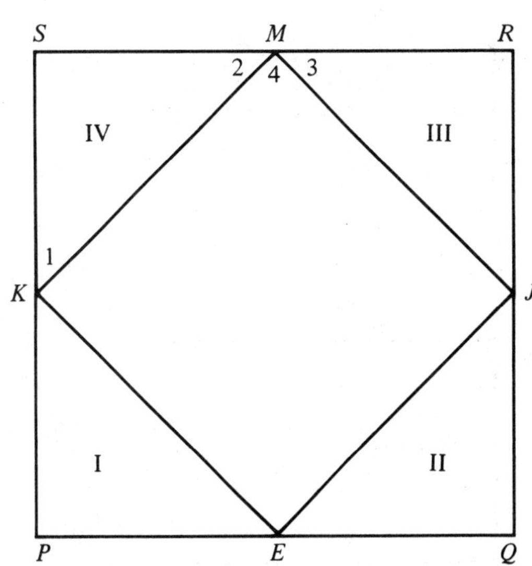

Statement	Reason
1. sq *PQRS*	1. ?
2. $\overline{PQ} \cong \overline{QR} \cong \overline{RS} \cong \overline{SP}$	2. ?
3. *E, J, M, K* midpts	3. ?
4. $\overline{PE} \cong \overline{EQ} \cong \overline{QJ} \cong \overline{JR} \cong \overline{RM} \cong \overline{MS} \cong \overline{SK} \cong \overline{KP}$	4. ?
5. $\measuredangle P \cong \measuredangle Q \cong \measuredangle R \cong \measuredangle S$	5. ?
6. $\triangle \text{I} \cong \triangle \text{II} \cong \triangle \text{III} \cong \triangle \text{IV}$	6. ?
7. $\overline{KE} \cong \overline{EJ} \cong \overline{JM} \cong \overline{MK}$	7. ?
8. *EJMK* ▱	8. ?
9. *EJMK* rh	9. ?
10. $\measuredangle 2 \cong \measuredangle 3$	10. ?
11. $\measuredangle 1 \cong \measuredangle 2$	11. ?
12. $\angle 1 + \angle 2 + \angle S = 180°$	12. ?
13. $\angle S = 90°$	13. ?
14. $\angle 1 + \angle 2 = 90°$	14. ?
15. $\angle 1 = \angle 2$, $\angle 2 = \angle 3$	15. ?
16. $\angle 1 = \angle 3$	16. ?
17. $\angle 3 + \angle 2 = 90°$	17. ?
18. $\angle 3 + \angle 2 + \angle 4 = 180°$	18. ?
19. $\angle 4 = 90°$	19. ?
20. $\measuredangle 4$ rt $\measuredangle$	20. ?
21. *EJMK* rect	21. ?
22. ∴ *EJMK* sq	22. ?

In exercises 13–30 copy the figure, the hypothesis, and the conclusion. Mark the figure and write a proof.

13. (Theorem 57)

Given
$\overline{HE} \parallel \overline{LP}$
$\overline{HE} \cong \overline{LP}$

To Prove
HELP ▱

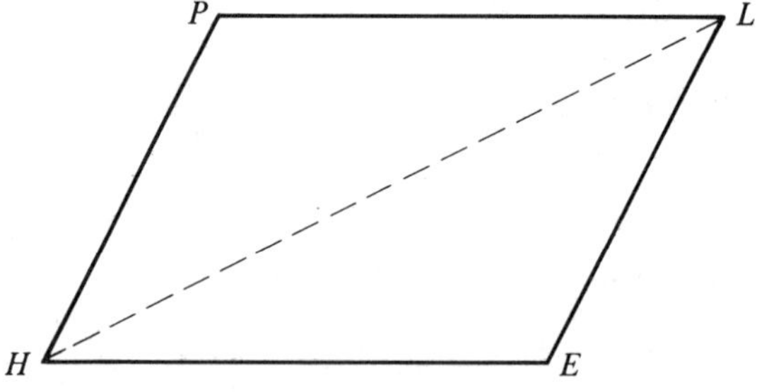

14. *Given*
▱*JECS*
K midpt $\overline{CS}$
A midpt $\overline{JE}$

To Prove
JACK ▱

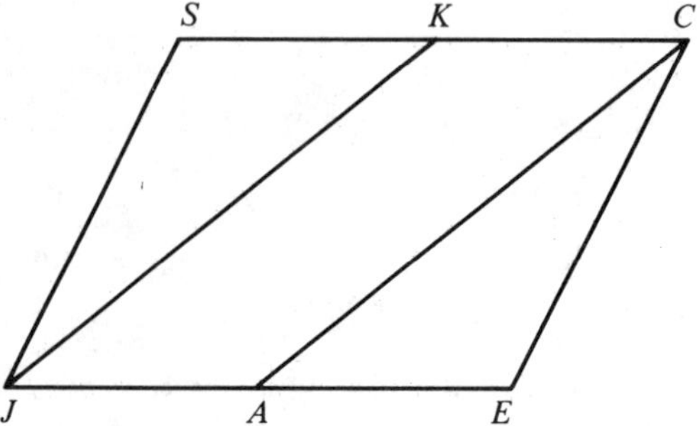

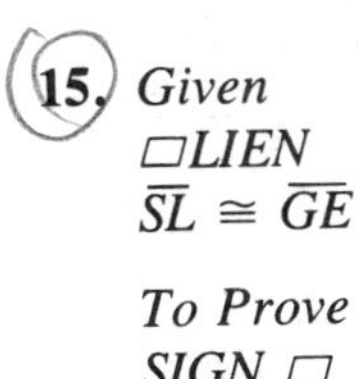

15. *Given*
▱*LIEN*
$\overline{SL} \cong \overline{GE}$

To Prove
SIGN ▱

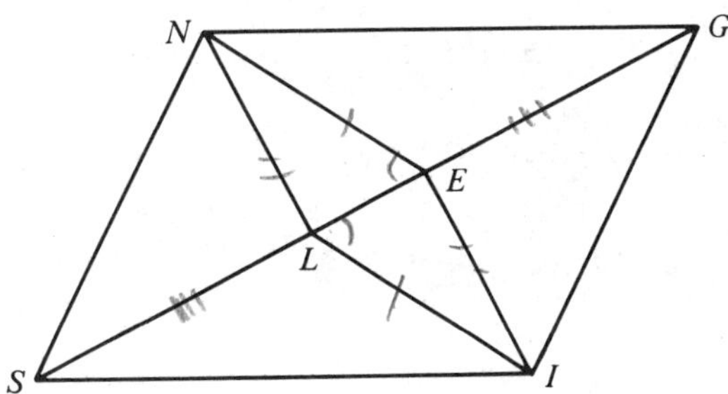

16. *Given*
▱*ABCD*
$\overline{AN} \cong \overline{CM}$

To Prove
MBND ▱

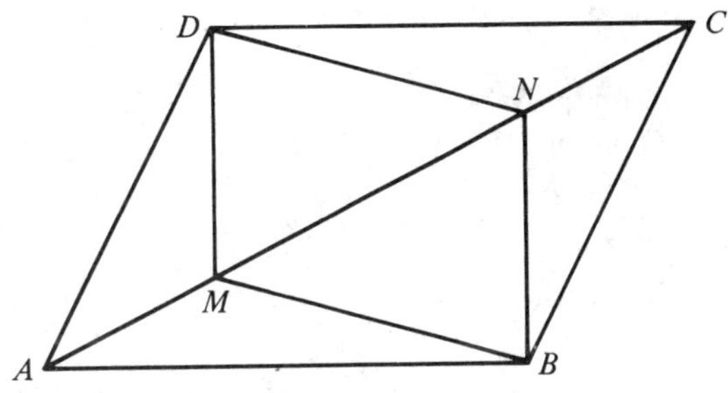

17. *Given*
$\overline{AE} \cong \overline{CE}$
$\overline{DE} \cong \overline{BE}$

To Prove
ABCD ▱

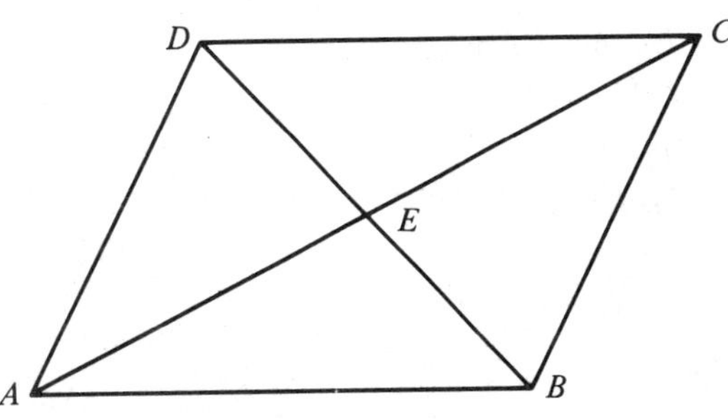

18. *Given*
▱*BING*
$\overline{BD} \parallel \overline{NE}$

To Prove
BEND ▱

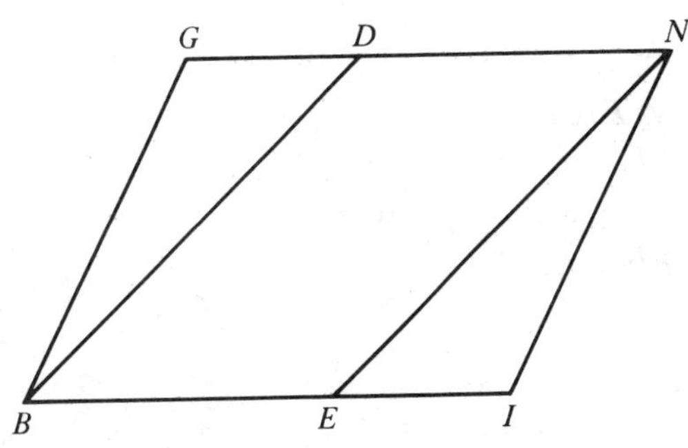

19. *Given*
rect *HERO* with midpts *F*, *L*, *I*, *P*

To Prove
FLIP rh

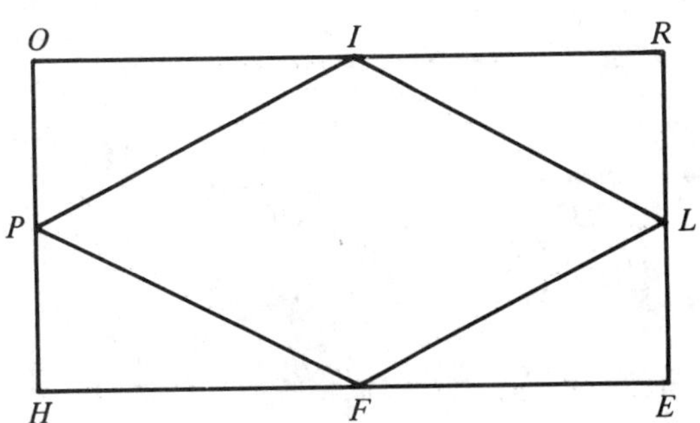

20. *Given*
$\overline{CO} \cong \overline{LT}$
$\overline{TL} \perp \overline{BA}$
$\angle 1 \cong \angle 2$

To Prove
COLT rect

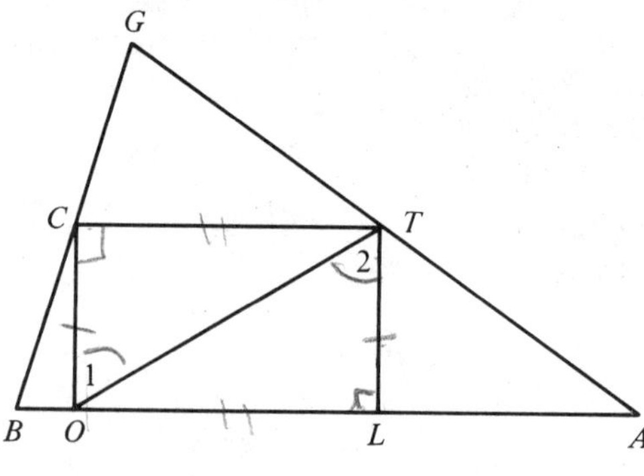

21. *Given*
▱*PQRS*
K midpt $\overline{SR}$
E midpt $\overline{QP}$
$\overline{PM} \cong \overline{RJ}$

To Prove
EJKM ▱

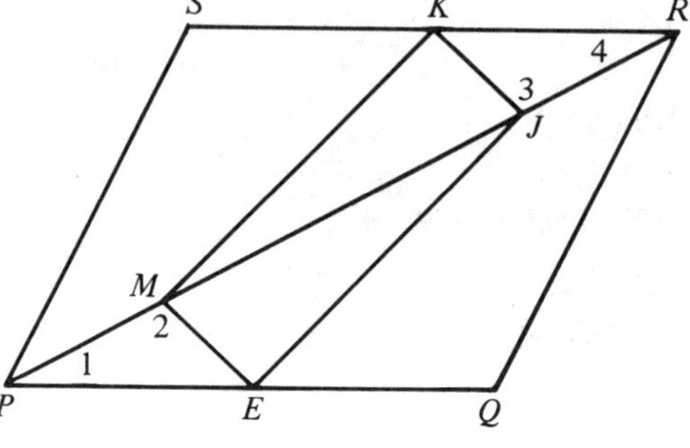

22. *Given*
$\overline{LE}$ and $\overline{PJ}$ bis ea other
E midpt $\overline{HJ}$

To Prove
HELP ▱

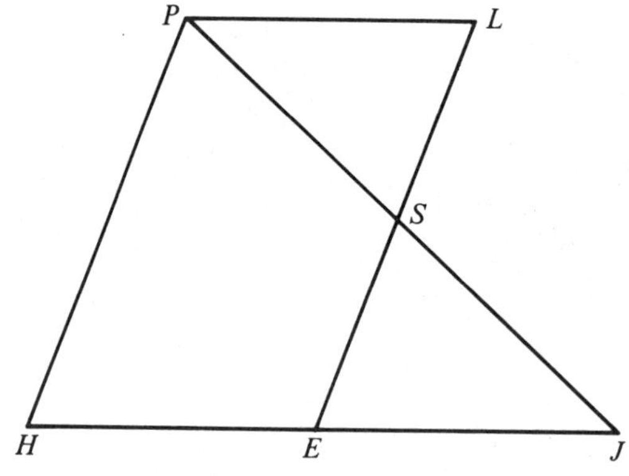

23. *Given*
sq *EJCK*
$\overline{EF} \cong \overline{CI} \cong \overline{CS} \cong \overline{EH}$

To Prove
FISH rect

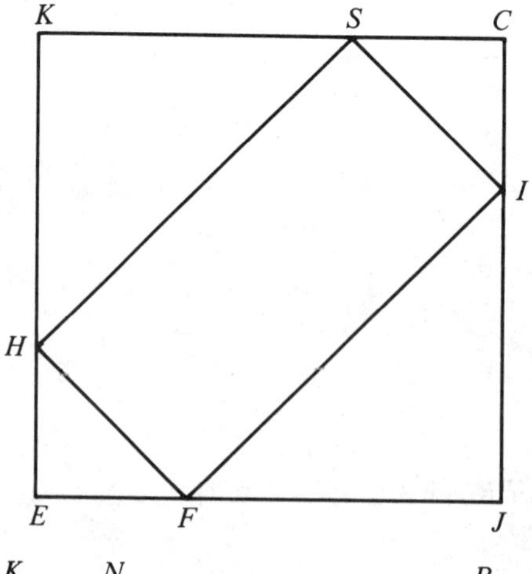

24. *Given*
▱*YORK*
$\overline{YN} \perp \overline{KR}$
$\overline{RA} \perp \overline{YO}$

To Prove
YARN rect

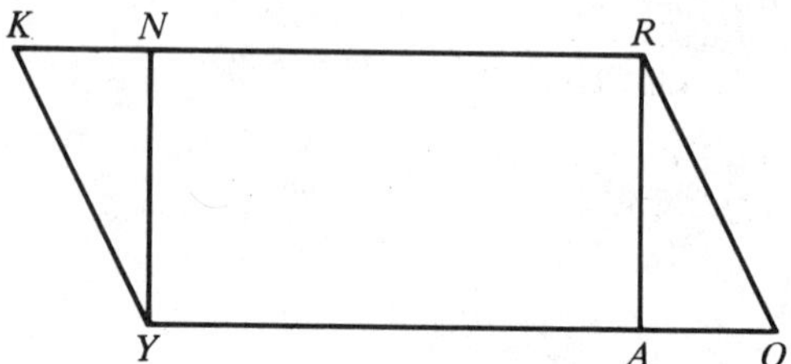

25. *Given*
N midpt $\overline{ST}$
M midpt $\overline{NG}$
M midpt $\overline{IT}$

To Prove
$SIGN$ ▱

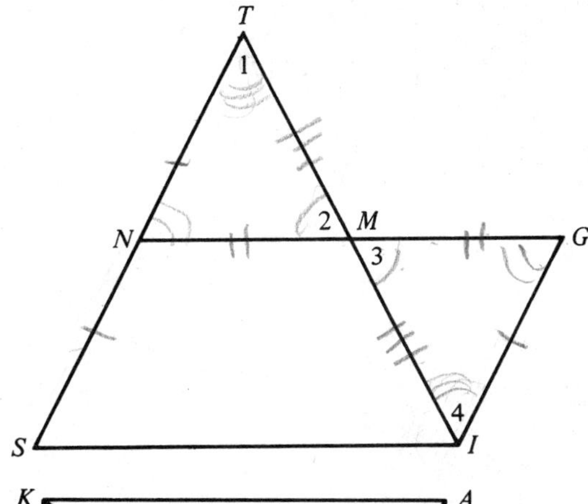

26. *Given*
sq $TRIM$
$\overline{RL} \cong \overline{IA} \cong \overline{MK} \cong \overline{TF}$

To Prove
$FLAK$ sq

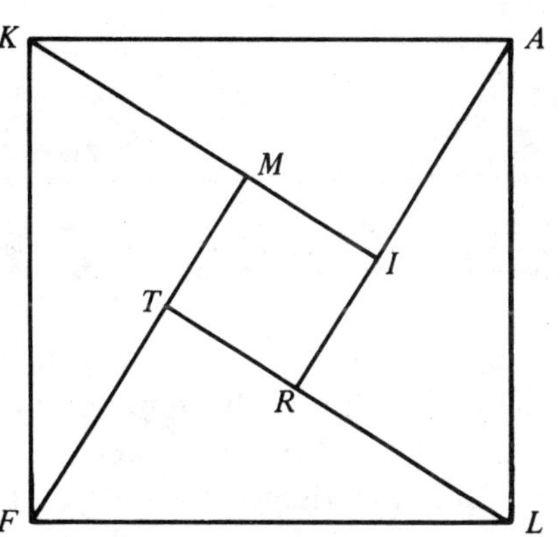

27. *Given*
▱$JAWS$
$\overline{AN}$ bis ∡JAW
$\overline{WD}$ bis ∡SWA

To Prove
$DAWN$ rh

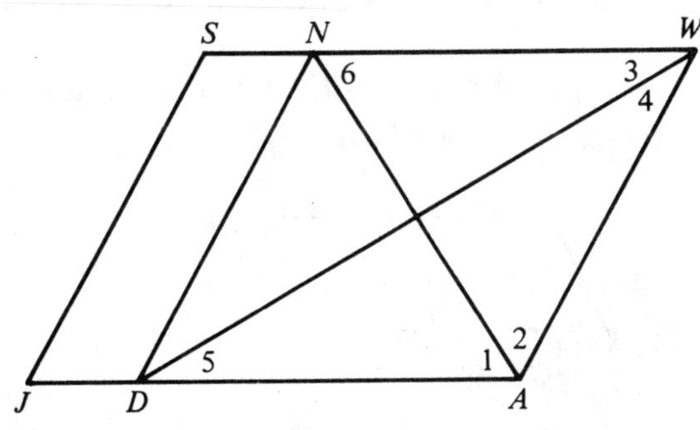

28. *Given*
∡S ≅ ∡I
∡L ≅ ∡M

To Prove
$SLIM$ ▱

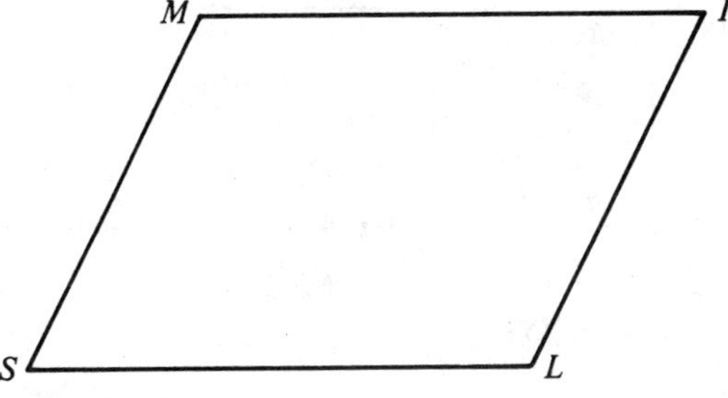

29. *Given*
▱$ECLD$
I midpt $\overline{DL}$
U midpt $\overline{CE}$

To Prove
$UJIS$ ▱

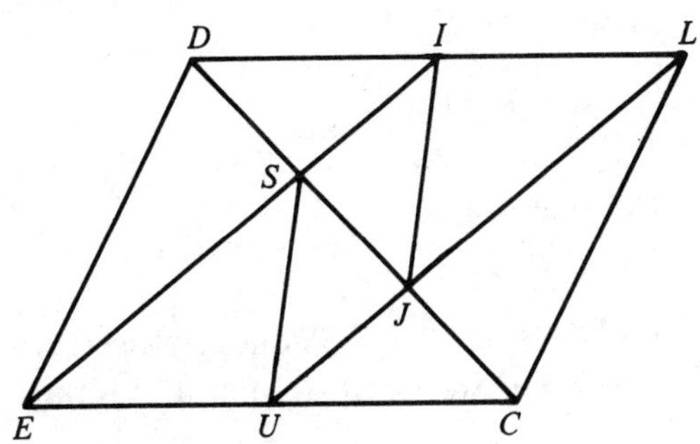

30. *Given*
sq *GRAB* with midpts *D*, *E*, *F*, *H*

To Prove
COLT rect

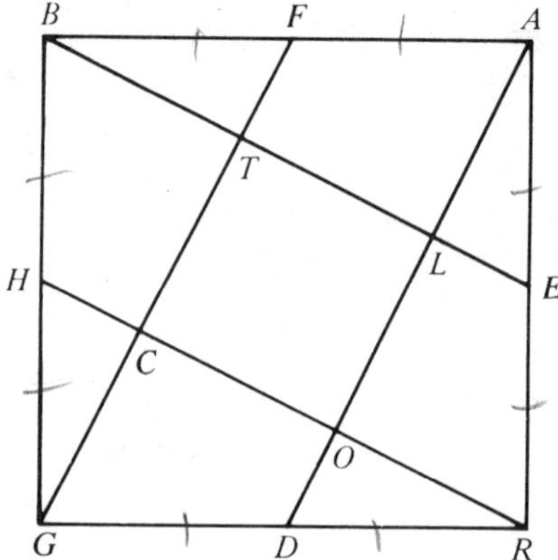

6.5 OTHER FOUR-LINE FIGURES

Recall that a trapezoid is a quadrilateral with only one pair of parallel sides. This fact limits the number of properties held by trapezoids. In the special case of the isosceles trapezoid, however, the base angles are congruent and so are the diagonals. We state and prove the first of these properties in Theorem 60, and leave the other as an exercise.

Theorem 60 The base angles of an isosceles trapezoid are congruent (base ∡s isos trap ≅).

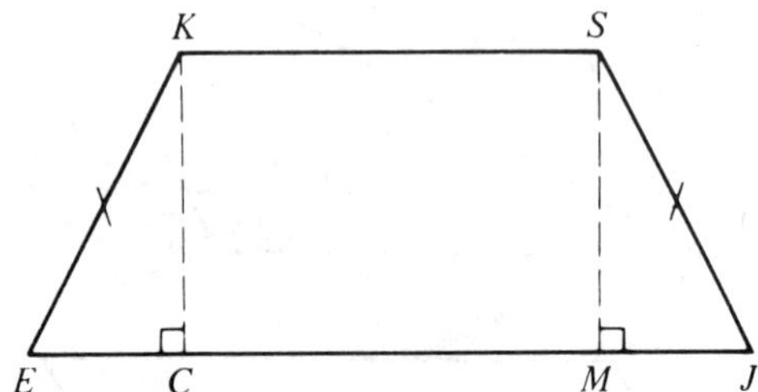

Given
isos trap *EJSK* ($\overline{EJ}$, $\overline{KS}$ bases)
$\overline{EK} \cong \overline{JS}$

To Prove
$\measuredangle E \cong \measuredangle J$

Statement	*Reason*
1. isos trap *EJSK* ($\overline{EJ}$, $\overline{KS}$ bases) $\overline{EK} \cong \overline{JS}$	1. given
2. $\overline{EJ} \parallel \overline{KS}$	2. trap iff 1 pr sides $\parallel$
3. Draw $\overline{KC} \perp \overline{EJ}$, $\overline{SM} \perp \overline{EJ}$.	3. 1 $\perp$ from pt to line
4. $KC = SM$	4. if lines $\parallel$, $\perp$ segs $=$
5. $\overline{KC} \cong \overline{SM}$	5. $\cong$ iff meas $=$
6. $\triangle KCE \cong \triangle SMJ$	6. hs $\cong$ hs
7. $\therefore \measuredangle E \cong \measuredangle J$	7. cpctc

We have frequently used triangles to prove facts about parallelograms. In Theorems 61–63 parallelograms are used to prove more facts about triangles.

Theorem 61 The line segment joining the midpoints of two sides of a triangle is half as long as the third side and parallel to it (midpt seg △ $\frac{1}{2}$ of and ∥ to 3d side).

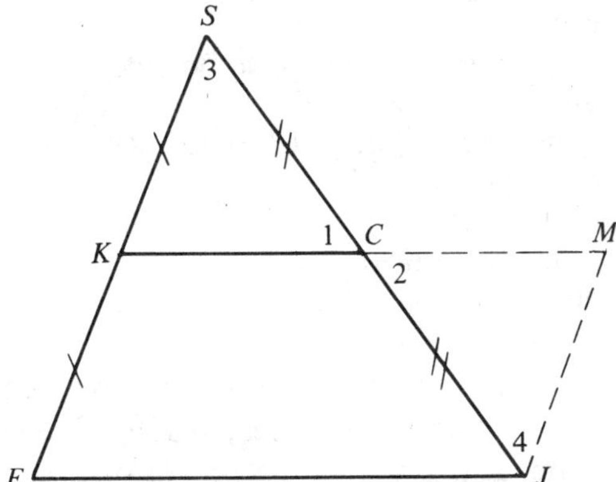

Given
K midpt $\overline{ES}$
C midpt $\overline{JS}$

To Prove
$KC = \frac{1}{2}EJ$
$\overline{KC} \parallel \overline{EJ}$

Statement	*Reason*
1. K midpt $\overline{ES}$, C midpt $\overline{JS}$	1. given
2. $\overline{KE} \cong \overline{SK}$, $\overline{SC} \cong \overline{CJ}$	2. midpt ÷ seg into 2 ≅ seg
3. Extend $\overline{KC}$ so $\overline{KC} \cong \overline{CM}$.	3. 2 pts determ line; can copy seg
4. $KC = CM$	4. ≅ iff meas =
5. Draw $\overline{MJ}$.	5. 2 pts determ line
6. ∡1 ≅ ∡2	6. vert ∡s ≅
7. $\triangle KCS \cong \triangle MCJ$	7. sas ≅ sas
8. $\overline{SK} \cong \overline{JM}$, ∡3 ≅ ∡4	8. cpctc
9. $\overline{KE} \cong \overline{JM}$	9. trans ≅
10. $\overline{ES} \parallel \overline{JM}$	10. $\not\cong$∡, lines ∥
11. $EJMK$ ▱	11. quad 1 pr opp sides ∥ and ≅ is ▱
12. ∴ $\overline{KC} \parallel \overline{EJ}$	12. ▱ iff opp sides ∥
13. $\overline{KM} \cong \overline{EJ}$	13. opp sides ▱ ≅
14. $KM = EJ$	14. ≅ iff meas =
15. ∴ $KC = \frac{1}{2}EJ$	15. $\frac{1}{2}$s of = are =

Theorem 61 of course applies to the midpoints of any two sides of a triangle. Its use to prove other facts is illustrated in Example 1.

EXAMPLE 1 Prove that if the consecutive midpoints of the sides of any quadrilateral are joined by line segments, then the line segments form a parallelogram.

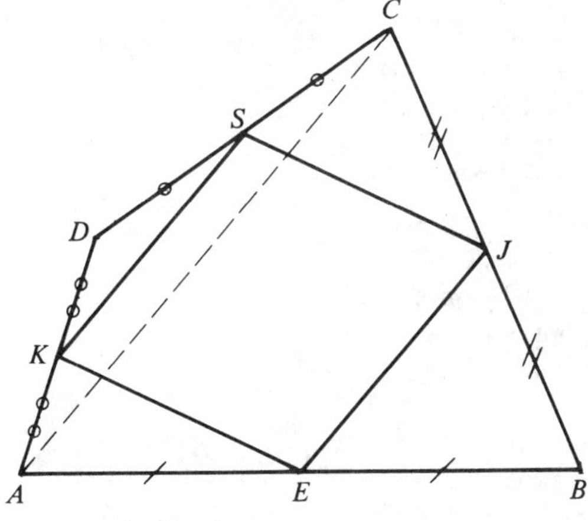

Given
quad $ABCD$
E midpt $\overline{AB}$
J midpt $\overline{BC}$
S midpt $\overline{CD}$
K midpt $\overline{DA}$

To Prove
$EJSK$ ▱

Statement	Reason
1. quad *ABCD*	1. given
2. Draw *AC*.	2. 2 pts determ line
3. *E* midpt $\overline{AB}$, *J* midpt $\overline{BC}$	3. given
4. $EJ = \frac{1}{2}AC$, $\overline{EJ} \parallel \overline{AC}$	4. midpt seg △ $\frac{1}{2}$ of and ∥ to 3d side
5. *S* midpt $\overline{CD}$, *K* midpt $\overline{DA}$	5. given
6. $SK = \frac{1}{2}AC$, $\overline{SK} \parallel \overline{AC}$	6. midpt seg △ $\frac{1}{2}$ of and ∥ to 3d side
7. $EJ = SK$	7. symm and trans =
8. $\overline{EJ} \cong \overline{SK}$	8. ≅ iff meas =
9. $\overline{EJ} \parallel \overline{SK}$	9. 2 lines ∥ 3d line ∥
10. ∴ *EJSK* ▱	10. quad 1 pr opp sides ∥ and ≅ is ▱

The proof of the next theorem is especially noteworthy because it involves congruent line segments, congruent angles, congruent triangles, parallel lines, and parallelograms. Thus, it brings together and displays the power of much of the theory that we have developed.

Theorem 62 If three parallel lines cut off congruent segments on one transversal, then they cut off congruent segments on every transversal (if 3 ∥ lines cut ≅ segs 1 *t*, then ≅ segs every *t*).

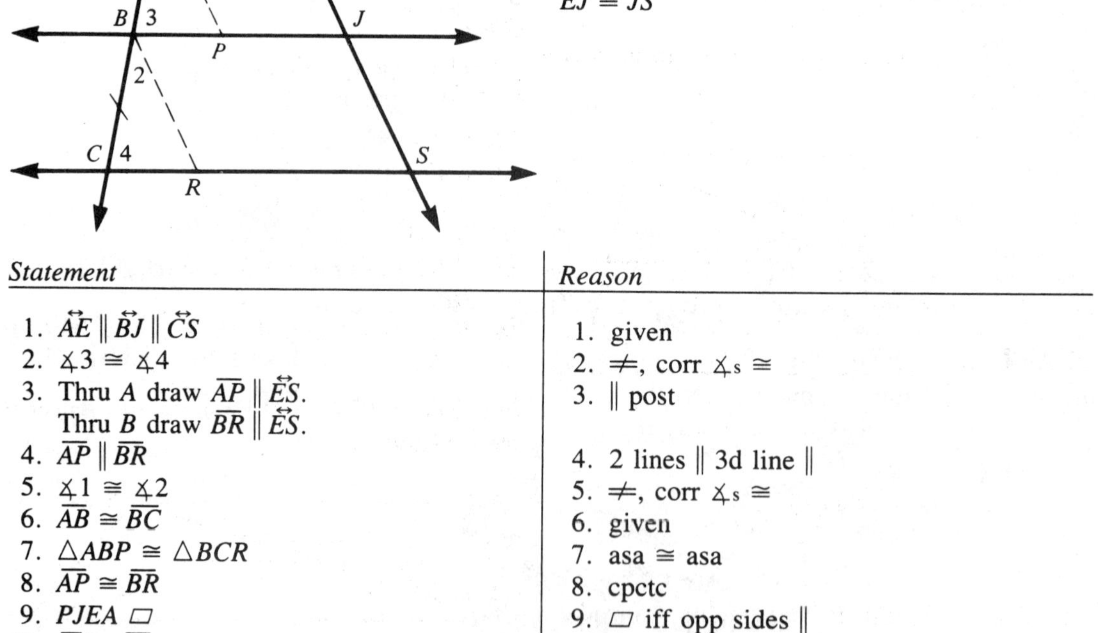

Given
$\overleftrightarrow{AE} \parallel \overleftrightarrow{BJ} \parallel \overleftrightarrow{CS}$
$\overline{AB} \cong \overline{BC}$

To Prove
$\overline{EJ} \cong \overline{JS}$

Statement	Reason
1. $\overleftrightarrow{AE} \parallel \overleftrightarrow{BJ} \parallel \overleftrightarrow{CS}$	1. given
2. ∡3 ≅ ∡4	2. ∦, corr ∡s ≅
3. Thru *A* draw $\overline{AP} \parallel \overleftrightarrow{ES}$. Thru *B* draw $\overline{BR} \parallel \overleftrightarrow{ES}$.	3. ∥ post
4. $\overline{AP} \parallel \overline{BR}$	4. 2 lines ∥ 3d line ∥
5. ∡1 ≅ ∡2	5. ∦, corr ∡s ≅
6. $\overline{AB} \cong \overline{BC}$	6. given
7. △*ABP* ≅ △*BCR*	7. asa ≅ asa
8. $\overline{AP} \cong \overline{BR}$	8. cpctc
9. *PJEA* ▱	9. ▱ iff opp sides ∥
10. $\overline{EJ} \cong \overline{AP}$	10. opp sides ▱ ≅
11. *RSJB* ▱	11. ▱ iff opp sides ∥
12. $\overline{BR} \cong \overline{JS}$	12. opp sides ▱ ≅
13. ∴ $\overline{EJ} \cong \overline{JS}$	13. trans ≅

Theorem 63 is a variation on the ideas involved in Theorem 61. The proof is left as an exercise.

Theorem 63 If a line is parallel to one side of a triangle and bisects a second side, then it bisects the third side also (line ∥ side △ and bis 2d, bis 3d).

EXERCISES FOR 6.5

In exercises 1–4 use Figure 6.11 to answer the questions.

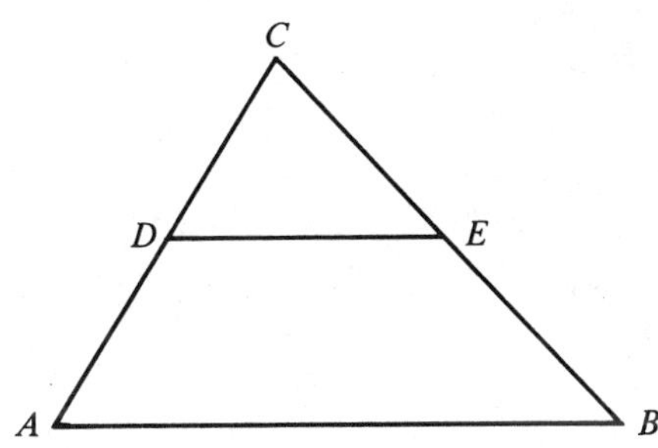

Figure 6.11

Given
D, *E* midpts

1. If DE = 7 in, find AB.
2. If AB = 23 cm, find DE.
3. If AB = $23\frac{3}{8}$ in, find DE.
4. If DE = $17\frac{2}{5}$ in, find AB.

In exercises 5–12 use Figure 6.12 to answer the questions.

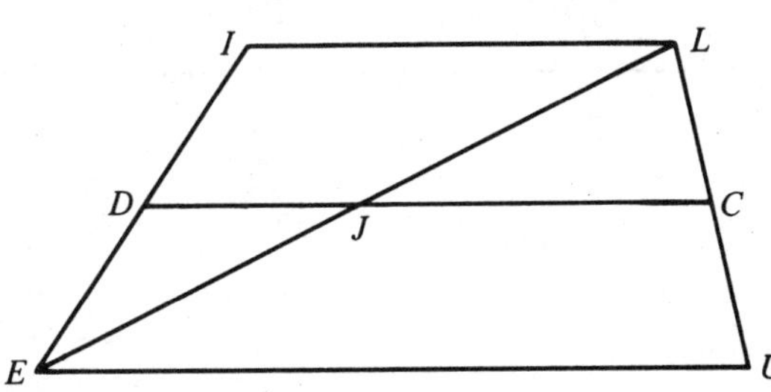

Figure 6.12

Given
trap $EULI$ ($\overline{EU}$, $\overline{IL}$ bases)
D, C midpts, J midpt $\overline{EL}$
$\overline{DC} \parallel \overline{EU}$

5. If IL = 43 cm, find DJ. (Hint: Consider $\triangle ELI$.)
6. If EU = 17 in, find JC. (Hint: Consider $\triangle EUL$.)
7. If JC = 12.5 cm, find EU.
8. If DJ = 6.3 cm, find IL.
9. If EU = 21 in and IL = 16 in, find DC.
10. If EU = 13.7 cm and IL = 5.9 cm, find DC.
11. If EU = $12\frac{1}{2}$ in and DC = $9\frac{5}{8}$ in, find IL.
12. If DC = 26.5 cm and IL = 21.6 cm, find EU.

In exercises 13–18 use Figure 6.13 to answer the questions.

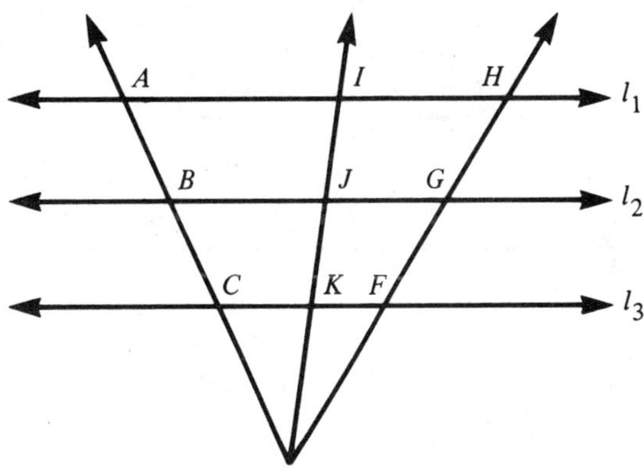

Figure 6.13

Given
$l_1 \parallel l_2 \parallel l_3$
$\overline{IJ} \cong \overline{JK}$

13. If AB = 14 cm, find AC.
14. If FG = $3\frac{1}{4}$ in, find FH.
15. If AC = 36 cm, find BC.
16. If GH = 22 in, find HF.
17. If BC = 4 in and GF = $6\frac{1}{2}$ in, find AC + HF.
18. If AC = 13 cm and HF = 22 cm, find AB + HG.

In exercises 19–25 use Figure 6.14 to answer the questions.

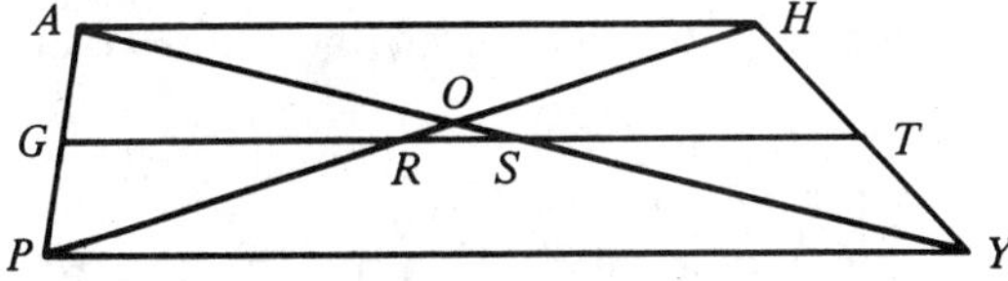

Figure 6.14

Given
trap $PYHA$ ($\overline{PY}$, $\overline{AH}$ bases)
G, T midpts
$\overline{GT} \parallel \overline{PY}$
PY = 24 in
AH = 18 in

19. Find GS.
20. Find RT.
21. Find GR.
22. Find ST.
23. Find RS.
24. Find RS if AH is changed to 12 in.
25. Find RS if PY is changed to 28 in.

In exercises 26–29 use Figure 6.15 to answer the questions.

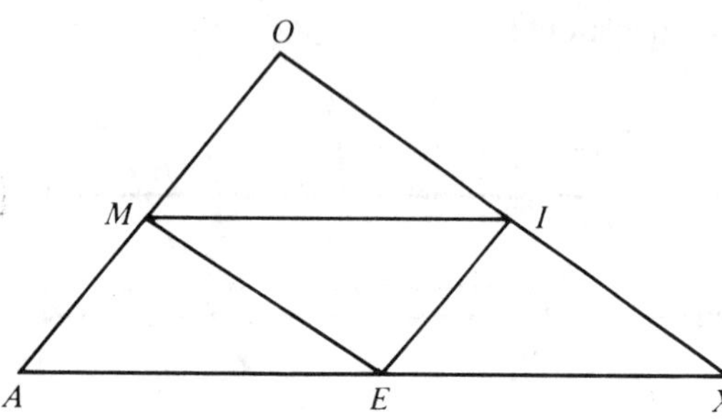

Figure 6.15

Given
E, I, M midpts

26. Find AO if $IE = 23$ cm.
27. Find ME if $OX = 47$ cm.
28. Find the perimeter (sum of lengths of sides) of $\triangle EIM$ if $AX = 12$ in, $XO = 9$ in, and $OA = 5$ in.
29. Find the perimeter of $\triangle AXO$ if $ME = 14$ cm, $EI = 11$ cm, and $IM = 18$ cm.

In exercises 30–32 use Figure 6.16 to answer the questions.

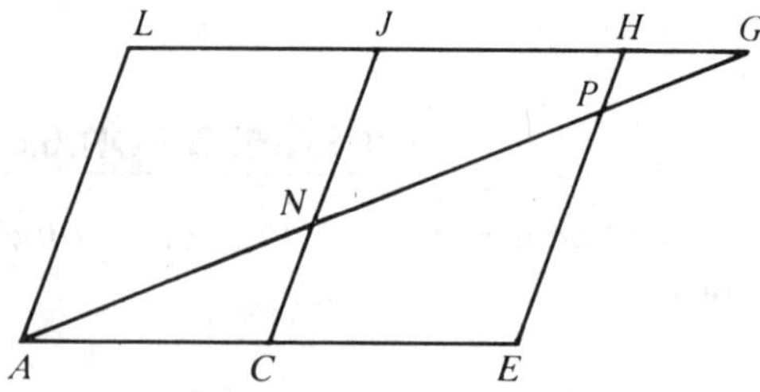

Figure 6.16

Given
$\overline{LA} \parallel \overline{JC} \parallel \overline{HE}$
$AC = CE$
$AP = 28$ cm
$JH = 12$ cm

30. Find LJ.
31. Find AN.
32. Find LH.

In exercises 33–35 use Figure 6.17 to answer the questions.

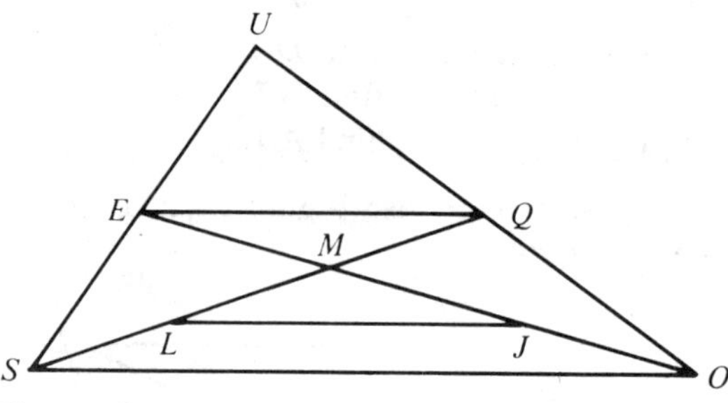

Figure 6.17

Given
$\overline{SQ}$ and $\overline{OE}$ medians
L midpt $\overline{SM}$
J midpt $\overline{OM}$

33. If $EQ = 6$ in, find SO.
34. If $LJ = 15$ cm, find SO.
35. If $SO = 23$ in, find $EQ + LJ$.

In exercises 36 and 37 copy the figure, mark it, and supply the missing reasons in each proof.

36. If a line is parallel to one side of a triangle and bisects a second side, then it bisects the third side also (Theorem 63).

Given
$\overleftrightarrow{KM} \parallel \overline{EJ}$
$\overleftrightarrow{KM}$ bis $\overline{ES}$

To Prove
$\overleftrightarrow{KM}$ bis $\overline{JS}$

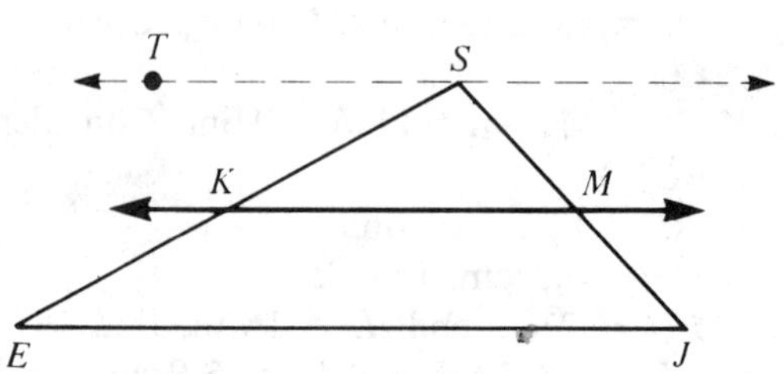

Statement	Reason
1. $\overleftrightarrow{KM} \parallel \overline{EJ}$	1. ?
2. $\overleftrightarrow{KM}$ bis $\overline{ES}$	2. ?
3. $\overline{EK} \cong \overline{KS}$	3. ?
4. Draw $\overleftrightarrow{TS} \parallel \overleftrightarrow{KM}$.	4. ?
5. $\overleftrightarrow{TS} \parallel \overline{EJ}$	5. ?
6. $\overline{JM} \cong \overline{MS}$	6. ?
7. $\therefore \overleftrightarrow{KM}$ bis $\overline{JS}$	7. ?

37. If a line is parallel to one base of a trapezoid and bisects a nonparallel side, then the line bisects the other nonparallel side also (compare with exercise 36).

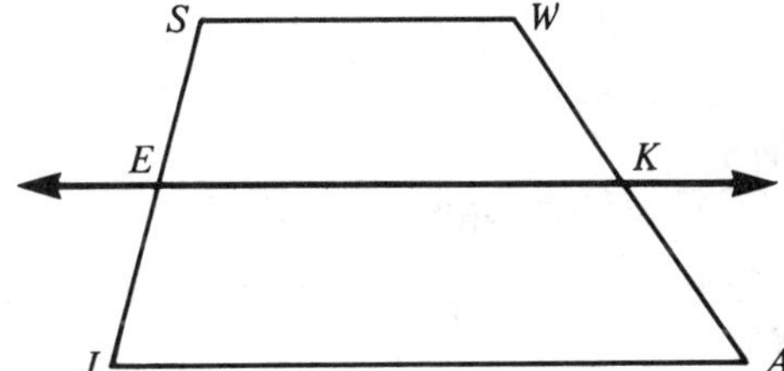

Given
trap *JAWS* ($\overline{JA}$, $\overline{SW}$ bases)
$\overleftrightarrow{EK} \parallel \overline{JA}$
$\overleftrightarrow{EK}$ bis $\overline{JS}$

To Prove
$\overleftrightarrow{EK}$ bis $\overline{AW}$

Statement	Reason
1. trap *JAWS* ($\overline{JA}$, $\overline{SW}$ bases)	1. ?
2. $\overline{JA} \parallel \overline{SW}$	2. ?
3. $\overleftrightarrow{EK} \parallel \overline{JA}$	3. ?
4. $\overleftrightarrow{EK} \parallel \overline{SW}$	4. ?
5. $\overleftrightarrow{EK}$ bis $\overline{JS}$	5. ?
6. $\overline{JE} \cong \overline{ES}$	6. ?
7. $\overline{AK} \cong \overline{KW}$	7. ?
8. $\therefore \overleftrightarrow{EK}$ bis $\overline{AW}$	8. ?

In exercises 38–46 copy the figure, the hypothesis, and the conclusion. Mark the figure and write a proof.

38. *Given*
$\overline{SQ}$ median
$\overline{OE}$ median
L midpt $\overline{SM}$
J midpt $\overline{OM}$

To Prove
$\overline{EQ} \parallel \overline{LJ}$

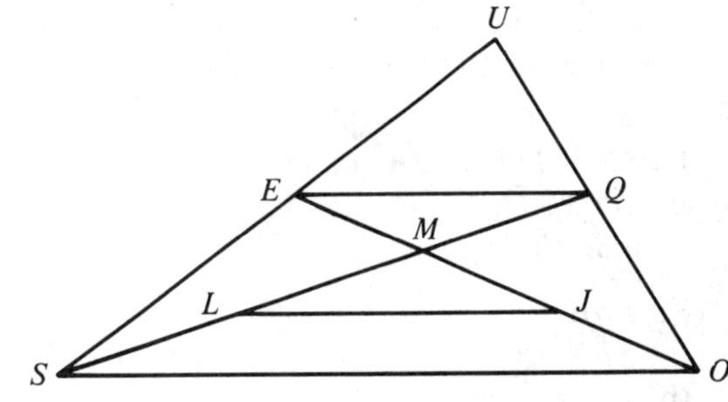

39. *Given*
quad *PTAO* with midpts *R, Y, H, G*

To Prove
$\overline{GH} \cong \overline{RY}$

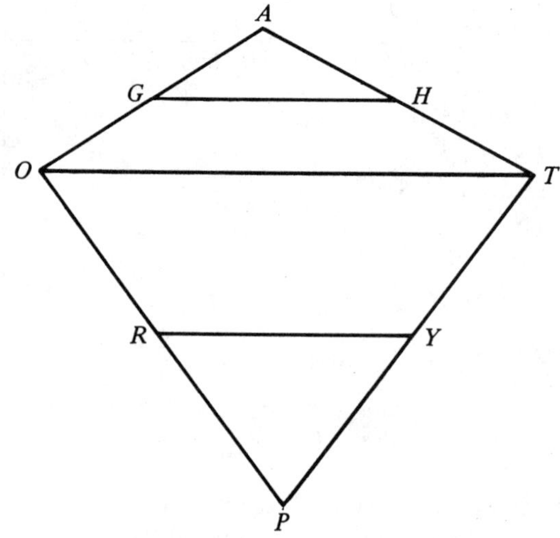

40. *Given*
rh *POST* with midpts *D, R, A, G*

To Prove
DRAG rect

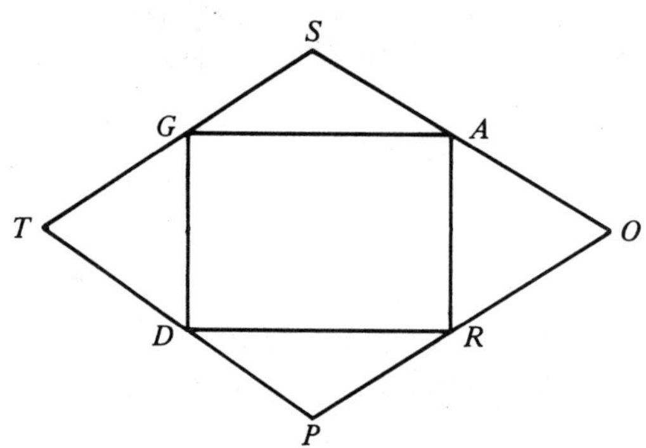

41. *Given*
isos trap *ABCD* ($\overline{AB}$, $\overline{DC}$ bases)

To Prove
$\overline{AC} \cong \overline{BD}$

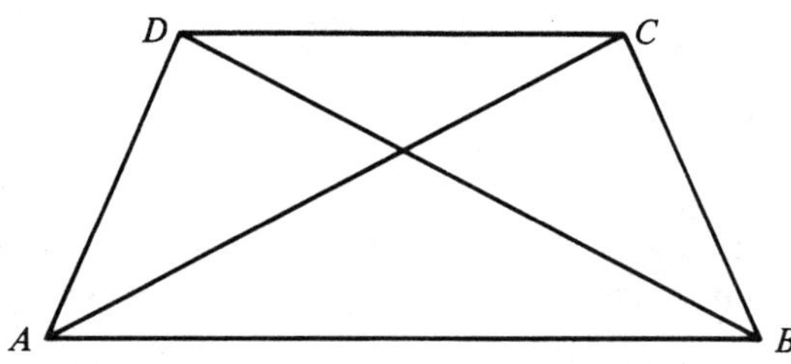

42. *Given*
isos trap *GOLD* ($\overline{GO}$, $\overline{DL}$ bases)
$\overline{EL} \cong \overline{RD}$
∡5 comp ∡4

To Prove
GORE rect

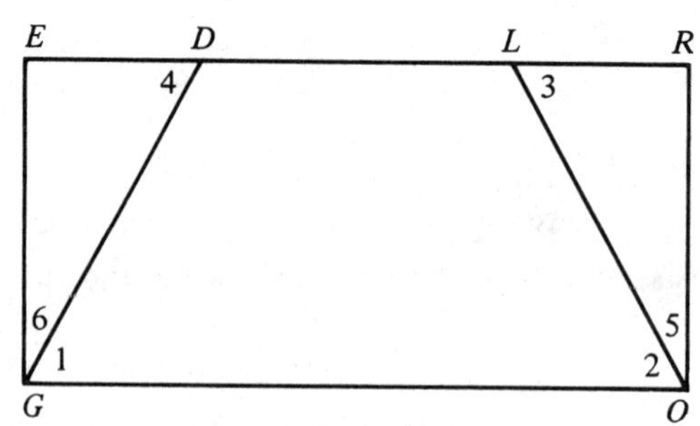

43. *Given*
trap *ABCD* ($\overline{AB}$, $\overline{DC}$ bases)
E midpt $\overline{AD}$
F midpt $\overline{BC}$

To Prove
(a) $\overline{EF} \parallel \overline{AB}$
(b) $EF = \frac{1}{2}(AB + DC)$

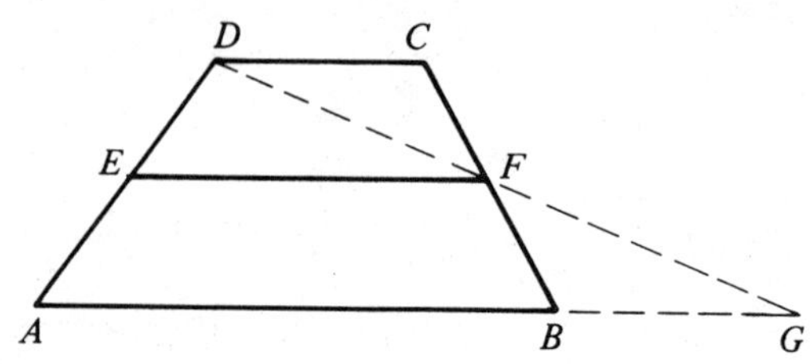

44. *Given*
isos trap $CORD$ ($\overline{CO}$, $\overline{DR}$ bases)
A midpt $\overline{CO}$
$\overline{DR} \cong \overline{AO}$
$\overline{CR}$ bis $\measuredangle C$

To Prove
$\overline{CR} \perp \overline{RO}$

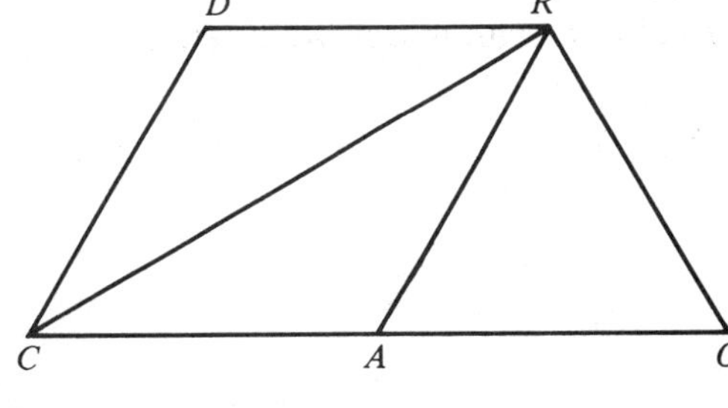

45. *Given*
$\triangle AIM$ with midpts X, O, E

To Prove
$\triangle XOE \cong \triangle MEO$

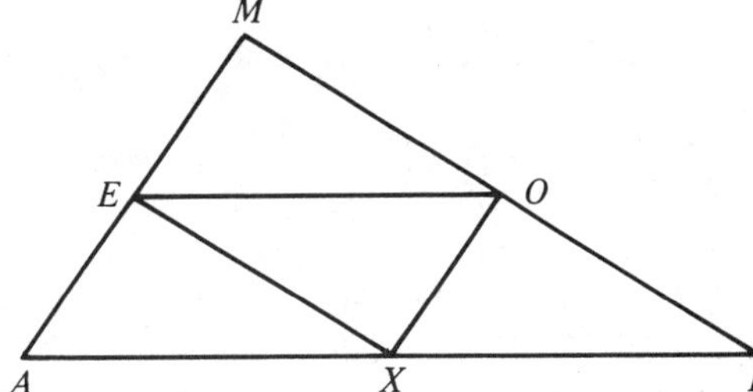

46. *Given*
L midpt $\overline{TA}$
O midpt $\overline{TN}$
V midpt $\overline{GN}$
E midpt $\overline{GA}$

To Prove
$LOVE$ ▱

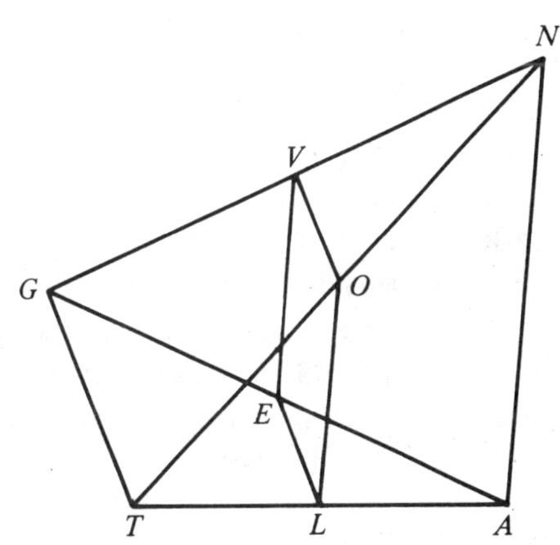

6.6

POLYGONS HAVING MORE THAN FOUR SIDES

If we were to continue our pattern in which each new figure studied contains one more line, then we would study figures containing five lines next. Instead, this section surveys several concepts concerning an entire family of figures: polygons. This progression of study works well because most problems about polygons can be solved using properties that have been developed for triangles and quadrilaterals. The definition of a polygon is a generalization of Definition 6.1 for quadrilaterals.

Definition 6.9 The union of line segments E_1E_2, E_2E_3, . . ., $E_{n-1}E_n$, E_nE_1 is a *polygon* iff E_1, E_2, . . ., E_n are coplanar points ($n > 2$) no three of which are collinear and each segment intersects exactly two others, one at each endpoint.

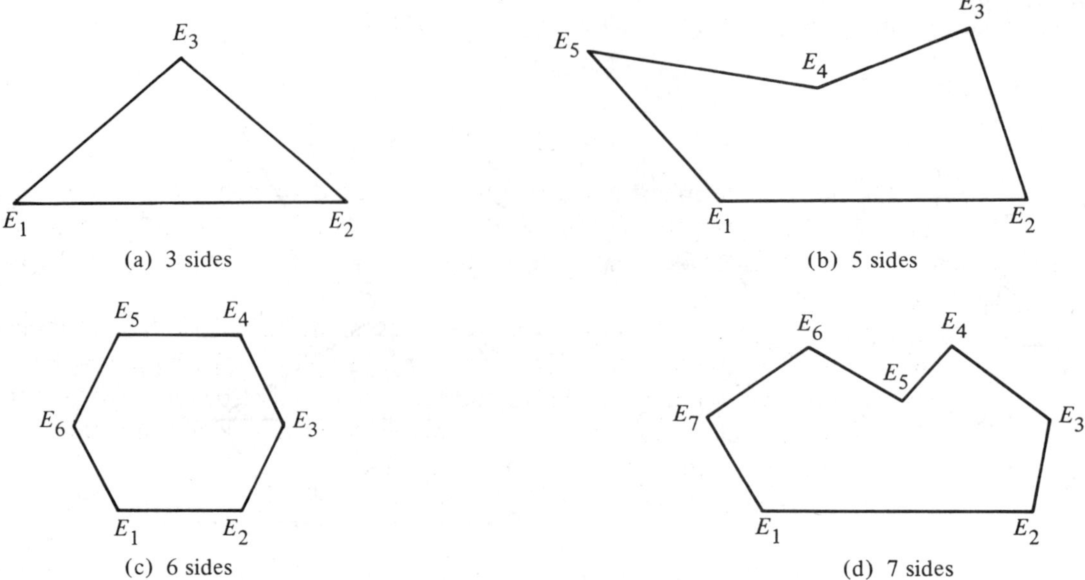

Figure 6.18

This definition looks imposing because it includes all n-sided polygons where $n > 2$. Thus, triangles ($n = 3$) and quadrilaterals ($n = 4$) are polygons. Figure 6.18 should clarify the definition. The subscript notation E_1, E_2, ... allows for polygons containing any number of sides greater than or equal to 3. Polygons with more than 26 sides, however, rarely occur so we use different letters to name polygons. To further clarify Definition 6.9 note that a set of n points ($n > 3$) may be joined to form figures that are *not* n-sided polygons. Two examples are shown in Figure 6.19.

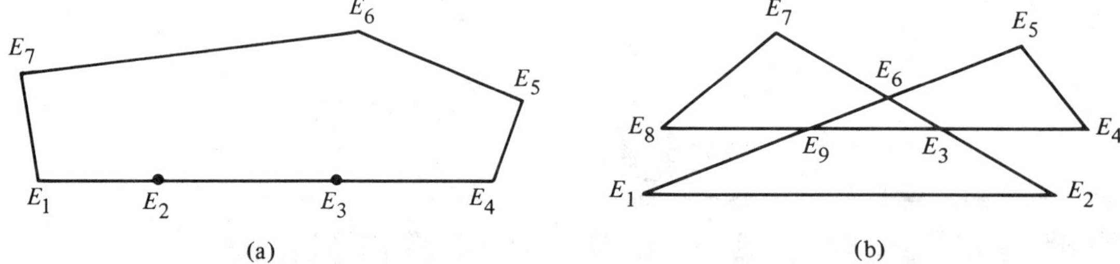

Figure 6.19 (a) Four points collinear. (b) Some sides intersect more than two others.

The terms *side, angle, vertex, consecutive vertices,* and *consecutive sides,* have the same meanings for polygons in general as they do for quadrilaterals. A *diagonal* of a polygon is a line segment joining any two nonconsecutive vertices. Figure 6.18(a) and (c) are *convex* polygons while (b) and (d) are *concave* polygons. Since convex polygons are by far the more important type, *we will use the term polygon to mean convex polygon unless otherwise stated.*

Special names are given to the most important polygons, according to the number of their sides as follows:

triangle	three sides
quadrilateral	four sides
pentagon	five sides
hexagon	six sides

heptagon	seven sides
octagon	eight sides
nonagon	nine sides
decagon	ten sides
dodecagon	twelve sides

The general term "n-gon" is sometimes used to name a polygon of n sides. This suggests the simple naming scheme of 3-gon, 4-gon, 5-gon, and so forth. These forms, however, are not normally used for the special cases listed above.

Polygons variously appear in architecture and design work. The Pentagon building in Washington, D.C., is a famous example. Highway signs are triangles, squares, rectangles, and octagons. Polygons also appear in nature. They may be seen in spider webs, bee hives, the wings of certain flies, and the crystalline structure of rocks and minerals.

Definition 6.10 describes an important special type of polygon.

Definition 6.10 A polygon is a *regular polygon* iff its sides are congruent and its angles are congruent (reg poly iff sides ≅ and ∡s ≅).

An equilateral triangle is also equiangular and so it is a regular polygon of three sides. A rectangle has all four of its angles congruent but it is not, in general, regular because its four sides are not usually congruent. The special rectangle called a square, however, is a regular polygon having four sides. A rhombus is not, in general, regular because its four angles are not usually congruent, although its four sides are. Example 1 is a proof involving a regular pentagon.

EXAMPLE 1

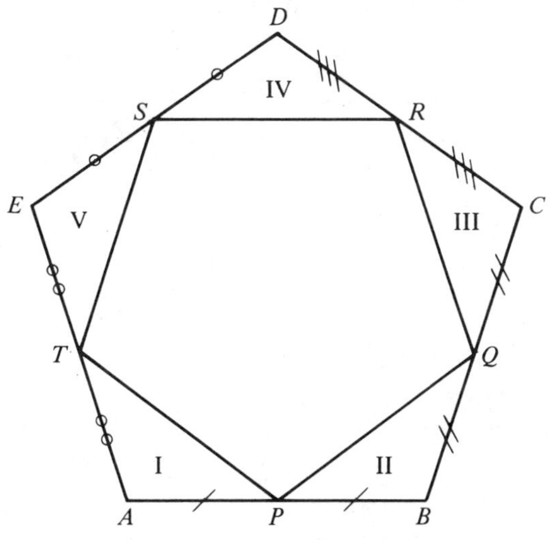

Given
ABCDE reg pentagon
P, Q, R, S, T midpts

To Prove
$\overline{TP} \cong \overline{PQ} \cong \overline{QR} \cong \overline{RS} \cong \overline{ST} \cong \overline{TP}$

Statement	*Reason*
1. *ABCDE* reg pentagon	1. given
2. $\measuredangle A \cong \measuredangle B \cong \measuredangle C \cong \measuredangle D \cong \measuredangle E$ $\overline{AB} \cong \overline{BC} \cong \overline{CD} \cong \overline{DE} \cong \overline{EA}$	2. reg poly iff sides ≅ and ∡s ≅
3. *P, Q, R, S, T* midpts	3. given

4. $\overline{AP} \cong \overline{PB}$, $\overline{BQ} \cong \overline{QC}$, $\overline{CR} \cong \overline{RD}$, $\overline{DS} \cong \overline{SE}$, $\overline{ET} \cong \overline{TA}$	4. midpt $\div$ seg into 2 $\cong$ segs
5. $\overline{AP} \cong \overline{PB} \cong \overline{BQ} \cong \overline{QC} \cong \overline{CR} \cong \overline{RD} \cong \overline{DS} \cong \overline{SE} \cong \overline{ET} \cong \overline{TA}$	5. $\frac{1}{2}$s of $\cong$ are $\cong$
6. $\triangle I \cong \triangle II \cong \triangle III \cong \triangle IV \cong \triangle V$	6. sas $\cong$ sas
7. $\therefore \overline{TP} \cong \overline{PQ} \cong \overline{QR} \cong \overline{RS} \cong \overline{ST}$	7. cpctc

Example 1 proves that *PQRST* is an equilateral pentagon. Is it also equiangular? If so, it is a regular pentagon. We now examine how to verify that this is indeed the case.

Figure 6.20 shows a hexagon divided into four triangles by the three diagonals from vertex *E*. It is clear that the sum of the angles of the hexagon is equal to the sum of the angles of the four triangles. This number is $4 \cdot 180° = 720°$ because the sum of the angles of each triangle is 180°. Note also that the number of triangles is 2 less than the number of sides.

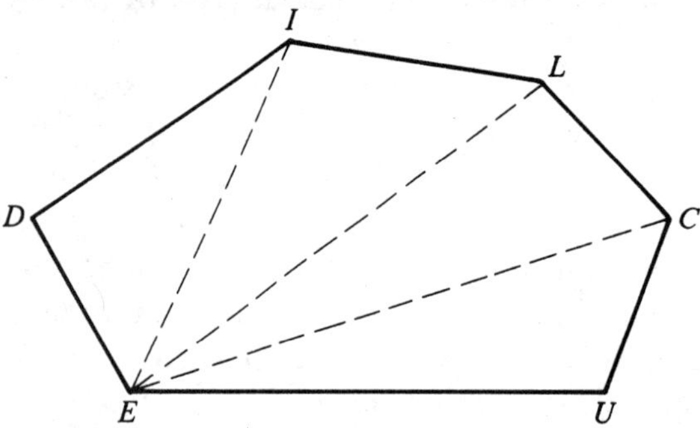

Figure 6.20

EXAMPLE 2 Find the sum of the measures of the angles in any octagon.

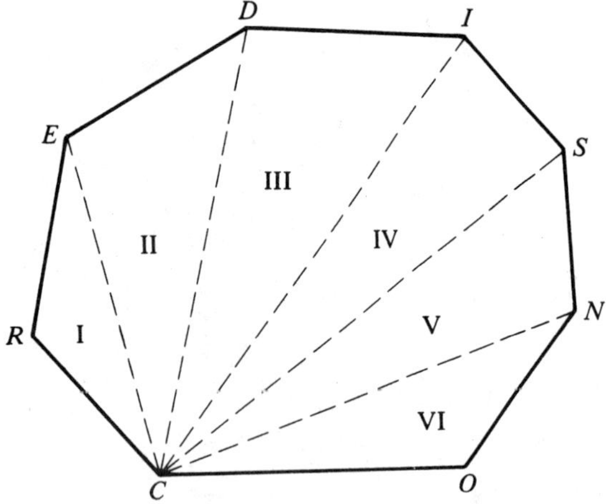

Answer

Octagon *CONSIDER* is divided into $8 - 2 = 6$ triangles by its diagonals from vertex *C*. Hence, the sum of its angles is $6 \cdot 180° = 1080°$.

Our discussion and Example 2 suggest that the diagonals from a vertex of an *n*-gon divide it into $(n - 2)$ triangles. This fact is the basis for theorem 64. The proof is omitted.

Theorem 64 The sum of the measures of the angles of an n-gon is $(n - 2) \cdot 180°$ ((n-2) 180° in reg poly).

This theorem is applied to a few cases in the table of polygons. Note the theorem's consistency with the previously proved results for triangles and quadrilaterals.

Polygon	Number of sides (n)	Sum of the Angles $(n - 2) \cdot 180°$
Triangle	3	$(3 - 2) \cdot 180° = 180°$
Quadrilateral	4	$(4 - 2) \cdot 180° = 360°$
Pentagon	5	$(5 - 2) \cdot 180° = 540°$
Hexagon	6	$(6 - 2) \cdot 180° = 720°$
Heptagon	7	$(7 - 2) \cdot 180° = 900°$
Octagon	8	$(8 - 2) \cdot 180° = 1080°$

EXAMPLE 3

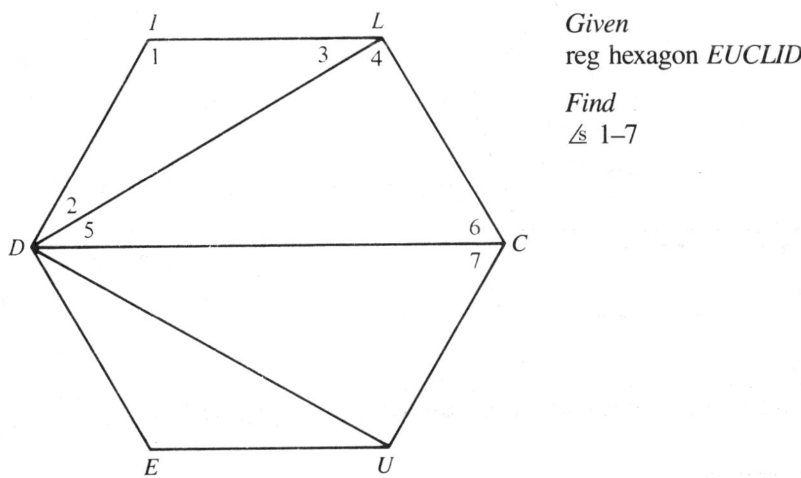

Given
reg hexagon *EUCLID*

Find
∡s 1–7

Answer

i. A regular hexagon has six congruent angles; hence, $\angle 1 = 720° \div 6 = 120°$.
ii. A regular hexagon has six congruent sides; hence, $\overline{DI} \cong \overline{LI}$ and $\angle 2 = \angle 3$. Also, $\angle 2 + \angle 3 = 180° - 120° = 60°$, so that $\angle 2 = \angle 3 = 30°$.
iii. $\angle 4 = 120° - 30° = 90°$.
iv. Since $\triangle UED \cong \triangle LID$ (why?), it follows that $\triangle UDC \cong \triangle LDC$ (sss ≅ sss) and $\angle 6 = \angle 7$. Also, $\angle 6 + \angle 7 = 120°$, so that $\angle 6 = \angle 7 = 60°$.
v. $\angle 5 = 180° - \angle 4 - \angle 6 = 180° - 90° - 60° = 30°$.

Figure 6.21 shows a regular hexagon and six of its *exterior angles*, ∡s 1–6. Since each of its (interior) angles measures 120° (Example 3), it follows that ∡s 1–6 each measure 60°, and that $\angle 1 + \angle 2 + \angle 3 + \angle 4 + \angle 5 + \angle 6 = 360°$. Although we omit the proof, it is true that the sum of n exterior angles of any n-gon is always 360°. This fact is further developed in the exercises for this section.

This section concludes with an important type of figure that contains more than four lines and is not a polygon. It involves a generalization of Theorem 62. If four or more parallel lines cut off congruent segments on one transversal, then they cut off congruent segments on every transversal. Although we will not prove this fact, it is applied in Example 4.

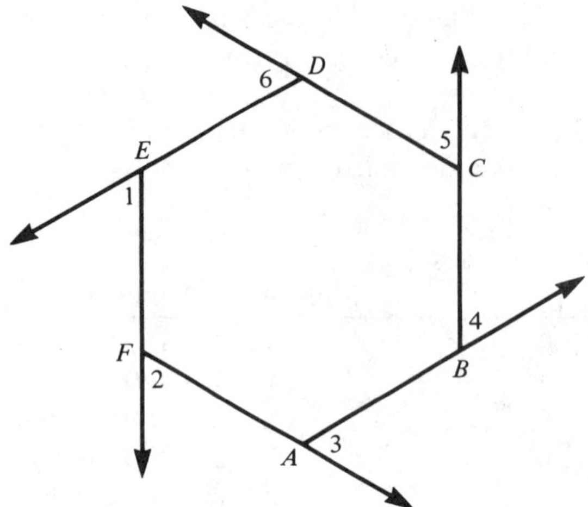

Figure 6.21

EXAMPLE 4

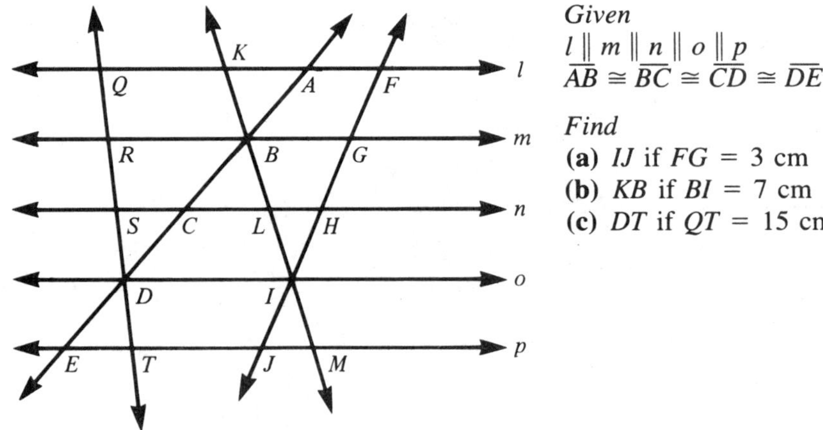

Given
$l \parallel m \parallel n \parallel o \parallel p$
$\overline{AB} \cong \overline{BC} \cong \overline{CD} \cong \overline{DE}$

Find
(a) IJ if $FG = 3$ cm
(b) KB if $BI = 7$ cm
(c) DT if $QT = 15$ cm

Answers
(a) $IJ = 3$ cm
(b) $KB = 7 \div 2 = 3.5$ cm
(c) $DT = 15 \div 4 = 3.75$ cm

Another application of Theorem 62 and its generalization described is shown in Construction 12. Any given line segment may be divided into two or more congruent parts using only a compass and straightedge. We demonstrate this for five parts, but the steps are indicated for any number n of congruent parts.

Construction 12 To divide a given line segment into n congruent parts ($n = 5$ is shown).

Given
line seg $\overline{AB}$

To Construct
points C, D, E, F such that
$\overline{AC} \cong \overline{CD} \cong \overline{DE} \cong \overline{EF} \cong \overline{FB}$

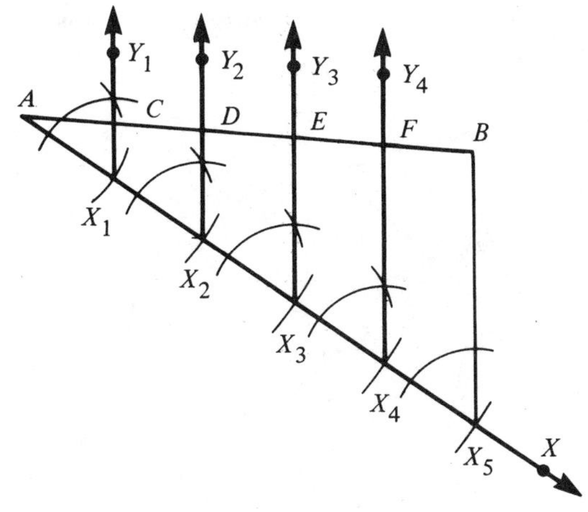

Steps

1. Draw any $\overrightarrow{AX}$.
2. With A as center and a convenient radius, mark an arc intersecting $\overrightarrow{AX}$. This determines point X_1. Repeat the process using X_1 as center and the *same* radius to determine point X_2.
3. Continue step 2 until n points, X_1, X_2, up to X_n, are determined.
4. Draw $\overline{BX_n}$.
5. Copy $\measuredangle AX_nB$ at each of the other X points as vertices (Construction 4). This determines rays $\overrightarrow{X_1Y_1}$, $\overrightarrow{X_2Y_2}$ and so on.
6. The intersections of the rays in step 5 with $\overline{AB}$ are the required points.

EXERCISES FOR 6.6

In exercises 1–20 answer true or false.

1. If four parallel lines cut off segments each 6 inches long on one transversal, they cut off segments each 6 inches long on any transversal.
2. A triangle is a polygon.
3. In a pentagon three diagonals can be drawn from any vertex.
4. A rhombus is a regular quadrilateral.
5. In hexagon $SOQUEL$, $\overline{QU}$ and $\overline{EL}$ are consecutive sides.
6. A pentagon has exactly five diagonals.
7. If four angles of a pentagon measure 121°12′13″, 83°15′49″, 101°37′44″, and 93°19′7″, then the fifth measures 139°35′7″.
8. The sum of the measures of the exterior angles of an equilateral triangle is 180°.
9. In regular hexagon $OBTUSE$, $\angle B = 108°$.
10. A hexagon is formed when any six points in a plane are joined by line segments.
11. An exterior angle of a regular pentagon measures 72°.
12. The sum of the angles of a heptagon is 900°.
13. The sum of the angles of an octagon is 1440°.
14. There exists an equiangular quadrilateral that is not a regular polygon.
15. If one angle of a regular polygon measures 135°, the polygon is a decagon.
16. Exactly three diagonals can be drawn from one vertex of a hexagon.
17. If an exterior angle of a regular polygon measures 40°, the polygon is a decagon.
18. It is possible to draw twenty different diagonals in an octagon.
19. If each interior angle of a regular polygon measures 140°, then the polygon is a nonagon.
20. There are 36° in the angle formed by the two diagonals drawn from one vertex in a regular pentagon.

In exercises 21 and 22 use Figure 6.22 to answer the questions.

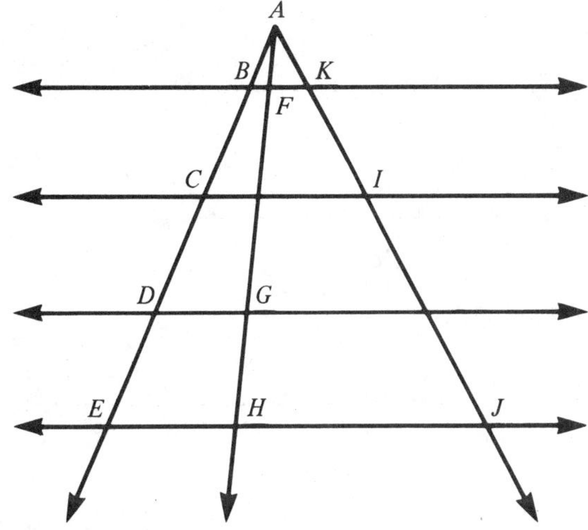

Figure 6.22

Given
$\overleftrightarrow{BF} \parallel \overleftrightarrow{CI} \parallel \overleftrightarrow{DG} \parallel \overleftrightarrow{EJ}$
$\overline{BC} \cong \overline{CD} \cong \overline{DE}$
$KJ = 36$ in
$GH = 10$ in

21. If $BC = 11$ in, find the sum $CE + FG$.
22. If $BC = 13$ in, find the sum $BD + IJ$.

In exercises 23 and 24 use Figure 6.23 to answer the questions.

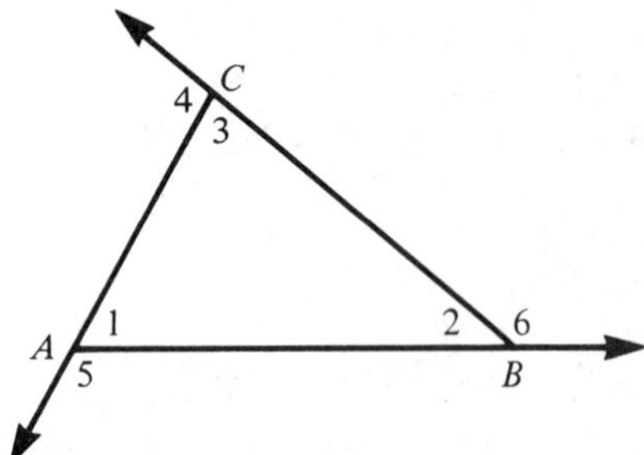

Figure 6.23

23. Write each of the following as the sum of two angle measures: (a) $\angle 4$, (b) $\angle 5$, and (c) $\angle 6$.

24. Using the answers to exercise 23 and the sum of the measures of the angles of a triangle, find the sum $\angle 4 + \angle 5 + \angle 6$.

In exercises 25–28 use Figure 6.24 to answer the questions.

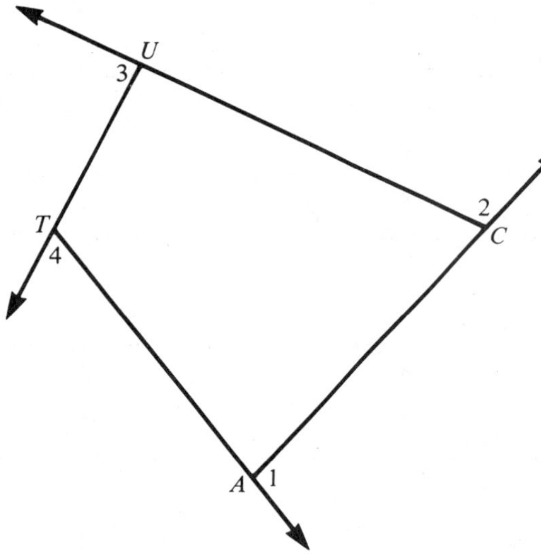

Figure 6.24

Given
quad *ACUT*
$\angle CAT = 82°23'$
$\angle ACU = 71°42'$
$\angle CUT = 92°17'$

25. How many diagonals can be drawn from *C*?

26. How many different diagonals can be drawn in the quadrilateral *ACUT*?

27. Find $\angle UTA$.

28. Find the sum $\angle 1 + \angle 2 + \angle 3 + \angle 4$.

In exercises 29–32 use Figure 6.25 to answer the questions.

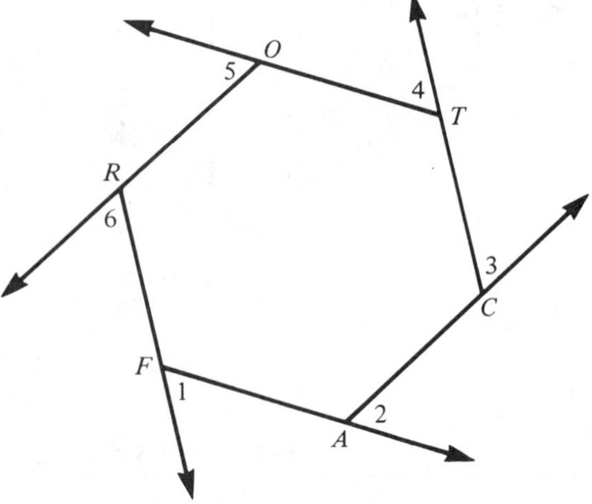

Figure 6.25

Given
regular hexagon *FACTOR*

29. Find $\angle ACT$.

30. How many diagonals can be drawn from *R*?

31. Find the sum $\angle 1 + \angle 2 + \angle 3 + \angle 4 + \angle 5 + \angle 6$.

32. According to your answers to exercises 24, 28, and 31, what does the sum of the exterior angles of a polygon appear to be? Is this always true?

In exercises 33–40 copy the figure, mark it, and find the requested measures.

33. *Given*
reg pentagon *APTOS*

Find
$\measuredangle$s 1–10

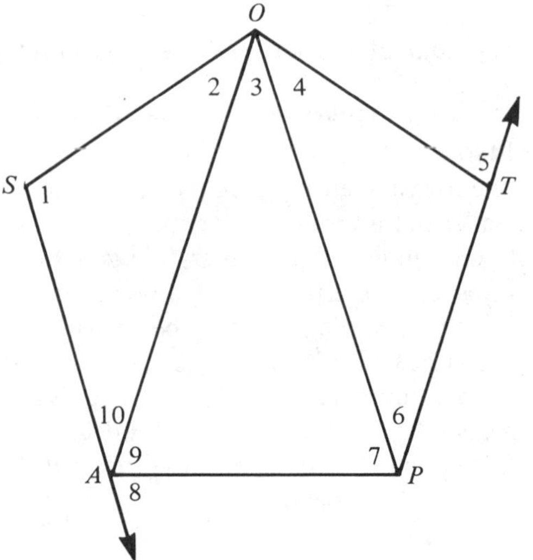

34. *Given*
reg hexagon *SOQUEL*

Find
∡s 1–10

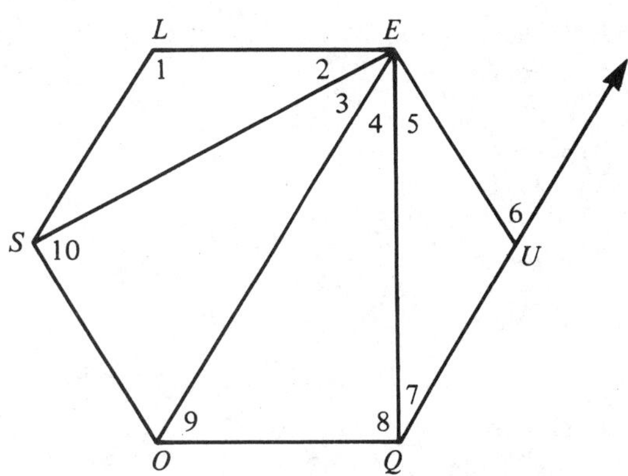

35. *Given*
▱*STOP*
$\overline{SJ}$ bis ∡*PST*
$\overline{TJ}$ bis ∡*STO*
$\overline{OK}$ bis ∡*TOP*
$\overline{PK}$ bis ∡*OPS*
∠*KPS* = 57°

Find
∡s 1–10

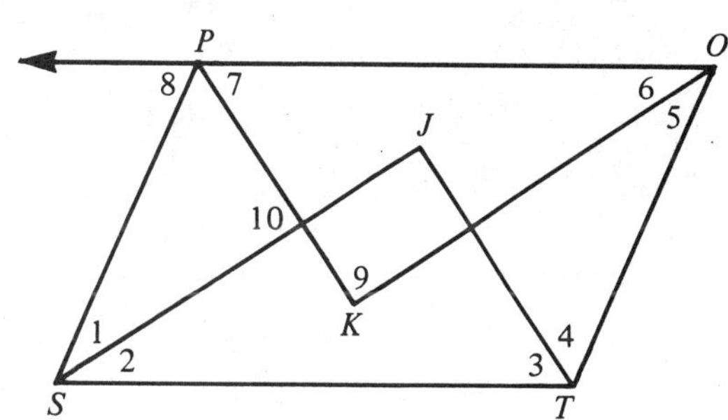

36. *Given*
reg octagon *TRIANGLE*
∡*REI* ≅ ∡*AEN*

Find
∡s 1–10

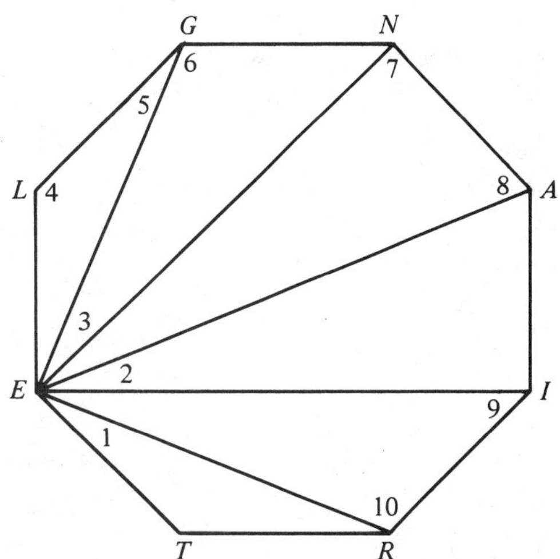

37. *Given*
rect *JAWS* with midpts *T*, *R*, *I*, *M*
∠*JTM* = 53°15′

Find
∡s 1–10

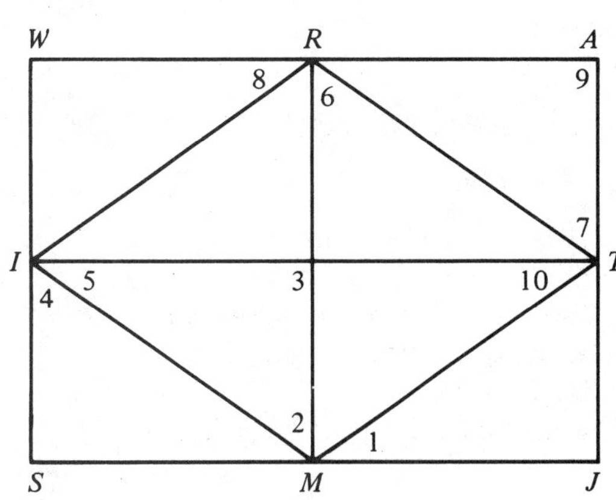

38. *Given*
▱$ECLD$
$\overline{IU} \parallel \overline{LC}$
$\angle DEL = 37°15'$
$\angle LDO = 47°$
$\angle LCE = 114°$
Find
$\angle$s 1–10

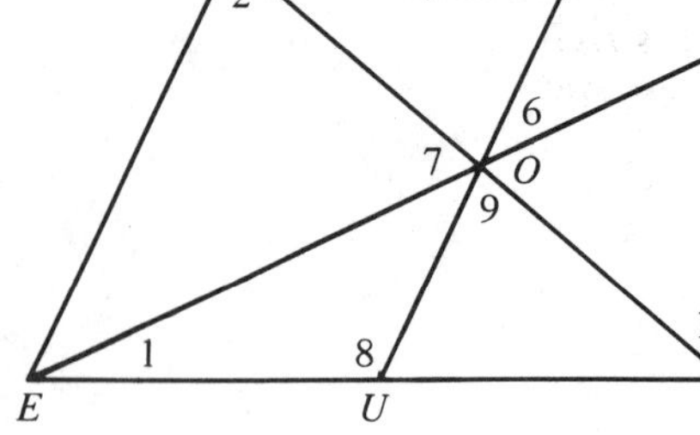

39. *Given*
reg pentagon $APTOS$

Find
$\angle$s 1–10

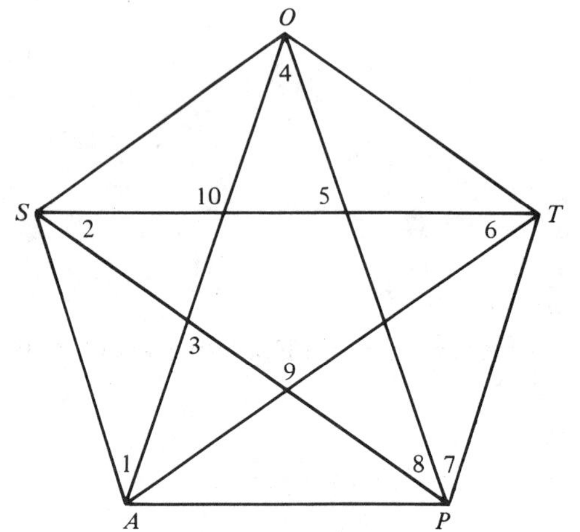

40. *Given*
reg pentagon $ANGEL$ with midpts T, R, I, M, S

Find
$\angle$s 1–10

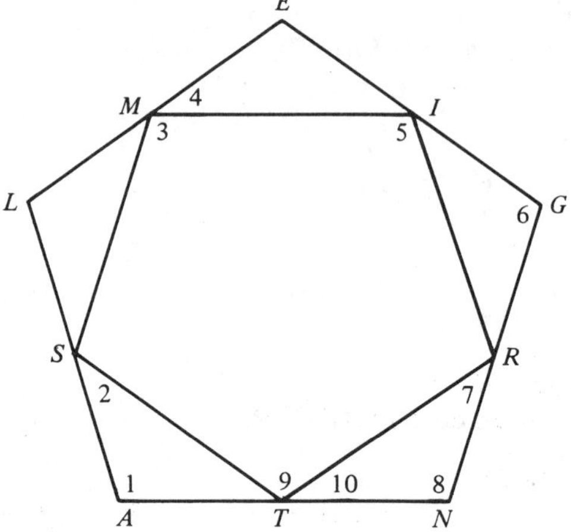

In exercises 41–45 copy the figure, the hypothesis, and the conclusion. Mark the figure and write a proof.

41. *Given*
reg hexagon $OBTUSE$

To Prove
$\overline{EU} \perp \overline{UT}$

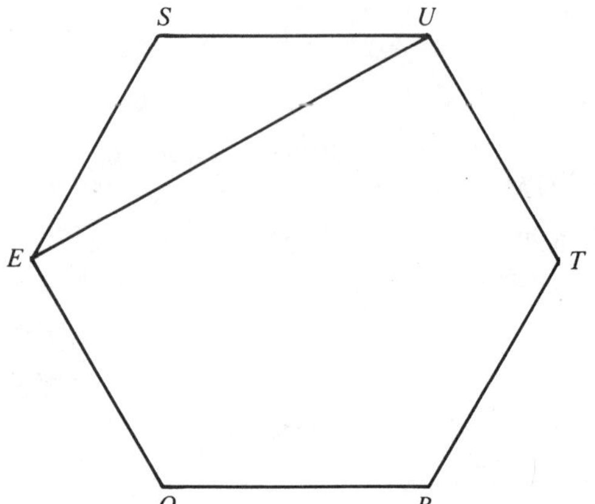

42. *Given*
reg pentagon $ANGLE$
$\overline{OJ} \perp$ bis $\overline{NG}$
$\overline{OK} \perp$ bis $\overline{AN}$

To Prove
$\measuredangle 1 \cong \measuredangle 2$

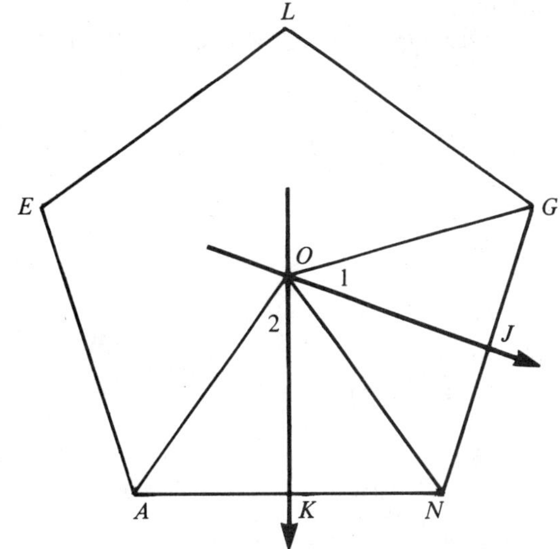

43. *Given*
reg pentagon $ACUTE$ with midpts G, I, V, O, N

To Prove
pentagon $GIVON$ equiang

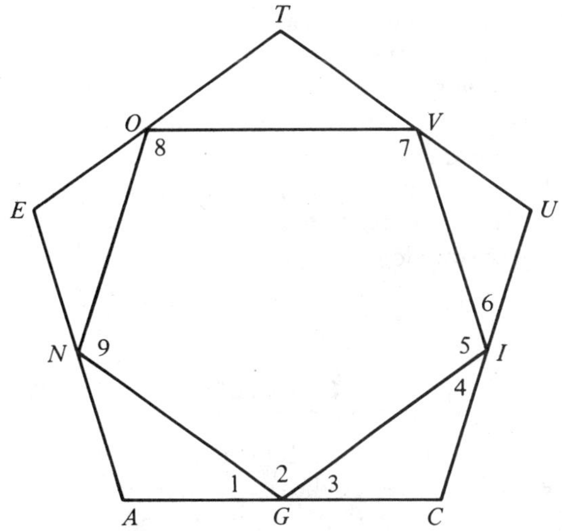

44. *Given*
reg hexagon $FACTOR$

To Prove
$\angle 1 + \angle 2 + \angle 3 + \angle 4 + \angle 5 + \angle 6 = 360°$

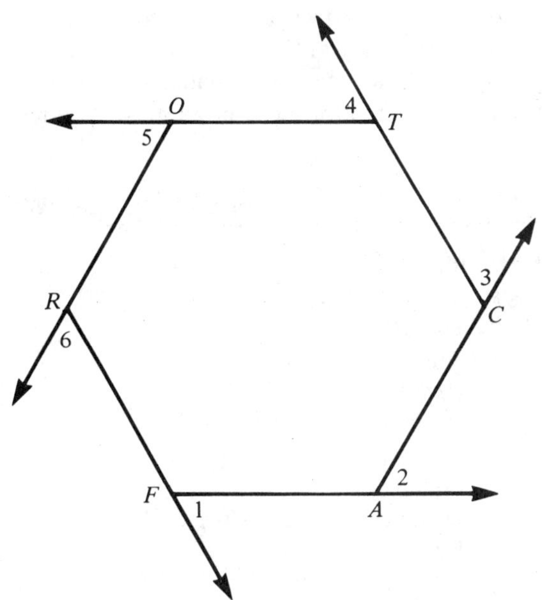

45. *Given*
reg hexagon *EUCLID* with midpts *W*, *A*, *T*, *S*, *O*, *N*

To Prove
WATSON equiang

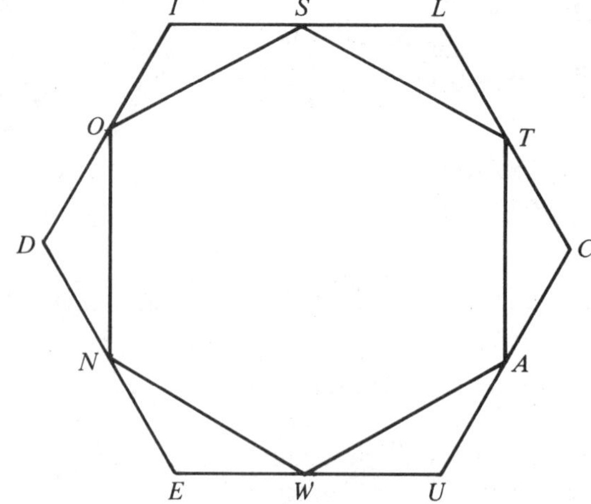

In exercises 46–50 use only a compass and straightedge.

46. Draw a line segment $\overline{AB}$ and divide it into five congruent parts (see Construction 12).

47. Draw a line segment $\overline{AB}$ and divide it into four congruent parts using the method of Construction 12.

48. Draw a line segment $\overline{AB}$ and divide it into four congruent parts using a geometric construction that is different from Construction 12.

49. (a) Construct a right triangle and trisect (divide into three congruent parts) the hypotenuse. (b) Draw line segments from the trisection points to the opposite vertex. Does this trisect the right angle?

50. (a) Draw an obtuse triangle and trisect the longest side. (b) Draw line segments from the trisection points to the opposite vertex. Does this trisect the obtuse angle?

CHAPTER 6 SUMMARY

Among the polygons with more than three sides, the quadrilateral is the most important, and special types such as rectangles and squares have many practical uses. To show that a quadrilateral is in fact a special type leads us to a detailed study of the parallelogram and its properties. Extensive use is made of congruent triangles to establish these properties. Among the polygons with more than four sides, the most useful are the regular ones. Finally, facts about congruent triangles and parallelograms enable us to prove interesting properties about midpoint lines in triangles and segments cut off of transversals by three or more parallel lines.

FACTS TO KNOW

1. Definitions
- **a.** Quadrilateral
- **b.** Diagonal
- **c.** Trapezoid
- **d.** Parallelogram
- **e.** Rhombus
- **f.** Rectangle
- **g.** Square
- **h.** Distance between two parallel lines
- **i.** Polygon
- **j.** Regular polygon

2. Theorems
- **a.** 360° in quad
- **b.** opp sides ▱ $\cong$
- **c.** opp ∡s ▱ $\cong$
- **d.** consec ∡s ▱ supp
- **e.** diags ▱ bis ea other
- **f.** if lines $\parallel$, $\perp$ seg $\cong$
- **g.** rect has 4 rt ∡s
- **h.** diags rect $\cong$
- **i.** rh has 4 $\cong$ sides
- **j.** diags rh bis ∡s

k. diags rh ⊥
l. quad opp sides ≅ is ▱
m. quad 1 pr opp sides ∥ and ≅ is ▱
n. ▱ diags ≅ is rect
o. ▱ diags ⊥ is rh
p. base ∡s isos trap ≅
q. midpt seg △ $\frac{1}{2}$ of and ∥ to 3d side
r. if 3 ∥ lines cut ≅ segs 1 *t*, then ≅ segs every *t*
s. line ∥ side △ and bis 2d side, bis 3d
t. sum ∡s *n*-gon is $(n - 2) \cdot 180°$

PROBLEMS TO MASTER

1. Recognize properties possessed by given types of quadrilaterals.
2. Prove that a quadrilateral is a special type.
3. Find the degree measures of angles in figures containing polygons.
4. Use facts about congruent triangles and quadrilaterals to write proofs.
5. Using a geometric construction, divide a line segment into two or more congruent parts.

7

CIRCLES

MAJOR TOPICS

- ⊙ The circle and associated arcs, lines, and angles
- ⊙ Degree measure of arcs
- ⊙ Properties relating central angles, arcs, and chords
- ⊙ Measures of inscribed angles and their arcs
- ⊙ Measures of angles and arcs formed by chords, tangents, and secants

HISTORICAL NOTE

NON-EUCLIDEAN GEOMETRIES

The story of the rise of non-Euclidean geometries is one of frustration and failure leading—after years of struggle—to ultimate success. The rejection in the early nineteenth century of the achievements of Lobachevski and Bolyai was the last defeat. Acceptance of their work, as is often the case, came soon after their deaths. Since that breakthrough, mathematicians have worked with skill and determination to place Euclidean geometry within the setting of a larger and more versatile geometric theory. As we have seen, the key that unlocked the door was Euclid's Parallel Postulate.

The assumption by Gauss, Lobachevski, and Bolyai, that through a point not on a line there is *more than one* parallel to that line led to the non-Euclidean system called hyberbolic geometry or Lobachevskian geometry (perhaps to atone for the original neglect of his work). Once this geometry became legitimate, other non-Euclidean systems began to appear. Chief among these was the elliptic or spherical geometry originated by the German mathematician Bernhard Riemann (1826–1866). A second type of elliptic geometry was later developed by Felix Klein (1849–1925), also of Germany. Their assumption was that through a point not on a line there is *no* parallel to that line. It is easy, of course, to dismiss such assumptions as absurd. What possible interpretation can there be for these geometries? Of what use are they?

Remember that Euclidean plane geometry concerns figures in a plane, an elementary term we do not define but that we visualize as a flat surface. Another undefined term is the straight line, which we use to determine the shortest distance between two points. Now suppose we deform a flat surface. What becomes of our straight lines and what is the shortest distance between two points? Make a fist of your hand and consider how you would determine the shortest distance on your hand between two points, say on either side of a knuckle or between two knuckles.

It turns out that Riemann's spherical geometry is, as the name suggests, the geometry of figures on the surface of a sphere. But here, the role of straight lines is played by *great circles,* that is, circles whose centers are at the center of the sphere. The shortest distance between two points is determined by the great circle joining them. Now, some theorems emerge that are indeed absurd in Euclidean geometry but that are perfectly reasonable in terms of a sphere. One such theorem asserts that the sum of the angles of a triangle is greater than 180°. Another asserts that two intersecting lines (i.e., great circles) determine a figure that has an area. Most importantly, lines are no longer of infinite extent: they are endless, yet finite!

A model for hyperbolic geometry is more difficult to construct. It may be accomplished using a surface called a "pseudosphere." Roughly speaking, this looks like two infinitely long, curving funnels with their rims glued together. Again, straight lines become the curves on the surface that determine the shortest distance between two points. Again, some "strange" theorems appear. For example, the sum of the angles of a triangle is now less than 180°.

Obviously, spherical geometry is of great practical use. We live on a surface that is approximately spherical. Ships and airplanes that traverse the shortest route between two places travel along great circles. Probably, Euclidean plane geometry was invented first only because it fits a small piece of the space in which we live. The wonder is that it took nearly 2000 years for people with their feet planted firmly on a spherical surface to open their minds to non-Euclidean geometry!

And what of the vast space beyond our earth? What geometric figure determines the shortest distance between our earth and a distant galaxy? What geometry fits the shape of the universe? Perhaps it has already been invented by some mathematician, freed by the pioneers of the nineteenth century to think and reason abstractly, unencumbered by purely utilitarian considerations.

7.1 INTRODUCTION

A polygon with a great many sides *suggests* the geometric figure that we examine in this chapter. The familiar circle, however, is *not* a polygon because a polygon has sides that are line segments and the circle does not. The many practical uses of the circle range from the wheel to the near-circular orbits of some communication satellites. Indeed, the mechanical uses of the circle have been known for thousands of years, and the ancient Greeks contributed significantly to our understanding of the circle's mathematical properties. The full moon, ripples in a pond when a stone is dropped in, and the shape of some bird's nests show some of the circles that appear in nature.

Our study of circles begins with some definitions, an explanation of the standard symbols used, and certain figures related to circles.

Definition 7.1 A *circle* is the set of all points in a plane that are a given distance from a given point in the plane. The given distance is the *radius* and the given point is the *center* (⊙ set of pts at given dis from given pt).

It is customary to name a circle with a single letter assigned to its center. Thus, in Figure 7.1 the center is labeled O and we refer to $\odot O$, read "circle O." Note that a circle is a *set of points,* one of which is E in Figure 7.1. The center, O, is *not* part of the circle. It belongs to a set of points called the *interior* of the circle. Thus, a circle divides a plane into three distinct subsets: the *interior,* the *circle itself,* and the *exterior*. Point P in Figure 7.1 is in the *exterior* of $\odot O$. Thus, a point is in the interior, on the circle, or in the exterior according to whether its distance from the center is less than, equal to, or greater than the radius, respectively.

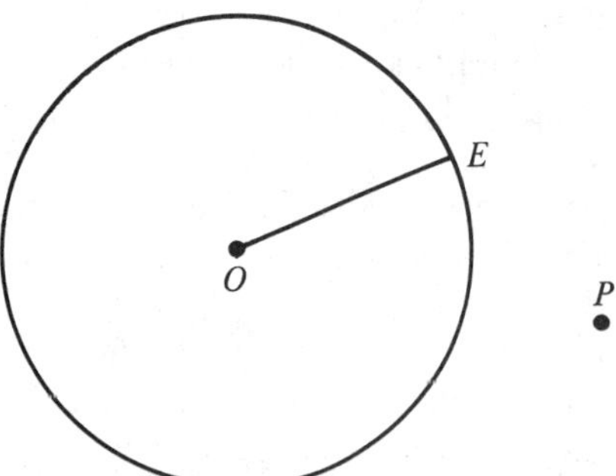

Figure 7.1 $\odot O$ with center O and radius OE.

The radius (plural, radii) of a circle is defined above as a *number*. As such it is the length of a great many line segments, one of which is $\overline{OE}$ for the circle in Figure 7.1. It is standard practice, however, for "radius" to also mean a line segment, as in the following definition.

Definition 7.2 A line segment is a *radius* of a circle iff one of its endpoints is the center and the other is a point of the circle.

You can usually determine which meaning of the word "radius" is intended by the context in which it is used.

Another term associated with circles also has a double meaning.

Definition 7.3 A line segment is a *diameter* of a circle iff its endpoints are points of the circle and it contains the center of the circle.

For any circle, the length of a diameter is twice the length of a radius. This *number,* the *length* of a diameter, is also referred to as the *diameter* of the circle. Thus, we say that a circle with a radius of 5 inches has a diameter of 10 inches. The "line segment" meaning of radius and diameter is used in Theorem 65.

Theorem 65 In any given circle all radii are congruent and all diameters are congruent (radii ⊙ ≅ and diams ⊙ ≅).

This theorem follows directly from Definitions 7.2 and 7.3. A formal proof is omitted.

It is easy to draw two circles such that a radius of one is clearly not congruent to a radius of the other. Figure 7.2 shows two circles having the same center. Since point A is in the interior of the outer circle, $OA < OB$ and $\overline{OA} \not\cong \overline{OB}$. Circles with the same center but different radii are given a special name, as follows.

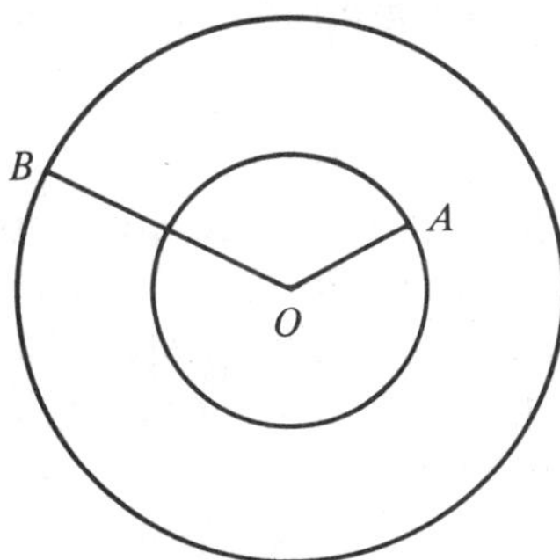

Figure 7.2

Definition 7.4 Two or more circles are *concentric* iff they have the same center.

Next, we define a type of line segment and two types of lines associated with circles.

Definition 7.5 A line segment is a *chord* of a circle iff its endpoints are points of the circle.

Definition 7.6 A line is a *secant* to a circle iff exactly two of its points are also points of the circle (sec inters ⊙ 2 pts).

Definition 7.7 A line is a *tangent* to a circle iff exactly one of its points is also a point of the circle. This point is called the *point of contact* or *point of tangency* (tan inters ⊙ 1 pt).

These terms are illustrated in Example 1. Note that a diameter is also a chord, but not all chords are diameters.

EXAMPLE 1 In the given figure, *name:*

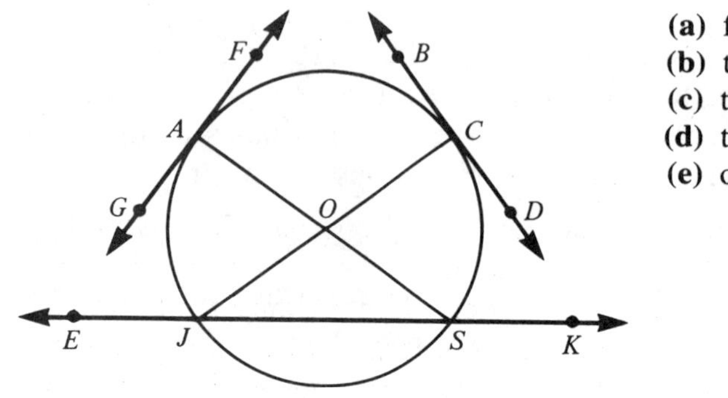

(a) four radii
(b) two diameters
(c) three chords
(d) two tangents
(e) one secant

Answers
(a) $\overline{OA}, \overline{OC}, \overline{OJ}, \overline{OS}$ **(b)** $\overline{AS}, \overline{JC}$ **(c)** $\overline{JS}, \overline{AS}, \overline{JC}$ **(d)** $\overleftrightarrow{GF}, \overleftrightarrow{BD}$ **(e)** $\overleftrightarrow{EK}$

Several types of angles associated with circles are seen in the figure for Example 1. Definition 7.8 describes the most fundamental of these angles.

Definition 7.8 An angle is a *central angle* of a circle iff its vertex is the center of the circle.

Thus, in Example 1 ∡AOJ, ∡JOS, ∡SOC, and ∡COA are all central angles of ⊙O. These angles "cut off" portions of the circle called *arcs* (this term has already been used in describing constructions). Formal definitions of three types of arcs follow. In Definitions 7.9 and 7.10, the central angles may be acute, right, or obtuse (i.e., measure less than 180°).

Definition 7.9 A *minor arc* is the set of points of a circle that are on a central angle or in its interior.

Definition 7.10 A *major arc* is the set of points of a circle that are on a central angle or in its exterior.

Definition 7.11 A *semicircle* is the set of points of a circle that are on, or are on one side of, a line containing a diameter.

These terms and the symbols used for them are illustrated in Example 2. To avoid confusion, two letters are used to name minor arcs, while three letters are used to name major arcs and semicircles.

EXAMPLE 2 In the given figure, *name:*

(a) two minor arcs
(b) two major arcs
(c) two semicircles

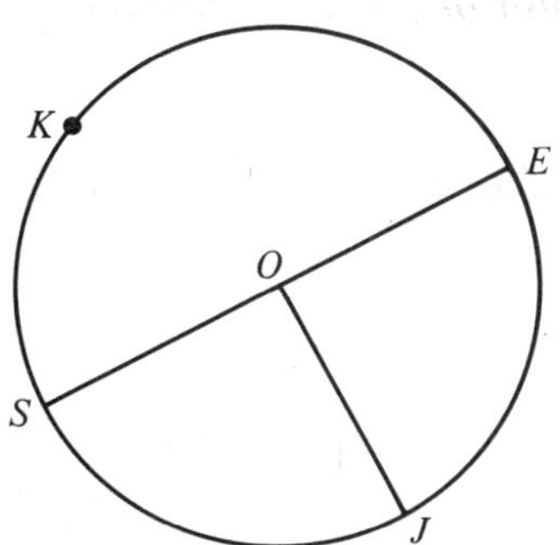

Answers
(a) $\overset{\frown}{SJ}$, $\overset{\frown}{JE}$ **(b)** $\overset{\frown}{SKJ}$, $\overset{\frown}{JKE}$ **(c)** $\overset{\frown}{SKE}$, $\overset{\frown}{SJE}$

Notation such as $\overset{\frown}{SJ}$ in Example 2 is read "arc SJ." Note that the three-letter notation leaves no doubt as to which arc is named. If necessary for clarity, minor arcs may also be named using three letters. In the figure for Example 2 other minor and major arcs may be named even though their central angles are not drawn. Thus $\overset{\frown}{KS}$, $\overset{\frown}{KJ}$, and $\overset{\frown}{KE}$ are minor arcs and $\overset{\frown}{KES}$, $\overset{\frown}{KEJ}$, and $\overset{\frown}{KSE}$ are major arcs.

There are some additional ways to use this arc terminology. In Figure 7.3 $\measuredangle AOB$ "intercepts" $\overset{\frown}{AB}$. Note that the intercepted arc is the *minor* arc associated with the central angle. More simply, for $\measuredangle AOB$ we refer to $\overset{\frown}{AB}$ as "its arc." Similarly, for the same angle we speak of chord $\overline{AB}$ as "its chord." In fact, this language is used in connection with any two of the following figures: $\measuredangle AOB$, $\overset{\frown}{AB}$, and chord $\overline{AB}$. Thus, for chord $\overline{AB}$ we refer to $\overset{\frown}{AB}$ as "its arc" and $\measuredangle AOB$ as "its central angle."

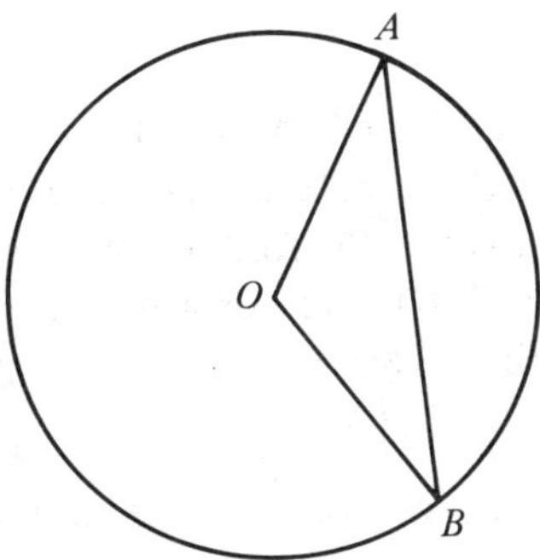

Figure 7.3

The concept of a central angle and its intercepted arc enables us to assign degree measures to arcs as follows.

Definition 7.12 The *degree measure* of

a. a *minor arc* is the measure of its central angle (meas min $\frown$ = cent $\angle$),
b. a *semicircle* is 180° (meas semi $\odot$ = 180°),
c. a *circle* is 360° (meas $\odot$ = 360°),
d. a *major arc* is 360° minus the measure of its associated minor arc (meas maj $\frown$ = 360° − min $\frown$).

The notation $\widehat{AB}$ names an arc (i.e., a set of points). To denote the degree measure of $\widehat{AB}$, we write $\widehat{AB}°$, a number, as illustrated in Example 3.

EXAMPLE 3

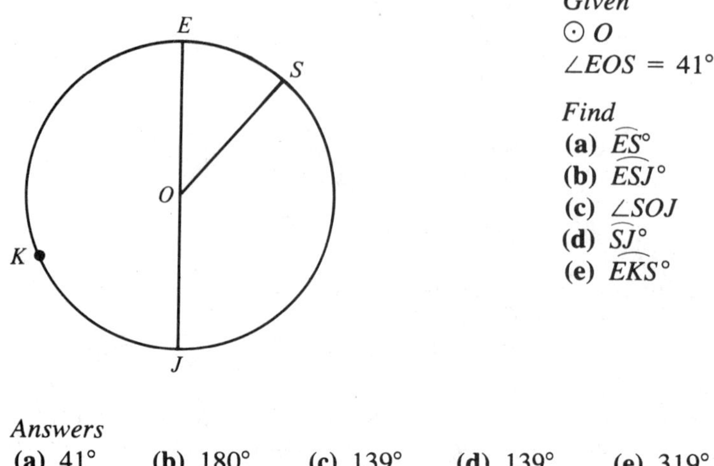

Given
$\odot O$
$\angle EOS = 41°$

Find
(a) $\widehat{ES}°$
(b) $\widehat{ESJ}°$
(c) $\angle SOJ$
(d) $\widehat{SJ}°$
(e) $\widehat{EKS}°$

Answers
(a) 41° **(b)** 180° **(c)** 139° **(d)** 139° **(e)** 319°

It is important to know that the degree measure of an arc is not a measure of the arc's length. Indeed, we have not yet shown how to find the length of an arc (Section 9.5, Theorem 107) or of a circle (Section 8.3, Theorem 90). It should be intuitively clear, however, that for the concentric circles in Figure 7.4, $\widehat{AB}° = \widehat{CD}°$ because the arcs have the same central angle, but certainly $\widehat{AB}$ is not as long as $\widehat{CD}$.

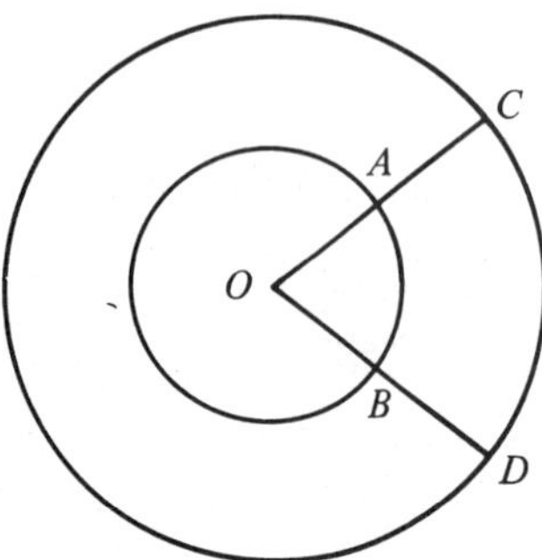

Figure 7.4

Another type of angle associated with circles is defined below.

Definition 7.13 An angle is an *inscribed angle* of a circle iff its vertex is a point of the circle and each of its sides contains another point of the circle.

In Figure 7.5(a), $\measuredangle SEJ$ is an inscribed angle of $\odot O$. We also say that $\measuredangle SEJ$ is *inscribed* in major arc $\widehat{SEJ}$ and *intercepts* minor arc $\widehat{SJ}$. The situation may be reversed as in Figure 7.5(b) where $\measuredangle ABC$ is an inscribed angle of $\odot P$. It is inscribed in minor arc $\widehat{AC}$ and intercepts major arc $\widehat{ADC}$. What is the relation between the degree measures of an inscribed angle and its intercepted arc? We discuss this and other relations involving angles and arcs of circles in the following sections of this chapter.

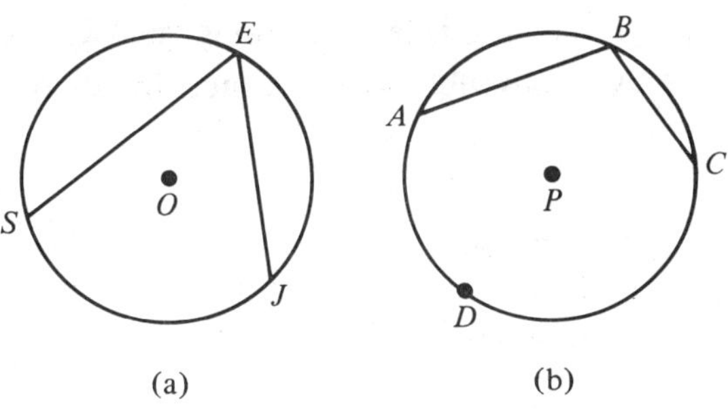

Figure 7.5

7.2

CENTRAL ANGLES, ARCS, AND CHORDS

There are some important properties about central angles, arcs, and chords that are associated with a given circle or with two circles that are the same size. But what is meant by "the same size"? Recall that this is the concept underlying the congruence relation previously defined for line segments and angles. We now extend this relation to circles.

Definition 7.14 Two *circles* are *congruent* iff their radii are congruent (⊙s ≅ iff radii ≅).

This definition uses the "line segment" meaning of radius. It follows directly that congruent circles have *equal* radii, where we are using the "distance" or "length" meaning of radius.

We also need to define congruent arcs. Note that this concept is restricted to two arcs in the same circle or in congruent circles, thus assuring that congruent arcs will have the same size and shape.

Definition 7.15 Two *arcs* of a circle or of congruent circles are *congruent* iff their degree measures are equal ($\frown$s ≅ iff meas =).

Theorem 66 follows directly from Definition 7.15. The proof is omitted.

Theorem 66 Any diameter divides a circle into two congruent semicircles (diam ÷ ⊙ into 2 ≅ semi ⊙s).

Since congruent arcs are defined in terms of numbers (degree measures), the addition, subtraction, multiplication, and division properties of congruence (Theorems 16–19) may be easily extended to include congruence between arcs. The "whole ≅ sum parts" property and concepts about bisection may be similarly extended. We will use these properties as needed in proofs.

We now state six theorems organized in pairs (theorem and converse) relating central angles, arcs, and chords in the same or congruent circles. The three proofs shown are for the "same circle" case. Proofs for the "congruent circles" case are similar. The proofs for the converses are left as exercises.

Theorem 67 If two minor arcs of a circle or of congruent circles are congruent, then their central angles are congruent (if ⌒s ≅, cent ∡s ≅).

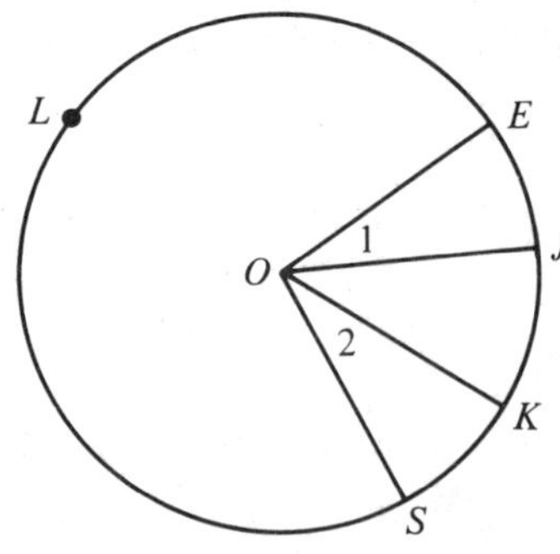

Given
⊙O, $\overset{\frown}{EJ} \cong \overset{\frown}{KS}$

To Prove
∡1 ≅ ∡2

Statement	*Reason*
1. ⊙ O, $\overset{\frown}{EJ} \cong \overset{\frown}{KS}$	1. given
2. $\overset{\frown}{EJ}° = \overset{\frown}{KS}°$	2. ⌒s ≅ iff meas =
3. $\angle 1 = \overset{\frown}{EJ}°$	3. meas min ⌒ = cent ∠
4. $\overset{\frown}{KS}° = \angle 2$	4. meas min ⌒ = cent ∠
5. $\angle 1 = \angle 2$	5. trans =
6. ∴ ∡1 ≅ ∡2	6. ≅ iff meas =

Theorem 67 is about two minor arcs given to be congruent. It is easy, however, to prove that if major arc $\overset{\frown}{ELJ}$ is congruent to major arc $\overset{\frown}{KLS}$, then ∡1 ≅ ∡2.

Theorem 68 *(Converse of Theorem 67.)* If two central angles in a circle or in congruent circles are congruent, then their arcs are congruent (if cent ∡s ≅, ⌒s ≅).

The next pair of theorems is similar to Theorems 67 and 68, with arcs replaced by chords.

Theorem 69 If two central angles in a circle or in congruent circles are congruent, then their chords are congruent (if cent ∡s ≅, chs ≅).

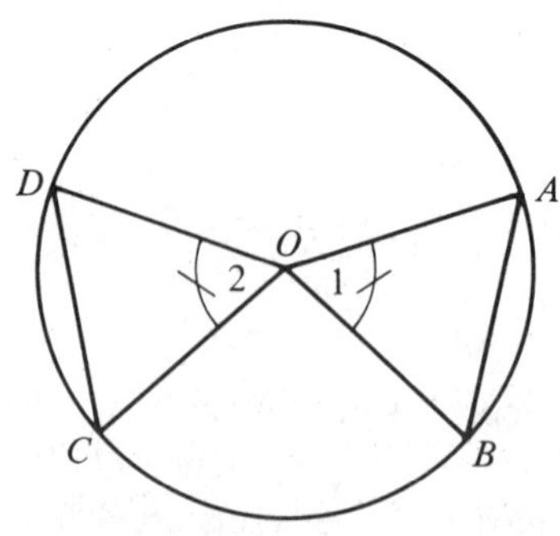

Given
⊙O
∡1 ≅ ∡2

To Prove
$\overline{AB} \cong \overline{DC}$

Statement	*Reason*
1. ⊙O, ∡1 ≅ ∡2	1. given
2. $\overline{OA} \cong \overline{OD}$, $\overline{OB} \cong \overline{OC}$	2. radii ⊙ ≅
3. $\triangle OAB \cong \triangle ODC$	3. sas ≅ sas
4. ∴ $\overline{AB} \cong \overline{DC}$	4. cpctc

In the above proof, it is not stated that $\overline{OA}$, $\overline{OD}$, $\overline{OB}$, and $\overline{OC}$ are radii. We will omit such identification statements for radii, diameters, chords, tangents, and secants in proofs. This shortcut causes no difficulty as long as the definitions of these terms are clearly understood and the center of the circle is given.

Theorem 70 *(Converse of Theorem 69.)* If two chords in a circle or in congruent circles are congruent, then their central angles are congruent (if chs $\cong$, cent $\measuredangle$s $\cong$).

The next pair of theorems relates chords and arcs in the same or congruent circles.

Theorem 71 If two chords in a circle or in congruent circles are congruent, then their arcs are congruent (if chs $\cong$, $\frown$s $\cong$).

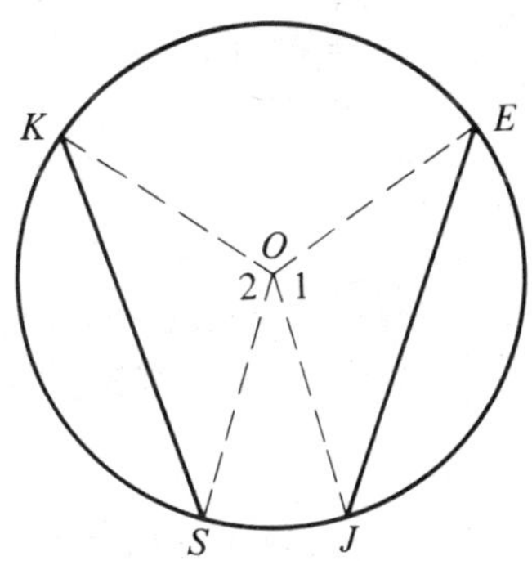

Given
$\odot O$
$\overline{EJ} \cong \overline{KS}$

To Prove
$\overset{\frown}{EJ} \cong \overset{\frown}{KS}$

Statement	*Reason*
1. $\odot O$, $\overline{EJ} \cong \overline{KS}$	1. given
2. Draw radii $\overline{OE}$, $\overline{OJ}$, $\overline{OS}$, $\overline{OK}$.	2. 2 pts determ line
3. $\overline{OE} \cong \overline{OK}$, $\overline{OJ} \cong \overline{OS}$	3. radii $\odot$ $\cong$
4. $\triangle OEJ \cong \triangle OKS$	4. sss $\cong$ sss
5. $\measuredangle 1 \cong \measuredangle 2$	5. cpctc
6. $\therefore \overset{\frown}{EJ} \cong \overset{\frown}{KS}$	6. if cent $\measuredangle$s $\cong$, $\frown$s $\cong$

Theorem 72 *(Converse of Theorem 71.)* If two minor arcs of a circle or of congruent circles are congruent, then their chords are congruent (if $\frown$s $\cong$, chs $\cong$).

It is also easy to show that if two major arcs of the same or congruent circles are congruent, then the chords for their associated minor arcs are congruent.

The foregoing six theorems are summarized in the following diagram:

$$\cong \text{central angles} \leftrightarrow \cong \text{arcs} \leftrightarrow \cong \text{chords}$$

Since the arrows point two ways, each of the three statements may represent either a hypothesis or a conclusion. These theorems, together with some from previous chapters, are applied in Examples 1 and 2.

EXAMPLE 1

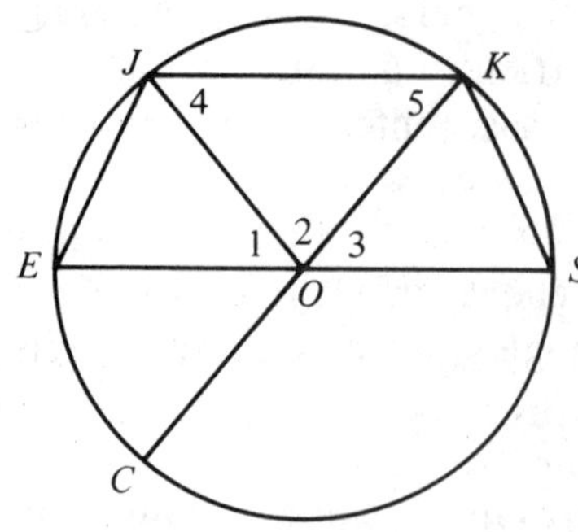

Given
⊙O
$\overline{ES} \parallel \overline{JK}$
$\overset{\frown}{JK}° = 78°$
$JE = 1.5$ cm

Find
(a) ∡s 1–5
(b) $\overset{\frown}{JE}°$, $\overset{\frown}{KS}°$, KS, $\overset{\frown}{JC}°$

Answers
Use the fact that ∡1 ≅ ∡4 ≅ ∡5 ≅ ∡3 (isos $\triangle OJK$ and alt int ∡s).
(a) $\angle 1 = 51°$ $\angle 2 = 78°$ $\angle 3 = 51°$ $\angle 4 = 51°$ $\angle 5 = 51°$
(b) $\overset{\frown}{JE}° = 51°$ $\overset{\frown}{KS}° = 51°$ $KS = 1.5$ cm $\overset{\frown}{JC}° = 102°$

EXAMPLE 2

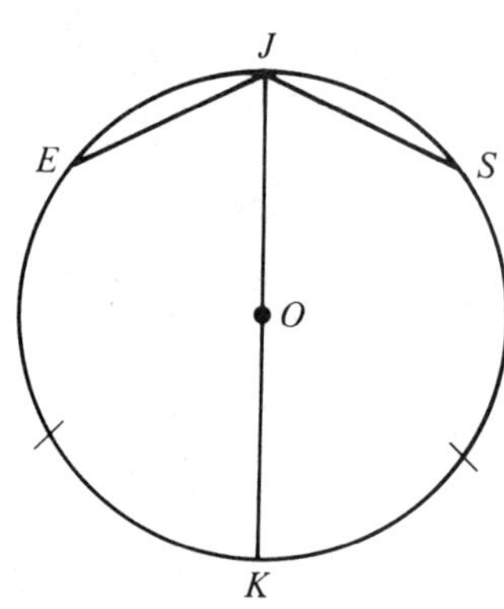

Given
⊙ O
$\overset{\frown}{EK} \cong \overset{\frown}{SK}$

To Prove
$\overline{EJ} \cong \overline{SJ}$

Statement	*Reason*
1. ⊙O	1. given
2. $\overset{\frown}{JEK} \cong \overset{\frown}{JSK}$	2. diam ÷ ⊙ into 2 ≅ semi ⊙s
3. $\overset{\frown}{EK} \cong \overset{\frown}{SK}$	3. given
4. $\overset{\frown}{JEK} - \overset{\frown}{EK} \cong \overset{\frown}{JSK} - \overset{\frown}{SK}$	4. ≅ − ≅, diffs ≅
5. $\overset{\frown}{EJ} \cong \overset{\frown}{JEK} - \overset{\frown}{EK}$ $\overset{\frown}{SJ} \cong \overset{\frown}{JSK} - \overset{\frown}{SK}$	5. whole ≅ sum parts
6. $\overset{\frown}{EJ} \cong \overset{\frown}{SJ}$	6. symm and trans ≅
7. ∴ $\overline{EJ} \cong \overline{SJ}$	7. if $\frown$s ≅, chs ≅

An alternate proof for Example 2 using central angles is suggested in the exercises.

EXERCISES FOR 7.1 AND 7.2

In exercises 1–20 answer true or false.

1. Circles are polygons with more than one billion sides.
2. If a central angle measures 135°, then its intercepted arc measures 135°.
3. If $\overline{EJ}$ is a chord of a circle, then $\overleftrightarrow{EJ}$ is a secant of the circle.
4. A semicircle is a major arc.
5. A round pizza is a better physical illustration of a circle than is a bicycle tire.
6. According to the definition of a tangent, a tangent is also a secant.
7. The word "radius" is defined to be either

a line segment or a length of a line segment.

8. A circle with a 7-inch radius has a diameter of 15 inches.
9. The double meanings for "radius" and "diameter" usually cause no confusion because the context in which the words are used clarifies the meaning intended.
10. A line always intersects a circle in two points.
11. An inscribed angle is a special central angle.
12. If $\odot O$ has a point J in its exterior, then $\overline{OJ}$ is a secant of the circle.
13. The same central angle for two concentric circles intercepts congruent arcs on the circles.
14. If $\overline{OE}$ and $\overline{OJ}$ are radii of a circle, then $\widehat{EJ}$ is always a minor arc.
15. If E and J are two points of $\odot O$, then $\angle EOJ = \frac{1}{2}\widehat{EJ}°$.
16. If an arc of a circle measures 60°, then the triangle formed by its central angle and chord is equilateral.
17. Congruent circles are circles with congruent centers.
18. In a circle, parallel chords are equidistant from the center.
19. In a circle, congruent central angles have congruent chords.
20. If inscribed $\measuredangle ABC$ is an acute angle then $\widehat{AC}$ must be a major arc.

In exercises 21–25 use Figure 7.6 to answer the questions.

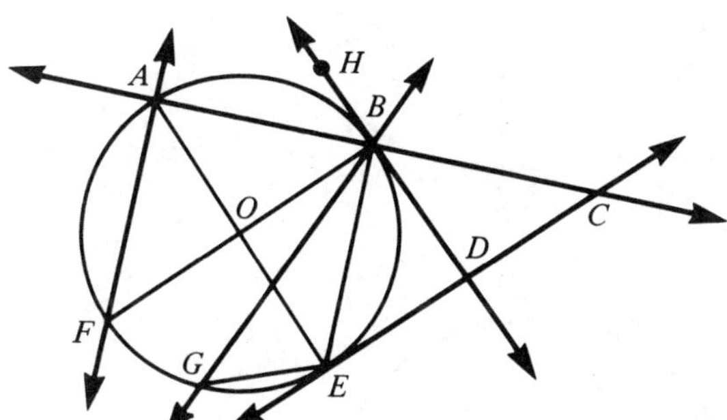

Figure 7.6

21. **(a)** Name seven chords.
    (b) Name two diameters.
22. **(a)** Name two tangents.
    (b) Name three secants.
23. **(a)** Name four central angles.
    (b) Name fourteen inscribed angles.
24. **(a)** Name two pairs of congruent arcs.
    (b) Name four pairs of inscribed angles that intercept the same arc.
25. **(a)** Name eleven angles formed by a tangent and a chord.
    (b) Name six angles formed by a tangent and a secant.

In exercises 26–33 explain what is wrong with the information as marked on the figure. Point O is the center of each circle.

26.

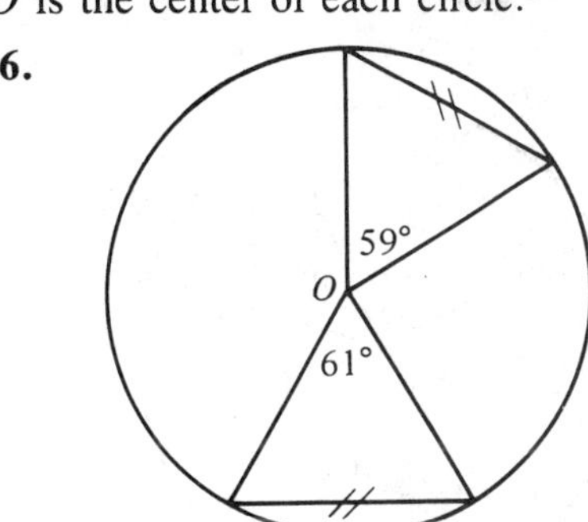

27.

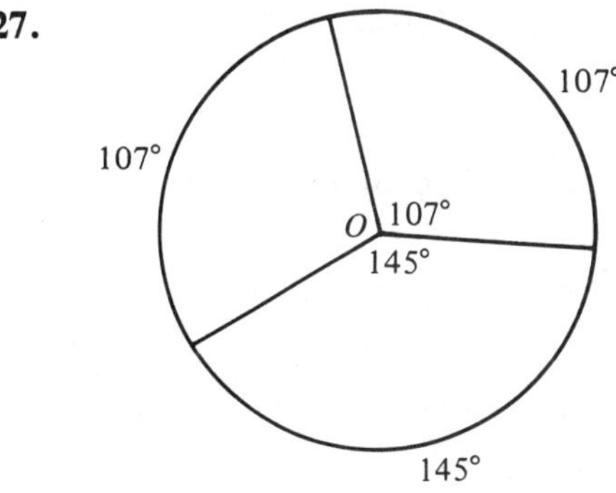

28.

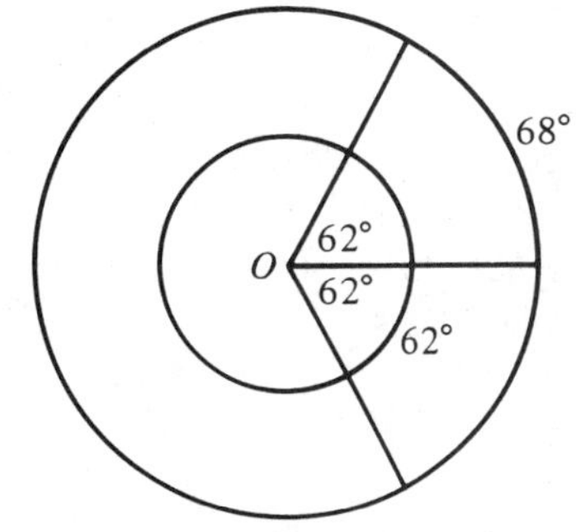

29.

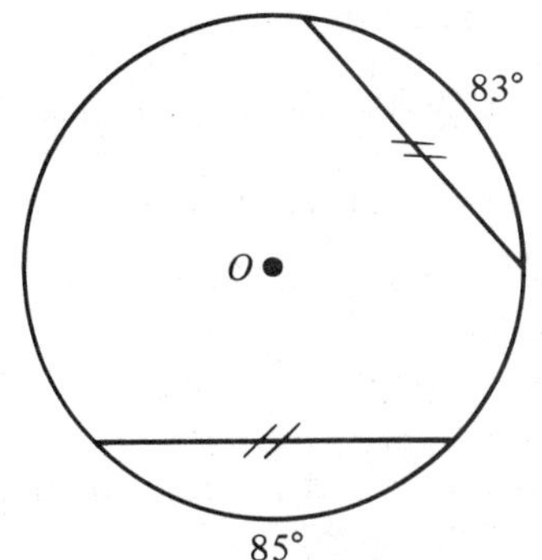

30.

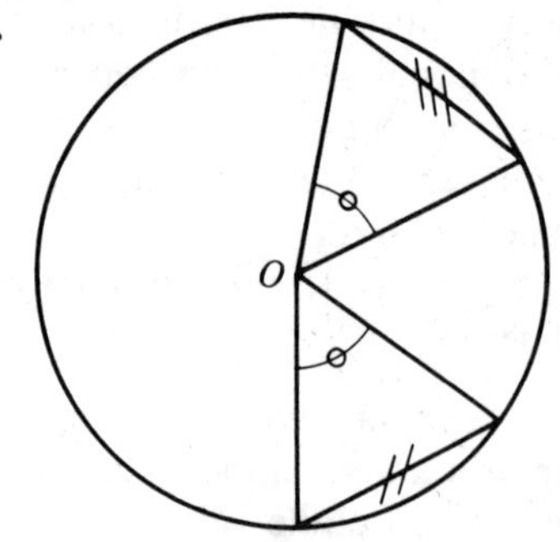

32.

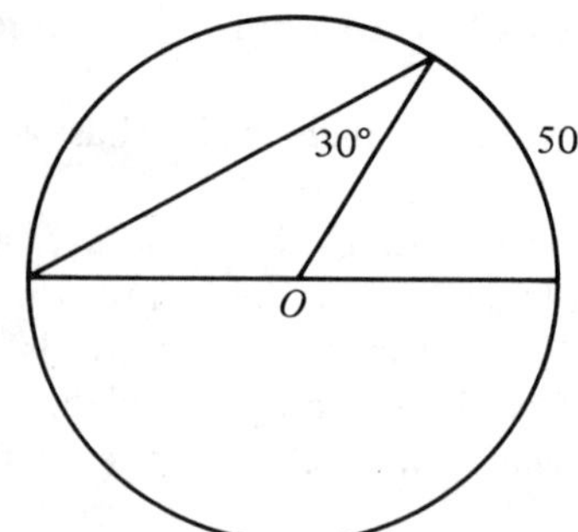

31.

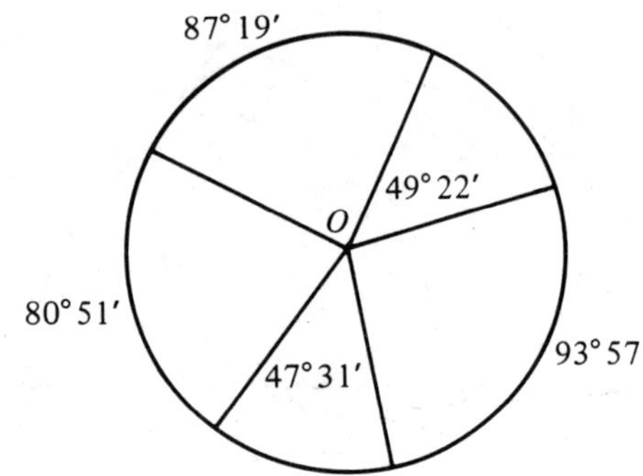

33.

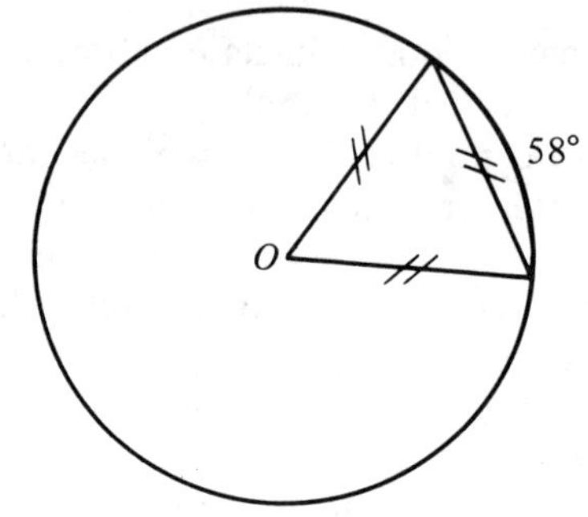

In exercises 34–42 copy the figure, mark it, and find the requested measures.

34. *Given*
⊙O
$\angle KOS = 31°$
$\angle EOJ = 82°$

Find
(a) $\overset{\frown}{KS}°$
(b) $\overset{\frown}{KSJ}°$
(c) $\overset{\frown}{SJ}°$
(d) $\overset{\frown}{JE}°$
(e) $\overset{\frown}{EK}°$

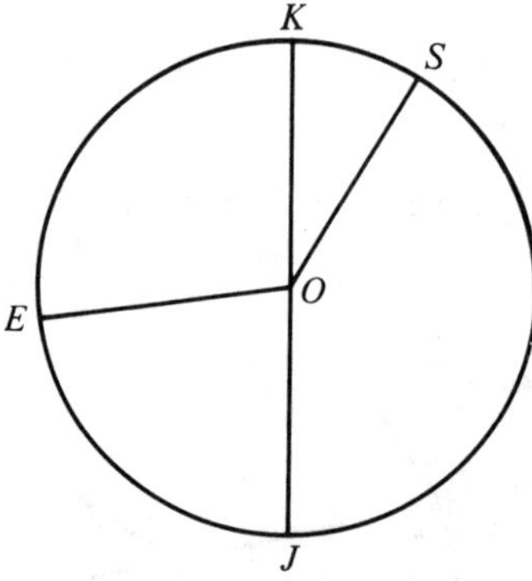

35. *Given*
⊙O
$\overline{EK} \parallel \overline{OS}$
$\angle KOS = 36°$

Find
(a) $\overset{\frown}{EK}°$
(b) $\overset{\frown}{KS}°$
(c) $\overset{\frown}{SJ}°$
(d) $\overset{\frown}{KJ}°$
(e) $\overset{\frown}{ES}°$

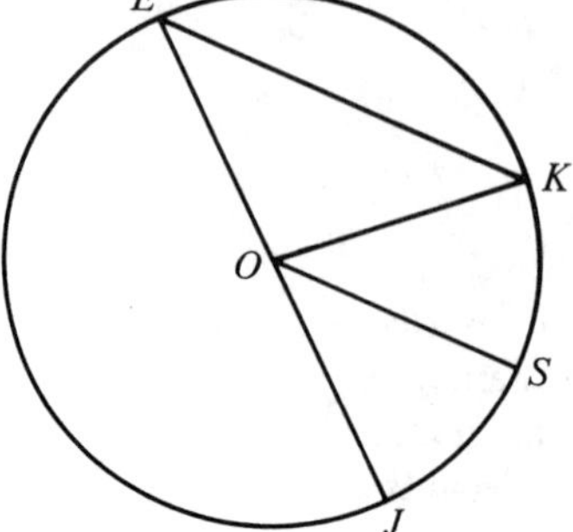

36. *Given*
$\odot O$
$\widehat{MT} = 128°$
$\widehat{RT}° = 69°$
$\widehat{IR}° = 101°$

Find
$\angle$s 1–10

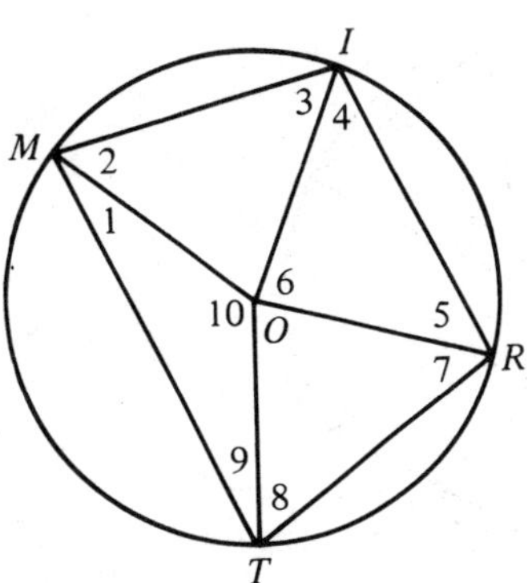

37. *Given*
$\odot O$
$\widehat{PS}° = 163°$

Find
$\angle$s 1–8

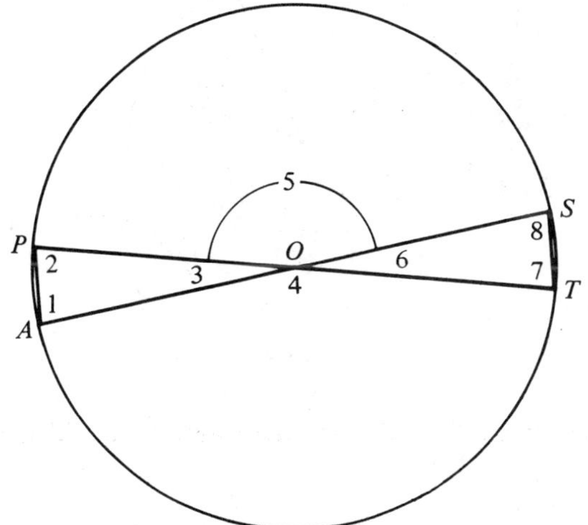

38. *Given*
$\odot O$
$\widehat{RA}° = 111°$
$\overline{PN} \parallel \overline{RO}$

Find
$\angle$s 1–8

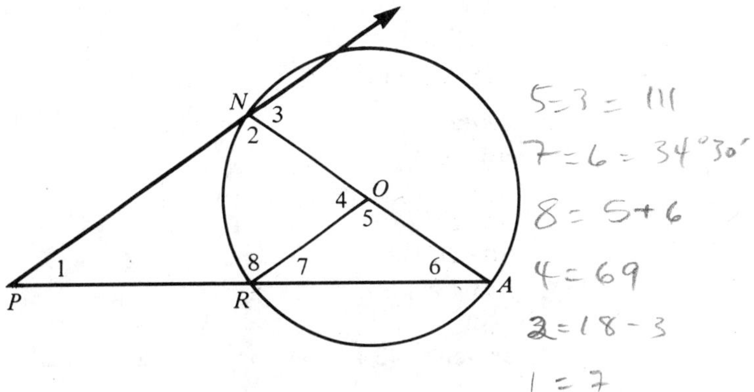

39. *Given*
$\odot O$
$\widehat{LE}° = 48°$
$\angle AOL = 66°$
$\angle AOT = 138°$

Find
$\angle$s 1–12

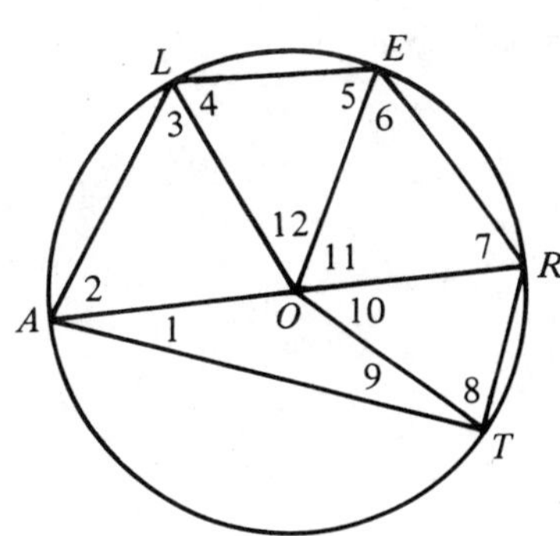

40. *Given*
$\odot O$
$\odot K$
$\widehat{DI}^\circ = 125^\circ$
$\widehat{IL}^\circ = 89^\circ$

Find
$\angle$s 1–10

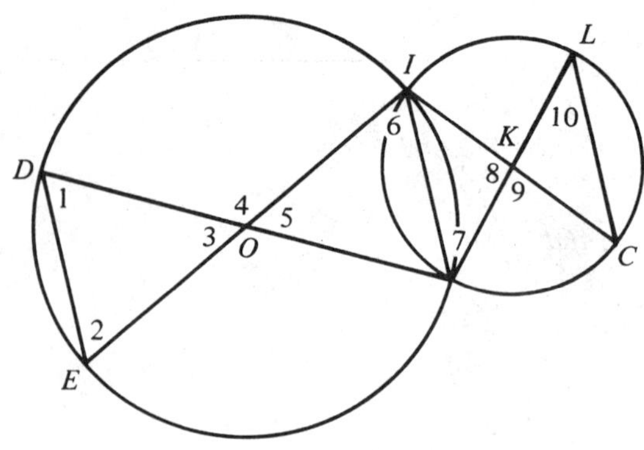

41. *Given*
$\odot O$
$\widehat{BF}^\circ = 99^\circ$

Find
$\angle$s 1–9

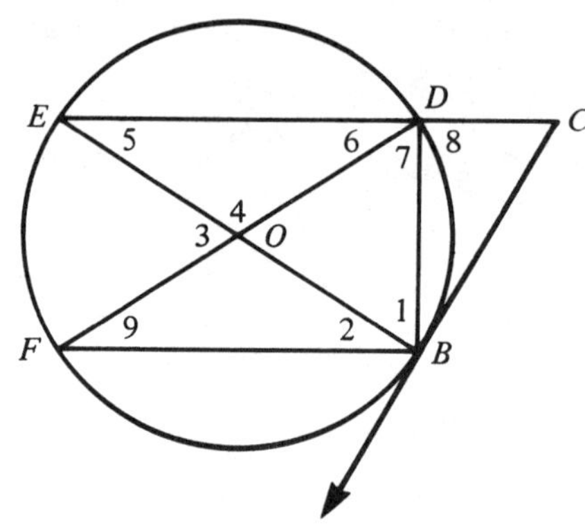

42. *Given*
concentric $\odot$s with center O
$\overline{OA} \perp \overline{BD}$
$\widehat{KM}^\circ = 47^\circ$
$\widehat{CF}^\circ = 57^\circ$
$\widehat{FH}^\circ = 111^\circ$

Find
$\angle$s 1–10

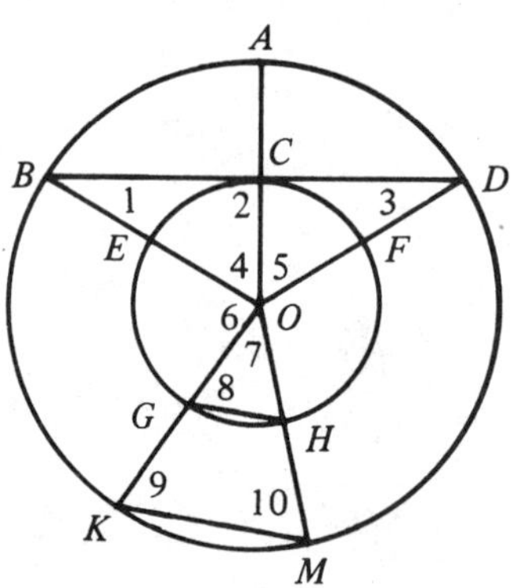

In exercises 43 and 44 copy the figure, mark it, and supply the missing reasons in each proof.

43. (Alternate proof, Example 2)

Given
$\odot O$
$\widehat{EK} \cong \widehat{SK}$

To Prove
$\overline{EJ} \cong \overline{SJ}$

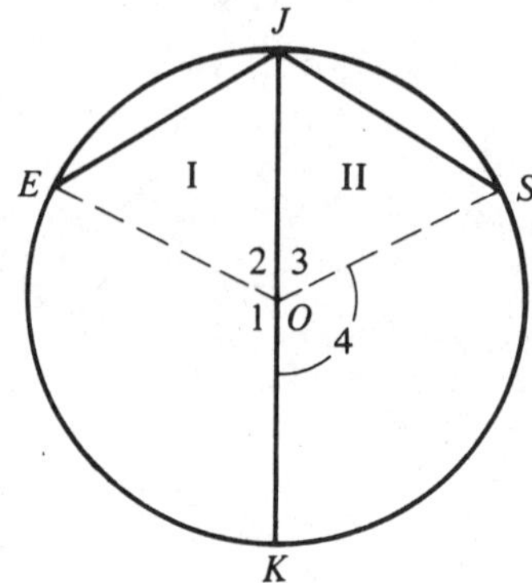

Statement	*Reason*
1. $\odot O$	1. ?
2. Draw $\overline{EO}$ and $\overline{SO}$.	2. ?
3. $\overline{EO} \cong \overline{SO}$	3. ?
4. $\widehat{EK} \cong \widehat{SK}$	4. ?
5. $\widehat{EK}^\circ = \widehat{SK}^\circ$	5. ?
6. $\angle 1 = \widehat{EK}^\circ$	6. ?
7. $\angle 4 = \widehat{SK}^\circ$	7. ?
8. $\widehat{SK}^\circ = \angle 4$	8. ?
9. $\angle 1 = \angle 4$	9. ?
10. $\measuredangle 1 \cong \measuredangle 4$	10. ?
11. $\measuredangle 2$ supp $\measuredangle 1$	11. ?
12. $\measuredangle 3$ supp $\measuredangle 4$	12. ?
13. $\measuredangle 2 \cong \measuredangle 3$	13. ?
14. $\therefore \overline{EJ} \cong \overline{SJ}$	14. ?

44. *Given*
$\odot O$
$\overline{AD} \cong \overline{BC}$

To Prove
$\widehat{AC} \cong \widehat{BD}$

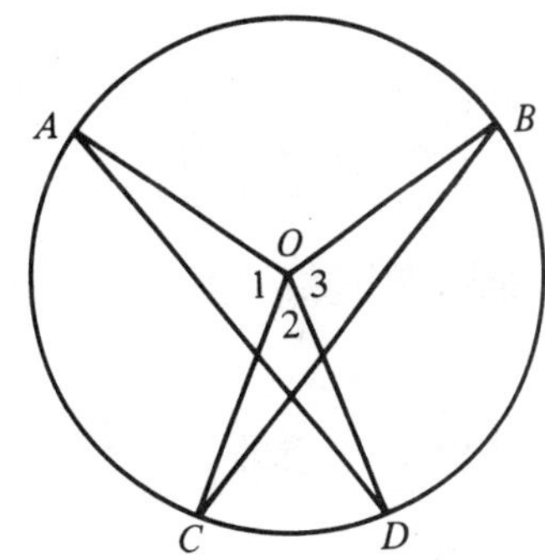

Statement	*Reason*
1. $\odot O$	1. ?
2. $\overline{AO} \cong \overline{BO}$	2. ?
3. $\overline{OD} \cong \overline{OC}$	3. ?
4. $\overline{AD} \cong \overline{BC}$	4. ?
5. $\triangle AOD \cong \triangle BOC$	5. ?
6. $\measuredangle AOD \cong \measuredangle BOC$	6. ?
7. $\measuredangle 2 \cong \measuredangle 2$	7. ?
8. $\measuredangle AOD - \measuredangle 2 \cong \measuredangle BOC - \measuredangle 2$	8. ?
9. $\measuredangle 1 \cong \measuredangle AOD - \measuredangle 2$	9. ?
10. $\measuredangle 3 \cong \measuredangle BOC - \measuredangle 2$	10. ?
11. $\measuredangle BOC - \measuredangle 2 \cong \measuredangle 3$	11. ?
12. $\measuredangle 1 \cong \measuredangle 3$	12. ?
13. $\therefore \widehat{AC} \cong \widehat{BD}$	13. ?

In exercises 45–55 copy the figure, the hypothesis, and the conclusion. Mark the figure and write a proof.

45. *Given*
⊙O
$\overset{\frown}{EJ} \cong \overset{\frown}{KS}$

To Prove
$\triangle I \cong \triangle II$

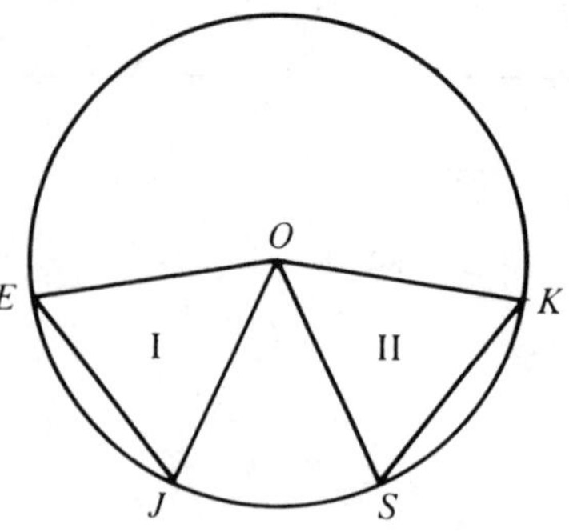

46. *Given*
⊙O
$\overset{\frown}{AC} \cong \overset{\frown}{BC}$

To Prove
$\measuredangle 1 \cong \measuredangle 2$

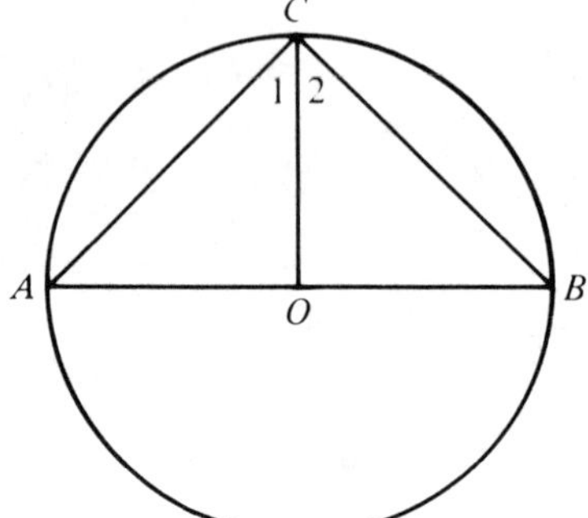

47. *Given*
⊙O
$\measuredangle EOK \cong \measuredangle JOS$

To Prove
$\overset{\frown}{ES} \cong \overset{\frown}{JK}$

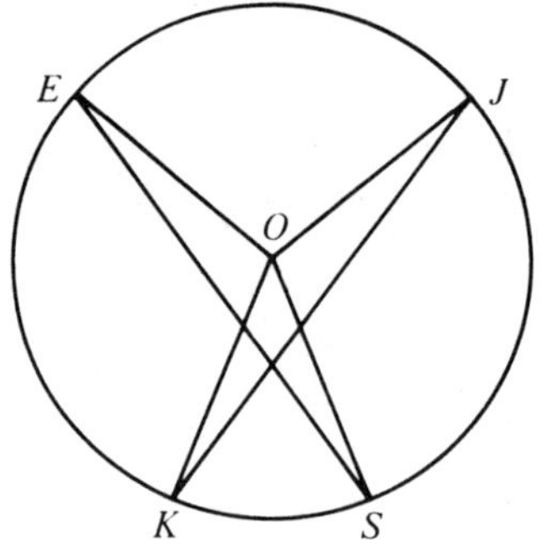

48. *Given*
⊙O
$\overline{EJ} \parallel \overline{SK}$

To Prove
$\overset{\frown}{ES} \cong \overset{\frown}{JK}$

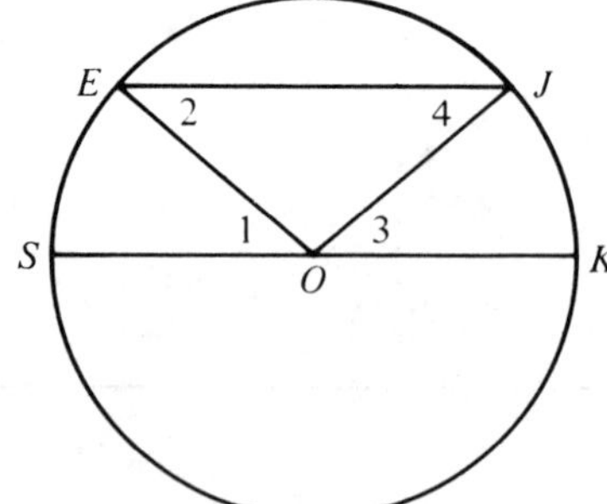

49. *Given*
⊙O
$\overset{\frown}{SJ} \cong \overset{\frown}{KJ}$

To Prove
$\measuredangle 1 \cong \measuredangle 2$

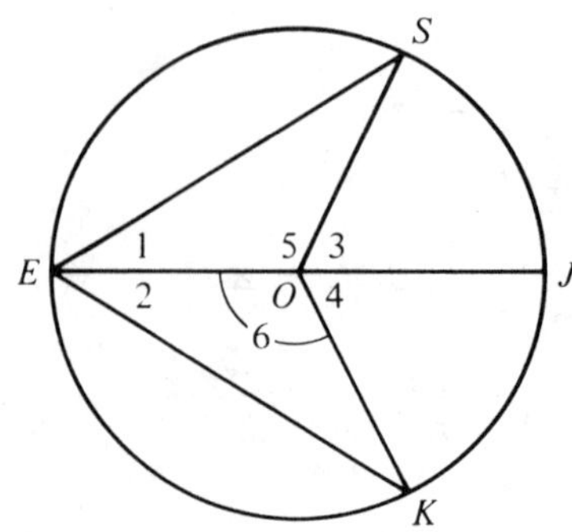

50. *Given*
$\odot O$
$\overline{EJ} \cong \overline{KS}$

To Prove
$\overline{EJ} \parallel \overline{KS}$

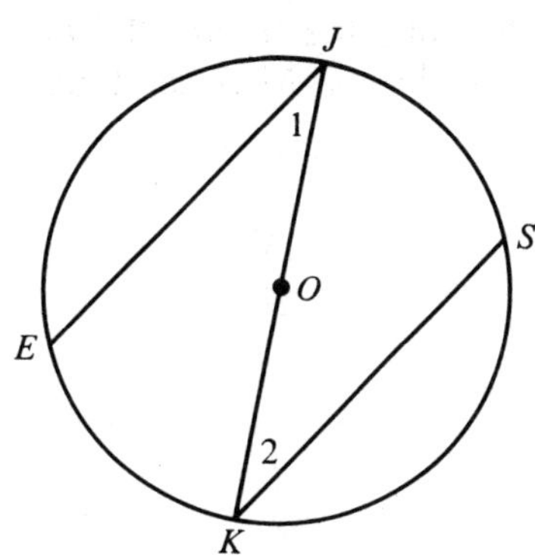

51. *Given*
$\odot O$
diams $\overline{GA}$, $\overline{LD}$

To Prove
GLAD rect

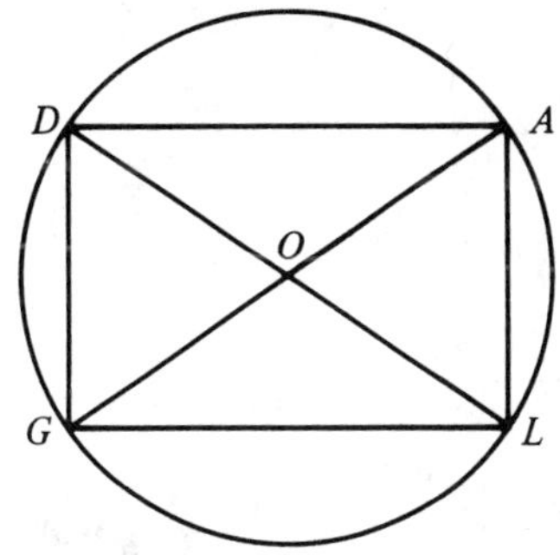

52. *Given*
$\odot O$
$\overline{OJ} \perp \overline{AB}$

To Prove
$\widehat{AJ} \cong \widehat{BJ}$

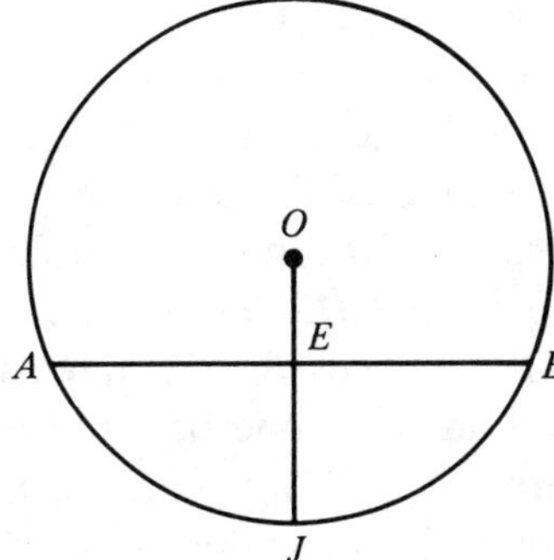

53. *Given*
$\odot O$
$\overline{DB} \cong \overline{CA}$

To Prove
$\overline{DA} \cong \overline{CB}$

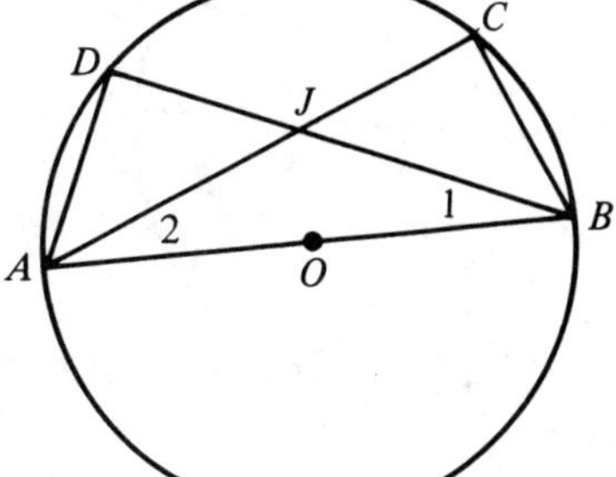

54. *Given*
⊙O
$\overline{AD} \parallel \overline{OC}$

To Prove
$\overset{\frown}{DC} \cong \overset{\frown}{CB}$

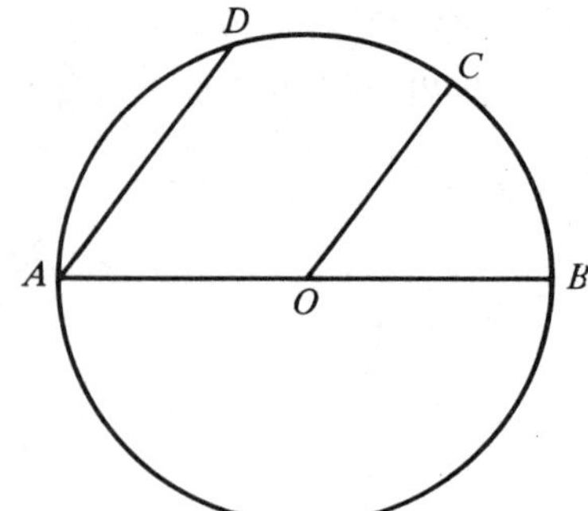

55. *Given*
⊙O
$\overset{\frown}{SB} \cong \overset{\frown}{BT} \cong \overset{\frown}{TP} \cong \overset{\frown}{PA}$

To Prove
$\overline{ST} \cong \overline{BP} \cong \overline{TA}$

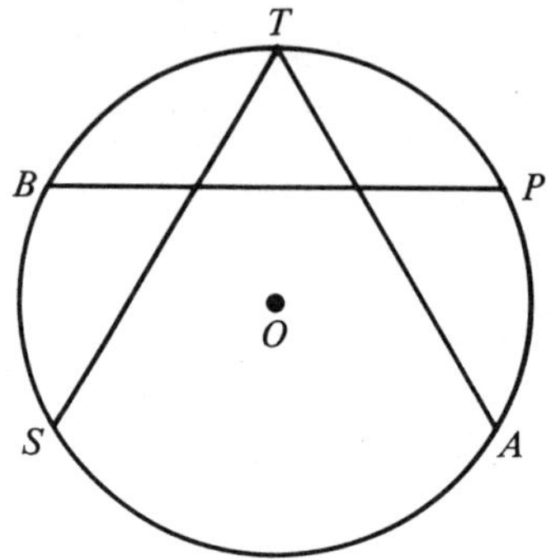

7.3 INSCRIBED ANGLES

Central angles played a major role in the previous section. This section develops several theorems about inscribed angles. There are three different types of inscribed angles when considered in relation to the center of the circle. First, one side of the angle may contain a diameter, as do $\measuredangle EJS$ and $\measuredangle SJK$ in Figure 7.7. Second, the circle's center may be in the angle's interior as is the case for $\measuredangle EJK$. Third, the center may be in the angle's exterior as it is for $\measuredangle ABC$. Theorem 73 states that for all three cases, the measure of an inscribed angle is one-half the degree measure of its intercepted arc. Thus, in Figure 7.7 $\angle EJS = \frac{1}{2}\overset{\frown}{ES}°$, $\angle EJK = \frac{1}{2}\overset{\frown}{EK}°$, and $\angle ABC = \frac{1}{2}\overset{\frown}{AC}°$. We prove the theorem by considering separately the three types of inscribed angles.

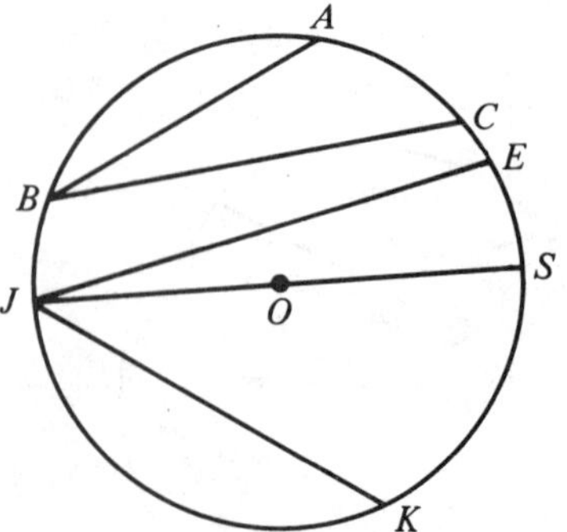

Figure 7.7

Theorem 73 The measure of an inscribed angle is equal to one-half the degree measure of its intercepted arc (inscr $\angle = \frac{1}{2}\frown^\circ$).

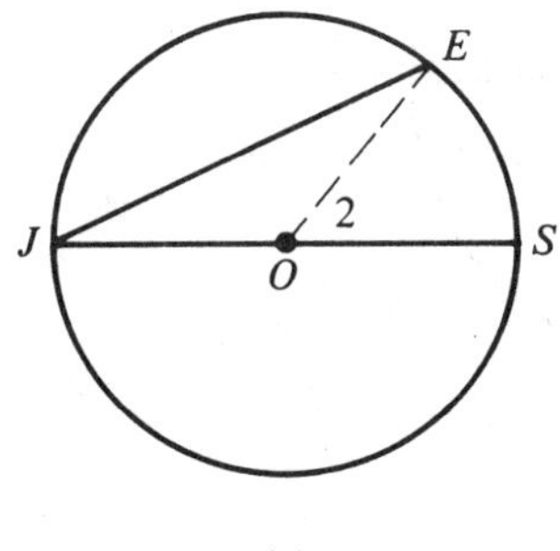

(a)

Given
$\odot O$
inscr $\measuredangle EJS$

To Prove
$\angle EJS = \frac{1}{2}\overset{\frown}{ES}^\circ$

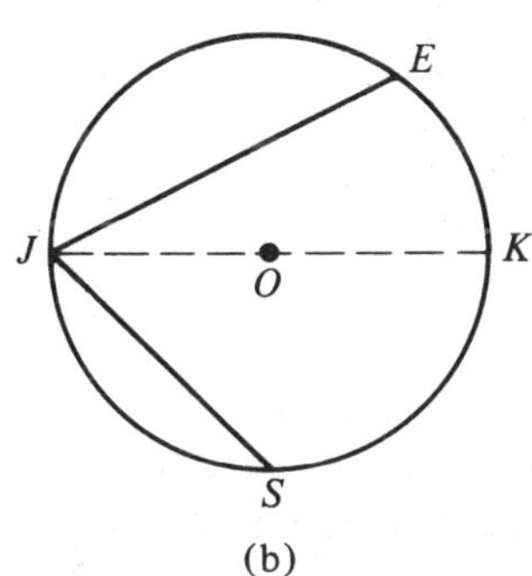

(b)

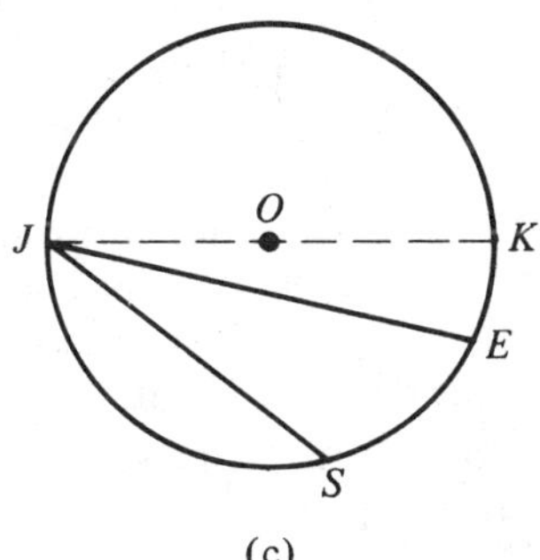

(c)

Statement	*Reason*
1. $\odot O$ and inscr $\measuredangle EJS$	1. given
(a) 2. Draw radius $\overline{OE}$.	2. 2 pts determ line
3. $\overline{OE} \cong \overline{OJ}$	3. radii $\odot \cong$
4. $\measuredangle J \cong \measuredangle E$	4. if 2 sides $\triangle \cong$, opp $\measuredangle$s $\cong$
5. $\angle J = \angle E$	5. $\cong$ iff meas $=$
6. $\angle J + \angle E = \angle 2$	6. ext $\angle$ = sum rem int $\measuredangle$s
7. $2\angle J = \angle 2$	7. subst and rearr props
8. $\angle 2 = \overset{\frown}{ES}^\circ$	8. meas min $\frown$ = cent $\angle$
9. $2\angle J = \overset{\frown}{ES}^\circ$	9. trans =
10. $\therefore \angle J = \frac{1}{2}\overset{\frown}{ES}^\circ$	10. $\frac{1}{2}$s of = are =
(b) 11. Draw diam $\overline{JK}$.	11. 2 pts determ line
12. $\angle EJK = \frac{1}{2}\overset{\frown}{EK}^\circ$, $\angle KJS = \frac{1}{2}\overset{\frown}{KS}^\circ$	12. inscr $\angle = \frac{1}{2}\frown^\circ$ (case [a])
13. $\angle EJK + \angle KJS = \frac{1}{2}\overset{\frown}{EK}^\circ + \frac{1}{2}\overset{\frown}{KS}^\circ$	13. = + =, sums =
14. $\angle EJK + \angle KJS = \frac{1}{2}(\overset{\frown}{EK}^\circ + \overset{\frown}{KS}^\circ)$	14. rearr props
15. $\angle EJS = \angle EJK + \angle KJS$ $\overset{\frown}{ES}^\circ = \overset{\frown}{EK}^\circ + \overset{\frown}{KS}^\circ$	15. whole = sum parts
16. $\therefore \angle EJS = \frac{1}{2}\overset{\frown}{ES}^\circ$	16. subst
(c) proof left as exercise	

In the proof of Theorem 73 note the use of (a) in the proof of (b). The proof of (c) is handled similarly.

The next theorem is a simple but important consequence of Theorem 73.

Theorem 74 If two inscribed angles in a circle intercept the same arc or congruent arcs, then the angles are congruent (inscr $\measuredangle$s interc same $\frown$ or $\cong$ $\frown$s are $\cong$).

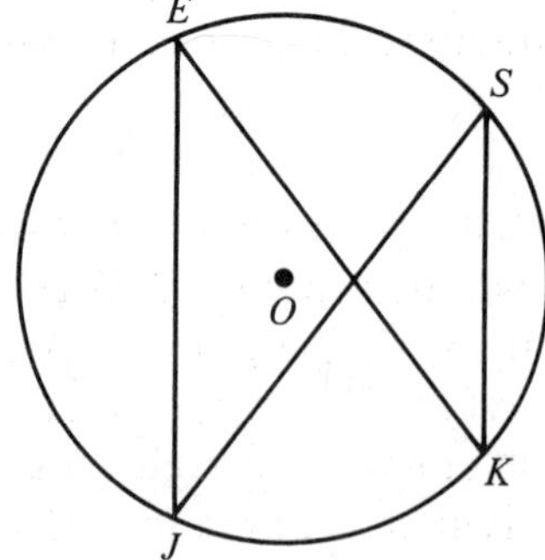

Given
$\odot O$
inscr $\measuredangle$s J and K

To Prove
$\measuredangle J \cong \measuredangle K$

Statement	*Reason*
1. $\odot O$, inscr $\measuredangle$s J, K	1. given
2. $\angle J = \frac{1}{2}\overset{\frown}{ES}^\circ$ $\angle K = \frac{1}{2}\overset{\frown}{ES}^\circ$	2. inscr $\angle = \frac{1}{2}\frown^\circ$
3. $\angle J = \angle K$	3. symm and trans =
4. $\therefore \measuredangle J \cong \measuredangle K$	4. $\cong$ iff meas =

The proof of Theorem 74 for the "congruent arcs" case is similar. Also, the converse of Theorem 74 is true. See exercise 39 for an example of its use.

An essential step in applying Theorem 74 is the identification of two inscribed angles that actually intercept the same arc or congruent arcs. One helpful device is marking with one color an arc and the sides of all the inscribed angles in the circle that intercept that arc. You may wish to try this in Example 1. Note that the new reason 2 in the proof of Example 1 is a natural extension of the discussion of bisection and Definitions 4.10–4.12 in Section 4.4

EXAMPLE 1

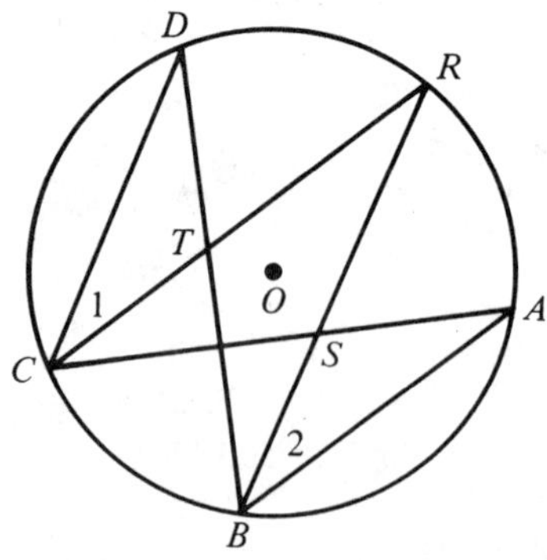

Given
$\odot O$
R midpt $\overset{\frown}{AD}$
$\overset{\frown}{AB} \cong \overset{\frown}{DC}$

To Prove
$\overline{BS} \cong \overline{CT}$

Statement	*Reason*
1. $\odot O$, R midpoint $\overset{\frown}{AD}$	1. given
2. $\overset{\frown}{AR} \cong \overset{\frown}{DR}$	2. midpt $\div$ $\frown$ into 2 $\cong$ $\frown$s
3. $\measuredangle 2 \cong \measuredangle 1$	3. inscr $\measuredangle$s interc $\cong$ $\frown$s are $\cong$
4. $\overset{\frown}{AB} \cong \overset{\frown}{DC}$	4. given
5. $\overline{AB} \cong \overline{DC}$	5. if $\frown$s $\cong$, chs $\cong$
6. $\measuredangle A \cong \measuredangle D$	6. inscr $\measuredangle$s interc same $\frown$ are $\cong$
7. $\triangle ABS \cong \triangle DCT$	7. asa $\cong$ asa
8. $\therefore \overline{BS} \cong \overline{CT}$	8. cpctc

The next theorem is really a corollary of Theorem 73. The Greek geometer Thales (640–546 B.C.), mentioned in Chapters 1 and 2, is generally credited with discovering this next theorem.

Theorem 75 If an inscribed angle intercepts a semicircle, then it is a right angle (inscr ∡ interc semi ⊙ is rt ∡).

The proof is simple and is omitted. It depends on the facts that, in Figure 7.8, $\widehat{EKS}° = 180°$ and $\angle EJS = \frac{1}{2}\widehat{EKS}°$. It is interesting to note ∡*EJS* is a right angle for every position of *J* on $\widehat{EJS}$ (other than the endpoints). It is also true that all triangles *EJS* are right triangles where $\overline{ES}$ is a diameter. Furthermore, the theorem provides a simple way to construct a right angle by drawing a circle. Finally, in Figure 7.8 we may say that ∡*EJS* is *inscribed in* semicircle $\widehat{EJS}$ and thus *any angle inscribed in a semicircle is a right angle*. Similarly, △*EJS* is inscribed in ⊙*O*.

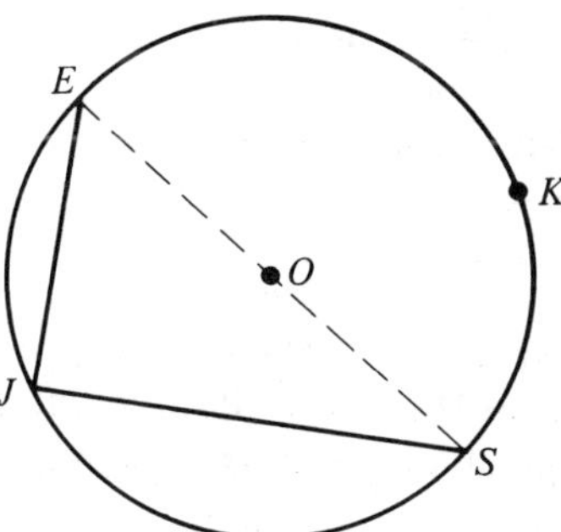

Figure 7.8

In general, *any polygon is inscribed in a circle* if and only if all its vertices are points of the circle; the *circle* is then said to be *circumscribed about the polygon*. Also, a *circle* is *inscribed in a polygon* if and only if it is tangent to each of the polygon's sides. These terms are illustrated in Figure 7.9.

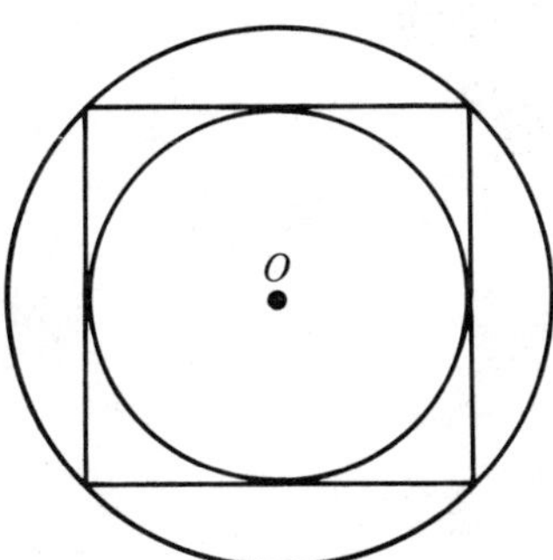

Figure 7.9 The square is inscribed in the larger circle. The larger circle is circumscribed about the square. The smaller circle is inscribed in the square.

The next theorem concerns a quadrilateral inscribed in a circle.

Theorem 76 If a quadrilateral is inscribed in a circle, then its opposite angles are supplementary (if quad inscr in ⊙, opp ∡s supp).

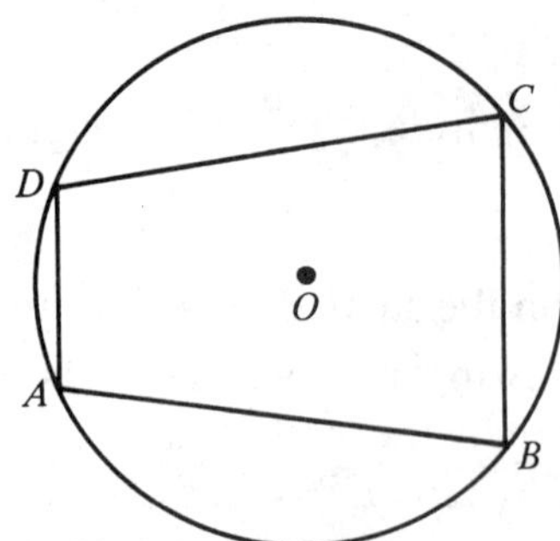

Given
⊙O
$ABCD$ inscr quad

To Prove
∡A supp ∡C
∡B supp ∡D

Statement	*Reason*
1. ⊙O with inscr quad $ABCD$	1. given
2. $\angle A = \frac{1}{2}\widehat{BCD}°$ $\angle C = \frac{1}{2}\widehat{BAD}°$	2. inscr $\angle = \frac{1}{2}$ ⌒°
3. $\angle A + \angle C = \frac{1}{2}\widehat{BCD}° + \frac{1}{2}\widehat{BAD}°$	3. = + =, sums =
4. $\angle A + \angle C = \frac{1}{2}(\widehat{BCD}° + \widehat{BAD}°)$	4. rearr props
5. $\widehat{BCD}° + \widehat{BAD}° = 360°$	5. whole = sum parts and meas ⊙ = 360°
6. $\angle A + \angle C = \frac{1}{2} \cdot 360° = 180°$	6. subst
7. ∴ ∡A supp ∡C	7. supp iff sum = 180°

The proof that ∡B is supplementary to ∡D is similar.

Inscribed angles may be used to prove part of a theorem about the arcs formed when parallel lines intersect a circle. There are three cases to consider.

Theorem 77 If two parallel lines intersect a circle, then the arcs of the circle between the parallel lines are congruent (if ∥ lines inters ⊙, ⌒s ≅).

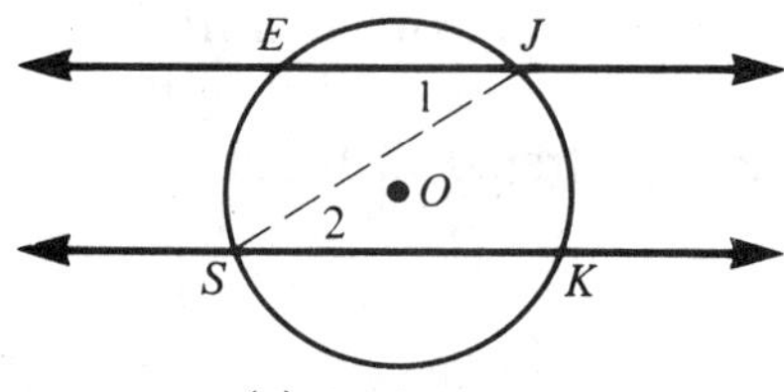

(a) two secants

Given
⊙ O
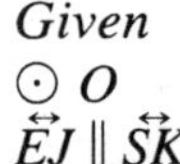
$\overleftrightarrow{EJ} \parallel \overleftrightarrow{SK}$

To Prove
(a) $\widehat{ES} \cong \widehat{JK}$
(b) $\widehat{SP} \cong \widehat{KP}$
(c) $\widehat{PAC} \cong \widehat{PBC}$

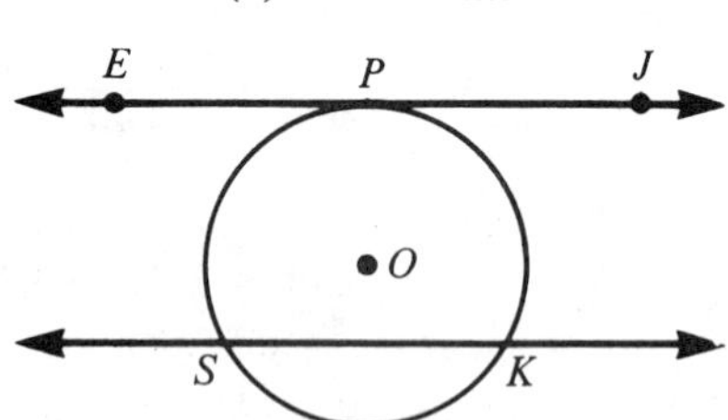

(b) secant and tangent

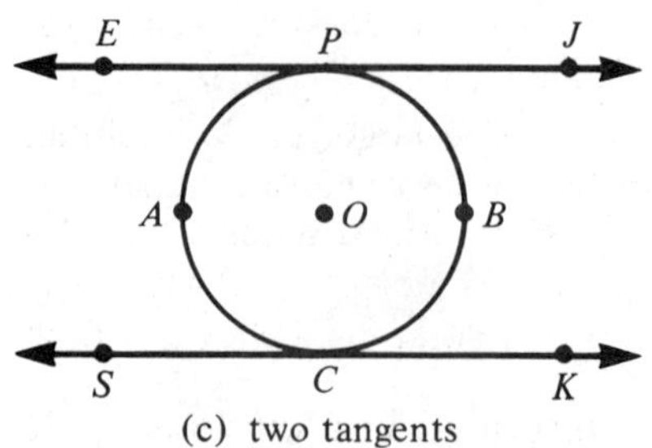

(c) two tangents

	Statement	*Reason*
	1. $\odot O$, $\overleftrightarrow{EJ} \parallel \overleftrightarrow{SK}$	1. given
(a)	2. Draw $\overline{SJ}$.	2. 2 pts determ line
	3. $\measuredangle 1 \cong \measuredangle 2$	3. $\not\Rightarrow$, alt int $\measuredangle$s $\cong$
	4. $\angle 1 = \angle 2$	4. $\cong$ iff meas $=$
	5. $\angle 1 = \frac{1}{2}\overset{\frown}{ES}^\circ$ $\angle 2 = \frac{1}{2}\overset{\frown}{JK}^\circ$	5. inscr $\angle = \frac{1}{2} \frown^\circ$
	6. $\frac{1}{2}\overset{\frown}{ES}^\circ = \frac{1}{2}\overset{\frown}{JK}^\circ$	6. symm and trans $=$
	7. $\overset{\frown}{ES}^\circ = \overset{\frown}{JK}^\circ$	7. $= \cdot =$, prods $=$
	8. $\therefore \overset{\frown}{ES} \cong \overset{\frown}{JK}$	8. $\cong$ iff meas $=$

Cases (b) and (c) may be proved using Theorem 84 of the next section. The proofs are left as exercises.

We conclude this section with an example using the foregoing theorems to find the measures of arcs and angles.

EXAMPLE 2

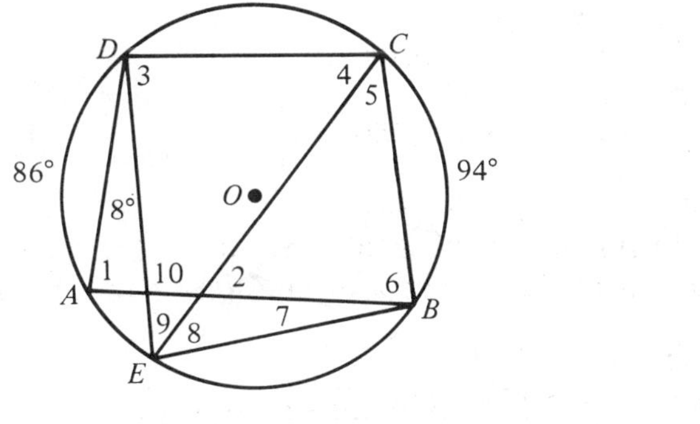

Given

$\odot O$

$\overline{BC} \parallel \overline{ED}$

$\overset{\frown}{BC}^\circ = 94^\circ$

$\overset{\frown}{AD}^\circ = 86^\circ$

$\angle ADE = 8^\circ$

Find

$\overset{\frown}{AE}^\circ$

$\overset{\frown}{DC}^\circ$

$\overset{\frown}{EB}^\circ$

$\measuredangle$s 1–10

Answers

Use the facts that $\overset{\frown}{EB}^\circ = \overset{\frown}{DC}^\circ$ (if $\parallel$ lines inters $\odot$, $\frown$s $\cong$) and $\overset{\frown}{AE}^\circ = 16^\circ$ (inscr $\angle = \frac{1}{2} \frown^\circ$).

$\overset{\frown}{AE}^\circ = 16^\circ$	$\angle 2 = 55^\circ$	$\angle 6 = 84^\circ$
$\overset{\frown}{DC}^\circ = 82^\circ$	$\angle 3 = 88^\circ$	$\angle 7 = 8^\circ$
$\overset{\frown}{EB}^\circ = 82^\circ$	$\angle 4 = 51^\circ$	$\angle 8 = 47^\circ$
$\angle 1 = 88^\circ$	$\angle 5 = 41^\circ$	$\angle 9 = 41^\circ$
		$\angle 10 = 96^\circ$

EXERCISES FOR 7.3

In exercises 1–20 answer true or false.

1. The measure of an inscribed angle can be greater than the measure of a central angle.

2. Two angles intercepting the same arc are congruent.

3. All points of a circle are in the exterior of a quadrilateral inscribed in it.

4. A circle can be constructed that contains any three points in a plane.

5. If quadrilateral $ABCD$ is inscribed in circle O and $\angle A = 78^\circ$, then $\angle C = 112^\circ$.

6. If two inscribed angles intercept the same arc, then the two angles are supplementary.

7. A pentagon whose vertices are points of a circle is inscribed in the circle.

8. If P, A, R, and K are four points of a circle with $\overline{PA}$ parallel and congruent to $\overline{KR}$, then $PARK$ is a rectangle.

9. If P, A, B, and C, in that order, are four points of a circle, then $\measuredangle PAC \cong \measuredangle PBC$.

10. If $EUCLID$ is an inscribed regular hexagon, then $\overset{\frown}{EU}^\circ = 68^\circ$.

11. If $\measuredangle EJS$ is an inscribed angle, then the measure of $\measuredangle EJS$ does not change if J names any other point on $\overset{\frown}{EJS}$ except E or S.

12. If a rectangle is inscribed in a circle, then

its diagonals are diameters of the circle.

13. An inscribed angle cannot have a diameter as one of its sides.

14. If an inscribed angle intercepts a semicircle, then it is a straight angle.

15. If a quadrilateral is inscribed in a circle, then its consecutive angles are supplementary.

16. When a circle is inscribed in a polygon, it is tangent to each of the polygon's sides.

17. If two parallel lines intersect a circle, three of the four arcs produced by the lines could have measures 112°, 132°, and 57°.

18. A line always intersects a circle in zero, one, or two points.

19. An angle inscribed in an arc that is less than a semicircle is an obtuse angle.

20. If $\triangle ABC$ is inscribed in a circle, then radii drawn to points A and B form an angle that is twice as large as $\measuredangle ACB$.

In exercises 21–28 explain what is wrong with the information marked on the figure. Point O is the center of each circle.

21.

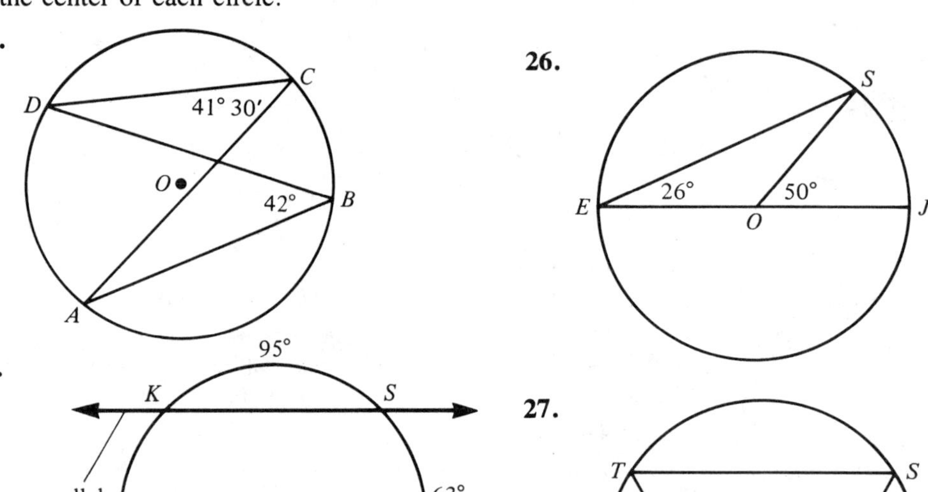

22.

23.

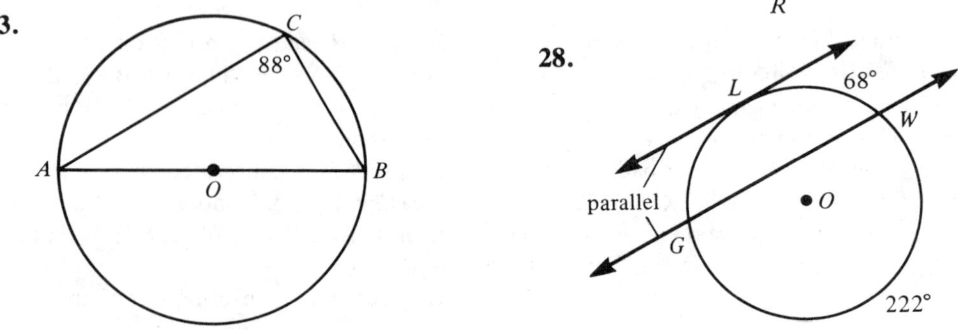

24.

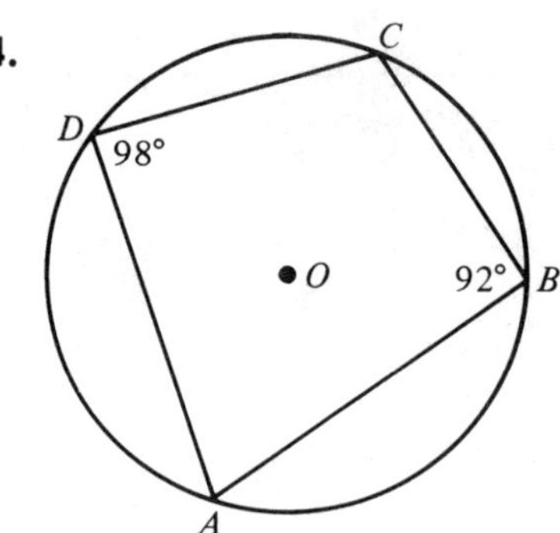

25.

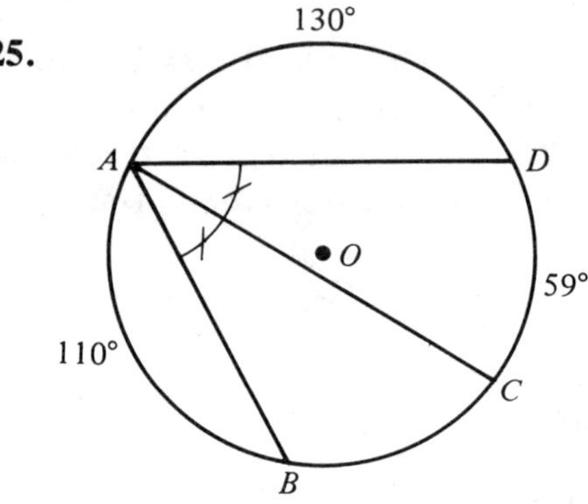

26.

27.

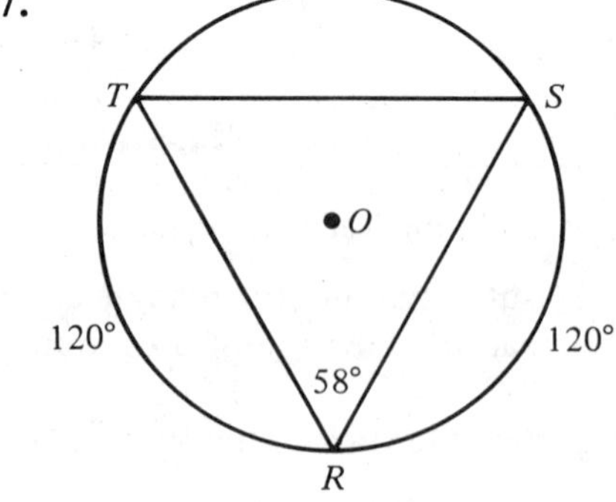

28.

In exercises 29–37 copy the figure, mark it, and find the requested measures.

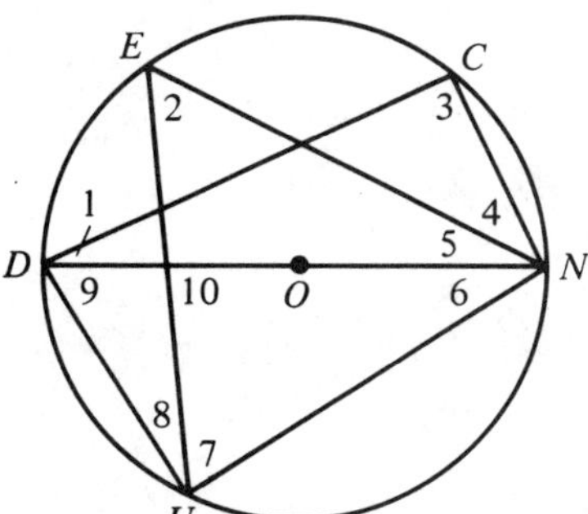

29. *Given*
$\odot O$
$\overset{\frown}{ED}° = 42°$
$\overset{\frown}{CN}° = 46°$
$\overset{\frown}{DU}° = 56°$

Find
$\measuredangle$s 1–10

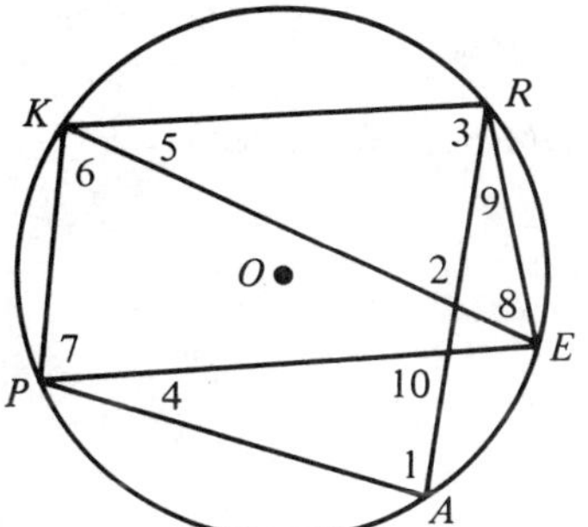

30. *Given*
$\odot O$
$\overline{KR} \parallel \overline{PE}$
$\overset{\frown}{KR}° = 91°$
$\overset{\frown}{PA}° = 87°$
$\overset{\frown}{AE}° = 17°$

Find
$\measuredangle$s 1–10

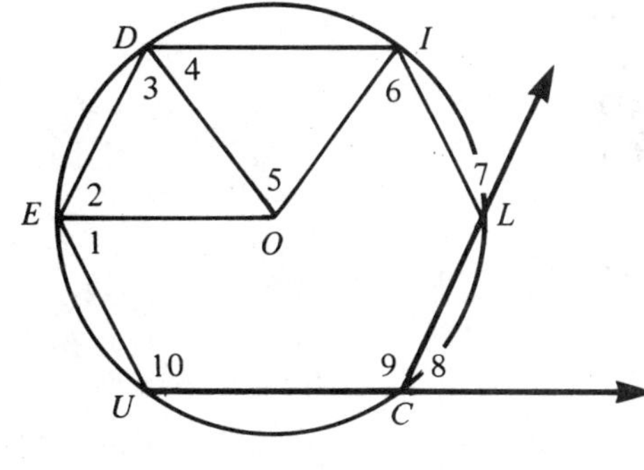

31. *Given*
$\odot O$
EUCLID inscr reg hexagon

Find
$\measuredangle$s 1–10

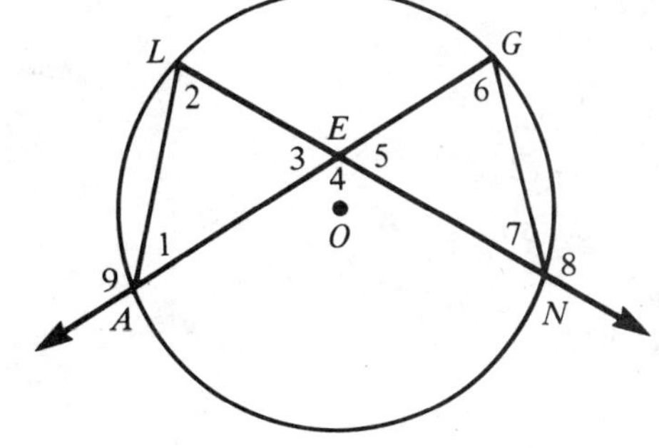

32. *Given* $\odot O$
$\overset{\frown}{LG}° = 88°$
$\overset{\frown}{AN}° = 151°$

Find
$\measuredangle$s 1–9

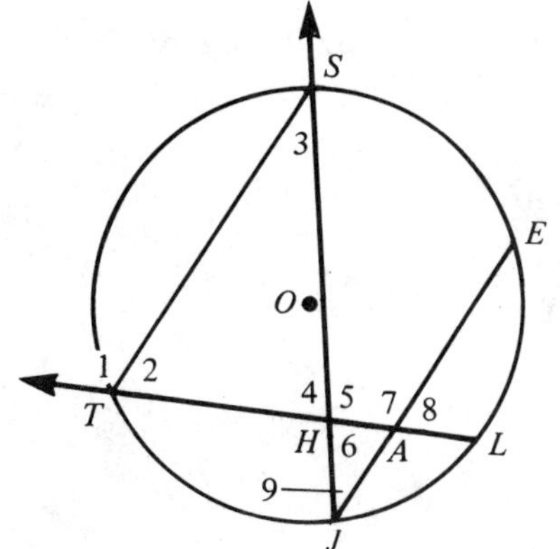

33. *Given*
$\odot O$
$\overline{TS} \parallel \overline{JE}$
$\overset{\frown}{SE}° = 72°$
$\overset{\frown}{LE}° = 56°$

Find
$\measuredangle$s 1–9

34. *Given*
$\odot O$
$\overset{\frown}{TP}° = 74°$
$\overset{\frown}{AE}° = 54°$

Find
$\measuredangle$s 1–8

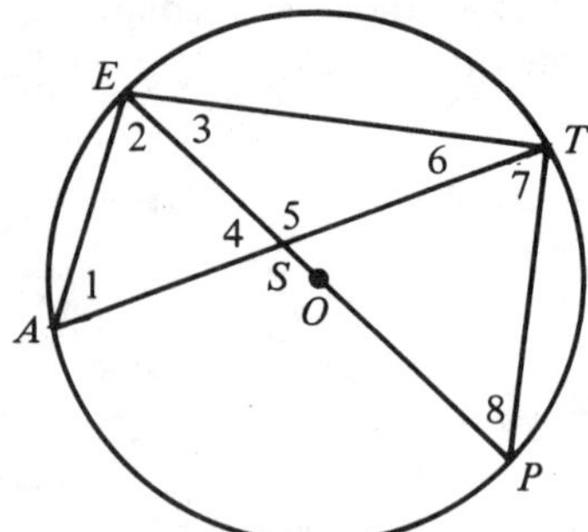

35. *Given*
$\odot O$
inscr trap *AXIM* ($\overline{AX}$, $\overline{MI}$ bases)
$\overset{\frown}{MI}° = 81°$
$\overset{\frown}{IX}° = 59°$

Find
$\measuredangle$s 1–10

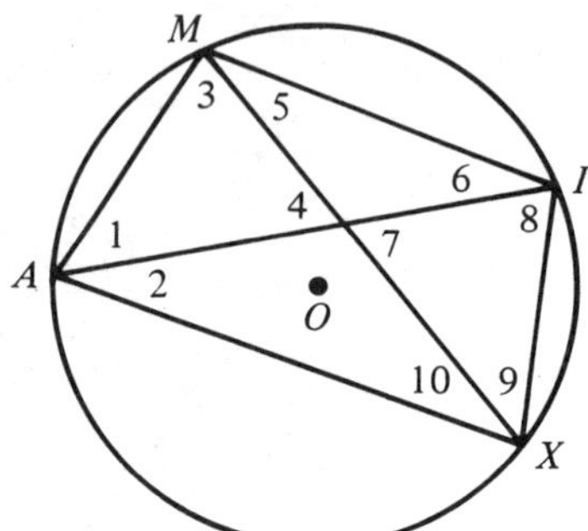

36. *Given*
$\odot O$
$\angle AOF = 111°$
$\overline{CB}$ bis $\measuredangle AOF$

Find
$\measuredangle$s 1–10

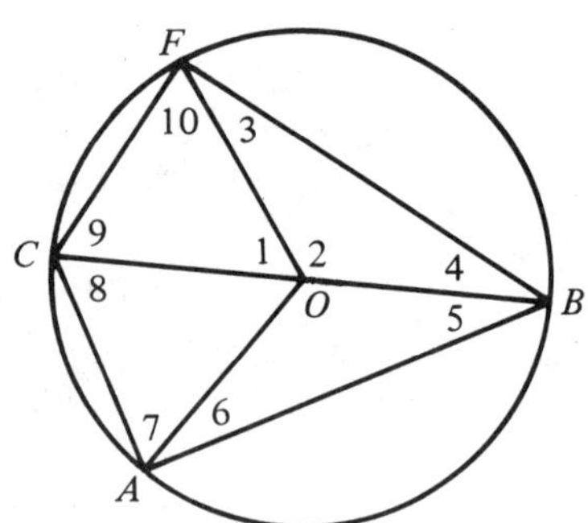

37. *Given*
$\odot O$
$\overline{PA} \cong \overline{YT}$
H midpt $\overset{\frown}{AT}$
$\overset{\frown}{AH}° = \frac{1}{3}\overset{\frown}{PY}°$
$\overset{\frown}{PA}° = 97°30'$

Find
$\measuredangle$s 1–10

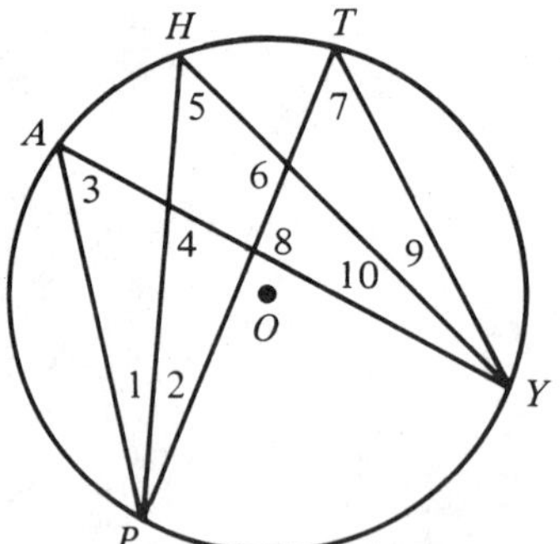

In exercise 38 and 39 copy the figure, mark it, and supply the missing reasons in each proof.

38. *Given*
$\odot O$
X midpt $\overline{AI}$

To Prove
$\overset{\frown}{EX} \cong \overset{\frown}{IX}$

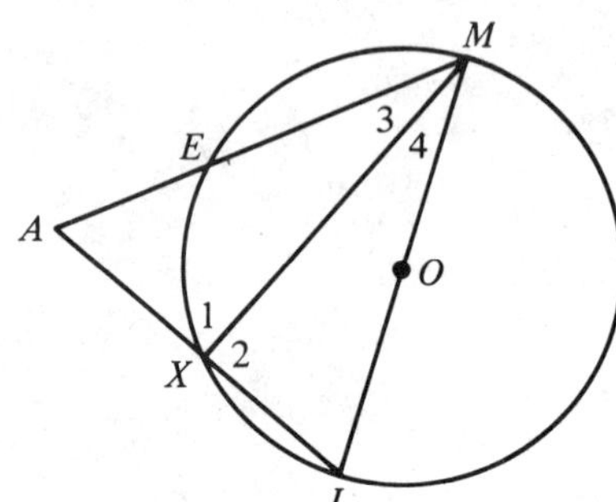

Statement	Reason
1. $\odot O$	1. ?
2. X midpt $\overline{AI}$	2. ?
3. $\overline{AX} \cong \overline{IX}$	3. ?
4. $\measuredangle 2$ rt $\measuredangle$	4. ?
5. $\angle 2 = 90°$	5. ?
6. $\measuredangle 1$ supp $\measuredangle 2$	6. ?
7. $\angle 1 + \angle 2 = 180°$	7. ?
8. $\angle 1 = 90°$	8. ?
9. $\angle 1 = \angle 2$	9. ?
10. $\measuredangle 1 \cong \measuredangle 2$	10. ?
11. $\overline{MX} \cong \overline{MX}$	11. ?
12. $\triangle AXM \cong \triangle IXM$	12. ?
13. $\measuredangle 3 \cong \measuredangle 4$	13. ?
14. $\therefore \widehat{EX} \cong \widehat{IX}$	14. ?

39. *Given*
$\odot O$
$\overline{AD}$ bis $\measuredangle BAC$
$\overline{AB} \parallel \overline{DE}$

To Prove
$\overline{AC} \cong \overline{DE}$

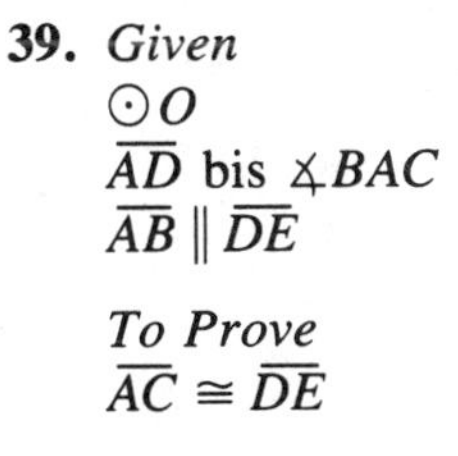

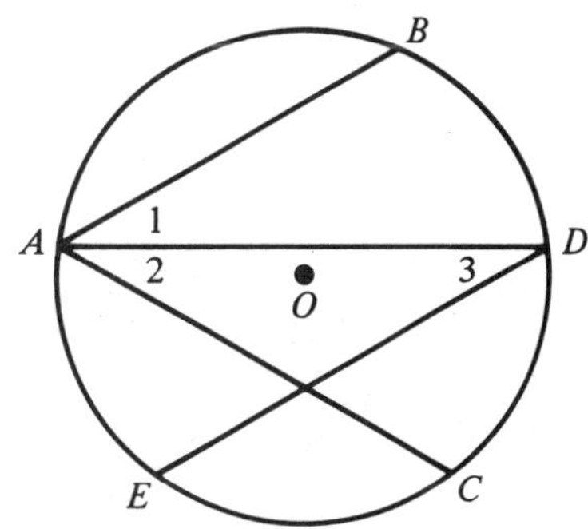

Statement	Reason
1. $\odot O$	1. ?
2. $\overline{AD}$ bis $\measuredangle BAC$	2. ?
3. $\measuredangle 1 \cong \measuredangle 2$	3. ?
4. $\overline{AB} \parallel \overline{DE}$	4. ?
5. $\measuredangle 3 \cong \measuredangle 1$	5. ?
6. $\measuredangle 3 \cong \measuredangle 2$	6. ?
7. $\widehat{AE} \cong \widehat{DC}$	7. If two angles inscribed in a circle are congruent, then their intercepted arcs are congruent.
8. $\widehat{EC} \cong \widehat{EC}$	8. ?
9. $\widehat{AE} + \widehat{EC} \cong \widehat{DC} + \widehat{EC}$	9. ?
10. $\widehat{AC} \cong \widehat{AE} + \widehat{EC}$	10. ?
11. $\widehat{DC} + \widehat{EC} \cong \widehat{DE}$	11. ?
12. $\widehat{AC} \cong \widehat{DE}$	12. ?
13. $\therefore \overline{AC} \cong \overline{DE}$	13. ?

In exercises 40–48 copy the figure, the hypothesis, and the conclusion. Mark the figure and write a proof.

40. *Given*
⊙O
$\measuredangle 1 \cong \measuredangle 2$

To Prove
$\triangle TIP \cong \triangle ITG$

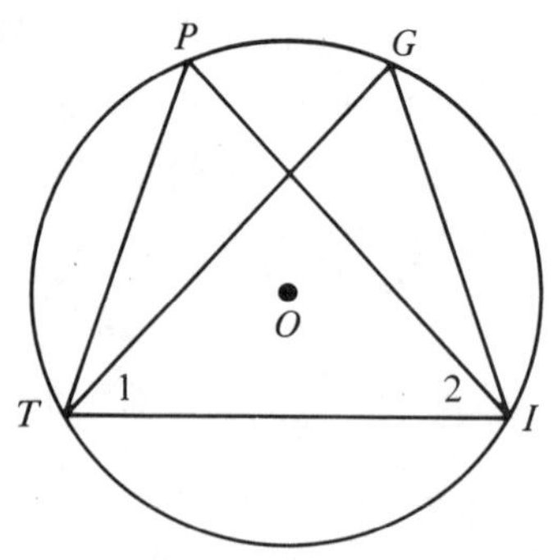

41. *Given*
⊙O
$\overset{\frown}{EJ} \cong \overset{\frown}{QP}$
$\overset{\frown}{ES} \cong \overset{\frown}{QR}$

To Prove
$\measuredangle 1 \cong \measuredangle 2$

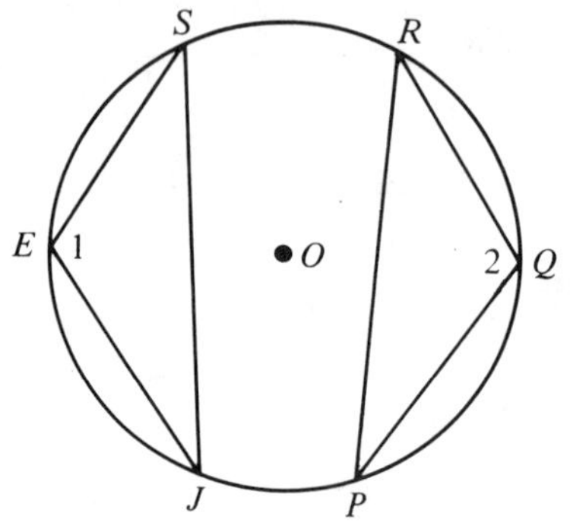

42. *Given*
⊙O
$\overset{\frown}{AB} \cong \overset{\frown}{DC}$

To Prove
$\triangle$I $\cong$ $\triangle$II

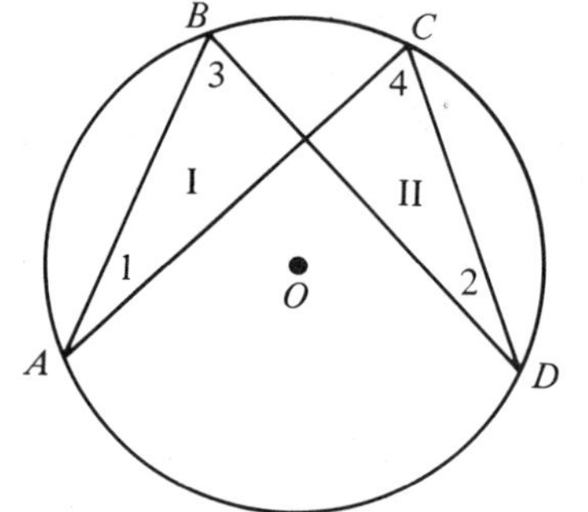

43. *Given*
⊙O
ABCD inscr trap ($\overline{AB}$, $\overline{DC}$ bases)

To Prove
$\measuredangle A \cong \measuredangle B$

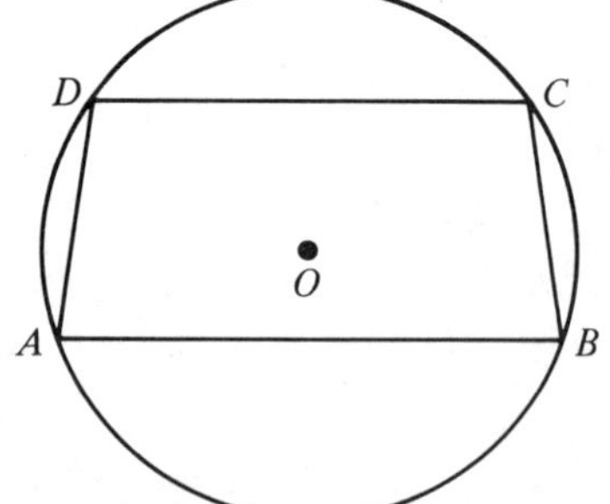

44. *Given*
⊙O
$\overset{\frown}{AD} \cong \overset{\frown}{BC}$

To Prove
$\overline{AC} \cong \overline{BD}$

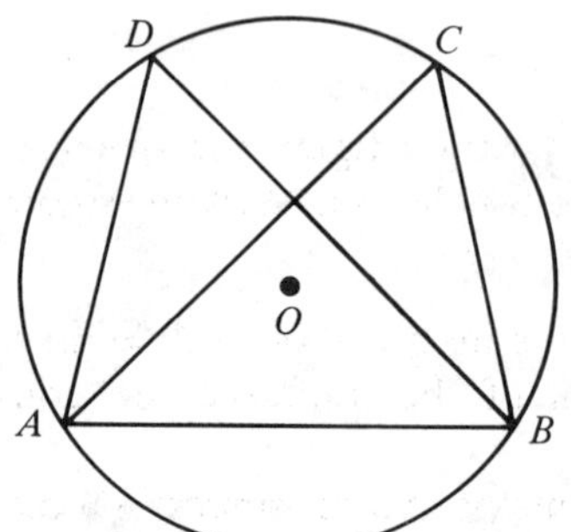

45. *Given*
$\odot O$
$\overset{\frown}{BC} \cong \overset{\frown}{EC}$

To Prove
C midpt $\overline{BD}$

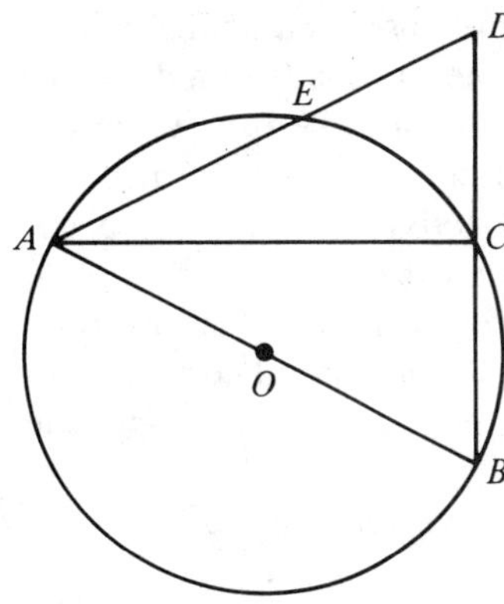

46. *Given*
$\odot O$
$\square SKMJ$

To Prove
$\triangle SKE$ isos

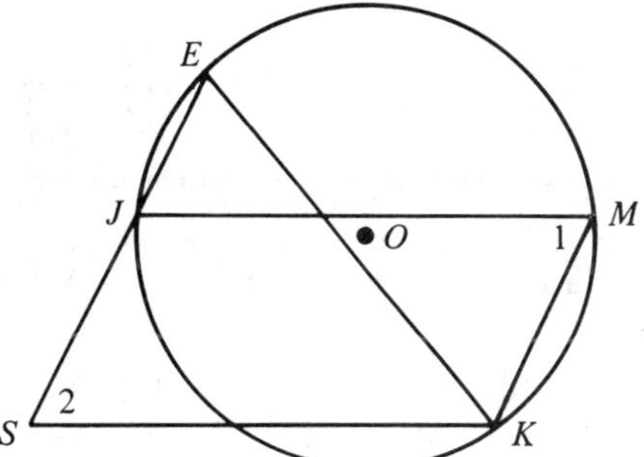

47. *Given*
$\odot O$
$\overset{\frown}{ES} \cong \overset{\frown}{EK}$

To Prove
$\overline{SJ} \cong \overline{KJ}$

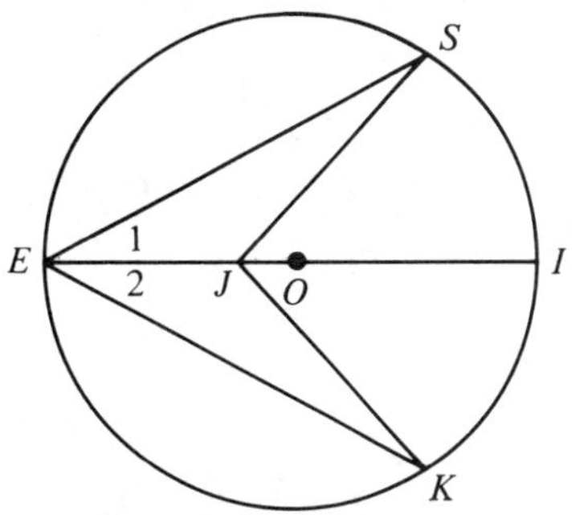

48. *Given*
$\odot O$
$\overline{CE} \perp \overline{AB}$
$\overline{AD} \perp \overline{BC}$

To Prove
$\overset{\frown}{BE} \cong \overset{\frown}{BD}$

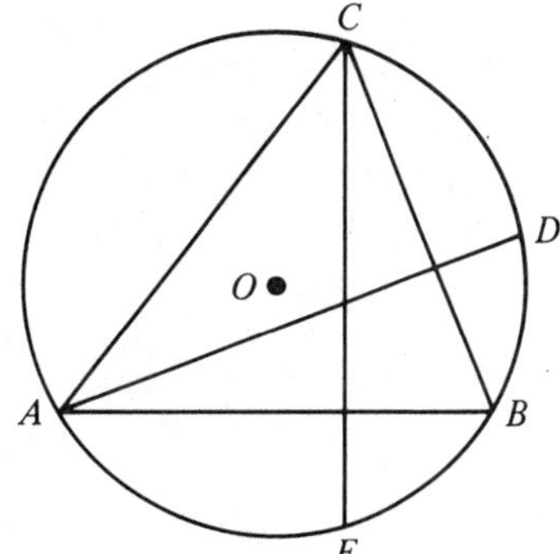

In exercises 49–54 draw a figure and write the hypothesis and the conclusion. Mark the figure and write a proof.

49. If a trapezoid is inscribed in a circle, then the diagonals of the trapezoid are congruent.

50. If the endpoints of two diameters in a circle are joined to form a quadrilateral, then the quadrilateral is a rectangle.

51. If a chord is parallel to a diameter in a circle and their endpoints are joined to form a quadrilateral, then the quadrilateral is an isosceles trapezoid.

52. In a circle, if two inscribed angles whose vertices are on the same side of a diameter intercept the same arc, then the three angles of one of the triangles formed are congruent, respectively, to the three angles of the other triangle.

53. If a quadrilateral is inscribed in a circle, then any angle of the quadrilateral is congruent to an exterior angle at the opposite vertex.

54. If a circle is drawn with one of the congruent sides of an isosceles triangle as a diameter, then the circle bisects the triangle's base.

In exercises 55–57 use only a compass and straightedge in the constructions.

55. Draw a circle and construct an inscribed square. (Hint: Use a property of the square's diagonals.)

56. Draw a circle and construct an inscribed regular hexagon. (Hint: A side is a chord of the circle. How large is the chord's central angle?)

57. Draw a circle and construct an inscribed equilateral triangle. (Hint: See exercise 56.)

7.4 CHORDS, TANGENTS, AND SECANTS

There are many interesting and useful properties involving chords, tangents, and secants, and the angles and arcs that they form. We begin with a theorem about a secant that contains the center of a circle and is perpendicular to a chord.

Theorem 78 If a secant contains the center of a circle and is perpendicular to a chord, then the secant bisects the chord and its arc (sec thru cen $\perp$ ch bis ch and $\frown$).

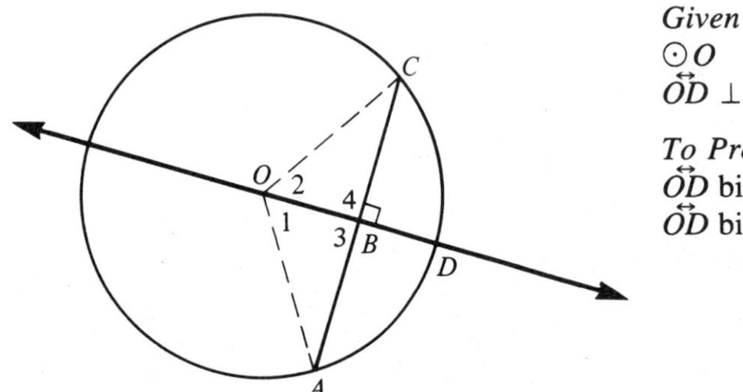

Given
$\odot O$
$\overleftrightarrow{OD} \perp \overline{AC}$

To Prove
$\overleftrightarrow{OD}$ bis $\overline{AC}$
$\overleftrightarrow{OD}$ bis $\overset{\frown}{AC}$

Statement	*Reason*
1. $\odot O$, $\overleftrightarrow{OD} \perp \overline{AC}$	1. given
2. $\angle 3$ and $\angle 4$ rt $\angle$s	2. $\perp$s form $\cong$ rt $\angle$s
3. Draw $\overline{OA}$ and $\overline{OC}$.	3. 2 pts determ line
4. $\overline{OA} \cong \overline{OC}$	4. radii $\odot$ $\cong$
5. $\overline{OB} \cong \overline{OB}$	5. refl $\cong$
6. $\triangle ABO \cong \triangle CBO$	6. hs $\cong$ hs
7. $\overline{AB} \cong \overline{CB}$	7. cpctc
8. $\therefore \overleftrightarrow{OD}$ bis $\overline{AC}$	8. bis $\div$ seg into 2 $\cong$ segs
9. $\angle 1 \cong \angle 2$	9. cpctc
10. $\overset{\frown}{AD} \cong \overset{\frown}{CD}$	10. if cent $\angle$s $\cong$, $\frown$s $\cong$
11. $\therefore \overleftrightarrow{OD}$ bis $\overset{\frown}{AC}$	11. bis $\div$ $\frown$ into 2 $\cong$ $\frown$s

You should be aware that Theorem 78 applies also to any subset of $\overleftrightarrow{OD}$, such as radius $\overline{OD}$.

Theorem 79 concerns chords that are equidistant from a circle's center. Recall that the distance from a point (the center) to a line (the chord) is the length of the perpendicular line segment joining the point and the line (Definition 3.16).

Theorem 79 If two chords of a circle (or of congruent circles) are equidistant from the center(s), then the chords are congruent (2 chs equidis from cen are ≅).

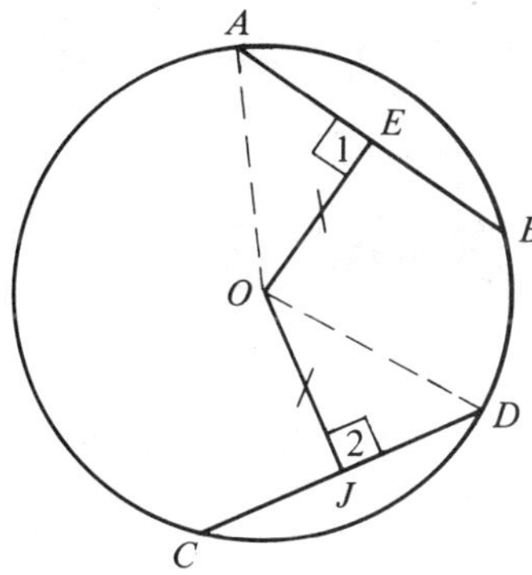

Given
$\odot O$
$\overline{OE} \cong \overline{OJ}$
$\overline{OE} \perp \overline{AB}$
$\overline{OJ} \perp \overline{CD}$

To Prove
$\overline{AB} \cong \overline{CD}$

Statement	*Reason*
1. $\odot O$, $\overline{OE} \cong \overline{OJ}$	1. given
2. Draw $\overline{OA}$ and $\overline{OD}$.	2. 2 pts determ line
3. $\overline{OA} \cong \overline{OD}$	3. radii $\odot$ ≅
4. $\overline{OE} \perp \overline{AB}$, $\overline{OJ} \perp \overline{CD}$	4. given
5. ∡1 rt ∡, ∡2 rt ∡	5. ⊥s form ≅ rt ∡s
6. $\triangle OEA \cong \triangle OJD$	6. hs ≅ hs
7. $\overline{AE} \cong \overline{DJ}$	7. cpctc
8. $\overline{OE}$ bis $\overline{AB}$, $\overline{OJ}$ bis $\overline{CD}$	8. sec thru cen ⊥ ch bis ch
9. ∴ $\overline{AB} \cong \overline{CD}$	9. doubles of ≅ are ≅

The proof for congruent circles is similar.

Statement 9 in the proof of Theorem 79 is a new shortcut. From statement 7 it follows that $AE = DJ$ and $2 \cdot AE = 2 \cdot DJ$. From statement 8 we have $2 \cdot AE = AB$ and $2 \cdot DJ = CD$. These equations prove that $AB = CD$ and thus $\overline{AB} \cong \overline{CD}$. All this is understood from reason 9 and we will use this shortcut as needed in subsequent work.

Theorem 80 (*Converse of Theorem 79.*) If two chords of a circle (or of congruent circles) are congruent, then the chords are equidistant from the center(s) of the circle(s). (2 ≅ chs are equidis from cen).

The proof of Theorem 80 is left as an exercise.

Example 1 uses two of the theorems in this section.

EXAMPLE 1

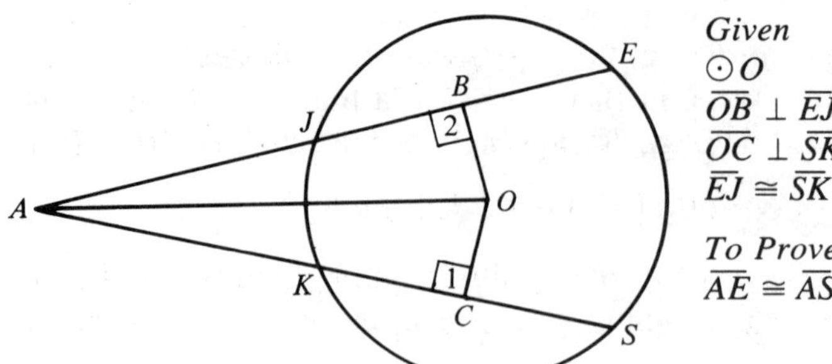

Given
$\odot O$
$\overline{OB} \perp \overline{EJ}$
$\overline{OC} \perp \overline{SK}$
$\overline{EJ} \cong \overline{SK}$

To Prove
$\overline{AE} \cong \overline{AS}$

Statement	*Reason*
1. $\odot O$, $\overline{OB} \perp \overline{EJ}$, $\overline{OC} \perp \overline{SK}$	1. given
2. $\overline{OB}$ bis $\overline{EJ}$, $\overline{OC}$ bis $\overline{SK}$	2. sec thru cen ⊥ ch bis ch
3. $\overline{EJ} \cong \overline{SK}$	3. given
4. $\overline{EB} \cong \overline{SC}$	4. $\frac{1}{2}$s of ≅ are ≅
5. $\measuredangle 1$ and $\measuredangle 2$ rt $\measuredangle$s	5. ⊥s form ≅ rt $\measuredangle$s
6. $\overline{OB} \cong \overline{OC}$	6. 2 ≅ chs are equidis from cen
7. $\overline{OA} \cong \overline{OA}$	7. refl ≅
8. $\triangle OBA \cong \triangle OCA$	8. hs ≅ hs
9. $\overline{AB} \cong \overline{AC}$	9. cpctc
10. $\overline{AB} + \overline{EB} \cong \overline{AC} + \overline{SC}$	10. ≅ + ≅, sums ≅
11. $\overline{AE} \cong \overline{AB} + \overline{EB}$ $\overline{AS} \cong \overline{AC} + \overline{SC}$	11. whole ≅ sum parts
12. ∴ $\overline{AE} \cong \overline{AS}$	12. symm and trans ≅

Theorem 81 states an important property of a tangent line to a circle. The proof is indirect.

Theorem 81 If a line is tangent to a circle, then it is perpendicular to the radius drawn to the point of contact (tan ⊥ rad to pt con).

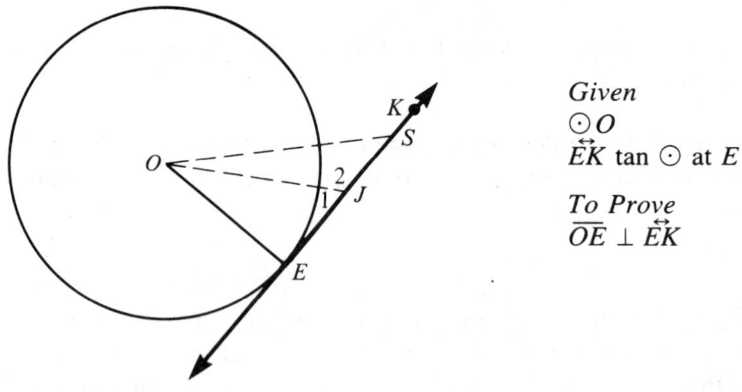

Given
$\odot O$
$\overleftrightarrow{EK}$ tan $\odot$ at E

To Prove
$\overline{OE} \perp \overleftrightarrow{EK}$

Assume that $\overline{OE}$ is not perpendicular to $\overleftrightarrow{EK}$. Then, by indirect proof:

Statement	*Reason*
1. $\odot O$, $\overleftrightarrow{EK}$ tan $\odot$ at E	1. given
2. Draw $\overline{OJ} \perp \overleftrightarrow{EK}$.	2. 1 ⊥ from pt to line
3. On $\overrightarrow{JK}$ opposite to $\overrightarrow{JE}$ construct $\overline{JS} \cong \overline{JE}$.	3. can copy seg
4. Draw $\overline{OS}$.	4. 2 pts determ line
5. $\measuredangle 1 \cong \measuredangle 2$	5. ⊥s form ≅ rt $\measuredangle$s
6. $\overline{OJ} \cong \overline{OJ}$	6. refl ≅

7. $\triangle OJE \cong \triangle OJS$	7. sas ≅ sas
8. $\overline{OE} \cong \overline{OS}$	8. cpctc
9. S is on ⊙, so $\overleftrightarrow{EK}$ inters ⊙ in 2 pts	9. ⊙ set of pts at given dis from given pt
10. $\overleftrightarrow{EK}$ inters ⊙ in exactly 1 pt	10. tan inters ⊙ 1 pt
11. ∴ $\overline{OE} \perp \overleftrightarrow{EK}$	11. statement 10 contradicts statement 9

Theorem 81 simplifies our proof of the next theorem.

Theorem 82 If two lines are tangent to a circle and contain a point in its exterior, then the line segments joining the point to the circle are congruent (tans to ⊙ ≅).

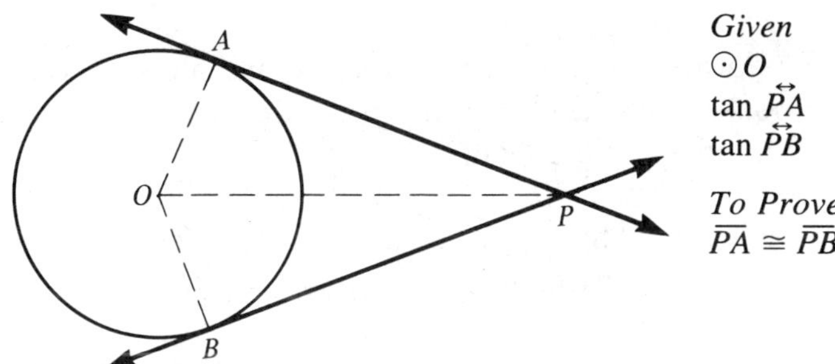

Given
⊙O
tan $\overleftrightarrow{PA}$
tan $\overleftrightarrow{PB}$

To Prove
$\overline{PA} \cong \overline{PB}$

Statement	*Reason*
1. ⊙O, tan $\overleftrightarrow{PA}$, tan $\overleftrightarrow{PB}$	1. given
2. Draw $\overline{OA}$ and $\overline{OB}$.	2. 2 pts determ line
3. $\overline{OA} \perp \overleftrightarrow{PA}$, $\overline{OB} \perp \overleftrightarrow{PB}$	3. tan ⊥ rad to pt con
4. ∡OAP and ∡OBP rt ∡s	4. ⊥s form ≅ rt ∡s
5. $\overline{OA} \cong \overline{OB}$	5. radii ⊙ ≅
6. Draw $\overline{OP}$.	6. 2 pts determ line
7. $\overline{OP} \cong \overline{OP}$	7. refl ≅
8. $\triangle OAP \cong \triangle OBP$	8. hs ≅ hs
9. ∴ $\overline{PA} \cong \overline{PB}$	9. cpctc

The three theorems and the example that follow concern angles formed by chords, tangents, and secants.

Theorem 83 If an angle is formed by two chords in a circle, then the measure of the angle is one-half the sum of the measures of the arcs intercepted by the angle and its vertical angle (2 chs $\angle = \frac{1}{2}$sum $\frown$°s).

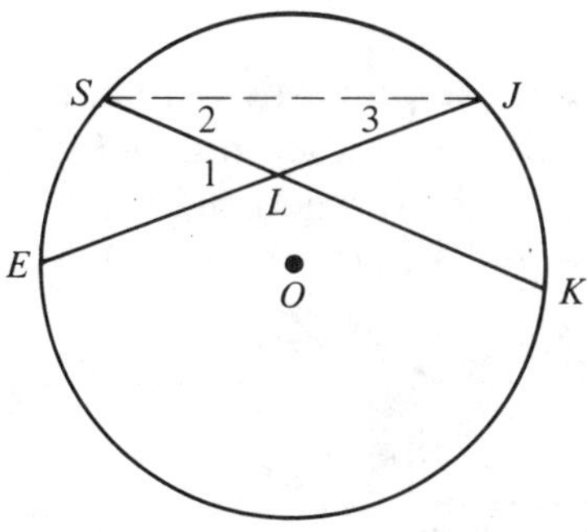

Given
⊙O
chs $\overline{EJ}$ and $\overline{SK}$ inters at L

To Prove
$\angle 1 = \frac{1}{2}(\overset{\frown}{JK}° + \overset{\frown}{SE}°)$

Statement	*Reason*
1. ⊙O, chs $\overline{EJ}$, $\overline{SK}$ inters at L	1. given
2. Draw $\overline{SJ}$.	2. 2 pts determ line

3. $\angle 2 = \frac{1}{2}\widehat{JK}°$ $\angle 3 = \frac{1}{2}\widehat{SE}°$	3. inscr $\angle = \frac{1}{2}\frown°$
4. $\angle 2 + \angle 3 = \frac{1}{2}\widehat{JK}° + \frac{1}{2}\widehat{SE}°$	4. = + =, sums =
5. $\angle 1 = \angle 2 + \angle 3$	5. ext $\angle$ = sum rem int $\angle$s
6. $\angle 1 = \frac{1}{2}\widehat{JK}° + \frac{1}{2}\widehat{SE}°$	6. trans =
7. $\therefore \angle 1 = \frac{1}{2}(\widehat{JK}° + \widehat{SE}°)$	7. rearr props

The conclusion in Theorem 83 holds for each of the four angles formed by the chords. The proofs for the other three are similar to the above proof for $\angle 1$.

Theorem 84 If an angle is formed by a tangent to a circle and a chord, one of whose endpoints is the point of contact, then the measure of the angle is one-half the measure of its intercepted arc (tan, ch $\angle = \frac{1}{2}\frown°$).

The angle in Theorem 84 is called "the angle formed by a tangent and a chord." Similar language names the angles in Theorem 85.

Theorem 85 If an angle is formed by two secants or a tangent and a secant or two tangents intersecting in the exterior of the circle, then the measure of the angle is one-half the difference of the measures of the intercepted arcs (2 secs $\angle = \frac{1}{2}$ diff $\frown°$s) (tan, sec $\angle = \frac{1}{2}$ diff $\frown°$s) (2 tan $\angle = \frac{1}{2}$ diff $\frown°$s).

Theorems 84 and 85 are illustrated in Figure 7.10. Their proofs are left as exercises.

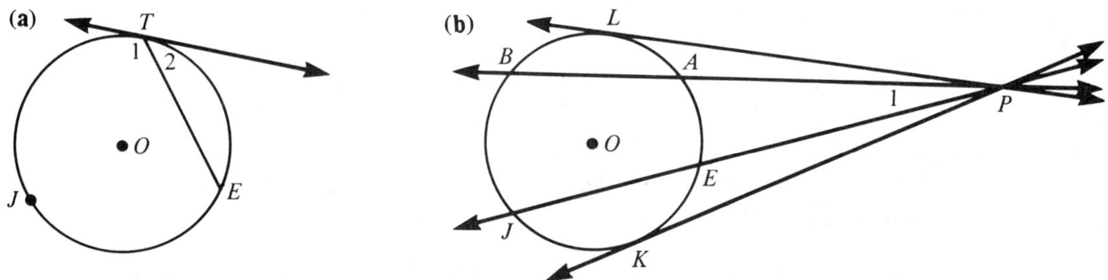

Figure 7.10 (a) Theorem 84; $\angle 1 = \frac{1}{2}\widehat{TJE}°$, $\angle 2 = \frac{1}{2}\widehat{TE}°$. (b) Theorem 85; $\angle 1 = \frac{1}{2}(\widehat{BJ}° - \widehat{AE}°)$, $\angle BPK = \frac{1}{2}(\widehat{BJK}° - \widehat{AK}°)$, $\angle LPK = \frac{1}{2}(\widehat{LBK}° - \widehat{LAK}°)$.

Figure 7.11 suggests a way to remember some of the properties of angles and arcs in circles. Note that the sizes of the angles decrease from left to right and that O is the circle's center. The following arcs and angles are shown in Figure 7.11:

Given arcs: 120°, 80°

Central angle: 120°

Angle formed by 2 chords: $100° = \dfrac{120° + 80°}{2}$

Inscribed angle: $60° = \frac{1}{2} \cdot 120°$

Angle formed by two secants: $20° = \dfrac{120° - 80°}{2}$

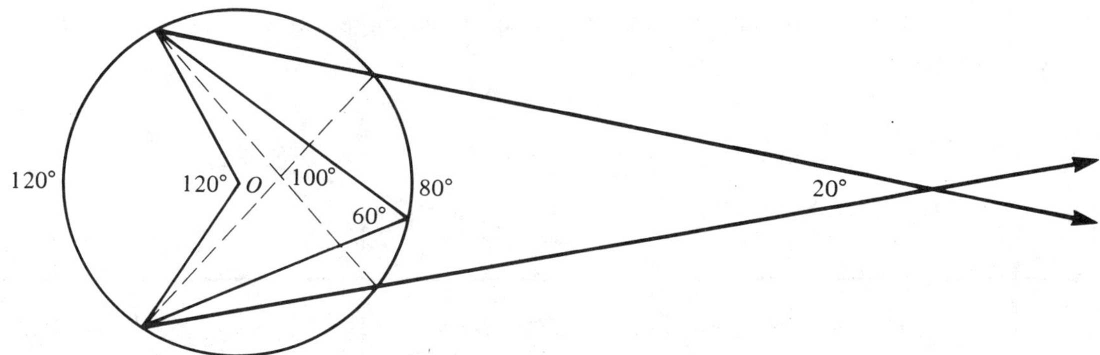

Figure 7.11

Example 2 illustrates many of the foregoing theorems.

EXAMPLE 2

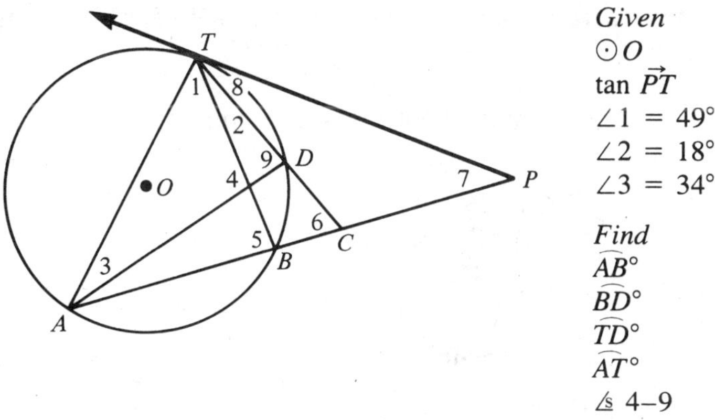

Given
$\odot O$
tan $\overrightarrow{PT}$
$\angle 1 = 49°$
$\angle 2 = 18°$
$\angle 3 = 34°$

Find
$\overset{\frown}{AB}°$
$\overset{\frown}{BD}°$
$\overset{\frown}{TD}°$
$\overset{\frown}{AT}°$
$\angle$s 4–9

Answers

$\overset{\frown}{AB}° = 98°$ (inscr $\angle = \frac{1}{2}\frown°$) $\overset{\frown}{BD}° = 36°$ (inscr $\angle = \frac{1}{2}\frown°$)

$\overset{\frown}{TD}° = 68°$ (inscr $\angle = \frac{1}{2}\frown°$) $\overset{\frown}{AT}° = 158°$ (360° in $\odot$)

$\angle 4 = \dfrac{158° + 36°}{2} = 97°$ (2 chs $\angle = \frac{1}{2}$sum $\frown°$s)

$\angle 5 = 79°$ (inscr $\angle = \frac{1}{2}\frown°$)

$\angle 6 = \dfrac{158° - 36°}{2} = 61°$ (2 secs $\angle = \frac{1}{2}$diff $\frown°$s)

$\angle 7 = \dfrac{158° - (36° + 68°)}{2} = 27°$ (tan, sec $\angle = \frac{1}{2}$diff $\frown°$s)

$\angle 8 = 34°$ (tan, ch $\angle = \frac{1}{2}\frown°$) $\angle 9 = 79°$ (inscr $\angle = \frac{1}{2}\frown°$)

The concept of tangency can be extended to two circles. If two circles have exactly one point in common, then they are said to be tangent to each other. Figure 7.12(a) shows circles O_1 and O_2 *tangent internally,* whereas circles O_1 and O_2 in Figure 7.12(b) are *tangent externally*. In both cases it can be shown that the *line of centers* $\overleftrightarrow{O_1O_2}$ contains the point P of tangency. Circles that are tangent internally have a common tangent line, $\overleftrightarrow{PQ}$ in Figure 7.12(a). Circles that are tangent externally have a common internal tangent line, $\overleftrightarrow{PQ}$ in Figure 7.12(b), and two common external tangent lines, $\overleftrightarrow{AB}$ and $\overleftrightarrow{CD}$ in Figure 7.12(b). Note in the latter case that $\overline{QA} \cong \overline{QP} \cong \overline{QB}$ according to Theorem 82 and the transitive property of congruence. Some problems about tangent circles and common tangent lines are included in the exercises of this section.

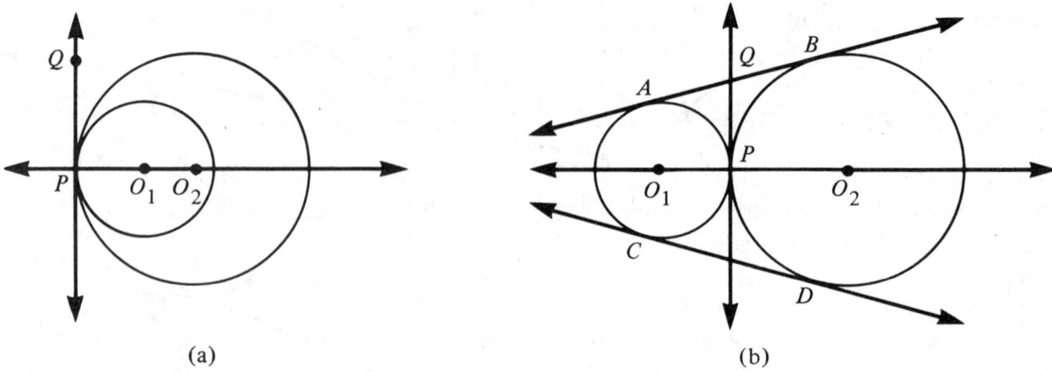

Figure 7.12

We conclude this section with a construction that motivates an important fact that we state as a postulate.

Construction 13 To construct a circle containing three given noncollinear points.

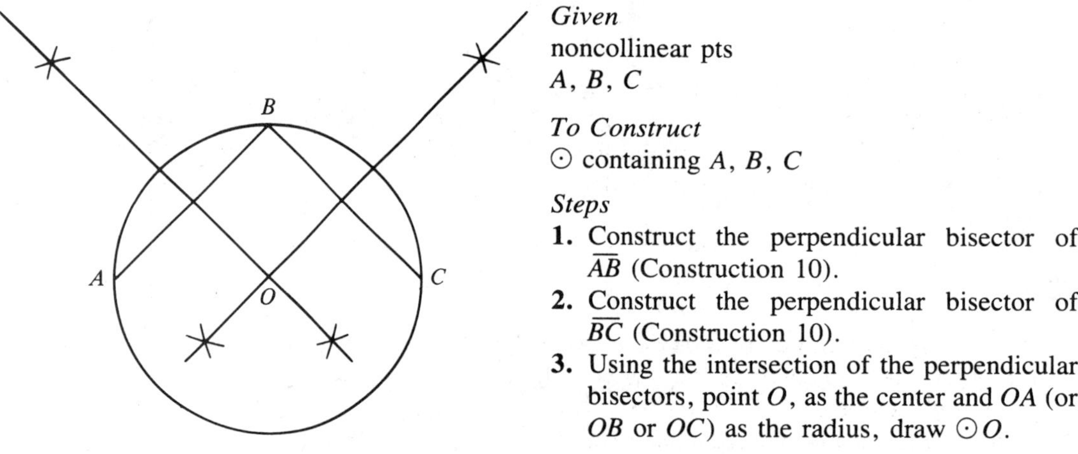

Given
noncollinear pts
A, *B*, *C*

To Construct
⊙ containing *A*, *B*, *C*

Steps
1. Construct the perpendicular bisector of $\overline{AB}$ (Construction 10).
2. Construct the perpendicular bisector of $\overline{BC}$ (Construction 10).
3. Using the intersection of the perpendicular bisectors, point *O*, as the center and *OA* (or *OB* or *OC*) as the radius, draw ⊙*O*.

Postulate 16 *The Circle Postulate*. There is one and only one circle that contains three given noncollinear points.

EXERCISES FOR 7.4

In exercises 1–20 answer true or false.

1. In a circle, any chord that bisects another chord must be perpendicular to it.
2. A diameter $\overline{AB}$ and a tangent $\overleftrightarrow{BP}$ of a circle are perpendicular to each other.
3. The measure of an angle formed by a tangent and a chord is one-half the measure of its intercepted arc.
4. If two chords intersect within a circle at right angles, then the sum of the lengths of either pair of arcs cut off by an angle and its vertical angle is half the circumference.
5. A diameter and a tangent to a circle are always perpendicular to each other.
6. In any circle, a radius that is perpendicular to a chord bisects the chord.
7. If two tangents are drawn to a circle from an exterior point, then the segments join-

ing the point to the circle have the same measure.

8. Inscribed angles and angles formed by a tangent and a chord both have measures equal to one-half the measure of their intercepted arcs.
9. An angle formed by a tangent and a chord cannot have a measure larger than a central angle of the same circle.
10. A secant of a circle that bisects a chord of the circle must be perpendicular to the chord.
11. If an angle formed by two chords in a circle measures 79°30′ and its intercepted arc measures 43°, then its vertical angle intercepts a 118° arc.
12. If an angle formed by two secants measures 23°30′ and one intercepted arc measures 21°, then the other intercepted arc measures 68°.
13. The distance from the center of a circle to a chord is defined as the length of the segment perpendicular to the chord joining the center and the chord.
14. In a circle, two chords having different lengths can be equidistant from the center of the circle.
15. If the measure of an arc of a circle is doubled, then the length of its chord is doubled.
16. If each side of a parallelogram is tangent to a circle, then the parallelogram is a rhombus.
17. If two congruent chords of a circle intersect, then each segment of one is congruent to a segment of the other.
18. If an angle formed by a tangent and secant to a circle measures 32°30′ and one intercepted arc measures 201°, then the other intercepted arc measures 135°30′.
19. The bisector of an angle of an inscribed quadrilateral and the bisector of the opposite exterior angle intersect at a point of the circle.
20. If two triangles are inscribed in the same circle with two angles of one congruent to two angles of the other, then the two triangles are congruent.

In exercises 21–28 explain what is wrong with the information marked on the figure. Point O is the center of each circle.

21.

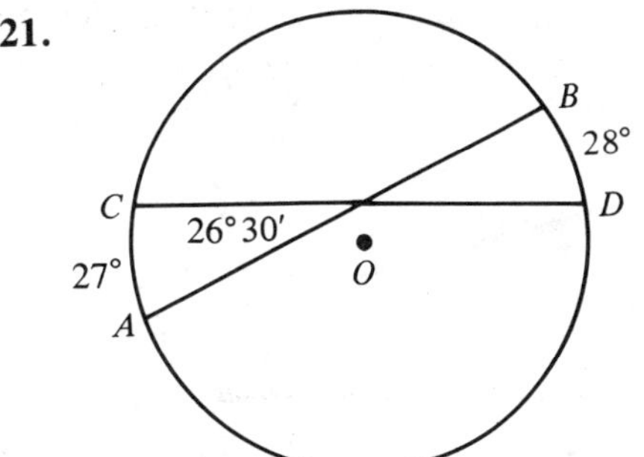

22.

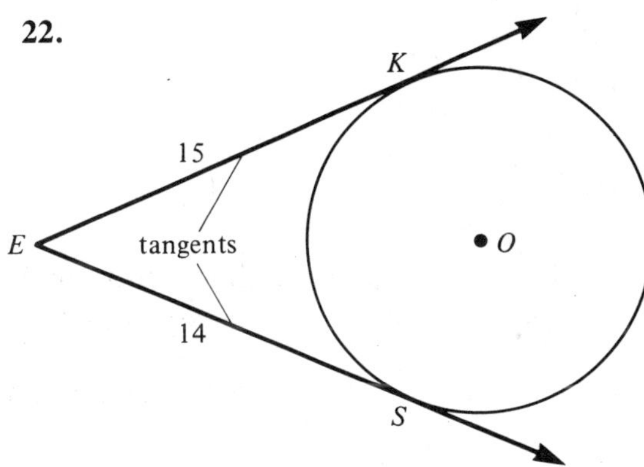

23.

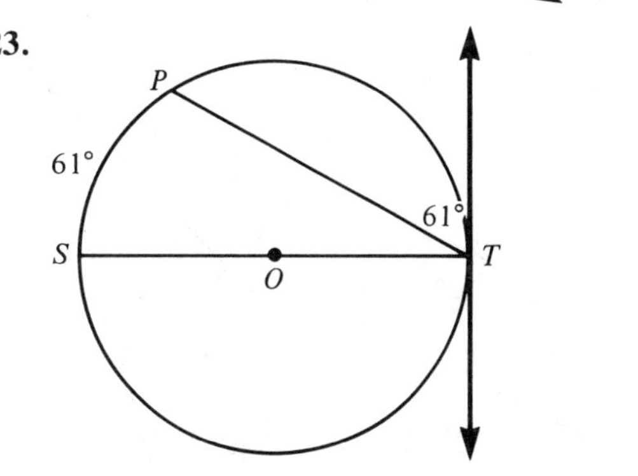

24.

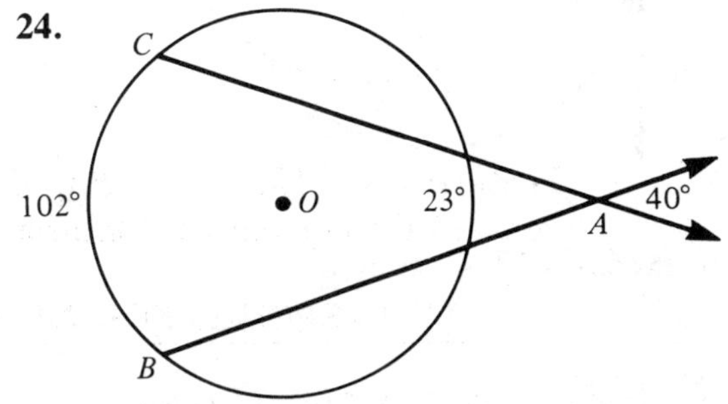

25.

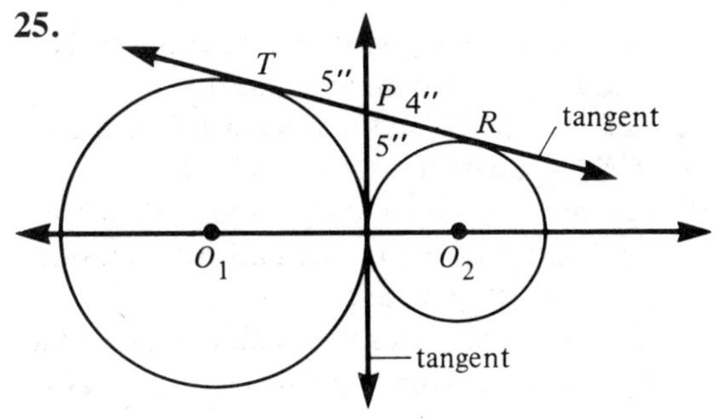

26.

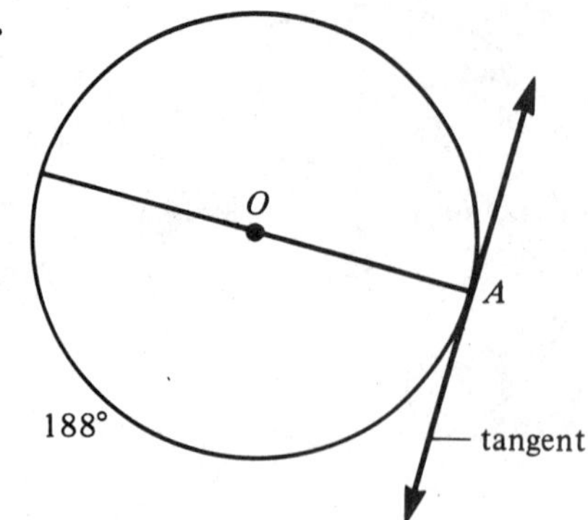

27.

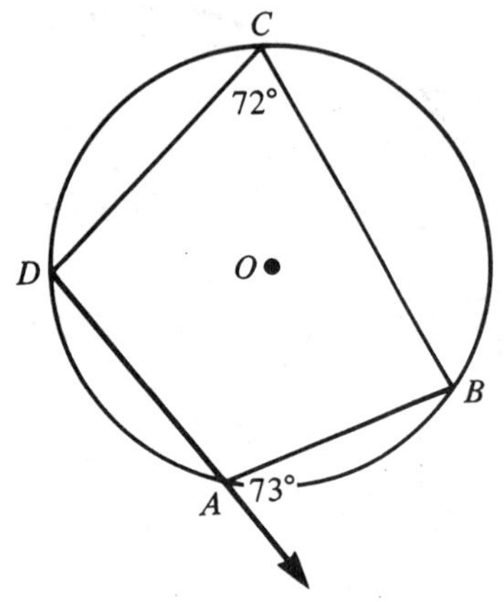

28.

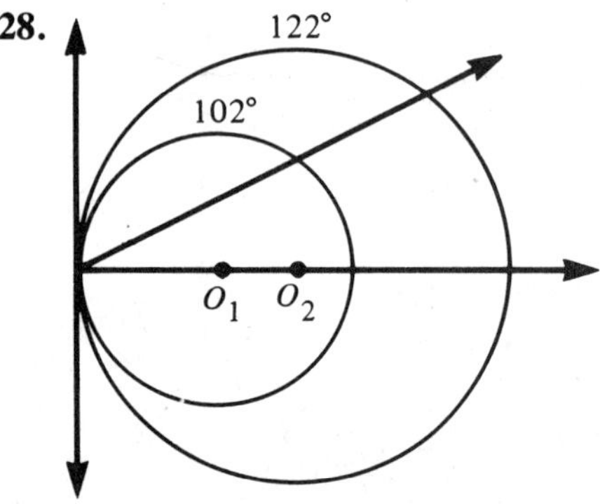

In exercises 29 and 30 use Figure 7.13 to answer the questions.

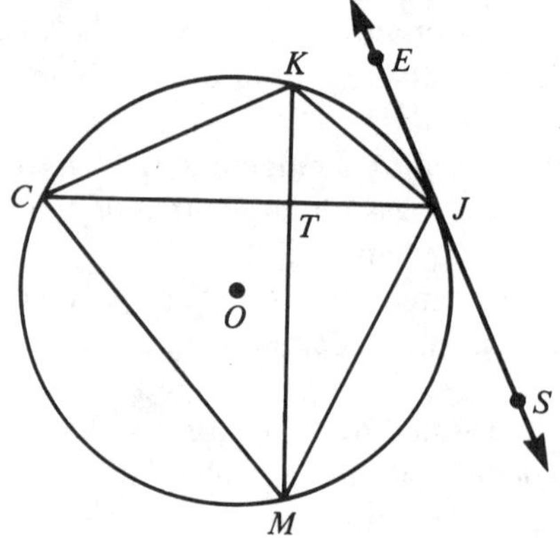

Figure 7.13

Given
⊙*O*
tan $\overleftrightarrow{ES}$

29. (a) Name two angles congruent to ∡*KJE*.
(b) Name two angles congruent to ∡*JCM*.

30. (a) Name three angles supplementary to ∡*KJS*.
(b) Name one angle supplementary to ∡*JCM*.

31. In (a)–(e) below, use a compass to draw *two* circles having exactly the indicated number of *common tangents*. Use a straightedge to estimate the location of the tangent lines (note this is not the same as *constructing* them).
(a) four **(b)** three **(c)** two **(d)** one **(e)** zero

32. Use a compass and straightedge to draw three circles having exactly one common tangent. Estimate the location of the tangent line.

In exercises 33–40 copy the given figure, mark it, and find the requested measures.

33. *Given*
⊙*O*
tan $\overleftrightarrow{ES}$
∠*CJM* = 64°
$\overset{\frown}{KJ}°$ = 36°
$\overset{\frown}{CK}°$ = 82°

Find
∡s 1–10

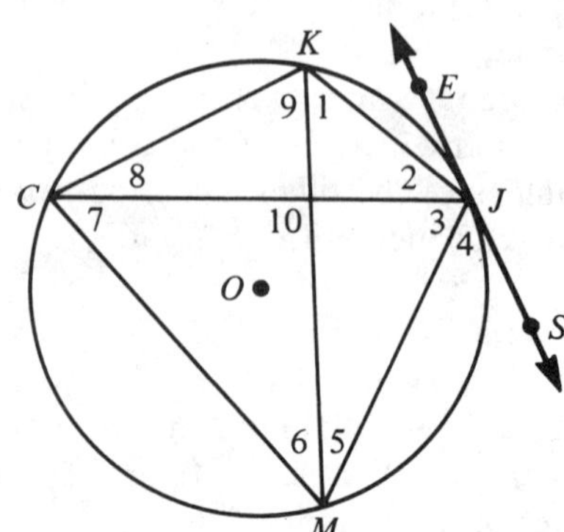

34. *Given*
$\odot O$
$\overset{\frown}{EJ}^\circ = 88^\circ$
$\overset{\frown}{KS}^\circ = 74^\circ$
$\angle 8 = \frac{1}{3}\angle 2$

Find
$\angle$s 1–8

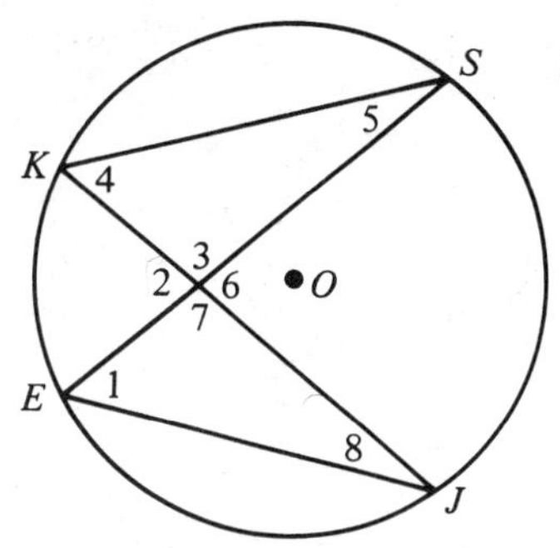

35. *Given*
$\odot O$
$\overline{TE} \perp \overline{RC}$
$\overset{\frown}{EC}^\circ = 78^\circ$

Find
$\angle$s 1–10

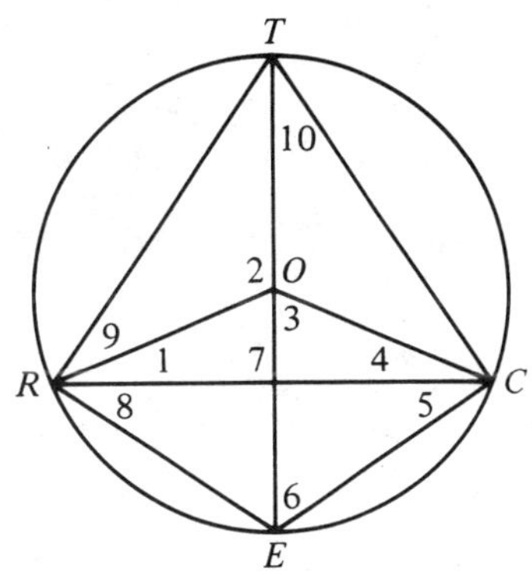

36. *Given*
$\odot O$
tans $\overleftrightarrow{PT}$, $\overrightarrow{AR}$
$\overset{\frown}{YH}^\circ = 101^\circ$
$\overset{\frown}{GS}^\circ = 121^\circ$

Find
$\angle$s 1–10

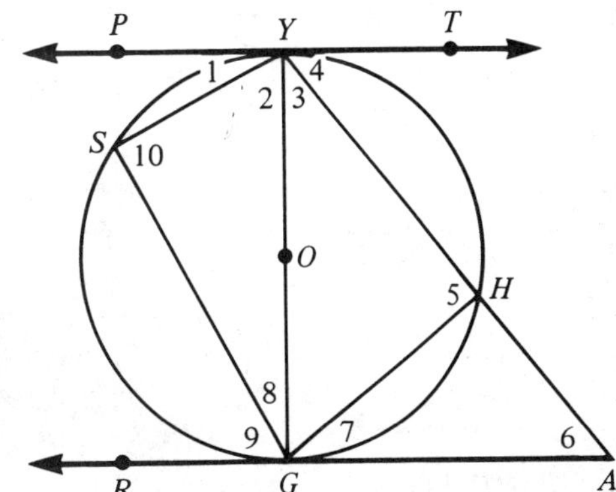

37. *Given*
$\odot O$
$\overleftrightarrow{EU} \parallel \overleftrightarrow{PI}$
$\angle EOP = 82^\circ$
$\overset{\frown}{PD}^\circ = 51^\circ$
$\overset{\frown}{CU}^\circ = 20^\circ$
D midpt $\overset{\frown}{PI}$

Find
$\angle$s 1–10

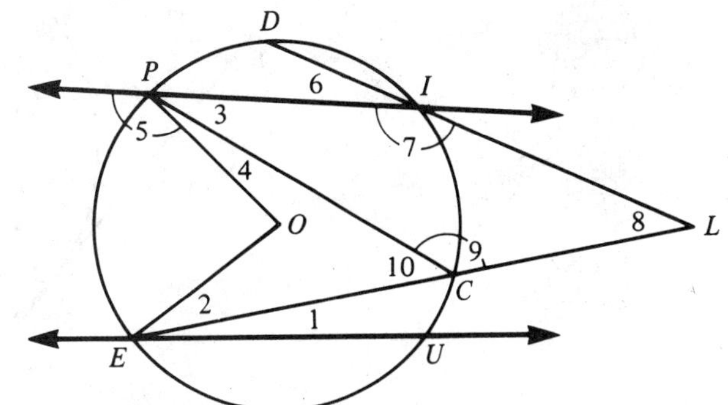

38. *Given*

$\odot O$

tans $\overrightarrow{PA}$, $\overrightarrow{PD}$

$\overset{\frown}{BA}° = 66°$

$\overset{\frown}{DE} \cong \overset{\frown}{EF} \cong \overset{\frown}{FA}$

$\overset{\frown}{DC}° = 66°$

$\overset{\frown}{CBA}° = 171°$

Find

$\measuredangle$s 1–9

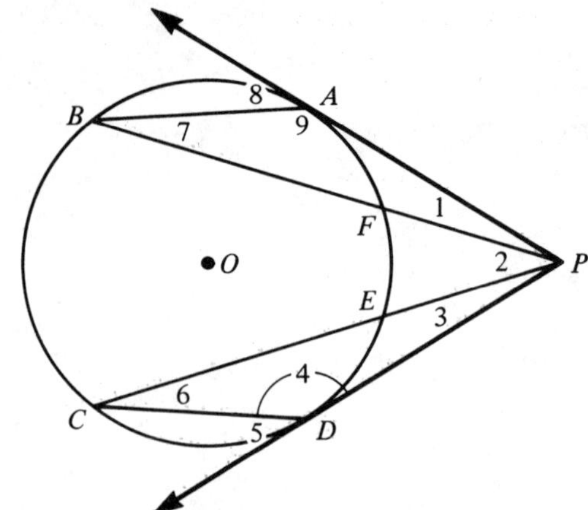

39. *Given*

$\odot O$

$\overrightarrow{EH}$ bis $\measuredangle TEL$

$\overleftrightarrow{HA}$ bis $\measuredangle LAS$

$\angle ATE = 78°$

$\angle TAL = 53°$

Find

$\measuredangle$s 1–10

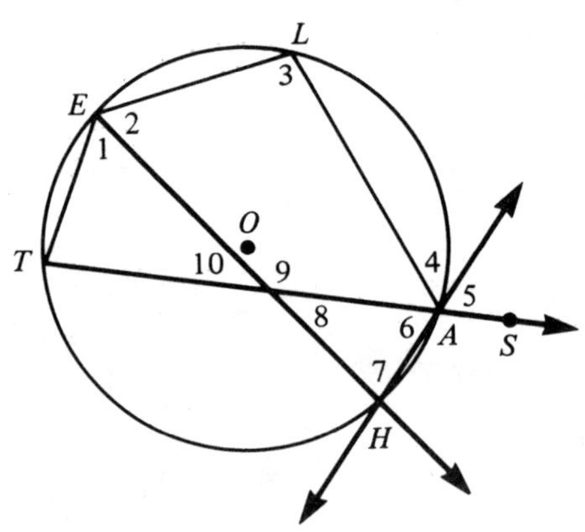

40. *Given*

$\odot O$

tans $\overleftrightarrow{BT}$, $\overrightarrow{PT}$, $\overrightarrow{PQ}$

$\angle BOA = 112°$

$\overset{\frown}{FE}° = 17°48'$

$\overset{\frown}{BC}° = 38°$

Find

$\measuredangle$s 1–20

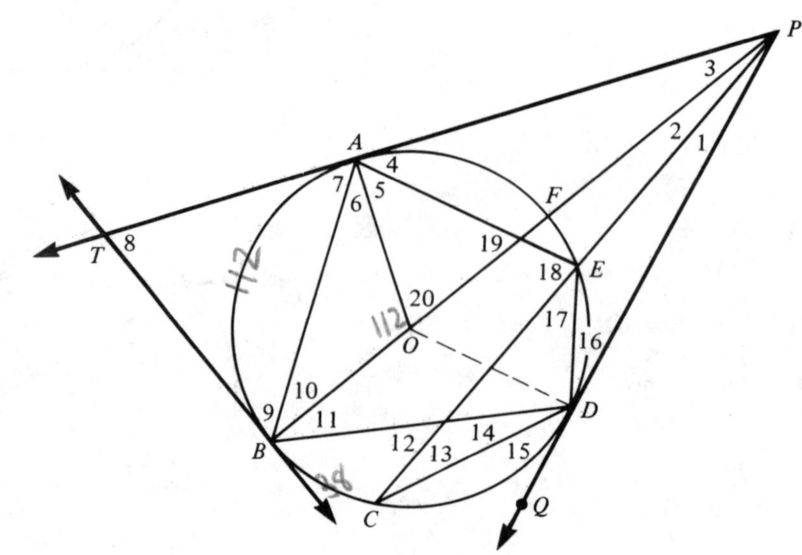

In exercises 41 and 42 copy the figure, mark it, and supply the missing reasons in each proof.

41. *Given*
$\overleftrightarrow{AG}$ tan $\odot$s O and K
$\overleftrightarrow{NL}$ tan $\odot$s O and K

To Prove
$\measuredangle 4$ rt $\measuredangle$

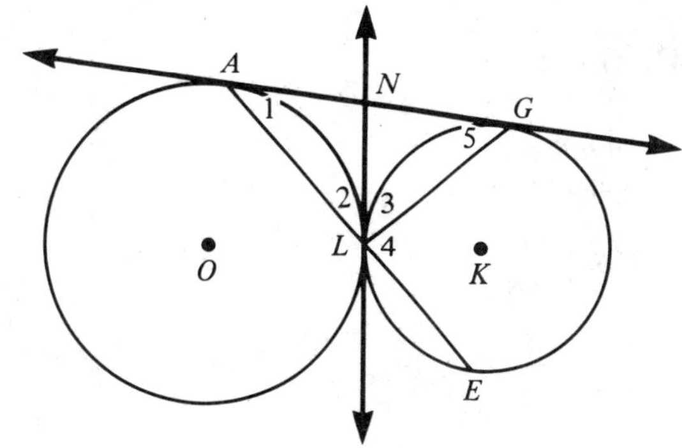

Statement	*Reason*
1. $\overleftrightarrow{AG}$ tan $\odot$s O and K $\overleftrightarrow{NL}$ tan $\odot$s O and K	1. ?
2. $\overline{NA} \cong \overline{NL}$	2. ?
3. $\measuredangle 1 \cong \measuredangle 2$	3. ?
4. $\angle 1 = \angle 2$	4. ?
5. $\overline{NL} \cong \overline{NG}$	5. ?
6. $\measuredangle 3 \cong \measuredangle 5$	6. ?
7. $\angle 3 = \angle 5$	7. ?
8. $\angle 1 + \angle 2 + \angle 3 + \angle 5 = 180°$	8. ?
9. $2 \cdot \angle 2 + 2 \cdot \angle 3 = 180°$	9. ?
10. $\angle 2 + \angle 3 = 90°$	10. ?
11. $\angle 2 + \angle 3 + \angle 4 = 180°$	11. ?
12. $\angle 4 = 90°$	12. ?
13. $\therefore \measuredangle 4$ rt $\measuredangle$	13. ?

42. (Theorem 80)

Given
$\odot O \cong \odot K$
$\overline{OE} \perp \overline{AB}$
$\overline{KS} \perp \overline{CD}$
$\overline{AB} \cong \overline{CD}$

To Prove
$\overline{OE} \cong \overline{KS}$

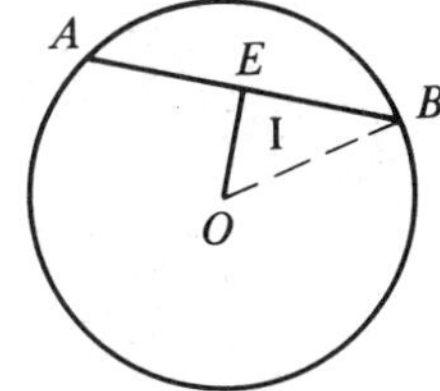

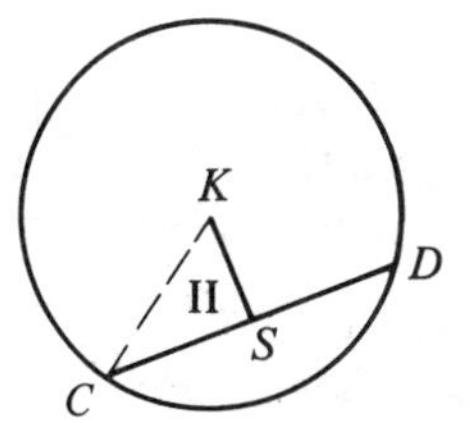

Statement	*Reason*
1. $\odot O \cong \odot K$	1. ?
2. Draw $\overline{OB}$, $\overline{KC}$.	2. ?
3. $\overline{OB} \cong \overline{KC}$	3. ?
4. $\overline{OE} \perp \overline{AB}$	4. ?
5. $\measuredangle OEB$ rt $\measuredangle$	5. ?
6. $\overline{KS} \perp \overline{CD}$	6. ?
7. $\measuredangle KSC$ rt $\measuredangle$	7. ?
8. $\overline{AB} \cong \overline{CD}$	8. ?
9. $\overline{AE} \cong \overline{BE}$	9. ?
10. $\overline{CS} \cong \overline{DS}$	10. ?
11. $\overline{BE} \cong \overline{CS}$	11. ?
12. $\triangle OEB \cong \triangle KSC$	12. ?
13. $\therefore \overline{OE} \cong \overline{KS}$	13. ?

In exercises 43–52 copy the figure, the hypothesis, and the conclusion. Mark the figure and write a proof.

43. *Given*
⊙O
diam $\overline{JT}$
tans $\overleftrightarrow{ES}$, $\overleftrightarrow{CR}$

To Prove
$\overleftrightarrow{ES} \parallel \overleftrightarrow{CR}$

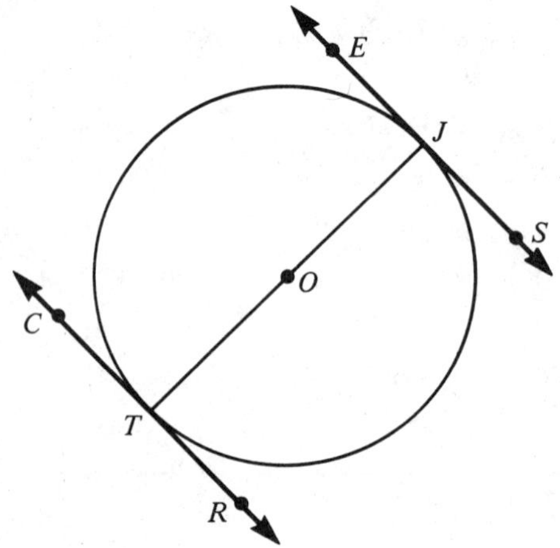

44. *Given*
⊙O
tans $\overline{BA}$, $\overline{BC}$

To Prove
$\overline{OB}$ ⊥ bis $\overline{AC}$

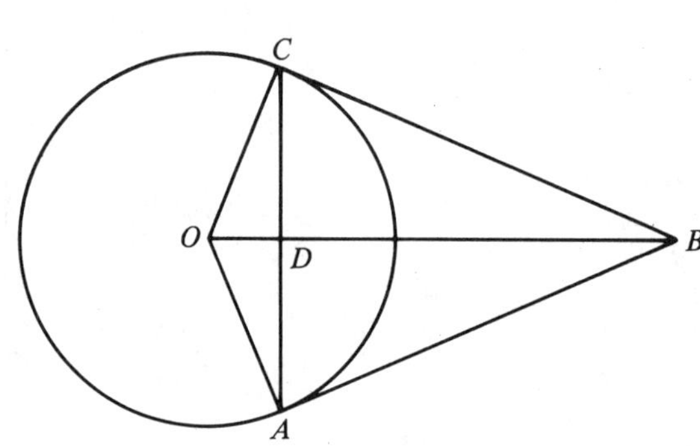

45. *Given*
⊙O
tans $\overline{AJ}$, $\overline{AK}$
$\overline{JA} \perp \overline{KA}$

To Prove
JAKO sq

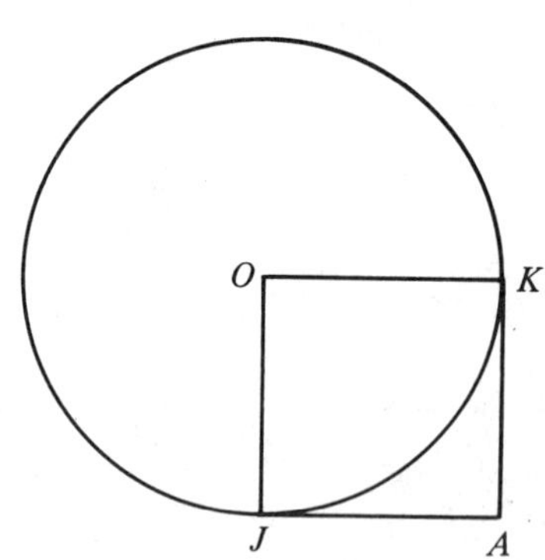

46. (Theorem 85)

Given
⊙O
secs $\overleftrightarrow{AC}$, $\overleftrightarrow{EC}$

To Prove
$\angle ACE = \frac{1}{2}(\widehat{AE}° - \widehat{BJ}°)$

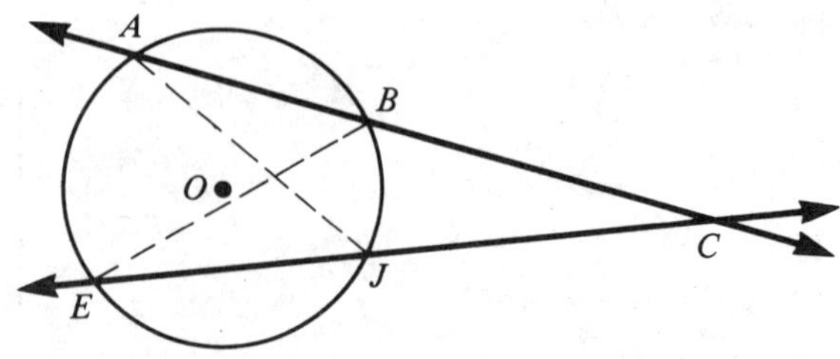

47. *Given*
$\odot O$
tan $\overline{EB}$
$\overline{CD} \parallel \overline{AB}$
$CD = \frac{1}{2}AB$

To Prove
$\angle E = 30°$

48. *Given*
$\odot O$
tan $\overleftrightarrow{AP}$
$\overline{AF}$ bis $\measuredangle BAC$

To Prove
$\overline{AP} \cong \overline{PE}$

49. *Given*
$\odot O$
$\overline{HP} \parallel \overleftrightarrow{RS}$

To Prove
$\measuredangle 1 \cong \measuredangle 2$

50. (Theorem 77b)

Given
$\odot O$
$\overleftrightarrow{AB} \parallel \overleftrightarrow{CD}$

To Prove
$\overset{\frown}{AC} \cong \overset{\frown}{AD}$

51. *Given*
$\odot O$
tans $\overleftrightarrow{JD}, \overline{CA}$

To Prove
$\overline{AJ} \cong \overline{CJ}$

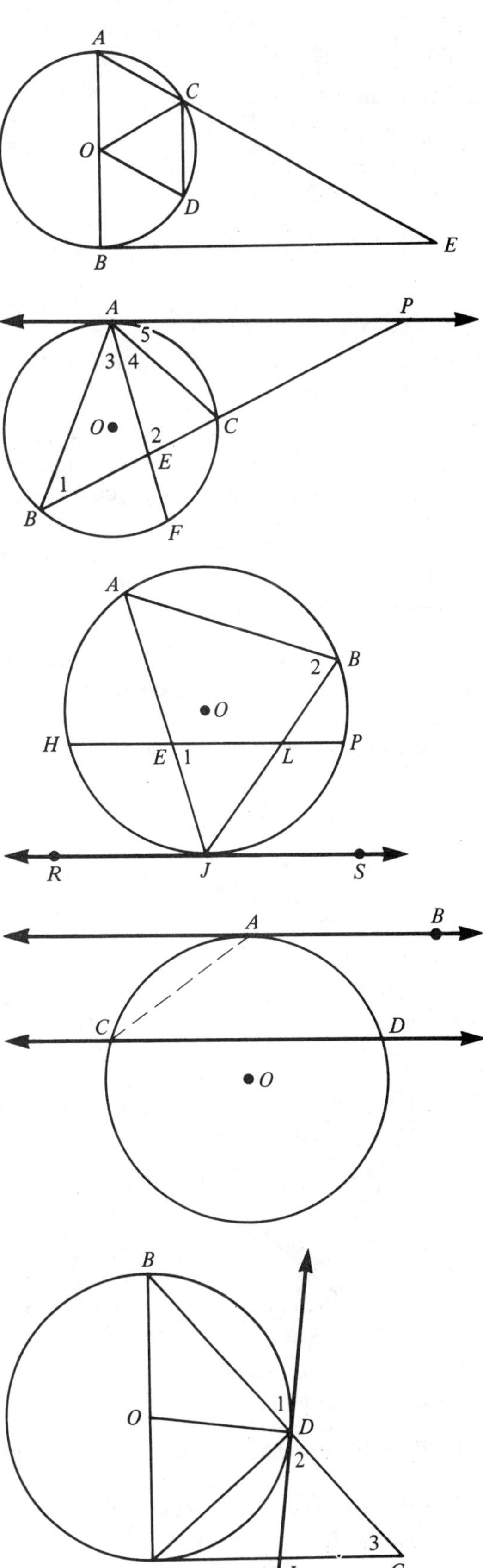

52. *Given*
⊙O and ⊙O'
$\overleftrightarrow{RM}$ tan ⊙s O and O' at S

To Prove
$\overline{EJ} \parallel \overline{AB}$

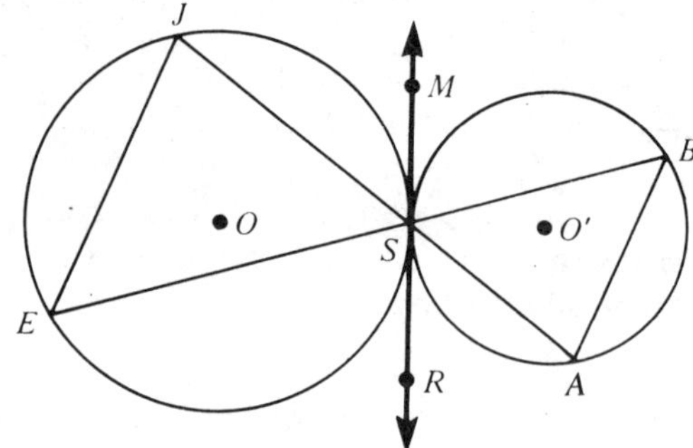

In exercises 53–56 draw a figure and write the hypothesis and the conclusion. Mark the figure and write a proof.

53. If two congruent chords of a circle intersect, then the segments of each formed by the intersection are congruent, respectively.

54. If each side of a parallelogram is tangent to a circle within it, then the parallelogram is a rhombus.

55. If a circle is drawn with one of the congruent sides of an isosceles triangle as a diameter, then the circle bisects the base of the triangle.

56. If $\overline{AB}$ and $\overline{DC}$ are parallel diameters of two externally tangent circles of equal radii, then the quadrilateral $ABCD$ is a rhombus.

In exercises 57–65 do the constructions using only a compass and straightedge. As illustrated in exercises 57, 58, and 61, a preliminary sketch may be helpful in determining the steps to use.

57. Construct the midpoint of an $\overparen{AB}$ of a circle.

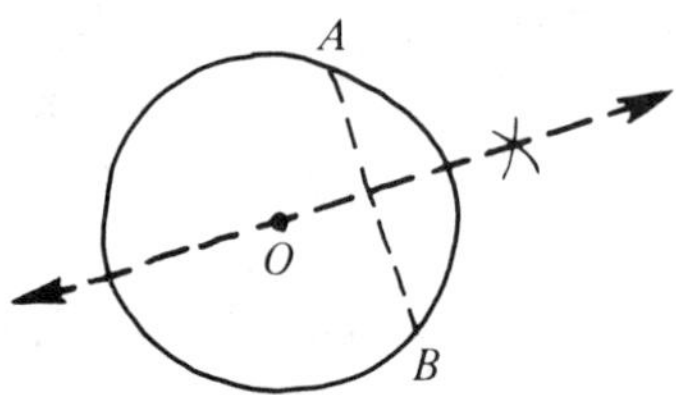

58. At a point P on a circle, construct the tangent to the circle.

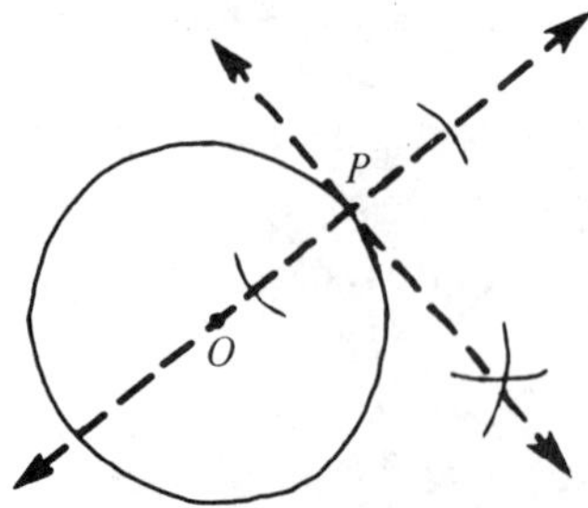

59. Through a point E in the interior of a circle, construct the chord whose midpoint is E. (Hint: Draw the diameter through E.)

60. If a wheel has been broken and only a piece of it remains, show how its diameter can be constructed. Represent the piece by an arc of a circle. (Hint: See Construction 13.)

61. Let E be any point on a line l and J be any point not on l. Construct the circle tangent to l at E and passing through J.

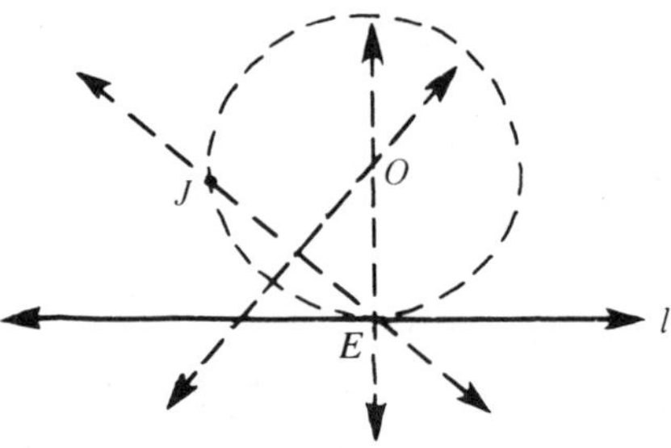

62. Through a point P in the exterior of a given circle construct the two tangents to the circle. (Hint: A tangent is perpendicular to the radius at the point of tangency, and an angle inscribed in a semicircle is a right angle.)

63. Construct the line perpendicular at B to a given line segment $\overline{AB}$: (a) by extending $\overline{AB}$ and using Construction 5 (to construct a line perpendicular to a given line through one of its points), and (b) without extending $\overline{AB}$. (Hint: Choose any point O not on $\overline{AB}$ and construct the circle with radius $\overline{OB}$.)

64. Construct a circle tangent to a given line and containing two given points on a line parallel to the given line.

65. Construct a circle, having a given radius r, that is tangent to a given circle O and to a given line l. (Hint: Construct a circle concentric with O whose radius is the sum of r and the radius of O.)

CHAPTER 7 SUMMARY

This chapter introduces a new figure, the circle, and the terms and notation that apply to it. Central and inscribed angles play a major role in developing the properties of circles and angles. As in previous chapters, congruent triangles serve as an essential tool. In this chapter they help to prove theorems involving radii, chords, tangents, and secants. The circle's properties, as described in this chapter, are the foundation for practical applications involving circles and circular motion.

FACTS TO KNOW

1. Definitions
   - a. Circle
   - b. Radius
   - c. Diameter
   - d. Concentric circles
   - e. Chord
   - f. Secant
   - g. Tangent
   - h. Central angle
   - i. Minor arc
   - j. Major arc
   - k. Semicircle
   - l. Degree measure
   - m. Inscribed angle
   - n. Congruent circles
   - o. Congruent arcs
2. The Circle Postulate
3. Theorems
   - a. radii ⊙ ≅ and diams ⊙ ≅
   - b. diam ÷ ⊙ into 2 ≅ semi ⊙s
   - c. if ⌒s ≅, cent ∡s ≅
   - d. if cent ∡s ≅, ⌒s ≅
   - e. if cent ∡s ≅, chs ≅
   - f. if chs ≅, cent ∡s ≅
   - g. if chs ≅, ⌒s ≅
   - h. if ⌒s ≅, chs ≅
   - i. inscr ∠ = $\frac{1}{2}$⌒°
   - j. inscr ∡s interc same ⌒ or ≅ ⌒s are ≅
   - k. inscr ∡ interc semi ⊙ is rt ∡
   - l. if quad inscr in ⊙, opp ∡s supp
   - m. if ‖ lines inters ⊙, ⌒s ≅
   - n. sec thru cen ⊥ ch bis ch and ⌒
   - o. 2 chs equidis from cen are ≅
   - p. 2 ≅ chs are equidis from cen
   - q. tan ⊥ rad to pt con
   - r. tans to ⊙ ≅
   - s. 2 chs ∠ = $\frac{1}{2}$sum ⌒°s
   - t. tan, ch ∠ = $\frac{1}{2}$⌒°
   - u. 2 secs ∠ = $\frac{1}{2}$diff ⌒°s
     tan, sec ∠ = $\frac{1}{2}$diff ⌒°s
     2 tan ∠ = $\frac{1}{2}$diff ⌒°s

PROBLEMS TO MASTER

1. Identify lines and angles associated with circles.
2. Find degree measures of angles in figures containing circles, triangles, polygons, and parallel lines.
3. Write proofs involving circle theorems.
4. Construct a circle containing three given noncollinear points.
5. Solve construction problems using previously given constructions.

8

AREA AND PERIMETER

MAJOR TOPICS

- Perimeter of a polygon
- Three postulates as the foundation for a polygon's area
- Definition of a rectangle's area based on covering it with unit squares
- Subdivision of polygons into triangles or rectangles to find areas by addition
- Approximations of areas using measurements
- The number π and the area of a circle

HISTORICAL NOTE

GEOMETRIC CONSTRUCTIONS

Classical Greek geometry (600–300 B.C.) raised many questions that had a later, unexpected impact on the development of mathematics. Among these are numerous construction problems involving lines, circles, and proportions, the most famous of which are "to trisect an angle," "to double a cube," and "to square a circle." To solve the first of these requires the division of any given angle into three congruent angles. To "double a cube" requires the construction of the edge of a second cube whose volume is twice that of a given one. And "to square a circle" requires the construction of a square whose area is equal to that of a given circle.

By the rules of the Greeks, geometric constructions are to be done using only a straightedge and compass. These self-imposed rules were due in part to the Greeks' wish to keep geometry simple and thus aesthetically pleasing. The philosopher Plato (427?–347 B.C.) believed that using more complicated instruments would reduce geometry to the world of the senses rather than elevate it to the abstract realm of thought.

It is true that these famous construction problems are not of practical importance. They can be solved with instruments only slightly more complicated than the straightedge and compass. Nonetheless, many people have worked on these problems ever since they were posed by the Greeks 2000 years ago. These years of labor demonstrate the persistence of the human intellect when faced with a challenge, particularly since we now know that with the restriction to compass and straightedge only these construction problems cannot be solved!

On the whole, it can be quite difficult to prove something *cannot* be done. In fact it was not until the early nineteenth century that certain algebraic concepts were developed enabling mathematicians to prove the impossibility of solving these three problems. This remarkable achievement was due largely to the work of the Italian Ruffini (1765–1822) and the Norwegian Niels Abel (1802–1829).

Briefly, the approach involves converting the geometric question into an equivalent algebraic problem. For example, a cube with an edge of one unit has a volume of one cubic unit. To double this cube we must find a length x such that $x^3 = 2$. In 1799 Gauss proved that such an equation has a solution; we express it as $\sqrt[3]{2}$, an irrational number. But can such a length be constructed? The answer is *no*, because it can be shown that the only irrational lengths that can be constructed with compass and straightedge only are those whose algebraic form involves square roots only. Hence, the impossibility of the construction is established.

The problem of trisecting an angle is perhaps the most famous of the three. Many solutions have been proposed, but all have failed in some way. One approach is to construct an isosceles triangle with the given angle opposite the base, then trisect the base and join the trisection points to the vertex of the given angle. This may look promising for an acute angle, but try it for an obtuse one! In fact, the algebraic equivalent of this problem is a cubic equation, and the impossibility of constructing a solution has been proved.

An algebraic equivalent for squaring the circle may be obtained by considering the given circle to have a radius of one unit and thus an area of π square units. We must then construct a length x such that $x^2 = \pi$, an equation having a root that may be donoted $\sqrt{\pi}$. The proof of the impossibility of constructing such a length is beyond the scope of elementary mathematics. It hinges on the nature of the number π.

Thus, the desire to solve these impractical problems of the Greek geometers led to many important developments in algebra. Indeed, the efforts of Ruffini and Abel followed by the work of the French mathematician Evariste Galois (1811–1832) began the development of modern algebra, a body of theory having many important applications. Rather than dismissing the ancient Greeks as impractical, it is more accurate to view their move toward simplicity and abstraction as visionary. Their questions have generated results of great importance in our present scientific age.

8.1
INTRODUCTION

Sizes of line segments are compared using their lengths, and sizes of angles are compared using their degree measures. Size comparisons between polygons are less straightforward. Associated with polygons, however, are two very useful numerical measures called *perimeter* and *area*. You are probably familiar with these as well as with some of the algebraic formulas used in connection with them. In this chapter we develop and define perimeter and area geometrically; we also use formulas as concise ways to express the results.

There are many practical uses of perimeter and area. Applications are found in activities such as surveying, construction, manufacturing, landscaping, and interior design. Indeed, the uses are so widespread that a clear understanding of these concepts is important for everyone. We begin with the concept of perimeter.

Definition 8.1 The *perimeter* of a polygon is the sum of the lengths of its sides.

In formulas for perimeters, P is used for the perimeter and lowercase letters are used for the lengths of the sides. Some illustrations are given in Figure 8.1 and Example 1.

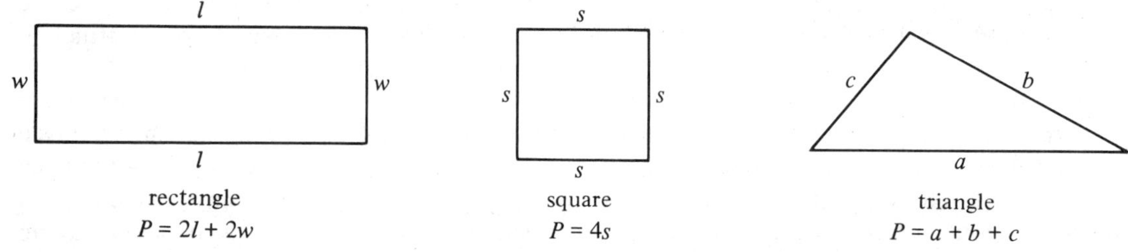

Figure 8.1

EXAMPLE 1 Find the perimeter of each polygon.

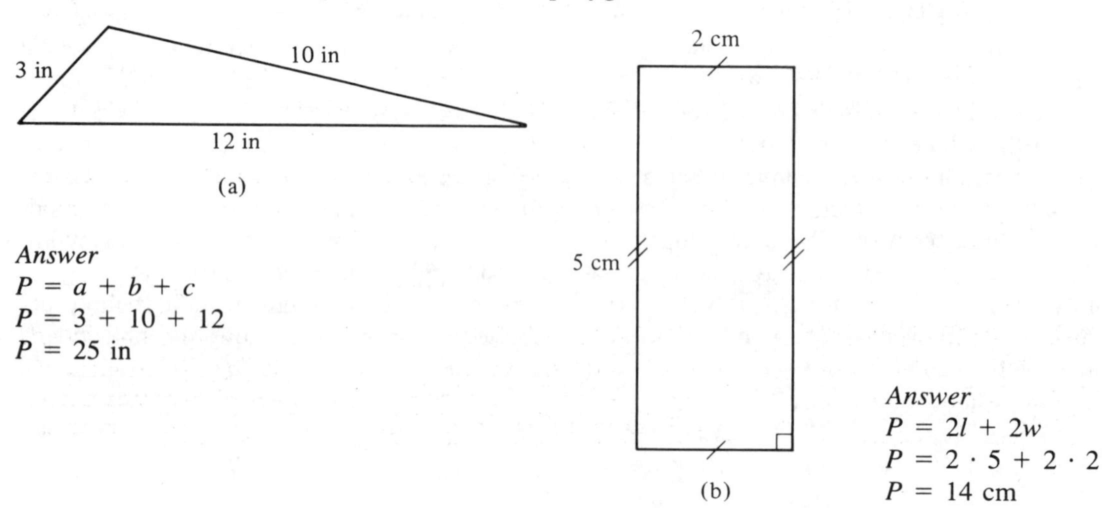

Answer
$P = a + b + c$
$P = 3 + 10 + 12$
$P = 25$ in

Answer
$P = 2l + 2w$
$P = 2 \cdot 5 + 2 \cdot 2$
$P = 14$ cm

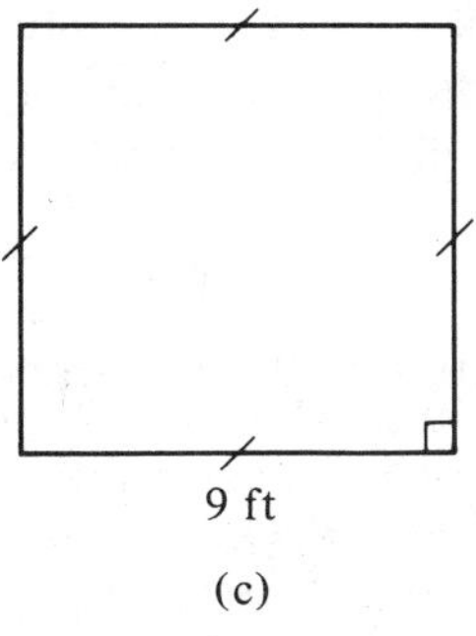

(c)

Answer
$P = 4s$
$P = 4 \cdot 9$
$P = 36$ ft

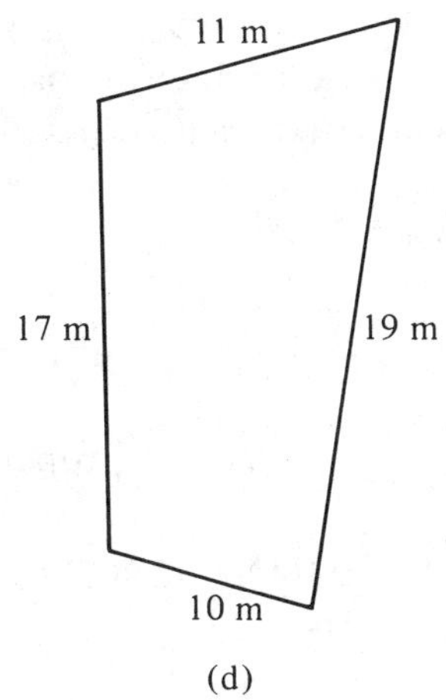

(d)

Answer
$P = a + b + c + d$
$P = 19 + 11 + 17 + 10$
$P = 57$ m

It is important when solving perimeter problems to (1) write an appropriate formula, (2) substitute the given lengths in the formula, and (3) assign the correct unit of measurement to the answer. These techniques are all shown in Example 1.

Our development of the area concept begins with the definition of a triangular region.

Definition 8.2 A *triangular region* is the union of a triangle and its interior.

Our objective is to assign a numerical measure called area not only to triangular regions, but also to such familiar figures as a parallelogram and its interior (this includes squares and rectangles), a trapezoid and its interior, and in general any polygon and its interior that can be divided into a finite number of triangular regions. Thus, if the area of a triangular region can be defined suitably, then the area of a region consisting of a finite number of triangular regions can be defined as the sum of the areas of the triangular regions. Our discussion suggests the following definition.

Definition 8.3 A *polygonal region* is the union of a finite number of coplanar triangular regions whose interiors have no points in common.

Figure 8.2 shows some polygonal regions divided into triangular regions whose interiors are shaded. Of course there is more than one way to make these divisions.

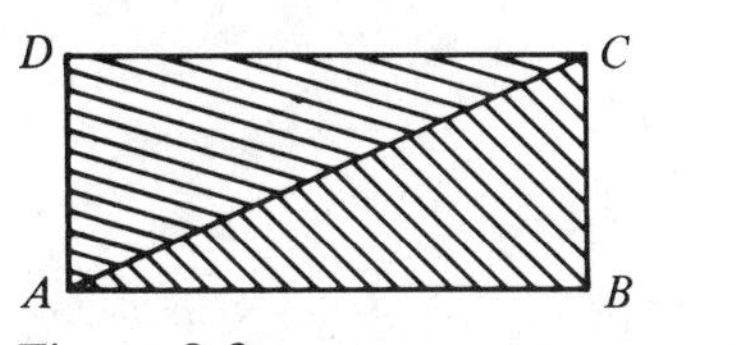

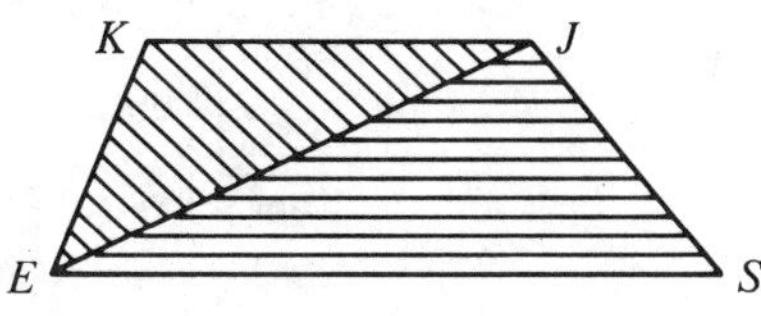

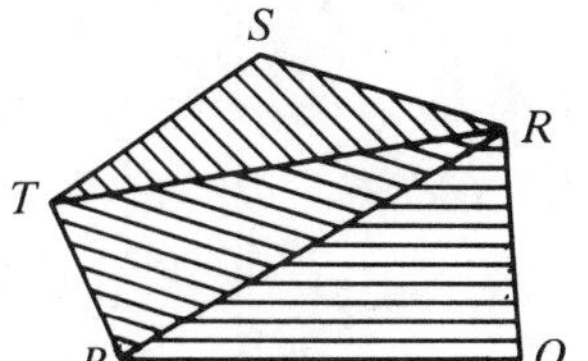

Figure 8.2

Before deciding how to assign an area to a polygonal region, we state three postulates on which to base our ideas. The first indicates the type of number to be used and asserts that a given polygonal region has a unique area.

Postulate 17 *The Area Postulate.* To each polygonal region there corresponds a unique positive real number called its area.

Postulates 18 and 19 state properties that area measures are to satisfy.

Postulate 18 Triangular regions bounded by congruent triangles have equal areas ($\cong \triangle$s, $=$ areas).

Postulate 19 If a polygonal region is the union of two or more polygonal regions with no interior points in common, then its area is the sum of their areas (area $\cup$ $=$ sum areas).

Our intuitive notion of area makes these postulates easy to accept. The task, then, is to develop a way to measure areas of polygonal regions that is consistent with these postulates. Before pursuing this, we mention an important agreement about word usage.

It is common practice to refer to the area of a triangular region as simply "the area of a triangle." This is not strictly accurate because a triangle is the set of points that are in its sides; the interior is not included. Nevertheless, we will adopt this common word usage and similar usage for other polygonal regions.

Since the foregoing discussion of area is based on triangles, the area of a triangle should be defined next. Although this logical approach is possible, it is more natural to begin with rectangles and assume that the result fits the above theory. We will do this and then proceed to define the areas of triangles and other polygons.

Area is measured in *square units* such as square inches, square centimeters, and square yards. A *unit square* is a square region whose sides are of length 1. Figure 8.3 shows two typical unit squares. A unit square has an area of 1 square unit. The area of a rectangle may be determined by *covering* it with unit squares according to Postulate 19 and counting their number (Figure 8.4). Note that fractional parts of unit squares may be involved. Note also that the number of unit squares may be found by multiplying the lengths of two consecutive sides. Hence we develop the following postulate.

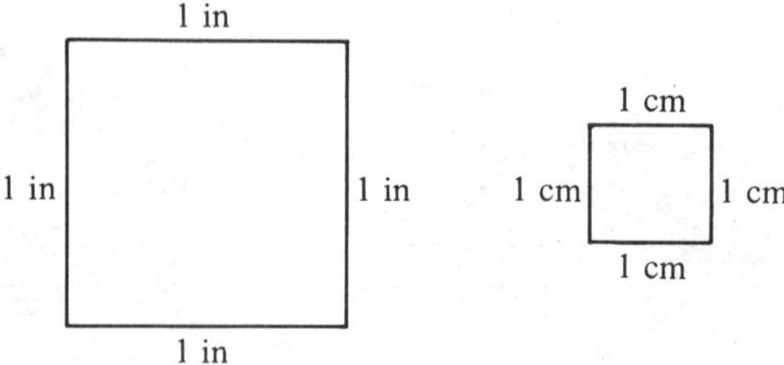

Figure 8.3

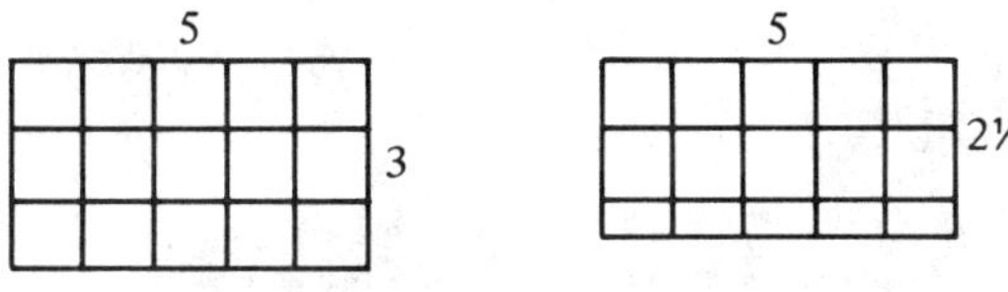

Figure 8.4

Postulate 20 The area of a rectangle is the product of the lengths of any two consecutive sides ($A(\text{rect}) = lw$ or bh).

In applying Postulate 20 it is to be understood that the lengths must be in the same unit of measurement. The two consecutive sides may be called "length and width" or "base and altitude." Postulate 20 also includes squares because they are special rectangles. These results are summarized in Figure 8.5 together with appropriate formulas in which the letter A is used to denote area.

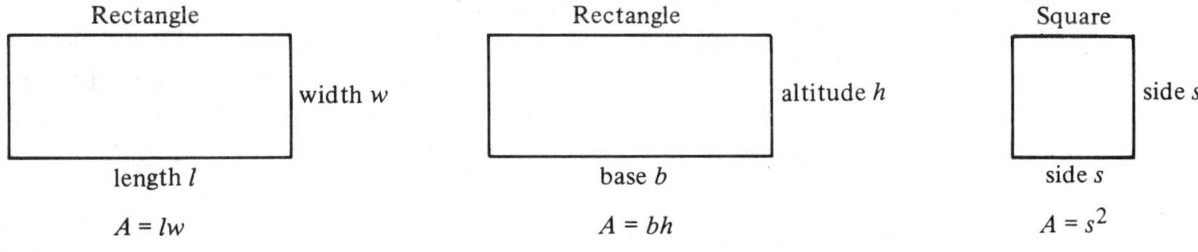

Figure 8.5

EXAMPLE 2 Find the area of each rectangle.

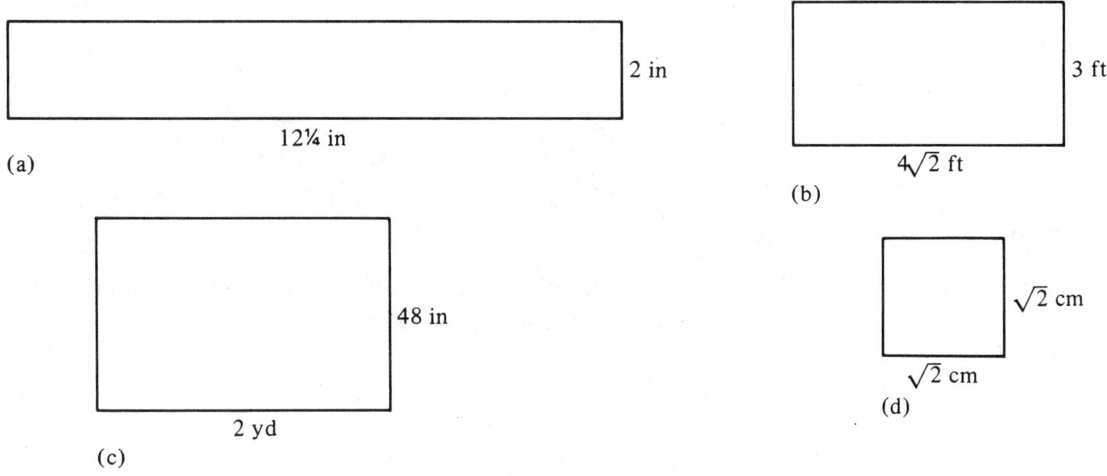

Answers

(a) $A = lw$
$A = 12\frac{1}{4} \cdot 2$
$A = 24\frac{1}{2}$ sq in

(b) $A = bh$
$A = 4\sqrt{2} \cdot 3$
$A = 12\sqrt{2}$ sq ft

(c) $A = lw$
$A = 2 \cdot 1\frac{1}{3}$
$A = 2\frac{2}{3}$ sq yd

(d) $A = s^2$
$A = (\sqrt{2})^2$
$A = 2$ sq cm

8.2

PARALLELOGRAMS, TRIANGLES, AND TRAPEZOIDS

In the previous section the symbol A was used to represent area. If we also wish to identify the figure involved, for example, $\triangle EJS$, we will write $A(\triangle EJS)$ or $A(EJS)$. Thus, if $EJKS$ names a rectangle, then we have the area formula $A(EJKS) = bh$ and if $ABCD$ names a square, then $A(ABCD) = s^2$. We next consider the area of another quadrilateral, namely, the parallelogram.

Any side of a parallelogram may be called its *base*. An *altitude* of the parallelogram is a line segment perpendicular to the base and with one endpoint in the line of the base and the other in the line of the opposite side (Figure 8.6). We abbreviate this informal definition as "alt $\perp$ base." The lengths of these perpendicular line segments are also called altitudes. Since perpendicular line segments joining two parallel lines all have the same length (Theorem 50), every parallelogram has exactly two "numerical" altitudes. They are the two distances between the two pairs of opposite sides. (In the special case of a rhombus, these two distances are equal.) These ideas are needed in the next theorem and Example 1.

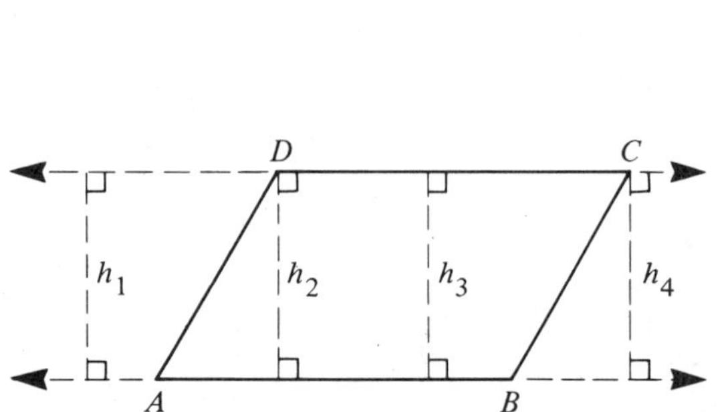

h_1, h_2, h_3, and h_4 are altitudes for base $\overline{AB}$ or base $\overline{DC}$

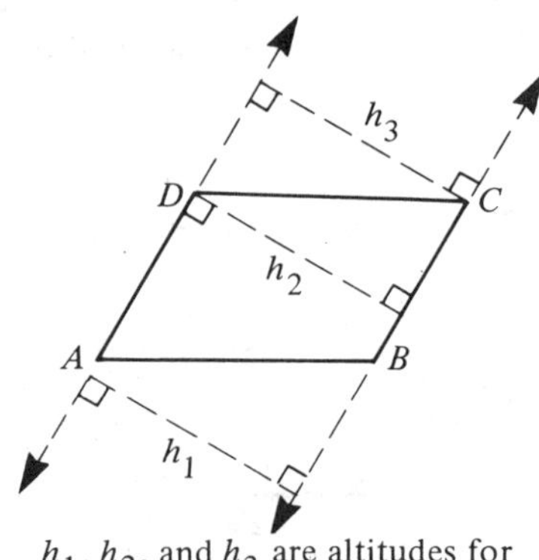

h_1, h_2, and h_3 are altitudes for base $\overline{AD}$ or base $\overline{BC}$

Figure 8.6

Theorem 86 The area of a parallelogram is the product of the lengths of any base and its corresponding altitude ($A(\square) = bh$).

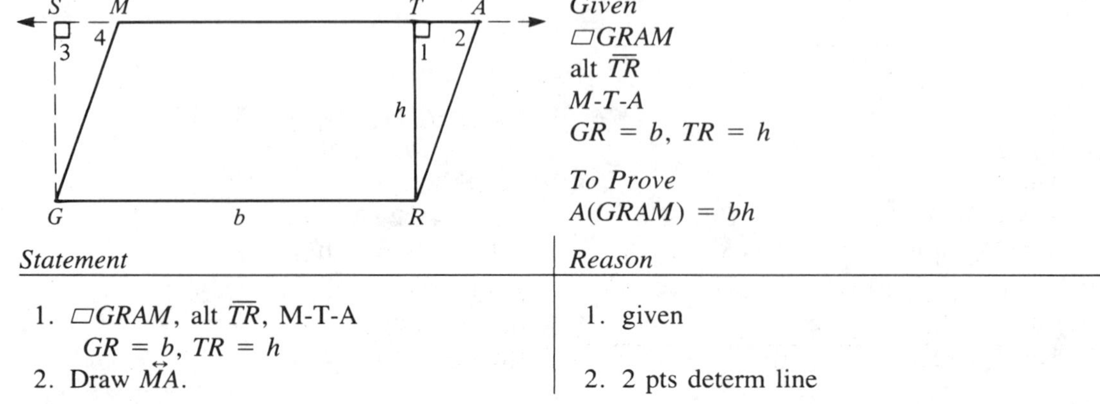

Given
$\square GRAM$
alt $\overline{TR}$
M-T-A
$GR = b$, $TR = h$

To Prove
$A(GRAM) = bh$

Statement	*Reason*
1. $\square GRAM$, alt $\overline{TR}$, M-T-A $GR = b$, $TR = h$	1. given
2. Draw $\overleftrightarrow{MA}$.	2. 2 pts determ line

	Statements		Reasons
3.	Draw $\overline{GS} \perp \overleftrightarrow{MA}$.	3.	1 ⊥ from pt to line
4.	∡3 rt ∡	4.	⊥s form rt ∡s
5.	$\overline{TR} \perp \overline{MA}$	5.	alt ⊥ base
6.	∡1 rt ∡	6.	⊥s form rt ∡s
7.	∡1 ≅ ∡3	7.	all rt ∡s ≅
8.	$\overline{RA} \parallel \overline{GM}$ and $\overline{GR} \parallel \overline{MA}$	8.	▱ iff opp sides ∥
9.	∡2 ≅ ∡4	9.	≠, corr ∡s ≅
10.	$\overline{RA} \cong \overline{GM}$	10.	opp sides ▱ ≅
11.	$\triangle RTA \cong \triangle GSM$	11.	aas ≅ aas
12.	$A(\triangle RTA) = A(\triangle GSM)$	12.	≅ △s, = areas
13.	$A(\triangle GSM) + A(GRTM) = A(GRTS)$	13.	area ∪ = sum areas
14.	$A(\triangle RTA) + A(GRTM) = A(GRTS)$	14.	subst
15.	$A(GRAM) = A(\triangle RTA) + A(GRTM)$	15.	area ∪ = sum areas
16.	$A(GRAM) = A(GRTS)$	16.	trans =
17.	$\overline{GS} \parallel \overline{RT}$	17.	2 lines ⊥ 3d line ∥
18.	*GRTS* ▱	18.	▱ iff opp sides ∥
19.	*GRTS* rect	19.	rect iff ▭
20.	$A(GRTS) = bh$	20.	$A(\text{rect}) = bh$
21.	$\therefore A(GRAM) = bh$	21.	trans =

In the above proof we have, roughly speaking, cut off $\triangle RTA$ from one end of the parallelogram and fitted it onto the other end. Note how the postulates concerning area provide a formal basis for this intuitively appealing point of view. Note, too, that the proof as written requires that point T be between M and A. There are, in fact, four other possible positions (Figure 8.7). Proofs that Theorem 86 is valid for these cases are left as exercises.

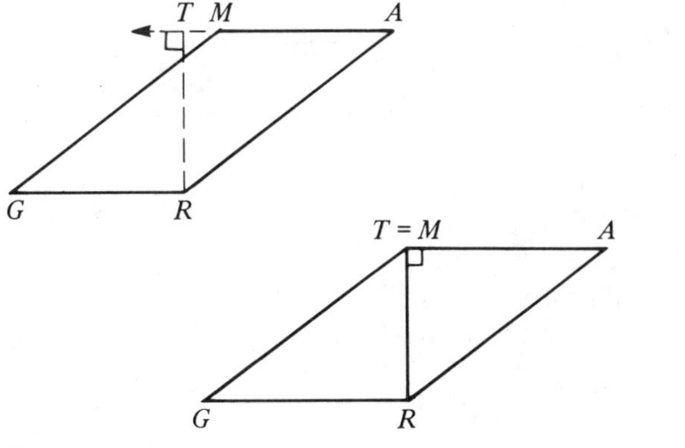

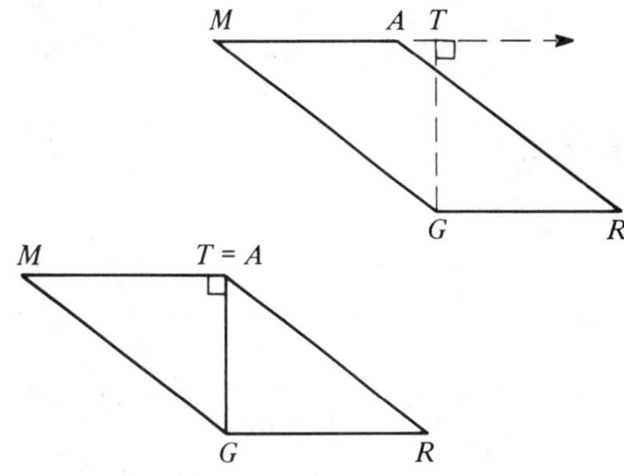

Figure 8.7

EXAMPLE 1

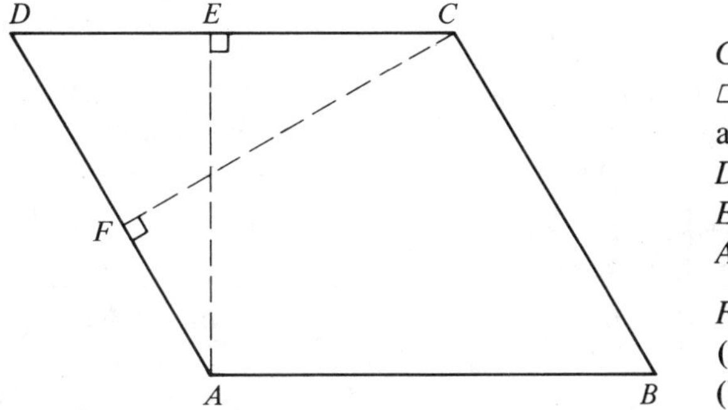

Given
▱*ABCD*
alts $\overline{EA}$, $\overline{FC}$
$DC = 30$ cm
$EA = 24$ cm
$AD = 27$ cm

Find
(a) $A(ABCD)$
(b) FC

Answers

(a) Using base $\overline{DC}$ and alt $\overline{EA}$

$$A(ABCD) = bh = 30 \cdot 24 = 720 \text{ sq cm}$$

(b) Using base $\overline{AD}$, alt $\overline{FC}$, and the answer to part (a)

$$A(ABCD) = bh$$
$$720 = 27 \cdot FC$$
$$\tfrac{720}{27} = FC$$
$$FC = \tfrac{80}{3} \text{ cm} = 26\tfrac{2}{3} \text{ cm}$$

We are now ready to state a theorem concerning the area of a triangle. Any side of a triangle may be used as its base; the corresponding altitude is the line segment from the opposite vertex that is perpendicular to the line containing the base.

Theorem 87 The area of a triangle is one-half the product of the lengths of any base and its corresponding altitude ($A(\triangle) = \tfrac{1}{2}bh$).

A formal proof of this theorem is indicated in the exercises. The plan of the proof is to construct a parallelogram whose area is twice that of the given triangle (Figure 8.8).

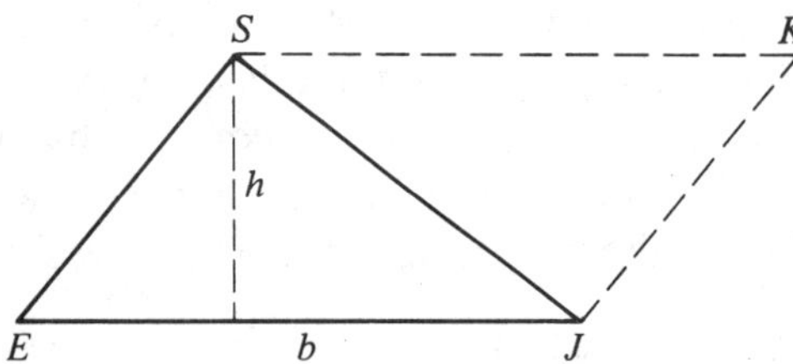

Figure 8.8 $\triangle SKJ \cong \triangle JES$; $A(EJKS) = bh$; $A(\triangle EJS) = \tfrac{1}{2}bh$.

EXAMPLE 2

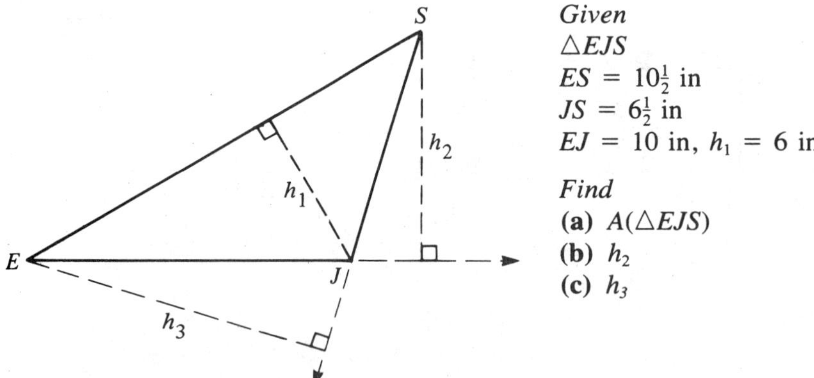

Given

$\triangle EJS$

$ES = 10\tfrac{1}{2}$ in

$JS = 6\tfrac{1}{2}$ in

$EJ = 10$ in, $h_1 = 6$ in

Find

(a) $A(\triangle EJS)$

(b) h_2

(c) h_3

Answers

(a) Using base $\overline{ES}$ and alt h_1

$$A(\triangle EJS) = \tfrac{1}{2}bh = \tfrac{1}{2} \cdot 10\tfrac{1}{2} \cdot 6 = \tfrac{63}{2}$$
$$A(\triangle EJS) = 31\tfrac{1}{2} \text{ sq in}$$

(b) Using base $\overline{EJ}$, alt h_2, and the area from (a)

$$A(\triangle EJS) = \tfrac{1}{2}bh$$
$$31\tfrac{1}{2} = \tfrac{1}{2} \cdot 10 \cdot h_2$$
$$\tfrac{1}{5} \cdot \tfrac{63}{2} = h_2$$
$$h_2 = 6\tfrac{3}{10} \text{ in}$$

(c) Using base $\overline{JS}$, alt h_3, and the area from (a)

$$A(\triangle EJS) = \tfrac{1}{2}bh$$
$$31\tfrac{1}{2} = \tfrac{1}{2} \cdot 6\tfrac{1}{2} \cdot h_3$$
$$\tfrac{63}{2} = \tfrac{13}{4} h_3$$
$$h_3 = 9\tfrac{9}{13} \text{ in}$$

Recall that a trapezoid has exactly one pair of opposite sides that are parallel. These parallel sides are called the *bases*. An *altitude* is a line segment that joins the lines containing the bases and is perpendicular to both of them. The words base and altitude are also used to refer to the *lengths* of the line segments in question. It follows that for a given trapezoid there are many line segments that are altitudes but they have equal lengths (Figure 8.9). Hence, there is only one "numerical" altitude.

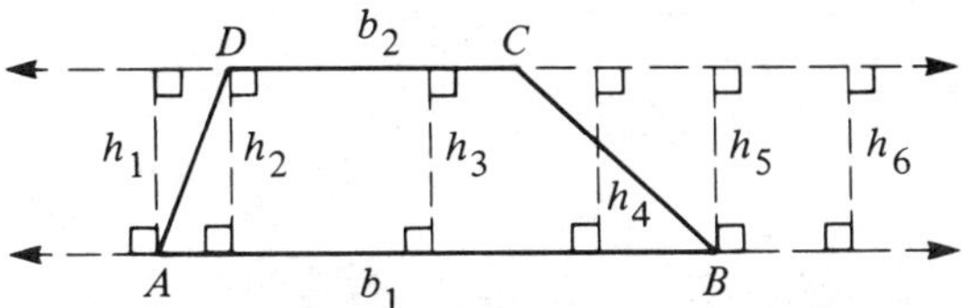

Figure 8.9 The bases are b_1 and b_2, the altitudes h_1 through h_6.

Theorem 88 The area of a trapezoid is one-half the product of the length of its altitude and the sum of the lengths of its bases ($A[\text{trap}] = \frac{1}{2}h[b_1 + b_2]$).

The proof is left as an exercise. A plan for a proof is indicated in Figure 8.10.

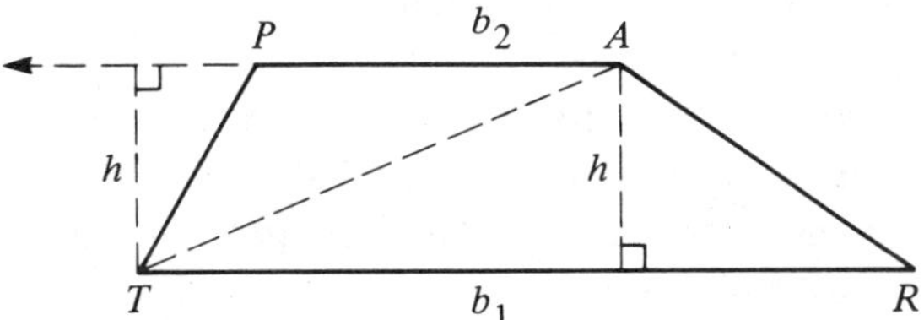

Figure 8.10 $A(\triangle TRA) = \frac{1}{2}b_1h$; $A(\triangle TAP) = \frac{1}{2}b_2h$; $A(TRAP) = \frac{1}{2}b_1h + \frac{1}{2}b_2h = \frac{1}{2}h(b_1 + b_2)$.

EXAMPLE 3

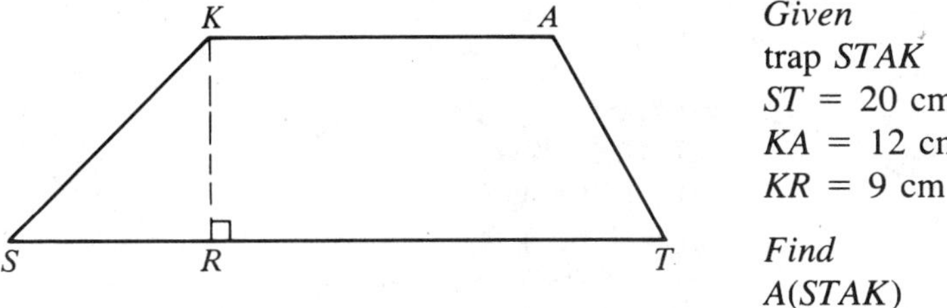

Given
trap *STAK*
$ST = 20$ cm
$KA = 12$ cm
$KR = 9$ cm

Find
$A(STAK)$

Answer

$$\begin{aligned} A(\text{trap}) &= \tfrac{1}{2}h(b_1 + b_2) \\ &= \tfrac{1}{2} \cdot 9 \cdot (20 + 12) \\ &= \tfrac{1}{2} \cdot 9 \cdot 32 \\ A(STAK) &= 144 \text{ sq cm} \end{aligned}$$

The parallelogram provides an interesting example showing that areas of triangles can be equal even if the triangles are *not* congruent.

EXAMPLE 4

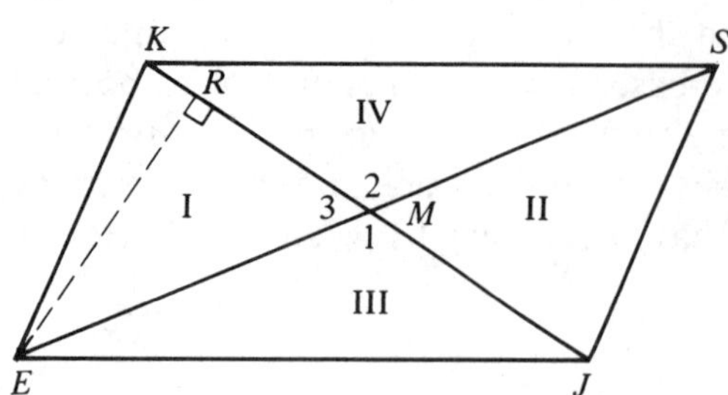

Given

▱$EJSK$

To Prove

$A(\triangle I) = A(\triangle II) = A(\triangle III) = A(\triangle IV)$

Statement	*Reason*
1. ▱$EJSK$	1. given
2. $\overline{KM} \cong \overline{JM}$, $\overline{EM} \cong \overline{SM}$	2. diags ▱ bis ea other
3. $\measuredangle 1 \cong \measuredangle 2$, $\measuredangle 3 \cong \measuredangle JMS$	3. vert $\measuredangle$s $\cong$
4. $\triangle I \cong \triangle II$, $\triangle III \cong \triangle IV$	4. sas $\cong$ sas
5. $A(\triangle I) = A(\triangle II)$, $A(\triangle III) = A(\triangle IV)$	5. $\cong$ $\triangle$s, = areas
6. Draw $\overline{ER} \perp \overline{JK}$.	6. 1 $\perp$ from pt to line
7. $A(\triangle I) = \frac{1}{2} \cdot KM \cdot ER$ $A(\triangle III) = \frac{1}{2} \cdot JM \cdot ER$	7. $A(\triangle) = \frac{1}{2}bh$
8. $KM = JM$	8. $\cong$ iff meas =
9. $A(\triangle III) = \frac{1}{2} \cdot KM \cdot ER$	9. subst
10. $A(\triangle I) = A(\triangle III)$	10. symm and trans =
11. $\therefore A(\triangle I) = A(\triangle II) = A(\triangle III) = A(\triangle IV)$	11. symm and trans =

Thus, there are four triangles of equal area although they are not all congruent to each other. The example contains another interesting result. Since $\overline{EM}$ is a median of $\triangle EJK$ and $A(\triangle I) = A(\triangle III)$, we see that a median divides a triangle into two triangles of equal area.

This section concludes with a numerical example illustrating several of the foregoing theorems.

EXAMPLE 5

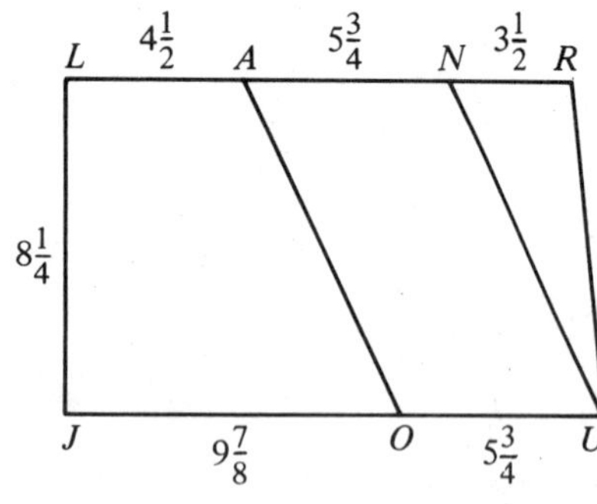

Given

$\overline{LJ} \perp \overline{JU}$

$\overline{LR} \parallel \overline{JU}$

Find

(a) $A(\triangle NRU)$

(b) $A(OUNA)$

(c) $A(JOAL)$

(d) $A(JURL)$

Answers

(a) Since NRU is a $\triangle$, $A = \frac{1}{2}bh$

$$A = \frac{1}{2} \cdot 3\frac{1}{2} \cdot 8\frac{1}{4}$$

$$A(\triangle NRU) = 14\frac{7}{16} \text{ sq units}$$

(b) Since $OUNA$ is a ▱, $A = bh$

$$A = 5\frac{3}{4} \cdot 8\frac{1}{4}$$

$$A(OUNA) = 47\frac{7}{16} \text{ sq units}$$

(c) Since *JOAL* is a trap, $A = \frac{1}{2}h(b_1 + b_2)$

$$A = \tfrac{1}{2} \cdot 8\tfrac{1}{4} \cdot (9\tfrac{7}{8} + 4\tfrac{1}{2})$$

$$A(JOAL) = 59\tfrac{19}{64} \text{ sq units}$$

(d) Since *JURL* is a trap, $A = \frac{1}{2}h(b_1 + b_2)$

$$A = \tfrac{1}{2} \cdot 8\tfrac{1}{4}(15\tfrac{5}{8} + 13\tfrac{3}{4})$$

$$A(JURL) = 121\tfrac{11}{64} \text{ sq units}$$

EXERCISES FOR 8.1 AND 8.2

In exercises 1–20 answer true or false.

1. A polygonal region includes the polygon itself.
2. Perimeter is a measure associated with a polygonal region.
3. A square unit is used to cover a polygon to measure its perimeter.
4. Area is a measure associated with a polygonal region.
5. If two triangles are congruent, then their areas are equal.
6. If two triangles have equal areas, then the triangles are congruent.
7. If $A(\square PLAN) = 50$ sq units, then $A(\triangle PLN) = 25$ sq units.
8. If the length of one side of a rectangular garden plot is 66 feet and the width is 2 yards, then the perimeter of the plot is 396 feet.
9. If the area of a square is 900 square centimeters, then each side measures 30 centimeters.
10. If the floor of a room is covered with small square tiles, then a count of the tiles gives a good approximation to the area of the floor.
11. If the area of a rectangle is 41 square inches and one side measures 12 inches, then the other side measures $3\frac{1}{2}$ inches.
12. If in trapezoid *ABCE*, the diagonals intersect in *M*, then $A(\triangle AME) = A(\triangle BMC)$.
13. If the area of a trapezoid is 112 square feet with bases 12 feet and 16 feet, then the altitude is 16 feet.
14. If the sum of the perimeters of a square and an equilateral triangle, whose sides have lengths equal to those of the square, is 42 feet, then each side measures 2 yards.
15. If a line segment is drawn from a vertex of a parallelogram to the midpoint of the opposite side, then the area of the triangle formed is one-fourth the area of the parallelogram.
16. If *P* is any point in the diagonal $\overline{AC}$ of parallelogram *ABCE*, then the $A(\triangle APB) = A(\triangle APE)$.
17. If two triangles have equal perimeters, then the triangles are congruent.
18. If an acute, a right, and an obtuse triangle have the same base and equal areas, then their third vertices (above the base) must all lie on a line parallel to the base.
19. If the diagonals of a rhombus measure 12 and 14 inches, then its area is 168 square inches.
20. If the base of a triangle is divided into five congruent parts and the points of division are joined to the opposite vertex, then the five triangles formed have equal areas.

In exercises 21–25 use Figure 8.11 to find the perimeter of each given polygon.

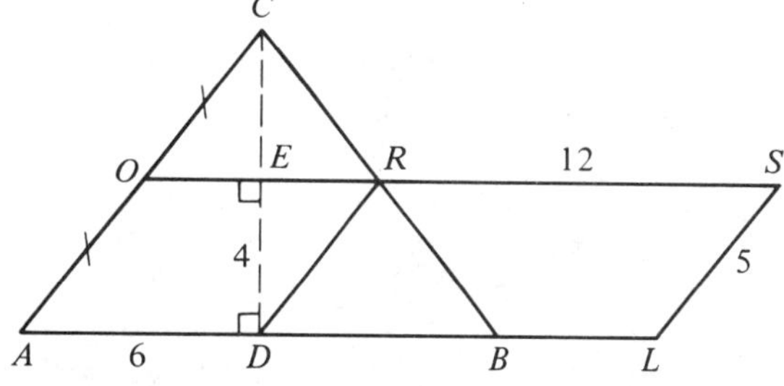

Figure 8.11

Given

$\square ALSO$, $\square DLSR$, $\overline{CD} \perp \overline{AB}$

$\triangle ABC$ isos ($\overline{AB}$ base), *O* midpt $\overline{AC}$

21. $\square ALSO$
22. $\triangle ABC$
23. trap *ABRO*
24. trap *DLSE*
25. polygon *ALSRC*

In exercises 26–30 use Figure 8.11 to find the area of each given polygon.

26. $\triangle COR$
27. $\square DLSR$
28. trap $BLSR$
29. $\triangle DRC$
30. polygon $ALSRC$

In exercises 31–34 use Figure 8.12 to answer the questions.

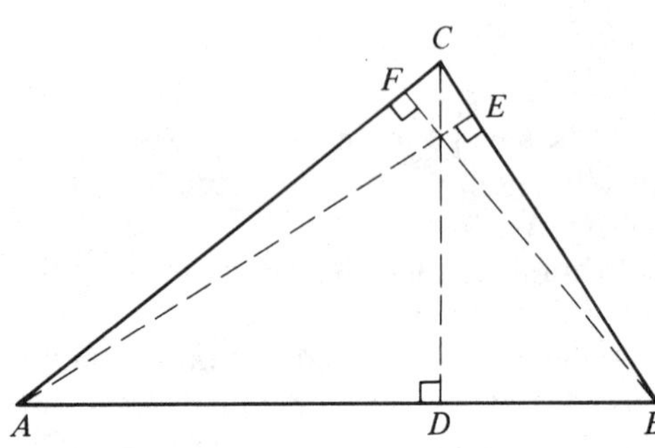

Figure 8.12

Given
$\triangle ABC$ with alts $\overline{CD}$, $\overline{AE}$, $\overline{BF}$

31. If $A(\triangle ABC) = 1512$ sq cm and $BF = 21$ cm, find AC.
32. If $AB = 24$ in, $CD = 20$ in, and $BC = 30$ in, find AE.
33. If $AE = 32$ cm, $BC = 48$ cm, and $CD = 24$ cm, find AB.
34. If $AC = 4\frac{1}{4}$ in, $BC = 9\frac{3}{4}$ in, and $AE = 6\frac{3}{8}$ in, find BF.

In exercises 35–38 use Figure 8.13 to answer the questions.

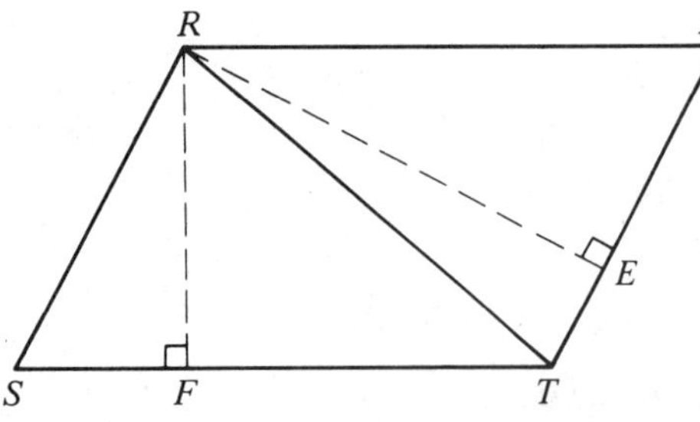

Figure 8.13

Given
$\square STAR$
alts $\overline{RF}$, $\overline{RE}$

35. If $A(STAR) = 540$ sq cm and $RE = 27$ cm, find TA.
36. If $A(\triangle TAR) = 144$ sq in and $RA = 18$ in, find RF.
37. If $RS = 21$ cm, $RE = 32$ cm, and $RF = 14$ cm, find RA.
38. If $RF = 3\frac{3}{8}$ in, $RA = 6\frac{3}{4}$ in, and $RE = 5\frac{1}{16}$ in, find SR.

In exercises 39 and 40 use Figure 8.14 to answer the questions.

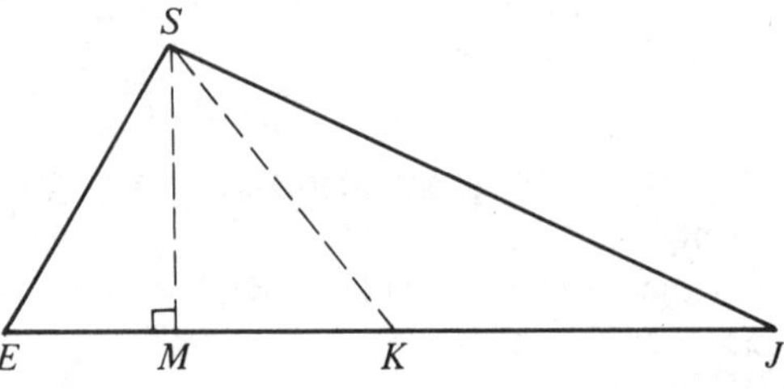

Figure 8.14

Given
med $\overline{SK}$
alt $\overline{SM}$

39. If $SM = 9$ cm and $KJ = 16$ cm, find (a) $A(\triangle EKS)$ and (b) $A(\triangle KJS)$.
40. If $A(\triangle EJS) = 646$ sq ft and $SM = 17$ ft, find EK.

In exercises 41–45 use Figure 8.15 to answer the questions.

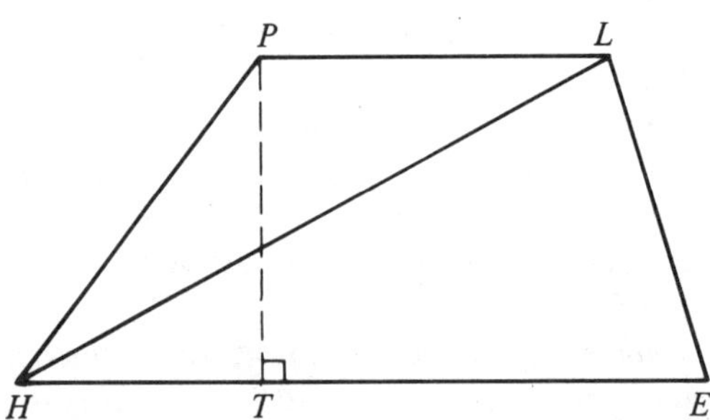

Figure 8.15

Given
trap $HELP$ ($\overline{HE}$, $\overline{PL}$ bases)
alt $\overline{PT}$

41. Find $A(HELP)$ if $PT = 18$ cm, $HE = 34$ cm, and $PL = 21$ cm.
42. Find $A(\triangle HTP)$ if $PT = 3\frac{3}{4}$ in, $HE = 12\frac{2}{3}$ in, and $TE = 8\frac{3}{4}$ in.
43. Find $A(\triangle HLP)$ if $PT = 4$ ft, $HE = 7$ ft, and $LP = 5$ ft.
44. Find PT if $A(HELP) = 150$ sq cm, $HE = 17$ cm, and $PL = 13$ cm.
45. Find HE if $A(HELP) = 212$ sq yd, $PT = 8$ yd, and $PL = 54$ ft.

In exercises 46–48 use Figure 8.16 to answer the questions.

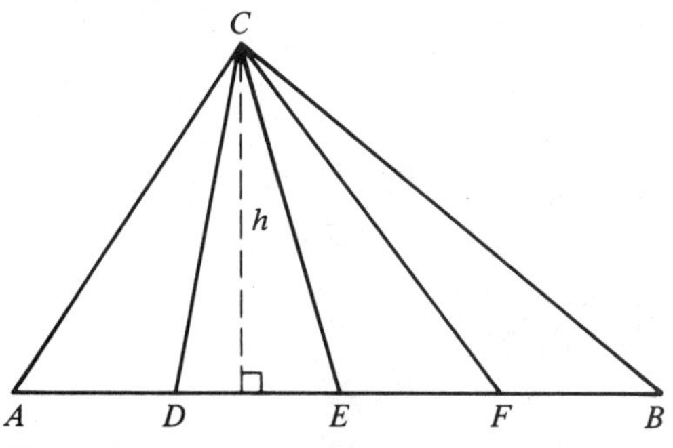

Figure 8.16

Given
$\overline{AD} \cong \overline{DE} \cong \overline{EF} \cong \overline{BF}$
h alt $\triangle ABC$

46. If $A(\triangle EFC) = 39$ sq in, find $A(\triangle ABC)$.

47. If $h = 11$ cm and $EF = 7$ cm, find $A(\triangle AFC)$.

48. If $A(\triangle ABC) = 448$ sq in and $h = 14$ in, find BF.

In exercises 49 and 50 use Figure 8.17 to answer the questions.

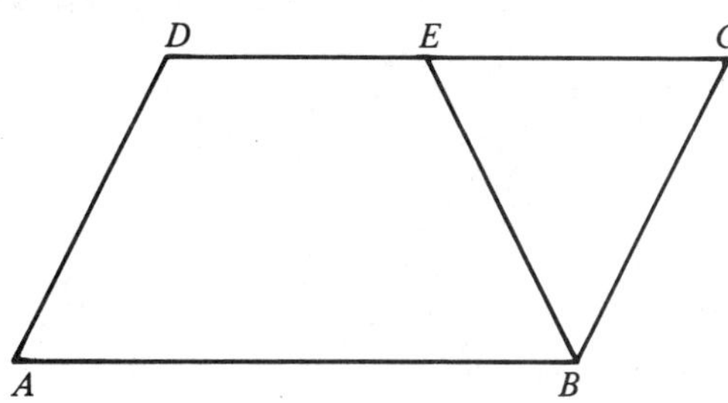

Figure 8.17

Given
$\square ABCD$
E midpt $\overline{DC}$

49. If $A(ABCD) = 323$ sq yd and $AB = 57$ ft, find $A(\triangle BCE)$.

50. If $A(\triangle BCE) = 112$ sq in, find $A(ABED)$.

51. If the diagonals of a square measure 20 inches, find the area of the square.

52. If the perimeter of a square is 100 centimeters, find the area of the square.

53. If the perimeter of a square is $24\sqrt{2}$ inches, find the length of a diagonal of the square.

54. Find the area of an isosceles right triangle if one leg is 14 feet long.

55. If two triangles have the same base and the altitude of one triangle is 6 inches longer than the altitude of the other, what is the length of the base if their areas differ by 30 square inches?

56. The area of a trapezoid with altitude 9 inches is 81 square inches. If one base measures 11 inches, what is the length of the other base?

57. If one base of a trapezoid is twice as long as its other base, the altitude is 6 feet, and the area is 45 square feet, what are the lengths of the two bases?

58. If the line joining the midpoints of the nonparallel sides of a trapezoid is 32 inches long and the altitude is 16 inches, find the area of the trapezoid.

59. Given $\overline{TA} \perp \overline{OP}$

(a) If $TA = 52$ cm and $OP = 74$ cm, find $A(APTO)$.

(b) Show that $A(APTO) = \frac{1}{2} \cdot TA \cdot OP$. (Hint: Find $A[\triangle OPT]$ and $A[\triangle OPA]$.)

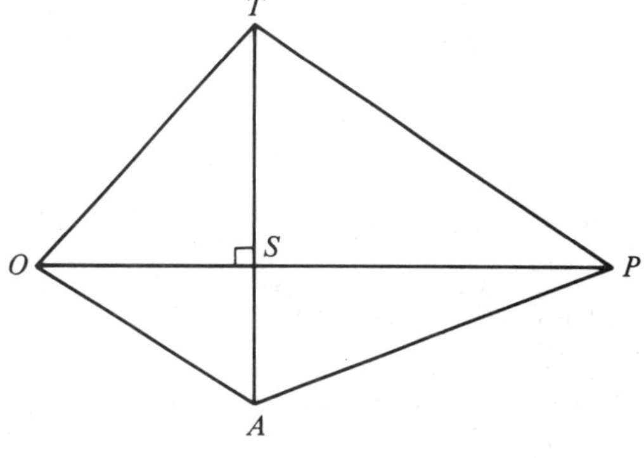

In exercises 60–62 copy the figure, mark it, and supply the missing reasons in each proof.

60. *Given*
$\square ABCD$
$\overline{EG} \parallel \overline{AB}$
$\overline{JH} \parallel \overline{AD}$

To Prove
$A(EFHD) = A(JBGF)$

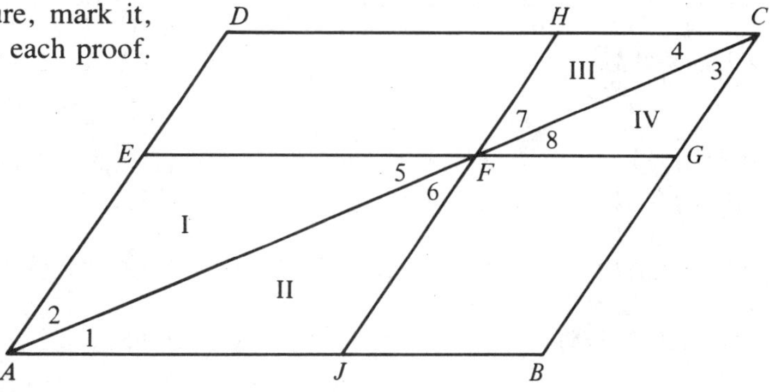

Statement	*Reason*
1. $\square ABCD$	1. ?
2. $\overline{CD} \cong \overline{AB}$, $\overline{AD} \cong \overline{CB}$	2. ?
3. $\overline{AC} \cong \overline{AC}$	3. ?
4. $\triangle ACD \cong \triangle CAB$	4. ?
5. $A(\triangle ACD) = A(\triangle CAB)$	5. ?
6. $\overline{EG} \parallel \overline{AB}$, $\overline{JH} \parallel \overline{AD}$	6. ?
7. $\measuredangle 5 \cong \measuredangle 1$, $\measuredangle 2 \cong \measuredangle 6$	7. ?
8. $\overline{AF} \cong \overline{AF}$	8. ?
9. $\triangle \text{I} \cong \triangle \text{II}$	9. ?
10. $A(\triangle \text{I}) = A(\triangle \text{II})$	10. ?
11. $\overline{AB} \parallel \overline{DC}$, $\overline{AD} \parallel \overline{BC}$	11. ?
12. $\overline{EG} \parallel \overline{DC}$, $\overline{JH} \parallel \overline{BC}$	12. ?
13. $\measuredangle 4 \cong \measuredangle 8$, $\measuredangle 7 \cong \measuredangle 3$	13. ?
14. $\overline{CF} \cong \overline{CF}$	14. ?
15. $\triangle \text{III} \cong \triangle \text{IV}$	15. ?
16. $A(\triangle \text{III}) = A(\triangle \text{IV})$	16. ?
17. $A(\triangle \text{I}) + A(\triangle \text{III}) = A(\triangle \text{II}) + A(\triangle \text{IV})$	17. ?
18. $A(\triangle ACD) = A(\triangle \text{I}) + A(\triangle \text{III}) + A(EFHD)$	18. ?
19. $A(\triangle CAB) = A(\triangle \text{II}) + A(\triangle \text{IV}) + A(JBGF)$	19. ?
20. $A(\triangle \text{I}) + A(\triangle \text{III}) + A(EFHD) = A(\triangle \text{II}) + A(\triangle \text{IV}) + A(JBGF)$	20. ?
21. $\therefore A(EFHD) = A(JBGF)$	21. ?

61. (Theorem 87)

Given
$\triangle EJS$
$EJ = b$
alt $SK = h$

To Prove
$A(\triangle EJS) = \frac{1}{2}bh$

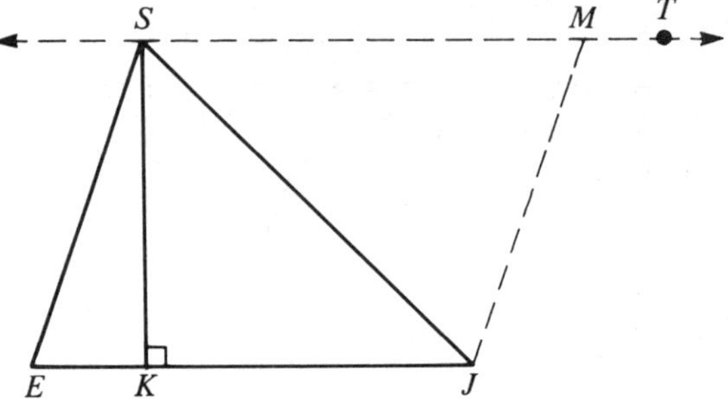

Statement	*Reason*
1. $\triangle EJS$, $EJ = b$, alt $SK = h$	1. ?
2. Thru S draw $\overleftrightarrow{ST} \parallel \overline{EJ}$.	2. ?
3. Construct $\overline{SM} \cong \overline{EJ}$.	3. ?
4. Draw $\overline{MJ}$.	4. ?
5. $EJMS$ $\square$	5. ?
6. $A(EJMS) = bh$	6. ?
7. $\overline{ES} \cong \overline{MJ}$	7. ?
8. $\overline{SJ} \cong \overline{SJ}$	8. ?
9. $\triangle EJS \cong \triangle MSJ$	9. ?
10. $A(\triangle EJS) = A(\triangle MSJ)$	10. ?
11. $A(\triangle EJS) + A(\triangle MSJ) = A(EJMS)$	11. ?
12. $A(\triangle EJS) + A(\triangle MSJ) = bh$	12. ?
13. $A(\triangle EJS) + A(\triangle EJS) = bh$	13. ?
14. $2 \cdot A(\triangle EJS) = bh$	14. ?
15. $\therefore A(\triangle EJS) = \frac{1}{2}bh$	15. ?

62. (Theorem 86)

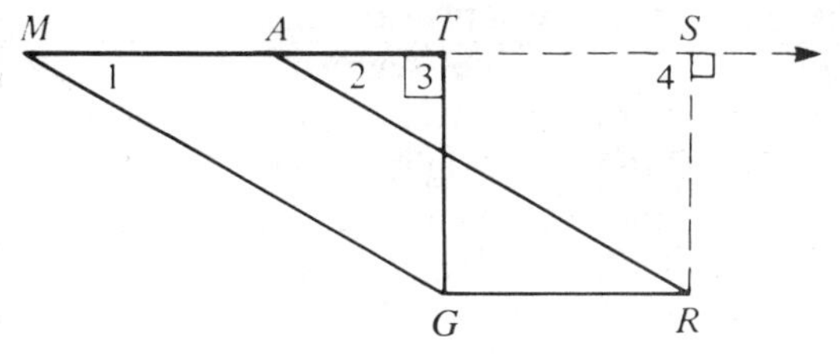

Given
$\square GRAM$
M-A-T
alt $\overline{GT}$
$GR = b$
$GT = h$

To Prove
$A(GRAM) = bh$

Statement	*Reason*
1. $\square GRAM$ with M-A-T alt $\overline{GT}$	1. ?
2. $\overline{GT} \perp \overline{MT}$	2. ?
3. $\measuredangle 3$ rt $\measuredangle$	3. ?
4. $GR = b$ and $GT = h$	4. ?
5. Draw $\overrightarrow{MT}$.	5. ?
6. Draw $\overline{RS} \perp \overrightarrow{MT}$.	6. ?
7. $\measuredangle 4$ rt $\measuredangle$	7. ?
8. $\measuredangle 4 \cong \measuredangle 3$	8. ?
9. $\overline{RA} \cong \overline{MG}$	9. ?
10. $\overline{MG} \parallel \overline{AR}$, $\overline{MA} \parallel \overline{GR}$	10. ?
11. $\measuredangle 2 \cong \measuredangle 1$	11. ?
12. $\triangle RSA \cong \triangle GTM$	12. ?
13. $A(\triangle RSA) = A(\triangle GTM)$	13. ?
14. $A(GRSM) = A(GRAM) + A(\triangle RSA)$	14. ?
15. $A(GRSM) = A(GRST) + A(\triangle GTM)$	15. ?
16. $A(GRAM) + A(\triangle RSA) = A(GRST) + A(\triangle GTM)$	16. ?
17. $A(GRAM) = A(GRST)$	17. ?
18. $\overline{GT} \parallel \overline{RS}$	18. ?
19. $GRST$ $\square$	19. ?
20. $GRST$ rect	20. ?
21. $A(GRST) = bh$	21. ?
22. $\therefore A(GRAM) = bh$	22. ?

In exercises 63–65 do the constructions using only a compass and straightedge. A preliminary sketch may be helpful in determining the steps to use as illustrated in three of the exercises.

63. **(a)** Draw an acute triangle KLM. Construct a right triangle KLT having the same area as $\triangle KLM$.

(b) Draw an obtuse triangle EJS. Construct an isosceles triangle EJK having the same area as $\triangle EJS$.

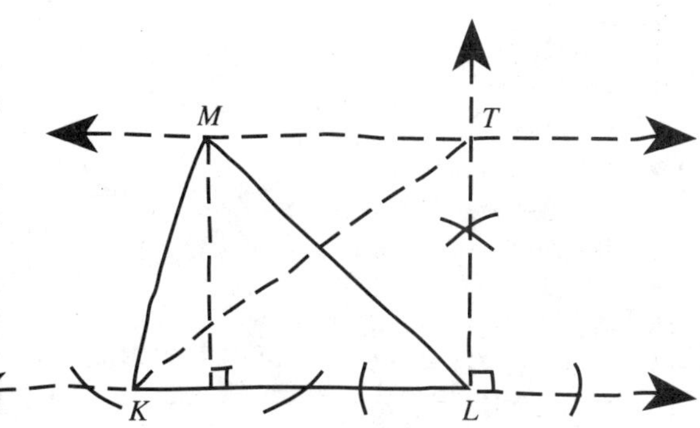

64. **(a)** Draw an obtuse triangle LAW. Construct a line segment that divides $\triangle LAW$ into two triangles of equal area.
(b) Construct a right triangle JMS. Construct two line segments that divide $\triangle JMS$ into three triangles of equal area.

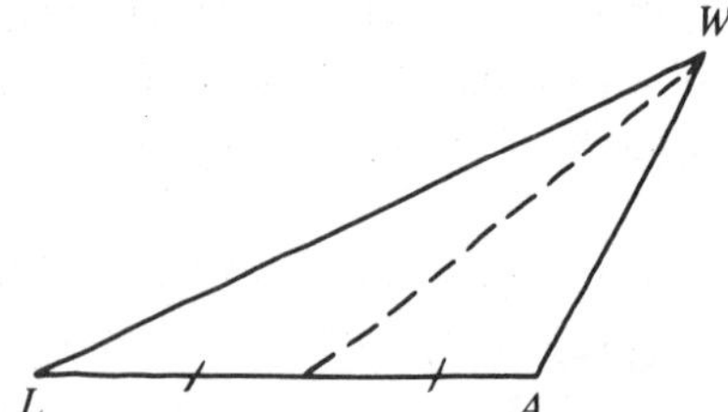

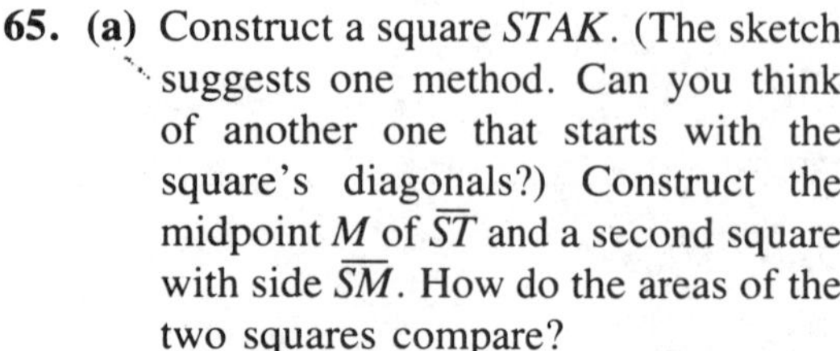

65. **(a)** Construct a square $STAK$. (The sketch suggests one method. Can you think of another one that starts with the square's diagonals?) Construct the midpoint M of $\overline{ST}$ and a second square with side $\overline{SM}$. How do the areas of the two squares compare?
(b) Construct a square $WYNT$. Trisect side $\overline{WY}$ and construct a second square with side $\frac{1}{3}WY$. How do the areas of the two squares compare?

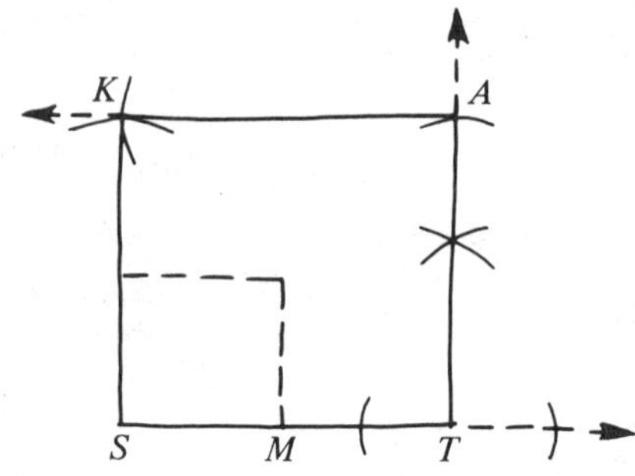

8.3
POLYGONS AND CIRCLES

Sections 8.1 and 8.2 developed formulas for the areas of rectangles, squares, parallelograms, triangles, and trapezoids. Using these results an area can be assigned to any polygonal region, or more briefly, to any polygon. This is done by dividing the given region into nonoverlapping regions of any of the above-mentioned types and then applying Postulate 19 (area ∪ = sum areas). Figure 8.18 shows a quadrilateral, a pentagon, and a hexagon that have been divided into triangles. The area of each polygon is the sum of the areas of the triangles into which it has been divided. Of course, such divisions can be done in more than one way. Figure 8.19 shows three congruent hexagons that are divided differently. Again, the area of each is the sum of the areas of the polygons into which it has been divided.

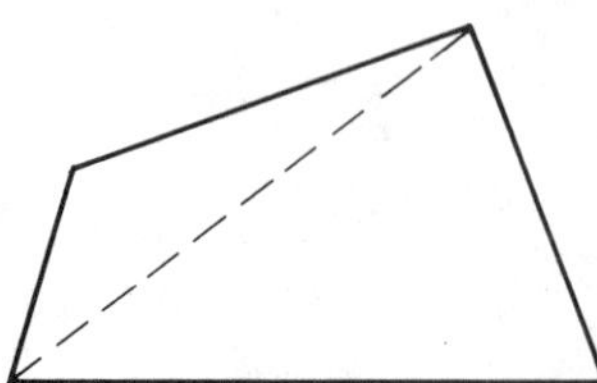
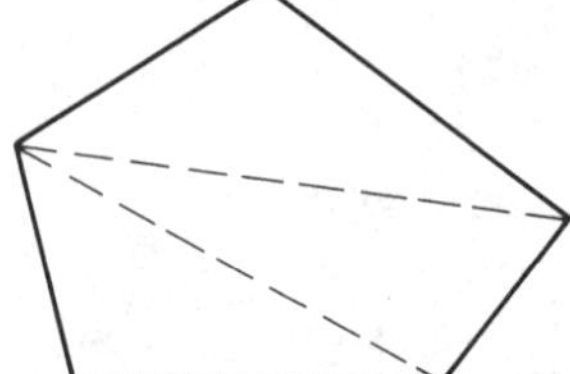
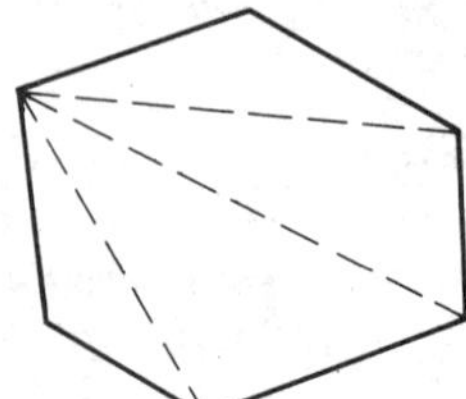

Figure 8.18

It should be clear that the above procedure yields the unique area of the polygon (the Area Postulate) only if the unique areas of the "subpolygons" can be found. This, in turn, requires determining the lengths of certain sides and altitudes. All this is possible if (1) enough information is given to specify a unique polygon, and (2) enough mathematics is known to calculate any other measures that are needed. The next chapter presents some facts about right triangles that may sometimes be helpful in accomplishing step (2). Step (2), however, is often best done using trigonometry, a subject that is not within the scope of this book. Example 1 contains a problem that can be solved at this stage of mathematical development. Note that the altitude of $\triangle$II is $30 - 21 = 9$ ft and that $RI = 64 - 15 - 12 = 37$ ft.

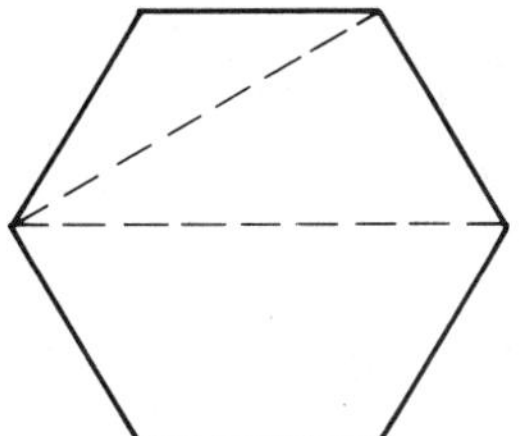
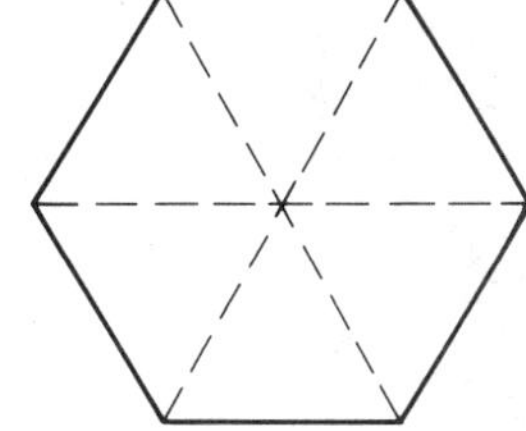
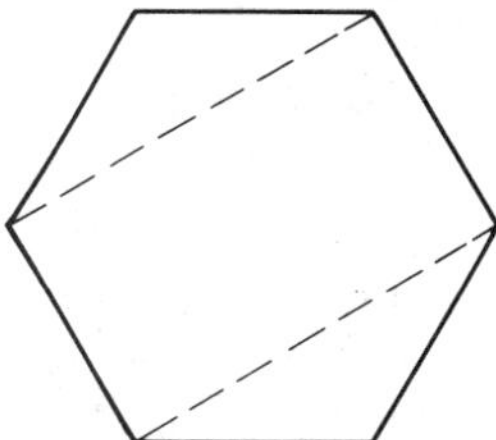

Figure 8.19

EXAMPLE 1

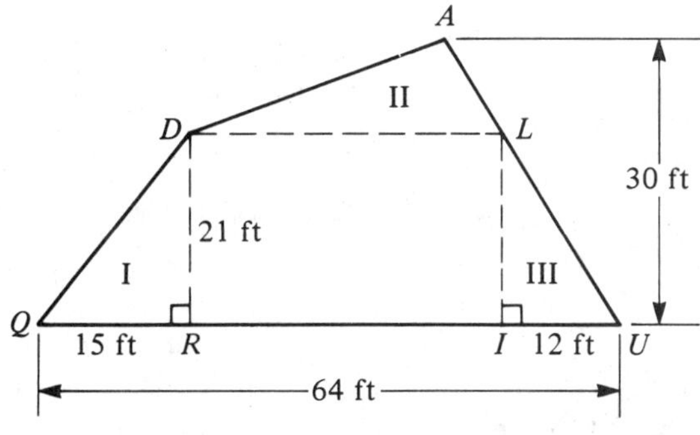

Given
quad $QUAD$

Find

(a) $A(QUAD)$ using three triangles and one rectangle

(b) $A(QUAD)$ using one triangle and one trapezoid

Answers

(a)

$$\begin{aligned}
A(\triangle) &= \tfrac{1}{2}bh \\
A(\triangle \text{I}) &= \tfrac{1}{2} \cdot 15 \cdot 21 \\
&= 157\tfrac{1}{2} \text{ sq ft} \\
A(\triangle \text{II}) &= \tfrac{1}{2} \cdot 37 \cdot 9 \\
&= 166\tfrac{1}{2} \text{ sq ft} \\
A(\triangle \text{III}) &= \tfrac{1}{2} \cdot 12 \cdot 21 \\
&= 126 \text{ sq ft} \\
A(\text{rect}) &= bh \\
A(RILD) &= 37 \cdot 21 = 777 \text{ sq ft} \\
A(QUAD) &= A(\triangle \text{I}) + A(\triangle \text{II}) + A(\triangle \text{III}) + A(RILD) \\
&= 157\tfrac{1}{2} + 166\tfrac{1}{2} + 126 + 777 \\
&= 1227 \text{ sq ft}
\end{aligned}$$

(b)

$$\begin{aligned}
A(\triangle) &= \tfrac{1}{2}\, bh \\
A(\triangle \text{II}) &= \tfrac{1}{2} \cdot 37 \cdot 9 \\
&= 166\tfrac{1}{2} \text{ sq ft} \\
A(\text{trap}) &= \tfrac{1}{2}h(b_1 + b_2) \\
A(QULD) &= \tfrac{1}{2} \cdot 21(64 + 37) \\
&= 1060\tfrac{1}{2} \text{ sq ft} \\
A(QUAD) &= A(\triangle \text{II}) + A(QULD) \\
&= 166\tfrac{1}{2} + 1060\tfrac{1}{2} \\
&= 1227 \text{ sq ft}
\end{aligned}$$

The above subdividing procedure also provides a practical way to *approximate* the area of a polygon as illustrated in Example 2. The symbol $\approx$ means "approximately equals."

EXAMPLE 2

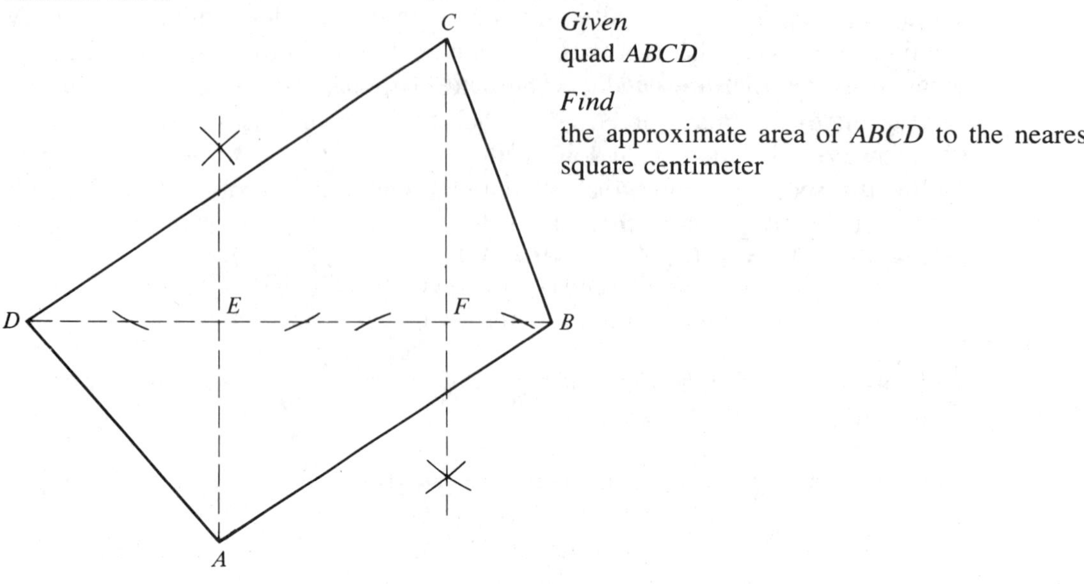

Given
quad $ABCD$

Find
the approximate area of $ABCD$ to the nearest square centimeter

Answer
Draw $\overline{BD}$, and using Construction 6, construct altitude $\overline{AE}$ of $\triangle ABD$ and altitude $\overline{CF}$ of $\triangle BCD$. With a ruler, find $BD \approx 7.0$ cm, $AE \approx 2.9$ cm, $CF \approx 3.8$ cm.

$A(\triangle) = \frac{1}{2}bh$	$A(\triangle) = \frac{1}{2}bh$	$A(ABCD) = A(\triangle ABD) + A(\triangle BCD)$
$A(\triangle ABD) \approx \frac{1}{2} \cdot (7.0) \cdot (2.9)$	$A(\triangle BCD) \approx \frac{1}{2}(7.0) \cdot (3.8)$	$A(ABCD) \approx 10.2 + 13.3$
$A(\triangle ABD) \approx 10.2$ sq cm	$A(\triangle BCD) \approx 13.3$ sq cm	$A(ABCD) \approx 23.5$ sq cm
		$A(ABCD) \approx 24$ sq cm

The area of a regular polygon may be found by the foregoing subdivision technique. There is, however, a special formula for regular polygons. Given any regular polygon, select three consecutive vertices and construct the circle that contains them (Construction 13, Section 7.4). By joining this circle's center to the polygon's vertices, a set of congruent triangles is formed. We omit a proof of this fact but illustrate the situation for a hexagon in Figure 8.20. It follows that the circle contains *all* of the vertices of the polygon.

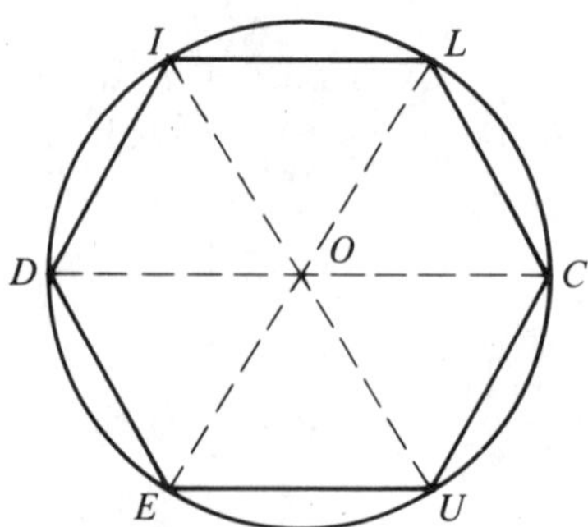

Figure 8.20

Recall from Section 7.3 that a polygon all of whose vertices are points of a circle is said to be *inscribed* in the circle, and the circle is said to be *circumscribed* about the polygon. For *regular* polygons we also have the following definitions.

Definition 8.4 The *center* of a regular polygon is the center of its circumscribed circle.

Definition 8.5 A *radius* of a regular polygon is a line segment joining its center to a vertex.

Since the radii of a regular polygon are congruent, their lengths are equal; we refer to this common length as the radius of the polygon.

Definition 8.6 An *apothem* of a regular polygon is a line segment from its center perpendicular to any side.

The apothems of a regular polygon are congruent and their common length may be referred to as the apothem of the polygon.

Definitions 8.4–8.6 are illustrated for a pentagon in Figure 8.21. Each triangle in this figure has area $\frac{1}{2}ba$, where b is the length of each of the polygon's sides and a is its apothem. Noting that $P = 5b$ where P is the pentagon's perimeter, we have $A(PENTA) = 5 \cdot \frac{1}{2} \cdot ba = \frac{1}{2}Pa$. This discussion suggests the following theorem. A formal proof is omitted.

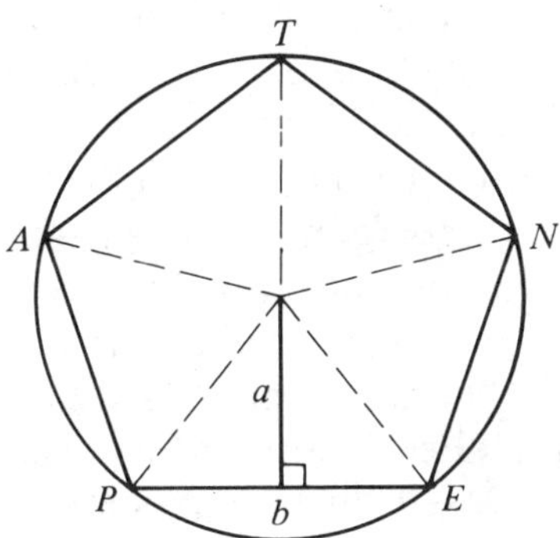

Figure 8.21

Theorem 89 The area of a regular polygon is one-half the product of its perimeter and its apothem ($A[\text{reg poly}] = \frac{1}{2}Pa$).

EXAMPLE 3

(a) Find the area of a regular hexagon whose sides are each 4 inches long and whose apothem is $2\sqrt{3}$ inches.

(b) Approximate the area to the nearest hundredth using $\sqrt{3} \approx 1.73$.

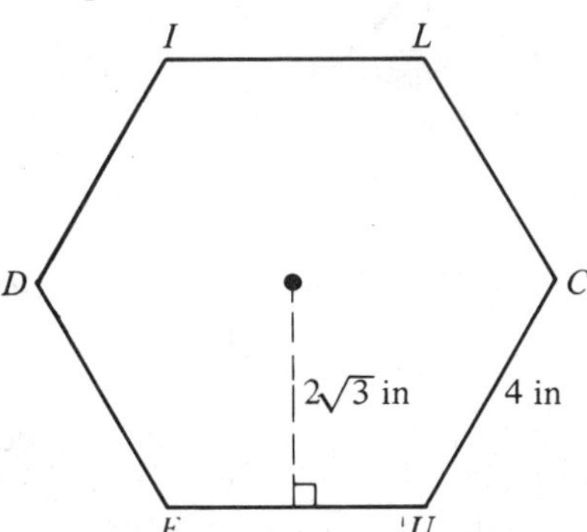

Answers

(a) $A = \frac{1}{2}Pa$

$A = \frac{1}{2} \cdot 6 \cdot 4 \cdot 2\sqrt{3}$

$A = 24\sqrt{3}$ sq in

(b) $A = 24\sqrt{3}$

$A \approx 24(1.73)$

$A \approx 41.52$ sq in

In Example 3, the apothem was given. It should be noted, however, that if the length of the sides of a regular polygon is known, then the apothem may be calculated using trigonometry. It is also worth noting that Theorem 89 provides a practical way to approximate a regular polygon's area by measuring the length of its sides and its apothem. Some problems using this technique are given in the exercises.

The *circumference* of a circle is analogous to the perimeter of a polygon. Intuitively, it is the circle's length, and it is reasonable to expect that given any circle there should be a way to assign a unique positive real number as its circumference. This, indeed, can be done but the mathematical development is too complex to present here. We can, however, give a brief discussion of the underlying idea, followed by a theorem stating how the circumference and diameter of a circle are numerically related.

The perimeter of an inscribed polygon is a natural approximation to the circumference of a circle. Figure 8.22 shows three congruent circles with polygons inscribed in them. It seems reasonable that the perimeter of the hexagon in (a) is smaller than the number that should be assigned as the circumference of the circle. In (b) a dodecagon is inscribed whose perimeter seems to be a better approximation to the circumference. To further improve the approximation, the number of sides may be increased as in (c). It can be shown that, given a circle, if a sequence of polygons with increasing numbers of sides is inscribed, then the sequence of corresponding perimeters approaches a unique positive real number that is defined as the circumference of the circle. It is this "approaching" or "limiting" process that gives rise to the irrational number symbolized by the Greek letter π (pi). The number π may be approximated as $\frac{22}{7}$ or 3.1416. Based on these results we have the following theorem which is stated without proof.

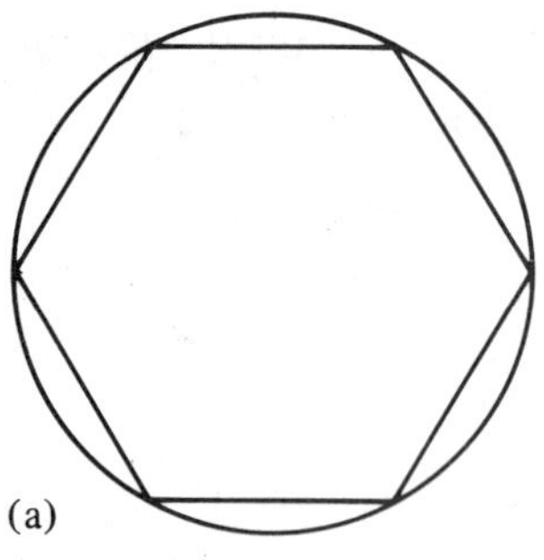
(a)

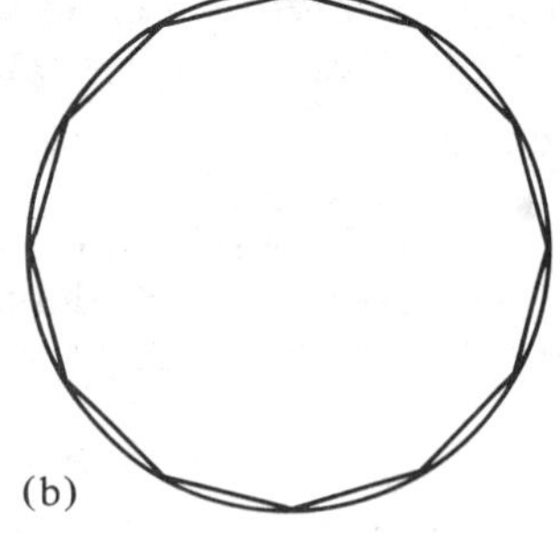
(b)

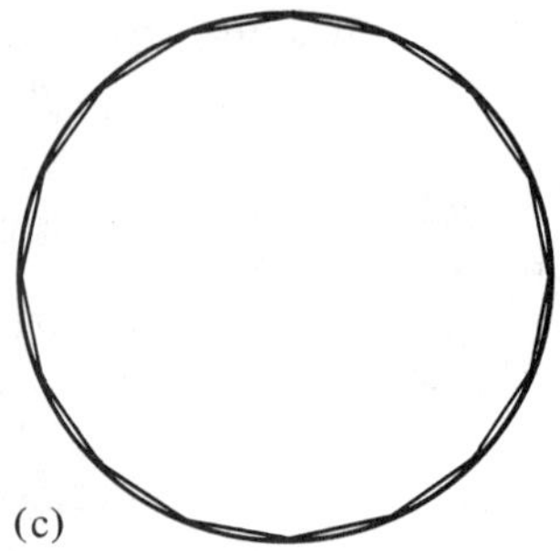
(c)

Figure 8.22

Theorem 90 The circumference of any circle is the product of π and its diameter ($C = \pi d$).

It follows that $C \div d = \pi$; that is, for every circle the circumference divided by the diameter is the number π. Also, since the diameter of any circle is twice the radius and since $C = \pi d$, we also have the formula $C = 2\pi r$.

EXAMPLE 4 A circle has a 14-inch diameter. Approximate its circumference using (a) $\pi \approx \frac{22}{7}$ and (b) $\pi \approx 3.14$.

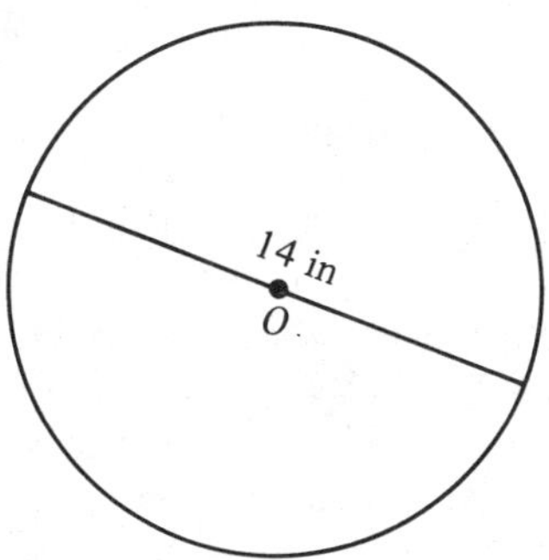

Answers

(a) $C = \pi d$
$C \approx \frac{22}{7} \cdot 14$
$C \approx 44$ in

(b) $C = \pi d$
$C \approx (3.14)(14)$
$C \approx 43.96$ in

The two answers in Example 4 are different because $\frac{22}{7} \neq 3.14$. In fact, $\frac{22}{7} = 3.142857142857 \cdots$, a repeating *non*terminating decimal. The number π, on the other hand, is a *non*repeating, *non*terminating decimal. To twelve places, it is 3.141592653590.

In the Greek language, π is the first letter of the word "periphereia," which means literally "to bear or carry around." Our word "periphery," meaning the boundary of a figure, is derived from this Greek word. Originally, π was used to represent the circumference of a circle, but in 1607 the English mathematician William Jones first used it to denote the constant ratio of the circumference of any circle divided by its diameter, and this usage continues today. This ratio was believed by the ancient Hebrews to be 3, as recorded in the Bible (I Kings 7:23 and II Chronicles 4:2), but much earlier the Egyptians were using the value 3.16 as recorded in the Ahmes Papyrus (1650 B.C.).

The number π is also used in calculating a circle's area. Again, consider the sequence of inscribed polygons as described above. It seems clear that the corresponding sequence of apothems approaches the radius of the circle and the sequence of areas approaches the area of the circle. Thus we are led to the following intuitively appealing equations:

$$\text{area of regular inscribed polygon} = \tfrac{1}{2}Pa$$
$$\text{area of circle} = \tfrac{1}{2} \cdot (2\pi r) \cdot r$$
$$\text{area of circle} = \pi r^2$$

This result suggests the following theorem, which is stated without proof.

Theorem 91 The area of a circle is the product of π and the square of its radius ($A = \pi r^2$).

EXAMPLE 5 A circle has a radius of $3\frac{1}{2}$ inches. (a) Find its area in terms of π. (b) Approximate its area using $\pi \approx 3.1416$. Round off the answer to three decimal places.

Answers

(a) $A = \pi r^2$
$A = \pi(\frac{7}{2})^2$
$A = \frac{49\pi}{4}$ sq in

(b) $A = \frac{49\pi}{4}$
$A \approx (12.25)(3.1416)$
$A \approx 38.484600$
$A \approx 38.485$ sq in

EXERCISES FOR 8.3

In exercises 1–20 answer true or false.

1. The area of a polygon can be found by subdividing the polygonal region into nonoverlapping triangular regions and adding the areas of the triangular regions.
2. Polygonal regions can be subdivided into smaller regions in exactly one way.
3. If a polygon is inscribed in a circle, then its vertices are points of the circle.
4. If the circumference of a circle is 12π centimeters, the radius of the circle is 12 centimeters.
5. If two pentagons have equal area, they are also congruent.
6. The apothem is the altitude of the triangle formed in a regular polygon by a side and by two radii of the circumscribed circle.
7. A circle with a 30-centimeter diameter has an area of 225π square centimeters.
8. If a regular pentagon is inscribed in a circle, then a central angle intercepting a side measures 72°.
9. If a regular hexagon is inscribed in a circle, then a side has the same measure as a radius.
10. A radius of a regular polygon is the same as a diagonal of the polygon.
11. If two regular polygons have the same perimeter, then they have the same area.
12. The three medians of a triangle divide the triangle into six smaller congruent triangles.
13. The three medians of a triangle divide the triangle into six smaller triangles of equal area.
14. If a square and a rectangle both have 32-inch perimeters and the rectangle has a 7-inch width, then the square has the greater area.
15. If the circumference of a circle is numerically equal to its area, then the radius is 2 units.
16. If the circumference of a circle is 10π units, then its area is 25π square units.
17. If the area of a circle is 432π square inches, then the area is also 3π square feet.
18. If two triangles have equal areas, the same base, and are on opposite sides of the base, then the segment joining their two vertices opposite the base is bisected by the line of the base.
19. The area of a circle circumscribed about a square of side 4 inches and diagonal $4\sqrt{2}$ inches has twice the area of the circle inscribed in the square (see Figure 7.9, Section 7.3).
20. If two concentric circles have diameters of 6 inches and 2 inches, then the area inside the larger circle and outside the smaller circle is 8 square inches.

In exercises 21–25 use Figure 8.23 to answer the questions.

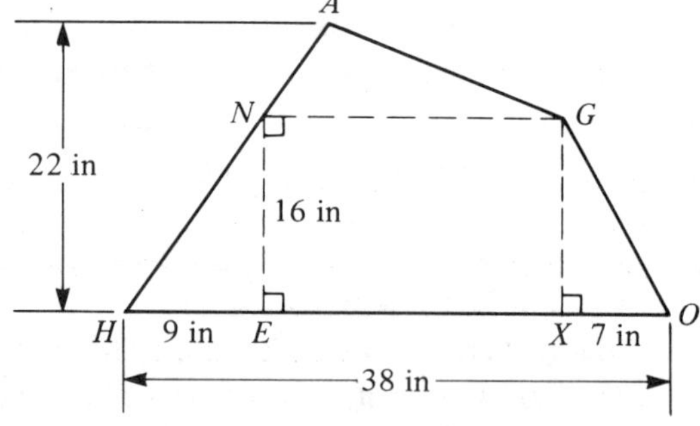

Figure 8.23

21. Find $A(HOGA)$ using three triangles and one rectangle.
22. Find $A(HOGA)$ using a triangle and a trapezoid.
23. Find $A(EXGAN)$ using a triangle and a rectangle.
24. Find $A(HXGA)$ using two triangles and a rectangle.
25. Find $A(EXGAN)$ using quad $HOGA$ and two triangles.

In exercises 26–29 use Figure 8.24 to answer the questions.

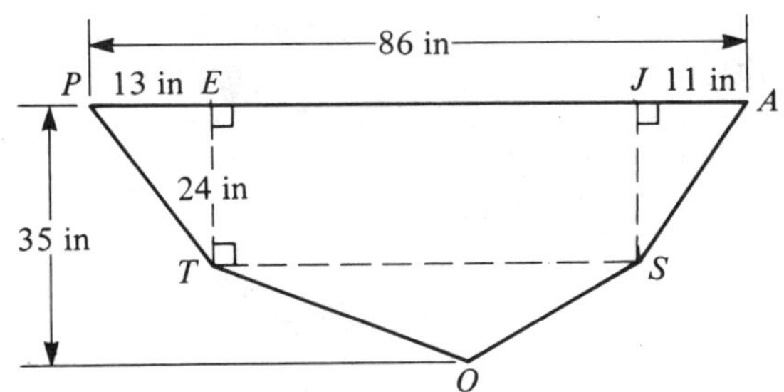

Figure 8.24

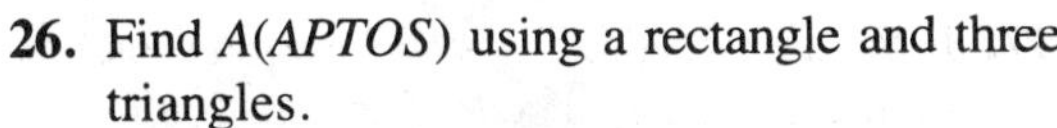

26. Find $A(APTOS)$ using a rectangle and three triangles.
27. Find $A(APTOS)$ using a trapezoid and one triangle.
28. Find $A(JPTOS)$ using a pentagon and one triangle.
29. Find $A(AETS)$ using a pentagon and two triangles.

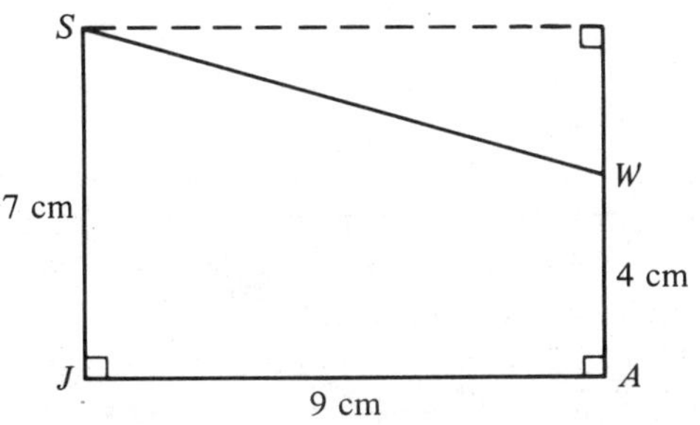

Figure 8.25

In exercises 30–32 use Figure 8.25 to answer the questions.

30. Find $A(JAWS)$ by adding the areas of a rectangle and a triangle.
31. $A(JAWS)$ by subtracting the areas of a rectangle and a triangle.
32. Find $A(JAWS)$ using the trapezoid formula for area.

In exercises 33–38 find $A(PQRS)$ or $A(PQRST)$.

33.

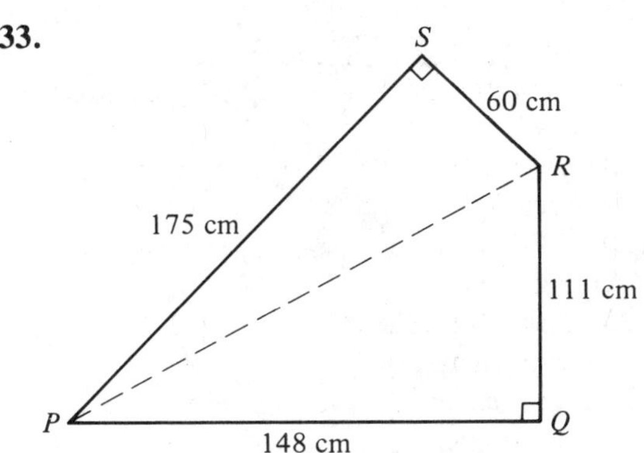

34.

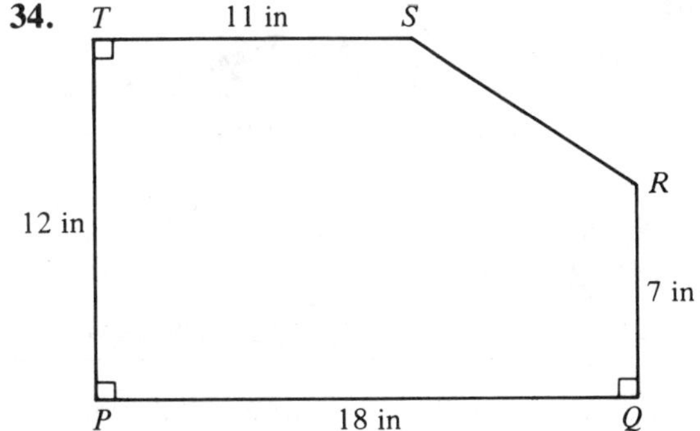

35.

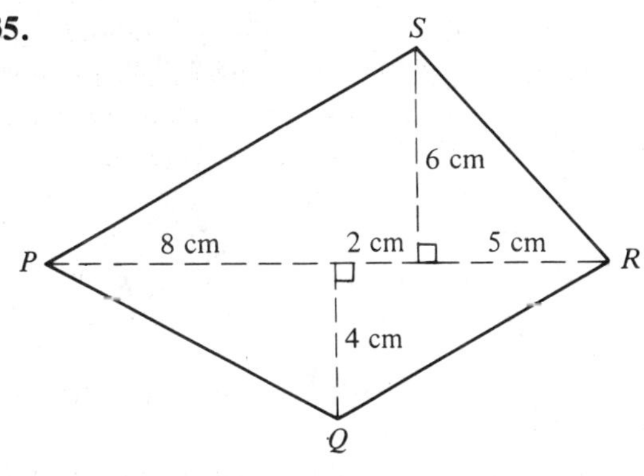

36.

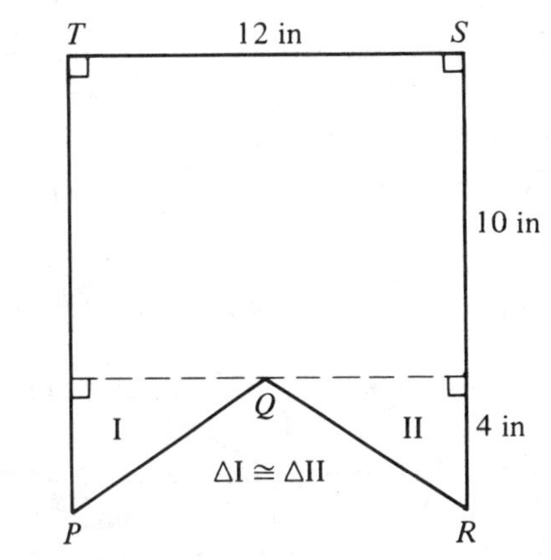

37.

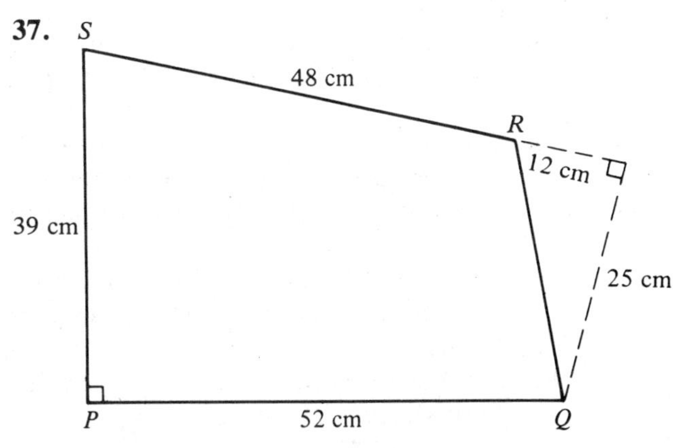

38.

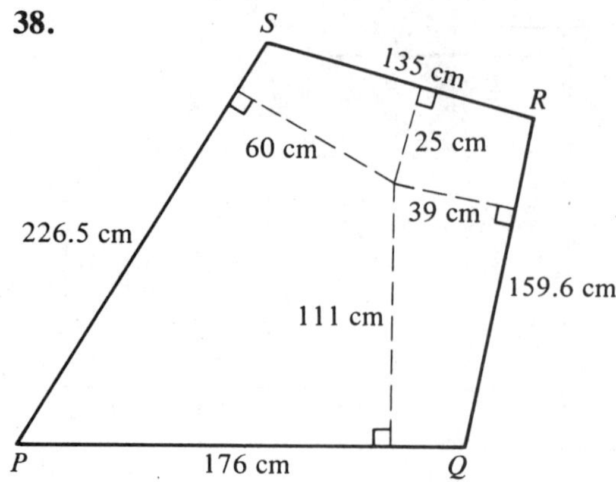

In exercises 39–44 approximate the areas of the polygons by subdividing the polygons into triangles, constructing altitudes and measuring the necessary segments. Use centimeters.

39.

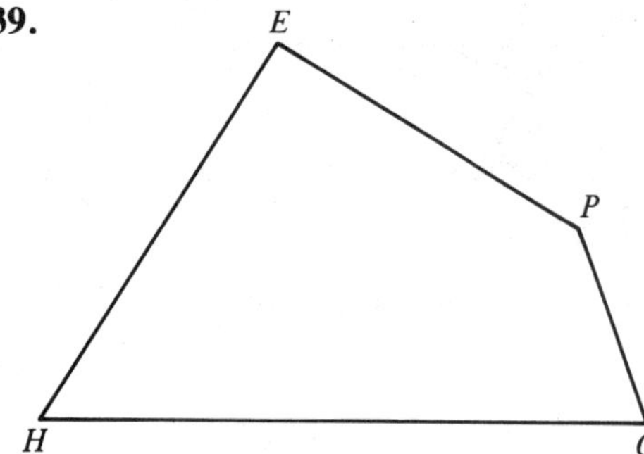

40.

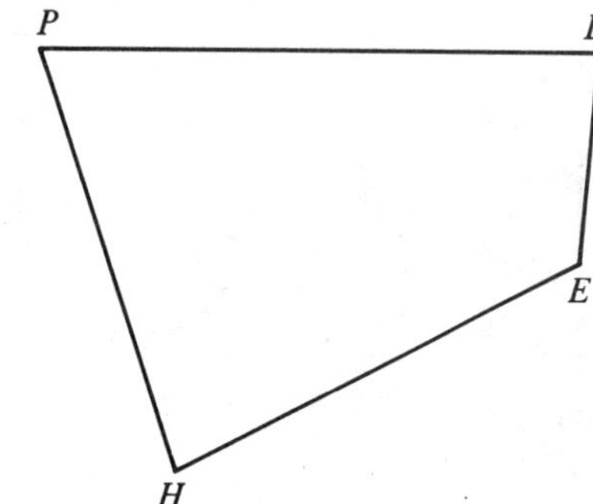

41.

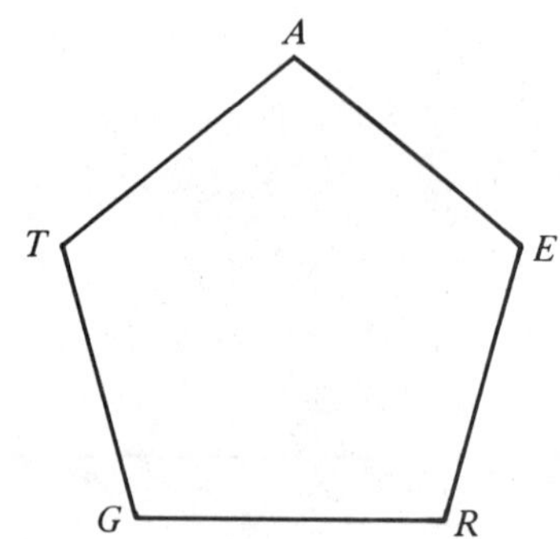

42.

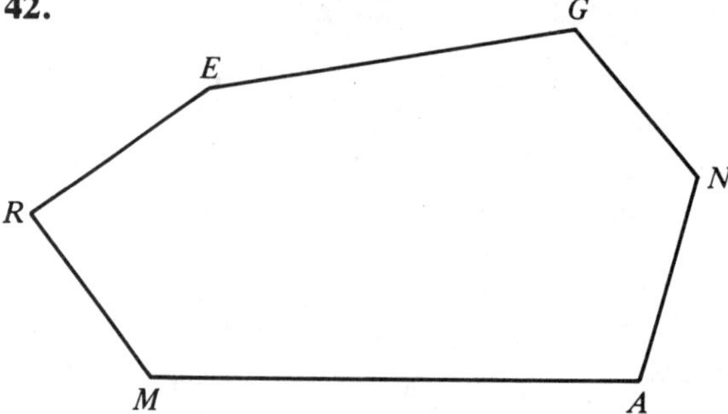

43. *Given*
⊙*O*
STAVE reg pentagon

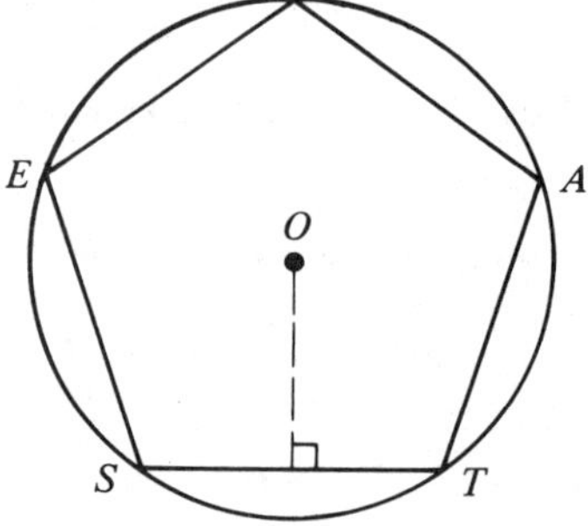

44. *Given*
⊙*O*
TANDEM reg hexagon

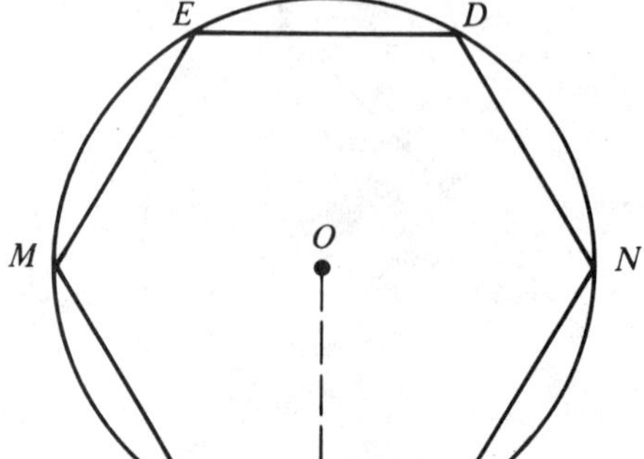

45. Given square *ABCD*, show using area formulas that $(b + c)^2 = b^2 + 2bc + c^2$, where b and c represent lengths as marked.

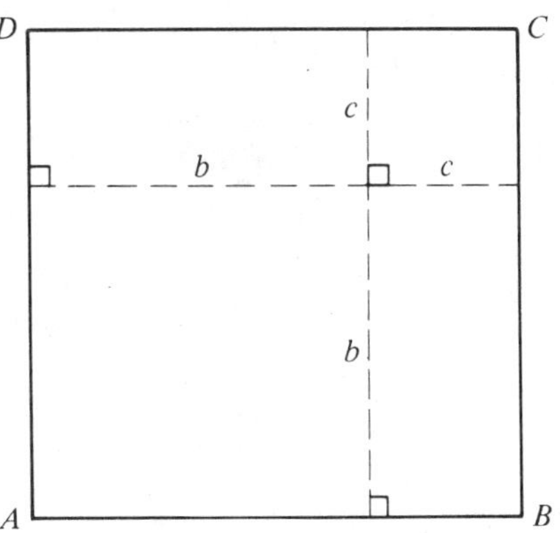

46. *Given*
$\odot O$ inscr in *ACEG*
$OB = 8$ in
$AC = 30$ in
$CE = 18$ in
$GE = 14$ in
$AG = 27$ in

Find
$A(ACEG)$

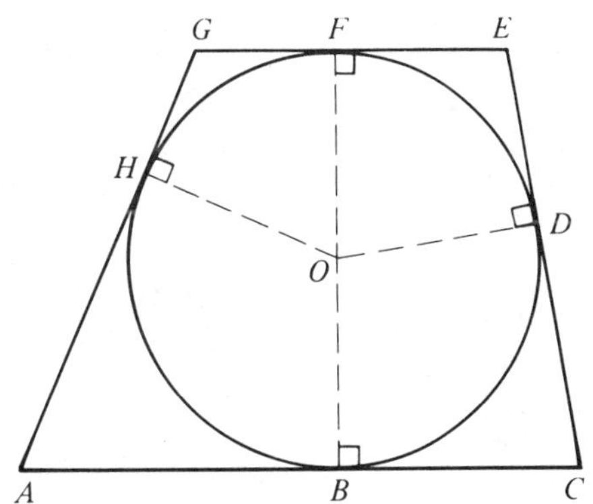

In exercises 47–54 find the areas of the shaded regions.

47. *Given*
rh *FISH*
$FS = 24$ cm
$IH = 18$ cm

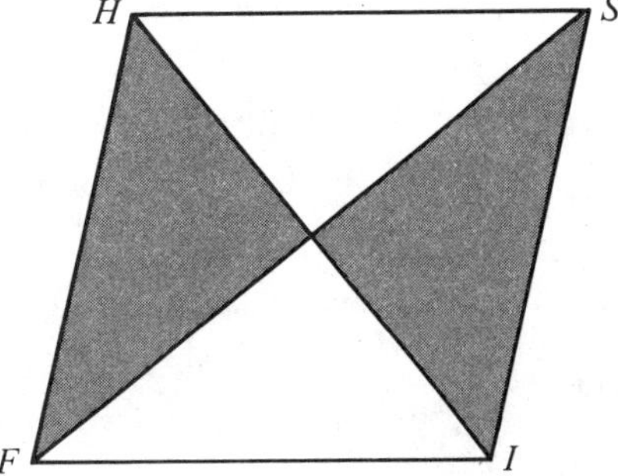

48. *Given*
▱*TOAD*
$\overline{LO} \perp \overline{DA}$
$TC = 14$ in
$DA = 16$ in
$LA = 4$ in
$LO = 9$ in

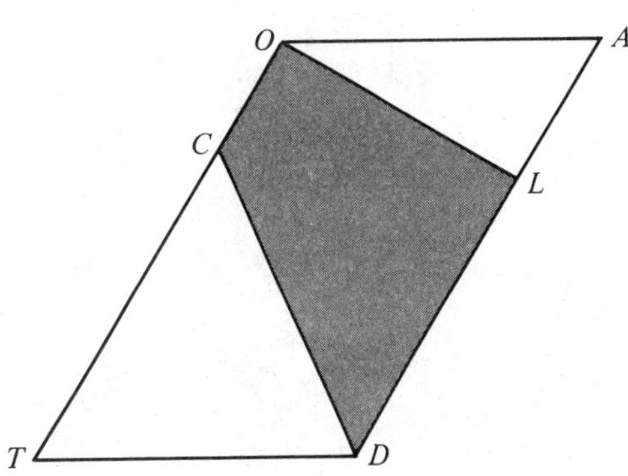

49. *Given*
rect *CROW*
rect *SILK*
$KL = 5$ in
$LI = 11$ in
$CR = 12$ in
$WC = 19$ in

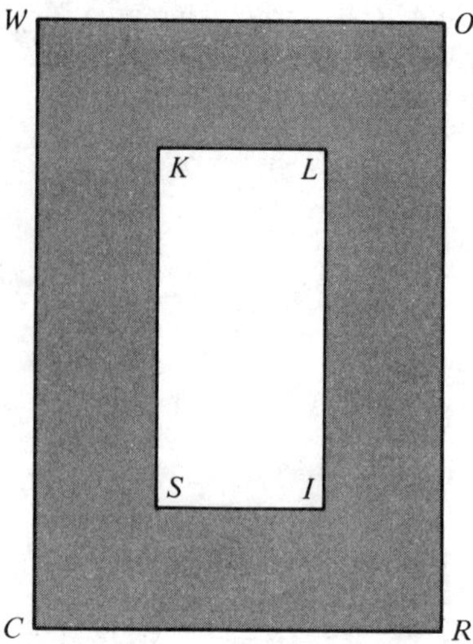

50. *Given*
$\square ABCD$
$A(ABCD) = 32$ sq in
$PB = \frac{1}{4}AB$
$BQ = \frac{1}{4}BC$
$DR = \frac{1}{4}DC$
$DS = \frac{1}{4}DA$

51. *Given*
rect *ABCD*
semi$\odot$ *O*
$OA = 6$ in
$\overline{AB}$, $\overline{BC}$, $\overline{CD}$ tans

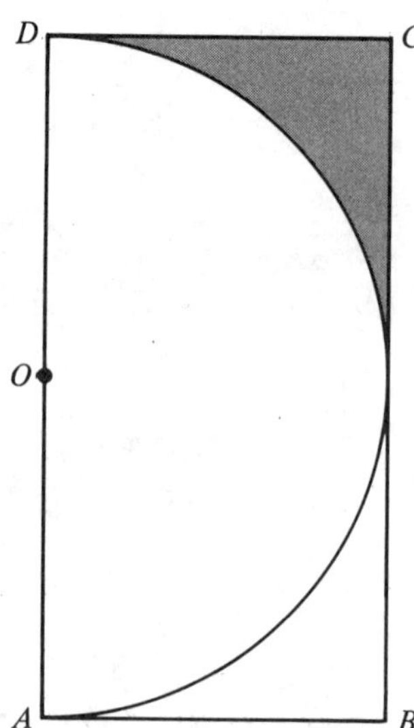

52. *Given*
rect $ECIR$

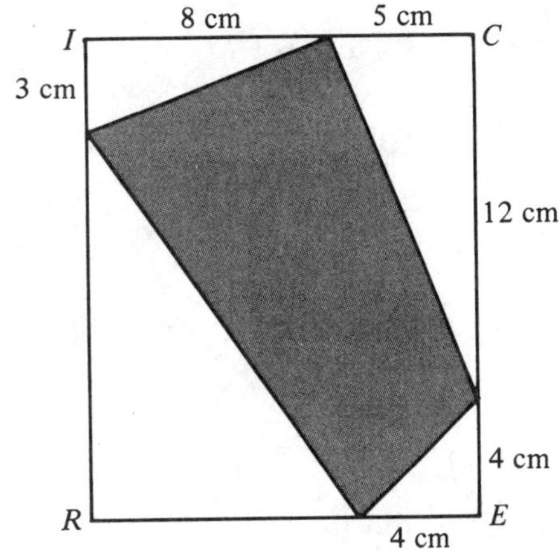

53. *Given*
concentric $\odot$s O
$\overline{EJ} \perp \overline{AB}$
$OC = 4$ in
$OJ = 9$ in

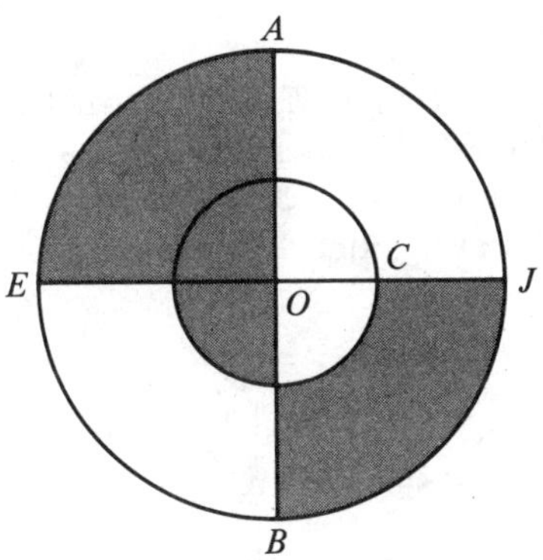

54. *Given*
$\odot O$
A, B, C, D, E, F centers of semi $\odot$s
$OG = 32$ in
$JB = BO = OE = EG$

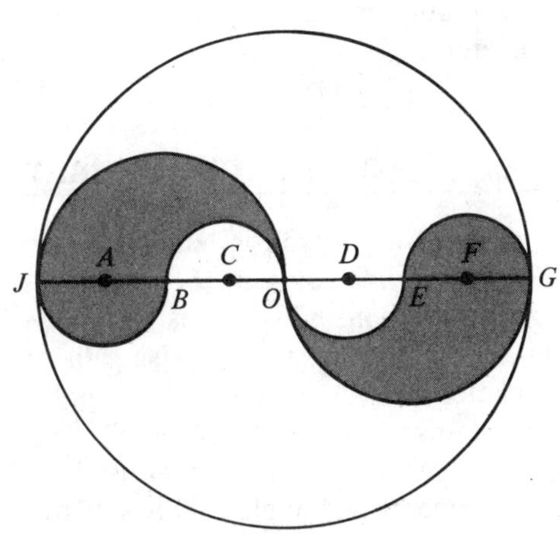

55. *Given*
$\square GONE$ with midpts S, C, A, M

Show
$A(SCAM) = \frac{1}{2}A(GONE)$

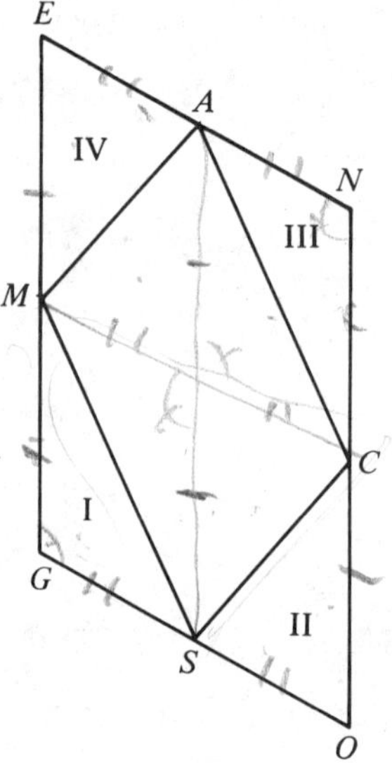

In exercises 56–60 do the constructions using only a compass and straightedge. A preliminary sketch may be helpful in determining the steps to use.

56. Draw an acute triangle EJS. Construct a rectangle with side $\overline{EJ}$ having the same area as $\triangle EJS$. Show why your construction gives equal areas. (Hint: See the figure.)

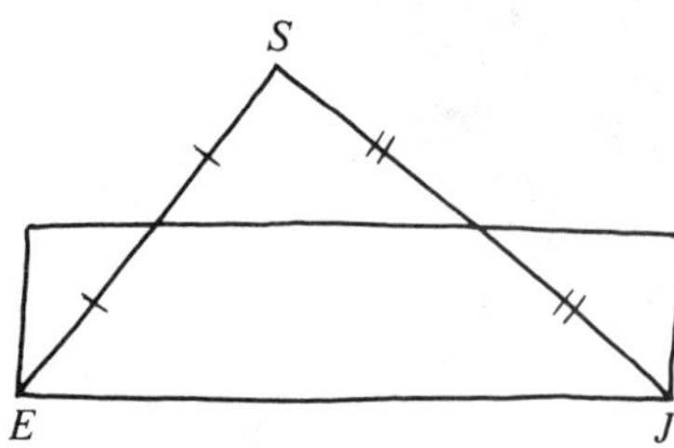

57. Construct a rectangle $ABCD$. Construct (a) an isosceles triangle having the same area as rect $ABCD$, and (b) a right triangle having the same area as rect $ABCD$. (Hint: See exercise 56.)

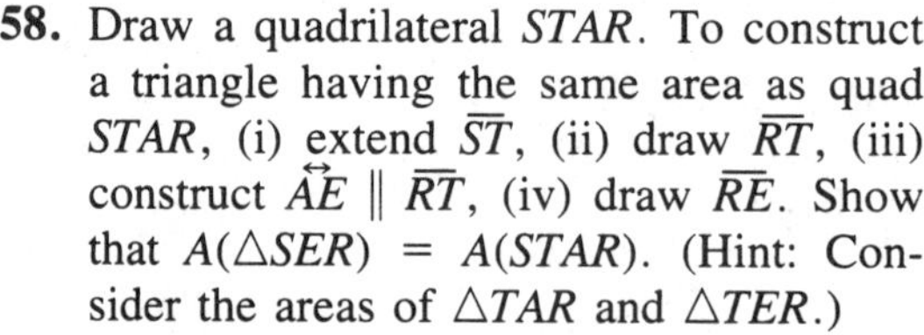

58. Draw a quadrilateral $STAR$. To construct a triangle having the same area as quad $STAR$, (i) extend $\overline{ST}$, (ii) draw $\overline{RT}$, (iii) construct $\overleftrightarrow{AE} \parallel \overline{RT}$, (iv) draw $\overline{RE}$. Show that $A(\triangle SER) = A(STAR)$. (Hint: Consider the areas of $\triangle TAR$ and $\triangle TER$.)

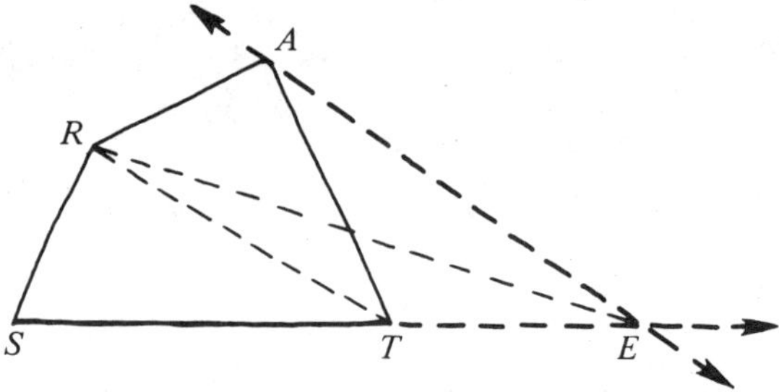

59. Construct a parallelogram $ABCD$. Use the method of exercise 58 to construct a triangle having the same area as $\square ABCD$.

60. Construct an isosceles trapezoid $ABCD$. Use the method of exercise 58 to construct a triangle having the same area as trap $ABCD$.

CHAPTER 8 SUMMARY

The perimeter of a polygon is based directly on the length of a line segment (Section 2.3). The area of a polygon, however, is a concept requiring a new set of postulates. Using these as a foundation, the development of a polygon's area begins by covering a rectangle with unit squares, a process similar to that used for measuring segments and angles. This leads to the area of a triangle and the area of a polygon as the sum of areas of triangles or rectangles. Formulas and approximations assist us in calculating these areas. Finally, formulas for the area and circumference of a circle are motivated and presented, but their derivations involve difficulties that must be left to more advanced courses.

FACTS TO KNOW

1. Definitions
   - **a.** Perimeter
   - **b.** Triangular region
   - **c.** Polygonal region
   - **d.** Center of a regular polygon
   - **e.** Radius of a regular polygon
   - **f.** Apothem
2. Postulates
   - **a.** The Area Postulate
   - **b.** $\cong$ $\triangle$s, = areas
   - **c.** Area $\cup$ = sum areas
   - **d.** A(rect) = lw or bh
3. Theorems
   - **a.** $A(\square) = bh$
   - **b.** $A(\triangle) = \frac{1}{2}bh$
   - **c.** $A(\text{trap}) = \frac{1}{2}h(b_1 + b_2)$
   - **d.** $A(\text{reg poly}) = \frac{1}{2}Pa$
   - **e.** $C = \pi d$
   - **f.** $A = \pi r^2$

PROBLEMS TO MASTER

1. Use formulas to find perimeters of polygons.
2. Use formulas to find areas of polygons.
3. Find areas by subdividing polygons or circles and adding or subtracting the areas of these subdivisions.
4. Use area formulas to find bases or altitudes.
5. Use formulas to find the area or circumference of a circle.
6. Solve construction problems using previously given constructions.

9

SIMILARITY

MAJOR TOPICS

- Ratio and proportion
- Properties of proportions
- Similar triangles
- RST properties of the similarity relation
- Proportionality of sides of similar triangles (csstp)
- The Pythagorean Theorem
- Practical and geometric applications of similar triangles and the Pythagorean Theorem

HISTORICAL NOTE

EUDOXUS

The discovery by the Pythagoreans of irrational numbers such as $\sqrt{2}$ dealt a devastating blow to their theory of similar figures and proportions. The basis of this theory was the assumption that any two line segments are commensurable; in other words, it is always possible to find a common measuring unit for any two lengths (see the Historical Note, Chapter 3). Thus, their discovery that the side of any square and its diagonal are *not* commensurable meant that a large part of their geometry had to be abandoned. This logical scandal was so upsetting to the Pythagoreans that they tried very hard—but in the end unsuccessfully—to keep it a secret.

This crisis in the foundation of Greek mathematics was not easily resolved. In about 370 B.C., however, a poor, young man named Eudoxus travelled from his home in Cnidus, a town in the southwestern part of Asia Minor, to Athens to study in Plato's Academy. Eudoxus formulated an ingenious definition for the equality of two ratios that was based only on whole numbers but that covered rational and irrational ratios as well. The ratios themselves he shrewdly left undefined for, as we know today, a proper definition would have required an understanding of the real numbers, which was unknown at that time. With his definition, Eudoxus bypassed the commensurability requirement of the Pythagoreans and resolved the crisis.

Eudoxus' work was so important that it became the basis for the fifth book in Euclid's *Elements*. Moreover, Eudoxus' mathematical insight was remarkable, for many years later in the middle of the nineteenth century, Eudoxus' geometrically oriented ideas were given fresh credibility through the theory of real numbers developed by the German mathematicians Karl Weierstrass (1815–1897) and Richard Dedekind (1831–1916).

Little is known about Eudoxus' early life except that he was so poor when he came to Athens that he could not afford to live in the city, and so daily he walked many dusty miles between Piraeus on the seashore and Plato's Academy. But Eudoxus' brilliance was noticed, and in time it brought him respect and a position as a teacher. He travelled in Egypt, Sicily, and Italy and attracted many students of his own. He studied and worked with Archytus, one of the important Pythagorean geometers of the time.

In addition to his work on proportions, Eudoxus was the first to prove that a cone and a pyramid have one-third the volume of a cylinder and a prism with the same base and height. He also devised a theory concerning infinite sequences of numbers, which anticipated certain concepts in calculus developed many centuries later.

When Eudoxus was still a student, Plato challenged the Academy to formulate a systematic theory that would account for the observed motions of the planets including their occasional retrograde (backward) motions in the heavens (the word planet means "wanderer" in Greek). So far, no one had given any unified explanation for the seemingly disorderly courses of the planets. Eudoxus devised a scheme involving a series of concentric spheres with the earth at the center. Each sphere rotated about a different axis and carried the spheres inside along as it rotated. By imagining that a planet was attached to the smallest of a system of four such spheres, Eudoxus was able to use the system's complicated motions to model the planet's apparent path across the sky. With a system of twenty-seven such spheres he accurately described the motions of the sun, the moon, the five planets, and the stars as then observed from the earth. For its time, Eudoxus' system was a monumental achievement; it is interesting that Eudoxus regarded his system as purely a mathematical theory having no physical reality.

The civilization of classical Greece is renowned for its intellectual achievements. Pythagoras, Euclid, Plato, and many others are names recognized the world over. It is unfortunate that Eudoxus is less well-known. His creative work in both astronomy and mathematics ranks him equally with the most original thinkers of his time.

9.1 INTRODUCTION

In previous chapters the congruence relations among line segments, angles, and triangles have played a central role, and it was pointed out that if two geometric figures are congruent, then they have the same shape and size. In this chapter we describe a relation that implies that two figures may have the same shape but not necessarily the same size. In Figure 9.1 only the third pair (c) of triangles have the same shape, and they are said to be *similar,* while the other pairs are not. Note that the two pairs of congruent angles (implying of course that the third pair is congruent) seem to insure this similarity. Note also that if the vertices of the congruent angles are matched, the corresponding pairs of sides are *not* congruent. Indeed, one triangle looks smaller than the other. The larger one, however, may be viewed as a photographic enlargement of the smaller, and this suggests that the corresponding pairs of sides are related in some way. In fact, they are algebraically proportional and for this reason we will review the concepts of ratio and proportion.

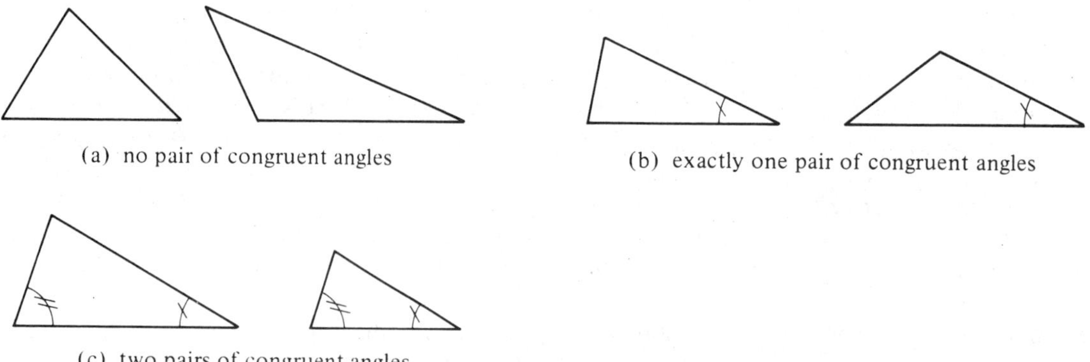

(a) no pair of congruent angles

(b) exactly one pair of congruent angles

(c) two pairs of congruent angles

Figure 9.1

Similar triangles have many practical applications. They may be used to find distances that are difficult or impossible to measure, as for example, the height of an Egyptian pyramid. They are the basis for right-triangle trigonometry and its many important applications. We will find similar triangles useful in proving, later in this chapter, the most famous of all geometric theorems, the Theorem of Pythagoras. The concept of similar figures is applied practically when models are made to study the design of something to be built. For example, airplane models are tested in wind tunnels to determine the best shape for the plane being designed. These are only a few of the many applications of the geometric relation called *similarity*.

Our first task is to develop a clear, mathematical way to compare the sizes of two numbers. For example, we might want to compare the length of a model of an object and the object's actual length. This may be done by means of a *ratio*.

Definition 9.1 The *ratio* of the real number a to the real number b, $b \neq 0$, is the size comparison of a to b expressed as the fraction a/b.

According to this definition, a ratio is a *number* with no units of measurement (such as inches) attached to it. In other words, to have a valid size comparison between two measurements a and b, the same units must be used for both. For example, to compare the lengths of the line segments $\overline{AB}$ and $\overline{CD}$, where $AB = 12$ cm and $CD = 2$ cm, we write the ratio 12 cm/2 cm $= \frac{6}{1}$, and we say that AB is to CD as 6 is to 1. This means that $\overline{AB}$ is six times as long as $\overline{CD}$. On the other hand, if $AB = 12$ in and $CD = 2$ ft, then 12 in/2 ft or $\frac{12}{2} = \frac{6}{1}$ is *not* a valid size comparison because the units are different. We may write $AB/CD = 12$ in/24 in $= \frac{1}{2}$, however, and this shows correctly that $\overline{AB}$ is one-half as long as $\overline{CD}$.

EXAMPLE 1 In (a)–(d) find the ratio of the first measurement to the second. State the size comparison.

(a) 34°, 17° **(b)** 15 feet, 9 yards **(c)** $16\frac{1}{4}$ inches, $6\frac{1}{2}$ inches **(d)** 5 inches, 5 gallons

Answers

(a) $\dfrac{34°}{17°} = \dfrac{2}{1}$; the first is twice the second.

(b) $\dfrac{15 \text{ ft}}{9 \cdot 3 \text{ ft}} = \dfrac{5 \cdot 3}{9 \cdot 3} = \dfrac{5}{9}$; the first is $\dfrac{5}{9}$ of the second.

(c) $\dfrac{16\frac{1}{4} \text{ in}}{6\frac{1}{2} \text{ in}} = \dfrac{65}{4} \div \dfrac{13}{2} = \dfrac{5}{2}$; the first is $2\frac{1}{2}$ times the second.

(d) This is not a valid size comparison because the units cannot be made the same.

According to Definition 9.1 and Example 1(d), $\frac{5 \text{ in}}{5 \text{ gal}}$ is not a ratio. Such fractions may be used (with care), however, in connection with *proportions* (Example 2(b), below).

Definition 9.2 A *proportion* is an equality between two ratios.

A simple example of a proportion is $\frac{1}{2} = \frac{2}{4}$. This equation may be read "one-half equals two-fourths" or "1 is to 2 as 2 is to 4." Since proportions are equations, algebra may be used to find an unknown number in a proportion as in the following example.

EXAMPLE 2

(a) Solve for x if $\dfrac{x}{15} = \dfrac{3}{10}$.

(b) If a map is drawn so that $1\frac{1}{4}$ inches represents 5 miles, how many miles does a map distance of 3 inches represent?

Answers

(a) $\dfrac{x}{15} = \dfrac{3}{10}$

clearing fractions gives

$$\frac{30}{1} \cdot \frac{x}{15} = \frac{30}{1} \cdot \frac{3}{10}$$
$$2x = 9$$
$$x = \frac{9}{2}$$

(b) Let $x =$ the number of miles represented by 3 inches.

$$\frac{1\frac{1}{4} \text{ in}}{5 \text{ mi}} = \frac{3 \text{ in}}{x \text{ mi}}$$
$$\frac{5}{4}x = 15$$
$$5x = 60$$
$$x = 12 \text{ mi}$$

Although the "ratios" used in Example 2(b) are not valid size comparisons, the proportion is correct because the units of the numerators are the same as the units of the denominators.

Proportions have some algebraic properties that can shorten the solutions to problems such as those in Example 2. These properties are stated below as theorems. The proofs are left as algebraic exercises. The equation $\frac{a}{b} = \frac{c}{d}$, also written $a:b = c:d$, represents any proportion, and the numbers a and d are called the *extremes,* whereas b and c are called the *means.*

Theorem 92 In a proportion, the product of the extremes equals the product of the means (prod extrms = prod mns).

Thus, if $\frac{a}{b} = \frac{c}{d}$ or $a:b = c:d$, then $ad = bc$.

Theorem 93 In a proportion, the means or extremes may be interchanged (interch mns or extrms).

Thus, if $\frac{a}{b} = \frac{c}{d}$, then $\frac{a}{c} = \frac{b}{d}$ or $\frac{d}{b} = \frac{c}{a}$.

Theorem 94 In a proportion, the ratios may be inverted (invert ratios).

Thus, if $\frac{a}{b} = \frac{c}{d}$, then $\frac{b}{a} = \frac{d}{c}$.

Theorem 95 *Addition Property of Proportions.* If $\frac{a}{b} = \frac{c}{d}$, then $\frac{a+b}{b} = \frac{c+d}{d}$ (add prop propor).

Theorem 96 *Subtraction Property of Proportions.* If $\frac{a}{b} = \frac{c}{d}$, then $\frac{a-b}{b} = \frac{c-d}{d}$ (subt prop propor).

EXAMPLE 3 Given $\frac{34}{38} = \frac{85}{95}$, (a) show that this is a proportion, (b) name the extremes, (c) name the means, (d) show that the product of the extremes equals the product of the means, and (e) use the Addition Property to write a new proportion.

Answers

(a) $\frac{34}{38} = \frac{2 \cdot 17}{2 \cdot 19} = \frac{17}{19}$

$\frac{85}{95} = \frac{5 \cdot 17}{5 \cdot 19} = \frac{17}{19}$

The ratios are equal.

(b) 34 and 95

(c) 38 and 85

(d) $34 \cdot 95 = 3230$

$38 \cdot 85 = 3230$

The products are equal.

(e) $\frac{34 + 38}{38} = \frac{85 + 95}{95}$

$\frac{72}{38} = \frac{180}{95}$

When the means in a proportion are the same number, that number is called the *mean proportional* or the *geometric mean* between the extremes. For example, in $\frac{3}{6} = \frac{6}{12}$, 6 is the mean proportional between 3 and 12. On the other hand, if two numbers are given as extremes, then there are two possible mean proportionals between them as shown in Example 4.

EXAMPLE 4 Find the mean proportionals between (a) 4 and 9 and (b) 5 and 15.

Answers

(a) $\frac{4}{x} = \frac{x}{9}$

$x^2 = 36$

$x = 6$ or -6

(b) $\frac{5}{x} = \frac{x}{15}$

$x^2 = \sqrt{75}$

$x = 75 = 5\sqrt{3}$

or $x = -\sqrt{75} = -5\sqrt{3}$

Next we examine a geometric theorem and corollary that involve ratio and proportion. Note that lengths of line segments now appear as the numbers in a proportion. The proof of the theorem is divided into three parts.

Theorem 97 If a line parallel to one side of a triangle intersects the other two sides in different points, it divides the sides in equal ratios (line $\parallel$ side $\triangle \div$ 2 sides in = ratios).

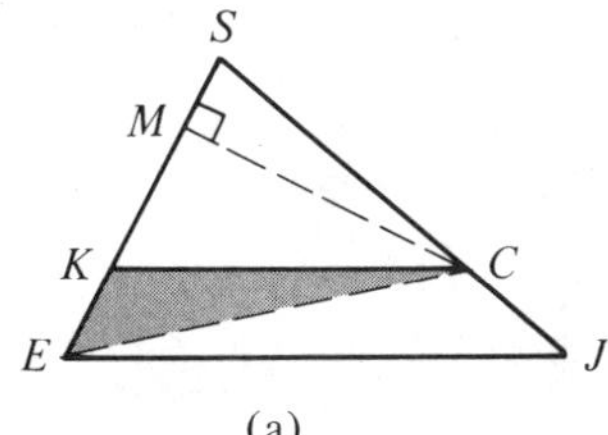

(a)

Given
$\triangle EJS$
$\overline{KC} \parallel \overline{EJ}$

To Prove
$\frac{SK}{KE} = \frac{SC}{CJ}$

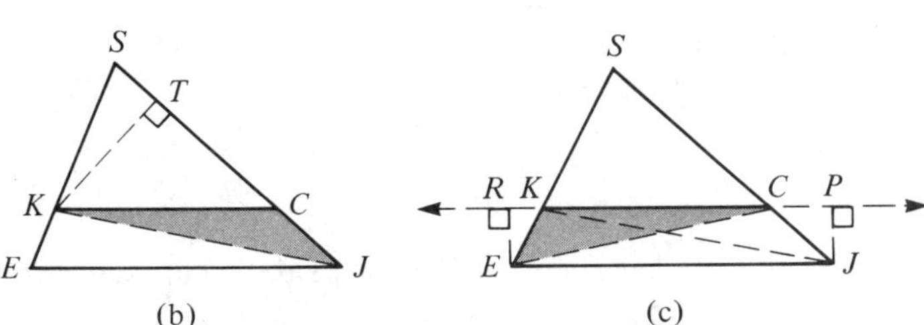

(b) (c)

	Statement	*Reason*
(a)	1. $\triangle EJS$, $\overline{KC} \parallel \overline{EJ}$	1. given
	2. Draw $\overline{CM} \perp \overline{SE}$.	2. 1 $\perp$ from pt to line
	3. $A(SKC) = \frac{1}{2} \cdot SK \cdot CM$	3. $A(\triangle) = \frac{1}{2}bh$
	4. Draw $\overline{EC}$.	4. 2 pts determ line
	5. $A(ECK) = \frac{1}{2} \cdot KE \cdot CM$	5. $A(\triangle) = \frac{1}{2}bh$
	6. $\frac{A(SKC)}{A(ECK)} = \frac{SK}{KE}$	6. $= \div =$, quot $=$
	7. $A(SKC) = \frac{SK}{KE} \cdot A(ECK)$	7. $= \cdot =$, prod $=$
(b)	8. Draw $\overline{KT} \perp \overline{SJ}$.	8. 1 $\perp$ from pt to line
	9. $A(SKC) = \frac{1}{2} \cdot SC \cdot KT$	9. $A(\triangle) = \frac{1}{2}bh$
	10. Draw $\overline{KJ}$.	10. 2 pts determ line
	11. $A(JCK) = \frac{1}{2} \cdot CJ \cdot KT$	11. $A(\triangle) = \frac{1}{2}bh$
	12. $\frac{A(SKC)}{A(JCK)} = \frac{SC}{CJ}$	12. $= \div =$, quot $=$
	13. $A(SKC) = \frac{SC}{CJ} \cdot A(JCK)$	13. $= \cdot =$, prod $=$

	14. $\frac{SK}{KE} \cdot A(ECK) = \frac{SC}{CJ} \cdot A(JCK)$	14. symm and trans =
(c)	15. Draw $\overleftrightarrow{KC}$.	15. 2 pts determ line
	16. Draw $\overline{ER} \perp \overleftrightarrow{KC}$, $\overline{PJ} \perp \overleftrightarrow{KC}$.	16. 1 ⊥ from pt to line
	17. $A(ECK) = \frac{1}{2} \cdot KC \cdot RE$	17. $A(\triangle) = \frac{1}{2}bh$
	18. $A(JCK) = \frac{1}{2} \cdot KC \cdot PJ$	18. $A(\triangle) = \frac{1}{2}bh$
	19. $\overline{RE} \cong \overline{PJ}$	19. if lines ∥, ⊥ seg ≅
	20. $RE = PJ$	20. ≅ iff meas =
	21. $A(ECK) = \frac{1}{2} \cdot KC \cdot PJ$	21. subst
	22. $A(ECK) = A(JCK)$	22. symm and trans =
	23. $\therefore \frac{SK}{KE} = \frac{SC}{CJ}$	23. = ÷ =, quot =

The following corollary of Theorem 97 is easy to prove using algebraic properties of proportions.

Theorem 98 If a line parallel to one side of a triangle intersects the other two sides in different points, it cuts segments proportional to the sides (line ∥ side △ cuts segs propor to sides).

This means that, in the figure for Theorem 97, $\frac{SK}{SE} = \frac{SC}{SJ}$ and $\frac{KE}{SE} = \frac{CJ}{SJ}$. Theorems 97 and 98 are illustrated in Example 5.

EXAMPLE 5

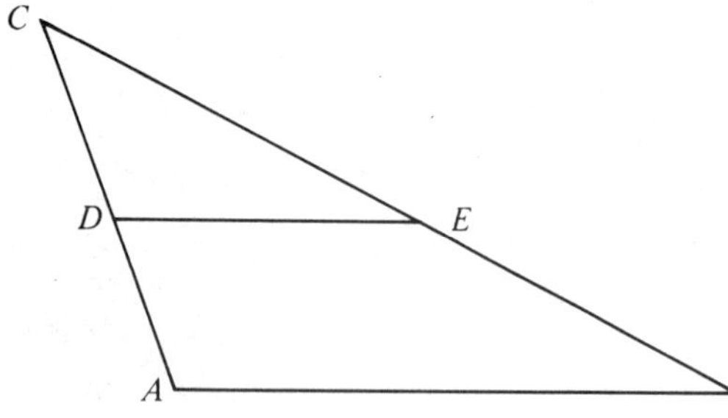

Given
$\overline{DE} \parallel \overline{AB}$
$AC = 26$ in
$AD = 12$ in
$BE = 18$ in

Find
EC

Answer

1. By Theorem 97 (line ∥ side △ ÷ 2 sides in = ratios):

$DC = AC - AD = 14$ in

$$\frac{DC}{AD} = \frac{EC}{BE}$$

$$\frac{14}{12} = \frac{EC}{18}$$

$$12 \cdot EC = 14 \cdot 18$$
$$EC = 21 \text{ in}$$

2. By Theorem 98 (line ∥ side △ cuts segs propor to sides):

$$\frac{AD}{AC} = \frac{BE}{BC}$$

$$\frac{12}{26} = \frac{18}{BC}$$

$$12 \cdot BC = 26 \cdot 18$$
$$BC = 39 \text{ in}$$
$$EC = BC - BE$$
$$EC = 39 - 18 = 21 \text{ in}$$

9.2 SIMILAR TRIANGLES

In the previous section we indicated informally that two triangles having the same shape but not necessarily the same size are said to be similar. The next definition states precisely what is meant by "same shape" and "similar."

Definition 9.3 Two triangles are *similar* iff there is a one-to-one correspondence between their vertices such that the three pairs of corresponding angles are congruent and the three pairs of corresponding sides are proportional (castc and csstp).

The abbreviation "castc" stands for "corresponding angles of similar triangles are congruent" and "csstp" means "corresponding sides of similar triangles are proportional." The notation for "$\triangle ABC$ is similar to $\triangle DEF$" is $\triangle ABC \sim \triangle DEF$.

In Figure 9.2, if $\triangle ABC \sim \triangle EJS$ with $ABC \leftrightarrow EJS$, then according to Definition 9.3, $\measuredangle A \cong \measuredangle E$, $\measuredangle B \cong \measuredangle J$, $\measuredangle C \cong \measuredangle S$, $\frac{AC}{ES} = \frac{AB}{EJ}$, $\frac{AC}{ES} = \frac{CB}{SJ}$, and $\frac{AB}{EJ} = \frac{CB}{SJ}$. The three proportions just given are usually written $\frac{AC}{ES} = \frac{AB}{EJ} = \frac{CB}{SJ}$.

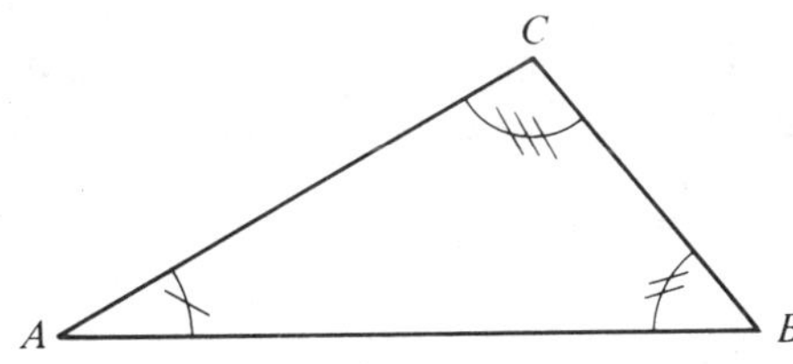

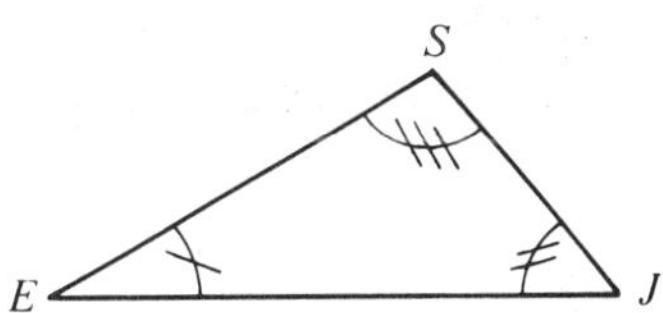

Figure 9.2

EXAMPLE 1

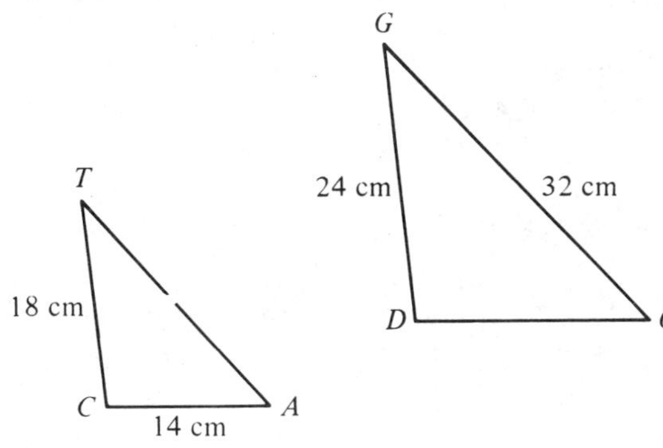

Given

$\triangle DOG \sim \triangle CAT$ with $DOG \leftrightarrow CAT$

$\angle D = 96°23'$

$\angle A = 48°11'$

$GD = 24$ cm

$TC = 18$ cm

$CA = 14$ cm

$GO = 32$ cm

Find

(a) $\angle G$

(b) TA

(c) DO

Answers

(a) since $\measuredangle O \cong \measuredangle A$

$\angle G = 180° - \angle D - \angle O$

$\angle G = 180° - 96°23' - 48°11'$

$\angle G = 35°26'$

(b) $\dfrac{GD}{TC} = \dfrac{GO}{TA}$

$\dfrac{24}{18} = \dfrac{32}{TA}$

$24 \cdot TA = 18 \cdot 32$

$TA = 24$ cm

(c) $\dfrac{GD}{TC} = \dfrac{DO}{CA}$

$\dfrac{24}{18} = \dfrac{DO}{14}$

$18 \cdot DO = 24 \cdot 14$

$DO = \dfrac{56}{3} = 18\tfrac{2}{3}$ cm

Recall that both the equals relation and the congruence relation have the reflexive, symmetric, and transitive properties. The similarity relation between triangles (and, indeed, between other geometric figures) also possesses these RST properties. We will not state these facts as theorems. They will be used to rearrange similarity statements as necessary, however. A brief informal justification of the properties follows.

1. Reflexive: $\triangle ABC \sim \triangle ABC$ because $\measuredangle A \cong \measuredangle A$, $\measuredangle B \cong \measuredangle B$, $\measuredangle C \cong \measuredangle C$, and $\frac{AB}{AB} = \frac{AC}{AC} = \frac{BC}{BC} = 1$.
2. Symmetric: If $\triangle ABC \sim \triangle EJS$, then $\triangle EJS \sim \triangle ABC$ because the congruences and proportions implied by the hypothesis are the ones needed to imply the conclusion.
3. Transitive: If $\triangle ABC \sim \triangle EJS$ and $\triangle EJS \sim \triangle KRM$, then $\triangle ABC \sim \triangle KRM$ because the transitive property for congruence applied to the congruences in the hypothesis and the transitive property for equality applied to the proportions in the hypothesis yield the congruences and proportions of the conclusion.

In Section 4.2 it was shown that two triangles can be proved congruent by establishing fewer than the six congruences required by the definition. The situation is similar when proving that two triangles are similar, as shown by the following important theorem.

Theorem 99 If two angles of one triangle are congruent to two angles of another triangle, then the triangles are similar (aa ≅ aa).

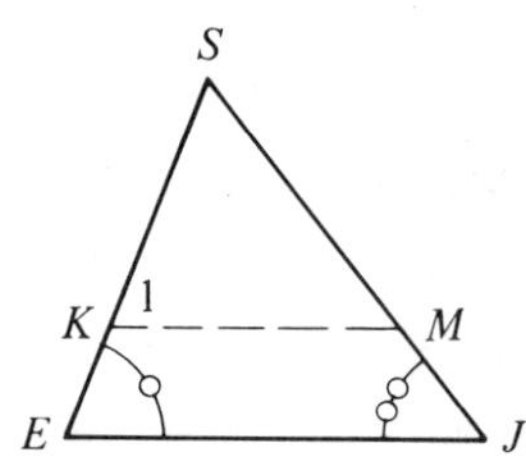

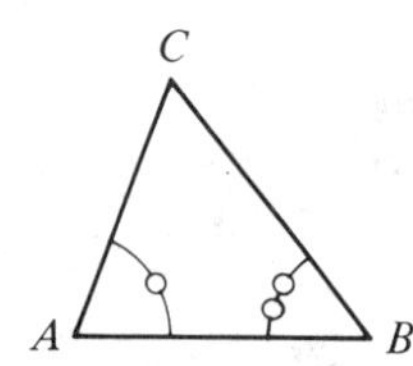

Given
$\measuredangle E \cong \measuredangle A$
$\measuredangle J \cong \measuredangle B$

To Prove
$\triangle EJS \sim \triangle ABC$

If the triangles are congruent, then they are similar. Let us assume they are not congruent and $SE > CA$. It can then be proved that $SJ > CB$ also, a fact we will assume for simplicity.

Statement	*Reason*
1. $\measuredangle E \cong \measuredangle A$, $\measuredangle J \cong \measuredangle B$	1. given
2. $\measuredangle S \cong \measuredangle C$	2. if aa ≅ aa, 3d ∡s ≅
3. Construct $\overline{SK} \cong \overline{CA}$, $\overline{SM} \cong \overline{CB}$.	3. can copy seg
4. Draw $\overline{KM}$.	4. 2 pts determ line
5. $\triangle SKM \cong \triangle CAB$	5. sas ≅ sas
6. $\measuredangle 1 \cong \measuredangle A$	6. cpctc
7. $\measuredangle E \cong \measuredangle 1$	7. symm and trans ≅
8. $\overline{KM} \parallel \overline{EJ}$	8. $\not\cong$∡, lines ∥
9. $\frac{SK}{SE} = \frac{SM}{SJ}$	9. line ∥ side △ cuts segs propor to sides
10. $SK = CA$, $SM = CB$	10. ≅ iff meas =
11. $\frac{CA}{SE} = \frac{CB}{SJ}$ similarly it can be proved that $\frac{CA}{SE} = \frac{BA}{JE}$ so that $\frac{CA}{SE} = \frac{CB}{SJ} = \frac{BA}{JE}$	11. subst
12. $\therefore \triangle EJS \sim \triangle ABC$	12. castc and csstp

Note that Theorem 99 is proved by showing that the given facts are sufficient to establish all the requirements of the definition of similar triangles. Now the theorem (rather than the definition) may be used to prove that two triangles are similar as shown in the next example.

EXAMPLE 2

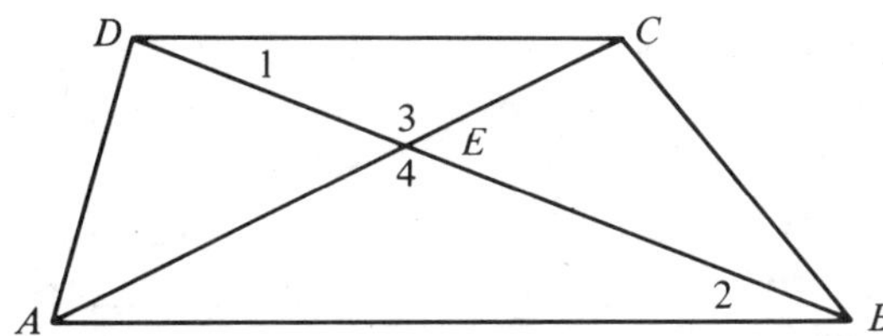

Given
trap $ABCD$ ($\overline{AB}$, $\overline{DC}$ bases)

To Prove
$\frac{DC}{BA} = \frac{DE}{BE}$

Statement	*Reason*
1. trap $ABCD$ ($\overline{AB}$, $\overline{DC}$ bases)	1. given
2. $\overline{AB} \parallel \overline{DC}$	2. trap iff 1 pr sides $\parallel$
3. $\measuredangle 1 \cong \measuredangle 2$	3. $\nparallel$, alt int $\measuredangle$s $\cong$
4. $\measuredangle 3 \cong \measuredangle 4$	4. vert $\measuredangle$s $\cong$
5. $\triangle DCE \sim \triangle BAE$	5. aa $\cong$ aa
6. $\therefore \frac{DC}{BA} = \frac{DE}{BE}$	6. csstp

In the above proof, $\triangle DCE$ and $\triangle BAE$ were chosen (rather than any other pair) because the proportion to be proved "fits" the correspondence $DCE \leftrightarrow BAE$ and these triangles can be proved similar using the given facts.

EXERCISES FOR 9.1 AND 9.2

In exercises 1–20 answer true or false.

1. A ratio is a size comparison between two real numbers.
2. Two congruent triangles are also similar triangles.
3. Two similar triangles are also congruent triangles.
4. A proportion is an equation in which two ratios are equal.
5. The equation $\frac{9}{16} = \frac{3}{4}$ is a proportion.
6. If $\frac{9}{6} = \frac{6}{4}$, 6 is called the third proportional between 9 and 4.
7. A mean proportional between 27 and 3 is 9.
8. If two angles of one triangle are congruent to two angles of a second triangle, then the triangles are similar.
9. Similar triangles have equal areas but different shapes.
10. Any two isosceles triangles are similar triangles.
11. If an acute angle of a right triangle is congruent to an acute angle of a second right triangle, then the two triangles are similar.
12. Two isosceles triangles are similar if their vertex angles are congruent.
13. Two equilateral triangles are not similar because their sides may have different lengths.
14. If two triangles are similar and the first triangle is an isosceles right triangle, then the second triangle is also an isosceles right triangle.
15. The diagonals of a trapezoid divide it into four triangles, two of which are similar while the other two have equal areas.
16. A line through two sides of a triangle divides the sides proportionally.
17. If $\triangle BIG \sim \triangle TOE$ with $BIG \leftrightarrow TOE$, then $\frac{BG}{TE} = \frac{TO}{BI}$.
18. If the three sides of one triangle are parallel, respectively, to three sides of a second triangle, then the triangles are similar.
19. If $\frac{xy}{4} = \frac{y}{8}$ ($y \neq 0$) is a proportion, then $x = \frac{1}{2}$.

20. The median to the base of a triangle bisects all segments parallel to the base, where the endpoints of the segments are points of the two sides.

In exercises 21–35 draw a figure where possible and answer the questions.

21. If $\frac{3}{x} = \frac{7}{63}$ is a proportion, find x.
22. Find the mean proportional between 6 and 24.
23. In the proportion $\frac{7}{11} = \frac{21}{33}$, name the means. Show that the product of the extremes is equal to the product of the means.
24. Given $\frac{6}{17} = \frac{18}{51}$, write a new proportion by (a) interchanging the means, (b) inversion, and (c) addition.
25. If $AB = 18$ in and $CD = 4$ ft, write the ratio of AB to CD.
26. Is $\frac{17}{3}:\frac{3}{5} = \frac{35}{12}:\frac{21}{68}$ a proportion? Why or why not?
27. The sides of a triangle measure 7, 10, and 12 feet, and the longest side of a similar triangle measures 18 feet. Find the lengths of the other two sides of the second triangle.
28. The sides of a right triangle measure 3, 4, and 5 inches. The hypotenuse of a similar right triangle measures 60 inches. Find the lengths of the other sides of the second right triangle.
29. The sides of a triangle measure 3, 5, and 7 inches. Find the lengths of the sides of three other triangles, each of which is similar to the first triangle and has one side 10.5 inches long.
30. If $2b = 5d$, what is the ratio of d to b?
31. If the ratio of AB to EJ is 0.75, what is the ratio of EJ to AB?
32. Two sides of a triangle have lengths of 12 inches and 16 inches. What is the ratio of the second side to the first if the sides are measured in yards?
33. The sides of a triangle measure 4, 5, and a inches. The corresponding sides of a similar triangle measure 6, b, and 8 inches. Find a and b.
34. A church steeple casts a shadow 100 feet long at the same time that a 6-foot post casts a shadow 7 feet long. How high is the steeple?
35. From a triangle of altitude 20 feet and base 50 feet, a small triangle is cut off by a line parallel to the base at a distance 4 feet from the vertex. What is the area of the remaining trapezoid?

In exercises 36–40 use Figure 9.3. Show all equations used.

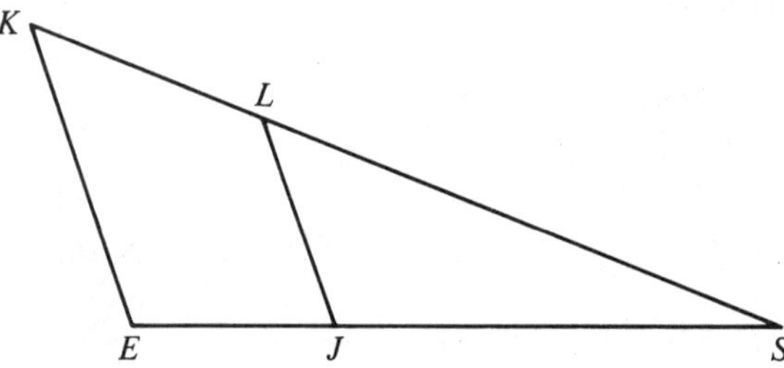

Figure 9.3

Given
$\overline{LJ} \parallel \overline{KE}$

36. Find EJ if $JS = 3$ in, $SL = 4$ in, and $LK = 6$ in.
37. Find JS if $ES = 24$ cm, $SL = 15$ cm, and $LK = 21$ cm.
38. If $\overline{EJ} \cong \overline{SL}$, find EJ if $LK = 3$ in and $JS = 27$ in.
39. If $ES = 20$ cm, $SL = 6$ cm, and $SK = 24$ cm, find EJ.
40. Find LK if $EJ = 3\frac{1}{2}$ in, $ES = 7\frac{1}{4}$ in, and $SL = 5\frac{1}{2}$ in.

In exercises 41–46 is $\triangle I \sim \triangle II$? Justify your answers.

41.

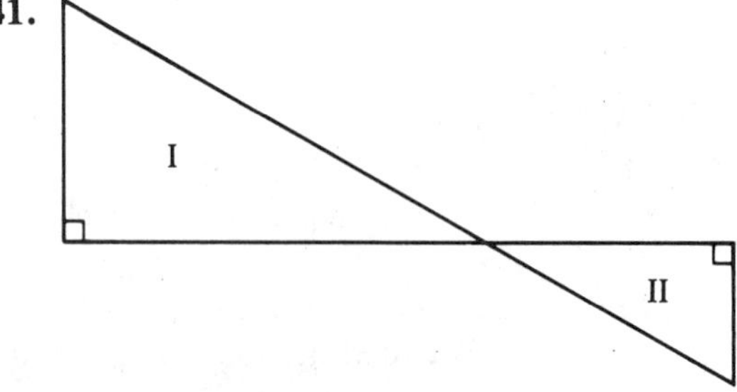

42.

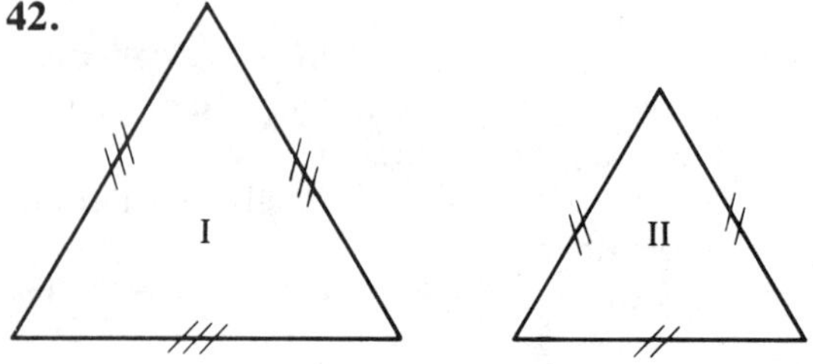

43.

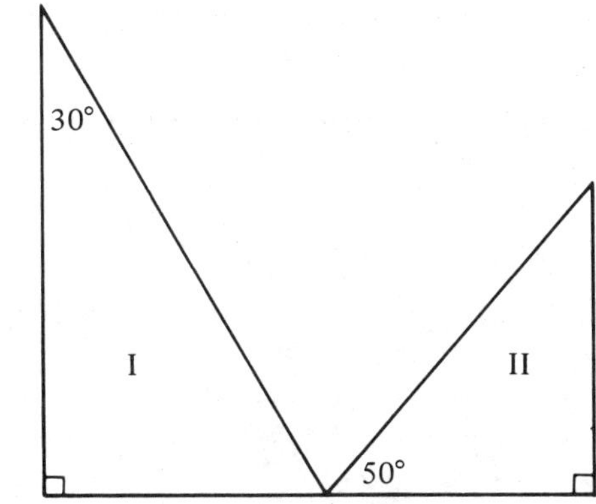

45.

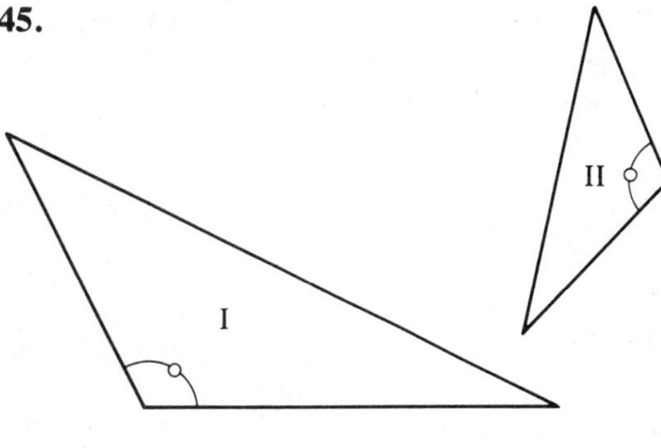

44.

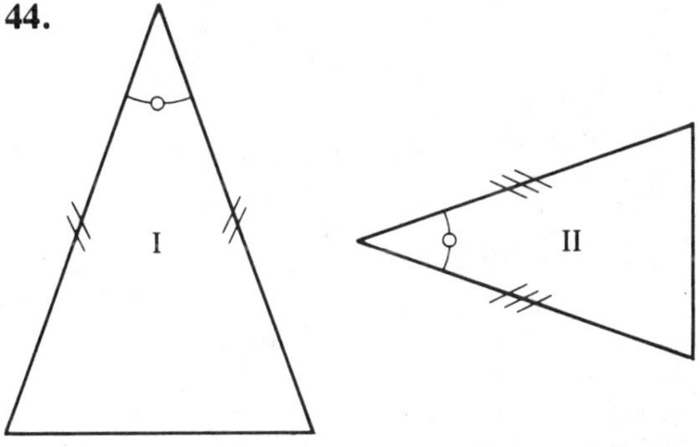

46.

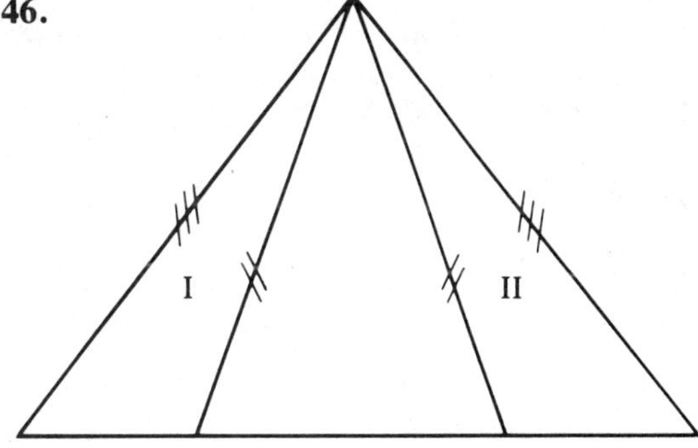

In exercises 47–55 copy the figure, the hypothesis, and the conclusion. Mark the figure and write a proof.

47. *Given*
$\overline{KS} \perp \overline{JS}$
$\overline{EJ} \perp \overline{JS}$

To Prove
$\triangle I \sim \triangle II$

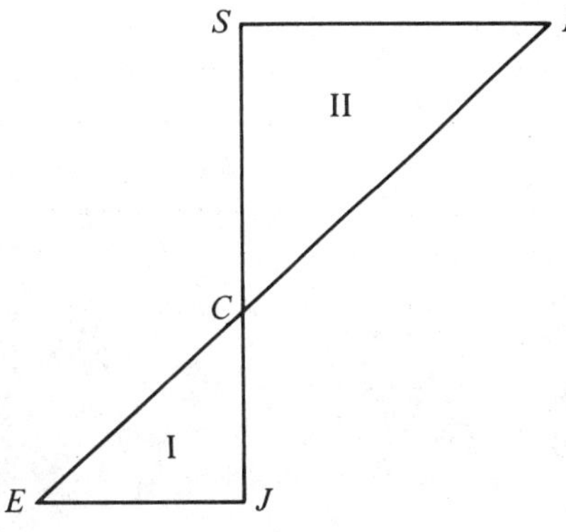

48. *Given*
$\overline{AE} \parallel \overline{CD}$

To Prove
$\triangle ABE \sim \triangle CBD$

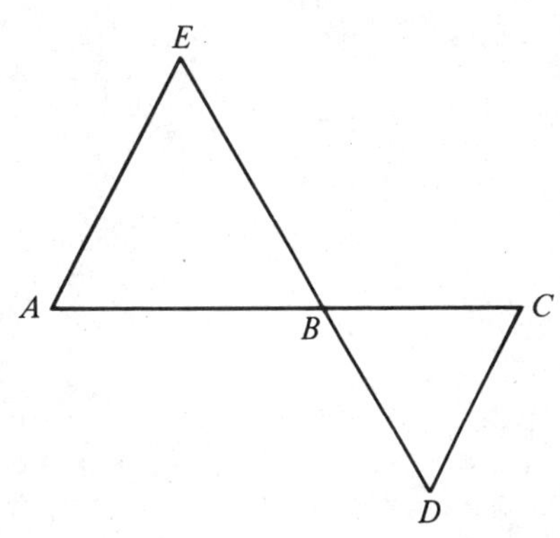

49. *Given*
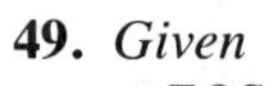
$\measuredangle FOS \cong \measuredangle L$

To Prove
$\triangle FOS \sim \triangle FLU$

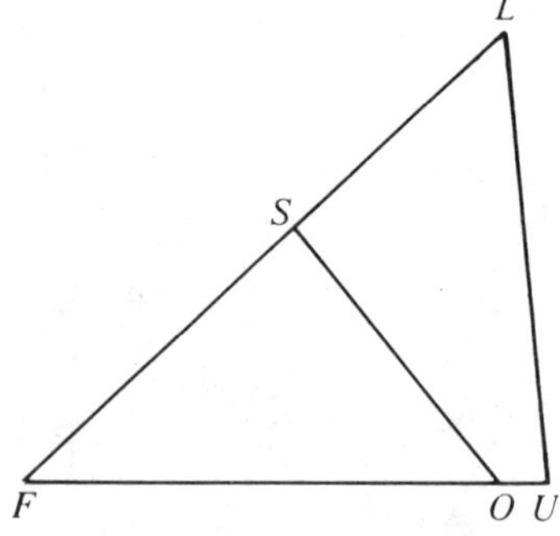

50. *Given*
alt $\overline{AE}$
alt $\overline{BD}$

To Prove
$\frac{AE}{BD} = \frac{CA}{CB}$

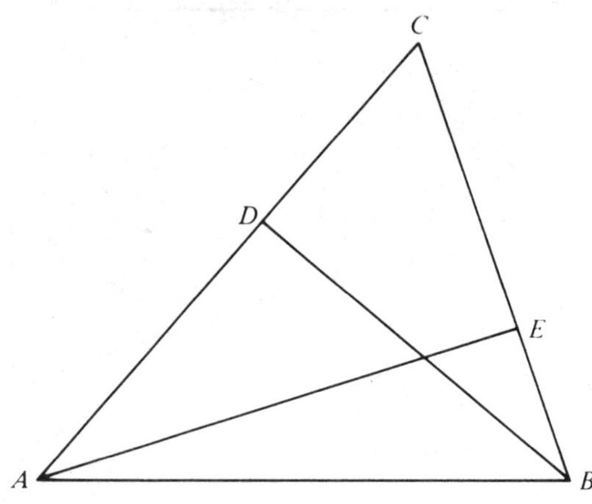

51. *Given*
rect $PQRS$
$\overline{TV} \perp \overline{PR}$

To Prove
$\triangle PVT \sim \triangle RQP$

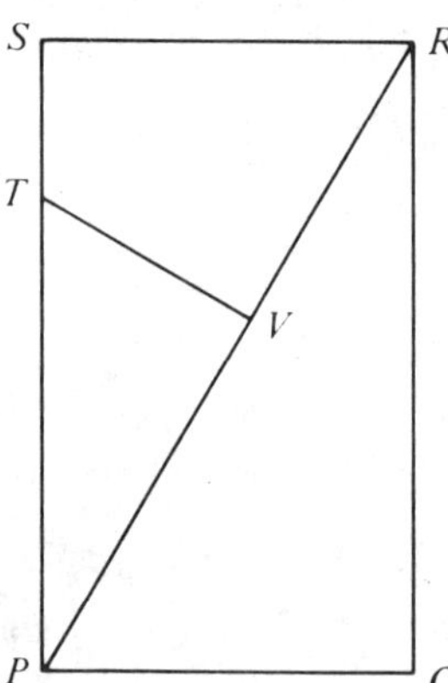

52. *Given*
$\odot O$
$\overline{KC} \perp \overline{EK}$

To Prove
$\triangle EJS \sim \triangle ECK$

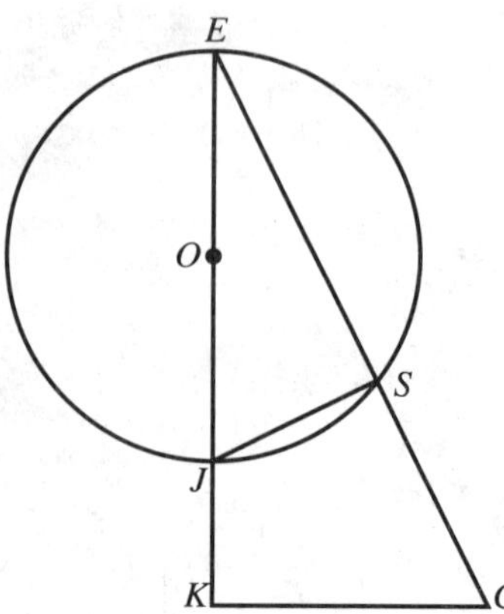

53. *Given*
trap *TANG* ($\overline{TA}$, $\overline{GN}$ bases)
To Prove
$\frac{GE}{AE} = \frac{NE}{TE}$

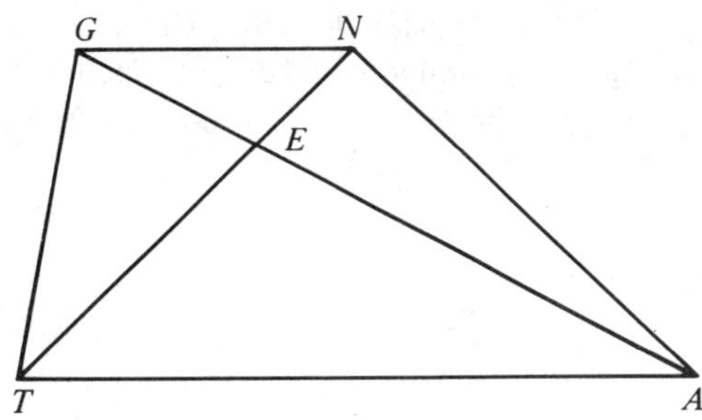

54. *Given*
$\odot O$
$\overline{CE}$ bis $\measuredangle ACB$

To Prove
$\frac{EB}{AD} = \frac{EC}{AC}$

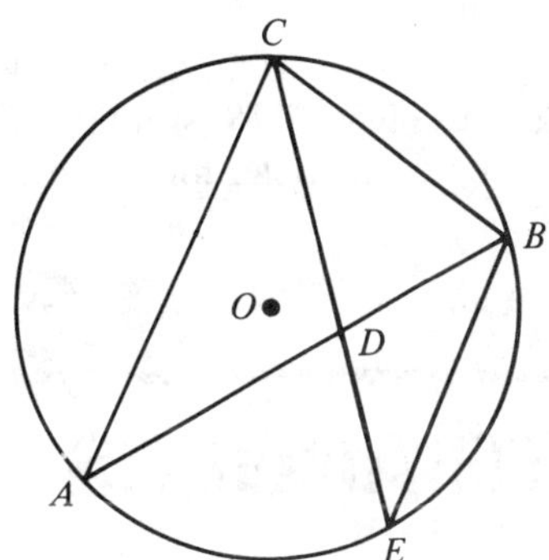

55. *Given*
$\overline{JS} \parallel \overline{KM}$
$\overline{SC} \parallel \overline{EK}$

To Prove
$\frac{EJ}{SC} = \frac{JS}{CM}$

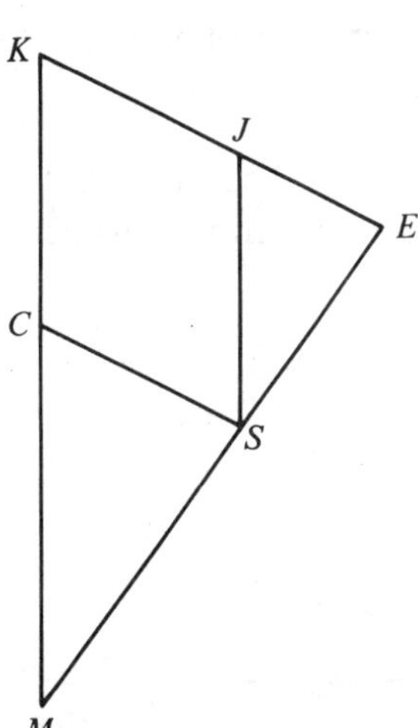

In exercises 56–60 do the constructions using only a compass and straightedge. A preliminary sketch may be helpful in determining the steps to use, as illustrated in two of the exercises.

56. Divide a given line segment $\overline{EJ}$ into two parts whose lengths are in the ratio 2:3.

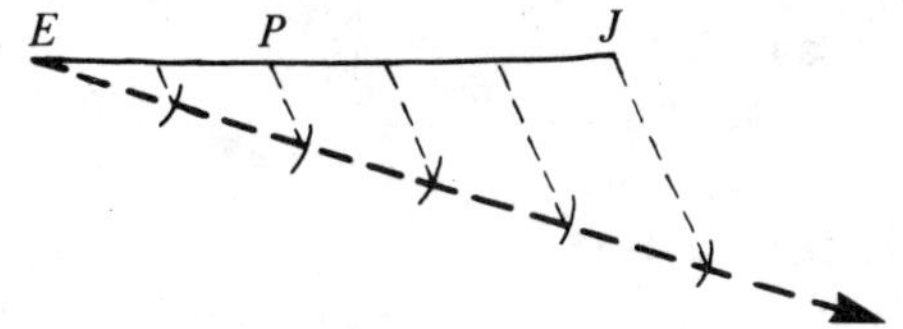

57. Divide a given line segment into three parts whose lengths are in the ratio 2:3:4. (Hint: See exercise 56.)

58. Given three line segments $\overline{AB}$, $\overline{CD}$, and $\overline{EF}$, construct a line segment $\overline{XY}$ such that $\frac{AB}{CD} = \frac{EF}{XY}$; that is, construct the *fourth proportional* to three given line segments. (Hint: See Theorem 97.)

59. Draw an acute triangle ABC. Construct a triangle EJS similar to $\triangle ABC$ and such that $\frac{AB}{EJ} = \frac{BC}{JS} = \frac{CA}{SE} = \frac{2}{3}$.

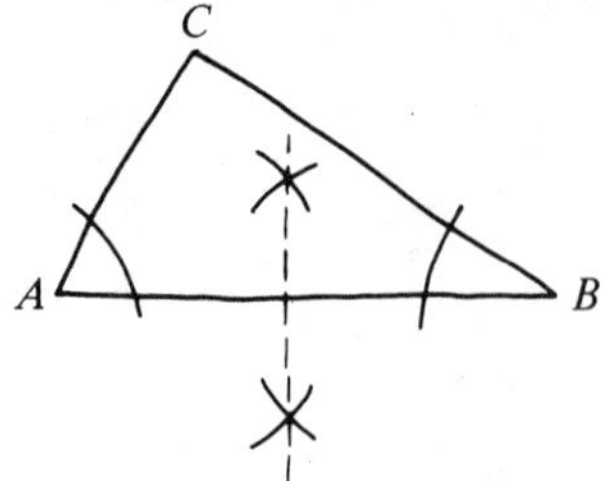

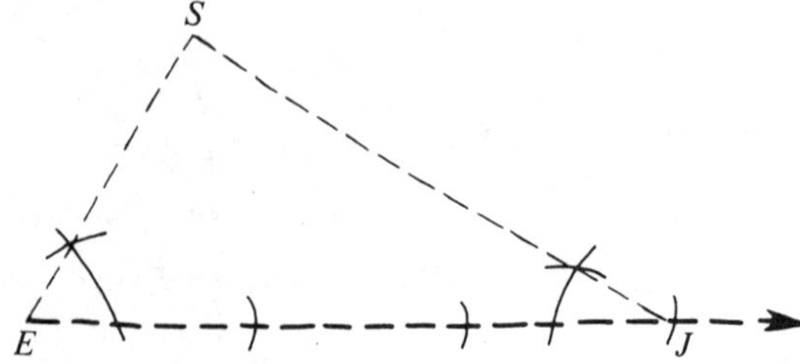

60. Construct a right triangle ABC. Construct a second right triangle KES similar to $\triangle ABC$ and having a perimeter three times that of $\triangle ABC$.

9.3 RIGHT TRIANGLES

Three special properties of right triangles are stated in the theorems of this section. The first two are about similarities and proportions concerning the altitude to the hypotenuse, while the third is the well-known Theorem of Pythagoras.

Theorem 100 The altitude to the hypotenuse of a right triangle forms two triangles that are similar to each other and to the original triangle (alt to hyp forms 3 ~ $\triangle$s).

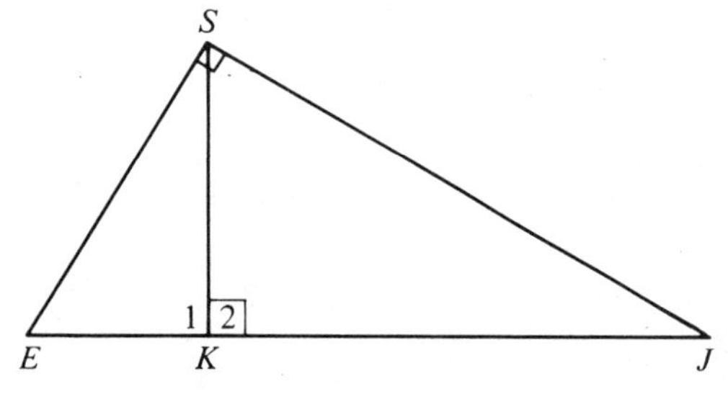

Given
rt $\triangle EJS$
rt $\measuredangle ESJ$
alt $\overline{SK}$

To Prove
(a) $\triangle ESK \sim \triangle EJS$
(b) $\triangle SJK \sim \triangle EJS$
(c) $\triangle ESK \sim \triangle SJK$

Statement	*Reason*
1. rt $\triangle EJS$, rt $\measuredangle ESJ$, alt $\overline{SK}$	1. given
2. $\overline{SK} \perp \overline{EJ}$	2. alt from vtx $\perp$ opp side
3. $\measuredangle 1 \cong \measuredangle ESJ$	3. $\perp$s form $\cong$ rt $\measuredangle$s
4. $\measuredangle E \cong \measuredangle E$	4. refl $\cong$
5. $\therefore$ (a) $\triangle ESK \sim \triangle EJS$	5. aa $\cong$ aa
6. $\measuredangle 2 \cong \measuredangle ESJ$	6. rt $\measuredangle$s $\cong$
7. $\measuredangle J \cong \measuredangle J$	7. refl $\cong$
8. $\therefore$ (b) $\triangle SJK \sim \triangle EJS$	8. aa $\cong$ aa
9. $\therefore$ (c) $\triangle ESK \sim \triangle SJK$	9. symm and trans ~

The next theorem is a corollary of Theorem 100.

Theorem 101 The altitude to the hypotenuse of a right triangle is the mean proportional between the segments into which it divides the hypotenuse, and each leg is the mean proportional between the hypotenuse and the segment of the hypotenuse adjacent to the leg (alt mn propor segs hyp, leg mn propor hyp adj seg).

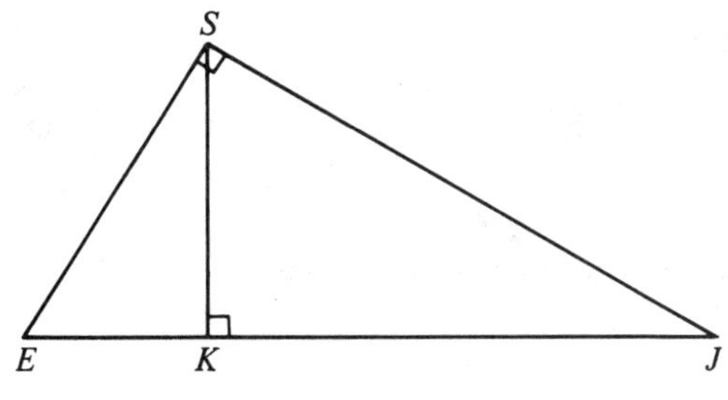

Given
rt $\triangle EJS$
rt $\measuredangle ESJ$
alt $\overline{SK}$

To Prove
(a) $\frac{EK}{SK} = \frac{SK}{JK}$
(b) $\frac{EJ}{ES} = \frac{ES}{EK}$
(c) $\frac{EJ}{SJ} = \frac{SJ}{KJ}$

Statement	*Reason*
1. rt $\triangle EJS$, rt $\measuredangle ESJ$, alt $\overline{SK}$	1. given
2. $\triangle ESK \sim \triangle SJK$	2. alt to hyp forms 3 $\sim$ $\triangle$s
3. $\therefore$ (a) $\frac{EK}{SK} = \frac{SK}{JK}$	3. csstp
4. $\triangle EJS \sim \triangle ESK$	4. alt to hyp forms 3 $\sim$ $\triangle$s
5. $\therefore$ (b) $\frac{EJ}{ES} = \frac{ES}{EK}$	5. csstp
6. $\triangle EJS \sim \triangle SJK$	6. alt to hyp forms 3 $\sim$ $\triangle$s
7. $\therefore$ (c) $\frac{EJ}{SJ} = \frac{SJ}{KJ}$	7. csstp

Theorem 101 is illustrated in Example 1. Note the use of the variables x, y, and z for ease in solving the proportions. It is also good practice to write the necessary proportions in terms of the labels $A, B, C, \ldots$, and then substitute the numbers and variables. Finally, note that only positive mean proportionals are required because the numbers to be found represent lengths.

EXAMPLE 1

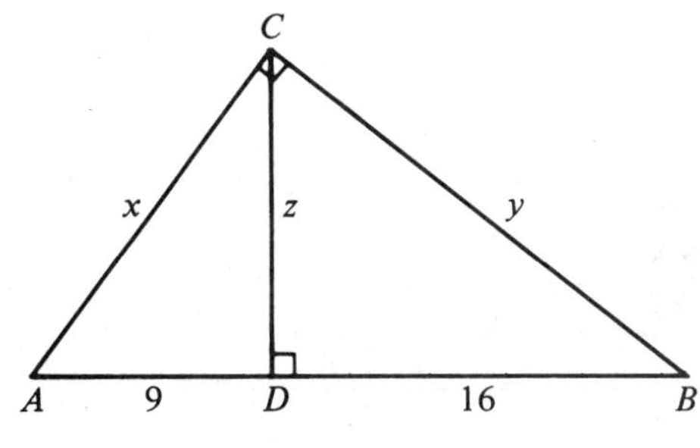

Given
rt $\triangle ABC$
$\angle C = 90°$
alt $\overline{CD}$
$AD = 9$ cm
$DB = 16$ cm

Find
(a) AC
(b) BC
(c) the perimeter of $\triangle ABC$
(d) CD
(e) the area of $\triangle ABC$

Answers

(a) $\frac{AB}{AC} = \frac{AC}{AD}$ ($\triangle ABC \sim \triangle ACD$)
$\frac{25}{x} = \frac{x}{9}$
$x^2 = 225$
$x = AC = 15$ cm

(b) $\frac{AB}{CB} = \frac{CB}{DB}$ ($\triangle ABC \sim \triangle CBD$)
$\frac{25}{y} = \frac{y}{16}$
$y^2 = 400$
$y = BC = 20$ cm

(c) $P = AC + BC + AB$
$P = 15 + 20 + 25$
$P = 60$ cm

(d) $\frac{AD}{CD} = \frac{CD}{BD}$ ($\triangle ACD \sim \triangle CBD$)
$\frac{9}{z} = \frac{z}{16}$
$z^2 = 144$
$z = CD = 12$ cm

(e) $A(\triangle) = \frac{1}{2}bh$
$A(\triangle ABC) = \frac{1}{2} \cdot AB \cdot CD$
$A(\triangle ABC) = \frac{1}{2} \cdot 25 \cdot 12$
$A(\triangle ABC) = 150$ sq cm

The fact that the altitude to the hypotenuse of a right triangle is the mean proportional between the segments into which it divides the hypotenuse (Theorem 101, first part) has some interesting applications in geometric construction problems. This is illustrated in Construction 14 and Example 2. Some further applications are included in the exercises.

Construction 14 To construct the mean proportional between two given line segments.

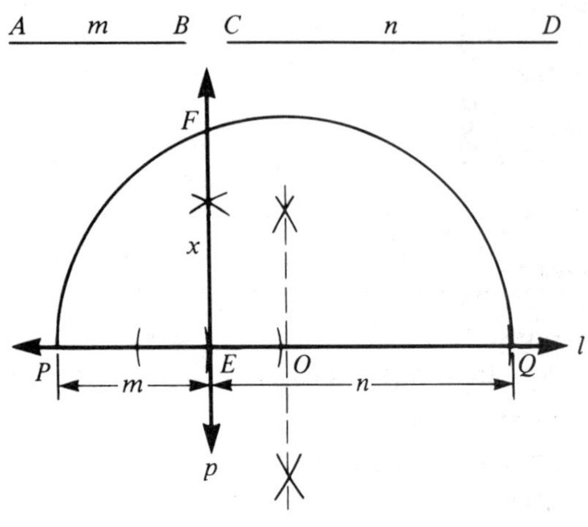

Given
$\overline{AB}$ with $AB = m$
$\overline{CD}$ with $CD = n$

To Construct

$\overline{EF}$ with $EF = x$ such that $\frac{m}{x} = \frac{x}{n}$

Steps

1. Draw any line l.
2. On l, construct $\overline{PE} \cong \overline{AB}$ and $\overline{EQ} \cong \overline{CD}$ (Construction 2).
3. Construct the midpoint O of $\overline{PQ}$ (Construction 1).
4. Draw a semicircle with center O and radius OQ.
5. Construct line $p \perp l$ at E (Construction 5).
6. The intersection F of line p and the semicircle determines the mean proportional $\overline{EF}$.

A proof of Construction 14 may be based on Theorem 101 by drawing $\overline{PF}$ and $\overline{FQ}$ and noting that $\triangle PFQ$ is a right triangle. This construction is applied in Example 2.

EXAMPLE 2 Construct a square having the same area as a given rectangle.

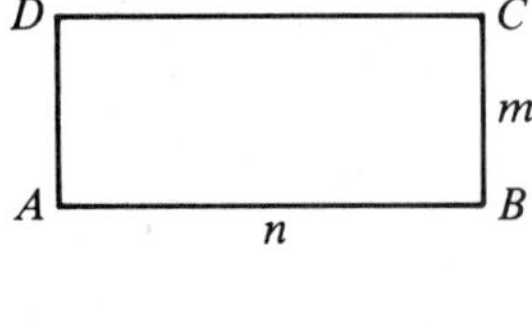

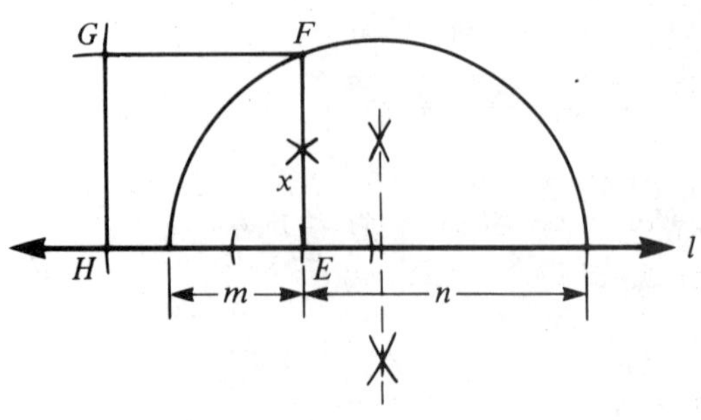

Given
rect $ABCD$

To Construct
sq $EFGH$ such that $A(EFGH) = A(ABCD)$

Steps

1. Let $BC = m$ and $AB = n$, and use Construction 14 to determine point F.
2. With radius EF and center E mark an arc intersecting l at H.
3. With radius EF and centers F and H, mark arcs intersecting at G.
4. Square $EFGH$ is correct because $\frac{m}{x} = \frac{x}{n}$ by Construction 14 and Theorem 101. It follows that $x^2 = mn$ and $A(EFGH) = A(ABCD)$.

The most famous theorem of plane geometry, named for the Greek geometer Pythagoras (584–495 B.C.), may be proved using the second part of

Theorem 101 as shown below. It has an enormous number of applications, both practical and theoretical.

Theorem 102 *The Pythagorean Theorem.* In any right triangle, the square of the hypotenuse is equal to the sum of the squares of the legs ($a^2 + b^2 = c^2$).

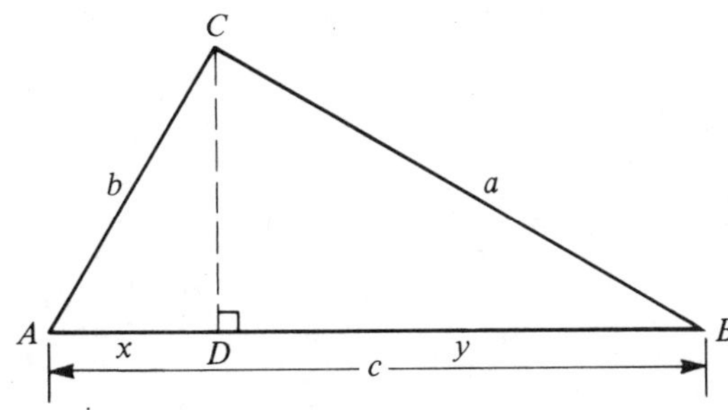

Given
rt $\triangle ABC$
rt $\measuredangle C$
Let $a = BC$, $b = AC$, $c = AB$, $x = AD$, and $y = DB$.

To Prove
$a^2 + b^2 = c^2$

Statement	*Reason*
1. rt $\triangle ABC$, rt $\measuredangle C$	1. given
2. Draw alt $\overline{CD}$.	2. 1 $\perp$ from pt to line
3. $\frac{c}{a} = \frac{a}{y}$	3. leg mn propor hyp adj seg
4. $a^2 = cy$	4. prod extrms = prod mns
5. $\frac{c}{b} = \frac{b}{x}$	5. leg mn propor hyp adj seg
6. $b^2 = cx$	6. prod extrms = prod mns
7. $a^2 + b^2 = cy + cx$	7. = + =, sums =
8. $a^2 + b^2 = c(y + x)$	8. rearr props
9. $c = y + x$	9. whole = sum parts
10. $\therefore a^2 + b^2 = c^2$	10. subst

Although we will not formally state and prove it, the converse of the Pythagorean Theorem is also true; that is, if the lengths a, b, and c of the three sides of a triangle are such that $a^2 + b^2 = c^2$, then the triangle is a right triangle with its right angle opposite side c.

We conclude this section with two examples that involve this famous theorem. Note the format used to solve each problem. It includes drawing a figure, labeling it, using variables to represent the lengths of the sides, and writing the equation used in the solution.

EXAMPLE 3

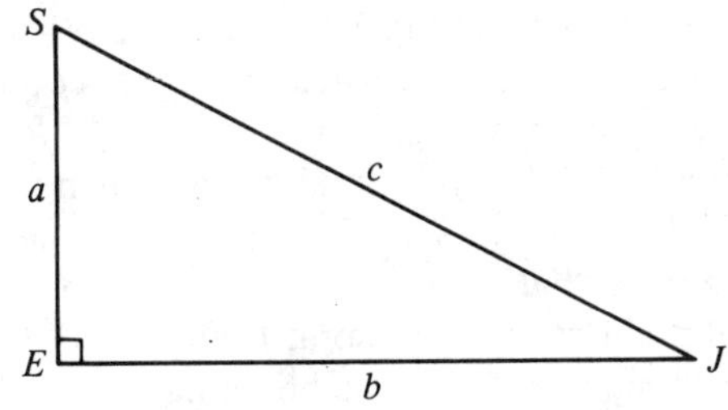

Given
rt $\triangle EJS$
rt $\measuredangle E$
Let $a = SE$, $b = EJ$, and $c = JS$.

Find
(a) JS if $SE = 5$ cm and $EJ = 12$ cm
(b) SE if $JS = 20$ in and $EJ = 16$ in
(c) EJ if $SJ = 15$ ft and $SE = 8$ ft

Answers

(a)
$c^2 = a^2 + b^2$
$c^2 = 5^2 + 12^2$
$c^2 = 25 + 144$
$c^2 = 169$
$c = JS = 13$ cm

(b)
$a^2 + b^2 = c^2$
$a^2 + 16^2 = 20^2$
$a^2 = 400 - 256$
$a^2 = 144$
$a = SE = 12$ in

(c)
$a^2 + b^2 = c^2$
$8^2 + b^2 = 15^2$
$b^2 = 225 - 64$
$b^2 = 161$
$b = EJ = \sqrt{161}$ ft
$EJ \approx 12.69$ ft

EXAMPLE 4 Find the area of an equilateral triangle with 20-inch sides.

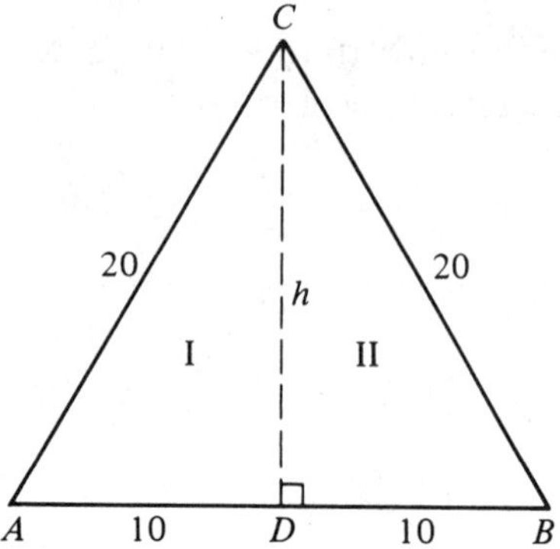

Answer

Construct alt CD in $\triangle ABC$. Then $\triangle I \cong \triangle II$ (why?) and $AD = DB = 10$ in.

We next find alt $CD = h$.

$$a^2 + b^2 = c^2$$
$$h^2 + 10^2 = 20^2$$
$$h^2 = 300$$
$$h = \sqrt{300} = 10\sqrt{3} \text{ in}$$

Now,

$$A = \tfrac{1}{2}bh$$
$$A = \tfrac{1}{2} \cdot 20 \cdot 10\sqrt{3}$$
$$A = 100\sqrt{3} \text{ sq in}$$
$$A \approx 173.2 \text{ sq in}$$

EXERCISES FOR 9.3

In exercises 1–20 answer true or false.

1. Two right triangles are always similar triangles.
2. Two isosceles right triangles are always similar triangles.
3. If two sides of a right triangle measure 7 centimeters and 24 centimeters, the hypotenuse measures 25 centimeters.
4. The diagonal of an 8-inch by 15-inch rectangle is 18 inches long.
5. The altitude to the hypotenuse of a right triangle forms two triangles that are similar.
6. In a proportion, the product of the extremes is always greater than the product of the means.
7. It is possible to have a right triangle whose sides measure $3\frac{3}{8}$, $4\frac{1}{2}$, and $5\frac{5}{8}$ inches.
8. If two angles of one triangle are congruent, respectively, to two angles of a second triangle and the third angles are supplementary, then the triangles are right triangles.
9. If $\overline{TO}$ is an altitude in right triangle TRY, then $\frac{RO}{TO} = \frac{TO}{OY}$.
10. If the hypotenuse of an isosceles right triangle measures $8\sqrt{2}$ inches, then each leg is 8 inches long.
11. A 61-foot ladder whose base is 11 feet from a wall reaches 60 feet up the wall.
12. If a vertical pole 24 feet long casts a 60-foot shadow, then a vertical pole 30 feet long casts a 75-foot shadow.
13. The set of similar right triangles in a plane is a subset of the set of congruent right triangles in that plane.
14. An altitude of an equilateral triangle with 30-inch sides is $15\sqrt{3}$ inches long.
15. If, with 210 feet of string out, a kite is 168 feet in the air, then the point directly below the kite is 126 feet from the kite flier, assuming that the string is straight and the ground is level.
16. If two right triangles are congruent, then they cannot be similar.

17. If an isosceles trapezoid has bases 11 and 17 feet long with its other sides both 5 feet long, then its area is 56 square feet.

18. The three sides of a right triangle could measure 9, 40, and 42 inches.

19. If the lengths of the legs of a right triangle are doubled, then the hypotenuse is increased four times.

20. If the lengths of three sides of a right triangle are consecutive integers, then one of the sides could be 4 inches.

In exercises 21–30 explain what is wrong in each figure.

21.

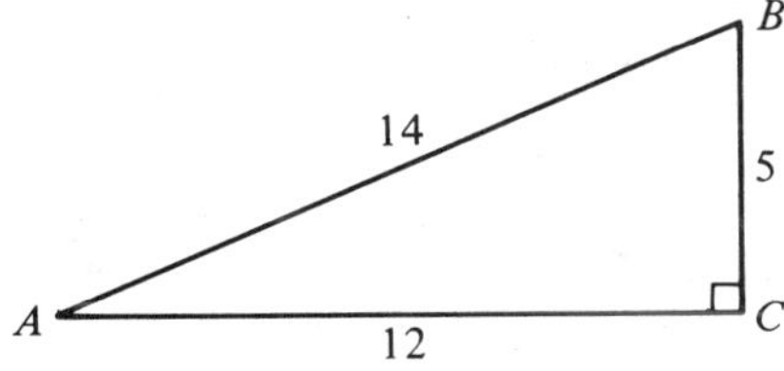

22.

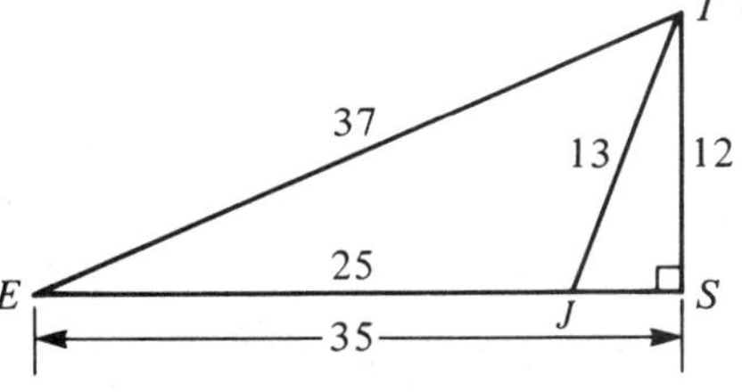

23.

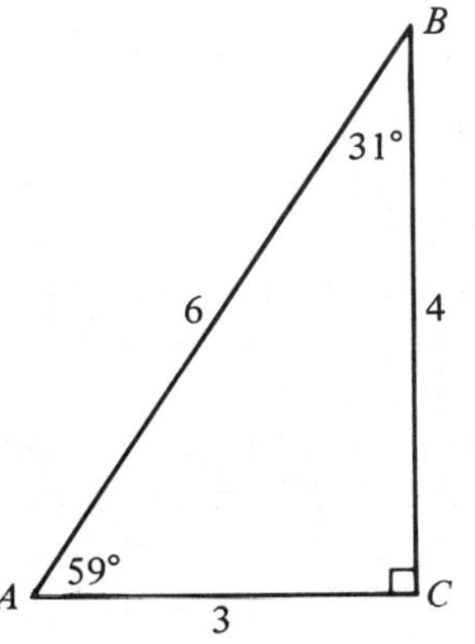

24.

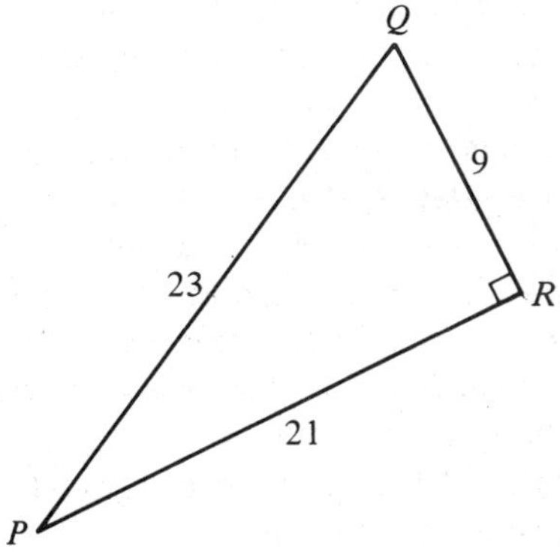

25.

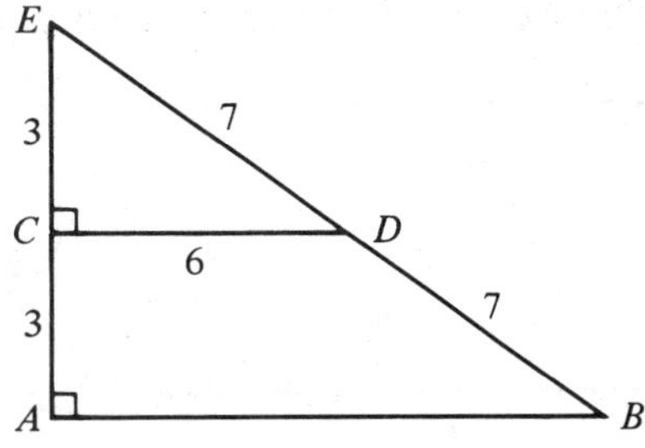

26.

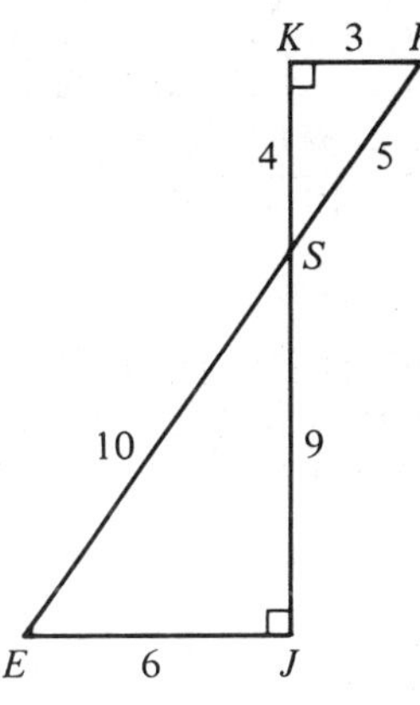

27.

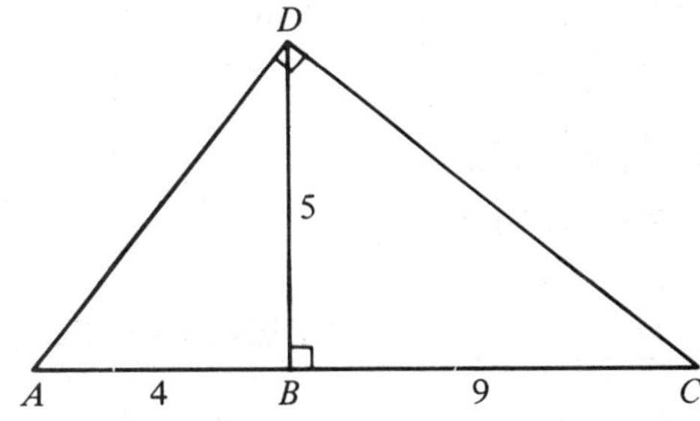

28.

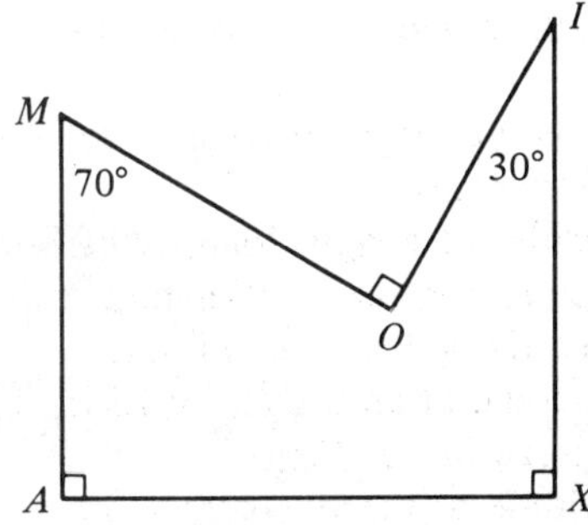

29.

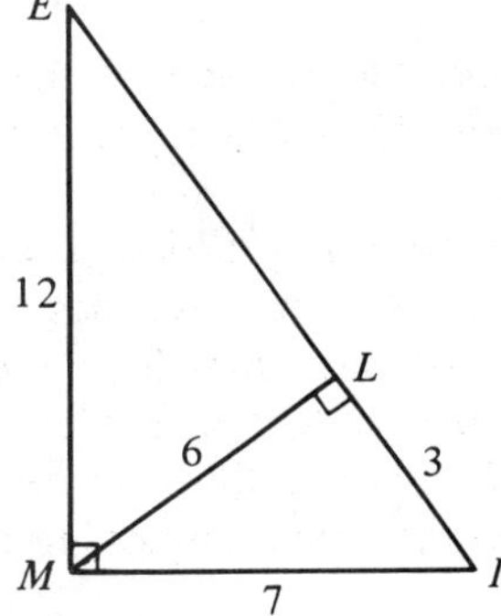

30.

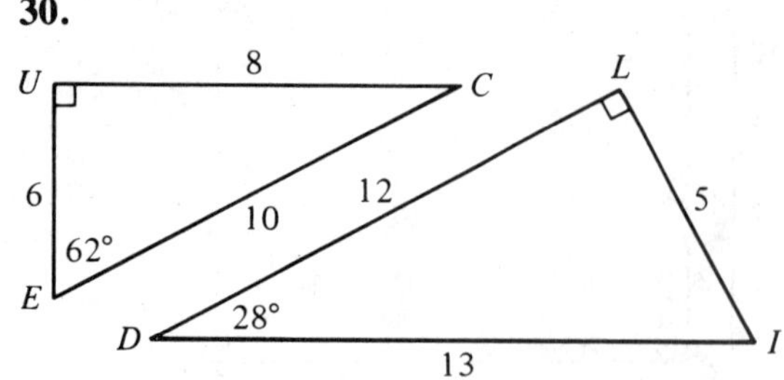

31. Name four pairs of similar right triangles, with corresponding vertices in order, that are not also congruent triangles.

Given
rh *ANGE*
$\overline{LG} \perp \overline{AG}$

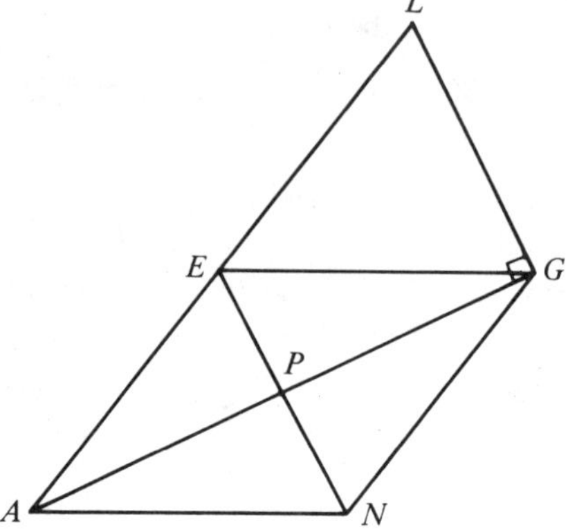

32. Name six pairs of similar right triangles with corresponding vertices in order.

Given
$\overline{GI} \perp \overline{RA}$
$\overline{RN} \perp \overline{GA}$
$\overline{TR} \perp \overline{RN}$
$\overline{TL} \perp \overline{GI}$

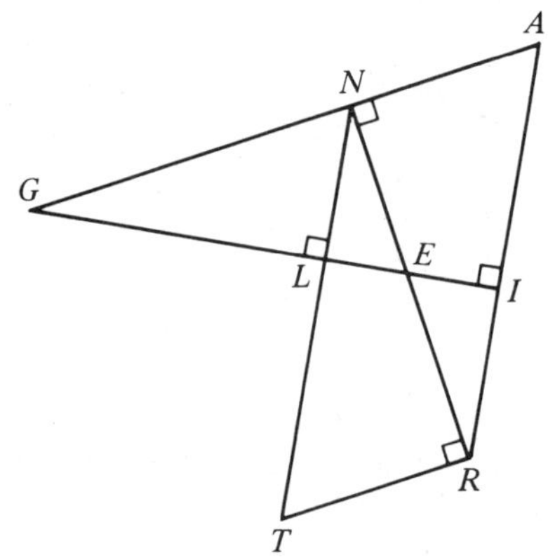

In exercises 33–36 use the given figures to answer the questions.

33. **(a)** Show that the area of the square on the hypotenuse is equal to the sum of the areas of the squares on the legs.
(b) Repeat part (a) using $AB = c$, $AC = b$, and $BC = a$.

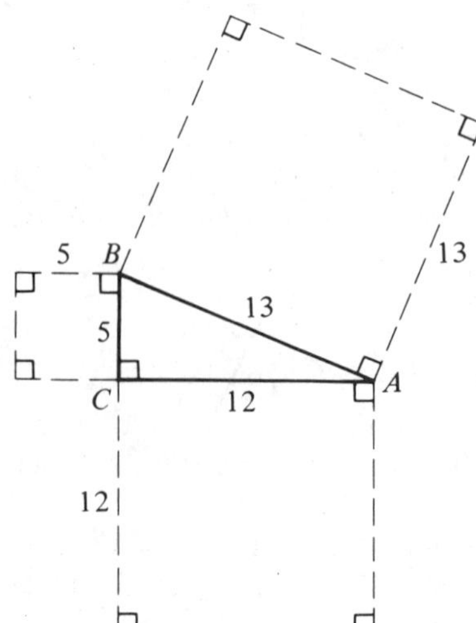

34. *Given*
sq *TINL*
sq *RAGE*
(a) Find c (without the Theorem of Pythagoras) by using the fact that the area of the large square is equal to the sum of the areas of $\triangle$s I–IV plus the area of the square *RAGE*.
(b) Repeat part (a) but replace 8 with a and 15 with b.

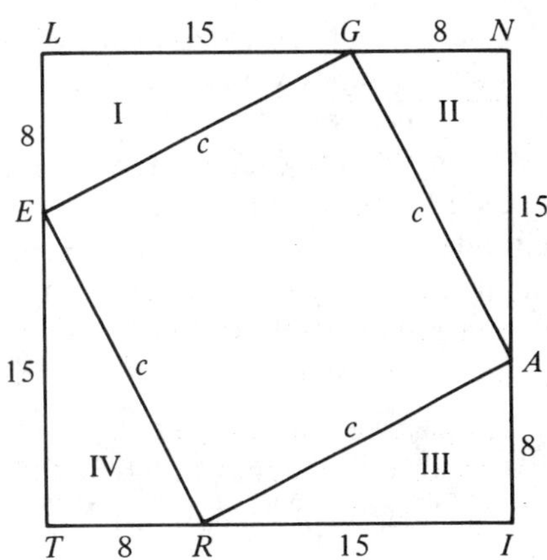

35. **(a)** Find c (without the Theorem of Pythagoras) by using the fact that the area of trapezoid *ANGL* equals the sum of the areas of the three right triangles.
(b) Repeat part (a) but replace 11 with a and 60 with b. (This proof of the Pythagorean Theorem is credited to James A. Garfield [1831–1881] the twentieth president of the United States.)

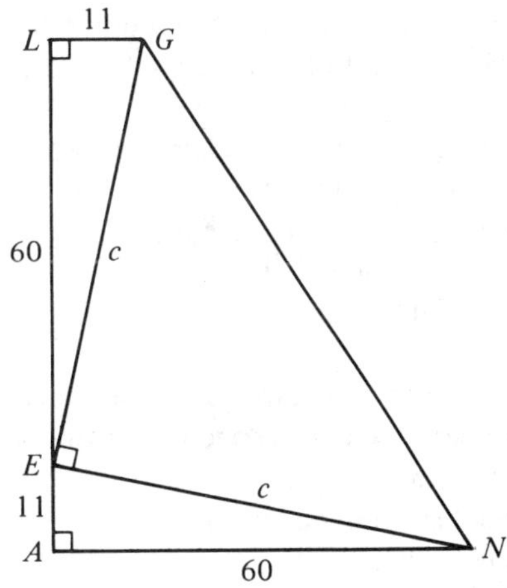

36. *Given*
sq *JAWS*, $SE = WP = AO = JH = 7$
sq *HOPE*, $SP = WO = AH = JE = 24$
(a) Find x by using the fact that the area of the large square equals the sum of the areas of the four triangles plus the area of the small square.
(b) How is the answer related to the lengths 24 and 7?
(c) In the *Given*, replace 7 with a and 24 with b. Let $SW = c$. Prove that $a^2 + b^2 = c^2$ using areas as in part (a). (This proof of the Pythagorean Theorem is credited to the Hindu mathematician Bhāskara [1114–1185] although he merely drew the figure and wrote below it the word "Behold!")

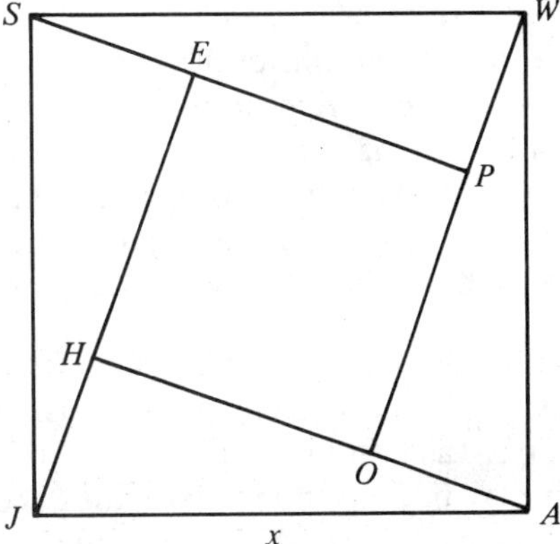

In exercises 37–50 draw a figure, label it, write an appropriate equation, and solve.

37. Find the length of the diagonal of a rectangle with a 14-inch width and a 48-inch length.

38. Find the length of the diagonal of a square each of whose sides measures 5 inches long.

39. Find the perimeter of a rhombus whose diagonals measure 12 inches and 16 inches, respectively.

40. Find the area of an isosceles triangle with a 60-inch base and 34-inch sides.

41. Find the lengths of the sides of an isosceles right triangle whose hypotenuse measures 32 inches.
42. Find the length of the side of a square having an 18-inch diagonal.
43. The altitude to the hypotenuse of a right triangle divides the hypotenuse into 16-inch and 9-inch segments. Find the length of the altitude and the perimeter of the triangle.
44. The hypotenuse of a right triangle measures 18 inches, and one of the legs measures 5 inches. Find the length of the other leg.
45. Find the length of a side of an equilateral triangle whose altitude measures 12 inches long.
46. If the sides of a triangle measure 61 inches, 60 inches, and 11 inches, is the largest angle an acute, right, or obtuse angle? Why?
47. If D is any point on side $\overline{AC}$ of $\triangle ABC$ with $\angle C = 90°$, show that $BD^2 + AC^2 = AB^2 + CD^2$.
48. If the two bases of a trapezoid measure 12 inches and 18 inches, respectively, the altitude measures 8 inches, and one of the nonparallel sides measures 10 inches, find the length of the fourth side.
49. If, in the trapezoid of exercise 48, the nonparallel sides are extended to form a triangle, find the perimeter of the triangle.
50. If the two legs of a right triangle measure 9 and 40 feet long, respectively, what is the length of the hypotenuse of another right triangle whose sides are three times as long? What is the ratio of the triangles' areas?

In exercises 51–54 do the constructions using only a compass and straightedge. A preliminary sketch may be helpful in determining the steps to follow as illustrated in two of the exercises.

51. Construct a parallelogram $ABCD$. Construct a square having the same area as $ABCD$. (Hint: See Example 2 of this section.)

52. (a) Construct a line segment $\sqrt{5}$ units long using Construction 14. (Hint: If $\frac{1}{x} = \frac{x}{5}$, then $x^2 = 5$ and $x = \sqrt{5}$.)
    (b) Construct a line segment $\sqrt{5}$ units long using the Pythagorean Theorem. (Hint: If $1^2 + 2^2 = x^2$, then $x^2 = 5$ and $x = \sqrt{5}$.)
53. (a) Construct a square whose area is twice that of a given square of side m.
    (b) Construct a square whose area is equal to the sum of the areas of two given squares.

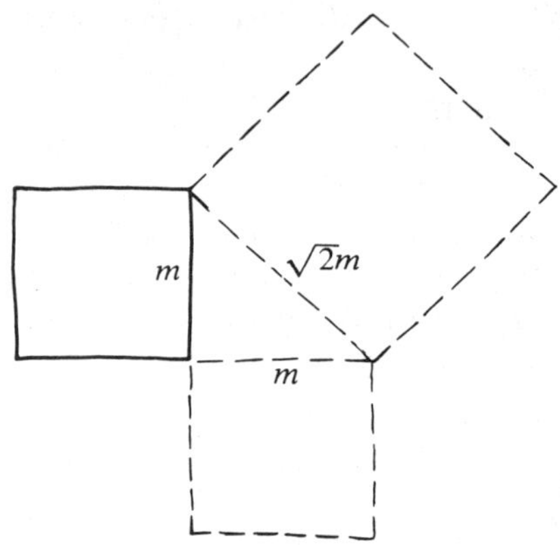

54. Construct a square having the same area as that of a given acute triangle ARC. (Hint: First construct a rectangle having the same area as $\triangle ARC$; then see Example 2 of this section.)

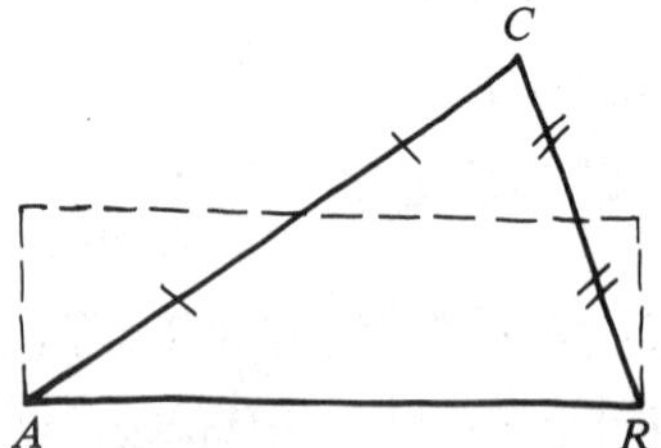

55. Our proof of the Pythagorean Theorem (Theorem 102) is an algebraic proof based on ratios and proportions involving corresponding sides of similar triangles. In this exercise we give a geometric proof based on areas (see also Exercise 33). This is probably how Pythagoras first proved the theorem. Supply the missing reasons in the proof.

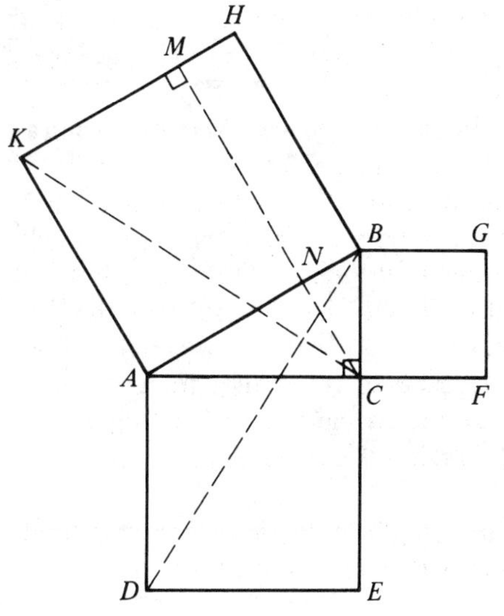

Given
rt $\triangle ABC$ (rt $\measuredangle C$)
sqs $ADEC$, $CFGB$, $ABHK$

To Prove
$A(\text{sq } ABHK) = A(\text{sq } ADEC) + A(\text{sq } CFGB)$

Statement	*Reason*
1. rt $\triangle ABC$ (rt $\measuredangle C$) sqs $ADEC$, $CFGB$, $ABHK$	1. ?
2. Construct $\overline{CM} \perp \overline{HK}$ and inters $\overline{AB}$ at N.	2. ?
3. Draw $\overline{CK}$ and $\overline{BD}$.	3. ?
4. $\measuredangle KAB$ and $\measuredangle DAC$ rt $\measuredangle$s	4. ?
5. $\measuredangle KAB \cong \measuredangle DAC$	5. ?
6. $\measuredangle BAC \cong \measuredangle BAC$	6. ?
7. $\measuredangle KAB + \measuredangle BAC \cong \measuredangle DAC + \measuredangle BAC$	7. ?
8. $\measuredangle KAC \cong \measuredangle KAB + \measuredangle BAC$ $\measuredangle BAD \cong \measuredangle DAC + \measuredangle BAC$	8. ?
9. $\measuredangle KAC \cong \measuredangle BAD$	9. ?
10. $\overline{KA} \cong \overline{BA}$, $\overline{AC} \cong \overline{AD}$	10. ?
11. $\triangle KAC \cong \triangle BAD$	11. ?
12. $A(\triangle KAC) = A(\triangle BAD)$	12. ?
13. $A(\triangle KAC) = \frac{1}{2} \cdot KA \cdot MK$ $A(\triangle BAD) = \frac{1}{2} \cdot AD \cdot DE$	13. ?
14. $\frac{1}{2} \cdot KA \cdot MK = \frac{1}{2} \cdot AD \cdot DE$	14. ?
15. $KA \cdot MK = AD \cdot DE$	15. ?
16. $A(ANMK) = KA \cdot MK$ $A(\text{sq } ADEC) = AD \cdot DE$	16. ?
17. $A(ANMK) = A(\text{sq } ADEC)$ Similarly, by drawing $\overline{CH}$ and $\overline{AG}$ it can be proved that $A(NBHM) = A(\text{sq } CFGB)$	17. ?
18. $A(ANMK) + A(NBHM) = A(\text{sq } ADEC) + A(\text{sq } CFGB)$	18. ?
19. $A(\text{sq } ABHK) = A(ANMK) + A(NBHM)$	19. ?
20. $\therefore A(\text{sq } ABHK) = A(\text{sq } ADEC) + A(\text{sq } CFGB)$	20. ?

9.4

MORE ABOUT SIMILAR TRIANGLES

We have seen that if two triangles are similar, then their corresponding sides are proportional. It is this proportionality of the sides that makes the theory of similar triangles so useful. Some practical applications are presented in Section 9.6. In this section we focus on proving that a proportion is true by first proving that an appropriate pair of triangles is similar.

EXAMPLE 1

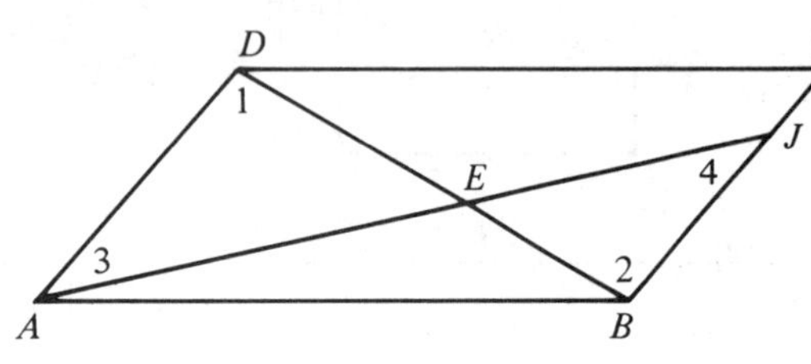

Given
▱$ABCD$

To Prove
(a) $\frac{DE}{BE} = \frac{AE}{JE}$
(b) $\frac{DE}{AE} = \frac{BE}{JE}$
(c) $DE \cdot JE = AE \cdot BE$

Statement	*Reason*
1. ▱$ABCD$	1. given
2. $\overline{AD} \parallel \overline{BC}$	2. ▱ iff opp sides ∥
3. ∡1 ≅ ∡2, ∡3 ≅ ∡4	3. ∥, alt int ∡s ≅
4. $\triangle AED \sim \triangle JEB$	4. aa ≅ aa
5. ∴ (a) $\frac{DE}{BE} = \frac{AE}{JE}$	5. csstp
6. ∴ (b) $\frac{DE}{AE} = \frac{BE}{JE}$	6. interch mns
7. ∴ (c) $DE \cdot JE = AE \cdot BE$	7. prod extrms = prod mns

Example 1 points out that more than one equation may be obtained from two pairs of corresponding sides of similar triangles. Note that the proof would have been more difficult to design if only equation (c) were in the conclusion because (c) is not a proportion. This type of problem appears in Example 2.

To discover a plan for the proof in Example 2, rearrange the equation $ES \cdot AC = KC \cdot KS$ into the proportion $\frac{ES}{KC} = \frac{KS}{AC}$, *before* looking for similar triangles. In so doing we are using prod extrms = prod mns in reverse. This proportion suggests trying to prove $\triangle ESK \sim \triangle KCA$.

EXAMPLE 2

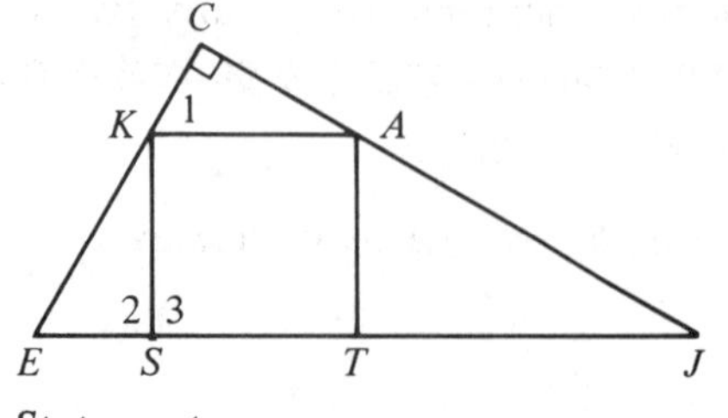

Given
sq $STAK$
rt $\triangle EJC$
rt ∡C

To Prove
$ES \cdot AC = KC \cdot KS$

Statement	*Reason*
1. sq $STAK$	1. given
2. ∡3 rt ∡	2. rect (sq) has 4 rt ∡s
3. $\overline{KS} \perp \overline{ET}$	3. ⊥ iff a rt ∡
4. ∡2 rt ∡	4. ⊥s form ≅ rt ∡s

5. rt $\triangle EJC$, rt $\measuredangle C$	5. given
6. $\measuredangle 2 \cong \measuredangle C$	6. rt $\measuredangle$s $\cong$
7. $\overline{KA} \parallel \overline{EJ}$	7. $\square$ (sq) iff opp sides $\parallel$
8. $\measuredangle E \cong \measuredangle 1$	8. $\nparallel$, corr $\measuredangle$s $\cong$
9. $\triangle ESK \sim \triangle KCA$	9. aa $\cong$ aa
10. $\frac{ES}{KC} = \frac{KS}{AC}$	10. csstp
11. $\therefore ES \cdot AC = KC \cdot KS$	11. prod extrms = prod mns

It is not always possible to prove that a given proportion is true given one pair of similar triangles. It may be necessary to find two pairs of similar triangles, and thus two proportions, that contain the same ratio. Example 3 illustrates this technique.

EXAMPLE 3

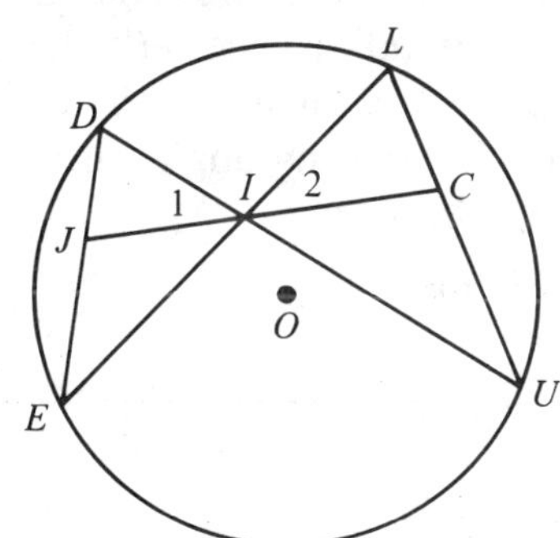

Given
$\odot O$
$\measuredangle 1 \cong \measuredangle 2$

To Prove
$\frac{DJ}{LC} = \frac{DE}{LU}$

Statement	*Reason*
1. $\odot O$, $\measuredangle 1 \cong \measuredangle 2$	1. given
2. $\measuredangle D \cong \measuredangle L$	2. inscr $\measuredangle$s interc same $\frown$ are $\cong$
3. $\triangle DJI \sim \triangle LCI$	3. aa $\cong$ aa
4. $\frac{DJ}{LC} = \frac{DI}{LI}$	4. csstp
5. $\measuredangle E \cong \measuredangle U$	5. inscr $\measuredangle$s interc same $\frown$ are $\cong$
6. $\triangle DEI \sim \triangle LUI$	6. aa $\cong$ aa
7. $\frac{DI}{LI} = \frac{DE}{LU}$	7. csstp
8. $\therefore \frac{DJ}{LC} = \frac{DE}{LU}$	8. trans =

The techniques illustrated in the foregoing examples can be used to prove some interesting and useful proportions as illustrated in the next two theorems.

Theorem 103 If two triangles are similar, the ratio of (a) any two corresponding altitudes, (b) any two corresponding medians, or (c) any two corresponding angle bisectors, is the same as the ratio of any two corresponding sides (corr alts, meds, $\measuredangle$ bis, $\sim \triangle$s propor corr sides).

Part (a) is proved below. Proofs for (b) and (c) are left as exercises.

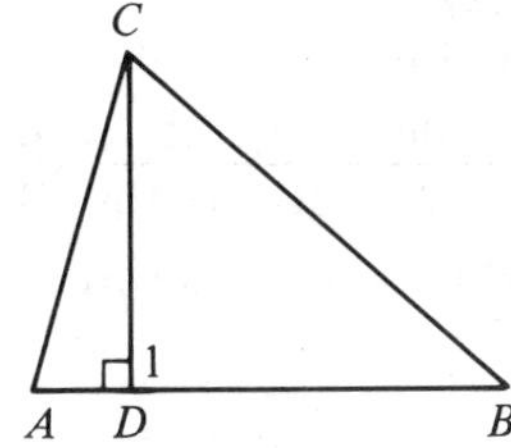

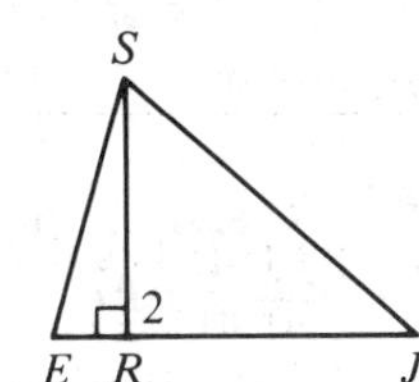

Given
$\triangle ABC \sim \triangle EJS$
alts $\overline{CD}$, $\overline{SR}$

To Prove
$\frac{CD}{SR} = \frac{BC}{JS} = \frac{AB}{EJ} = \frac{CA}{SE}$

Statement	Reason
1. $\triangle ABC \sim \triangle EJS$	1. given
2. $\frac{BC}{JS} = \frac{AB}{EJ} = \frac{CA}{SE}$	2. csstp
3. $\measuredangle B \cong \measuredangle J$	3. castc
4. alt $\overline{CD}$, alt $\overline{SR}$	4. given
5. $\overline{CD} \perp \overline{AB}$, $\overline{SR} \perp \overline{EJ}$	5. alt from vtx $\perp$ opp side
6. $\measuredangle 1 \cong \measuredangle 2$	6. $\perp$s from $\cong$ rt $\measuredangle$s
7. $\triangle CDB \sim \triangle SRJ$	7. aa $\cong$ aa
8. $\frac{CD}{SR} = \frac{BC}{JS}$	8. csstp
9. $\therefore \frac{CD}{SR} = \frac{BC}{JS} = \frac{AB}{EJ} = \frac{CA}{SE}$	9. trans =

Theorem 104 If two triangles are similar, the ratio of their areas is the same as the ratio of (a) the squares of any two corresponding sides, (b) the squares of any two corresponding altitudes, (c) the squares of any two corresponding medians, or (d) the squares of any two corresponding angle bisectors (areas $\sim$ $\triangle$s propor sqs corr sides, alts, meds, $\measuredangle$ bis).

Part (b) is proved below. Note how the use of Theorem 103(a) in step 2 of this proof leads to the substitution and the conclusion in step 5. Parts (a), (c), and (d) may be proved using Theorem 103 in a similar way. The proofs are left as exercises.

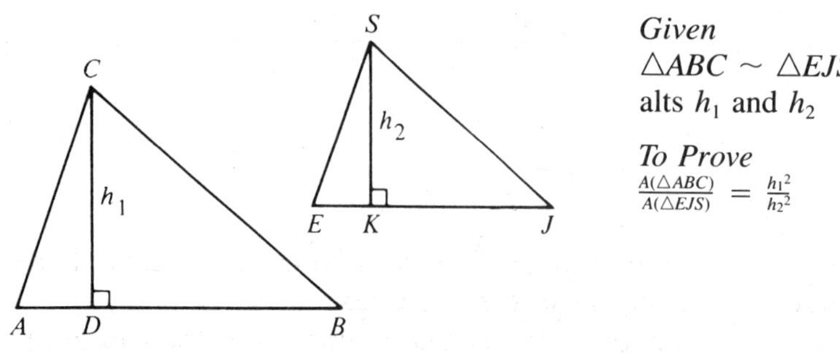

Given
$\triangle ABC \sim \triangle EJS$
alts h_1 and h_2

To Prove
$\frac{A(\triangle ABC)}{A(\triangle EJS)} = \frac{h_1^2}{h_2^2}$

Statement	Reason
1. $\triangle ABC \sim \triangle EJS$, alts h_1 and h_2	1. given
2. $\frac{AB}{EJ} = \frac{h_1}{h_2}$	2. corr alts $\sim$ $\triangle$s propor corr sides
3. $A(\triangle ABC) = \frac{1}{2} \cdot AB \cdot h_1$ $A(\triangle EJS) = \frac{1}{2} \cdot EJ \cdot h_2$	3. $A(\triangle) = \frac{1}{2}bh$
4. $\frac{A(\triangle ABC)}{A(\triangle EJS)} = \frac{AB}{EJ} \cdot \frac{h_1}{h_2}$	4. $= \div =$, quot $=$
5. $\therefore \frac{A(\triangle ABC)}{A(\triangle EJS)} = \frac{h_1}{h_2} \cdot \frac{h_1}{h_2} = \frac{h_1^2}{h_2^2}$	5. subst

Example 4 contains some numerical applications of the two theorems above. It is important to understand that in the first part of Example 4(a), the *ratio* of the corresponding altitudes is being calculated, not the actual lengths of the altitudes. Similarly, the *ratio* of the areas, not the areas themselves, is being calculated in the second part of Example 4(a).

EXAMPLE 4

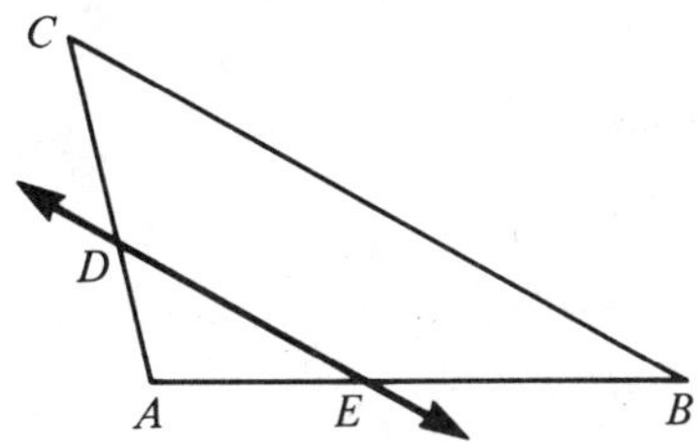

Given
$DE \parallel CB$

(a) If $ED = 10$ in and $BC = 25$ in, find for $\triangle AED$ and $\triangle ABC$ the ratio of their corresponding altitudes and the ratio of their areas.

(b) If $A(\triangle AED):A(\triangle ABC) = 4:49$ and $AE = 6$ in, find AB.

Answers

(a) Since $\triangle AED \sim \triangle ABC$ (why?), then

$$\text{ratio of altitudes} = \frac{ED}{BC} = \frac{10}{25} = \frac{2}{5} \text{ (Theorem 103: corr alts} \sim \triangle\text{s propor corr sides)}$$

$$\text{ratio of areas} = \frac{ED^2}{BC^2} = \frac{2^2}{5^2} = \frac{4}{25}$$

(Theorem 104: areas ~ △s propor sqs corr sides)

(b) Let $x = AB$. Then, since $\triangle AED \sim \triangle ABC$,

$$\frac{AE^2}{AB^2} = \frac{A(\triangle AED)}{A(\triangle ABC)} \quad \text{(Theorem 104: areas} \sim \triangle\text{s propor sqs corr sides)}$$

$$\frac{6^2}{x^2} = \frac{4}{49}$$

$$4x^2 = 36 \cdot 49$$

$$x^2 = \frac{36 \cdot 49}{4}$$

$$x^2 = 441$$

$$x = 21 \text{ in}$$

More applications of Theorems 103 and 104, as well as some parts of the proofs that are omitted above, appear in the exercises.

The final theorem of this section contains a consequence of the similarity relation that is probably not intuitively obvious.

Theorem 105 An angle bisector in a triangle divides the opposite side into segments that have the same ratio as the other two sides (∡ bis ÷ opp side same ratio other 2 sides).

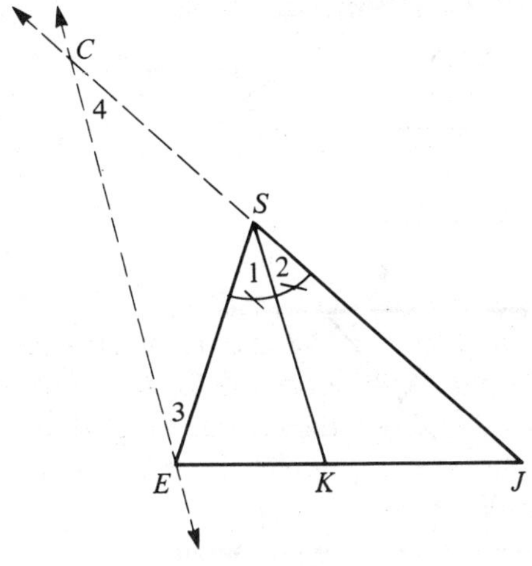

Given
$\triangle EJS$
$\overline{SK}$ bis $\measuredangle ESJ$

To Prove
$\frac{EK}{KJ} = \frac{ES}{SJ}$

Statement	*Reason*
1. $\triangle EJS$, $\overline{SK}$ bis $\measuredangle ESJ$	1. given
2. $\measuredangle 1 \cong \measuredangle 2$	2. bis $\div$ $\measuredangle$ into 2 $\cong$ $\measuredangle$s
3. Draw $\overrightarrow{JS}$.	3. 2 pts determ line
4. Draw $\overleftrightarrow{EC} \parallel \overline{SK}$.	4. $\parallel$ post
5. $\frac{EK}{KJ} = \frac{CS}{SJ}$	5. line $\parallel$ side $\triangle$ $\div$ 2 sides in $=$ ratios
6. $\measuredangle 3 \cong \measuredangle 1$	6. $\nparallel$, alt int $\measuredangle$s $\cong$
7. $\measuredangle 2 \cong \measuredangle 4$	7. $\nparallel$, corr $\measuredangle$s $\cong$
8. $\measuredangle 3 \cong \measuredangle 4$	8. trans $\cong$
9. $\overline{ES} \cong \overline{CS}$	9. if 2 $\measuredangle$s $\triangle$ $\cong$, opp sides $\cong$
10. $ES = CS$	10. $\cong$ iff meas $=$
11. $\therefore \frac{EK}{KJ} = \frac{ES}{SJ}$	11. subst

Note that, in Theorem 105, $\triangle EKS$ is not in general similar to $\triangle JKS$.

EXERCISES FOR 9.4

In exercises 1–10 name the theorem (most are from Section 9.1) or axiom that justifies each statement.

1. If $\frac{EJ}{AJ} = \frac{ES}{AB}$, then $\frac{EJ}{ES} = \frac{AJ}{AB}$.
2. If $\frac{EJ}{AJ} = \frac{ES}{AB}$, then $EJ \cdot AB = AJ \cdot ES$.
3. If $\frac{ES}{AB} = \frac{JS}{JB}$, then $ES \cdot JB = AB \cdot JS$.
4. If $\frac{ES}{AB} = \frac{JS}{JB}$, then $\frac{ES}{JS} = \frac{AB}{JB}$.
5. If $\frac{EJ}{AJ} = \frac{ES}{AB}$, then $\frac{EJ + AJ}{AJ} = \frac{ES + AB}{AB}$.
6. If $\frac{EJ}{AJ} = \frac{ES}{AB}$, then $\frac{EJ - AJ}{AJ} = \frac{ES - AB}{AB}$.
7. If $\frac{JB}{JS} = \frac{AB}{ES}$, then $\frac{JS}{JB} = \frac{ES}{AB}$.
8. If $\frac{AJ}{EJ} = \frac{JB}{JS}$, then $\frac{EJ}{AJ} = \frac{JS}{JB}$.
9. If $\frac{AK}{EK} = \frac{CK}{SK}$ and $\frac{CK}{SK} = \frac{KB}{KJ}$, then $\frac{AK}{EK} = \frac{KB}{KJ}$.
10. If $\frac{JK}{BK} = \frac{SK}{CK}$ and $\frac{EK}{AK} = \frac{SK}{CK}$, then $\frac{JK}{BK} = \frac{EK}{AK}$.
11. If $ES \cdot JB = AB \cdot JS$, does $\frac{ES}{AB} = \frac{JS}{JB}$? Why or why not?
12. If $EJ \cdot JB = AJ \cdot ES$, does $\frac{EJ}{AJ} = \frac{ES}{JB}$? Why or why not?

In exercises 13–15 copy the figure, mark it, and write a proportion from which the conclusion will follow.

13. *Given*
$\measuredangle A \cong \measuredangle 1$
$\measuredangle C \cong \measuredangle 2$

To Prove
$AB \cdot DE = AC \cdot DB$

14. *Given*
$l \parallel m$

To Prove
$SE \cdot SK = ST \cdot SJ$

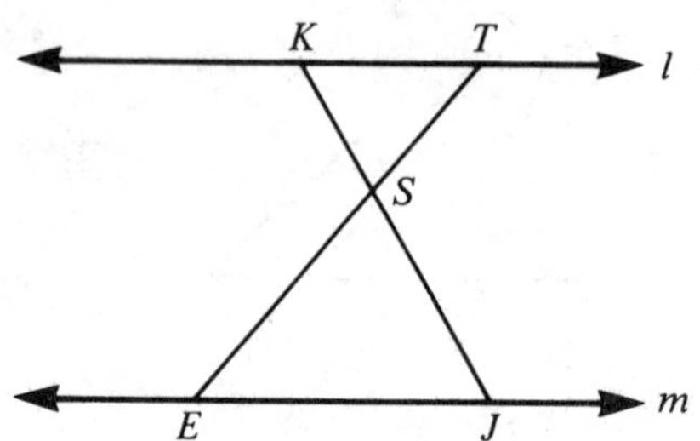

15. *Given*
$\odot O$
$\overset{\frown}{ST} \cong \overset{\frown}{KE}$

To Prove
$ST \cdot SK = KE \cdot SK$

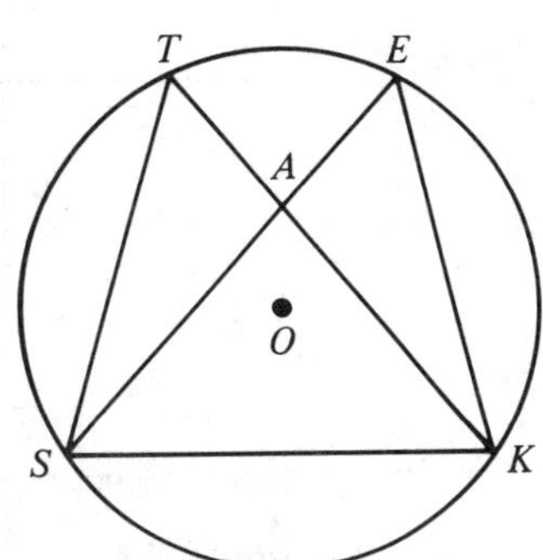

In exercises 16 and 17 copy the figure, mark it, and supply the missing reasons in each proof.

16. *Given*
$\overline{DE} \parallel \overline{IU}$
$\overline{IE} \parallel \overline{LU}$

To Prove
$DI \cdot UL = IL \cdot EI$

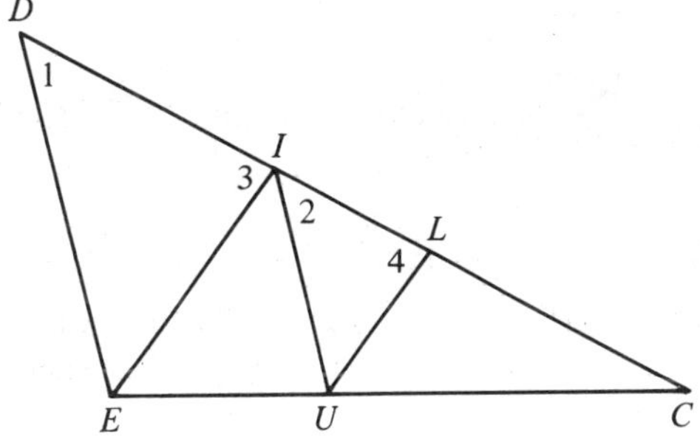

Statement	*Reason*
1. $\overline{DE} \parallel \overline{IU}$	1. ?
2. $\measuredangle 1 \cong \measuredangle 2$	2. ?
3. $\overline{IE} \parallel \overline{LU}$	3. ?
4. $\measuredangle 3 \cong \measuredangle 4$	4. ?
5. $\triangle DEI \sim \triangle IUL$	5. ?
6. $\frac{DI}{IL} = \frac{EI}{UL}$	6. ?
7. $\therefore DI \cdot UL = IL \cdot EI$	7. ?

17. *Given*
$\overleftrightarrow{EJ} \parallel \overline{SQ}$
O midpt $\overline{SQ}$

To Prove
$LE \cdot QU = LS \cdot EU$

(To develop a plan for this proof, note that if $\frac{LE}{LS} = \frac{EU}{QU}$, then $LE \cdot QU = LS \cdot EU$.)

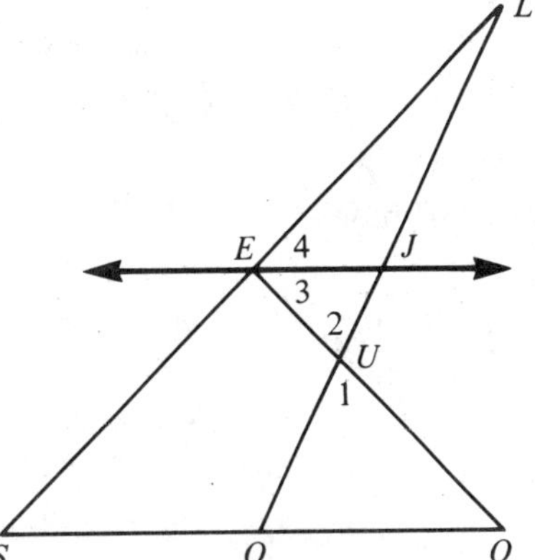

Statement	*Reason*
1. $\overleftrightarrow{EJ} \parallel \overline{SQ}$	1. ?
2. $\measuredangle 3 \cong \measuredangle Q$	2. ?
3. $\measuredangle 2 \cong \measuredangle 1$	3. ?
4. $\triangle JEU \sim \triangle OQU$	4. ?
5. $\frac{JE}{OQ} = \frac{EU}{QU}$	5. ?
6. $\measuredangle 4 = \measuredangle S$	6. ?
7. $\measuredangle L = \measuredangle L$	7. ?

8. $\triangle LEJ \sim \triangle LSO$	8. ?
9. $\frac{LE}{LS} = \frac{JE}{OS}$	9. ?
10. O midpt $\overline{SQ}$	10. ?
11. $OS = OQ$	11. ?
12. $\frac{LE}{LS} = \frac{JE}{OQ}$	12. ?
13. $\frac{LE}{LS} = \frac{EU}{QU}$	13. ?
14. $\therefore LE \cdot QU = LS \cdot EU$	14. ?

In exercises 18–30 copy the figure, the hypothesis, and the conclusion. Mark the figure and write a proof.

18. *Given*
rect $ABCD$
$\overline{EJ} \perp \overline{AC}$

To Prove
$\frac{DA}{AC} = \frac{JE}{EA}$

19. *Given*
$\overline{SJ} \perp \overline{EJ}$
$\overline{RT} \perp \overline{ES}$
$\overline{RE} \perp \overline{EJ}$

To Prove
$\frac{SJ}{EJ} = \frac{ET}{RT}$

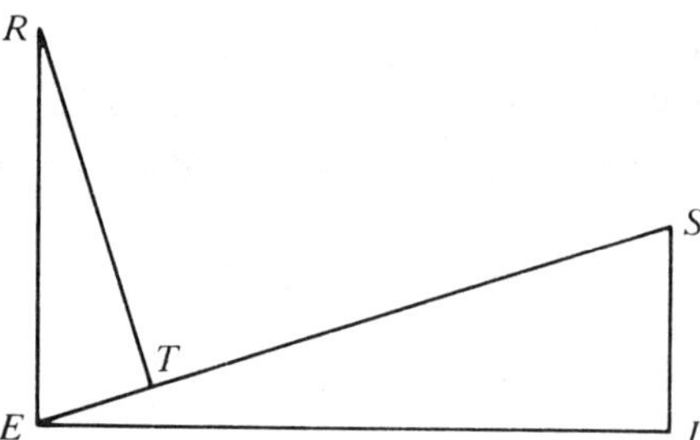

20. *Given*
$\overline{SP}$ bis $\measuredangle AST$
$\triangle SPO$ isos ($\overline{SP}$ base)

To Prove
$AT \cdot OP = PT \cdot SA$

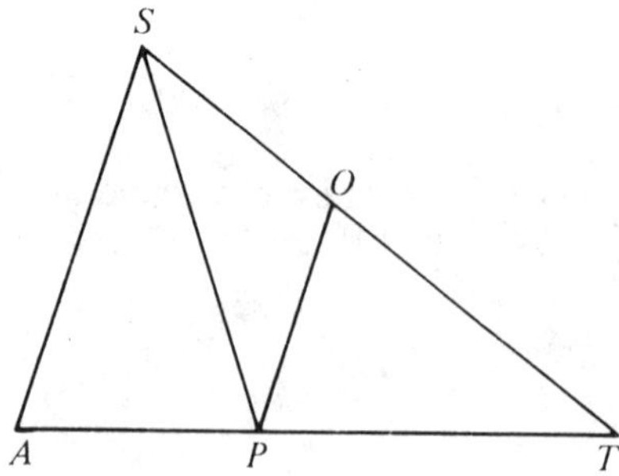

21. *Given*
R midpt $\overline{OF}$
T midpt $\overline{OC}$
A midpt $\overline{FC}$

To Prove
$\frac{OC}{OF} = \frac{AR}{AT}$

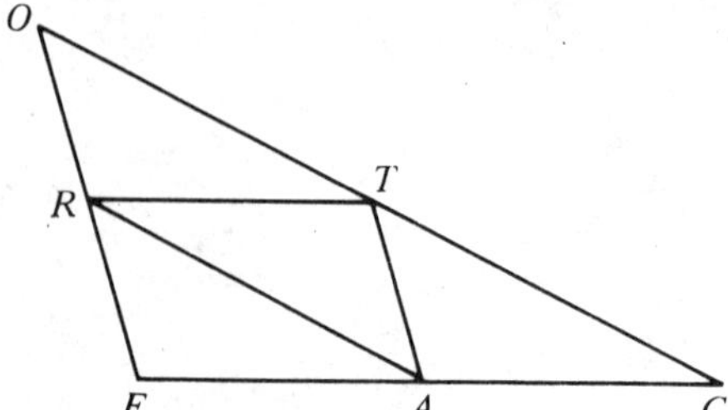

22. *Given*
$\odot O$
M midpt $\overset{\frown}{KS}$
inscr trap $EJSK$ ($\overline{EJ}$, $\overline{KS}$ bases)

To Prove
$\frac{EC}{KC} = \frac{JR}{SR}$

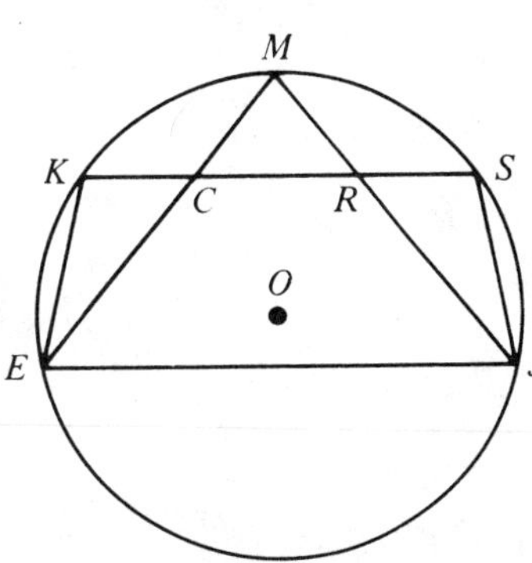

23. *Given*
$\odot O$
$\overline{AD}$ bis $\angle BAC$

To Prove
$AC \cdot BD = AD \cdot PC$

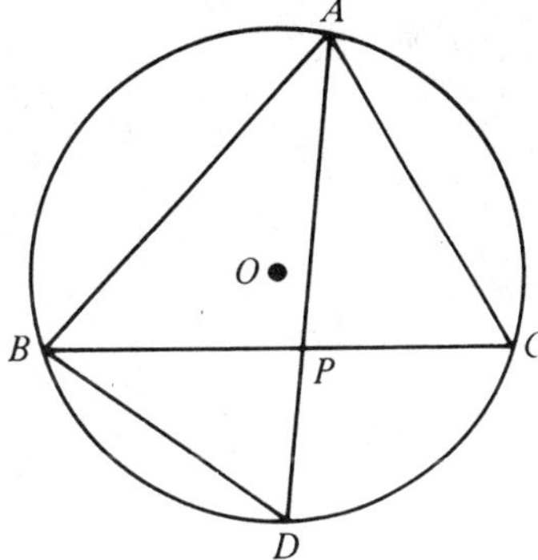

24. *Given*
$\odot O$
S midpt $\overset{\frown}{AK}$

To Prove
$AS \cdot JA = AE \cdot JS$

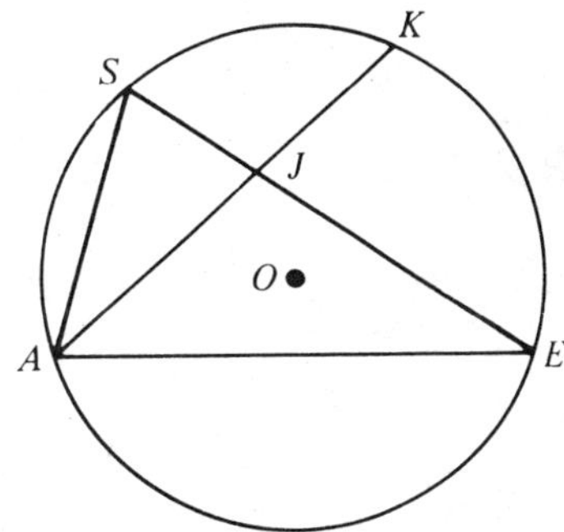

25. *Given*
$\triangle ABC$ isos ($\overline{BC}$ base)
$\overline{BD} \perp \overline{AC}$
$\overline{EC} \perp \overline{BC}$
M midpt $\overline{BE}$

To Prove
$\triangle ABC \sim \triangle MCE$

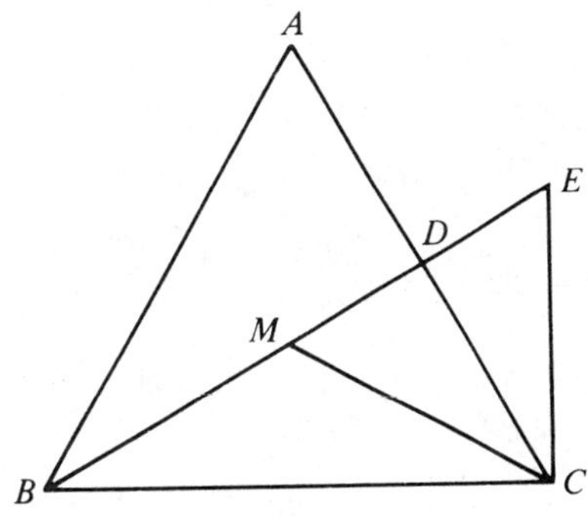

26. *Given*
$\odot O$
tan $\overleftrightarrow{JE}$

To Prove
$\frac{PE}{JE} = \frac{JE}{TE}$

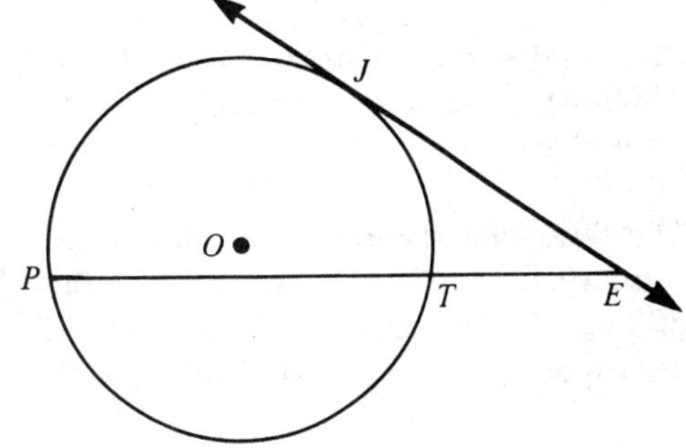

27. *Given*

□STAR

To Prove
$RE \cdot RE = EJ \cdot EK$

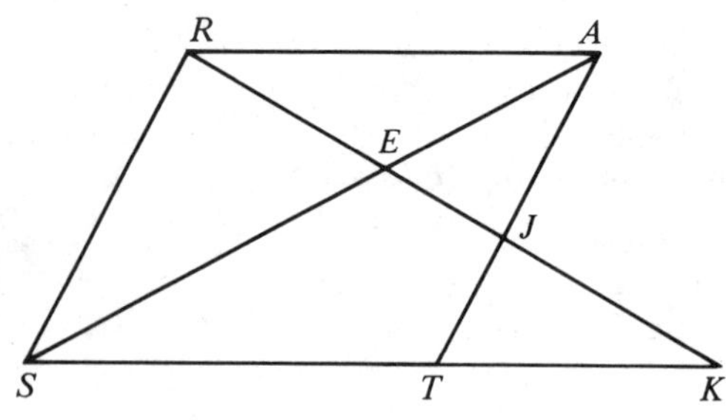

28. *Given*
$\odot O$
$\overline{IU}$ bis $\measuredangle WTE$

To Prove
$\frac{WI}{IE} = \frac{CU}{UA}$

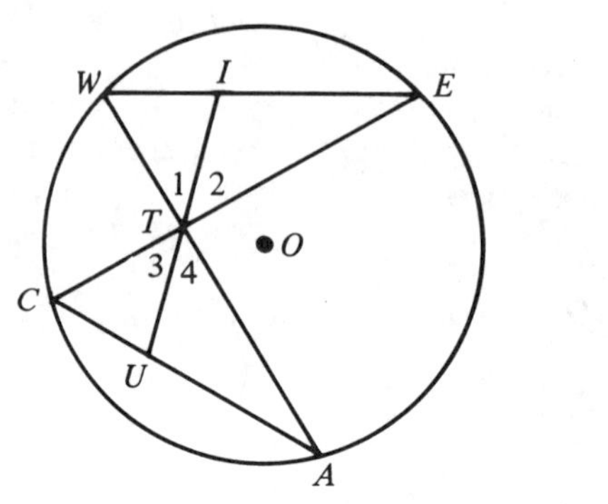

29. *Given*
$\overleftrightarrow{EM}$ tan $\odot O$
$\overleftrightarrow{EM} \parallel \overline{CS}$

To Prove
$JS \cdot JS = JC \cdot JK$

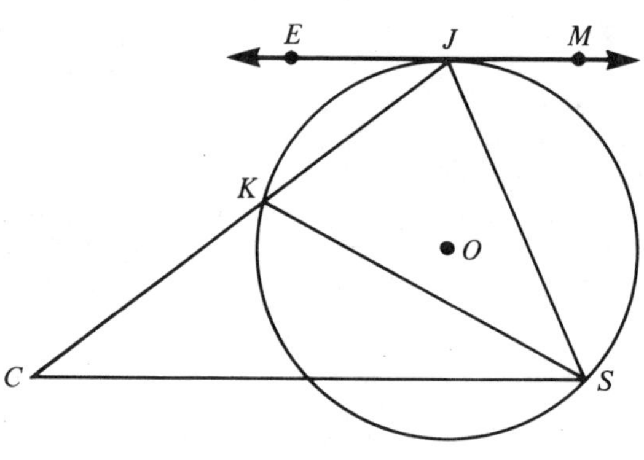

30. *Given*
□ELID

To Prove
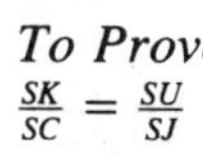
$\frac{SK}{SC} = \frac{SU}{SJ}$

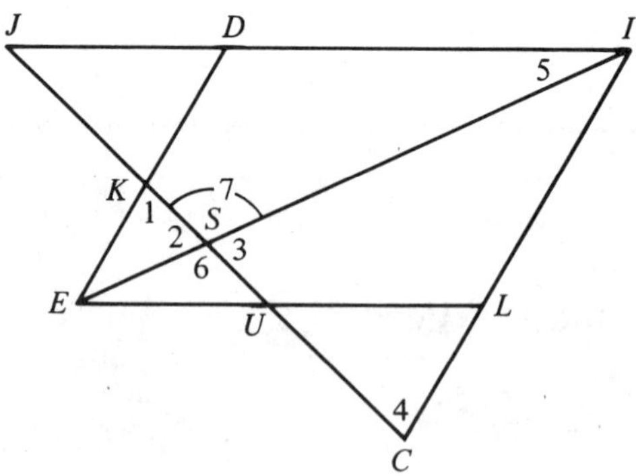

In exercises 31–40 use Theorems 103–105 and the techniques of Example 4 (Section 9.4) to answer the questions.

31. The ratio of corresponding sides of two similar triangles is 2 : 3. What is the ratio of their (a) corresponding altitudes, (b) corresponding medians, and (c) areas?

32. The ratio of corresponding medians of two similar triangles is 4 : 9. What is the ratio of their (a) areas, (b) corresponding sides, and (c) corresponding angle bisectors?

33. The ratio of the areas of two similar triangles is 16 : 25. What is the ratio of their (a) corresponding sides, (b) corresponding medians, and (c) corresponding altitudes?

34. The ratio of the areas of two similar triangles is 4:9. If the longest side of the smaller triangle measures 16 inches, find the length of the longest side of the larger triangle.

35. The lengths of the sides of a triangle measure 2, 3, and 4 inches. Find the lengths of the sides of a similar triangle whose area is four times as great.

36. The sides of a triangle measure 12, 16, and 20 centimeters. How long are the sides of a similar triangle whose area measures 150 square centimeters? (Hint: These must be what type of triangle?)

37. The sides of $\triangle EJS$ measure $2\frac{3}{4}$, $3\frac{1}{8}$, and $3\frac{9}{16}$ feet, and the sides of $\triangle LAW$ measure $5\frac{1}{2}$, $6\frac{1}{4}$, and $7\frac{1}{8}$ feet. What is the ratio of their (a) corresponding altitudes (shorter to longer) and (b) areas (smaller to larger)?

38. The areas of two similar triangles measure 80 square feet and 125 square feet, respectively. If a side of the larger triangle is 30 feet long, find the length of the corresponding side of the smaller triangle.

39. In acute triangle EJS, $SE = 12$ in, $\overline{EJ} \parallel \overline{KC}$ where $S\text{-}K\text{-}E$ and $S\text{-}C\text{-}J$, and $SK = 4$ in. Find $A(\text{trap } EJCK):A(\triangle KCS)$. (Hint: Use the fact that $\triangle EJS \sim \triangle KCS$ to first find $A[\triangle EJS]:A[\triangle KCS]$.)

40. If in $\triangle DEF$, $\overline{FK}$ bisects $\measuredangle DFE$ where $D\text{-}K\text{-}E$, $DE = 18$ cm, $EF = 15$ cm, and $DF = 12$ cm, find DK and KE.

In exercises 41–44 draw a figure, and write the hypothesis and the conclusion. Mark the figure and write a proof.

41. Theorem 103(c).

42. Theorem 103(b).

43. Theorem 104(a).

44. Theorem 104(d).

45. Use the given figure, hypothesis, and conclusion to prove that the ratio of the perimeters of two similar triangles is the same as the ratio of any two corresponding sides.

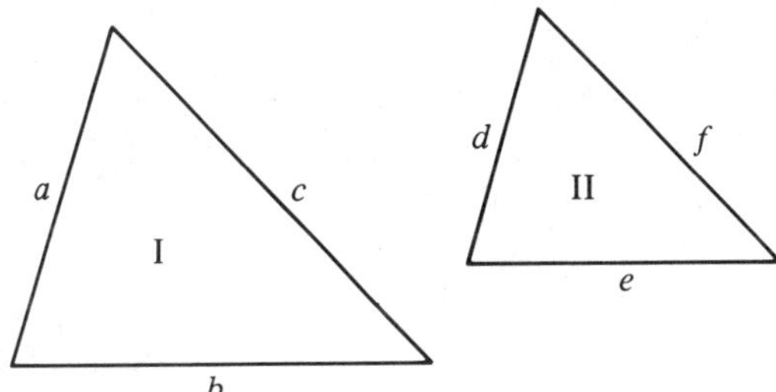

Given
$\triangle I \sim \triangle II$
a, b, c, d, e, and f lengths as shown

To Prove
$$\frac{a+b+c}{d+e+f} = \frac{a}{d}$$

(Hint: Write $\frac{a}{d} = k$ or $a = kd$, etc., and add.)

9.5 CIRCLES, SIMILARITY, AND SECTORS

Any two circles are similar in the sense that they have the same shape. As with similar triangles, there are some very useful proportions that can be written concerning two circles. Figure 9.4 shows $\odot O_1$, $\odot O_2$, and formulas

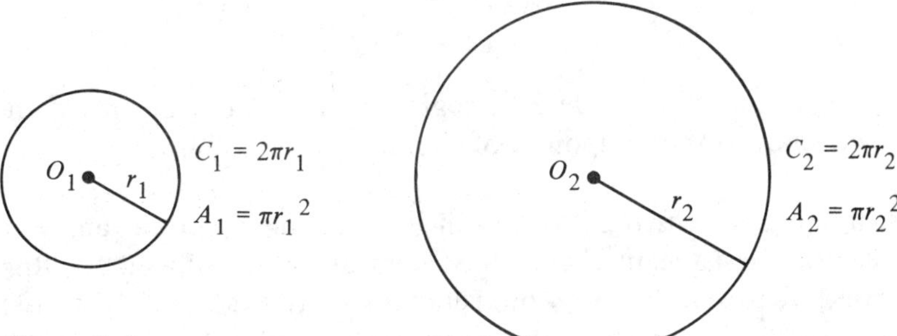

Figure 9.4

for their circumferences and areas. Comparing the circumferences as a ratio we find:

$$\frac{C_1}{C_2} = \frac{2\pi r_1}{2\pi r_2} \quad \text{or} \quad \frac{C_1}{C_2} = \frac{r_1}{r_2}$$

Thus, if $r_1 = 2$ in and $r_2 = 4$ in, $C_1/C_2 = r_1/r_2 = \frac{2}{4} = \frac{1}{2}$, and we see, without computing the circumferences, that C_1 is one-half of C_2 just as r_1 is one-half of r_2.

Next, comparing the areas as a ratio, we find:

$$\frac{A_1}{A_2} = \frac{\pi r_1^2}{\pi r_2^2} \quad \text{or} \quad \frac{A_1}{A_2} = \frac{r_1^2}{r_2^2} = \left(\frac{r_1}{r_2}\right)^2$$

Now, if $r_1 = 2$ in and $r_2 = 4$ in, then $A_1/A_2 = (\frac{2}{4})^2 = (\frac{1}{2})^2 = \frac{1}{4}$, which means that A_1 is *one-fourth* of A_2 although r_1 is *one-half* of r_2. In general, if $r_2 = 2r_1$, then

$$\frac{A_1}{A_2} = \left(\frac{r_1}{r_2}\right)^2 = \left(\frac{r_1}{2r_1}\right)^2 = \left(\frac{1}{2}\right)^2 = \frac{1}{4}$$

The above discussion shows that if the radius of a circle is doubled so is the circumference, whereas the new area is *four* times that of the original. If the radius were tripled, what would be the effect on the circumference? What would it be on the area?

Next, consider a geometric figure determined by an arc and two radii of a circle. This figure can be made familiar by imagining that Figure 9.5 represents two 9-inch pies, the first cut into eight pieces of equal size and the second cut into six of equal size. A hungry person would surely select a piece from the second pie rather than the first because each piece in the second has a larger area than one from the first. This area may be related to the area of the entire pie by means of a ratio. Also, the length of the curved edge (arc) of the piece may be related to the circumference by a ratio. We begin by defining the geometric figure in question.

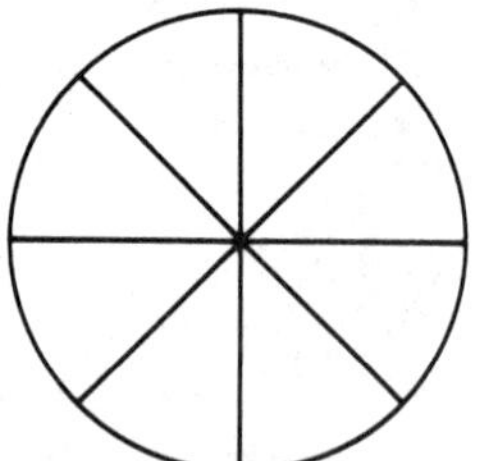
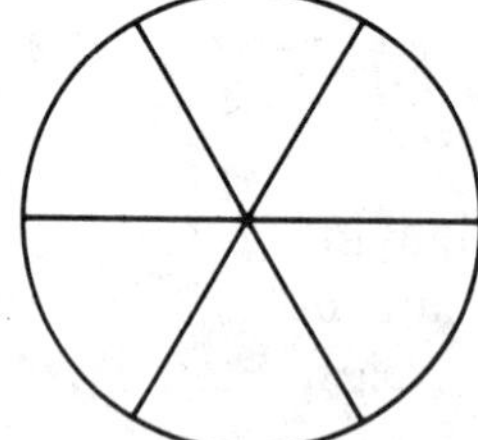

Figure 9.5

Definition 9.4 A *sector* of a circle is a region bounded by an arc of the circle and the two radii to the endpoints of the arc.

In a sector, the angle formed by two radii is of course a central angle of the circle. To cut the first pie in Figure 9.5, central angles of 360° ÷ 8 = 45° should be used. The second pie would have central angles of 360° ÷ 6 = 60°. The next two theorems show that the central angle plays a key role in relating the area and arc length of a sector to the area and circumference of the circle. Instead of formal proofs, brief algebraic arguments are given to justify each theorem.

Theorem 106 The area of a sector of radius r whose angle has measure $a°$ is $\frac{a}{360} \cdot \pi r^2$ ($A_s = \frac{a}{360} \cdot \pi r^2$).

To justify this, assume that $\frac{A_s}{A} = \frac{a}{360}$, where A is the area of the circle. We may then write $A_s = \frac{a}{360} \cdot \pi r^2$.

Theorem 107 The length of the arc of a sector of radius r whose angle has measure $a°$ is $\frac{a}{360} \cdot 2\pi r$ ($L = \frac{a}{360} \cdot 2\pi r$).

Assuming that $\frac{L}{C} = \frac{a}{360}$ where C is the circumference of the circle, then $L = \frac{a}{360} \cdot 2\pi r$.

EXAMPLE 1

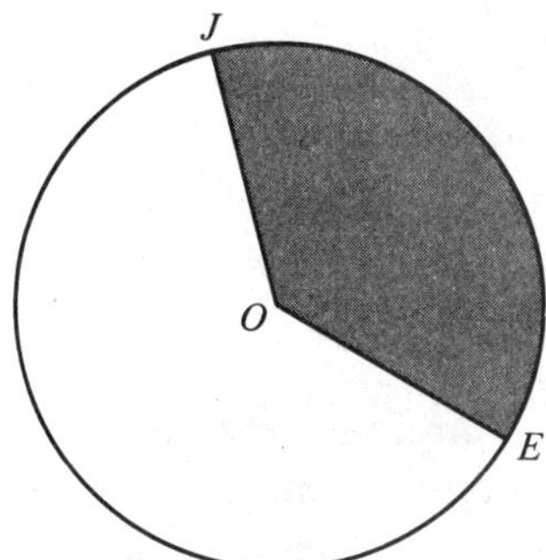

Given

$\odot O$

$\angle JOE = 135°$

$OJ = 8$ in

Find

(a) area of $\odot O$

(b) area of shaded sector

(c) circumference of $\odot O$

(d) $\overset{\frown}{JE}°$

(e) $L(\overset{\frown}{JE})$

Leave answers (a), (b), (c), and (e) in terms of π.

Answers

(a) $A = \pi r^2$

$A = \pi \cdot 8^2$

$A = 64\pi$ sq in

(b) $A_s = \dfrac{a}{360} \cdot \pi r^2$

$A = \dfrac{135}{360} \cdot \pi \cdot 64$

$A = 24\pi$ sq in

(c) $C = 2\pi r$

$C = 2 \cdot \pi \cdot 8$

$C = 16\pi$ in

(d) $\overset{\frown}{JE}° = \angle JOE$

$\overset{\frown}{JE}° = 135°$

(e) $L = \dfrac{a}{360} \cdot 2\pi r$

$L(\overset{\frown}{JE}) = \dfrac{135}{360} \cdot 16\pi$

$L(\overset{\frown}{JE}) = 6\pi$ in

Note in Example 1 that $\frac{a}{360} = \frac{135}{360} = \frac{3}{8}$. Thus, A_s is $\frac{3}{8}$ of the circle's area and $L(\overset{\frown}{JE})$ is $\frac{3}{8}$ of the circle's circumference.

Segments of chords, tangents, and secants of circles have some interesting properties that are consequences of the theory of similar triangles. These involve multiplications of lengths of line segments and are proved using the methods of Section 9.4.

Theorem 108 If two chords intersect in a circle, the product of the lengths of the segments of one chord is equal to the product of the lengths of the segments of the other chord (prods segs 2 chs =).

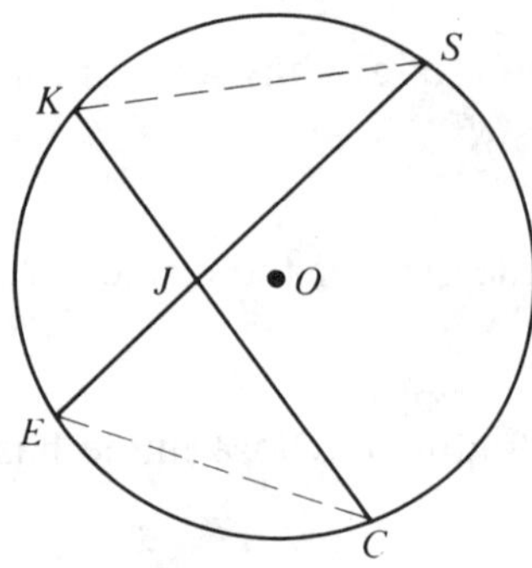

Given
⊙O
chs $\overline{KC}$, $\overline{ES}$ inters at J

To Prove
$EJ \cdot JS = KJ \cdot JC$

Statement	*Reason*
1. ⊙O, chs $\overline{KC}$ and $\overline{ES}$ inters at J	1. given
2. Draw $\overline{KS}$ and $\overline{EC}$.	2. 2 pts determ line
3. $\measuredangle E \cong \measuredangle K$, $\measuredangle C \cong \measuredangle S$	3. inscr $\measuredangle$s interc same ⌒ are ≅
4. $\triangle EJC \sim \triangle KJS$	4. aa ≅ aa
5. $\frac{EJ}{KJ} = \frac{JC}{JS}$	5. csstp
6. $\therefore EJ \cdot JS = KJ \cdot JC$	6. prod extrms = prod mns

In Theorem 109 the term *secant segment* is used. In the figure for the theorem, $\overline{MS}$ and $\overline{ES}$ are secant segments.

Theorem 109 If two secant segments are drawn to a circle from an external point, then the product of the lengths of one secant segment, and its external part is equal to the product of the lengths of the other secant segment and its external part (prods 2 secs and segs =).

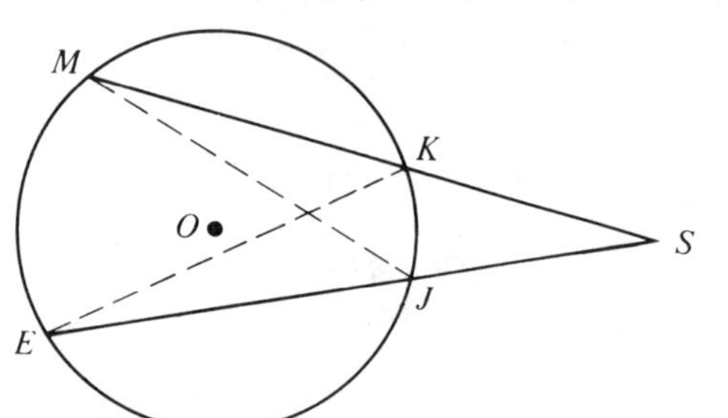

Given
⊙O
sec segs $\overline{MS}$ and $\overline{ES}$

To Prove
$MS \cdot KS = ES \cdot JS$

Statement	*Reason*
1. ⊙ O, sec segs $\overline{MS}$ and $\overline{ES}$	1. given
2. Draw $\overline{EK}$ and $\overline{MJ}$.	2. 2 pts determ line
3. $\measuredangle M \cong \measuredangle E$	3. inscr $\measuredangle$s interc same ⌒ are ≅
4. $\measuredangle S \cong \measuredangle S$	4. refl ≅
5. $\triangle MJS \sim \triangle EKS$	5. aa ≅ aa
6. $\frac{MS}{ES} = \frac{JS}{KS}$	6. csstp
7. $\therefore MS \cdot KS = ES \cdot JS$	7. prod extrms = prod mns

These two theorems are used in Examples 2 and 3.

EXAMPLE 2

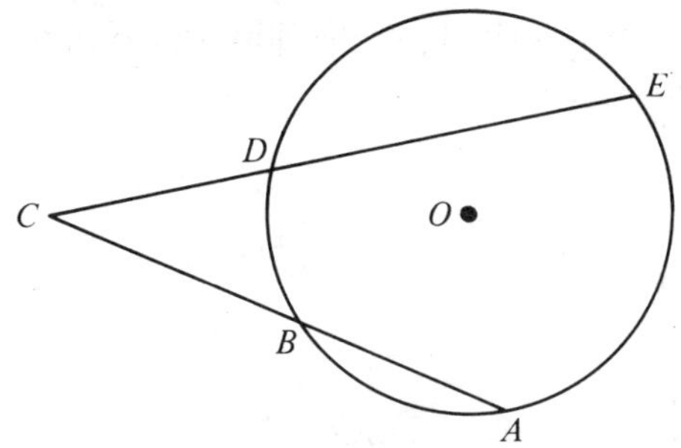

Given
$\odot O$
$EC = 12$ in
$ED = 7$ in
$BC = 6$ in

Find
AB

Answer
$DC = EC - ED = 5$ in
$AC \cdot BC = EC \cdot DC$ (prods 2 secs and segs =)
$AC \cdot 6 = 12 \cdot 5$
$AC = \frac{60}{6} = 10$ in
$AB = AC - BC = 4$ in

EXAMPLE 3

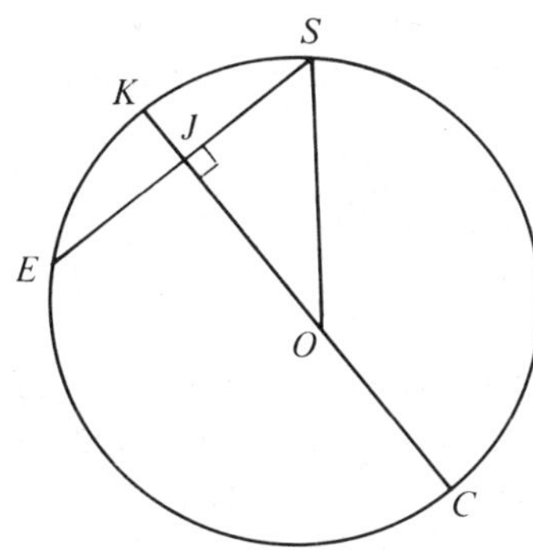

Given
$\odot O$
$\overline{KC} \perp \overline{ES}$
$ES = 18$ cm
$KJ = 3$ cm

Find
OS

Answer
$EJ = JS = \frac{18}{2} = 9$ (sec thru center $\perp$ ch bis ch)
$KJ \cdot JC = EJ \cdot JS$ (prods segs 2 chs =)
$3 \cdot JC = 9 \cdot 9$
$JC = \frac{9 \cdot 9}{3} = 27$
$KC = KJ + JC = 30$
$OS = OC = \frac{1}{2} \cdot KC = 15$ cm

The proof of Theorem 110 is omitted (but see exercise 26, Section 9.4, in which a proof is requested). A figure and the conclusion, however, are shown in Figure 9.6(a). The term *tangent segment* in Theorem 110 refers to $\overline{ST}$ in the figure.

Theorem 110 If a tangent segment and a secant segment are drawn to a circle from an external point, then the length of the tangent segment is the mean proportional between the lengths of the secant segment and its external part (tan seg mn propor sec segs).

The similarity between Theorems 110 and 109 can be seen in Figure 9.6(b) by replacing both *ES* and *JS* by *TS*.

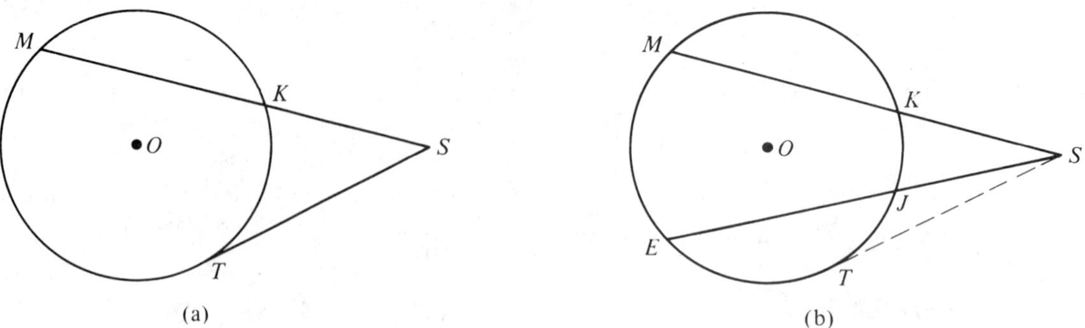

Figure 9.6 (a) Theorem 110; $MS/TS = TS/KS$ or $MS \cdot KS = TS \cdot TS$. (b) Theorem 109; $MS \cdot KS = ES \cdot JS$.

Theorem 110 is used below in a geometric construction that is of great historical interest. A line segment is said to be divided by a point into *extreme and mean ratio* when the length of the longer part is the mean proportional between the entire length and the length of the shorter part. This division is called the "Golden Section" or the "Divine Proportion," and a rectangle whose length and width are the parts of a line segment so divided is called a "Golden Rectangle" (Figure 9.7).

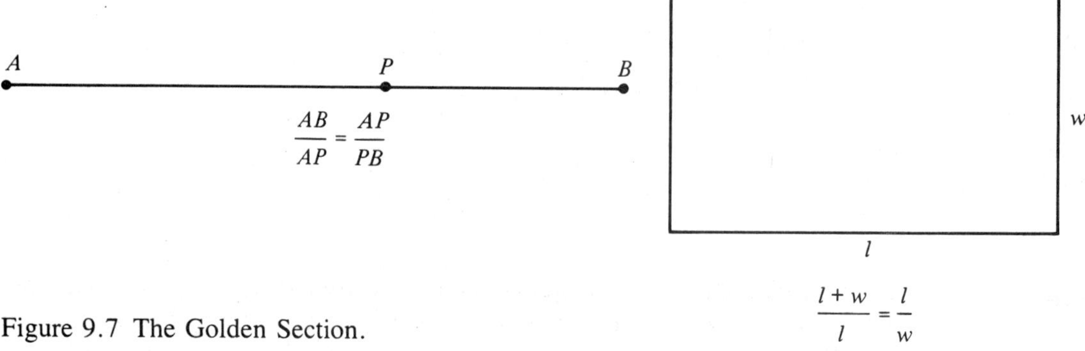

Figure 9.7 The Golden Section.

The ratio in the Golden Section is called the *Golden Ratio*. It is an irrational number (see exercise 60 of this section) but $\frac{5}{8}$ is a close approximation. The classical Greeks greatly admired this ratio, and it was widely used in their architecture, sculpture, pottery, and paintings. They considered the Golden Rectangle to be the rectangle most pleasing to the eye. The Golden Ratio can also be found in the work of many later artists, in particular, the Italian painters Leonardo da Vinci (1452–1519) and Raphael (1483–1520). But perhaps most remarkable, the Golden Ratio can be found in nature. It appears in the spiral patterns of pine cones, sunflower seed heads, and the shells of the chambered nautilus.

Construction 15 To divide a line segment in extreme and mean ratio.

Given

$\overline{AB}$

To Construct

point P on $\overline{AB}$ such that $\frac{AB}{AP} = \frac{AP}{PB}$

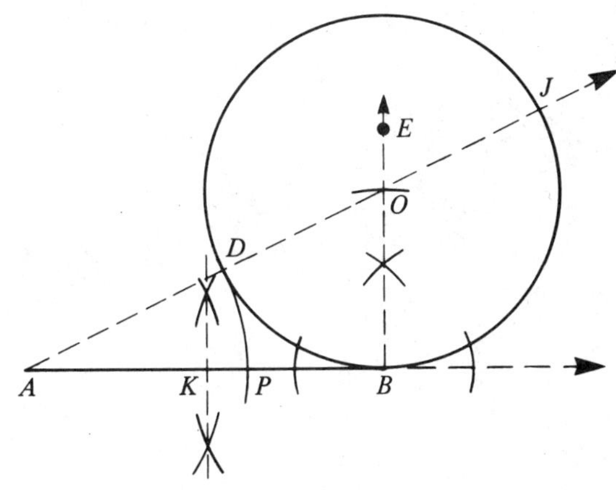

Steps

1. Construct $\overrightarrow{BE} \perp \overline{AB}$ at B (Construction 5).
2. Construct the midpoint K of $\overline{AB}$ (Construction 1).
3. Construct point O on $\overrightarrow{BE}$ such that $\overline{BO} \cong \overline{BK}$ (Construction 2).
4. Draw $\odot O$ with radius OB.
5. Draw $\overrightarrow{AO}$ intersecting $\odot O$ at D.
6. With center A and radius AD, draw an arc intersecting $\overline{AB}$ at the required point P.

Construction 15 may be informally proved as follows. Note that $\overline{AB}$ is tangent to $\odot O$ and that $\overrightarrow{AO}$ is extended to intersect $\odot O$ at J.

$\frac{AJ}{AB} = \frac{AB}{AD}$ (tan seg mn propor sec segs)

$\frac{AJ - AB}{AB} = \frac{AB - AD}{AD}$ (subt prop propor)

$AB = DJ$ and $AD = AP$ (by construction)

$\frac{AJ - DJ}{AB} = \frac{AB - AP}{AD}$ (subst)

$\frac{AD}{AB} = \frac{PB}{AD}$ (whole = sum parts)

$\frac{AP}{AB} = \frac{PB}{AP}$ (subst)

$\therefore \frac{AB}{AP} = \frac{AP}{PB}$ (invert ratios)

The construction of the Golden Section is used in other geometric constructions including that for a regular pentagon. The early Greek geometers knew of this construction for it appears in Euclid's *Elements;* the Golden Ratio may be found in the five-pointed star symbol of the Society of Pythagoreans.

EXERCISES FOR 9.5

In exercises 1–20 answer true or false.

1. Any two circles are similar.
2. If the radius of a circle is doubled, then its area is also doubled.
3. A sector of a circle is the same as the central angle of the circle.
4. The area of a sector is given by $\frac{a}{360} \cdot \pi r^2$, where r is the radius and $a°$ is the measure of its angle.
5. If the area of a sector of a circle is twice that of another sector in the same circle, then the central angle of the first is twice that of the second.
6. If two sectors of a circle have central angles of 45° and 120°, then the ratio of their areas is 3:8.
7. Given that two polygons are similar if and only if their corresponding angles are congruent and corresponding sides are proportional, then any two rectangles are similar.
8. Any two rhombuses are similar.
9. Any two squares are similar.
10. If an angle of one rhombus is congruent to an angle of a second rhombus, then the rhombuses are similar.

11. If the circumference of a circle is quadrupled, then the radius is doubled.
12. If a wall clock has a 15-inch minute hand, then the tip of the hand travels 4π inches in 8 minutes.
13. If a 60° arc of a circle has a 2-inch chord, then the radius of the circle is 4 inches long.
14. If two quadrilaterals are similar and one is a rectangle, then the other is also.
15. The ratio of the circumference of a circle to its diameter is the same for all circles.
16. If a 60° arc of a circle has a 2-inch chord, then the area of its sector is $\frac{2}{3}\pi$ square inches.
17. If two quadrilaterals are similar and the diagonals of the first are perpendicular to each other, then the diagonals of the second are also perpendicular.
18. If two chords, $\overline{AB}$ and $\overline{CD}$, of a circle intersect at E, then $AE \cdot EB = CE \cdot ED$.
19. If the radius of a circle is tripled, then the area of the circle is also tripled.
20. If two secant segments, $\overline{ES}$ and $\overline{AS}$, intersect a circle at J and B, then $EJ \cdot JS = AB \cdot BS$.

In exercises 21–41 find the unknown measure x.

21.

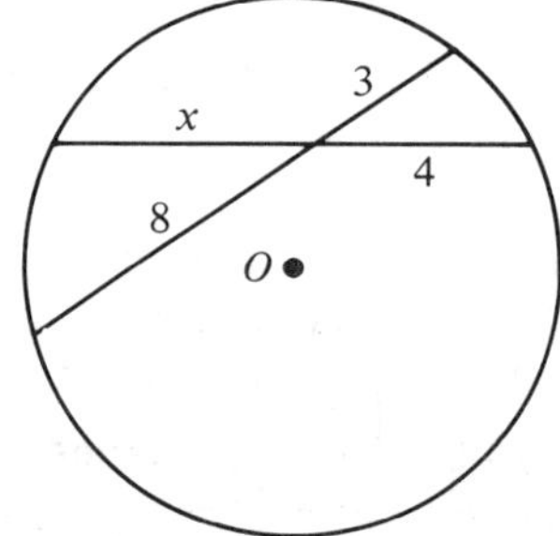

22.

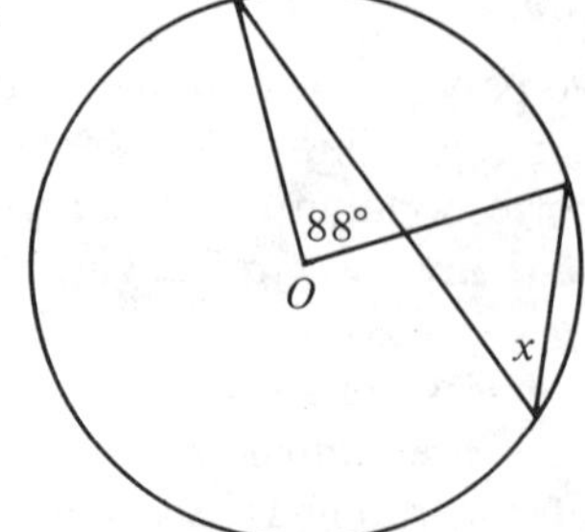

23.

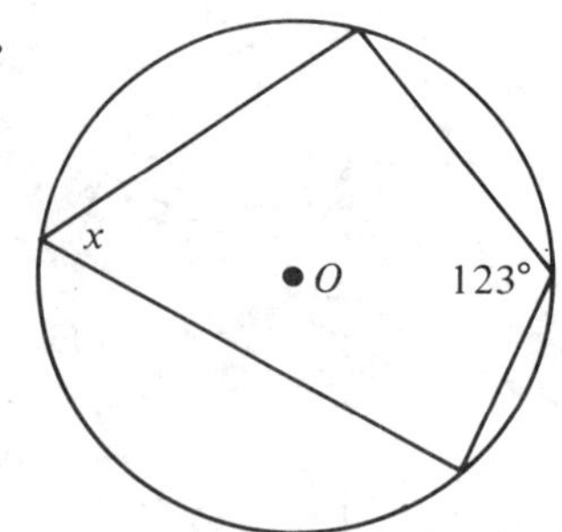

24.

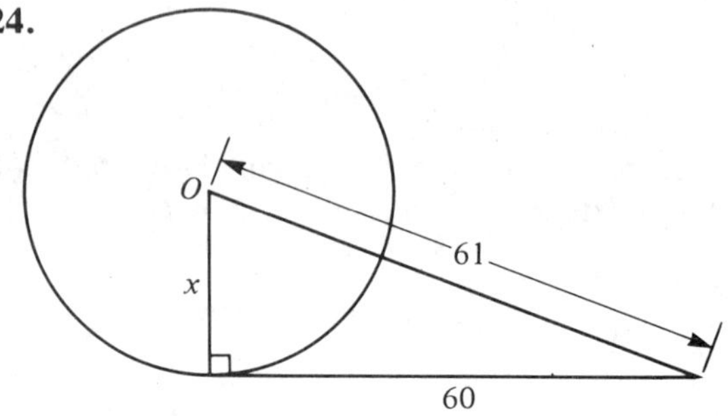

25.

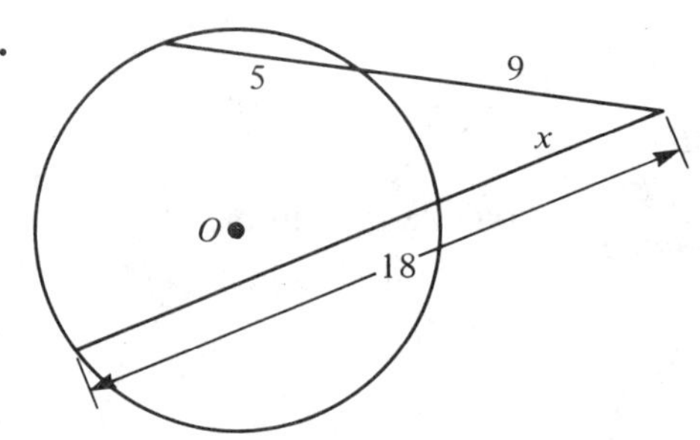

26.

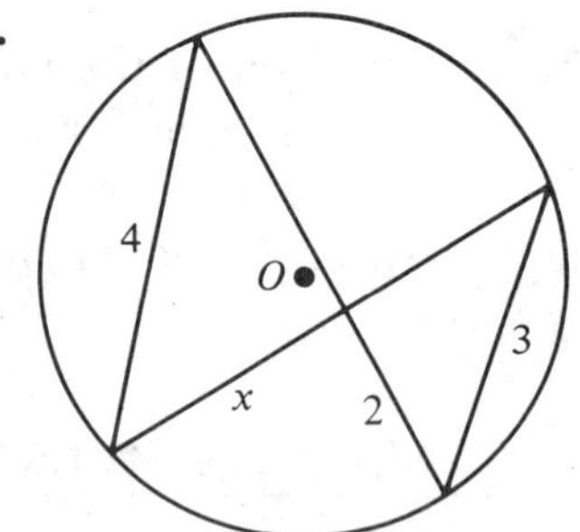

27.

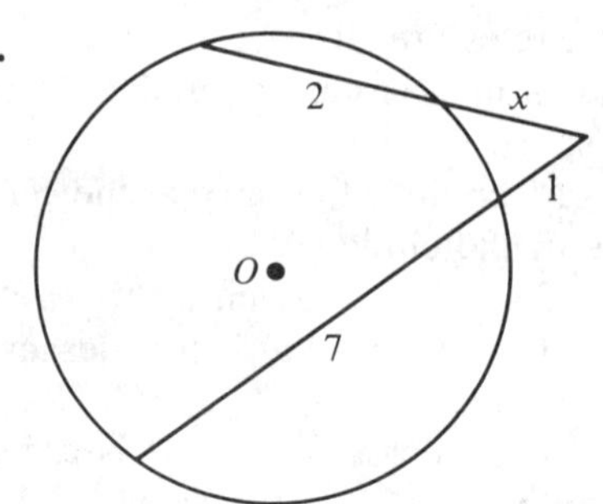

28.

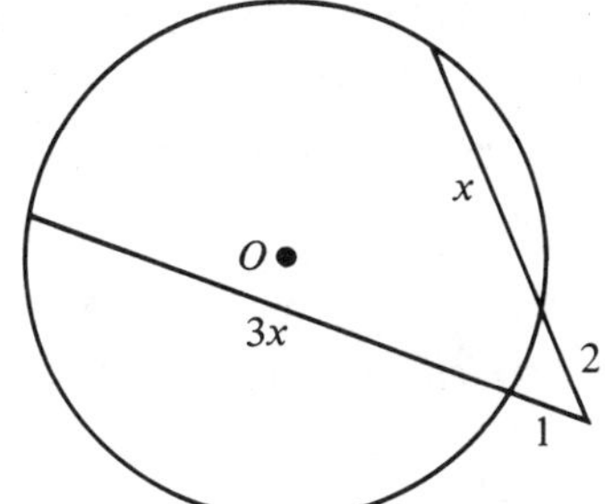

29.

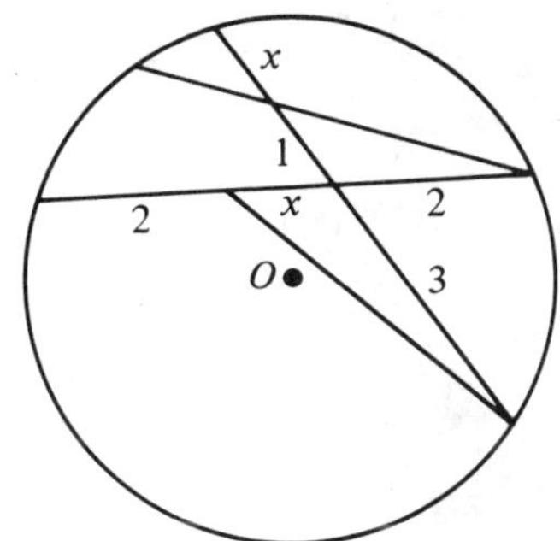

30.

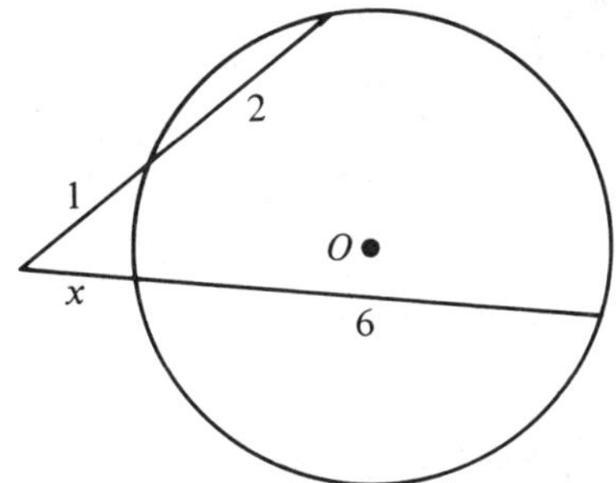

31.

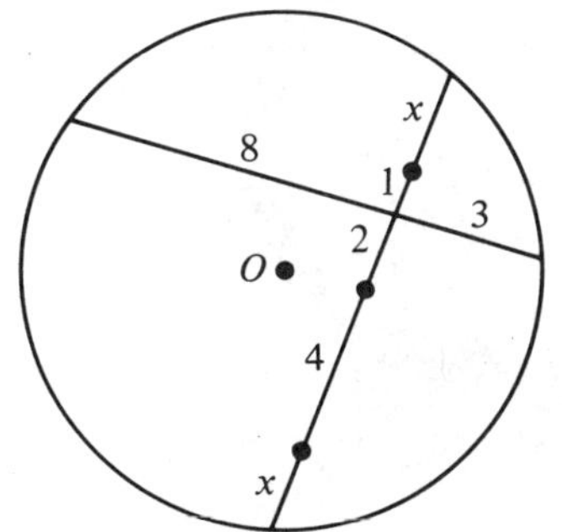

32.

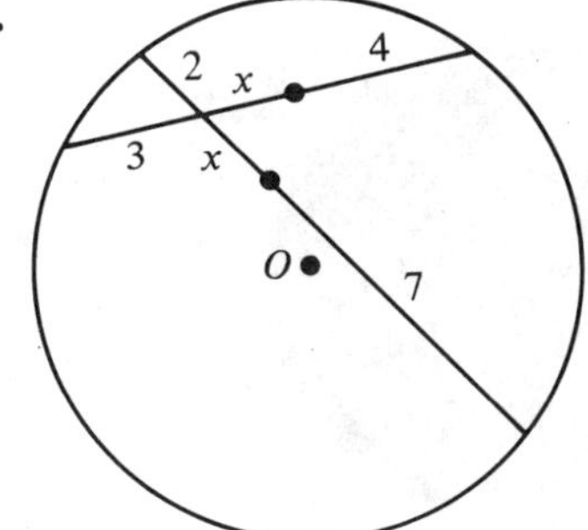

33.

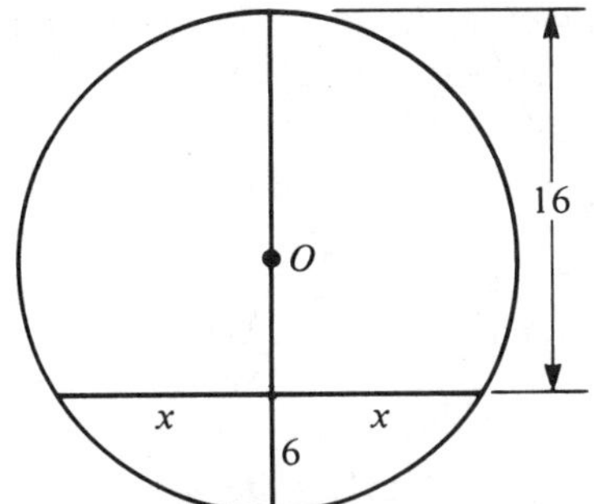

34.

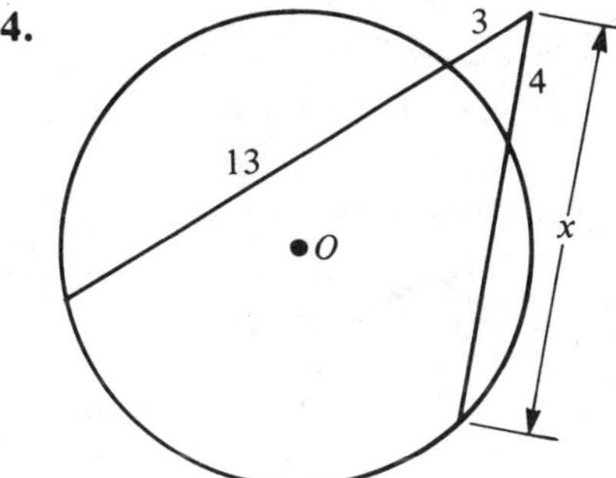

35.

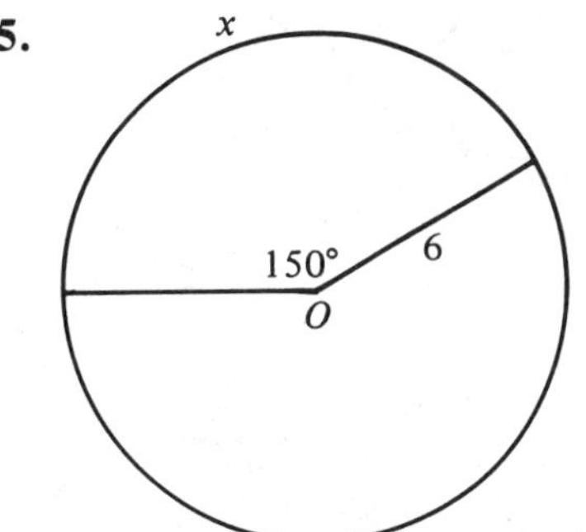

36.

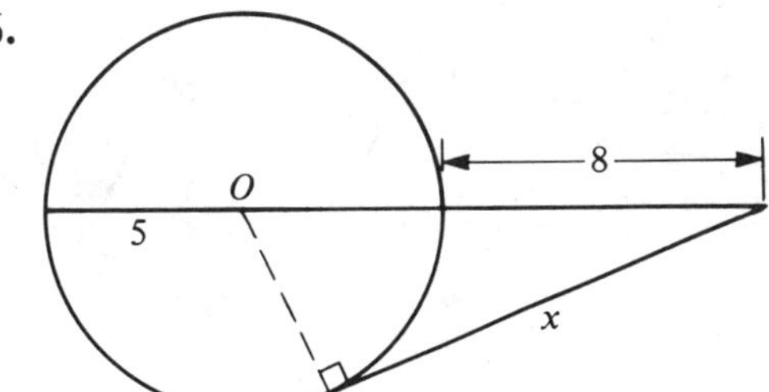

37.

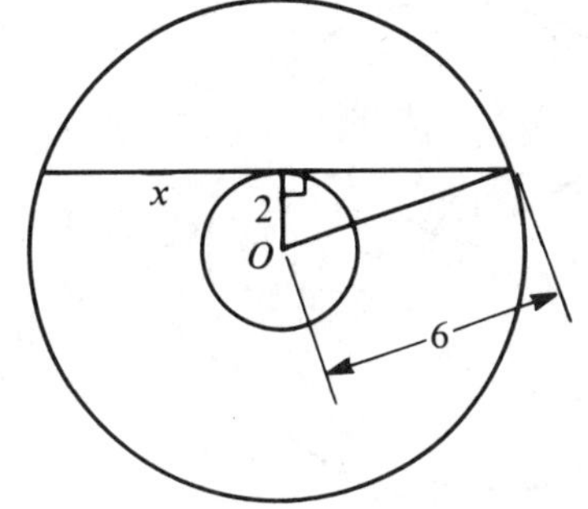

38.

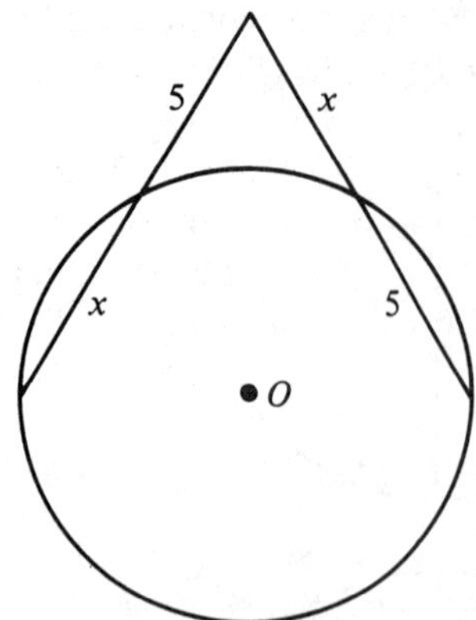

In exercises 42–50 find the areas of the shaded regions.

42.

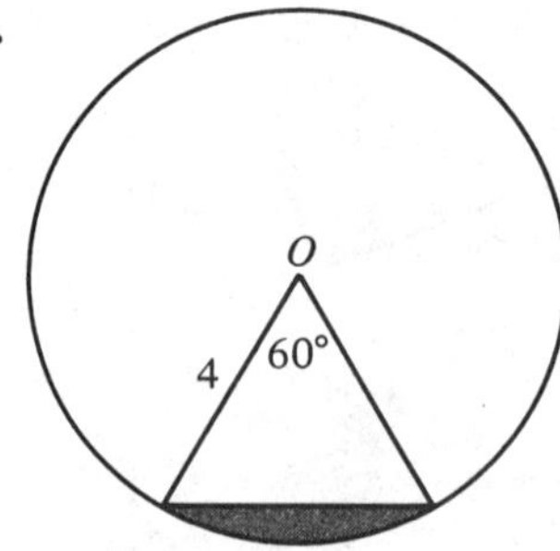

39.

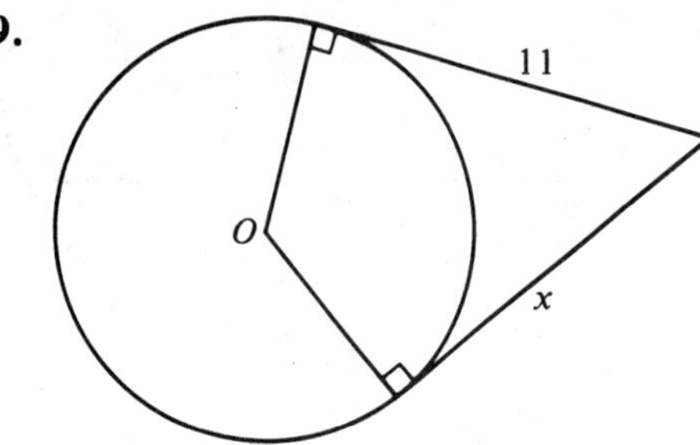

43.

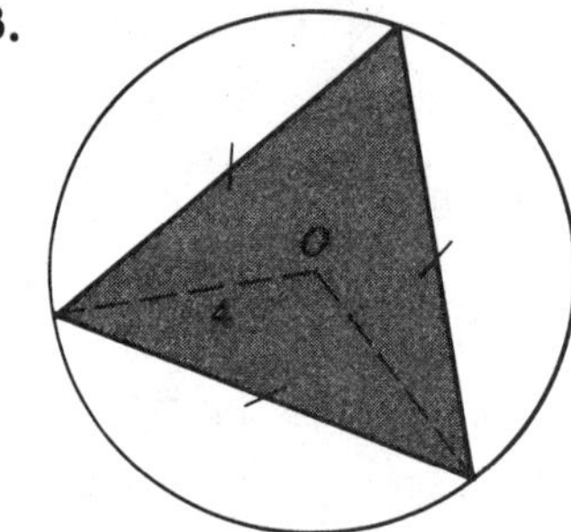

40.

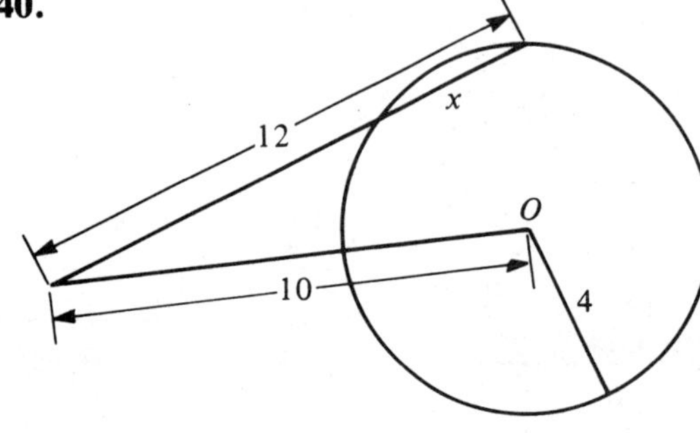

44.

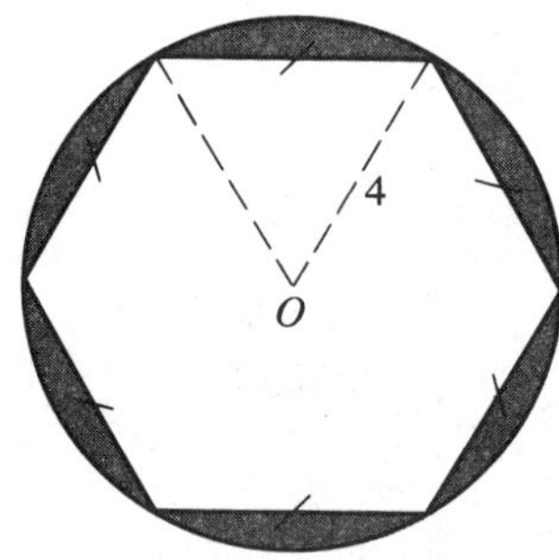

41.

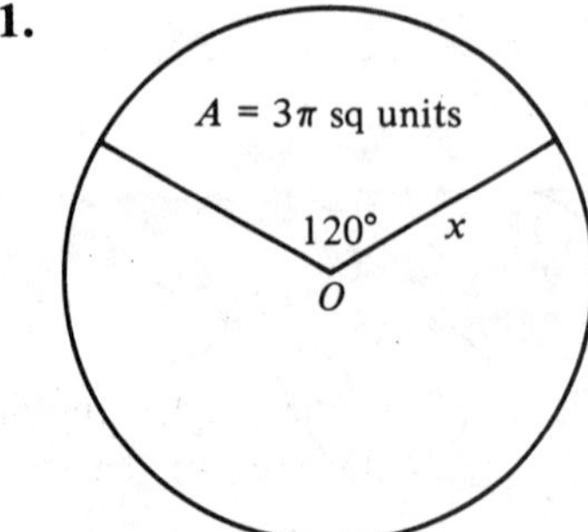

45.

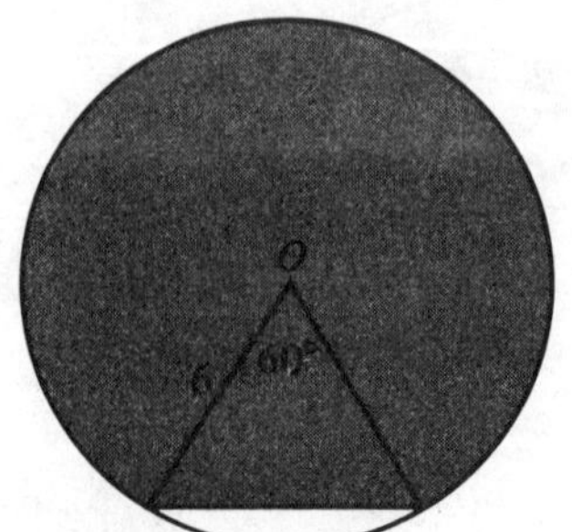

46.

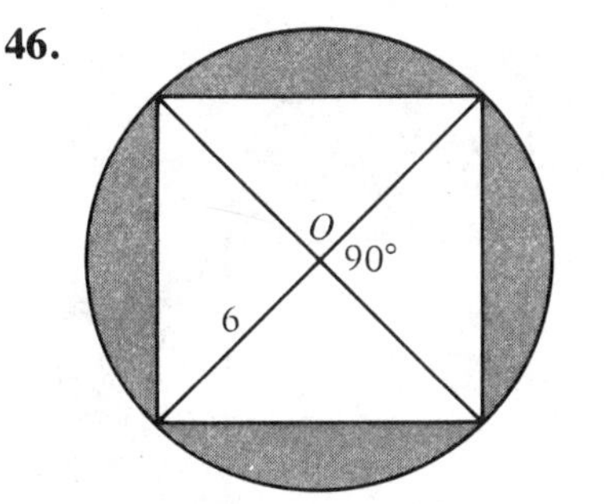

47.

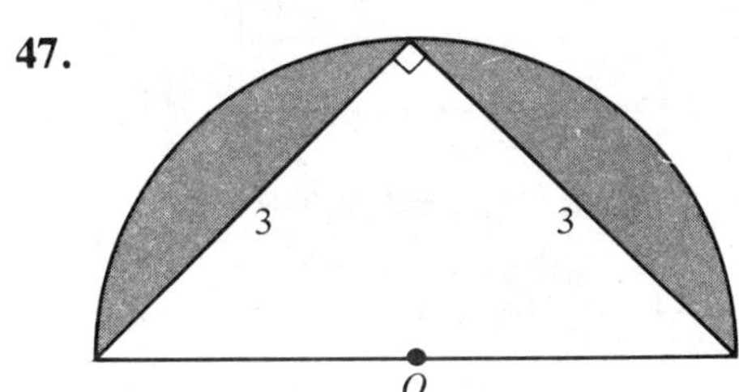

48.

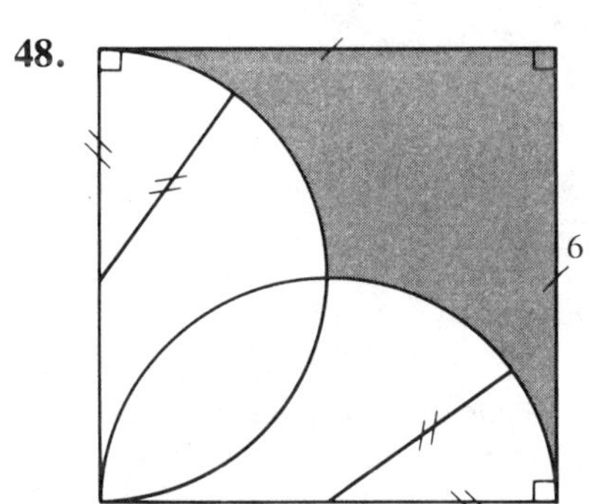

49.

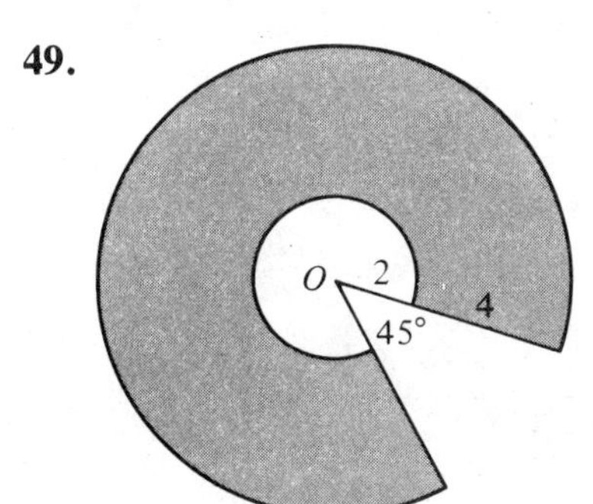

50.

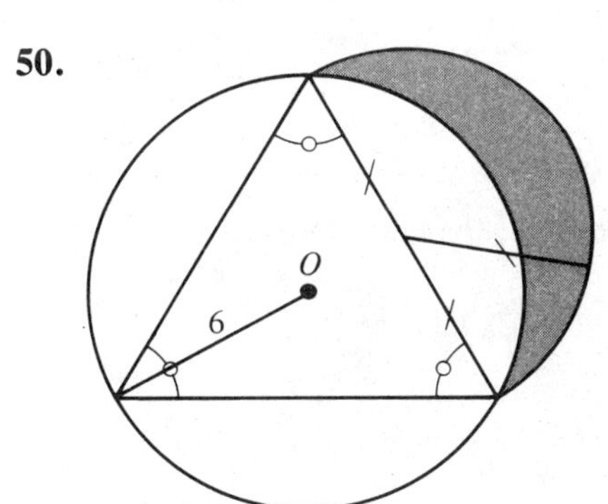

In exercises 51–55 the crescents (shaded areas) in Figure 9.8 are called the *Lunes of Hippocrates* after the early Greek geometer and physician Hippocrates (460–377 B.C.). These curious figures and the problem of finding their areas likely grew out of attempts to "square the circle" (see Historical Note, Chapter 8).

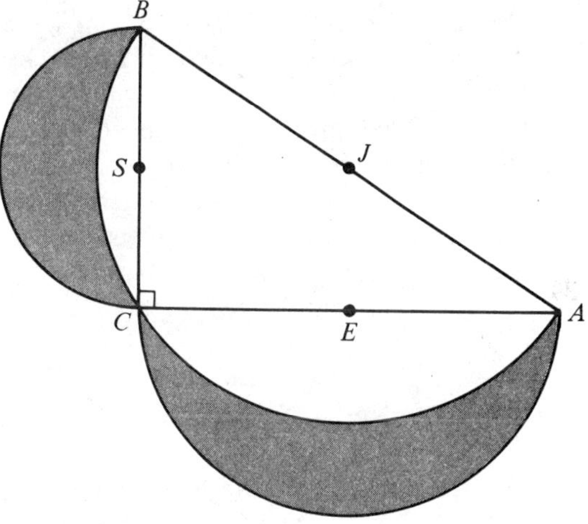

Figure 9.8

Given
rt $\triangle ABC$
E, J, S midpts of sides and centers of semicircles

51. *Given*
$BC = 5$
$CA = 12$

Find
area of shaded regions

52. *Given*
$BC = 8$
$BA = 17$

Find
area of shaded regions

53. *Given*
$BA = c$
$BC = a$
$CA = b$

Find
area of shaded regions

54. Show that the area of the shaded regions (Figure 9.8) equals the area of the triangle.

55. *Given*
sq *ABCD* inscr in ⊙*O*
sides diams of semicircles
$AB = 9$ in

(a) Find the area of the shaded regions.
(b) Compare (a) to the area of the square.

(The results in 54 and 55(b) were historically the first demonstrations that figures bounded by straight lines can have the same areas as figures bounded by curves. Hippocrates had "squared" the lune, and this probably convinced geometers that the circle could also be squared. At least he eliminated the argument that it was impossible because a circle is curved, and so the search, doomed as it was to failure, continued for centuries.)

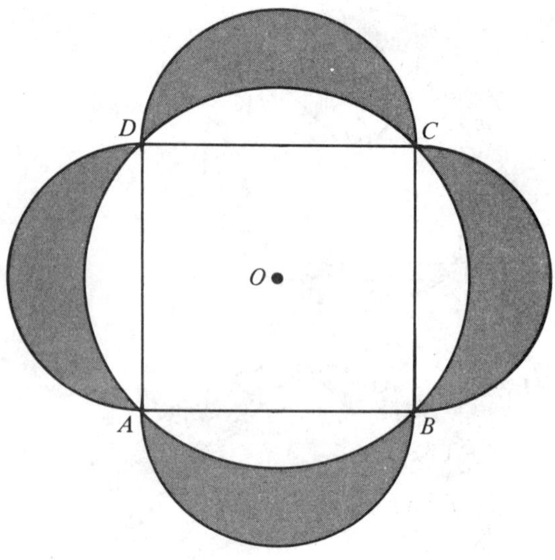

In exercises 56–59 do the constructions using only a compass and straightedge.

56. Construct a circle whose circumference is twice that of a given circle. (Hint: Consider the radii.)

57. Construct a circle whose circumference is one-third that of a given circle.

58. Construct a circle whose circumference is equal to the sum of the circumferences of two given circles.

59. Construct a circle whose area is equal to twice the area of a given circle. (Hint: Compare radii and use the Pythagorean Theorem to construct the new radius.)

60. Supply the missing reasons in the following derivation that shows that the Golden Ratio is $\frac{\sqrt{5}-1}{2}$.

The Golden Rectangle in which $\frac{w}{l} = \frac{\sqrt{5}-1}{2} \approx 0.618 \approx \frac{5}{8}$.

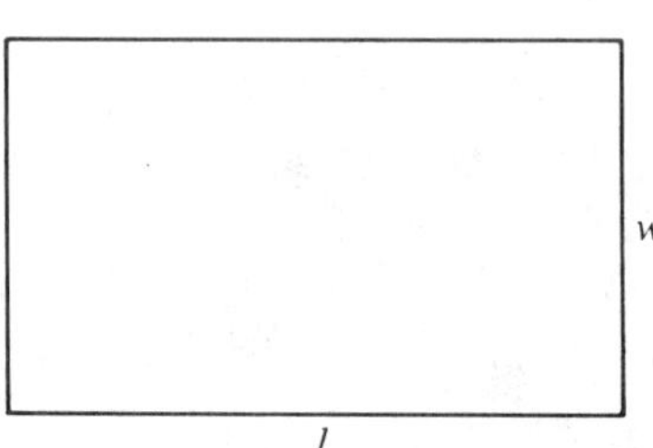

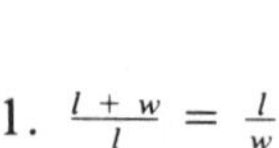

1. $\frac{l+w}{l} = \frac{l}{w}$	1. given
2. $(l+w)\cdot w = l \cdot l$	2. ?
3. $w^2 + lw = l^2$	3. ?
4. $w^2 + lw + \frac{1}{4}l^2 = l^2 + \frac{1}{4}l^2$	4. ?
5. $(w + \frac{1}{2}l)^2 = \frac{5}{4}l^2$	5. ?
6. $w + \frac{1}{2}l = \frac{\sqrt{5}}{2}l$	6. if $a = b$, then $\sqrt{a} = \sqrt{b}$
7. $w = \frac{\sqrt{5}}{2}l - \frac{1}{2}l$	7. ?
8. $w = (\frac{\sqrt{5}}{2} - \frac{1}{2})l$	8. ?
9. $\therefore \frac{w}{l} = \frac{\sqrt{5}-1}{2}$	9. ?

9.6
APPLICATIONS

Similar figures, especially triangles, have many important applications. The same is true for the Pythagorean Theorem. For example, both are basic to the development of trigonometry and its many practical uses. This section presents some problems that can be solved by using similar triangles and proportions or by using the Pythagorean Theorem. These problems are of two types: arithmetic and algebraic. In the arithmetic cases we are interested in finding a *number* such as the length of a line segment. Examples 1–3 are of this type. Note that the format used includes drawing a figure, labeling it, writing the equation to be used, and then solving it.

EXAMPLE 1 A girl casts a shadow that is 12 feet long at the same time that a telephone pole casts a shadow 224 feet long. If the girl is 5 feet 6 inches tall, what is the height of the telephone pole?

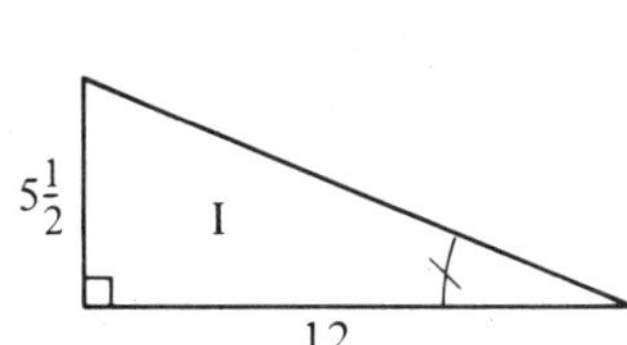

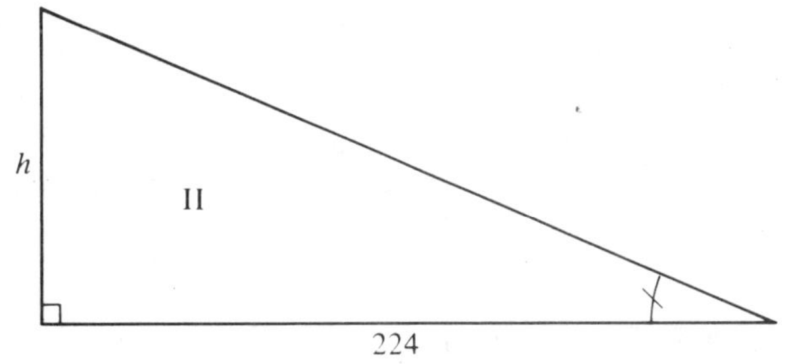

Answer

$\triangle I \sim \triangle II$ (aa ≅ aa)

$$\frac{h}{5\frac{1}{2}} = \frac{224}{12}$$

$$h = \frac{11}{2} \cdot \frac{224}{12}$$

$$h = \frac{308}{3} = 102\tfrac{2}{3} = 102 \text{ ft } 8 \text{ in}$$

EXAMPLE 2 If the top of a 17-foot ladder touches a house so that its base is 8 feet from the wall, how high on the wall does it reach?

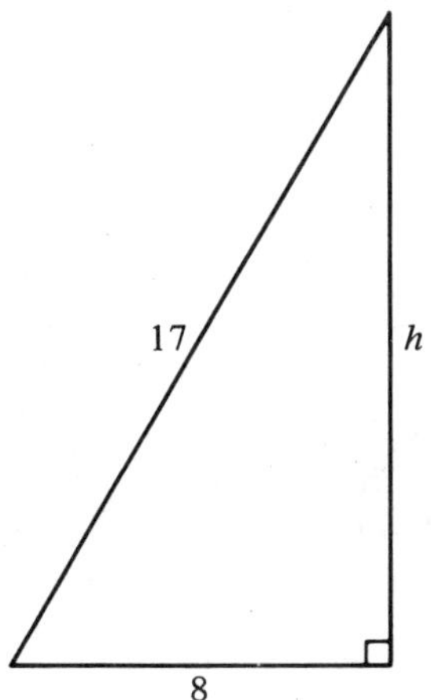

Answer

$a^2 + b^2 = c^2$ (Pythagorean Theorem)

$$h^2 + 8^2 = 17^2$$

$$h^2 = 289 - 64$$

$$h^2 = 225$$

$$h = 15 \text{ ft}$$

EXAMPLE 3 Find the distance across the canal using the information on the figure.

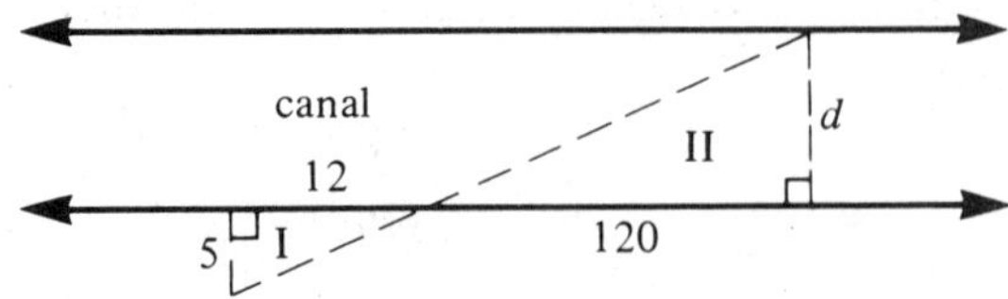

Answer

$\triangle II \sim \triangle I$ (aa $\cong$ aa)

$$\frac{d}{5} = \frac{120}{12}$$

$$d = 10 \cdot 5 = 50 \text{ ft}$$

Examples 1–3 demonstrate some techniques for *indirect measurement*. The length desired is not actually measured; rather it is calculated using an appropriate equation into which more accessible measurements are substituted. Note that a geometric figure is drawn to represent the physical situation and that properties of the figure are then used to obtain the result.

Examples 4 and 5 are algebraic problems. Here we are not interested in calculating a measurement, but rather we want an equation *relating* two measurements. These measurements are unknown and indeed are subject to change, but the equation found must be true at all times.

EXAMPLE 4 A man 6 feet tall is walking in a straight line away from a 15-foot lamppost. Find an equation relating the height of the lamppost, the height of the man, the length of his shadow, and the distance from the head-end of his shadow to the base of the lamppost.

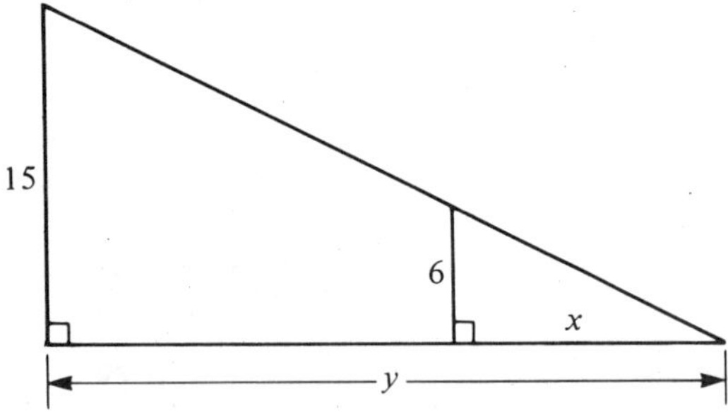

Answer

Since the two triangles are similar,

$$\frac{y}{x} = \frac{15}{6} \quad \text{or} \quad y = \frac{5}{2}x$$

It is interesting to note in Example 4 that if the man's rate of walking is known, it is possible to find the rate at which the head-end of his shadow is moving by using mathematics studied in calculus and the equation derived above.

EXAMPLE 5 An airplane, flying at an altitude of 1200 feet, is chasing a helicopter flying at an altitude of 1000 feet. Find an equation relating the vertical distance between them, the horizontal distance between them, and the line-of-sight distance between them.

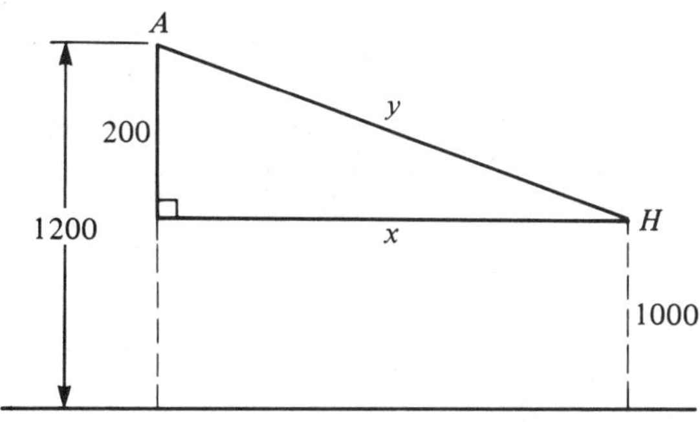

Answer

$$c^2 = a^2 + b^2 \quad \text{(Pythagorean Theorem)}$$
$$y^2 = x^2 + 200^2$$
or $$y = \sqrt{x^2 + 40{,}000}$$

If the speeds of the two aircraft in Example 5 are known, it is possible to calculate their closing speed, that is, the rate at which y is decreasing, by using calculus and the equation derived above.

EXERCISES FOR 9.6

In exercises 1–14 use the fact that two polygons are similar if their corresponding angles are congruent and their corresponding sides are proportional. (a) Are the indicated pairs of polygons similar? (b) State why they are similar or give an example showing why they are not similar.

1. any two congruent triangles
2. any two isosceles triangles
3. any two squares
4. any two rhombuses
5. any two rectangles
6. any two isosceles triangles whose vertex angles are congruent
7. any rectangle and square
8. any square and rhombus
9. any two equilateral triangles
10. any two right triangles with a pair of acute angles congruent
11. any two right triangles
12. any two pentagons
13. any two regular pentagons
14. any two regular hexagons

In exercises 15–30 find the unknown measure x.

15.

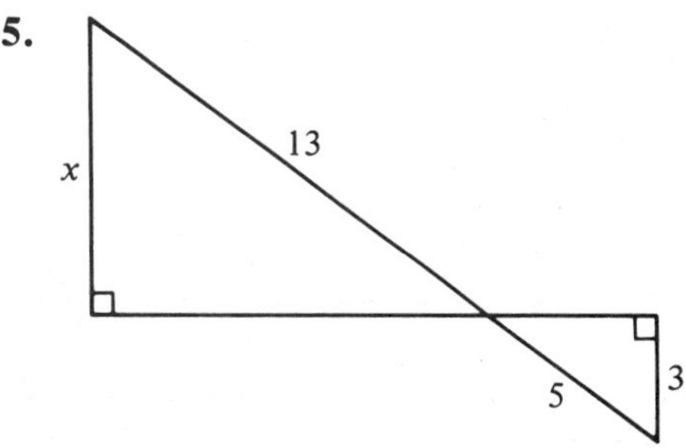

16.

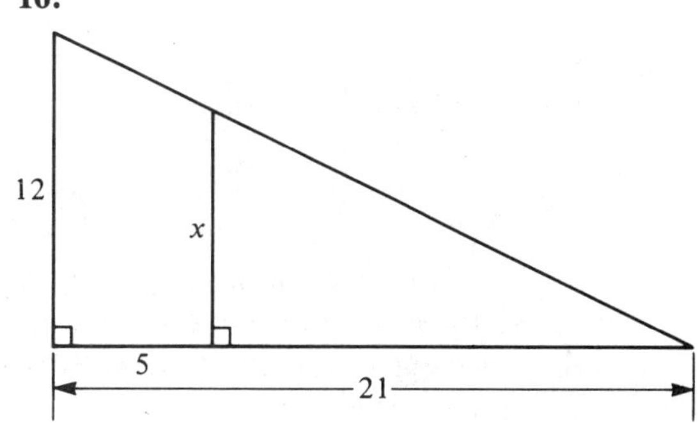

17.

9 x

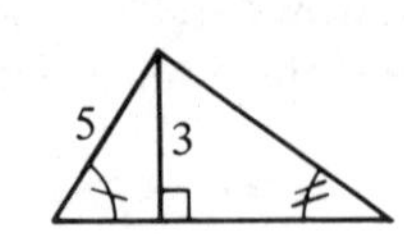

18.

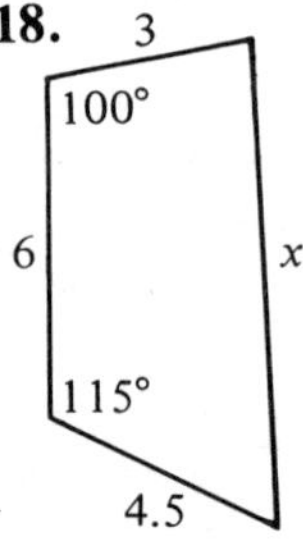

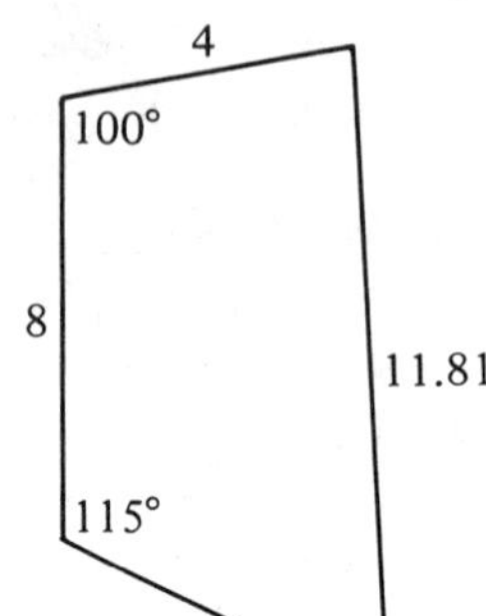

19.

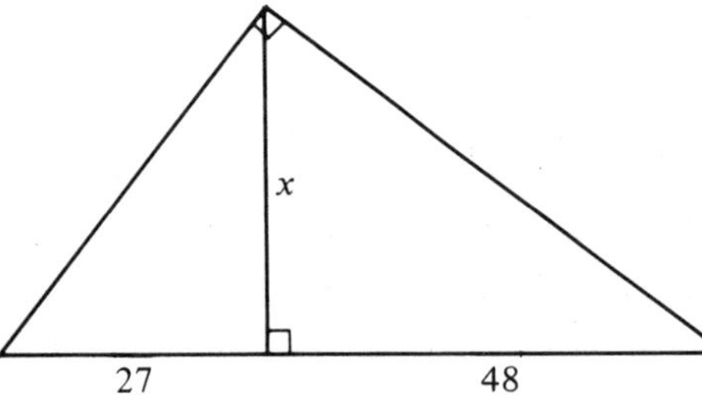

20.

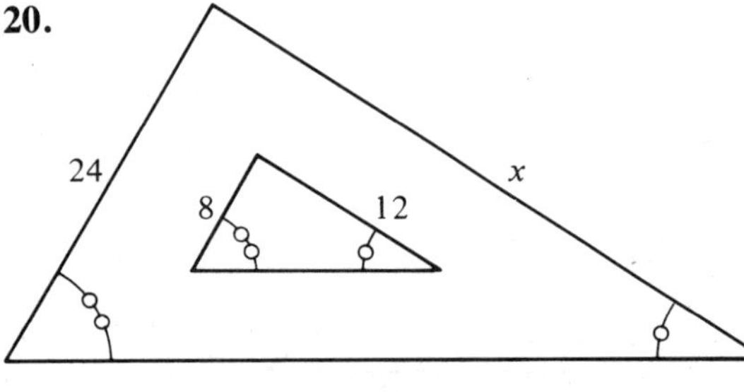

21.

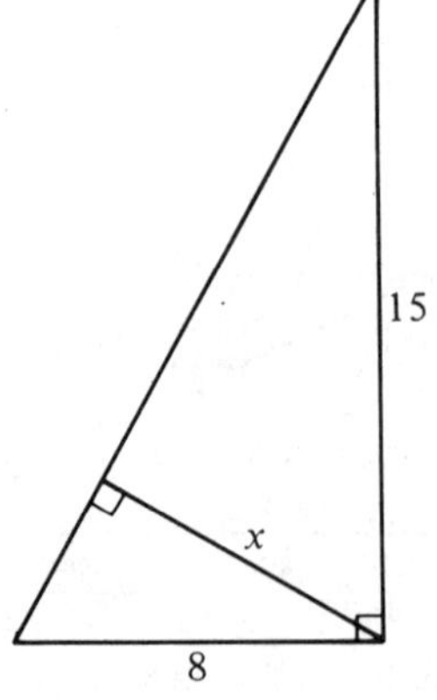

22.

x

12

23.

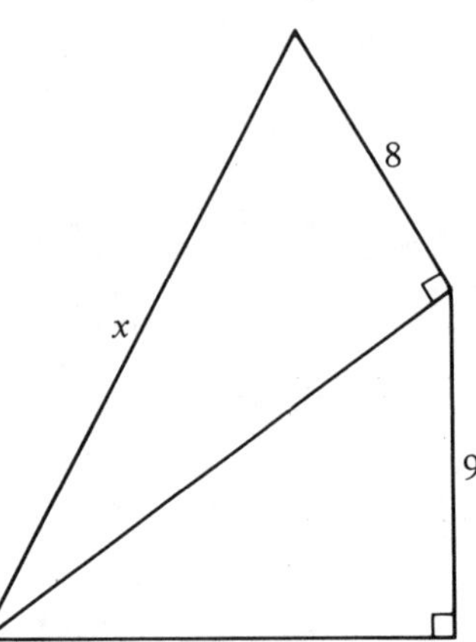

24.

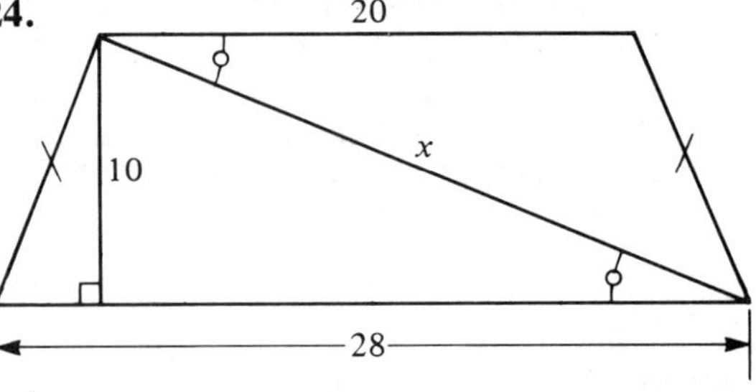

25.

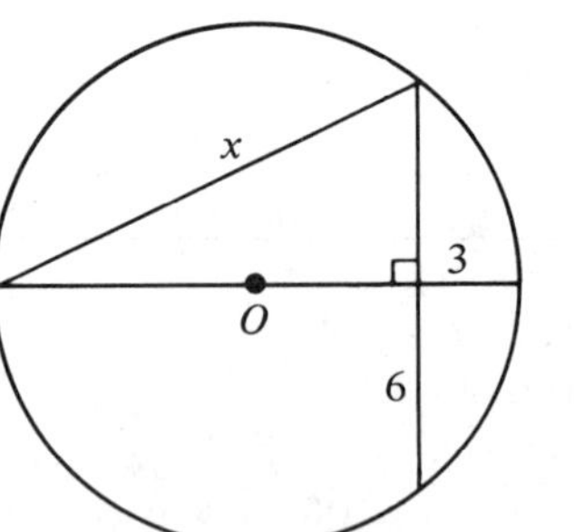

26.

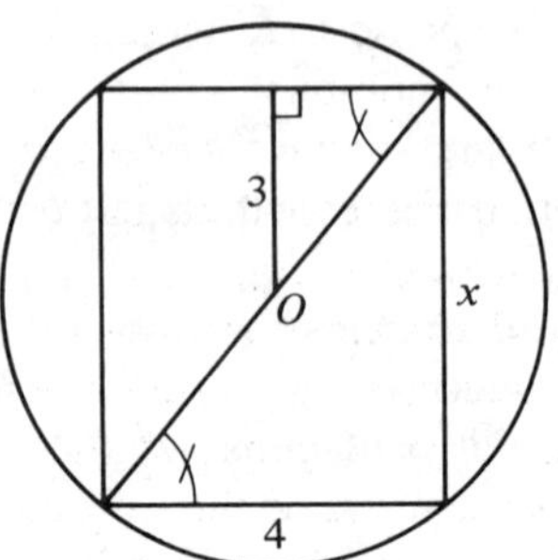

27.

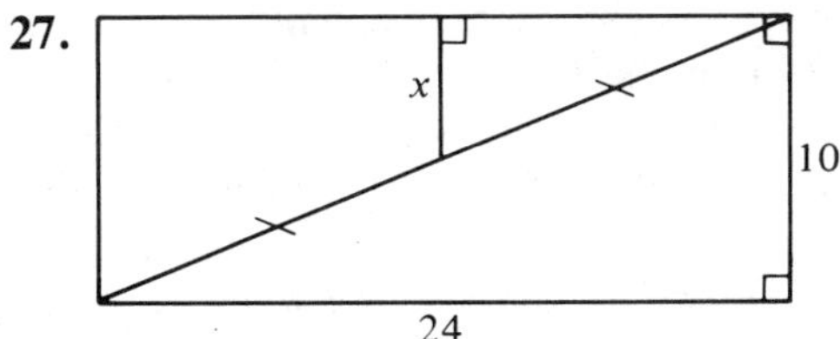

28.

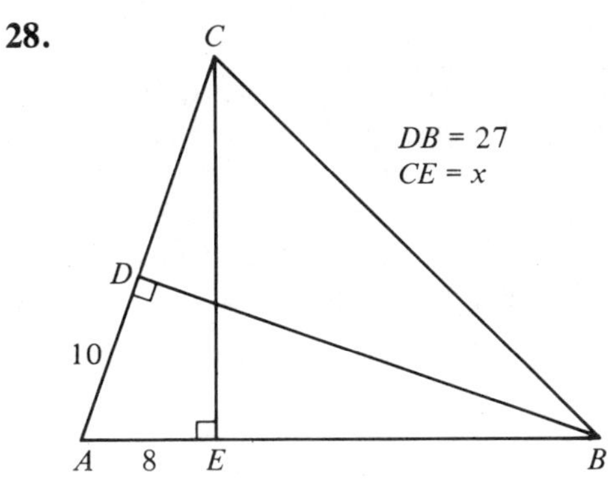

29.

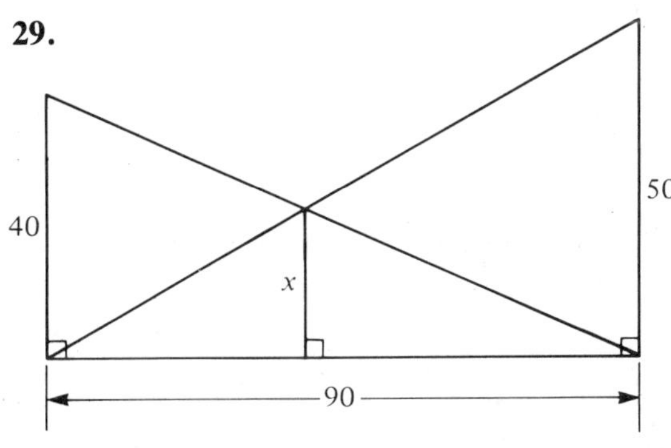

30.

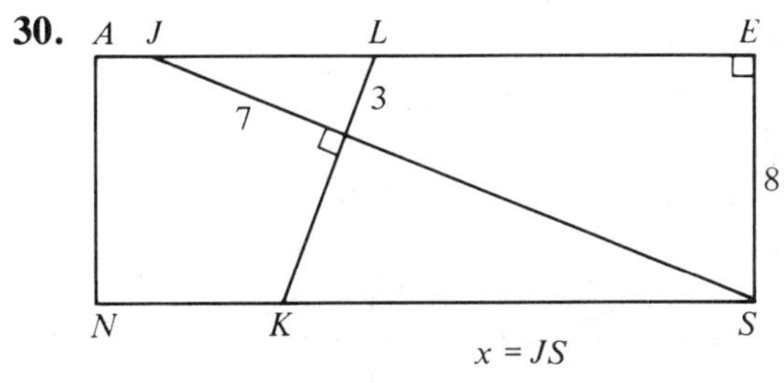

In exercises 31–46 draw a figure, label it, write an appropriate equation, and solve.

31. A chord 48 inches long is 10 inches from the center of a circle. Find the circle's radius.

32. Two vertical poles stand 24 feet apart on level ground. If the poles are 15 feet and 33 feet high, respectively, how long is a straight rope that joins their tops?

33. If the radius of a circle is tripled in length, how does the circumference of the larger circle compare to that of the original circle? How do the areas compare?

34. A circle of radius 4 inches is inscribed in a regular hexagon. A second regular hexagon is inscribed in the circle. Find the ratios of the circumference of the circle to each of the perimeters of the two hexagons. Find the ratios of their areas.

35. A contractor is replacing a pipeline whose diameter measures 2 inches. The new pipeline is to have a carrying capacity that is four times that of the old one. What diameter pipe must be used? (Carrying capacity depends directly on the cross-sectional area.)

36. The lengths of the minute hands of two tower clocks measure 6 and 8 feet, respectively. What is the ratio of the circumferences of the clock's faces? What is the ratio of their areas?

37. Semicircles are drawn on the sides of a 5-inch by 12-inch by 13-inch right triangle so that the sides of the triangles are the diameters of the semicircles. Find the areas of the semicircles. How does the sum of the areas of the two smaller semicircles compare to that of the larger semicircle?

38. An arc of length $\frac{\pi^2}{4}$ is part of a circle of radius π. What is the degree measure of the central angle subtended by this arc?

39. A tangent is drawn to a circle of radius 15 inches from a point that is 25 inches from the center of the circle. Find the length of the tangent segment.

40. Two concentric circles have radii that measure 6 and 10 inches, respectively. Find the length of a chord of the larger circle that is tangent to the smaller circle.

41. A building casts an 85-foot shadow at the same time a 25-foot pole casts a 17-foot shadow. Find the height of the building.

42. Find the area and the arc length of the sector of a circle whose central angle measures 108° if the radius of the circle measures 15 inches.

43. The distance from the midpoint of a chord 16 centimeters long to the midpoint of its arc is 6 centimeters. Find the radius of the circle.

44. The bases of a trapezoid measure 8 feet and 12 feet, respectively, and the nonparallel sides measure 4 feet and 5 feet, respectively. How far must each of the two sides be extended so that they intersect?

45. The base of an isosceles triangle measures 9 inches long and its perimeter measures 33 inches. If the perimeter of a similar isosceles triangle measures 22 inches, find the length of its base.

46. What length must a ladder have to reach a window 35 feet above the ground if the lower end of the ladder must be 12 feet from the building?

47. A man 6 feet tall walks toward a street light whose bulb is 15 feet above the ground. To find the rate at which his shadow is moving, we first need an equation relating the length l of his shadow and the distance d its endpoint is from the street light. Draw and label a figure and write the equation.

48. A man is approaching a wall 10 feet high. To find the rate at which the distance d from his feet to the wall's top is changing, we first need an equation relating the distance x from his feet to the wall and the distance d to the top of the wall. Draw and label a figure and write the equation.

49. A ship leaves a port sailing due west while a second ship leaves the same port sailing due south. To find the rate at which they are separating, we first need an equation relating the distance z between them, the distance x the first ship travels, and the distance y the second ship travels. Draw and label a figure and write the equation.

50. The given figure represents a cross-section of a conical water tank with radius r_1, and depth h_1 that may be filled to any depth h_2. Write a relation involving r_1, h_1, r_2, and h_2 that is true for any depth h_2.

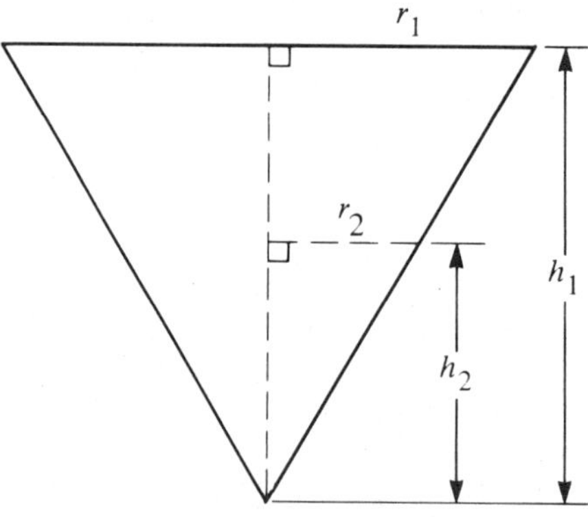

51. *Given*
$\overline{ST} \parallel \overline{AP}$
If $ST = 57$ ft, $SA = 48$ ft, and $AP = 133$ ft, find the distance OS across the river.

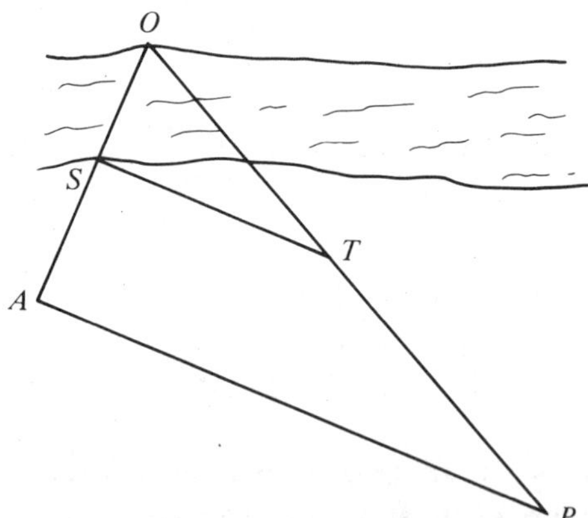

52. As for similar triangles (Theorem 104), the ratio of the areas of two similar polygons is the same as the ratio of the squares of any two corresponding sides. Use this fact to answer the following questions:

(a) If the shortest sides of two similar pentagons measure 9 inches and 15 inches, respectively, and the area of the smaller pentagon measures 75 square inches, what is the area of the larger pentagon?

(b) If corresponding sides of two similar polygons measure 16 inches and 30 inches, respectively, how long is the corresponding side of a third polygon that is similar to the first two and whose area is equal to the sum of their areas?

53. *Given*
concentric circles with center O
$\overline{ES}$ tan at J

(a) If $SE = 17$ units, find the area of the region between the circles.
(b) If the area of the small circle is two-thirds of the area of the large circle and the radius of the large circle measures 4 inches, what is the radius of the small circle?

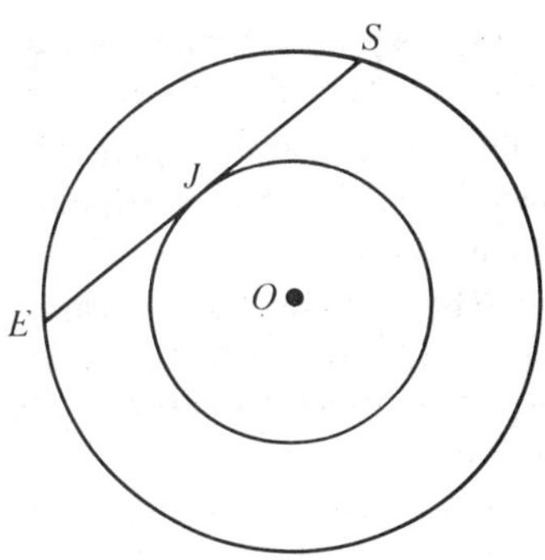

54. *Given*
$\odot O$
$\overline{EA} \cong \overline{AB} \cong \overline{BJ}$
C, A, B, D centers of semicircles
$EJ = 12$ in

(a) Find the area of each of the shaded regions.
(b) Find the perimeter of each of the shaded regions.
(c) Let $EJ = 3a$ units and compare the area of the upper shaded region with that of the nonshaded region.
(d) Let $EJ = 3a$ units and compare the perimeters of the three regions (two shaded, one nonshaded).

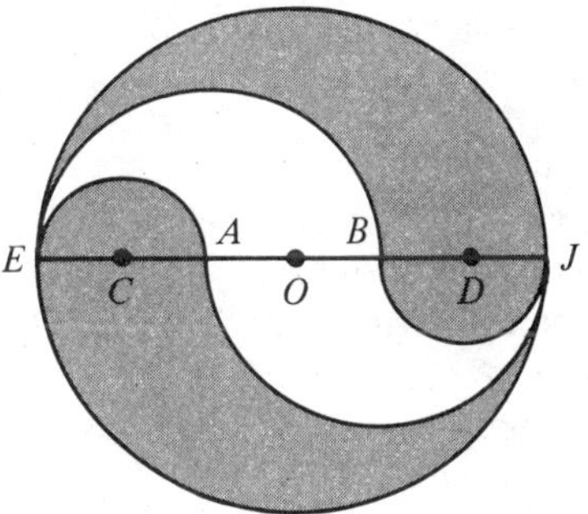

55. This figure is called an arbelos or shoemaker's knife.

Given
K, O, S centers of semicircles
$OJ = 12$ in
$SJ = 9$ in
$\overline{LT} \perp \overline{EJ}$

(a) Find the area of the shaded region.
(b) Find x. (Hint: See Construction 14.)
(c) Find the area of a circle whose diameter is equal to the answer to part (b). Compare it with the area of the shaded region.
(d) Let $ET = a$ units, $TJ = b$ units, and show that the area of the shaded region is the same as the area of a circle whose diameter is x units. (Archimedes was the first to show that these two areas are equal.)

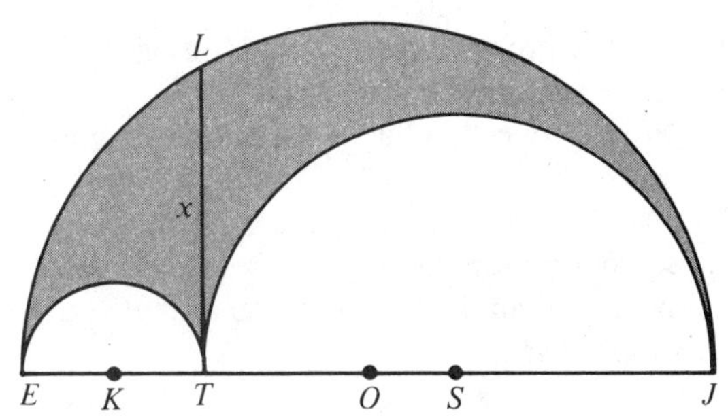

CHAPTER 9 SUMMARY

The similarity relation and the congruence relation developed in previous chapters provide two of the fundamental problem-solving techniques of geometry. The fact that corresponding sides of similar figures are proportional is the key to applications of the similarity relation and to the proof of the famous and widely used Pythagorean Theorem. The chapter concludes by presenting a few of the many types of practical and geometric problems that can be solved using similar triangles or the Pythagorean Theorem.

FACTS TO KNOW

1. Definitions
   - **a.** Ratio
   - **b.** Proportion
   - **c.** Similar triangles
   - **d.** Sector of a circle

2. Theorems
   - **a.** prod extrms = prod mns
   - **b.** interch mns or extrms
   - **c.** invert ratios
   - **d.** add prop propor
   - **e.** subt prop propor
   - **f.** line ∥ side △ ÷ 2 sides in = ratios
   - **g.** line ∥ side △ cuts segs propor to sides
   - **h.** aa ≅ aa
   - **i.** alt to hyp forms 3 ~ △s
   - **j.** alt mn propor segs hyp, leg mn propor hyp adj seg
   - **k.** $a^2 + b^2 = c^2$
   - **l.** corr alts, meds, ∡ bis ~ △s propor corr sides
   - **m.** areas ~ △s propor sqs corr sides, alts, meds, ∡ bis
   - **n.** ∡ bis ÷ opp side same ratio other 2 sides
   - **o.** $A_s = \frac{a}{360} \cdot \pi r^2$
   - **p.** $L = \frac{a}{360} \cdot 2\pi r$
   - **q.** prods segs 2 chs =
   - **r.** prods 2 secs and segs =
   - **s.** tan seg mn propor sec segs

PROBLEMS TO MASTER

1. Write and simplify ratios.
2. Solve a proportion for a missing part.
3. Prove triangles similar.
4. Prove proportions using similar triangles (csstp).
5. Use $a^2 + b^2 = c^2$ to find a missing side.
6. Solve proportions about sides, altitudes, medians, angle bisectors, and areas of similar triangles.
7. Find arcs and areas of sectors of a circle.
8. Solve practical problems using similar triangles or the Pythagorean Theorem.
9. Construct the mean proportional between two given line segments.
10. Divide a line segment in extreme and mean ratio.
11. Solve construction problems using previously given constructions.

10

SOLID GEOMETRY

MAJOR TOPICS

- Surfaces, lines, and planes as basic figures in three dimensions
- Depiction of three-dimensional figures
- Polyhedrons, prisms, and pyramids
- Volume and the covering process
- Role of axioms and postulates in overcoming difficulties in measuring volume
- Lateral area, total area, and volume of prisms, pyramids, and right circular cylinders
- Volume and surface area of spheres

HISTORICAL NOTE

ARCHIMEDES

When Euclid wrote *Elements* (300 B.C.), Alexandria was becoming the commercial and intellectual hub of the Mediterranean world. In succeeding years, a new mathematics began to evolve. While the earlier Greeks were interested mainly in theoretical abstractions, the Alexandrians were willing to apply their talents to practical problems as well. The man whose work best characterizes the Alexandrian age was Archimedes (287–212 B.C.), one of the most extraordinary intellects the world has known. No classical mathematical treatise surpasses those of Archimedes in importance of content or elegance of style. He, Gauss, and Newton are generally considered the three greatest mathematicians of all time.

Archimedes was born in Syracuse on the island of Sicily, the son of an astronomer named Pheidias. Archimedes studied in Alexandria where he had many friends among the mathematicians, but he lived most of his life in Syracuse where he did the bulk of his creative work. All of Archimedes' treatises contain fresh contributions to mathematical knowledge. They include such topics as the equilibrium of plane figures; areas of parabolic segments; theorems about spirals, spheres, cylinders, paraboloids, and many other solids; measurements of circles; and the physics of floating bodies. In his treatise "The Sand Reckoner" Archimedes develops a practical notation for very large numbers. In "The Method" he describes a way to discover geometric formulas that anticipates—by nearly 2000 years—the underlying concepts of integral calculus.

Archimedes' achievements were not limited to the theoretical, however. He had practical talents as well, his efforts thus perfectly reflecting the new Alexandrian school of mathematics. He built a miniature planetarium that portrayed the motions of the heavenly bodies, invented a water pump, and designed a system of compound pulleys that enabled him to launch a heavily laden ship from dry dock while he was seated in a chair on the beach. When the Romans besieged Syracuse in 214 B.C., they were thwarted for two years by ingenious devices designed by Archimedes. Catapults hurled rocks on the attackers, and huge cranes lifted the Roman ships out of the water and shook them to pieces. Concave mirrors focused the sun's heat on approaching ships and set them ablaze.

Archimedes' theoretical work was influenced by the practicalities of the Alexandrian age for he was very interested in measurement. He proved that the area of a circle is half its circumference multiplied by its radius; he also computed the number π to be between $3\frac{10}{71}$ and $3\frac{1}{7}$. Of all his accomplishments he was most proud of his discovery that the ratio of the volume of a sphere inscribed in a cylinder to the volume of the cylinder is 2:3 and that the ratio of their surface areas is also 2:3. On his tombstone by his own request was carved the figure of a sphere inscribed in a cylinder and the ratio 2:3.

History includes many colorful stories about Archimedes. After discovering the laws of levers he is reputed to have declared, "Give me a place to stand on and I will move the earth." Perhaps the most famous story is about a crown of gold ordered by the King of Syracuse. Suspecting that the maker had substituted cheaper metals, the King asked Archimedes to determine if the crown was pure gold without destroying it. While lying in the city baths, Archimedes hit on the key to the problem (now called the First Law of Hydrostatics): A body immersed in a fluid is buoyed up by a force equal to the weight of the fluid displaced. He was so excited by his discovery that he rose from the bath and, forgetting to dress, ran home through the streets shouting, "Eureka, eureka!" ("I have found it, I have found it!")

During his lifetime, Archimedes represented the popular image of the learned man, much as Einstein did in his lifetime. Included in this image was a tendency toward absent mindedness. Perhaps it is rather a faculty of genius to focus one's entire attention on the question at hand to the exclusion of everything else. The Roman biographer Plutarch writes that when Syracuse was finally invaded by General Marcellus and his Roman legions in 212 B.C., Archimedes was so intent on a problem that he did not notice that the city had fallen. When a soldier ordered him to report to Marcellus, Archimedes refused to go until he had solved his problem. This so enraged the soldier that he thereupon killed Archimedes. Plutarch tells two other versions of the story, but whatever the truth, history seems clear that Marcellus was genuinely distressed at the death of so great a man and ordered an elaborate tomb bearing the inscription Archimedes had requested. Such was the still-enduring fame of Archimedes, a mathematician and genius of the highest order.

10.1 INTRODUCTION

Chapters 2–9 concern geometric figures that are in a plane. Such figures are said to be two-dimensional. This chapter introduces three-dimensional figures; that is, certain figures that are not in a plane. The study of such figures is called *space geometry* or *solid geometry*. Our development of the subject is informal. We do not rigorously define every term; instead, we rely on informal descriptions, figures, and the context to explain many concepts. Theorems are stated and explained but not proved. This approach enables us to cover briefly topics that are important in later work in mathematics and science.

A key concept in space geometry is that of a *surface*. An example is a plane, a term that was left undefined but was described in Section 2.1 as a flat surface that extends without end in all directions. When drawing a plane that is not in the plane of the paper, a part of it is shown in perspective as in Figure 10.1(a). Figure 10.1 also shows that a surface may consist of parts of planes as in (b) or it may be curved as in (c).

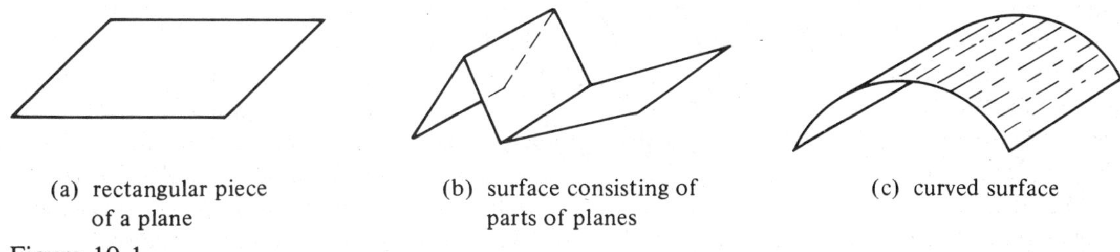

(a) rectangular piece of a plane (b) surface consisting of parts of planes (c) curved surface

Figure 10.1

An important type of figure in plane geometry is the set of points formed by the union of a closed boundary (such as a rectangle or circle) and its interior. The three-dimensional counterpart of such figures is a set of points that is the union of a *closed surface* and its interior. Such sets of points are called *geometric solids*. Two familiar physical examples are a brick, Figure 10.2(a), and a piece of a broom handle, Figure 10.2(b). Again, these three-dimensional figures are drawn on a flat surface in perspective.

(a) (b)

Figure 10.2

The major objectives of this chapter are to develop some important relations between lines and planes in space, and to describe certain useful surfaces and solids and ways to calculate their areas and volumes. The chapter should also help you to visualize three-dimensional figures and draw two-dimensional views of them.

10.2

LINES AND PLANES IN SPACE

The first postulate in our development of plane geometry states essentially that two points determine one and only one line. Just as the line is the simplest "curve" in a plane, the plane is the simplest surface in space. Therefore, we now list four figures that determine a unique plane in space. Recall that two parallel lines are by definition coplanar (Definition 5.1). This fact is included for completeness in Postulate 21, part (3), below.

Postulate 21 One and only one plane is determined by each of the following: (1) three noncollinear points (3 noncol pts determ pl), (2) two intersecting lines (2 inters lines determ pl), (3) two parallel lines (2 $\parallel$ lines determ pl), and (4) a line and a point not on the line (l and P off l determ pl).

Figure 10.3 illustrates each of the four cases.

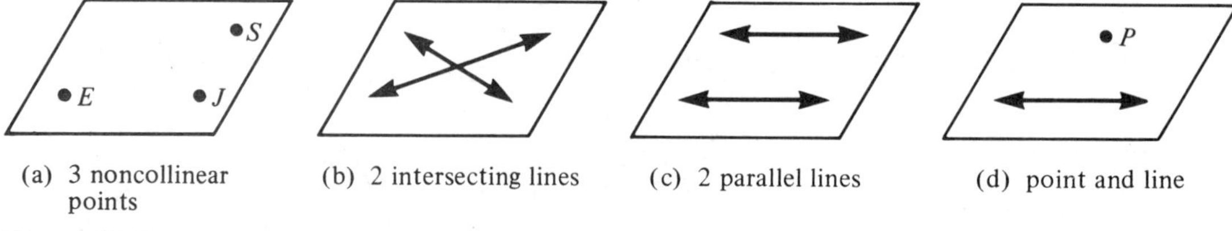

(a) 3 noncollinear points (b) 2 intersecting lines (c) 2 parallel lines (d) point and line

Figure 10.3

It is important to identify certain relationships involving lines and planes in space. Most of these can be seen in the drawing of the box in Figure 10.4 as follows:

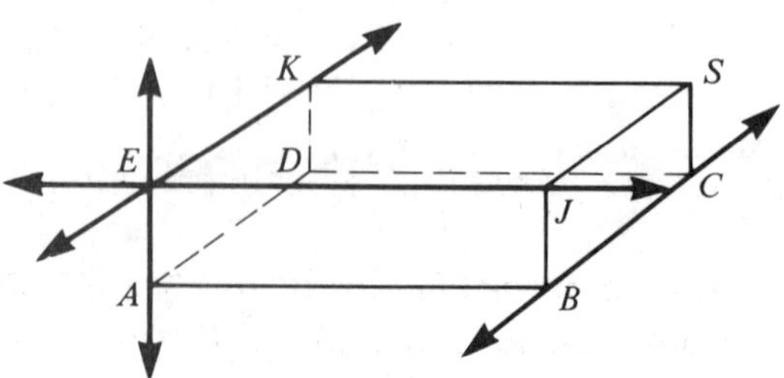

Figure 10.4

1. *Skew lines*. $\overleftrightarrow{EJ}$ and $\overleftrightarrow{BC}$ are an example. As mentioned in Chapter 5 (Section 5.1), these lines do not intersect, but neither are they parallel for they are not coplanar.
2. *A line parallel to a plane*. $\overleftrightarrow{EK}$ is parallel to plane *ABCD* and also to plane *BCSJ*. Note that $\overleftrightarrow{EK}$ intersects neither of these planes despite the fact that they extend without end.
3. *A line perpendicular to a plane*. $\overleftrightarrow{AE}$ is perpendicular to planes *ABCD* and *EJSK*. Some careful thought is required, however, to properly define this concept because when a line intersects a plane no angles are formed, so we cannot say the line and plane form a right angle. A suitable definition appears below.
4. *A plane parallel to a plane*. Plane *EJSK* is parallel to plane *ABCD*. Note that, as with a line parallel to a plane, these parallel planes do not intersect despite the fact that they extend without end.
5. *A plane perpendicular to a plane*. Plane *BCSJ* is perpendicular to plane *EJSK*. Again, think carefully about a suitable definition of this concept (see below).
6. *Two planes that are not parallel intersect in a line*. Plane *ABJE* intersects plane *EJSK* in $\overleftrightarrow{EJ}$, for example.

With the above discussion as a guide, definitions for four of the line and plane relationships may be stated as follows.

Definition 10.1 A line and a plane are *parallel* iff their intersection is empty.

Definition 10.2 A line and a plane are *perpendicular* iff they intersect and the line is perpendicular to every line in the plane that passes through the point of intersection ($l \perp$ pl is $\perp$ all l in pl thru inters).

Figure 10.5 illustrates Definition 10.2.

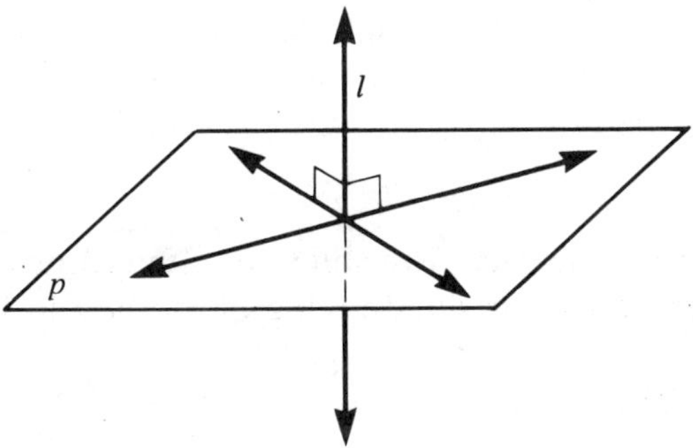

Figure 10.5 Line $l \perp$ plane p.

Definition 10.3 Two planes are *parallel* iff their intersection is empty.

Definition 10.4 Two planes are *perpendicular* iff one plane contains a line that is perpendicular to the other plane ($\text{pl}_1 \perp \text{pl}_2$ iff l in $\text{pl}_1 \perp \text{pl}_2$).

Figure 10.6 illustrates Definition 10.4.

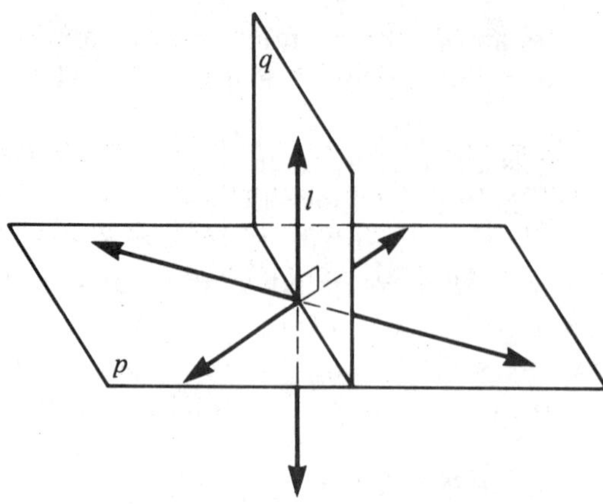

Figure 10.6 Plane $q \perp$ plane p since line l is in q and $l \perp p$.

One other relationship between two planes that does not appear in the drawing of the box (Figure 10.4) is shown in Figure 10.7. Two planes that are neither parallel nor perpendicular are said to be oblique.

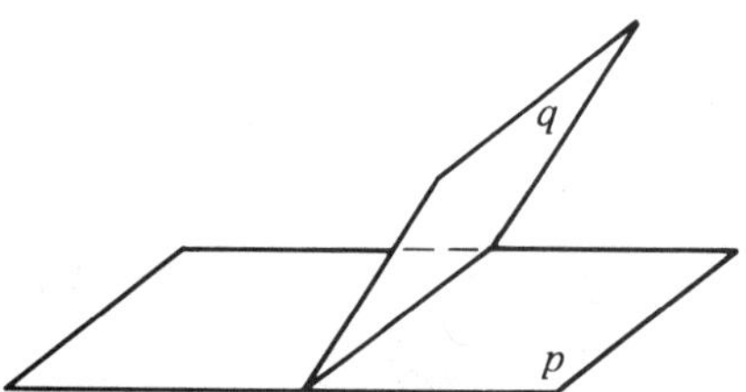

Figure 10.7 Planes p and q are oblique.

The two examples that conclude this section illustrate some of the concepts just presented.

EXAMPLE 1 Answer true or false and draw a figure to illustrate each answer. (a) If two planes are each perpendicular to a third plane, then the two planes are perpendicular. (b) If two planes are each parallel to a third plane, then the two planes are parallel. (c) If two lines are in parallel planes, then the two lines are parallel.

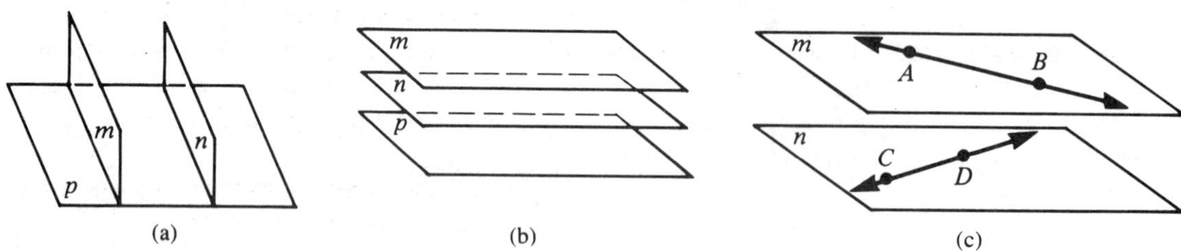

Answers
(a) False; $m \perp p$, $n \perp p$, and $m \parallel n$.
(b) True; $m \parallel p$, $n \parallel p$, and $m \parallel n$.
(c) False; $m \parallel n$ and $\overleftrightarrow{AB} \nparallel \overleftrightarrow{CD}$.

As illustrated in Example 1 it is usually easier to show a statement to be false than to show one to be true. Parts (a) and (c) are easily shown to be false by exhibiting examples in which each is false. Part (b) is in fact true, but the figure is not necessarily conclusive for it may not show all possible arrangements of the planes. The figure and our concept of parallelism, however, are probably convincing in this case. (A formal proof is, of course, possible.)

Although there are very few proofs in this chapter, one is included in Example 2 to show how theorems from plane geometry can be used in a three-dimensional problem. Note how the technique of proving triangles congruent is applied although the triangles are in different planes.

EXAMPLE 2

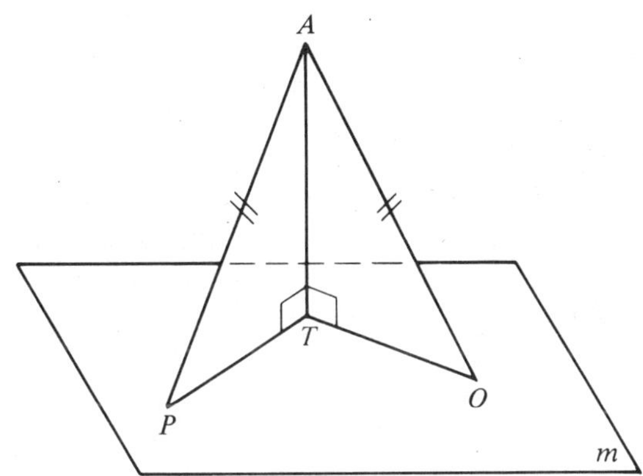

Given
$\overline{AT} \perp$ pl m
$\overline{AP} \cong \overline{AO}$

To Prove
$\measuredangle P \cong \measuredangle O$

Statement	*Reason*
1. $\overline{AT} \perp$ pl m	1. given
2. $\overline{AT} \perp \overline{TP}$, $\overline{AT} \perp \overline{TO}$	2. $l \perp$ pl is $\perp$ all l in pl thru inters
3. $\measuredangle ATP$ and $\measuredangle ATO$ rt $\measuredangle$s	3. $\perp$s form $\cong$ rt $\measuredangle$s
4. $\overline{AP} \cong \overline{AO}$	4. given
5. $\overline{AT} \cong \overline{AT}$	5. reflex $\cong$
6. $\triangle ATP \cong \triangle ATO$	6. hs $\cong$ hs
7. $\measuredangle P \cong \measuredangle O$	7. cpctc

EXERCISES FOR 10.1 AND 10.2

In exercises 1–20 answer true or false.

1. Plane geometry is the study of three-dimensional figures.
2. Two planes perpendicular to the same plane are parallel to each other.
3. If each of three lines is perpendicular to the other two, then the three lines pass through a single point.
4. A plane is defined as a flat surface.
5. If one plane is perpendicular to a second plane, then any line in the first plane is perpendicular to the second plane.
6. A line not in a given plane either parallels the plane or intersects the plane in exactly one point.
7. Three points determine a plane.
8. If a line is parallel to a given plane, then every plane containing the line is also parallel to the given plane.
9. If two planes intersect, then their points of intersection form a line.
10. If a given line is perpendicular to a plane, then any line through their point of intersection is also perpendicular to the given line.
11. Two planes parallel to the same plane are perpendicular to each other.
12. A line in one of two parallel planes is always either parallel or skew to a line in the other plane.
13. If two intersecting lines are both parallel to a given plane, then the plane determined by the lines is also parallel to the given plane.
14. The "is-parallel-to" relation in the set of all planes is reflexive, symmetric, and transitive.

15. The "is-perpendicular-to" relation in the set of all planes is symmetric and transitive but not reflexive.
16. A plane is an example of a curved surface.
17. An ordinary brick is an example of a set of points called a geometric solid.
18. In space, two lines perpendicular to the same line are parallel.
19. If four points A, B, C, D in space are joined in order with $\overline{AB} \perp \overline{BC}$, then $ABCD$ must be in one plane.
20. If two lines are parallel, any plane containing one of the lines but not the other line is always parallel to the other line.

Since facts and techniques from plane geometry are used in proving facts in space geometry, care must be taken when applying properties of two-dimensional figures to three-dimensional figures. In exercises 21–30 state whether each statement applies to plane geometry only, space geometry only, or to both.

21. If three sides of one triangle are congruent, respectively, to three sides of a second triangle, then the triangles are congruent.
22. If two angles of one triangle are congruent, respectively, to two angles of a second triangle, then the triangles are similar.
23. A line perpendicular to one of two parallel lines is perpendicular to the other also.
24. Through a point on a line, one and only one line can be drawn perpendicular to the given line.
25. Through a point on a line, many lines can be drawn perpendicular to the given line.
26. Two points, each equidistant from the endpoints of a line segment, determine the perpendicular bisector of that line segment.
27. If each of two intersecting lines has a line drawn perpendicular to it, then the perpendiculars will intersect.
28. If two parallel lines are cut by a transversal, then the alternate interior angles are congruent.
29. If two lines are each parallel to a third line, then the two lines are parallel.
30. Corresponding parts of congruent triangles are congruent.

Exercises 31–40 are about *dihedral angles*. These are angles formed by two intersecting planes. They are measured by the angle of intersection formed in a third plane perpendicular to the line of intersection of the two planes. Dihedral angles are named using four letters. In the figure, ∡*E-JS-K* names the "upper right" dihedral angle formed by planes q and m. Refer to Figure 10.8 in exercises 31–40.

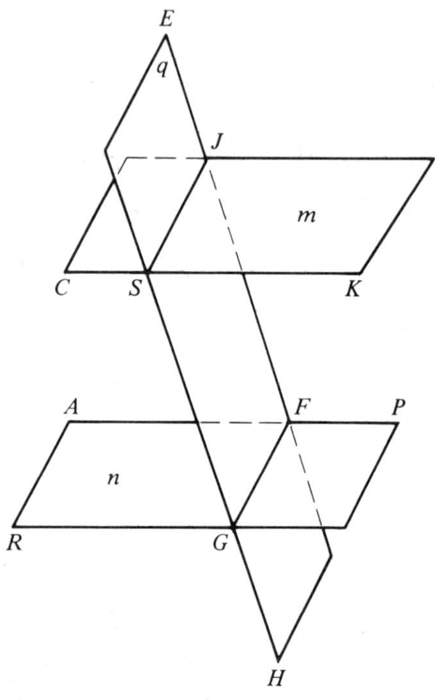

Figure 10.8

31. Name four pairs of *vertical* dihedral angles.
32. Name two pairs of *alternate interior* dihedral angles.
33. Name four pairs of *supplementary* dihedral angles using $\overline{JS}$.
34. Name four *linear pairs* of dihedral angles using $\overline{FG}$.
35. Name four pairs of *corresponding* dihedral angles.
36. If plane m is parallel to plane n, how is ∡*K-SJ-F* related to ∡*S-GF-P?*
37. If plane m is parallel to plane n and $\angle E\text{-}JS\text{-}C = 71°$, what is $\angle S\text{-}GF\text{-}P$?
38. If $\angle H\text{-}GF\text{-}A = 115°$ and $\angle C\text{-}SJ\text{-}E = 55°$, is plane m parallel to plane n?
39. If plane m is parallel to plane n and $\angle A\text{-}FG\text{-}H = 109°$, what is $\angle E\text{-}JS\text{-}K$?
40. The pair ∡*P-FG-H* and ∡*E-JS-C* are what type of angles?

In exercises 41 and 42 copy the figure, mark it, and supply the missing reasons in each proof.

41. *Given*
$\overline{SJ} \perp$ pl q
$\overline{JS} \perp$ pl p
$\overline{JS}$ bis $\overline{EK}$ at R

To Prove
$\overline{JE} \cong \overline{SK}$

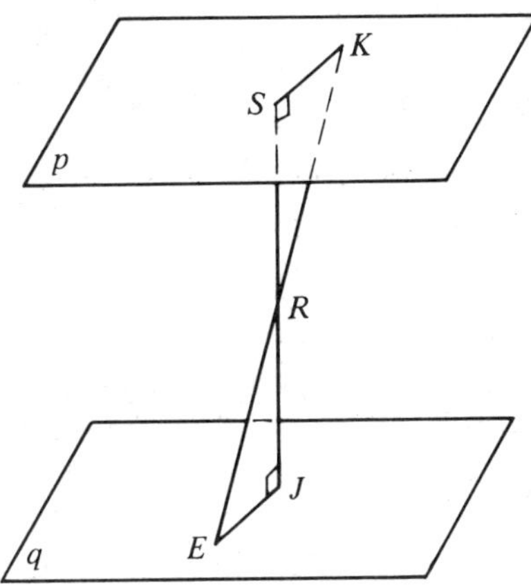

Statement	*Reason*
1. $\overline{SJ} \perp$ pl q	1. ?
2. $\overline{SJ} \perp \overline{EJ}$	2. ?
3. $\measuredangle EJR$ rt $\measuredangle$	3. ?
4. $\overline{JS} \perp$ pl p	4. ?
5. $\overline{JS} \perp \overline{KS}$	5. ?
6. $\measuredangle KSR$ rt $\measuredangle$	6. ?
7. $\measuredangle EJR \cong \measuredangle KSR$	7. ?
8. $\overline{JS}$ bis $\overline{EK}$ at R	8. ?
9. $\overline{ER} \cong \overline{KR}$	9. ?
10. $SKEJ$ forms pl	10. ?
11. $\measuredangle ERJ \cong \measuredangle KRS$	11. ?
12. $\triangle EJR \cong \triangle KSR$	12. ?
13. $\therefore \overline{JE} \cong \overline{SK}$	13. ?

42. *Given*
$\overline{KO} \perp$ pl p at O
rh $AXIO$ in pl p
$\overline{MX} \cong \overline{EX}$

To Prove
$\measuredangle MKO \cong \measuredangle EKO$

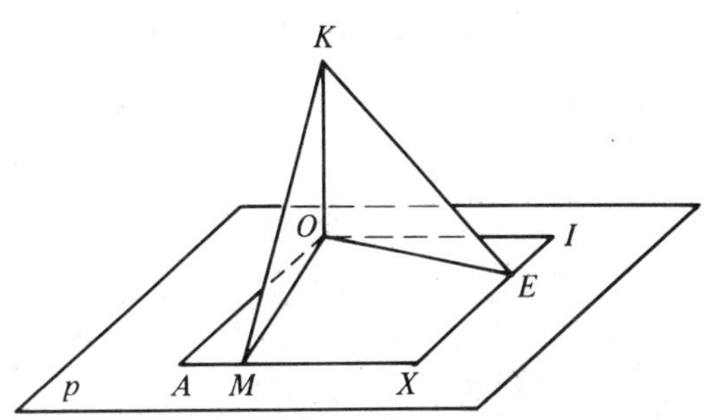

Statement	*Reason*
1. $\overline{KO} \perp$ pl p at O	1. ?
2. $\overline{KO} \perp \overline{OM}$	2. ?
3. $\measuredangle KOM$ rt $\measuredangle$	3. ?
4. $\overline{KO} \perp \overline{OE}$	4. ?
5. $\measuredangle KOE$ rt $\measuredangle$	5. ?
6. $\measuredangle KOM \cong \measuredangle KOE$	6. ?
7. rh $AXIO$ in pl p	7. ?
8. $\overline{AO} \cong \overline{IO}$	8. ?
9. $\overline{AX} \cong \overline{IX}$	9. ?
10. $\overline{MX} \cong \overline{EX}$	10. ?
11. $\overline{AX} - \overline{MX} \cong \overline{IX} - \overline{EX}$	11. ?
12. $\overline{AM} \cong \overline{AX} - \overline{MX}$	12. ?
13. $\overline{IE} \cong \overline{IX} - \overline{EX}$	13. ?

14. $\overline{AM} \cong \overline{IE}$	14. ?
15. $\measuredangle A \cong \measuredangle I$	15. ?
16. $\triangle AMO \cong \triangle IEO$	16. ?
17. $\overline{OM} \cong \overline{OE}$	17. ?
18. $\overline{KO} \cong \overline{KO}$	18. ?
19. $\triangle KOM \cong \triangle KOE$	19. ?
20. $\therefore \measuredangle MKO \cong \measuredangle EKO$	20. ?

In exercises 43–50 copy the figure, the hypothesis, and the conclusion. Mark the figure and write a proof.

43. *Given*
$\overline{ER} \perp$ pl p at R
$\measuredangle EIR \cong \measuredangle ECR$

To Prove
$\overline{IR} \cong \overline{CR}$

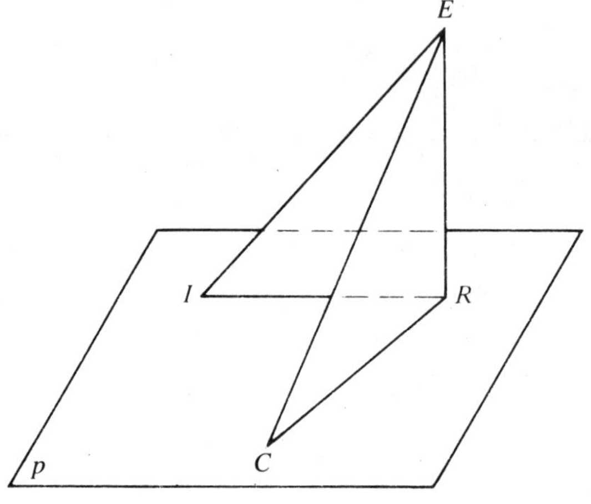

44. *Given*
$\triangle ABC$ in pl q
P, O, S, T midpts

To Prove
$POST$ ▱

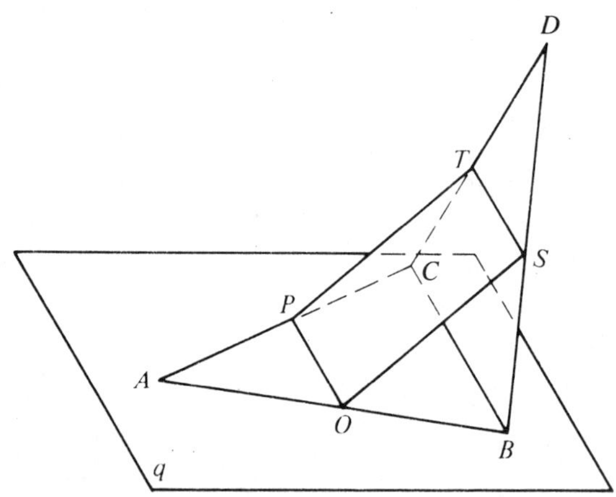

45. *Given*
$\overline{EJ} \perp$ pl p
$\measuredangle S \cong \measuredangle K$

To Prove
$\overline{SJ} \cong \overline{KJ}$

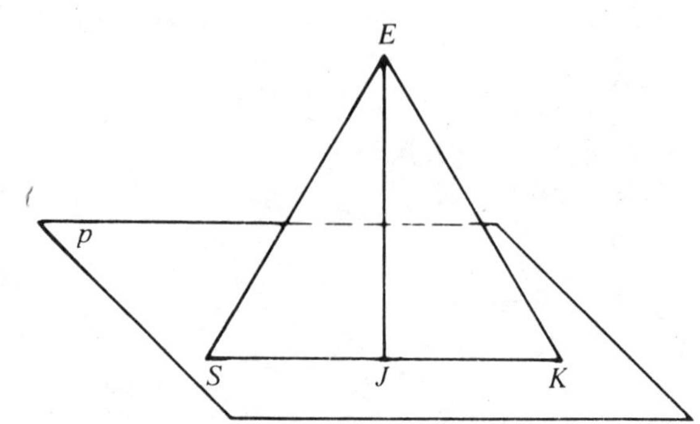

46. *Given*
$\overline{OR} \perp$ pl p
$\overline{PS}$ bis $\overline{OR}$

To Prove
$\overline{OS} \cong \overline{RS}$

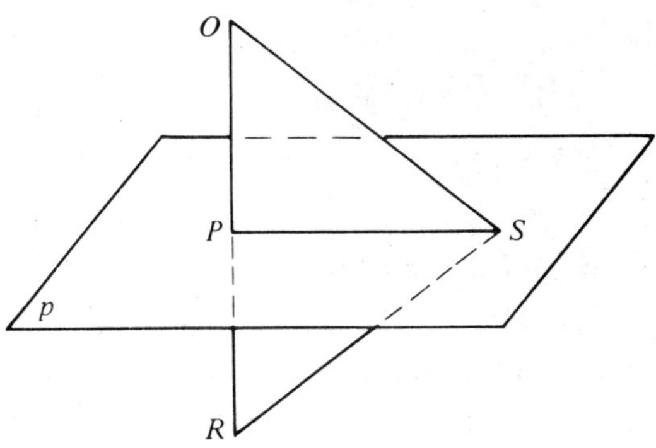

47. *Given*
$\overline{EJ} \perp$ pl p
$\overline{JS} \perp \overline{CM}$
$\overline{JS}$ bis $\overline{CM}$

To Prove
$\triangle ECM$ isos

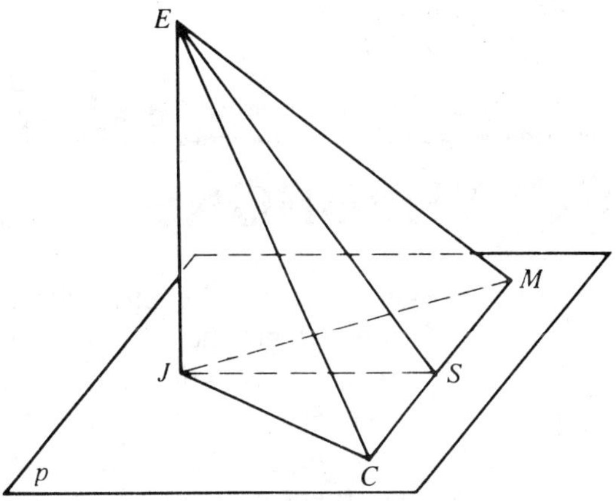

48. *Given*
sq $STAK$ in pl p
$\overline{OE} \perp$ pl p

To Prove
$\overline{OS} \cong \overline{OT} \cong \overline{OA} \cong \overline{OK}$

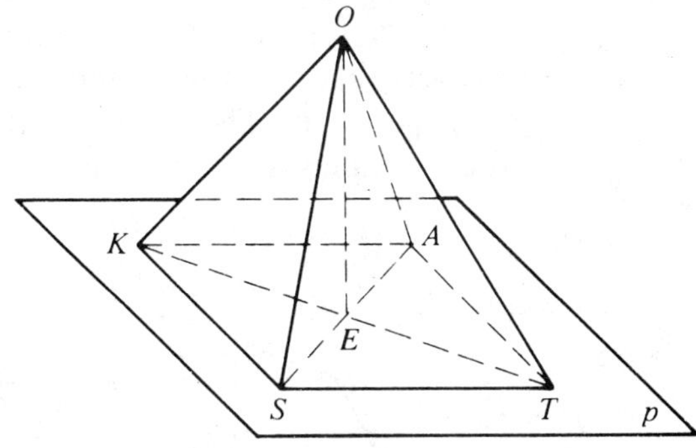

49. *Given*
$\odot O$ on pl p
$\overline{SO} \perp$ pl p

To Prove
$\triangle EJS$ isos

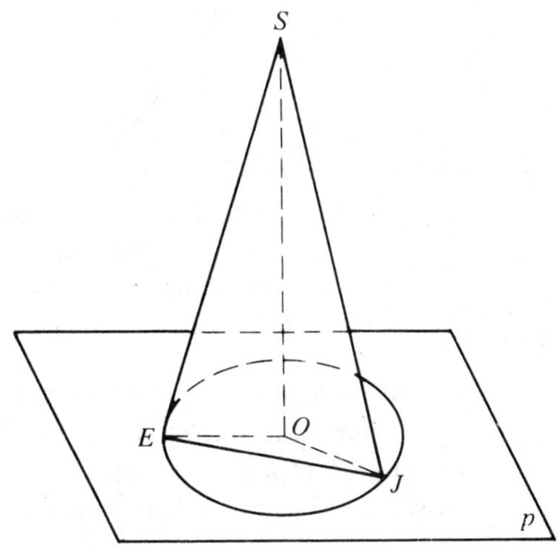

50. *Given*
sq $ABCD$ on pl p
$\overline{BF} \cong \overline{BG}$
$\overline{ED} \perp$ pl p

To Prove
$\overline{EF} \cong \overline{EG}$

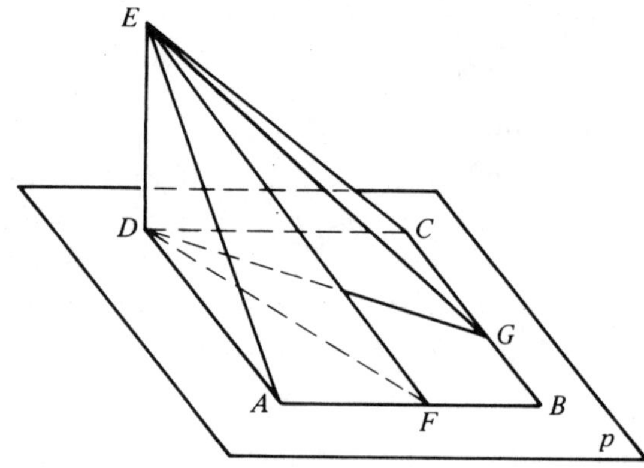

10.3
POLYHEDRONS

Polyhedrons are the three-dimensional counterparts of the two-dimensional polygons. A polyhedron is a surface consisting of parts of intersecting planes each of which is called a *face*. In this section we discuss prisms and pyramids, only two of the many types of polyhedrons.

A *prism* is a polyhedron two of whose faces, called *bases,* are bounded by congruent polygons in parallel planes and whose remaining faces, called *lateral faces,* are bounded by parallelograms. A drawing of a *triangular prism* appears in Figure 10.9, together with some important terminology. Note, however, that the bases need not be triangles; they may be any type of congruent polygon. The name of the bases is used to name the prism. Some more examples are shown in Figure 10.10 and 10.11.

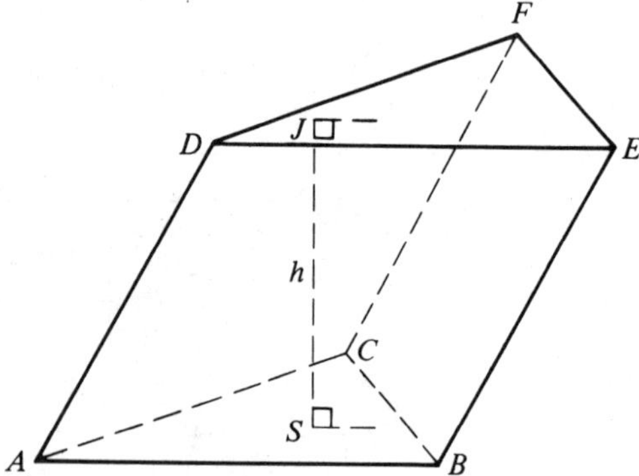

Figure 10.9 Triangular prism. $\triangle ABC$ and $\triangle DEF$ are the bases; A, B, C, D, E, and F are the vertices; $\overline{AD}$, $\overline{BE}$, and $\overline{CF}$ are the lateral edges; ▱s $ABED$, $BEFC$, and $CFDA$ are the lateral faces; $\overline{JS}$ is an altitude (length h).

An important type of prism is one whose bases are parallelograms. Such prisms are called *parallelepipeds*. Their bases may of course be rectangles or squares (special parallelograms). Some examples of parallelepipeds are shown in Figure 10.10(b) and 10.11(a) and (d).

An *altitude* of a prism is any line segment perpendicular to the parallel bases. Since all the altitudes of a prism are congruent, their common length, denoted h, is called *the altitude* of the prism. A *right prism* is one whose lateral edges are also altitudes. If this is not the case, the prism is *oblique*. A *regular prism* is a right prism whose bases are regular polygons. A regular triangular prism (bases equilateral triangles) is shown in Figure 10.10(a). Another important type of right prism is the *rectangular parallelepiped* or *rectangular right prism*. In everyday language, such prisms are called rectangular boxes (Figure 10.10[b]).

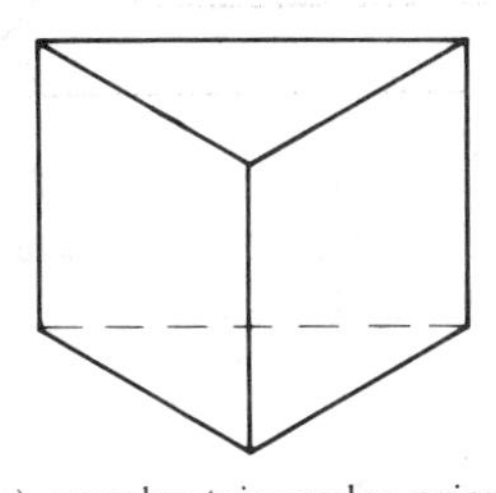

(a) regular triangular prism

(b) rectangular right prism or rectangular parallelepiped (rectangular box) with section $ABCD$

Figure 10.10

If a plane intersects a prism, then the lines of intersection form a *section* of the prism. Figure 10.10(b) shows a section of a rectangular prism. If the plane is perpendicular to all the lateral edges, then it forms a *right* section of the prism.

In summary, several examples of prisms are shown in Figure 10.11.

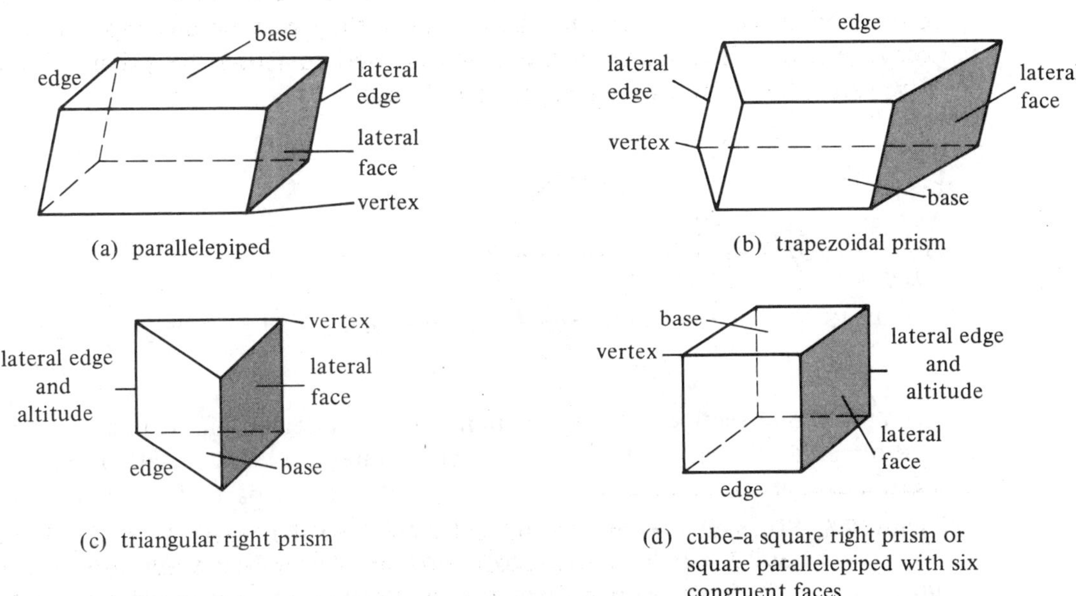

(a) parallelepiped

(b) trapezoidal prism

(c) triangular right prism

(d) cube–a square right prism or square parallelepiped with six congruent faces

Figure 10.11

A *pyramid* is a polyhedron whose *base* is bounded by a polygon and whose *lateral faces* are bounded by triangles, formed by line segments, that join each vertex of the base to a point not in the plane of the base. Figure 10.12 is a drawing of a square pyramid.

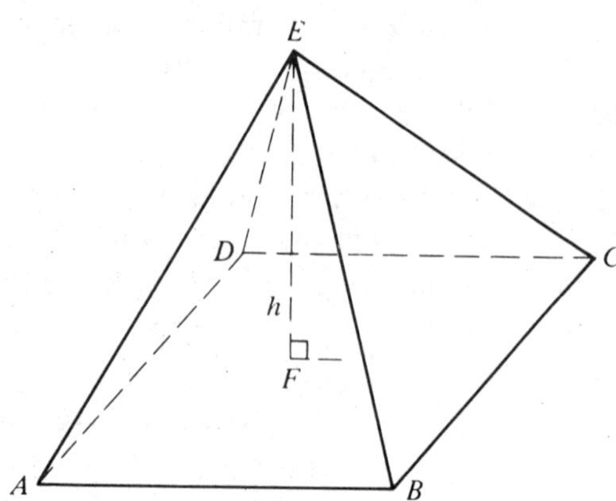

Figure 10.12 Square pyramid. Square $ABCD$ is the base; E is the vertex; $\overline{AE}$, $\overline{BE}$, $\overline{CE}$, and $\overline{DE}$ are the lateral edges; $\triangle$s AEB, BEC, CED, and DEA are the lateral faces; $\overline{EF}$ (length h) is the altitude.

Of course, the base of a pyramid may be any polygon. The name of the base is used to name the pyramid. A *regular pyramid* is one whose base is a regular polygon and whose lateral edges are congruent. It can be proved that the lateral faces of a regular pyramid are congruent triangles and that the altitude joins its vertex to the center of its base. The slant height l of a regular pyramid is the altitude from the pyramid's vertex of any of its lateral faces (Figure 10.13).

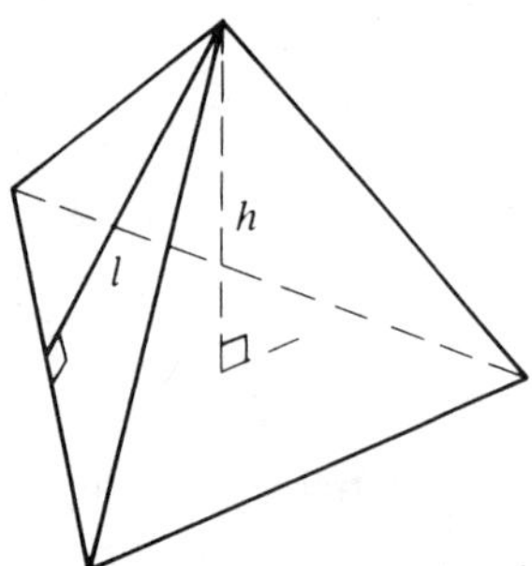

Figure 10.13 Regular triangular pyramid with altitude h and slant height l.

If a plane intersects a pyramid, then the lines of intersection form a *section* of the pyramid (Figure 10.14[a]). If the plane intersects all the lateral edges in distinct points and is parallel to the base and if the part of the pyramid between the vertex and the section is discarded, then a *frustum* of a pyramid is formed (Figure 10.14[b]). The terms *bases, lateral faces, altitude,* and *slant height* have their obvious meanings for a frustum of a pyramid. Note that the lateral faces are trapezoids and the slant height is the altitude of the trapezoids.

The *lateral area* (LA) of a prism, pyramid, or frustum of a pyramid is the sum of the areas of its lateral faces. The *total area* (TA) is the sum of the lateral area and the area(s) of the base(s). These concepts are illustrated in Examples 1–3.

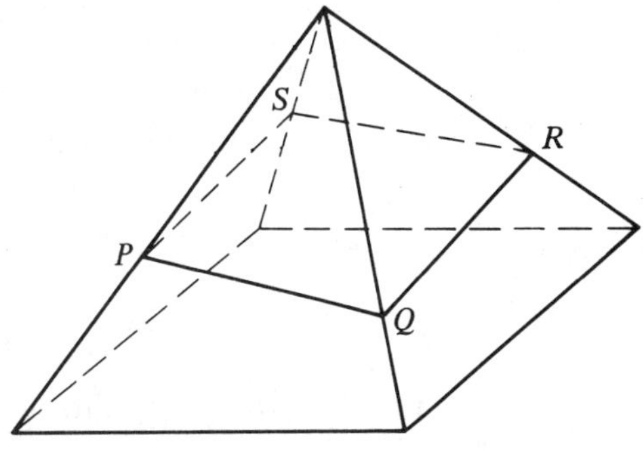

(a) pyramid and section $PQRS$

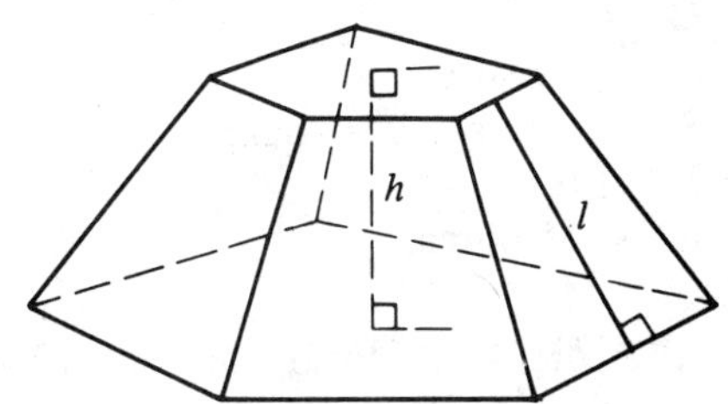

(b) frustum of a pyramid with altitude h and slant height l

Figure 10.14

EXAMPLE 1 Find (a) the *LA* and (b) the *TA* to the nearest square inch of the given regular triangular prism. Use $\sqrt{3} \approx 1.73$.

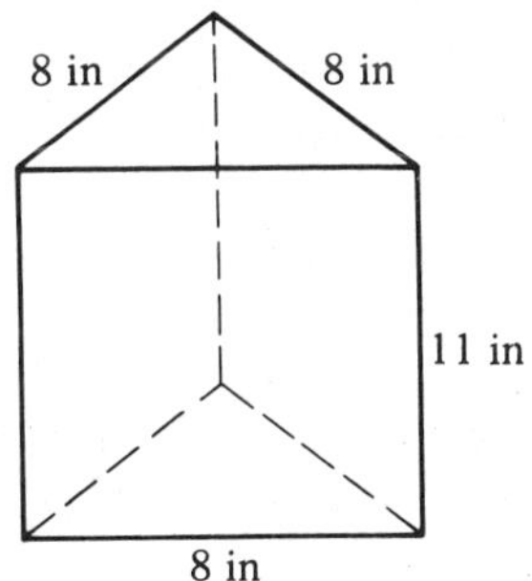

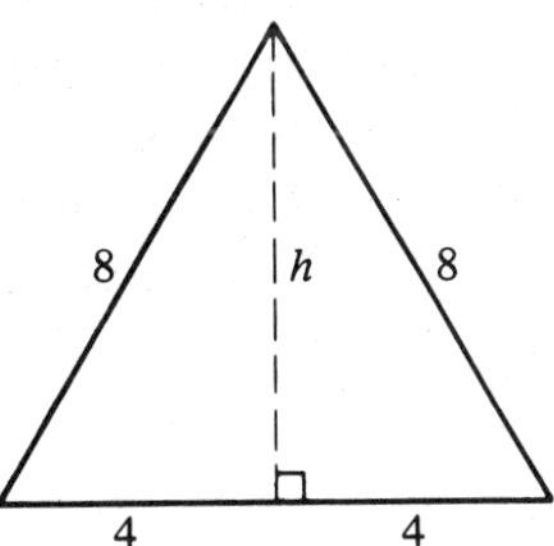

Answers

(a) Since the lateral faces are congruent rectangles, then
$LA = 3 \cdot bh$
$LA = 3 \cdot 11 \cdot 8$
$LA = 264$ sq in

(b) Since the bases are congruent equilateral triangles, then
$a^2 + b^2 = c^2$
$h^2 + 4^2 = 8^2$
$h^2 = 64 - 16$
$h^2 = 48$ or $h = 4\sqrt{3}$ in
$A = \frac{1}{2}bh$
$A = \frac{1}{2} \cdot 8 \cdot 4 \cdot \sqrt{3}$
$A = 16\sqrt{3}$ sq in
$TA = 264 + 2 \cdot 16\sqrt{3}$
$TA = 264 + 32\sqrt{3} \approx 319$ sq in

EXAMPLE 2 Find the *LA* and *TA* of the given regular square pyramid.

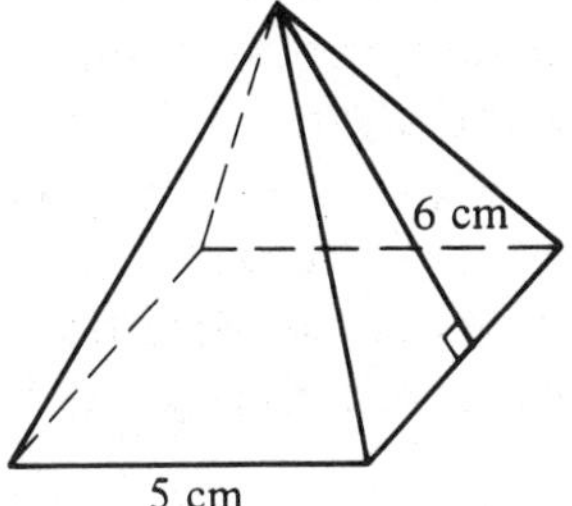

Answers
Since the faces are triangles,
$LA = 4 \cdot \frac{1}{2} \cdot bl$
$LA = 2 \cdot 5 \cdot 6$
$LA = 60$ sq cm
Since the base is a square,
$TA = 60 + 5^2$
$TA = 85$ sq cm

EXAMPLE 3 Find the LA and TA of the given frustum of a regular square pyramid.

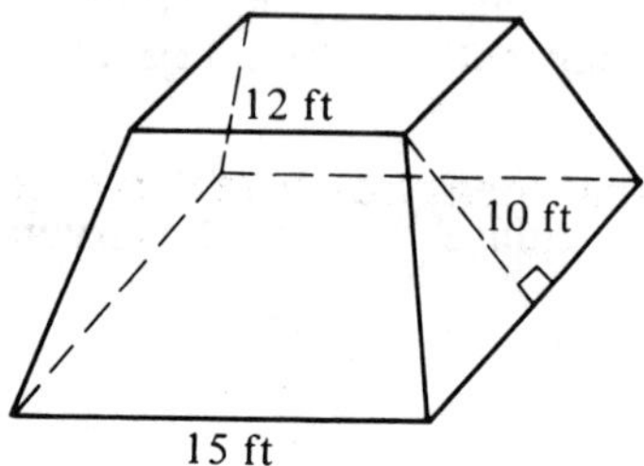

Answers
Since the faces are trapezoids,
$LA = 4 \cdot \frac{1}{2} \cdot l(b_1 + b_2)$
$LA = 2 \cdot 10 \cdot (12 + 15)$
$LA = 20 \cdot 27$
$LA = 540$ sq ft
Since the bases are squares,
$TA = 540 + 12^2 + 15^2$
$TA = 540 + 144 + 225$
$TA = 909$ sq ft

There is a formula for the lateral area of a *regular* pyramid according to the following theorem.

Theorem 111 The lateral area of a regular pyramid is one-half the product of the perimeter of its base and its slant height ($LA = \frac{1}{2}Pl$).

While we will not prove this theorem for all cases, the following figure shows it to be correct for a regular triangular pyramid.

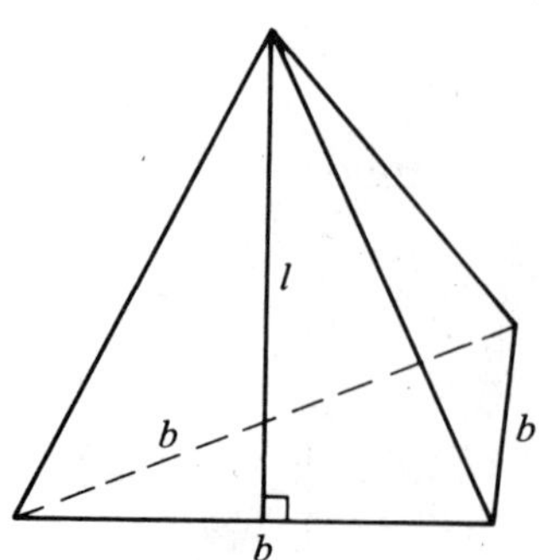

$LA = 3 \cdot \frac{1}{2}bl$
$LA = \frac{1}{2}(3b)l$
$LA = \frac{1}{2}Pl$

This section concludes with an application of the Pythagorean Theorem in three-dimensional figures. Figure 10.15 shows a rectangular right prism (rectangular box) and one of its *diagonals*. (How many does it have?) Example 4 shows how the length of such a diagonal may be calculated.

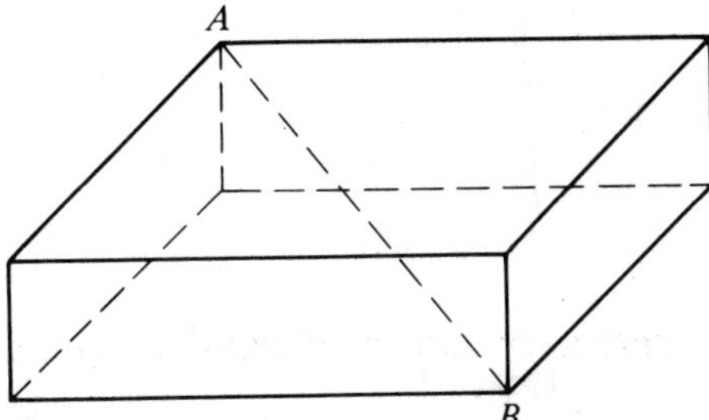

Figure 10.15 *A* and *B* are opposite vertices; $\overline{AB}$ is a diagonal.

EXAMPLE 4 A rectangular room 8 feet high has a floor that measures 9 feet by 12 feet. Find the length x of the longest rod that can fit in the room.

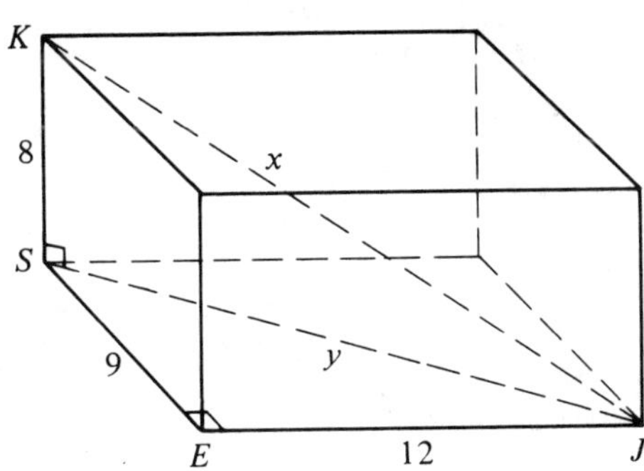

Answer

In right triangle *EJS*, y is the length of the hypotenuse. Hence,

$y^2 = 9^2 + 12^2$
$y^2 = 81 + 144$
$y^2 = 225$
$y = 15$ ft

In right triangle *SJK*, x is the length of the hypotenuse (the rod). Hence,

$x^2 = 8^2 + y^2$
$x^2 = 64 + 225$
$x^2 = 289$
$x = 17$ ft

EXERCISES FOR 10.3

In exercises 1–10 name (a) the type of polyhedron, (b) the bases, (c) the vertices, (d) the lateral edges, and (e) the lateral faces.

1.

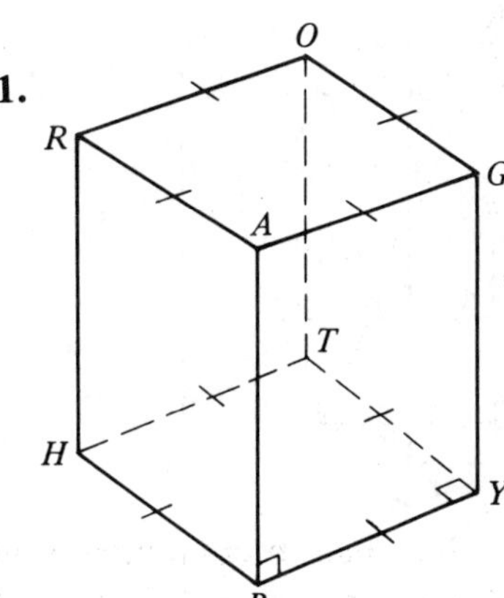

2.

O
I
A
X

3.

O
R
T
F
C
A

4.

T
D
I
U
A

5.

R
L
S
N
P
A
T
G
C
O

6.

Q
P
R
D
F
A
C
E
T
S
B
I

7.

O
D
C
E
B
A

8.

L
E
Q
U
P
A
O
S

9.

K
E
S
J

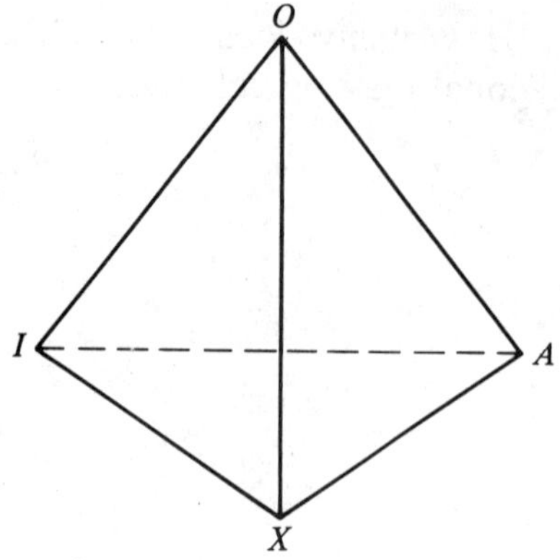

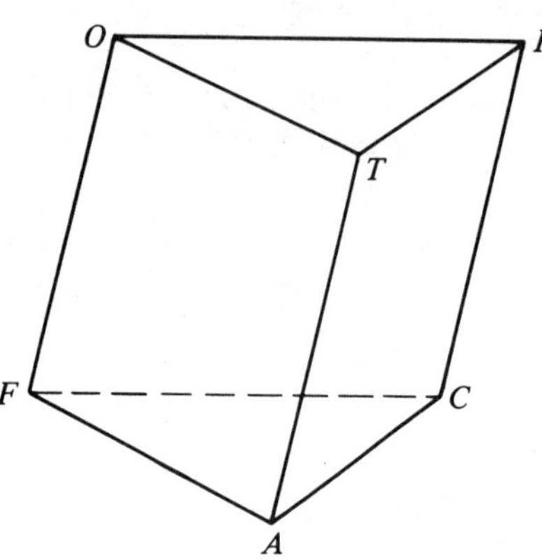

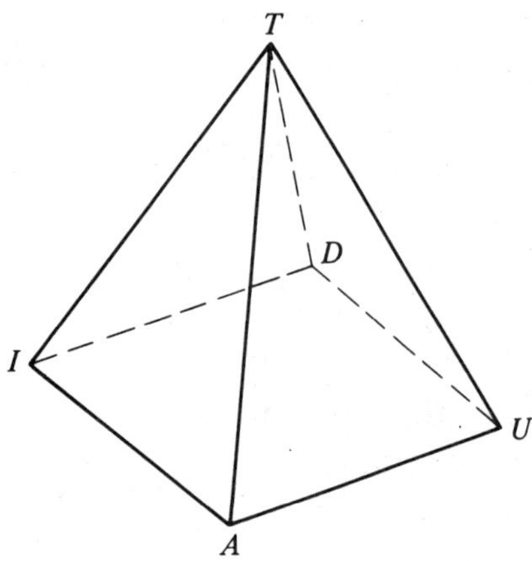

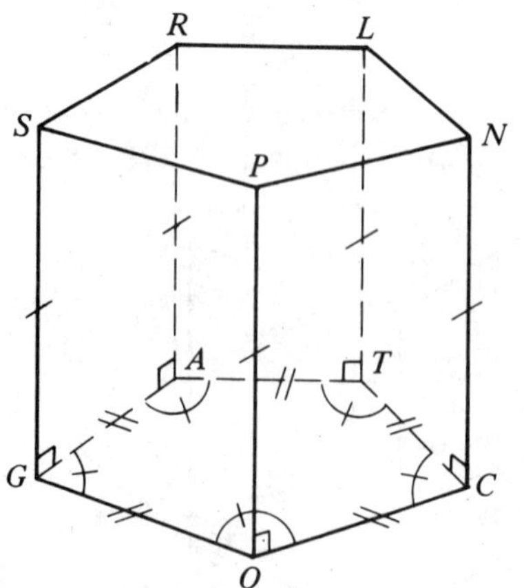

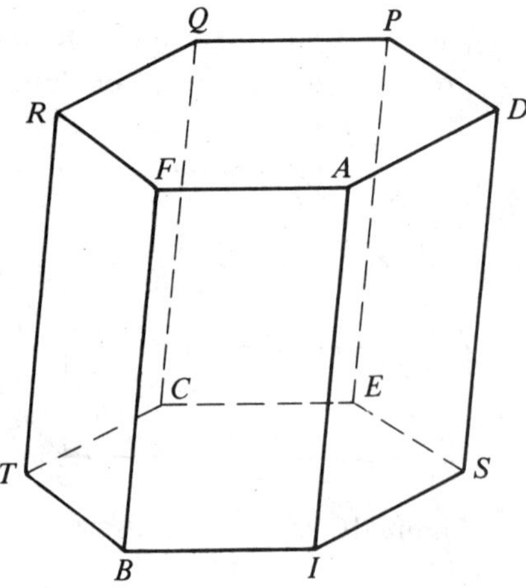

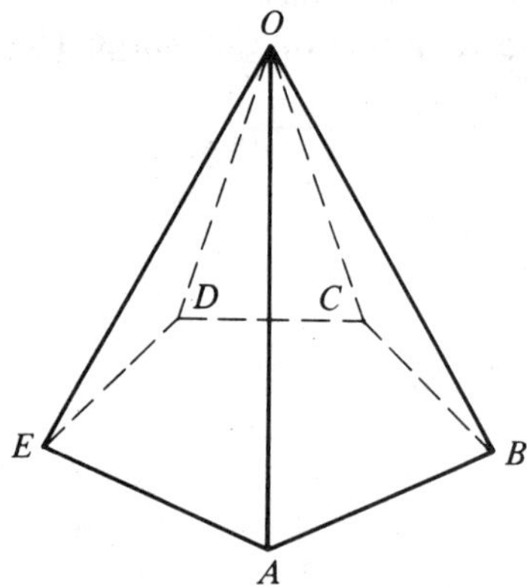

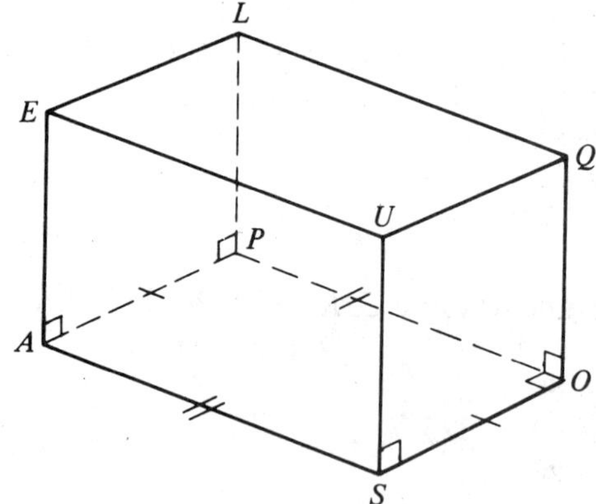

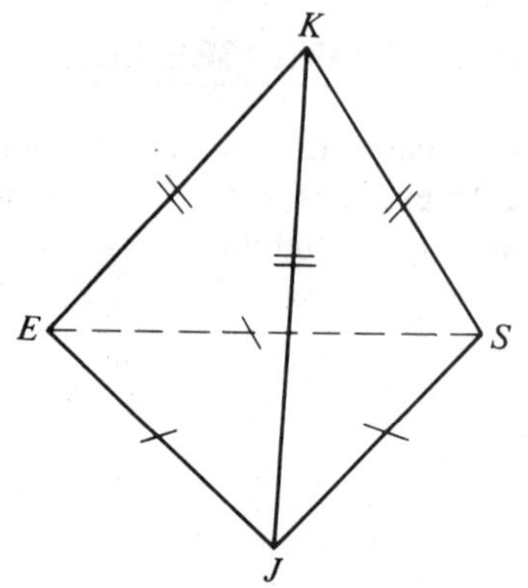

10.

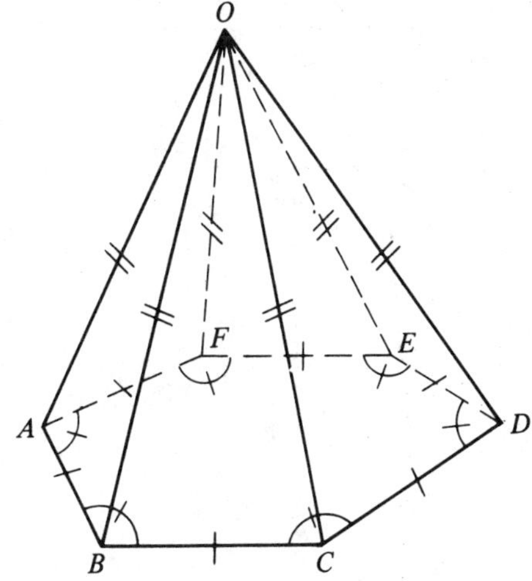

In exercises 11–20 find (a) the lateral area and (b) the total area.

11. *Given*
rect parallelepiped
$SW = 5$ in
$WN = 11$ in

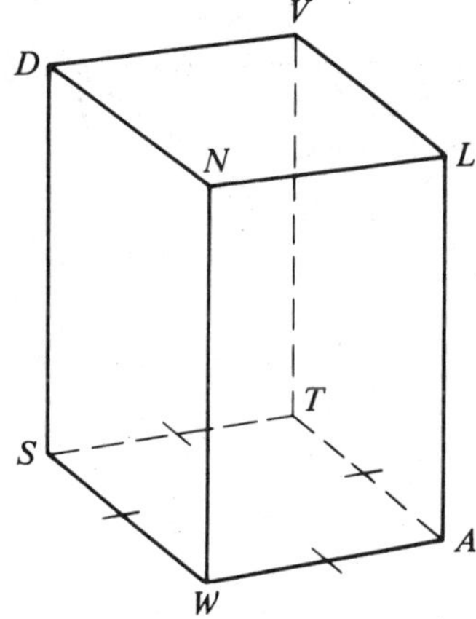

12. *Given*
reg triang pyramid
$AC = 10$ in
$AO = 13$ in

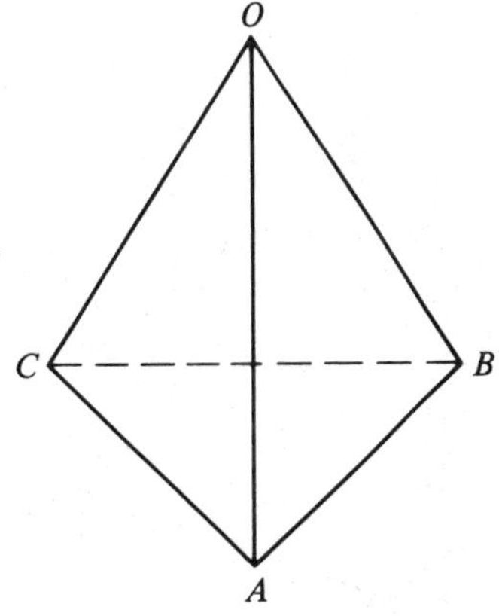

13. *Given*
reg sq pyramid
$AP = 8$ in
$l = 15$ in

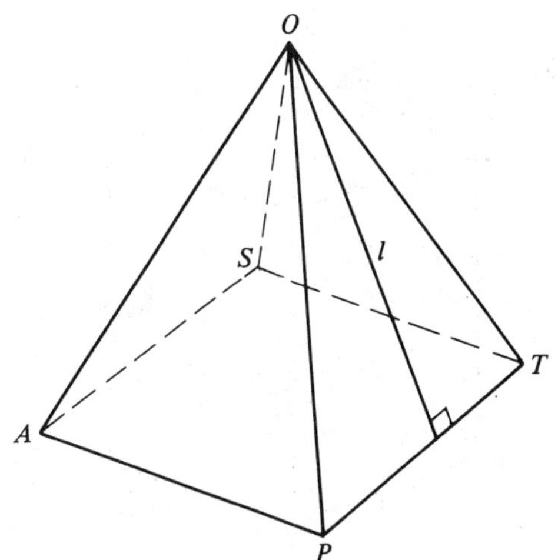

14. *Given*
reg hexagonal prism
B center of base
$EF = 9$ in
$FA = 4$ in

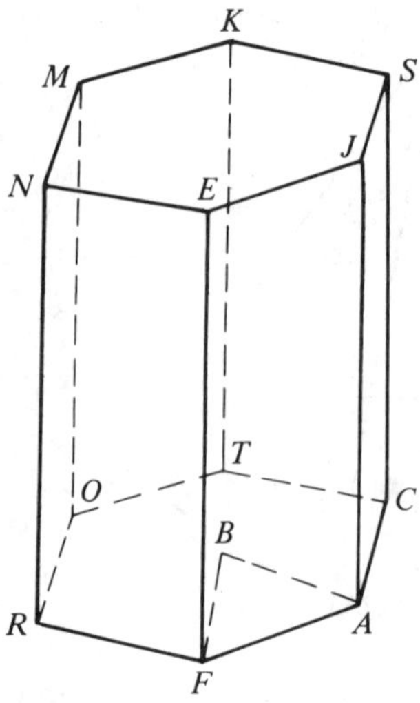

15.
Given
reg triang prism
$TR = 18$ cm
$GT = 28$ cm

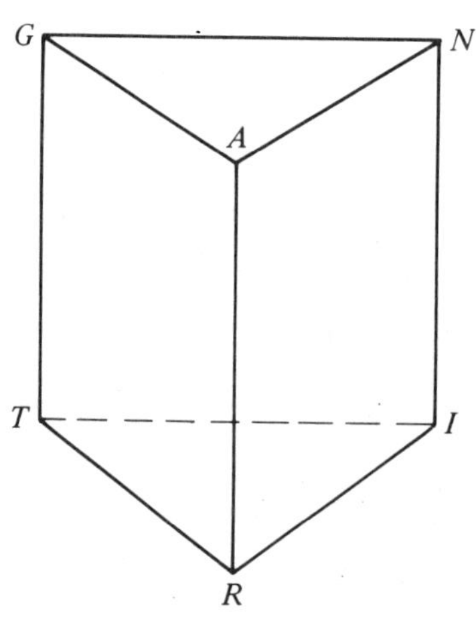

16. *Given*
reg hexagonal pyramid
B center of base
$OP = 8$ ft
$PA = 5$ ft

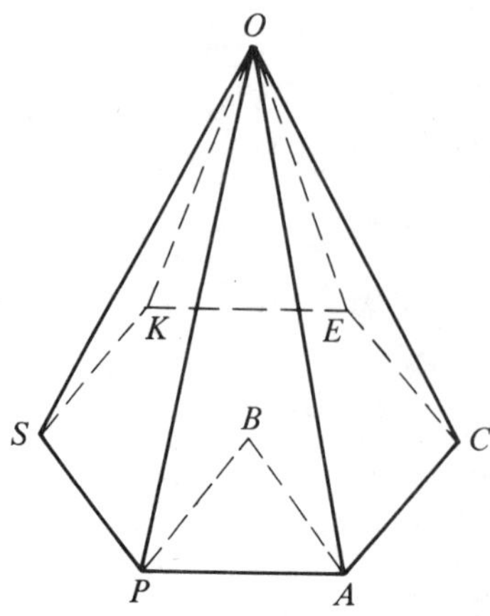

17. *Given*
reg sq pyramid
$EK = 34$ ft
$KO = 30$ ft

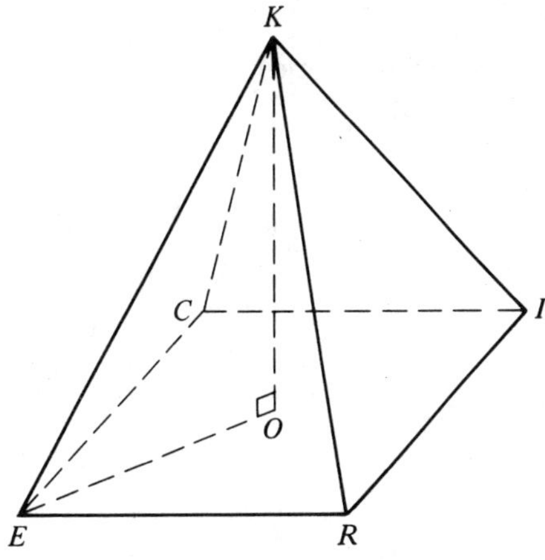

18. *Given*
sq pyramid
$MO = 6$ in
$XI = 6$ in

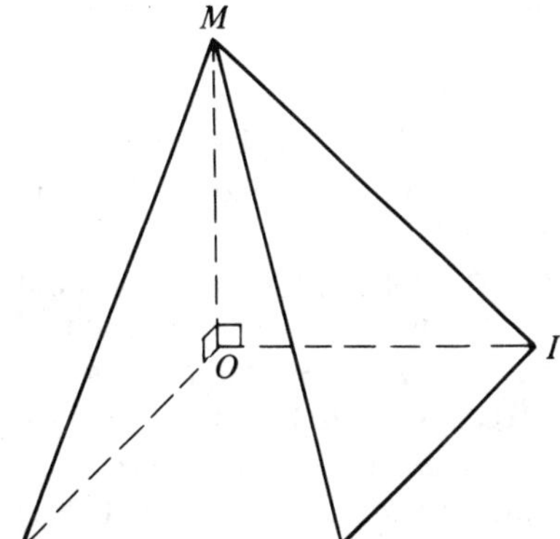

19. *Given*
reg triang pyramid
$PC = 61$ cm
$PO = 60$ cm
$CO = \frac{2}{3}CD$

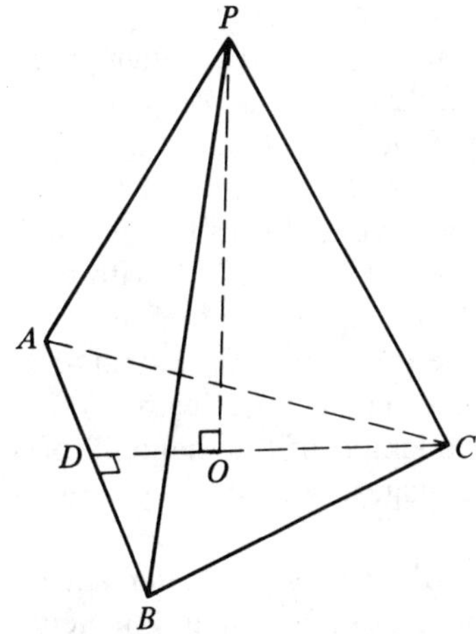

20. *Given*
reg hexagonal pyramid
$RO = 3\sqrt{3}$ in
$YT = 8$ in

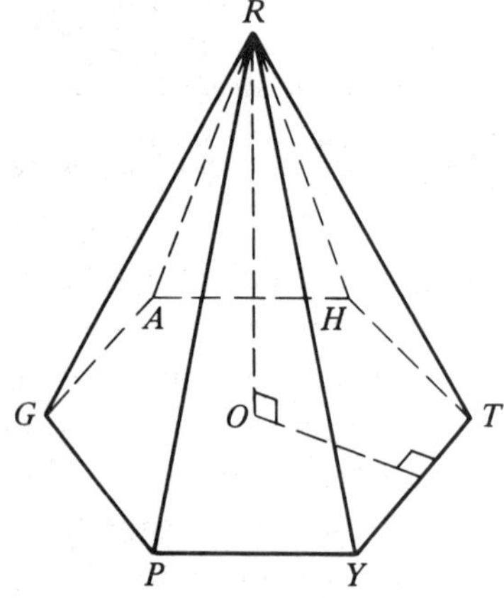

In exercises 21–35 draw a figure, label it, write the necessary equations, and solve.

21. If the total area of a cube is 96 square inches, find the length of an edge.

22. The dimensions of a rectangular parallelepiped are 6 feet by 7 feet by 9 feet. Find the edge of a cube that has the same total area.

23. The base of a regular pyramid is an equilateral triangle whose sides are each 12 centimeters long, and the lateral edges each measure 10 centimeters. Find the total area.

24. A regular pyramid has a square base whose sides are each 40 centimeters long. If each lateral edge measures 29 centimeters, find the lateral area.

25. A yardstick fits exactly into a cubical box as one of its diagonals. Find the total area of the inside of the box.

26. The altitude of a regular triangular prism is 10 feet. The edges of its bases are each 6 feet long. Find the total area.

27. The altitude of a regular triangular prism is 20 yards. The edges of its bases are each 15 feet long. Find the lateral area.

28. The inside dimensions of a rectangular box are 6 inches by 9 inches by 18 inches. How much will it cost to line the box with copper at $25.60 per square foot, if an additional $\frac{1}{24}$ of the total area of the inside of the box is necessary for the seams?

29. Show that the length of the diagonal of a cube whose edges are of length e is $e\sqrt{3}$.

30. Find the lateral area of a regular square pyramid whose slant height is 26 inches and whose altitude is 24 inches.

31. A solid is composed of a cube with 30-inch edges surmounted by a regular square pyramid of slant height 39 inches and whose base is the top face of the cube. Find the total area of the solid.

32. The diagonal of one cube is three times as long as the edge of a second cube. What is the ratio of the total area of the larger cube to that of the smaller?

33. The slant height of a frustum of a regular pyramid is 41 feet and its bases are squares with sides of 15 feet and 33 feet, respectively. Find the lateral area and the total area of the frustum.

34. For a convex polyhedron, Euler's formula states that $V - E + F = 2$, where V is the number of vertices, E is the number of edges, and F is the number of faces. Verify this formula for (a) a triangular prism, (b) a square pyramid, and (c) a prism whose bases are pentagons, by drawing a figure and counting the vertices, edges, and faces. (See Appendix D for a brief discussion of the Swiss mathematician Leonhard Euler [1707–1783], the discoverer of this formula.)

35. Verify Euler's formula (exercise 34) for (a) a cube, (b) a pyramid whose base is a hexagon, and (c) a regular tetrahedron (four faces that are equilateral triangles) by drawing the figures and counting the vertices, edges, and faces.

10.4

VOLUMES OF PRISMS AND PYRAMIDS

As indicated in Section 10.1 a geometric solid is the union of a closed surface and its interior. When we refer to the volume of a prism or a pyramid we really mean the volume of the geometric solid bounded by a prism or a pyramid. For convenience and to conform to common usage, however, we will use the briefer language. Keep in mind, though, that the volume of a polyhedron is a measure assigned to a set of points on the polyhedron and in its interior, just as the area of a polygon is a measure assigned to the set of points on the polygon and in its interior.

Recall that a measure is assigned to a set of points by covering it with a unit measure. For volume, the unit measure is a cube whose edges are all of length 1. Such a cube is called a *unit cube*. Figure 10.16 shows a unit cube and a rectangular right prism (rectangular parallelepiped or rectangular box) covered with unit cubes. Evidently, exactly $4 \cdot 3 \cdot 2 = 24$ unit cubes cover this solid, and so the volume is 24 cubic units. Not all such rectangular boxes can be covered by a whole number of unit cubes, of course, but the example suggests that the appropriate number of unit cubes may be calculated as the product of the three dimensions: length times width times height (altitude).

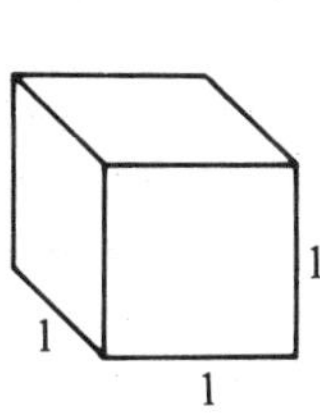

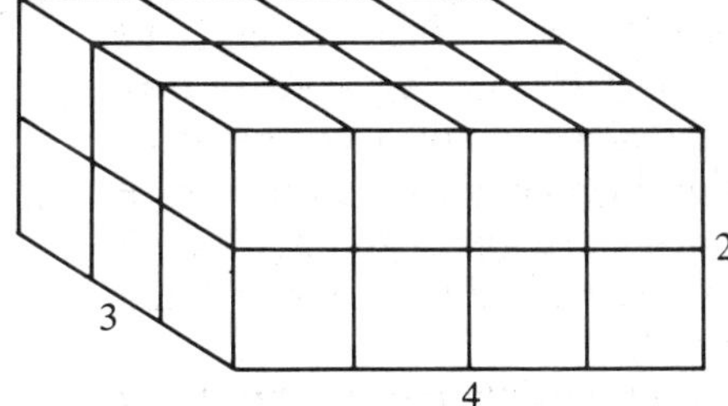

Figure 10.16

As shown in Figure 10.17, this product is equal to the product of the area of one of the box's faces, taken as a base, and the altitude to that base. This suggests the following postulate.

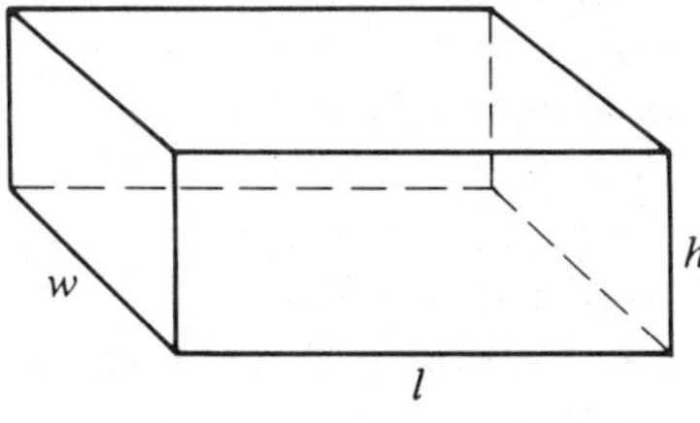

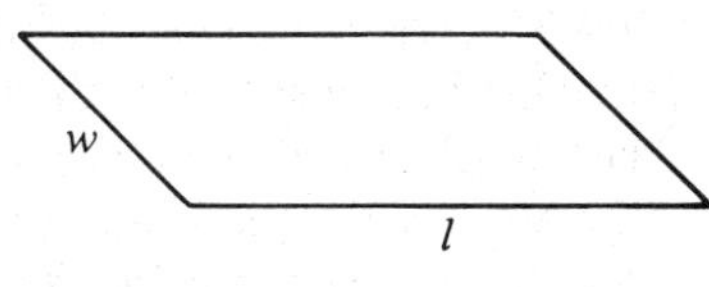

Figure 10.17

Postulate 22 The volume of a rectangular right prism or rectangular parallelepiped is the product of the area of its base and its altitude ($V = lwh$).

Of course, this postulate includes the special case of a cube. With each dimension of the cube denoted e, however, we write the volume formula as $V = e^3$. (Indeed, this is the origin of the way in which the exponent 3 is normally read.)

Based on Postulate 22, we can prove the following theorem.

Theorem 112 The volume of any prism is the product of the area of one of its bases and its altitude ($V = Bh$).

To gain some insight into this theorem, consider a pack of cards as representing a rectangular box. The volume of this box is the sum of the volumes of the cards. If the cards are pushed to form a new prism (Figure 10.18) that is not a right prism, but has the same base and altitude, it should be clear that the volume is unchanged. Furthermore, if we "cut" from a rectangular prism a new prism with, for example, a triangular base whose area is one-half that of the original base, it is reasonable that the new volume should be one-half of the volume of the original prism. Our discussion is illustrated in the next example.

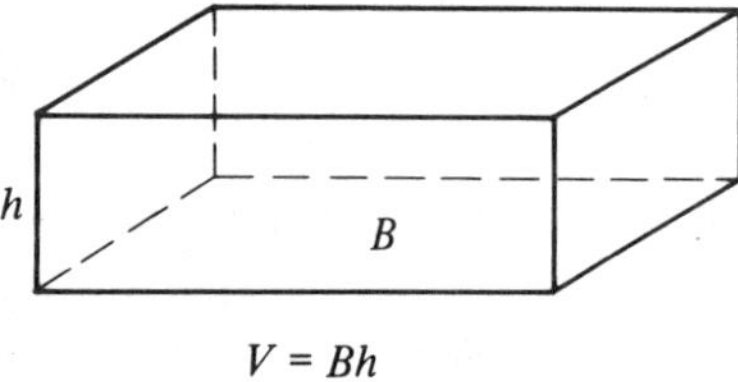

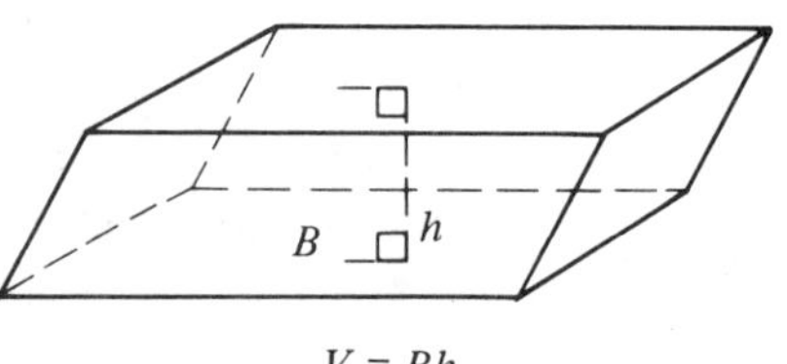

Figure 10.18

EXAMPLE 1 Find the volume of the given solids.

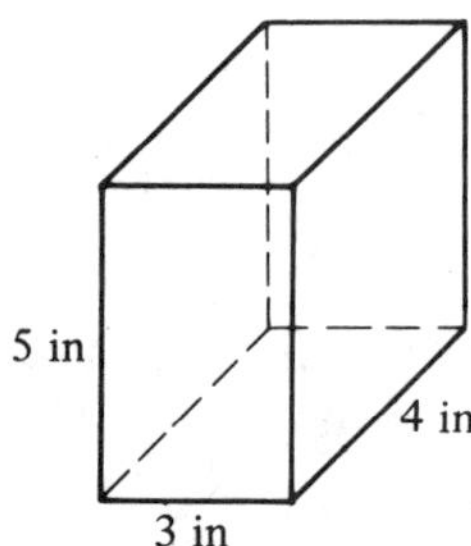

(a) rectangular right prism

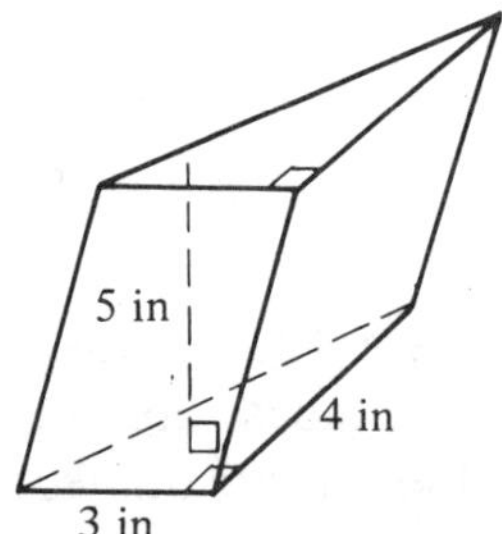

(b) triangular prism (bases right triangles)

Answers

(a) $V = lwh$
$V = 4 \cdot 3 \cdot 5$
$V = 60$ cu in

(b) $V = Bh$
$V = \frac{1}{2} \cdot 4 \cdot 3 \cdot 5$
$V = 30$ cu in

Next, consider the volume of a pyramid. Figure 10.19 shows a triangular prism and a way that it can be divided into three triangular pyramids $ABCE$, $ACED$, and $DEFC$. It can be shown that these three pyramids have equal volumes. Since the volume of the prism is Bh, it follows that the volume of each pyramid is $\frac{1}{3}Bh$. The next theorem states that this is correct for all pyramids.

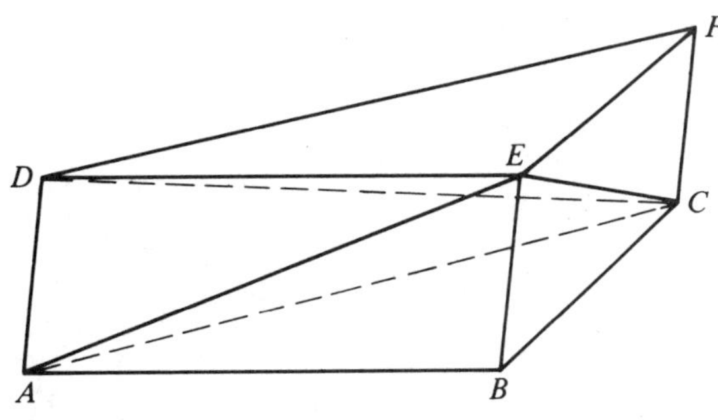

Figure 10.19

Theorem 113 The volume of any pyramid is one-third the product of the area of its base and its altitude ($V = \frac{1}{3}Bh$).

EXAMPLE 2 Find the volume of the given solids.

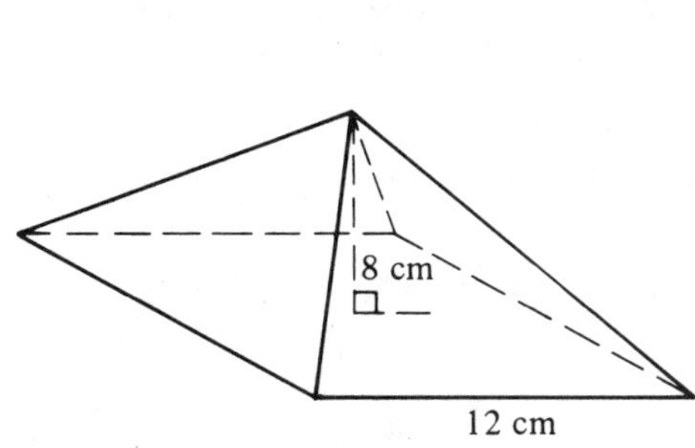

(a) square pyramid

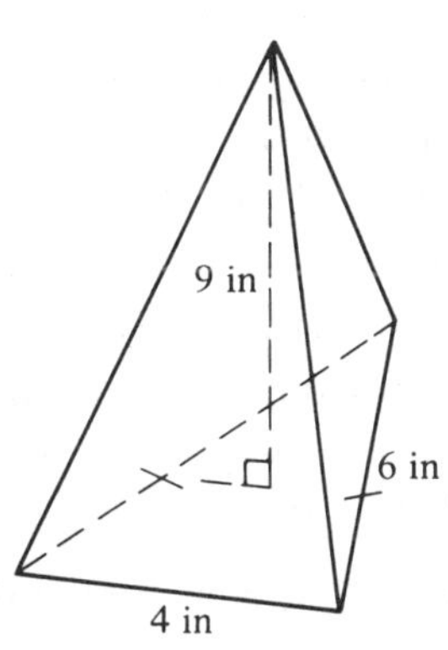

(b) isosceles triangular pyramid

Answers

(a) $V = \frac{1}{3}Bh$ $\quad V = \frac{1}{3} \cdot 12^2 \cdot 8$ $\quad V = \frac{1}{3} \cdot 144 \cdot 8$ $\quad V = 384$ cu cm

(b)

$x^2 + 2^2 = 6^2$
$x^2 = 36 - 4$
$x = \sqrt{32} = 4\sqrt{2}$ in

$B = \frac{1}{2}bx$
$B = \frac{1}{2} \cdot 4 \cdot 4 \cdot \sqrt{2}$
$B = 8\sqrt{2}$ sq in

$V = \frac{1}{3}Bh$
$V = \frac{1}{3} \cdot 8 \cdot \sqrt{2} \cdot 9$
$V = 24\sqrt{2}$
$V \approx 33.6$ cu in

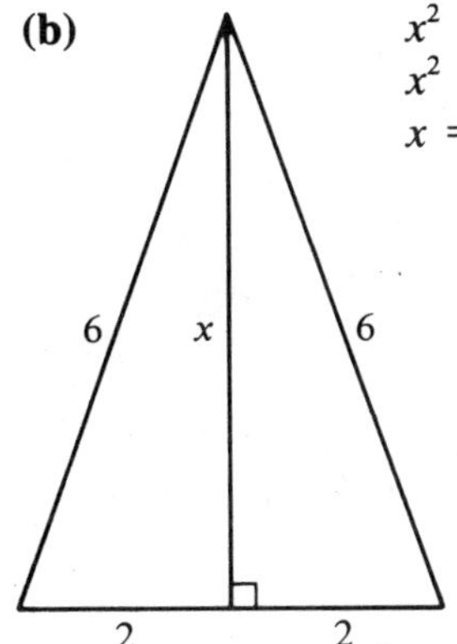

(b) base of pyramid

There is a theory about similar polyhedrons that is a natural extension of that for similar triangles (Chapter 9). Although the theory is beyond the scope of this text, we will mention an aspect of it concerning areas and volumes. Two polyhedrons are *similar* if they have the same number of faces, similar each to each, and similarly placed and if their corresponding dihedral angles (exercises 31–40, Section 10.2) are congruent. Figure 10.20 shows two similar triangular pyramids.

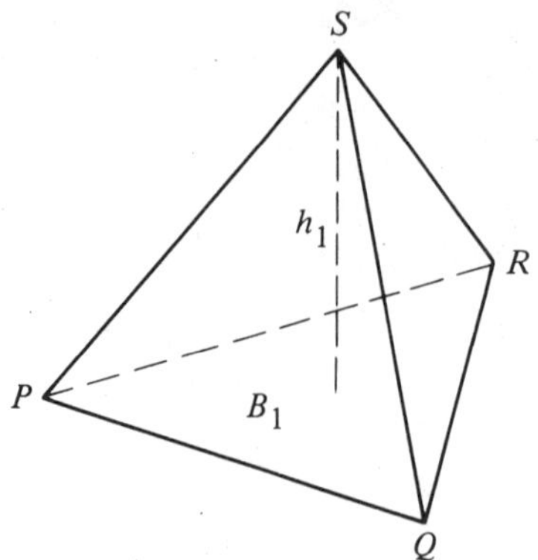

Figure 10.20

Recall that if two triangles are similar, then corresponding sides and corresponding altitudes are proportional and the ratio of their areas is the same as the ratio of the squares of any two corresponding sides or corresponding altitudes (Theorem 104). It is intuitively reasonable that these facts extend to polyhedrons thus:

> If two polyhedrons are similar, then corresponding edges and corresponding altitudes are proportional and the ratio of their total areas is the same as the ratio of the squares of any two corresponding edges or corresponding altitudes.

Furthermore, we have this important fact:

> If two polyhedrons are similar, then the ratio of their volumes is the same as the ratio of the cubes of any two corresponding edges or corresponding altitudes.

To gain some understanding of this, note that for the triangular pyramids in Figure 10.20 we have

1. $\dfrac{V_1}{V_2} = \dfrac{\cancel{\frac{1}{3}}B_1h_1}{\cancel{\frac{1}{3}}B_2h_2}$ (volume formula)
2. $\dfrac{B_1}{B_2} = \dfrac{PQ^2}{EJ^2}$ (bases are similar triangles)
3. $\dfrac{h_1}{h_2} = \dfrac{PQ}{EJ}$ (ratio of altitudes of similar pyramids equals ratio of corresponding edges)
4. $\dfrac{V_1}{V_2} = \dfrac{PQ^2}{EJ^2} \cdot \dfrac{PQ}{EJ} = \dfrac{PQ^3}{EJ^3}$ (substitution of (2) and (3) into (1))

EXAMPLE 3 If the edges of two similar polyhedrons are in the ratio 2:5, what is the ratio of their volumes?

Answer

$$\frac{V_1}{V_2} = \frac{e_1^3}{e_2^3} = \left(\frac{e_1}{e_2}\right)^3 = \left(\frac{2}{5}\right)^3 = \frac{8}{125}$$

The final example of this section shows a practical application of volume. Other applied problems appear in the exercises.

EXAMPLE 4 A grocer packs soapboxes whose dimensions are 3 inches by 6 inches by 10 inches in a cubical carton whose edge e is $2\frac{1}{2}$ feet long. How many boxes can he put in the carton?

Answer

$V(\text{box}) = lwh$
$= 6 \cdot 3 \cdot 10$
$V(\text{box}) = 180$ cu in
Since $e = 2\frac{1}{2}$ ft, or 30 in,
$V(\text{carton}) = e^3$
$= 30^3$
$V(\text{carton}) = 27{,}000$ cu in
By dividing we have

$$\frac{V(\text{carton})}{V(\text{box})} = \frac{27{,}000}{180} = 150 \text{ boxes}$$

Some comments about Example 4 are in order. First, from an arithmetic point of view, we worked too hard. It would have been easier to write:

$$\frac{V(\text{carton})}{V(\text{box})} = \frac{\overset{5}{\cancel{30}} \cdot \overset{10}{\cancel{30}} \cdot \overset{3}{\cancel{30}}}{\underset{1}{\cancel{6}} \cdot \underset{1}{\cancel{3}} \cdot \underset{1}{\cancel{10}}} = 150 \text{ boxes}$$

More important, note that the numbers are carefully rigged. Not only is the answer a whole number, but also 30 inches (the edge of the carton) is divisible by all three dimensions of the box. This means the 150 boxes will, in fact, fit into the carton. But suppose the boxes were 2 inches by 9 inches by 10 inches. The volume computations would be unchanged, but the answer, 150 boxes, would be wrong! Do you see why? This indicates the care that must be exercised in interpreting numbers and the arithmetic that is done with them.

EXERCISES FOR 10.4

In exercises 1–20 copy the figure, label it with the given measures, write the necessary formulas, and find the requested measures.

1. *Given*
pyramid $O\text{-}APT$
$A(\triangle APT) = 21$ sq in
$\overline{OE}$ alt
$OE = 15$ in

Find
volume of pyramid

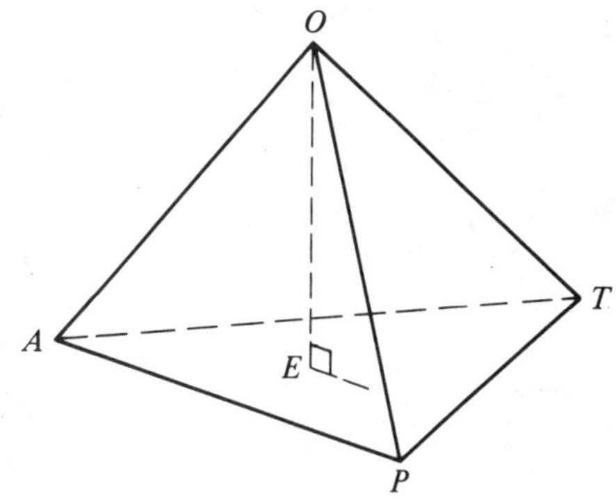

2. *Given*
rect parallelepiped
$AB = 7$ in
$BC = 15$ in
$GD = 13$ in

Find
volume of parallelepiped

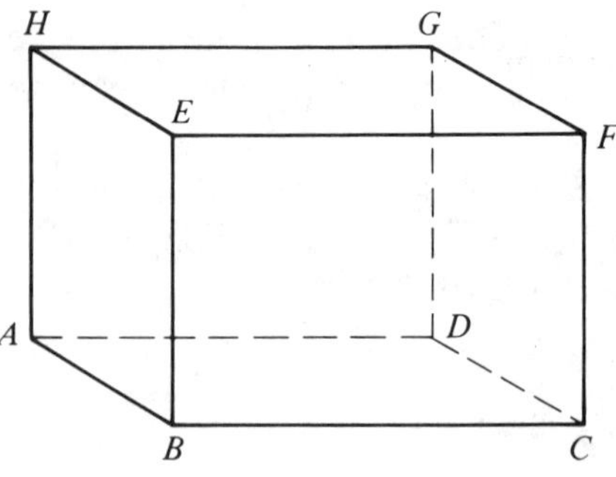

3. *Given*
cube
$EJ = 8$ in

Find
volume of cube

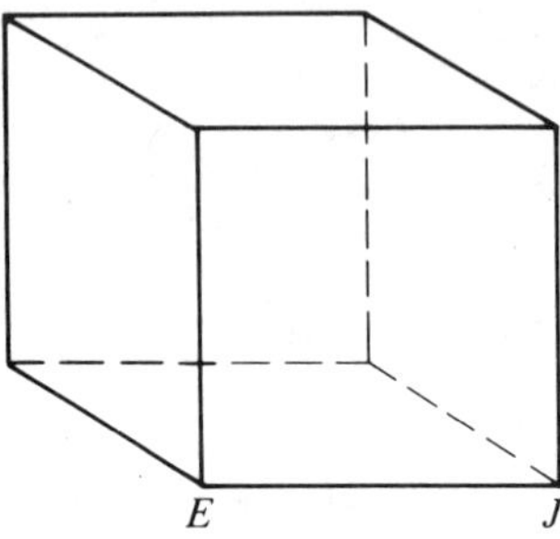

4. *Given*
pyramid *O-JAWS*
sq *JAWS*
$\overline{OE}$ alt
$SW = 15$ cm
$OE = 23$ cm

Find
volume of pyramid

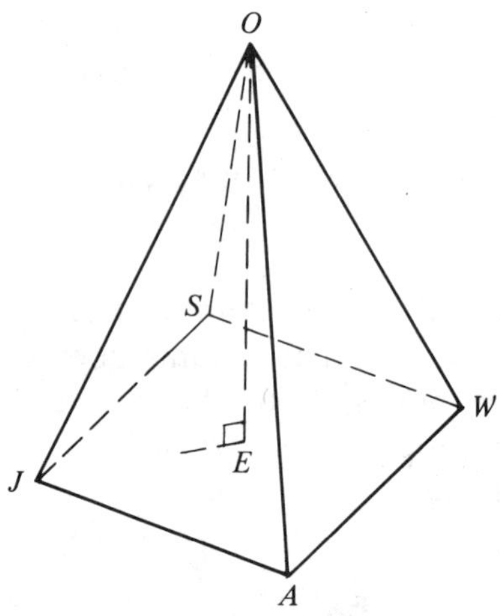

5. *Given*
pyramid *O-ANGLE*
$\overline{OJ}$ alt
$A(\text{base}) = 8\sqrt{3}$ sq ft
$OJ = 2\sqrt{3}$ ft

Find
volume of pyramid

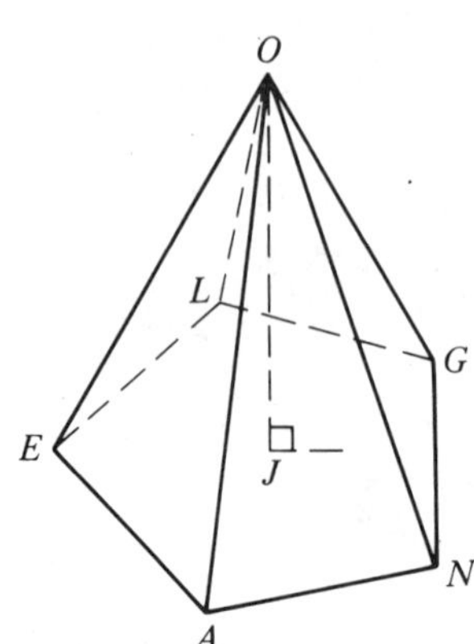

6. *Given*
triang rt prism
$A(\text{base}) = 57$ sq cm
$AB = 32$ cm

Find
volume of prism

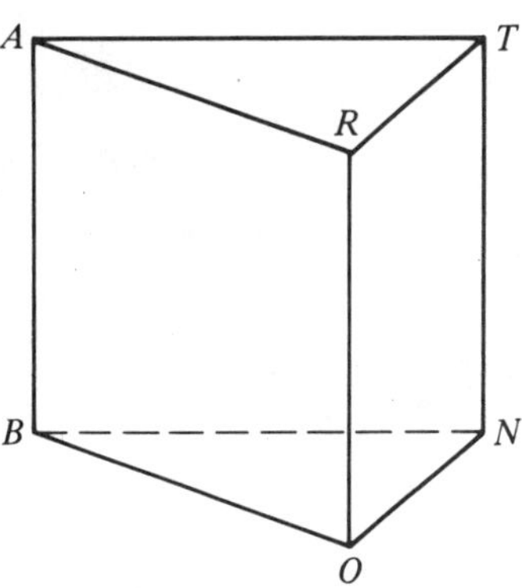

7. *Given*
pentagonal rt prism
$A(\text{base}) = 52$ sq in
$h = 37$ in

Find
volume of prism

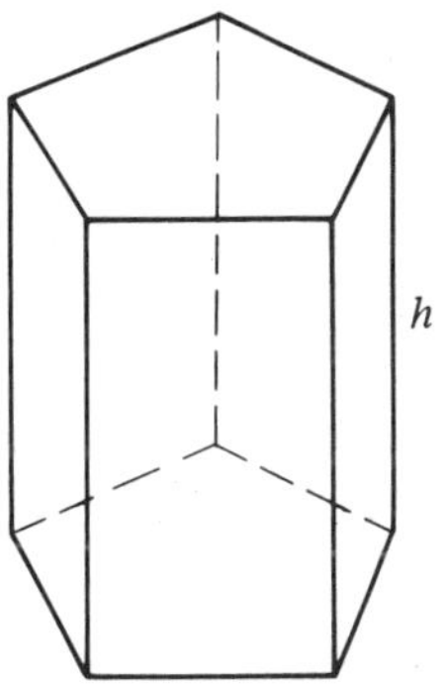

8. *Given*
reg sq pyramid *E-FACT*
$\overline{EO}$ alt
$EA = 17$ cm
$OA = 8$ cm

Find
volume of pyramid

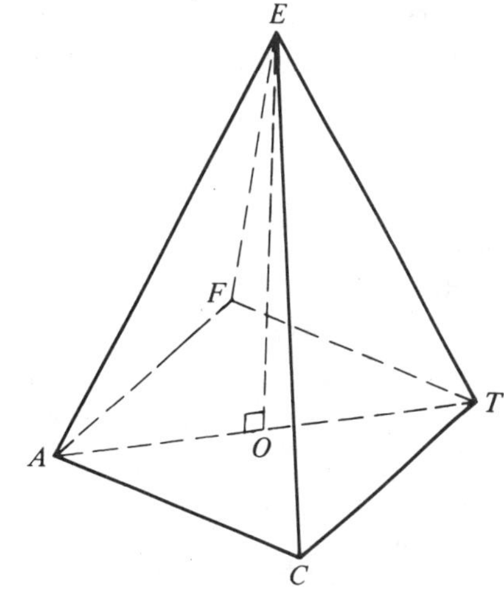

9. *Given*
reg triang pyramid *E-CAT*
$\overline{TR} \perp \overline{AC}$
$\overline{EO}$ alt
$ET = 61$ cm
$TO = 11$ cm
$TO = \frac{2}{3}TR$

Find
volume of pyramid

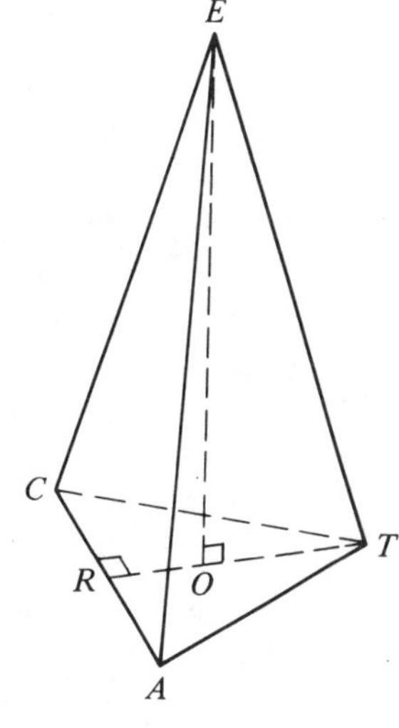

10. *Given*
reg sq pyramid *O-STAK*
$\overline{OE}$ alt
$\overline{OR} \perp \overline{ST}$
$ER = 8$ in
$OR = 17$ in

Find
volume of pyramid

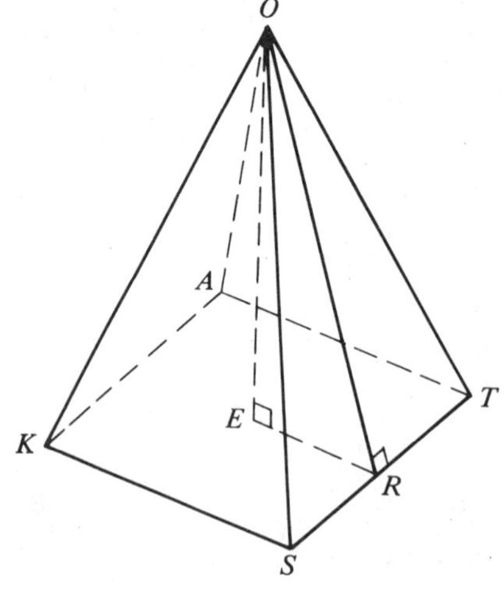

11. *Given*
rect parallelepiped
$PT = 15$ ft
$RT = 17$ ft
$YT = 9$ ft

Find
volume of parallelepiped

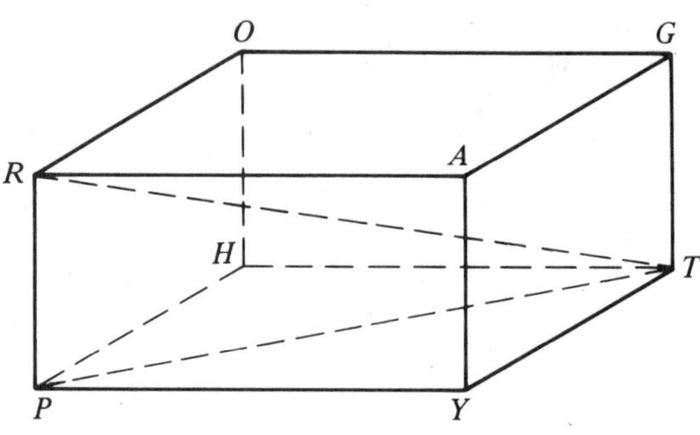

12. *Given*
triang rt prism
ΔLIN isos ($\overline{LI}$ base)
$\overline{MN} \perp \overline{LI}$
$LI = 12$ in
$LS = 37$ in
$MN = 9$ in

Find
volume of prism

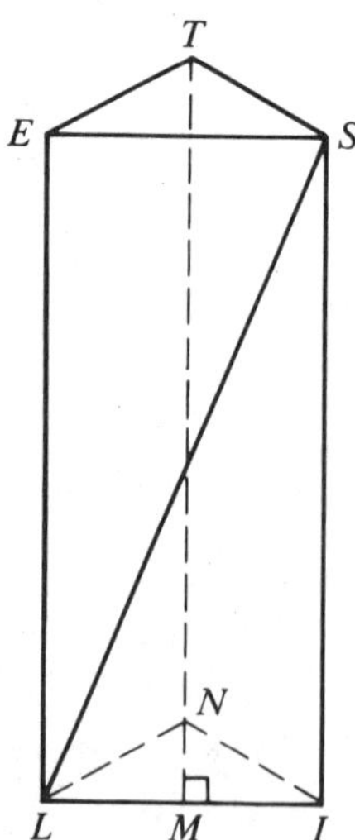

13. *Given*
trapezoidal rt prism ($\overline{AB} \parallel \overline{DC}$)
$\overline{AR} \perp \overline{DC}$
$AB = 3$ ft
$DC = 5$ ft
$AR = 2$ ft
$BF = 10$ ft

Find
volume of prism

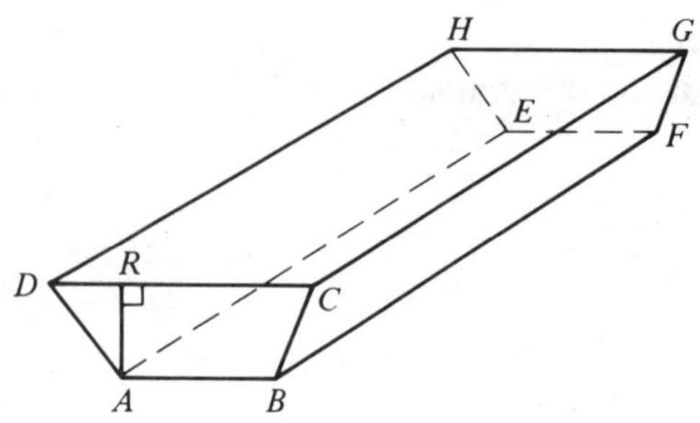

In exercises 14 and 15 refer to Figure 10.21.

14. *Given*
reg hexagonal pyramid
$PY = 9$ in
$EP = 15$ in
$\overline{EO}$ alt
$\overline{OR} \perp \overline{GP}$

Find
volume of pyramid

15. *Given*
reg hexagonal pyramid
$ER = 37$ cm
$EO = 35$ cm

Find
volume of pyramid

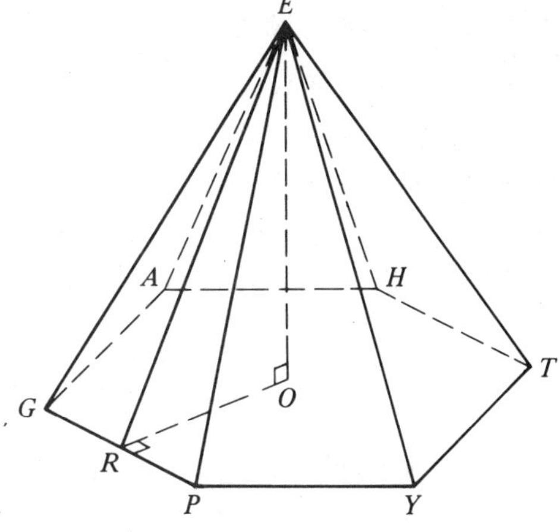

Figure 10.21

In exercises 16 and 17 refer to Figure 10.22.

16. *Given*
reg sq pyramid O-$DECA$
$\overline{OT}$ alt
pl $PGRI \parallel$ pl $DECA$
$OC = 10$ in
$RC = 5$ in
$TC = 6$ in

Find
volume of frustum of pyramid

17. *Given*
reg sq pyramid O-$DECA$
pl $PGRI \parallel$ pl $DECA$
$\overline{OT}$ alt
$\overline{OQ} \perp \overline{DE}$
$OQ = 30$ cm
$OV = 20$ cm
$DE = 36$ cm

Find
volume of frustum of pyramid

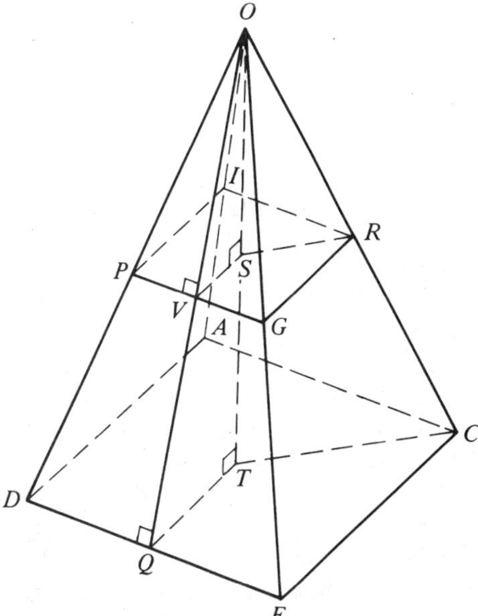

Figure 10.22

18. *Given*
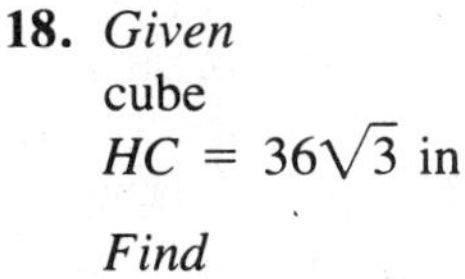
cube
$HC = 36\sqrt{3}$ in

Find
volume of cube

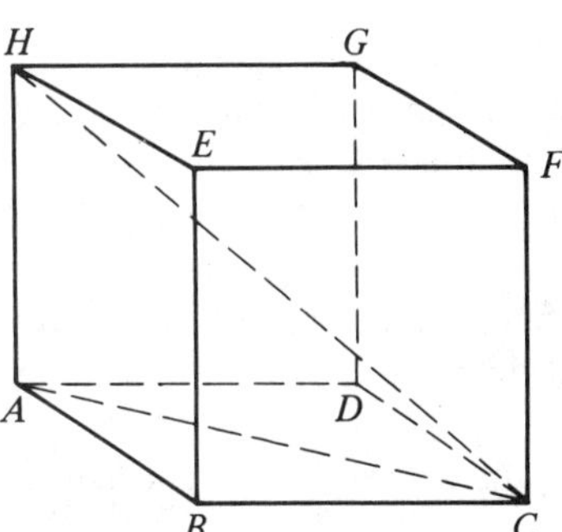

19. *Given*
cube
$DE = 75\sqrt{3}$ cm

Find
volume of pyramid *D-EUC*

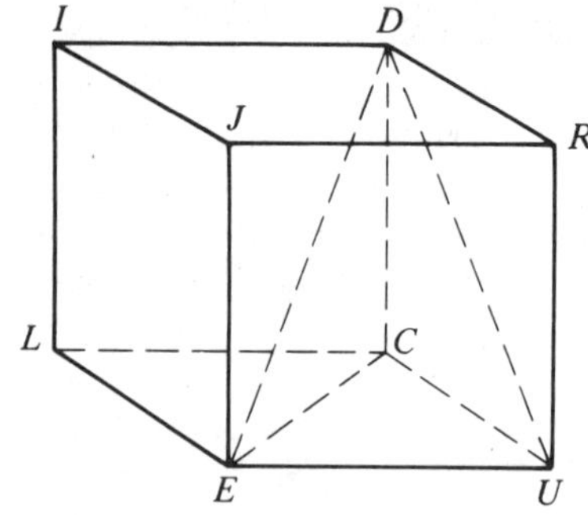

20. *Given*
reg sq pyramid *O-JAWS*
$\overline{OE}$ alt
$JA = a$ units
$\overline{OE} \cong \overline{JW}$

Find
volume of pyramid

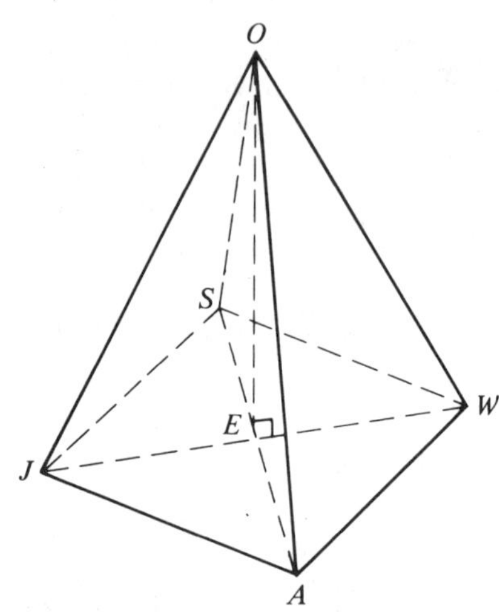

In exercises 21–40 draw a figure, label it, write the necessary equations, and solve.

21. Find the volume of a rectangular parallelepiped with dimensions 3 feet by 5 feet by 7 feet.

22. If the ratio of the volumes of two similar triangular pyramids is 27:64, what is the ratio of any two corresponding edges? If an edge of the smaller pyramid is 18 inches long, how long is the corresponding edge of the larger pyramid?

23. The edges of the bases of a regular triangular prism are each 10 inches long and the altitude is 7 inches. Find the volume of the prism.

24. The edges of the bases of a regular hexagonal prism are each 4 feet long and the altitude measures 27 inches. Find the volume of the prism.

25. If the edge of an ice cube measures 4 centimeters, find the number of cubes that will fit into a rectangular ice tray with dimensions 24 centimeters by 32 centimeters by 20 centimeters.

26. A yardstick fits exactly into a cubical box as one of its diagonals. Find the volume of the box.

27. A regular square pyramid has slant height 26 centimeters and altitude 24 centimeters. Find the volume of the pyramid.

28. The lengths of three edges of a rectangular parallelepiped are 12, 16, and 20 centimeters. Choose two diagonals and show that they have the same length.

29. Find the volume of a regular square pyramid if each base edge and each lateral edge is 12 centimeters long.

30. The dimensions of a rectangular parallelepiped are 4 inches by 8 inches by 16 inches. Find the length of the diagonal of a cube with the same volume.

31. The lateral area of a regular triangular prism is 48 square inches. If its altitude is 4 inches, find the volume of the prism.

32. If the number of cubic inches in the volume of a cube equals the number of square inches in its total area, find the length of the diagonal of one of the faces of the cube.

33. An electronics firm packages an odd-sized product into 2-inch-by-3-inch-by-15-inch boxes. How many of the boxes can be packed in a carton 3 feet by 3 feet by $3\frac{3}{4}$ feet? Show how to pack them.

34. If a regular hexagonal pyramid has a lateral edge of 29 inches and a base edge of 20 inches, find the volume of the pyramid.

35. The dimensions of a rectangular parallelepiped are 6, 8, and 10 inches. A plane is passed through the midpoints of three edges that meet at a vertex. Find the volume of the smaller solid that is cut off by the plane.

36. A square pyramid is inscribed in a rectangular parallelepiped; that is, they have the same base and the pyramid's vertex is in the upper base of the parallelepiped. If the base edge measures 12 inches and the altitude measures 25 inches, find the volume of the solid that is inside the parallelepiped and outside the pyramid.

37. How many ice cubes with $1\frac{1}{4}$-inch edges can be stored in a cubical freezing compartment with 1-foot edges? Show how to store them.

38. A swimming pool has the shape of a trapezoidal right prism, 3 feet deep at one end and 10 feet at the other. It is 30 feet long and 18 feet wide. How many gallons of water does it take to fill the pool? (1 cu ft = 7.48 gal)

39. A concrete staircase has steps in the form of triangular right prisms whose ends are right triangles (see the figure). If the staircase has eight steps, how much concrete does it contain?

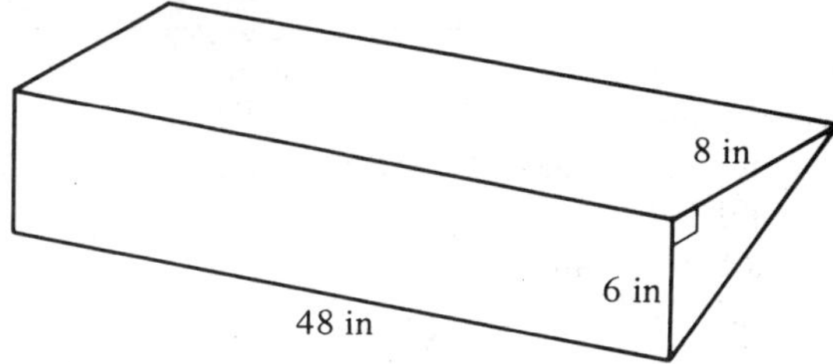

40. If the lengths of all edges of a regular triangular prism are b units, find its volume in terms of b.

10.5 CYLINDERS, CONES, AND SPHERES

The purpose of this section is to describe certain curved surfaces and geometric solids bounded by curved surfaces and to state how to calculate their areas and volumes. There is a major difficulty in deriving formulas for such areas and volumes, however. Recall that to measure area, for example, the figure in question is covered with unit squares and these are parts of a *plane*. How, then, can a curved surface be covered in this manner? Similarly, how can a geometric solid that is bounded by a *curved* surface be covered with unit cubes? The answer of course is that in the ordinary geometric sense these things *cannot* be done! Yet intuitively it seems that there should be a way to assign measure to the areas and volumes of such surfaces and solids. That this is indeed possible is demonstrated in calculus where the difficulties are overcome using the concept of a limit. Here we simply state the appropriate formulas without proof.

We begin by describing a circular cylindrical surface. Let $\odot O$ in a plane p be intersected by a line l not in p (Figure 10.23). The union of all lines parallel to l and intersecting $\odot O$ is a *circular cylindrical surface*. Note that this surface extends without end. The outer surface of a water pipe is a good representation of a portion of such a surface.

Next consider a plane q that is parallel to the plane p of Figure 10.23. Plane q and the cylindrical surface intersect in a section of the surface. The union of this section and its interior with $\odot O$ and its interior and the part of the cylindrical surface *between* the two circles is a *circular cylinder* (Figure

10.24). The two circular regions (circles and their interiors) are the *bases,* and the part of the cylindrical surface between them is the *lateral surface.* Thus, a circular cylinder is the circular counterpart of a prism.

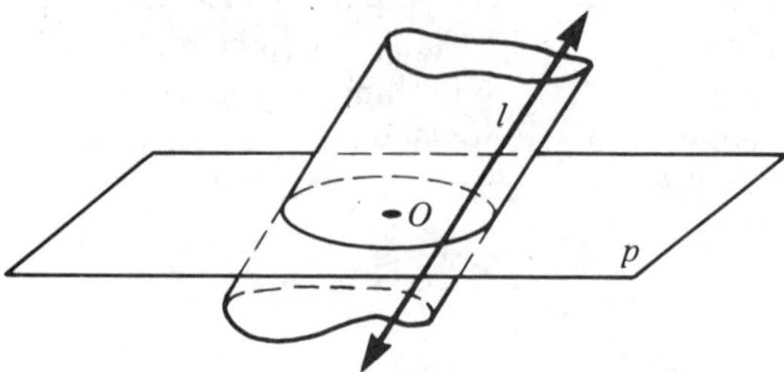

Figure 10.23

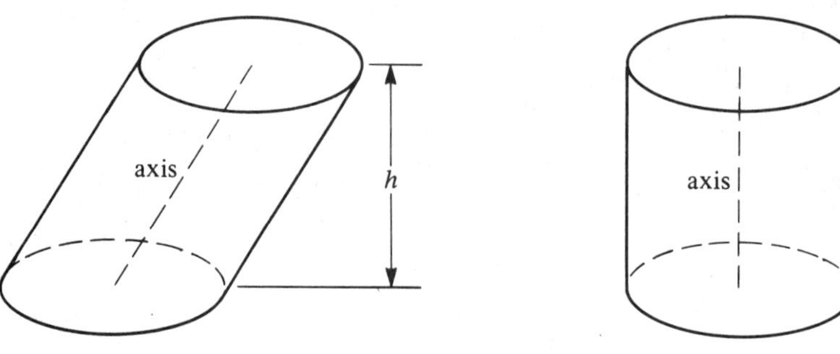

(a) oblique circular cylinder (b) right circular cylinder

Figure 10.24

The line segment joining the centers of the bases is the *axis* of the cylinder. In a *right* cylinder the axis is perpendicular to the bases (Figure 10.24[b]); in an *oblique* cylinder it is not (Figure 10.24[a]). The length of a line segment perpendicular to the planes of the bases is the altitude h of the cylinder.

We are now ready to state theorems and formulas about the area and volume of a right circular cylinder. The notations LA and TA have the same meanings as for a prism, and the volume applies to the solid bounded by a right circular cylinder. Also, keep in mind that the area of a circle is πr^2 and the circumference is $2\pi r$, where r is the circle's radius.

Theorem 114 The lateral area of a right circular cylinder is the product of the circumference of one of its bases and its altitude ($LA = 2\pi rh$). The total area is the sum of the lateral area and twice the area of one of its bases ($TA = 2\pi rh + 2\pi r^2$).

We may gain an understanding of Theorem 114 from Figure 10.25.

Figure 10.25 $LA = 2\pi rh$; $TA = LA + 2\pi r^2$.

Theorem 115 The volume of a right circular cylinder is the product of the area of one of its bases and its altitude ($V = \pi r^2 h$).

EXAMPLE 1 A tuna can is a right circular cylinder as shown. Find, to the nearest tenth, (a) the area of the label, (b) the area of the metal in the can, and (c) the volume of tuna in the can. Use $\pi \approx 3.14$.

Answers

(a) $LA = 2\pi rh$
$LA = 2 \cdot \pi \cdot (1.7) \cdot (1.5)$
$LA = 5.1\pi$ sq in
$LA \approx 16.0$ sq in

(b) $TA = LA + 2\pi r^2$
$TA = 5.1\pi + 2 \cdot \pi \cdot (1.7)^2$
$TA = 5.1\pi + 5.78\pi$
$TA = 10.88\pi$ sq in
$TA \approx 34.2$ sq in

(c) $V = \pi r^2 h$
$V = \pi \cdot (1.7)^2 \cdot (1.5)$
$V = 4.335\pi$ cu in
$V \approx 13.6$ cu in

Next, consider $\odot O$ in plane p and point V not in plane p as shown in Figure 10.26. The union of all lines such as l containing V and $\odot O$ is a *circular conical* surface. Again, we have a surface that extends without end. The part of the surface above V in Figure 10.26 is one *nappe* of the surface; the other nappe is below V. The union of $\odot O$ and its interior with the part of the conical surface between $\odot O$ and V is a *circular cone*. Point V is the *vertex*, $\odot O$ and its interior is the *base*, $\overline{OV}$ is the *axis*, and the length of a perpendicular line segment joining V to the plane $\odot O$ is the *altitude*. In a *right circular cone* the axis is perpendicular to the base (Figure 10.27[b]); in an oblique circular cone it is not (Figure 10.27[a]). Clearly, a circular cone is the circular counterpart of a pyramid. Just as a regular pyramid has a slant height, so does a right circular cone: it is the length l of a line segment joining V to a point of $\odot O$ (Figure 10.27).

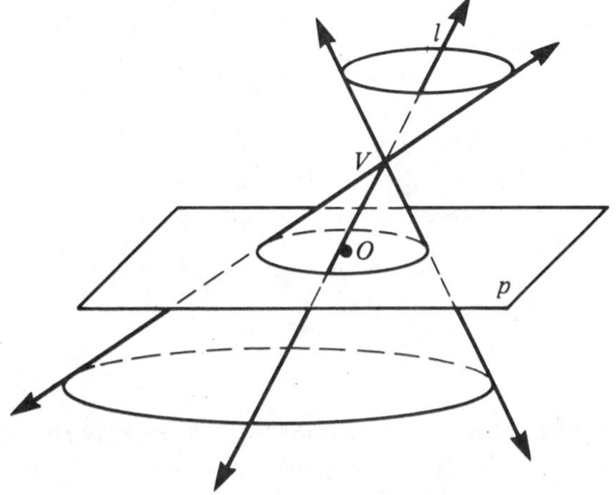

Figure 10.26

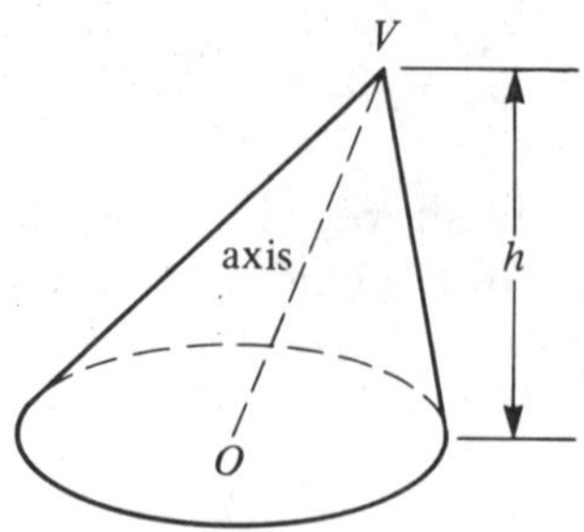

(a) oblique circular cone

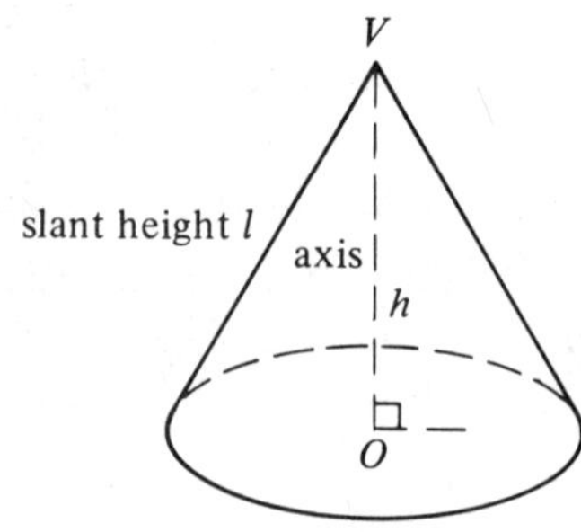

(b) right circular cone

Figure 10.27

The meanings of *LA*, *TA*, and volume of a right circular cone should be clear from previous contexts; formulas for their calculation are given in the theorems below.

Theorem 116 The lateral area of a right circular cone is one-half the product of the circumference of its base and its slant height ($LA = \frac{1}{2} \cdot 2\pi rl = \pi rl$). The total area is the sum of the lateral area and the area of its base ($TA = \pi rl + \pi r^2$).

The similarity between the *LA* theorem above and Theorem 111 concerning the *LA* of a pyramid should be evident.

Theorem 117 The volume of a right circular cone is one-third the product of the area of its base and its altitude ($V = \frac{1}{3}\pi r^2 h$).

Compare Theorem 117 with Theorem 113 about the volume of a pyramid.

EXAMPLE 2 For the given right circular cone, find (a) *LA*, (b) *TA*, and (c) the volume (leave answers in terms of π).

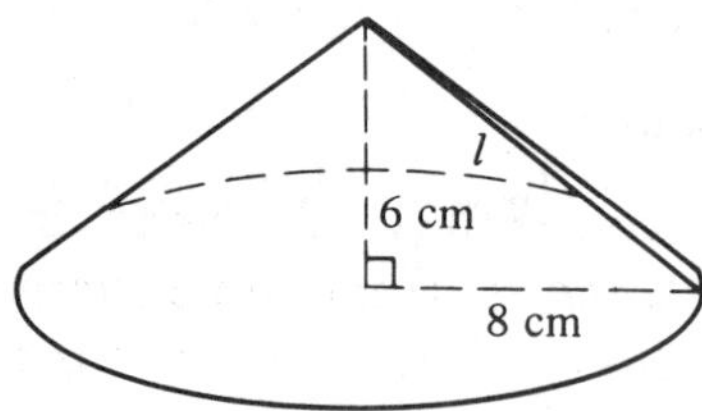

Answers

(a) $l^2 = r^2 + h^2$
$l^2 = 8^2 + 6^2$
$l^2 = 100$
$l = 10$ cm
$LA = \pi rl$
$LA = \pi \cdot 8 \cdot 10$
$LA = 80\pi$ sq cm

(b) $TA = LA + \pi r^2$
$TA = 80\pi + \pi \cdot 8^2$
$TA = 80\pi + 64\pi$
$TA = 144\pi$ sq cm

(c) $V = \frac{1}{3}\pi r^2 h$
$V = \frac{1}{3} \cdot \pi \cdot 8^2 \cdot 6 = 128\pi$ cu cm

Another important curved surface is the sphere. A *sphere* is the set of all points in space that are at a given distance called the *radius* from a given point called the *center*. A plane intersects a sphere in either a point or a circle.

A plane that contains the sphere's center forms a cross section called a *great circle*. A great circle divides a sphere into two congruent parts called *hemispheres*. Circular cross sections formed by planes not containing the center are called *small circles*. A plane that intersects a sphere in exactly one point is *tangent* to the sphere. The point of intersection is the *point of contact*. A radius drawn to the point of contact is perpendicular to the tangent plane. These definitions and relationships are illustrated in Figure 10.28.

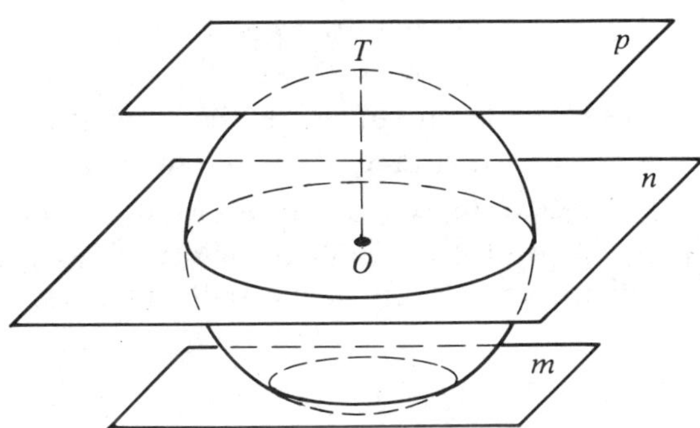

Figure 10.28 Plane p is tangent to sphere O at T. $OT \perp p$. Plane n intersects sphere O in a great circle. Plane m intersects sphere O in a small circle.

Theorem 118 If a sphere has radius r, then its surface area $S = 4\pi r^2$ and its volume $V = \frac{4}{3}\pi r^3$.

Thus, a volleyball with a 6-inch radius has a surface area $S = 4 \cdot \pi \cdot 6^2 = 144\pi$ sq in and a volume $V = \frac{4}{3} \cdot \pi \cdot 6^3 = 288\pi$ cu in. Using $\pi \approx 3.14$ we obtain $S \approx 452$ sq in and $V \approx 904$ cu in.

An interesting corollary of Theorem 118 is that the surface area of a sphere equals the area of four of its great circles. Also, it can be shown using Theorems 117 and 118 that the volume of a sphere is twice the volume of a cone whose base matches a great circle and whose altitude matches a diameter (see exercise 56, this section).

The concluding examples show more complicated applications of the formulas of this section.

EXAMPLE 3 An open storage tank has the form of the lateral surface of a right circular cylinder mounted on the lateral surface of a right circular cone. If the dimensions are as shown, find, to the nearest whole number, (a) the volume of liquid in the tank if the surface is 4 feet below the top, and (b) the surface area of the tank.

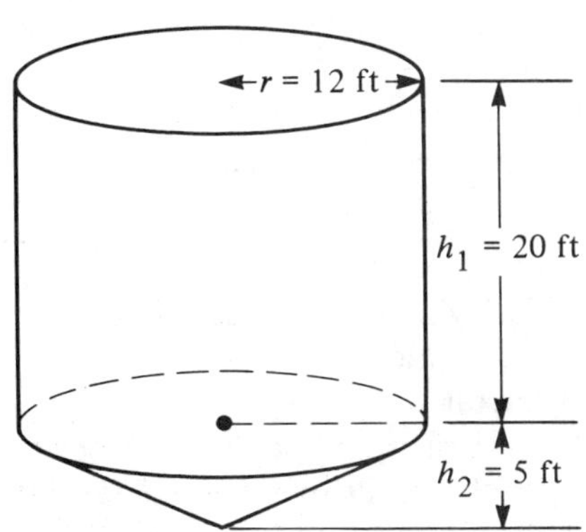

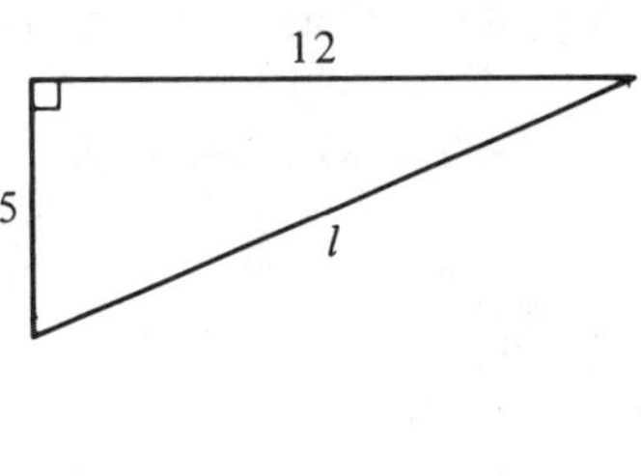

Answers

(a) $V = V(\text{cone}) + V(\text{cyl of liquid})$
$V = \frac{1}{3}\pi r^2 h_2 + \pi r^2 (h_1 - 4)$
$V = \frac{1}{3} \cdot \pi \cdot 12^2 \cdot 5 + \pi \cdot 12^2 \cdot 16$
$V = 240\pi + 2304\pi$
$V = 2544\pi$ cu ft
$V \approx 7988$ cu ft

(b) $l^2 = 5^2 + 12^2$
$l^2 = 169$
$l = 13$ ft
$LA = LA(\text{cyl}) + LA(\text{cone})$
$LA = 2\pi r h_1 + \pi r l$
$LA = 2 \cdot \pi \cdot 12 \cdot 20 + \pi \cdot 12 \cdot 13$
$LA = 480\pi + 156\pi$
$LA = 636\pi$ sq ft
$LA \approx 1997$ sq ft

EXAMPLE 4 A student is trying to use a ruler to measure the diameters of some congruent spherical ball bearings. Finding this difficult, the student measures the diameter of a handy cylindrical jar as 16 centimeters, puts some water in the jar, and drops in nine of the ball bearings. The water level rises $1\frac{1}{2}$ centimeters. Show how these measurements can be used to find the diameter of each of the ball bearings.

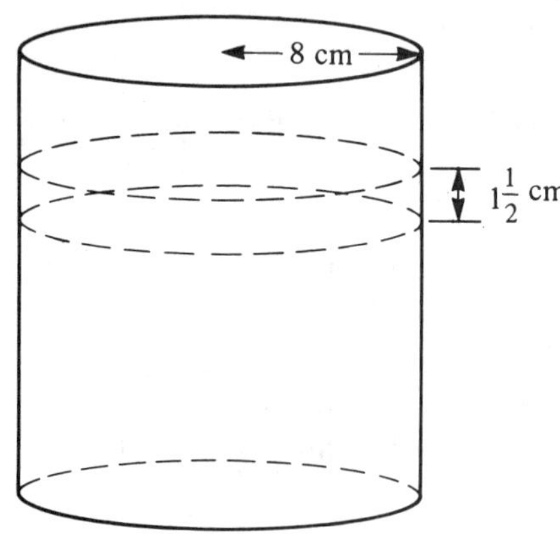

Answer

volume displaced in cylinder:
$V_1 = \pi r^2 h$
$V_1 = \pi \cdot 8^2 \cdot 1\frac{1}{2}$
$V_1 = 96\pi$ cu cm

volume of the nine spheres:
$V_2 = 9 \cdot \frac{4}{3} \cdot \pi \cdot r^3$
$V_2 = 12\pi r^3$ cu cm
$V_2 = V_1$
$12\pi r^3 = 96\pi$
$r^3 = 8$
$r = 2$ cm
$\therefore$ diameter of each is 4 centimeters

Although the method above was clever, the student could have made the measurement directly with the ruler and two flat surfaces using the concept of tangent planes. Can you see how?

EXERCISES FOR 10.5

In exercises 1–20 answer true or false.

1. A geometric solid is the union of a closed surface and its interior.
2. A right circular cylinder is an example of a cylindrical surface.
3. A solid is assigned a measure called its volume by covering it with segments each one unit in length.
4. The part of a cylindrical surface between the two bases of a circular cylinder is the cylinder's lateral surface.
5. The axis of a right circular cylinder is perpendicular to the bases of the cylinder.

6. The lateral area of a cone is the same as the total area of the cone.
7. The slant height of a cone is the same as the altitude of the cone.
8. The volume of a cone having the same base and altitude as a cylinder is one-half that of the cylinder.
9. If the areas of the bases of a cone and a pyramid are equal and the altitude of the cone is twice that of the pyramid, then the volume of the cone is twice that of the pyramid.
10. Spheres are special right circular cylinders.
11. If the radius of a sphere is 9 inches, then its surface area and volume have the same numerical measure.
12. The ratio of the volumes of a cone and a cylinder that have the same base and equal altitudes is the same as the ratio of the volumes of a pyramid and a prism that have the same base and equal altitudes.
13. If the slant height of a cone measures 61 feet and its radius measures 11 feet, then its altitude measures 57 feet.
14. The surface area of a sphere is the same as the area of a circle whose radius is equal to the diameter of the sphere.
15. If three spheres have the sides of a right triangle as diameters, then the sum of the surface areas of the two spheres on the legs equals the surface area of the sphere on the hypotenuse.
16. If three spheres have as diameters three edges of a rectangular right prism that meet at a vertex, then the sum of the surface areas of the spheres equals the surface area of the sphere having as a diameter a diagonal of the prism.
17. The volume of a right circular cylinder is equal to one-fourth the diameter of the bases multiplied by its lateral surface area.
18. If the radius of a sphere is doubled, then its volume is multiplied by a factor of four.
19. If the lateral area of a right circular cone is two-thirds of the total area, then the slant height is the same as the diameter of the base.
20. If a cube and a sphere have the same surface area, then the cube has the greater volume.

In exercises 21–32 find the ratio of the volume of solid I to that of solid II given the regular prisms, regular pyramids, right circular cylinders, right circular cones, and spheres as shown. Centers are labeled "O."

21.

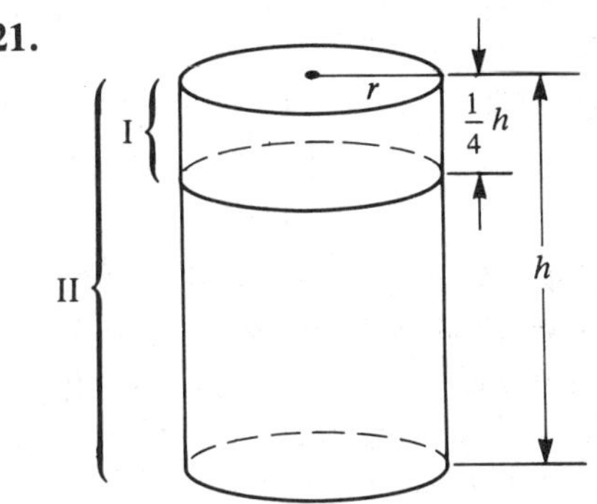

22.

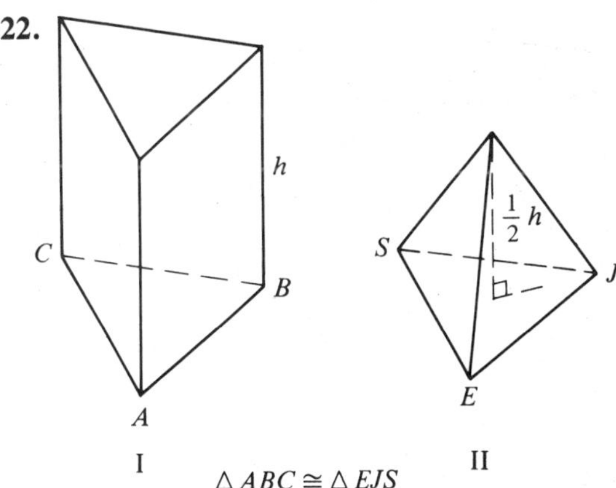

$\triangle ABC \cong \triangle EJS$

23.

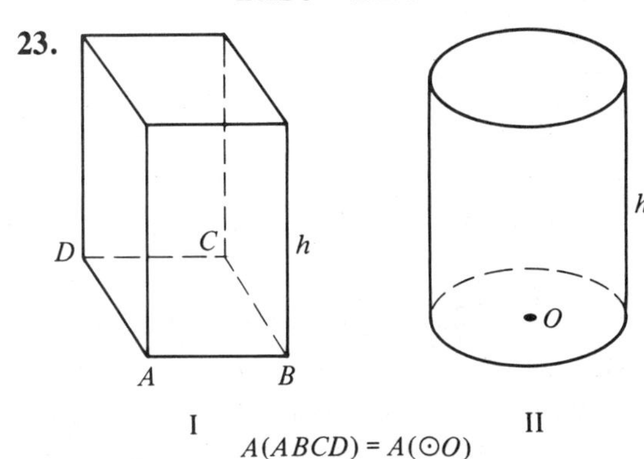

$A(ABCD) = A(\odot O)$

24.

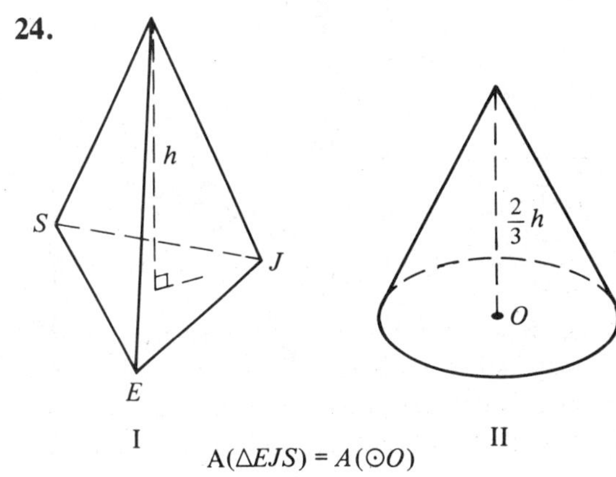

$A(\triangle EJS) = A(\odot O)$

25.

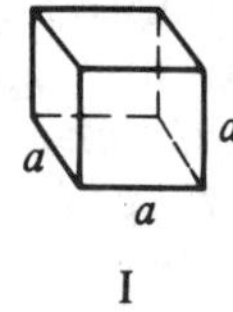

I

3a

3a

3a

II

26.

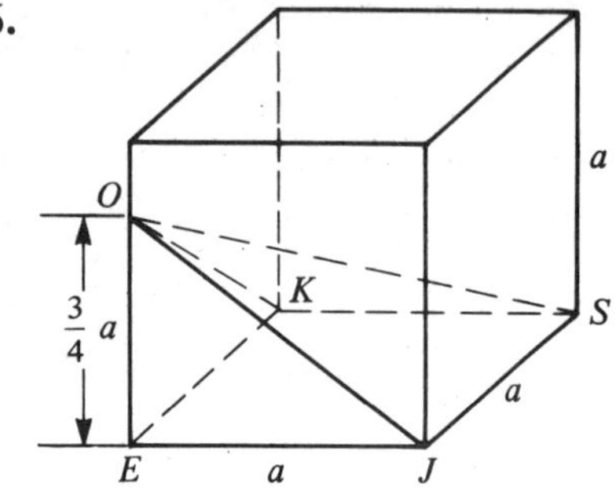

I is pyramid *O–EJSK*
II is the cube

27.

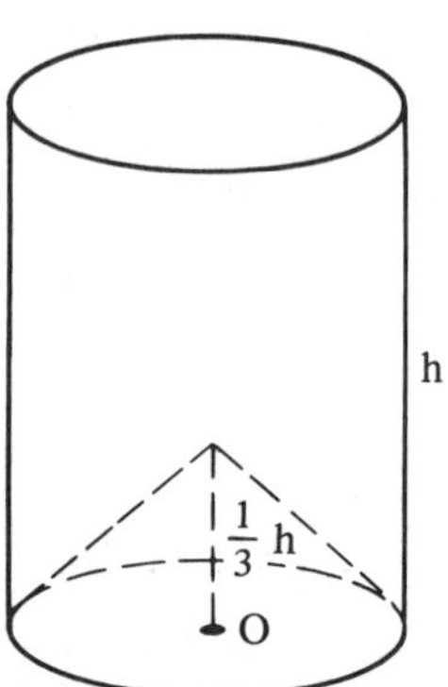

I is the cone
II is the part of the cylinder above the cone

28.

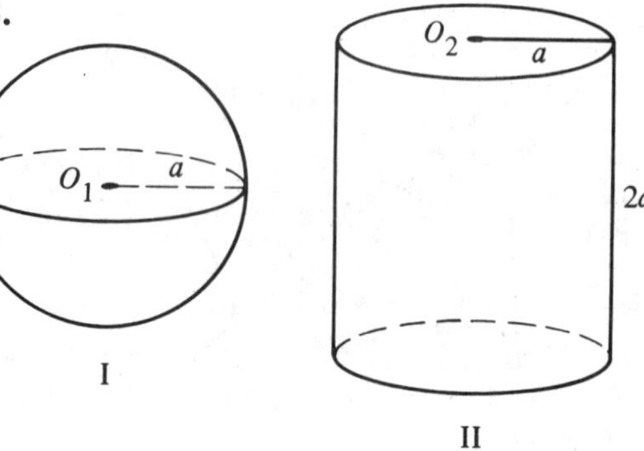

I

II

29.

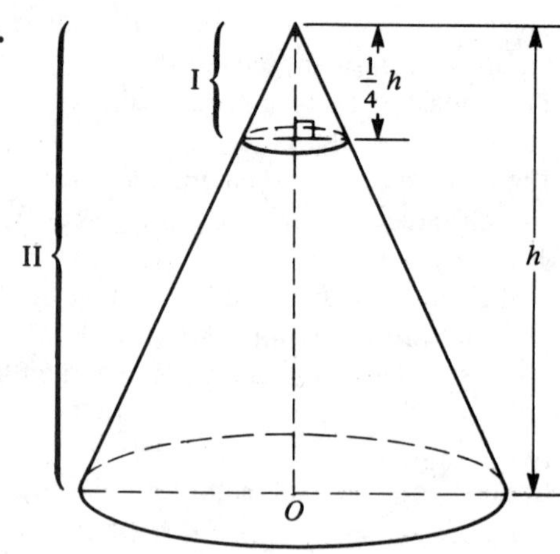

30.

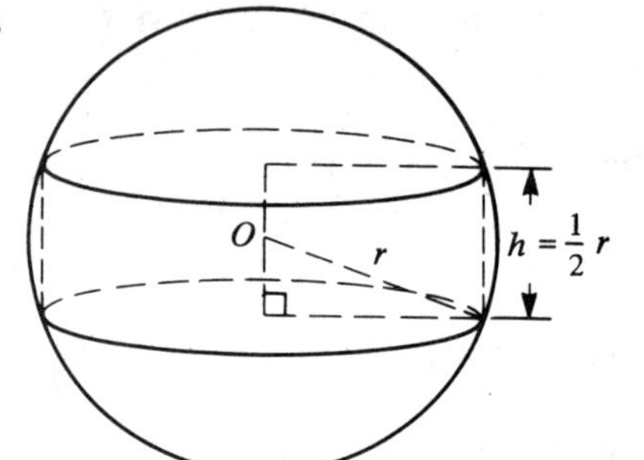

I is the inscribed cylinder
II is the sphere

31.

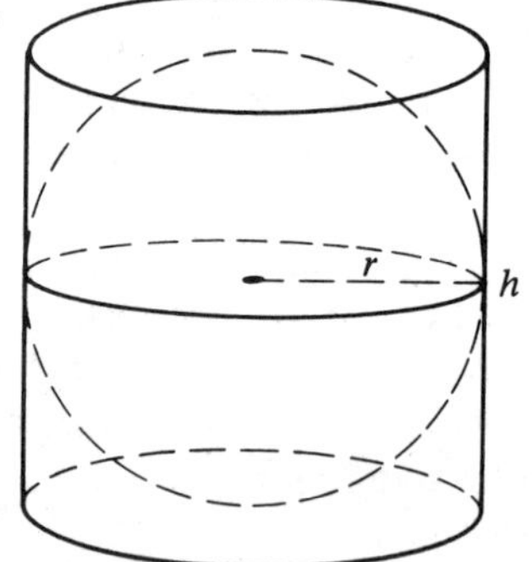

I is the inscribed sphere
II is the cylinder

32.

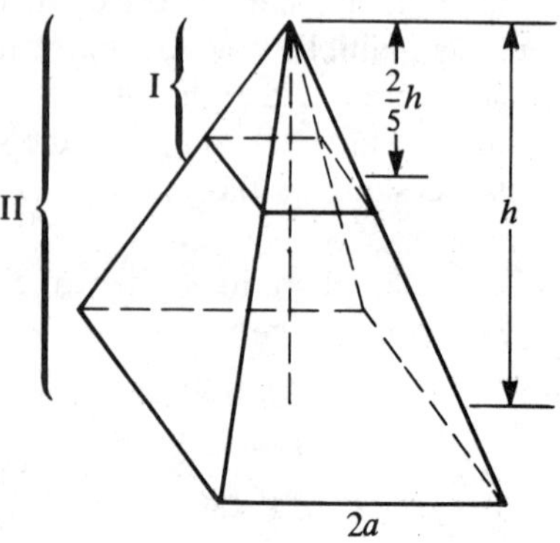

33. A 15-inch-by-10-inch rectangle is rotated about its longer side. Find the lateral area and the volume of the solid formed.
34. A right triangle with 8-inch and 15-inch legs is rotated about its shorter leg. Find the total area and the volume of the solid formed.
35. If a blacktop roller is 4 feet long and has a diameter of 36 inches, how many square feet of pavement does it cover in 200 revolutions?
36. Find the surface area and the volume of a sphere of diameter 24 inches.
37. Two concentric spheres of radii 10 and 14 inches, respectively, form a spherical shell. Find the volume of the shell.
38. A milk tank is in the shape of a right circular cylinder $10\frac{1}{2}$ inches in diameter and 3 feet high. How many gallons of milk does it hold? (Use $\pi = \frac{22}{7}$ and 231 cu in = 1 gal.)
39. The total area of a right circular cylinder is 130π sq ft, and the radius of the base is 5 feet. Find the altitude of the cylinder.
40. The altitude of a right circular cylinder is twice the radius of the base. What is the ratio of the lateral area to the total area of the cylinder?
41. A concrete pipe 24 feet long has an inside diameter of 2 feet. If the thickness of the concrete is 3 inches, what is the volume of the concrete in the pipe?
42. A solid is composed of a right circular cylinder of radius 6 feet and altitude 14 feet surmounted by a cone with the same base and whose altitude is 8 feet. Find the surface area of the solid.
43. The number of square feet in the total surface area of a right circular cylinder is equal numerically to the number of cubic feet in its volume. The altitude is four times the radius of the base. Find the volume of the cylinder.
44. A great circle of a sphere has a radius of 8 inches. Find the ratio of the area of a hemisphere of this sphere to the area of a great circle of the sphere.
45. The radius of the base of a right circular cylinder measures 8 centimeters and the altitude measures 15 centimeters. A right circular cone is inscribed in the cylinder; that is, they have the same base and the vertex of the cone is in the upper base of the cylinder. What is the volume of the solid inside the cylinder and outside the cone?
46. Find the volume of a sphere that will just fit into a cubical box whose inside edges are 10 inches long.
47. The volume of a certain sphere is numerically equal to its surface area. Find the radius of the sphere.
48. A cube and a sphere have the same surface area. Which has the greater volume? Show why.
49. Find the ratio of the lateral area of a right circular cylinder to the surface area of a sphere inscribed in it. Also find the ratio of their volumes.
50. Show that the lateral area of the frustum of a right circular cone is $LA = \pi L(r_1 + r_2)$, where L is the slant height of the frustum and r_1 and r_2 are the base radii. (Hint: Extend the frustum into a cone, subtract lateral areas, and use similar triangles.)
51. Use the formula in exercise 50 to find the lateral area of a frustum of a right circular cone of altitude 12 feet and base radii of 8 feet and 13 feet, respectively.
52. Show that the volume of the frustum of a right circular cone is given by $V = \frac{1}{3}\pi h(r_1^2 + r_1r_2 + r_2^2)$, where h is the frustum's altitude and r_1 and r_2 are the base radii. (Hint: Extend the frustum into a cone, subtract the volumes, and use similar triangles.)
53. Use the formula in exercise 52 to find the volume of the frustum of the right circular cone given in exercise 51.
54. An ice cream cone has the form of a frustum of a right circular cone with base diameters 2 inches and $1\frac{1}{2}$ inches, respectively, and with altitude $2\frac{1}{2}$ inches. If two spherical scoops of ice cream with diameters $1\frac{3}{4}$ inches each are put in the cone and allowed to melt, would the cone be able to hold the liquid?
55. The volume of a frustum of a right circular cone is 2200π cubic feet. The slant height is 13 feet and the altitude is 12 feet. Find the radii of the bases. (Hint: Carefully draw a figure and use the formula in exercise 52.)
56. Show that the volume of a sphere is twice the volume of a cone whose base matches a great circle and whose altitude matches a diameter.

CHAPTER 10 SUMMARY

This chapter presents a brief development of solid geometry. The definitions, postulates, and theorems are explained intuitively and as extensions of concepts from plane geometry. Visualizing three-dimensional figures and drawing them in two dimensions also aids in understanding the development. The concepts of volume and surface area, like the concepts of length, angle measure, and area in two dimensions, are based on postulates and the unit-covering process. This foundation leads to formulas for the volume, lateral area, and total area of many solids bounded by plane surfaces. Similar formulas for cylinders, cones, and spheres are presented but, as with circle formulas, their derivation involves difficulties that must be left to more advanced courses.

FACTS TO KNOW

1. Definitions
   - **a.** Line parallel to plane
   - **b.** Line perpendicular to plane
   - **c.** Parallel planes
   - **d.** Perpendicular planes

2. Postulates
   - **a.** One and only one plane is determined by (1) three noncollinear points, (2) two intersecting lines, (3) two parallel lines, and (4) a line and a point not on the line
   - **b.** $V(\text{rect box}) = lwh$

3. Theorems
   - **a.** $LA(\text{pyr}) = \frac{1}{2}Pl$
   - **b.** $V(\text{prism}) = Bh$
   - **c.** $V(\text{pyr}) = \frac{1}{3}Bh$
   - **d.** $LA(\text{cyl}) = 2\pi rh$
   - **e.** $TA(\text{cyl}) = 2\pi rh + 2\pi r^2$
   - **f.** $V(\text{cyl}) = \pi r^2 h$
   - **g.** $LA(\text{cone}) = \pi rl$
   - **h.** $TA(\text{cone}) = \pi rl + \pi r^2$
   - **i.** $V(\text{cone}) = \frac{1}{3}\pi r^2 h$
   - **j.** $S(\text{sph}) = 4\pi r^2$
   - **k.** $V(\text{sph}) = \frac{4}{3}\pi r^3$

PROBLEMS TO MASTER

1. Make two-dimensional drawings of three-dimensional figures.

2. Prove triangles congruent in three-dimensional figures.

3. Use formulas to find lateral areas, total areas, and volumes of prisms, pyramids, cones, and cylinders.

4. Use formulas to find surface areas and volumes of spheres.

5. Solve practical problems using three-dimensional figures and formulas.

Appendix A

THE SYSTEM OF REAL NUMBERS

AXIOMS FOR ADDITION

Closure for Addition
If $x, y \in R$, then there is a unique $z \in R$ such that $x + y = z$.
Commutative for Addition
If $x, y \in R$, then $x + y = y + x$.
Associative for Addition
If $x, y, z \in R$, then $(x + y) + z = x + (y + z)$.
Additive Identity
There is in R a unique number called zero, written 0, such that for any $x \in R$, $x + 0 = x$.
Additive Inverse
Corresponding to each $x \in R$, there is a unique $y \in R$, called the additive inverse (or opposite) of x, such that $x + y = 0$.

AXIOMS FOR MULTIPLICATION

Closure for Multiplication
If $x, y \in R$, then there is a unique $z \in R$, such that $x \cdot y = z$.
Commutative for Multiplication
If $x, y \in R$ then $x \cdot y = y \cdot x$.
Associative for Multiplication
If $x, y, z \in R$, then $(x \cdot y) \cdot z = x \cdot (y \cdot z)$.
Multiplicative Identity
There is in R a unique number called one, written 1, such that for any $x \in R$, $x \cdot 1 = x$.
Multiplicative Inverse
Corresponding to each $x \in R$ except 0, there is a unique $y \in R$, called the multiplicative inverse of x, such that $x \cdot y = 1$.

GENERAL AXIOMS

Distributive
If $x, y, z \in R$, then $x \cdot (y + z) = x \cdot y + x \cdot z$.
Completeness
There exists a one-to-one correspondence between the elements of R and the points on a line.

AXIOMS FOR ORDER

Trichotomy
If $x, y \in R$, then one and only one of the following is true: $x < y$, $x = y$, or $y < x$.
Transitive for Order
If $x, y, z \in R$, $x < y$, and $y < z$, then $x < z$.
Addition for Order
If $x, y, z \in R$ and $x < y$, then $x + z < y + z$.
Multiplication for Order
If $x, y, z \in R$, $x < y$ and $z > 0$, then $xz < yz$.

ADDITIONAL PROPERTIES USED IN GEOMETRY

Although these properties may be proved as theorems, they are stated here as Axioms 11–17, as in Section 1.5.

Axiom 11 *Addition of Equals* (= + =, sums =)
If $a = b$ and $c = d$, then $a + c = b + d$.

Axiom 12 *Subtraction of Equals* (= − =, diff =)
If $a = b$ and $c = d$, then $a - c = b - d$.

Axiom 13 *Multiplication of Equals* (= · =, prod =)
If $a = b$ and $c = d$, then $a \cdot c = b \cdot d$.

Axiom 14 *Division of Equals* (= ÷ =, quot =)
If $a = b$ and $c = d$, $c \neq 0$, $d \neq 0$, then $a \div c = b \div d$.

Axiom 15 *Whole Greater than Part* (whole > part)
If $x, y, z \in R$, $z > 0$, and $x = y + z$, then $x > y$.

Axiom 16 *Addition of Inequalities* ($< + <$, sums $<$ or $> + >$, sums $>$)
If $a < b$ and $c < d$, then $a + c < b + d$, or if $a > b$ and $c > d$, then $a + c > b + d$.

Axiom 17 *Substitution* (subst)
If a and b name two mathematical expressions such that $a = b$, then a may replace b or b may replace a in any mathematical statement.

Appendix B

DEFINITIONS, POSTULATES, AND THEOREMS IN THIS TEXT

DEFINITIONS

1.1 A set A is a *subset* of a set B, written $A \subseteq B$ iff every element of A is also an element of B.

1.2 Let A, B, and C name three sets and the symbol $\cup$ name the set operation called *union*. Then $A \cup B = C$ iff C contains all those elements and only those elements that are either in A or in B or in both.

1.3 Let A, B, and C name three sets and the symbol $\cap$ name the set operation called *intersection*. Then $A \cap B = C$ iff C contains all those elements and only those elements that are in both A and B.

1.4 A number is called a *rational number* iff it can be written as a fraction a/b, where $a, b \in J$, but $b \neq 0$.

1.5 Let c be a positive rational number. Then (1) $\sqrt{c} = x$ iff $x^2 = c$ and x is positive, (2) $-\sqrt{c} = x$ iff $x^2 = c$ and x is negative, and (3) $\sqrt{0} = 0$.

1.6 The numbers represented by the nonterminating, nonrepeating decimals are called *irrational* numbers. The set of irrational numbers is named set I.

1.7 The numbers represented by the terminating, the nonterminating repeating, and the nonterminating, nonrepeating decimals are called *real numbers*. The set of real numbers is named set R. Symbolically, $R = \{x | x$ has a decimal numeral$\}$.

1.8 Let $x \in R$ and let $|x|$ denote the *absolute value* of x. Then (1) $|x| = x$ if $x > 0$, (2) $|x| = 0$ if $x = 0$, and (3) $|x| = (-1) \cdot x$ if $x < 0$.

1.9 Let P and Q name two points on a number line, with x the coordinate of P and y the coordinate of Q. Then the *distance* between P and Q is $PQ = |x - y| = |y - x|$.
2.1 *Space* is the set of all points.
2.2 A *geometric figure* is any nonempty subset of space.
2.3 A set of three or more points is *collinear* iff it is a subset of a line.
2.4 A set of points is a *line segment* iff it consists of two points and all the points between them.
2.5 A set of points is a *ray* iff it is the union of a half line and its endpoint.
2.6 The *length,* or *measure,* of a line segment is the distance between its endpoints.
2.7 Point J is called the *midpoint* of ES iff E-J-S and $EJ = JS$ (midpt iff 2 lengths =).
2.8 A line, half line, ray, or line segment is a *bisector* of a given line segment iff it contains the midpoint and no other points of that given segment (bis seg iff contains midpt).
2.9 Two line segments are *congruent* (denoted ≅) iff their lengths (measures) are equal (≅ iff meas =).
3.1 A set of points is an *angle* iff it is the union of two rays having the same endpoint.
3.2 Let $\overrightarrow{OA}$, $\overrightarrow{OB}$, and $\overrightarrow{OC}$ name three rays with the same endpoint O. Then $\overrightarrow{OB}$ is *between* $\overrightarrow{OA}$ and $\overrightarrow{OC}$ iff B is in the interior of ∡AOC.
3.3 Two angles are called *adjacent angles* iff they have the same vertex and a common side between their other two sides (adj ∡s iff same vtx and com side betw).
3.4 Two angles are called *vertical angles* iff the sides of one are rays opposite to the sides of the other (vert ∡s formed by opp rays).
3.5 Two angles are a *linear pair* iff they have a common side and the other two sides are opposite rays (lin pr iff com side and opp rays).
3.6 The *degree measure* of an angle is the angular distance between its sides.
3.7 $\overrightarrow{JK}$ is called the *midray* of ∡EJS iff K is in the interior of ∡EJS and ∠EJK = ∠KJS (midray iff 2 ∠s =).
3.8 Either the midray of an angle or the line determined by the midray is a *bisector* of the angle (midray or its line is ∡ bis) and (∡ has 1 and only 1 bis).
3.9 An angle is an *acute angle* iff its measure is greater than 0° but less than 90°.
3.10 An angle is a *right angle* iff its measure is 90° (rt ∠ = 90°).
3.11 An angle is an *obtuse angle* iff its measure is greater than 90° but less than 180°.
3.12 Two angles are *supplementary* iff the sum of their measures is 180° (supp iff sum = 180°).
3.13 Two angles are *complementary* iff the sum of their measures is 90° (comp iff sum = 90°).
3.14 Two angles are *congruent* (denoted ≅) iff their measures are equal (≅ iff meas =).
3.15 Two lines or subsets of lines are *perpendicular* (denoted ⊥) iff they intersect and form a right angle (⊥ iff a rt ∡).
3.16 The *distance from a point to a line* is the length of the perpendicular line segment joining the point and the line (dis pt to line is length of ⊥ seg).
4.1 A figure is a *triangle* iff it is the union of three line segments determined by three noncollinear points.

4.2 A triangle is *scalene* iff no two of its sides are congruent.

4.3 A triangle is *isosceles* iff at least two of its sides are congruent (isos △ iff 2 ≅ sides).

4.4 A triangle is *equilateral* iff all three of its sides are congruent (equilat △ iff 3 ≅ sides).

4.5 A triangle is *acute* iff all three of its angles are acute.

4.6 A triangle is *right* iff one of its angles is a right angle (rt △ iff a rt ∡).

4.7 A triangle is *obtuse* iff one of its angles is an obtuse angle.

4.8 A triangle is *equiangular* iff all three of its angles are congruent (equiang △ iff 3 ≅ ∡s).

4.9 Two triangles are *congruent* iff there is a one-to-one correspondence between their vertices such that the three pairs of corresponding sides are congruent and the three pairs of corresponding angles are congruent (cpctc).

4.10 A point is the *midpoint* of a line segment iff it divides it into two congruent line segments (midpt ÷ seg into 2 ≅ segs).

4.11 A line, half line, ray, or line segment is a *bisector* of a line segment iff it divides it into two congruent line segments (bis ÷ seg into 2 ≅ segs).

4.12 A ray or the line it determines is a *bisector* of an angle iff it divides it into two congruent angles (bis ÷ ∡ into 2 ≅ ∡s).

4.13 A line segment is a *median* of a triangle iff its endpoints are a vertex and the midpoint of the opposite side (med from vtx to midpt opp side).

4.14 An *altitude* of a triangle is a line segment from one vertex perpendicular to the line containing the opposite side (alt from vtx ⊥ opp side).

4.15 An angle is an *exterior angle* of a triangle iff it forms a linear pair with one of the angles of the triangle (ext ∡ of △ iff lin pr with 1 ∡).

4.16 A *remote interior angle* associated with an exterior angle of a triangle is either one of the interior angles not forming a linear pair with the exterior angle.

4.17 A line is the *perpendicular bisector* of a line segment iff it bisects the given segment and is perpendicular to it (⊥ bis iff bis seg and is ⊥).

5.1 Two coplanar lines, l and m, are *parallel* (abbreviated $l \parallel m$) iff $l \cap m = \emptyset$.

5.2 Two *nonadjacent* angles formed by two lines and a transversal are

1. *Alternate interior angles* iff they are interior angles whose interiors are on opposite sides of the transversal (alt int ∡s iff int ∡s opp sides t).
2. *Alternate exterior angles* iff they are exterior angles whose interiors are on opposite sides of the transversal (alt ext ∡s iff ext ∡s opp sides t).
3. *Corresponding angles* iff one is an interior angle, the other is an exterior angle, and their interiors are on the same side of the transversal (corr ∡s iff 1 int, 1 ext, same side t).

6.1 The union of four line segments $\overline{EJ}$, $\overline{JS}$, $\overline{SK}$, and $\overline{EK}$ is a *quadrilateral* iff E, J, S, and K are coplanar points no three of which are collinear and each segment intersects exactly two others, one at each endpoint.

6.2 A line segment is a *diagonal* of a quadrilateral iff its endpoints are opposite vertices.

6.3 A quadrilateral is a *trapezoid* iff exactly one pair of its opposite sides are parallel (trap iff 1 pr sides ∥).

6.4 A quadrilateral is a *parallelogram* iff both pairs of opposite sides are parallel (▱ iff opp sides ∥).

6.5 A parallelogram is a *rhombus* iff it has a pair of adjacent sides that are congruent (rh iff ▱).

6.6 A parallelogram is a *rectangle* iff it has a right angle (rect iff ▭).

6.7 A rectangle is a *square* iff it has a pair of adjacent sides that are congruent (sq iff ▭).

6.8 The *distance between two parallel lines* is the length of any perpendicular line segment joining the lines.

6.9 The union of line segments $\overline{E_1E_2}$, $\overline{E_2E_3}$, . . . , $\overline{E_{n-1}E_n}$, $\overline{E_nE_1}$ is a *polygon* iff E_1, E_2, . . . , E_n are n coplanar points ($n > 2$) no three of which are collinear and each segment intersects exactly two others, one at each endpoint.

6.10 A polygon is a *regular polygon* iff its sides are congruent and its angles are congruent (reg poly iff sides ≅ and ∡s ≅).

7.1 A *circle* is the set of all points in a plane that are a given distance from a given point in the plane. The given distance is the *radius* and the given point is the *center* (⊙ set of pts at given dis from given pt).

7.2 A line segment is a *radius* of a circle iff one of its endpoints is the center and the other is a point of the circle.

7.3 A line segment is a *diameter* of a circle iff its endpoints are points of the circle and it contains the center of the circle.

7.4 Two or more circles are *concentric* iff they have the same center.

7.5 A line segment is a *chord* of a circle iff its endpoints are points of the circle.

7.6 A line is a *secant* to a circle iff exactly two of its points are also points of the circle (sec inters ⊙ 2 pts).

7.7 A line is a *tangent* to a circle iff exactly one of its points is also a point of the circle. This point is called the *point of contact or point of tangency* (tan inters ⊙ 1 pt).

7.8 An angle is a *central angle* of a circle iff its vertex is the center of the circle.

7.9 A *minor arc* is the set of points of a circle that are on a central angle or in its interior.

7.10 A *major arc* is the set of points of a circle that are on a central angle or in its exterior.

7.11 A *semicircle* is the set of points of a circle that are on, or on one side of, a line containing a diameter.

7.12 The *degree measure* of a

a. *minor arc* is the measure of its central angle (meas min ⌒ = cent ∠),

b. *semicircle* is 180° (meas semi ⊙ = 180°),

c. *circle* is 360° (meas ⊙ = 360°),

d. *major arc* is 360° minus the measure of its associated minor arc (meas maj ⌒ = 360° − min ⌒).

7.13 An angle is an *inscribed angle* of a circle iff its vertex is a point of the circle and each of its sides contains another point of the circle.

7.14 Two *circles* are *congruent* iff their radii are congruent (⊙s ≅ iff radii ≅).

7.15 Two *arcs* of a circle or of congruent circles are *congruent* iff their degree measures are equal (⌒s ≅ iff meas =).

8.1 The *perimeter* of a polygon is the sum of the lengths of its sides.

8.2 A *triangular region* is the union of a triangle and its interior.

8.3 A *polygonal region* is the union of a finite number of coplanar triangular regions whose interiors have no points in common.

8.4 The *center* of a regular polygon is the center of its circumscribed circle.

8.5 A *radius* of a regular polygon is a line segment joining its center to a vertex.

8.6 An *apothem* of a regular polygon is a line segment from its center perpendicular to any side.

9.1 The *ratio* of the real number a to the real number b, $b \neq 0$, is the size comparison of a to b expressed as the fraction a/b.
9.2 A *proportion* is an equality between two ratios.
9.3 Two triangles are *similar* iff there is a one-to-one correspondence between their vertices such that the three pairs of corresponding angles are congruent and the three pairs of corresponding sides are proportional (castc and csstp).
9.4 A *sector* of a circle is a region bounded by an arc of the circle and the two radii to the endpoints of the arc.
10.1 A line and a plane are *parallel* iff their intersection is empty.
10.2 A line and a plane are *perpendicular* iff they intersect and the line is perpendicular to every line in the plane that passes through the point of intersection ($l \perp$ pl is $\perp$ all l in pl thru inters).
10.3 Two planes are *parallel* iff their intersection is empty.
10.4 Two planes are *perpendicular* iff one plane contains a line that is perpendicular to the other plane ($pl_1 \perp pl_2$ iff l in $pl_1 \perp pl_2$).

POSTULATES

CHAPTER 2

1. Any two points determine exactly one line (2 pts determ line).
2. Any line contains at least two points.
3. *The Ruler Postulate*. The points of any line may be placed in one-to-one correspondence with the real numbers, and a unique positive number may be assigned as the distance between two given points.
4. If $\overline{ES}$ is a line segment and J is a point such that E-J-S, then $EJ + JS = ES$ (whole = sum parts).
5. Given any $\overline{EJ}$ and any $\overrightarrow{AB}$, there exists a unique point S on $\overrightarrow{AB}$ such that $\overline{AS} \cong \overline{EJ}$ (can copy seg).

CHAPTER 3

6. *The Protractor Postulate*. The rays in a half rotation around a point may be placed in one-to-one correspondence with the real numbers from zero to 180, inclusive, and a unique positive number may be assigned as the angular distance between two given rays.
7. If K is any point in the interior of $\measuredangle EJS$, then $\angle EJK + \angle KJS = \angle EJS$ (whole = sum parts).
8. The measure of a straight angle is 180° (st $\angle$ = 180°).
9. Given any $\measuredangle EJS$ and $\overrightarrow{ML}$, there exists a $\overrightarrow{MK}$ such that $\measuredangle LMK \cong \measuredangle EJS$ (can copy $\measuredangle$).
10. There is one and only one line perpendicular to a given line through one of its points (1 $\perp$ thru pt on line).
11. There is one and only one line perpendicular to a given line through a point not on the given line (1 $\perp$ from pt to line).

CHAPTER 4

12. If there is a correspondence between two triangles such that the three sides of one are congruent to the corresponding parts of the other, then the triangles are congruent (sss ≅ sss).
13. If there is a correspondence between two triangles such that two sides and the included angle of one are congruent to the corresponding parts of the other, then the triangles are congruent (sas ≅ sas).
14. If there is a correspondence between two triangles such that two angles and the included side of one are congruent to the corresponding parts of the other, then the triangles are congruent (asa ≅ asa).

Alternate for 4 and 7. The whole of a line segment or angle is congruent to the "sum" of its parts (whole ≅ sum parts).

CHAPTER 5

15. *The Parallel Postulate*. There is one and only one line parallel to a given line and containing a given point not on that line (∥ post).

CHAPTER 7

16. *The Circle Postulate*. There is one and only one circle that contains three given noncollinear points.

CHAPTER 8

17. *The Area Postulate*. To each polygonal region there corresponds a unique positive real number called its area.
18. Triangular regions bounded by congruent triangles have equal areas (≅ △s, = areas).
19. If a polygonal region is the union of two or more polygonal regions with no interior points in common, then its area is the sum of their areas (area ∪ = sum areas).
20. The area of a rectangle is the product of the lengths of any two consecutive sides (A[rect] = lw or bh).

CHAPTER 10

21. One and only one plane is determined by each of the following: (1) three noncollinear points (3 noncol pts determ pl), (2) two intersecting lines (2 inters lines determ pl), (3) two parallel lines (2 ∥ lines determ pl), and (4) a line and a point not on the line (l and P off l determ pl).
22. The volume of a rectangular right prism or rectangular parallelepiped is the product of the area of its base and its altitude ($V = lwh$).

THEOREMS

CHAPTER 2

1. If $\overline{EJ}$ is any line segment, then $\overline{EJ} \cong \overline{EJ}$ (refl ≅).
2. If $\overline{EJ}$ and $\overline{KS}$ are line segments and $\overline{EJ} \cong \overline{KS}$, then $\overline{KS} \cong \overline{EJ}$ (symm ≅).

3. If $\overline{EJ}$, $\overline{KS}$, and $\overline{CM}$ are line segments such that $\overline{EJ} \cong \overline{KS}$ and $\overline{KS} \cong \overline{CM}$, then $\overline{EJ} \cong \overline{CM}$ (trans ≅).

CHAPTER 3

4. If two angles are a linear pair, then the two angles are supplementary (lin pr supp).
5. If ∡E is any angle, then ∡E ≅ ∡E (refl ≅).
6. If ∡E and ∡J are angles such that ∡E ≅ ∡J, then ∡J ≅ ∡E (symm ≅).
7. If ∡E, ∡J, and ∡S are angles such that ∡E ≅ ∡J and ∡J ≅ ∡S, then ∡E ≅ ∡S (trans ≅).
8. If two angles are complementary to the same (or congruent) angle(s), then the two angles are congruent (∡s comp same ∡ [or ≅ ∡s] are ≅).
9. If two angles are supplementary to the same (or congruent) angle(s), then the two angles are congruent (∡s supp same ∡ [or ≅ ∡s] are ≅).
10. If two angles are vertical, then they are congruent (vert ∡s ≅).
11. All right angles are congruent (rt ∡s ≅).
12. If two lines are perpendicular, then they form four congruent right angles (⊥s form ≅ rt ∡s).

CHAPTER 4

13. If △EJS is any triangle, then △EJS ≅ △EJS (refl ≅).
14. If △EJS and △CKM are triangles such that △EJS ≅ △CKM, then △CKM ≅ △EJS (symm ≅).
15. If △EJS, △CAM, and △LRW are such that △EJS ≅ △CAM and △CAM ≅ △LRW, then △EJS ≅ △LRW (trans ≅).
16. *Addition Property of Congruence.* If congruent line segments (or angles) are "added" to congruent line segments (or angles), the "sums" are congruent (≅ + ≅, sums ≅).
17. *Subtraction Property of Congruence.* If congruent line segments (or angles) are "subtracted" from congruent line segments (or angles), the "differences" are congruent (≅ − ≅, diff ≅).
18. *Multiplication Property of Congruence.* If congruent line segments (or angles) are "multiplied" by a positive number, the "products" are congruent (≅ · pos, prod ≅).
19. *Division Property of Congruence.* If congruent line segments (or angles) are "divided" by a positive number, the "quotients" are congruent (≅ ÷ pos, quot ≅) and ($\frac{1}{2}$s of ≅ are ≅).
20. If two sides of a triangle are congruent, then the angles opposite the congruent sides are congruent (if 2 sides △ ≅, opp ∡s ≅).
21. If two angles of a triangle are congruent, then the sides opposite the congruent angles are congruent (if 2 ∡s △ ≅, opp sides ≅).
22. An equilateral triangle is also equiangular (if equilat △, then equiang △).
23. The measure of an exterior angle of a triangle is greater than the measure of either remote interior angle (ext ∠ > rem int ∠).
24. If the lengths of two sides of a triangle are unequal, then the measures of the angles opposite them are unequal and the larger angle is opposite the longer side (2 sides △ ≠, opp ∡s ≠ same order).

25. If the measures of two angles of a triangle are unequal, then the lengths of the sides opposite them are unequal and the longer side is opposite the larger angle (2 $\angle$s $\triangle$ $\neq$, opp sides $\neq$ same order).
26. The sum of the lengths of any two sides of a triangle is greater than the length of its third side (sum 2 sides $\triangle > $ 3d side).
27. If a point is on the perpendicular bisector of a line segment, then it is equidistant from the line segment's endpoints.
28. If a point is equidistant from the endpoints of a line segment, then it is on the perpendicular bisector of the line segment.
    27 and 28: (pt on $\perp$ bis of seg iff equidis from endpts)

CHAPTER 5

29. If two lines and a transversal form congruent alternate interior angles, then the two lines are parallel ($\not\cong$, lines $\|$).
30. If two lines and a transversal form congruent alternate exterior angles, then the two lines are parallel ($\not\cong$, lines $\|$).
31. If two lines and a transversal form congruent corresponding angles, then the two lines are parallel ($\not\cong$, lines $\|$).
32. If two lines and a transversal form supplementary interior angles on the same side of the transversal, then the two lines are parallel ($\not\cong$, lines $\|$).
33. If two lines are perpendicular to a third line, then they are parallel (2 lines $\perp$ 3d line $\|$).
34. If two parallel lines are cut by a transversal, then both pairs of alternate interior angles are congruent ($\neq$, alt int $\angle$s $\cong$).
35. If two parallel lines are cut by a transversal, then both pairs of alternate exterior angles are congruent ($\neq$, alt ext $\angle$s $\cong$).
36. If two parallel lines are cut by a transversal, then all four pairs of corresponding angles are congruent ($\neq$, corr $\angle$s $\cong$).
37. If two parallel lines are cut by a transversal, then both pairs of interior angles on the same side of the transversal are supplementary ($\neq$, int $\angle$s same side t supp).
38. If two lines are each parallel to a third line, then the two lines are parallel to each other (2 lines $\|$ 3d line $\|$).
39. The sum of the measures of the angles of a triangle is 180° (180° in $\triangle$).
40. If there is a correspondence between two triangles such that two angles of one are congruent to the corresponding parts of the other, then the third angles are congruent (if aa $\cong$ aa, 3d $\angle$s $\cong$).
41. If there is a correspondence between two triangles such that two angles and a side of one are congruent to the corresponding parts of the other, then the triangles are congruent (aas $\cong$ aas).
42. The acute angles in a right triangle are complementary (acute $\angle$s rt $\triangle$ comp).
43. The measure of an exterior angle of a triangle is equal to the sum of the measures of the two remote interior angles (ext $\angle$ = sum rem int $\angle$s).
44. If there is a correspondence between two right triangles such that the hypotenuse and a leg of one are congruent to the corresponding parts of the other, then the triangles are congruent (hs $\cong$ hs).

CHAPTER 6

45. The sum of the measures of the angles of a quadrilateral is 360° (360° in quad).

46. The opposite sides of a parallelogram are congruent (opp sides ▱ ≅).
47. The opposite angles of a parallelogram are congruent (opp ∡s ▱ ≅).
48. Any two consecutive angles of a parallelogram are supplementary (consec ∡s ▱ supp).
49. The diagonals of a parallelogram bisect each other (diags ▱ bis ea other).
50. If two lines are parallel, then every perpendicular line segment joining one to the other has the same length (if lines ∥, ⊥ seg ≅).
51. The four angles of a rectangle are right angles (rect has 4 rt ∡s).
52. The diagonals of a rectangle are congruent (diags rect ≅).
53. The four sides of a rhombus are congruent (rh has 4 ≅ sides).
54. The diagonals of a rhombus bisect the angles of the rhombus (diags rh bis ∡s).
55. The diagonals of a rhombus are perpendicular to each other (diags rh ⊥).
56. If both pairs of opposite sides of a quadrilateral are congruent, then the quadrilateral is a parallelogram (quad opp sides ≅ is ▱).
57. If one pair of opposite sides of a quadrilateral is both parallel and congruent, then the quadrilateral is a parallelogram (quad 1 pr opp sides ∥ and ≅ is ▱).
58. If the diagonals of a parallelogram are congruent, then the parallelogram is a rectangle (▱ diags ≅ is rect).
59. If the diagonals of a parallelogram are perpendicular, then the parallelogram is a rhombus (▱ diags ⊥ is rh).
60. The base angles of an isosceles trapezoid are congruent (base ∡s isos trap ≅).
61. The line segment joining the midpoints of two sides of a triangle is half as long as the third side and parallel to it (midpt seg △ $\frac{1}{2}$ of and ∥ to 3d side).
62. If three parallel lines cut off congruent segments on one transversal, then they cut off congruent segments on every transversal (if 3 ∥ lines cut ≅ segs 1 t, then ≅ segs every t).
63. If a line is parallel to one side of a triangle and bisects a second side, then it bisects the third side also (line ∥ side △ and bis 2d, bis 3d).
64. The sum of the measures of the angles of an n-gon is $(n - 2) \cdot 180°$.

CHAPTER 7

65. In any given circle all radii are congruent and all diameters are congruent (radii ⊙ ≅ and diams ⊙ ≅).
66. Any diameter divides a circle into two congruent semicircles (diam ÷ ⊙ into 2 ≅ semi⊙s).
67. If two minor arcs of a circle or of congruent circles are congruent, then their central angles are congruent (if ⌒s ≅, cent ∡s ≅).
68. If two central angles in a circle or in congruent circles are congruent, then their arcs are congruent (if cent ∡s ≅, ⌒s ≅).
69. If two central angles in a circle or in congruent circles are congruent, then their chords are congruent (if cent ∡s ≅, chs ≅).
70. If two chords in a circle or in congruent circles are congruent, then their central angles are congruent (if chs ≅, cent ∡s ≅).
71. If two chords of a circle or of congruent circles are congruent, then their arcs are congruent (if chs ≅, ⌒s ≅).
72. If two minor arcs of a circle or of congruent circles are congruent, then their chords are congruent (if ⌒s ≅, chs ≅).

73. The measure of an inscribed angle is equal to one-half the degree measure of its intercepted arc (inscr ∠ = $\frac{1}{2}$⌒°).
74. If two inscribed angles in a circle intercept the same arc or congruent arcs, then the angles are congruent (inscr ∡s interc same ⌒ or ≅ ⌒s are ≅).
75. If an inscribed angle intercepts a semicircle, then it is a right angle (inscr ∡ interc semi⊙ is rt ∡).
76. If a quadrilateral is inscribed in a circle, then its opposite angles are supplementary (If quad inscr in ⊙, opp ∡s supp).
77. If two parallel lines intersect a circle, then the arcs of the circle between the parallel lines are congruent (if ∥ lines inters ⊙, ⌒s ≅).
78. If a secant contains the center of a circle and is perpendicular to a chord, then the secant bisects the chord and its arc (sec thru cen ⊥ ch bis ch and ⌒).
79. If two chords of a circle (or of congruent circles) are equidistant from the center(s), then the chords are congruent (2 chs equidis from cen are ≅).
80. If two chords of a circle (or of congruent circles) are congruent, then the chords are equidistant from the center(s) of the circle(s) (2 ≅ chs are equidis from cen).
81. If a line is tangent to a circle, then it is perpendicular to the radius drawn to the point of contact (tan ⊥ rad to pt con).
82. If two lines are tangent to a circle and contain a point in its exterior, then the line segments joining the point to the circle are congruent (tans to ⊙ ≅).
83. If an angle is formed by two chords in a circle, then the measure of the angle is one-half the sum of the measures of the arcs intercepted by the angle and its vertical angle (2 chs ∠ = $\frac{1}{2}$sum ⌒°s).
84. If an angle is formed by a tangent to a circle and a chord, one of whose endpoints is the point of contact, then the measure of the angle is one-half the measure of its intercepted arc (tan, ch ∠ = $\frac{1}{2}$⌒°).
85. If an angle is formed by two secants or a tangent and a secant or two tangents intersecting in the exterior of the circle, then the measure of the angle is one-half the difference of the measures of the intercepted arcs (2 secs ∠ = $\frac{1}{2}$diff ⌒°s) (tan, sec ∠ = $\frac{1}{2}$diff ⌒°s) (2 tan ∠ = $\frac{1}{2}$diff ⌒°s).

CHAPTER 8

86. The area of a parallelogram is the product of the lengths of any base and its corresponding altitude (A[▱] = bh).
87. The area of a triangle is one-half the product of the lengths of any base and its corresponding altitude (A[△] = $\frac{1}{2}bh$).
88. The area of a trapezoid is one-half the product of the length of its altitude and the sum of the lengths of its bases (A[trap] = $\frac{1}{2}h[b_1 + b_2]$).
89. The area of a regular polygon is one-half the product of its perimeter and its apothem (A[reg poly] = $\frac{1}{2}Pa$).
90. The circumference of any circle is the product of π and its diameter ($C = \pi d$).
91. The area of a circle is the product of π and the square of its radius ($A = \pi r^2$).

CHAPTER 9

92. In a proportion, the product of the extremes equals the product of the means (prod extrms = prod mns).

93. In a proportion, the means or extremes may be interchanged (interch mns or extrms).
94. In a proportion, the ratios may be inverted (invert ratios).
95. If $\frac{a}{b} = \frac{c}{d}$, then $\frac{a+b}{b} = \frac{c+d}{d}$ (add prop propor).
96. If $\frac{a}{b} = \frac{c}{d}$, then $\frac{a-b}{b} = \frac{c-d}{d}$ (subt prop propor).
97. If a line parallel to one side of a triangle intersects the other two sides in different points, it divides the sides in equal ratios (line ∥ side △ ÷ 2 sides in = ratios).
98. If a line parallel to one side of a triangle intersects the other two sides in different points, it cuts segments proportional to the sides (line ∥ side △ cuts segs propor to sides).
99. If two angles of one triangle are congruent to two angles of another triangle, then the triangles are similar (aa ≅ aa).
100. The altitude to the hypotenuse of a right triangle forms two triangles that are similar to each other and to the original triangle (alt to hyp forms 3 ~ △s).
101. The altitude to the hypotenuse of a right triangle is the mean proportional between the segments into which it divides the hypotenuse, and each leg is the mean proportional between the hypotenuse and the segment of the hypotenuse adjacent to the leg (alt mn propor segs hyp, leg mn propor hyp adj seg).
102. *The Pythagorean Theorem*. In any right triangle, the square of the hypotenuse is equal to the sum of the squares of the legs ($a^2 + b^2 = c^2$).
103. If two triangles are similar, the ratio of (a) any two corresponding altitudes, (b) any two corresponding medians, or (c) any two corresponding angle bisectors is the same as the ratio of any two corresponding sides (corr sides, alts, meds, ∡ bis ~ △s propor).
104. If two triangles are similar, the ratio of their areas is the same as the ratio of (a) the squares of any two corresponding sides, (b) the squares of any two corresponding altitudes, (c) the squares of any two corresponding medians, or (d) the squares of any two corresponding angle bisectors (areas ~ △s propor sqs corr sides, alts, meds, ∡ bis).
105. An angle bisector in a triangle divides the opposite side into segments that have the same ratio as the other two sides (∡ bis ÷ opp side same ratio other 2 sides).
106. The area of a sector of radius r whose angle has measure $a°$ is $\frac{a}{360} \cdot \pi r^2$ ($A_s = \frac{a}{360}\pi r^2$).
107. The length of the arc of a sector of radius r whose angle has measure $a°$ is $\frac{a}{360} \cdot 2\pi r$ ($L = \frac{a}{360} 2\pi r$).
108. If two chords intersect in a circle, the product of the lengths of the segments of one chord is equal to the product of the lengths of the segments of the other chord (prods segs 2 chs =).
109. If two secant segments are drawn to a circle from an external point, then the product of the lengths of one secant segment and its external part is equal to the product of the lengths of the other secant segment and its external part (prods 2 secs and segs =).
110. If a tangent segment and a secant segment are drawn to a circle from an external point, then the length of the tangent segment is the mean proportional between the lengths of the secant segment and its external part (tan seg mn propor sec segs).

CHAPTER 10

111. The lateral area of a regular pyramid is one-half the product of the perimeter of its base and its slant height ($LA = \frac{1}{2}Pl$).
112. The volume of any prism is the product of the area of one of its bases and its altitude ($V = Bh$).
113. The volume of any pyramid is one-third the product of the area of its base and its altitude ($V = \frac{1}{3}Bh$).
114. The lateral area of a right circular cylinder is the product of the circumference of one of its bases and its altitude ($LA = 2\pi rh$). The total area is the sum of the lateral area and twice the area of one of its bases ($TA = 2\pi rh + 2\pi r^2$).
115. The volume of a right circular cylinder is the product of the area of one of its bases and its altitude ($V = \pi r^2 h$).
116. The lateral area of a right circular cone is one-half the product of the circumference of its base and its slant height ($LA = \frac{1}{2} \cdot 2\pi rl = \pi rl$). The total area is the sum of its lateral area and the area of its base ($TA = \pi rl + \pi r^2$).
117. The volume of a right circular cone is one-third the product of the area of its base and its altitude ($V = \frac{1}{3}\pi r^2 h$).
118. If a sphere has radius r, then its surface area $S = 4\pi r^2$ and its volume $V = \frac{4}{3}\pi r^3$.

Appendix C

LOCI

The word loci (pronounced lō′-sī) is the plural of the Latin word locus, which means place or location. Sometimes it is necessary in geometry to specify the location of all points satisfying one or more conditions. In this text we have shown how the concept of a set of points, the operations of union and intersection, and set notation can be used for this purpose. We have also used intersections of arcs and lines to construct a set of points satisfying certain conditions. The words locus and loci may also be used in these circumstances. A locus is a set of points such that:

1. Every point in the set satisfies certain conditions.
2. Every point that satisfies the conditions is in the set.

These two requirements are the content of the following definition.

Definition C.1 A *locus of points* is a geometric figure formed by all those points, and only those points, that satisfy one or more given conditions.

Theorems 27 and 28 in Section 4.7 may be conveniently stated in locus terminology. Theorem 27 establishes that every point on the perpendicular bisector of a line segment is equidistant from the segment's endpoints, and Theorem 28 (the converse) asserts that every point that is equidistant from a line segment's endpoints is on the perpendicular bisector of the segment. Thus, the perpendicular bisector of a line segment is the locus of points equidistant from the segment's endpoints.

Next we state five theorems concerning loci of points. It should be clear from the foregoing discussion that each of these is in fact a theorem and its converse, and thus a two-part proof is required for a locus theorem. We will omit proofs at first, however, in order to concentrate on developing the locus concept. An example of a proof is given at the end of this section and more proofs are requested in the exercises. The following five theorems are quite simple and their correctness should be evident. They are *fundamental loci,* and examples of their use in finding more complicated loci are given below.

It is to be understood that *all locus statements in this appendix are about figures in a plane*.

Theorem C.1 The locus of points at a given distance from a given line is a pair of lines parallel to the given line at the given distance from it.

Theorem C.2 The locus of points equidistant from two given parallel lines is a line parallel to each of them and midway between them.

The above theorems are illustrated in Figure C.1.

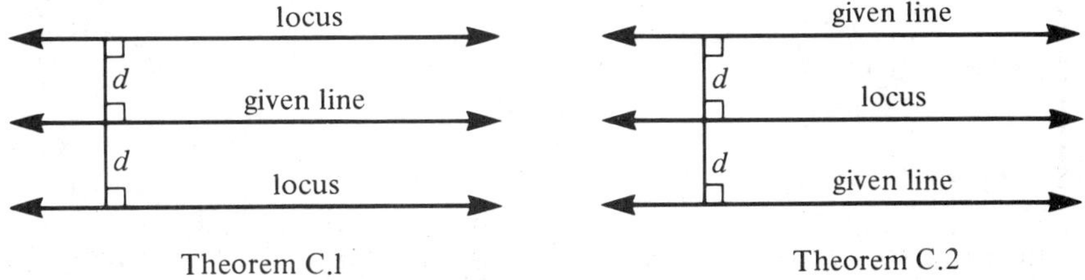

Figure C.1

The next theorem is the locus equivalent of the definition of a circle (Definition 7.1). Thus, it is a direct consequence of Definition C.1 above and Definition 7.1.

Theorem C.3 The locus of points at a given distance from a given point is a circle whose center is the given point and whose radius is the given distance.

Theorems C.4 and C.5 below require a definition of the distance from a point to a circle (Figure C.2).

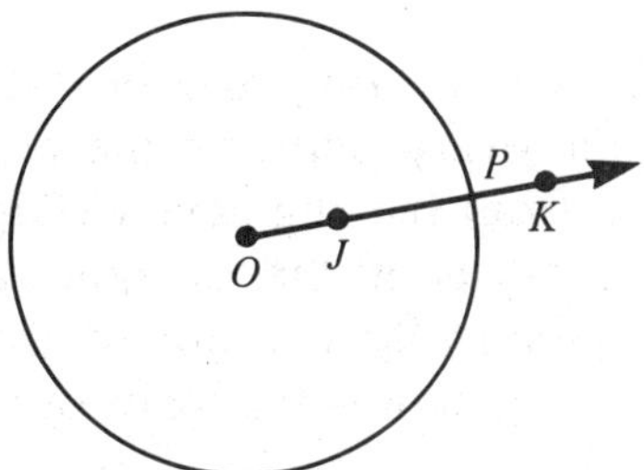

Figure C.2 The distance from J to $\odot O$ is JP. The distance from K to $\odot O$ is KP.

Definition C.2 The distance from a point A to a circle with center O is AP where P is the intersection of $\overrightarrow{OA}$ and $\odot O$.

Figure C.3 shows a given circle with radius $OP = r$ and the locus of points at a given distance d less than r from it. This illustrates the next theorem.

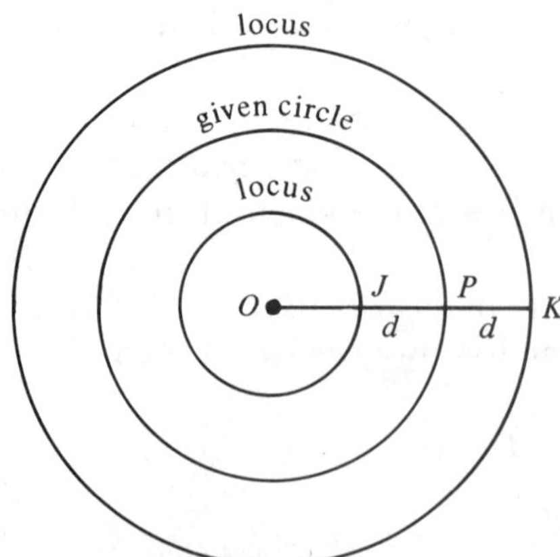

Figure C.3 (Theorem C.4.) Let $OP = r$, then $OJ = r - d$, $OK = r + d$.

Theorem C.4 The locus of points at a given distance d from a given circle with radius r, where $d < r$, is a pair of circles concentric with the given circle and whose radii are $r - d$ and $r + d$, respectively.

Figure C.4 illustrates Theorem C.5. It shows the locus of points equidistant from two given concentric circles. The locus is a third concentric circle whose radius is the average of the radii of the given circles.

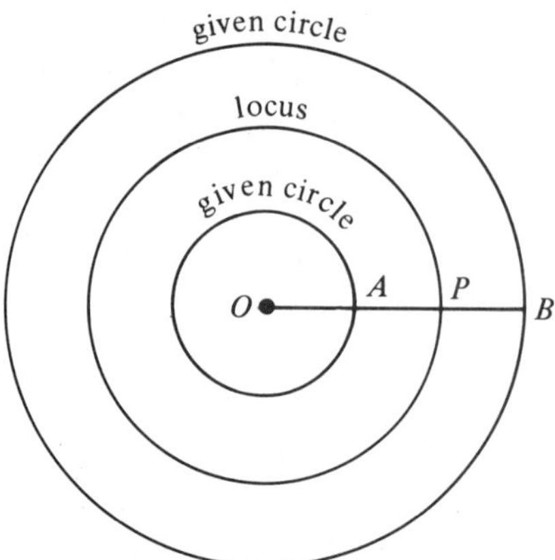

Figure C.4 Let $OA = r$ and $OB = R$, then $OP = r + AP$, $AP = \frac{1}{2}(R - r) = \frac{1}{2}R - \frac{1}{2}r$, $OP = r + \frac{1}{2}R - \frac{1}{2}r = \frac{1}{2}r + \frac{1}{2}R$, $OP = \frac{r + R}{2}$.

Theorem C.5 The locus of points equidistant from a given pair of concentric circles with radii r and R, respectively, is a circle concentric with the given circles and whose radius is $\frac{r + R}{2}$.

The fundamental loci in Theorems C.1–C.5 can be used to determine other loci as indicated in the examples below.

EXAMPLE 1 Draw and describe the locus of points that are (a) one fourth of an inch from the sides and in the exterior of a given rectangle, and (b) the midpoints of the radii of a given circle.

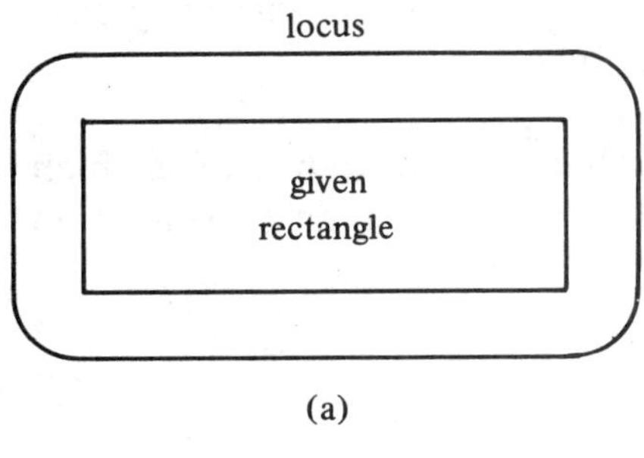

(a)

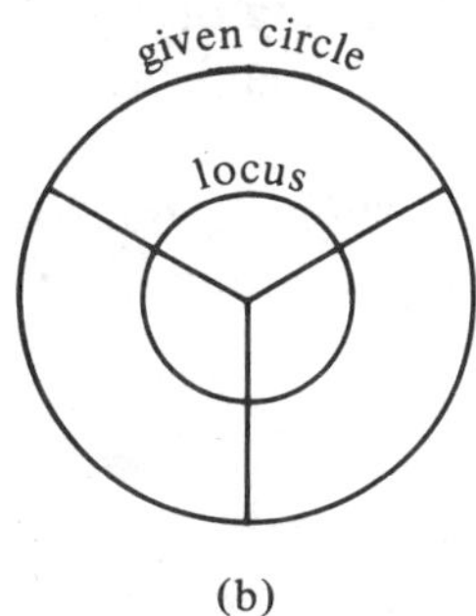

(b)

Answers

(a) The locus is formed by four line segments parallel to and $\frac{1}{4}$ inch from the sides and four quarter circles with centers at the vertices and radius $\frac{1}{4}$ inch.

(b) The locus is a circle concentric with the given circle and whose radius is one-half of the radius of the given circle.

It is sometimes useful to view a locus as the path traced by a point that moves such that one or more conditions are satisfied. For instance, the locus in Example 1(b) would be traced by the midpoint of a radius rotating, like the spoke of a wheel, about the center. This viewpoint is evident in many ways in our technical world. A graph shown on an oscilloscope, electronic scoreboards that spell out words, some animated cartoons, and computer graphics may be seen as loci traced by moving points.

As stated in Definition C.1, a locus of points may be required to satisfy one or more conditions. Such a locus may be found by first drawing independently the locus for each given condition. The points of intersections, if any, of these loci form the required locus as illustrated in the next two examples. In the first of these we use the fact that the locus of points equidistant from the sides of an angle is the bisector of the angle. This fact is proved as Theorem C.6 below.

EXAMPLE 2 Draw and describe the locus of points that are equidistant from the sides of $\measuredangle E$ and from vertices J and S for a given $\triangle EJS$.

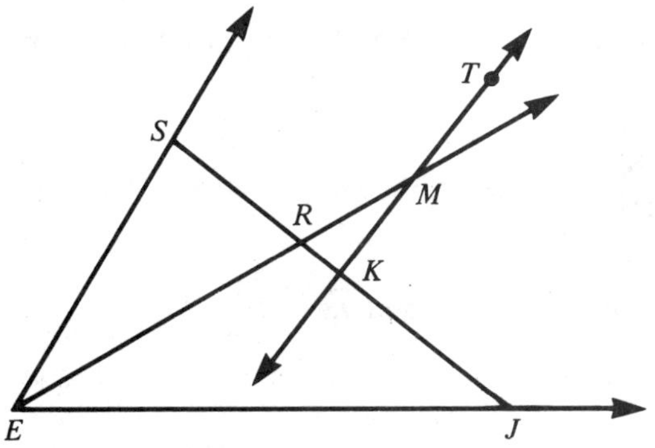

Answer

The locus of points equidistant from sides $\overrightarrow{EJ}$ and $\overrightarrow{ES}$ of $\measuredangle E$ is the bisector $\overrightarrow{ER}$ of $\measuredangle JES$. The locus of points equidistant from J and S is the perpendicular bisector $\overleftrightarrow{KT}$ of $\overline{JS}$. Hence, the required locus is point M, the intersection of $\overrightarrow{ER}$ and $\overleftrightarrow{KT}$.

Note in the above example that the locus, M, may be outside, on, or inside the triangle, depending on the type of triangle that is given. Is there any case in which the locus could be more than one point?

EXAMPLE 3 Draw and describe the locus of points that are one fourth of an inch from circle O and from a given line $\overleftrightarrow{OP}$ where the radius of $\odot O$ is three fourths of an inch.

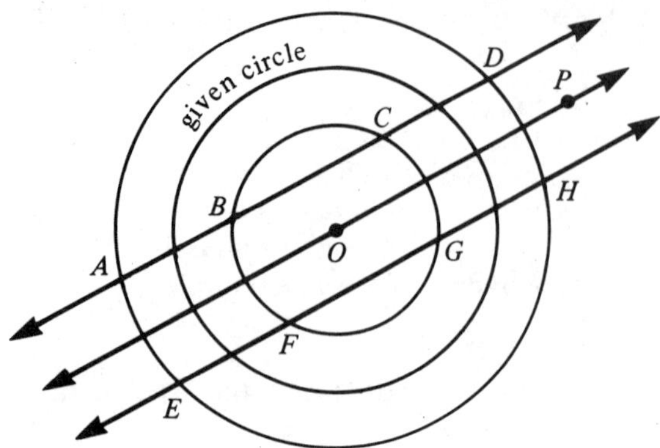

Answer
The locus of points $\frac{1}{4}$ inch from $\odot O$ is a pair of circles concentric with O and with radii $\frac{1}{2}$ inch and 1 inch, respectively. The locus of points $\frac{1}{4}$ inch from $\overleftrightarrow{OP}$ is a pair of lines parallel to and $\frac{1}{4}$ inch from $\overleftrightarrow{OP}$. The intersections of these loci, points A, B, C, D, E, F, G, and H, form the required locus.

In the foregoing development, no attempt was made to prove that the loci obtained were in fact the correct ones. As explained previously, such proofs require two parts; that is, to prove that a set of points is a required locus, it must be shown that (1) every point in the set satisfies the given condition or conditions, and (2) every point that satisfies the given condition or conditions is in the set. Our discussion of loci concludes with a sample of such a proof.

Theorem C.6 The locus of points equidistant from the sides of an angle is the bisector of the angle.

Part 1: If P is any point on the bisector of $\measuredangle EJS$, then P is equidistant from $\overrightarrow{JE}$ and $\overrightarrow{JS}$.

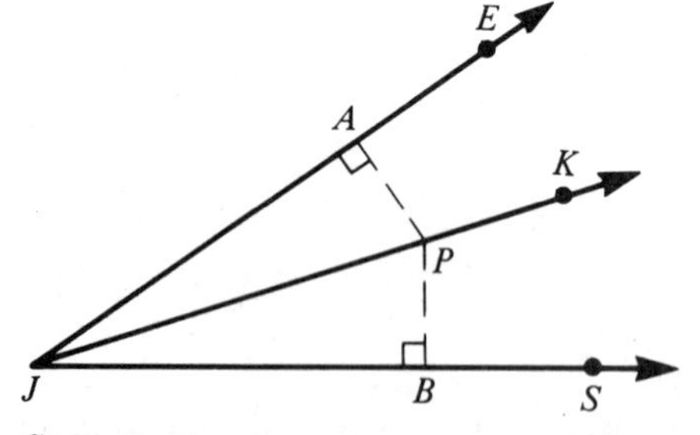

Given
$\overrightarrow{JK}$ bis $\measuredangle EJS$
P any pt on $\overrightarrow{JK}$

To Prove
P equidis from $\overrightarrow{JE}$ and $\overrightarrow{JS}$

Statement	*Reason*
1. $\overrightarrow{JK}$ bis $\measuredangle EJS$	1. given
2. $\measuredangle EJK \cong \measuredangle SJK$	2. bis $\div$ $\measuredangle$ into 2 $\cong$ $\measuredangle$s
3. P any pt on $\overrightarrow{JK}$	3. given
4. Draw $\overline{PA} \perp \overrightarrow{JE}$ and $\overline{PB} \perp \overrightarrow{JS}$.	4. 1 $\perp$ from pt to line
5. $\measuredangle PAJ$ and $\measuredangle PBJ$ rt $\measuredangle$s.	5. $\perp$s form rt $\measuredangle$s
6. $\measuredangle PAJ \cong \measuredangle PBJ$	6. rt $\measuredangle$s $\cong$

7. $\overline{JP} \cong \overline{JP}$	7. refl $\cong$
8. $\triangle JPA \cong \triangle JPB$	8. aas $\cong$ aas
9. $\overline{PA} \cong \overline{PB}$	9. cpctc
10. $PA = PB$	10. $\cong$ iff meas $=$
11. $\therefore P$ equidis from $\overrightarrow{JE}$ and $\overrightarrow{JS}$	11. dis pt to line is length of $\perp$ seg

Part 2: If P is any point that is equidistant from $\overrightarrow{JE}$ and $\overrightarrow{JS}$, then P is on the bisector of $\measuredangle EJS$.

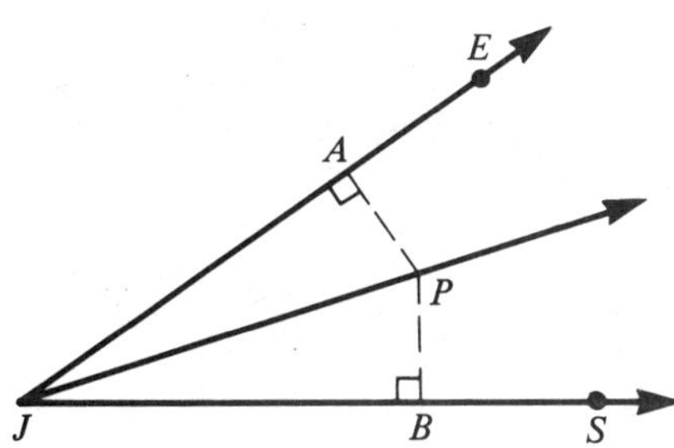

Given
P equidis from $\overrightarrow{JE}$ and $\overrightarrow{JS}$

To Prove
$\overrightarrow{JP}$ bis $\measuredangle EJS$

Statement	*Reason*
1. P equidis from $\overrightarrow{JE}$ and $\overrightarrow{JS}$	1. given
2. Draw $\overline{PA} \perp \overrightarrow{JE}$ and $\overline{PB} \perp \overrightarrow{JS}$.	2. 1 $\perp$ from pt to line
3. $PA = PB$	3. dis pt to line is length of $\perp$ seg
4. $\overline{PA} \cong \overline{PB}$	4. $\cong$ iff meas $=$
5. $\overline{JP} \cong \overline{JP}$	5. refl $\cong$
6. $\measuredangle JAP$ and $\measuredangle JBP$ rt $\measuredangle$s	6. $\perp$s form rt $\measuredangle$s
7. $\triangle JPA \cong \triangle JPB$	7. hs $\cong$ hs
8. $\measuredangle PJA \cong \measuredangle PJB$	8. cpctc
9. $\therefore \overrightarrow{JP}$ bis $\measuredangle EJS$	9. bis $\div$ $\measuredangle$ into 2 $\cong$ $\measuredangle$s

In summary, the purpose of this appendix is to explain and illustrate the language and viewpoint of loci. This language is of interest because of its frequent usage in the historical development of geometry. It is also of value as a concise way to describe a set of points determined by certain specific conditions.

EXERCISES FOR APPENDIX C

In exercises 1–16, (a) draw the locus of points that satisfy the given condition, and (b) describe the locus.

1. 2 inches from a point B
2. 1 inch from a line l
3. equidistant from two lines l and m, which are 1 inch apart
4. $\frac{1}{2}$ inch from a circle O of radius 1 inch
5. equidistant from two concentric circles of radii 2 inches and 3 inches, respectively
6. the vertices of right angles of right triangles with a given hypotenuse $\overline{AB}$
7. the centers of circles tangent to a line l at a given point A on l
8. the midpoints of line segments that are parallel to the hypotenuse $\overline{AB}$ of a right triangle ABC and whose endpoints are on $\overline{AC}$ and $\overline{BC}$
9. the vertices S of triangles EJS with a given side $\overline{EJ}$ and given area K
10. the centers of circles tangent to two intersecting lines l and m
11. the midpoints of chords $\overline{AB}$ of a circle O where $\overline{AB}$ has a given length AB
12. the midpoints of segments $\overline{BX}$ such that X is any point on a triangle BRT

13. the vertices P of triangles PLW such that $\overline{LW}$ is 4 inches long and the median to $\overline{LW}$ is 3 inches long

14. the midpoints of chords $\overline{AB}$ of a circle O such that A is a given point on the circle

15. the midpoints of legs $\overline{BC}$ of right triangles ABC with given hypotenuse $\overline{AB}$

16. the points P in the exterior of two externally tangent circles such that the tangent segments from P to the circles are congruent

In exercises 17–24 draw the locus of points satisfying all the given conditions.

17. 3 inches from J and $1\frac{1}{2}$ inches from l where J is a given point on a line l

18. equidistant from 3 noncollinear points A, B, and C

19. equidistant from the sides of $\measuredangle L$ and $1\frac{1}{2}$ inches from M for equilateral triangle KLM whose sides are each 2 inches long

20. equidistant from the sides of angle E and from vertices J and S for isosceles triangle EJS ($\overline{JS}$ base) (compare with Example 2)

21. equidistant from J and S and 2 inches from the midpoint of $\overline{EJ}$ for equilateral triangle EJS whose sides are each 4 inches long

22. equidistant from two intersecting lines and 2 inches from their point of intersection

23. $\frac{3}{4}$ inch from P and equidistant from two given lines that intersect at Q where points P and Q are 1 inch apart

24. equidistant from two concentric circles and two points E and J where E is on one of the circles and J is on the other

25. If line l is tangent at B to circle O whose radius is 4 inches, draw and describe the locus of points two inches from the circle and (a) 1 inch from l, (b) 2 inches from l, (c) 3 inches from l.

26. Draw and describe the locus of the vertices of the right angles of right triangles having a given line segment 4 inches long as hypotenuse and whose altitudes to the hypotenuse are $1\frac{1}{2}$ inches long.

In exercises 27–29 for each of parts (1) and (2), as in the proof of Theorem C.6, draw a figure, write the hypothesis, the conclusion, and a proof.

27. The locus of the vertices of the right triangles with given hypotenuse $\overline{AB}$ is a circle, less its two endpoints, with diameter $\overline{AB}$.

28. The locus of points equidistant from two intersecting lines l and m is the pair of perpendicular lines that bisect the angles formed by l and m.

29. The locus of the midpoints of legs $\overline{BC}$ of right triangles ABC with given hypotenuse $\overline{AB}$ is a circle, less its two endpoints, with center O on $\overline{AB}$ such that $OB = \frac{1}{4}AB$.

30. What is the locus of the midpoints of the chords that can be drawn through a given point P in the interior of a given circle O? Prove that your answer is correct.

31. What is the locus of the intersections of the diagonals of the rhombuses with a given line segment $\overline{AB}$ as one side? Prove that your answer is correct.

Appendix D

CONCURRENT LINES AND TRIANGLES

In section 4.5 it is stated but not proved that the three bisectors of the angles of any triangle intersect in a point, that is, they are *concurrent*. The medians, the altitudes, and the perpendicular bisectors of the sides have the same property. In this appendix we prove these facts and also explain some interesting and important properties of these points of intersection. We begin with a definition.

Definition D.1 Two or more lines or subsets of lines are *concurrent* iff they intersect at one point (lines concurr iff inters 1 pt).

In Figure D.1 lines l, m, and n are concurrent because they intersect in one point O; whereas, lines p, q, and r are not concurrent because they do not intersect in one point. (Lines p and q, however, *are* concurrent. The same is true for q and r and for p and r.)

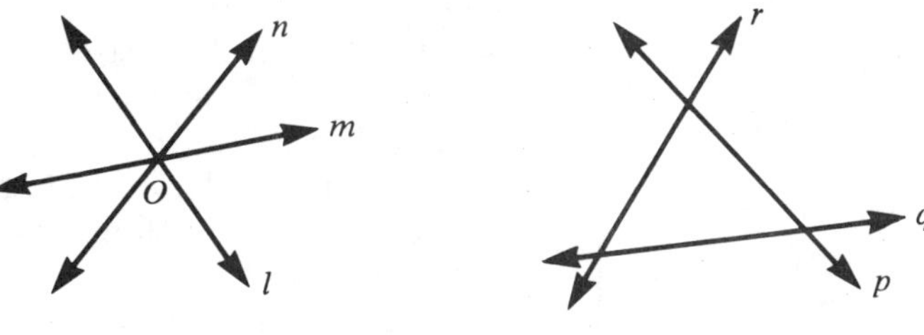

Figure D.1

The main content of this appendix rests in four theorems that are stated and proved below. It is to be understood that *all theorems in this appendix are about figures in a plane*. The proofs given here contain some shortcuts not used in the text that require a knowledge of the fundamentals of plane geometry. For example, it is assumed that the reader knows the meaning of terms such as supplementary angles, angle bisector, perpendicular bisector, altitude, and median. Also, reasons that may be new or unfamiliar are written in full. This is the case for theorems from Appendixes C and D, which are also referred to by number. Finally, some parts of the proofs are indirect. In particular, to prove that two rays or lines intersect, we assume that they are parallel. This leads to a contradiction and we conclude that they are not parallel, that is, that they must intersect.

Theorem D.1 The bisectors of the angles of a triangle are concurrent in a point equidistant from the sides of the triangle.

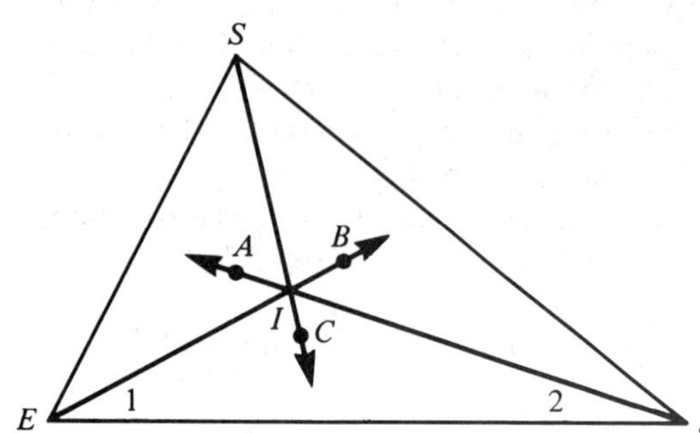

Given
$\triangle EJS$
$\overrightarrow{EB}$ bis $\measuredangle SEJ$
$\overrightarrow{JA}$ bis $\measuredangle EJS$
$\overrightarrow{SC}$ bis $\measuredangle JSE$

To Prove
$\overrightarrow{EB}$, $\overrightarrow{JA}$, $\overrightarrow{SC}$ concurr at a point I
I equidis from $\overline{EJ}$, $\overline{JS}$, $\overline{SE}$

Statement	*Reason*
1. $\triangle EJS$ $\overrightarrow{EB}$ bis $\measuredangle SEJ$ $\overrightarrow{JA}$ bis $\measuredangle EJS$ $\overrightarrow{SC}$ bis $\measuredangle JSE$	1. given
Assume $\overrightarrow{EB} \parallel \overrightarrow{JA}$, then	
2. $\angle 1 + \angle 2 = 180°$	2. $\nparallel$, int $\measuredangle$s same side t supp
3. $\angle 1 = \frac{1}{2}\angle SEJ$, $\angle 2 = \frac{1}{2}\angle EJS$	3. bis $\div$ $\measuredangle$ into 2 $\cong$ $\measuredangle$s
4. $\frac{1}{2}\angle SEJ + \frac{1}{2}\angle EJS = 180°$	4. subst
5. $\angle SEJ + \angle EJS = 360°$	5. doubles of =s are =
6. Statement 5 is a contradiction.	6. 180° in $\triangle$
7. $\overrightarrow{EB}$ and $\overrightarrow{JA}$ intersect; let I name the point of intersection	7. If two lines are not parallel, then they intersect.
8. $\therefore I$ equidis from $\overline{EJ}$, $\overline{JS}$, $\overline{SE}$	8. If a point is on the bisector of an angle, then it is equidistant from the sides of the angle (Theorem C.6).
9. I is on $\overrightarrow{SC}$	9. If a point is equidistant from the sides of an angle, then it is on the bisector of the angle (Theorem C.6).
10. $\therefore$ $\overrightarrow{EB}$, $\overrightarrow{JA}$, $\overrightarrow{SC}$ concurrent at I	10. lines concurr iff inters 1 pt

Since the point I of Theorem D.1 is equidistant from the sides of the triangle, line segments from I perpendicular to the sides will be congruent. With their common length as a radius and I as the center, a circle may be drawn that will be tangent to the sides of the triangle. This circle is *inscribed* in the triangle, and its center, the intersection of the angle bisectors, is called the *incenter* of the triangle.

Construction D.1 To construct the incenter and the inscribed circle for a triangle.

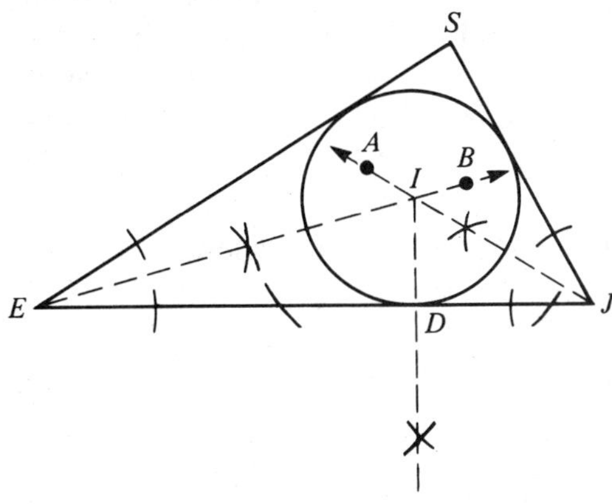

Given
$\triangle EJS$

To Construct
incenter I
inscribed $\odot I$

Steps
1. Construct the bisector $\overrightarrow{EB}$ of $\angle SEJ$ (Construction 3).
2. Construct the bisector $\overrightarrow{JA}$ of $\angle EJS$ (Construction 3). The intersection I of $\overrightarrow{EB}$ and $\overrightarrow{JA}$ is the incenter of $\triangle EJS$.
3. Construct the perpendicular $\overrightarrow{ID}$ from I to $\overline{EJ}$ (Construction 6).
4. With I as center and ID as a radius, draw $\odot I$, the inscribed circle for $\triangle EJS$.

The proof of Construction D.1 is omitted; it is based on Theorem D.1.

Theorem D.2 The perpendicular bisectors of the sides of a triangle are concurrent in a point equidistant from the vertices of the triangle.

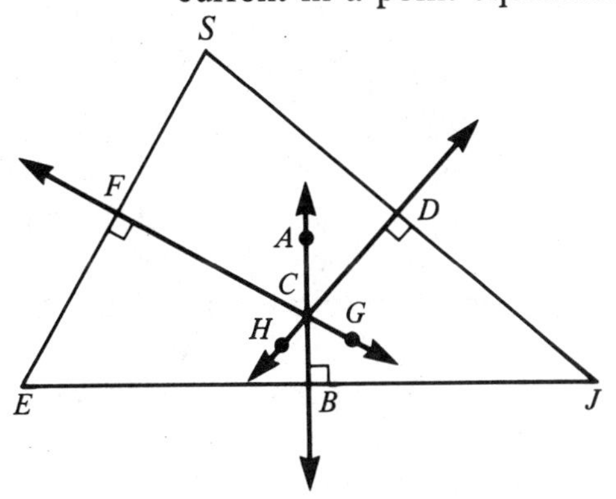

Given
$\triangle EJS$
$\overleftrightarrow{AB} \perp$ bis $\overline{EJ}$
$\overleftrightarrow{HD} \perp$ bis $\overline{JS}$
$\overleftrightarrow{GF} \perp$ bis $\overline{SE}$

To Prove
$\overleftrightarrow{AB}$, $\overleftrightarrow{HD}$, $\overleftrightarrow{GF}$ concurr at a point C
C equidis from E, J, and S

Statement	*Reason*
1. $\triangle EJS$ $\overleftrightarrow{AB} \perp$ bis $\overline{EJ}$ $\overleftrightarrow{HD} \perp$ bis $\overline{JS}$ $\overleftrightarrow{GF} \perp$ bis $\overline{SE}$ Assume $\overleftrightarrow{AB} \parallel \overleftrightarrow{HD}$, then	1. given
2. $\overline{EJ} \parallel \overline{JS}$	2. If two lines are perpendicular to two parallel lines, then they are parallel.
3. Statement 2 is a contradiction.	3. A figure is a triangle iff it is the union of three line segments determined by three noncollinear points.
4. $\overleftrightarrow{AB}$ and $\overleftrightarrow{HD}$ intersect; let C name the point of intersection	4. If two lines are not parallel, then they intersect.
5. $\therefore$ C equidis from E, J, and S	5. pt on $\perp$ bis of seg iff equidis from endpts
6. C is on $\overleftrightarrow{GF}$	6. pt on $\perp$ bis of seg iff equidis from endpts
7. $\therefore$ $\overleftrightarrow{AB}$, $\overleftrightarrow{HD}$, $\overleftrightarrow{GF}$ concurr at C	7. lines concurr iff inters 1 pt

Since the point C of Theorem D.2 is equidistant from the vertices of the triangle, line segments from C to the vertices will be congruent. With their common length as a radius and C as the center, a circle may be drawn that will pass through the three vertices. This circle is *circumscribed* about the triangle, and its center, the intersection of the perpendicular bisectors of the sides, is the *circumcenter* of the triangle. The triangle is, of course, inscribed in its circumscribed circle.

Construction D.2 To construct the circumcenter and the circumscribed circle for a triangle.

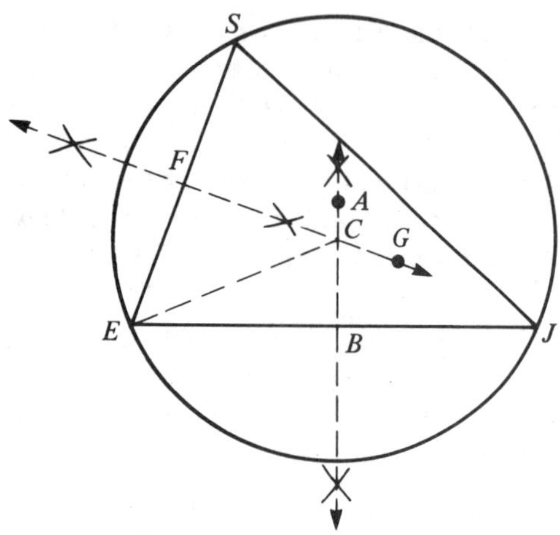

Given
$\triangle EJS$

To Construct
circumcenter C
circumscribed $\odot C$

Steps

1. Construct the perpendicular bisector $\overleftrightarrow{AB}$ of $\overline{EJ}$ (Construction 10).
2. Construct the perpendicular bisector $\overleftrightarrow{GF}$ of $\overline{SE}$ (Construction 10). The intersection C of $\overleftrightarrow{AB}$ and $\overleftrightarrow{GF}$ is the circumcenter of $\triangle EJS$.
3. With C as center and CE as a radius, draw $\odot C$, the circumscribed circle for $\triangle EJS$.

Construction D.2 is a direct consequence of Theorem D.2 and a proof is omitted. Note, however, that in the figure an acute triangle is given and the circumcenter is in the triangle's interior. There are some exercises at the end of this appendix concerning the location of the circumcenter of a right and of an obtuse triangle. Also, although this construction will work for any triangle, there is a much shorter one for a right triangle based on the fact that if a right triangle is inscribed in a circle, then its hypotenuse is a diameter of the circle (see exercise 8).

The next theorem provides an example of the way in which the proof of a new theorem may sometimes be based directly on one that has just been established.

Theorem D.3 The altitudes of a triangle are concurrent.

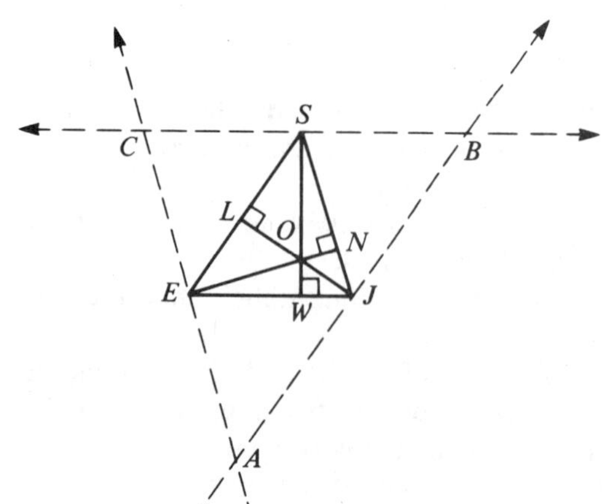

Given
$\triangle EJS$
alts $\overline{EN}$, $\overline{JL}$, $\overline{SW}$

To Prove
$\overline{EN}$, $\overline{JL}$, $\overline{SW}$ concurr at a point O

Statement	*Reason*
1. $\triangle EJS$ alts $\overline{EN}$, $\overline{JL}$, $\overline{SW}$	1. given
2. Draw $\overleftrightarrow{EA} \parallel \overline{JS}$, $\overleftrightarrow{JB} \parallel \overline{SE}$, and $\overleftrightarrow{SC} \parallel \overline{EJ}$.	2. $\parallel$ post
3. $EJBS$ and $EJSC$ ▱s	3. ▱ iff opp sides $\parallel$
4. $\overline{BS} \cong \overline{EJ}$, $\overline{EJ} \cong \overline{SC}$	4. opp sides ▱ $\cong$
5. $\overline{BS} \cong \overline{SC}$	5. trans $\cong$
6. $\overline{SW} \perp \overline{BC}$	6. If a line is perpendicular to one of two parallel lines, then it is perpendicular to the other one also.
7. $\overline{SW} \perp$ bis $\overline{BC}$ Similarly, it can be proved that $\overline{EN} \perp$ bis $\overline{CA}$ $\overline{JL} \perp$ bis $\overline{AB}$	7. $\perp$ bis iff bis seg and is $\perp$
8. $\therefore$ $\overline{EN}$, $\overline{JL}$, $\overline{SW}$ concurr	8. The perpendicular bisectors of the sides of a triangle ($\triangle ABC$ in the figure) are concurrent (Theorem D.2).

The intersection of the altitudes (O in the figure for Theorem D.3) is called the *orthocenter* of the triangle. The prefix ortho comes from the Greek word orthos, which means straight or upright. In mathematics the word orthogonal means "at right angles." Thus, the term orthocenter is used here because the altitudes meet the sides of the triangle at right angles. In the figure for Theorem D.3, $\triangle EJS$ is acute and its orthocenter is in its interior. There are some questions in the exercises about the location of the orthocenter of a right and of an obtuse triangle. Finally, note that it is easy to construct the orthocenter of a triangle by constructing perpendiculars from two of its vertices to the opposite sides (Construction 6).

Theorem D.4 The medians of a triangle are concurrent in a point that is two thirds of the distance from each vertex to the midpoint of the opposite side (meds concurr $\frac{2}{3}$ dis vtx to opp side).

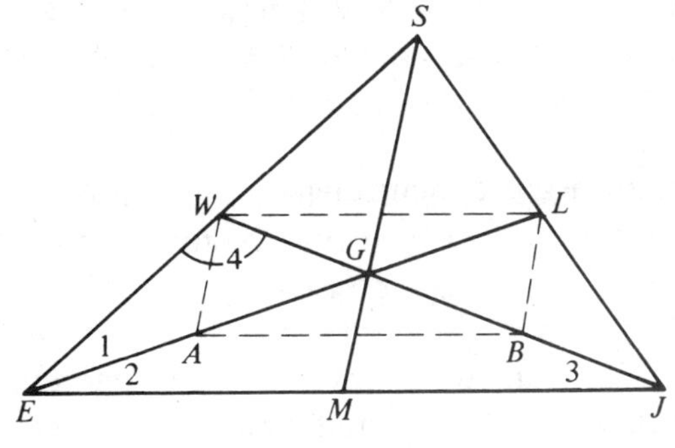

Given
$\triangle EJS$
meds $\overline{EL}$, $\overline{JW}$, $\overline{SM}$

To Prove
$\overline{EL}$, $\overline{JW}$, $\overline{SM}$ concurr at a point G
$EG = \frac{2}{3}EL$
$JG = \frac{2}{3}JW$
$SG = \frac{2}{3}SM$

Part 1: Proof for $\overline{EL}$ and $\overline{JW}$.

Statement	*Reason*
1. $\triangle EJS$, meds $\overline{EL}$, $\overline{JW}$	1. given
2. $\angle 1 + \angle 2 + \angle 3 + \angle 4 = 180°$	2. 180° in $\triangle$
3. $\angle 2 + \angle 3 < 180°$	3. whole $>$ part
Assume $\overline{EL} \parallel \overline{JW}$, then 4. $\angle 2 + \angle 3 = 180°$	4. $\neq$, int $\measuredangle$s same side t supp

Statement	Reason
5. Statement 4 is a contradiction.	5. If $x, y \in R$, then one and only one of the following is true: $x < y$, $x = y$, or $y < x$ (Trichotomy Axiom).
6. $\overline{EL}$ and $\overline{JW}$ intersect; let G name the point of intersection	6. If two lines are not parallel, then they intersect.
7. let A be midpt $\overline{EG}$ so $EA = AG$ let B be midpt $\overline{JG}$ so $JB = BG$	7. A line segment has one and only one midpoint.
8. Draw $\overline{AB}$, $\overline{BL}$, $\overline{WL}$, $\overline{AW}$.	8. 2 pts determ line
9. $\overline{WL} \parallel \overline{EJ}$, $WL = \frac{1}{2}EJ$ $\overline{AB} \parallel \overline{EJ}$, $AB = \frac{1}{2}EJ$	9. midpt seg $\triangle$ $\frac{1}{2}$ of and $\parallel$ to 3d side
10. $\overline{WL} \parallel \overline{AB}$	10. 2 lines $\parallel$ 3d line are $\parallel$
11. $\overline{WL} \cong \overline{AB}$	11. trans = and $\cong$ iff meas =
12. $ABLW$ ▱	12. quad 1 pr opp sides $\parallel$ and $\cong$ is ▱
13. $AG = GL$, $BG = GW$	13. The diagonals of a parallelogram bisect each other.
14. $EA = AG = GL$	14. trans =
15. $EG = 2EA$, $EL = 3EA$	15. whole = sum parts
16. $\frac{EG}{EL} = \frac{2}{3}$	16. = ÷ =, quot =
17. $\therefore EG = \frac{2}{3}EL$	17. = · =, prod =

Similarly, it can be proved that $JG = \frac{2}{3}JW$.

Part 2: proof that $\overline{EL}$, $\overline{JW}$, and $\overline{SM}$ are concurrent at G and that $SG = \frac{2}{3}SM$. The details are omitted. They are similar to part 1. An outline is

1. Show that $\overline{EL}$ and $\overline{SM}$ intersect in a point G'.
2. Let P be the midpoint of SG' and prove that $AMLP$ is a parallelogram.
3. Using ▱$AMLP$ prove that $EG' = \frac{2}{3}EL$. Hence, G' and G are the same point, and $\overline{EL}$, $\overline{JW}$, and $\overline{SM}$ are concurrent at G.
4. Using ▱$AMLP$, prove $SG = \frac{2}{3}SM$.

The intersection of the medians of a triangle is called the *centroid* of the triangle. The centroid may be constructed by constructing the midpoints of two sides of the triangle and drawing their corresponding medians. The centroid of a triangular plate of uniform thickness and composition is the *center of gravity* of the plate. It is the point at which the plate will balance in a horizontal position.

The historical notes in this text trace the enormous efforts by mathematicians from the time of Euclid (300 B.C.) until the nineteenth century to solve the parallel postulate controversy and to solve certain construction problems. Perhaps because of this, very little progress in geometry was made during those years. Among the few notable achievements, however, is a theorem proved in the seventeenth century by the Italian mathematician and engineer Giovanni Ceva (chā´vä). Because the theorem is about concurrent lines in a triangle, Ceva's name is applied to line segments such as altitudes, medians, and angle bisectors as follows.

Definition D.2 A line segment is a *cevian* iff one of its endpoints is a vertex of a triangle and the other is a point of the opposite side that is not a vertex.

Thus, in the figure for Theorem D.4, $\overline{EL}$, $\overline{JW}$, and $\overline{SM}$ are cevians.

Theorem D.5 *(Ceva's Theorem.)* The three cevians to the points P, Q, R on the respective sides of a triangle ABC are concurrent iff $\frac{AR}{RB} \cdot \frac{BP}{PC} \cdot \frac{CQ}{QA} = 1$.

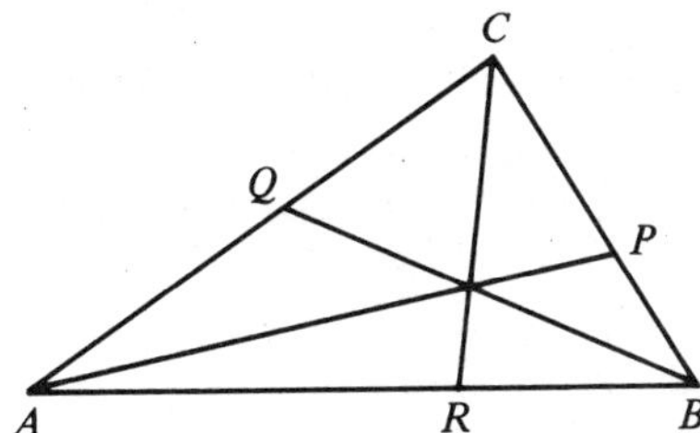

Because of the "iff", this is a theorem and its converse. We will prove that if the cevians are concurrent, then the equation shown is true. The proof of the converse is left as an exercise.

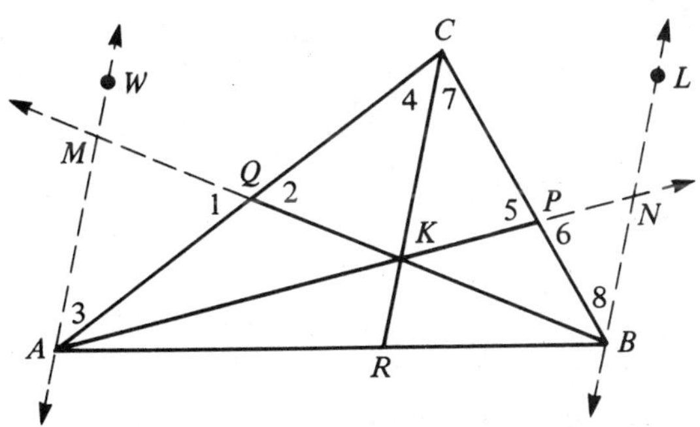

Given
$\triangle ABC$
cevians $\overline{AP}$, $\overline{BQ}$, $\overline{CR}$ concurr at K

To Prove
$\frac{AR}{RB} \cdot \frac{BP}{PC} \cdot \frac{CQ}{QA} = 1$

Statement	*Reason*
1. $\triangle ABC$ cevians $\overline{AP}$, $\overline{BQ}$, $\overline{CR}$ concurr at K	1. given
2. Draw $\overleftrightarrow{AW} \parallel \overline{CR}$ and $\overleftrightarrow{BL} \parallel \overline{CR}$.	2. $\parallel$ post
3. Draw $\overrightarrow{AP}$ inters $\overleftrightarrow{BL}$ at N and $\overrightarrow{BQ}$ inters $\overleftrightarrow{AW}$ at M.	3. 2 pts determ line
4. $\measuredangle 2 \cong \measuredangle 1$, $\measuredangle 6 \cong \measuredangle 5$	4. vert $\measuredangle$s $\cong$
5. $\measuredangle 4 \cong \measuredangle 3$, $\measuredangle 8 \cong \measuredangle 7$	5. $\parallel$, alt int $\measuredangle$s $\cong$
6. $\triangle CQK \sim \triangle AQM$, $\triangle BPN \sim \triangle CPK$	6. aa $\cong$ aa
7. $\frac{CQ}{QA} = \frac{CK}{AM}$, $\frac{BP}{PC} = \frac{BN}{CK}$	7. csstp
8. $\measuredangle KAR \cong \measuredangle KAR$, $\measuredangle KBR \cong \measuredangle KBR$	8. refl $\cong$
9. $\measuredangle ARK \cong \measuredangle ABN$, $\measuredangle BRK \cong \measuredangle BAM$	9. $\parallel$, corr $\measuredangle$s $\cong$
10. $\triangle ARK \sim \triangle ABN$, $\triangle BRK \sim \triangle BAM$	10. aa $\cong$ aa
11. $\frac{AR}{AB} = \frac{RK}{BN}$, $\frac{AB}{RB} = \frac{AM}{RK}$	11. csstp
12. $\frac{CQ}{QA} \cdot \frac{AR}{\cancel{AB}} \cdot \frac{\cancel{AB}}{RB} \cdot \frac{BP}{PC} = \frac{\cancel{CK}}{\cancel{AM}} \cdot \frac{\cancel{RK}}{\cancel{BN}} \cdot \frac{\cancel{AM}}{\cancel{RK}} \cdot \frac{\cancel{BN}}{\cancel{CK}}$	12. $= \cdot =$, prod $=$
13. $\therefore \frac{AR}{RB} \cdot \frac{BP}{PC} \cdot \frac{CQ}{QA} = 1$	13. rearr props

In a sense, Ceva's Theorem is a unification of Theorems D.1, D.3, and D.4. In fact, it is possible to prove the concurrency of the angle bisectors, altitudes, and medians using the converse of the part of Ceva's Theorem proved above. Some numerical examples of this theorem appear in the exercises.

We conclude this appendix with a brief discussion of a remarkable figure that is part of the folklore of geometry and which is the subject of the cover of this textbook. Recall that three noncollinear points determine a unique circle (The Circle Postulate). In any triangle, the circle determined by the midpoints of the sides passes through the feet of the altitudes (their endpoints on the sides) and through the midpoints of the segments connecting the vertices to the orthocenter (the intersection of the altitudes). Since there are nine such points, shown as open dots in Figure D.2, the circle is called the *nine-point circle*.

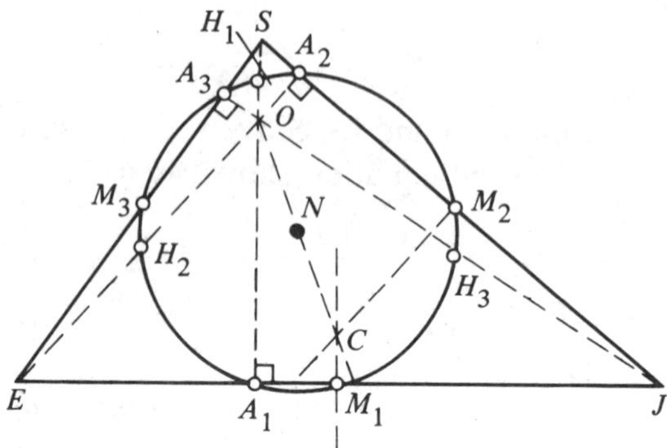

Figure D.2 M_1, M_2, M_3 midpoints of sides
A_1, A_2, A_3, feet of altitudes
H_1, H_2, H_3 midpoints of $\overline{SO}$, $\overline{EO}$, $\overline{JO}$
O orthocenter
C circumcenter
N center of nine-point circle and midpoint of $\overline{OC}$

In addition to the curious fact that the nine points described above are on a single circle, other interesting properties of this figure have been discovered. For example, the radius of the nine-point circle is one-half that of the circumcircle. Also, not only is the center of the nine-point circle the midpoint of the segment connecting the orthocenter and the circumcenter, but also the centroid is collinear with these points as well. This line of collinearity is named the Euler line after the renowned Swiss mathematician Leonhard Euler (1707–1783) who studied the properties of the nine-point circle. Indeed, Euler was one of the most prolific mathematicians of all time and his name is attached to almost every branch of mathematics. Recall "Euler's formula" in exercises 34 and 35, Section 10.3. Also, all scientific calculators have built in them the irrational number 2.718 · · ·. This is the important Euler's constant of calculus and is denoted e in his honor. It is notable that the wide-ranging interests of a mathematician of such stature included geometry and the nine-point circle.

EXERCISES FOR APPENDIX D

Use only a compass and straightedge to do the constructions in exercises 1–20. In exercises 1–4 construct a triangle of the indicated type and its *inscribed* circle.

1. scalene acute

2. isosceles

3. equilateral

4. right

In exercises 5–8 construct a triangle of the indicated type and its *circumscribed* circle.

5. scalene acute
6. isosceles obtuse
7. equilateral
8. right (Use a short method and state the location of the circumcenter.)

In exercises 9–12 construct a triangle of the indicated type and the indicated point.

9. acute, orthocenter
10. right, orthocenter (State the location of the orthocenter.)
11. acute, centroid
12. right, centroid

In exercises 13–16 construct an *obtuse* triangle and the indicated point. State the location of the point relative to the triangle.

13. incenter
14. circumcenter
15. orthocenter
16. centroid
17. (a) Construct an isosceles triangle and its incenter, circumcenter, orthocenter, and centroid. Which of these points coincide?
(b) Repeat part (a) for an equilateral triangle.
18. Construct an acute triangle EJS and the bisector of $\measuredangle S$. Draw $\overrightarrow{SE}$ and $\overrightarrow{SJ}$ and construct the bisectors of the exterior angles at E and J. Extend the three angle bisectors to their point of concurrence. This point is one of the three *excenters* of the triangle.
19. Follow the instructions in exercise 18 for a triangle with an obtuse angle at S.
20. Draw a large scalene acute triangle and construct its nine-point circle (see Figure D.2).

In exercises 21–25 the questions refer to Figure D.3.

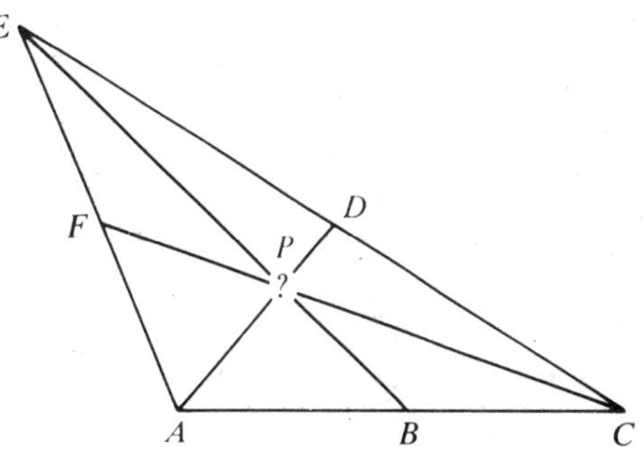

Figure D.3

21. Let $\overline{AD}$, $\overline{CF}$, and $\overline{EB}$ be medians.
(a) What is their point P of concurrence called?
(b) If $AD = EP = 6$ in, find AP, PD, and PB.
22. If $\overline{AD}$, $\overline{CF}$, and $\overline{EB}$ are medians with $FP = 3$ in, $BP = 4$ in, and $AP = 8$ in, find EB, AD, and CF.
23. If $\frac{EF}{FA} = \frac{16}{9}$, $\frac{AB}{BC} = \frac{3}{4}$, and $\frac{CD}{DE} = \frac{9}{12}$, are the three cevians concurrent? Why?
24. If $EF = FA$, $AB = 4$, $BC = 12$, and $CD = 18$, what is the length of $\overline{DE}$ for the three cevians to be concurrent?
25. If $AB = 3$ cm, $BC = 2$ cm, $CD = 4$ cm, $DE = 5$ cm, and $EA = 9$ cm, find EF and FA such that the three cevians will be concurrent.

In exercises 26–30 copy the figure, the hypothesis, and the conclusion. Mark the figure and write a proof.

26. *Given*
meds $\overline{AE}$, $\overline{BD}$
$\overline{AE} \cong \overline{BD}$

To Prove
$\triangle ABF$ isos

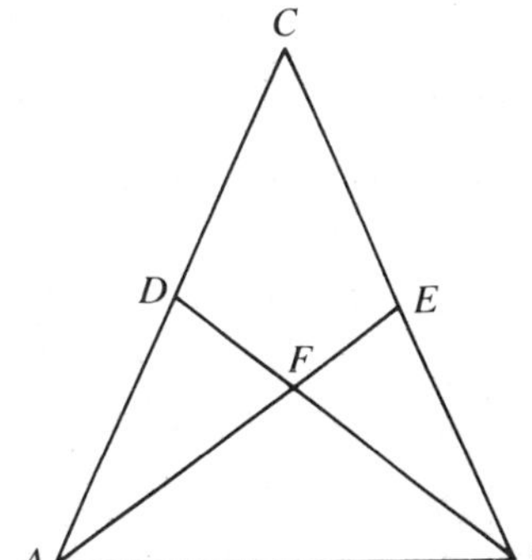

27. *Given*
meds $\overline{WA}$, $\overline{NB}$
$\measuredangle 1 \cong \measuredangle 2$

To Prove
$\overline{LN} \cong \overline{LW}$

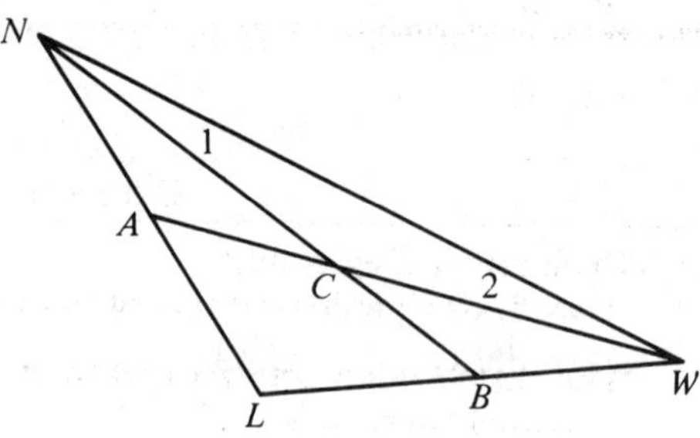

28. *Given*
meds $\overline{JB}$, $\overline{FC}$, $\overline{KA}$
H midpt $\overline{OF}$

To Prove
$\overline{AH} \cong \overline{OB}$
(Hint: Draw $\overline{BH}$.)

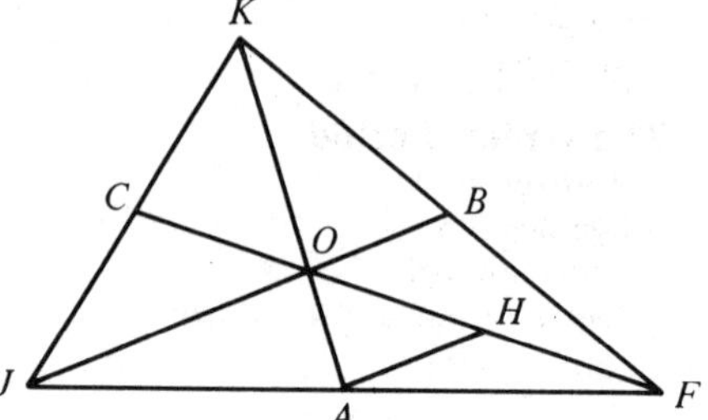

29. *Given*
$\square PQRS$
T midpt $\overline{SP}$

To Prove
$SY = \frac{1}{3}SQ$
(Hint: Consider $\triangle SPR$ and its medians.)

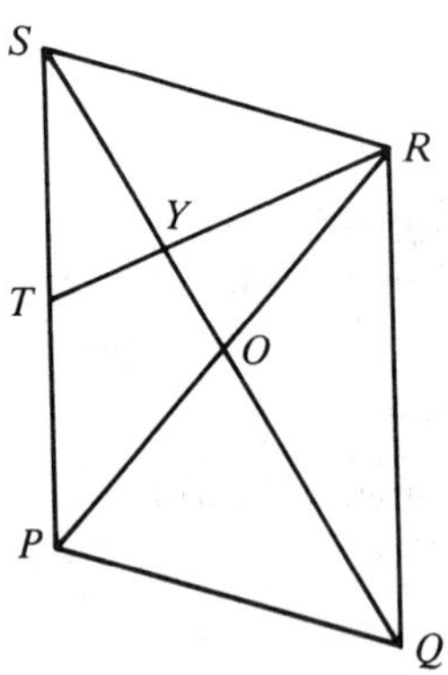

30. *Given*
meds $\overline{NJ}$, $\overline{LS}$,. $\overline{WE}$
rt $\measuredangle NAL$

To Prove
$\overline{WA} \cong \overline{NL}$
(Hint: Consider the circle with center E and radius EL.)

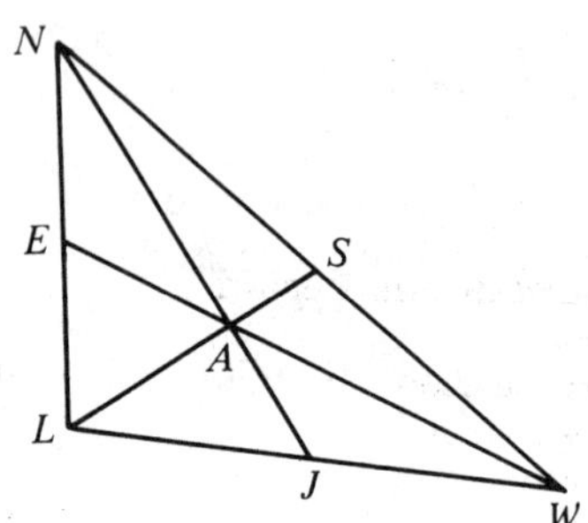

Appendix E

Geometric Date Line

Period	Date	Mathematicians
Prehistoric Beginnings Geometric forms in paintings and carvings	20,000 B.C.	
The Babylonian and Egyptian Period Practical geometry Formulas and rules Pyramids and temples Canals Surveying	1800 B.C.	Ahmes (1650?)
The Greek Period Abstraction Organization Deductive logic Proofs	600 B.C.	Thales (640–546) Pythagoras (584–495) Eudoxus (408–355) Euclid (330–275) Archimedes (287–212) Apollonius (262–200)
	0	
		Ptolemy (100–168) Proclus (412–485) Nasir-ed-din (1201–1272)
The Algebra Period Analytic geometry Equations for curves Graphing Projective geometry	A.D. 1600	Kepler (1571–1630) Desargues (1593–1662) Descartes (1596–1650) Fermat (1601–1655) Pascal (1623–1662)
The Non-Euclidean Period Hyperbolic geometry Elliptic geometry Riemannian geometries Finite geometries Topology	A.D. 1700	Saccheri (1667–1733) Euler (1707–1783) Lambert (1728–1777) Legendre (1752–1833) Gauss (1777–1855) Moebius (1790–1868) Lobachevski (1793–1856) Bolyai (1802–1860) Cayley (1821–1895) Riemann (1826–1866) Klein (1849–1925)
The Foundations Period Set theory Irrational numbers Undefined terms Definitions Axioms Postulates	A.D. 1850	Boole (1815–1864) Dedekind (1831–1916) Cantor (1845–1918) Whitehead (1861–1947) Hilbert (1862–1943) Russell (1872–1970) Godel (1906–1978)

ANSWERS TO SELECTED EXERCISES

EXERCISES FOR 1.1 AND 1.2

1. T **3.** T **5.** F **7.** F
9. T **11.** F **13.** T **15.** F
17. T **19.** F **27.** T **29.** F
31. F **33.** T **35.** T **37.** Ø
39. E **41.** U **43.** {a, e, i, o}
45. {a, e, i, o, u, j, k, l, m, n}
47. $A \subseteq B$ **49.** $A = \emptyset$

51.

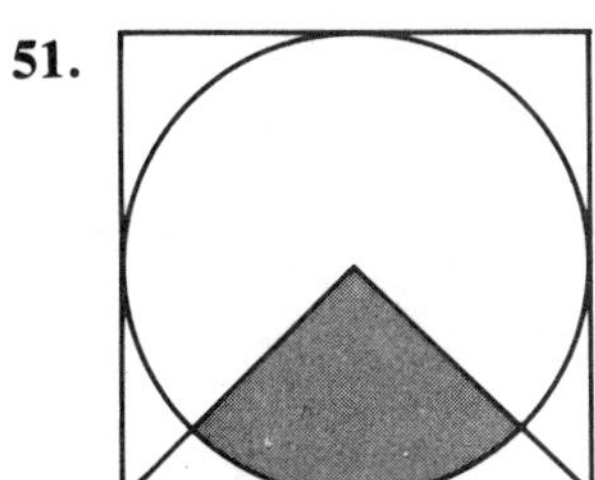

53. same as 51

55.

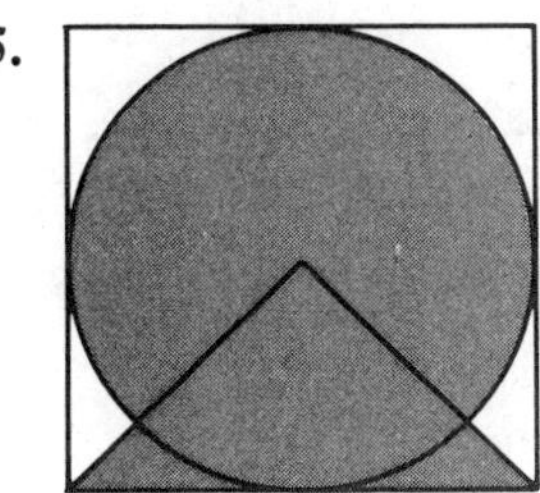

57.

59.

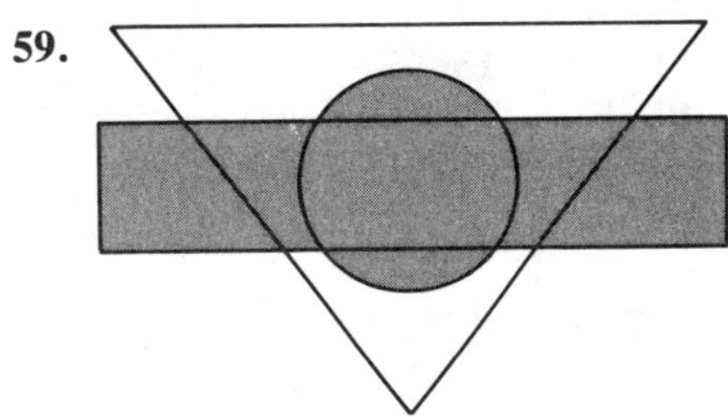

61. same as 59
63. same as 57

65.

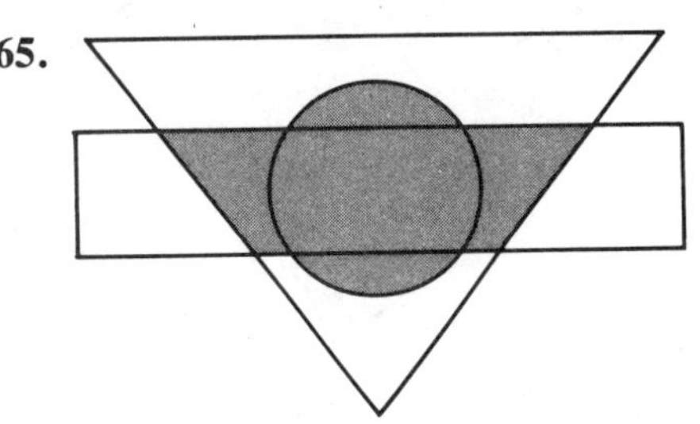

EXERCISES FOR 1.3

1. T **3.** T **5.** T **7.** T
9. F **11.** F **13.** F **15.** F
17. F **19.** T **21.** 0.875, terminating
23. 0.714285714285· · ·, nonterminating, repeating
25. −0.846153846153· · ·, nonterminating repeating
27. $\subseteq$ **29.** $\notin$ **31.** $\notin$ **33.** $\not\subseteq$
35. $\subseteq$ **37.** $\cup$ **39.** $\cap$ **41.** $\cap$
43. $\cup$ **45.** $\cap$ **47.** $(\frac{-2}{3})^2 = \frac{4}{9}$

EXERCISES FOR 1.4

1. F **3.** T **5.** F **7.** T
9. F **11.** T **13.** F **15.** T
17. F **19.** F **21.** -3 **23.** *C*
25. *L* **27.** 9 **29.** *G* **31.** 11 units
33. 4 units **35.** 15 units
41. $\frac{1}{4} < \frac{3}{4}$, but $\frac{3}{4} \not< \frac{1}{4}$
43. $\sqrt{2} < \pi$, but $\pi \not< \sqrt{2}$
45. Five is 3 units to the left of 8 on the number line, but 8 is *not* 3 units to the left of 5 on the number line.
47. Suppose *A* is distinct from *B*, so that *B* is distinct from *A*. Then *A* is not distinct from *A*.
49. $|-7| = 7$ but $|7| \neq -7$
51. *R*, *T*, not *S*
53. *R*, *T*, not *S*
55. *S*, not *R* or *T*

EXERCISES FOR 1.5

1. T **3.** T **5.** T **7.** T
9. F **11.** T **13.** T **15.** F
17. F **19.** T
29. Commutative for Multiplication
31. Addition of Inequalities
33. Distributive
35. Substitution
37. Addition of Inequalities
39. Associative for Addition
41. Commutative for Addition
43. Completeness
45. Commutative for Addition
47. Associative for Addition, Commutative for Addition, Associative for Addition, Distributive
49. Associative for Multiplication, Commutative for Addition, Associative for Addition, Distributive

EXERCISES FOR 2.1 AND 2.2

1. T **3.** F **5.** F **7.** T
9. F **11.** F **13.** T **15.** T
17. F **19.** F **21.** *K*, *J*, *H*, *S* **23.** *S*
25. *E*, *K*, *J* **27.** $\overline{AB}$, $\overline{AC}$, $\overline{AD}$, $\overline{BC}$
29. $\{A\}$, $\{D\}$, $\{A, D\}$, $\overline{AD}$, $\overrightarrow{AD}$, $\overset{\circ\!\!\longrightarrow}{AD}$, $\overrightarrow{DA}$, $\overset{\circ\!\!\longrightarrow}{DA}$, $\overleftrightarrow{AD}$, Ø
31. $\overline{PR}$ **33.** Ø **35.** $\overrightarrow{PR}$ **37.** $\overline{QT}$
39. $\overline{PR} \cup \overrightarrow{ST}$ **41.** $\overline{AE}$ **43.** $\{G\}$
45. $\{F, G, H\}$
47. C A D B
49. C A B
51.

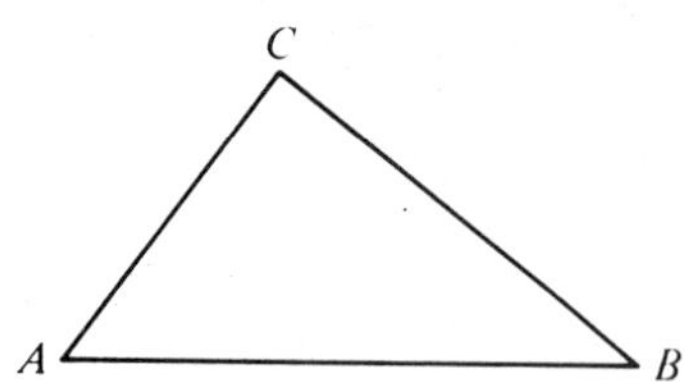

53.

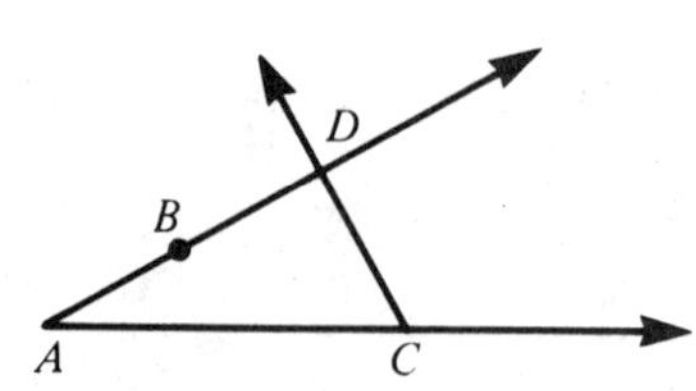

55.

57.

59.

EXERCISES FOR 2.3

1. T **3.** F **5.** T **7.** F
9. F **11.** T **13.** T **15.** T
17. F **19.** T **21.** −2
23. 1 **25.** 10 units **27.** 7 units
29. *G*, 4 **31.** −6, 9
33. 5 units **35.** $\overline{XN}$, $\overline{HG}$ **37.** $6\frac{1}{2}$
39. 8 **41.** −9 and 25
43. They are not collinear.
45. *S*, *O*, *Q*, *U*, *E*, *L*

EXERCISES FOR 2.4

1. T **3.** T **5.** F **7.** F
9. F **11.** T **13.** T **15.** T
17. F **19.** F

21. 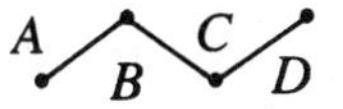

23. 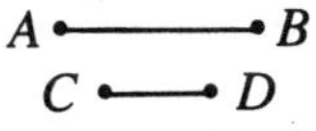

$AB > CD$, but $CD \not> AB$

25. 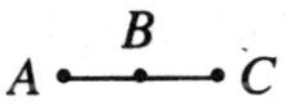

$\overline{AB} \subseteq \overline{AC}$, but $\overline{AC} \not\subseteq \overline{AB}$

27. 

A on same segment as *B*; *B* on same segment as *C*; but *A* not on same segment as *C*.

29. 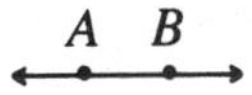

$\overset{\circ}{\overrightarrow{AB}}$ does not extend in opposite direction to $\overrightarrow{AB}$.

31. *S* only **33.** *S* only **35.** *R*, *S* only

EXERCISES FOR 2.5

1. T **3.** F **5.** F **7.** T
9. T **11.** F **13.** T **15.** T
17. T **19.** T
21. $\overline{AB} \cong \overline{DE}$, $\overline{BC} \cong \overline{EF}$
23. $\overline{PT} \cong \overline{MR}$, $\overline{MP} \cong \overline{LM}$, $\overline{OM} \cong \overline{RN}$
25. $\overline{AR} \cong \overline{RP}$, $\overline{RO} \cong \overline{OP} \cong \overline{AO}$
27. 1. given 2. given
3. ≅ iff meas = 4. refl ≅
5. ≅ iff meas =
6. = + =, sums =
7. whole = sum parts
8. whole = sum parts
9. trans = 10. ≅ iff meas =

29. 1. given 2. given
3. ≅ iff meas = 4. given
5. ≅ iff meas =
6. = − =, diff =
7. whole = sum parts
8. whole = sum parts 9. trans =
10. ≅ iff meas =

31. g, h, b, i, a, d, c, f, j, e

33.

1. *E-J-S*	1. given
2. $EJ = ES - JS$	2. whole = sum parts
3. *K-C-M*	3. given
4. $CM = KM - KC$	4. whole = sum parts
5. $\overline{ES} \cong \overline{KM}$	5. given
6. $ES = KM$	6. ≅ iff meas =
7. $\overline{JS} \cong \overline{KC}$	7. given
8. $JS = KC$	8. ≅ iff meas =
9. $ES - JS = KM - KC$	9. = − =, diff =
10. $KM - KC = CM$	10. symm =
11. $EJ = CM$	11. trans =
12. $\therefore \overline{EJ} \cong \overline{CM}$	12. ≅ iff meas =

35.

1. $\overline{ES}$ inters $\overline{LW}$ at J	1. given
2. J midpt $\overline{ES}$	2. given
3. $EJ = JS$	3. midpt iff 2 lengths =
4. J midpt $\overline{LW}$	4. given
5. $LJ = JW$	5. midpt iff 2 lengths =
6. $\overline{ES} \cong \overline{LW}$	6. given
7. $ES = LW$	7. $\cong$ iff meas =
8. $\frac{1}{2}ES = \frac{1}{2}LW$	8. $\frac{1}{2}$s of = are =
9. $ES = EJ + JS$ $LW = LJ + JW$	9. whole = sum parts
10. $ES = JS + JS$ $LW = JW + JW$	10. subst
11. $ES = 2JS$ $LW = 2JW$	11. rearr props
12. $\frac{1}{2}ES = JS$ $\frac{1}{2}LW = JW$	12. = ÷ =, quot =
13. $JS = \frac{1}{2}ES$	13. symm =
14. $JS = JW$	14. trans =
15. $\therefore \overline{JS} \cong \overline{JW}$	15. $\cong$ iff meas =

EXERCISES FOR 3.1 AND 3.2

1. T **3.** F **5.** T **7.** F
9. T **11.** F **13.** F **15.** T
17. T **19.** F
21. **(a)** $\measuredangle UDC$ **(b)** $\measuredangle CDL$
23. **(a)** $\overrightarrow{DC}$ **(b)** $\overrightarrow{DU}$
25. **(a)** $\measuredangle 3$, $\measuredangle 4$, $\measuredangle CDI$
(b) $\measuredangle EDI$, $\measuredangle UDI$, $\measuredangle CDI$
27. T **29.** T
31. 2 and 14, 11 and 12, 9 and 10, 6 and 7
33. 1 and 2, 1 and 14, 5 and 8, 5 and 11
35. 1 and 2, 2 and 3, 6 and 8, 6 and 10, 7 and 9, 8 and 9, 11 and 13, 12 and 13
37. 2, 3, 4, 6, 7, 8, 10, 12, 13, 14
39. 1 and 2, 1 and 3, 11 and 12
41. $\measuredangle BED$ **43.** $\measuredangle ACE$ **45.** $\overleftrightarrow{BF}$
47. $\{D\}$ **49.** $\measuredangle EBF$
51. $\measuredangle$s 1, 2, 6, 7, 9, 10, 12, 13, 14, 15, 16
53. 3, 4, 5, 17
55. 1 and 2, 3 and 4, 8 and 11, 9 and 12, 10 and 13
57. 9 and 10, 12 and 13, 9 and 13, 10 and 12
59. no common side **61.** 32°33′
63. 20°45′37″ **65.** 89°48′31″
67. $(180 - b)°$ **69.** 68°48′49″
71. 213°18′43″
73. 46°56′31″, 136°56′31″, 90°, yes
75. 60°
77. They are complementary.
79. 18°

EXERCISES FOR 3.3

1. T **3.** F **5.** T **7.** F
9. T **11.** F **13.** F **15.** T
17. F **19.** F **21.** T **23.** T
25. F **27.** F **29.** F **31.** S
33. S and T **35.** S **37.** S
39. **(a)** 26°20′ **(b)** 29°38′
41. 1. given 2. $\cong$ iff meas = 3. symm = 4. $\cong$ iff meas =
43. 1. given
2. supp iff sum = 180°
3. given
4. supp iff sum = 180°
5. symm =
6. trans =
7. refl =
8. = − =, diff =
9. $\cong$ iff meas =
45. $\overrightarrow{PC}$ and $\overrightarrow{PE}$, $\overrightarrow{PF}$ and $\overrightarrow{PE}$, $\overrightarrow{PF}$ and $\overrightarrow{PA}$, $\overrightarrow{PC}$ and $\overrightarrow{PA}$, $\overrightarrow{PB}$ and $\overrightarrow{PD}$
47. $\measuredangle APB$ and $\measuredangle BPC$, $\measuredangle BPC$ and $\measuredangle CPD$

EXERCISES FOR 3.4

1. ∡1 ≅ ∡5, ∡4 ≅ ∡8, ∡3 ≅ ∡7

3. ∡1 ≅ ∡4, ∡2 ≅ ∡5, ∡3 and ∡6 rt ∡s

5. ∡1 ≅ ∡4, ∡2 and ∡5 rt ∡s, ∡3 ≅ ∡6

7. ∠1 = 21°30′, ∠2 = 21°30′, ∠3 = 137°, ∠4 = 21°30′, ∠5 = 21°30′

9. ∠1 = 63°, ∠2 = 63°, ∠3 = 27°, ∠4 = 63°, ∠5 = 27°

11. ∠1 = ∠3 = ∠5 = ∠7 = 65°, ∠2 = ∠4 = ∠6 = ∠8 = 115°

13. ∠1 = 28°, ∠2 = 90°, ∠3 = 62°, ∠4 = 28°, ∠5 = 62°

15. ∠1 = ∠3 = ∠6 = ∠8 = 135°, ∠2 = ∠4 = ∠5 = ∠7 = 45°

17. ∠1 = 74°30′, ∠2 = 31°, ∠3 = 90°, ∠4 = 105°30′, ∠5 = 59°, ∠6 = 59°, ∠7 = 74°30′, ∠8 = 31°, ∠9 = 74°30′, ∠10 = 31°

19. 1. vert ∡s formed by opp rays
2. vert ∡s ≅
3. vert ∡s formed by opp rays
4. vert ∡s ≅ 5. given
6. midray or its line is ∡ bis
7. midray iff 2 ∡s =
8. ≅ iff meas = 9. trans ≅
10. ≅ iff meas =
11. midray or its line is ∡ bis

21. b, h, d, a, c, g, e

23.

1. ∡*TOE* and ∡*MON* vert ∡s	1. vert ∡s formed by opp rays
2. ∡*TOE* ≅ ∡*MON*	2. vert ∡s ≅
3. ∠*TOE* = ∠*MON*	3. ≅ iff meas =
4. ∡*HOE* ≅ ∡*AON*	4. given
5. ∠*HOE* = ∠*AON*	5. ≅ iff meas =
6. ∠*TOE* − ∠*HOE* = ∠*MON* − ∠*AON*	6. = − =, diff =
7. ∠*HOT* = ∠*TOE* − ∠*HOE* ∠*AOM* = ∠*MON* − ∠*AON*	7. whole = sum parts
8. ∠*MON* − ∠*AON* = ∠*AOM*	8. symm =
9. ∠*HOT* = ∠*AOM*	9. trans =
10. ∴ ∡*HOT* ≅ ∡*AOM*	10. ≅ iff meas =

27.

1. ∡*EJS* st ∡	1. opp rays form st ∡
2. ∠*EJS* = 180°	2. st ∠ = 180°
3. ∠1 + ∠2 + ∠3 + ∠4 = ∠*EJS*	3. whole = sum parts
4. ∠1 + ∠2 + ∠3 + ∠4 = 180°	4. trans =
5. ∡1 ≅ ∡3	5. given
6. ∠1 = ∠3	6. ≅ iff meas =
7. ∡2 ≅ ∡4	7. given
8. ∠2 = ∠4	8. ≅ iff meas =
9. ∠3 + ∠2 + ∠3 + ∠2 = 180°	9. subst
10. 2 · ∠2 + 2 · ∠3 = 180°	10. rearr props
11. ∠2 + ∠3 = 90°	11. = ÷ =, quot =
12. ∠*RJC* = ∠2 + ∠3	12. whole = sum parts
13. ∠*RJC* = 90°	13. trans
14. ∡*RJC* rt ∡	14. rt ∠ = 90°
15. ∴ $\overrightarrow{JR} \perp \overrightarrow{JC}$	15. ⊥ iff a rt ∡

EXERCISES FOR 4.1 AND 4.2

1. F **3.** T **5.** F **7.** T
9. T **11.** F **13.** T **15.** F
17. F **19.** F

21. **(a)** △*ETS*, △*EHS*, △*ELS*, △*TLH*
(b) △*ETL*, △*HLS*, △*ETH*, △*SHT*
(c) △*SAT*

23. **(a)** ∡*A* **(b)** ∡*ADB*

25. **(a)** ∡*DBC* **(b)** ∡*A*

27. **(a)** $\overline{SJ} \cong \overline{MK}$, $\overline{EJ} \cong \overline{CK}$, ∡*J* ≅ ∡*K*
(b) △I ≅ △II **(c)** sas ≅ sas

29. **(a)** $\overline{KS} \cong \overline{JE}$, $\overline{KE} \cong \overline{JS}$, $\overline{KJ} \cong \overline{KJ}$
(b) △I ≅ △II **(c)** sss ≅ sss

31. **(a)** $\overline{AE} \cong \overline{DF}$, $\overline{EC} \cong \overline{FB}$, $\overline{BC} \cong \overline{BC}$
(b) cannot conclude △I ≅ △II

33. **(a)** ∡*A* ≅ ∡*C*, $\overline{AD} \cong \overline{CD}$, $\overline{DB} \cong \overline{DB}$
(b) cannot conclude △I ≅ △II

35. **(a)** ∡*SEK* ≅ ∡*SJK*, $\overline{ES} \cong \overline{JS}$, $\overline{SK} \cong \overline{SK}$
(b) cannot conclude △I ≅ △II

37. **(a)** ∡*CUL* ≅ ∡*DEI*, ∡*CLU* ≅ ∡*DIE*, $\overline{UE} \cong \overline{IL}$, $\overline{UI} \cong \overline{UI}$
(b) △I ≅ △II **(c)** asa ≅ asa

39. The *corresponding* parts are not ≅.

41. 1. given 2. given
3. midray iff 2 ∡s =
4. ≅ iff meas = 5. refl ≅
6. sas ≅ sas

43. 1. given 2. ≅ iff meas =
3. given
4. ≅ iff meas = 5. = − =, diff =
6. whole = sum parts
7. whole = sum parts
8. symm = 9. trans =
10. ≅ iff meas = 11. symm ≅
12. refl ≅
13. asa ≅ asa

45. c, a, e, f, d, b

49.

Statement	Reason
1. △*RAM* isos ($\overline{RM}$ base)	1. given
2. $\overline{AR} \cong \overline{AM}$	2. isos △ iff 2 ≅ sides
3. ∡*R* ≅ ∡*M*	3. given
4. $\overline{RP} \cong \overline{MN}$	4. given
5. *RP* = *MN*	5. ≅ iff meas =
6. *NP* = *NP*	6. refl =
7. *RP* − *NP* = *MN* − *NP*	7. = − =, diff =
8. *RN* = *RP* − *NP* *MP* = *MN* − *NP*	8. whole = sum parts
9. *MN* − *NP* = *MP*	9. symm =
10. *RN* = *MP*	10. trans =
11. $\overline{RN} \cong \overline{MP}$	11. ≅ iff meas =
12. ∴ △*RAN* ≅ △*MAP*	12. sas ≅ sas

53.

Statement	Reason
1. $\overline{IU} \perp \overline{EC}$	1. given
2. ∡*IUC* rt ∡	2. ⊥ iff a rt ∡
3. $\overline{EL} \perp \overline{IC}$	3. given
4. ∡*ELC* rt ∡	4. ⊥ iff a rt ∡
5. ∡*ELC* ≅ ∡*IUC*	5. rt ∡s ≅
6. $\overline{CL} \cong \overline{CU}$	6. given
7. ∡*C* ≅ ∡*C*	7. refl ≅
8. ∴ △*ECL* ≅ △*ICU*	8. asa ≅ asa

EXERCISES FOR 4.3

1. ∠1 = 63°, ∠2 = 63°, ∠3 = 58°30′, ∠4 = 58°30′, ∠5 = 54°

3. ∠1 = 16°, ∠2 = 16°, ∠3 = 16°, ∠4 = 16°, ∠5 = 58°, ∠6 = 106°, ∠7 = 90°, ∠8 = 74°, ∠9 = 106°, ∠10 = 58°.

5. ∠1 = 110°30′, ∠2 = 69°30′, ∠3 = 69°30′, ∠4 = 55°15′, ∠5 = 55°15′, ∠6 = 124°45′, ∠7 = 55°15′, ∠8 = 69°30′, ∠9 = 41°, ∠10 = 69°30′

7. **(a)** $\triangle VGE$ and $\triangle VNI$
(b) $\overline{VE} \cong \overline{VI}$, $\measuredangle V \cong \measuredangle V$, $\overline{VG} \cong \overline{VN}$
(c) $\triangle VGE \cong \triangle VNI$ (d) sas $\cong$ sas

9. **(a)** $\triangle ADB$ and $\triangle BEA$
(b) $\overline{AD} \cong \overline{BE}$, $\overline{BD} \cong \overline{AE}$, $\overline{AB} \cong \overline{AB}$
(c) $\triangle ADB \cong \triangle BEA$ (d) sss $\cong$ sss

11. yes, sas $\cong$ sas **13.** no, ssa$\not\cong$ssa
15. yes, asa $\cong$ asa
17. 1. given 2. given 3. refl $\cong$ 4. sss $\cong$ sss 5. cpctc
19. d, i, a, e, j, b, g, k, f, m, c, l, h

25.

Statements	Reasons
1. $\triangle EJS$ isos ($\overline{EJ}$ base)	1. given
2. $\overline{JS} \cong \overline{ES}$	2. isos $\triangle$ iff 2 $\cong$ sides
3. $\measuredangle 8 \cong \measuredangle 5$	3. given
4. $\measuredangle S \cong \measuredangle S$	4. refl $\cong$
5. $\triangle JKS \cong \triangle ETS$	5. asa $\cong$ asa
6. $\therefore \overline{SK} \cong \overline{ST}$	6. cpctc

29.

Statements	Reasons
1. S midpt $\overline{ET}$	1. given
2. $TS = SE$	2. midpt iff 2 lengths =
3. $\overline{TS} \cong \overline{SE}$	3. $\cong$ iff meas =
4. L midpt EA	4. given
5. $LA = EL$	5. midpt iff 2 lengths =
6. $\overline{LA} \cong \overline{EL}$	6. $\cong$ iff meas =
7. $\overline{SH} \cong \overline{LA}$	7. given
8. $\overline{SH} \cong \overline{EL}$	8. trans $\cong$
9. H midpt $\overline{TA}$	9. given
10. $TH = HA$	10. midpt iff 2 lengths =
11. $\overline{TH} \cong \overline{HA}$	11. $\cong$ iff meas =
12. $\overline{HA} \cong \overline{SL}$	12. given
13. $\overline{TH} \cong \overline{SL}$	13. trans $\cong$
14. $\triangle THS \cong \triangle SLE$	14. sss $\cong$ sss
15. $\therefore \measuredangle 1 \cong \measuredangle 2$	15. cpctc

EXERCISES FOR 4.4

1. $\cong + \cong$, sums $\cong$
3. whole $\cong$ sum parts
5. $\frac{1}{2}$s of $\cong$ are $\cong$
7. bis $\div$ $\measuredangle$ into 2 $\cong$ $\measuredangle_s$
9. $\cong \cdot$ pos, prod $\cong$
11. 1. given 2. $\cong$ iff meas = 3. refl $\cong$ 4. $\cong$ iff meas = 5. = + =, sums = 6. whole = sum parts 7. whole = sum parts 8. trans = 9. $\cong$ iff meas = 10. given 11. isos $\triangle$ iff 2 $\cong$ sides 12. given 13. isos $\triangle$ iff 2 $\cong$ sides 14. sss $\cong$ sss 15. cpctc

13. 1. given 2. midpt iff 2 lengths = 3. $\cong$ iff meas = 4. given 5. given 6. $\cong$ iff meas = 7. refl $\cong$ 8. $\cong$ iff meas = 9. = + =, sums = 10. whole = sum parts 11. whole = sum parts 12. trans = 13. $\cong$ iff meas = 14. sas $\cong$ sas 15. cpctc
15. j, f, a, h, c, i, k, d, e, g, b

19.

Statements	Reasons
1. $\overline{HA} \cong \overline{EL}$	1. given
2. $\overline{AL} \cong \overline{AL}$	2. refl $\cong$
3. $\overline{HA} + \overline{AL} \cong \overline{EL} + \overline{AL}$	3. $\cong + \cong$, sums $\cong$
4. $\overline{HL} \cong \overline{HA} + \overline{AL}$ $\overline{EL} + \overline{AL} \cong \overline{EA}$	4. whole $\cong$ sum parts
5. $\overline{HL} \cong \overline{EA}$	5. trans' $\cong$
6. $\overline{TH} \perp \overline{HE}$	6. given
7. $\measuredangle THL$ rt $\measuredangle$	7. $\perp$ iff a rt $\measuredangle$
8. $\overline{SE} \perp \overline{HE}$	8. given
9. $\measuredangle SEA$ rt $\measuredangle$	9. $\perp$ iff a rt $\measuredangle$
10. $\measuredangle THL \cong \measuredangle SEA$	10. rt $\measuredangle$s $\cong$
11. $\measuredangle 2 \cong \measuredangle 1$	11. given
12. $\triangle THL \cong \triangle SEA$	12. asa $\cong$ asa
13. $\therefore \overline{HT} \cong \overline{ES}$	13. cpctc

27.

Statements	Reasons
1. $\overline{AS} \cong \overline{PT}$	1. given
2. $\triangle APO$ isos ($\overline{AP}$ base)	2. given
3. $\overline{AO} \cong \overline{PO}$	3. isos $\triangle$ iff 2 $\cong$ sides
4. $\overline{AO} - \overline{AS} \cong \overline{PO} - \overline{PT}$	4. $\cong - \cong$, diff $\cong$
5. $\overline{SO} \cong \overline{AO} - \overline{AS}$ $\overline{PO} - \overline{PT} \cong \overline{TO}$	5. whole $\cong$ sum parts
6. $\overline{SO} \cong \overline{TO}$	6. trans $\cong$
7. $\overline{TO} \cong \overline{SO}$	7. symm $\cong$
8. $\measuredangle O \cong \measuredangle O$	8. refl $\cong$
9. $\triangle ATO \cong \triangle PSO$	9. sas $\cong$ sas
10. $\therefore \overline{AT} \cong \overline{PS}$	10. cpctc

EXERCISES FOR 4.5

1. F **3.** T **5.** F **7.** F
9. F **11.** T **13.** F **15.** T
17. T **19.** T

21. $\angle 1 = 116°$, $\angle 2 = 64°$, $\angle 3 = 58°$, $\angle 4 = 32°$, $\angle 5 = 90°$, $\angle 6 = 90°$, $\angle 7 = 64°$, $\angle 8 = 58°$, $\angle 9 = 58°$, $\angle 10 = 64°$

23. $\angle 1 = 144°$, $\angle 2 = 36°$, $\angle 3 = 72°$, $\angle 4 = 108°$, $\angle 5 = 72°$, $\angle 6 = 72°$, $\angle 7 = 108°$, $\angle 8 = 72°$, $\angle 9 = 36°$

25. $\angle 1 = 30°$, $\angle 2 = 120°$, $\angle 3 = 60°$, $\angle 4 = 60°$, $\angle 5 = 120°$, $\angle 6 = 30°$, $\angle 7 = 60°$, $\angle 8 = 90°$

27. 1. given 2. alt from vtx $\perp$ opp side 3. $\perp$s form $\cong$ rt $\measuredangle$s 4. refl $\cong$ 5. given 6. bis $\div$ $\measuredangle$ into 2 $\cong$ $\measuredangle$s 7. asa $\cong$ asa 8. cpctc 9. isos $\triangle$ iff 2 $\cong$ sides

31.

Statements	Reasons
1. $\triangle ACD$ isos ($\overline{AC}$ base)	1. given
2. $\overline{AD} \cong \overline{CD}$	2. isos $\triangle$ iff 2 $\cong$ sides
3. $\overline{DB}$ bis $\measuredangle ADC$	3. given
4. $\measuredangle ADB \cong \measuredangle CDB$	4. bis $\div$ $\measuredangle$ into 2 $\cong$ $\measuredangle$s
5. $\overline{DB} \cong \overline{DB}$	5. refl $\cong$
6. $\triangle ADB \cong \triangle CDB$	6. sas $\cong$ sas
7. $\measuredangle ABD \cong \measuredangle CBD$	7. cpctc
8. $\angle ABD = \angle CBD$	8. $\cong$ iff meas $=$
9. $\measuredangle ABD$ and $\measuredangle CBD$ lin pr	9. lin pr iff com side and opp rays
10. $\measuredangle ABD$ supp $\measuredangle CBD$	10. lin pr supp

11. $\angle ABD + \angle CBD = 180°$	11. supp iff sum = 180°
12. $\angle CBD + \angle CBD = 180°$	12. subst
13. $2 \cdot \angle CBD = 180°$	13. rearr props
14. $\angle CBD = 90°$	14. = ÷ =, quot =
15. ∡CBD rt ∡	15. rt ∠ = 90°
16. $\overline{DB} \perp \overline{AC}$	16. ⊥ iff a rt ∡
17. ∴ $\overline{DB}$ alt	17. alt from vtx ⊥ opp side

45.

1. $\overline{KE} \cong \overline{CJ}$	1. given
2. $\overline{EC} \cong \overline{JK}$	2. given
3. Draw $\overline{KC}$.	3. 2 pts determ line
4. $\overline{KC} \cong \overline{KC}$.	4. refl ≅
5. $\triangle KCE \cong \triangle CKJ$.	5. sss ≅ sss
6. ∴ ∡E ≅ ∡J	6. cpctc

51. 1. given 2. given 3. given 4. given 7. sss ≅ sss 8. cpctc

EXERCISES FOR 4.6

1. ext ∠ > rem int ∠
3. 2 sides △ ≠, opp ∠s ≠ same order
5. sum 2 sides △ > 3d side
7. 2 ∠s △ ≠, opp sides ≠ same order
9. ext ∠ > rem int ∠
11. 2 ∠s △ ≠, opp sides ≠ same order
13. sum 2 sides △ > 3d side
15. ext ∠ > rem int ∠
17. ext ∠ > rem int ∠
19. 2 sides △ ≠, opp ∠s ≠ same order
21. **(a)** 2, 4, 5, 7, 9, 11
(b) vertical with ∡8
23. 1, 3, 6, 8, 10, 12
25. **(a)** $\angle 10 > \angle 8$ (b) $\angle 10 > \angle 3$
27. **(a)** no, sum 2 sides △ > 3d side
(b) yes, 2 sides △ ≠, opp ∠s ≠ same order
29. 8, 3, 10
31. 1. given 2. if 2 sides △ ≅, opp ∡s ≅ 3. ≅ iff meas = 4. ext ∠ > rem int ∠ 5. ext ∠ > rem int ∠ 6. subst 7. trans > 8. 2 ∠s △ ≠, opp sides ≠ same order
33. 1. given 2. isos △ iff 2 ≅ sides 3. if 2 sides △ ≅, opp ∡s ≅ 4. ≅ iff meas = 5. whole = sum parts 6. whole > part 7. subst

39.

1. $\overline{CU} \cong \overline{EU}$	1. given
2. ∡CEU ≅ ∡ECU	2. if 2 sides △ ≅, opp ∡s ≅
3. $\angle CEU = \angle ECU$	3. ≅ iff meas =
4. $\angle LCE > \angle CEU$	4. ext ∠ > rem int ∠
5. $\angle LCE > \angle ECU$	5. subst
6. $\angle ECU > \angle ELC$	6. ext ∠ > rem int ∠
7. $\angle LCE > \angle ELC$	7. trans >
8. ∴ $EL > EC$	8. 2 ∠s △ ≠, opp sides ≠ same order

EXERCISES FOR 4.7

1. F **3.** T **5.** T **7.** F
9. F **11.** T **13.** T **15.** T
17. F **19.** T
21. **(a)** ∡1 ≅ ∡2, ∡3 ≅ ∡4, ∡CKI ≅ ∡CKE
(b) $\overline{CK} \cong \overline{CK}$, $\triangle CKI \cong \triangle CKE$, $\overline{CI} \cong \overline{CE}$, ∡$CIK$ ≅ ∡CEK, $\overline{IK} \cong \overline{EK}$, ∡$IKR$ ≅ ∡EKR, $\triangle IKR \cong \triangle EKR$, $\overline{IR} \cong \overline{ER}$, ∡$IRK$ ≅ ∡ERK
23. $\angle 1 = 29°$, $\angle 2 = 61°$, $\angle 3 = 61°$, $\angle 4 = 37°$, $\angle 5 = 82°$, $\angle 6 = 98°$, $\angle 7 = 53°$,

$\angle 8 = 53°$, $\angle 9 = 98°$, $\angle 10 = 37°$

25. $\angle 1 = 137°30'$, $\angle 2 = 42°30'$, $\angle 3 = 42°30'$, $\angle 4 = 68°45'$, $\angle 5 = 68°45'$, $\angle 6 = 68°45'$, $\angle 7 = 68°45'$, $\angle 8 = 42°30'$, $\angle 9 = 42°30'$, $\angle 10 = 137°30'$

27. $\angle 1 = 36°7'30''$, $\angle 2 = 36°7'30''$, $\angle 3 = 17°45'$, $\angle 4 = 17°45'$, $\angle 5 = 126°7'30''$, $\angle 6 = 126°7'30''$, $\angle 7 = 107°45'$, $\angle 8 = 36°7'30''$

29. $\angle 1 = 66°$, $\angle 2 = 90°$, $\angle 3 = 78°$, $\angle 4 = 24°$, $\angle 5 = 78°$, $\angle 6 = 78°$, $\angle 7 = 78°$, $\angle 8 = 66°$, $\angle 9 = 36°$, $\angle 10 = 24°$

31. 1. given 2. midpt ÷ seg into 2 ≅ segs 3. given 4. given 5. sas ≅ sas 6. cpctc 7. if 2 ∡s △ ≅, opp sides ≅ 8. sas ≅ sas 9. cpctc 10. ≅ − ≅, diff ≅ 11. whole ≅ sum parts 12. whole ≅ sum parts 13. trans ≅

35.	
1. $\overline{CE} \perp$ bis $\overline{AB}$	1. given
2. ∡3 ≅ ∡4	2. ⊥s form ≅ rt ∡s
3. $\overline{AE} \cong \overline{BE}$	3. bis ÷ seg into 2 ≅ segs
4. $\overline{DE} \cong \overline{DE}$	4. refl ≅
5. $\triangle AED \cong \triangle BED$	5. sas ≅ sas
6. $\overline{AD} \cong \overline{BD}$	6. cpctc
7. $\overline{CE} \cong \overline{CE}$	7. refl ≅
8. $\triangle AEC \cong \triangle BEC$	8. sas ≅ sas
9. $\overline{AC} \cong \overline{BC}$	9. cpctc
10. $\overline{CD} \cong \overline{CD}$	10. refl ≅
11. $\triangle ADC \cong \triangle BDC$	11. sss ≅ sss
12. ∴ ∡5 ≅ ∡6	12. cpctc

45.	
1. $\overline{EC} \cong \overline{UC}$	1. given
2. $\overline{CI} \cong \overline{CL}$	2. given
3. ∡1 ≅ ∡2	3. given
4. ∡LCI ≅ ∡LCI	4. refl ≅
5. ∡1 + ∡LCI ≅ ∡2 + ∡LCI	5. ≅ + ≅, sums ≅
6. ∡ECI ≅ ∡1 + ∡LCI ∡2 + ∡LCI ≅ ∡UCL	6. whole ≅ sum parts
7. ∡ECI ≅ ∡UCL	7. trans ≅
8. $\triangle ECI \cong \triangle UCL$	8. sas ≅ sas
9. ∴ ∡4 ≅ ∡3	9. cpctc

EXERCISES FOR 5.1 AND 5.2

1. T **3.** T **5.** T **7.** T
9. T **11.** T **13.** F **15.** F
17. F **19.** T

21. 1 and 8, 2 and 4, 3 and 7, 4 and 7, 6 and 7

23. 3 and 4, 7 and 9, 3 and 12, 2 and 7, 6 and 12, 4 and 5, 5 and 6, 1 and 10, 4 and 12

25. $\overleftrightarrow{EC}$ and $\overleftrightarrow{JD}$, $\overleftrightarrow{ES}$ and $\overleftrightarrow{CT}$, $\overleftrightarrow{CT}$ and $\overleftrightarrow{DG}$, $\overleftrightarrow{ES}$ and $\overleftrightarrow{DG}$

27. **(a)** no, intersects 1 pt
(b) yes, intersects 2 pts

29. **(a)** yes, 1 ext ∡ and 1 int ∡ on same side trans
(b) no, ∡9 has $\overline{CD}$ as side not $\overleftrightarrow{BC}$

31. 1. given 2. isos △ iff 2 ≅ sides 3. if 2 sides △ ≅, opp ∡s ≅ 4. vert ∡s formed by opp rays 5. vert ∡s ≅ 6. given 7. isos △ iff 2 ≅ sides 8. if 2 sides △ ≅, opp ∡s ≅ 9. trans ≅ 10. alt int ∡s iff int ∡s opp sides t 11. ∡̸≅, lines ∥

33. e, c, f, a, d, g, b

35. d, a, f, h, g, n, l, k, i, e, o, j, m, c, p, b

39. 1. $\overline{AE}$ bis $\measuredangle OAP$	1. given
2. $\measuredangle 1 \cong \measuredangle 2$	2. bis $\div$ $\measuredangle$ into 2 $\cong$ $\measuredangle$s
3. $\triangle AEO$ isos ($\overline{AE}$ base)	3. given
4. $\overline{OA} \cong \overline{OE}$	4. isos $\triangle$ iff 2 $\cong$ sides
5. $\measuredangle 3 \cong \measuredangle 1$	5. if 2 sides $\triangle$ $\cong$, opp $\measuredangle$s $\cong$
6. $\measuredangle 3 \cong \measuredangle 2$	6. trans $\cong$
7. $\measuredangle 3$, $\measuredangle 2$ alt int $\measuredangle$s	7. alt int $\measuredangle$s iff int $\measuredangle$s opp sides *t*
8. $\therefore \overline{OS} \parallel \overline{AP}$	8. $\ncong$, lines $\parallel$

47. 1. $\overline{OP}$ $\perp$ bis $\overline{AT}$	1. given
2. $\overline{AS} \cong \overline{TS}$	2. $\perp$ bis iff bis seg and is $\perp$
3. $\measuredangle ASO \cong \measuredangle ASP \cong \measuredangle TSO$	3. $\perp$s form $\cong$ rt $\measuredangle$s
4. $\overline{AT}$ bis $\measuredangle OAP$	4. given
5. $\measuredangle OAS \cong \measuredangle PAS$	5. bis $\div$ $\measuredangle$ into 2 $\cong$ $\measuredangle$s
6. $\overline{AS} \cong \overline{AS}$	6. refl $\cong$
7. $\triangle OAS \cong \triangle PAS$	7. asa $\cong$ asa
8. $\measuredangle AOS \cong \measuredangle APS$	8. cpctc
9. $\overline{OS} \cong \overline{OS}$	9. refl $\cong$
10. $\triangle ASO \cong \triangle TSO$	10. sas $\cong$ sas
11. $\measuredangle AOS \cong \measuredangle TOS$	11. cpctc
12. $\measuredangle TOS \cong \measuredangle AOS$	12. symm $\cong$
13. $\measuredangle TOS \cong \measuredangle APS$	13. trans $\cong$
14. $\measuredangle TOS$, $\measuredangle APS$ alt int $\measuredangle$s	14. alt int $\measuredangle$s iff int $\measuredangle$ opp sides *t*
15. $\therefore \overline{OT} \parallel \overline{AP}$	15. $\ncong$, lines $\parallel$

EXERCISES FOR 5.3

1. 1 and 2, 8 and 10, 6 and 5, 1 and 3, 8 and 5

3. 2 and 4, 7 and 6, 10 and 11, 7 and 11

5. 1 and 4, 2 and 3, 9 and 10, 4 and 7, 8 and 6

7. 11 and 3, 1 and 5, 2 and 6, 9 and 7, 1 and 9, 3 and 8, 5 and 7, 4 and 10

9. $\measuredangle GAP$ and $\measuredangle TYH$, $\measuredangle APG$ and $\measuredangle YHT$

11. $\angle 1 = 50°36'30''$, $\angle 2 = 50°36'30''$, $\angle 3 = 129°23'30''$, $\angle 4 = 78°47'$, $\angle 5 = 101°13'$, $\angle 6 = 129°23'30''$, $\angle 7 = 50°36'30''$, $\angle 8 = 50°36'30''$, $\angle 9 = 101°13'$, $\angle 10 = 78°47'$

13. $\angle 1 = 112°8'$, $\angle 2 = 67°52'$, $\angle 3 = 112°8'$, $\angle 4 = 112°8'$, $\angle 5 = 112°8'$, $\angle 6 = 112°8'$, $\angle 7 = 67°52'$, $\angle 8 = 112°8'$, $\angle 9 = 67°52'$, $\angle 10 = 112°8'$

15. $\angle 1 = 122°37'$, $\angle 2 = 57°23'$, $\angle 3 = 65°14'$, $\angle 4 = 114°46'$, $\angle 5 = 65°14'$, $\angle 6 = 57°23'$, $\angle 7 = 57°23'$, $\angle 8 = 65°14'$, $\angle 9 = 57°23'$

17. $\angle 1 = 35°$, $\angle 2 = 90°$, $\angle 3 = 55°$, $\angle 4 = 55°$, $\angle 5 = 55°$, $\angle 6 = 90°$, $\angle 7 = 55°$, $\angle 8 = 70°$, $\angle 9 = 55°$, $\angle 10 = 125°$, $\angle 11 = 55°$, $\angle 12 = 35°$

19. $\angle 1 = 62°$, $\angle 2 = 90°$, $\angle 3 = 62°$, $\angle 4 = 31°$, $\angle 5 = 28°$, $\angle 6 = 31°$, $\angle 7 = 28°$, $\angle 8 = 31°$, $\angle 9 = 28°$, $\angle 10 = 28°$

21. $\angle 1 = 37°23'$, $\angle 2 = 24°34'$, $\angle 3 = 73°12'$, $\angle 4 = 44°51'$, $\angle 5 = 82°14'$, $\angle 6 = 97°46'$, $\angle 7 = 37°23'$, $\angle 8 = 24°34'$, $\angle 9 = 82°14'$, $\angle 10 = 44°51'$

23.
1. given
2. corr $\measuredangle$s iff 1 int, 1 ext, same side t
3. $\neq$, corr $\measuredangle$s $\cong$
4. alt int $\measuredangle$s iff int $\measuredangle$s opp sides t
5. $\neq$, alt int $\measuredangle$s $\cong$ 6. given
7. isos $\triangle$ iff 2 $\cong$ sides
8. if 2 sides $\triangle$ $\cong$, opp $\measuredangle$s $\cong$
9. symm $\cong$ 10. trans $\cong$
11. bis $\div$ $\measuredangle$ into 2 $\cong$ $\measuredangle$s

25. m, e, h, i, c, g, k, a, f, b, l, n, j, d

31. 1. $\overleftrightarrow{ES} \parallel \overline{CM}$	1. given
2. $\measuredangle EJK$, $\measuredangle JKM$ alt int $\measuredangle$s	2. alt int $\measuredangle$s iff int $\measuredangle$s opp sides *t*
3. $\measuredangle EJK \cong \measuredangle JKM$	3. $\neq$, alt int $\measuredangle$s $\cong$
4. $\overrightarrow{JR}$ bis $\measuredangle EJK$	4. given
5. $\measuredangle 1 \cong \measuredangle 2$	5. bis $\div$ $\measuredangle$ into 2 $\cong$ $\measuredangle$s

6. $\overrightarrow{KT}$ bis $\measuredangle JKM$	6. given
7. $\measuredangle 3 \cong \measuredangle 4$	7. bis $\div$ $\measuredangle$ into 2 $\cong$ $\measuredangle$s
8. $\measuredangle 2 \cong \measuredangle 3$	8. $\frac{1}{2}$s of $\cong$ are $\cong$
9. $\measuredangle 2$, $\measuredangle 3$ alt int $\measuredangle$s	9. alt int $\measuredangle$s iff int $\measuredangle$s opp sides t
10. $\therefore \overrightarrow{JR} \parallel \overrightarrow{KT}$	10. $\not\measuredangle$, lines $\parallel$

39.

1. $IC > RC$	1. given
2. $\angle IRC > \angle I$	2. 2 sides $\triangle \neq$, opp $\measuredangle$s $\neq$ same order
3. $\overline{EJ} \parallel \overline{RC}$	3. given
4. $\measuredangle IRC$, $\measuredangle E$ corr $\measuredangle$s	4. corr $\measuredangle$s iff 1 int $\measuredangle$, 1 ext $\measuredangle$ same side t
5. $\measuredangle IRC \cong \measuredangle E$	5. $\neq$, corr $\measuredangle$s $\cong$
6. $\angle IRC = \angle E$	6. $\cong$ iff meas $=$
7. $\therefore \angle E > \angle I$	7. subst

EXERCISES FOR 5.4

1. F **3.** F **5.** T **7.** T
9. T **11.** T **13.** F **15.** F
17. F **19.** F
21. $\angle 1 = 58°$, $\angle 2 = 64°$, $\angle 3 = 22°$, $\angle 4 = 72°$, $\angle 5 = 94°$, $\angle 6 = 86°$, $\angle 7 = 36°$, $\angle 8 = 86°$, $\angle 9 = 22°$, $\angle 10 = 94°$
23. $\angle 3 = 41°27'$, $\angle 4 = 44°$, $\angle 5 = 79°$, $\angle 6 = 41°$, $\angle 7 = 57°$, $\angle 8 = 79°$, $\angle 9 = 38°$, $\angle 10 = 85°$, $\angle 11 = 57°$
25. $\angle 1 = 58°$, $\angle 2 = 122°$, $\angle 3 = 45°$, $\angle 4 = 45°$, $\angle 5 = 45°$, $\angle 6 = 77°$, $\angle 7 = 45°$, $\angle 8 = 135°$, $\angle 9 = 45°$, $\angle 10 = 58°$, $\angle 11 = 90°$, $\angle 12 = 32°$
27. $\angle 1 = 56°$
29. 1. given 2. $\neq$, alt int $\measuredangle$s $\cong$
3. $\cong$ iff meas $=$
4. lin pr supp 5. supp iff sum $= 180°$
6. subst 7. supp iff sum $= 180°$
8. lin pr supp 9. supp iff sum $= 180°$
10. subst 11. supp iff sum $= 180°$
35. 1. given 2. vert $\measuredangle$s $\cong$
3. $\neq$, alt int $\measuredangle$s $\cong$
4. trans $\cong$ 5. vert $\measuredangle$s $\cong$
6. $\neq$, alt int $\measuredangle$s $\cong$ 7. trans $\cong$
8. vert $\measuredangle$s $\cong$ 9. trans $\cong$
10. vert $\measuredangle$s $\cong$ 11. trans $\cong$
33. i, e, a, h, f, c, d, j, g, b

37.

1. $\overleftrightarrow{ES} \parallel \overleftrightarrow{CM}$	1. given
2. $\measuredangle SJK$ supp $\measuredangle JKM$	2. $\neq$, int $\measuredangle$s same side t supp
3. $\angle SJK + \angle JKM = 180°$	3. supp iff sum $= 180°$
4. $\angle SJK = \angle 1 + \angle 2$ $\angle JKM = \angle 3 + \angle 4$	4. whole $=$ sum parts
5. $\angle 1 + \angle 2 + \angle 3 + \angle 4 = 180°$	5. subst
6. $\overrightarrow{JR}$ bis $\measuredangle SJK$	6. given
7. $\measuredangle 1 \cong \measuredangle 2$	7. bis $\div$ $\measuredangle$ into 2 $\cong$ $\measuredangle$s
8. $\angle 1 = \angle 2$	8. $\cong$ iff meas $=$
9. $\overrightarrow{KR}$ bis $\measuredangle JKM$	9. given
10. $\measuredangle 3 \cong \measuredangle 4$	10. bis $\div$ $\measuredangle$ into 2 $\cong$ $\measuredangle$s
11. $\angle 3 = \angle 4$	11. $\cong$ iff meas $=$
12. $\angle 2 + \angle 2 + \angle 3 + \angle 3 = 180°$	12. subst
13. $2 \cdot \angle 2 + 2 \cdot \angle 3 = 180°$	13. rearr props
14. $\angle 2 + \angle 3 = 90°$	14. $= \div =$, quot $=$
15. $\angle 2 + \angle 3 + \angle JRK = 180°$	15. $180°$ in $\triangle$
16. $\angle JRK = 90°$	16. $= - =$, diff $=$
17. $\therefore \measuredangle JRK$ rt $\measuredangle$	17. rt $\angle = 90°$

41.

1. $\overline{CA} \perp \overline{AB}$	1. given
2. $\measuredangle CAB$ rt $\measuredangle$	2. $\perp$ iff a rt $\measuredangle$
3. $\overline{BE} \perp \overline{CE}$	3. given

4. $\measuredangle BEC$ rt $\measuredangle$	4. $\perp$ iff a rt $\measuredangle$
5. $\measuredangle CAB \cong \measuredangle BEC$	5. rt $\measuredangle$s $\cong$
6. $\overline{CD} \cong \overline{BD}$	6. given
7. $\measuredangle CDA \cong \measuredangle BDE$	7. vert $\measuredangle$s $\cong$
8. $\triangle CAD \cong \triangle BED$	8. aas $\cong$ aas
9. $\therefore \overline{CA} \cong \overline{BE}$	9. cpctc

EXERCISES FOR 6.1 AND 6.2

1. F **3.** F **5.** F **7.** F
9. T **11.** F **13.** F **15.** F
17. F **19.** T
21. **(a)** $\overline{RS}$ and $\overline{AT}$, $\overline{RA}$ and $\overline{ST}$ **(b)** $\measuredangle ARS$ and $\measuredangle ATS$, $\measuredangle RST$ and $\measuredangle RAT$
23. three
25. parallelogram **27.** isosceles trapezoid
29. rhombus
31. $\angle 1 = 113°43'$, $\angle 2 = 66°17'$, $\angle 3 = 66°17'$, $\angle 4 = 113°43'$, $\angle 5 = 113°43'$, $\angle 6 = 66°17'$, $\angle 7 = 66°17'$, $\angle 8 = 113°43'$, $\angle 9 = 66°17'$, $\angle 10 = 47°26'$, $\angle 11 = 66°17'$, $\angle 12 = 113°43'$
33. $\angle 1 = 49°$, $\angle 2 = 49°$, $\angle 3 = 41°$, $\angle 4 = 41°$, $\angle 5 = 49°$, $\angle 6 = 49°$, $\angle 7 = 41°$, $\angle 8 = 41°$, $\angle 9 = 90°$, $\angle 10 = 90°$, $\angle 11 = 90°$, $\angle 12 = 90°$
35. $\angle 1 = 37°30'$, $\angle 2 = 52°30'$, $\angle 3 = 90°$, $\angle 4 = 52°30'$, $\angle 5 = 90°$, $\angle 6 = 37°30'$, $\angle 7 = 37°30'$, $\angle 8 = 52°30'$, $\angle 9 = 52°30'$, $\angle 10 = 90°$
37. 1. given 2. opp sides $\square$ $\cong$ 3. given 4. $\cong - \cong$, diff $\cong$ 5. whole $\cong$ sum parts 6. whole $\cong$ sum parts 7. symm $\cong$ 8. trans $\cong$ 9. opp $\measuredangle$s $\square$ $\cong$ 10. given 11. sas $\cong$ sas 12. cpctc
39. b, g, a, e, c, i, k, j, f, h, l, d

43.

1. $\square JACK$	1. given
2. $\overline{JK} \cong \overline{CA}$	2. opp sides $\square$ $\cong$
3. $\measuredangle K \cong \measuredangle A$	3. opp $\measuredangle$s $\square$ $\cong$
4. $\overline{JA} \cong \overline{CK}$	4. opp sides $\square$ $\cong$
5. O midpt $\overline{JA}$	5. given
6. $\overline{AO} \cong \overline{OJ}$	6. midpt $\div$ seg into 2 $\cong$ segs
7. S midpt $\overline{CK}$	7. given
8. $\overline{KS} \cong \overline{SC}$	8. midpt $\div$ seg into 2 $\cong$ segs
9. $\overline{KS} \cong \overline{AO}$	9. $\frac{1}{2}$s of $\cong$ are $\cong$
10. $\triangle JKS \cong \triangle CAO$	10. sas $\cong$ sas
11. $\therefore \measuredangle 1 \cong \measuredangle 2$	11. cpctc

49.

1. $\square ECLD$	1. given
2. $\overline{EC} \parallel \overline{LD}$	2. $\square$ iff opp sides $\parallel$
3. $\measuredangle UEJ \cong \measuredangle ILR$	3. $\nparallel$, alt int $\measuredangle$s $\cong$
4. $\overline{EC} \cong \overline{LD}$	4. opp sides $\square$ $\cong$
5. U midpt $\overline{EC}$	5. given
6. $\overline{EU} \cong \overline{UC}$	6. midpt $\div$ seg into 2 $\cong$ segs
7. I midpt $\overline{DL}$	7. given
8. $\overline{LI} \cong \overline{ID}$	8. midpt $\div$ seg into 2 $\cong$ segs
9. $\overline{EU} \cong \overline{LI}$	9. $\frac{1}{2}$s of $\cong$ are $\cong$
10. $\overline{DE} \cong \overline{CL}$	10. opp sides $\square$ $\cong$
11. $\measuredangle DEU \cong \measuredangle CLI$	11. opp $\measuredangle$s $\square$ $\cong$
12. $\triangle DEU \cong \triangle CLI$	12. sas $\cong$ sas
13. $\measuredangle EUJ \cong \measuredangle LIR$	13. cpctc
14. $\triangle EUJ \cong \triangle LIR$	14. asa $\cong$ asa
15. $\therefore \overline{JU} \cong \overline{RI}$	15. cpctc

EXERCISES FOR 6.3

1. a, b, c
3. a, b, c, d, e, f, g, h, i, j, k
5. a, b, c, d, h, j
7. a, b, c, d, e, g, h, j
9. 1 and 5, 2 and 6, 3 and 7, 4 and 8
11. $\overline{BU} \cong \overline{US}$, $\overline{US} \cong \overline{ST}$, $\overline{ST} \cong \overline{TB}$, $\overline{TB} \cong \overline{BU}$, $\overline{BR} \cong \overline{RS}$, $\overline{TR} \cong \overline{RU}$, $\overline{BU} \cong \overline{ST}$, $\overline{TB} \cong \overline{US}$
13. ∡1 ≅ ∡9, ∡2 ≅ ∡8, ∡4 ≅ ∡11, ∡3 ≅ ∡10
15. $\overline{KE} \cong \overline{ET}$, $\overline{SE} \cong \overline{EA}$, $\overline{KT} \cong \overline{SA}$, $\overline{KE} \cong \overline{EA}$, $\overline{KE} \cong \overline{SE}$, $\overline{AE} \cong \overline{ET}$, $\overline{SE} \cong \overline{ET}$
17. △*SEK*, △*KEA*, △*KST*, △*SKA*, △*KAT*, △*STA*, △*EAT*, △*SET*
19. ∠1 = 38°, ∠2 = 104°, ∠3 = 76°, ∠4 = 142°, ∠5 = 38°, ∠6 = 32°, ∠7 = 72°, ∠8 = 76°, ∠9 = 38°, ∠10 = 38°, ∠11 = 110°, ∠12 = 70°, ∠13 = 110°, ∠14 = 70°, ∠15 = 32°, ∠16 = 72°
21. ∠1 = 49°, ∠2 = 49°, ∠3 = 41°, ∠4 = 41°, ∠5 = 41°, ∠6 = 41°, ∠7 = 49°, ∠8 = 49°, ∠9 = 90°, ∠10 = 139°
23. ∠1 = 37°30′, ∠2 = 81°, ∠3 = 136°30′, ∠4 = 55°30′, ∠5 = 43°30′, ∠6 = 87°, ∠7 = 43°30′, ∠8 = 136°30′, ∠9 = 99°, ∠10 = 43°30′
25. ∠1 = 68°, ∠2 = 68°, ∠3 = 22°, ∠4 = 22°, ∠5 = 34°, ∠6 = 90°, ∠7 = 90°, ∠8 = 22°, ∠9 = 22°, ∠10 = 34°, ∠11 = 68°, ∠12 = 68°, ∠13 = 112°, ∠14 = 34°, ∠15 = 34°
27. 1. given 2. rect (sq) has 4 rt ∡s
3. ⊥ iff a rt ∡ 4. ⊥s form ≅ rt ∡s
5. rt ∡s ≅ 6. ≇, lines ∥
7. ≠, alt int ∡s ≅ 8. given
9. midpt ÷ seg into 2 ≅ segs
10. aas ≅ aas 11. cpctc
12. opp sides ▱ (sq) ≅
13. trans ≅
14. midpt ÷ seg into 2 ≅ segs

31.

Statement	Reason
1. sq *RJMN*	1. given
2. $\overline{NR} \cong \overline{RJ}$	2. rh (sq) has 4 ≅ sides
3. $\overline{RT} \cong \overline{JH}$	3. given
4. $\overline{NR} + \overline{RT} \cong \overline{RJ} + \overline{JH}$	4. ≅ + ≅, sums ≅
5. $\overline{NT} \cong \overline{NR} + \overline{RT}$ $\overline{RJ} + \overline{JH} \cong \overline{RH}$	5. whole ≅ sum parts
6. $\overline{NT} \cong \overline{RH}$	6. trans ≅
7. ∡*RNM*, ∡*NRJ* rt ∡s	7. rect (sq) has 4 rt ∡s
8. $\overline{TN} \perp \overline{OM}$ $\overline{HR} \perp \overline{TN}$	8. ⊥ iff a rt ∡
9. ∡*ONR*, ∡*TRH* rt ∡s	9. ⊥ iff a rt ∡
10. ∡*ONR* ≅ ∡*TRH*	10. rt ∡s ≅
11. $\overline{OM} \cong \overline{TN}$	11. given
12. $\overline{NM} \cong \overline{NR}$	12. rh (sq) has 4 ≅ sides
13. $\overline{OM} - \overline{NM} \cong \overline{TN} - \overline{NR}$	13. ≅ − ≅, diff ≅
14. $\overline{ON} \cong \overline{OM} - \overline{NM}$ $\overline{TN} - \overline{NR} \cong \overline{TR}$	14. whole ≅ sum parts
15. $\overline{ON} \cong \overline{TR}$	15. trans ≅
16. △*ONT* ≅ △*TRH*	16. sas ≅ sas
17. ∴ $\overline{OT} \cong \overline{TH}$	17. cpctc

37.

Statement	Reason
1. sq *ABDE*	1. given
2. ∡*EDB* rt ∡	2. rect (sq) has 4 rt ∡s
3. ∠*EDB* = 90°	3. rt ∠ = 90°
4. $\overline{DA}$ bis ∡*EDB*	4. diag rh (sq) bis ∡s
5. ∠*BDA* = $\frac{1}{2}$ · ∠*EDB*	5. bis ÷ ∡ into 2 = ∡s
6. $\frac{1}{2}$ · ∠*EDB* = 45°	6. = · =, prod =
7. ∠*BDA* = 45°	7. trans =
8. $\overline{CF} \perp \overline{AD}$	8. given
9. ∡*CFD* rt ∡	9. ⊥ iff a rt ∡

Statement	Reason
10. $\angle CFD = 90°$	10. rt $\angle$ = 90°
11. $\angle BDA + \angle CFD = 135°$	11. = + =, sums =
12. $\angle BDA + \angle CFD + \angle DCF = 180°$	12. 180° in $\triangle$
13. $\angle DCF = 45°$	13. = − =, diff =
14. $\angle BDA = \angle DCF$	14. trans =
15. $\measuredangle BDA \cong \measuredangle DCF$	15. $\cong$ iff meas =
16. $\overline{FC} \cong \overline{FD}$	16. if 2 $\measuredangle$s $\triangle$ $\cong$, opp sides $\cong$
17. $\therefore \triangle FCD$ isos	17. isos $\triangle$ iff 2 $\cong$ sides

EXERCISES FOR 6.4

1. rhombus **3.** square
5. quadrilateral
7. isosceles trapezoid **9.** parallelogram
11. 1. given 2. opp sides ▱ $\cong$
3. given 4. $\cong$ − $\cong$, diff $\cong$
5. whole $\cong$ sum parts
6. whole $\cong$ sum parts
7. trans $\cong$
8. opp $\measuredangle$s ▱ $\cong$ 9. opp sides ▱ $\cong$
10. given 11. $\cong$ − $\cong$, diff $\cong$
12. whole $\cong$ sum parts
13. whole $\cong$ sum parts
14. trans $\cong$
15. sas $\cong$ sas 16. cpctc
17. opp $\measuredangle$s ▱ $\cong$ 18. sas $\cong$ sas
19. cpctc 20. quad opp sides $\cong$ is ▱

15.

Statement	Reason
1. ▱$LIEN$	1. given
2. $\overline{NL} \cong \overline{IE}$	2. opp sides ▱ $\cong$
3. $\overline{NL} \parallel \overline{IE}$	3. ▱ iff opp sides $\parallel$
4. $\measuredangle NLS \cong \measuredangle IEG$	4. $\nparallel$, alt ext $\measuredangle$s $\cong$
5. $\overline{SL}$;$\cong$ $\overline{GE}$	5. given
6. $\triangle NLS \cong \triangle IEG$	6. sas $\cong$ sas
7. $\overline{NS} \cong \overline{IG}$	7. cpctc
8. $\measuredangle NSL \cong \measuredangle IGE$	8. cpctc
9. $\overline{NS} \parallel \overline{IG}$	9. $\not\measuredangle$, lines $\parallel$
10. $\therefore SIGN$ ▱	10. quad 1 pr opp sides $\parallel$ and $\cong$ is ▱

23.

Statement	Reason
1. sq $EJCK$	1. given
2. $\measuredangle E \cong \measuredangle J \cong \measuredangle C \cong \measuredangle K$	2. rect (sq) has 4 $\cong$ rt $\measuredangle$s
3. $\overline{EJ} \cong \overline{JC} \cong \overline{CK} \cong \overline{KE}$	3. rh (sq) has 4 $\cong$ sides
4. $\overline{EF} \cong \overline{CI} \cong \overline{CS} \cong \overline{EH}$	4. given
5. $\triangle EFH \cong \triangle CSI$	5. sas $\cong$ sas
6. $\overline{HF} \cong \overline{IS}$	6. cpctc
7. $\overline{EJ} - \overline{EF} \cong \overline{JC} - \overline{CI} \cong \overline{CK} - \overline{CS} \cong \overline{KE} - \overline{EH}$	7. $\cong$ − $\cong$, diff $\cong$
8. $\overline{FJ} \cong \overline{EJ} - \overline{EF}$ $\overline{JI} \cong \overline{JC} - \overline{CI}$ $\overline{SK} \cong \overline{CK} - \overline{CS}$ $\overline{KH} \cong \overline{KE} - \overline{EH}$	8. whole $\cong$ sum parts
9. $\overline{FJ} \cong \overline{JI} \cong \overline{SK} \cong \overline{KH}$	9. trans $\cong$
10. $\triangle FJI \cong \triangle SKH$	10. sas $\cong$ sas
11. $\overline{HS} \cong \overline{IF}$	11. cpctc
12. $FISH$ ▱	12. quad opp sides $\cong$ is ▱
13. $\measuredangle EFH \cong \measuredangle EHF$ $\measuredangle JFI \cong \measuredangle JIF$	13. if 2 sides $\triangle$ $\cong$, opp $\measuredangle$s $\cong$
14. $\angle EFH = \angle EHF$ $\angle JFI = \angle JIF$	14. $\cong$ iff meas =
15. $\angle E + \angle EFH + \angle EHF = 180°$ $\angle J + \angle JFI + \angle JIF = 180°$	15. 180° in $\triangle$

16. $\angle E = 90°$ $\angle J = 90°$	16. rt $\angle$ = 90°
17. $\angle EFH + \angle EHF = 90°$ $\angle JFI + \angle JIF = 90°$	17. = − =, diff =
18. $\angle EFH + \angle EFH = 90°$ $\angle JFI + \angle JFI = 90°$	18. subst
19. $2 \cdot \angle EFH = 90°$ $2 \cdot \angle JFI = 90°$	19. rearr props
20. $\angle EFH = 45°$ $\angle JFI = 45°$	20. = ÷ =, quot =
21. $\measuredangle EFH + \measuredangle HFI + \measuredangle JFI \cong \measuredangle EFJ$	21. whole ≅ sum parts
22. $\angle EFH + \angle HFI + \angle JFI = \angle EFJ$	22. ≅ iff meas =
23. $\angle EFJ = 180°$	23. st $\angle$ = 180°
24. $\angle EFH + \angle HFI + \angle JFI = 180°$	24. trans =
25. $\angle HFI = 90°$	25. = − =, diff =
26. $\measuredangle HFI$ rt $\measuredangle$	26. rt $\angle$ = 90°
27. ∴ *FISH* rect	27. rect iff ⊡

EXERCISES FOR 6.5

1. 14 in **3.** $11\frac{11}{16}$ in **5.** 21.5 cm **7.** 25 cm **9.** $18\frac{1}{2}$ in **11.** $6\frac{3}{4}$ in **13.** 28 cm **15.** 18 cm **17.** 21 in **19.** 12 in **21.** 9 in **23.** 3 in **25.** 5 in **27.** 23.5 cm **29.** 86 cm **31.** 14 cm **33.** 12 in **35.** 23 in

37. 1. given 2. trap iff 1 pr sides ∥
3. given 4. 2 lines ∥ 3d line are ∥
5. given 6. bis ÷ seg into 2 ≅ segs
7. if 3 ∥ lines cut ≅ seg 1 t, then ≅ segs every t
8. bis ÷ seg into 2 ≅ segs

39.

1. quad *PTAO* with midpts *R*, *Y*, *H*, *G*	1. given
2. $GH = \frac{1}{2}OT$ $RY = \frac{1}{2}OT$	2. midpt seg △ = $\frac{1}{2}$ of and ∥ to 3d side
3. $\frac{1}{2}OT = RY$	3. symm =
4. $GH = RY$	4. trans =
5. ∴ $\overline{GH} \cong \overline{RY}$	5. ≅ iff meas =

45.

1. $\triangle AIM$ with midpts *X*, *O*, *E*	1. given
2. $EO = \frac{1}{2}AI$ and $\overline{EO} \parallel \overline{AI}$	2. midpt seg △ = $\frac{1}{2}$ of and ∥ to 3d side
3. $\overline{AX} \cong \overline{XI}$	3. midpt ÷ seg into 2 ≅ segs
4. $AX = XI$	4. ≅ iff meas =
5. $\overline{AX} + \overline{XI} \cong \overline{AI}$	5. whole ≅ sum parts
6. $AX + XI = AI$	6. ≅ iff meas =
7. $AX + AX = AI$	7. subst
8. $2AX = AI$	8. rearr props
9. $AX = \frac{1}{2}AI$	9. = ÷ =, quot =
10. $EO = AX$	10. symm and trans =
11. $\overline{EO} \cong \overline{AX}$	11. ≅ iff meas =
12. $\overline{EX} \cong \overline{EX}$	12. refl ≅
13. $\measuredangle XEO \cong \measuredangle EXA$	13. ≠, alt int $\measuredangle$s ≅
14. $\triangle XOE \cong \triangle EAX$	14. sas ≅ sas
15. $\measuredangle EAX \cong \measuredangle MEO$	15. ≠, corr $\measuredangle$s ≅

16. $\overline{EA} \cong \overline{ME}$	16. midpt $\div$ seg into 2 $\cong$ segs
17. $\triangle EAX \cong \triangle MEO$	17. sas $\cong$ sas
18. $\therefore \triangle XOE \cong \triangle MEO$	18. trans $\cong$

EXERCISES FOR 6.6

1. F **3.** F **5.** F **7.** F
9. F **11.** T **13.** F **15.** F
17. F **19.** T **21.** 42 in
23. **(a)** $\angle 4 = \angle 1 + \angle 2$ **(b)** $\angle 5 = \angle 2 + \angle 3$ **(c)** $\angle 6 = \angle 1 + \angle 3$
25. one **27.** $113°38'$
29. $120°$ **31.** $360°$
33. $\angle 1 = 108°$, $\angle 2 = 36°$, $\angle 3 = 36°$, $\angle 4 = 36°$, $\angle 5 = 72°$, $\angle 6 = 36°$, $\angle 7 = 72°$, $\angle 8 = 72°$, $\angle 9 = 72°$, $\angle 10 = 36°$
35. $\angle 1 = 33°$, $\angle 2 = 33°$, $\angle 3 = 57°$, $\angle 4 = 57°$, $\angle 5 = 33°$, $\angle 6 = 33°$, $\angle 7 = 57°$, $\angle 8 = 66°$, $\angle 9 = 90°$, $\angle 10 = 90°$
37. $\angle 1 = 36°45'$, $\angle 2 = 53°15'$, $\angle 3 = 90°$, $\angle 4 = 53°15'$, $\angle 5 = 36°45'$, $\angle 6 = 53°15'$, $\angle 7 = 53°15'$, $\angle 8 = 36°45'$, $\angle 9 = 90°$, $\angle 10 = 36°45'$
39. $\angle 1 = 36°$, $\angle 2 = 36°$, $\angle 3 = 72°$, $\angle 4 = 36°$, $\angle 5 = 72°$, $\angle 6 = 36°$, $\angle 7 = 36°$, $\angle 8 = 36°$, $\angle 9 = 108°$, $\angle 10 = 108°$

43.

1. reg pentagon *ACUTE* with midpts *G, I, V, O, N*	1. given
2. $\overline{AC} \cong \overline{CU} \cong \overline{UT} \cong \overline{TE} \cong \overline{EA}$ $\measuredangle A \cong \measuredangle C \cong \measuredangle U \cong \measuredangle T \cong \measuredangle E$	2. reg pent iff sides $\cong$ and $\measuredangle$s $\cong$
3. $\overline{AG} \cong \overline{GC}$, $\overline{CI} \cong \overline{IU}$, $\overline{UV} \cong \overline{VT}$ $\overline{TO} \cong \overline{OE}$, $\overline{EN} \cong \overline{NA}$	3. midpt $\div$ seg into 2 $\cong$ segs
4. $\overline{AG} \cong \overline{GC} \cong \overline{CI} \cong \overline{IU} \cong \overline{UV} \cong \overline{VT} \cong \overline{TO} \cong \overline{OE} \cong \overline{EN} \cong \overline{NA}$	4. $\frac{1}{2}$s of $\cong$ are $\cong$
5. $\triangle AGN \cong \triangle CIG \cong \triangle UVI \cong \triangle TOV \cong \triangle ENO$	5. sas $\cong$ sas
6. $\measuredangle 1 \cong \measuredangle 4$, $\measuredangle 3 \cong \measuredangle 6$	6. cpctc
7. $\measuredangle 3 \cong \measuredangle 4$	7. if 2 sides $\triangle \cong$, opp $\measuredangle$s $\cong$
8. $\measuredangle 1 \cong \measuredangle 3 \cong \measuredangle 4 \cong \measuredangle 6$	8. symm and trans $\cong$
9. $\measuredangle AGC \cong \measuredangle 1 + \measuredangle 2 + \measuredangle 3$ $\measuredangle CIU \cong \measuredangle 4 + \measuredangle 5 + \measuredangle 6$	9. whole $\cong$ sum parts
10. $\measuredangle AGC \cong \measuredangle CIU$	10. st $\measuredangle$s $\cong$
11. $\measuredangle 1 + \measuredangle 2 + \measuredangle 3 \cong \measuredangle 4 + \measuredangle 5 + \measuredangle 6$	11. symm and trans $\cong$
12. $\measuredangle 2 \cong \measuredangle 5$	12. $\cong - \cong$, diff $\cong$
Similarly, $\measuredangle$s 7, 8, 9 can be proved $\cong$ to $\measuredangle$s 2 and 5	
13. $\therefore$ pentagon *GIVON* equiang	13. pent equiangular iff all $\measuredangle$s $\cong$

EXERCISES FOR 7.1 AND 7.2

1. F **3.** T **5.** F **7.** T
9. T **11.** F **13.** F **15.** F
17. F **19.** T
21. **(a)** $\overline{AB}$, $\overline{AE}$, $\overline{AF}$, $\overline{BE}$, $\overline{BG}$, $\overline{BF}$, $\overline{EG}$
(b) $\overline{AE}$, $\overline{BF}$
23. **(a)** $\measuredangle AOB$, $\measuredangle BOE$, $\measuredangle EOF$, $\measuredangle FOA$
(b) $\measuredangle ABE$, $\measuredangle ABG$, $\measuredangle ABF$, $\measuredangle FBG$, $\measuredangle FBE$, $\measuredangle GBE$, $\measuredangle AEG$, $\measuredangle BEG$, $\measuredangle BEA$, $\measuredangle EGB$, $\measuredangle AFB$, $\measuredangle FAE$, $\measuredangle EAB$, $\measuredangle FAB$
25. **(a)** $\measuredangle HBA$, $\measuredangle HBF$, $\measuredangle HBG$, $\measuredangle HBE$, $\measuredangle DBA$, $\measuredangle DBF$, $\measuredangle DBG$, $\measuredangle DBE$, $\measuredangle DEB$, $\measuredangle DEA$, $\measuredangle DEG$
(b) $\measuredangle HBA$, $\measuredangle HBG$, $\measuredangle DBA$, $\measuredangle DBG$, $\measuredangle ACE$, $\measuredangle HBC$
27. sum $\frown$s $\neq 360°$
29. $\cong$ chs do not have $\cong$ $\frown$s
31. sum $\frown$s $\neq 360°$
33. equilateral $\triangle$ has $60°$ $\measuredangle$s, so arc must be $60°$
35. **(a)** $108°$ **(b)** $36°$ **(c)** $36°$
(d) $72°$ **(e)** $144°$
37. $\angle 1 = 81°30'$, $\angle 2 = 81°30'$, $\angle 3 = 17°$, $\angle 4 = 163°$, $\angle 5 = 163°$, $\angle 6 = 17°$, $\angle 7 = 81°30'$, $\angle 8 = 81°30'$

39. $\angle 1 = 21°$, $\angle 2 = 57°$, $\angle 3 = 57°$, $\angle 4 = 66°$, $\angle 5 = 66°$, $\angle 6 = 57°$, $\angle 7 = 57°$, $\angle 8 = 69°$, $\angle 9 = 21°$, $\angle 10 = 42°$, $\angle 11 = 66°$, $\angle 12 = 48°$

41. $\angle 1 = 49°30'$, $\angle 2 = 40°30'$, $\angle 3 = 81°$, $\angle 4 = 99°$, $\angle 5 = 40°30'$, $\angle 6 = 40°30'$, $\angle 7 = 49°30'$, $\angle 8 = 90°$, $\angle 9 = 40°30'$

43. 1. given 2. 2 pts determ line
3. radii $\odot$ ≅ 4. given
5. $\frown$s ≅ iff meas =
6. meas min $\frown$ = cent $\angle$
7. meas min $\frown$ = cent $\angle$
8. symm = 9. trans =
10. ≅ iff meas = 11. lin pr supp
12. lin pr supp
13. $\measuredangle$s supp ≅ $\measuredangle$s are ≅
14. if cent $\measuredangle$s ≅, chs ≅

47.

Statements	Reasons
1. $\odot O$	1. given
2. $\measuredangle EOK \cong \measuredangle JOS$	2. given
3. $\measuredangle KOS \cong \measuredangle KOS$	3. refl ≅
4. $\measuredangle EOK + \measuredangle KOS \cong \measuredangle JOS + \measuredangle KOS$	4. ≅ + ≅, sums ≅
5. $\measuredangle EOS \cong \measuredangle EOK + \measuredangle KOS$ $\measuredangle JOS + \measuredangle KOS \cong \measuredangle JOK$	5. whole ≅ sum parts
6. $\measuredangle EOS \cong \measuredangle JOK$	6. trans ≅
7. $\therefore \overset{\frown}{ES} \cong \overset{\frown}{JK}$	7. if cent $\measuredangle$s ≅, $\frown$s ≅

53.

Statements	Reasons
1. $\odot O$	1. given
2. $\overset{\frown}{ADB} \cong \overset{\frown}{ADB}$	2. refl ≅
3. $\overline{DB} \cong \overline{CA}$	3. given
4. $\overset{\frown}{DB} \cong \overset{\frown}{CA}$	4. if chs ≅, $\frown$s ≅
5. $\overset{\frown}{ADB} - \overset{\frown}{DB} \cong \overset{\frown}{ADB} - \overset{\frown}{CA}$	5. ≅ − ≅, diff ≅
6. $\overset{\frown}{DA} \cong \overset{\frown}{ADB} - \overset{\frown}{DB}$ $\overset{\frown}{ADB} - \overset{\frown}{CA} \cong \overset{\frown}{CB}$	6. whole ≅ sum parts
7. $\overset{\frown}{DA} \cong \overset{\frown}{CB}$	7. trans ≅
8. $\therefore \overline{DA} \cong \overline{CB}$	8. if $\frown$s ≅, chs ≅

EXERCISES FOR 7.3

1. T **3.** F **5.** F **7.** T
9. T **11.** T **13.** F **15.** F
17. F **19.** T

21. $\measuredangle C$ should be ≅ to $\measuredangle B$

23. $\measuredangle C$ should be a rt $\measuredangle$

25. $\overset{\frown}{BC}° = 61°$ instead of $59°$

27. $\angle R = 60°$ instead of $58°$

29. $\angle 1 = 23°$, $\angle 2 = 62°$, $\angle 3 = 90°$, $\angle 4 = 46°$, $\angle 5 = 21°$, $\angle 6 = 28°$, $\angle 7 = 69°$, $\angle 8 = 21°$, $\angle 9 = 62°$, $\angle 10 = 83°$

31. $\angle 1 = 60°$, $\angle 2 = 60°$, $\angle 3 = 60°$, $\angle 4 = 60°$, $\angle 5 = 60°$, $\angle 6 = 60°$, $\angle 7 = 60°$, $\angle 8 = 60°$, $\angle 9 = 120°$, $\angle 10 = 120°$

33. $\angle 1 = 116°$, $\angle 2 = 64°$, $\angle 3 = 36°$, $\angle 4 = 80°$, $\angle 5 = 100°$, $\angle 6 = 80°$, $\angle 7 = 116°$, $\angle 8 = 64°$, $\angle 9 = 36°$

35. $\angle 1 = 40°30'$, $\angle 2 = 29°30'$, $\angle 3 = 80°30'$, $\angle 4 = 59°$, $\angle 5 = 29°30'$, $\angle 6 = 29°30'$, $\angle 7 = 59°$, $\angle 8 = 80°30'$, $\angle 9 = 40°30'$, $\angle 10 = 29°30'$

37. $\angle 1 = 16°30'$, $\angle 2 = 16°30'$, $\angle 3 = 49°30'$, $\angle 4 = 66°$, $\angle 5 = 49°30'$, $\angle 6 = 114°$, $\angle 7 = 49°30'$, $\angle 8 = 97°30'$, $\angle 9 = 16°30'$, $\angle 10 = 16°30'$

39. 1. given 2. given
3. bis ÷ $\measuredangle$ into 2 ≅ $\measuredangle$s 4. given
5. ≠, alt int $\measuredangle$s ≅ 6. trans ≅
8. refl ≅ 9. ≅ + ≅, sums ≅
10. whole ≅ sum parts
11. whole ≅ sum parts
12. trans ≅ 13. if $\frown$s ≅, chs ≅

41.

1. $\odot O$	1. given
2. $\overset{\frown}{EJ} \cong \overset{\frown}{QP}$	2. given
3. $\overline{EJ} \cong \overline{QP}$	3. if $\frown$s $\cong$, chs $\cong$
4. $\overset{\frown}{ES} \cong \overset{\frown}{QR}$	4. given
5. $\overline{ES} \cong \overline{QR}$	5. if $\frown$s $\cong$, chs $\cong$
6. $\overset{\frown}{EJ} + \overset{\frown}{ES} \cong \overset{\frown}{QP} + \overset{\frown}{QR}$	6. $\cong + \cong$, sums $\cong$
7. $\overset{\frown}{SJ} \cong \overset{\frown}{EJ} + \overset{\frown}{ES}$ $\overset{\frown}{QP} + \overset{\frown}{QR} \cong \overset{\frown}{RP}$	7. whole $\cong$ sum parts
8. $\overset{\frown}{SJ} \cong \overset{\frown}{RP}$	8. trans $\cong$
9. $\overline{SJ} \cong \overline{RP}$	9. if $\frown$s $\cong$, chs $\cong$
10. $\triangle EJS \cong \triangle QPR$	10. sss $\cong$ sss
11. $\therefore \measuredangle 1 \cong \measuredangle 2$	11. cpctc

45.

1. $\odot O$	1. given
2. $\overset{\frown}{BC} \cong \overset{\frown}{EC}$	2. given
3. $\measuredangle BAC \cong \measuredangle DAC$	3. inscr $\measuredangle$s interc $\cong$ $\frown$s are $\cong$
4. $\overline{AC} \cong \overline{AC}$	4. refl $\cong$
5. $\measuredangle ACB$ rt $\measuredangle$	5. inscr $\measuredangle$ interc semi$\odot$ is rt $\measuredangle$
6. $\overline{AC} \perp \overline{BD}$	6. $\perp$ iff a rt $\measuredangle$
7. $\measuredangle ACD$ rt $\measuredangle$	7. $\perp$s form $\cong$ rt $\measuredangle$s
8. $\measuredangle ACB \cong \measuredangle ACD$	8. rt $\measuredangle$s $\cong$
9. $\triangle ACB \cong \triangle ACD$	9. asa $\cong$ asa
10. $\overline{CB} \cong \overline{CD}$	10. cpctc
11. $\therefore C$ midpt $\overline{BD}$	11. midpt $\div$ seg into 2 $\cong$ segs

EXERCISES FOR 7.4

1. F **3.** T **5.** F **7.** T
9. F **11.** F **13.** T **15.** F
17. T **19.** T

21. $\angle AOC$ should be 54°30′

23. $\overset{\frown}{PS}°$ should be 58°

25. *PR* should be 5 inches

27. $\angle DCB$ should be 73°

29. (a) $\measuredangle KCJ$, $\measuredangle KMJ$ **(b)** $\measuredangle MKJ$, $\measuredangle MJS$

31.

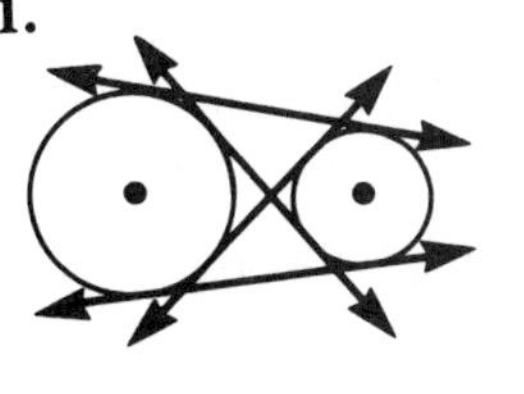
(a)

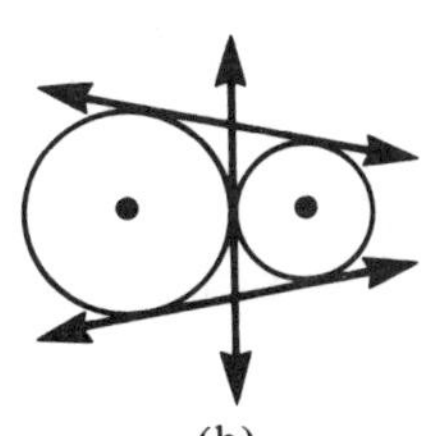
(b)

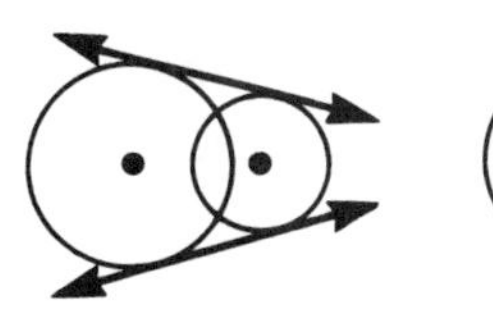
(c)

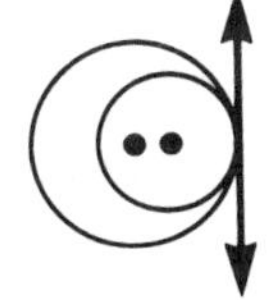
(d)

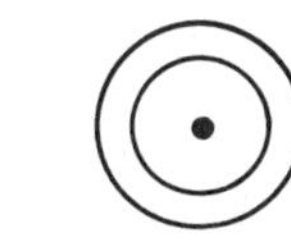
(e)

33. $\angle 1 = 57°$, $\angle 2 = 41°$, $\angle 3 = 64°$, $\angle 4 = 57°$, $\angle 5 = 18°$, $\angle 6 = 41°$, $\angle 7 = 57°$, $\angle 8 = 18°$, $\angle 9 = 64°$, $\angle 10 = 82°$

35. $\angle 1 = 12°$, $\angle 2 = 102°$, $\angle 3 = 78°$, $\angle 4 = 12°$, $\angle 5 = 39°$, $\angle 6 = 51°$, $\angle 7 = 90°$, $\angle 8 = 39°$, $\angle 9 = 39°$, $\angle 10 = 39°$

37. $\angle 1 = 10°$, $\angle 2 = 33°$, $\angle 3 = 31°$, $\angle 4 = 8°$, $\angle 5 = 141°$, $\angle 6 = 25°30'$, $\angle 7 = 154°30'$, $\angle 8 = 35°30'$, $\angle 9 = 139°$, $\angle 10 = 41°$

39. $\angle 1 = 63°30'$, $\angle 2 = 63°30'$, $\angle 3 = 102°$, $\angle 4 = 63°30'$, $\angle 5 = 63°30'$, $\angle 6 = 63°30'$, $\angle 7 = 78°$, $\angle 8 = 38°30'$, $\angle 9 = 141°30'$, $\angle 10 = 38°30'$

41. 1. given 2. tans to $\odot$ $\cong$
3. if 2 sides $\triangle$ $\cong$, opp $\measuredangle$s $\cong$
4. $\cong$ iff meas = 5. tans to $\odot$ $\cong$
6. if 2 sides $\triangle$ $\cong$, opp $\measuredangle$s $\cong$
7. $\cong$ iff meas = 8. 180° in $\triangle$
9. subst 10. $\frac{1}{2}$s of = are =
11. st $\angle$ = 180°
12. = − =, diff = 13. rt $\angle$ = 90°

45.

Statements	Reasons
1. $\odot O$	1. given
2. tan $\overline{AJ}$	2. given
3. $\overline{OJ} \perp \overline{AJ}$	3. tan $\perp$ rad to pt con
4. tan $\overline{AK}$	4. given
5. $\overline{OK} \perp \overline{AK}$	5. tan $\perp$ rad to pt con
6. $\overline{JA} \perp \overline{KA}$	6. given
7. $\overline{OJ} \parallel \overline{KA}$	7. 2 lines $\perp$ 3d line $\parallel$
8. $\overline{OK} \parallel \overline{JA}$	8. 2 lines $\perp$ 3d line $\parallel$
9. $JAKO$ ▱	9. ▱ iff opp sides $\parallel$
10. $\overline{OJ} \cong \overline{OK}$	10. radii $\odot$ $\cong$
11. $JAKO$ rh	11. rh iff ▱
12. $\measuredangle OJA$ rt $\measuredangle$	12. $\perp$ iff a rt$\measuredangle$
13. $\therefore$ $JAKO$ sq	13. sq iff ▱ with rt $\measuredangle$

51.

Statements	Reasons
1. $\odot O$	1. given
2. tans $\overleftrightarrow{JD}$, $\overline{CA}$	2. given
3. $\overline{AJ} \cong \overline{JD}$	3. tans to $\odot$ $\cong$
4. $\angle 1 = \frac{1}{2}\overset{\frown}{BD}°$	4. tan, ch $\angle = \frac{1}{2}\frown°$
5. $\overset{\frown}{BD} \cong \overset{\frown}{ADB} - \overset{\frown}{AD}$	5. whole $\cong$ sum parts
6. $\overset{\frown}{BD}° = \overset{\frown}{ADB}° - \overset{\frown}{AD}°$	6. $\cong$ iff meas $=$
7. $\angle 1 = \frac{1}{2}(\overset{\frown}{ADB}° - \overset{\frown}{AD}°)$	7. subst
8. $\measuredangle 2 \cong \measuredangle 1$	8. vert $\measuredangle$s $\cong$
9. $\angle 2 = \angle 1$	9. $\cong$ iff meas $=$
10. $\angle 2 = \frac{1}{2}(\overset{\frown}{ADB}° - \overset{\frown}{AD}°)$	10. trans $=$
11. $\angle 3 = \frac{1}{2}(\overset{\frown}{AB}° - \overset{\frown}{AD}°)$	11. tan, sec $\angle = \frac{1}{2}$diff $\frown$°s
12. $\overset{\frown}{ADB} \cong \overset{\frown}{AB}$	12. diam $\div$ $\odot$ into 2 $\cong$ semi$\odot$s
13. $\overset{\frown}{ADB}° = \overset{\frown}{AB}°$	13. $\cong$ iff meas $=$
14. $\angle 3 = \frac{1}{2}(\overset{\frown}{ADB}° - \overset{\frown}{AD}°)$	14. subst
15. $\angle 2 = \angle 3$	15. symm and trans $=$
16. $\measuredangle 2 \cong \measuredangle 3$	16. $\cong$ iff meas $=$
17. $\overline{DJ} \cong \overline{CJ}$	17. if 2 $\measuredangle$s $\triangle$ $\cong$, opp sides $\cong$
18. $\therefore$ $\overline{AJ} \cong \overline{CJ}$	18. trans $\cong$

EXERCISES FOR 8.1 AND 8.2

1. T **3.** F **5.** T **7.** T
9. T **11.** F **13.** F **15.** T
17. F **19.** F **21.** 46 units
23. 28 units **25.** 50 units
27. 48 sq units
29. 12 sq units
31. 144 cm **33.** 64 cm
35. 20 cm
37. 48 cm
39. **(a)** 72 sq cm **(b)** 72 sq cm
41. 495 sq cm **43.** 10 sq ft
45. 35 yd **47.** 115.5 sq cm
49. 80.75 sq yd **51.** 200 sq in
53. 12 in **55.** 10 in
57. 5 ft, 10 ft **59.** **(a)** 1924 sq cm
61. 1. given 2. $\parallel$ post 3. can copy seg
4. 2 pts determ line
5. quad 1 pr opp sides $\parallel$ and $\cong$ is ▱
6. A(▱) $= bh$ 7. opp sides ▱ $\cong$
8. refl $\cong$ 9. sss $\cong$ sss
10. $\cong$ $\triangle$s, $=$ areas
11. area $\cup$ $=$ sum areas
12. trans $=$ 13. subst
14. rearr props 15. $\frac{1}{2}$s of $=$s are $=$

EXERCISES FOR 8.3

1. T **3.** T **5.** F **7.** T
9. T **11.** F **13.** T **15.** T
17. T **19.** T **21.** 546 sq in
23. 418 sq in **25.** 418 sq in
27. 2117 sq in **29.** 1620 sq in
31. 49.5 sq cm **33.** 13,464 sq cm
35. 75 sq cm **37.** 1614 sq cm
39. 13.0 sq cm **41.** 10.7 sq cm
43. 9.6 sq cm **47.** 108 sq cm
49. 173 sq in **51.** $(37 - 9\pi)$ sq in
53. $\frac{81\pi}{2}$ sq in

EXERCISES FOR 9.1 AND 9.2

1. T **3.** F **5.** F **7.** T
9. F **11.** T **13.** F **15.** T
17. F **19.** T **21.** 27
23. means are 11 and 21, $7 \cdot 33 = 11 \cdot 21 = 231$
25. $\frac{3}{8}$ **27.** 10.5 ft, 15 ft
29. 10.5 in, 7.5 in, 4.5 in; 10.5 in, 6.3 in, 14.7 in; 10.5 in, 17.5 in, 24.5 in
31. $\frac{4}{3}$ **33.** $a = 5\frac{1}{3}$ in, $b = 7\frac{1}{2}$ in
35. 480 sq ft **37.** 10 cm
39. 12.8 sq cm **41.** yes, aa ≅ aa
43. no, only 1 pr ∡s ≅
45. no, only 1 pr ∡s ≅

47.

1. $\overline{SK} \perp \overline{JS}$	1. given
2. ∡*KSC* rt ∡	2. ⊥ iff a rt ∡
3. $\overline{EJ} \perp \overline{JS}$	3. given
4. ∡*EJC* rt ∡	4. ⊥ iff a rt ∡
5. ∡*KSC* ≅ ∡*EJC*	5. rt ∡s ≅
6. ∡*SCK* ≅ ∡*JCE*	6. vert ∡s ≅
7. ∴ △I ~ △II	7. aa ≅ aa

53.

1. trap *TANG*	1. given
2. $\overline{GN} \parallel \overline{TA}$	2. trap iff 1 pr sides ∥
3. ∡*NGE* ≅ ∡*TAE* ∡*GNE* ≅ ∡*ATE*	3. ≠, alt int ∡s ≅
4. △*ENG* ~ △*ETA*	4. aa ≅ aa
5. ∴ $\frac{GE}{AE} = \frac{NE}{TE}$	5. csstp

EXERCISES FOR 9.3

1. F **3.** T **5.** T **7.** T
9. T **11.** T **13.** F **15.** T
17. T **19.** F
21. $12^2 + 5^2 = 169 \neq 14^2$
23. $3^2 + 4^2 = 25 \neq 6^2$
25. $3^2 + 6^2 = 45 \neq 7^2$ **27.** $\frac{4}{5} \neq \frac{5}{9}$
29. $3^2 + 6^2 = 45 \neq 7^2$
31. △*AGL* ~ △*APE*, △*AGL* ~ △*APN*, △*AGL* ~ △*GPE*, △*AGL* ~ △*GPN*
33. **(a)** $5^2 + 12^2 = 169 = 13^2$
(b) $a^2 + b^2 = c^2$
35. **(a)** 61 **(b)** $\sqrt{a^2 + b^2}$
37. 50 in **39.** 40 in
41. $16\sqrt{2}$ in **43.** 12 in, 60 in
45. $8\sqrt{3}$ in **49.** 72 in
55. 1. given 2. 1 ⊥ from pt to line
3. 2 pts determ line
4. rect (sq) has 4 rt ∡s
5. rt ∡s ≅ 6. refl ≅
7. ≅ + ≅, sums ≅
8. whole ≅ sum parts
9. trans ≅ 10. rh (sq) has 4 ≅ sides
11. sas ≅ sas 12. ≅ △s, = areas
13. $A(\triangle) = \frac{1}{2}bh$ 14. trans =
15. = · =, prod = 16. *A*(rect) = *lw*
17. trans = 18. = + =, sums =
19. area ∪ = sum areas 20. trans =

EXERCISES FOR 9.4

1. interch mns
3. prod extrms = prod mns
5. add prop propor **7.** invert ratios
9. trans =
11. yes, = ÷ =, quot =
13. $\frac{AB}{DB} = \frac{AC}{DE}$ **15.** $\frac{ST}{KE} = \frac{SK}{SK}$

17. 1. given 2. $\neq$, alt int $\measuredangle$s $\cong$
3. vert $\measuredangle$s $\cong$ 4. aa. $\cong$ aa
5. csstp 6. $\neq$, corr $\measuredangle$s $\cong$
7. refl $\cong$ 8. aa $\cong$ aa
9. csstp 10. given
11. midpt iff 2 lengths = 12. subst
13. trans = 14. prod extrms = prod mns

21.

Statements	Reasons
1. R midpt $\overline{OF}$, T midpt $\overline{OC}$	1. given
2. $\overline{RT} \parallel \overline{FC}$	2. midpt seg $\triangle$ $\frac{1}{2}$ of and $\parallel$ to 3d side
3. $\measuredangle TRA \cong \measuredangle FAR$	3. $\neq$, alt int $\measuredangle$s $\cong$
4. A midpt $\overline{FC}$	4. given
5. $\overline{RA} \parallel \overline{OC}$	5. midpt seg $\triangle$ $\frac{1}{2}$ of and $\parallel$ to 3d side
6. $\measuredangle FAR \cong \measuredangle FCO$	6. $\neq$, corr $\measuredangle$s $\cong$
7. $\measuredangle TRA \cong \measuredangle FCO$	7. trans $\cong$
8. $\overline{TA} \parallel \overline{OF}$	8. midpt seg $\triangle$ $\frac{1}{2}$ of and $\parallel$ to 3d side
9. $\measuredangle CAT \cong \measuredangle CFO$	9. $\neq$, corr $\measuredangle$s $\cong$
10. $\measuredangle RTA \cong \measuredangle CAT$	10. $\neq$, alt int $\measuredangle$s $\cong$
11. $\measuredangle RTA \cong \measuredangle CFO$	11. trans $\cong$
12. $\triangle TRA \sim \triangle FCO$	12. aa $\cong$ aa
13. $\frac{AT}{OF} = \frac{AR}{OC}$	13. csstp
14. $\therefore \frac{OC}{OF} = \frac{AR}{AT}$	14. interch mns or extrms

27.

Statements	Reasons
1. $\square STAR$	1. given
2. $\overline{RS} \parallel \overline{TA}$	2. $\square$ iff opp sides $\parallel$
3. $\measuredangle RSE \cong \measuredangle JAE$ $\measuredangle SRE \cong \measuredangle AJE$	3. $\neq$, alt int $\measuredangle$s $\cong$
4. $\triangle RSE \sim \triangle JAE$	4. aa $\cong$ aa
5. $\frac{RE}{EJ} = \frac{ES}{EA}$	5. csstp
6. $\overline{RA} \parallel \overline{SK}$	6. $\square$ iff opp sides $\parallel$
7. $\measuredangle ARE \cong \measuredangle SKE$ $\measuredangle RAE \cong \measuredangle KSE$	7. $\neq$, alt into $\measuredangle$s $\cong$
8. $\triangle ARE \sim \triangle SKE$	8. aa $\cong$ aa
9. $\frac{ES}{EA} = \frac{EK}{RE}$	9. csstp
10. $\frac{RE}{EJ} = \frac{EK}{RE}$	10. trans =
11. $\therefore RE \cdot RE = EJ \cdot EK$	11. prod extrms = prod mns

31. **(a)** $\frac{2}{3}$ **(b)** $\frac{2}{3}$ **(b)** $\frac{4}{9}$
33. **(a)** $\frac{4}{5}$ **(b)** $\frac{4}{5}$ **(b)** $\frac{4}{5}$
35. 4 in, 6 in, 8 in
37. **(a)** $\frac{1}{2}$ **(b)** $\frac{1}{4}$
39. $\frac{8}{1}$

EXERCISES FOR 9.5

1. T **3.** F **5.** T **7.** F
9. T **11.** F **13.** F **15.** T
17. T **19.** F **21.** 6 **23.** 57°
25. 7 **27.** 2 **29.** 1 **31.** 2
33. $4\sqrt{6}$ **35.** 5π **37.** $4\sqrt{2}$
39. 11 **41.** 3
43. $12\sqrt{3}$ sq units
45. $(30\pi + 9\sqrt{3})$ sq units
47. $(\frac{9\pi}{4} - \frac{9}{2})$ sq units
49. 28π sq units **51.** 30 sq units
53. $\frac{a^2\pi}{8} + \frac{b^2\pi}{8} + \frac{ab}{2} - \frac{c^2\pi}{8}$
55. **(a)** 81 sq units **(b)** same area

EXERCISES FOR 9.6

1. **(a)** $\sim$ **(b)** aa $\cong$ aa
3. **(a)** $\sim$
(b) corr $\measuredangle$s $\cong$ and corr sides propor
5. **(a)** not $\sim$
(b) 1 by 2 rect is not $\sim$ to 1 by 3 rect because $\frac{1}{1} \neq \frac{2}{3}$
7. **(a)** not $\sim$
(b) 1-by-1 sq not $\sim$ to 1-by-2 rect because $\frac{1}{1} \neq \frac{1}{2}$
9. **(a)** $\sim$ **(b)** aa $\cong$ aa
11. **(a)** not $\sim$
(b) 30°, 60°, 90° rt $\triangle$ is not $\sim$ 45°, 45°, 90° rt $\triangle$ because $\measuredangle$s not $\cong$
13. **(a)** $\sim$
(b) corr $\measuredangle$s $\cong$ and corr sides propor
15. $\frac{39}{5}$ **17.** $\frac{27}{5}$ **19.** 36
21. $\frac{120}{17}$ **23.** 17 **25.** $6\sqrt{5}$
27. 5 **29.** $\frac{200}{9}$ **31.** 26 in
33. C is tripled, A is nine times larger
35. 4 in **37.** $\frac{25\pi}{8}$, 18π, $\frac{169\pi}{8}$; equal
39. 20 in **41.** 125 ft
43. $\frac{25}{3}$ cm **45.** 6 in
47. $2d = 5l$ **49.** $z^2 = x^2 + y^2$
51. 36 ft
53. **(a)** $\frac{289\pi}{4}$ sq units **(b)** $\frac{4\sqrt{6}}{3}$ in
55. **(a)** 27π sq in **(b)** $6\sqrt{3}$ in
(c) 27π sq in

EXERCISES FOR 10.1 AND 10.2

1. F **3.** T **5.** F **7.** F
9. T **11.** F **13.** T **15.** F
17. T **19.** F **21.** both
23. plane only **25.** space only
27. plane only **29.** both
31. $\measuredangle E\text{-}JS\text{-}C$ and $\measuredangle F\text{-}JS\text{-}K$, $\measuredangle E\text{-}JS\text{-}K$ and $\measuredangle C\text{-}SJ\text{-}F$, $\measuredangle P\text{-}FG\text{-}S$ and $\measuredangle H\text{-}GF\text{-}A$, $\measuredangle A\text{-}FG\text{-}S$ and $\measuredangle P\text{-}FG\text{-}H$
33. $\measuredangle C\text{-}SJ\text{-}E$ and $\measuredangle E\text{-}JS\text{-}K$, $\measuredangle C\text{-}SJ\text{-}E$, and $\measuredangle C\text{-}SJ\text{-}F$; $\measuredangle C\text{-}SJ\text{-}F$ and $\measuredangle F\text{-}JS\text{-}K$, $\measuredangle F\text{-}JS\text{-}K$ and $\measuredangle K\text{-}SJ\text{-}E$
35. $\measuredangle E\text{-}JS\text{-}C$ and $\measuredangle S\text{-}GF\text{-}A$, $\measuredangle E\text{-}JS\text{-}K$ and $\measuredangle S\text{-}GF\text{-}P$, $\measuredangle H\text{-}GF\text{-}P$ and $\measuredangle F\text{-}JS\text{-}K$, $\measuredangle H\text{-}GF\text{-}A$ and $\measuredangle F\text{-}JS\text{-}C$
37. 109° **39.** 109°
41. 1. given
2. $l \perp$ pl is $\perp$ all l in pl thru inters
3. $\perp$ iff a rt $\measuredangle$ 4. given
5. $l \perp$ pl is $\perp$ all l in pl thru inters
6. $\perp$ iff a rt $\measuredangle$ 7. rt $\measuredangle$s $\cong$
8. given 9. bis $\div$ seg into 2 $\cong$ segs
10. 2 inters lines determ pl
11. vert $\measuredangle$s $\cong$
12. aas $\cong$ aas 13. cpctc

43.

1. $\overline{ER} \perp$ pl p at R	1. given
2. $\overline{ER} \perp \overline{IR}$, $\overline{ER} \perp \overline{CR}$	2. $l \perp$ pl is $\perp$ all l in pl thru inters
3. $\measuredangle ERI$, $\measuredangle ERC$ rt $\measuredangle$s	3. $\perp$ iff a rt $\measuredangle$
4. $\measuredangle ERI \cong \measuredangle ERC$	4. rt $\measuredangle$s $\cong$
5. $\overline{ER} \cong \overline{ER}$	5. refl $\cong$
6. $\measuredangle EIR \cong \measuredangle ECR$	6. given
7. $\triangle EIR \cong \triangle ECR$	7. aas $\cong$ aas
8. $\therefore \overline{IR} \cong \overline{CR}$	8. cpctc

47.

1. $\overline{EJ} \perp$ pl p	1. given
2. $\overline{EJ} \perp \overline{JM}$, $\overline{EJ} \perp \overline{JC}$	2. $l \perp$ pl is $\perp$ all l in pl thru inters
3. $\measuredangle EJM$, $\measuredangle EJC$ rt $\measuredangle$s	3. $\perp$ iff a rt $\measuredangle$
4. $\measuredangle EJM \cong \measuredangle EJC$	4. rt $\measuredangle$s $\cong$
5. $\overline{JS} \perp \overline{CM}$	5. given
6. $\measuredangle JSC \cong \measuredangle JSM$	6. $\perp$s form $\cong$ rt $\measuredangle$s
7. $\overline{JS}$ bis $\overline{CM}$	7. given
8. $\overline{SM} \cong \overline{SC}$	8. bis $\div$ seg into 2 $\cong$ segs
9. $\overline{JS} \cong \overline{JS}$	9. refl $\cong$
10. $\triangle JSM \cong \triangle JSC$	10. sas $\cong$ sas
11. $\overline{JM} \cong \overline{JC}$	11. cpctc
12. $\overline{EJ} \cong \overline{EJ}$	12. refl $\cong$
13. $\triangle EJM \cong \triangle EJC$	13. sas $\cong$ sas
14. $\overline{EM} \cong \overline{EC}$	14. cpctc
15. $\therefore \triangle ECM$ isos	15. isos $\triangle$ iff 2 $\cong$ sides

EXERCISES FOR 10.3

1. **(a)** square right prism
(b) sq *ROGA* and sq *HTYP*
(c) *R, O, G, A, H, T, Y, P*
(d) $\overline{RH}$, $\overline{AP}$, $\overline{GY}$, $\overline{OT}$
(e) rect *RAPH*, rect *AGYP*, rect *GOTY*, rect *ORHT*

3. **(a)** triangular prism **(b)** $\triangle FAC$, $\triangle OTR$
(c) *O, R, T, F, A, C*
(d) $\overline{OF}$, $\overline{TA}$, $\overline{RC}$
(e) ▱*OTAF*, ▱*TRCA*, ▱*ROFC*

5. **(a)** regular pentagonal prism
(b) reg pentagon *ATCOG*, reg pentagon *RLNPS*
(c) *S, R, L, N, P, G, A, T, C, O*
(d) $\overline{SG}$, $\overline{RA}$, $\overline{LT}$, $\overline{NC}$, $\overline{PO}$
(e) rect *SPOG*, rect *PNCO*, rect *NLTC*, rect *LRAT*, rect *RSGA*

7. **(a)** pentagonal pyramid
(b) pentagon *ABCDE*
(c) *A, B, C, D, E, O*
(d) $\overline{AO}$, $\overline{BO}$, $\overline{CO}$, $\overline{DO}$, $\overline{EO}$
(e) $\triangle ABO$, $\triangle BCO$, $\triangle CDO$, $\triangle DEO$, $\triangle EAO$

9. **(a)** regular triangular pyramid
(b) $\triangle JES$ **(c)** *J, E, S, K*
(d) $\overline{EK}$, $\overline{JK}$, $\overline{SK}$
(e) $\triangle EJK$, $\triangle JSK$, $\triangle SEK$

11. **(a)** 220 sq in **(b)** 270 sq in
13. **(a)** 240 sq in **(b)** 304 sq in
15. **(a)** 1512 sq cm
(b) $(1512 + 162\sqrt{3})$ sq cm
17. **(a)** $64\sqrt{514}$ sq ft
(b) $(64\sqrt{514} + 512)$ sq ft
19. **(a)** $\frac{33\sqrt{43,563}}{4}$ sq cm
(b) $(\frac{33\sqrt{43,563}}{4} + \frac{363\sqrt{3}}{4})$ sq cm
21. 4 in
23. $(144 + 36\sqrt{3})$ sq cm **25.** 18 sq ft
27. 300 sq yd **31.** 6840 sq in
33. $LA = 3936$ sq ft, $TA = 5250$ sq ft
35. **(a)** $8 - 12 + 6 = 2$
(b) $7 - 12 + 7 = 2$
(c) $4 - 6 + 4 = 2$

EXERCISES FOR 10.4

1. 105 cu in **3.** 512 cu in
5. 16 cu ft **7.** 1924 cu in
9. $1815\sqrt{3}$ cu cm **11.** 864 cu ft
13. 80 cu ft **15.** $3360\sqrt{3}$ cu cm
17. 7296 cu cm **19.** 70,312.5 cu cm
21. 105 cu ft **23.** $175\sqrt{3}$ cu in
25. 240 cubes **27.** 3200 cu cm
29. $288\sqrt{2}$ cu cm **31.** $16\sqrt{3}$ cu in
33. 648 boxes **35.** 10 cu in
37. 729 ice cubes **39.** 9216 cu in

EXERCISES FOR 10.5

1. T **3.** F **5.** T **7.** F
9. T **11.** F **13.** F **15.** T
17. T **19.** T **21.** $\frac{1}{4}$ **23.** $\frac{1}{1}$
25. $\frac{1}{27}$ **27.** $\frac{1}{8}$ **29.** $\frac{1}{64}$ **31.** $\frac{2}{3}$
33. $LA = 300\pi$ sq in, $V = 1500\pi$ cu in
35. 2400π sq ft **37.** $\frac{6976\pi}{3}$ cu in
39. 8 ft **41.** $\frac{27\pi}{2}$ cu ft
43. $\frac{125\pi}{2}$ cu ft **45.** 640π cu cm
47. 3 units **49.** $\frac{1}{1}, \frac{3}{2}$
51. 273π sq ft **53.** 1348π cu ft
55. $r_1 = \frac{-5 + 5\sqrt{29}}{2}$, $r_2 = \frac{5 + 5\sqrt{29}}{2}$

EXERCISES FOR APPENDIX C

1. **(b)** circle of radius 2 inches centered at *B*
3. **(b)** line parallel to and $\frac{1}{2}$ inch from both *l* and *m*
5. **(b)** circle concentric with given circles and of radius $2\frac{1}{2}$ inches
7. **(b)** union of two half lines perpendicular to *l* with *A* as endpoint of both
9. **(b)** two lines each parallel and $\frac{2K}{EJ}$ units from $\overline{EJ}$
11. **(b)** circle centered at *O* with radius the distance from *O* to midpoints of the chords

13. **(b)** circle of radius 3 inches centered at midpoint of $\overline{LW}$ except endpoints of diameter containing L and W

15. **(b)** circle centered at point one fourth of distance from B to A with radius $\frac{1}{4}AB$ except endpoints of diameter containing B

EXERCISES FOR APPENDIX D

21. **(a)** centroid
(b) $AP = 4$ in, $PD = 2$ in, $PB = 3$ in

23. yes, $\frac{16}{9} \cdot \frac{3}{4} \cdot \frac{9}{12} = 1$

25. $EF = \frac{45}{11}$ cm, $FA = 4\frac{10}{11}$ cm

INDEX

aa ≅ aa, 336
aas ≅ aas, 187
Abbreviations in proofs, 41
Abel, Niels, 299
Absolute value, 15
Acute angle, 60
Acute triangle, 89
Addition
  of congruences, 113
  of equals, 22, 41
  of inequalities, 22, 41, 136
  property of order, 142
  rearrangement properties of, 20, 22
Adjacent angles, 55
Adjacent sides in quadrilateral, 201
Alexander the Great, 87
Alternate exterior angles, 162
Alternate interior angles, 162, 165
Altitude
  of circular cone, 415
  of circular cylinder, 414
  of frustum of pyramid, 394
  of parallelogram, 304
  of prism, 393
  of pyramid, 394
  of rectangle, 303
  of trapezoid, 307
  of triangle, 125, 306
Angle(s), 53
  acute, 60
  adjacent, 55
  alternate exterior, 162
  alternate interior, 162, 165
  base, of isosceles trapezoid, 202
  base, of isosceles triangle, 89
  bisector of, 60, 113
  central, of circle, 256
  complementary, 61
  complement of, 61
  congruent, 65
  copying an, 66
  corresponding, 162
  dihedral, 388
  exterior, 161
  exterior of, 54–55
  inscribed, 258, 273
  interior, 161
  interior of, 54–55
  measuring, 56–59
  midray of, 60
  notation for, 53
  obtuse, 60
  of polygon, 240
  of quadrilateral, 201
  right, 60
  sides of, 53
  straight, 54, 61
  supplementary, 61
  supplement of, 61
  of triangle, 89
  vertex of, 53
  vertex, of isosceles triangle, 89
  vertical, 56
Angle bisector of triangle, 124
Angular distance, 58
Apothem, 317
Archimedes, 3, 382–383
Arc(s), 256–257
  congruent, 259
  in constructions, 35
  degree measure of, 257–258
  of sector of circle, 362–363
Area, 302
  of circle, 319
  lateral, 394
  of parallelogram, 304
  of polygon, 314–317
  postulate, 302
  of rectangle, 303
  of sector of circle, 363
  total, 394
  of trapezoid, 307
  of triangle, 306
Arithmetic, geometric, 2
asa ≅ asa, 94
Associative property
  for addition, 20
  for multiplication, 21
Auxiliary lines, 125
Axioms
  for order, 21–22, 136
  for real numbers, 20–23, 41–42, A-1–A-3
Axis
  of circular cone, 415
  of circular cylinder, 414
Base(s)
  of circular cone, 415
  of circular cylinder, 414
  of frustum of pyramid, 394
  of isosceles triangle, 89
  of parallelogram, 304
  of prism, 392
  of pyramid, 393–394
  of rectangle, 303
  of trapezoid, 202, 307
  of triangle, 306
Base angles
  of isosceles trapezoid, 202
  of isosceles triangle, 89
Between
  for points, 28
  for rays, 55
  as undefined term, 28
Bisector
  of angle, 60, 113
  of arc, 282
  of chord, 282
  of line segment, 35, 41, 112
  perpendicular, 147, 148, 153
Bolyai, Janos, 173, 199, 253

castc, 335
Center(s)
  of circle, 254
  line of, 287
  of regular polygon, 317
  of sphere, 416
Central angle, 256
Centroid of triangle, A-28
Ceva, Giovanni, A-28
  theorem of, A-29
Cevian, A-28
Chord of circle, 255
Circle(s), 254
  arc of, 256
  area of, 319
  center of, 254
  chord of, 255
  circumference of, 318
  circumscribed, 316–317
  concentric, 255
  congruent, 259
  degree measure of, 257
  diameter of, 255

exterior of, 254
externally tangent, 287
interior of, 254
internally tangent, 287
nine-point, A-30
postulate, 288
radius of, 254
secant of, 255
sector of, 362
similar, 361
tangent of, 256
Circumcenter of triangle, A-26
Circumference of circle, 318
Circumscribed circle, 273
for triangle, A-26
Closed surface, 383
Collinear, 29
Common tangent line, 287
Commutative property
for addition, 20
for multiplication, 21
Complementary angles, 61
Complement of angle, 61
Completeness property, 22
Concentric circles, 255
Conclusion in proof, 4, 41
Concurrent lines, 88, A-23
Cone, circular, 415
area of, 416
volume of, 416
Congruence, 90
addition property of, 113
division property of, 114
multiplication property of, 114
RST properties of, 37–38, 66, 91–92
subtraction property of, 113
Congruent angles, 65
ways to prove, 115
Congruent arcs, 259
Congruent circles, 259
Congruent line segments, 37, 41
ways to prove, 115
Congruent triangles, 91
construction of, 92–94
postulates about, 93–94
Conical surface, 415
Consecutive angles of polygon, 201, 240
Consecutive sides of polygon, 201, 240
Consecutive vertices of polygon, 201, 240
Constructions, geometric, 4, 35
bisector of angle, 60, 135
bisector of line segment, 35
circle containing three points, 288
circumcenter of triangle, A-26
circumscribed circle for triangle, A-26
congruent triangles, 92–94
copying angle, 66
copying line segment, 39
divide line segment into congruent parts, 244
divide line segment into extreme and mean ratio, 366–367
famous, 299
incenter of triangle, A-25
inscribed circle for triangle, A-25
mean proportional, 344
midpoint of line segment, 35
parallel to line, 162–163
perpendicular bisector of line segment, 148, 153
perpendicular to line, 69, 70, 135
Converse of theorem, 126
Convex polygon, 200, 240
Convex set, 55
Coordinate of point, 15
Coplanar, 161
Copying
angle, 66
line segment, 39
Corollary, 127
Corresponding angles, 162
Corresponding parts, 91
Counterexample, 39
Covering a line segment, 32–33
cpctc, 91
csstp, 335
Cube, 393
volume of, 404
Cylinder, circular, 413–414
area of, 414
volume of, 415
Cylindrical surface, 413

da Vinci, Leonardo, 366
Decagon, 241
Decimals, types of, 12
Dedekind, Richard, 329
Deductive reasoning, 26
Definitions, complete list, A-1–A-8
Degree measure
of angle, 57–59
of arc, 257–258
of circle, 257
of semicircle, 257
Diagonal of polygon, 201, 240
Diameter of circle, 255
Dihedral angle, 388
Distance
angular, 58
between parallel lines, 206
between points, 16, 33
from point to line, 70
Distributive property, 21
Division
of congruences, 114
of equals, 22, 41
Divine Proportion, 366
Dodecagon, 241
Doubling a cube, 299

Elements, 3
and Golden Ratio, 367
history of, 87, 329, 382
and Parallel Postulate, 199
Elements in a set, 6
Empty set, 6, 7
Endpoint, 29
Equals relation, 14
properties of, 17, 22, 41
Equiangular triangle, 90
Equilateral triangle, 89
Euclid, 3, 87, 160, 172
Euclidean geometry, 3
Eudoxus, 329
Euler, Leonhard, 402, A-30
Exterior
of angle, 54–55
of circle, 254
of triangle, 89
Exterior angles, 161
of polygon, 243
of triangle, 136
Externally tangent circles, 287
Extreme and mean ratio, 366–367
Extremes of proportion, 332

Face, 392
Figure, geometric, 27
Fractional parts, 15
Frustum of pyramid, 394

Galois, Evariste, 299
Garfield, James A., 349
Gauss, Karl Friedrich, 173, 199, 253
Geometric constructions, 4
Geometric date line, A-33
Geometric figure, 27
Geometric mean, 332
Geometric solid, 383
Geometry, 2
elliptic, 253
Euclidean, 3
hyperbolic, 253
Lobachevskian, 253
non-Euclidean, 173
plane, 3
solid, 383
spherical, 173, 253
Golden Ratio, 366
Golden Rectangle, 366
Golden Section, 366
Great circle, 417

Half line, 29
Hemisphere, 417
Heptagon, 241
Hexagon, 240
Hippocrates, 371
hs ≅ hs, 188
Hypotenuse of right triangle, 90
Hypothesis, 4, 41

If and only if (iff), 7
Incenter of triangle, A-24–A-25
Included angles, 89
Indirect proof, 139
Inequalities, addition property of, 22
Inscribed angle, 258
Inscribed circle, 273
for triangle, A-24–A-25
Inscribed polygon, 273
Integer, 10
Intercepted arc, 257
Interior
of angle, 54–55
of circle, 254
of triangle, 89
Interior angles, 161
Internally tangent circles, 287
Intersection
of lines, 29–30
of planes, 385
of sets, 8
Irrational numbers, 12, 15
discovery of, 2, 52
Isosceles trapezoid, 202
Isosceles triangle, 89

Jones, William, 319

Klein, Felix, 253

Lateral area, 394
of regular pyramid, 396
of right circular cone, 416
of right circular cylinder, 414
Lateral edges
of prism, 392
of pyramid, 394
Lateral faces
of frustum of pyramid, 394
of prism, 392
of pyramid, 393–394
Lateral surface of circular cylinder, 414
Legs
of isosceles triangle, 89
of right triangle, 90
Length
of arc of sector of circle, 363
of line segment, 33
of rectangle, 303
Line(s), 27
of centers, 287
concurrent, 88, A-23
notation for, 28
number, 14–15
parallel, 161–163
parallel to plane, 385
perpendicular, 69
perpendicular to plane, 385
postulates for, 28, 42
segment of, 29
skew, 385
Linear pair, 56
Line segment(s), 29
bisector of, 35, 41, 112
congruent, 37, 41
copying a, 39, 42
covering a, 32
length of, 33–34
measure of, 32–34
midpoint of, 34–35, 41, 112
notation for, 29
perpendicular bisector of, 147-148
Lobachevski, Nikolai Ivanovich, 173, 199, 253
Locus, 147, A-16
Lunes of Hippocrates, 371

Mathematical system, 3–4
Major arc, 256, 257
Mean proportional, 332, 344
Means of a proportion, 332
Measure
of angle, 59
of arc, 257
area, 302
of circle, circumference, 318
of circle, degrees, 257
degree, 57–58
of line segment, 32–34
perimeter, 300–301
of semicircle, 257
Median of triangle, 124
Midpoint of line segment, 34, 35, 41, 112
Midray of angle, 60
Minor arc, 256, 257
Minutes, in measuring angles, 57
Multiplication
of congruences, 114
of equals, 22, 41
property of order, 142
rearrangement properties of, 21, 22

Nappe, 415
n-gon, 241
sum of angles, 243
Nine-point circle, A-30
Nonagon, 241
Non-Euclidean geometries, 173, 253
Nonterminating decimal, 12
Null set, 6, 7
Number(s)
in geometry, 10
integer, 10
irrational, 2, 12, 15, 52
rational, 10, 12
real, 13
whole, 10
Number line, 14–15
distance on, 16

Oblique cylinder, 414
Oblique planes, 386
Oblique prism, 393
Obtuse angle, 60
Obtuse triangle, 90
Octagon, 241
Opposite angles
in quadrilateral, 201
in triangle, 89
Opposite rays, 54
Opposite sides in quadrilateral, 201
Opposite vertices in quadrilateral, 201
Order relation, 14
Order, Transitive Property of, 21
Orthocenter of triangle, A-27

Parallelepiped, 392
rectangular, 393
Parallel lines, 161–163
distance between, 206
to plane, 385
Parallelogram, 202
altitude of, 304
area of, 304
base of, 304
Parallel Postulate, 172–173
history of, 160, 199
Pentagon, 240
Perimeter, 300
Perpendicular bisector of line segment, 147, 148, 153
Perpendicular lines, 69–70
to a plane, 385
Pi, 318–319
Plane(s), 27, 384
oblique, 386
parallel to plane, 385
perpendicular to plane, 385
Point, 26
of contact, 256
coordinate of, 15
of tangency, 256
Polygon, 239–241
area of, 314
inscribed in circle, 316
origin of term, 200
Polygonal region, 301
Polyhedron(s), 392
similar, 405–406
Postulates, 4, 28
complete list, A-8–A-9
Prism, 392–393
area of, 394
volume of, 403, 404
Proclus, 26, 160
Proofs
abbreviations in, 41
auxiliary lines in, 125
conclusion in, 41
by contradiction, 140
direct, 138–139
hypothesis in, 41
indirect, 139
reasons in, 41
shortcuts in, 68, 112–115, 185, 214–215, 261, 283
writing, 40–41, 42, 76, 146
Proportion, 331–332
Protractor, 57–58
postulate, 59
Ptolemy, 87
Pyramid, 393–394
area of, 394
volume of, 404–405
Pythagoras, 3, 52
Pythagoreans, Order of, 52, 329
Pythagorean Theorem, 345
applications of, 373, 375, 396–397
converse of, 345

Quadrilateral, 200–201
special types of, 202–203

Radius
of circle, 254–255
in constructions, 35
of regular polygon, 317
of sphere, 416
Raphael, 366
Ratio, 330
Rational number, 10, 12
Ray(s), 29
opposite, 54
Real number(s), 13
absolute value of, 15
axioms for, 20–23, A-1–A-3
Rearrangement properties, 21, 41
Reasons in proofs, 41
Rectangle, 203
altitude of, 303
area of, 303
base of, 303
length of, 303
width of, 303
Rectangular parallelepiped, 393
Rectangular right prism, 393
volume of, 403
Reflexive property
of congruence of angles, 66
of congruence of line segments, 38
of congruence of triangles, 91
of equals, 17, 41
Regular polygon, 241
apothem of, 317
area of, 316, 317
center of, 317
radius of, 317

Regular prism, 393
Regular pyramid, 394
  lateral area of, 396
  volume of, 405
Relation(s)
  equals, 14
  geometric, 3
  numerical, 3
  order, 14
Remote interior angle, 136
Repeating decimal, 12
Rhombus, 202
Riemann, Bernhard, 253
Right angle, 60
Right circular cone, 415
  area of, 416
  volume of, 416
Right circular cylinder, 414
  area of, 414
  volume of, 415
Right prism, 393
Right section of prism, 393
Right triangle, 89
RST properties, 17
  checking validity of, 17–18
  of congruence of angles, 66
  of congruence of line segments, 37–38, 42
  of congruence of triangles, 91–92
  of similarity relation, 336
Ruffini, 299
Ruler Postulate, 33

Saccheri, Girolamo, 160, 199
sas ≅ sas, 93
Scalene triangle, 89
Secant segment, 364
Secant to circle, 255
Seconds, in measuring angles, 57
Section
  of prism, 393
  of pyramid, 394
Sector of circle, 362
  area of, 363
  length of arc of, 363
Semicircle, 256
  degree measure of, 257
Set(s), 6
  convex, 55
  elements in a, 6
  empty, 6, 7
  naming, 6, 30
  notation for, 7
  null, 6, 7
  operations with, 8
  subset of a, 6
Set-builder notation, 7
Sides
  of angle, 53
  of polygon, 240
  of quadrilateral, 201
  of triangle, 88
Similarity relation, 336
Similar polyhedrons, 405–406
Similar triangles, 330, 335
  applications of, 373, 374
Skew lines, 385
Slant height
  of frustum of pyramid, 394
  of regular pyramid, 394
  of right circular cone, 415
Small circle of sphere, 417
Solid, geometric, 383
Solid geometry, 383
Space, 27
Space geometry, 383
Sphere, 416–417
Spherical geometry, 173
Square, 203
Square root, 11
Squaring the circle, 299, 371
sss ≅ sss, 93
Straight angle, 54
  measure of, 61
Subset, 6
Substitution, 23, 42
Subtraction
  of congruences, 113
  of equals, 22, 41
Supplementary angles, 61
Supplement of an angle, 61
Surface, 383
  circular conical, 415
  circular cylindrical, 413
Surface area of sphere, 417
Symmetric Property
  of congruence of angles, 66
  of congruence of line segments, 38
  of congruence of triangles, 91
  of equals, 17, 41
System, mathematical, 3–4

Tangent circles, 287
Tangent plane, 417
Tangent segment, 365
Tangent to circle, 256
Terminating decimal, 12
Terms, undefined, 4
Thales, 3, 52, 103, 273
Theorem(s), 4
  complete list, A-9–A-15
Transitive property
  of congruence of angles, 66
  of congruence of line segments, 38
  of congruence of triangles, 92
  of equals, 17, 41
  of order, 21, 41, 136
Transversal, 161
Trapezoid, 202
  altitude of, 307
  bases of, 202, 307
  isosceles, 202
Triangle(s), 88
  acute, 89
  altitude of, 125, 306
  angle bisector of, 124
  angles of, 89
  area of, 306
  base of, 306
  centroid of, A-28
  circumcenter of, A-26
  circumscribed circle of, A-26
  congruent, 91
  equiangular, 90
  equilateral, 89
  exterior of, 89
  exterior angle of, 136
  incenter of, A-24
  inequalities in, 136–138
  inscribed circle of, A-24–A-25
  interior of, 89
  isosceles, 89
  matching, 91
  median of, 124
  notation for, 88
  obtuse, 90
  orthocenter of, A-27
  right, 89
  scalene, 89
  sides of, 88
  similar, 330, 335
  vertices of, 88
Triangle Inequality Theorem, 138
Triangular prism, 392
Triangular region, 301
Trisecting an angle, 299
Total area, 394
  of right circular cone, 416
  of right circular cylinder, 414

Undefined terms, 4
Union of sets, 8
Unit angle, 56–57
Unit cube, 403
Unit length, 32
Unit line segment, 56
Unit square, 302

Vertex
  of angle, 53
  of circular cone, 415
  of pyramid, 394
Vertex angle of isosceles triangle, 89
Vertical angles, 56
Vertices
  of polygon, 240
  of prism, 392
  of quadrilateral, 201
  of triangle, 88
Volume, 403
  of cube, 404
  of rectangular right prism, 403
  of right circular cone, 416
  of right circular cylinder, 415
  of prism, 404
  of pyramid, 405
  of sphere, 417

Weierstrass, Karl, 329
Whole greater than part, 22, 41, 136
Whole number, 10
Width of rectangle, 303

B C D E F G H 3 I 4 J 5